Detecting Women

Detecting Women

A Reader's Guide and Checklist
for Mystery Series Written by Women

3rd edition

Willetta L. Heising

PURPLE
MOON
PRESS

For information address: Purple Moon Press, 3319 Greenfield Road, Suite 317, Dearborn, Michigan 48120-1212.

Phone 313-593-1033
Fax 313-593-4087
E-mail <purplemoon@prodigy.net> or <willetta@purplemoonpress.com>

ISBN: 0-9644593-5-3 (hardcover)
ISBN: 0-9644593-6-1 (paperback)

Printed on recycled paper and bound in the USA by
Malloy Lithographing, Inc. of Ann Arbor, Michigan.

Cover design, electronic prepress and text design by
Jacqué Consulting & Design of Dearborn, Michigan.

The paper used in this publication meets the minimum requirements of American National Standard for Information Sciences—Permanence of Paper for Printed Library Materials. ANSI Z39.48-1984

First printing November 1999

Publisher's Cataloging-in-Publication
(Provided by Quality Books, Inc.)

Heising, Willetta L.
    Detecting women : a reader's guide and checklist for mystery series written by women / Willetta L. Heising. – 3rd ed.
        p. cm.
    Includes bibliographical references and index.
    ISBN: 0-9644593-5-3 (hardcover)
    ISBN: 0-9644593-6-1 (paperback)

    1. Detective and mystery stories, American—Bibliography.
    2. Detective and mystery stories, English—Bibliography
    3. American fiction—Women authors—Bibliography.
    4. English fiction—Women authors—Bibliography. I. Title

Z1231.D47H45 2000
016.813/0872/099287   QB199-523

Author's Note

Any good reference is a work in progress and *Detecting Women* is no exception, even the third time around. Constant changes were a fact of life during production of this book. New series were announced, titles were changed, publication dates came and went, while spellings, locations and countless details were in a perpetual state of flux. No sooner were errors corrected than new ones popped up to take their places among the more than 100,000 facts presented in this third edition of *Detecting Women*.

We would like to say that you will find perfect consistency among the various chapters in this book, but we know that is not the case. The most up-to-date information is always presented in Chapter 1, the Master List. If you find conflicting information elsewhere in the book, you should always assume the Master List, including profile text, character description, title list and awards information, is the most current and accurate data we have collected. Almost 200 new titles (1999 and 2000) that were not part of the original data base have been mentioned within the author profiles, so that readers can make additions to their personal checklists

A wise friend once suggested a few errors be scattered about so as not to disappoint those who take great pleasure in finding them. We have happily obliged.

Acknowledgments

The list of people who helped make the 3rd edition of *Detecting Women* a reality is a long one. But two stand out above the rest—Linda L. Eddy and Doris Ann Norris. Week after week, month after month, for almost two years, they soldiered on. Doris Ann tracked down the hard-to-find and the impossible, and I have 2,000 e-mail messages from her to prove it. Linda organized an acre of files, proofread and cross-checked till her vision blurred, and cheerfully kept me from jumping off the Ambassador Bridge. Many days these two women were all that stood between me and I-Give-Up. If you enjoy this book, be sure to tell Linda and Doris Ann thank you. I owe them both—big time. Thank you, Linda. Thank you, Doris Ann.

Other heroes include Susan Eggers (the Queen of British mysteries), who more than once read six books in a weekend to answer my questions; Allen J. Hubin, who generously checked every entry in the *Detecting Women Pocket Guide* against his data base; and Alice Ann Carpenter and John Leininger, who pulled out-of-print books off their shelves to provide jacket copy for my files.

To the dream team at Jacqué Consulting & Design, who outdid themselves once again, my heartfelt thanks. Jackie McClure, Robert Smiley, Carol Romano, Jackie Mayberry and Chris Shamus, thank you.

To Patrice Smith, Lynn Rohkohl and the production staff at Malloy Lithographing, who leaped tall buildings in a single bound, moved mountains, and walked on water, I couldn't have done it without you.

To those who sent letters, phoned, faxed, and e-mailed their enthusiasm and support, you have my sincerest gratitude.

A special thank you to syndicated cartoonist Bill Holbrook for creating the fingerprint illustration on our cover.

Thank you one and all.

We did it!

To my senior partners

Whose love and support
has made all things possible.
I thank God every day for the
richest blessing of my life,
which is you.

Contents

HOW TO USE THIS BOOK

No matter what your preference for hunting mysteries—by author, character, mystery type, background, setting, book title, publication date or awards won—*Detecting Women* has a list for you. Complete with boxes to check for every series title, the Master List is designed to keep track of books you've read, books you own, books you intend to buy, books you especially like, or anything about mystery series written by women that you would like to keep track of.

Chapter 1—Master List

In the Master List, a total of 690 author entries appear in alphabetical order by last name, according to the name under which each mystery series is published. Pseudonymous authors are identified with a [P] and 225 authors not previously featured in *Detecting Women* are designated with a ☀ new ☀ . Each author entry shows the series titles published under that name. For example, Grand Master Barbara Mertz is listed as both Elizabeth Peters and Barbara Michaels, and Gwendoline Butler is listed separately as Jennie Melville. An author profile with information about the author's life and work is followed by series character(s) and book titles in order of publication. The parenthetical date following the title is intended to be the earliest date of publication.

Books first published in Britain, Canada or Australia often appear a year or more later in the United States. Also, U.S. titles sometimes differ from the British, Canadian or Australian titles. Some books have not yet been published in the United States. There may also be differences between hardcover and paperback editions. Whenever more than one title is known, both titles will be listed, with a notation indicating whether the second title is U.S., British or an alternate title. APA is used to indicate "also published as."

When an author has more than one series detective, the characters are listed in alphabetical order by first name. A short character description, including the primary series setting, follows the character's name. This may not be the setting for every book in the series, but it is typically the home base of the protagonist.

When a book has been nominated or has received recognition for a major prize or award in the mystery field, the book title appears in boldface type followed by the specific nomination or award and a star. If you are looking for award-winning authors, or books nominated for mystery awards, just scan the pages of

Chapter 1 looking for bold, starred titles. Solid stars ★ indicate award winners and open stars ☆ identify nominations. Because these awards are a fairly recent phenomenon, you should not overlook titles which predate awards. A description of the various mystery awards can be found following Awards List 3 at the back of Chapter 8, Mystery Book Awards. Please note that awards and nominations in this 3rd edition include only those awards through 1998, for books published in 1997. Awards conferred in 1999 do not appear.

In this third edition, for the most part, we have included only those women series writers who were alive in 1998. After the data base had been closed in mid 1998, we learned of the death of several authors. Rather than remove them, we chose to leave them in. The deceased Mary Jane Latsis (Emma Lathen), Kate Ross and Rebecca Rothenberg are also included.

Chapter 2—Mystery Types

A total of 815 mystery series presented in *Detecting Women* have been subdivided into four basic groups based on standard classifications for police procedurals, private eye novels, espionage, and traditional mysteries featuring amateur detectives. Rather than restricting the last group solely to amateur detectives, we have applied the mystery backgrounds for traditional mysteries to police and private eye series as well. You'll find historical police and private eye series from ancient Rome to 21st century. Detectives with disabilities, single parents, Jewish, black, gay and lesbian detectives, and others have been identified wherever possible. We have tried to cross-reference background and type whenever the background is important to the series. For example, historical private eye series appear in the P.I. section and again in the appropriate historical section. Thus, you will find Suzanne Robinson's Lord Meren series, and Lindsey Davis' Falco series listed with private investigators, as well as in the 'Historical, ancient' section.

Mystery backgrounds include:

Academic

Advertising & Public Relations

Animals, cats

_____ , dogs

_____ , horses

_____ , other

new Archaeology & Anthropology

new Architecture & Engineering

Art & Antiques

Authors & Writers

Black

Books & Libraries

Botanical

Business & Finance

Computers & Technology

Criminals

Cross Genre

new Detectives with Disabilities

Domestic

Ecclesiastical & Religious

Environment & Wilderness

Ethnic

new Fashion

new Forensic

Gay & Lesbian

Gourmet & Food

Government & Politics

new Historical, prehistory

_____ , ancient

_____ , 11th century

_____ , 12th century

_____ , 14th century

_____ , 15th century

_____ , 16th century

_____ , 17th century

_____ , 18th century

_____ , 19th century

_____ , 1900s

_____ , 1910s

_____ , 1920s

_____ , 1930s

_____ , 1940s

_____ , 1950s

_____ , 1960s

_____ , 1970s

_____ , other

new Historical Figures

Hotels & Inns

new Humor

new Jewish

Journalism, magazine

_____ , newspaper

_____ , photography

_____ , radio & television

Legal, attorney

_____ , judge

new _____ , prosecutor

Medical

Military

Miscellaneous

Movies & Filmmaking

Music

Native American

Paranormal

new Psychology & Psychiatry

new Real Estate

Romantic

new Royals & Aristocrats

new Science

Senior Sleuths

new Sherlockian

new Single Parent

Small Town

new Social Services

Sports

Suburban

Theatre & Performing Arts

Travel

Although we have identified gay & lesbian detectives, black, Jewish, other ethic detectives, and detectives with disabilities, these are never the only categories in which they are listed. Black cops and private eyes are listed first as cops and P.I.s and secondly as black detectives.

The Cross Genre category includes fantasy and horror, science fiction, and western private eyes. This is not meant to be an exhaustive list of cross genre detective fiction, but rather a sampling of series you might not be familiar with.

In Chapters 2 through 4 we use a series shorthand for date of the first book in the series and number of books in the series. When you see '72-20, for example, you will know the series begins in 1972 and currently stands at 20 books, as does Marcia Muller's Sharon McCone series. This two-part column, included in all table-format lists (types, series characters and settings), makes it easy to spot the long-running series.

Whenever a collection of short stories featuring a series character appears in the series list, it will appear in the order in which it was published, but will not be numbered. Anthologies are not considered to be series installments. For example, *Renowned Be Thy Grave* (1998)—P.M. Carlson's short story collection introducing Bridget Mooney—is listed as 'ss' rather than #1 in the series. The shorthand for this series is '98-ss.

Chapter 3—Series Characters

This list will prove useful for those who know a character's first name but not the author's. Whenever the series character is a pair, each of the partners is listed separately. For example, both Annie Laurance and Max Darling from Carolyn Hart's Death on Demand series appear in the character listing, first under Annie and later under Max. The partner's name is always attached so you know the character is part of a series pair.

Chapter 4—Settings

Settings identified in the Master List and Chapter 4 are not necessarily the setting for each book in the series, but typically the home base of the series character(s).

When world travel is part of the story line, we attempt to classify the series as such. When the setting changes from book to book, we choose what appears to be the most frequent setting. When there are several books in a series, each with different settings, we try to specify the current location. Locations outside the United States are presented alphabetically by country. Within each country, state or province, cities and towns appear in alphabetical order, with fictional towns included as if they were real. Unspecified locations are grouped together at the beginning of each section.

Chapter 5—Title Chronology

Within the chronological list, all 3,777 series titles are arrayed by year—presented in alphabetical order according to the author's last name. Whenever a title is the first in a series, it is marked with a **1** in front of the title. Black header bars separate the decades, and beginning with 1990, underscores are provided between letters of the alphabet according to the author's last name for each year's titles. Titles nominated or receiving mystery book awards are marked with open and solid stars. Because these prizes are a fairly recent phenomenon, stars do not appear until 1961.

Chapter 6—Alphabetical List of Titles

In the alphabetical list of titles, all 3,777 series titles are listed in alphabetical order. Whenever the first word in the title is an article (A, An, The), it has been dropped, so that the second word controls the title's placement. When a title is the first in a series, it is identified by a **1**. Alternate titles are listed as part of the entry for the first appearance of a particular work. Titles are also starred to indicate award winners and nominees.

Chapter 7—Pseudonyms

A discussion of the use of pseudonyms appears at the beginning of Chapter 7.

Chapter 8—Mystery Book Awards

More than 400 awards and nominations are presented in Chapter 8 in three formats. Only those awards and nominations given to series mysteries written by women are included here. You will not find awards or nominations for nonseries novels or for authors not included in this data base. List 1 shows winners and nominees in alphabetical order by conferring agency and award name. List 2 reconfigures the same information year by year for each award category, starting with Best First Novel, from the most recent awards to the earliest. List 3 is an alphabetical list of the same awards and nominations by author's last name.

Index

The index includes authors (last name first) and series characters (first name first). Index entries for authors included in the Master List are marked with a black square bullet ■. The first index entry for each author is typically her location in the Master List. Multiple mentions of an author on a single page are not separately identified.

How You Can Help

Any edition of a reference book of this scope is bound to contain errors, some of which come from errors in other reference sources. Without reading at least one book in each of the 815 series identified in this data base, it is doubtful we could be entirely certain of each character's occupation, the series setting, or even the correct mystery type and background. It's surprising how often a book's dust jacket will contain misinformation about the story. And many out of print titles are hard to find.

If you have personal knowledge you would like to share, we hope you will get in touch with us and help correct omissions or errors. Please provide documentation when you contact us about errors. A photocopy of a book's copyright page is often the best documentation for certain errors. When you suggest authors for inclusion in future editions, please provide a title list or tell us how to get in touch with the author. It is never too early to send title lists, character descriptions, awards and biographical information for future editions.

A special thank you to all who continue to provide information, support and enthusiasm for our Detecting series of mystery reader's guides. We couldn't do it without you.

Master List 1

◼ ADAMS, Deborah

Seventh-generation Tennesseean, Deborah Adams, is the creator of an Agatha-nominated series featuring Jesus Creek, Tennessee, population 430. A misread highway sign was her inspiration for the small-town home of an ensemble cast of alternating narrators for these rollicking whodunits. Youngest charter member of Carroll County's Historical Society at age 14, Adams lists endurance riding among her current interests. She and her horse Sundance completed a 25-mile trail ride for novices in 1995. Despite a raging thunderstorm on the edge of a hurricane, they proudly finished the race and were not last. "Cast Your Fate to the Wind" (*Malice Domestic 3*) won her a 1995 Macavity Award for best short story shared with Jan Burke. Adams' more recent short stories appear in *Funny Bones* (1997), *Murder, They Wrote 2* (1998) and *Canine Capers* (1999). She teaches online courses through Nashville State Technical Institute—Writing the Mystery Novel, Writing Short Stories and Tarot for Beginners.

Jesus Creek TN...eccentric small town...Jesus Creek, Tennessee

- ❑ ❑ 1 - **All the Great Pretenders (1992) Agatha nominee** ☆
- ❑ ❑ 2 - All the Crazy Winters (1992)
- ❑ ❑ 3 - All the Dark Disguises (1993)
- ❑ ❑ 4 - All the Hungry Mothers (1993)
- ❑ ❑ 5 - All the Deadly Beloved (1995)
- ❑ ❑ 6 - All the Blood Relations (1997)
- ❑ ❑ . . . .
- ❑ ❑ . . . .

◼ ADAMS, Jane

Jane Adams writes a Norwich police series featuring Detective Inspector Mike Croft, introduced in *The Greenway* (1995). A Creasey nominee for best first novel, the book takes its title from an ancient sheltered pathway. A missing child case set in a seaside village, the series opener includes a strong supporting cast—a former Norwich detective, the retired vicar, a journalist and a black psychiatrist named Maria. In addition to her police series, Adams is the author of *Bird* (1997), a novel of psychological suspense featuring a young woman who tries to uncover her grandfather's death bed secret. With a degree in sociology, this Leicester native once sang lead vocal in a folk rock band. She says one of her dreams is to travel the length of the Silk Road on a motorbike. Other interests include pen and ink drawing, aikido and tae kwan do.

Mike Croft...detective inspector...Norwich, England

- ❑ ❑ 1 - **The Greenway (1995) Creasey nominee** ☆
- ❑ ❑ 2 - Cast the First Stone (1996)
- ❑ ❑ 3 - Fade to Grey (1998)
- ❑ ❑ . . . .
- ❑ ❑ . . . .

■ ADAMSON, M.J.

Denver author Mary Jo Adamsom, writing as M.J. Adamson, is the author of a police series set in Puerto Rico, featuring N.Y.P.D. homicide detective Balthazar Marten and Puerto Rican cop Sixto Cardenas. The Spanish-speaking Marten is sent to Puerto Rico on an exchange program while recovering from the bombing which killed his young wife. Book 5 in this series, *May's Newfangled Mirth* (1989), was named a Notable Book of the Year by *The New York Times Book Review*. Along with fellow Denver novelist Yvonne Montgomery, Adamson has written historical romance (*Bridey's Mountain*) as Yvonne Adamson. After growing up in Illinois, she started graduate work in English at U.C.L.A. and later earned a Ph.D. from the University of Denver. After living in London, Los Angeles, several cities in Northern California, southeast Missouri and central Wyoming, she prefers these days spending winters in Puerto Rico and summers in Colorado.

Balthazar Marten & Sixto Cardenas...NYPD homicide detective & Puerto Rican cop...Puerto Rico

❑ ❑   1 - Not Till a Hot January (1987)
❑ ❑   2 - A February Face (1987)
❑ ❑   3 - Remember March (1988)
❑ ❑   4 - April When They Woo (1988)
❑ ❑   5 - May's Newfangled Mirth (1989)
❑ ❑   . . . .
❑ ❑   . . . .

■ AIRD, Catherine [P]

Catherine Aird is the pseudonym of Kinn Hamilton McIntosh, creator of Inspector C.D. Sloan, aptly nicknamed "Seedy" by his friends. Launched in 1966 with *The Religious Body*, the series is set in the fictitious county of Calleshire. Included in that first book is a map depicting all the geographical features and fictional landmarks of Calleshire—towns, farms, factories, schools, and, of course, Berebury police headquarters. Each detective's character is fully described in the series opener, and after more than 30 years of police work, they've thankfully changed not one bit. Supporting cast members include Sloan's annoying boss, Superintendent Leeyes, "Defective" Constable William Crosby and the strangely humorous pathologist, Dr. Dabbe. Aird is also the author of *A Most Contagious Game* (1967), involving a secret room, a murdered wife and a 200-year-old skeleton. A past Chairman of the British Crime Writer's Association, she lives in Kent, England.

Christopher Dennis "Seedy" Sloan...CID department head...Berebury, West Calleshire, England

❑ ❑   1 - The Religious Body (1966)
❑ ❑   2 - Henrietta Who? (1968)
❑ ❑   3 - The Complete Steel (1969)
❑ ❑   - U.S.-The Stately Home Murder
❑ ❑   4 - A Late Phoenix (1970)
❑ ❑   5 - His Burial Too (1973)
❑ ❑   6 - Slight Mourning (1975)
❑ ❑   7 - Parting Breath (1977)
❑ ❑   8 - Some Die Eloquent (1979)
❑ ❑   9 - Passing Strange (1980)
❑ ❑   10 - Last Respects (1982)
❑ ❑   11 - Harm's Way (1984)
❑ ❑   12 - A Dead Liberty (1986)
❑ ❑   13 - The Body Politic (1990)
❑ ❑   14 - A Going Concern (1993)
❑ ❑   15 - After Effects (1996)
❑ ❑   ss - Injury Time [16 stories] (1997)
❑ ❑   16 - Stiff News (1998)
❑ ❑   . . . .
❑ ❑   . . . .

■ ALBERT, Susan Wittig

Former Texas university professor and administrator, Susan Wittig Albert, writes an Agatha- and Anthony-nominated series that tells a corporate leave-taking story not unlike her own. Albert's fictional creation, former fast-track attorney China Bayles, ditches the big-city rat race for an herb shop in the west Texas Hill Country. Once a fast tracker herself, Albert now writes full time. She holds a Ph.D. from Berkeley and is the author of numerous books and articles about literature and writing, including *Work of Her Own, A Woman's Guide to Success off the Career Track* (1992) and *Writing From Life: Telling Your Soul's Story* (1997). Albert's Story Circle Network is a not-for-profit organization that encourages women to tell their stories using the framework provided in *Writing From Life*. With husband Bill Albert, she writes a Victorian mystery series under the pseudonym Robin Paige. Together they have also written more than 60 novels for young readers.

China Bayles...herb shop owner & former attorney...Pecan Springs, Texas
- ❑ ❑   1 - **Thyme of Death (1992) Agatha & Anthony nominee** ☆☆
- ❑ ❑   2 - Witches' Bane (1993)
- ❑ ❑   3 - Hangman's Root (1994)
- ❑ ❑   4 - Rosemary Remembered (1995)
- ❑ ❑   5 - Rueful Death (1996)
- ❑ ❑   6 - Love Lies Bleeding (1997)
- ❑ ❑   7 - Chile Death (1998)
- ❑ ❑   . . . .
- ❑ ❑   . . . .

■ ALEXANDER, Skye

A professional astrologer for more than 20 years, Skye Alexander has used unconventional techniques to help police in seven states solve crimes. Armed with experience from several publishing houses as editor, publicist, copywriter, book designer and sales director, she is now publishing her own mysteries. Using PhotoShop and PageMaker, she even designed the cover and interior layout for *Hidden Agenda* (1997), winner of the Kiss of Death Award from Romance Writers of America. This Magical Mystery Series opener features Boston astrologer Charlotte McCrea, who is visiting her hometown when two witches are murdered. "Feminist New Age romantic mystery" is how the author describes book 1. Alexander's nonfiction classic, *Planets in Signs* (1988), has been praised as the "best and most complete book available on the subject." After growing up in the rural South, where she had a newspaper column at age 15, the author now lives in Gloucester, Massachusetts.

Charlotte McCrae...Boston astrologer...Clearwater, North Carolina
- ❑ ❑   1 - **Hidden Agenda (1997) Kiss of Death winner** ★
- ❑ ❑   2 - Hide in Plain Sight (1999)
- ❑ ❑   3 - Rose-Colored Glasses (2000)
- ❑ ❑   . . . .
- ❑ ❑   . . . .

■ ALLEN, Irene [P]

Irene Allen is the pseudonym of Elsa Kirsten Peters, a Harvard- and Princeton-educated geologist and creator of a Quaker mystery series featuring Elizabeth Elliot, a 60-something widowed meeting clerk in Cambridge, Massachusetts. The series opener, *Quaker Silence* (1992), involves the brutal slaying of a wealthy Quaker, while book 2 takes Elizabeth to Harvard University, where a friend is the prime suspect in the death of a respected paleontologist accused of sexual harassment. Elizabeth ends up in big trouble herself in book 3, when a pacifist husband and wife face I.R.S. eviction for refusal to pay war taxes. The wife turns up dead and the police accuse Elizabeth. But she's off to Seattle in *Quaker Indictment* (1998) to visit a college friend who asks her help in gathering evidence against a nuclear facility accused of releasing radioactive material into the landscape. The author lives in Washington State.

Elizabeth Elliot...widowed Quaker meeting clerk...Cambridge, Massachusetts
- ❑ ❑   1 - Quaker Silence (1992)
- ❑ ❑   2 - Quaker Witness (1993)
- ❑ ❑   3 - Quaker Testimony (1996)
- ❑ ❑   4 - Quaker Indictment (1998)
- ❑ ❑   . . . .
- ❑ ❑   . . . .

■ ALLEN, Kate [P]

Cat lover Kate Allen is the pseudonymous author of a police series featuring lesbian "leather" cop Alison Kaine, diagnosed with fibromyalgia syndrome in book 3, a condition she shares with her creator. In their review of this installment, *Kirkus Reviews* praised "Allen's mastery of superlatively bitchy arguments." Her nonseries mystery, *I Knew You Would Call* (1995), features a Basque-American phone psychic named Marta Goicochea, in a complicated but often funny story of incest survival, abusive lesbian relationships and child custody battles. Allen is currently writing a cross-genre mystery featuring a rich lesbian vampire who works in an all-night plasma bank and is the daughter of an antiques dealer. The owner of four animal-rescue cats, the oldest of which is 20, Allen is a collector of cat fabrics, cat earrings and other cat stuff. A resident of Denver, Colorado, she enjoys quilt-making and likes to two-step.

Alison Kaine...lesbian leather cop...Denver, Colorado

- ❏ ❏   1 - Tell Me What You Like (1993)
- ❏ ❏   2 - Give My Secrets Back (1995)
- ❏ ❏   3 - Takes One To Know One (1996)
- ❏ ❏   4 - Just a Little Lie (1999)
- ❏ ❏   . . . .
- ❏ ❏   . . . .

■ AMATO, Angela and Joe Sharkey

Angela Amato and Joe Sharkey are co-authors of *Lady-Gold* (1998), introducing undercover New York cop Gerry Conte babysitting a young mobster-turned-informant. Like her fictional counterpart, Amato left the force to become a Legal Aid attorney, but not before getting undercover experience as one of the N.Y.P.D.'s original female decoy cops. Posing as a prostitute made front-page news in New York when it was revealed the brothel under investigation was billing sexual services to Blue Cross and other insurance providers. In addition to her criminal practice in New York and Florida, Amato is executive producer of the Paramount film adaptation of *LadyGold* and has created a television series for a major network. Her collaborator Joe Sharkey, author of *Bedlam* (1994), *Above Suspicion* (1996) and other nonfiction books, is a columnist for *The New York Times*. He lives in New Jersey.

Gerry Conte...undercover cop turned defense attorney...New York, New York

- ❏ ❏   1 - LadyGold (1998)
- ❏ ❏   2 - Jackpot (1999)
- ❏ ❏   . . . .
- ❏ ❏   . . . .

■ AMEY, Linda

Linda Amey of Austin, Texas is a mortician and funeral home director, as well as the author of a mystery series featuring Austin funeral director Blair Emerson. The series debuts with *Bury Her Sweetly* (1992) and later moves to Emerson's home town of Live Oak in *Dead of Night* (1995). When daughter Brandi, kidnapped as a toddler, is returned 11 years later (obsessive-compulsive and afraid to be touched), Emerson hopes the small-town friendliness of Live Oak will act as therapy for the traumatized girl. Unfortunately, a string of arson fires and a stalker heighten the tension, with a hated environmentalist and a troubled teenager adding to the blaze. An "engrossing storyteller," according to *Booklist*, Amey is also the author of four mystery suspense novels published by a Christian press. She operates the family mortuary business with her husband.

Blair Emerson...funeral director...Austin, Texas

- ❏ ❏   1 - Bury Her Sweetly (1992)
- ❏ ❏   2 - At Dead of Night (1995)
- ❏ ❏   . . . .
- ❏ ❏   . . . .

■ ANDREAE, Christine

Freelance writer and adjunct English professor Christine Andreae is also the creator of a mystery series featuring camp cook and poet Lee Squires. To escape the summer heat of Washington, D.C., Squires signs on as substitute cook for a Montana trail ride through the Bob Marshall Wilderness in *Trail of Murder* (1992), nominated for an Edgar Award for best first novel. She cooks at a dude ranch on the Eastern front of the Rockies in *Grizzly* (1994) and later joins a llama trek in the Mission Mountains in *Small Target* (1996). A descendant of French fur trappers in the early American West, Andreae says she grew up in the East on a steady diet of *Gunsmoke, Roy Rogers* and *The Lone Ranger*. From her home base in the Shenandoah Valley of Virginia, the author spends as much time as possible in Montana.

Lee Squires...camp cook & poet...Montana
❑	❑	1 - **Trail of Murder (1992) Edgar nominee** ☆
❑	❑	2 - Grizzly, A Murder (1994)
❑	❑	3 - A Small Target (1996)
❑	❑	. . . .
❑	❑	. . . .

■ ANDREWS, Sarah

Geologist Sarah Andrews has researched her Em Hansen mysteries in the badlands of Wyoming, on the sand dunes of Ecuador and Australia, under condos in Long Beach, and next to airstrips where B-52 bombers practiced take-offs and landings. In her first appearance, Em is working on a Wyoming drilling rig, looking for oil in Tensleep sandstone—a 400-million-year-old formation rich in petroleum. Book 2 takes her to the Denver headquarters of Blackfeet Oil Company, while a serious downturn in the oil business sends her to the unemployment line in book 3. Here she investigates the suspicious death of a senator's daughter, a California geologist and environmental consultant in Santa Rosa. Still unemployed in book 4, Em tries to help the daughter of a former boss recover from the trauma of witnessing her mother's murder. After working for the federal government, commercial oil producers and environmental services, Andrews now writes full time.

Em Hansen...oil company geologist...Wyoming
❑	❑	1 - Tensleep (1994)
❑	❑	2 - A Fall in Denver (1995)
❑	❑	3 - Mother Nature (1997)
❑	❑	4 - Only Flesh and Bones (1998)
❑	❑	. . . .
❑	❑	. . . .

■ ARNOLD, Catherine [P]

Catherine Arnold is the pseudonym of Theresa Sandberg for her Florida legal mysteries featuring Karen Perry-Mondori, a five-foot two-inch 37-year-old rising legal star married to a brilliant Tampa neurosurgeon. First seen in the paperback original *Due Process* (1996), Perry-Mondori is up against murder, sex and plenty of courtroom double-dealing. While neighbors in a posh community turn against each other after a brutal slaying, she defends a man accused of a crime he may not have committed. In *Imperfect Justice* (1997), this Miami native, who worked her way through college and law school as a waitress, takes on yet another client she suspects is guilty. When a former big-time crime boss faces a charge of drug possession, the deadly conspiracy reaches the highest levels of government. Arnold is a trial lawyer in Palm Harbor, Florida.

Karen Perry-Mondori...criminal defense attorney...Tampa, Florida
❑	❑	1 - Due Process (1996)
❑	❑	2 - Imperfect Justice (1997)
❑	❑	3 - Wrongful Death (1999)
❑	❑	. . . .
❑	❑	. . . .

■ ARNOLD, Margot [P]

Margot Arnold is the pseudonym of Petronelle Cook for her mysteries featuring 60-something academic sleuths, American anthropologist Penelope Spring and British archaeologist Tobias Glendower. Arnold brings her lifelong interest in archaeology, anthropology and travel to the globe-trotting adventures of Penny and Sir Toby. While *Zadok's Treasure* (1979) takes them to Israel and the tomb of King Solomon's high priest, *The Menehune Murders* (1989) finds them chasing Hawaiian leprechauns (menehunes). Arnold has also written several novels of romantic suspense. As Petronelle Cook, she is the author of *Queen Consorts of England: The Power Behind the Throne* (1993), a study of the true lives of the wives of English Kings, with detailed biographies arranged chronologically, genealogical charts and notes on succession. A longtime resident of Cape Cod, the author was educated at Oxford and has lived and traveled extensively abroad. She currently makes her home in Pennsylvania.

Penny Spring & Toby Glendower...anthropologist & archeologist

- ❏ ❏ 1 - Exit Actors, Dying (1979)
- ❏ ❏ 2 - Zadock's Treasure (1979)
- ❏ ❏ 3 - The Cape Cod Caper (1980)
- ❏ ❏ 4 - Death of a Voodoo Doll (1982)
- ❏ ❏ 5 - Lament for a Lady Laird (1982)
- ❏ ❏ 6 - Death on a Dragon's Tongue (1982)
- ❏ ❏ 7 - The Menehune Murders (1989)
- ❏ ❏ 8 - Toby's Folly (1990)
- ❏ ❏ 9 - The Catacomb Conspiracy (1991)
- ❏ ❏ 10 - Cape Cod Conundrum (1992)
- ❏ ❏ 11 - Dirge for a Dorset Druid (1994)
- ❏ ❏ 12 - The Midas Murders (1995)
- ❏ ❏ . . . .
- ❏ ❏ . . . .

■ ATHERTON, Nancy

Nancy Atherton's Aunt Dimity creation was first a Christmas gift for an editor friend who later found her an agent. In a 1998 *Troutworks* interview, Atherton tells about tracing the origins of 'Dimity' to Georgette Heyer, whose characters often wore dresses of dimity, and Dorothy L. Sayers, who named the smallest bell Dimity in "The Nine Tailors." Atherton has heard from two women named Dimity—a Delaware librarian and a 19-year-old who wanted to change her name until reading these books. A serious fan of figure skating, World War I history, P.D. James and Tony Hillerman, Atherton says she is an eleventh-hour dropout from the University of Chicago Ph.D. program in English. A former freelance proofreader and a rare book bibliographer, she has worked at a dude ranch, ski lodge and day care center. Born in Chicago and raised in Oak Park, she currently lives in Downstate Illinois.

Aunt Dimity...romantic ghost...England

- ❏ ❏ 1 - Aunt Dimity's Death (1992)
- ❏ ❏ 2 - Aunt Dimity and the Duke (1994)
- ❏ ❏ 3 - Aunt Dimity's Good Deed (1996)
- ❏ ❏ 4 - Aunt Dimity Digs In (1998)
- ❏ ❏ . . . .
- ❏ ❏ . . . .

■ AYRES, Noreen

Noreen Ayres, of Houston, Texas, is the creator of forensic expert Smokey Brandon, ex-cop and former exotic dancer turned civilian employee of the Orange County sheriff's department. Armed with a .38 Colt revolver, Smokey has a fondness for Blues and Budweiser, not always in that order. Optioned for film and television, Ayres' creation has been called "tough, hip, visceral and lusty enough to make both Wambaugh and Spillane sit up" (*Kirkus Reviews*). A former technical writer and editor of aircraft maintenance manuals and computer reference guides, Ayres has a master's degree in English and has won awards for short fiction and poetry. She has worked as a fish cleaner, bookbinder, sign painter, insurance rater, trademark docket clerk, church secretary, proofreader, personnel clerk, brokerage receptionist and science teacher, but never as an exotic dancer. Her story is featured in Cynthia Kersey's *Unstoppable: 45 Powerful Stories of Perseverance and Triumph from People Just Like You* (1998).

Samantha "Smokey" Brandon...sheriff's forensic expert...Orange County, California
- ❑ ❑ 1 - A World the Color of Salt (1992)
- ❑ ❑ 2 - Carcass Trade (1994)
- ❑ ❑ . . . .
- ❑ ❑ . . . .

■ BABBIN, Jacqueline

Jacqueline Babbin, former producer of the ABC-TV daytime drama *All My Children,* is the creator of a mystery series featuring Clovis Kelly, ex-N.Y.P.D. homicide detective first grade turned television crime consultant. After writing his own best-seller, Kelly lands a role in the soap opera when visiting the set during the commission of a crime. The series opener, *Prime Time Corpse* (1972), was re-printed more than 15 years later as *Bloody Special* when the sequel, *Bloody Soaps*, was published in 1989. Babbin started her career as assistant to theatrical agent Audrey Wood and later worked on the original Broadway production of "Streetcar Named Desire." She spent 14 years with David Susskind, as both story editor and producer, and subsequently produced and won an Emmy for the NBC-drama *Sybil*, starring Joanne Woodward and Sally Field. Along with Ragdoll cats, Bowzer and Amos, Babbin lives in Connecticut.

Clovis Kelly...homicide cop turned crime consultant...New York, New York
- ❑ ❑ 1 - Prime Time Corpse (1972)
- ❑ ❑ - APA-Bloody Special (1989)
- ❑ ❑ 2 - Bloody Soaps (1989)
- ❑ ❑ . . . .
- ❑ ❑ . . . .

■ BABSON, Marian

American-born author Marian Babson has lived in London most of her life and writes mysteries in the traditional English style, often featuring Americans in London or Londoners visiting the United States. In addition to more than 25 nonseries novels, she has written two mystery series. The first features Doug Perkins, co-owner of a London public relations firm. Babson's second series features a humorous cast of characters headed by a pair of aging Hollywood movie queens—Evangeline Sinclair and Trixie Dolan—looking to jump-start their careers on the London stage. Currently writing a collection of mysteries known as Babson's Cats, the author says she has no plans to write a continuing character, but a cat will always be center stage. Recent titles include *A Company of Cats* (1999), published in Britain as *The Multiple Cat, Paws for Alarm* (1998), *Canapés for the Kitties* (1997), published in the U.K. as *Miss Petunia's Last Case*, and *Whiskers and Smoke* (1997), previously published as *A Trail of Ashes* [1984].

Douglas Perkins...public relations agent...London, England
- ❑ ❑ 1 - Cover-up Story (1971)
- ❑ ❑ 2 - Murder on Show (1972)
- ❑ ❑ - U.S.-Murder at the Cat Show (1989)
- ❑ ❑ 3 - Tourists are for Trapping (1989)
- ❑ ❑ 4 - In the Teeth of Adversity (1990)
- ❑ ❑ . . . .
- ❑ ❑ . . . .

Evangeline Sinclair & Trixie Dolan...aging American ex-movie queens...London, England
- ❑ ❑ 1 - Reel Murder (1986)
- ❑ ❑ 2 - Encore Murder (1989)
- ❑ ❑ 3 - Shadows in Their Blood (1993)
- ❑ ❑ 4 - Even Yuppies Die (1993)
- ❑ ❑ 5 - Break a Leg, Darlings (1995)
- ❑ ❑ . . . .
- ❑ ❑ . . . .

■ BACON-SMITH, Camille

Folklorist and fantasy-horror writer Camille Bacon-Smith returned to college for a B.A. at the age of 30 and went on to earn a Ph.D. in folklore from the University of Pennsylvania, where her dissertation on fan behavior became the Hugo-nominated *Enterprising Women, Television Fandom and the Creation of Modern Myth* (1992). Her mystery series features an unlikely trio of Philadelphia investigators and art recovery specialists—daemons Kevin Bradley and Lily Ryan, and Evan Davis, Kevin's accidental offspring. With Society Hill offices decorated in period-authentic Hepplewhite and French Aubusson, their daily rate of $1500 plus expenses is payable in advance, one week at a time. While writing her nonseries novel, *The Face of Time* (1996), Bacon-Smith lived briefly in Thorgill, on the shoulder of Rose Moor, where she sent her new Scotland Yard detectives in search of a serial killer. She currently teaches at Temple University and runs a website and e-mail list for professional folklorists.

Kevin Bradley...daemon art recovery specialist...Philadelphia, Pennsylvania

- ❏ ❏ 1 - Eye of the Daemon (1996)
- ❏ ❏ 2 - Eyes of the Empress (1998)
- ❏ ❏ . . . .
- ❏ ❏ . . . .

■ BAILEY, Michele

An Englishwoman living in Brussels, Michele Bailey has written a trio of mysteries featuring 30-something Matilda Haycastle, a beautiful and socially-eclectic office temp living in Brussels. The only installment to be published in the U.S., *Dreadful Lies* is a "fascinatingly layered view of expatriate life in a great foreign capital," according to *Kirkus Reviews*, which went on to say that "Matilda's love affair with her surly policeman generates a chemical burn quite rare in these politically correct times." Thanks to a father in the R.A.F., Bailey lived all over the British Isles and the Middle East while growing up. Thanks to her French mother, she is bilingual and worked in London, Paris and Geneva before moving to Brussels in 1976. Author of a one-act play titled "Going All the Way," Bailey previously worked as a secretary and pharmaceutical market researcher, in addition to running her own business.

Matilda Haycastle...30-something office temp...Brussels, Belgium

- ❏ ❏ 1 - Dreadful Lies (1994)
- ❏ ❏ 2 - The Cuckoo Case (1995)
- ❏ ❏ 3 - Haycastle's Cricket (1996)
- ❏ ❏ . . . .
- ❏ ❏ . . . .

■ BAKER, Nikki [P]

Ohio native Nikki Baker is the pseudonymous author of a mystery series featuring black lesbian stockbroker Virginia Kelly, whose first appearance finds her in mid-fling with a high-powered Chicago lawyer. A business school friend needs help when her lover's bullet-riddled body is found behind a gay bar. Although the police suspect a hate crime, Ginny thinks otherwise, knowing the dead woman was being threatened with arrest on embezzlement charges. A Provincetown vacation with chain-smoking friend Naomi provides the backdrop for book 2, and it's trouble at a class reunion in book 3. A planned fourth installment, *The Ultimate Exit Strategy*, has not been published. Baker earned a B.S. from Purdue University and an M.B.A. from the University of Chicago. She told *Contemporary Authors* that her primary motivation in writing *In the Game* was to create a reflection of her experience as an affluent, educated, late baby-boom, black lesbian.

Virginia Kelly...black lesbian stockbroker...Chicago, Illinios

- ❏ ❏ 1 - In the Game (1991)
- ❏ ❏ 2 - The Lavender House Murder (1992)
- ❏ ❏ 3 - Long Goodbyes (1993)
- ❏ ❏ 4 - Ultimate Exit Strategy (1996)
- ❏ ❏ . . . .
- ❏ ❏ . . . .

■ BANKS, Carolyn

Carolyn Banks is the creator of five comic mysteries featuring Texas equestrienne sleuth Robin Vaughan. Introduced in *Death by Dressage* (1993), Robin makes her final appearance in *A Horse To Die For* (1996). A horse-loving Texan herself, Banks is the owner of a mare named Emma Peel who used to toss Banks about the way her fictional heroine tossed villains about. Author of *A Horse Lover's Guide to Texas* (1988) and a frequent reviewer of mysteries for *Washington Post Book World*, Banks previously wrote a monthly true crime column for the now-defunct *CrimeBeat* magazine. Her first novel, *Mr. Right* (1979), has been republished in 1999 with a cover description considered a put-down 20 years ago—"smartass parafeminist psycho-erotic thriller." Other scary, sexy novels from Banks include *The Darkroom* (1980), *The Girls on the Row* (1983) and *Patchwork* (1987). She is currently writing an erotic thriller titled *His*.

Robin Vaughan...equestrienne sleuth...Texas

- ❏ ❏ 1 - Death by Dressage (1993)
- ❏ ❏ 2 - Groomed for Death (1994)
- ❏ ❏ 3 - Murder Well-Bred (1995)
- ❏ ❏ 4 - Death on the Diagonal (1996)
- ❏ ❏ 5 - A Horse To Die For (1996)
- ❏ ❏ . . . .
- ❏ ❏ . . . .

■ BANKS, Jacqueline Turner

Children's book author Jacqueline Turner Banks has launched her own mystery series from a small press headed by her publisher-husband Reginald. In addition to *Maid in the Shade* (1998), ReGeJe Press released five other titles their first year, including thriller, romance and horror novels, as well as a juvenile mystery and a hard-to-classify work of adult fiction. Banks' college-educated black cleaning woman, Ruby Gordon, is "a woman of substance, possessed of a quirky good humor delightfully expressed," says *Publishers Weekly*. A Flint, Michigan native and University of Michigan graduate, Banks became a certified hypnotherapist while researching a novel about paranormal phenomenon. Daughter of a Genesee County deputy sheriff, she has worked as a probation officer, assistant registrar at a school for the blind and teacher. Her juvenile books, published by Houghton Mifflin, feature 6th grade Kentucky twins, Judge and Jury Jenkins, seen most recently in *Egg Drop Blues* (1995).

Ruby Gordon...college-educated black cleaning woman...Oakland, California

- ❏ ❏ 1 - Maid in the Shade (1998)
- ❏ ❏ 2 - Barely Maid (1999)
- ❏ ❏ . . . .
- ❏ ❏ . . . .

■ BANNISTER, Jo

Former newspaper editor Jo Bannister has written science fiction, thrillers and four mystery series, including her earliest featuring mystery-writing physician Clio Rees, who marries the local chief inspector. Her newest series introduces Primrose Holland, ex-pathologist turned agony aunt (advice columnist), whose column, "The Primrose Path," has enthusiasm, intelligence and heart, but no tact whatsoever. Bannister's primary and best-known mysteries are six considerably darker ones featuring Castlemere police Superintendent Frank Shapiro, Inspector Liz Graham and her assistant Sergeant Cal Donovan. American photojournalist Mickey Flynn is featured in a pair of high-action novels. Bannister's nonseries novels include a locked-floor mystery titled *The Lazarus Hotel* (1997). Born in Lancashire, Bannister left school at the age of 16 and was hired as the office junior at the *County Down Spectator*. When she left 20 years later to write full time, she had been the paper's editor for five years. She lives in Northern Ireland.

Clio Rees & Harry Marsh...physician novelist & chief inspector...England

- ❏ ❏ 1 - Striving With Gods (1984)
- ❏ ❏ 2 - Gilgamesh (1989)
- ❏ ❏ 3 - The Going Down of the Sun (1990)
- ❏ ❏ . . . .
- ❏ ❏ . . . .

Frank Shapiro, Cal Donovan & Liz Graham...police officers...Castlemere, England

- ❑ ❑　1 - A Bleeding of Innocents (1993)
- ❑ ❑　2 - Sins of the Heart (1994)
- ❑ ❑　　- U.S.-Charisma
- ❑ ❑　3 - Burning Desires (1995)
- ❑ ❑　　- U.S.-A Taste for Burning
- ❑ ❑　4 - No Birds Sing (1996)
- ❑ ❑　5 - Broken Lines (1998)
- ❑ ❑　6 - The Hireling's Tale (1999)
- ❑ ❑　. . . . .
- ❑ ❑　. . . . .

Mickey Flynn...American photojournalist...London, England

- ❑ ❑　1 - Shards (1990)
- ❑ ❑　2 - Death and Other Lovers (1991)
- ❑ ❑　. . . . .
- ❑ ❑　. . . . .

Primrose Holland...newspaper advice columnist...Skipley, England

- ❑ ❑　1 - The Primrose Convention (1998)
- ❑ ❑　. . . . .
- ❑ ❑　. . . . .

■ BARNES, Linda

Linda Barnes is best known for her red-headed cab-driving private eye, Carlotta Carlyle, first seen in the Edgar-award winning short story, "Lucky Penny" (1985), followed by the Anthony-, Edgar- and Shamus-nominated *A Trouble of Fools* (1987). The six-foot one-inch Carlotta is a natural at volleyball, and like her five-foot ten-inch creator, passionate about blues guitar. Last seen in book 8, *Flashpoint* (1999), Carlotta returns in *The Big Dig* (2000). Barnes' amateur sleuth, Michael Spraggue, is passionate about the theatre world, much like the author who once taught high school drama and worked briefly as a playwright. Spraggue's delightful Aunt Mary is the bonus in this series, introduced in 1982 and recently reissued in paperback. Sadly, Barnes won't be writing any more Spraggue books because she says he was getting too depressed. To keep him supplied with cases, she was killing everyone around him. Born and raised in Detroit, Barnes lives in Boston, where she earned a B.A. in fine arts from Boston University.

Carlotta Carlyle...6'1" cab-driving ex-cop P.I....Boston, Massachusetts

- ❑ ❑　1 - **A Trouble of Fools (1987) Anthony, Edgar & Shamus nominee** ☆☆☆
- ❑ ❑　2 - The Snake Tattoo (1989)
- ❑ ❑　3 - Coyote (1990)
- ❑ ❑　4 - Steel Guitar (1991)
- ❑ ❑　5 - Snapshot (1993)
- ❑ ❑　6 - Hardware (1995)
- ❑ ❑　7 - Cold Case (1997)
- ❑ ❑　. . . . .
- ❑ ❑　. . . . .

Michael Spraggue...wealthy actor ex-private eye...Boston, Massachusetts

- ❑ ❑　1 - Blood Will Have Blood (1982)
- ❑ ❑　2 - Bitter Finish (1983)
- ❑ ❑　3 - Dead Heat (1984)
- ❑ ❑　4 - Cities of the Dead (1986)
- ❑ ❑　. . . . .
- ❑ ❑　. . . . .

■ BARR, Nevada

Agatha and Anthony award-winner Nevada Barr is the creator of tough-talking, 40-something Anna Pigeon, federal law enforcement ranger for the National Park Service. Her adventures take readers inside 1-Guadalupe Mountains (TX), 2-Isle Royale (MI), 3-Mesa Verde (CO), 4-Lassen Volcanic (CA), 5-Cumberland Island Seashore (GA), 6-Carlsbad Caverns (NM) and 7-Ellis Island national parks. As yet untitled, Anna's next adventure will feature Natchez Trace Parkway (MS), site of Barr's last ranger assign-

ment. Like Anna, Barr has a sister named Molly, who is not a Manhattan psychologist, but a retired commercial airline pilot. After eight years on duty, Barr recently hung up her ranger hat to write full-time from her home in Mississippi. Before her days with the Park Service, armed with a master's degree in theatre, she was a working actor for 18 years in New York and Minneapolis. And yes, Nevada is the name her parents gave her. It's where she was born.

Anna Pigeon...U. S. park ranger...National Parks
- ❏ ❏ 1 - **Track of the Cat (1993) Agatha & Anthony winner ★★**
- ❏ ❏ 2 - A Superior Death (1994)
- ❏ ❏ 3 - Ill Wind (1995)
- ❏ ❏ 4 - Firestorm (1996)
- ❏ ❏ 5 - Endangered Species (1997)
- ❏ ❏ 6 - Blind Descent (1998)
- ❏ ❏ 7 - Liberty Falling (1999)
- ❏ ❏ . . . .
- ❏ ❏ . . . .

■ BARRETT, Kathleen Anne

Milwaukee native Kathleen Anne Barrett introduced 40-something attorney Beth Hartley in *Milwaukee Winters Can Be Murder* (1996), the first of her three-book series featuring an amateur sleuth who operates a legal research firm out of the eastside mansion inherited from her Aunt Sarah. After proving in book 1 that her secretary's younger brother did not commit suicide, Beth is asked for help in book 2 by a young neighbor whose C.P.A. father has been murdered. In

book 3, Beth is hired by an old friend from law school who turns up dead before she can start the assignment. After earning accounting and law degrees from Marquette University, Barrett practiced law in Milwaukee and Philadelphia firms and later worked at a Charlottesville, Virginia legal research firm. A former student at the Wisconsin Conservatory of Music, she currently lives in a New Jersey suburb of Philadelphia.

Beth Hartley...attorney turned legal researcher...Milwaukee, Wisconsin
- ❏ ❏ 1 - Milwaukee Winters Can Be Murder (1996)
- ❏ ❏ 2 - Milwaukee Summers Can Be Deadly (1997)
- ❏ ❏ 3 - Milwaukee Autumns Can Be Lethal (1998)
- ❏ ❏ . . . .
- ❏ ❏ . . . .

■ BARRETT, Margaret [P] and Charles Dennis

Margaret Barrett is the pseudonym of Manhattan A.D.A. Anne Rudman who teamed with screenwriter and novelist Charles Dennis to write a pair of mysteries featuring Assets & Forfeiture A.D.A. Susan Given, introduced in *Given the Crime* (1998). While engaged in a custody battle with her psychiatrist husband over adopted daughters Polly and Ivy, Given makes the connection between a gangland slaying, a C.I.A. informant and a dead prostitute. As she is fond of saying, "Crime never

sleeps." Calling it great entertainment, *Kirkus* noted "this kickoff barrels along on a gift for witty dialogue that sounds like a top T.V. crime show." Over-worked and overstressed in book 2, Given is up against "enough felonious subplots for an entire season of Lawyer on the Edge." Like her fictional counterpart, Barrett is an assistant district attorney in the Assets & Forfeiture Division, charged with putting forfeited criminal property to work policing the city of New York.

Susan Given...asset forfeiture prosecutor...New York, New York
- ❏ ❏ 1 - Given the Crime (1998)
- ❏ ❏ 2 - Given the Evidence (1998)
- ❏ ❏ . . . .
- ❏ ❏ . . . .

BARRON, Stephanie [P]

Stephanie Barron is the pseudonym of Colorado author and former C.I.A. intelligence analyst Francine (Stephanie) Mathews nee Barron. Majoring in European history at Princeton, she focused on the Napoleonic era, but it was her love of Tolstoy and Jane Austen that prompted Barron to bring them together in a mystery series with Jane-as-detective in Regency England. Telling the story by means of journal entries, book 1 begins at a country manor house party in 1802, shortly after our 27-year-old heroine turns down what may be her last proposal of marriage. "This is Jane Austen for the 1990s," said a *Booklist* reviewer, "complete with a blunt and ardent feminism." Coming next in the popular series are *Jane and the Genius of the Place* (1999) and *Jane and the Stillroom Maid* (2000). A sixth installment is under contract. As Francine Mathews the author also writes the Meredith Folger mysteries set on Nantucket.

Jane Austen...19th century British novelist...Bath, England
- ❏ ❏ 1 - Jane and the Unpleasantness at Scargrave Manor (1996)
- ❏ ❏ 2 - Jane and the Man of the Cloth (1997)
- ❏ ❏ 3 - Jane and the Wandering Eye (1998)
- ❏ ❏ ....
- ❏ ❏ ....

BARTHOLOMEW, Nancy [P]

A practicing psychotherapist with a graduate degree in social work, Nancy Bartholomew is the creator of exotic dancer Sierra Lavotini and her hairless Chihuahua Fluffy, introduced in *The Miracle Strip* (1998). A good Catholic girl from Philadelphia, Sierra is the most popular dancer at The Tiffany Gentlemen's Club in Panama City, Florida, far from the watchful eyes of her fireman father and three-firemen-and-a-cop brothers. Crazy trailer park neighbors, out-of-control bikers, wannabe mobsters and a handsome detective round out the cast of Sierra's debut. While working at a Philadelphia drug clinic, Bartholomew (a rebel preacher's kid herself), once collared rehab clients by beating them in pickup basketball games. With no dancing experience of her own, Bartholomew learned the ropes from Nova Whyte, one of Atlanta's premier dancers. A former country and western singer, Bartholomew launches a second series in early 2000 with *Your Cheatin' Heart*, introducing Greensboro, North Carolina beautician-turned-singer Maggie Reid.

Sierra Lavotini...exotic dancer...Panama City, Florida
- ❏ ❏ 1 - The Miracle Strip (1998)
- ❏ ❏ 2 - Dragstrip (1999)
- ❏ ❏ ....
- ❏ ❏ ....

BEATON, M.C. [P]

M.C. Beaton is the mystery-writing pseudonym of Scotland native Marion Chesney whose Hamish Macbeth series features a village constable in the highlands of Scotland. Now the subject of a BBC television series, the idea for Hamish (HAY-mish) first came to her while learning to fly cast for salmon in Northern Scotland. Her newer series introduces Agatha Raisin who, like the author, lives in a charming Cotswold cottage. Best known as a romance writer, she has written more than 100 novels of historical romance, under her own name and various pseudonyms including Helen Crampton, Ann Fairfax, Jennie Tremaine and Charlotte Ward. Of her Regency novels, one reviewer declared that nobody writes Jane Austen like Marion Chesney. Noted for her historical accuracy and fondness for such period details as clothing, decor, cuisine and manners, it is no surprise that Chesney was once women's fashion editor of *Scottish Field* magazine.

Agatha Raisin...retired London advertising exec...Carsely, England
- ❏ ❏ 1 - Agatha Raisin and the Quiche of Death (1992)
- ❏ ❏ 2 - Agatha Raisin and the Vicious Vet (1993)
- ❏ ❏ 3 - Agatha Raisin and the Potted Gardener (1994)

❑ ❑   4 - Agatha Raisin and the Walkers of Dembley (1995)
❑ ❑   5 - Agatha Raisin and the Murderous Marriage (1996)
❑ ❑   6 - Agatha Raisin and the Terrible Tourist (1997)
❑ ❑   7 - Agatha Raisin and the Wellspring of Death (1998)
❑ ❑   8 - Agatha Raisin and the Wizard of Evesham (1999)
❑ ❑   . . . .
❑ ❑   . . . .

Hamish Macbeth…Scottish police constable…Lochdubh, Scotland
❑ ❑   1 - Death of a Gossip (1985)
❑ ❑   2 - Death of a Cad (1987)
❑ ❑   3 - Death of an Outsider (1988)
❑ ❑   4 - Death of a Perfect Wife (1989)
❑ ❑   5 - Death of a Hussy (1990)
❑ ❑   6 - Death of a Snob (1991)
❑ ❑   7 - Death of a Prankster (1992)
❑ ❑   8 - Death of a Glutton (1993)
❑ ❑   9 - Death of a Travelling Man (1993)
❑ ❑   10 - Death of a Charming Man (1994)
❑ ❑   11 - Death of a Nag (1995)
❑ ❑   12 - Death of a Macho Man (1996)
❑ ❑   13 - Death of a Dentist (1997)
❑ ❑   14 - Death of a Scriptwriter (1998)
❑ ❑   . . . .
❑ ❑   . . . .

■ BEAUFORT, Simon [P]

Simon Beaufort is the joint pseudonym of the already-pseudonymous Susanna Gregory and her husband, Cambridge history lecturer Beau Riffenburgh, for their medieval mysteries featuring Crusader knight, Sir Geoffrey de Mappestone. In the series opener, Geoffrey is sent to Jerusalem by his liege lord to investigate the killings of priests and knights. After 20 years abroad, Geoffrey is ordered home by King Henry I to spy on his own family in book 2. The knight's father and his favorite sister Enide are the first to die. The London-born Gregory, who once worked with the coroner's office, conducts academic research on marine pollution. In addition to her Matthew Bartholomew mysteries as Susanna Gregory, she has written books on medieval castles and cathedrals. The American-born Riffenburgh, whose Cambridge Ph.D. is in imperial history, is currently journal editor for the Scott Polar Research Institute. A former N.F.L. historian, he has written several books and hundreds of articles about football, including *The Official History of Pro Football* (1990).

Geoffrey de Mappestone…brave knight of the Crusades…England
❑ ❑   1 - Murder in the Holy City (1998)
❑ ❑   2 - A Head for Poisoning (1999)
❑ ❑   . . . .
❑ ❑   . . . .

■ BECK, K.K.

Previously the pseudonym of Seattle native Katherine Marris, K.K. Beck is now the legal name of Katherine Beck. With a background in advertising, public relations and trade magazine publishing, she has written more than 15 mysteries, including two continuing series and numerous standalone novels. Introduced in *Death in a Deck Chair* (1984), 1920s Stanford University coed, Iris Cooper, and her wealthy aunt Hermione are on the final leg of their 'round-the-world cruise. Former lounge singer and middle-age widow, Jane da Silva, is first seen in *A Hopeless Case* (1992), where she collects money from her uncle's estate as payment for taking over his work solving crimes for those who can't afford a private investigator. Beck's most recent mysteries are standalones—*We Interrupt this Broadcast* (1997) and *The Revenge of Kali-Ra* (1999). Once a contestant on "Jeopardy," she is married to mystery author Michael Dibdin. They live in Seattle, Washington.

Iris Cooper...1920s Stanford University co-ed...Palo Alto, California
- ❑ ❑ 1 - Death in a Deck Chair (1984)
- ❑ ❑ 2 - Murder in a Mummy Case (1985)
- ❑ ❑ 3 - Peril Under the Palms (1989)
- ❑ ❑ . . . .
- ❑ ❑ . . . .

Jane da Silva...former lounge singer...Seattle, Washington
- ❑ ❑ 1 - A Hopeless Case (1992)
- ❑ ❑ 2 - Amateur Night (1993)
- ❑ ❑ 3 - Electric City (1994)
- ❑ ❑ 4 - Cold Smoked (1995)
- ❑ ❑ . . . .
- ❑ ❑ . . . .

■ BEDFORD, Jean

Widely-anthologized short-story writer Jean Bedford has written three novels featuring private enquiry agent Anna Southwood, first seen in *To Make a Killing* (1990). Later installments include *Worse Than Death* (1992) and *Signs of Murder* (1993). Small and pale, with frizzy red hair, Anna sometimes shares a Sydney office with Toby, her fat, white, green-eyed cat. Born in England, Bedford moved to Australia the following year and after growing up in Victoria, earned degrees from Monash University and the University of Papua New Guinea. A journalist and publisher's editor, she has taught creative writing and English as a second language. Editor of *Moonlight Becomes You* (1996), number 6 in the Crimes for Summer anthologies, Bedford has produced Southwood stories for several of these collections, including *Love Lies Bleeding* (1994), number 5 in the series. Married to mystery author Peter Corris, she divides her time between Sydney and Australia's Illawarra Coast.

Anna Southwood...private enquiry agent...Sydney, Australia
- ❑ ❑ 1 - To Make a Killing (1990)
- ❑ ❑ 2 - Worse Than Death (1992)
- ❑ ❑ 3 - Signs of Murder (1993)
- ❑ ❑ . . . .
- ❑ ❑ . . . .

■ BEECHAM, Rose [P]

Rose Beecham is the creator of an ex-New York City lesbian cop turned Detective Inspector in New Zealand, first seen in *Introducing Amanda Valentine* (1992). In book 2, the D.I. has just returned from a one-year leave of absence in New York and is looking forward to life in the slow lane Down Under. Unfortunately, she's just in time for the year's most sensational homicide involving the daughter of the former ambassador to the United States. While a voracious media fuels the scandal, the dead woman's powerful family fights to cover up the facts in the case. In book 3, the son of a Baptist preacher is murdered in Wellington. This less than angelic former choir boy was president of Melbourne-based Spectrum Television, a gay and lesbian broadcasting firm. When the investigation leads Amanda to Australia she is strongly attracted to her designated police contact, Det. Sgt. Mary Devine.

Amanda Valentine...lesbian detective inspector...Wellington, New Zealand
- ❑ ❑ 1 - Introducing Amanda Valentine (1992)
- ❑ ❑ - APA-The Garbage Dump Murders
- ❑ ❑ 2 - Second Guess (1994)
- ❑ ❑ 3 - Fair Play (1995)
- ❑ ❑ . . . .
- ❑ ❑ . . . .

■ BELFORT, Sophie [P]

Sophie Belfort is the pseudonym of historian Kate Auspitz, creator of a Boston mystery series featuring Molly Rafferty, professor of Renaissance and Reformation history, and her love interest, homicide detective Nick Hannibal. Introduced in *The Lace Curtain Murders* (1986), Molly makes her third appearance in

Eyewitness to Murder (1992) which takes her to an academic conference in Krakow, Poland. World renowned scholar Caleb Tuttle, once Molly's mentor, is poisoned after urging that a local priest be extradited to the now-independent Ukraine and tried for war crimes. Professor Tuttle was eyewitness to an act of genocide involving the priest during the Second World War. No surprise that Molly suspects foul play when Tuttle dies shortly after incriminating film footage of the priest's involvement is recovered from Eastern Europe. "Worth reading for its unusual plot and setting" as well as "literate style, au courant politics and flashes of wit," said *Kirkus Reviews*.

Molly Rafferty...college history professor...Boston, Massachusetts
- ❏ ❏   1 - The Lace Curtain Murders (1986)
- ❏ ❏   2 - The Marvell College Murders (1991)
- ❏ ❏   3 - Eyewitness to Murder (1992)
- ❏ ❏   ....
- ❏ ❏   ....

■ BELL, Nancy

Agatha nominee Nancy Bell is the creator of "deliciously funny" Texas grandmother Biggie Weatherford, the richest woman in Job's Crossing. When *People* magazine picked Biggie's first case as a Page-Turner of Week, she was hailed as "an eccentric of Lone Star proportions." Series regulars include 10-year-old grandson J.R., who acts as narrator, and housekeeper Willie Mae, a Cajun voodoo woman, and the best cook in Texas, whose recipe for gumbo is included in book 1. *Booklist* called it "St. Mary Mead seasoned with Maggody and given a Texas accent." Food plays a big part in this series, especially in book 3 where the opening of an all-chicken restaurant finds one of its 300-pound owners dead under the kitchen table, covered in gravy and garnished with parsley. A native of East Texas, Bell lives in Austin where she is housemother to the sorority sisters of Alpha Chi Omega at the University of Texas.

Biggie Weatherford & J.R....grandmother & nephew sidekick...Job's Crossing, Texas
- ❏ ❏   1 - **Biggie and the Poisoned Politician (1996) Agatha nominee** ☆
- ❏ ❏   2 - Biggie and the Mangled Mortician (1997)
- ❏ ❏   3 - Biggie and the Fricasseed Fat Man (1998)
- ❏ ❏   ....
- ❏ ❏   ....

■ BELL, Pauline

Former school teacher and mother-of-a-constable Pauline Bell has written eight Yorkshire police mysteries featuring D.C.I. Thomas Browne, Sergeant Jerry Hunter and D.C. Benedict "Benny" Mitchell. The brash, young Mitchell is frequently at odds with his disapproving sergeant, starting with *The Dead Do Not Praise* (1990). While engaged in the murder investigation of an unpopular headmistress at a school he once attended, Benny still has time to set his sights on the D.C.I.'s daughter Virginia. Their developing relationship is a running thread in these mysteries and they become engaged in book 2. Virginia is away at Oxford in book 3 and Benny becomes involved with a special constable who ends up one of the victims when a serial killer starts eliminating sopranos during the choral society's Christmas concert preparations. It's a drama teacher who's found dead in book 5, during a school production of "A Midsummer Night's Dream."

Benny Mitchell...brash detective constable...Cloughton, Yorkshire, England
- ❏ ❏   1 - The Dead Do Not Praise (1990)
- ❏ ❏   2 - Feast into Mourning (1991)
- ❏ ❏   3 - No Pleasure in Death (1992)
- ❏ ❏   4 - The Way of a Serpent (1993)
- ❏ ❏   5 - Downhill to Death (1994)
- ❏ ❏   6 - Sleeping Partners (1995)
- ❏ ❏   7 - A Multitude of Sins (1997)
- ❏ ❏   8 - Blood Ties (1998)
- ❏ ❏   ....
- ❏ ❏   ....

■ BENJAMIN, Carole Lea

Award-winning author of eight books about dog behavior and training, Carol Lea Benjamin is a former detective who puts her knowledge and experience to use writing mysteries about private investigator Rachel Alexander and her pitbull sidekick, Dashiell. Introduced in the Shamus award-winning *This Dog for Hire* (1996), former dog trainer Rachel is hired to find the killer of a champion Basenji's owner. They sort out the apparent suicide of her cousin in book 2, with only an Akita witness to the young woman's fall from the window of a t'ai chi dojo. In book 3, the twosome is hired to provide security for a dog-training conference. Benjamin's well-respected training manuals include *Mother Knows Best, The Natural Way to Train Your Dog* (1985), used successfully by mystery author Harlan Coben with his Bearded Collie, Chloe. Along with two very smart and well-behaved dogs, Benjamin and her husband live in New York's Greenwich Village.

Rachel Alexander & Dash...dog trainer turned P.I. & pitbull sidekick...New York, New York

- ❏ ❏   1 - **This Dog for Hire (1996) Shamus winner ★**
- ❏ ❏   2 - The Dog Who Knew Too Much (1997)
- ❏ ❏   3 - A Hell of a Dog (1998)
- ❏ ❏   . . . .
- ❏ ❏   . . . .

■ BENKE, Patricia D.

California Appeals Court judge Patricia D. Benke brings more than 20 years of criminal law experience to her legal mysteries featuring San Diego chief assistant district attorney Judith Thornton, introduced in *Guilty by Choice* (1995). The first woman to hold this position, 37-year-old Judith is up against an ambitious defense attorney whose child-killer client will go free unless she can convince a traumatized witness to testify. This single-mother prosecutor is expected to make her fourth paperback appearance in *Cruel Justice* (1999). Before her appointment to the appellate court, Benke served as deputy attorney general for the State of California and judge in both municipal and superior court in San Diego. A graduate of San Diego State and the University of San Diego School of Law, Benke teaches criminal law at Western State University and writes frequently for law journals and the media. She lives in San Diego, California.

Judith Thornton...chief assistant district attorney...San Diego, California

- ❏ ❏   1 - Guilty By Choice (1995)
- ❏ ❏   2 - False Witness (1996)
- ❏ ❏   3 - Above the Law (1997)
- ❏ ❏   . . . .
- ❏ ❏   . . . .

■ BENNETT, Liza

Liza Bennett is the author of two paperback mysteries featuring Peg Goodenough, creative director at Peabody & Quinlan, a Madison Avenue advertising agency. Daughter of an acclaimed abstract expressionist painter, Peg attended art schools all over the world, but much to her mother's dismay, chose graphic design over a painting career. In *Madison Avenue Murder* (1989), she juggles a fried chicken photo shoot, while her boss gets carved up in Soho, literally. In *Seventh Avenue Murder* (1990), the head of a women's clothing manufacturer hangs herself with pantyhose material from a new hosiery line and N.Y.P.D. homicide detective Dante Cursio is not happy to hear Peg thinks it's murder. The detective's got his hands full with the arrival of his eight-year-old daughter visiting from England, and Peg's getting more advice than she needs from a 79-year-old psychic neighbor.

Peg Goodenough...ad agency creative director...New York, New York

- ❏ ❏   1 - Madison Avenue Murder (1989)
- ❏ ❏   2 - Seventh Avenue Murder (1990)
- ❏ ❏   . . . .
- ❏ ❏   . . . .

■ BERENSON, Laurien

Laurien Berenson writes mysteries using the dog show world as a backdrop for the sleuthing activities of Melanie Travis, special education teacher, dog lover and single mother of five-year-old Davey. In the series opener, Uncle Max dies unexpectedly while working in his breeding kennel, and Melanie's Aunt Peg decides they should investigate. She also wants to know what happened to Max's missing champion poodle. Author of 18 books, including two romance novels written as Laurien Blair, young adult and

mystery fiction, Berenson has more than 20 years' experience as a dog breeder and exhibitor. While her mother bred and showed dogs, her grandmother was a dog show judge. Berenson currently owns six miniature poodles who are three generations of the same family. Her nonfiction work has appeared in a variety of magazines and *The New York Times*. Formerly a resident of New Canaan, Connecticut, she now lives in Atlanta, Georgia.

Melanie Travis...special ed teacher and dog lover...Connecticut
- ❑ ❑ 1 - A Pedigree To Die For (1995)
- ❑ ❑ 2 - Underdog (1996)
- ❑ ❑ 3 - Dog Eat Dog (1996)
- ❑ ❑ 4 - Hair of the Dog (1997)
- ❑ ❑ 5 - Watchdog (1998)
- ❑ ❑ 6 - Hush Puppy (1999)
- ❑ ❑ . . . .
- ❑ ❑ . . . .

■ BERNE, Karin [P]

Karin Berne is the joint pseudonym of Sue Bernell and Michaela Karni, Albuquerque, New Mexico authors of Victorian romance novels, magazine features, television scripts and screenplays. During the mid-'80s they wrote three paperback mysteries featuring 38-year-old, newly-divorced Ellie Gordon, office manager for an Orange County, California law firm. First seen in *Bare Acquaintances* (1985), Ellie was lauded as "literate and bright as Kate Fansler, witty (and sexy)," by New Mexico's own Tony Hillerman. In book 2, Ellie puts

her sleuthing smarts and smart mouth to work when one of her best friends, public relations executive at a controversial nuclear power plant, is suspected in the death of her handsome, male chauvinist boss. It seems his death by electrocution was wired into a tangle of office intrigue and sexual politics. Writing together as Diana Burke, Bernell and Karni also wrote *The Heart of the Matter* (1980) and *The Impoverished Heiress* (1981).

Ellie Gordon...law firm office manager...Orange County, California
- ❑ ❑ 1 - Bare Acquaintances (1985)
- ❑ ❑ 2 - Shock Value (1985)
- ❑ ❑ 3 - False Impressions (1986)
- ❑ ❑ . . . .
- ❑ ❑ . . . .

■ BERRY, Carole

Carole Berry's fictional sleuth is a Manhattan office temp with a love for tap dancing. Each of Bonnie Indermill's work assignments provides a new supporting cast, including her eighth adventure, *Death of a Downsizer* (1999), where Bonnie foolishly looks for job security. *The Death of a Dancing Fool* (1996) finds her back on the dance floor with old friend turned club owner, "Fast Eddie" Fong. Although newly-engaged and contemplating life in the suburbs, Bonnie can't

resist an invitation to return to the Manhattan club scene. One wild night later, she's investigating a celebrity death and answering questions from the police. Like her fictional sleuth, Berry has had a number of jobs—waitress, teacher, publisher's assistant, office manager, sales clerk and temporary typist. But unlike her heroine, she has been employed for many years by the same New York City law firm where she works as a legal secretary.

Bonnie Indermill...tap-dancing Manhattan office temp...New York, New York
- ❑ ❑ 1 - The Letter of the Law (1987)
- ❑ ❑ 2 - The Year of the Monkey (1988)

❑ ❑   3 - Good Night, Sweet Prince (1990)
❑ ❑   4 - Island Girl (1991)
❑ ❑   5 - The Death of a Difficult Woman (1994)
❑ ❑   6 - The Death of a Dancing Fool (1996)
❑ ❑   7 - Death of a Dimpled Darling (1997)
❑ ❑   . . . .
❑ ❑   . . . .

■ BISHOP, Claudia [P]

Claudia Bishop is the pseudonym of Mary Stanton, for her bed and breakfast series featuring sisters Sarah and Meg Quilliam. While Sarah serves as manager of the Hemlock Falls Inn, Meg toils as the establishment's chef. After growing up in Hawaii and Japan, Stanton started her writing career with nonfiction articles for national magazines. After the sale of her process assessment business in 1994, she started writing fiction full-time. A former singer, actor, insurance claims adjuster and advertising copywriter, she also writes young adult fantasy, including scripts for the television series *Princess Gwenevere and the Jewel Riders*. Under the name Anne Craig, she wrote a hardboiled suspense novel. In addition to her adult mysteries as Bishop, she currently writes young adult science fiction mysteries, including *My Aunt the Monster* (1997) and *Next Door to a Witch* (1997). She divides her time between Upstate New York and South Florida.

Sarah & Meg Quilliam...inn owner & chef sisters...Hemlock Falls, New York

❑ ❑   1 - A Taste for Murder (1994)
❑ ❑   2 - A Dash of Death (1995)
❑ ❑   3 - A Pinch of Poison (1995)
❑ ❑   4 - Murder Well-Done (1996)
❑ ❑   5 - Death Dines Out (1997)
❑ ❑   6 - A Touch of the Grape (1998)
❑ ❑   . . . .
❑ ❑   . . . .

■ BLACK, Cara

Inveterate traveler and adventurer Cara Black once lived in Paris, the setting for her debut mystery featuring 30-something French-American investigator Aimée Leduc (em-MAY luh-DEW), owner of the detective agency founded by her grandfather, a former Suréte inspector. Leduc's offices are located on the rue du Louvre and she lives in an inherited 17th century apartment on Ile. St. Louis. Her partner, Rene Friant, is a genius computer hacker and a dwarf. Their first case involves a 50-year-old encrypted photograph and an old Jewish woman whose body is found with a swastika carved in her forehead. Black has spent time in Japan, hitched across Europe, and ridden a motorcycle (purchased in Sicily after one lesson in Italian) from Tunisia to Morocco. After selling her blood in Kuwait (for the fare), she hopped a freighter to Bombay and once cleaned newspaper offices in Basel, Switzerland. Currently she lives with her family in San Francisco.

Aimée Leduc...French-American private eye...Paris, France

❑ ❑   1 - Murder in the Marais (1999)
❑ ❑   2 - Murder in the Chabris (2000)
❑ ❑   . . . .
❑ ❑   . . . .

■ BLACK, Veronica [P]

Veronica Black is a pseudonym of English romance writer Maureen Peters for her ten-book mystery series featuring British investigative nun, Sister Joan, first seen in *Vow of Silence* (1990). From her home base at the Convent of the Daughters of Compassion, high in the Cornish Moors, Sister Joan is frequently joined on her detecting adventures by Brother Cuthbert and Detective Sergeant Mill. A founding member of the Romantic Novelists Association, Peters has written more than 60 novels under a variety of pseudonyms, including Catherine Darby, Judith Rothman, Sharon Whitby and Veronica Black. Her first published novel, *Elizabeth the Beloved*, appeared under her own name in 1965. A former teacher of English to retarded children, Peters includes among her interests theatre, the Tudor period and hagiography. Born in North Wales where she graduated from University College,

the author says she writes everything in longhand, often working eight to ten hours a day.

Sister Joan...British investigative nun...Cornwall, England

❑ ❑   1 - A Vow of Silence (1990)
❑ ❑   2 - A Vow of Chastity (1992)
❑ ❑   3 - A Vow of Sanctity (1993)
❑ ❑   4 - A Vow of Obedience (1993)
❑ ❑   5 - A Vow of Penance (1994)
❑ ❑   6 - A Vow of Devotion (1994)
❑ ❑   7 - A Vow of Fidelity (1995)
❑ ❑   8 - A Vow of Poverty (1996)
❑ ❑   9 - A Vow of Adoration (1997)
❑ ❑ 10 - A Vow of Compassion (1998)
❑ ❑ . . . .
❑ ❑ . . . .

■ BLANC, Suzanne

Suzanne Blanc won the 1962 Edgar for best first novel with *The Green Stone*, which introduced Inspector Miguel Menendez of Mexico's San Luis Potosi police. The green stone of the title is an emerald that changes the lives of all who possess it. An educated Indian who speaks four languages, Menendez is an anomaly in both time and place, notes Nina King in her *Crimes of the Scene* (1997). He has a "machine-like brain and the face of a grim Aztec idol." The inspector has a

daughter he adores, but an unhappy marriage to a devoutly religious wife whose mother disliked him from the start. Two subsequent novels complete the series—*The Yellow Villa* (1964) and *The Rose Window* (1967)—both featuring American women tourists as central characters, similar to the series opener. A later standalone novel, *The Sea Troll* (1969), is set aboard a passenger-cargo ship sailing the Pacific.

Miguel Menendez...Aztec police inspector...San Luis Potosi, Mexico

❑ ❑ 1 - **The Green Stone (1961) Edgar winner ★**
❑ ❑ 2 - The Yellow Villa (1964)
❑ ❑ 3 - The Rose Window (1967)
❑ ❑ . . . .
❑ ❑ . . . .

■ BLAND, Eleanor Taylor

Eleanor Taylor Bland is the creator of mystery fiction's first black woman homicide detective, Marti MacAlister. A former Chicago cop and widowed mother of two, Marti moves 60 miles out of the city to join the suburban Lincoln Prairie police force after the death of her husband. In book 6, she and her partner Vik immediately suspect foul play when a young woman's body is found along the rocky Lake Michigan shore. With no strong evidence to implicate

the dead woman's drug-dealing boyfriend, they pursue other leads while a killer from Marti's past threatens to reappear. Bland has managed to produce a book each year since the series was introduced in 1992, despite working nine-to-five as an auditor. She says it works because Marti is always several chapters ahead of her. A native of Boston, Bland lives in Waukegan, Illinois where she is an active supporter of numerous civic and social programs.

Marti MacAlister...widowed black police detective...Lincoln Prairie, Illinios

❑ ❑ 1 - Dead Time (1992)
❑ ❑ 2 - Slow Burn (1993)
❑ ❑ 3 - Gone Quiet (1994)
❑ ❑ 4 - Done Wrong (1995)
❑ ❑ 5 - Keep Still (1996)
❑ ❑ 6 - See No Evil (1998)
❑ ❑ 7 - Tell No Tales (1999)
❑ ❑ . . . .
❑ ❑ . . . .

■ BLOCK, Barbara

Barbara Block writes an animal mystery series featuring the recently-widowed owner of a Syracuse, New York pet shop known as Noah's Ark. Introduced in *Chutes and Adders*, Robin Light is a soft-hearted, tough-minded amateur sleuth who can't seem to stay out of trouble. With *The Scent of Murder* (1997), *Booklist* selected her as one of its Top Five Lesser-Known Female Sleuths. A blue-haired gothic teenager wants to board her albino ferret, Mr. Bones, and before Robin

knows it, she's drawn into the underworld of runaways, addicts and strippers. An ex-Manhattanite whose pets have included a number of reptiles and other exotic wildlife, Block lives in Syracuse. In addition to her mysteries, she has written how-to books for six major job markets—*How to Be Happily Employed in Boston (Dallas-Fort Worth, Phoenix, St. Louis, San Francisco, Washington, D.C.), Step-by-Step Guide(s) to Finding the Job that is Right for You.*

Robin Light...pet store owner...Syracuse, New York

  ❑ ❑ 1 - Chutes and Adders (1994)
  ❑ ❑ 2 - Twister (1994)
  ❑ ❑ 3 - In Plain Sight (1996)
  ❑ ❑ 4 - The Scent of Murder (1997)
  ❑ ❑ 5 - Vanishing Act (1998)
  ❑ ❑ . . . .
  ❑ ❑ . . . .

■ BOLITHO, Janie

British author Janie Bolitho (bo-LITH-o) has written eight mysteries featuring D.C.I. Ian Roper in the quiet fictional village of Rickenham Green. First seen in *Kindness Can Kill* (1993), Roper is an intelligent man, well-liked and respected by his team. He is happily married with two grown children. Bolitho's newer series introduces recently-widowed Rose Trevelyan, soon to make her third appearance in *Crushed in Cornwall* (1999). An attractive woman in her late 40s,

Rose is both a painter and photographer. Although her work as an artist does not directly solve crimes, her powers of observation and knowledge of art are key to the investigations. While she has a relationship with local D.I. Jack Pearce in the series opener, she meets a mysterious artist in *Framed in Cornwall* (1998). Bolitho makes her home in the Cornish countryside, where she plans to write a new book each year for both her series.

Ian Roper...detective chief inspector...Rickenham Green, England

  ❑ ❑ 1 - Kindness Can Kill (1993)
  ❑ ❑ 2 - Ripe for Revenge (1994)
  ❑ ❑ 3 - Motive for Murder (1994)
  ❑ ❑ 4 - Dangerous Deceit (1995)
  ❑ ❑ 5 - Finger of Fate (1996)
  ❑ ❑ 6 - Sequence of Shame (1996)
  ❑ ❑ 7 - Absence of Angels (1997)
  ❑ ❑ 8 - Exposure of Evil (1998)
  ❑ ❑ . . . .
  ❑ ❑ . . . .

Rose Trevelyan...widowed painter and photographer...Cornwall, England

  ❑ ❑ 1 - Snapped in Cornwall (1997)
  ❑ ❑ 2 - Framed in Cornwall (1998)
  ❑ ❑ . . . .
  ❑ ❑ . . . .

■ BORTHWICK, J.S. [P]

J.S. Borthwick is the pseudonym of Joan Scott Creighton from Thomaston, Maine, creator of series pair Sarah Deane and Alex McKenzie—Boston graduate student in English literature and bird-watching Boston physician. Their adventures begin in

Texas with the death of Sarah's boyfriend, but they return to home ground after successfully solving their first case. Later in the series, the pair marries and Sarah becomes a professor. In book 8, *The Garden Plot* (1997), Sarah heads to Europe at the invitation of her

her Aunt Julia, to join a garden tour lead by an old friend. When the tour leader turns up dead before the group boards their plane, husband Alex stays home to investigate while Sarah stays with the very strange tour group. Borthwick describes herself as the "old lady of Medium Egg Cozies—yolk runny, white firm." The *Rockland Courier-Gazette* called her "more than a barrel of clams at high tide."

Sarah Deane & Alex McKenzie...English professor & internist...Boston, Massachusetts
- ❑ ❑ 1 - The Case of the Hook-Billed Kites (1982)
- ❑ ❑ 2 - The Down East Murders (1985)
- ❑ ❑ 3 - The Student Body (1986)
- ❑ ❑ 4 - Bodies of Water (1990)
- ❑ ❑ 5 - Dude on Arrival (1992)
- ❑ ❑ 6 - The Bridled Groom (1994)
- ❑ ❑ 7 - Dolly Is Dead (1995)
- ❑ ❑ 8 - The Garden Plot (1997)
- ❑ ❑ 9 - My Body Lies Over the Ocean (1999)
- ❑ ❑ . . . .
- ❑ ❑ . . . .

■ BORTON, D.B. [P]

D.B. Borton is the pseudonym of Ohio Wesleyan English professor Dr. Lynette Carpenter, creator of Cincinnati private-eye-in-training Cat Caliban, introduced in *One for the Money* (1993). After 38 years of marriage, Cat buys an apartment building and starts work on her investigator's license. Along the way she manages to demolish all the stereotypes about mothers and women of a certain age. In 1999, writing as Della Borton, Carpenter launched a new series featuring small-town movie theatre owner Gilda Liberty and her large, eccentric, movie-mad family, first seen in *Fade to Black*. Carpenter teaches American literature, film, composition and women's studies and has written film and literary criticism for academic journals. A native of Houston, she earned a B.A. at the University of Texas and M.A. and Ph.D. degrees from Indiana University. Her familiarity with Cincinnati is a result of having taught at the University of Cincinnati during the early '80s.

Cat Caliban...60-something P.I.-in-training...Cincinnati, Ohio
- ❑ ❑ 1 - One for the Money (1993)
- ❑ ❑ 2 - Two Points for Murder (1993)
- ❑ ❑ 3 - Three Is a Crowd (1994)
- ❑ ❑ 4 - Four Elements of Murder (1995)
- ❑ ❑ 5 - Five Alarm Fire (1996)
- ❑ ❑ 6 - Six Feet Under (1997)
- ❑ ❑ . . . .
- ❑ ❑ . . . .

Gilda Liberty...small-town movie theater proprietor...Eden, Ohio
- ❑ ❑ 1 - Fade to Black [as Della Borton] (1999)
- ❑ ❑ . . . .
- ❑ ❑ . . . .

■ BOWEN, Gail

Ellis award winner Gail Bowen is the creator of Canadian political science professor, Joanne Kilbourn, introduced in *Deadly Appearances* (1990) as the widow of a cabinet minister. In addition to her teaching, the professor works as a T.V. political commentator and actively participates in provincial politics. A series of two-hour television movies starring Kate Nelligan is scheduled to start filming in late 1998 with book 1. In the T.V. scripts, Kilbourn will teach criminal justice, rather than political science. Book 4 in this series, *A Colder Kind of Death* (1994) won the Ellis Award for best novel from the Crime Writers of Canada. After earning her M.A. at the University of Waterloo, Bowen headed West, where she is currently assistant professor of English at the Saskatchewan Indian Federated College of the University of Regina. A native of Toronto and mother of three, she has taught Anglican church school for 25 years.

Joanne Kilbourn...political science professor...Regina, Saskatchewan, Canada

- ❑ ❑ 1 - Deadly Appearances (1990)
- ❑ ❑ 2 - Love and Murder (1991)
- ❑ ❑   - APA-Murder at the Mendel
- ❑ ❑ 3 - The Wandering Soul Murders (1993)
- ❑ ❑ 4 - **A Colder Kind of Death (1994) Ellis winner ★**
- ❑ ❑ 5 - A Killing Spring (1996)
- ❑ ❑ 6 - A Verdict in Blood (1998)
- ❑ ❑ . . . .
- ❑ ❑ . . . .

■ BOWEN, Rhys [P]

Rhys (Rees) Bowen spent childhood summers in a Welsh village much like the setting for her mysteries featuring appealing young constable Evan Evans, introduced in *Evans Above* (1997). Nestled among the Snowdonia mountains of North Wales, Llanfair boasts two competitive ministers, one lascivious barmaid and three other Evans—Evans-the-Meat, Evans-the-Milk and Evans-the-Post. "Evan Evans is like a nice nutbrown ale," said Black Bird Mysteries, "good flavor, great color and a humorous taste." After writing almost 100 books under her own name (Janet Quin-Harkin), primarily for children and young adults, Bowen chose her Welsh grandfather's name as a pseudonym. Born in Bath and educated in England, Austria and Germany, she went to work after college for the B.B.C., where she found her niche in the drama department. While working for Australian broadcasting in Sydney, she met her Englishman husband. They've lived in Marin County, California for more than 20 years.

Evan Evans...village constable...Llanfair, N Wales

- ❑ ❑ 1 - Evans Above (1997)
- ❑ ❑ 2 - Evan Help Us (1998)
- ❑ ❑ 3 - Evanly Choirs (1999)
- ❑ ❑ . . . .
- ❑ ❑ . . . .

■ BOWERS, Elisabeth

Canadian author Elisabeth Bowers has written a pair of mysteries set in Vancouver, British Columbia, featuring private eye Meg Lacey, who runs her own investigations service. Meg's college-age son lives at home with his divorced mother, while an older daughter is now on her own. The series opener, *Ladies' Night* (1988), is followed by *No Forwarding Address* (1991) where Meg takes a missing persons case that turns into domestic and child abuse and later double murder. A *Kirkus* reviewer praised "the exquisitely delineated scenes between Meg and her college-age son, in the throes of his first love affair, and her career-minded daughter, a new convert to feminism." According to *Canadian Crime Fiction* (1996), Bowers turned to writing full-time, after a varied career. Born and raised in Vancouver, she lives with her family on the Gulf Islands off the west coast of British Columbia.

Meg Lacey...single mother private eye...Vancouver, British Columbia, Canada

- ❑ ❑ 1 - Ladies' Night (1988)
- ❑ ❑ 2 - No Forwarding Address (1991)
- ❑ ❑ . . . .
- ❑ ❑ . . . .

■ BOYLAN, Eleanor

Eleanor Boylan is the creator of the Agatha-nominated Clara Gamadge series featuring a character who first appeared as the wife of Henry Gamadge, a New York bibliophile created by Boylan's aunt, Elizabeth Daly, said to be the favorite American writer of Agatha Christie. By 1989 when Boylan's series begins, Clara has become Henry's widow. The family adventures continue, but this time around, Clara's the one doing the detecting. Her widowed cousin Charlie Saddlier (Sadd for short), is a real stickler for correct grammar and precise English whenever providing his able assistance. Her two adult children, son Henry Junior and daughter Paula, their respective spouses and Clara's three grandchildren are also featured. A bonus of this series is that they all like each other and play genuine supporting roles. Boylan is a New York native who lives on Anna Maria Island in Florida where she also writes short stories for mystery magazines.

Clara Gamadge...widow of Henry the forgery expert...New York, New York

- ❏ ❏ 1 - **Working Murder (1989) Agatha nominee** ☆
- ❏ ❏ 2 - Murder Observed (1990)
- ❏ ❏ 3 - Murder Machree (1992)
- ❏ ❏ 4 - Pushing Murder (1993)
- ❏ ❏ 5 - Murder Crossed (1996)
- ❏ ❏ ....
- ❏ ❏ ....

■ BRAUN, Lilian Jackson

Former *Detroit Free Press* feature writer Lilian Jackson Braun is widely acknowledged as originator of the current cat craze in mysteries with her Cat Who series. Newspaper columnist Jim Qwilleran and his Siamese cats Koko and Yum Yum have been sleuthing in fictional Pickax City for more than 30 years and Michigan fans have long claimed Moose County as part of that state's Upper Peninsula. The first three books appeared in the late '60s, but almost 20 years passed before Braun revived the series with her Edgar-nominated *The Cat Who Saw Red* (1986). The following year *The Cat Who Played Brahms* (1987) was nominated for an Anthony award. Along with Siamese cats Koko III and Pitti Sing, Braun and husband currently live in North Carolina, where local residents have included such famous retirees as poet Carl Sandburg and television icon Buffalo Bob and his pal Howdy Doody.

Jim Qwilleran, Koko & Yum Yum...ex-police reporter & cats...Upper Peninsula, Michigan

- ❏ ❏ 1 - The Cat Who Could Read Backwards (1966)
- ❏ ❏ 2 - The Cat Who Ate Danish Modern (1967)
- ❏ ❏ 3 - The Cat Who Turned On and Off (1968)
- ❏ ❏ 4 - **The Cat Who Saw Red (1986) Edgar nominee** ☆
- ❏ ❏ 5 - **The Cat Who Played Brahms (1987) Anthony nominee** ☆
- ❏ ❏ 6 - The Cat Who Played Post Office (1987)
- ❏ ❏ 7 - The Cat Who Knew Shakespeare (1988)
- ❏ ❏ 8 - The Cat Who Sniffed Glue (1988)
- ❏ ❏ 9 - The Cat Who Went Underground (1989)
- ❏ ❏ 10 - The Cat Who Talked to Ghosts (1990)
- ❏ ❏ 11 - The Cat Who Lived High (1990)
- ❏ ❏ 12 - The Cat Who Knew a Cardinal (1991)
- ❏ ❏ 13 - The Cat Who Moved a Mountain (1992)
- ❏ ❏ 14 - The Cat Who Wasn't There (1993)
- ❏ ❏ 15 - The Cat Who Came to Breakfast (1994)
- ❏ ❏ 16 - The Cat Who Went into the Closet (1994)
- ❏ ❏ 17 - The Cat Who Blew the Whistle (1995)
- ❏ ❏ 18 - The Cat Who Said Cheese (1996)
- ❏ ❏ 19 - The Cat Who Tailed a Thief (1997)
- ❏ ❏ 20 - The Cat Who Sang for the Birds (1998)
- ❏ ❏ 21 - The Cat Who Saw Stars (1999)
- ❏ ❏ ....
- ❏ ❏ ....

■ BRENNAN, Carol

Public relations consultant Carol Brennan spent two years selling luxury Manhattan real estate before writing her second mystery featuring PR consultant Liz Wareham. After finding her client skewered to his desk with a Chinese dagger in *Headhunt* (1991), Liz enters the high-end real estate world in *Full Commission* (1992). She is hired by the Rooney Property Company to provide damage control when a prankster with an odd sense of humor starts playing lethal tricks on people who have nothing in common except that they're trying to sell their Manhattan apartments. Brennan's second series features 29-year-old actress Emily Silver, whose parents died in an alleged murder-suicide when she was nine. While working to uncover new evidence in the case, Emily's boyfriend is killed and she is left to search on her own. Brennan, who lives in Dutchess County, New York, has also worked as a speech therapist, a spokesperson and an actress.

Emily Silver...New York actress...New York, New York

❑ ❑ 1 - In the Dark (1994)
❑ ❑ 2 - Chill of Summer (1995)
❑ ❑ . . . .
❑ ❑ . . . .

Liz Wareham...40-ish public relations consultant...New York, New York

❑ ❑ 1 - Headhunt (1991)
❑ ❑ 2 - Full Commission (1992)
❑ ❑ . . . .
❑ ❑ . . . .

■ BRIGHTWELL, Emily [P]

Emily Brightwell is the pseudonymous author of a mystery series featuring Victorian Scotland Yard Inspector Gerald Witherspoon and his sleuthing housekeeper, Mrs. Hepzibah Jeffries. The supporting staff at Upper Edmonton Gardens includes Smythe, the burly, kind-hearted coachman; Mrs. Goodge, the gray-headed, bespectacled cook; Betsy, the pretty blonde maid, and Wiggins, the 19-year-old, blue-eyed footman. Plump and kindly Mrs. Jeffries, auburn-haired but gray at the temples, has been called "the Miss Marple of Victorian mysteries." Although Inspector Witherspoon has not an inkling, the staff is quite certain their beloved inspector would still be a clerk in the records room, if it weren't for their snooping skills. Although not born to wealth, the inspector acquired a fortune and his huge house upon the death of Aunt Euphemia. The 13-book paperback series was originated by The Berkley Publishing Group which owns the copyrights, but Southern Californian Cheryl Arguile is the sole author.

Insp. Witherspoon & Mrs. Jeffries...Victorian inspector & his housekeeper...London, England

❑ ❑ 1 - The Inspector and Mrs. Jeffries (1993)
❑ ❑ 2 - Mrs. Jeffries Dusts for Clues (1993)
❑ ❑ 3 - The Ghost and Mrs. Jeffries (1993)
❑ ❑ 4 - Mrs. Jeffries Takes Stock (1994)
❑ ❑ 5 - Mrs. Jeffries on the Ball (1994)
❑ ❑ 6 - Mrs. Jeffries on the Trail (1995)
❑ ❑ 7 - Mrs. Jeffries Plays the Cook (1995)
❑ ❑ 8 - Mrs. Jeffries and the Missing Alibi (1996)
❑ ❑ 9 - Mrs. Jeffries Stands Corrected (1996)
❑ ❑ 10 - Mrs. Jeffries Takes the Stage (1997)
❑ ❑ 11 - Mrs. Jeffries Questions the Answer (1997)
❑ ❑ 12 - Mrs. Jeffries Reveals Her Art (1998)
❑ ❑ 13 - Mrs. Jeffries Takes the Cake (1998)
❑ ❑ . . . .
❑ ❑ . . . .

■ BRILL, Toni [P]

Toni Brill is the pseudonym of husband-and-wife writing team Anthony and Martha Olcott, authors of a pair of very funny mysteries featuring children's author and former college Russian teacher, Midge Cohen. Five-foot four-inch Midge, the tallest Cohen woman ever born, is the only daughter of quintessential Jewish mother, Pearl. Lucky Midge lives in a three-room Brooklyn apartment inherited from her Aunt Dora, whose bequest also included a plug-in fireplace, a collection of ceramic shepherdesses and $120,000.

In *Date with a Dead Doctor* (1991), a gangly, balding urologist needs some Russian letters translated, but Midge just wants to get back to Tammy and Tanesia, the clever Girl Scout heroines of her Camp Poncatoncas mysteries. When Dr. Leon Skripnik is found dead the following day, Pearl drags her daughter to the funeral and she is still scouting marriage prospects for Midge in *Date with a Plummeting Publisher* (1993).

Midge Cohen...children's author fluent in Russian...Brooklyn, New York

❑ ❑ 1 - Date With a Dead Doctor (1991)
❑ ❑ 2 - Date With a Plummeting Publisher (1993)
❑ ❑ . . . .
❑ ❑ . . . .

■ BROD, D.C.

Illinois author D.C. Brod is Deborah Cobban Brod, creator of the Quint McCauley series set in the western suburbs of Chicago. Described as a medium-boiled private eye, the ex-big city cop first appeared in the 1989 short story, "The Night the Lights Went Out at the Tattersall Tavern," published in *Alfred Hitchcock's Mystery Magazine.* McCauley starts the four-book series as a department store security chief and turns to private work in book 2, *Error in Judgment*

(1990). Thanks to her good fortune to marry a patron of the arts, Brod says she is free to write full-time. She has completed a modern-day Arthurian novel set in Southern England and Wales and among her numerous short stories are two which appeared in *Cat Crimes 3* (1994) and *Lethal Ladies* (1996). She and her husband live in St. Charles, Illinois, with their cat Travis McGee.

Quint McCauley...ex-cop turned private eye...Chicago suburb, Illinois
❑ ❑ 1 - Murder in Store (1989)
❑ ❑ 2 - Error In Judgment (1990)
❑ ❑ 3 - Masquerade in Blue (1991)
❑ ❑   - APA-Framed in Blue
❑ ❑ 4 - Brothers in Blood (1993)
❑ ❑   . . . .
❑ ❑   . . . .

■ BROWN, Lizbie [P]

Lizbie Brown is the pseudonym of Mary Marriott, creator of two quilting mysteries featuring American widow Elizabeth Blair from Turkey Creek, Virginia, transplanted to Bath, England. Elizabeth had originally come to West Country to research her ancestors after the death of her husband. But she fell in love with the honey-colored Regency terraces of Bath and decided to open the Martha Washington quilt shop in Pierrepont Mews. How fortuitous that a dashing and handsome private detective has offices above her

shop. In *Turkey Tracks* (1995), Elizabeth is drafted by the fictional Wetherburn Museum to lecture on the history of patchwork, after the curator's sister is shot dead in the museum. Meanwhile, animal rights activists dressed in turkey costumes are targeting Elizabeth's shop in support of turkey liberation. The author, who lives in Bristol, was brought up in Cornwall and previously lived in Bath. As Lizbie Brown she also wrote *Golden Dolly* (1988).

Elizabeth Blair...American widow quilt shop owner...Bath, England
❑ ❑ 1 - Broken Star (1992)
❑ ❑ 2 - Turkey Tracks (1995)
❑ ❑   . . . .
❑ ❑   . . . .

■ BROWN, Molly

British author Molly Brown first appeared on the American scene with the U.S. publication of *Cracker: To Say I Love You* (1996), based on the A&E television mystery series. She spent three years researching Restoration London for her next book, *Invitation to a Funeral* (1997), which introduced real-life spy-turned-playwright Aphra Behn in a tale *Booklist* hailed as "stunningly original, deliciously funny, and breathtakingly suspenseful." Aphra's next adventure will be based on a short story ("The Lemon Juice Plot") that

first appeared in *Royal Crimes.* Nell Gwyn brings Aphra a stolen book that leads them to a chemist's lab and evidence of a plot to kill the French Catholic mistress of Charles II. Brown has worked as a stand-up comic and began writing to kill time during a long break in rehearsals for a play. Her first novel (*Virus*) was a young-adult science-fiction thriller. She is currently finishing a near-future black-comedy thriller (*Aries Grove*).

Aphra Behn...17th century spy turned playwright...London, England
❑ ❑ 1 - Invitation to a Funeral (1997)
❑ ❑ 2 - The Lemon Juice Plot (2000)
❑ ❑   . . . .
❑ ❑   . . . .

■ BROWN, Rita Mae

Emmy-nominated screenwriter Rita Mae Brown is a best-selling author, poet, political activist and adopted mother of Sneaky Pie, her tiger cat collaborator. Their mystery series features post-mistress Mary Minor Haristeen (Harry to her friends) of Crozet (rhymes with crochet), Virginia, and her tiger cat, Mrs. Murphy. A 1998 television movie inspired by the series starred Ricki Lake as Harry, with Blythe Danner as the voice of Mrs. Murphy. Book 7, *Cat on the Scent* (1999), will feature a Civil War enactment, while *Sneaky Pie's Cookbook for Mystery Lovers* (1999) will feature recipes for humans and felines alike. A Pennsylvania native, Brown earned a B.A. in classics and English from New York University and a Ph.D. in political science from the Institute for Policy Studies in Washington DC, where she later worked as a research fellow. Her "exuberantly raunchy" autobiographical novel, *Rubyfruit Jungle*, first published in 1973, has sold more than one million copies. She lives in Charlottesville, Virginia.

Mary Minor Haristeen...small-town postmistress...Crozet, Virginia

- ❑ ❑ 1 - Wish You Were Here (1990)
- ❑ ❑ 2 - Rest in Pieces (1992)
- ❑ ❑ 3 - Murder at Monticello (1994)
- ❑ ❑ 4 - Pay Dirt (1995)
- ❑ ❑ 5 - Murder, She Meowed (1996)
- ❑ ❑ 6 - Murder on the Prowl (1998)
- ❑ ❑ . . . .
- ❑ ❑ . . . .

■ BRYAN, Kate [P]

Kate Bryan is the mystery pseudonym of 1998 Spur award-winning western fiction author Ellen Recknor, who has also penned romance novels as Caitlin Adams Bryan, Ellen Archer and Phoebe Fitzjames. Her third Kate Bryan mystery, *Murder on the Barbary Coast* (1999), brings back ex-Pinkerton detective Maggie Maguire, a partner with her cousin Grady in 1870s San Francisco. Their agency, Discreet Inquiries, makes use of Maggie's many skills, including martial arts, knife-throwing, trick horse riding and mesmerism. An Iowa native who once worked as a wildlife painter and equine artist, Recknor has recently written a historical mystery and is working on another western, a comic thriller and a comic paranormal mystery. She shares her Scottsdale, Arizona, home with cats Murphy, Rocket and Rudi; a redfoot tortoise named Baby; Blue, the Australian Shepherd; and whippet half-brothers Dylan and Peri, whose job it is to keep the couch from floating to the ceiling.

Maggie Maguire...ex-Pinkerton agent...San Francisco, California

- ❑ ❑ 1 - Murder at Bent Elbow (1998)
- ❑ ❑ 2 - A Record of Death (1998)
- ❑ ❑ . . . .
- ❑ ❑ . . . .

■ BUCHANAN, Edna

Tenth-grade dropout Edna Buchanan won a Pulitzer Prize for her police-beat reporting for *The Miami Herald* and went on to create a best-selling Edgar-nominated mystery series featuring Cuban-American police reporter Britt Montero. In a 1994 review, *Booklist* credits Buchanan with capturing "every shade of sleaze in Miami's neon rainbow." The intrepid Montero, along with ace photographer sidekick, Lottie, will make her sixth appearance in *Garden of Evil* (1999). Buchanan is also the author of true crime and autobiographical works including *The Corpse Had a Familiar Face* (1987), *Nobody Lives Forever* (1990) and *Never Let Them See You Cry* (1992). Her standalone thriller, *Pulse* (1998), features successful Miami businessman Frank Douglas, who is determined to reinvent himself after a heart transplant. The donor's wife is convinced her husband was murdered and teams with Frank to investigate. A native of Paterson, New Jersey, Buchanan moved to Miami after visiting on vacation. She says it's been a love affair ever since.

Britt Montero...Cuban-American crime reporter...Miami, Florida

- ❑ ❑ 1 - Contents Under Pressure (1992)
- ❑ ❑ 2 - **Miami, It's Murder (1994) Edgar nominee** ☆
- ❑ ❑ 3 - Suitable for Framing (1995)
- ❑ ❑ 4 - Act of Betrayal (1996)
- ❑ ❑ 5 - Margin of Error (1997)
- ❑ ❑ . . . .
- ❑ ❑ . . . .

■ BUCKLEY, Fiona [P]

Fiona Buckley is the pseudonym of a British historical novelist who says she first became interested in history at the age of 15 when she saw the MGM movie *Ivanhoe*. Published in both England and the U.S., Buckley's mysteries feature young widow Ursula Blanchard, who joins Elizabeth I's Ladies of the Presence Chamber in *To Shield the Queen* (1997). Ursula's lively debut is filled with "vivid characters, religious conflict, subplots, and power plays," according to *Kirkus Reviews*. Book 2, *The Doublet Affair*

(1998), begins as Ursula is having a lesson in lock-picking under the watchful eye of her majesty's secretary of state. An eye and ear for suspicious dealings has gained Ursula additional income as a spy, but she longs to leave court to join her daughter and French husband. However, the Queen refuses Ursula's petition to leave England, and assigns her to mind the children of a couple suspected of plotting treason. The plucky sleuth's third adventure will be *Queen's Ransom* (2000).

Ursula Blanchard...lady-in-waiting to Elizabeth I ...London, England
- ❏ ❏ 1 - The Robsart Mystery (1997)
- ❏ ❏ - U.S.-To Shield the Queen
- ❏ ❏ 2 - The Doublet Affair (1998)
- ❏ ❏ . . . .
- ❏ ❏ . . . .

■ BUCKSTAFF, Kathryn

Kathryn Buckstaff has written a pair of mysteries featuring Florida travel reporter Emily Stone, who heads for Branson, Missouri, in *No One Dies in Branson* (1994), to report on the Hot Country music awards. No sooner has Emily overheard Stella Love announce that "she's sucked her last sugar daddy at the hands of her one-eyed mentor" (*Kirkus Reviews*), than the starlet takes a header off her ex-sugar daddy's balcony. The sheriff calls it an accident, but Emily suspects otherwise. In *Evil Harmony* (1996), Emily's still in

Branson, in love with country singing star Marty Rose, whose associates begin dying mysteriously. Buckstaff has also written *Branson and Beyond: A Country Music Lover's Guide to Visiting Branson MO, Nashville TN and Pigeon Forge TN* (1995) and *Branson Backstage: A Photographic Look at the Branson Experience* (1996). She lives in Branson and writes frequently about the small town that draws more than 5 million visitors annually.

Emily Stone...Florida-based travel writer...Branson, Missouri
- ❏ ❏ 1 - No One Dies in Branson (1994)
- ❏ ❏ 2 - Evil Harmony (1996)
- ❏ ❏ . . . .
- ❏ ❏ . . . .

■ BUGGÉ, Carole

Actor-singer-composer-playwright Carole Buggé published her first addition to the Baker Street canon in 1998 (*The Star of India*) and her Holmes and Watson will return in *The Haunting of Torre Abbey* (2000). Buggé's second series debuts in late 1999 with *Who Killed Blanche DuBois*, introducing New York City mystery editor Claire Rawlings and her precocious 12-year-old ward Meredith Lawrence. Despite the ancient Norwegian surname, Buggé (BYEW-gay) was born in Germany of American parents and counts two

signers of the Declaration of Independence (John Adams and Richard Stockton) among her ancestors. A graduate of Duke University with majors in English and German, she has worked as a French cook, toured with an improvisational comedy group and written four musicals, including "Treason" about Benedict Arnold. A trained pianist, she also writes the music. In her spare time she likes to bike, hike, kayak, collect wild mushrooms and ride her Chestnut Morgan, Cora, in Putnam County. She lives in New York City.

Claire Rawlings...book editor with 12-yr-old ward...New York, New York
- ❏ ❏ 1 - Who Killed Blanche Dubois (1999)
- ❏ ❏ 2 - Murder at Ravenscroft (1999)
- ❏ ❏ 3 - The Secret Drawer Society (2000)
- ❏ ❏ . . . .
- ❏ ❏ . . . .

Sherlock Holmes...consulting detective...London, England

❏ ❏   1 - The Star of India (1998)
❏ ❏   . . . .
❏ ❏   . . . .

■ BURDEN, Pat

Pat Burden is the creator of a cozy English mystery series featuring retired Detective Chief Superintendent Henry Bassett, perfectly content in his Herefordshire cottage, tending his pigs, chickens and garden. Perfect peace for the widowed Bassett is sitting in his large wrap-around leather armchair, a nitecap whiskey in one hand, a book in the other, with his golden Labrador pup snoring contentedly at his feet. The series opener, *Screaming Bones* (1990), features the bizarre crime that upsets Bassett's domesticity. An Agatha nominee for best first traditional mystery, this "splendidly complicated puzzle" is "rich in enjoyable characters, handsome scenery and sleek prose," according to *Financial Times*. Born in Birmingham, England, Burden has been both a medical and dental nurse and secretary, and once worked in public relations for British Rail and a national bus company. She lives in an isolated Herefordshire cottage with her husband and their Labrador.

Henry Bassett...retired cop...Herefordshire, England

❏ ❏   1 - **Screaming Bones (1990) Agatha nominee** ☆
❏ ❏   2 - Wreath of Honesty (1990)
❏ ❏   3 - Bury Him Kindly (1992)
❏ ❏   4 - Father, Forgive Me (1993)
❏ ❏   . . . .
❏ ❏   . . . .

■ BURKE, Jan

Jan Burke's first manuscript was bought unagented and unsolicited by Simon & Schuster, and later earned Agatha and Anthony nominations for best first mystery novel, along with accolades from President Clinton, who mentioned *Goodnight, Irene* (1993) in a television interview. The Macavity award-winning author and her investigative reporter Irene Kelly, who live and work on the Southern California coast, make their seventh appearance in 1999 in *Bones*, with a case involving forensic anthropologists and cadaver dogs. When her 1994 short story "Unharmed" won the *Ellery Queen Mystery Magazine* Readers Award, Burke was the first woman to win this honor. The story also won a Macavity award, shared with Deborah Adams. A Houston (TX) native, Burke grew up in Orange County (CA) and earned a B.A. in history from California State University, Long Beach. A former manufacturing plant manager, she previously wrote a book column for the *Long Beach Press-Telegram* and chaired several promotional programs for Sisters in Crime.

Irene Kelly...newspaper reporter...Las Piernas, California

❏ ❏   1 - **Goodnight, Irene (1993) Agatha & Anthony nominee** ☆☆
❏ ❏   2 - Sweet Dreams, Irene (1994)
❏ ❏   3 - Dear Irene, (1995)
❏ ❏   4 - Remember Me, Irene (1996)
❏ ❏   5 - **Hocus (1997) Agatha & Macavity nominee** ☆☆
❏ ❏   6 - Liar (1998)
❏ ❏   . . . .
❏ ❏   . . . .

■ BUSHELL, Agnes

Maine author Agnes Bushell wrote for a variety of underground papers during the 1970s and was part of a women's collective that founded Littoral Books, publisher of the first anthology of Maine women's poetry. She later introduced a pair of lesbian private eyes in Portland, Maine, whose first case, *Shadowdance* (1989), involves Russian exiles and local feminists. Wilson and Wilder make a return appearance in *Death by Crystal* (1993). Bushell has also written *Local Deities* (1990) and *The Enumerator* (1997), a political thriller set in San Francisco during the heights of the AIDS crisis. The enumerator is a health official who collects information about sexual habits in an effort to track the spread of H.I.V. infections. Born in Queens, New York, Bushell attended the University of Chicago and later earned a B.A. from the University of Maine at Orono. A former instructor at the Portland School of Art, she lives in Portland.

Wilson & Wilder...lesbian private eye duo...Portland, Maine

❏ ❏ 1 - Shadowdance (1989)
❏ ❏ 2 - Death by Crystal (1993)
❏ ❏ . . . .
❏ ❏ . . . .

■ BUTLER, Gwendoline

Silver Dagger winner Gwendoline Butler has published more than 60 novels since 1956, including her 27-book series featuring John Coffin, now Chief Commander of the Second City of London. Along with his actress wife, Stella Pinero, Coffin lives in a converted church located in a fictional area of South London. Stella is kidnapped by a gang of terrorists who plan to blackmail her into passing on police intelligence by spying on her husband in book 26, *Coffin's Game* (1998), published in the U.S. as *Coffin's Games*. Coffin's 27th case, available in the U.K. in 1999, is *Coffin's Ghost*. Butler's 1973 Silver Dagger winner, *A Coffin for Pandora*, is not part of the Coffin series, but rather a Victorian mystery set in 1880s Oxford where Butler was once a university student and later a teacher. Under the pseudonym Jennie Melville, she writes a long-running police series featuring a woman officer named Charmian Daniels, as well as numerous titles of romantic suspense and historical fiction.

John Coffin...Scotland Yard commander...London, England

❏ ❏ 1 - Dead in a Row (1957)
❏ ❏ 2 - The Dull Dead (1958)
❏ ❏ 3 - The Murdering Kind (1958)
❏ ❏ 4 - Death Lives Next Door (1960)
❏ ❏ 5 - Make Me a Murderer (1961)
❏ ❏ 6 - Coffin in Oxford (1962)
❏ ❏ 7 - A Coffin for Baby (1963)
❏ ❏ 8 - Coffin Waiting (1964)
❏ ❏ 9 - A Nameless Coffin (1966)
❏ ❏ 10 - Coffin Following (1968)
❏ ❏ 11 - Coffin's Dark Number (1969)
❏ ❏ 12 - A Coffin From the Past (1970)
❏ ❏ 13 - A Coffin for the Canary (1974)
❏ ❏   - U.S.-Sarsen Place
❏ ❏ 14 - Coffin on the Water (1986)
❏ ❏ 15 - Coffin in Fashion (1987)
❏ ❏ 16 - Coffin Underground (1988)
❏ ❏ 17 - Coffin in the Black Museum (1989)
❏ ❏ 18 - Coffin in the Museum of Crime (1989)
❏ ❏ 19 - Coffin and the Paper Man (1991)
❏ ❏ 20 - Coffin on Murder Street (1992)
❏ ❏ 21 - Cracking Open a Coffin (1993)
❏ ❏ 22 - A Coffin for Charley (1994)
❏ ❏ 23 - The Coffin Tree (1994)
❏ ❏ 24 - A Dark Coffin (1995)
❏ ❏ 25 - A Double Coffin (1996)
❏ ❏ 26 - Coffin's Game (1998)
❏ ❏   - U.S.-Coffin's Games
❏ ❏ . . . .
❏ ❏ . . . .

■ BYFIELD, Barbara Ninde

Children's author and illustrator Barbara Ninde Byfield is best-known for *The Book of Weird* (1973), first published as *The Glass Harmonica* (1967). This "most desirable lexicon of the fantastical," reissued in 1994, includes Byfield's own line art. She wrote and illustrated seven children's books and served as illustrator for *The Cable Car and the Dragon* (1972) by Herb Caen, among others. Byfield's first mystery, written with Frank L. Tedeschi, includes her illustrations of the cathedral interior where a wealthy, influential rector is bludgeoned in *Solemn High Murder*

(1975). The Rev. Simon Bede, assistant to the Archbishop of Canterbury, is in New York on church business. With the help of world-famous photographer Helen Bullock, he discovers the rector may not have been the man Bede thought he knew. A sketch map of the resort setting for book 2 (Michigan's Upper Peninsula) is another Byfield illustration. Simon and Helen vacation in the Berkshires in book 3 and travel to Marrakesh with a film crew in book 4.

Simon Bede & Helen Bullock...Episcopal priest & phototographer...New York, New York

- ❏ ❏ 1 - Solemn High Murder [NY] (1975)
- ❏ ❏ 2 - Forever Wilt Thou Die [MI] (1976)
- ❏ ❏ 3 - A Harder Thing Than Triumph [MA] (1977)
- ❏ ❏ 4 - A Parcel of Their Fortunes [Morocco] (1979)
- ❏ ❏ . . . .
- ❏ ❏ . . . .

■ CAIL, Carol

Carol Cail has written three mysteries featuring Boulder investigative reporter Maxey Burnell, first seen in *Private Lies* (1993) when her boss dies in a fiery explosion. In book 2 Maxey finds herself co-owner, with her infuriatingly irresponsible ex-husband, of Boulder's weekly newspaper. Maxey visits her Nebraska hometown in book 3, a "novel about small-town Americana that also satisfies as a whodunit," said *Kirkus*. Cail's Harlequin romance novels as Kara Galloway include *Sleight of Heart* (1990) and *Love at*

Second Sight (1991). Born in Indiana, she earned B.Ed. and M.Ed. degrees at the University of Arkansas and University of Kentucky before moving to Colorado where she has lived since 1978. Once the owner of an Ohio flower shop, Cail has reviewed cookbooks for *Home Cooking* magazine, taught adult education courses in writing for Boulder community schools, served as an associate editor for the Writer's Digest School and owned and operated a Longmont, Colorado office supply company.

Maxey Burnell...investigative reporter...Boulder, Colorado

- ❏ ❏ 1 - Private Lies (1993)
- ❏ ❏ 2 - Unsafe Keeping (1995)
- ❏ ❏ 3 - If Two of Them Are Dead (1996)
- ❏ ❏ . . . .
- ❏ ❏ . . . .

■ CALLOWAY, Kate

Kate Calloway is the creator of rookie lesbian private eye Cassidy James of Cedar Hills, Oregon, introduced in *First Impressions* (1996). When the victim's beautiful niece is a suspect in his death, she hires Cassidy to find the killer in a quiet Oregon lakeside resort town. In *Second Fiddle* (1996), it's not just the two gay men who've hired Cassidy that are getting threatening letters. Cassidy's ex-lover from the series opener returns in *Third Degree* (1997), but it's the home invasions she is hired to investigate that are her biggest

problem. A week at an Oregon wilderness retreat would normally be just what the doctor ordered in *Fourth Down* (1998), but someone is trying to kill the head physician at a Portland women's clinic and rich benefactor of an influential lesbian organization. Calloway divides her time between Southern California and the Pacific Northwest. Her hobbies include cooking, wine-tasting, boating, song-writing and her two cats. Calloway's friends say that Cassidy James is not entirely fictional.

Cassidy James...rookie lesbian private eye...Cedar Hills, Oregon

- ❏ ❏ 1 - First Impressions (1996)
- ❏ ❏ 2 - Second Fiddle (1996)
- ❏ ❏ 3 - Third Degree (1997)

❑ ❑ 4 - Fourth Down (1998)
❑ ❑ 5 - Fifth Wheel (1998)
❑ ❑ 6 - Sixth Sense (1999)
❑ ❑ 7 - Seventh Heaven (1999)
❑ ❑ . . . .
❑ ❑ . . . .

■ CANNELL, Dorothy

Agatha award-winner Dorothy Cannell (rhymes with panel) was born in Nottingham, England, but moved to the U.S. in 1963. From her home in Peoria, Illinois she writes the "deliciously malicious" Agatha and Anthony award-nominated series featuring Ellie (Giselle) Simons and Ben (Bentley T.) Haskell. The dotty Tramwell sisters, Hyacinth and Primrose, join the cast in book 2 and pop in an out of the series as owners of Flowers Detection Agency. At the outset, Ellie is an unmarried, overweight interior decorator who hires a professional escort to hunt family treasure. She ends up marrying him and inheriting Merlin Court when she loses 60 pounds in six months' time as a condition of her uncle's will. Ben, the lucky escort, is an aspiring chef who becomes a cookbook author and restaurateur. In book 9, *The Trouble with Harriet* (1999), Ellie's long-absent father turns up on her doorstep with his sweetie's ashes in an urn. Cannell's short stories include the Agatha award-winning "The Family Jewels" from *Malice Domestic 3*.

Ellie & Ben Haskell...interior decorator & writer-chef...Chitterton Fells, England

❑ ❑ 1 - The Thin Woman (1984)
❑ ❑ 2 - Down the Garden Path (1985)
❑ ❑ 3 - **The Widow's Club (1988) Agatha & Anthony nominee** ☆☆
❑ ❑ 4 - Mum's the Word (1990)
❑ ❑ 5 - Femmes Fatal (1992)
❑ ❑ 6 - How To Murder Your Mother-in-law (1994)
❑ ❑ 7 - How To Murder the Man of Your Dreams (1995)
❑ ❑ 8 - The Spring Cleaning Murders (1998)
❑ ❑ . . . .
❑ ❑ . . . .

■ CANNON, Taffy

Writing as Taffy Cannon, Eileen E. Cannon is the author of a three-book series featuring Los Angeles attorney Nan Robinson, who works as an investigator for the California State Bar, starting with *A Pocketful of Karma* (1993). After launching her Irish Eyes Travel series with *Guns and Roses* (2000), Cannon will complete *The Tumbleweed Murders* (2001), a botanical mystery left unfinished by the late Rebecca Rothenberg. Cannon has also written the 1975 Academy Award-nominated screenplay for *Doubletalk.*, *Convictions: A Novel of the Sixties* (1985), and a young adult mystery, *Mississippi Treasure Hunt* (1996). A professional feminist, Cannon is a former carnival barker. As a *Jeopardy* contestant she once wagered everything on the Daily Double Women Writers, and correctly identified Shirley Jackson as the author of "The Lottery." Cannon earned an undergraduate degree with distinction in political science and an M.A.T. from Duke University. The Chicago native lives in Carlsbad, California.

Nan Robinson...state bar investigator...Los Angeles, California

❑ ❑ 1 - A Pocketful of Karma (1993)
❑ ❑ 2 - Tangled Roots (1995)
❑ ❑ 3 - Class Reunions are Murder (1996)
❑ ❑ . . . .
❑ ❑ . . . .

■ CARLSON, P.M.

Former psychology and statistics professor P(atricia) M(cElroy) Carlson is the creator of New York statistician sleuth Maggie Ryan. The eight-book series, nominated four times for mystery awards, opens with Maggie as a college student and follows her through marriage and motherhood. Owing to a publisher oversight, the Edgar-nominated *Murder in the Dog Days* was released in January 1991 despite the fact that it precedes *Murder Misread*, published several weeks earlier in December 1990. Carlson has also written a pair of mysteries featuring Marty Hopkins, a young Indiana sheriff and mother. Her Bridget

Mooney short stories, including two Agatha nominees, are collected in *Renowned Be They Grave* (1998), where the guttersnipe turned actress meets President Grant and Sarah Bernhardt, among others. Born in Guatemala, where her father was as an engineer, Carlson divides her time between Brooklyn and Ithaca, New York. A past president of Sisters in Crime, she holds B.A., M.A. and Ph.D. degrees from Cornell University.

Bridget Mooney...Victorian actress...New York, New York
- ❑ ❑ ss - Renowned Be Thy Grave (1998)
- ❑ ❑ . . . .

Maggie Ryan...coed turned statistician mom...New York, New York
- ❑ ❑ 1 - Audition for Murder (1985)
- ❑ ❑ **2 - Murder Is Academic (1985) Anthony nominee** ☆
- ❑ ❑ 3 - Murder Is Pathological (1986)
- ❑ ❑ **4 - Murder Unrenovated (1988) Anthony & Macavity nominee** ☆☆
- ❑ ❑ 5 - Rehearsal for Murder (1988)
- ❑ ❑ **6 - Murder in the Dog Days (1991) Edgar nominee** ☆
- ❑ ❑ 7 - Murder Misread (1990)
- ❑ ❑ 8 - Bad Blood (1991)
- ❑ ❑ . . . .
- ❑ ❑ . . . .

Marty LaForte Hopkins...deputy sheriff mom...Southern Indiana
- ❑ ❑ 1 - Gravestone (1992)
- ❑ ❑ 2 - Bloodstream (1995)
- ❑ ❑ . . . .
- ❑ ❑ . . . .

■ CARTER, Charlotte

new

Charlotte Carter's fictional detective Nanette Hayes is "young, tall, black, beautiful and defiantly bald," armed with attitude and a master's degree in French. "A Spike Lee heroine in a Woody Allen world," Nan is a former child prodigy who plays tenor sax on Manhattan street corners. Never mind that her mother thinks she teaches college French. First seen in *Rhode Island Red* (1997), Nan dreams of living in France and translating Rimbaud. Instead she ends up with an undercover cop dead in her living room and $60,000 stuffed in her sax. After a trip to Paris in search of her Aunt Viv in *Coq au Vin* (1999), Nan will return to New York for book 3, *Drumsticks* (2000). Carter describes herself as a so-so poet before turning to detective fiction, having done some ghost-writing with another New York writer. She has lived in Chicago, Montreal, Paris and Tangier, where she went in the 1980s to study with Paul Bowles, author of *The Sheltering Sky* and composer of the *Summer and Smoke* muscial score for his friend Tennessee Williams.

Nanette Hayes...young black tenor sax player...New York, New York
- ❑ ❑ 1 - Rhode Island Red (1997)
- ❑ ❑ 2 - Coq au Vin (1999)
- ❑ ❑ . . . .
- ❑ ❑ . . . .

■ CASTLE, Jayne [P]

new

Jayne Castle is one of several pseudonyms of romance author Jayne Ann Krentz. Among her more than 120 published novels since 1979 are 24 *New York Times* bestsellers. Her work as Jayne Castle includes four paperback mysteries featuring Guinevere Jones, owner and operator of Camelot Services, a Seattle temp agency. Starting with *The Desperate Game* (1986), Gwen's love interest is Zac Justis, owner of Free Enterprise Security. Krentz also writes under her own name and as Jayne Bentley, Amanda Glass, Amanda Quick, Stephanie James and Jayne Taylor. With a bachelor's degree in history from the University of California, Santa Cruz, and a master's degree in library science from San Jose State University, Krentz has worked as a librarian in both corporate and academic libraries. She is editor and contributor to *Dangerous Men and Adventurous Women: Romance Writers on the Appeal of the Romance* (1992) from the University of Pennsylvania Press. A native of San Diego, California, she lives in Seattle, Washington.

Guinevere Jones...office-temps business owner...Seattle, Washington

- ❑ ❑ 1 - The Desperate Game (1986)
- ❑ ❑ 2 - The Chilling Deception (1986)
- ❑ ❑ 3 - The Sinister Touch (1986)
- ❑ ❑ 4 - The Fatal Fortune (1986)
- ❑ ❑ . . . .
- ❑ ❑ . . . .

■ CAUDWELL, Sarah [P]

Sarah Caudwell is the pseudonym of English barrister Sarah Cockburn for her "intricate but elegant and hilarious" mysteries featuring Oxford professor, Hilary Tamar. A medieval law specialist, Tamar is frequently called on to assist junior members of the Chancery Bar practicing in London. Introduced in *Thus Was Adonis Murdered* (1981), the cast has appeared in two subsequent novels, but has not been heard from since 1989. Much to the consternation of Caudwell's fans, book 4 in the Anthony award-winning series has been promised annually since 1997 and has yet to be published. Readers continue to puzzle over whether the brilliant professor is a man or a woman, and Caudwell refuses to settle the debate. Her prose has been described as "luscious, funny, charming, literate and sexy" but never "easy." Before studying law at St. Ann's College, Oxford, Caudwell earned a degree in Classics from Aberdeen University. Her distinguished parents are writer Claud Cockburn and actress- journalist Jean Ross.

Hilary Tamar...medieval law specialist...London, England

- ❑ ❑ 1 - Thus Was Adonis Murdered (1981)
- ❑ ❑ 2 - The Shortest Way to Hades (1985)
- ❑ ❑ 3 - **The Sirens Sang of Murder (1989) Anthony winner ★ Agatha nominee ☆**
- ❑ ❑ 4 - The Sibyl in Her Grave (1999)
- ❑ ❑ . . . .
- ❑ ❑ . . . .

■ CAVERLY, Carol

Carol Caverly spent many years on a Wyoming ranch and uses her background and experience for mysteries featuring Chicago magazine editor Thea Barlow. In the series opener, *All the Old Lions* (1994), Thea is editing a manuscript about an 1880s Wyoming brothel for *Western True Adventure* magazine. When someone tries to stop the story, Thea becomes a target. In book 2, *Frogskin and Muttonfat* (1996), Thea travels to Wyoming to interview 82-year-old Kid Corcoran, last of the old time bandits, just released from prison. Corcoran says he just wants to live out his days in peace, but resentful locals are convinced he's come back to retrieve a stash of stolen jade. Barlow learns that Wyoming jade fields may be mined out, but memories of jumped claims and murder are alive and thriving. Caverly is working on a third book in the series, *Dead in Hog Heaven*. Caverly lives in Colorado Springs where she works at Aurora Public Library as the librarian responsible for selection of the juvenile collection.

Thea Barlow...Western magazine editor...Wyoming

- ❑ ❑ 1 - All the Old Lions (1994)
- ❑ ❑ 2 - Frogskin and Muttonfat (1996)
- ❑ ❑ . . . .
- ❑ ❑ . . . .

■ CERCONE, Karen Rose

Karen Rose Cercone has written three Pittsburgh mysteries featuring turn-of-the-century police detective Milo Kachigan and social worker and political activist Helen Sorby. Each installment focuses on the social turmoil caused by the industries that powered Pittsburgh—steel, railroads, electricity and coal. Milo and Helen join forces in *Steel Ashes* (1997) to investigate a tenement fire that has claimed the lives of two poor immigrants in 1905. In *Blood Tracks* (1998) Milo hears about the murder of an engineer at the Westinghouse plant where Helen is working. Set during the bitter coal strikes of 1906, *Coal Bones* (1999) finds the intrepid Helen working as a reporter, chasing her story between the elegant homes of Oakmont and the muddy coal patches of the Allegheny Valley. A professor of geoscience at Indiana University of Pennsylvania, Cercone holds an A.B. degree from Bryn Mawr and a Ph.D. from the University of Michigan. Writing as L.A. Graf, she has co-authored with Julia Ecklar seven Star Trek novels including *War Dragons* (1998).

Helen Sorby & Milo Kachigan...social worker & policeman in 1905...Pittsburgh, Pennsylvania

- ❑ ❑   1 - Steel Ashes (1997)
- ❑ ❑   2 - Blood Tracks (1998)
- ❑ ❑   3 - Coal Bones (1999)
- ❑ ❑   . . . .
- ❑ ❑   . . . .

■ CHAPMAN, Sally

Sally Chapman spent nine years with I.B.M. and was well-acquainted with life in Silicon Valley before writing four mysteries featuring computer fraud investigator Juliet Blake, introduced in *Raw Data* (1991). With hunky love interest Vic Paoli, Julie forms Data9000 Investigations and the pair takes a missing-persons case in *Love Bytes* (1994). The best-known virtual reality programmer in the business has disappeared along with half a million dollars of his employer's money. In *Cyberkiss* (1996), Julie and Vic go undercover as programmers at a high-tech pharmaceuticals company in a case of cybersex stalking. When last seen in *Hardwired* (1997), Julie and Vic are on their way to Johnson Space Center in Houston to find the hacker trying to sabotage an upcoming N.A.S.A. mission. Writing as Annie Griffin, Chapman has launched a new series featuring 60-something sisters in *A Very Eligible Corpse* (1998). Sensible Hannah Malloy is a Marin County gardener and poet, but her sex-crazed sister Kiki is something else.

Juliet Blake...computer fraud investigator...Silicon Valley, California

- ❑ ❑   1 - Raw Data (1991)
- ❑ ❑   2 - Love Bytes (1994)
- ❑ ❑   3 - Cyberkiss (1996)
- ❑ ❑   4 - Hardwired (1997)
- ❑ ❑   . . . .
- ❑ ❑   . . . .

■ CHAPPELL, Helen

Award-winning journalist Helen Chappell has made a career of writing about the Eastern Shore of Maryland in fiction and nonfiction, from mysteries to book-length collections of short-short stories first published in *The Baltimore Sun*. Her mythical shore-marsh village of Oysterback has also appeared in stage and radio plays and will eventually become a novel. While working as a reporter for a now-defunct small-town paper, Chappell's favorite beat was crime and the courts. During endless hours watching trials and talking with law enforcement officers, she collected the story ideas that launched reporter-sleuth Hollis Ball, introduced with the ghost of her ex-husband Sam Wescott, in *Slow Dancing with the Angel of Death* (1996). In book 4, *Giving Up the Ghost* (1999), Hollis judges a competition of Elvis impersonators. In addition to more than 30 novels, Chappell's non-fiction includes *The Chesapeake Book of the Dead: Tombstones, Epitaphs, Histories, Reflections and Oddments of the Region* (1999). She and her cat William collect white ironstone china.

Hollis Ball & Sam Wescott...reporter & her ex-husband's ghost...Santimoke County, Maryland

- ❑ ❑   1 - Slow Dancing With the Angel of Death (1996)
- ❑ ❑   2 - Dead Duck (1997)
- ❑ ❑   3 - Ghost of a Chance (1998)
- ❑ ❑   . . . .
- ❑ ❑   . . . .

■ CHARLES, Kate [P]

Kate Charles is the pseudonym of Carol Chase, an American expatriate living in England, who brings personal experience as a parish administrator to her ecclesiastical mystery series. Solicitor David Middleton-Brown and artist Lucy Kingsley meet in *A Drink of Deadly Wine* (1991), when David is hired by a priest being blackmailed. Anglican politics and church art and architecture play dominant roles in the six-book series once described as "Barbara Pym meets P.D. James." Charles has described her 1996 open-heart surgery as a life-changing experience, triggering a directional change in her writing.

The non-series novel, *Unruly Passions* (1998), is the result. Born in Cincinnati, Charles earned a B.A. from Illinois State University and an M.L.S. from Indiana University. Having worked as a promotion assistant and record librarian for a Cincinnati radio station, she currently writes full time from her home outside London. A former chairman of the Crime Writers' Association, Charles admits her favorite hobby is visiting churches.

Lucy Kingsley & David Middleton-Brown...artist & solicitor...London, England

- ❑ ❑ 1 - A Drink of Deadly Wine (1991)
- ❑ ❑ 2 - The Snares of Death (1993)
- ❑ ❑ 3 - Appointed To Die (1994)
- ❑ ❑ 4 - A Dead Man Out of Mind (1995)
- ❑ ❑ 5 - Evil Angels Among Them (1995)
- ❑ ❑ . . . .
- ❑ ❑ . . . .

■ CHASE, Elaine Raco

Agatha nominee Elaine Raco Chase wrote a dozen romance novels during the 1980s, published in 14 languages and 24 countries, with over three million copies in print. She turned to mystery writing with the introduction of investigative reporter Nikki Holden and private eye Roman Cantrell, a pair of Florida investigators who annoy the daylights out of each other. Seen first in *Dangerous Places* (1987), the two return in *Dark Corners* (1988). With Anne Wingate, Chase is co-editor of the Agatha-nominated *Amateur Detectives, A Writer's Guide to How Private Citizens Solve Criminal Cases* (1996), part of the Howdunit Series from Writer's Digest Books. Editor of the short story anthology *Partners in Crime* (1994), Chase contributed two essays to *The Fine Art of Murder* (1993). A past president of Sisters in Crime, she has worked as an audio-visual librarian for a Schenectady television station and copywriter for an Albany advertising agency. Born in Schenectady, New York, she lives in Fairfax, Virginia.

Nikki Holden & Roman Cantrell...investigative reporter & private eye...Miami, Florida

- ❑ ❑ 1 - Dangerous Places (1987)
- ❑ ❑ 2 - Dark Corners (1988)
- ❑ ❑ . . . .
- ❑ ❑ . . . .

■ CHISHOLM, P.F. [P]

Award-winning historical novelist Patricia Finney, writing as P.F. Chisholm, has created a fictional detective role for Sir Robert Carey, a real-life cousin of Queen Elizabeth I. Introduced in *A Famine of Horses* (1994), the Elizabethan nobleman is part Cary Grant, part Harrison Ford, according to a Chisholm fan. "A charismatic hero with a sense of honor and a sense of humor," said *Kirkus*. Finney was only 17 years old when she completed her first novel, *A Shadow of Gulls* (1977), published two years later. Set in second century Ireland, the book and its sequel are based on the Ulster cycle of Celtic Hero Tales. Her recent historical fiction includes *Firedrake's Eye* (1997) and *Unicorn's Blood* (1998). Finney hopes to write screenplays, science fiction, children's books and history. She also intends to learn several languages, including Hungarian, so she can translate the novels of her Hungarian grandmother, Dr. Lilla Veszy-Wagner. Born in London, where she now lives, Finney earned a B.A. with honors at Wadham College, Oxford.

Robert Carey...Elizabethan nobleman...England

- ❑ ❑ 1 - A Famine of Horses (1994)
- ❑ ❑ 2 - A Season of Knives (1995)
- ❑ ❑ 3 - A Surfeit of Guns (1996)
- ❑ ❑ 4 - A Plague of Angels (1998)
- ❑ ❑ . . . .
- ❑ ❑ . . . .

CHITTENDEN, Margaret

Writing five days a week since 1970, Margaret Chittenden has published more than 30 novels, including mystery, suspense, romance and mainstream, children's books and How To Write Your Novel (1995). Her San Francisco mystery series features 30-something, orange-haired divorcee, Charlie Plato, and sexy television actor, Zack Hunter, owners of a country-western tavern, CHAPS. In the series opener, Dying To Sing (1996), a skeleton is uncovered outside CHAPS after an earthquake. Zack's political opponent in the City Council race turns up dead in Dead Men Don't Dance (1997) and Charlie investigates to clear Zack's name. "An assortment of nifty characters and a knack for storytelling," said a Booklist reviewer about Don't Forget To Die (1999). Chittenden once worked as a clerical officer in London's Ministry of Works and as a production company accountant at Pinewood Studios. Her two dozen romance novels include nine written as Rosalind Carson. Born in London, she has lived in Japan, California and Washington State.

Charlie Plato & Zack Hunter...country-western tavern owners...San Francisco, California

- ❏ ❏ 1 - Dying To Sing (1996)
- ❏ ❏ 2 - Dead Men Don't Dance (1997)
- ❏ ❏ 3 - Dead Beat and Deadly (1998)
- ❏ ❏ 4 - Don't Forget To Die (1999)
- ❏ ❏ . . . .
- ❏ ❏ . . . .

CHRISTMAS, Joyce

Joyce Christmas is the author of two mystery series featuring women of accomplishment who find themselves in sleuthing roles—New York socialite Lady Margaret Priam and retired Connecticut office manager Betty Trenka. An English noblewoman living in Manhattan, Lady Margaret makes her tenth appearance in 2000. Her friends are socialites and royalty but her romantic interest is in police detective Sam de Vere. Betty Trenka's fourth appearance in Mood To Murder (1999) finds her temping in the principal's office at East Moulton High. After graduation from Radcliffe College, Christmas spent a year in Vienna and Rome. She returned to an editorial post at The Writer magazine in Boston where she worked for six years. Author of several children's plays, she has ghost-written a dozen nonfiction books and written PR and advertising copy. Currently an executive with a hotel technology consulting firm, Christmas edits a monthly industry newsletter and writes for hotel trade magazines. She lives in New York City.

Betty Trenka...retired office manager...Connecticut

- ❏ ❏ 1 - This Business Is Murder (1993)
- ❏ ❏ 2 - Death at Face Value (1995)
- ❏ ❏ 3 - Downsized to Death (1997)
- ❏ ❏ . . . .
- ❏ ❏ . . . .

Margaret Priam...English noblewoman...New York, New York

- ❏ ❏ 1 - Suddenly in Her Sorbet (1988)
- ❏ ❏ 2 - Simply To Die For (1989)
- ❏ ❏ 3 - A Fete Worse than Death (1990)
- ❏ ❏ 4 - A Stunning Way To Die (1991)
- ❏ ❏ 5 - Friend or Faux (1991)
- ❏ ❏ 6 - It's Her Funeral (1992)
- ❏ ❏ 7 - A Perfect Day for Dying (1994)
- ❏ ❏ 8 - Mourning Gloria (1996)
- ❏ ❏ 9 - Going Out in Style (1998)
- ❏ ❏ . . . .
- ❏ ❏ . . . .

■ CHURCHILL, Jill [P]

Jill Churchill is the pseudonym of Janice Young Brooks, Agatha and Macavity award-winning author of two mystery series and a dozen historical novels. She chose her mystery pseudonym with the expectation her books would be shelved alongside Agatha Christie's, and her cozy mysteries feature suburban Chicago single mother Jane Jeffry, a young Miss Marple with kids, a dog and a very busy schedule. Jane's first adventure, *Grime & Punishment* (1989), was an Agatha and Macavity award-winner as well as an Anthony nominee for best first mystery. When last seen in book 11, *A Groom with a View* (1999), Jane and her best friend Shelley Nowack are masquerading as wedding planners when things go not-so-blissfully awry. Churchill's new series, beginning with *Anything Goes* (1999), is set in the Hudson River Valley of Upstate New York during the 1930s. Lily and Robert Brewster, once rich, now poor, have inherited a Grace and Favor mansion with the stipulation they live in it for ten years and become self-supporting.

Jane Jeffry...suburban single mother...Chicago, Illinois
❏ ❏   1 - **Grime & Punishment (1989) Agatha & Macavity winner ★★ Anthony nominee ☆**
❏ ❏   2 - A Farewell to Yarns (1991)
❏ ❏   3 - A Quiche Before Dying (1993)
❏ ❏   4 - The Class Menagerie (1993)
❏ ❏   5 - A Knife to Remember (1994)
❏ ❏   6 - From Here to Paternity (1995)
❏ ❏   7 - Silence of the Hams (1996)
❏ ❏   8 - War and Peas (1996)
❏ ❏   9 - Fear of Frying (1997)
❏ ❏   10 - The Merchant of Menace (1998)
❏ ❏   11 - A Groom with a View (1999)
❏ ❏   . . . .
❏ ❏   . . . .

Lily & Robert Brewster...sister & brother inn owners in 1930...Voorburg-on-Hudson, New York
❏ ❏   1 - Anything Goes (1999)
❏ ❏   . . . .
❏ ❏   . . . .

■ CLAIRE, Edie

Edie Claire is the creator of suburban Pittsburgh advertising copywriter Leigh Koslow, introduced in *Never Buried* (1999) when an embalmed body is found swinging in her cousin's backyard hammock. Leigh's part-time job at the city zoo in *Never Sorry* (1999) turns dicey when an old boyfriend's leg is found in the tiger cage. And a charismatic preacher meets an untimely end at the local animal shelter in *Never Preach Past Noon* (2000). The supporting cast includes Leigh's imperious Persian cat, Mao Tse; her college roommate and Avalon's six-foot two-inch police-woman, Maura Polanski; Leigh's veterinarian father and her overprotective mother. After growing up in small towns in Missouri and Kentucky, Claire graduated from Rhodes College in Memphis and earned her D.V.M. degree at Auburn University in Alabama. She worked in a small animal clinic for several years before deciding she enjoyed freelance medical writing more than hands-on veterinary practice. Her Pittsburgh household includes a husband, two kids, two dogs and a Himalayan cat.

Leigh Koslow...advertising copywriter...Pittsburgh, Pennsylvania
❏ ❏   1 - Never Buried (1999)
❏ ❏   2 - Never Sorry (1999)
❏ ❏   3 - Never Preach Past Noon (2000)
❏ ❏   . . . .
❏ ❏   . . . .

■ CLARK, Carol Higgins

Carol Higgins Clark, daughter of best-selling suspense writer Mary Higgins Clark, once worked as her mother's research assistant and typist. But critics agree that the younger Clark's style is lighter and more humorous than her mother's. Her fictional private eye, Regan Reilly, is the daughter of a famous mystery novelist mother and funeral director father. Regan's debut in *Decked* (1992) was nominated for Agatha and Anthony awards as best first novel. Book 2, *Snagged* (1993), finds Regan and her parents at a Miami hotel where conventions are being held for funeral directors and pantyhose executives. It's off to Aspen in book 3, *Iced* (1995), where a reformed jewel thief she had recommended for a house-sitting job disappears along with some valuable paintings. When last seen in *Twanged* (1998), Regan is working as a bodyguard for a country music star with Irish roots. A graduate of Mount Holyoke College, Clark has acted professionally on stage, film and television. She lives in New York City.

Regan Reilly...P.I. and novelist's daughter...Los Angeles, California
- ❑ ❑ 1 - **Decked (1992) Agatha & Anthony nominee** ☆☆
- ❑ ❑ 2 - Snagged (1993)
- ❑ ❑ 3 - Iced (1995)
- ❑ ❑ 4 - Twanged (1998)
- ❑ ❑ . . . .
- ❑ ❑ . . . .

■ CLARKE, Anna

British author Anna Clarke has written more than 25 mysteries, many of them set in the literary world. Her series detective is Paula Glenning, a writer and professor of English at the University of London, is introduced in *Last Judgment* (1985). Glenning's ninth and most recent appearance is *The Case of the Anxious Aunt* (1996). Born in Cape Town, South Africa, where her parents were educators, Clarke earned bachelor's degrees in both arts and sciences from London universities. In her late 20s she worked as a private secretary at the publishing firm of Victor Gollancz. Her first published work was *Clinical Papers and Essays on Psychoanalysis* (1955) which she translated and co-edited. Although she had originally planned a career in mathematics, Clarke's academic life was interrupted by a long and severe illness, followed by a need to earn a living. Her first mystery, *The Darkened Room* (1968), was published when she was 49 years old. At the age of 56 she earned her M.A. degree from Sussex University.

Paula Glenning...British professor & writer...London, England
- ❑ ❑ 1 - Last Judgment (1985)
- ❑ ❑ 2 - Cabin 3033 (1986)
- ❑ ❑ 3 - The Mystery Lady (1986)
- ❑ ❑ 4 - Last Seen in London (1987)
- ❑ ❑ 5 - Murder in Writing (1988)
- ❑ ❑ 6 - The Whitelands Affair (1989)
- ❑ ❑ 7 - The Case of the Paranoid Patient (1991)
- ❑ ❑ 8 - The Case of the Ludicrous Letters (1994)
- ❑ ❑ 9 - The Case of the Anxious Aunt (1996)
- ❑ ❑ . . . .
- ❑ ❑ . . . .

■ CLAYTON, Mary

Born and raised in Cornwall, Mary Clayton read history at Oxford University. As a Fulbright Fellow she later taught history at the University of Michigan in Ann Arbor. Beginning with *Pearls Before Swine* (1995) she introduced ex-Inspector John Reynolds of the Devon and Cornwall Constabulary, prematurely retired to devote more time to writing detective novels. Described as tall and athletic, Reynolds looks closer to 40 than 55. Gardening, hiking and writing occupy his time since his wife left him six years earlier, but P.C. Derrymore, a big fan of the ex-Inspector's books, soon curtails Reynolds' retirement. At the opening of *The Prodigal's Return* (1997), Reynolds is summoned by his ex-wife to the scene of a murder where she becomes a suspect. As Mary Lide and Mary Lomer, Clayton has written historical novels and sagas, including *Command of the King* (1991) and *The Homecoming* (1993) as Lide and *Rowlands Castle Past and Present* (1988) as Lomer. She divides her time between the U.S. and Europe.

John Reynolds...ex-inspector turned crime writer...Cornwall, England

- ❏ ❏   1 - Pearls Before Swine (1995)
- ❏ ❏   2 - Dead Men's Bones (1996)
- ❏ ❏   3 - The Prodigal's Return (1997)
- ❏ ❏   4 - The Word Is Death (1997)
- ❏ ❏   5 - Death Is the Inheritance (1998)
- ❏ ❏   . . . .
- ❏ ❏   . . . .

■ CLEARY, Melissa [P]

Melissa Cleary is the pseudonymous author of ten paperback mysteries for dog lovers, featuring college film instructor Jackie Walsh and her ten-year-old son Peter. In the series opener, *A Tail of Two Murders* (1992), a beautiful Alsatian shepherd (a retired police dog named Jake) turns up in their backyard with a bullet wound in his leg. In *First Pedigree Murder* (1994) Jackie and Jake investigate a murder at the university radio station. Murder strikes again at Rodgers U. in *Dead and Buried* (1994), when the school's security chief is murdered. Jackie's friend Marcella is working undercover at the local zoo in *Murder Most Beastly*

(1996) when a zookeeper is killed. When last seen in book 10, *And Your Little Dog, Too* (1998), a stray terrier leads Jackie to the body of a homeless woman. The Melissa Cleary name is owned by Berkely Publishing Group and according to a knowledgeable source, the series has recently been taken over by the third Melissa Cleary, Shamus nominee Bridget McKenna, beginning with book 10. McKenna has also written the Melissa Cleary stories in *Canine Crimes* (1998) and *Canine Christmas* (1999), edited by Jeffrey Marks.

Jackie Walsh & Jake...film instructor & ex-police dog...Palmer, Ohio

- ❏ ❏   1 - A Tail of Two Murders (1992)
- ❏ ❏   2 - Dog Collar Crime (1993)
- ❏ ❏   3 - Hounded to Death (1993)
- ❏ ❏   4 - Skull and Dog Bones (1994)
- ❏ ❏   5 - First Pedigree Murder (1994)
- ❏ ❏   6 - Dead and Buried (1994)
- ❏ ❏   7 - The Maltese Puppy (1995)
- ❏ ❏   8 - Murder Most Beastly (1996)
- ❏ ❏   9 - Old Dogs (1997)
- ❏ ❏ 10 - And Your Little Dog, Too (1998)
- ❏ ❏   . . . .
- ❏ ❏   . . . .

■ CLEEVES, Ann

Former probation officer Ann Cleeves once worked as a cook for a Bird Observatory on Fair Isle, where she was introduced to bird-watching and her future husband, a conservation officer for the Royal Society for the Protection of Birds. Her eight bird-watching mysteries feature George Palmer-Jones, a retired official of the Home Office, and his wife Molly, a former social worker, introduced in *A Bird in the Hand* (1986). During the course of the series, the couple establishes an inquiry agency specializing in missing

teenagers. Cleeves' second series, set in the North East, features Inspector Stephen Ramsay of the Northumberland police, introduced in *A Lesson in Dying* (1990), where the local headmaster is murdered at a the school's Halloween party. Cleeves' 15th mystery, *The Crow Trap* (1999), features an environmental survey team of three women, including a botanist and a police inspector investigating a suicide. Raised in North Devon, where her father was the school teacher, Cleeves lives in Northumberland.

George & Molly Palmer-Jones...ex-Home Office bird-watcher & wife...Surrey, England

- ❏ ❏   1 - A Bird in the Hand (1986)
- ❏ ❏   2 - Come Death and High Water (1987)
- ❏ ❏   3 - Murder in Paradise (1989)
- ❏ ❏   4 - A Prey To Murder (1989)
- ❏ ❏   5 - Sea Fever (1991)
- ❏ ❏   6 - Another Man's Poison (1992)

❏ ❏ 7 - The Mill on the Shore (1994)
❏ ❏ 8 - High Island Blues (1996)
❏ ❏ . . . .
❏ ❏ . . . .

Stephen Ramsay...impulsive police inspector...Northumberland, England

❏ ❏ 1 - A Lesson in Dying (1990)
❏ ❏ 2 - Murder in My Backyard (1991)
❏ ❏ 3 - A Day in the Death of Dorothea Cassidy (1992)
❏ ❏ 4 - Killjoy (1995)
❏ ❏ 5 - The Healers (1995)
❏ ❏ 6 - The Baby Snatcher (1997)
❏ ❏ . . . .
❏ ❏ . . . .

■ COBURN, Laura

Former L.A.P.D. reserve officer Laura Coburn has written four paperback mysteries featuring single-mother police detective Kate Harrod, introduced in *A Desperate Call* (1995). Scots-Irish Kate once thought she might become a librarian. Instead, she's the newly-appointed homicide chief of San Madera, a fictional Southern California city. When her 8-year-old son's friend goes missing, Kate discovers the boy was last seen playing baseball in her yard. *An Uncertain Death* (1996) involves the suspicious death of 16-year-old star athlete, while Kate agonizes over a missing infant and a dead babysitter in *A Lying Silence* (1997). Kate's fourth case, *A Missing Suspect* (1998), finds the beautiful wife of a prominent businessman drowned in her own bathtub. Coburn served as a reserve officer for the L.A.P.D. for more than six years and handled battery and assault-with-deadly-weapons investigations while assigned to West Los Angeles Homicide. A former journalist with the *Richmond Times-Dispatch*, she lives in Carmel, California.

Kate Harrod...single-mother police detective...San Madera, California

❏ ❏ 1 - A Desperate Call (1995)
❏ ❏ 2 - An Uncertain Death (1996)
❏ ❏ 3 - A Lying Silence (1997)
❏ ❏ 4 - A Missing Suspect (1998)
❏ ❏ . . . .
❏ ❏ . . . .

■ CODY, Liza [P]

Silver Dagger award-winning author of ten mysteries, American-born Liza Cody is perhaps the only crime novelist ever to study painting at the Royal Academy School of Art and work at Madame Tussaud's Wax Museum. First seen in the Creasey award-winning *Dupe* (1980), Cody's Anna Lee is the only female operative with Brierly Security. Adapted for British cable television, this series has been twice nominated for Edgar awards. Cody's newer detective is "big, ugly and irresistible" Eva Wylie, a junkyard security guard and small-time criminal known as "The London Lassassin" on the female pro wrestling circuit. Introduced in the Silver Dagger-winning *Bucket Nut* (1992), Eva spent her adolescence surviving on the streets of London. Although she does occasional work for Anna Lee, Eva lives a solitary existence, "suspicious of anyone who tries to join her." Born Liza Nassim, Cody has worked as a painter, furniture-maker, photographer and graphic designer. She lives in Somerset, near crime writer Michael Z. Lewin.

Anna Lee...investigator for security firm...London, England

❏ ❏ 1 - **Dupe (1980) Creasey winner ★ Edgar nominee** ☆
❏ ❏ 2 - Bad Company (1982)
❏ ❏ 3 - Stalker (1984)
❏ ❏ 4 - Head Case (1985)
❏ ❏ 5 - **Under Contract (1986) Gold Dagger nominee** ☆
❏ ❏ 6 - **Backhand (1991) Edgar nominee** ☆
❏ ❏ . . . .
❏ ❏ . . . .

Eva Wylie…wrestler & security guard…London, England

❏ ❏	1 -	**Bucket Nut (1992) Silver Dagger winner ★**
❏ ❏	2 -	Monkey Wrench (1994)
❏ ❏	3 -	Musclebound (1997)
❏ ❏		. . . .
❏ ❏		. . . .

■ COEL, Margaret

Historian Margaret Coel is the creator of Jesuit missionary, John Aloysius O'Malley, and Arapaho attorney, Vicky Holden, introduced in *The Eagle Catcher* (1995). When the Wind River Reservation chief is murdered, O'Malley must prove the man's son innocent, while fighting a strong attraction to attorney Holden. The Arapaho know there's a Ghost Walker among them when a body disappears from a roadside ditch in book 2. In O'Malley and Holden's fifth case, *The Lost Bird* (1999), the priest thinks a bullet that killed his assistant may have been meant for him. Among Coel's nonfiction books are *Chief Left Hand* (1981), *Goin' Railroading* (1986) and *450 Best Sales Letters for Every Selling Situation* (1991). She has written on the American West for numerous publications, including the *New York Times* and *National Observer*. A Colorado native and descendant of Colorado pioneers, Coel holds a B.A. from Marquette University. A one-time graduate student at the University of Colorado and Oxford University, she lives in Boulder, Colorado.

John Aloysius O'Malley & Vicky Holden…Jesuit missionary & Arapaho attorney…
Wind River Reservation, Wyoming

❏ ❏	1 -	The Eagle Catcher (1995)
❏ ❏	2 -	The Ghost Walker (1996)
❏ ❏	3 -	The Dream Stalker (1997)
❏ ❏	4 -	The Story Teller (1998)
❏ ❏		. . . .
❏ ❏		. . . .

■ COGAN, Priscilla

Licensed clinical psychologist and former mental health agency director Priscilla Cogan writes novels of discovery where readers assume the role of detective alongside Northern Michigan therapist Meggie O'Connor, newly-divorced and turning 40. Elderly Lakota medicine woman Winona Pathfinder is O'Connor's teacher-guide, while the medicine man and storyteller named Hawk, a cousin of Winona's, becomes her love interest. Plans are underway for an HBO movie based on *Winona's Web* and Cogan is at work on the third novel in her trilogy examining the archetypal themes of life, love and death. A graduate of Carleton College, she holds a Ph.D. from the California School of Professional Psychology. Although retired from her psychotherapy practice, Cogan previously specialized in multiple personality disorder. Married to a Cherokee psychologist, she has studied Lakota medicine since 1978. A Boston native, Cogan divides her time between Massachusetts and Michigan, where she spends her summers.

Meggie O'Connor…practicing psychologist…Leelanau Peninsula, Michigan

❏ ❏	1 -	Winona's Web (1997)
❏ ❏	2 -	Compass of the Heart (1998)
❏ ❏		. . . .
❏ ❏		. . . .

■ COHEN, Anthea [P]

Anthea Cohen is the pseudonym of British nurse and medical writer Doris Simpson, author of 15 mysteries featuring hospital staff nurse Agnes Carmichael, a woman whose approach to problem-solving is homicidal. Introduced as an awkward, slightly pathetic women, Sister Carmichael will no longer be bullied and in the series opener, *Angel of Vengeance* (1982), she clashes violently with the parents involved in a case of suspected child abuse. In book 2, Carmichael and her colleagues are up against a despotic nursing supervisor with a passion for blackmail. For the first time in her life, Carmichael falls in love in book 3. Poor Agnes is recovering from a breakdown and long rehabilitation in book 4 when her precious kitties, Tibbles and Torty, are missing after her lovely cottage is vandalized. In a 1992 *Contemporary Authors* interview, then 79-year-old Cohen listed her hobby as "visiting discotheques." Before training as a nurse, the Isle of Wight resident worked as an antiques buyer and shoe salesperson.

Agnes Carmichael...hospital staff nurse...England

❏	❏	1 - Angel of Vengeance (1982)
❏	❏	2 - Angel Without Mercy (1982)
❏	❏	3 - Angel of Death (1984)
❏	❏	4 - Fallen Angel (1984)
❏	❏	5 - Guardian Angel (1985)
❏	❏	6 - Hell's Angel (1986)
❏	❏	7 - Ministering Angel (1986)
❏	❏	8 - Destroying Angel (1988)
❏	❏	9 - Angel Dust (1989)
❏	❏	10 - Recording Angel (1991)
❏	❏	11 - Angel in Action (1992)
❏	❏	12 - Angel in Love (1993)
❏	❏	13 - Angel in Autumn (1995)
❏	❏	14 - Dedicated Angel (1997)
❏	❏	15 - Angel of Retribution (1998)
❏	❏	. . . .
❏	❏	. . . .

■ COKER, Carolyn

Carolyn Coker is the author of five mysteries featuring art historian and restorer Andrea Perkins, first seen in *The Other David* (1984). On leave from her teaching position at Harvard, Andrea is working in Florence at the Galleria dell' Academia when an old priest gives her a painting that turns out to be one of only two portraits executed by Michelangelo. It's a portrait of the young man who posed for Michelangelo's David. According to Marcia Muller in *1001 Midnights* (1986), Coker provides "a fascinating glimpse into the art world, from the techniques of the masters to computer technology." Muller found the ending of book 1 "not only surprising but thoroughly satisfying." Coker's 1985 novel, *Back Toward Lisbon*, was published under the name Allison Cole. After earning a B.A. from the University of Oklahoma, Coker did graduate work at Southern Methodist University and Tulane. She has extensive television experience, both on camera and off. A native of Oklahoma, Coker lives in Southern California.

Andrea Perkins...art historian & restorer...Boston, Massachusetts

❏	❏	1 - The Other David (1984)
❏	❏	2 - The Vines of Ferrara (1986)
❏	❏	3 - The Hand of the Lion (1987)
❏	❏	4 - The Balmoral Nude (1990)
❏	❏	5 - Appearance of Evil (1993)
❏	❏	. . . .
❏	❏	. . . .

■ COLEMAN, Evelyn

Award-winning author of six children's books, Evelyn Coleman is the creator of black Atlanta journalist Patricia Conley, introduced in *What's a Woman Gotta Do* (1998). The morning after Conley has been stood up at the altar, police detectives want to know why her abandoned car is found dripping with blood. Her ex-fiancé is missing, but Conley had seen him holding hands with another woman shortly after the un-ceremony. Why has he left Conley a safe deposit box brimming with cash and a rare red diamond? The intrepid reporter returns in *When the Gods Take a Wife* (1999). Among her children's titles, Coleman's personal favorite is *The Foot Warmer and the Crow* (1994), about a slave who gets his freedom using wit and wisdom. The original woodcuts from Daniel Minter's illustrations are on display at Microsoft Headquarters in Redmond, Washington. Coleman's *White Socks Only* was the "Outstanding Book" among *Smithsonian Magazine's* Notable Books for Children in 1996. A native of North Carolina, she lives in Atlanta.

Pat Conley...black woman journalist...Atlanta, Georgia

❑ ❑   1 - What's a Woman Gotta Do? (1998)
❑ ❑   2 - When the Gods Take a Wife (1999)
❑ ❑   . . . .
❑ ❑   . . . .

■ COMFORT, B.

Writing as B. Comfort, Barbara Comfort is the creator of 70-something Vermont artist and painter, Tish McWhinny, and her loyal pug Lulu. Introduced in *Phoebe's Knee* (1986), Tish is "Miss Marple without the cuteness," said Margaret Maron. Two earlier mysteries, *Vermont Village Murder* (1982) and *Green Mountain Murder* (1984), feature 30-something Liz Bell. A portrait and landscape painter who has exhibited in galleries from Boston to Honolulu, Comfort studied painting at New York's National Academy, the Cape School of Art and the Ecole des Beaux Arts. One of Portraits, Inc.'s first and youngest painters, her smallest painting was a one- by two-inch oil of a green olive, commissioned by a martini drinker. Comfort fell in love with Vermont during the 1940s when she spent a month in Landgrove in exchange for a portrait. Today she paints during the summer at her Vermont studio under the watchful eye of her eight-foot outdoor replica of the Statue of Liberty. Winters are spent writing in Greenwich Village.

Tish McWhinny...70-something artist-painter...Lofton, Vermont

❑ ❑   1 - Phoebe's Knee (1986)
❑ ❑   2 - Grave Consequences (1989)
❑ ❑   3 - The Cashmere Kid (1993)
❑ ❑   4 - Elusive Quarry (1995)
❑ ❑   5 - A Pair for the Queen (1998)
❑ ❑   . . . .
❑ ❑   . . . .

■ CONANT, Susan

Susan Conant has written a dozen mysteries featuring 30-something dog trainer Holly Winter and her lovable Malamute Rowdy, first seen in *A New Leash on Death* (1989). As a columnist for *Dog's Life Magazine*, Holly is covering an Alaskan Malamute show where both a prize dog-owner and a judge are murdered in *Stud Rites* (1996). "A frisky look at mayhem unleashed," said *Publishers Weekly*. In book 11, *The Barker Street Regulars* (1998), Holly encounters an animal psychic during Rowdy's training to be a nursing home therapy dog. "Appealing characters and snappy dialogue," said *Booklist*. A graduate of Radcliffe College, Conant earned her Ed.D. from Harvard University. Her nonfiction books include *Living with Chronic Fatigue: New Strategies for Coping with and Conquering CFS* (1990) Conant and her husband, along with two cats and two Alaskan Malamutes (including one named Rowdy), live in Newton, Massachusetts. Since 1988 she has served as state coordinator of the Alaskan Malamute Protection League.

Holly Winter...dog trainer & magazine columnist...Cambridge, Massachusetts

❑ ❑   1 - A New Leash on Death (1989)
❑ ❑   2 - Dead and Doggone (1990)
❑ ❑   3 - A Bite of Death (1991)
❑ ❑   4 - Paws Before Dying (1992)
❑ ❑   5 - Gone to the Dogs (1992)
❑ ❑   6 - Bloodlines (1992)
❑ ❑   7 - Ruffly Speaking (1993)
❑ ❑   8 - Black Ribbon (1995)
❑ ❑   9 - Stud Rites (1996)
❑ ❑   10 - Animal Appetite (1997)
❑ ❑   11 - The Barker Street Regulars (1998)
❑ ❑   . . . .
❑ ❑   . . . .

■ CONNOR, Beverly

While Beverly Connor was supposed to be writing a doctoral dissertation in instructional design, she started writing novels instead. Her fictional alter ego, Dr. Lindsay Chamberlain, first seen in *A Rumor of Bones* (1996), is the result. A renowned forensic archaeologist, Lindsay is a professor at the University of Georgia, specializing in bone identification and archaeology of the Southeastern United States. In *Questionable Remains* (1997) she is working at a site-excavation visited by Spanish Conquistadors 500 years earlier. *Dressed To Die* (1998) takes place on campus where she finds a 60-year old skeleton that may have been hidden by her archaeologist grandfather. Book 4 of Connor's planned five-book series is *Skeleton Crew* (1999). With a master's degree in archaeology from the University of Georgia, Connor has worked on archaeological digs in the Southeastern U.S. and done laboratory research on archaeological artifacts. A native of East Tennessee, she lives in the woods of Oglethorpe County, Georgia.

Lindsay Chamberlain...forensic archaeologist...Athens, Georgia

- ❑ ❑   1 - A Rumor of Bones (1996)
- ❑ ❑   2 - Questionable Remains (1997)
- ❑ ❑   3 - Dressed To Die (1998)
- ❑ ❑   ....
- ❑ ❑   ....

■ COOK, Judith

Award-winning investigative reporter Judith Cook is the creator of Dr. Simon Forman, Elizabethan physician, horoscope caster and solver of mysteries, introduced in his 1591 casebook, *Death of a Lady's Maid* (1997). Forman's third casebook, *Blood on the Borders,* was released in the U.K. in early 1999. Although many of Cook's nonfiction books have been published in the U.S., her Dr. Forman mysteries are not yet available from an American publisher. Born and raised in Manchester, Cook began her career as a journalist for *The Guardian*. Her nonfiction books include *To Brave Every Danger* (1993), the epic life of Mary Bryant, highwaywoman and convicted felon, being made into an MGM movie. A part-time lecturer on Elizabethan and Jacobean theatre at Exeter University, Cook has written books about Chaucer and Shakespeare and a historical thriller about the mysterious death of Elizabethan playwright Christopher Marlowe, *The Slicing Edge of Death* (1993). She lives in the Cornwall fishing port of Newlyn.

Simon Forman...Elizabethan physician-astrologer...London, England

- ❑ ❑   1 - Death of a Lady's Maid (1997)
- ❑ ❑   2 - Murder at the Rose (1998)
- ❑ ❑   ....
- ❑ ❑   ....

■ COOPER, Natasha [P]

Natasha Cooper is the pseudonym of English romance novelist Daphne Wright, author of seven books featuring an amateur sleuth who leads a double life as Willow King and Cressida Woodruffe. Civil service administrator, Willow King, works Tuesday through Thursday for the Department of Old Age Pensions (DOAP). Her wardrobe and apartment are as drab as her job. When she leaves the office on Thursday evenings, a manicure, make-up and new hair transform King into romance novelist Cressida Woodruffe. Her glamorous home comes with a housekeeper-cook who leaves cold lobster salad in her fridge. In 1998 Cooper introduced a second series featuring family law barrister, Trish Maguire, first seen in *Creeping Ivy*. When her cousin's four-year-old daughter disappears, even Trish is a suspect. Book 2, *Fault Lines,* was published in the U.K. in 1999. Cooper worked for ten years as an editor before leaving to write full time. She reviews books for *The Times* and the *New Law Journal*.

Trish Maguire...family law barrister...London, England

- ❑ ❑   1 - Creeping Ivy (1998)
- ❑ ❑   ....
- ❑ ❑   ....

Willow King…civil-servant romance-novelist…London, England

- ❑ ❑ 1 - Festering Lilies (1990)
- ❑ ❑   - U.S.-A Common Death
- ❑ ❑ 2 - Poison Flowers (1991)
- ❑ ❑ 3 - Bloody Roses (1992)
- ❑ ❑ 4 - Bitter Herbs (1993)
- ❑ ❑ 5 - Rotten Apples (1995)
- ❑ ❑ 6 - Fruiting Bodies (1996)
- ❑ ❑ 7 - Sour Grapes (1997)
- ❑ ❑ . . . .
- ❑ ❑ . . . .

■ COOPER, Susan Rogers

Susan Rogers Cooper has written more than a dozen mysteries in three different series set in the American Southwest. Her first novel, *The Man in the Green Chevy* (1988), introduced Prophesy County, Oklahoma sheriff's deputy, Milt Kovak, who unexpectedly meets the woman who will change his life in book 4, *Chasing Away the Devil* (1991). You'll want to read this delightful series just for the titles, especially *Houston in the Rear View Mirror* (1990). Cooper later introduced E.J. (Eloise Janine) Pugh, 5-foot 11-inch, red-haired Texas housewife and romance novelist in *One, Two,*

What Did Daddy Do? (1992). Although Cooper never intended E.J. to be a series character, the small-town mom makes her fifth appearance in *A Crooked Little House* (1999). The supporting cast includes E.J.'s mother-in-law Vera, husband Willis, and their three kids. Cooper's third series features Kimmey Kruse, a young stand-up comic first seen in *Funny as a Dead Comic* (1993). Born in Michigan, Cooper lives in Austin where she has trained volunteers for several crisis agencies.

E. J. Pugh…housewife-mom romance writer…Black Cat Ridge, Texas

- ❑ ❑ 1 - One, Two, What Did Daddy Do? (1992)
- ❑ ❑ 2 - Hickory, Dickory Stalk (1996)
- ❑ ❑ 3 - **Home Again, Home Again (1997) Edgar nominee** ☆
- ❑ ❑ 4 - There Was a Little Girl (1998)
- ❑ ❑ 5 - A Crooked Little House (1999)
- ❑ ❑ . . . .
- ❑ ❑ . . . .

Kimmey Kruse…stand-up comic…Austin, Texas

- ❑ ❑ 1 - Funny as a Dead Comic (1993)
- ❑ ❑ 2 - Funny as a Dead Relative (1994)
- ❑ ❑ . . . .
- ❑ ❑ . . . .

Milton Kovak…chief deputy…Prophesy County, Oklahoma

- ❑ ❑ 1 - The Man in the Green Chevy (1988)
- ❑ ❑ 2 - Houston in the Rear View Mirror (1990)
- ❑ ❑ 3 - Other People's Houses (1990)
- ❑ ❑ 4 - Chasing Away the Devil (1991)
- ❑ ❑ 5 - Dead Moon on the Rise (1994)
- ❑ ❑ 6 - Doctors and Lawyers and Such (1995)
- ❑ ❑ . . . .
- ❑ ❑ . . . .

■ CORNWELL, Patricia

Former crime reporter Patricia Cornwell spent six years in the Virginia Medical Examiner's Office as a technical writer and computer analyst before launching her multiple-award-winning series featuring Virginia Medical Examiner, Dr. Kay Scarpetta,

introduced in *Postmortem* (1990). Working closely with Richmond police and the Behavioral Sciences Division of the F.B.I., Scarpetta's supporting cast includes homicide captain Pete Marino and her niece Lucy, F.B.I. agent turned helicopter pilot and fire investigator for the Bureau of Alcohol, Tobacco and Firearms. Their tenth adventure, *Black Notice* (1999), with a first printing of 1,000,000 copies, takes Scarpetta to Belgium and France. Cornwell's second series features a Charlotte police trio transferred to Richmond in book 2, *Southern Cross* (1999). Her 1997 biography of mentor Ruth Graham is a revision of an earlier edition. Cornwell recently donated $1.5 million to help create the Virginia Institute of Forensic Science and Medicine, the nation's first institution to train forensic scientists and pathologists. A licensed helicopter pilot, she lives in New York City and Richmond, Virginia.

Andy Brazil...reporter and volunteer cop...Charlotte, North Carolina

- ❑ ❑ 1 - Hornet's Nest (1997)
- ❑ ❑ 2 - Southern Cross (1999)
- ❑ ❑ . . . .
- ❑ ❑ . . . .

Kay Scarpetta...chief medical examiner...Richmond, Virginia

- ❑ ❑ 1 - **Postmortem (1990) Anthony, Creasey, Edgar & Macavity winner ★★★★**
- ❑ ❑ 2 - Body of Evidence (1991)
- ❑ ❑ 3 - All That Remains (1992)
- ❑ ❑ 4 - **Cruel and Unusual (1993) Gold Dagger winner ★**
- ❑ ❑ 5 - The Body Farm (1994)
- ❑ ❑ 6 - From Potter's Field (1995)
- ❑ ❑ 7 - Cause of Death (1996)
- ❑ ❑ 8 - Unnatural Exposure (1997)
- ❑ ❑ 9 - Point of Origin (1998)
- ❑ ❑ . . . .
- ❑ ❑ . . . .

■ CORPI, Lucha

new

Award-winning poet Lucha (LOO-cha) Corpi is the creator of Chicana activist Gloria Damasco, introduced in *Eulogy for a Brown Angel* (1992). Discovering the body of a murdered child on the streets of Los Angeles in 1970 triggers Gloria's awareness of her extrasensory abilities. Believing the crime will never be solved, she eventually returns to her family in Oakland, but keeps collecting information about the case. After *Cactus Blood* (1995), Gloria returns in *Black Widow's Wardrobe* (1999). In addition to her children's book, *Where Fireflies Dance* (1997), and an autobiographical novel, *Delia's Song* (1988), Corpi has also edited a collection of contemporary Latina essays, *Mascaras* (1997). Born in Veracruz, Mexico, Corpi emigrated to Berkeley, California as a student-wife at age 19. For more than 25 years she has taught adult education in the Oakland Public Schools. Corpi earned a B.A. from the University of California, Berkeley and an M.A. from San Francisco State University. She lives in Oakland, California.

Gloria Damasco...Chicana activist with ESP...Oakland, California

- ❑ ❑ 1 - Eulogy for a Brown Angel (1992)
- ❑ ❑ 2 - Cactus Blood (1995)
- ❑ ❑ . . . .
- ❑ ❑ . . . .

■ CRAIG, Alisa [P]

Award-winning Canadian-born author Charlotte MacLeod has written 32 adult mysteries in four different series since 1978. Her two American series are published under her own name, while two Canadian series appear under the name Alisa Craig. Her more traditional Canadian mysteries feature Royal Canadian Mounted Police (R.C.M.P.) officer Madoc Rhys and his wife Janet, introduced in *A Pint of Murder* (1980). The zaniest character names in mystery fiction inhabit Craig's Grub-and-Stakers series, set in Lobelia Falls, Ontario. These comic mysteries tell the adventures of Dittany Henbit Monk and her husband Osbert, a writer of westerns, along with his romance-novelist aunt, Arethusa. As Alisa Craig, she has also written the nonseries mystery, *The Terrible Tide* (1983). A Nero Wolfe award-winner, she has earned two Edgar nominations, an Agatha nomination, and lifetime achievement recognition from Malice Domestic in 1998. Born in Bath, New Brunswick, she lived for many years in the Boston area. Owing to failing health, she has retired to Maine.

Dittany Henbit Monk & Osbert Monk...garden club member & author of westerns...
Lobelia Falls, Ontario, Canada
- ❏ ❏ 1 - The Grub-and-Stakers Move a Mountain (1981)
- ❏ ❏ 2 - The Grub-and-Stakers Quilt a Bee (1985)
- ❏ ❏ 3 - The Grub-and-Stakers Pinch a Poke (1988)
- ❏ ❏ 4 - The Grub-and-Stakers Spin a Yarn (1990)
- ❏ ❏ 5 - The Grub-and-Stakers House a Haunt (1993)
- ❏ ❏ . . . .
- ❏ ❏ . . . .

Madoc & Janet Rhys...RCMP inspector & wife...New Brunswick, Canada
- ❏ ❏ 1 - A Pint of Murder (1980)
- ❏ ❏ 2 - Murder Goes Mumming (1981)
- ❏ ❏ 3 - A Dismal Thing To Do (1986)
- ❏ ❏ 4 - Trouble in the Brasses (1989)
- ❏ ❏ 5 - The Wrong Rite (1992)
- ❏ ❏ . . . .
- ❏ ❏ . . . .

■ CRAMER, Rebecca

Rebecca Cramer is the creator of fourth-grade mission-school teacher Linda Bluenight, introduced in *Mission to Sonora* (1998). Before taking the Tohono O'odham Indian Reservation school assignment ten years earlier, Bluenight worked as a forensic anthropologist for the Kansas City police department. While hiking in the Santa Catalina Mountains, Bluenight's teenage son Matty finds the body of a millionaire land developer and Bluenight is asked to examine the body. Fluent in Spanish and Hopi, Cramer recently completed the screenplay for *Mission to Sonora*. She earned a B.A. in sociology and history from State University of New York, Stony Brook, and master's degrees in both sociology and anthropology from the University of Iowa. Currently in her 25th year teaching in the anthropology department at Johnson County Community College in Overland Park, Kansas, Cramer has been a visiting scholar in both anthropology and Indian Studies at the University of Arizona.

Linda Bluenight...anthropologist turned teacher...Tucson, Arizona
- ❏ ❏ 1 - Mission to Sonora (1998)
- ❏ ❏ 2 - View From Frog Mountain (2000)
- ❏ ❏ . . . .
- ❏ ❏ . . . .

■ CRANE, Hamilton [P]

Writing as Hamilton Crane, Sarah J. Mason is the author of 14 books in the long-running Miss Seeton series featuring English spinster and retired art teacher, Emily Dorothea Seeton. Started in 1968 by Heron Carvic, who wrote five novels before his death, the series was dormant for 15 years until the pseudonymous Hampton Charles produced three installments in 1990. "Hamilton was my hall of residence at St. Andrews, and Crane seemed appropriate to follow Heron," said Mason about her choice of pseudonym. Mason's contribution to the series begins with book 9, *Miss Seeton Cracks the Case* (1991), and ends with book 22, *Miss Seeton's Finest Hour* (1999), where a much younger Miss Seeton attracts the interest of the Ministry of Information in 1940. Writing under her own name, Mason has published six books featuring Allingham police officers Trewley and Stone. After attending university in Scotland, Mason lived in New Zealand for a year before returning home to England. She lives with her husband outside London.

Emily D. Seeton...retired British art teacher...Kent, England
- ❏ ❏ 1 - **Picture Miss Seeton (1968) Edgar nominee** ☆
- ❏ ❏ 2 - Miss Seeton Draws the Line (1969)
- ❏ ❏ 3 - Witch Miss Seeton (1971)
- ❏ ❏   - Brit.-Miss Seeton, Bewitched
- ❏ ❏ 4 - Miss Seeton Sings (1973)

❑ ❑ 5 - Odds on Miss Seeton (1975)
❑ ❑ 6 - Miss Seeton, by Appointment [Hampton Charles] (1990)
❑ ❑ 7 - Advantage Miss Seeton[Hampton Charles] (1990)
❑ ❑ 8 - Miss Seeton at the Helm [Hampton Charles] (1990)
❑ ❑ 9 - Miss Seeton Cracks the Case (1991)
❑ ❑ 10 - Miss Seeton Paints the Town (1991)
❑ ❑ 11 - Miss Seeton Rocks the Cradle (1992)
❑ ❑ 12 - Hands up, Miss Seeton (1992)
❑ ❑ 13 - Miss Seeton by Moonlight (1992)
❑ ❑ 14 - Miss Seeton Plants Suspicion (1993)
❑ ❑ 15 - Miss Seeton Goes to Bat (1993)
❑ ❑ 16 - Starring Miss Seeton (1994)
❑ ❑ 17 - Miss Seeton Undercover (1994)
❑ ❑ 18 - Miss Seeton Rules (1994)
❑ ❑ 19 - Sold to Miss Seeton (1995)
❑ ❑ 20 - Sweet Miss Seeton (1996)
❑ ❑ 21 - Bonjour, Miss Seeton (1997)
❑ ❑ 22 - Miss Seeton's Finest Hour (1999)
❑ ❑ . . . .
❑ ❑ . . . .

■ CRESPI, Camilla [P]

Born in Prague to an American mother and Italian father who served in the diplomatic corps, Camilla T. Crespi came to the U.S. as a teenager and later earned a degree from Barnard College. She then returned to Italy where she worked for 17 years in the movie industry, dubbing films for directors such as Fellini, Germi, Visconti, Wertmuller and others. After returning to the U.S., Crespi worked in a small New York advertising agency for a boss who refused to give her a raise. She did the sensible thing and created food-loving Italian Simona Griffo, who works in a New York advertising agency, starting with *The Trouble with a Small Raise* (1991) where the boss dies. Age 34 in the series opener, Simona will turn 40 in book 8. The first three books in the series appeared under the name Trella Crespi, but the author name was changed to Camilla T. Crespi with book 4. Each book but the first contains a recipe for salad or pasta. Past president of the New York chapter of Mystery Writers of America, Crespi lives in New York City.

Simona Griffo...gourmet cook ad executive...New York, New York
❑ ❑ 1 - The Trouble With a Small Raise (1991)
❑ ❑ 2 - The Trouble With Moonlighting (1991)
❑ ❑ 3 - The Trouble With Too Much Sun (1992)
❑ ❑ 4 - The Trouble With Thin Ice (1993)
❑ ❑ 5 - The Trouble With Going Home (1995)
❑ ❑ 6 - The Trouble With a Bad Fit (1996)
❑ ❑ 7 - The Trouble With a Hot Summer (1997)
❑ ❑ . . . .
❑ ❑ . . . .

■ CROMBIE, Deborah

Macavity award-winner Deborah Crombie writes a British police series featuring Scotland Yard Detective Superintendent Duncan Kincaid and his partner, Sergeant Gemma (JEM-uh) James, introduced in the Agatha and Macavity award-nominated *A Share in Death* (1993). While Kincaid's background is "inoffensively upper-class," single-mother James has humbler beginnings. A *New York Times* Notable Book, *Dreaming of the Bones* (1997), was a Macavity winner and Edgar and Agatha nominee. Their sixth case, *Kissed a Sad Goodbye* (1999), is another "compelling story from start to finish," according to *Kirkus*. Crombie worked in advertising and publishing in Texas before moving to Edinburgh, Scotland and Chester, England. She lives with her husband, a police communications specialist, and teenage daughter in a 1905 Craftsman bungalow in the historic district of McKinney, Texas, north of Dallas. A secret fan of the *X-Files*, she recently started piano lessons.

Duncan Kincaid & Gemma James...Scotland Yard detective partners...London, England

❏ ❏ 1 - **A Share in Death (1993) Agatha & Macavity nominee** ☆☆
❏ ❏ 2 - All Shall Be Well (1994)
❏ ❏ 3 - Leave the Grave Green (1995)
❏ ❏ 4 - Mourn Not Your Dead (1996)
❏ ❏ 5 - **Dreaming of the Bones (1997) Macavity winner ★**
Agatha & Edgar nominee ☆☆

❏ ❏ . . . .
❏ ❏ . . . .

■ CROSS, Amanda [P]

Long-time feminist and scholar Carolyn G. Heilbrun published her Edgar-nominated first mystery, *In the Last Analysis*, in 1964 under the name Amanda Cross, to protect her standing at Columbia University. Her identity remained secret until she was granted tenure in 1972. Doyenne of the American literary mystery, Heilbrun once described her fictional alter ego, Kate Fansler, as "richer, thinner, braver" than her Nero Wolfe award-winning creator. Twelve novels and a Fansler short story collection are peppered with Heilbrun's social commentary, satiric wit and clever literary allusions. A Phi Beta Kappa graduate of Wellesley College, she earned M.A. and Ph.D. degrees from Columbia University. Past president of the Modern Language Association, she taught English and humanities at Brooklyn College and Columbia University for more than 30 years. Heilbrun's nonfiction includes *The Last Gift of Time: Life Beyond Sixty* (1997), a 1995 biography of Gloria Steinem, *Hamlet's Mother and Other Women* (1990) and the feminist classic *Writing a Woman's Life* (1988). She lives in New York City.

Kate Fansler...feminist English professor...New York, New York

❏ ❏ 1 - **In the Last Analysis (1964) Edgar nominee** ☆
❏ ❏ 2 - The James Joyce Murder (1967)
❏ ❏ 3 - Poetic Justice (1970)
❏ ❏ 4 - The Theban Mysteries (1972)
❏ ❏ 5 - The Question of Max (1976)
❏ ❏ 6 - **Death in a Tenured Position (1981) Nero Wolfe winner ★**
❏ ❏ - Brit.-A Death in the Faculty
❏ ❏ 7 - Sweet Death, Kind Death (1984)
❏ ❏ 8 - No Word From Winifred (1986)
❏ ❏ 9 - A Trap for Fools (1989)
❏ ❏ 10 - The Players Come Again (1990)
❏ ❏ 11 - An Imperfect Spy (1995)
❏ ❏ ss - The Collected Stories [10 stories] (1997)
❏ ❏ 12 - The Puzzled Heart (1998)

❏ ❏ . . . .
❏ ❏ . . . .

■ CROWLEIGH, Ann [P]

Ann Crowleigh is the joint pseudonym of Barbara Cummings and Jo-Ann Power for two historical mysteries set in Victorian London's Mayfair district. Introduced in *Dead as Dead Can Be* (1993), twin sisters Mirinda and Clare Clively find evidence of a 30-year-old murder at the family estate. In *Wait for the Dark* (1993) they stumble across the corpse of a young Chinese man and use their aristocratic wits to solve the crime. The sisters were last seen in "The Ghost of Christmas Past," a short story in *Murder Under the Tree* (1998). Cummings and Power are co-authors of *Prime Time* (1992), winner of a Reviewers' Choice award from *Romantic Times*. Author of 13 novels and short fiction, including young adult and historical romance and mystery, Cummings' short story appears in *In Our Dreams* (1998). Power writes historical romance with mystery and suspense sub-plots, including her American Beauties trilogy, *Never Say Never* (1999), *Never Again* (1998) and *Never Before* (1998). Cummings lives in Maryland and Power in Texas, where she owns a PR firm specializing in book and author promotion.

Mirinda & Clare Clively...Victorian twin sisters...London, England

- ❑ ❑ 1 - Dead as Dead Can Be (1993)
- ❑ ❑ 2 - Wait for the Dark (1993)
- ❑ ❑ . . . .
- ❑ ❑ . . . .

■ CRUM, Laura

Laura Crum grew up in Northern California horse country, where she has been a regular competitor on the cutting and team-roping circuit, training and showing cowhorses for more than 20 years. She writes mysteries featuring 30-something Santa Cruz horse veterinarian, Gail McCarthy, introduced in *Cutter* (1994). Set in the cutthroat world of cowhorse competition, McCarthy's first adventure features an "appealingly offbeat background," said *Kirkus*, with a "plot that races nicely to a satisfying finish,"

according to *Publishers Weekly*. In book 3, *Roughstock* (1997), McCarthy attends a Lake Tahoe equine seminar where one of her fellow horse vets ends up dead and another is accused of murder. With only her horses and dog for company, McCarthy sets off on a solo pack trip in book 5, *Slickrock* (1999). Finding an abnormal number of accidents along the way, she gradually realizes she is being hunted on the trail. Owner of three quarter horses and a pair of Queensland heelers, Crum lives in Capitola, California.

Gail McCarthy...horse veterinarian...Santa Cruz, California

- ❑ ❑ 1 - Cutter (1994)
- ❑ ❑ 2 - Hoofprints (1996)
- ❑ ❑ 3 - Roughstock (1997)
- ❑ ❑ 4 - Roped (1998)
- ❑ ❑ . . . .
- ❑ ❑ . . . .

■ CURZON, Clare [P]

Clare Curzon began writing imaginative stories at the age of five, but didn't see publication of her first novel until 36 years later. The book, written as Rhona Petrie, was *Death in Deakins Wood* (1963), her first police procedural featuring Inspector Marcus MacLurg. During the 1970s she wrote a number of dark suspense novels as Marie Buchanan, the most successful of which was *Anima* (1972). She is best known in the U.S. as Clare Curzon, author of more than a dozen Thames Valley mysteries featuring Detective

Superintendent Mike Yeadings, first seen in *I Give You Five Days* (1983). As director of the Serious Crimes Squad, Yeadings makes his 14th appearance in *Cold Hands* (1999). Born in Sussex, Curzon earned a B.A. with honors from the University of London where she studied European languages and psychology. She has worked throughout Europe as an interpreter, translator, language teacher, probation officer and social secretary. Author of more than 30 novels, she is Eileen-Marie Duell Buchanan.

Mike Yeadings...Serious Crime Squad superintendent...Thames Valley, England

- ❑ ❑ 1 - I Give You Five Days (1983)
- ❑ ❑ 2 - Masks and Faces (1984)
- ❑ ❑ 3 - The Trojan Hearse (1985)
- ❑ ❑ 4 - The Quest for K (1986)
- ❑ ❑ 5 - Three-Core Lead (1988)
- ❑ ❑ 6 - The Blue-Eyed Boy (1990)
- ❑ ❑ 7 - Cat's Cradle (1992)
- ❑ ❑ 8 - First Wife, Twice Removed (1993)
- ❑ ❑ 9 - Death Prone (1994)
- ❑ ❑ 10 - Nice People (1995)
- ❑ ❑ 11 - Past Mischief (1996)
- ❑ ❑ 12 - Close Quarters (1997)
- ❑ ❑ 13 - All Unwary (1998)
- ❑ ❑ . . . .
- ❑ ❑ . . . .

■ CUTLER, Judith

After teaching for many years in a large inner-city college, Judith Cutler began writing mysteries featuring Sophie Rivers, lecturer at an under-funded multicultural college in Birmingham. Introduced in *Dying Fall* (1995), Sophie is a younger, more fit version of her creator, who shares her love of music and passion for deprived kids struggling against a system stacked against them. Sophie's sixth adventure, *Dying To Score* (1999), finds her on vacation with a new love interest who becomes a prime suspect in the death of an unpopular rival cricketer. Cutler has launched a new series featuring former Metropolitan Police detective Kate Power, first seen in *Power on Her Own* (1998) when she makes a new start with the Birmingham CID. Kate returns in *Staying Power* (1999). Secretary of the Crime Writers' Association, she serves as trustee of the Birmingham Symphony and Orchestra Benevolent Society. She lives in Birmingham where she earned a B.A. with honors from the University of Birmingham.

Sophie Rivers...college lecturer and amateur singer...Birmingham, England

- ❑ ❑ 1 - Dying Fall (1995)
- ❑ ❑ 2 - Dying To Write (1996)
- ❑ ❑ 3 - Dying on Principle (1996)
- ❑ ❑ 4 - Dying for Millions (1997)
- ❑ ❑ 5 - Dying for Power (1998)
- ❑ ❑ . . . .
- ❑ ❑ . . . .

■ DAHEIM, Mary

Seattle native and former journalist Mary Daheim (rhymes with daytime) writes two Agatha-nominated mystery series, with more than 25 titles published since 1991. Her Judith McMonigle Flynn series features a Seattle bed & breakfast owner who marries a homicide detective. *Legs Benedict* (1999) is the 14th installment. Daheim's Alpine series features small-town newspaper editor and publisher, Emma Lord, whose 12th appearance is *The Alpine Legacy* (1999). Although the western Washington town of Alpine no longer exists, its thriving mill, owned by a cousin of Mark Twain's, was in operation until the late '20s. When the logging operation shut down, Alpine was burned to the ground to prevent transients from starting forest fires. In the intervening years, a second stand of trees has completely obliterated the original town, but Daheim's mother grew up in Alpine, and the author felt the town deserved to live again. Daheim has also published seven historical novels. A graduate of the University of Washington, she lives in Seattle.

Emma Lord...small-town newspaper owner-editor...Alpine, Washington

- ❑ ❑ 1 - **The Alpine Advocate (1992) Agatha nominee** ☆
- ❑ ❑ 2 - The Alpine Betrayal (1993)
- ❑ ❑ 3 - The Alpine Christmas (1993)
- ❑ ❑ 4 - The Alpine Decoy (1994)
- ❑ ❑ 5 - The Alpine Escape (1995)
- ❑ ❑ 6 - The Alpine Fury (1995)
- ❑ ❑ 7 - The Alpine Gamble (1996)
- ❑ ❑ 8 - The Alpine Hero (1997)
- ❑ ❑ 9 - The Alpine Icon (1997)
- ❑ ❑ 10 - The Alpine Journey (1998)
- ❑ ❑ 11 - The Alpine Kindred (1998)
- ❑ ❑ . . . .
- ❑ ❑ . . . .

Judith McMonigle Flynn...bed & breakfast owner...Seattle, Washington

- ❑ ❑ 1 - **Just Desserts (1991) Agatha nominee** ☆
- ❑ ❑ 2 - Fowl Prey (1991)
- ❑ ❑ 3 - Holy Terrors (1992)
- ❑ ❑ 4 - Dune To Death (1993)
- ❑ ❑ 5 - Bantam of the Opera (1993)
- ❑ ❑ 6 - Fit of Tempera (1994)

❑	❑	7 - Major Vices (1995)
❑	❑	8 - Murder, My Suite (1995)
❑	❑	9 - Auntie Mayhem (1996)
❑	❑	10 - Nutty as a Fruitcake (1996)
❑	❑	11 - September Mourn (1997)
❑	❑	12 - Wed and Buried (1998)
❑	❑	13 - Snow Place To Die (1998)
❑	❑	. . . .
❑	❑	. . . .

■ DAIN, Catherine

Two-time Shamus nominee Catherine Dain is the creator of Freddie O'Neal, hard-boiled Reno private eye with a love of flying, a weakness for Keno and a gun in her cowboy boot. When last seen in book 7, *Dead Man's Hand* (1997), Freddie has killed her teenage attacker, but later agrees to help his family. Under her previous name, Judith Garwood, Dain is the author of a *Make Friends with Murder* (1992). After earning a degree in theatre arts from U.C.L.A., she worked as a television editor and newscaster. With an M.B.A. from the University of Southern California, she moved into editorial and teaching positions at several Southern California universities. Former managing editor of *New Management* magazine, she has edited books on leadership and business for U.S.C.'s International Business Education and Research Center. Raised in Reno, she lives in Ventura, California where she works as a tarot reader and teacher at a metaphysical store. Her next mystery, *Angel in the Dark* (2000), features a New Age amateur detective.

Freddie O'Neal...plane-flying keno-playing P.I....Reno, Nevada

❑	❑	1 - **Lay It on the Line (1992) Shamus nominee** ☆
❑	❑	2 - Sing a Song of Death (1993)
❑	❑	3 - Walk a Crooked Mile (1994)
❑	❑	4 - **Lament for a Dead Cowboy (1994) Shamus nominee** ☆
❑	❑	5 - Bet Against the House (1995)
❑	❑	6 - The Luck of the Draw (1996)
❑	❑	7 - Dead Man's Hand (1997)
❑	❑	. . . .
❑	❑	. . . .

■ D'AMATO, Barbara

Barbara D'Amato has written musical comedies, true crime, and mysteries featuring an investigative journalist, a forensic pathologist and Chicago police detectives. *The Doctor, The Murder, The Mystery* (1992), her Anthony award-winning true crime, was featured on *Unsolved Mysteries*. Freelance magazine writer, Cat Marsala, investigates Chicago's 'hard' stories, most recently domestic violence and police corruption in *Hard Evidence* (1999). Writing as Malacai Black, D'Amato is the author of the Anthony-nominated *On My Honor* (1989). After starring in the technothriller *KILLER.app* (1996), Chicago cops Suze Figueroa and Norm Bennis are minor characters in *Good Cop, Bad Cop* (1998). With *Help Me Please* (1999), D'Amato introduces Chicago police detective Polly Kelly. Before earning B.A. and M.A. degrees at Northwestern University, D'Amato worked as an assistant surgical orderly, a carpenter for stage magic illusions, an assistant tiger handler and a criminal law researcher. Past president of Sisters in Crime, she is president of Mystery Writers of America. Born in Grand Rapids, Michigan, D'Amato lives in Chicago.

Cat Marsala...freelance investigative journalist...Chicago, Illinois

❑	❑	1 - Hardball (1990)
❑	❑	2 - Hard Tack (1991)
❑	❑	3 - Hard Luck (1992)
❑	❑	4 - **Hard Women (1993) Nero Wolfe nominee** ☆
❑	❑	5 - Hard Case (1994)
❑	❑	6 - **Hard Christmas (1995) Anthony & Macavity nominee** ☆☆
❑	❑	7 - Hard Bargain (1997)
❑	❑	. . . .
❑	❑	. . . .

Gerritt DeGraaf...forensic pathologist...Chicago, Illinois
- ❏ ❏ 1 - The Hands of Healing Murder (1980)
- ❏ ❏ 2 - The Eyes on Utopia Murders (1981)
- ❏ ❏ ....
- ❏ ❏ ....

Suze Figueroa & Norm Bennis...pair of cops...Chicago, Illinois
- ❏ ❏ 1 - KILLER.app (1996)
- ❏ ❏ 2 - Good Cop, Bad Cop (1998)
- ❏ ❏ ....
- ❏ ❏ ....

■ DAMS, Jeanne M.

Agatha award-winner Jeanne M. Dams has published six mysteries since the 1995 arrival of her best-first, *The Body in the Transept*, introducing widowed American Dorothy Martin, who stumbles over a dead Canon on Christmas Eve while visiting England. When last seen, the hat-loving Dorothy is newly wed in book 5, *The Victim in Victoria Station* (1999). Beginning with *Death in Lacquer Red* (1999), Dams introduces Swedish housemaid Hilda Johansson, working at Tippecanoe mansion, home of the wealthy Studebakers of South Bend, Indiana in 1900. Despite the attempts of those who would like to gentrify her name, the author says she is just plain Jeanne (rhymes with gene) Dams. Except for three years in Southern California, she is a life-long resident of South Bend, where she earned an M.A. in English literature from the University of Notre Dame. She has worked as an elementary school teacher, advertising copywriters and university administrator. A frequent visitor to England, Dams owns even more hats than Dorothy Martin.

Dorothy Martin...60-something American widow...Sherebury, England
- ❏ ❏ 1 - **The Body in the Transept (1995) Agatha winner ★ Macavity nominee ☆**
- ❏ ❏ 2 - Trouble in the Town Hall (1996)
- ❏ ❏ 3 - Holy Terror in the Hebrides (1997)
- ❏ ❏ 4 - Malice in Miniature (1998)
- ❏ ❏ ....
- ❏ ❏ ....

Hilda Johansson...turn-of-the-century Swedish housemaid...South Bend, Indiana
- ❏ ❏ 1 - Death in Lacquer Red (1999)
- ❏ ❏ 2 - A Red, White and Blue Murder (2000)
- ❏ ❏ ....
- ❏ ❏ ....

■ DANK, Gloria

Gloria Dank's four Connecticut mysteries feature curmudgeonly child-hating children's book author, Bernard Woodruff, and his goofy brother-in-law, Arthur "Snooky" Randolph. When last seen in *The Misfortunes of Others* (1993), Snooky has come for a visit with sister Maya, in the throes of morning sickness, and Bernard painting the nursery chocolate brown, to welcome their first child. With her physicist father Milton, Dank is the author of several mysteries for young adults, including *The Computer Caper* (1983), *A UFO Has Landed* (1983), *The 3-D Traitor* (1984), *The Treasure Code* (1985) and *The Computer Game Murder* (1985). Dank has also written *The Forest of App* (1983), a fantasy novel for young adults. A Phi Beta Kappa and summa cum laude graduate of Princeton University, Dank was a George C. Marshall scholar during her studies at Cambridge University in England. After graduate school she worked briefly as a programmer and research analyst for a computer consulting company.

Bernard Woodruff & Snooky Randolph...children's author & his brother-in-law...Connecticut
- ❏ ❏ 1 - Friends Till the End (1989)
- ❏ ❏ 2 - Going Out in Style (1990)
- ❏ ❏ 3 - As the Sparks Fly Upward (1992)
- ❏ ❏ 4 - The Misfortunes of Others (1993)
- ❏ ❏ ....
- ❏ ❏ ....

■ DANKS, Denise

Denise Danks has written four mysteries featuring London computer journalist Georgina Powers, introduced in *The Pizza House Crash* (1989), published in the U.S. as *User Deadly* (1991). Reporting for *Technology Week*, Georgina investigates the death of her cousin Julian, a software developer with ties to her ex-husband and his latest mistress. "Feisty characters and tidy plotting," said *Kirkus*. Following *Better Off Dead* (1991), available only in the U.K., Georgina becomes the object of a sadist's virtual reality fantasy in *Frame Grabber* (1992). In book 4, *Wink a Hopeful Eye* (1993), the game is high stakes computer-chip poker, hailed by *Kirkus Reviews* as "a video-game version of *The Big Sleep* programmed by David Mamet—incessantly brutal and funny." A journalist specializing in information technology, Danks spent 1994 traveling and researching in the U.S. as a Raymond Chandler Fulbright Award winner. Her new crime novel, *Torso* (1999), features an English couple living a wild Los Angeles lifestyle.

Georgina Powers...British computer journalist...London, England

❏ ❏	1 -	The Pizza House Crash (1989)
❏ ❏	-	U.S.-User Deadly
❏ ❏	2 -	Better Off Dead (1991)
❏ ❏	3 -	Frame Grabber (1992)
❏ ❏	4 -	Wink a Hopeful Eye (1993)
❏ ❏	. . . .
❏ ❏	. . . .

■ DAVIDSON, Diane Mott

Diane Mott Davidson is the creator of Colorado's culinary sleuth Goldy Bear Schultz, owner of Goldilocks' Catering, "Where everything is just right." The series debut, *Catering to Nobody* (1990), was nominated for Agatha, Anthony and Macavity awards as best first mystery. In addition to Goldy's catering adventures, the books contain original recipes created especially for the series. Among the supporting cast are Goldy's son Arch and her husband, police detective Tom Schultz, one ex-husband, and best friend Marla, who happens to be another ex-wife of the same ex-husband. Before writing full time, Davidson was a prep school teacher, volunteer counselor, tutor and licensed lay preacher in the Episcopal church. She also worked as a caterer and completed what she describes as "the police academy without pushups." Born in Honolulu and raised in Maryland and Virginia, Davidson earned a B.A. from Stanford and an M.F.A. from Johns Hopkins. She lives in Evergreen, Colorado, her inspiration for Aspen Meadow.

Goldy Bear Schultz...detecting caterer...Aspen Meadow, Colorado

❏ ❏	1 -	**Catering to Nobody (1990) Agatha, Anthony & Macavity nominee** ☆☆☆
❏ ❏	2 -	Dying for Chocolate (1992)
❏ ❏	3 -	Cereal Murders (1993)
❏ ❏	4 -	The Last Suppers (1994)
❏ ❏	5 -	Killer Pancake (1995)
❏ ❏	6 -	The Main Corpse (1996)
❏ ❏	7 -	The Grilling Season (1997)
❏ ❏	8 -	Prime Cut (1998)
❏ ❏	. . . .
❏ ❏	. . . .

■ DAVIS, Dorothy Salisbury

Seven-time Edgar nominee Dorothy Salisbury Davis is the author of more than 20 mystery novels, past president of Mystery Writers of America and a founding director of Sisters in Crime. Named Grand Master in 1985 and honored with a lifetime achievement Anthony Award in 1989, Davis holds five best-novel Edgar nominations and two for best short story. While the majority of her work is nonseries, she has written three mysteries featuring D.A.'s investigator, Jasper Tully, and his Scottish housekeeper, Mrs. Norris; and four with Julie Hayes, former New York City actress turned columnist who tells fortunes in Times Square. Davis cites as her best work *A Gentle Murderer* (1951), *The Pale Betrayer* (1965) and *God Speed the Night* (1958). Her 1969 novel *Where the Dark Streets Go* was filmed for CBS television as *Broken Vows* in 1986. A graduate of Barat College in Lake Forest, Illinois, she started her writing career as research librarian and trade magazine editor for Swift & Company. A native of Chicago, Davis lives in Palisades, New York.

Jasper Tully & Mrs. Norris...DA's investigator & Scottish housekeeper...New York, New York
- ❏ ❏   1 - Death of an Old Sinner (1957)
- ❏ ❏   2 - A Gentleman Called (1958)
- ❏ ❏   3 - Old Sinners Never Die (1959)
- ❏ ❏   . . . .
- ❏ ❏   . . . .

Julie Hayes...actress turned columnist and fortuneteller...New York, New York
- ❏ ❏   1 - A Death in the Life (1976)
- ❏ ❏   2 - Scarlet Night (1980)
- ❏ ❏   3 - Lullaby of Murder (1984)
- ❏ ❏   4 - The Habit of Fear (1987)
- ❏ ❏   . . . .
- ❏ ❏   . . . .

■ DAVIS, Kaye

Criminalist Kaye Davis has worked for 20 years in a regional crime lab for the Texas Department of Public Safety, with special expertise in drug and paint analysis and tire-track and shoeprint evidence. A participant in numerous crime scene investigations, she has testified in court more than 350 times. Starting with *Devil's Leg Crossing* (1997), Davis has put her experience to use writing lesbian mysteries featuring independent crime scene specialist, Maris Middleton. In the series opener, Maris is hired by Lauren O'Conner, an agent on leave from the F.B.I., to assist in the search for Lauren's missing 16-year-old niece. A sadistic serial killer, with ties to similar crimes 15 years earlier, is on the loose in book 2, *Possessions* (1998). While Lauren is away for training at the F.B.I. Academy in book 3, *Until the End* (1998), Maris becomes involved with a homicide case linked to a pattern of revenge and retribution dating back 50 years. The duo returns in book 4, *Shattered Illusions* (1999). Davis lives in the Dallas area.

Maris Middleton...lesbian forensic chemist...Texas
- ❏ ❏   1 - Devil's Leg Crossing (1997)
- ❏ ❏   2 - Possessions (1998)
- ❏ ❏   3 - Until the End (1998)
- ❏ ❏   . . . .
- ❏ ❏   . . . .

■ DAVIS, Lindsey

Lindsey Davis is the creator of Marcus Didius Falco, plebeian private eye and staunch republican, who finds himself, much to his own discomfort, in the employ of Emperor Vespasian in 70 A.D. Rome. Falco travels to Britain to work undercover in a silver mine in the series opener, *Silver Pigs* (1989). In the course of his investigation, he meets and falls in love with the patrician Helena Justina, a senator's daughter who becomes his sleuthing sidekick. "Roman history and culture are nice accessories for the more durable tool that Davis employs—hilariously good writing," said *Washington Post Book World*. Falco and Helena's tenth adventure, *Two for the Lions* (1998), was named the first winner of the C.W.A. Ellis Peters Historical Dagger in 1999. Created in memory of Ellis Peters, the award is sponsored by Peters' estate and her two main publishers, Headline and Little, Brown. Born and raised in Birmingham, Davis joined the civil service after reading English at Oxford. She lives in London where she writes full time.

Marcus Didius Falco...1st century Roman private eye...Rome, Italy
- ❏ ❏   1 - The Silver Pigs (1989)
- ❏ ❏   2 - Shadows in Bronze (1990)
- ❏ ❏   3 - Venus in Copper (1991)
- ❏ ❏   4 - The Iron Hand of Mars (1992)
- ❏ ❏   **5 - Poseidon's Gold (1993) Last Laugh nominee** ☆
- ❏ ❏   6 - Last Act in Palmyra (1994)
- ❏ ❏   7 - Time To Depart (1995)

❑ ❑   8 - A Dying Light in Corduba (1996)
❑ ❑   9 - Three Hands in the Fountain (1997)
❑ ❑   10 - Two for the Lions (1998)
❑ ❑   11 - One Dead Virgin (1999)
❑ ❑   . . . .
❑ ❑   . . . .

■ DAVIS, Val [P]

Val Davis is the joint pseudonym of wife-and-husband writing team, Angela and Robert Irvine, for their mysteries featuring archaeologist Nicolette Scott, an untenured Berkeley professor specializing in ruins of the recent past. A passion for uncovering lost aircraft leads Nick to the New Mexico desert, where a downed B-17 bomber, with bodies of the crew still aboard, is found in *Track of the Scorpion* (1996). With a B.A. in English and a master's in computer engineering, Angela Irvine taught Apollo astronauts how to use their spacecraft's on-board computers during the 1960s. Her short stories in *Ellery Queen Mystery Magazine* feature a character from her husband's Moroni Traveler series. Two-time Edgar nominee and former Los Angeles T.V.-news director, Robert Irvine once studied archaeology. The couple lives in Carmel, California, where they have written the screenplay for book 1. When writing together, they work out the plot jointly. He writes the first draft; she the second. They pass notes back and forth, but do not speak to each other while writing.

Nicolette Scott...UC-Berkeley archaeologist...New Mexico

❑ ❑   1 - Track of the Scorpion (1996)
❑ ❑   2 - Flight of the Serpent (1998)
❑ ❑   3 - Wake of the Hornet (2000)
❑ ❑   . . . .
❑ ❑   . . . .

■ DAWKINS, Cecil

A Southern writer transplanted to the desert Southwest, Cecil Dawkins is the author of four Santa Fe mysteries, including two featuring Ginevra Prettifield, part-Sioux and assistant director of the prestigious Waldheimer Museum. When a Rembrandt is stolen and a Remington sculpture is used as a deadly weapon, Prettifield investigates in *The Santa Fe Rembrandt* (1993). An enraged bear in the Sangre de Cristos Mountains is part of Gin's second adventure in *Rare Earth* (1995). Dawkins' other Santa Fe mysteries are *Clay Dancers* (1994) and *Turtle Truths* (1997), set partly in Jamaica. Before writing mysteries she produced an award-winning volume of short stories, *The Quiet Enemy* (1963); a play adapted from the stories of Flannery O'Connor, *The Displaced Person* (1966); and two literary novels, *The Live Goat* (1971) and *Charleyhorse* (1985). A graduate of the University of Alabama, Dawkins earned an M.A. from Stanford University. A former Guggenheim fellow, the Alabama native lives in Santa Fe, New Mexico.

Ginevra Prettifield...art museum assistant director...Santa Fe, New Mexico

❑ ❑   1 - The Santa Fe Rembrandt (1993)
❑ ❑   2 - Rare Earth (1995)
❑ ❑   . . . .
❑ ❑   . . . .

■ DAWSON, Janet

Janet Dawson's first mystery was published when she won the 1989 St. Martin's Press Private Eye Writers of America contest for best first private eye novel. Later nominated for Anthony, Shamus and Macavity awards, *Kindred Crimes* (1990) introduced P.I. Jeri (Jerusha) Howard, ex-wife of Oakland homicide detective Sid Vernon. In book 8, Jeri goes undercover in the legal department of a food processing firm in *Where the Bodies are Buried* (1998). Paralegal Rob Lawter, ready to expose a Bates cover-up, takes a header out his fifth-floor living-room window shortly after hiring Jeri. She had cashed his retainer check, but Rob asked her to wait for more details. With a dead client and minimal information, Jeri forges ahead. A journalism graduate of the University of Colorado, Dawson earned an M.A. in history from California State University, Hayward. She has worked as a newspaper reporter, an enlisted journalist and an officer in the U.S. Navy. Born in Purcell, Oklahoma on Halloween, she lives in Alameda, California.

Jeri Howard...private eye...Oakland, California

- ❏ ❏ 1 - **Kindred Crimes (1990) SMP/PWA winner** ★
  Anthony, Macavity & Shamus nominee ☆☆☆
- ❏ ❏ 2 - Till the Old Men Die (1993)
- ❏ ❏ 3 - Take a Number (1993)
- ❏ ❏ 4 - Don't Turn Your Back on the Ocean (1994)
- ❏ ❏ 5 - Nobody's Child (1995)
- ❏ ❏ 6 - A Credible Threat (1996)
- ❏ ❏ 7 - Witness to Evil (1997)
- ❏ ❏ 8 - Where the Bodies Are Buried (1998)
- ❏ ❏ . . . .
- ❏ ❏ . . . .

■ DAY, Dianne

Macavity award-winner Dianne Day writes mysteries featuring Caroline Fremont Jones, the 20-something owner of a turn-of-the-century San Francisco typewriting service. Armed with her typewriting machine and a degree from Wellesley, Fremont has left Boston for Baghdad-by-the-Bay and business success at ten cents a page. Among her first clients in award-winning *The Strange Files of Fremont Jones* (1995) is the mysterious Edgar Allen Partridge. By book 4, Fremont and Michael Archer are partners in a fledgling investi-gations firm and their first client involves them in a case of spiritualism and mesmerism. Day has written eight novels of romantic suspense, including those under the retired pseudonyms of Madelyn Sanders and Diana Bane. A Stanford University graduate, she holds a master's degree in clinical psychology and has worked as a psychologist, psychotherapist and health services administrator. Day lives on the Monterey peninsula, not far from the Point Pinos Lighthouse brought to life in *The Bohemian Murders* (1997).

Fremont Jones...1900s typewriting-business owner...San Francisco, California

- ❏ ❏ 1 - **The Strange Files of Fremont Jones (1995) Macavity winner** ★
- ❏ ❏ 2 - Fire and Fog (1996)
- ❏ ❏ 3 - The Bohemian Murders (1997)
- ❏ ❏ 4 - Emperor Norton's Ghost (1998)
- ❏ ❏ 5 - Death Train to Boston (1999)
- ❏ ❏ 6 - Beacon Street Mourning (2000)
- ❏ ❏ . . . .
- ❏ ❏ . . . .

■ DAY, Marele

Marele Day unleashed Australia's first woman private eye with the publication of her first novel, *The Life and Crimes of Harry Lavender* (1988), introducing Claudia Valentine. Her Sydney P.I.'s third appearance, *The Last Tango of Delores Delgado* (1992), was a Shamus award-winner for best original paperback. Day's most recent novel is the nonmystery *Lambs of God* (1998), a story of three nuns of an enclosed order, long forgotten by society. An honors graduate of the University of Sydney, Day grew up in Sydney but has traveled extensively, and lived in Italy, France and Ireland. She once took a voyage by yacht from Cairns to Singapore where she was nearly shipwrecked in the Java Sea. Her work experience ranges from fruit picking to academic teaching. Currently a freelance editor, she is the author of *Successful Promotion by Writers* in "The Art of Self Promotion" series, and editor of *How To Write Crime* (1996), to which she contributed Chapter 11, "Taking Care of Business."

Claudia Valentine...private investigator...Sydney, Australia

- ❏ ❏ 1 - The Life and Crimes of Harry Lavender (1988)
- ❏ ❏ 2 - The Case of the Chinese Boxes (1990)
- ❏ ❏ 3 - **The Last Tango of Delores Delgado (1992) Shamus winner** ★
- ❏ ❏ 4 - The Disappearance of Madalena Grimaldi (1994)
- ❏ ❏ . . . .
- ❏ ❏ . . . .

■ DELOACH, Nora

Nora DeLoach is the creator of black mother-daughter sleuthing team, Otis, South Carolina social worker Candi (Grace) Covington and her Atlanta paralegal daughter Simone. Nicknamed for her golden brown complexion (the color of candied sweet potatoes), 50-something Mama is a case worker for the county welfare department and a renowned cook. Beginning with *Mama Solves a Murder* (1994), 20-something Simone serves as narrator of their collaborative adventures. While the first four mysteries were published by a small press specializing in Afro-American books, the series was picked up by Bantam Books starting with book 5, *Mama Stalks the Past* (1997), in hardcover. When last seen in book 6, *Mama Rocks the Empty Cradle* (1998), Simone arrives in Otis to provide some much-needed assistance after Mama's bunion surgery. Under Candi's watchful eye, Simone discovers enough long-buried secrets to keep them both busy. "The touch is light, the food is rich, and the African American cast is recognizable," said *Booklist*.

Candi & Simone Covington...black social worker & paralegal daughter...Otis, South Carolina
- ❏ ❏   1 - Mama Solves a Murder (1994)
- ❏ ❏   2 - Mama Traps a Killer (1995)
- ❏ ❏   3 - Mama Saves a Victim (1997)
- ❏ ❏   4 - Mama Stands Accused (1997)
- ❏ ❏   5 - Mama Stalks the Past (1997)
- ❏ ❏   6 - Mama Rocks the Empty Cradle (1998)
- ❏ ❏   . . . .
- ❏ ❏   . . . .

■ DENGLER, Sandy

Author of more than 40 books, many of them for juveniles, Sandy Dengler has written two adult mystery series featuring law enforcement officers. In 1993 she introduced U.S. park ranger Jack Prester in *Death Valley*, the first of her four-book national parks series. The same year she introduced Sgt. Joe Rodriguez of the Phoenix police department in *Cat Killer*, another first-of-four. Dengler's newest detective is a Neanderthal shaman named Gar, who discovers a headless body in *Hyaenas* (1998). The dead man's tribe tells Gar evil spirits will destroy his family if he does not find the killer. Armed with an M.S. in desert ecology from Arizona State University, Dengler has milked scorpions and hiked barefoot to the bottom of the Grand Canyon. Wife of a now-retired park ranger, Dengler has lived in national parks across the country, where she has taught first-aid for the Red Cross, and served as a paleontologist's assistant, horse wrangler, naturalist and emergency medical technician. The Denglers live in Norman, Oklahoma.

Gar...Neanderthal shaman...Germany
- ❏ ❏   1 - Hyaenas (1998)
- ❏ ❏   2 - Wolves (2000)
- ❏ ❏   . . . .
- ❏ ❏   . . . .

Jack Prester...U.S. park ranger...National Parks
- ❏ ❏   1 - Death Valley (1993)
- ❏ ❏   2 - A Model Murder (1993)
- ❏ ❏   3 - Murder on the Mount (1994)
- ❏ ❏   4 - The Quick and the Dead (1995)
- ❏ ❏   . . . .
- ❏ ❏   . . . .

Joe Rodriguez...police sergeant...Phoenix, Arizona
- ❏ ❏   1 - Cat Killer (1993)
- ❏ ❏   2 - Mouse Trapped (1993)
- ❏ ❏   3 - The Last Dinosaur (1994)
- ❏ ❏   4 - Gila Monster (1994)
- ❏ ❏   . . . .
- ❏ ❏   . . . .

■ DENTINGER, Jane

Armed with an "encyclopedic knowledge of theater history and gift for witty dialogue," Jane Dentinger bumps off various members of the acting fraternity in her six mysteries featuring Broadway actor and director Jocelyn O'Roarke. Introduced in book 1, *Murder on Cue* (1983), is the elder statesman of Josh's supporting cast—wise and wonderful Frederick Revere, former king of Broadway and Hollywood matinee idol. The cast's last appearance in *Who Dropped Peter Pan?* (1995) is "packed with theater buzz, hip chatter, plot zig-zags and relentlessly colorful characters," said *Kirkus*. Freddie makes a solo appearance in "The Last of Laura Dane," in *Jessica Fletcher Presents: Murder, They Wrote* (1998). After completing a B.F.A. in acting and directing from Ithaca College, Dentinger worked in regional theatre, Off Broadway and Joe Papp's Shakespeare in the Park as an actor, director and acting coach. Editor for Doubleday's Mystery Guild Book Club, she recently completed her first stage play, a theatre mystery in two acts set in 1940.

Jocelyn O'Roarke...Broadway actor and director...New York, New York
- ❏ ❏ 1 - Murder on Cue (1983)
- ❏ ❏ 2 - First Hit of the Season (1984)
- ❏ ❏ 3 - Death Mask (1988)
- ❏ ❏ 4 - Dead Pan (1992)
- ❏ ❏ 5 - The Queen Is Dead (1994)
- ❏ ❏ 6 - Who Dropped Peter Pan? (1995)
- ❏ ❏ . . . .
- ❏ ❏ . . . .

■ DERESKE, Jo

Drawing on 20 years' experience as a university and corporate librarian and researcher, Jo Dereske writes two mystery series—one set in Washington, the other in her home state of Michigan. Her library mysteries feature the exasperating Miss Helma Zukas, whose seventh appearance is *Miss Zukas in Death's Shadow* (1999). Introduced in *Savage Cut* (1996) is questioned-documents expert Ruby Crane, single mother of a brain-injured 14-year-old. Returning to Michigan after a 17-year absence, Ruby thinks her inherited lakeside cottage in western Michigan is the best place for daughter Jesse to begin her recovery. Thanks to Federal Express, Ruby can continue working for her former boss, a Palo Alto, California private detective. Raised in Walhalla, Michigan (population 300), where her house (seven avid readers) was a regular book-mobile stop, Dereske attended a one-room school until age nine. Author of three fantasy novels for children, she holds B.A. and M.L.S. degrees from Western Michigan University. She lives in Bellingham, Washington.

Helma Zukas...public librarian...Bellehaven, Washington
- ❏ ❏ 1 - Miss Zukas and the Library Murders (1994)
- ❏ ❏ 2 - Miss Zukas and the Island Murders (1995)
- ❏ ❏ 3 - Miss Zukas and the Stroke of Death (1996)
- ❏ ❏ 4 - Miss Zukas and the Raven's Dance (1996)
- ❏ ❏ 5 - Out of Circulation (1997)
- ❏ ❏ 6 - Final Notice (1998)
- ❏ ❏ . . . .
- ❏ ❏ . . . .

Ruby Crane...questioned-documents expert...Western Michigan
- ❏ ❏ 1 - Savage Cut (1996)
- ❏ ❏ 2 - Cut and Dry (1997)
- ❏ ❏ 3 - Short Cut (1998)
- ❏ ❏ . . . .
- ❏ ❏ . . . .

■ DEWHURST, Eileen

Since publication of her first mystery, *Death Came Smiling* (1975), Eileen Dewhurst has written 20 crime novels, including more than a dozen in four series—two featuring male police inspectors and two with London actresses. Helen Markham Johnson, an actress recruited by the British Secret Service for her role-playing skills, appears in two espionage novels. A decade later came Phyllida Moon, hired to play a television private eye, beginning with *Now You See Her* (1995). After appearing as a secondary character in *Curtain Fall* (1977), Neil Carter of the Metropolitan

Police is featured in four subsequent novels. In *Death in Candie Garden* (1992), Dewhurst introduces Guernsey D.I. Tim Le Page and veterinarian Anna Weston, last seen in book 3, *Death of a Stranger* (1999). After earning B.A. and M.A. degrees from St. Anne's College, Oxford, Dewhurst held various administrative posts at London and Liverpool universities and worked as a freelance journalist. Born in Liverpool, she lives near York where she enjoys painting and solving cryptic crosswords.

Helen Markham Johnson...actress recruited by Secret Service...London, England
- ❏ ❏ 1 - Whoever I Am (1982)
- ❏ ❏ 2 - Playing Safe (1985)
- ❏ ❏ ....
- ❏ ❏ ....

Neil Carter...Scotland Yard detective...London, England
- ❏ ❏ 1 - Curtain Fall (1977)
- ❏ ❏ 2 - Drink This (1980)
- ❏ ❏ 3 - Trio in Three Flats (1981)
- ❏ ❏ 4 - There Was a Little Girl (1984)
- ❏ ❏ 5 - A Nice Little Business (1987)
- ❏ ❏ ....
- ❏ ❏ ....

Tim LePage...local detective inspector...Guernsey, England
- ❏ ❏ 1 - Death in Candie Gardens (1992)
- ❏ ❏ 2 - Alias the Enemy (1997)
- ❏ ❏ ....
- ❏ ❏ ....

Phyllida Moon...television private eye...London, England
- ❏ ❏ 1 - Now You See Her (1995)
- ❏ ❏ 2 - The Verdict on Winter (1996)
- ❏ ❏ 3 - Roundabout (1998)
- ❏ ❏ ....
- ❏ ❏ ....

■ DIETZ, Denise

Denise Dietz is the creator of diet group leader Ellie Bernstein, who attracts the attention of homicide Lt. Peter Miller when she tries to find out who's killing members of her Weight Winner's club in *Throw Darts at a Cheesecake* (1992). Dietz says her writing is inspired by her experience as a waitress, Weight Watchers lecturer, professional singer, newspaper reporter and film extra at Paramount. As Denise Dietz Wiley she is the author of two history-mystery-romance novels, *Dream Dancer* (1997), and *The*

Rainbow's Foot (1998), a generational saga she spent ten years writing and researching. In 1998 she published two electronic books, including her first Ingrid Beaumont mystery, *Footprints in the Butter*, featuring a 50-something amateur sleuth and her canine sidekick, Hitchcock. Writing as Deni Dietz, she is the author of the western historical, *Promises to Keep*. A graduate of the University of Wisconsin, Dietz lives in Colorado Springs where she is writing a third Ellie Bernstein mystery and cheering for the Denver Broncos.

Ellie Bernstein...diet group leader...Colorado Springs, Colorado
- ❏ ❏ 1 - Throw Darts at a Cheesecake (1992)
- ❏ ❏ 2 - Beat up a Cookie (1994)
- ❏ ❏ ....
- ❏ ❏ ....

■ DIXON, Louisa

As Mississippi's first woman Commissioner of Public Safety, Louisa Dixon had oversight responsibility for the state highway patrol, narcotics bureau, crime lab, medical examiner's office and law enforcement officers' training academy. Before her appointment was confirmed by the State Senate in 1989, no woman had ever overseen state police operations in Mississippi, or any other state in the Nation. Her Laura Owen mysteries, beginning with *Next to Last Chance* (1998), are a broadly fictionalized account of many of the situations she encountered during her three years as director. A clinical psychology major at Ohio State University, Dixon earned her J.D. in Omaha, Nebraska where she clerked for two federal judges and did criminal legal research. She later worked for the Department of Energy in Washington and the State Auditor's Office in Mississippi, where she directed investigations into fraud and misuse of public funds. Raised in Connecticut, she lives in Jackson, Mississippi with her attorney husband and ten-year-old son.

Laura Owen...state public safety commissioner...Jackson, Mississippi

❑ ❑ 1 - Next to Last Chance (1998)
❑ ❑ 2 - Outside Chance (1999)
❑ ❑ 3 - No Chance (2000)
❑ ❑ . . . .
❑ ❑ . . . .

■ DOBSON, Joanne

An active scholar of American literature and professor of English for 15 years, Joanne Dobson writes mysteries featuring English professor and literary sleuth Karen Pelletier, introduced in the Agatha award-nominated *Quieter Than Sleep* (1997). The 30-something working-class single mother teaches at posh Enfield College in Massachusetts, where she is suspected of killing a departmental colleague in the series opener. Karen thinks a recently-unearthed 19th century secret may have pushed someone to murder. "The reality of academic hysteria is perfectly captured," said reviewer Dick Adler. A founding member of the Emily Dickinson International Society, Dobson once served as a tour guide at the Dickinson homestead in Amherst and published a 1989 scholarly book about Dickinson. With a Ph.D. from the University of Massachusetts at Amherst, she has taught at Amherst College, Tufts University and Fordham University, where she is currently a professor of English. She lives in Putnam County, New York.

Karen Pelletier...single-mother English professor...Enfield, Massachusetts

❑ ❑ 1 - **Quieter Than Sleep (1997) Agatha nominee** ☆
❑ ❑ 2 - The Northbury Papers (1998)
❑ ❑ 3 - The Raven and the Nightingale (1999)
❑ ❑ . . . .
❑ ❑ . . . .

■ DOMINIC, R.B. [P]

R.B. Dominic is the joint pseudonym of Mary Jane Latsis (1927-1997) and Martha Henissart for their seven mysteries featuring Ohio Democratic congressman Ben Safford, introduced in *Murder Sunny Side Up* (1968). Each installment features a different aspect of life inside the U.S. House of Representatives. When one of Safford's constituents is nominated for the Supreme Court, an opposition member of the Senate Judiciary Committee is murdered while jogging in book 3, *There Is No Justice* (1971). A nuclear power plant is proposed for Safford's district in book 5, *Murder Out of Commission* (1976), and an Atomic Energy Commission safety inspector is murdered after a simple meeting turns violent. Latsis and Henissart are best-known for their work as Emma Lathen—two dozen mysteries featuring Wall Street banker, John Putnam Thatcher. The long-running series won Gold and Silver Daggers and a 1970 Edgar award nomination. In 1997 the authors were recognized by Malice Domestic for lifetime achievement.

Ben Safford...Democratic Congressman from Ohio...Washington, District of Columbia

❑ ❑ 1 - Murder Sunny Side Up (1968)
❑ ❑ 2 - Murder in High Place (1970)

❏　❏　　3 - There is No Justice (1971)
❏　❏　　　- Brit.-Murder Out of Court
❏　❏　　4 - Epitaph for a Lobbyist (1974)
❏　❏　　5 - Murder Out of Commission (1976)
❏　❏　　6 - The Attending Physician (1980)
❏　❏　　7 - Unexpected Developments (1984)
❏　❏　　　- Brit.-A Flaw in the System
❏　❏　　. . . . .
❏　❏　　. . . . .

■ DONALD, Anabel

Anabel Donald is the creator of London television researcher and part-time private eye Alex Tanner, introduced in *An Uncommon Murder* (1993). "Sparkling writing, plus a gripping mystery," said the *Sunday Telegraph*. After moving back and forth across the Atlantic in search of a missing young man in *The Loop* (1996), Alex is back in London in book 5, *Destroy Unopened* (1999), where she is hired to find out who was sending love letters to her widowed client's husband. Donald's first novel, *Hannah at Thirty-Five*

(1984), was followed by several other mainstream novels and historical romance written as Serena Galt and Kate Rhys. Born in India where her father was a diplomat, Donald was educated at a convent boarding school in Oxford and later earned B.A. and M.Litt. degrees at St. Anne's College, Oxford. During the late '60s she taught English literature at the University of Texas at Austin and then returned to England where she worked as a lecturer and headmistress in London, Malvern and Doncaster.

Alex Tanner...TV researcher and part-time P.I....London, England
❏　❏　　1 - An Uncommon Murder (1993)
❏　❏　　2 - In at the Deep End (1994)
❏　❏　　3 - The Glass Ceiling (1995)
❏　❏　　4 - The Loop (1996)
❏　❏　　5 - Destroy Unopened (1999)
❏　❏　　. . . . .
❏　❏　　. . . . .

■ DOUGLAS, Carole Nelson

Former newspaper journalist Carole Nelson Douglas is the author of more than 30 novels of mystery, science fiction, fantasy, romance, historical and mainstream. Diva-detective Irene Adler, the only woman to outwit Sherlock Holmes, is featured in four books starting with *Good Night, Mr. Holmes* (1990). Best known among cat lovers is Douglas' cozy-noir series with Las Vegas publicist Temple Barr, and Midnight Louie, the big, black tomcat sleuth with his own fan newsletter. Louie's 10th adventure, *Cat in an Indigo Mood* (1999),

includes Nose E., the drug-sniffing Maltese dog introduced in a Louie short story. Book 10 is the first to include four human points of view (Temple, Matt, Lt. Molina and Max Kinsella) plus Louie's. A restored version of Louie's earliest romantic adventures is *The Cat and the King of Clubs* (1999). And Louie meets Elvis in book 11, *Cat in a Jeweled Jumpsuit* (2000). Douglas and her artist husband live in Fort Worth, Texas, along with seven cats, one dog, and her large collection of cat shoes, cat purses and cat jewelry.

Irene Adler...19th century American diva...Paris, France
❏　❏　　1 - Good Night, Mr. Holmes (1990)
❏　❏　　2 - Good Morning, Irene (1990)
❏　❏　　3 - Irene at Large (1992)
❏　❏　　4 - Irene's Last Waltz (1994)
❏　❏　　. . . . .
❏　❏　　. . . . .

Kevin Blake...psychiatrist...Minnesota
❏　❏　　1 - Probe (1985)
❏　❏　　2 - Counterprobe (1990)
❏　❏　　. . . . .
❏　❏　　. . . . .

Temple Barr & Midnight Louie...PR freelancer & tomcat sleuth ...Las Vegas, Nevada

- ❏ ❏ 1 - Catnap (1992)
- ❏ ❏ 2 - Pussyfoot (1993)
- ❏ ❏ 3 - Cat on a Blue Monday (1994)
- ❏ ❏ 4 - Cat in a Crimson Haze (1995)
- ❏ ❏ 5 - Cat in a Diamond Dazzle (1996)
- ❏ ❏ 6 - Cat With an Emerald Eye (1996)
- ❏ ❏ 7 - Cat in a Flamingo Fedora (1997)
- ❏ ❏ 8 - Cat in a Golden Garland (1997)
- ❏ ❏ 9 - Cat on a Hyacinth Hunt (1998)
- ❏ ❏ . . . .
- ❏ ❏ . . . .

■ DOUGLAS, Lauren Wright

Lambda award winner Lauren Wright Douglas has written six mysteries featuring lesbian private eye Caitlin Reece of Victoria, British Columbia. Focusing on crimes against women, children and animals, Caitlin takes clients only by referral. She has no office, and never leaves home without her .357 Magnum. The strong supporting cast includes Maggie the doctor, Sandy the cop, Gray the Vietnamese animal psychologist, and Lester the electronics expert. As Zenobia N. Vole, Douglas is the author of *Osten's Bay* (1988). She has also written *In the Blood* (1989), a science fiction novel. Born in Ontario, Canada, Douglas grew up in a military family and spent part of her childhood in Europe. A graduate of Carleton University, she later studied at the University of Toronto where she was editor of the University of Toronto *Bulletin*. A former California resident, Douglas lives on the Oregon coast where she writes the Allison O'Neil mysteries featuring a displaced Californian who inherits an Oregon bed & breakfast from an aunt.

Allison O'Neil...lesbian B & B owner...Lavner Bay, Oregon

- ❏ ❏ 1 - Death at Lavender Bay (1996)
- ❏ ❏ 2 - Swimming at Cat Cove (1997)
- ❏ ❏ . . . .
- ❏ ❏ . . . .

Caitlin Reece...lesbian private eye...Victoria, British Columbia, Canada

- ❏ ❏ 1 - The Always Anonymous Beast (1987)
- ❏ ❏ 2 - **Ninth Life (1989) Lambda winner ★**
- ❏ ❏ 3 - The Daughters of Artemis (1991)
- ❏ ❏ 4 - A Tiger's Heart (1992)
- ❏ ❏ 5 - Goblin Market (1993)
- ❏ ❏ 6 - A Rage of Maidens (1994)
- ❏ ❏ . . . .
- ❏ ❏ . . . .

■ DRAKE, Alison [P]

Alison Drake is a pseudonym of T.J. MacGregor, author of more than 20 books, including mystery and suspense novels and nonfiction. Writing as Alison Drake, she has created a four-book series featuring Florida homicide detective Aline Scott, introduced in *Tango Key* (1988). The detective's beat is the fictional island of Tango Key, a tropical paradise shaped roughly like a cat's head, 11 miles long and seven miles across at its widest point. Her house is on stilts and she keeps a pet skunk named Wolfe. In book 4, *High Strangeness* (1992), she has moved to an 1871 lighthouse on the remote western slope of the island with her lover Kincaid, an insurance investigator. Wolfe grudgingly shares his new domain with a stray tabby cat named Unojo (Spanish for one eye) and an injured screech owl named Boo. Born and raised in Caracas, Venezuela, the author lives in South Florida with her husband, writer Rob MacGregor. A former social worker and Spanish teacher, she is a professional tarot card reader and astrologer.

Aline Scott...homicide detective...Tango Key, Florida

- ❏ ❏ 1 - Tango Key (1988)
- ❏ ❏ 2 - Fevered (1988)

❏ ❏   3 - Black Moon (1989)
❏ ❏   4 - High Strangeness (1992)
❏ ❏   . . . .
❏ ❏   . . . .

■ DREHER, Sarah

Prize-winning playwright Sarah Dreher is a clinical psychologist who writes mysteries featuring Boston-based travel agent and lesbian amateur sleuth Stoner McTavish, introduced in *Stoner McTavish* (1985). The seven-book series includes Stoner's collection of colorful friends and relatives, from eccentric Aunt Hermione, to lover Gwen, and business partner Marylou—the travel agent who's afraid of flying. In book 5, *Otherworld* (1993), the merry band accompanies Marylou's mother, the eminent Dr. Edith Kesselbaum, to a psychiatric convention at Disney World. When last seen in book 7, *Shaman's Moon* (1998), hungry ghosts in the New Age town of Shelburne Falls have marked Aunt Hermione as their next prey. Dreher's nonmystery *Solitaire and Brahms* (1997) is a novel of the early '60s that she says she began writing 35 years ago. By the time of publication, only about two sentences were left from her original version. Dreher lives in Amherst, Massachusetts.

Stoner McTavish...lesbian travel agent...Boston, Massachusetts

❏ ❏   1 - Stoner McTavish (1985)
❏ ❏   2 - Something Shady (1986)
❏ ❏   3 - Gray Magic (1987)
❏ ❏   4 - A Captive in Time (1990)
❏ ❏   5 - Otherworld (1993)
❏ ❏   6 - Bad Company (1995)
❏ ❏   7 - Shaman's Moon (1998)
❏ ❏   . . . .
❏ ❏   . . . .

■ DREYER, Eileen

Former trauma nurse and licensed death investigator Eileen Dreyer (rhymes with flyer) is the author of 25 novels, including five medical thrillers under her own name and 20 romance novels as the award-winning Kathleen Korbel. Her first hardcover novel, *Brain Dead* (1997), features a forensic nurse and a burned-out Pulitzer Prize-winning journalist on the trail of suspicious deaths among the elderly of Puckett, Missouri. Dreyer's debut mystery series, introducing trauma nurse and death investigator, Molly Burke, opens with a rash of lawyer suicides in the Anthony award-nominated *Bad Medicine* (1995). Dreyer's other medical thrillers are *If Looks Could Kill* (1992), *Nothing Personal* (1994) and *Man To Die For* (1997). After 17 years in the emergency rooms of major St. Louis hospitals, she writes full time, alternating romance and mystery titles. A member of the Romance Writers Hall of Fame and diehard Cardinals fan, Dreyer was at Busch Stadium the night Mark McGwire hit his record-breaking 62nd home run in 1998.

Molly Burke...death investigator...St. Louis, Missouri

❏ ❏   1 - **Bad Medicine (1995) Anthony nominee** ☆
❏ ❏   2 - Bad Reaction (2000)
❏ ❏   . . . .
❏ ❏   . . . .

■ DRURY, Joan M.

Publisher and philanthropist Joan M. Drury has written three mysteries featuring San Francisco-based newspaper columnist, Tyler Jones, introduced in *The Other Side of Silence* (1993). Accompanied by her Golden retriever, Agatha Christie, Tyler goes home to Stony River, Minnesota in the Edgar-nominated *Silent Words* (1996), to honor her mother's deathbed wish that she shake some family skeletons. In *Closed in Silence* (1998), Tyler joins five University of Michigan friends on a deserted island in Puget Sound to celebrate their 20th reunion. As owner and publisher, Drury makes all acquisitions for Spinster's Ink, the San Francisco feminist press she acquired in 1992. Now based in Duluth, Spinster's has more than 50 titles in print. Drury is the founder and executive director of Harmony Women's Fund, a supporter of women's social service and arts endeavors such as Norcroft, the women's writing retreat located not far from the fictional Stony River on the northern shores of Lake Superior. Drury lives in Duluth.

Tyler Jones...lesbian activist newspaper columnist...San Francisco, California

- ❏ ❏ 1 - The Other Side of Silence (1993)
- ❏ ❏ **2 - Silent Words (1996) Edgar nominee** ☆
- ❏ ❏ 3 - Closed in Silence (1998)
- ❏ ❏ . . . .
- ❏ ❏ . . . .

■ DUFFY, Margaret

Margaret Duffy's first mystery was the opener for an action-packed six-book series featuring British special agents Ingrid Langley and Major Patrick Gillard. Ingrid, a former agent turned novelist, gets called back to serve with her ex-husband, still recovering from his Falklands War injuries. One American reviewer aptly noted the author's "wonderful sense of humor and frighteningly insightful view of male-female relation-ships," which make these books "impossible to put down." Duffy's second series introduces Joanna McKenzie, former C.I.D. turned private detective, and her ex-boss and old flame, D.C.I. James Carrick. In book 2, *Prospect of Death* (1995), which includes an appearance by Patrick Gillard, Joanna must clear the Chief Inspector's name after he is found intoxicated at the wheel of his crashed car with no recall of the accident. When last seen in book 4, *A Fine Target* (1998), Carrick investigates his own brother's death. Born in Essex, England, where her mother was a court dressmaker, Duffy lives in Scotland.

Ingrid Langley & Patrick Gillard...novelist secret agent & army major...England

- ❏ ❏ 1 - A Murder of Crows (1987)
- ❏ ❏ 2 - Death of a Raven (1988)
- ❏ ❏ 3 - Brass Eagle (1989)
- ❏ ❏ 4 - Who Killed Cock Robin? (1990)
- ❏ ❏ 5 - Rook-Shoot (1991)
- ❏ ❏ 6 - Gallows-Bird (1993)
- ❏ ❏ . . . .
- ❏ ❏ . . . .

Joanna MacKenzie & James Carrick...ex-CID detective & Det. Chief Insp....Bath, England

- ❏ ❏ 1 - Dressed To Kill (1994)
- ❏ ❏ 2 - Prospect of Death [incl Patrick Gillard] (1995)
- ❏ ❏ 3 - Music in the Blood (1997)
- ❏ ❏ 4 - A Fine Target (1998)
- ❏ ❏ . . . .
- ❏ ❏ . . . .

■ DUFFY, Stella

London theatre and radio performer Stella Duffy is the creator of South London detective Saz Martin, introduced in *Calendar Girl* (1994). A Trans-Atlantic case of drug-smuggling, gambling and high-class prostitution finds Saz chasing a woman known only as September. An "unusual, cleverly constructed recital of deception in relationships," said the *San Francisco Examiner*. "The downbeat denouement packs an unexpected, morbid wallop." Saz agrees to curtail danger in book 4, *Fresh Flesh* (1999), when she and her partner decide to have a baby. In *Singling Out the Couples* (1998), Duffy has written a modern fairy tale about a heartless princess on Notting Hill who delights in breaking up loving couples, until she falls in love and discovers a tiny heart growing in her chest. Duffy is the author of *Eating Cake* (1999) and a one-woman show titled "The Tedious Predictability of Falling in Love". Born in the U.K., she grew up in New Zealand and now lives in London where she teaches improvisational comedy.

Saz Martin...lesbian private eye...London, England

- ❏ ❏ 1 - Calendar Girl (1994)
- ❏ ❏ 2 - Wavewalker (1996)
- ❏ ❏ 3 - Beneath the Blonde (1997)
- ❏ ❏ . . . .
- ❏ ❏ . . . .

■ DUNANT, Sarah

Silver Dagger winner Sarah Dunant has written three mysteries featuring Hannah Wolfe, a contract private investigator for a London agency, starting with the case of missing ballet dancer in *Birth Marks* (1992). Hannah is hired to baby-sit the rebellious teenage daughter of a noted research scientist targeted by a radical animal rights group in the award-winning *Fat Lands* (1993). A fancy health spa is being sabotaged in *Under My Skin* (1995) and Hannah checks-in to investigate. Dunant's nonseries crime novels include *Transgressions* (1998) and *Snowstorms in a Hot Climate* (1988). Well-known in England as a BBC television host, Dunant presided over *The Late Show*, described as *The Tonight Show* for intellectuals. Appearing in her T.V. host persona, Dunant is a featured character in *Living Proof* (1995), book 7 in John Harvey's popular Charlie Resnick series. The Nottingham inspector investigates the murder of a foul-mouthed American woman mystery writer at a local crime convention.

Hannah Wolfe...contract private investigator...London, England
- ❑ ❑ 1 - Birth Marks (1992)
- ❑ ❑ **2 - Fat Lands (1993) Silver Dagger winner ★**
- ❑ ❑ 3 - Under My Skin (1995)
- ❑ ❑ . . . .
- ❑ ❑ . . . .

■ DUNBAR, Sophie [P]

Sophie Dunbar's "delightfully irreverent, slightly wacky and sizzlingly sexy" first novel, *Behind Eclaire's Doors* (1993), introduces Danish-Cajun hairdresser, Evangeline Claire Jenerette, and her corporate attorney husband, Dan Louis Claiborne. Although their second adventure, *Redneck Riviera* (1998), was published after book 3, you'll want to read them in the proper order, so as not to miss any of the steamy fun. The Claibornes live in an authentically-restored Garden District townhouse, with Claire's beauty shop occupying the ground floor. More French country cottage than hair salon, Eclaire features tapestries, terra cotta, oil portraits on rough plaster walls, and the occasional murder. In book 4, *Shiveree* (1999), Claire and Dan's best friends are getting married in one of the city's swankiest hotels. Faster than you can hum "Here Comes the Bride," all hell breaks loose and supermodel-turned-detective, Nectarine Savoy, has a murder investigation on her hands. A New Orleans native, the author lives with her husband in Southern California.

Claire Claiborne...beauty salon owner...New Orleans, Louisiana
- ❑ ❑ 1 - Behind Eclaire's Doors (1993)
- ❑ ❑ 2 - Redneck Riviera (1998)
- ❑ ❑ 3 - A Bad Hair Day (1996)
- ❑ ❑ 4 - Shiveree (1999)
- ❑ ❑ 5 - Senseless Ax of Beauty (2000)
- ❑ ❑ . . . .
- ❑ ❑ . . . .

■ DUNLAP, Susan

Two-time Anthony nominee and author of 17 books, Susan Dunlap has written series mysteries featuring all three detective types—police, private eye and amateur. California homicide detective and former beat cop, Jill Smith, contends with unusual crimes, quirky suspects and radical-chic politics Berkeley-style. Former San Francisco medical examiner turned private investigator, Kiernan O'Shaughnessy lives at the beach near La Jolla with an ex-football player houseman who is a gourmet cook, while ex-PR executive Vejay Haskell reads meters for Pacific Gas & Electric in Northern California's picturesque Russian River area. Dunlap has edited several anthologies and is a frequent short story contributor. After growing up in New York, she earned B.A. and M.A.T. degrees in English from Bucknell University and the University of North Carolina. She has done social work in New York City, Baltimore and Contra Costa County, California, and taught Hatha Yoga. A founding member and past president of Sisters in Crime, she lives near San Francisco.

Jill Smith...homicide detective...Berkeley, California

❏ ❏   1 - Karma (1981)
❏ ❏   2 - As a Favor (1984)
❏ ❏   3 - Not Exactly a Brahmin (1985)
❏ ❏   4 - Too Close to the Edge (1987)
❏ ❏   5 - A Dinner To Die For (1987)
❏ ❏   6 - Diamond in the Buff (1990)
❏ ❏   7 - Death and Taxes (1992)
❏ ❏   8 - Time Expired (1993)
❏ ❏   9 - Sudden Exposure (1996)
❏ ❏ 10 - Cop Out (1997)
❏ ❏   . . . .
❏ ❏   . . . .

Kiernan O'Shaughnessy...medical examiner turned P.I....La Jolla, California

❏ ❏   1 - **Pious Deception (1989) Anthony nominee** ☆
❏ ❏   2 - **Rogue Wave (1991) Anthony nominee** ☆
❏ ❏   3 - High Fall (1994)
❏ ❏   4 - No Immunity (1998)
❏ ❏   . . . .
❏ ❏   . . . .

Vejay Haskell...utility meter reader...Northern California

❏ ❏   1 - An Equal Opportunity Death (1983)
❏ ❏   2 - The Bohemian Connection (1985)
❏ ❏   3 - The Last Annual Slugfest (1986)
❏ ❏   . . . .
❏ ❏   . . . .

■ DUNN, Carola

Author of more than 30 Regency novels since 1980, Carola Dunn writes mysteries featuring the Honourable Daisy Dalrymple, an aristocratic young woman of the 1920s, who writes magazine features about stately English homes for *Town and Country*. The series is "heaven for those who miss Allingham and Sayers...perfect hammock reading that never insults your intelligence or twists your brain—a neat trick to pull off, it's a portrait under glass of another era, said one newspaper reviewer. Recently-engaged to her Scotland Yard D.C.I. beau, Daisy investigates a rash of poison-pen letters threatening residents of her sister Violet's Kent village in book 7, *Styx and Stones* (1999). Armed with a degree in French and Russian from Manchester University, Dunn traveled extensively throughout Europe, Canada, Israel, Samoa and Fiji. Born in London, she came to the U.S. at age 22 and lived for a number of years in San Diego, where her various jobs included market research, building design and construction labor. She lives in Oregon.

Daisy Dalrymple...1920s aristocratic feature writer...Hampshire, England

❏ ❏   1 - Death at Wentwater Court (1994)
❏ ❏   2 - The Winter Garden Mystery (1995)
❏ ❏   3 - Requiem for a Mezzo (1996)
❏ ❏   4 - Murder on the Flying Scotsman (1997)
❏ ❏   5 - Damsel in Distress (1997)
❏ ❏   6 - Dead in the Water (1998)
❏ ❏   . . . .
❏ ❏   . . . .

■ DUNNETT, Dorothy

Renowned historical novelist Dorothy Dunnett is best known for her six-volume Lymond Saga featuring Francis Crawford of Lymond, a 16th century Scottish rebel introduced in *The Game of Kings* (1961), recently re-released in a freshened text. "Byron crossed with Lawrence of Arabia," raved a London critic. Between historical novels, Dunnett penned seven espionage thrillers featuring American portrait painter and yachtsman, Johnson Johnson. Owner of a yacht named Dolly, the bifocaled government agent attracts a succession of birds who serve as the books' narrators. An operatic soprano handles the Scottish-set

Dolly and the Singing Bird (1968), while a blue-blooded chef takes over when the action moves to Spain in *Dolly and the Cookie Bird* (1970). Other exotic series locales include Italy, the Bahamas and Morocco. The first four books were published under the author's maiden name, Dorothy Halliday, in England. An established portrait painter and sailing enthusiast, she lives with her husband, author, newspaper editor and playwright, Sir Alastair Dunnett, in Edinburgh.

Johnson Johnson...British agent and yachtsman

❑ ❑ 1 - The Photogenic Soprano (1968)
❑ ❑   - Brit.-Dolly and the Singing Bird
❑ ❑ 2 - Murder in the Round (1970)
❑ ❑   - Brit.-Dolly and the Cookie Bird
❑ ❑ 3 - Match for a Murderer (1971)
❑ ❑   - Brit.-Dolly and the Doctor Bird
❑ ❑ 4 - Murder in Focus (1972)
❑ ❑   - Brit.-Dolly and the Starry Bird
❑ ❑ 5 - Split Code (1976)
❑ ❑   - Brit.-Dolly and the Nanny Bird
❑ ❑ 6 - Tropical Issue (1983)
❑ ❑   - Brit.-Dolly and the Bird of Paradise
❑ ❑ 7 - Moroccan Traffic (1992)
❑ ❑   - Brit.-Send a Fax to the Kasbah
❑ ❑   . . . .
❑ ❑   . . . .

■ DYMMOCH, Michael Allen [P]

When Michael Allen Dymmoch (DIM-ick) won the 1992 St. Martin's Press Malice Domestic Contest for best first traditional mystery, publication of her first novel, *The Man Who Understood Cats* (1993), was assured. Stressed-out Chicago cop, John Thinnes, and successful, urbane and unabashedly gay psychiatrist, Jack Caleb, are introduced in the book that a Los Angeles Times reviewer called "continuously surprising, ingeniously plotted, swiftly advancing, yet sensitively observed." The cats in question are Caleb's—one black, the other orange—Freud and B.F. Skinner. In book 2, *Death of a Blue Mountain Cat* (1995), Thinnes relies heavily on Caleb's knowledge of the art world when a Native American artist is murdered at an ultraconservative art museum. In *Incendiary Designs* (1998), Caleb rescues a trapped patrolman from a police car about to be torched at the beginning of a long, hot urban summer. With degrees in chemistry and law enforcement, Dymmoch is a professional driver who lives and works in the northern suburbs of Chicago.

John Thinnes & Jack Caleb...cop & gay psychiatrist...Chicago, Illinois

❑ ❑ **1 - The Man Who Understood Cats (1993) SMP/MD winner ★**
❑ ❑ 2 - The Death of Blue Mountain Cat (1995)
❑ ❑ 3 - Incendiary Designs (1998)
❑ ❑   . . . .
❑ ❑   . . . .

■ ECCLES, Marjorie

Marjorie Eccles has written 11 books featuring Detective Superintendent Gil Mayo, introduced in *Cast a Cold Eye* (1988). Joined by his new sergeant, the intelligent and attractive Abigail Moon, starting with book 6, Mayo is a Yorkshireman transplanted to the Midlands, working from divisional police headquarters across from the town hall in fictional Lavenstock. Not yet published in the U.S., Mayo's latest appearance is book 11, *The Superintendent's Daughter* (1999). In book 10, *Killing Me Softly*, Mayo and Moon investigate members of the Hertfordshire force who seem to be involved in a series of robberies. Before turning to crime writing, Eccles penned seven romantic suspense novels under the pseudonyms Judith Bordill and Jennifer Hyde. Like Gil Mayo, Eccles was born in Yorkshire and later moved to the Midlands where she lived for 30 years. A graduate of the Open University, she currently makes her home in a picturesque village on the edge of the Chilterns in a Victorian house with a large garden.

Gil Mayo...detective chief inspector...Midlands, England

  ❑ ❑   1 - Cast a Cold Eye (1988)
  ❑ ❑   2 - Death of a Good Woman (1989)
  ❑ ❑   3 - Requiem for a Dove (1990)
  ❑ ❑   4 - More Deaths Than One (1990)
  ❑ ❑   5 - Late of This Parish (1992)
  ❑ ❑   6 - The Company She Kept (1993)
  ❑ ❑   7 - An Accidental Shroud (1994)
  ❑ ❑   8 - A Death of Distinction (1995)
  ❑ ❑   9 - A Species of Revenge (1996)
  ❑ ❑ 10 - Killing Me Softly (1998)
  ❑ ❑   . . . .
  ❑ ❑   . . . .

■ EDGHILL, Rosemary [P]

Rosemary Edghill is the pseudonym of eluki bes sha-har, author of more than 15 novels of romance, fantasy, science fiction and mystery. Her Karen Hightower mysteries feature a 30-something Manhattan graphics designer, also known as Bast the white witch, first seen in *Speak Daggers to Her* (1994). The three Hightower mysteries are collected in a single volume, *Bell, Book, and Murder* (1998). Edghill's most recent novel is *The Shadow of Albion* (1999), written in collaboration with Andre Norton. *Kirkus* called it an "alternate-world historical romantic fantasy" with "swirling intrigues, restrained magics, subtle spies, and dauntless heroines: jolly good." Edghill describes it as "James Bond meets Jane Austen in a Regency that never was." She and Norton are working on a sequel. As eluki bes shahar she has written several X-Men novels, including *Smoke and Mirrors* (1997) and in collaboration with Tom Defalco, *Time's Arrow: The Future* (1998). Born in Alameda, California, she lives in New York's Mid-Hudson Valley.

Karen Hightower aka Bast...white witch graphic designer...New York, New York

  ❑ ❑   1 - Speak Daggers to Her (1994)
  ❑ ❑   2 - Book of Moons (1995)
  ❑ ❑   3 - The Bowl of Night (1996)
  ❑ ❑   . . . .
  ❑ ❑   . . . .

■ EDWARDS, Grace F.

In her Anthony award-nominated first mystery featuring Mali Anderson, a 31-year-old ex-cop from Harlem, Grace Edwards "captures the rhythm of life on the streets." When first seen in *If I Should Die* (1997), Mali has been fired after only two years on the force, when she punched out a fellow officer for sexual slurs. Living with her jazz musician father, Mali is raising her orphaned 11-year-old nephew and working toward a Ph.D. in social work. In book 2, *A Toast Before Dying* (1998), Mali is hired by a wealthy white woman to investigate the murder of a beautiful bartender and aspiring singer. A serial killer is on the loose in Harlem in book 3, *No Time To Die* (1999). Edwards' first novel, *In the Shadow of the Peacock* (1988) was published under the name Grace Yearwood. Born and raised in Harlem, Edwards earned an M.A. in creative writing at City University of New York. She has reviewed books for the *Los Angeles Times* and taught at The Writers Voice in New York City. A member of the Harlem Writers Guild, she lives in Brooklyn.

Mali Anderson...black ex-cop in Harlem...New York, New York

  ❑ ❑   **1 - If I Should Die (1997) Anthony nominee** ☆
  ❑ ❑   2 - A Toast Before Dying (1998)
  ❑ ❑   . . . .
  ❑ ❑   . . . .

EDWARDS, Ruth Dudley

Ruth Dudley Edwards is the creator of a laugh-out-loud series featuring career civil servant Robert Amiss and his good friend, police Supt. James Milton. One reviewer described these adventures as well-plotted mysteries with a cast of characters straight out of a Pink Panther movie. After resigning his civil service appointment in disgust at the end of book 2, Amiss begins a series of temporary posts, enabling Supt. Milton to make use of Amiss' investigative skills and Edwards to satirize a whole host of British institutions. In *Clubbed to Death* (1992), short-listed for the Last Laugh award, Amiss goes undercover as a waiter at a gentleman's club. Also short-listed for the Last Laugh is *Ten Lords A-Leaping* (1996), where ten lords have simultaneous heart attacks. When last seen in book 8, *Publish and Be Murdered* (1998), Amiss is managing a 200-year-old right-wing magazine of economics and politics. A prize-winning biographer and historian, Edwards once worked for the British Post Office and Department of Industry. Born and educated in Ireland, she has lived in England since 1965.

James Milton & Robert Amiss...police superintendent & ex-civil servant...London, England

- ❑ ❑ 1 - **Corridors of Death (1981) Creasey nominee** ☆
- ❑ ❑ 2 - St. Valentine's Day Murders (1985)
- ❑ ❑ 3 - The English School of Murder (1990)
- ❑ ❑   - APA-The School of English Murder
- ❑ ❑ 4 - **Clubbed to Death (1992) Last Laugh nominee** ☆
- ❑ ❑ 5 - Matricide at St. Martha's (1994)
- ❑ ❑ 6 - **Ten Lords A-Leaping (1996) Last Laugh nominee** ☆
- ❑ ❑ 7 - Murder in a Cathedral (1996)
- ❑ ❑ 8 - Publish and Be Murdered (1998)
- ❑ ❑   . . . .
- ❑ ❑   . . . .

EICHLER, Selma

Selma Eichler is the creator of queen-size private investigator Desiree Shapiro, whose husband Ed choked on a chicken bone and died after only five years of marriage. Although the 5-foot two-inch Desiree had been a Manhattan P.I. more than 20 years before catching her first murder case, she had handled mostly divorce and insurance matters, with some child custody and missing persons thrown in. But that was before a poor grocery delivery kid was accused of murdering an elderly woman during a botched robbery in book 1, *Murder Can Kill Your Social Life* (1994). When last seen in *Murder Can Singe Your Old Flame* (1999), Desiree is just getting over an unhappy love affair when her former sweetie shows up, begging her to investigate the death of his recent bride. The short-lived Mrs. was a stewardess who may have uncovered a drug smuggler among her fellow attendants. A former advertising copywriter, Eichler lives in Manhattan where she has been known to try out recipes for Desiree on husband Lloyd.

Desiree Shapiro...5'2" queen-size P.I....New York, New York

- ❑ ❑ 1 - Murder Can Kill Your Social Life (1994)
- ❑ ❑ 2 - Murder Can Ruin Your Looks (1995)
- ❑ ❑ 3 - Murder Can Stunt Your Growth (1996)
- ❑ ❑ 4 - Murder Can Wreck Your Reunion (1997)
- ❑ ❑ 5 - Murder Can Spook Your Cat (1998)
- ❑ ❑ 6 - Murder Can Singe Your Old Flame (1999)
- ❑ ❑   . . . .
- ❑ ❑   . . . .

ELKINS, Charlotte & Aaron

Charlotte Elkins was the American art librarian at a San Francisco museum when husband Aaron sold his first mystery novel in 1982. Since then they have co-authored the 1992 Agatha award-winning short story "Nice Gorilla" and launched a mystery series featuring novice golf pro Lee Ofsted and homicide detective Graham Sheldon. Charlotte creates the plot, setting and characters for the series, while Aaron serves as in-house editor. "I give him ten pages and he gives me back twenty, so we rarely have disagreements," she told *Contemporary Authors*. As Emily Spenser, she has written five romance novels. In addition to their collaborative fiction, Aaron writes two mystery series—one featuring anthropologist-detective Gideon Oliver and the other art curator-sleuth Chris Norgren. Published in six languages,

the award-winning series have been filmed for television. Born in Houston, Charlotte earned an M.L.S. from San Jose State University. A former professor of anthropology, Aaron holds an Ed.D. from the University of California, Berkeley. They live in Washington State.

Lee Ofsted & Graham Sheldon...woman golf pro & homicide detective...Washington
- ❏ ❏ 1 - A Wicked Slice (1989)
- ❏ ❏ 2 - Rotten Lies (1995)
- ❏ ❏ 3 - Nasty Breaks (1997)
- ❏ ❏ ....
- ❏ ❏ ....

■ ELROD, P.N.

P.N. Elrod is Patricia N. Elrod, author of four vampire series, including the Vampire Files set in 1930s gangland Chicago. Ace reporter Jack Fleming is transformed into a good-guy vampire by the lovely Maureen. After being gunned down by a contract killer in book 1, *Bloodlist* (1990), Jack returns in search of Maureen in *Lifeblood* (1990), only to discover he's being stalked by a vampire hunter. Philosophical about his situation, Jack realizes he will never grow old or die, can sleep all day and gets to hunt down his own

murderer. Elrod says she chose Jack's name by pairing Jack Chalker with Ian Fleming. She sees Nicholas Cage or Tom Amandes playing the part. In book 8, *The Dark Sleep* (1999), Jack's got some mob money nobody seems to be missing. The supporting cast includes Jack's girlfriend, nightclub singer Bobbi Smythe, and his P.I. partner and good friend, Englishman Charles Escott, named in honor of a Sherlock Holmes alias. Rumored to be a passionate collector of Barbie dolls, Elrod lives in Richardson, Texas.

Jack Fleming...'30s reporter turned vampire...Chicago, Illinois
- ❏ ❏ 1 - Bloodlist (1990)
- ❏ ❏ 2 - Lifeblood (1990)
- ❏ ❏ 3 - Bloodcircle (1990)
- ❏ ❏ 4 - Art in the Blood (1991)
- ❏ ❏ 5 - Fire in the Blood (1991)
- ❏ ❏ 6 - Blood on the Water (1992)
- ❏ ❏ 7 - A Chill in the Blood (1998)
- ❏ ❏ ....
- ❏ ❏ ....

■ EMERSON, Kathy Lynn

Author of more than 20 books since 1984, Kathy Lynn Emerson alternates between contemporary and historical fiction with an occasional nonfiction project for variety. Her favorite century is the 16th, the setting for her Lady Appleton mysteries. An expert on poisonous herbs, Susanna is the wife of Elizabethan courtier and intelligence-gatherer, Sir Robert Appleton. In book 1, *Face Down in the Marrow-Bone Pie* (1997), Susanna travels to Robert's childhood home in Lancashire, against his wishes, where she finds murder and family secrets. In book 3, *Face Down*

Among the Winchester Geese (1999), it's 1563 and a mysterious Frenchwoman comes calling at the London home Robert has leased for his wife. Emerson's nonfiction books include *The Writer's Guide to Everyday Life in Renaissance England* (1996). As Kaitlyn Gorton she has written three romance novels. A graduate of Bates College, she holds an M.A. from Old Dominion University. A former librarian, lecturer and English instructor at various colleges, Emerson lives in rural Maine.

Susanna Appleton...Elizabethan herbalist noblewoman ...England
- ❏ ❏ 1 - Face Down in the Marrow-Bone Pie (1997)
- ❏ ❏ 2 - Face Down Upon an Herbal (1998)
- ❏ ❏ 3 - Face Down Among the Winchester Geese (1999)
- ❏ ❏ 4 - Face Down Beneath the Eleanor Cross (2000)
- ❏ ❏ ....
- ❏ ❏ ....

ENGLISH, Brenda

Brenda English is the creator of Northern Virginia police reporter Sutton McPhee, first seen in *Corruption of Faith* (1997), when her younger sister Cara, a church secretary, is found murdered in a bank parking lot. Police are baffled. When last seen in book 3, *Corruption of Justice* (1999), Sutton is riding with a beat cop in order to write a day-in-the-life feature. When the young cop ends up dead, she gets a bigger story than she planned. A journalism graduate of the University of Georgia, majoring in radio, T.V. and film-produc-tion, English worked for a Florida television station as a film editor and reporter, before moving to the *Tallahassee Democrat* as a print reporter. While her husband worked at the *Detroit Free Press*, English spent five years at the now-defunct *Ypsilanti Press* before moving to Northern Virginia where she was publications manager at Fairfax Hospital for a dozen years. A native of Georgia, where she grew up on a farm south of Savannah, she lives with her husband and daughter in the Tidewater area of Virginia.

Sutton McPhee...police reporter...Fairfax County, Virginia

- ❏ ❏   1 - Corruption of Faith (1997)
- ❏ ❏   2 - Corruption of Power (1998)
- ❏ ❏   ....
- ❏ ❏   ....

ENNIS, Catherine

Former medical illustrator Catherine Ennis has written seven novels, including her first, *To the Lightning* (1988), published at the age of 51. A science fiction romance, the story features two women caught in a lightning storm and transported to a primitive, uninhabited world in their VW station wagon. Ennis has also written two mysteries featuring Dr. Bernadette Hebert, a Louisiana crime lab expert, introduced in *Clearwater* (1991). Dr. Bernie returns in *Chatauqua* (1993). Ennis' most recent novel, *The Naked Eye* (1998), features prominent wildlife photographer, Katherine Duncan, drawn to the dangers of the Louisiana swampland. A Southerner by birth, Ennis still lives in the deep South where she enjoys gardening, gourmet cooking and working on her Model A Ford coupe. In addition to her experience as a medical illustrator, she has worked as a wholesale florist and research office manager, spent several years on the arts and crafts show circuit, and started her own business using her art background.

Bernadette Hebert...lesbian crime lab expert...Louisiana

- ❏ ❏   1 - Clearwater (1991)
- ❏ ❏   2 - Chatauqua (1993)
- ❏ ❏   ....
- ❏ ❏   ....

EPSTEIN, Carole

Carole Epstein misspent her youth as a fashion model in London and then came home to Montreal where she spent 20 years running a business that manufactured belts for the apparel industry, at one time the largest such manufacturer in North America. Her mysteries feature 40-something businesswoman Barbara Simons, downsized from her high-level Montreal job at PanCanada Airlines in *Perilous Friends* (1996). "Susan Isaacs goes Canadian in this piquant first novel," said the *Kirkus* reviewer. In *Perilous Relations* (1997), Barbara and her T.V.-reporter friend Joanne investigate the murder of Barbara's former boss. Epstein has also worked as an art gallery assistant and production assistant on what she describes as "two really bad films." Her most unusual vacation took her, two friends and four Cayapo Indians to deepest Brazil, one hour by canoe from the nearest village and another hour by plane to the nearest civilization. These days Epstein spends the winter months in Florida and returns to Montreal for the summer.

Barbara Simons...downsized business executive...Montreal, Quebec, Canada

- ❏ ❏   1 - Perilous Friends (1996)
- ❏ ❏   2 - Perilous Relations (1997)
- ❏ ❏   ....
- ❏ ❏   ....

■ EVANOVICH, Janet

"Raucous, rambunctious Jersey girl Stephanie Plum," the Bounty Hunter from Hell, is the comic creation of Jersey girl Janet Evanovich. "Hilarious dialogue, oddball characters, and eye-popping action," says *Booklist* about her fifth adventure, *High Five* (1999). Stephanie is "a righteous babe if ever there was one." Four-time nominee for best first mystery, the series opener introduced Cousin Vinnie of Vincent Plum Bail Bonds, Grandma Mazur, Detective Joe Morelli, Ranger, and Rex the hamster. When asked if she is

Stephanie Plum, Evanovich says they're both from New Jersey, love Cheetos and have owned a hamster. Although their common history includes learning to drive in a 1953 powder blue Buick, Steph is not autobiographical, insists Evanovich, who has never killed anyone and did not lose her virginity in a bakery. Before writing mysteries, she penned 12 funny romance novels, including three as Steffie Hall. A graduate of Douglass College with a degree in art, Evanovich lives in New Hampshire.

Stephanie Plum...lingerie buyer turned bounty hunter...Trenton, New Jersey

❏	❏	1 -	**One for the Money (1994) Creasey winner ★**
			Agatha, Edgar, Last Laugh & Shamus nominee ☆☆☆☆
❏	❏	2 -	**Two for the Dough (1996) Last Laugh winner ★**
❏	❏	3 -	**Three To Get Deadly (1997) Silver Dagger winner ★**
❏	❏	4 -	Four To Score (1998)
❏	❏		. . . .
❏	❏		. . . .

■ EVANS, Geraldine

Geraldine Evans has written three mysteries featuring marriage-phobic Detective Inspector Joseph Rafferty and his well-educated Welsh sergeant, Dafyd (David) Llewellyn. In the series opener, *Dead Before Morning* (1993), the Yorkshire policemen are called to a posh private psychiatric facility where a nude young woman has been found dead on the hospital grounds. Their list of suspects includes the social-climbing hospital director, Dr. Melville-Briggs, his do-gooder wife, and his mistress, all of whom appear to have

airtight alibis. In book 2, *Down Among the Dead Men* (1994), Rafferty suspects their newest homicide is the work of a copycat killer. Rich and beautiful Barbara Longman has been lured to a lovely meadow on the pretext someone was about to destroy wildflowers she had fought to protect. Rafferty and Llewellyn were last seen in book 3, *Death Line* (1995), published only in Britain. London-born of Irish parents, Evans lives in Surrey with her husband. She once helped run a vehicle repair shop.

Joseph Rafferty & Dafyd Llewellyn...D.I.& his Welsh sergeant...Yorkshire, England

❏	❏	1 -	Dead Before Morning (1993)
❏	❏	2 -	Down Among the Dead Men (1994)
❏	❏	3 -	Death Line (1995)
❏	❏		. . . .
❏	❏		. . . .

■ EYRE, Elizabeth [P]

Elizabeth Eyre is one of the pseudonyms of London-born authors Jill Staynes and Margaret Storey, writing partners for two mystery series. As Elizabeth Eyre, they write a Renaissance Italy series featuring Sigismondo da Roca, "unofficial Mr. Fix-it for papal bigwigs and the aristocracy," and his "dim-witted but exceedingly loyal servant" Benno. Introduced in *Death of a Duchess* (1992), Sigismondo was last seen in book 6, *Dirge for a Doge* (1996), when a Venetian nobleman is stilettoed in his locked palazzo study.

"An exquisitely crafted blend of history, humor, and suspense," said *Booklist*. As Susannah Stacey, Staynes and Storey have written eight contemporary English mysteries featuring Inspector Robert Bone, including the Agatha-nominated series opener, *Goodbye Nanny Gray* (1987). After their days together at St. Paul's School in London, Staynes earned a B.A. at St. Anne's, Oxford, while Storey went on to Girton College, Cambridge where she earned B.A. and M.A. degrees. Staynes lives in London and Storey in Kent.

Sigismondo...agent of a Renaissance duke...Venice, Italy

❏	❏	1 -	Death of a Duchess (1992)
❏	❏	2 -	Curtains for the Cardinal (1993)
❏	❏	3 -	Poison for the Prince (1994)

❑ ❑   4 - Bravo for the Bride (1994)
❑ ❑   5 - Axe for an Abbot (1996)
❑ ❑   6 - Dirge for a Doge (1997)
❑ ❑   . . . .
❑ ❑   . . . .

■ FAIRSTEIN, Linda

As director of the Sex Crimes Prosecution Unit for the Manhattan District Attorney's Office, Linda Fairstein has been waging war against rape for more than 20 years. Starting with her Macavity-nominated first mystery, *Final Jeopardy* (1996), she takes readers behind the scenes with "smart, sexy, indefatigable and relentlessly likable" Alexandra Cooper (*Library Journal*), who works the same job as Fairstein. When last seen in *Cold Hit* (1999), Coop and wisecracking N.Y.P.D. detectives, Chapman and Wallace, are on a circuitous chase through the rarefied Manhattan art world. "Fairstein once again uses her own experience and knowledge of the city to strong advantage," raved *Publishers Weekly* in a starred review. A graduate of Vassar College and the University of Virginia Law School, Fairstein has also written a nonfiction book, *Sexual Violence: Our War Against Rape* (1993). Her script for HBO's 1999 "Happily Ever After" cartoon series features a farmer's clever daughter as a detective in "Aesop's Fables: A Whodunit Musical."

Alexandra Cooper...chief sex crimes prosecutor...New York, New York

❑ ❑   1 - **Final Jeopardy (1996) Macavity nominee** ☆
❑ ❑   2 - Likely To Die (1997)
❑ ❑   3 - Cold Hit (1999)
❑ ❑   . . . .
❑ ❑   . . . .

■ FALLON, Ann C.

Yeats scholar Ann C(onnerton) Fallon has written five contemporary Irish mysteries featuring Dublin solicitor James Fleming, introduced in *Blood is Thicker* (1990). A comfortably well-off bachelor with an upper-middle class background and a love of railway travel, Fleming has a law practice that affords him some unusual opportunities for sleuthing. In book 3, *Dead Ends* (1992), he has gone to the Cromlech Lodge to draw up a will for the owner. After a guest topples down the main staircase and dies on the dining room floor, Fleming's inquiry turns up an old diary telling of the lodge's previous incarnation as a "home for the bewildered." Fleming's fifth appearance in *Hour of Our Death* (1995) involves a woman with a vision of the Blessed Virgin. While earning a Ph.D. in English from Brandeis University, Fallon wrote her doctoral dissertation on *The Speckled Bird*, an unpublished novel of William Butler Yeats (1865-1939).

James Fleming...train-loving solicitor...Dublin, Ireland

❑ ❑   1 - Blood Is Thicker (1990)
❑ ❑   2 - Where Death Lies (1991)
❑ ❑   3 - Dead Ends (1992)
❑ ❑   4 - Potter's Field (1993)
❑ ❑   5 - Hour of Our Death (1995)
❑ ❑   . . . .
❑ ❑   . . . .

■ FARMER, Jerrilyn

Television writer Jerrilyn Farmer is the creator of Hollywood chef, Madeline Bean, owner of Madeline Bean Catering, and her best friend and business partner, Wesley Westcott. As caterers to the stars, Maddie and Wes specialize in exotic food and over-the-top events, such as the Halloween dinner for 600 guests of a notorious film producer in the series opener, *Sympathy for the Devil* (1998). After preparing breakfast for the Pope and 2,000 bigwigs in *Immaculate Reception* (1999), they tackle a *Killer Wedding* (2000) in book 3. Farmer moved to Los Angeles from suburban Chicago in search of an acting job, but found a Hollywood writing career instead. A staff writer on *Jeopardy!*, she has created questions for more than a dozen T.V. game shows, including *Supermarket Sweep*, still running on Lifetime. In addition to celebrity interview specials, she has written comedy specials for Dana Carvey and Martin Short. Farmer lives in Glendale, California.

Madeline Bean...Hollywood party planner...Los Angeles, California
- ❏ ❏ 1 - Sympathy for the Devil (1998)
- ❏ ❏ 2 - Immaculate Reception (1999)
- ❏ ❏ . . . .
- ❏ ❏ . . . .

■ FARRELL, Gillian B.

Gillian B. Farrell brings an intimate knowledge of the theatre and private eye worlds to her mysteries featuring New York actress, Annie McGrogan. Recently returned from Los Angeles in *Alibi for an Actress* (1992), Annie and ex-cop turned P.I. Sonny Gandolfo are hired to protect a sexy soap star from a threatening fan. After winning a movie role that takes her to Upstate New York's Mohonk Mountain House, Annie ends up the prime suspect when the director is murdered in *Murder and a Muse* (1994). An actor in Los Angeles and New York, Farrell has worked as a private detective in New York City, where she served divorce papers on a Mafia Don and assisted Bernie Goetz with his defense. Farrell is married to Edgar award-winning author Larry Beinhart, whose *American Hero* (1993) inspired the 1997 film, *Wag the Dog*, starring Dustin Hoffman and Robert DeNiro. Born in New York City, she lives with her family in Woodstock, New York.

Annie McGrogan...actor-P.I. returned from LA...New York, New York
- ❏ ❏ 1 - Alibi for an Actress (1992)
- ❏ ❏ 2 - Murder and a Muse (1994)
- ❏ ❏ . . . .
- ❏ ❏ . . . .

■ FARRELLY, Gail E.

Accounting professor Gail E. Farrelly is the creator of finance instructor Lisa King, introduced in *Beaned in Boston: Murder at a Finance Convention* (1995). In book 2, *Duped by Derivatives* (1999), Lisa takes a leave from teaching to work at a New York investment management firm. Also returning in book 2 are Boston policeman Roy Clarkson, who opens a Manhattan detective agency, and feisty Katie Maguire, who trades in her Boston chambermaid's uniform and signs on as Clarkson's secretary-receptionist and sole associate at Clarkson and Associates. Associate professor of accounting at Rutgers University, Farrelly is a financial communications consultant and co-author of *Shaping the Corporate Image* (1992). Author of numerous articles on financial reporting issues, she holds a Ph.D. in accounting from George Washington University. Her sister Rita K. Farrelly, author of *Not in Bronxville* (1998), also writes mysteries.

Lisa King...finance professor and CPA...Boston, Massachusetts
- ❏ ❏ 1 - Beaned in Boston (1995)
- ❏ ❏ 2 - Duped by Derivatives (1999)
- ❏ ❏ . . . .
- ❏ ❏ . . . .

■ FAWCETT, Quinn [P]

Quinn Fawcett is the shared pseudonym of Chelsea Quinn Yarbro and Bill Fawcett, collaborators on two historical mystery series. Beginning with *The Adventures of Mycroft Holmes* (1994), their series featuring Sherlock's elder brother is the first Mycroft series to be authorized by Dame Jean Conan Doyle. The smarter brother's fourth appearance is *The Flying Scotsman* (1999). Their French series features Madame Victoire Vernet, devoted wife of a young French policeman in the time of Napoleon. When Madame's husband is wrongly accused of theft and murder, she single-mindedly sets out to clear his name with an investigation that leads from the safety of her boudoir to an assassination plot against the Emperor himself. Yarbro is a prolific author of science fiction, horror, mystery and children's books. She lives in Berkeley, California. A well-known editor of military history and science fiction, Fawcett makes his home in Lake Zurich, Illinois.

Mycroft Holmes...Sherlock Holmes' older brother...London, England
- ❏ ❏ 1 - The Adventures of Mycroft Holmes (1994)
- ❏ ❏ 2 - Against the Brotherhood (1997)
- ❏ ❏ 3 - Embassy Row (1998)
- ❏ ❏ . . . .
- ❏ ❏ . . . .

Victoire Vernet...wife of Napoleonic gendarme...Paris, France

❏ ❏	1 -	Napoleon Must Die (1993)
❏ ❏	2 -	Death Wears a Crown (1993)
❏ ❏		. . . .
❏ ❏		. . . .

■ FEDDERSEN, Connie

Award-winning romance writer Connie Feddersen is the author of more than 50 novels, with over eight million books in print, including her mysteries featuring sexy C.P.A. Amanda Hazard and small-town police chief, Nick Thorn, in Vamoose, Oklahoma. After the first Vamoose fatality is found *Dead in the Water* (1993), victims of foul play are later found in the cellar, the melon patch, the dirt, the mud, the driver's seat and the hay. Feddersen writes historical and western romance as Connie Drake, Debra Falcon,

Carol Finch and Gina Robins. A physical education and science major at Oklahoma State University, she taught school in Kansas before marrying former teacher and basketball coach Ed Feddersen, who painted the artwork (using his wife as a model) for the cover of book 3. The Feddersens live on a working ranch in Oklahoma where they raise cattle and farm wheat. Many of the scenes in her mysteries are inspired by actual incidents on their ranch.

Amanda Hazard...sexy small-town CPA...Vamoose, Oklahoma

❏ ❏	1 -	Dead in the Water (1993)
❏ ❏	2 -	Dead in the Cellar (1994)
❏ ❏	3 -	Dead in the Melon Patch (1995)
❏ ❏	4 -	Dead in the Dirt (1996)
❏ ❏	5 -	Dead in the Mud (1997)
❏ ❏	6 -	Dead in the Driver's Seat (1998)
❏ ❏		. . . .
❏ ❏		. . . .

■ FEMLING, Jean

Self-described newspaper addict Jean Femling is the creator of a Southern California mystery series featuring Orange County insurance claims investigator, Martha Brant, introduced in *Hush, Money* (1989). Martha, who answers to the name Moz, is half-Filipino. Often mistaken for Mexican, she regularly encounters racial prejudice and discrimination. Motivated by her employer's offer of a hefty reward for any agent providing proof of insurance fraud, Moz, who lives in a

garage apartment, has her eye on a small two-bedroom house in rural Silverado Canyon. In *Getting Mine* (1991), Moz investigates an automobile accident insurance scam, a story inspired by current newspaper headlines. Femling worked full-time as a computer trainer for her local community college district, while writing her Moz Brant mysteries on weekends and holidays. She lives in Costa Mesa, California where she is working on another Moz mystery.

Martha Brant...insurance claims investigator...Orange County, California

❏ ❏	1 -	Hush, Money (1989)
❏ ❏	2 -	Getting Mine (1991)
❏ ❏		. . . .
❏ ❏		. . . .

■ FENNELLY, Tony

Former Bourbon Street showgirl Tony Fennelly spent ten years writing and completed eight full-length books before selling *The Glory Hole Murders* (1985), earning her a best first novel Edgar nomination and launching her Matt Sinclair series. Books 1 and 2 were reprinted as *Murder With a Twist* (1991). The gay epileptic New Orleans D.A. turned furniture store owner has become a cult favorite, translated into German, Japanese, Danish and Czech. Fennelly's newer series features ex-stripper turned *Times-*

Picayune gossip columnist, Margo Fortier, introduced in *The Hippie in the Wall* (1994). Margo's third adventure, set on a cruise ship, titled *Don't Blame the Snake* by Fennelly, has been published in Germany as *Kreuzfahrt Mit Bis* (1999), *Cruise with a Bite*. A University of New Orleans graduate, Fennelly has studied at Fricke School of Music and worked as an exotic dancer, barmaid, welfare case worker and actress. Born in New Jersey, she lives in New Orleans.

Margo Fortier...ex-stripper turned columnist...New Orleans, Louisiana

❏ ❏ 1 - The Hippie in the Wall (1994)
❏ ❏ 2 - 1-900-DEAD (1997)
❏ ❏ . . . .
❏ ❏ . . . .

Matthew Arthur Sinclair...gay epileptic D.A. turned store owner...New Orleans, Louisiana

❏ ❏ 1 - **The Glory Hole Murders (1985) Edgar nominee** ☆
❏ ❏ 2 - The Closet Hanging (1987)
❏ ❏ 3 - Kiss Yourself Goodbye (1989)
❏ ❏ . . . .
❏ ❏ . . . .

■ FERGUSON, Frances [P]

Frances Ferguson is the pseudonym of Barbara-Serene Perkins, creator of D.S. Jane Perry, a well-educated, widely-traveled general's daughter, who joins the Metropolitan Police C.I.D. directly from university. Expecting some prejudice on the job, the French-speaking Perry drops Rees from her hyphenated name (Rees-Perry) to appear less posh. From the outset in *Missing Person* (1993), the bias runs deeper than anticipated and Perry applies for a transfer. The woman D.C.I. at her new post in Canterbury is promptly transferred, leaving Perry with "the male chauvinist pig of all time" as her new boss, according to Carol Harper in *Deadly Pleasures*. How lucky that her best friend from school, a woman neurosurgeon, lives nearby. Writing as Barbara Perkins, the author writes romantic fiction, much of which features the medical world. Originally trained as a nurse, Ferguson is studying to be a Shiatsu practitioner. She lives in East Kent.

Jane Perry...French-speaking detective sergeant...Canterbury, Kent, England

❏ ❏ 1 - Missing Person (1993)
❏ ❏ 2 - No Fixed Abode (1994)
❏ ❏ 3 - Identity Unknown (1995)
❏ ❏ 4 - With Intent To Kill (1996)
❏ ❏ . . . .
❏ ❏ . . . .

■ FERRIS, Monica [P]

Monica Ferris is the pseudonym of Anthony and Edgar award nominee Mary Pulver Kuhfeld for needlework mysteries featuring 50-something Betsy Devonshire, introduced in *Crewel World* (1999). Each book includes a needlework pattern designed specifically for the series. After creating a lovely Minnesota town full of interesting characters, Ferris realized she lacked the depth of knowledge to sustain believability in a sleuth who owned a needlework business. So she promptly murdered the intended protagonist and substituted her visiting sister Betsy, who inherits the shop and stays to solve the crime. "When you read about Betsy's frustration with learning to knit and deciphering *Quicken*, you are hearing me," says Ferris, who is working on her first sweater. As Mary Monica Pulver, she has written five mysteries featuring Peter and Kori Brichter. Born in Terre Haute, Indiana, Kuhfeld lives in St. Louis Park, Minnesota.

Betsy Devonshire...needlework shop owner...Excelsior, Minnesota

❏ ❏ 1 - Crewel World (1999)
❏ ❏ 2 - Framed in Lace (1999)
❏ ❏ . . . .
❏ ❏ . . . .

■ FICKLING, G.G. [P]

G.G. Fickling is the shared pseudonym of journalists Gloria G. and Forrest E. "Skip" Fickling, creators of Honey West, "the sexiest private eye ever to pull a trigger!" Beginning with *This Girl for Hire* (1957), much is made of Honey's sexual attributes, including her measurements (38-22-36) on the back cover. "There is a certain prefeminist charm in seeing the hard-boiled Honey at work in a man's world," said Bill Crider in *1001 Midnights* (1986), "despite Lt. Mark Storm and his attempts to persuade her to leave the brainwork to the men." Honey was a big success, complete with her own television series starring Anne Francis. The Ficklings also created $1000-a-day Los Angeles private eye Erik March, first seen in the Honey West series opener. Erik's three solo appearances were followed by his and Honey's last stand in *Stiff as a Broad* (1972). Gloria Fickling was a *Look* magazine fashion editor and *Women's Wear Daily* correspondent; her husband a sportswriter and broadcaster.

Erik March...macho private eye...Los Angeles, California

- ❏ ❏ 1 - Naughty But Dead (1962)
- ❏ ❏ 2 - The Case of the Radioactive Redhead (1963)
- ❏ ❏ 3 - The Crazy Mixed-Up Nude (1964)
- ❏ ❏ . . . .
- ❏ ❏ . . . .

Honey West...sexiest P.I. ever to pull a trigger...Los Angeles, California

- ❏ ❏ 1 - This Girl for Hire [includes Erik March] (1957)
- ❏ ❏ 2 - Girl on the Loose (1958)
- ❏ ❏ 3 - A Gun for Honey (1958)
- ❏ ❏ 4 - Girl on the Prowl (1959)
- ❏ ❏ 5 - Honey in the Flesh (1959)
- ❏ ❏ 6 - Dig a Dead Doll (1960)
- ❏ ❏ 7 - Kiss for a Killer (1960)
- ❏ ❏ 8 - Blood and Honey (1961)
- ❏ ❏ 9 - Bombshell (1964)
- ❏ ❏ 10 - Honey on Her Tail (1971)
- ❏ ❏ 11 - Stiff as a Broad [includes Erik March] (1972)
- ❏ ❏ . . . .
- ❏ ❏ . . . .

■ FIEDLER, Jacqueline

Commercial artist Jacqueline Fiedler writes what she calls animal "mytheries," puzzle stories arising from animal myths and folklore, with each book featuring a different species. Her amateur detective is Chicago-area wildlife artist Caroline Canfield, 30-something daughter of a Los Angeles television actress. Along with Spooks the Silver Persian and Evie the Everlast punching bag, Canfield lives in an 1879 church converted into her residence and "It's a Wild Life'" art studio, complete with a small cemetery. In the series opener, *Tiger's Palette* (1998), Caroline is hired to complete a huge mural for the zoo's white tiger exhibit, after her mentor plunges to his death from a scaffold. Snowbound at a remote wolf research center with some Internet pals in *Sketches with Wolves* (2000), Caroline must unmask the murderer among them. A frequent visitor to zoos and wildlife refuges, Fiedler operates her own design and illustration studio in Chicago.

Caroline Canfield...wildlife artist...River Ridge, Illinois

- ❏ ❏ 1 - Tiger's Palette (1998)
- ❏ ❏ 2 - Sketches With Wolves (2000)
- ❏ ❏ . . . .
- ❏ ❏ . . . .

■ FITZWATER, Judy

Judy Fitzwater writes mysteries featuring aspiring mystery novelist Jennifer Marsh, introduced in the aptly-titled *Dying To Get Published* (1998). Eight diligently-crafted manuscripts have earned Jennifer nothing but a large collection of rejection letters, so she dreams up a killer of an idea for her next attempt. After serving as a reluctant witness for the prosecution in *Dying To Get Even* (1999), Jennifer and her writing group pals return in book 3, *Dying for a Clue* (1999). Fitzwater says the members of her own writing group want to know why they don't get into the fun situations she scripts for Jennifer's cohorts. Thanks to growing up in an Air Force family, Fitzwater has lived in Georgia, Hawaii, Kentucky, Maine, New York, New Jersey, North Carolina, Oklahoma and Texas. With a B.A. in English, she later earned a master's in counseling. Fitzwater lives in Maryland with her husband, two daughters, and their Norwich terrier, Hunter.

Jennifer Marsh…aspiring mystery novelist…Atlanta, Georgia
- ❏ ❏ 1 - Dying To Get Published (1998)
- ❏ ❏ 2 - Dying To Get Even (1999)
- ❏ ❏ . . . .
- ❏ ❏ . . . .

■ FLETCHER, Jessica and Donald Bain

More than a dozen mysteries in the Murder-She-Wrote series based on television crime-solver, Jessica Fletcher, have been published since 1989 by Jessica Fletcher and Donald Bain. After solving two Colorado murders in book 12, *Murder at the Powderhorn Ranch* (1999), Jessica heads to New York, where one of her mysteries has been turned into a Broadway play in book 13, *Knock 'Em Dead* (1999). A ghostwriter since the early '60s, Bain has written at least 75 books, some carrying his byline, as well as articles, speeches and columns for corporate executives. According to a 1997 column in the *Rocky Mountain News*, Bain's first best-seller (and his second book) was *Coffee, Tea or Me?* (1968), the first of four stewardess adventures by the non-existent Trudy Baker and Rachel Jones. The series sold 17 million copies. Although Bain has agreed not to disclose which books he ghostwrites, it is said he has written at least some of the mysteries attributed to Margaret Truman.

Jessica Fletcher…60-something mystery writer…Cabot Cove, Maine
- ❏ ❏ 1 - Gin and Daggers (1989)
- ❏ ❏ 2 - Manhattans & Murder (1994)
- ❏ ❏ 3 - Rum & Razors (1995)
- ❏ ❏ 4 - Martinis & Mayhem (1995)
- ❏ ❏ 5 - A Deadly Judgment (1996)
- ❏ ❏ 6 - A Palette for Murder (1996)
- ❏ ❏ 7 - The Highland Fling Murders (1997)
- ❏ ❏ 8 - Brandy & Bullets (1997)
- ❏ ❏ 9 - Murder on the QE2 (1997)
- ❏ ❏ 10 - Murder in Moscow (1998)
- ❏ ❏ 11 - A Little Yuletide Murder (1998)
- ❏ ❏ . . . .
- ❏ ❏ . . . .

■ FLORA, Kate Clark

Kate Clark Flora has written five mysteries featuring Massachusetts educational consultant Thea Kozak, introduced in *Chosen for Death* (1994). This mystery about a law student, involving legal questions of inheritance, was triggered by an anguished birth mother's letter to Ann Landers. When last seen in *Death in Paradise* (1998), Thea is attending an educational seminar in Hawaii. "Fans of Thea's battle-hardened style know they can count on the knives coming out early and often," said *Kirkus*. Flora has also written *Silent Buddy* (1995), featuring high school biology teacher Ross McIntyre in a small-town Maine case of drug smuggling. Writing as Katharine Clark, she is the author of *Steal Away* (1998), "a tricky thriller" about the search for a kidnapped child. The daughter of a chicken farmer, Flora is a former assistant attorney general for the state of Maine. A graduate of Northeastern University law school, she lives in Concord, Massachusetts.

Thea Kozak…educational consultant…Boston, Massachusetts
- ❏ ❏ 1 - Chosen for Death (1994)
- ❏ ❏ 2 - Death in a Funhouse Mirror (1995)
- ❏ ❏ 3 - Death at the Wheel (1996)
- ❏ ❏ 4 - An Educated Death (1997)
- ❏ ❏ 5 - Death in Paradise (1998)
- ❏ ❏ . . . .
- ❏ ❏ . . . .

■ FORREST, Katherine V.

Two-time Lambda award winner Katherine V. Forrest is the creator of lesbian homicide detective Kate Delafield, tough and demanding ex-Marine leader of an L.A.P.D. homicide investigation team, introduced in *Amateur City* (1984). "Few mystery writers combine such an intelligent take on the issues with such solid storytelling," said *Publishers Weekly*. Kate's second case, *Murder at the Nightwood Bar* (1986), is a forthcoming Hollywood film, *River's Edge*, by director Tim Hunter. The La Brea Tar Pits become a crime scene in book 7, *Sleeping Bones* (1999). Forrest is the author of *Curious Wine* (1983), the all-time best-selling love story published by Naiad Press, where Forrest works as an editor. Co-editor of several lesbian anthologies, she has also written a fantasy science-fiction lesbian romance titled *Daughters of a Coral Dawn*.(1984). Born in Windsor, Ontario, Forrest attended Wayne State University and the University of California, Los Angeles. She lives in California.

Kate Delafield...LAPD lesbian homicide detective...Los Angeles, California
- ❏ ❏ 1 - Amateur City (1984)
- ❏ ❏ 2 - Murder at the Nightwood Bar (1986)
- ❏ ❏ **3 - The Beverly Malibu (1989) Lambda winner ★**
- ❏ ❏ **4 - Murder by Tradition (1991) Lambda winner ★**
- ❏ ❏ 5 - Liberty Square (1996)
- ❏ ❏ 6 - Apparition Alley (1997)
- ❏ ❏ . . . .
- ❏ ❏ . . . .

■ FOWLER, Earlene

Three-time Agatha award nominee Earlene Fowler has written seven mysteries featuring folk art museum curator and ex-rancher, Benni (Albenia) Harper, and sexy Latino Police Chief, Gabe Ortiz, of San Celina, a fictional artsy ranching community on California's Central Coast. Future installments in the quilt-patterned series will include books 8 and 9, *Arkansas Traveler* (2001) and *Steps to the Altar* (2002). Fowler confirms that she ages her characters just two years during the first seven books, in order to keep Benni's feisty, lovable grandmother, Dove, comfortably in her mid-70s. A native Californian raised in La Puente, Fowler was born to a Southern mother and a Western father, both the offspring of talented quilters and needlewomen. A lover of quilts, folk art, dogs, chicken-fried steak, country western music and cowboy boots, she owns 23 pairs of boots, including the purple ones that match her pick-up truck. Fowler lives in Fountain Valley, California.

Benni Harper...folk art museum curator...San Celina, California
- ❏ ❏ **1 - Fool's Puzzle (1994) Agatha nominee ☆**
- ❏ ❏ 2 - Irish Chain (1995)
- ❏ ❏ **3 - Kansas Troubles (1996) Agatha nominee ☆**
- ❏ ❏ **4 - Goose in the Pond (1997) Agatha nominee ☆**
- ❏ ❏ 5 - Dove in the Window (1998)
- ❏ ❏ 6 - Mariner's Compass (1999)
- ❏ ❏ 7 - Seven Sisters (2000)
- ❏ ❏ . . . .
- ❏ ❏ . . . .

■ FRANKEL, Valerie

Valerie Frankel is the author of four New York mysteries featuring tough-talking, gun-toting private investigator, Wanda Mallory, owner of the Do It Right Detective Agency in Times Square. "A little raunchy, quite funny, and very entertaining," said the *Tulsa World* about Mallory's debut in *Deadline for Murder* (1991). When last seen in *A Body To Die For* (1995), Mallory has joined Brooklyn's trendiest health club to investigate the suspected infidelities of the club's owner. A graduate of Dartmouth College where she wrote a weekly column for the school paper, Frankel got her first magazine job as a fact checker for *New York Woman* in 1987. An editor at *Mademoiselle* magazine, she is co-author with Ellen Tien of *The I Hate My Job Handbook: How To Deal With Hell at Work* (1996) and *Prime Time Style: The Ultimate T.V. Guide to Fashion Hits and Misses* (1997). Born in Newark, New Jersey, Frankel she lives in Brooklyn, New York.

Wanda Mallory...detective agency owner...New York, New York
- ❑ ❑ 1 - A Deadline for Murder (1991)
- ❑ ❑ 2 - Murder on Wheels (1992)
- ❑ ❑ 3 - Prime Time for Murder (1994)
- ❑ ❑ 4 - A Body To Die For (1995)
- ❑ ❑ . . . .
- ❑ ❑ . . . .

■ FRASER, Anthea

Anthea Fraser has published more than 30 novels, translated into seven languages, including her long-running series featuring Detective Chief Inspector David Webb, introduced in *A Shroud for Delilah* (1984). Tall and lanky, the divorced D.C.I. likes to sketch and paint. Called Spiderman by his colleagues, Webb is 46 when the series opens. The town of Shillingham and the county of Broadshire are fictional additions to southwest England. Beginning with book 5, *The Nine Bright Shiners* (1987), Fraser began using verses of "Green Grow the Rushes O" for her titles, although out of sequence with the folk song's verses. Book 9, *The Lily-White Boys* (1991) was retitled in the U.S. as *I'll Sing You Two-O* (1996). Installments 15 and 16, published by Severn House, are *Eleven That Went Up to Heaven* (1999) and *The Twelve Apostles* (1999). Fraser has also written as Vanessa Graham and Lorna Cameron. Born in Lancashire to a director-father and a novelist-mother, she lives in Hertfordshire, England.

David Webb...detective chief inspector...Wiltshire, England
- ❑ ❑ 1 - A Shroud for Delilah (1984)
- ❑ ❑ 2 - A Necessary End (1985)
- ❑ ❑ 3 - Pretty Maids All in a Row (1986)
- ❑ ❑ 4 - Death Speaks Softly (1987)
- ❑ ❑ 5 - The Nine Bright Shiners (1987)
- ❑ ❑ 6 - Six Proud Walkers (1988)
- ❑ ❑ 7 - The April Rainers (1989)
- ❑ ❑ 8 - Symbols at Your Door (1990)
- ❑ ❑ 9 - The Lily-White Boys (1991)
- ❑ ❑   - U.S.-I'll Sing You Two-O (1996)
- ❑ ❑ 10 - Three, Three the Rivals (1992)
- ❑ ❑ 11 - The Gospel Makers (1994)
- ❑ ❑ 12 - The Seven Stars (1995)
- ❑ ❑ 13 - One Is One and All Alone (1996)
- ❑ ❑ 14 - The Ten Commandments (1997)
- ❑ ❑ . . . .
- ❑ ❑ . . . .

■ FRASER, Antonia

Lady Antonia Fraser's long-running series featuring glamorous media personality and investigative journalist, Jemima Shore, has been the subject of two television series, for which Fraser has written a number of scripts. Introduced in *Quiet as a Nun* (1977), Jemima Shore was last seen in *Political Death* (1994), when her source for an exposé about a '60s political scandal dies in a suspicious fall. Author of more than two dozen books, Fraser has written at least ten volumes of historical non-fiction, including critically-acclaimed historical biographies such as *Mary, Queen of Scots* (1969) and *The [Six] Wives of Henry VIII* (1992). As noted in *Contemporary Authors*, she is the eldest child of highly educated and politically active parents, the Earl and Countess of Longford, who were also writers. Raised at Oxford where her father was a don, she earned B.A. and M.A. Oxford degrees in history. Past chairman of the British Crime Writers' Association, she lives in London with her husband, dramatist Harold Pinter.

Jemima Shore...British TV interviewer...London, England
- ❑ ❑ 1 - Quiet as a Nun (1977)
- ❑ ❑ 2 - The Wild Island (1978)
- ❑ ❑ 3 - A Splash of Red (1981)

    ❑ ❑   4 - Cool Repentance (1982)
    ❑ ❑   5 - Oxford Blood (1985)
    ❑ ❑   ss - Jemima Shore's First Case & Other Stories (1986)
    ❑ ❑   6 - Your Royal Hostage (1987)
    ❑ ❑   7 - The Cavalier Case (1991)
    ❑ ❑   ss - Jemima Shore at the Sunny Grave [9 stories] (1993)
    ❑ ❑   8 - Political Death (1994)
    ❑ ❑   . . . .
    ❑ ❑   . . . .

■ FRAZER, Margaret [P]

Margaret Frazer was the joint pseudonym of Gail Frazer and Mary Pulver Kuhfeld for the first six installments of their Edgar-nominated medieval mystery series featuring Benedictine nun, Dame Frevisse (FRAY-viss). A niece of Thomas Chaucer, one of the richest and most powerful commoners in England, Dame Frevisse is hosteler of the priory at St. Frideswide in 1431 Oxfordshire when the series begins with *The Novice's Tale* (1992). Starting with the Edgar-nominated book 7, *The Prioress' Tale* (1997),

Frazer says she is "entirely to blame" for the exploits of Dame Frevisse. The nun's ninth and tenth adventures are *The Reeve's Tale* (1999) and *The Squire's Tale* (2000). Frazer's short stories have appeared in *Royal Whodunnits* (1999), *Shakespearean Detectives* (1998) and *Shakespearean Whodunnits* (1997) and other anthologies. Kuhfeld also writes mysteries as Mary Monica Pulver and Monica Ferris. Both Frazer and Kuhfeld live near Minneapolis.

Dame Frevisse...15th century Benedictine nun...Oxfordshire, England
    ❑ ❑   1 - The Novice's Tale (1992)
    ❑ ❑   2 - **The Servant's Tale (1993) Edgar nominee** ☆
    ❑ ❑   3 - The Outlaw's Tale (1994)
    ❑ ❑   4 - The Bishop's Tale (1994)
    ❑ ❑   5 - The Boy's Tale (1995)
    ❑ ❑   6 - The Murderer's Tale (1996)
    ❑ ❑   7 - **The Prioress' Tale (1997) Edgar nominee** ☆
    ❑ ❑   8 - The Maiden's Tale (1998)
    ❑ ❑   . . . .
    ❑ ❑   . . . .

■ FRENCH, Linda [P]

Linda French is the creator of five-foot three-inch history professor Teddy (Teodora) Morelli and her six-foot pro-wrestler sister, Tabor the Amazon, assistant basketball coach at the University of Washington. The unlikely sisters are introduced in *Talking Rain* (1998). After saving sister Daisy from a charge of murder-by-coffee in book 2, Teddy gets strong-armed into writing a biography of the university's latest donor in *Steeped in Murder* (1999). Writing as Linda French Mariz,

French is the author of two Laura Ireland mysteries. A former Georgia state backstroke record-holder, she works out daily with a local swim team and recently purchased a black rubber wetsuit for swimming in Puget Sound. Born in New Orleans and raised in Atlanta, she has lived in the Pacific Northwest for 20 years. Trained in American history, French has worked as a community college instructor, grants administrator and creative writing teacher.

Teddy Morelli...college history professor...Seattle, Washington
    ❑ ❑   1 - Talking Rain (1998)
    ❑ ❑   2 - Coffee To Die For (1998)
    ❑ ❑   3 - Steeped in Murder (1999)
    ❑ ❑   . . . .
    ❑ ❑   . . . .

FRIEDMAN, Mickey

Mickey Friedman is Michaele Thompson Friedman, author of two mysteries featuring Georgia Lee Maxwell, a Florida society editor who moves to Paris on a whim and begins writing a New York magazine column, "Paris Patter." On a visit to the Musee Bellefroide in *Magic Mirror* (1988), Georgia Lee witnesses the killing of a guard by two thieves who steal the mirror used by Nostradamus to divine the future. The book was published in England as *Deadly Reflections*. In *A Temporary Ghost* (1989), she travels to Provence to ghostwrite the story of a woman who is thought to have murdered her wealthy husband. Friedman has also written *Hurricane Season* (1983), *The Fault Tree* (1984), *Paper Phoenix* (1986), *Venetian Mask* (1987) and *Riptide* (1994). As publications chair of Mystery Writers of America, she compiled the top 100 mystery novels of all time, selected by M.W.A. members, and published as *The Crown Crime Companion* (1995).

Georgia Lee Maxwell...freelance writer...Paris, France
- ❏ ❏ 1 - Magic Mirror (1988)
- ❏ ❏   - Brit.-Deadly Reflections
- ❏ ❏ 2 - A Temporary Ghost (1989)
- ❏ ❏ . . . .
- ❏ ❏ . . . .

FRITCHLEY, Alma

First-time novelist Alma Fritchley introduces mystery fiction's first chicken-farmer amateur sleuth with Letty Campbell in *Chicken Run* (1997). Billed as a lesbian comedy thriller, Letty's debut has crime, sex, big cars, money, drugs and plenty of chickens. After inheriting the Yorkshire farm from her aunt, Letty lets ex-girl-friend Julia Rossi rent some fallow acreage for an auction of stratospherically-priced classic cars. "Hilarious," said the *Evening Standard*. "A gentle lesbian love story with down-home British lunacy," proclaimed *Kirkus*. While her new love-interest, librarian Anne Marple, is away on a lecture tour in *Chicken Feed* (1998), Letty is besieged with visiting friends and relations at Calderton Brook Farm. The resulting mayhem was described by one reviewer as "a weekend run of Fawlty Towers at an unlicensed lesbian hostelry." Fritchley, who lives in Manchester, says she began writing to amuse her lover, who is still laughing.

Letty Campbell...lesbian chicken farmer...Manchester, England
- ❏ ❏ 1 - Chicken Run (1997)
- ❏ ❏ 2 - Chicken Feed (1998)
- ❏ ❏ 3 - Chicken Out (1999)
- ❏ ❏ . . . .
- ❏ ❏ . . . .

FROMER, Margot J.

Margot J. Fromer brings her medical writing background and 20 years of nursing experience to her mystery series featuring Amanda Knight, R.N., director of nursing at Washington D.C.'s fictional J.F.K. Memorial Hospital, starting with *Scalpel's Edge* (1991). Fromer's best ideas for poisonings have come while doing research for serious medical articles. With life becoming more and more bizarre, so are her ideas for fiction, she says. Fromer's academic career includes a B.S. from Boston University, M.A. and M.Ed. degrees from Columbia University and doctoral study at Georgetown University. A frequent lecturer and workshop presenter, she has taught nursing at several colleges and universities and authored nursing and health books, journal articles and scores of magazine and newspaper features. Recent books include *Healthy Living With Diabetes* (1998) and *The Endometriosis Survival Guide* (1998). Born in New York City, she lives in Silver Spring, Maryland.

Amanda Knight...hospital director of nursing...Washington, District of Columbia
- ❏ ❏ 1 - Scalpel's Edge (1991)
- ❏ ❏ 2 - Night Shift (1993)
- ❏ ❏ . . . .
- ❏ ❏ . . . .

■ FROMMER, Sara Hoskinson

Sara Hoskinson Frommer (rhymes with Homer) writes small-town Midwestern mysteries featuring music and murder in Oliver, Indiana, a fictional college town quite a bit smaller than Bloomington, where Frommer plays viola in the community orchestra. Amateur detective Joan Spencer is director of the senior citizens' center, manager of the local symphony orchestra, and the widowed mother of a grown son and daughter. In book 4, *The Vanishing Violinist* (1999), Joan's wedding planing is interrupted by a missing Stradivarius and a disappearing violinist at the International Violin Competition of Indianapolis—the Olympics for violinists. Frommer is also the author of 16 easy-to-read short story books written for adults, including several mysteries. Born in Chicago to Hoosier parents, she grew up in Hawaii and Illinois and has lived in Indiana most of her adult life. An Oberlin College and Brown University graduate, she is an experienced quilter.

Joan Spencer...symphony orchestra manager...Oliver, Indiana

- ❑ ❑ 1 - Murder in C Major (1986)
- ❑ ❑ 2 - Buried in Quilts (1994)
- ❑ ❑ 3 - Murder & Sullivan (1997)
- ❑ ❑ . . . .
- ❑ ❑ . . . .

■ FULTON, Eileen

Eileen Fulton is best known as the scheming Lisa Miller of the CBS daytime drama *As the World Turns*, a role she has played since 1960. Eight time married in her 40 years on screen, she has been widowed, raped, held hostage and nearly killed. She is also the author of six mysteries featuring Nina McFall, star of *The Turning Seasons*, and Lt. Dino Rossi, N.Y.P.D., first seen when the soap's despotic producer is murdered in *Take One for Murder* (1988). Fulton's seventh novel and first romance introduces daytime television newcomer Amanda Baker, a naïve Midwestern girl who lands her dream job after being left at the altar in *Soap Opera* (1999). A frequent cabaret and stage performer, Fulton has her own line of costume jewelry on the Home Shopping Network. She has also co-authored two autobiographies, *How My World Turns* (1970) and *As My World Still Turns: The Uncensored Memoirs of America's Soap Opera Queen* (1995).

Nina McFall & Dino Rossi...TV soap star & NYPD lieutenant...New York, New York

- ❑ ❑ 1 - Take One for Murder (1988)
- ❑ ❑ 2 - Death of a Golden Girl (1988)
- ❑ ❑ 3 - Dying for Stardom (1988)
- ❑ ❑ 4 - Lights, Camera, Death (1988)
- ❑ ❑ 5 - A Setting for Murder (1988)
- ❑ ❑ 6 - Fatal Flashback (1989)
- ❑ ❑ . . . .
- ❑ ❑ . . . .

■ FURIE, Ruthe

Two-time Shamus nominee Ruthe Furie worked as a journalist, artist and teacher before writing mysteries featuring fledgling Buffalo private detective Fran Kirk. First seen the Shamus-nominated *If Looks Could Kill* (1995), Fran is a former battered wife who turns her life around. She's "plain and earnest, just like Buffalo," says Furie. A New York natural food farm is the scene of Fran's insurance investigation in the Shamus-nominated *Natural Death* (1996). For *A Deadly Paté* (1996), Furie did research while visiting her daughter in Vaudois en Brie, where old homes have walls two feet thick and Roman roads can be found under back yard gardens. Raised in Brooklyn, Furie spent 19 years in Buffalo, where she reared her children and earned her college degrees. She has worked at the *New York Daily News*, *The Buffalo News*, and *The Hackensack Record*. Writing as Ruth Stout, she co-authored *Hell Gate* (1990) with her former husband.

Fran Kirk...ex-battered wife turned fledgling P.I....Buffalo, New York

- ❑ ❑ 1 - **If Looks Could Kill (1995) Shamus nominee** ☆
- ❑ ❑ 2 - **Natural Death (1996) Shamus nominee** ☆
- ❑ ❑ 3 - A Deadly Paté (1996)
- ❑ ❑ . . . .
- ❑ ❑ . . . .

■ FYFIELD, Frances [P]

Silver Dagger winner Frances Fyfield is the pseudonym of Frances Hegarty, a practicing criminal prosecutor for London's Metropolitan Police and the Crime Prosecution Service. With 20 years' experience, she still works one day a week as a prosecutor, but considers herself a full-time writer. Fyfield's first legal series features Helen West, a Crown Prosecutor in domestic violence court, introduced in *A Question of Guilt* (1988), the Edgar, Anthony and Agatha award nominee for best first novel in 1989. Fyfield's second

series introduces Sarah Fortune, solicitor with a prestigious British firm, whose third appearance, *Staring at the Light* (1999), is guaranteed to terrify anyone planning to visit the dentist. A nonseries thriller, *Blind Date* (1998), features an ex-police detective recovering from an acid attack. Writing as Frances Hegarty, Fyfield is the author of *The Playroom* (1991) and *Half Light* (1993). An English honors graduate of Newcastle University, her passion is collecting paintings.

Helen West...London Crown prosecutor...London, England
- ❏ ❏ 1 - **A Question of Guilt (1988) Agatha, Anthony & Edgar nominee** ☆☆☆
- ❏ ❏ 2 - Trial by Fire (1990)
- ❏ ❏   - U.S.-Not That Kind of Place
- ❏ ❏ 3 - **Deep Sleep (1991) Silver Dagger winner** ★
- ❏ ❏ 4 - Shadow Play (1993)
- ❏ ❏ 5 - A Clear Conscience (1994)
- ❏ ❏ 6 - Without Consent (1996)
- ❏ ❏ . . . .
- ❏ ❏ . . . .

Sarah Fortune...lawyer in prestigious British firm...London, England
- ❏ ❏ 1 - Shadows on the Mirror (1989)
- ❏ ❏ 2 - Perfectly Pure and Good (1994)
- ❏ ❏ . . . .
- ❏ ❏ . . . .

■ GALLISON, Kate

Kate Gallison has written two New Jersey mystery series, one featuring a Trenton private eye and the other an Episcopal parish priest. The Trenton P.I., Nick Magaracz, is introduced in *Unbalanced Accounts* (1986), when he is hired to locate several hundred missing government checks. Mother Lavinia Grey is newly-assigned by the Department of Missions to embattled St. Bede's, a "functionally dead" church sitting on extremely valuable real estate in the series opener, *Bury the Bishop* (1995). When last seen in book

5, *Grave Misgivings* (1998), Vinnie befriends a man and his daughter, found wandering in the local cemetery. "A quirky, entertaining story," said *Publishers Weekly*. At various times in her career, Gallison has worked as a *Washington Post* library clerk, AT&T accounting clerk, New Jersey Treasury Department computer programmer-analyst, and research firm technical writer. Born in Philadelphia, Gallison grew up in Illinois and New Jersey. A graduate of Edison College, she lives in Lambertville, New Jersey.

Lavinia Grey...Episcopal vicar...Fishersville, New Jersey
- ❏ ❏ 1 - Bury the Bishop (1995)
- ❏ ❏ 2 - Devil's Workshop (1996)
- ❏ ❏ 3 - Unholy Angels (1996)
- ❏ ❏ 4 - Hasty Retreat (1997)
- ❏ ❏ 5 - Grave Misgivings (1998)
- ❏ ❏ . . . .
- ❏ ❏ . . . .

Nick Magaracz...private investigator...Trenton, New Jersey
- ❏ ❏ 1 - Unbalanced Accounts (1986)
- ❏ ❏ 2 - The Death Tape (1987)
- ❏ ❏ 3 - The Jersey Monkey (1992)
- ❏ ❏ . . . .
- ❏ ❏ . . . .

■ GARCIA-AGUILERA, Carolina

Cuban-born Carolina (car-oh-LEE-nah) Garcia-Aguilera (au-ghee-LEHR-ah), president of her own Miami investigations firm for ten years, is the creator of fictional private eye Lupe Solano, daughter of a wealthy Cuban-American family, introduced in *Bloody Waters* (1996). Brash, sexy, smart and proud of her Cuban heritage, Lupe drives a Mercedes convertible and carries a Beretta while investigating illegal adoptions (book 1), the death of a close friend (book 2), and a 40-year-old mystery that goes back to the night before Castro captured Havana (book 3). When last seen in book 4, *A Miracle in Paradise*, (1999), Lupe has been hired by her sister's Mother Superior to substantiate or expose an announced religious miracle in Miami. Series regulars include Lupe's comic assistant Leonardo, attorney-boyfriend Tommy McDonald, sister Lourdes (a nun) and other Solano family. Fluent in three languages, Garcia-Aguilera holds a B.A. in history and political science from Rollins College and an M.B.A. in finance from the University of South Florida.

Lupe Solano...Cuban-American princess P.I....Miami, Florida
- ❏ ❏ 1 - Bloody Waters (1996)
- ❏ ❏ 2 - Bloody Shame (1997)
- ❏ ❏ 3 - Bloody Secrets (1998)
- ❏ ❏ ....
- ❏ ❏ ....

■ GEASON, Susan

Susan Geason's Syd Fish mysteries set in Sydney, Australia feature a failed journalist and sacked political minder turned private investigator, introduced in *Shaved Fish* (1990). Her politically incorrect P.I. came to his present calling via the yellow press and politics, hence his strong stomach, moral flexibility and comfort with sleaze, says Geason. With Paul R. Wilson she is the author of five crime prevention books for the Australian Institute of Criminology, most recently *Preventing Retail Crime* (1992). Geason has also written a literary study, *Regarding Jane Eyre* (1997), and a crime novel featuring a Sydney policewoman, *Wildfire* (1995). Born in Tasmania, Geason has lived in Brisbane, Canberra and Toronto, where she earned an M.A. in political theory from the University of Toronto. A former journalist with the *National Times*, she worked as a policy adviser in Canberra's Parliament House and for the New South Wales Premier. Geason lives in Sydney, where she works as a freelance writer, researcher, speechwriter and book reviewer.

Syd Fish...politically incorrect P.I....Sydney, Australia
- ❏ ❏ 1 - Shaved Fish (1990)
- ❏ ❏ 2 - Dogfish (1991)
- ❏ ❏ 3 - Sharkbait (1993)
- ❏ ❏ ....
- ❏ ❏ ....

■ GEORGE, Anne

Former Alabama State Poet, Anne George, writes the Southern Sisters mysteries, featuring sensible Patricia Anne Hollowell and flashy Mary Alice Crane, a pair of 60-something Alabama sisters. Before writing her Agatha award-winning first novel, *Murder on a Girls' Night Out* (1996), George put the sisters in a short story, and a one-act play at the University of Alabama. All the incidents in her books, except the murders, are taken straight from her own life, insists George. Although friends and family recognize each other, she is relieved they don't recognize themselves. When last seen in book 6, *Murder Shoots the Bull* (1999), the sisters have been invited to join an investment club. Co-founder of the Druid Press, George has published four volumes of poetry, including the Pulitzer prize-nominated *Some of It Is True* (1993). Her mainstream novel, *This One and Magic Life* (1999), spans five decades in the lives of three Mobile siblings. Born in Montgomery, George lives in Birmingham, Alabama.

Mary Alice Crane & Patricia Anne Hollowell...60-something sister sleuths...Birmingham, Alabama

- ❑ ❑   1 - **Murder on a Girls' Night Out (1996) Agatha winner ★**
- ❑ ❑   2 - Murder on a Bad Hair Day (1996)
- ❑ ❑   3 - Murder Runs in the Family (1997)
- ❑ ❑   4 - Murder Makes Waves (1997)
- ❑ ❑   5 - Murder Gets a Life (1998)
- ❑ ❑   . . . .
- ❑ ❑   . . . .

■ GEORGE, Elizabeth

American author Elizabeth George writes best-selling crime novels featuring aristocratic Scotland Yard Inspector Thomas Lynley (Earl of Asherton) and his working class partner, Sergeant Barbara Havers, last seen in book 10, *In Pursuit of the Proper Sinner* (1999). Series regulars include Lynley's best friend, crippled forensic pathologist Simon Allcourt-St. James, who is married to one of Lynley's former girlfriends. Simon's laboratory assistant and former lover, Lady Helen Clyde, has an on-again off-again relationship with Inspector Lynley. Written in 42 days between the end of a research trip to England and the beginning of the school year, *A Great Deliverance* (1988) won Anthony and Agatha best-first novel awards. Winner of Le Grand Prix de Littérature Policiére, the book also earned Edgar and Macavity nominations. Born in Ohio and raised in California, George earned a B.A. in English and an M.A. in counseling and later taught high school English for 13 years. She lives in London and Huntington Beach, California.

Thomas Lynley & Barbara Havers...Scotland Yard inspector & detective sergeant...London, England

- ❑ ❑   1 - **A Great Deliverance (1988) Anthony & Agatha winner ★★**
  Edgar & Macavity nominee ☆☆
- ❑ ❑   2 - Payment in Blood (1989)
- ❑ ❑   3 - Well-Schooled in Murder (1990)
- ❑ ❑   4 - A Suitable Vengeance (1991)
- ❑ ❑   5 - For the Sake of Elena (1992)
- ❑ ❑   6 - Missing Joseph (1993)
- ❑ ❑   7 - Playing for the Ashes (1994)
- ❑ ❑   8 - In the Presence of the Enemy (1996)
- ❑ ❑   9 - Deception on His Mind (1997)
- ❑ ❑   . . . .
- ❑ ❑   . . . .

■ GILL, B.M. [P]

Gold Dagger winner and three-time Edgar nominee Barbara Margaret Trimble wrote 21 novels, including a dozen romantic thrillers as Margaret Blake and Barbara Gilmour before publishing her first crime novel as B.M. Gill. The political thriller, *Target Westminster* (1977), was followed by Gill's first Edgar-nominated novel, *Death Drop* (1979). Police inspector Tom Maybridge is featured in only three novels, beginning with *Victims* (1981), published in the U.S. as *Suspect*. Maybridge returns in *Seminar for Murder* (1985), a locked room mystery involving the murder of a loathsome author at a convention of crime writers. His final appearance in *The Fifth Rapunzel* (1991) was Gill's last published novel. She won a Gold Dagger and second Edgar nomination for *The Twelfth Juror* (1984), and her third Edgar nomination for *Nursery Crimes* (1986). Trained as a chiropodist and primary school teacher, the Welsh native alternated work in both fields for more than 30 years, before her 1981 retirement from the National Health Service.

Tom Maybridge...detective chief inspector...England

- ❑ ❑   1 - Victims (1981)
- ❑ ❑   - U.S.-Suspect
- ❑ ❑   2 - Seminar for Murder (1985)
- ❑ ❑   3 - The Fifth Rapunzel (1991)
- ❑ ❑   . . . .
- ❑ ❑   . . . .

■ GILMAN, Dorothy

A former drawing and creative writing teacher, Dorothy Gilman wrote a dozen children's books as Dorothy Gilman Butters, before launching her mystery series featuring the C.I.A.'s most unlikely agent, a New Jersey grandmother turned Connecticut matron. Beginning with *The Unexpected Mrs. Pollifax* (1966), white-haired Emily Pollifax travels the globe, narrowly escaping danger, one quick step ahead of her pursuers. In her 13th adventure, *Mrs. Pollifax, Innocent Tourist* (1997), she heads to the Middle east to retrieve a manuscript written by a murdered dissident. "Three parts expert tour-guide, one part game intrigue—the whole mixture gently stirred, never shaken," said *Kirkus*. Book 14 is *Mrs. Pollifax Veiled* (2000). Among Gilman's seven other books are *Thale's Folly* (1999), "a sweetly entertaining fairy tale" about a novelist who rediscovers his creative self, and *New Kind of Country* (1978), Gilman's tale of rediscovery in a small Nova Scotia lobstering village, after the end of her 20-year marriage.

Emily Pollifax...grandmother CIA agent

- ❏ ❏ 1 - The Unexpected Mrs. Pollifax (1966)
- ❏ ❏ 2 - The Amazing Mrs. Pollifax (1970)
- ❏ ❏ 3 - The Elusive Mrs. Pollifax (1971)
- ❏ ❏ 4 - A Palm for Mrs. Pollifax (1973)
- ❏ ❏ 5 - Mrs. Pollifax on Safari (1976)
- ❏ ❏ 6 - Mrs. Pollifax on the China Station (1983)
- ❏ ❏ 7 - Mrs. Pollifax and the Hong Kong Buddha (1985)
- ❏ ❏ 8 - Mrs. Pollifax and the Golden Triangle (1988)
- ❏ ❏ 9 - Mrs. Pollifax and the Whirling Dervish (1990)
- ❏ ❏ 10 - Mrs. Pollifax and the Second Thief (1993)
- ❏ ❏ 11 - Mrs. Pollifax Pursued (1995)
- ❏ ❏ 12 - Mrs. Pollifax and the Lion Killer (1996)
- ❏ ❏ 13 - Mrs. Pollifax, Innocent Tourist (1997)
- ❏ ❏ . . . .
- ❏ ❏ . . . .

■ GILPATRICK, Noreen

Malice Domestic award winner Noreen Gilpatrick has written two police novels featuring Seattle detective Kate MacLean introduced in *Final Design* (1993). When an attractive businesswoman is poisoned in her graphics studio, MacLean is named detective-in-charge on her first homicide investigation. Returning in *Shadow of Death* (1995), Kate misses her ex-partner Sam who has taken a desk job and is attempting a reconciliation with his wife. Prior to starting her mystery writing career, Gilpatrick worked in both print and broadcast media, including a stint on the staff of *Psychology Today*. She once owned her own advertising agency in Seattle and lived on an island in Puget Sound. She has worked as a press aide for a gubernatorial candidate, and a producer and program specialist for a PBS affiliate in Kentucky. Her first novel, The *Piano Man* (1991), won the Malice Domestic award for best first traditional mystery. "Ms. Gilpatrick knows exactly how to raise goose flesh," noted *The New York Times Book Review*.

Kate MacLean...police detective...Seattle, Washington

- ❏ ❏ 1 - Final Design (1993)
- ❏ ❏ 2 - Shadow of Death (1995)
- ❏ ❏ . . . .
- ❏ ❏ . . . .

■ GIRDNER, Jaqueline

Jaqueline Girdner has written ten comic mysteries featuring Marin County, California vegetarian and gag gift wholesaler Kate Jasper, introduced in *Adjusted to Death* (1991). After solving a case of murder at her chiropractor's office in the series opener, Kate travels to a health spa in book 2, *The Last Resort* (1991), when her ex-husband is under suspicion for the mud bath murder of his new girlfriend. When an author drops dead in front of a book-signing audience in book 9, *Death Hits the Fan* (1998), Kate wants to know why the woman had called out her name. Kate agrees to accompany her friend Barbara on a visit to a local psychic in book 10, *Murder on the Astral Plane* (1999). They hope to discover the secret to repairing Kate's bad karma. A former family law attorney, psychiatric aide, and business owner, Girdner has owned a pinball refurbishing business, a mill-end yarn emporium and Jest Cards, a greeting card company. She lives in Marin County, where she practices tai chi and eats plenty of vegetables.

Kate Jasper...gag gift wholesaler...Marin County, California
- ❏ ❏ 1 - Adjusted to Death (1991)
- ❏ ❏ 2 - The Last Resort (1991)
- ❏ ❏ 3 - Murder Most Mellow (1992)
- ❏ ❏ 4 - Fat-Free and Fatal (1993)
- ❏ ❏ 5 - Tea-Totally Dead (1994)
- ❏ ❏ 6 - A Stiff Critique (1995)
- ❏ ❏ 7 - Most Likely To Die (1996)
- ❏ ❏ 8 - A Cry for Self Help (1997)
- ❏ ❏ 9 - Death Hits the Fan (1998)
- ❏ ❏ 10 - Murder on the Astral Plane (1999)
- ❏ ❏ 11 - Murder, My Deer (2000)
- ❏ ❏ . . . .
- ❏ ❏ . . . .

■ GIROUX, E.X. [P]

Canadian author Doris Shannon published ten novels under her own name before taking the pseudonym E.X. Giroux for the first of her ten mysteries featuring London barrister Robert (Robby) Forsythe and his "crisply efficient" secretary Abigail (Sandy) Sanderson. In *A Death for Adonis* (1984) Robby comes out of early retirement to investigate a 25-year-old murder. Sandy takes the lead in *A Death for a Doctor* (1986), when she is recruited by the police to impersonate a cousin of the murder victim. She is primary again in *Death of a Dietician* (1988), when she is invited to a murder weekend at a private island resort. After vacationing in British Columbia in *Death for a Dancing Doll* (1991), Robby is recuperating from knee surgery in the final installment, *A Death for a Dodo* (1993), when he befriends a group of patients whose collective past includes unsolved murders. Born in Elmira, New York, Giroux attended college in Ontario and once worked as a clerk for Royal Bank of Canada. She lives in lives in Vancouver, British Columbia.

Robert Forsythe & Abigail Sanderson...barrister & his secretary...London, England
- ❏ ❏ 1 - A Death for Adonis (1984)
- ❏ ❏ 2 - A Death for a Darling (1985)
- ❏ ❏ 3 - A Death for a Dancer (1986)
- ❏ ❏ 4 - A Death for a Doctor (1986)
- ❏ ❏ 5 - A Death for a Dilletante (1987)
- ❏ ❏ 6 - A Death for a Dietician (1988)
- ❏ ❏ 7 - A Death for a Dreamer (1989)
- ❏ ❏ 8 - A Death for a Double (1990)
- ❏ ❏ 9 - A Death for a Dancing Doll (1991)
- ❏ ❏ 10 - A Death for a Dodo (1993)
- ❏ ❏ . . . .
- ❏ ❏ . . . .

■ GLASS, Leslie

Former *New York* magazine columnist Leslie Glass writes police novels featuring Chinese-American N.Y.P.D. Detective Sergeant April Woo, last seen in *Stealing Time* (1999). April's romantic involvement with her former supervisor, Mexican-American Detective Sergeant Mike Sanchez, brings out the worst in April's old-style Chinese mother, Skinny Dragon, who never gives up trying to find a suitable Chinese husband for "worm daughter." An important point of view in Glass' Time series is provided by April's friend and colleague, psychoanalyst Dr. Jason Frank. Glass has also written *Getting Away With It* (1976) and *Modern Love* (1983). Actively involved with a number of forensic and psychologic projects as an advisor to the John Jay College of Criminal Justice, Glass is president of the Glass Institute for Psychodynamic and Social Research. The only mystery writer who serves as a Trustee of the New York City Police Foundation, Glass is a graduate of Sarah Lawrence College. She lives in New York City and Sarasota, Florida.

April Woo…Chinese-American police detective…New York, New York
- ❏ ❏ 1 - Burning Time (1993)
- ❏ ❏ 2 - Hanging Time (1995)
- ❏ ❏ 3 - Loving Time (1996)
- ❏ ❏ 4 - Judging Time (1998)
- ❏ ❏ . . . .
- ❏ ❏ . . . .

■ GLEN, Alison [P]

Alison Glen is the joint pseudonym of Ohio writing partners, Louise Vetter and Cheryl Meredith Lowry, for two mysteries featuring freelance Columbus writer Charlotte Sams. When first seen in *Showcase* (1992), Charlotte wants to know who killed her cousin Phil, an expert in Chinese art. Shortly after telling Charlotte that the Museum's Imperial jade necklace is a fake, Phil is found dead. In book 2, *Trunk Show* (1995), Charlotte gets involved with murder at the Columbus Zoo, when the elephant keeper is found dead. Director of Conflict Management Services in Columbus, Lowry is quick to point out that she does not recommend murder as a method of conflict resolution. Senior research specialist emeritus at Ohio State University, Vetter is an enthusiastic Earthwatch volunteer. She has been part of expeditions to dig up mammoth bones near Oxford, England, and other artifacts on Easter Island, Grand Turk Island, and at the Norman cathedral of St. Albans in England.

Charlotte Sams…freelance writer…Columbus, Ohio
- ❏ ❏ 1 - Showcase (1992)
- ❏ ❏ 2 - Trunk Show (1995)
- ❏ ❏ . . . .
- ❏ ❏ . . . .

■ GODFREY, Ellen

A Canadian resident for many years, American author Ellen Godfrey has written mysteries set in both Canada and the United States. Mirroring her own experience as the president of a computer software company are Godfrey's mysteries featuring Toronto headhunter Jane Tregar, introduced in *Murder Behind Locked Doors* (1988). A pair of earlier Ontario mysteries featured Polish-born octogenarian anthropologist, Rebecca Rosenthal. Godfrey's true crime book, *By Reason of Doubt* (1982), winner of a special Edgar award, was also an Edgar nominee for best fact crime. Godfrey's newest mysteries feature high-school dropout Janet Barkin who runs The Women's Rescue Center in Evanston, Illinois. Starting with *Murder on the Loose* (1999), these books are part of a collection for adult literacy students. With a B.A. in history and anthropology from Stanford University, Godfrey taught English as a second language in Ghana. Born in Chicago, she lived in Ontario before moving to current home in Victoria, British Columbia.

Jane Tregar…corporate headhunter…Toronto, Ontario, Canada
- ❏ ❏ 1 - Murder Behind Locked Doors (1988)
- ❏ ❏ 2 - Georgia Disappeared (1991)
- ❏ ❏ . . . .
- ❏ ❏ . . . .

Janet Barkin…high school dropout…Evanston, Illinois
- ❏ ❏ 1 - Murder on the Loose (1999)
- ❏ ❏ 2 - Murder on the Lover's Bridge (1999)
- ❏ ❏ 3 - Murder in the Shadows (1999)
- ❏ ❏ . . . .
- ❏ ❏ . . . .

Rebecca Rosenthal…80-year-old Polish-born anthropologist…Toronto, Ontario, Canada
- ❏ ❏ 1 - The Case of the Cold Murderer (1976)
- ❏ ❏ 2 - Murder Among the Well-to-do (1977)
- ❏ ❏ . . . .
- ❏ ❏ . . . .

■ GOLDSTONE, Nancy

Ex-New Yorker Nancy Goldstone ditched a high-paying job and moved to the Berkshires to write novels, including a pair of mysteries featuring single mother and mystery novelist Elizabeth Halperin, introduced in *Mommy and the Murder* (1995). When her estranged husband is murdered at a Halloween party, Elizabeth turns to the mothers in her toddler's play group for help in proving her innocence. Goldstone also wrote *Trading Up* (1988) and *Bad Business* (1991). With husband Larry, Goldstone co-authored *Used and Rare:* *Travels in the Book World* (1997), an account of their love affair with book collecting, which started with Nancy's $10 purchase of a definitive translation of *War and Peace*. "A sort of Year in Provence for book lovers," said *Kirkus*. In their sequel, *Slightly Chipped* (1999), the Goldstones "investigate the wildly high prices for first editions of recent mysteries, skewer the Edgar Awards, cover a Sotheby's auction and explore the workings of book dealers on the Internet," according to *Publishers Weekly*.

Elizabeth Halperin...single-mother mystery writer...Berkshires, Massachusetts
- ❑ ❑ 1 - Mommy and the Murder (1995)
- ❑ ❑ 2 - Mommy and the Money (1997)
- ❑ ❑ ....
- ❑ ❑ ....

■ GOM, Leona

Poet, playwright and novelist Leona Gom has written two mysteries featuring a Canadian Army wife of mixed Indian heritage, introduced in *After-Image* (1996). Living on a Canadian Army base in Germany, Vicky Bauer is struggling to stay sober and finish a master's thesis on women in film. She returns to Canada in book 2. Gom has published three other novels, six volumes of poetry, and two full-length radio plays produced by the CBC. For ten years she was editor of *Event* literary magazine. Her most unusual job was carving tombstones in Edmonton. Gom spent the first 20 years of her life on a isolated farm in Northern Alberta, where her parents were homesteaders. With no electricity or plumbing, and very little contact with the outside world, she rode horseback to school, across several miles of wilderness. Gom earned B.Ed. and M.A. degrees with honors from the University of Alberta and currently teaches creative writing at the University of British Columbia. She lives in a Vancouver suburb, near the U.S. border.

Vicky Bauer...Army wife of mixed Indian heritage...Canada
- ❑ ❑ 1 - After-Image [Germany] (1996)
- ❑ ❑ 2 - Double Negative (1998)
- ❑ ❑ ....
- ❑ ❑ ....

■ GORDON, Alison

Alison Gordon became the first full-time woman beat writer in the major leagues when she was hired by Canada's largest newspaper, the *Toronto Star*, to cover the Toronto Blue Jays in 1979. She held the job for five years and then wrote *Foul Balls: Five Years in the American League* (1984). Her fictional alter ego, sportswriter Kate Henry, covers the make-believe Toronto Titans, starting with *The Dead Pull Hitter* (1988). Born in New York City to a Canadian father and American mother, Gordon spent her teenage years in Tokyo, Cairo and Rome, where her father was a United Nations information officer. Gordon's parents were working as editors at Farrar & Rinehart when they met, and both their fathers were writers. Writing as Ralph Connor, her paternal grandfather was a bestselling novelist, while her maternal grandfather, Isaac Anderson (1868-1961), was the mystery reviewer for *The New York Times Book Review* for 25 years. Before his retirement in 1949, Anderson reviewed more than 5,280 mysteries, including the work of Hammett and Chandler.

Kate Henry...baseball newswriter...Toronto, Ontario, Canada
- ❑ ❑ 1 - The Dead Pull Hitter (1988)
- ❑ ❑ 2 - Safe at Home (1990)
- ❑ ❑ 3 - Night Game (1992)

❑ ❑   4 - Striking Out (1995)
❑ ❑   5 - Prairie Hardball (1997)
❑ ❑   6 - Suicide Squeeze (2000)
❑ ❑   . . . .
❑ ❑   . . . .

■ GOSLING, Paula

Gold Dagger winner Paula Gosling was born and raised in Detroit, Michigan, where she graduated from Wayne State University and worked in advertising before moving to England to meet the Beatles. Her first novel, *A Running Duck* (*Fair Game* in the U.S.). won the 1978 Creasey award and was later made into a 1986 Sylvester Stallone film, *Cobra*, and a 1995 Cindy Crawford movie, *Fair Game*. The first of Gosling's Michigan mysteries featuring Jack Stryker and Kate Trevorne, *Monkey Puzzle*, was awarded a Gold Dagger for best crime novel in 1985. Three years later she was elected chairman of the British Crime Writers' Association. Set in Blackwater Bay like the Stryker and Trevorne novels, *A Few Dying Words* (1994) introduces new lead characters. The latest in this series, *Death and Shadows* (1999) and *Underneath Every Stone* (2000), are available in the U.K., but don't yet have an American publisher. As Ainslie Skinner, she has also written *Mind's Eye* (1980), published in the U.S. as *The Harrowing*. Gosling lives in Bath.

Matt Gabriel...sheriff...Blackwater Bay, Michigan
❑ ❑   1 - The Body in Blackwater Bay (1992)
       [incl. Stryker & Trevorne]
❑ ❑   2 - A Few Dying Words (1994)
❑ ❑   3 - The Dead of Winter (1995)
❑ ❑   4 - Death and Shadows (1999)
❑ ❑   . . . .
❑ ❑   . . . .

Jack Stryker & Kate Trevorne...homicide cop & English professor...Michigan
❑ ❑   1 - **Monkey Puzzle (1985) Gold Dagger winner ★**
❑ ❑   2 - Backlash (1989)
❑ ❑   . . . .
❑ ❑   . . . .

Luke Abbott...English cop...England
❑ ❑   1 - The Wychford Murders (1986)
❑ ❑   2 - Death Penalties (1991)
❑ ❑   . . . .
❑ ❑   . . . .

■ GRAFTON, Sue

Four-time Anthony award winner Sue Grafton has been writing alphabet mysteries featuring Southern California private eye Kinsey Millhone since 1982. Last seen in *"O" is for Outlaw* (1999), the twice-divorced ex-cop with blue-collar roots is still eating peanut butter and pickle sandwiches. After speeding through the first half of the alphabet, Grafton has slowed her pace somewhat. Her current schedule should result in the arrival of book 26 for Kinsey's May 5 birthday in 2016. Although Grafton will have just turned 76, lucky Kinsey (who ages one year every two and a half books) will be turning 40, just ten years older than she was in the series opener. In Grafton's Hollywood days, she wrote screenplays and television scripts in collaboration with husband Steven F. Humphrey. Grafton's father, a Louisville, Kentucky bond attorney, started his own mystery series with *The Rat Began to Gnaw the Rope* (1943). Despite plans to produce a ten-book series, he published only two titles, and the standalone *Beyond a Reasonable Doubt* (1950).

Kinsey Millhone...blue-collar ex-cop P.I....Santa Teresa, California
❑ ❑   1 - **"A" is for Alibi (1982) Anthony winner ★ Shamus nominee ☆**
❑ ❑   2 - **"B" is for Burglar (1985) Anthony & Shamus winner ★★**
❑ ❑   3 - **"C" is for Corpse (1986) Anthony winner ★ Shamus nominee ☆**
❑ ❑   4 - **"D" is for Deadbeat (1987)**
❑ ❑   5 - **"E" is for Evidence (1988) Anthony nominee ☆**

❑ ❑   6 - "F" is for Fugitive (1989)
❑ ❑   7 - **"G" is for Gumshoe (1990) Anthony & Shamus winner ★★**
❑ ❑   8 - "H" is for Homicide (1991)
❑ ❑   9 - "I" is for Innocent (1992)
❑ ❑   10 - "J" is for Judgment (1993)
❑ ❑   11 - **"K" is for Killer (1994) Shamus winner ★**
                 Anthony & Gold Dagger nominee ☆☆
❑ ❑   12 - "L" is for Lawless (1995)
❑ ❑   13 - "M" is for Malice (1996)
❑ ❑   14 - "N" is for Noose (1998)
❑ ❑   . . . .
❑ ❑   . . . .

■ GRAHAM, Caroline

Caroline Graham writes a gentle police series featuring mild-mannered Chief Inspector Tom Barnaby and his trusty sidekick, Sergeant Troy, introduced in *The Killings at Badger's Drift* (1987). The Macavity award-winning series opener, nominated for Agatha and Anthony awards, has since been filmed for British and American television as part of the five-episode *Midsomer Murders*. Barnaby investigates a seemingly motiveless murder in the village of Ferne Basset in book 6, *A Place of Safety* (1999). A playwright and broadcaster with experience in both stage and television, Graham has worked as an actress, stage manager and professional dancer. The author of two books for children, she has also written several nonmysteries, including *Camilla: The King's Mistress: A Love Story* (1994), updated with new material in 1995. After earning a B.A. from Open University, Graham later received an M.A. from Birmingham University in writing for the theatre. Born in Warwickshire, she lives in Suffolk, England.

Tom Barnaby…chief inspector…Causton, England
❑ ❑   1 - **The Killings at Badger's Drift (1987) Macavity winner ★**
                 Agatha & Anthony nominee ☆☆
❑ ❑   2 - Death of a Hollow Man (1989)
❑ ❑   3 - Death in Disguise (1992)
❑ ❑   4 - **Written in Blood (1994) Last Laugh nominee ☆**
❑ ❑   5 - Faithful Unto Death (1996)
❑ ❑   . . . .
❑ ❑   . . . .

■ GRANGER, Ann

Ann Granger has worked around the world in diplomatic service, much like her series protagonist, foreign service officer Meredith Mitchell. Working for the Foreign Office in London, Mitchell commutes each day by train from her terraced cottage in the Cotswolds. The series cast prominently features Chief Inspector Alan Markby, who would like nothing better than to see her retire from the service and join him full time in Bamford. Despite her reservations about police work, Mitchell can never resist the temptation to sleuth. The duo was last seen in book 10, *Beneath These Stones* (1999). Granger also writes the Fran Varaday series, featuring a young unlicensed London investigator who aspires to an acting career. Under her married name, Ann Hulme, Granger published 16 historical romance novels during the 1980s. Granger met her husband while working in the British Embassy in Prague and together they received postings to places as far apart as Munich and Lusaka. Today they live near Oxford in Beicester, England.

Alan Markby & Meredith Mitchell…D.I. & Foreign Service officer…Cotswolds, England
❑ ❑   1 - Say It With Poison (1991)
❑ ❑   2 - A Season for Murder (1992)
❑ ❑   3 - Cold in the Earth (1993)
❑ ❑   4 - Murder Among Us (1993)
❑ ❑   5 - Where Old Bones Lie (1993)
❑ ❑   6 - A Fine Place for Death (1994)
❑ ❑   7 - Flowers for His Funeral (1994)
❑ ❑   8 - A Candle for a Corpse (1995)

❏ ❏   9 - A Touch of Mortality (1996)
❏ ❏ 10 - A Word After Dying (1996)
❏ ❏ 11 - Call the Dead Again (1998)
❏ ❏ . . . .
❏ ❏ . . . .

Fran Varaday...unlicensed young investigator...London, England
❏ ❏ 1 - Asking for Trouble (1997)
❏ ❏ 2 - Keeping Bad Company (1997)
❏ ❏ 3 - Running Scared (1998)
❏ ❏ . . . .
❏ ❏ . . . .

■ GRANT, Anne Underwood

Former advertising agency owner Anne Underwood Grant has written three Sydney Teague mysteries featuring a Charlotte, North Carolina single mother of two and owner of an ad agency. In Sydney's first outing, *Multiple Listing* (1998), the always-competitive real estate market in heat-drenched Charlotte has turned cut-throat. "A super ending tops off this series debut," said *Publishers Weekly*. When her newest client, the inventor of a synthetic nicotine substitute, turns up dead, Sydney knows he did not commit suicide in *Smoke Screen* (1998). In book 3, *Cuttings* (1999), Sydney's agency is handling a floral convention when a world-class designer dies. A Phi Beta Kappa graduate of the University of North Carolina at Chapel Hill, Grant has owned a garden design business, worked for the North Carolina Arts Council and spent ten years with her own ad agency. After many years in Charlotte, Grant sold her home and moved to a mountain cabin outside Asheville, North Carolina to devote more time to her writing.

Sydney Teague...single-mother ad agency owner...Charlotte, North Carolina
❏ ❏ 1 - Multiple Listing (1998)
❏ ❏ 2 - Smoke Screen (1998)
❏ ❏ 3 - Cuttings (1999)
❏ ❏ . . . .
❏ ❏ . . . .

■ GRANT, Linda [P]

Three-time Anthony nominee Linda Grant is the creator of San Francisco Aikido black belt Catherine Sayler, a private investigator and corporate crime specialist, introduced in *Random Access Murder* (1988). Catherine's assistant Jesse, a young computer whiz who later becomes her partner, adds a convincing technical dimension to their cases. When last seen in book 6, *Vampire Bytes* (1998), Catherine has been hired to investigate a live-action vampire computer game played on the streets of Palo Alto. "Frightening enough to inspire nightmares," said *Booklist*. Grant's short fiction includes her Martha Washington story in *First Lady Murders* (1999). After college Grant spent two years with the Peace Corps in Ethiopia, taught high school English, wrote training materials for community action agencies, conducted computer classes and trained teachers. Under her own name, Linda VerLee Williams, she is the author of *Teaching for the Two-Sided Mind* (1983). A past president of Sisters in Crime, she lives in Berkeley, California.

Catherine Sayler...single-mother corporate P.I....San Francisco, California
❏ ❏ **1 - Random Access Murder (1988) Anthony nominee** ☆
❏ ❏ 2 - Blind Trust (1990)
❏ ❏ **3 - Love nor Money (1991) Anthony nominee** ☆
❏ ❏ 4 - A Woman's Place (1994)
❏ ❏ **5 - Lethal Genes (1996) Anthony nominee** ☆
❏ ❏ 6 - Vampire Bytes (1998)
❏ ❏ . . . .
❏ ❏ . . . .

■ GRANT-ADAMSON, Lesley

Lesley Grant-Adamson has two mystery series set in London, including her early novels featuring celebrity gossip columnist, Rain Morgan, introduced in *Patterns in the Dust* (1985), published in the U.S. as *Death on Widow's Walk*. Good-looking con man Jim Rush, first seen in *A Life of Adventure* (1992), is a young American gambler inveigling his way into English society. London Irish private eye Laura Flynn appears only in *Flynn* (1991), retitled as *Too Many Questions* for U.S. publication. Grant-Adamson has been a trade journal editor, a feature writer for The *Guardian*, one of England's leading national newspapers, and a freelance writer of television documentaries and short stories for broadcast on the BBC. She and her journalist husband Andrew Grant-Adamson lived for several years in an olive grove in the Alpujarra region of Andalusia and wrote a portrait of the area, *A Season in Spain* (1995). Her recent novels of psychological suspense are *Lipstick and Lies* (1998), *The Girl in the Case* (1997) and *Evil Acts* (1996).

Jim Rush...American on the run from British police...England
- ❑ ❑   1 - A Life of Adventure (1992)
- ❑ ❑   2 - Dangerous Games (1994)
- ❑ ❑   . . . .
- ❑ ❑   . . . .

Rain Morgan...Fleet Street gossip columnist...London, England
- ❑ ❑   1 - Patterns in the Dust (1985)
- ❑ ❑   - U.S.-Death on Widow's Walk
- ❑ ❑   2 - The Face of Death (1985)
- ❑ ❑   3 - Guilty Knowledge (1986)
- ❑ ❑   4 - Wild Justice (1987)
- ❑ ❑   5 - Curse the Darkness (1990)
- ❑ ❑   . . . .
- ❑ ❑   . . . .

■ GRAVES, Sarah [P]

Sarah Graves is the pseudonym of Mary Kittredge for her Jacobia "Jake" Triptree mysteries set in the remote seacoast village of Eastport, Maine, beginning with *The Dead Cat Bounce* (1998). *"This Old House* meets *Murder, She Wrote,"* said the Amazon reviewer. Jake has left a Wall Street money manager's position and a brain surgeon ex-husband to remodel a 200-year-old derelict of a house and save her 16-year-old son Sam from the bad influence of his city friends. In book 2, *Triple Witch* (1999), the first murder victim is local bad boy Kenny Mumford, an old flame of Jake's sleuthing partner Ellie White. As Mary Kittredge, the author has written nine mysteries in two Connecticut series— one featuring freelance writer Charlotte Kent and the other, R.N. and medical investigator Edwina Crusoe. Formerly a hospital respiratory therapist in New Haven, Connecticut, the author has moved to Eastport, Maine where she is remodeling the 1823 Federal style house that helped inspire her newest mysteries.

Jacobia Triptree...ex-investment banker...Eastport, Maine
- ❑ ❑   1 -The Dead Cat Bounce (1998)
- ❑ ❑   2 - Triple Witch (1999)
- ❑ ❑   3 - A Blonde for a Shilling (1999)
- ❑ ❑   . . . .
- ❑ ❑   . . . .

■ GRAY, Dulcie [P]

Dulcie Gray is the stage and author name of Dulcie Winifred Catherine Dennison, who starred in 41 London plays and toured South Africa, Australia, Hong Kong and Berlin. In addition to feature-length films, she has made over 500 radio and T.V. appearances, including her 1985-86 television role in *Howard's Way*. Gray is the author of more than 20 books, including 17 crime novels, two short story collections, stage and radio plays, a nonfiction book, a juvenile mystery, horror stories, and newspaper and magazine articles, all published during her successful acting career. Inspector Superintendent Cardiff appears only twice, in *Epitaph for a Dead Actor* (1960) and *Died in the Red* (1967). While most of Gray's books are set in England, several feature more exotic locales. *For Richer, For Richer* (1970) is set in Morocco, *Baby Face* (1959) in South Africa, and *Murder in Melbourne* (1958) in Australia. Born in Kuala Lumpur, Malaya, Gray was educated in England and Malaya and at London's Academy des Beaux Arts.

Insp. Supt. Cardiff...inspector superintendent...England

   ❏ ❏   1 - Epitaph for a Dead Actor (1960)
   ❏ ❏   2 - Died in the Red (1967)
   ❏ ❏   . . . .
   ❏ ❏   . . . .

■ GRAY, Gallagher [P]

Gallagher Gray is the pseudonym of Katy Munger, a North Carolina native who lived for 16 years in New York City, where she worked in the personnel department of a private bank on Wall Street. As Gallagher Gray, her mysteries feature a retired law firm personnel manager, T.S. Hubbert, and his 84-year-old, still stylish Auntie Lil, a former dress designer who calls her nephew Theodore. On the first day of his retirement from Sterling and Sterling, 55-year-old T.S. is called back to work in the series opener, *Partners in Crime* (1991), when one of the bigwigs is found murdered in the Partners' Room. "Deftly plotted and well-paced," said the *San Francisco Chronicle*. "Gray's writing style is delightful," said *Associated Press*. Under her own name, Munger writes the Shamus-nominated Casey Jones private eye series beginning with *Legwork* (1997). Munger grew up in Raleigh and graduated from the University of North Carolina at Chapel Hill. She lives in Raleigh with her husband Greg and their daughter Zuzu.

Theodore S. Hubbert & Auntie Lil...retired personnel manager & dress designer...New York, New York

   ❏ ❏   1 - Partners in Crime (1991)
   ❏ ❏   2 - A Cast of Killers (1992)
   ❏ ❏   3 - Death of a Dream Maker (1995)
   ❏ ❏   4 - A Motive for Murder (1996)
   ❏ ❏   . . . .
   ❏ ❏   . . . .

■ GREEN, Christine

Christine Green has written two series, beginning with her Creasey award-nominated debut novel, *Deadly Errand* (1991), introducing Kate Kinsella, a 30-something nurse turned medical investigator. Kate's friend and office landlord operates Humbertstone's funeral parlor on the building's ground floor. When last seen in book 4, *Deadly Partners* (1996), Kate is befriended by three vodka-swilling octogenarians during her search for a missing hotel owner on the Isle of Wight. Green's second series features Chief Inspector Connor O'Neill and his young partner, Detective Sergeant Fran Wilson, introduced in *Death in the Country* (1993). The townspeople of Fowchester are strangely unwilling to help the police when a severed arm is discovered in the series opener. Trained in London as a nurse and midwife, Green turned briefly to teaching before reverting to medicine, where she has worked as a district nurse and health visitor. Her two daughters are also nurses. Born in Luton, Green lives in Wolverhampton, England.

Connor O'Neill & Fran Wilson...village chief insp. & detective sgt....Fowchester, England

   ❏ ❏   1 - Death in the Country (1993)
   ❏ ❏   2 - Die in My Dreams (1995)
   ❏ ❏   3 - Fatal Cut (1999)
   ❏ ❏   . . . .
   ❏ ❏   . . . .

Kate Kinsella...nurse and medical investigator...Longborough, England

   ❏ ❏   **1 - Deadly Errand (1991) Creasey nominee** ☆
   ❏ ❏   2 - Deadly Admirer (1992)
   ❏ ❏   3 - Deadly Practice (1994)
   ❏ ❏   4 - Deadly Partners (1996)
   ❏ ❏   . . . .
   ❏ ❏   . . . .

■ GREEN, Edith Pinero

Edith Pinero Green is the creator of Dearborn V. Pinch, an enterprising old boy with a sharp eye for the ladies. Known for helping friends with problems they do not wish to take to the police, 70-something Mr. Pinch is visited by an old flame in the series opener, *Rotten Apples* (1977). Antoinette Ormach is part of the Rotten Apple Corps, formed 40 years earlier by eleven people who had each committed a minor crime. As members start dying under suspicious circumstances, Antoinette fears she may be next. When she is murdered, Pinch feels obligated to expose the rotten apple. Green's publishers called Mr. Pinch "the world's oldest and cleverest detective," while others labeled him "the horniest old man in mystery fiction." *The New York Times Book Review* proclaimed Pinch "a querulous old boy with the morals of a tomcat." A New Jersey native, Green earned a B.A. at the New School for Social Research and later worked for a New York advertising agency. She has also written nonseries mysteries and historical romance.

Dearborn V. Pinch...70-something ladies man...New York, New York

- ❏ ❏ 1 - Rotten Apples (1977)
- ❏ ❏ 2 - Sneaks (1979)
- ❏ ❏ 3 - Perfect Fools (1982)
- ❏ ❏ . . . .
- ❏ ❏ . . . .

■ GREEN, Kate

Children's author Kate Green is the creator of professional psychic Theresa Fortunato, who assists L.A.P.D. homicide lieutenant Oliver Jardine in the Edgar-nominated *Shattered Moon* (1986). The second installment, *Black Dreams* (1993), winner of a Minnesota Book Award, is "a compelling story, told with intelligence and skill," said *Booklist*. "In the hands of a less talented author, Theresa's gift would seem little more than a gimmick; here, it deepens characterization," added *Kirkus*. Green has also written two suspense thrillers, *Shooting Star* (1992), featuring a Santa Fe P.I. Harm Bohland, and *Night Angel* (1989). Among her children's books are the Fossil Family Tales series, the continuing adventures of a dinosaur family, and A *Number of Animals* (1994), in collaboration with British engraver Christopher Wormell. After graduating from the University of Minnesota, Green earned an M.A. from Boston University. She is a published poet and teaches a graduate course in writing at Hamline University.

Theresa Fortunato & Oliver Jardine...professional psychic & LAPD detective...Los Angeles, California

- ❏ ❏ 1 - **Shattered Moon (1986) Edgar nominee** ☆
- ❏ ❏ 2 - Black Dreams (1993)
- ❏ ❏ 3 - Angel Falls (1997)
- ❏ ❏ . . . .
- ❏ ❏ . . . .

■ GREENWOOD, D.M.

D.M. Greenwood is Diane M. Greenwood, author of nine Anglican church mysteries featuring the Reverend Theodora Braithwaite, a deaconess when first seen in *Clerical Errors* (1991). "Greenwood has a fresh, clever, and civilized style," said *Kirkus*. When Rev. Braithwaite is sent to the country cathedral of Bow St. Aelfric in book 3, *Idol Bones* (1993), she finds a hotbed of petty politics, a pagan idol of two-faced Janus unearthed on church grounds, and one dead Dean. When last seen in book 9, *Foolish Ways* (1999), deacon Braithwaite is on hand to assist the police when a young priest is found dead at the "Millennial Message" conference of clerical and lay workers. With a classics degree from Oxford University and a theology degree from London University, Greenwood has taught at a number of schools, including St. Paul's Girls' School in London. An ecclesiastical civil servant for more than 15 years, she currently works for the diocese of Rochester. Greenwood lives overlooking the Thames in Greenwich, England.

Theodora Braithwaite...British woman clergy...London, England

- ❏ ❏ 1 - Clerical Errors (1991)
- ❏ ❏ 2 - Unholy Ghosts (1992)
- ❏ ❏ 3 - Idol Bones (1993)

❏ ❏   4 - Holy Terrors (1994)
❏ ❏   5 - Every Deadly Sin (1995)
❏ ❏   6 - Mortal Spoils (1996)
❏ ❏   7 - Heavenly Vices (1997)
❏ ❏   8 - A Grave Disturbance (1998)
❏ ❏   . . . .
❏ ❏   . . . .

■ GREENWOOD, Kerry

Australian Kerry Greenwood has written ten novels featuring wealthy 1920s Londoner, Phryne (FREE-nee) Fisher, who moves to Melbourne and takes up a bit of detection. Always armed with a Beretta .32, Phryne drives her own gigantic red Hispano-Suiza, last seen in *Death Before Wicket* (1999). Her name comes from Herodotus' histories, where Phryne was the courtesan of ancient Thebes, a very clever and wealthy woman. During her trial for impersonating a goddess (a capital crime in ancient Greece), her counsel had run out of arguments when he ripped off her garment, displaying her naked form to the jury and asked, "Could anyone this beautiful have done anything wrong?" Phryne, of course, was acquitted. A playwright, singer and qualified solicitor, Greenwood works part-time as a public defender for Sunshine Legal Aid in Melbourne. Her previous jobs include director, producer, translator, costume maker and cook. She lives in suburban Melbourne with a registered wizard and quite a few cats.

Phryne Fisher...1920s Londoner...Melbourne, Australia
❏ ❏   1 - Cocaine Blues (1989)
❏ ❏   - U.S.-Death by Misadventure
❏ ❏   2 - Flying Too High (1990)
❏ ❏   3 - Murder on the Ballarat Train (1991)
❏ ❏   4 - Death at Victoria Dock (1992)
❏ ❏   5 - The Green Mill Murder (1993)
❏ ❏   6 - Blood and Circuses (1994)
❏ ❏   7 - Ruddy Gore (1995)
❏ ❏   8 - Urn Burial (1996)
❏ ❏   9 - Raisins and Almonds (1997)
❏ ❏   . . . .
❏ ❏   . . . .

■ GREGORY, Susanna [P]

new

The pseudonymous Susanna Gregory writes 14th century mysteries featuring Dr. Matthew Bartholomew, a Cambridge physician and forensic sleuth, introduced in *A Plague on Both Your Houses* (1996). A Master of Medicine and trainer of physicians, Matthew is assisted by his good friend Brother Michael, a portly monk and Senior Proctor at Michaelhouse. After traveling to Suffolk in book 5, *A Wicked Deed* (1999), Matthew and Brother Michael return in *A Masterly Murder* (2000). Using the joint pseudonym of Simon Beaufort, Gregory co-authors mysteries about a Crusader knight with her American-born husband, a Cambridge history lecturer. Once a coroner's officer in Yorkshire, Gregory has also written several nonfiction books on medieval castles and cathedrals. After earning degrees from the universities of Lancaster and Durham, she completed a Ph.D. at Cambridge University, where she is currently a fellow conducting research on marine pollution. A London native, Gregory and her husband live near Cambridge.

Matthew Bartholomew...14th century physician and teacher...Cambridge, England
❏ ❏   1 - A Plague on Both Your Houses (1996)
❏ ❏   2 - An Unholy Alliance (1996)
❏ ❏   3 - A Bone of Contention (1997)
❏ ❏   4 - A Deadly Brew (1998)
❏ ❏   . . . .
❏ ❏   . . . .

■ GRETH, Roma

Award-winning playwright Roma Greth has written more than 40 plays, including several mysteries in three acts first published as LeRoma Greth. Her plays featuring historical, religious and mysteries themes have been performed in Atlanta, Los Angeles, New York City, Syracuse, and various theatres in the Philadelphia area. She is the author of two mysteries featuring 40-something Hana Shaner, a carpet company heiress who lives on a large estate, complete with butler, in the Pennsylvania Dutch town of Conover.

Hana makes her debut in *Now You Don't* (1988) and returns in *Plain Murder* (1989). She is also the central character in short stories published in *Death Knell* (1994), *Death Knell II* (1996) and *Death Knell III* (1998). Greth has also written advertising copy, as well as newspaper and magazine articles. She lives in the Pennsylvania Dutch country that was the setting for her play, *Clean Murder*, performed in a staged reading at the Mid-Atlantic Mystery Book Fair and Convention in Philadelphia in 1997.

Hana Shaner...40-something heiress...Conover, Pennsylvania
- ❏ ❏ 1 - Now You Don't (1988)
- ❏ ❏ 2 - Plain Murder (1989)
- ❏ ❏ . . . .
- ❏ ❏ . . . .

■ GRIFFIN, Annie [P]

Annie Griffin is the pseudonym used by Sally Chapman for her Marin County mysteries featuring an unlikely pair of 60-something sisters, sensible poet and gardener, Hannah Malloy, and self-absorbed, sex-crazed Kiki Goldstein, introduced in *A Very Eligible Corpse* (1998). With Kiki as the prime suspect in two murders, Hannah must investigate. When a former grade B movie director is poisoned in book 2, *Date with a Perfect Dead Man* (1999), Hannah feels guilty for having invited him to a town festival. Set in Hill

Creek, California, a thinly-disguised Mill Valley, the series pokes fun at the yuppie pretensions and New Age sympathies of Marin County's more eccentric residents. Where else can you find a supermarket with a foot reflexology section, or gurus on cable access television, asks Chapman. After working at I.B.M. for nine years, Chapman was well-acquainted with life in Silicon Valley, a background put to good use in her mysteries featuring computer fraud investigators, Juliet Blake and Vic Paoli.

Hannah Malloy & Kiki Goldstein...unlikely pair of 60-something sisters...Marin County, California
- ❏ ❏ 1 - A Very Eligible Corpse (1998)
- ❏ ❏ 2 - Date With the Perfect Dead Man (1999)
- ❏ ❏ . . . .
- ❏ ❏ . . . .

■ GRIMES, Martha

Nero Wolfe award winner Martha Grimes is the author of 19 novels, including 16 books featuring Inspector Richard Jury of Scotland Yard. Each Jury novel takes its name and at least part of its setting from an English pub or country inn, starting with *The Man with a Load of Mischief* (1981). Grimes says that unless she has the name of the pub first, she cannot write the book. Recurring characters include Jury's sidekick Melrose Plant, an aristocratic professor of French romantic poetry, and Plant's "obnoxious,

snobby, interfering," American-born Aunt Agatha. In book 16, *The Lamorna Wink* (1999), Plant takes center stage when he goes to Cornwall to check out an intriguing house. Professor of English at Montgomery College in Tacoma Park, Grimes holds B.A. and M.A. degrees from the University of Maryland. She makes annual research trips to England and occasionally teaches detective fiction at Johns Hopkins University. Her non-Jury novels set in the U.S. include *End of the Pier* (1992) and *Biting the Moon* (1999).

Richard Jury...Scotland Yard inspector...London, England
- ❏ ❏ 1 - The Man With a Load of Mischief (1981)
- ❏ ❏ 2 - The Old Fox Deceived (1982)
- ❏ ❏ **3 - The Anodyne Necklace (1983) Nero Wolfe winner ★**
- ❏ ❏ 4 - The Dirty Duck (1984)
- ❏ ❏ 5 - Jerusalem Inn (1984)

❑ ❑ 6 - Help the Poor Struggler (1985)
❑ ❑ 7 - The Deer Leap (1985)
❑ ❑ 8 - I Am the Only Running Footman (1986)
❑ ❑ 9 - The Five Bells and Bladebone (1987)
❑ ❑ 10 - The Old Silent (1989)
❑ ❑ 11 - The Old Contemptibles (1990)
❑ ❑ 12 - The Horse You Came in On (1993)
❑ ❑ 13 - Rainbow's End (1995)
❑ ❑ 14 - The Case Has Altered (1997)
❑ ❑ 15 - The Stargazey (1998)
❑ ❑ . . . .
❑ ❑ . . . .

■ GRIMES, Terris McMahan

Two-time Anthony award winner Terris McMahan Grimes is the creator of amateur sleuth Theresa Galloway, a black urban professional and mother of two, with a husband, a demanding job as a state personnel officer, and a mother who's always getting into other people's business. The series opener, *Somebody Else's Child* (1996), walked away with Anthony honors for best first novel and best original paperback, as well as a Chester Himes award and an Agatha nomination. In book 2, *Blood Will Tell* (1997),

a stranger claiming to be Theresa's long-lost brother moves into her mother's home and promptly turns up dead. Born in Arkansas, Grimes grew up in Oakland and has lived in Sacramento for 20 years. A career bureaucrat, she works as a land agent for the state of California and holds a B.A. in English from California State University in Chico. Like her fictional sleuth, Grimes has worked as a personnel officer, has a husband and two children. But she does not drive a BMW, nor has she ever been in a fight or solved a murder.

Theresa Galloway...black married-mother civil servant...Sacramento, California
❑ ❑ 1 - **Somebody Else's Child (1996) Anthony winners ★★ Agatha nominee** ☆
❑ ❑ 2 - Blood Will Tell (1997)
❑ ❑ 3 - Other Duties As Required (2000)
❑ ❑ . . . .
❑ ❑ . . . .

■ GRINDLE, Lucretia

Lucretia Grindle has written two English mysteries featuring widowed C.I.D. Detective Inspector H.W. Ross, introduced in *The Killing of Ellis Martin* (1993). Ross and his fiercely loyal Welsh assistant, Owen Davies, want to know who killed Ellis Martin, a well-heeled young local known for annoying her neighbors. "For fans of English country mysteries, this is a must," said a *Mystery News* review of Grindle's debut novel. Having just completed the senior command course at the Police College in Bramshill, the newly-promoted

Detective Superintendent is spending ten days in August at Gleneagles in the Scottish Highlands, a long overdue vacation of fly-fishing for salmon on the river Spey, in book 2, *So Little to Die For* (1994). The day after dining with actress Claudia Furnival, her twin sister, and their husbands, Ross learns all four have been viciously murdered. When a local shepherd is arrested for the crime, Ross and Sergeant Davies decide to do a little snooping on their own.

H.W. Ross...detective superintendent...England
❑ ❑ 1 - The Killing of Ellis Martin (1993)
❑ ❑ 2 - So Little To Die For (1994)
❑ ❑ . . . .
❑ ❑ . . . .

■ GUIVER, Patricia

Patricia Guiver (GUY-ver) is the author of a pet detective series featuring British widow Delilah Doolittle, whose specialty is locating missing pets in Surf City, California. In the series opener, *Delilah Doolittle and*

the Purloined Pooch (1997), the pet detective and her loyal assistant, a Doberman pinscher named Watson, find a corpse in the doghouse of a missing German shepherd. In book 3, Delilah and Watson are on the trail of a missing Abyssinian, when the cat owner's next-door neighbor is murdered. Known to friends and colleagues as the Dear Abby of the animal world, Guiver has written a newspaper pet column, and hosted Paw Prints, a Southern California cable television program. She is also the author of Animal Connections, a directory of Southern California animal resources. Raised in Surrey, England, Guiver lives in Huntington Beach, California, where she heads the Orange County chapter of the S.P.C.A., and shares her home with a Yorkshire terrier named Paddington, three cats and a cockatiel.

Delilah Doolittle...British widow pet detective...Surf City, California
- ❑ ❑ 1 - Delilah Doolittle and the Purloined Pooch (1997)
- ❑ ❑ 2 - Delilah Doolittle and the Motley Mutts (1998)
- ❑ ❑ 3 - Delilah Doolittle and the Careless Coyote (1998)
- ❑ ❑ ....
- ❑ ❑ ....

■ GUNN, Elizabeth

Minnesota native Elizabeth Gunn writes mysteries featuring divorced police detective Jake Hines of Rutherford, Minnesota, a fictional town of 100,000 about 80 miles southeast of the Twin Cities. First seen in *Triple Play* (1997), the detective with straight black hair and a nose like Montezuma, had been abandoned at birth, and never knew his parents. In the series opener, mutilated corpses left on local softball diamonds may be tied to the apparent suicide of the recreation director. Jake's supporting cast includes his mentor and chief of detectives, their linguistically-challenged coroner, and Jake's love interest, St. Paul fingerprint expert Trudy Hanson. Following *Par Four* (1998), Jake returns in *Five Card Stud* (2000). A graduate of the University of Minnesota, Gunn lived in Montana before selling the family motel business and heading to the Gulf of Mexico and the Caribbean for an extended sailing adventure. An accomplished diver, Gunn worked as a travel writer before moving to Tucson, Arizona to write mysteries.

Jake Hines...small town police detective...Rutherford, Minnesota
- ❑ ❑ 1 - Triple Play (1997)
- ❑ ❑ 2 - Par Four (1998)
- ❑ ❑ ....
- ❑ ❑ ....

■ GUNNING, Sally

Sally Gunning lives and works on Cape Cod, where her family roots go back many generations. It's the perfect place for the directionally dyslexic, says Gunning. The worst that can happen when you take a wrong turn is that 20 minutes later you'll run into one or another body of water. Then you've arrived, or you turn around. Her ten-book series featuring Peter Bartholomew is set on the fictional island of Nashtoba, a mixture of old and new Cape Cod. Owner of the odd-jobs company, Factotum, Bartholomew is introduced in *Hot Water* (1990) and each subsequent title finds him dealing with water of another sort. When last seen in book 10, *Fire Water* (1999), Pete tops the lists of suspects when a human skull found in his marsh turns out to belong to an old flame who disappeared 15 years earlier. After earning a degree in sociology from the University of Rhode Island, Gunning worked as a museum tour guide, cruise ship stewardess, bank accountant, and office manager for a small town medical practice.

Peter Bartholomew...odd-jobs company owner...Cape Cod, Massachusetts
- ❑ ❑ 1 - Hot Water (1990)
- ❑ ❑ 2 - Under Water (1992)
- ❑ ❑ 3 - Ice Water (1993)
- ❑ ❑ 4 - Troubled Water (1993)
- ❑ ❑ 5 - Rough Water (1994)
- ❑ ❑ 6 - Still Water (1995)
- ❑ ❑ 7 - Deep Water (1996)
- ❑ ❑ 8 - Muddy Water (1997)
- ❑ ❑ 9 - Dirty Water (1998)
- ❑ ❑ 10 - Fire Water (1999)
- ❑ ❑ ....
- ❑ ❑ ....

■ GUR, Batya

Batya Gur has written the first mystery novel from a best-selling Israeli author to reach an American audience. *The Saturday Morning Murder:A Psychoanalytic Case* was translated from Hebrew for U.S. publication in 1992. "A splendid, intriguing mystery," said *Time* magazine. When a senior analyst at the Jerusalem Psychoanalytic Institute is murdered, Chief Inspector Michael Ohayon, deputy head of the Investigations Division of the Jerusalem Subdistrict, quickly deduces that each member of the Institute staff is a likely suspect. The tall Moroccan-born detective, previously a Cambridge University Ph.D. candidate in medieval history, once aroused the envy of fellow students with his ability to recount the names of all the popes and royal dynasties of Europe. These days, Ohayon keeps such finely-tuned gifts to himself. Following the Anthony award-nominated *Murder on a Kibbutz: A Communal Case* (1994), Ohayon returns in book 4, *Murder Duet: A Musical Case* (1999). Gur is a professor of literature in Jerusalem.

Michael Ohayon...Moroccan-born chief inspector...Jerusalem, Israel
- ❑ ❑ 1 - The Saturday Morning Murder (1992)
- ❑ ❑ 2 - Literary Murder (1993)
- ❑ ❑ **3 - Murder on a Kibbutz (1994) Anthony nominee** ☆
- ❑ ❑ 4 - Murder Duet (1999)
- ❑ ❑ . . . .
- ❑ ❑ . . . .

■ HADDAD, C.A.

Writing as C.A. Haddad, Carolyn A. Haddad has published seven crime novels, including two featuring Chicago computer snoop Becky Belski, introduced in *Caught in the Shadows* (1992). Becky's assignment, for the consulting firm Resources, is to dig up enough dirt on socialite Lionel Aberdeen to keep his wife's divorce action out of court. Along the way, she discovers a connection to William Townsend, killed 25 years earlier by his second wife—none other than Becky's mother. The "appealingly hardheaded Becky finds herself digging deeper into her own family mystery," said *Kirkus*. She returns in *Root Canal* (1994). Haddad's other crime fiction includes two espionage novels set in the Middle East featuring David Haham, *Bloody September* (1976) and *Operation Apricot* (1978). She also wrote *The Moroccan* (1975), set in Israel, *The Academic Factor* (1980), set in Bulgaria, and a Holocaust novel, *A Mother's Secret* (1988). Haddad lives in Chicago.

Becky Belski...computer investigator...Chicago, Illinois
- ❑ ❑ 1 - Caught in the Shadows (1992)
- ❑ ❑ 2 - Root Canal (1994)
- ❑ ❑ . . . .
- ❑ ❑ . . . .

David Haham...government agent...Middle East
- ❑ ❑ 1 - Bloody September (1976)
- ❑ ❑ 2 - Operation Apricot (1978)
- ❑ ❑ . . . .
- ❑ ❑ . . . .

■ HADDAM, Jane [P]

Jane Haddam (rhymes with Adam) is the pseudonym of Orania Papazoglou for her 16-book series featuring retired Philadelphia F.B.I. agent Gregor Demarkian, introduced in the Edgar and Anthony award-nominated *Not A Creature Was Stirring* (1990). Demarkian travels to Litchfield County, Connecticut to assist local authorities with the investigation of a debutante's murder in book 16, *Skeleton Key* (2000). Writing as Papazoglou she has published two psychological thrillers and a five-book series featuring Patience Campbell McKenna, a romance novelist turned crime writer. Before turning to mystery writing, Papazoglou edited *Greek Accent* magazine and freelanced for *Glamour*, *Mademoiselle* and *Working Woman*. Under the name Ann Paris she has written *Graven Image* (1987), set in Greece, and *Arrowheart* (1988), set in France. A graduate of Vassar College, she was married to three-time Edgar award-winner and columnist William DeAndrea (1952-1996). She lives in Connecticut with her two sons.

Gregor Demarkian...former FBI department head...Philadelphia, Pennsylvania

❏ ❏   1 - **Not a Creature Was Stirring (1990) Anthony & Edgar nominee** ☆☆
❏ ❏   2 - Precious Blood (1991)
❏ ❏   3 - Act of Darkness (1991)
❏ ❏   4 - Quoth the Raven (1991)
❏ ❏   5 - A Great Day for the Deadly (1992)
❏ ❏   6 - Feast of Murder (1992)
❏ ❏   7 - A Stillness in Bethlehem (1992)
❏ ❏   8 - Murder Superior (1993)
❏ ❏   9 - Bleeding Hearts (1994)
❏ ❏ 10 - Dear Old Dead (1994)
❏ ❏ 11 - Festival of Deaths (1994)
❏ ❏ 12 - Fountain of Death (1995)
❏ ❏ 13 - And One To Die On (1996)
❏ ❏ 14 - Baptism in Blood (1996)
❏ ❏ 15 - Deadly Beloved (1997)
❏ ❏   . . . .
❏ ❏   . . . .

■ HADDOCK, Lisa

Lisa Haddock has written two lesbian mysteries featuring Oklahoma newspaper copy editor Carmen Ramirez, introduced in *Edited Out* (1994). The 24-year-old daughter of an Irish mother and Puerto Rican father, Carmen was raised by her courageous, stubborn, loving and homophobic grandmother, who has recently rejected Carmen for resuming her "perverted" lifestyle. When Carmen is assigned to assist in updating a two-year-old story about the apparent suicide of a lesbian school teacher, she finds more questions than answers in the "solved" case. As a student at the University of Tulsa, Haddock served as news editor, managing editor and editor-in-chief of the *Collegian*. She has also worked as a clerk at the *St. Louis Globe-Democrat*, copy editor at the *Tulsa World*, and copy and layout editor at *The Record* in Hackensack, New Jersey. Born in Tulsa, Oklahoma, Haddock earned B.A. (with honors) and M.A. degrees from the University of Tulsa. She lives in New York.

Carmen Ramirez...lesbian newspaper copy editor...Frontier City, Oklahoma

❏ ❏   1 - Edited Out (1994)
❏ ❏   2 - Final Cut (1995)
❏ ❏   . . . .
❏ ❏   . . . .

■ HADLEY, Joan [P]

Joan Hadley is the pseudonym used by Joan Hess for her pair of horticultural mysteries featuring bachelor botanist and former spy Theo Bloomer, introduced in *Night-Blooming Cereus* (1986), set in Israel. A plant-loving retiree with a nose for crime-solving, Bloomer makes a second appearance in *Deadly Ackee* (1990), when he "chaperones his obnoxiously upscale niece Dorrie and her chums on a one-week Jamaican holiday at a hillside resort outside Montego Bay." The unusual murder weapon is the poisonous-when-unripe ackee fruit. A fifth-generation resident of Fayetteville, Arkansas, Hess has published more than 20 adult mysteries in two Arkansas series under her own name, as well as two young adult mysteries. A six-time nominee for Agatha and Anthony awards, she holds a B.A. in art from the University of Arkansas and an M.A. in education from Long Island University. After working in real estate sales for six years, she late taught art to three- and four-year-olds in a private preschool.

Theo Bloomer...retired florist and former spy

❏ ❏   1 - Night-Blooming Cereus (1986)
❏ ❏   2 - Deadly Ackee (1988)
❏ ❏   . . . .
❏ ❏   . . . .

■ HAFFNER, Margaret

Canadian biologist Margaret Haffner has written two mysteries featuring Ontario scientist Catherine Edison, introduced in *A Murder of Crows* (1992), set in the fictional town of Kingsport, a thinly-disguised Kingston. In *A Killing Frost* (1994), Edison and her daughter Morgan travel to the small Ontario town of Atawan. While the man acquitted in Tracy Tomachuk's strangulation death is attempting to re-establish himself, Edison uncovers the truth about Tracy's murder. Haffner's nonseries mystery, *Snowblind* (1993), is set in the Arctic. She has also written a children's book, *Fearless Jake* (1995). Born and raised in Kingston, Ontario, she earned a degree in biology from the University of Toronto. According to *Canadian Crime Fiction* (1996), Haffner has worked in plant biotechnology research in England and Canada, and currently heads the tissue culture laboratory at the Harrow Research Centre of the Department of Agriculture and Agrifood Canada near Windsor, Ontario. Born and raised in Kingston, she lives in Windsor.

Catherine Edison...scientist and single mother...Kingsport, Ontario, Canada

- ❑ ❑ 1 - A Murder of Crows (1992)
- ❑ ❑ 2 - A Killing Frost (1994)
- ❑ ❑ ....
- ❑ ❑ ....

■ HAGER, Jean

Jean Hager writes three mystery series, including two about contemporary Cherokee life in Oklahoma. Half-Cherokee police chief Mitch Bushyhead, who grew up and married outside the tribe, copes with raising a teenage daughter alone, after the death of his wife. Another Cherokee series focuses on Molly Bearpaw, civil rights investigator for the Native American Advocacy Council. Hager's Iris House series features Tess Darcy, proprietor of an elegant bed and breakfast in Victoria Springs, Missouri. Tess is busy planning her wedding in book 6, *Weigh Dead* (1999). Since the publication of her first two books (children's mysteries) in 1970, Hager has produced more than 50 novels under a variety of pseudonyms, including Marlaine Kyle, Jeanne Stephens, and *Playboy* house names Amanda McAllister and Sara North. Author and publisher of *How To Write And Market Your Mystery Novel* (1998), Hager is a former high school English teacher who has been writing full time since 1975. One-sixteenth Cherokee, she lives in Tulsa, Oklahoma.

Mitch Bushyhead...police chief of Cherokee descent...Buckskin, Oklahoma

- ❑ ❑ 1 - The Grandfather Medicine (1989)
- ❑ ❑ 2 - Night Walker (1990)
- ❑ ❑ 3 - Ghostland (1992)
- ❑ ❑ 4 - The Fire Carrier (1996)
- ❑ ❑ 5 - Masked Dancers (1998)
- ❑ ❑ ....
- ❑ ❑ ....

Molly Bearpaw...Cherokee civil rights investigator...Tahlequah, Oklahoma

- ❑ ❑ 1 - Ravenmocker (1992)
- ❑ ❑ 2 - The Redbird's Cry (1994)
- ❑ ❑ 3 - Seven Black Stones (1995)
- ❑ ❑ 4 - The Spirit Caller (1997)
- ❑ ❑ ....
- ❑ ❑ ....

Tess Darcy...Ozarks bed & breakfast owner...Victoria Springs, Missouri

- ❑ ❑ 1 - Blooming Murder (1994)
- ❑ ❑ 2 - Dead and Buried (1995)
- ❑ ❑ 3 - Death on the Drunkard's Path (1996)
- ❑ ❑ 4 - The Last Noel (1997)
- ❑ ❑ 5 - Sew Deadly (1998)
- ❑ ❑ ....
- ❑ ❑ ....

■ HALL, Linda

Linda Hall has written three mysteries featuring Royal Canadian Mounted Police Corporal Roger Sheppard, introduced in *August Gamble* (1995). The father of teenagers, Sheppard struggles to balance the demands of his job with the needs of his family. While the first two books are set in Alberta, Sheppard is transferred to a small town in New Brunswick for the final installment, *April Operation* (1997). Hall's "Coast of Maine" suspense trilogy from Multnomah Publishers begins with *Margaret's Peace* (1998). After the death of her daughter and the breakup of her marriage, Margaret returns to the family home in Maine where she relives her sister's death and faces long-buried secrets. *Island of Refuge* (1999) involves a similar coastal setting, but different characters. The trilogy concludes with *Katheryn's Secret* (2000). Hall's first novel, *The Josiah Files* (1993), science fiction with mystery elements, is set in 2194. After growing up in the U.S., Hall became a Canadian citizen in 1981. She teaches fiction writing at the University of New Brunswick.

Roger Sheppard...RCMP officer and family man...Alberta, Canada
- ❏ ❏ 1 - August Gamble (1995)
- ❏ ❏ 2 - November Veil (1996)
- ❏ ❏ 3 - April Operation (1997)
- ❏ ❏ . . . .
- ❏ ❏ . . . .

■ HALL, Patricia [P]

British journalist Maureen O'Connor, writing as Patricia Hall, is the author of six mysteries featuring Bradfield reporter Laura Ackroyd and Detective Chief Inspector Michael Thackeray, first seen in *Death by Election* (1993). Newly-arrived in Bradfield, Thackeray meets Ackroyd when she discovers disturbing connections between an election campaign to "out" sitting officials and a murder on the moor. "A satisfyingly ugly study of English local politics," said *Kirkus*. In book 6, *Dead on Arrival* (1999), Laura has witnessed the murder of a young African in London and is horrified at the lack of police interest. Back in Bradfield, Thackeray is dealing with a police scandal. Hall's first novel, *The Poison Pool* (1991), features Yorkshire village Inspector Alex Sinclair and social worker Kate Weston. The daughter of a headmaster, Hall was raised in West Yorkshire and read English literature at Birmingham University, where she edited the student newspaper. She has worked at *The Guardian*, the BBC, and the *London Evening Standard*.

Laura Ackroyd & Michael Thackeray...investigative reporter & police inspector...
Bradfield, Yorkshire, England
- ❏ ❏ 1 - Death by Election (1993)
- ❏ ❏ 2 - Dying Fall (1994)
- ❏ ❏ 3 - In the Bleak Midwinter (1995)
- ❏ ❏   - U.S.-Dead of Winter
- ❏ ❏ 4 - Perils of the Night (1997)
- ❏ ❏ 5 - The Italian Girl (1998)
- ❏ ❏ . . . .
- ❏ ❏ . . . .

■ HAMBLY, Barbara

Author of more than 30 novels, Barbara Hambly has written two cross-genre mystery series, including a pair of books featuring professor James Asher, a part-time spy in London at the time of Sherlock Holmes. Asher's detecting skills are sought by London's oldest vampire in *Those Who Hunt the Night* (1988). With *A Free Man of Color* (1997), Hambly introduces Benjamin January, a Paris-trained Creole surgeon in 1830s New Orleans. "A stunning mystery, magically rich and poignant," said reviewers. January's third case is *Graveyard Dust* (1999). Past president of Science Fiction Writers of America, Hambly has written the Darwath Series, Windrose Chronicles, Sunwolf, Sun-Cross and Star Trek series. With an M.A. in medieval history from the University of California, she later studied at universities in France and Australia. A Black Belt in karate, Hambly has worked as a karate instructor and competed in national tournaments. Her hobbies include painting, historical and fantasy costuming and carpentry.

Benjamin January...1830s Paris-trained black doctor...New Orleans, Louisiana

❏ ❏   1 - A Free Man of Color (1997)
❏ ❏   2 - Fever Season (1998)
❏ ❏   . . . .
❏ ❏   . . . .

James Asher...professor and part-time spy...London, England

❏ ❏   1 - Those Who Hunt the Night (1988)
❏ ❏   2 - Traveling With the Dead (1995)
❏ ❏   . . . .
❏ ❏   . . . .

■ HAMILTON, Laurell K.

In Laurell K. Hamilton's fictional alternate world, St. Louis reanimator and vampire hunter Anita Blake, an expert on creatures of the night, works as an investigator for Animators, Inc., starting with *Guilty Pleasures* (1993). Anita is a sassy, savvy private eye cast in a romantic-horror-mystery series—lots of fun, even for people who wouldn't be caught dead (pardon the expression) reading a vampire novel. In the series' first hardcover installment (book 8), *Blue Moon* (1998), Anita's ex-fiancé Richard has been jailed on a rape charge and he asks for her help. She knows he's a monster (the alpha werewolf), but he's no rapist and she needs to get him out of jail before the blue moon causes him more problems. The Animators gang returns in early 2000 in book 9, *Obsidian Butterfly*. Hamilton begins a new series in late 2000 with *Kiss of Shadows*, a hardcover first edition. Hamilton has also written *Nightseer* (1998), *Nightshade* (Star Trek, the Next Generation, No. 24), and *Death of a Darklord* (Ravenloft, No. 11).

Anita Blake...reanimator and vampire hunter...St. Louis, Missouri

❏ ❏   1 - Guilty Pleasures (1993)
❏ ❏   2 - The Laughing Corpse (1994)
❏ ❏   3 - Circus of the Damned (1995)
❏ ❏   4 - The Lunatic Cafe (1996)
❏ ❏   5 - Bloody Bones (1996)
❏ ❏   6 - The Killing Dance (1997)
❏ ❏   7 - Burnt Offerings (1998)
❏ ❏   8 - Blue Moon (1998)
❏ ❏   . . . .
❏ ❏   . . . .

■ HAMILTON, Lyn

Canadian author Lyn Hamilton has two jobs linked to her passion for ancient history, mythology and archaeology. By day she is director of cultural programs for the Province of Ontario. At night she writes archaeological mysteries featuring Lara McClintock, a Toronto antiquities dealer, introduced in *The Xibalba* (she-bal-BA) *Murders* (1997), an Ellis nominee for best first mystery. Hamilton made several trips to the Yucatan for book 1 and lived for more than two months on Malta for book 2. As part of her research for book 3, she spent time at an excavation site in the northern coastal desert of Peru where, U.S. and Canadian archaeologists were searching Moche cemetery sites. During two study trips for book 4, *The Celtic Riddle* (2000), she searched for the mythic center of Ireland. With a degree in English, Hamilton has studied anthropology and takes courses in ancient languages at the University of Toronto. Formerly a public relations and corporate communications professional, she lives in Toronto.

Lara McClintock...antiquities dealer and shop owner...Toronto, Ontario, Canada

❏ ❏   **1 - The Xibalba Murders [Mexico] (1997) Ellis nominee** ☆
❏ ❏   2 - The Maltese Goddess [Malta] (1998)
❏ ❏   3 - The Moche Warrior [Peru] (1999)
❏ ❏   4 - The Celtic Riddle [Ireland] (2000)
❏ ❏   . . . .
❏ ❏   . . . .

■ HANEY, Lauren [P]

Writing as Lauren Haney, amateur Egyptologist Betty Winkelman is the author of three Egyptian mysteries featuring ex-charioteer Lieutenant Bak, Commander of the Medjay police, introduced in *The Right Hand of Amon* (1997). It is the 18th Dynasty of Queen Maatkare Hatshepsut and Lt. Bak is a loyal servant of the royal house of Egypt in the frontier fortress city of Buhen in Lower Nubia. A man of honor and ability, Bak must oversee the corps assigned to escort the golden idol (the god of Amon) on its journey up the Nile to heal the ailing son of a powerful tribal king. In book 2, *A Face Turned Backward* (1999), Bak receives a new assignment when valuable elephant tusks are found to be bypassing royal coffers. The lieutenant's third adventure is *A Vile Justice* (1999). A frequent contributor to *K.M.T.*, the premier newsletter on ancient Egypt, Haney travels to Egypt and other sites of ancient ruins, at every opportunity. Previously a technical editor in California's aerospace and construction industries, she lives in New Mexico.

Lt. Bak...ex-charioteer turned Medjay police head...Buhen, Egypt
- ❏ ❏ 1 - The Right Hand of Amon (1997)
- ❏ ❏ 2 - A Face Turned Backward (1999)
- ❏ ❏ . . . .
- ❏ ❏ . . . .

■ HARDWICK, Mollie

Author of more than 60 books, Mollie Hardwick is well-known for her novelizations from popular BBC television series such as *Upstairs, Downstairs* and *The Duchess of Duke Street*, co-authored with husband Michael Hardwick (1924-1991). In addition to their T.V. novelizations, the Hardwicks co-wrote more than 20 books, including plays, novels and nonfiction about Sherlock Holmes, Charles Dickens and Bernard Shaw. Hardwick once commented that the two shared an almost identical writing style, allowing them to write a book together and argue later as to who wrote certain passages. Hardwick's mysteries feature antiques-seller Doran Fairweather, who marries vicar Rodney Chelmarsh, the man with a quote from literature or Scripture for every occasion. Art, antiques, religion and literature figure prominently in these perfect cozies, starting with *Malice Domestic* (1986). Hardwick has also written plays, historical novels, biographies, children's books, and several books as Mary Atkinson.

Doran Fairweather...British antiques dealer...Kent, England
- ❏ ❏ 1 - Malice Domestic (1986)
- ❏ ❏ 2 - Parson's Pleasure (1987)
- ❏ ❏ 3 - Uneaseful Death (1988)
- ❏ ❏ 4 - The Bandersnatch (1989)
- ❏ ❏ 5 - Perish in July (1989)
- ❏ ❏ 6 - The Dreaming Damozel (1990)
- ❏ ❏ 7 - Come Away, Death (1997)
- ❏ ❏ . . . .
- ❏ ❏ . . . .

■ HARRIS, Charlaine

Daughter of a librarian and a school principal, Charlaine Harris has written six mysteries featuring 20-something librarian Aurora (Roe) Teagarden, first seen in the Agatha award-nominated *Real Murders* (1990). In later installments Roe marries an older man, joins her mother's real estate firm, and tries her hand at selling houses. Harris' second series introduces rape survivor and beginning karate student Lily Bard, who cleans houses for a living, starting with *Shakespeare's Landlord* (1996). "An engaging puzzler, gripping and full of surprises," said *Publishers Weekly*. Coming next is book 4, *Shakespeare's Trollop* (2000). Harris earned a B.A. in English and communication arts from Rhodes College in Memphis. A student of goju karate, she is the mother of three and presides over a household that includes two large dogs, a duck and two ferrets. Before writing full time, Harris worked as a typesetter for several commercial printers and Federal Express. Born in Mississippi, she lives in Arkansas.

Aurora Teagarden...librarian turned real estate agent...Lawrenceton, Georgia

- ❑ ❑   1 - **Real Murders (1990) Agatha nominee** ☆
- ❑ ❑   2 - A Bone To Pick (1992)
- ❑ ❑   3 - Three Bedrooms, One Corpse (1994)
- ❑ ❑   4 - The Julius House (1995)
- ❑ ❑   5 - Dead Over Heels (1996)
- ❑ ❑   6 - A Fool and His Honey (1999)
- ❑ ❑   . . . .
- ❑ ❑   . . . .

Lily Bard...30-something cleaning woman...Shakespeare, Arkansas

- ❑ ❑   1 - Shakespeare's Landlord (1996)
- ❑ ❑   2 - Shakespeare's Champion (1997)
- ❑ ❑   3 - Shakespeare's Christmas (1998)
- ❑ ❑   . . . .
- ❑ ❑   . . . .

■ HARRIS, Lee [P]

Writing as Lee Harris, Syrell (suh-RELL) Rogovin (ruh-GO-vin) Leahy (LAY-hee) is the author 11 mysteries featuring former nun Christine Bennett, who lives in a suburb of New York City and investigates crimes with answers buried in the past. Each title, beginning with the Edgar award-nominated *The Good Friday Murder* (1992), is tied to a different holiday. The 30-something Bennett takes her name from the Buffalo, New York high school (Bennett High) that claims at least two mystery writers among its graduates—Lee Harris and Lawrence Block. During the '70s and '80s, Harris wrote mainstream novels under her own name, including her first novel, *A Book of Ruth* (1975). A graduate of Cornell University, she studied in Germany as a Fulbright scholar and later earned an M.A. from Columbia University. According to *Contemporary Authors*, she once worked as a linguistic researcher for I.B.M. and wrote training materials for AT&T. A native of Brooklyn, New York, she lives in New Jersey.

Christine Bennett...former nun...Oakwood, New York

- ❑ ❑   1 - **The Good Friday Murder (1992) Edgar nominee** ☆
- ❑ ❑   2 - The Yom Kippur Murder (1992)
- ❑ ❑   3 - The Christening Day Murder (1993)
- ❑ ❑   4 - The St. Patrick's Day Murder (1994)
- ❑ ❑   5 - The Christmas Night Murder (1994)
- ❑ ❑   6 - The Thanksgiving Day Murder (1995)
- ❑ ❑   7 - The Passover Murder (1996)
- ❑ ❑   8 - The Valentine's Day Murder (1997)
- ❑ ❑   9 - The New Year's Eve Murder (1997)
- ❑ ❑ 10 - The Labor Day Murder (1998)
- ❑ ❑ 11 - The Father's Day Murder (1999)
- ❑ ❑   . . . .
- ❑ ❑   . . . .

■ HARRISON, Jamie

Jamie Harrison has written four mysteries featuring Jules Clement, a 30-something archaeologist-turned-sheriff in Blue Deer, Montana, where his father was county sheriff when Jules was in high school. Just north of Yellowstone National Park, Blue Deer has a mix of rural independents and artsy types, all of whom are suspicious of Sheriff Clement. The series opener, *The Edge of the Crazies* (1995), refers to the Crazy Mountains and to the zany cast of this psychological thriller disguised as a humorous police mystery. Harrison has said she plans to keep book 4, *Blue Deer Thaw* (2000), open-ended enough that she can pick up again with Jules, or one of the other characters, in the future. She intends to write a screenplay or a mainstream novel next. A Michigan native and University of Michigan graduate, Harrison is the daughter of novelist Jim Harrison. After spending a summer on the edge of the Crazies, Harrison and her husband elected to stay and have lived in Montana for more than ten years. She reports they have two dogs, two cats and a yard that looks like Alice and Peter's.

Jules Clement...30-something archaeologist turned sheriff...Blue Deer, Montana
- ❏ ❏   1 - The Edge of the Crazies (1995)
- ❏ ❏   2 - Going Local (1996)
- ❏ ❏   3 - An Unfortunate Prairie Occurance (1998)
- ❏ ❏   . . . .
- ❏ ❏   . . . .

■ HARROD-EAGLES, Cynthia

Well-known British historical novelist Cynthia Harrod-Eagles is the creator of an eight-book mystery series she never intended to write. The first Bill Slider novel, *Orchestrated Death* (1991), was a gift for her sister after repeated laments that "no one writes mysteries anymore like Dorothy L. Sayers." D.I. Slider of Shepherd's Bush C.I.D. solves his eighth case, *Blood Sinister*, in the 1999 U.K. edition of the author's 51st book. Her historical, fantasy and romance fiction includes at least 22 titles in her Dynasty series, spanning British history from the Middle Ages forward. Writing as Emma Woodhouse and Elizabeth Bennett, Harrod-Eagles has ten more novels. Born and raised in the Shepherd's Bush area of London, she grew up about about half a mile from the home and fictional killing ground of Agatha Christie. An honors graduate of University College, London, Harrod-Eagles plays in several amateur orchestras. In addition to music, her passions are gardening, history, horses, architecture and the English countryside.

Bill Slider...Shepherd's Bush CID inspector...London, England
- ❏ ❏   1 - Orchestrated Death (1991)
- ❏ ❏   2 - Death Watch (1992)
- ❏ ❏   3 - Death To Go (1993)
- ❏ ❏   - APA-Necrochip
- ❏ ❏   4 - Grave Music (1994)
- ❏ ❏   - Brit.-Dead End
- ❏ ❏   5 - Blood Lines (1996)
- ❏ ❏   6 - Killing Time (1996)
- ❏ ❏   7 - Shallow Grave (1998)
- ❏ ❏   . . . .
- ❏ ❏   . . . .

■ HART, Carolyn G.

Two-time Agatha and Anthony award winner Carolyn G. Hart has written 30 novels, including her popular Death on Demand series featuring South Carolina mystery bookstore owner Annie Laurance and her sleuthing partner and husband Max Darling, last seen in book 11, *White Elephant Dead* (1999). Chock full of mystery personalities and crime fiction lore, these books have won a virtual trophy case of awards and nominations. With *Dead Man's Island* (1993), Hart introduced veteran journalist Henrietta O'Dwyer Collins, known to her friends as Henrie O, portrayed by Barbara Eden in a television movie. Book 6, *Death on the River Walk* (1999), takes Henrie O to San Antonio. Hart has written five juvenile mysteries, including her first book, *The Secret of the Cellars* (1964). An Oklahoma native and Phi Beta Kappa journalism graduate of the University of Oklahoma, she has also worked as a newspaper reporter and professional writing professor. A founding past president of Sisters in Crime, she lives in Oklahoma City.

Annie Laurance & Max Darling...bookstore owner & investigator...Broward's Rock, South Carolina
- ❏ ❏   1 - **Death on Demand (1987) Anthony & Macavity nominee** ☆☆
- ❏ ❏   2 - Design for Murder (1987)
- ❏ ❏   3 - **Something Wicked (1988) Anthony & Agatha winner** ★★
- ❏ ❏   4 - **Honeymoon With Murder (1988) Anthony winner** ★
- ❏ ❏   5 - **A Little Class on Murder (1989) Macavity winner** ★
           Anthony & Agatha nominee ☆☆
- ❏ ❏   6 - **Deadly Valentine (1990) Agatha & Macavity nominee** ☆☆
- ❏ ❏   7 - **The Christie Caper (1991) Anthony, Agatha & Macavity nominee** ☆☆☆
- ❏ ❏   8 - **Southern Ghost (1992) Anthony & Agatha nominee** ☆☆
- ❏ ❏   9 - The Mint Julep Murder (1995)
- ❏ ❏ 10 - Yankee Doodle Dead (1998)
- ❏ ❏   . . . .
- ❏ ❏   . . . .

Henrietta O'Dwyer Collins...70-something reporter...Oklahoma

- ❏ ❏ 1 - **Dead Man's Island (1993) Agatha winner ★**
- ❏ ❏ 2 - **Scandal in Fair Haven (1994) Agatha nominee ☆**
- ❏ ❏ 3 - Death in Lovers' Lane (1997)
- ❏ ❏ 4 - Death in Paradise (1998)
- ❏ ❏ . . . .
- ❏ ❏ . . . .

■ HART, Ellen [P]

Ellen Hart is the pseudonym of Patricia Ellen Boenhardt (BAIN-hart), whose 12 years as a sorority house kitchen manager at the University of Minnesota inspired her first murderous thoughts. Her two-time Lambda award-winning Jane Lawless series features a Minneapolis restaurant owner and her college friend Cordelia Thorn, artistic director of a St. Paul theatre, first seen in *Hallowed Murder* (1989). Hart later introduced a gourmet journalism series featuring magazine editor and food critic Sophie Greenway and her hus-

band Bram Baldric, a radio talk-show host. While Sophie reconnects with an old boyfriend, Bram gets involved with another woman in book 5, *Slice and Dice* (2000). Stay tuned for book 6 in 2001. Born in Minneapolis where she still lives, Hart is a gourmet cook and former chef. Armed with a B.A. in theology, she teaches mystery writing for the University of Minnesota and The Loft, the nation's largest independent writing community. Among her former students are Deborah Woodworth and new author K.J. Erickson.

Jane Lawless...lesbian restaurateur...Minneapolis, Minnesota

- ❏ ❏ 1 - Hallowed Murder (1989)
- ❏ ❏ 2 - Vital Lies (1991)
- ❏ ❏ 3 - Stage Fright (1992)
- ❏ ❏ 4 - A Killing Cure (1993)
- ❏ ❏ 5 - **A Small Sacrifice (1994) Lambda winner ★**
- ❏ ❏ 6 - Faint Praise (1995)
- ❏ ❏ 7 - **Robber's Wine (1996) Lambda winner ★**
- ❏ ❏ 8 - Wicked Games (1998)
- ❏ ❏ . . . .
- ❏ ❏ . . . .

Sophie Greenway...food critic and magazine editor...Minneapolis, Minnesota

- ❏ ❏ 1 - This Little Piggy Went To Murder (1994)
- ❏ ❏ 2 - For Every Evil (1995)
- ❏ ❏ 3 - The Oldest Sin (1996)
- ❏ ❏ 4 - Murder in the Air (1997)
- ❏ ❏ . . . .
- ❏ ❏ . . . .

■ HARTZMARK, Gini

Edgar nominee Gini Hartzmark has written six mysteries featuring Katherine Prescott Milholland, a blueblood Chicago attorney specializing in mergers and acquisitions, starting with *Principal Defense* (1992). Smart, funny Milholland takes on her sixth case in *Dead Certain* (2000), when the sale of her family's charitable hospital to a greedy corporation has Kate's aristocratic mother up in arms. A graduate of the University of Chicago, Hartzmark wrote business and economics textbooks before turning to fiction.

A former feature writer for Chicago newspapers and national magazines, Hartzmark lives in Arizona where she sets the thermostat to 68 degrees and puts on a sweater to remind her of Chicago. The daughter of a pathologist, she once worked in the coroner's office taking blood samples from corpses. Her college job in a primate research lab introduced her to hundreds of monkeys who all had names, including the dental school monkeys (with braces) named for fantasy and science fiction characters.

Katherine Prescott Milholland...blueblood corporate attorney...Chicago, Illinois

- ❏ ❏ 1 - **Principal Defense (1992) Edgar nominee ☆**
- ❏ ❏ 2 - Final Option (1994)

❏	❏	3 - Bitter Business (1995)
❏	❏	4 - Fatal Reaction (1997)
❏	❏	5 - Rough Trade (1999)
❏	❏	. . . .
❏	❏	. . . .

■ HATHAWAY, Robin

Malice Domestic winner Robin Hathaway modeled her amateur detective, Dr. Andrew B. Fenimore, after her own husband, an old-fashioned cardiologist in private practice, who drives an ancient car and occasionally buys his clothes in thrift shops. The fictional cardiologist is a 45-year-old Philadelphia bachelor whose investigations revolve around Main Line socialites and the Lenni-Lenape Indians of South Jersey. "Nebbishy but nice," said *Kirkus*. When Hathaway received the news that she had won the 1997 St. Martin's Press Malice Domestic contest for best first traditional mystery, she "got one gigantic migraine that lasted for three days, but worth every minute," she said. A second cousin to Grand Master Helen McCloy (1904-1993), Hathaway remembers the fun her mother and McCloy used to have discussing mysteries. For 25 years, Hathaway ran a printing and publishing firm called Barnhouse Press, with one press in the barn and another in her kitchen. She lives in New York City and Bayside, New Jersey.

Andrew Fenimore...old-fashioned cardiologist...Philadelphia, Pennsylvania

❏	❏	1 - **The Doctor Digs a Grave (1998) SMP/MD winner ★**
❏	❏	2 - The Doctor Makes a Dollhouse Call (2000)
❏	❏	. . . .
❏	❏	. . . .

■ HAYDEN, G. Miki

G. Miki Hayden spent childhood summers in southwest Michigan, the setting for her mystery series featuring psychiatrist Dr. Dennis Astin, introduced in *By Reason of Insanity* (1998). As Center City's acting medical examiner, Astin wants to know who killed a young nurse found beaten in the park. He doesn't buy the police theory that a homeless schizophrenic is responsible. While the setting is fictitious, as are all the hospitals Hayden writes about, she says the issues are real. During her 20 years as a working journalist she has frequently written about the medical field. Her first novel, *Pacific Empire* (1998), was featured on the 1998 *New York Times* recommended summer reading list. An alternative history of the Second World War, the book is a collection of nine interconnected stories that can stand alone, but together form a novel that tells what might have happened if Japan had won the war in the Pacific. Born in Illinois, Hayden grew up in Florida. She lives in New York City.

Dennis Astin...psychopharmacologist...Center City, Michigan

❏	❏	1 - By Reason of Insanity (1998)
❏	❏	2 - Too Old for Murder (1999)
❏	❏	. . . .
❏	❏	. . . .

■ HAYMON, S.T.

Silver Dagger winner Sylvia Theresa Haymon (1918-1995), writing as S.T. Haymon, wrote eight mysteries featuring Norwich Detective Inspector, Benjamin Jurnet of the Angleby C.I.D., introduced in *Death and the Pregnant Virgin* (1980). Jurnet's ambivalence about his religious identity and his eventual conversion to Judaism are woven throughout the series. After winning a Silver Dagger for *Ritual Murder* (1982), Haymon turned up the heat in *Stately Homicide* (1984), where Jurnet finds himself taking a stately home tour of Bullen Hall. Lost love letters from Anne Boleyn to her brother George Bullen have been sequestered by the incoming curator, who has discovered his predecessor's plans to write a book about the incestuous relationship. Guess which curator ends up dead in the Bullen Hall moat—attacked and partially eaten by giant eels? Haymon wrote two volumes of memoirs—*Opposite the Cross Keys: An East Anglican Childhood* (1988) and *The Quivering Tree* (1990)—and two biographies, including one of Prince Charles.

Benjamin Jurnet...Angleby CID detective inspector...Norwich, England

- ❑ ❑ 1 - Death and the Pregnant Virgin (1980)
- ❑ ❑ 2 - **Ritual Murder (1982) Silver Dagger winner ★**
- ❑ ❑ 3 - Stately Homicide (1984)
- ❑ ❑ 4 - Death of a God (1987)
- ❑ ❑ 5 - A Very Particular Murder (1989)
- ❑ ❑ 6 - Death of a Warrior Queen (1991)
- ❑ ❑ 7 - A Beautiful Death (1993)
- ❑ ❑ 8 - Death of a Hero (1996)
- ❑ ❑ . . . .
- ❑ ❑ . . . .

■ HAYTER, Sparkle

Sparkle Hayter writes laugh aloud mysteries featuring cable news reporter Robin Hudson, last seen in book 4, *The Chelsea Girl Murders* (2000). Born and raised in western Canada, Hayter moved to New York in 1980 where she graduated from N.Y.U. Film School. After five years at CNN, where she worked as assignment editor, producer, field producer and writer, Hayter spent 10 months backpacking alone across Europe, Asia, India and Pakistan. While riding trains around India she ran out of reading material and wrote the first draft of *What's a Girl Gotta Do?* The manuscript languished in a drawer for several years before she rewrote it, and won the Ellis Award for best first mystery. After twelve months covering the Afghan war as a television correspondent, Hayter returned to New York and did stand-up comedy for two years. A Bugs Bunny fanatic (she's got a tattoo), she collects fish, eyeballs, pen and pencil boxes, and Dana Girls mysteries. Her father insists she was not named after the *Dick Tracy* comic strip character, Sparkle Plenty.

Robin Hudson...cable news reporter...New York, New York

- ❑ ❑ 1 - **What's a Girl Gotta Do? (1994) Ellis winner ★**
- ❑ ❑ 2 - **Nice Girls Finish Last (1996) Ellis nominee ☆**
- ❑ ❑ 3 - Revenge of the Cootie Girls (1997)
- ❑ ❑ 4 - The Last Manly Man (1998)
- ❑ ❑ . . . .
- ❑ ❑ . . . .

■ HEBDEN, Juliet [P]

John Harris, writing as Mark Hebden (1916-1991), published more than 70 novels during his lifetime, including 17 mysteries featuring that quirky Burgundian, Chief Inspector Evariste Clovis Desire Pel of the French Police Judiciare. Daughter Juliet Harris, writing as Juliet Hebden, has added five new tales since 1993, bringing the Pel pantheon to 22 installments. The Gauloise-addicted Pel has a hate-hate relationship with his housekeeper, Madame Routy, who does not cook. She watches television non-stop (at high volume) from the only comfortable chair in the house. After meeting a wealthy heiress in book 2, Inspector Pel timidly pursues her until he proposes in book 7. The large supporting cast includes a handsome ladies-man as Pel's second-in-command, and a young cadet who happens to be the housekeeper's nephew. A punk Huguenot with "spiky blonde hair" and the confidence to stand up to Pel joins the detective team in book 22. "Hilarious," said *Amazon*. Juliet Harris lives in France with her six children.

Clovis Pel...curmudgeonly police inspector...Burgundy, France

- ❑ ❑ 1 - Death Set to Music [by Mark Hebden] (1979)
- ❑ ❑ - APA-Pel and the Parked Car (1995)
- ❑ ❑ 2 - Pel and Faceless Corpse [by Mark Hebden] (1979)
- ❑ ❑ 3 - Pel Under Pressure [by Mark Hebden] (1980)
- ❑ ❑ 4 - Pel is Puzzled [by Mark Hebden] (1981)
- ❑ ❑ 5 - Pel and the Stagehound [by Mark Hebden] (1982)
- ❑ ❑ 6 - Pel and the Bombers [by Mark Hebden] (1982)
- ❑ ❑ 7 - Pel and the Predators [by Mark Hebden] (1984)
- ❑ ❑ 8 - Pel and the Pirates [by Mark Hebden] (1984)
- ❑ ❑ 9 - Pel and the Prowler [by Mark Hebden] (1985)

MASTER LIST

❏	❏	10 - Pel and the Paris Mob [by Mark Hebden] (1986)
❏	❏	11 - Pel Among the Pueblos [by Mark Hebden] (1987)
❏	❏	12 - Pel and the Touch of Pitch [by Mark Hebden] (1987)
❏	❏	13 - Pel and the Picture of Innocence [by Mark Hebden] (1989)
❏	❏	14 - Pel and the Party Spirit [by Mark Hebden] (1989)
❏	❏	15 - Pel and the Missing Persons [by Mark Hebden] (1990)
❏	❏	16 - Pel and the Promised Land [by Mark Hebden] (1991)
❏	❏	17 - Pel and the Sepulchre [by Mark Hebden] (1992)
❏	❏	18 - Pel Picks up the Pieces (1993)
❏	❏	19 - Pel and the Perfect Partner (1994)
❏	❏	20 - Pel and the Patriarch (1996)
❏	❏	21 - Pel and the Precious Parcel (1997)
❏	❏	22 - Pel is Provoked (1998)
❏	❏	. . . .
❏	❏	. . . .

■ HENDERSON, Lauren

Lauren Henderson is the creator of savvy London sculptor Sam (Samantha) Jones, introduced in the U.K. with *Dead White Female* (1995). "We've always had the reprobate hero: this is the female counterpart who might eat him for breakfast," said the *Mail on Sunday*. When one of Sam's gym colleagues is found dead in *Too Many Blondes* (1996), she is asked to investigate. "Wonderfully politically incorrect, Henderson is the dominatrix of the British crime scene," said *Time Out*. Henderson's U.S. publisher elected to begin publication with book 3, *Black Rubber Dress*, in mid-1999, to be followed by book 4, *Freeze My Margarita*, in early 2000 and book 5, *The Strawberry Tattoo*, later that year. If the series finds an American audience, books 1 and 2 may follow. London born and bred, Henderson read English at Cambridge University and then worked as a freelance journalist for several magazines, including the indie music publication, *Lime Lizard*. An inveterate traveler, she divides her time between a flat in Tuscany and London.

Sam Jones...20-something sculptress...London, England

❏	❏	1 - Dead White Female (1995)
❏	❏	2 - Too Many Blondes (1996)
❏	❏	3 - Black Rubber Dress (1997)
❏	❏	4 - Freeze My Margarita (1998)
❏	❏	. . . .
❏	❏	. . . .

■ HENDRICKSEN, Louise

Louise Hendricksen shares a keen interest in forensic science with her protagonist, Dr. Amy Prescott, a state crime lab scientist with the Western Washington Crime Laboratory in Seattle. Amy's father, Dr. B.J. Prescott, is the medical examiner on Lomitas Island in Puget Sound. As the series progresses, the immensely-likable pair establishes a forensic investigations business on the shores of Puget Sound in Western Washington. Amy and her father, along with ace reporter Simon Kittredge, investigate the strange disappearance of cousin Oren Prescott and his fiancée in the series opener, *With Deadly Intent* (1993). When Simon Kittredge vanishes in book 2, *Grave Secrets* (1994), Amy teams up with Native American detective Nathan Blackthorne, a man of a hundred disguises. When last seen in *Lethal Legacy* (1995), Amy investigates the murder of a trusted colleague's wife. Prior to writing full time, Hendricksen worked in a primary care clinic laboratory. She lives with her husband Gene in Renton, Washington.

Amy Prescott...crime lab physician...Seattle, Washington

❏	❏	1 - With Deadly Intent (1993)
❏	❏	2 - Grave Secrets (1994)
❏	❏	3 - Lethal Legacy (1995)
❏	❏	. . . .
❏	❏	. . . .

■ HENRY, Sue

Anthony and Macavity award winner Sue Henry lives in Anchorage, Alaska, the setting for her six-book series featuring Alaska State Trooper, Alex Jensen, and champion sled-dog racer, Jessie Arnold. Their first adventure, *Murder on the Iditarod Trail* (1991), won Anthony and Macavity awards for best first novel, and later became the subject of a CBS television movie, *The Cold Heart of a Killer*, filmed (in part) in Alaska with Corbin Bernsen and Kate Jackson. Book 2, *Termination Dust* (1995), takes place in Klondike Gold

Rush country, with a 100-year-old mystery complicating a modern murder. When last seen in book 6, *Murder on the Yukon Quest* (1999), Jessie is back on the racing circuit, this time in the toughest race of all—1,000 treacherous miles starting in the Yukon Territory and ending in Fairbanks. A 25-year resident of Alaska, Henry retired recently from her administrative position at the University of Alaska. In addition to working on her next novel, she teaches mystery writing at the University of Alaska.

Jessie Arnold & Alex Jensen...sled dog racer & Alaska state trooper...Anchorage, Alaska

❏	❏	1 - **Murder on the Iditarod Trail (1991) Anthony & Macavity winner ★★**
❏	❏	2 - Termination Dust (1995)
❏	❏	3 - Sleeping Lady (1996)
❏	❏	4 - Death Takes Passage (1997)
❏	❏	5 - Deadfall (1998)
❏	❏	. . . .
❏	❏	. . . .

■ HERNDON, Nancy

Former advertising copywriter Nancy Herndon has written seven mysteries featuring Texas police detective Elena Jarvis with the Crimes Against Persons unit of the Los Santos police department. Three chapters of the series opener, *Acid Bath* (1995), were first published as short stories in the third and fourth *WomanSleuth Anthologies*. When last seen in book 7, *Casanova Crimes* (1999), Elena investigates the death of a campus Casanova. Herndon's six romance novels as Elizabeth Chadwick include *Reluctant Lovers* (1993), featuring a

suffragette-business woman, and *Virgin Fire* (1991), about a 19th century woman lawyer who wheels and deals in the Spindletop oil fields. A native of St. Louis, Missouri, Herndon was Phi Beta Kappa at the University of Missouri, where she earned B.A. degrees in both English and journalism. After earning an M.A from Rice University, she taught at New York University, Florida Atlantic University, and the Universities of Mississippi and Texas. She lives in El Paso.

Elena Jarvis...wise-cracking police detective...Los Santos, Texas

❏	❏	1 - Acid Bath (1995)
❏	❏	2 - Widows' Watch (1995)
❏	❏	3 - Lethal Statues (1996)
❏	❏	4 - Hunting Game (1996)
❏	❏	5 - Time Bombs (1997)
❏	❏	6 - C.O.P. Out (1998)
❏	❏	. . . .
❏	❏	. . . .

■ HERON, Echo

A critical care nurse in coronary and emergency medicine for 17 years, Echo Heron has written three medical mysteries featuring charge nurse Adele Monsarrat, introduced in *Pulse* (1998). Adele investigates when a popular young nurse dies in the recovery room after a routine appendectomy. Heron's debut fiction was the standalone novel *Mercy* (1993). Her first nonfiction, *Intensive Care: The Story of a Nurse* (1987), a *New York Times* bestseller, recounts her years at a major San Francisco hospital. The second volume of her true

story is *Condition Critical: The Story of a Nurse Continues* (1994). Heron has also written *Tending Lives: Nurses on the Medical Front* (1998), first-person stories from more than 40 nurses in a variety of fields, including five involved with the aftermath of the Oklahoma City bombing. Before making the transition from nurse to full-time writer, Heron moved to Monserrat as the |caretaker of a vacation home rarely used by its owners. Today she lives in Chicago with her cat Mooshie.

Adele Monsarrat...hospital registered nurse...Marin County, California
- ❏ ❏ 1 - Pulse (1998)
- ❏ ❏ 2 - Panic (1998)
- ❏ ❏ 3 - Paradox (1998)
- ❏ ❏ . . . .
- ❏ ❏ . . . .

■ HESS, Joan

Six-time Agatha and Anthony award nominee Joan Hess has written a dozen installments for each of her two series set in small Arkansas towns. Her first mystery, *Strangled Prose* (1986), introduced 30-something widowed bookstore owner, Claire Malloy, mother of an annoying teenage daughter named Caron. Police chief Arly Hanks of Maggody, Arkansas (population 755), along with a large cast of quirky characters, debut in *Malice in Maggody* (1987), written in less than six weeks as divorce therapy. While await- ing book 12, *Murder@Maggody.com* (2000), fans can visit the Maggody website at www.maggody.com and check out the town map sketched by the author. A fifth-generation resident of Fayetteville, Arkansas, Hess has written two botanical mysteries as Joan Hadley, award-winning short stories, three young adult mysteries and a romance novel (*No Martians, Please*) that was sold but never published. She holds a B.A. in art from the University of Arkansas and an M.A. in education from Long Island University.

Arly Hanks...small-town police chief...Maggody, Arkansas
- ❏ ❏ 1 - Malice in Maggody (1987)
- ❏ ❏ **2 - Mischief in Maggody (1988) Anthony & Agatha nominee ☆☆**
- ❏ ❏ 3 - Much Ado in Maggody (1989)
- ❏ ❏ 4 - Madness in Maggody (1990)
- ❏ ❏ 5 - Mortal Remains in Maggody (1991)
- ❏ ❏ 6 - Maggody in Manhattan (1992)
- ❏ ❏ **7 - O Little Town of Maggody (1993) Anthony & Agatha nominee ☆☆**
- ❏ ❏ 8 - Martians in Maggody (1994)
- ❏ ❏ **9 - Miracles in Maggody (1995) Agatha nominee ☆**
- ❏ ❏ 10 - The Maggody Militia (1997)
- ❏ ❏ 11 - Misery in Maggody (1998)
- ❏ ❏ . . . .
- ❏ ❏ . . . .

Claire Malloy...small-town bookstore owner...Farberville, Arkansas
- ❏ ❏ **1 - Strangled Prose (1986) Anthony nominee ☆**
- ❏ ❏ 2 - The Murder at the Murder at the Mimosa Inn (1986)
- ❏ ❏ 3 - Dear Miss Demeanor (1987)
- ❏ ❏ 4 - A Really Cute Corpse (1988)
- ❏ ❏ 5 - A Diet To Die For (1989)
- ❏ ❏ 6 - Roll Over and Play Dead (1991)
- ❏ ❏ 7 - Death by the Light of the Moon (1992)
- ❏ ❏ 8 - Poisoned Pins (1993)
- ❏ ❏ 9 - Tickled to Death (1994)
- ❏ ❏ 10 - Busy Bodies (1995)
- ❏ ❏ 11 - Closely Akin to Murder (1996)
- ❏ ❏ 12 - A Holly, Jolly Murder (1997)
- ❏ ❏ . . . .
- ❏ ❏ . . . .

■ HIGHSMITH, Domini

Domini Highsmith has published 13 novels, including three medieval thrillers set in East Yorkshire, England during the late 12th century. A raging storm mysteri- ously heals Father Simeon of a crippling affliction, and when a hooded stranger rides into Beverley with a newborn baby, Simeon hides the child from cruel designs of fellow clergy. Simeon and nurse Elvira become the little boy's guardians in *Keeper at the Shrine* (1995). When last seen in *Master of the Keys* (1996), cor- rupt priests have plunged the town into anarchy.

Highsmith says her Beverley series is based on historical fact, inspired by the Unknown Priest whose tomb stands in the North Transept of Beverley Minster. Her novels as Domini Wiles include five thrillers set in San Francisco, New York and Paris, and a sixth as Amy Van Hassen. Other fiction as Domini Highsmith includes two semi-autobiographical novels set in post-war Bradford and a pair of historical sagas set in the Wye Valley. The Yorkshire native lives in the shadow of Beverley Minster.

Father Simeon & Elvira...medieval priest & nurse...East Yorkshire, England
- ❏ ❏   1 - Keeper at the Shrine (1994)
- ❏ ❏   2 - Guardian at the Gate (1995)
- ❏ ❏   3 - Master of the Keys (1996)
- ❏ ❏   . . . .
- ❏ ❏   . . . .

■ HIGHTOWER, Lynn S.

Lynn S. Hightower has written eight mysteries, including four futuristic police novels starring homicide detective David Silver and his Elaki partner, String, a seven-foot stingray who smells like fresh limes, introduced in *Alien Blues* (1992). "Complex... snappy...original," said *Asimov's Science Fiction*. Hightower's Shamus award-winning *Satan's Lambs* (1993) introduced Lexington private eye Lena Padget. A three-book series featuring Cincinnati homicide detective Sonora Blair opens with *Flashpoint* (1995), where Blair matches wits with a female serial killer. "Miraculously fresh and harrowing fiction," said *Kirkus*. Book 4, *The Debt Collector*, was released in the U.K. in 1999 and will appear in the U.S. in 2000. A graduate of the University of Kentucky, Hightower once listed her hobbies as canoeing, riding horses and eating M&Ms. At various times she has shared home and office with an iguana named Earl, several cats and Griffin the Golden Retriever. Born in Chattanooga, Tennessee, Hightower lives in Lexington, Kentucky.

David Silver & String...homicide cop & alien partner...USA
- ❏ ❏   1 - Alien Blues (1992)
- ❏ ❏   2 - Alien Eyes (1993)
- ❏ ❏   3 - Alien Heat (1994)
- ❏ ❏   4 - Alien Rites (1995)
- ❏ ❏   . . . .
- ❏ ❏   . . . .

Lena Padget...private investigator...Lexington, Kentucky
- ❏ ❏   1 - **Satan's Lambs (1993) Shamus winner ★**
- ❏ ❏   . . . .
- ❏ ❏   . . . .

Sonora Blair...homicide detective...Cincinnati, Ohio
- ❏ ❏   1 - Flashpoint (1995)
- ❏ ❏   2 - Eyeshot (1995)
- ❏ ❏   3 - No Good Deed (1998)
- ❏ ❏   . . . .
- ❏ ❏   . . . .

■ HOFF, B.J.

Christian author B.J. Hoff has written more than 20 novels, including five mysteries featuring Daniel and Jennifer Kaine, first published in the late 1980s. Starting with *Storm at Daybreak* (1986), the series was repackaged by Tyndale House as the Daybreak Mysteries and re-released in 1996 and 1997. In book 1, Jennifer Terry is hired as Kaine's executive assistant at his West Virginia Christian radio station. Immediately attracted to her new boss, Jennifer discovers that the former Olympic gold-medal swimmer, blinded in an accident caused by a drunk driver, is receiving threatening phone calls. Daniel and Jennifer befriend a renowned Christian singer, in seclusion since the death of her fiancé in a plane crash, while on their honeymoon in book 2, *The Domino Image* (1987), also published as *The Captive Voice* (1995). A former church music director, Hoff has written poetry, inspirational books, and more than a dozen historical novels based on the experience of Irish immigrants to America. She lives in Lancaster, Ohio.

Daniel & Jennifer Kaine...Christian radio station owner & exec asst...West Virginia

❑ ❑   1 - Storm at Daybreak (1986)
❑ ❑   2 - The Domino Image (1987)
❑ ❑   - APA-The Captive Voice (1995)
❑ ❑   3 - The Tangled Web (1988)
❑ ❑   4 - Vow of Silence (1988)
❑ ❑   5 - Dark River Legacy (1990)
❑ ❑   . . . .
❑ ❑   . . . .

■ HOLBROOK, Teri

Teri Holbrook collected seven award nominations for the first two books in her series featuring Southern historian Gale Grayson, who divides her time between her hometown in Georgia and England. A very pregnant Gale is introduced in *A Far and Deadly Cry* (1995) shortly after the death of her ecoterrorist husband, Tom, an English poet. When the babysitter is killed on her way to Gale's home, Scotland Yard has lots of questions, forcing Gale to investigate when the village turns against her. Gale returns home in the four-time award nominated, *The Grass Widow* (1996), but is back in England for *Sad Water* (1999). After earning a degree in anthropology and linguistics from The College of William and Mary, Holbrook worked as a journalist for five years. Along with her husband, syndicated cartoonist Bill Holbrook, she shares child-rearing duties in a complicated schedule allowing both of them to work full time from home offices and keep up with two young daughters. She is a fifth-generation native of Atlanta.

Gale Grayson...American expatriate historian...England

❑ ❑   **1 - A Far and Deadly Cry (1995) Anthony, Agatha & Macavity nominee** ☆☆☆
❑ ❑   **2 - The Grass Widow (1996) Anthony, Agatha, Edgar &**
                                   Macavity nominee ☆☆☆☆
❑ ❑   3 - Sad Water (1999)
❑ ❑   . . . .
❑ ❑   . . . .

■ HOLLAND, Isabelle

Author of more than 50 novels for children and adults, Isabelle Holland has written a six-book series featuring psychologist Claire Aldington, an Episcopal priest at wealthy St. Anselm's Church in Manhattan. A widow with a problem teenage step-daughter, Rev. Aldington first appears in *The Lost Madonna* (1983). Born in Basel, Switzerland where her father was the American consul, Holland lived in Guatemala City and Liverpool before moving to New Orleans, where she graduated from Tulane University. Her first published short story appeared in the English children's magazine, *Tiger Tim*, when Holland was 13. Her books for young adults have been internationally recognized, beginning with her first novel, the semi-autobiographical *Cecily* (1967), about an awkward young teen at an English boarding school. Her third novel, *The Man Without a Face* (1972), was adapted for film by Mel Gibson in 1993. Holland lives in New York City where she has worked in magazine and book publishing for many years.

Claire Aldington...Episcopal priest...New York, New York

❑ ❑   1 - The Lost Madonna (1983)
❑ ❑   2 - A Death at St. Anselm's (1984)
❑ ❑   3 - Flight of the Archangel (1985)
❑ ❑   4 - A Lover Scorned (1986)
❑ ❑   5 - A Fatal Advent (1989)
❑ ❑   6 - The Long Search (1990)
❑ ❑   . . . .
❑ ❑   . . . .

■ HOLMS, Joyce

Joyce Holms has written four mysteries featuring young Edinburgh law student Fizz Fitzgerald and her solicitor-boss, Tam Buchanan, introduced in *Payment* *Deferred* (1996), when a convicted child molester asks their help in regaining custody of his daughter. "Despite the serious nature of its subject matter the book is very funny; both tense and comic; a brilliant debut," said *Crime Time*. "Deft, daft and definitely delicious," said Val McDermid in the *Manchester Evening News*. When last seen in *Thin Ice* (1999), it's the week before Christmas and Tam is hoping for a quiet break, only to become involved in a child kidnapping. Thanks to her low boredom threshold,

Holms has lived in 13 houses. Her more interesting jobs include running a hotel on the island of Arran in southwest Scotland, teaching window-dressing and working in an Edinburgh detective agency. During the summer months she runs a bed & breakfast in the Central Highlands of Scotland. Born and raised in Glasgow, she lives in Edinburgh and Killin.

Tam Buchanan & Fizz...older Scottish attorney & law student...Edinburgh, Scotland

❑ ❑ 1 - Payment Deferred (1996)
❑ ❑ 2 - Foreign Body (1997)
❑ ❑ 3 - Bad Vibes (1998)
❑ ❑ ....
❑ ❑ ....

■ HOLT, Hazel

After graduating with honors from Newnham College, Cambridge, Hazel Holt went to work for the International African Institute in London where she began a 30-year friendship with novelist Barbara Pym. Holt was named official biographer and literary executor when Pym died in 1980, and three nonfiction books resulted, including the Pym biography, *A Lot to Ask* (1991). Holt's first fiction, published when she was 60, introduced 50-something Sheila Malory, a widowed literary magazine writer from the English seaside

village of Taviscombe, in *Mrs. Malory Investigates* (1989). In book 2, Mrs. Malory travels to Oxford where she investigates the murder of a librarian. A former reviewer and feature writer for *Stage and Television Today*, Holt is the mother of novelist Tom Holt. Visitors to the Somerset village where Holt lives on the western coast of England will recognize actual place names from the Mrs. Malory mysteries. The Holts' thatched cottage is her husband's birthplace and has been in the family for more than 100 years.

Sheila Malory...British literary magazine writer...Devon, England

❑ ❑ 1 - Mrs. Malory Investigates (1989)
❑ ❑   - Brit.-Gone Away
❑ ❑ 2 - The Cruellest Month (1991)
❑ ❑ 3 - The Shortest Journey (1992)
❑ ❑ 4 - Mrs. Malory and the Festival Murders (1993)
❑ ❑   - Brit.-Uncertain Death
❑ ❑ 5 - Mrs. Malory: Detective in Residence (1994)
❑ ❑   - Brit.-Murder on Campus
❑ ❑ 6 - Mrs. Malory Wonders Why (1995)
❑ ❑   - Brit.-Superfluous Death
❑ ❑ 7 - Mrs. Malory: Death of a Dean (1996)
❑ ❑ 8 - Mrs. Mallory and the Only Good Lawyer (1997)
❑ ❑ ....
❑ ❑ ....

■ HOLTZER, Susan

When Susan Holtzer moved to San Francisco in 1990, few residents of Ann Arbor, Michigan knew they were about to be targeted for murder, starting with three bumped off in a single week during *Something To Kill For* (1994), winner of the St. Martin's Press Malice Domestic contest for best first traditional mystery. After 30 years in Ann Arbor, Holtzer is well acquainted with the town's lively mix of academics, artists, students and business people, and its reputation for the best garage sales in America. Divorced computer

programmer Anneke (AH-nuh-key) Haagen (rhymes with noggin) and local cop and former pro linebacker, Karl Genesco, star in the 'Go Blue' series, where they marry in book 6, *The Wedding Game* (2000), and honeymoon in book 7. Holtzer earned B.A. and M.A. degrees in journalism from the University of Michigan, where she worked on *The Michigan Daily*, married a *Daily* staffer and edited the paper's centennial anthology in 1990. She and her husband own a small educational publishing company.

Anneke Haagen...computer consultant...Ann Arbor, Michigan
- ❏ ❏ 1 - **Something To Kill For (1994) SMP/MD winner ★**
- ❏ ❏ 2 - Curly Smoke (1995)
- ❏ ❏ 3 - Bleeding Maize and Blue (1996)
- ❏ ❏ 4 - Black Diamond (1997)
- ❏ ❏ 5 - The Silly Season (1999)
- ❏ ❏ . . . .
- ❏ ❏ . . . .

■ HOOPER, Kay

Kay Hooper is the author of more than 60 books with over four million copies in print, including two private eye novels featuring Lane Montana, a finder of lost things, and Trey Fortier, an Atlanta homicide detective, introduced in *Crime of Passion* (1991). In the Shamus-nominated sequel, *House of Cards* (1991), Lane takes the handsome lieutenant to meet her family, but a murder takes center stage at the reunion. In the late '80s, Hooper wrote 11 spy novels featuring a government agent named Hagen, starting with

In Serena's Web (1987). Her recent American gothic suspense includes her first hardcover title, *Amanda* (1995), followed by *After Caroline* (1996), *Finding Laura* (1997) and *Haunting Rachel* (1998). These romantic thrillers are basically mysteries, says Hooper, in that the heroine is always trying to solve an important puzzle in her life. Eleven romance novels published as Kay Robbins in the early '80s are currently being re-released under the Hooper name. A California native, she lives in North Carolina.

Hagen...government agent...USA
- ❏ ❏ 1 - In Serena's Web (1987)
- ❏ ❏ 2 - Raven on the Wing (1987)
- ❏ ❏ 3 - Rafferty's Wife (1987)
- ❏ ❏ 4 - Zach's Law (1987)
- ❏ ❏ 5 - The Fall of Lucas Kendrick (1988)
- ❏ ❏ 6 - Unmasking Kelsey (1988)
- ❏ ❏ 7 - Outlaw Derek (1988)
- ❏ ❏ 8 - Shades of Gray (1988)
- ❏ ❏ 9 - Captain's Paradise (1988)
- ❏ ❏ 10 - It Takes a Thief (1989)
- ❏ ❏ 11 - Aces High (1989)
- ❏ ❏ . . . .
- ❏ ❏ . . . .

Lane Montana & Trey Fortier...finder of lost things & homicide detective...Atlanta, Georgia
- ❏ ❏ 1 - Crime of Passion (1991)
- ❏ ❏ 2 - **House of Cards (1991) Shamus nominee ☆**
- ❏ ❏ . . . .
- ❏ ❏ . . . .

■ HORANSKY, Ruby [P]

Writing as Ruby Horansky, Rebecca Holland is the author of two mysteries featuring 30-something six-foot N.Y.P.D. homicide detective, Nikki Trakos, introduced in *Dead Ahead* (1990). When a small-time gambler is shot to death on the Brooklyn waterfront, Trakos has three days to crack the case before her chauvinist boss brings in a more experienced (i.e., male) investigator. Why was the dead man carrying a phone number for the wealthy tycoon who died in a boating accident 48 hours earlier? "A solidly entertaining and

engrossing mystery; Horansky has constructed a tight plot and keeps the reader guessing," said *Booklist*. Struggling with personal turmoil in book 2, *Dead Center* (1994), Trakos is working with a new partner when she's put in charge of a murder case involving a widely-admired City Council member. "Nifty, out-of-the-past intrigue unpacked with authority and punch," said *Kirkus*. Under her own name, Holland has also written *Danger on Cue* (1981). She lives in Brooklyn, New York.

Nikki Trakos...6-ft. NYPD homicide detective...Brooklyn, New York
- ❏ ❏ 1 - Dead Ahead (1990)
- ❏ ❏ 2 - Dead Center (1994)
- ❏ ❏ . . . .
- ❏ ❏ . . . .

■ HORNSBY, Wendy

Wendy Hornsby writes sizzling California mysteries and award-winning short stories, including her 1991 Edgar winner, "Nine Sons." Hornsby's first two mysteries featured history professor Kate Teague and homicide detective Roger Tejeda, starting with *No Harm* (1987). A longer-running series stars documentary film maker Maggie MacGowen, first seen in *Telling Lies* (1992). The supporting cast includes Maggie's teenage daughter Casey, homicide detective Mike Flint, and his college-age son Michael. Based on an actual L.A.P.D. case, *77th Street Requiem* (1995), earned Hornsby a starred review in *Publishers Weekly*. When last seen in *A Hard Light* (1997), Maggie is filming a documentary on teenage criminals that leads back to the final days of the Vietnam War. A Southern California native with graduate degrees in ancient and medieval history, Hornsby teaches at Long Beach City College. She recently completed a standalone novel and is looking forward to the release of a collection of her short stories in 2000.

Kate Teague & Roger Tejeda...college professor & homicide detective...Los Angeles, California

- ❏ ❏ 1 - No Harm (1987)
- ❏ ❏ 2 - Half a Mind (1990)
- ❏ ❏ . . . .
- ❏ ❏ . . . .

Maggie MacGowen...documentary filmmaker...Los Angeles, California

- ❏ ❏ 1 - Telling Lies (1992)
- ❏ ❏ 2 - Midnight Baby (1993)
- ❏ ❏ 3 - Bad Intent (1994)
- ❏ ❏ 4 - 77th Street Requiem (1995)
- ❏ ❏ 5 - A Hard Light (1997)
- ❏ ❏ . . . .
- ❏ ❏ . . . .

■ HOROWITZ, Renee B.

Renee B. Horowitz has written two mysteries featuring 50-something widowed pharmacist Ruthie Kantor Morris, introduced in *Rx for Murder* (1997), when a patient dies mysteriously. As the pharmacy manager for a Scottsdale, Arizona supermarket, Ruthie must find out who is responsible for the death of a teenager, when the pharmacy is accused of a fatal prescription error in book 2, *Deadly Rx* (1997). After earning a Ph.D. in comparative literature from the University of Colorado, Horowitz spent six years as a technical writer in the engineering industry. She currently teaches at Arizona State University, where she is professor of information and management technology. Her behind-the-scenes look at the world of pharmacy comes from husband Arthur, who is a pharmacy manager for an Arizona supermarket chain. While her father and father-in-law are both pharmacists, Horowitz says she opted out of the field when she found out she'd have to dissect frogs. The New York native lives in Scottsdale, Arizona.

Ruthie Kantor Morris...widowed pharmacist...Scottsdale, Arizona

- ❏ ❏ 1 - Rx for Murder (1997)
- ❏ ❏ 2 - Deadly Rx (1997)
- ❏ ❏ . . . .
- ❏ ❏ . . . .

■ HOWE, Melodie Johnson

Los Angeles native Melodie Johnson Howe dreamed of becoming a movie star and novelist. After attending Stephens College in Columbia, Missouri and the University of Southern California, she was discovered by Universal Studios and signed as a contract player. While working in television, movies and commercials, she studied writing at U.C.L.A. and published *The Mother Shadow* (1989), nominated for Edgar, Agatha and Anthony awards as best first novel. Elegant private eye Claire Conrad and her very independent assistant Maggie Hill travel to New York City for their second adventure in *Beauty Dies* (1994). While preparing for a return flight to Los Angeles, Claire and Maggie receive a strange message from a young woman who is later stabbed to death. They stay in New York to investigate. As a writing instructor at U.C.L.A. Extension, Howe coached future authors such as Jerrilyn Farmer, who started her first mystery in Howe's class. She lives near Santa Barbara with husband, legendary music producer Bones Howe.

Claire Conrad & Maggie Hill...elegant P.I. & assistant...Los Angeles, California

- ❏ ❏ **1 - The Mother Shadow (1989) Anthony, Agatha & Edgar nominee** ☆☆☆
- ❏ ❏ 2 - Beauty Dies (1994)
- ❏ ❏ . . . .
- ❏ ❏ . . . .

■ HOWELL, Lis

British television executive Lis Howell has written three mysteries featuring London television producer Kate Wilkinson, introduced in *After the Break* (1995). Between projects and on the outs with her sweetheart, Reverend John Maple, Kate travels to a village in the Lake District to work on an independent film about rural regeneration in book 2, *The Director's Cut* (1996). "When Kate decides her little film should show the town's dark side, what started out as a lightly diverting sudser turns into a wickedly delicious commentary on the rot that underlie a picture-postcard facade," said *Publishers Weekly*. "Howell shows her steady hand, leavening the suspense with humor." When last seen in *A Job To Die For* (1997), Kate has landed the prestigious job of setting up a new cable television channel. Former programming director of the London-based breakfast station GMTV, Howell is senior vice-president of Flextech, a major European satellite-television programmer, where she was previously vice-president of programming.

Kate Wilkinson...television producer...London, England

- ❏ ❏ 1 - After the Break (1995)
- ❏ ❏ 2 - The Director's Cut (1996)
- ❏ ❏ 3 - A Job To Die For (1997)
- ❏ ❏ . . . .
- ❏ ❏ . . . .

■ HUFF, Tanya

Canadian Tanya Huff has written a five-book series featuring ex-cop Vicki Nelson, a Toronto P.I. specializing in otherworldly crimes. First seen in *Blood Price* (1992), Nelson is no Canadian Kinsey Millhone. Her former significant other is Henry Fitzroy (bastard son of Henry VIII), who died at 17 in 1536. A Toronto-based vampire, Fitzroy writes bodice-ripping romance novels. In book 5, *Blood Debt* (1997), he needs Vicki's help when a ghost invades his inner sanctum. Born in Nova Scotia, Huff earned a degree in radio and television arts from Toronto's Ryerson Polytechnic University. As T.S. Huff and Terri Hanover, her short fiction includes "The Chase Is On," a space opera. Her Magdelene stories about the most powerful wizard in the world include "Third Time Lucky," "And Who Is Joah?" (nominated for a 1987 Aurora award) and "The Last Lesson," all featured in *Amazing Short Stories*. A former science fiction bookstore manager in Toronto, Huff served three years in the Canadian Naval Reserve. She lives in rural Ontario.

Vicki Nelson...ex-cop turned P.I. with vampire lover...Toronto, Ontario, Canada

- ❏ ❏ 1 - Blood Price (1992)
- ❏ ❏ 2 - Blood Trail (1992)
- ❏ ❏ 3 - Blood Lines (1993)
- ❏ ❏ 4 - Blood Pact (1993)
- ❏ ❏ 4 - Blood Debt (1997)
- ❏ ❏ . . . .
- ❏ ❏ . . . .

■ HYDE, Eleanor

Eleanor Hyde is the creator of 30-something New York fashion magazine editor Lydia Miller, whose holiday weekend in the Hamptons turns disastrous in *In Murder We Trust* (1995). When Lydia finds her millionaire host dead in the swimming pool, she becomes the prime murder suspect when it is disclosed that she is the man's chief beneficiary. In *Animal Instinct* (1996), Lydia takes a sabbatical from her magazine duties to volunteer at a private animal shelter, where she uncovers a conspiracy involving animal abduction. Hyde's first novel was *Those Who Stayed Behind* (1981). Former copyeditor for the American Institute of Physics, she studied at the Sorbonne, University of Paris and the Université Laval. Author of a 1996 one-act play produced at the Harold Clurman Theatre, she has published short fiction in *Cosmopolitan*, *Redbook*, *Ladies Home Journal* and *McCall's* magazines. Born in Ohio, Hyde lives in New York City where she heads a mentor program sponsored by Mystery Writers of America.

Lydia Miller...30-something fashion editor...New York, New York

❏ ❏	1 - In Murder We Trust (1995)
❏ ❏	2 - Animal Instincts (1996)
❏ ❏	. . . .
❏ ❏	. . . .

■ IAKOVOU, Takis and Judy

Restaurant owners Takis (TOCK-is) and Judy Iakovou (ee-uh-KO-voo) have created a pair of sleuthing Georgia café owners strikingly similar to themselves, although they are quick to point out that no one has ever died in one of their restaurants, nor have their detecting skills been used to unmask a killer. Nick and Julia Lambros are owners of the Oracle Café in the college town of Delphi, introduced in *So Dear to Wicked Men* (1996). Nick is a Greek immigrant and Julia a part-time speech pathologist. While he is olive oil to her vinegar, they "radiate warmth and charm," according to *Kirkus*. The supporting cast includes their sparkplug of a little dog, a gentle giant Cretan cook, and octogenarian Miss Alma. When Nick and Julia take a Florida vacation in book 3, *There Lies a Hidden Scorpion* (1999), a Greek wedding turns into a deadly family feud. Restaurant owners for 20 years, the Iakovous are proprietors of the Silver Screen Grill in Crawford and The Checkered Cloth Café in Arnoldsville, Georgia.

Nick & Julia Lambros...college-town cafe owners...Delphi, Georgia

❏ ❏	1 - So Dear to Wicked Men (1996)
❏ ❏	2 - Go Close Against the Enemy (1998)
❏ ❏	. . . .
❏ ❏	. . . .

■ JACKSON, Hialeah [P]

Hialeah Jackson is the pseudonym of Polly Whitney for her South Florida mysteries featuring security specialists Annabelle Hardy-Maratos and her Cuban-born second-in-command, Dave "the Monkeyman" Enamorado, in *The Alligator's Farewell* (1998) and *Farewell, Conch Republic* (1999). Once married and teaching at Yale, the recently-deaf Annabelle has inherited her father's Miami detective agency. As Polly Whitney, the author writes the Agatha award-nominated Until series, set in New York City. As P.L. Whitney, she has written *This Is Graceanne's Book* (1999), a mainstream novel set in the 1960s world of a nine-year-old boy. After earning an M.A. in English from Yale University, Whitney worked as a crime reporter and photographer for the *New Haven Register*. Before turning to novel-writing she taught English for four years at a Miami prep school. Married to a network television producer, Whitney is a native of St. Louis and divides her time among Midtown Manhattan, Northern New Jersey and Florida.

Annabelle Hardy-Maratos & Dave the Monkeyman...security specialists...Miami, Florida

❏ ❏	1 - The Alligator's Farewell (1998)
❏ ❏	2 - Farewell, Conch Republic (1999)
❏ ❏	. . . .
❏ ❏	. . . .

■ JACKSON, Marian J.A. [P]

Writing under her maiden name, Marian Rogers writes historical mysteries as Marian J.A. Jackson. Set at the turn of the century, her series features American heiress Abigail Patience Danforth, who aspires to be the world's first female consulting detective. Miss Danforth asks the advice of Sir Arthur Conan Doyle, who is less than enthusiastic about her plans. When Mark Twain gives his approval, the die is cast. Much of the first installment takes place in England, but book 2 sends Abigail back to New York, where she and companion, Maude Cunningham, board a train for their adventure out West. Book 5, *The Sunken Treasure* (1994), finds Abigail and Maude on a yacht sailing from Panama to New Orleans, with Abigail wondering how she'll unlock the secrets of Houdini. For eight years Rogers managed the technical services department of the Institute of Electrical and Electronics Engineers in New York City. A native of Birmingham, Alabama, she lives in New York, where she has served in the local police auxiliary organization.

Abigail Patience Danforth...19th century American heiress detective
- ❏ ❏ 1 - The Punjat's Ruby (1990)
- ❏ ❏ 2 - The Arabian Pearl (1990)
- ❏ ❏ 3 - The Cat's Eye (1991)
- ❏ ❏ 4 - Diamond Head (1992)
- ❏ ❏ 5 - The Sunken Treasure (1994)
- ❏ ❏ . . . .
- ❏ ❏ . . . .

■ JACOBS, Jonnie

Jonnie Jacobs was a high school English teacher and counselor and later an attorney with a large San Francisco law firm before writing her first mystery. Jacobs' six novels comprise two three-book series, beginning with *Murder Among Neighbors* (1994), introducing amateur sleuth and suburban mother Kate Austen. After the breakup of Kate's marriage in the series opener, she meets nice-guy police detective Mike Stone, who becomes her love interest. Jacobs' second series, set in the fast-track world of young attorneys, is harder-edged than her first, with single San Francisco attorney Kali O'Brien making her debut in *Shadow of Doubt* (1996). In book 3, *Motion To Dismiss* (1999), Kali's client is a sick friend's husband accused of rape. After graduation from the University of California, Berkeley, Jacobs earned a law degree at Boalt Hall School of Law, and master's degrees in English and counseling from the University of Michigan and San Jose State University. She lives with her husband and two sons in Northern California.

Kali O'Brien...attorney...Gold Country, California
- ❏ ❏ 1 - Shadow of Doubt (1996)
- ❏ ❏ 2 - Evidence of Guilt (1997)
- ❏ ❏ 3 - Motion To Dismiss (1999)
- ❏ ❏ . . . .
- ❏ ❏ . . . .

Kate Austen...suburban single mother...Walnut Hills, California
- ❏ ❏ 1 - Murder Among Neighbors (1994)
- ❏ ❏ 2 - Murder Among Friends (1995)
- ❏ ❏ 3 - Murder Among Us (1998)
- ❏ ❏ . . . .
- ❏ ❏ . . . .

■ JACOBS, Nancy Baker

Nancy Baker Jacobs is one of only a few private eye writers who can claim actual experience as a working private investigator. Her three-book series features Minneapolis P.I. Devon MacDonald, introduced in *The Turquoise Tattoo* (1991), voted one of the year's ten best hardboiled mysteries by Japan's Maltese Falcon Society, when it was published there in 1994. In the series opener, Devon is hired by a Jewish doctor who once donated his sperm to a local sperm bank and now must find a half-sibling for a possible bone marrow donation before his son dies of leukemia. Devon locates a potential donor, who turns out to be the son of an Aryan supremacist. Jacobs' five suspense novels are *Rocking the Cradle* (1996), *Daddy's Gone A-Hunting* (1995), *Cradle and All* (1995), *See Mommy Run* (1992), and *Deadly Companion* (1986). A former newspaper reporter, scriptwriter, and college professor, she has written six nonfiction books as Nancy C. Baker. A former Minnesotan, Jacobs lives on the Monterey Peninsula in California.

Devon MacDonald...ex-teacher private eye...Minneapolis, Minnesota
- ❏ ❏ 1 - The Turquoise Tattoo (1991)
- ❏ ❏ 2 - A Slash of Scarlet (1992)
- ❏ ❏ 3 - The Silver Scalpel (1993)
- ❏ ❏ . . . .
- ❏ ❏ . . . .

■ JAFFE, Jody

Jody Jaffe has written three equestrian mysteries featuring Natalie Gold, a Charlotte newspaper reporter on the North Carolina horse show circuit, beginning with *Horse of a Different Killer* (1995), nominated for Agatha and Macavity awards as best first mystery. "Shades of Arthur Conan Doyle's Silver Blaze," raved *Kirkus*. Despite Nattie's Philadelphia Yankee heritage, she knows horses, having scrimped and saved to buy her own aptly-named hunter, Brenda Starr. In *Chestnut Mare, Beware* (1996), Jaffe "satirizes both the newspaper business and the horsy set without slowing her galloping plot by a single stride," said *People* magazine when they picked book 2 as a Page-Turner of the Week. While riding and showing hunters for more than 25 years, Jaffe spent ten years as a reporter on *The Charlotte Observer*, where she once out-ranked co-worker Patricia Cornwell. A graduate of Cornell University, Jaffe is married to Charlie Shepard, who won a Pulitzer Prize for his work uncovering the P.T.L. scandal. They live in Maryland.

Natalie Gold...reporter on horse show circuit...Charlotte, North Carolina

- ❏ ❏ 1 - **Horse of a Different Killer (1995) Agatha & Macavity nominee** ☆☆
- ❏ ❏ 2 - Chestnut Mare, Beware (1996)
- ❏ ❏ 3 - In Colt Blood (1998)
- ❏ ❏ . . . .
- ❏ ❏ . . . .

■ JAKEMAN, Jane

Art historian Jane Jakeman writes 19th century historical mysteries featuring Lord Ambrose Malfine, introduced in *Let There Be Blood* (1997). Badly scarred, both emotionally and physically, on the battlefields of Greece, Lord Ambrose returns to his rural West Country mansion in 1830 to heal his wounds in seclusion. His faithful manservant Belos is instructed to turn away all callers, but Ambrose must intervene when a local farmer and his son are shot dead with dueling pistols. Ambrose travels to Egypt to rescue a spirited West Country heiress in book 2, *The Egyptian Coffin* (1998), and returns home for a case of poisoning in book 3, *Fool's Gold* (1998). After studying English at the University of Birmingham, Jakeman earned a doctorate from Oxford University in the architectural history of Islamic Cairo. On staff at the Bodleian Library, she lives in Oxford, where she writes about art, food and travel for British magazines and newspapers. Jakeman has traveled extensively in the Mediterranean and Middle East.

Ambrose Malfine...lord and heir to a decaying estate...West Country, England

- ❏ ❏ 1 - Let There Be Blood (1997)
- ❏ ❏ 2 - The Egyptian Coffin (1998)
- ❏ ❏ 3 - Fool's Gold (1998)
- ❏ ❏ . . . .
- ❏ ❏ . . . .

■ JAMES, P.D.

Baroness James of Holland Park is known to millions of readers as P.D. James. She is also Phyllis Dorothy James White, who spent 30 years in British Civil Service, including the Police and Criminal Law Departments of the Home Office. The recipient of numerous prizes and honors, including a 1991 Life Peerage, James has been awarded a Diamond Dagger for lifetime achievement, three Silver Daggers, and multiple Edgar nominations. At least six of her novels have been filmed and broadcast on British and American television and she has served as a magistrate and governor of the BBC. James' well-known series characters are Commander Adam Dalgleish of Scotland Yard, a published poet, and Cordelia Gray, who have made appearances in each other's books. Cordelia is introduced in the Edgar-nominated *An Unsuitable Job for a Woman* (1972), when she inherits a private enquiry firm from her former partner. James has also written *The Children of Men* (1992), a novel about 21st century dystopia.

Adam Dalgleish...published poet of Scotland Yard...London, England

- ❏ ❏ 1 - Cover Her Face (1962)
- ❏ ❏ 2 - A Mind To Murder (1963)
- ❏ ❏ 3 - Unnatural Causes (1967)

❑ ❑   4 - **Shroud for a Nightingale (1971) Silver Dagger winner ★ Edgar nominee ☆**
❑ ❑   5 - **The Black Tower (1975) Silver Dagger winner ★**
❑ ❑   6 - Death of an Expert Witness (1977)
❑ ❑   7 - **A Taste for Death (1986) Silver Dagger & Macavity winner ★★**
❑ ❑   8 - Devices and Desires (1989)
❑ ❑   9 - Original Sin (1994)
❑ ❑ 10 - A Certain Justice (1998)
❑ ❑   . . . .
❑ ❑   . . . .

Cordelia Gray…fledgling P.I.…London, England
❑ ❑   1 - **An Unsuitable Job for a Woman (1972) Edgar nominee ☆**
❑ ❑   2 - The Skull Beneath the Skin (1982)
❑ ❑   . . . .
❑ ❑   . . . .

■ JANCE, J.A.

J.A. Jance is Judith A. Jance, creator of the best-selling Seattle series featuring Jonas Piedmont Beaumont, better known as J.P., introduced in *Until Proven Guilty* (1985). The once hard-drinking Seattle homicide cop with the high-rise condo and fast car makes his 14th appearance in *Breach of Duty* (1999). Jance writes a second law enforcement series featuring Joanna Brady, first appearing in *Desert Heat* (1993), where she faces some tough decisions after the death of her husband in Cochise County, Arizona. Jance's psycho-logical thriller, *Hour of the Hunter* (1991), will be joined by a sequel, *Kiss of the Bees*, in 2000. She has written three titles in the Children's Safety series, including *Welcome Home, Stranger* (1986). Before writing full time, Jance taught high school English, worked as a school librarian on an Arizona Indian reservation, and sold life insurance for more than ten years. Born in South Dakota and raised in Arizona, she is a graduate of the University of Arizona. Jance lives with her husband in Seattle.

J.P. Beaumont…homicide detective…Seattle, Washington
❑ ❑   1 - Until Proven Guilty (1985)
❑ ❑   2 - Injustice for All (1986)
❑ ❑   3 - Trial by Fury (1986)
❑ ❑   4 - Taking the Fifth (1987)
❑ ❑   5 - Improbable Cause (1988)
❑ ❑   6 - A More Perfect Union (1988)
❑ ❑   7 - Dismissed With Prejudice (1989)
❑ ❑   8 - Minor in Possession (1990)
❑ ❑   9 - Payment in Kind (1991)
❑ ❑ 10 - Without Due Process (1992)
❑ ❑ 11 - Failure To Appear (1993)
❑ ❑ 12 - Lying in Wait (1994)
❑ ❑ 13 - Name Withheld (1995)
❑ ❑ 14 - Breach of Duty (1999)
❑ ❑   . . . .
❑ ❑   . . . .

Joanna Brady…single-mother sheriff…Cochise County, Arizona
❑ ❑   1 - Desert Heat (1993)
❑ ❑   2 - Tombstone Courage (1994)
❑ ❑   3 - Shoot, Don't Shoot (1995)
❑ ❑   4 - Dead to Rights (1996)
❑ ❑   5 - Skeleton Canyon (1997)
❑ ❑   6 - Rattlesnake Crossing (1998)
❑ ❑   7 - Outlaw Mountain (1999)
❑ ❑   . . . .
❑ ❑   . . . .

■ JENNINGS, Maureen

Born in England, Maureen Jennings immigrated to Canada, where she writes 1890s Canadian mysteries featuring Toronto's first and only police detective, Inspector William Murdoch. The series opener, *Except the Dying* (1997), was nominated for Anthony and Ellis awards as best first novel and received a commendation from Heritage Toronto. "An exhilarating first novel," raved *Publishers Weekly*. The *New York Times Book Review* praised the "vividness of its period setting and lifelike characters caught up in its broad social sweep." Book 3, *Poor Tom Is Cold*, is scheduled for 2000 release. Jennings' two historical mystery plays feature John Wilson Murray, Provincial Detective for Ontario from 1876 to 1906 in *No Traveller Returns*, and *The Black Ace*, performed at Solar Stage in 1990 and 1999. Owing to many hours spent in the Ontario Archives, Jennings is an expert on Toronto crime in 1895, having read the police commissioner's report and a complete record of coroner's inquest reports for the entire year. She lives in Toronto.

William Murdoch...Victorian police inspector...Toronto, Ontario, Canada
- ❏ ❏   1 - **Except the Dying (1997) Anthony & Ellis nominee** ☆☆
- ❏ ❏   2 - Under the Dragon's Tail (1998)
- ❏ ❏   . . . .
- ❏ ❏   . . . .

■ JOHN, Cathie [P]

Cathie John is the pseudonym of Cathie and John Celestri, who publish their own mysteries featuring Cincinnati gourmet caterer, Kate Cavanaugh, a 43-year-old breast cancer survivor introduced in *Add One Dead Critic* (1997). Owner of 'Round the World Catering, six-foot three-inch Kate has a busy schedule in book 2, *Beat a Rotten Egg to the Punch* (1998), with an Iranian wedding reception, Italian stag party and a booth at Taste of Cincinnati. A graduate of the culinary program at Rhode Island School of Design, Canadian-born Cathie Celestri is a breast cancer survivor. Once a student at Toronto's Royal Conservatory of Music with aspirations to become a symphony flutist, she has worked in restaurants and catering. A former architecture student at Fordham University, Brooklyn-born John Celestri has been animating movies, television and videos since his first paying job in the 1975 film *Tubby the Tuba*. One of his recent animations is the villainous Kralahome in *The King and I*. The Celestris live in Loveland, Ohio.

Kate Cavanaugh...gourmet caterer...Cincinnati, Ohio
- ❏ ❏   1 - Add One Dead Critic (1997)
- ❏ ❏   2 - Beat a Rotten Egg to the Punch (1998)
- ❏ ❏   3 - Carve a Witness to Shreds (1999)
- ❏ ❏   4 - Debone a Killer's Alibi (2000)
- ❏ ❏   . . . .
- ❏ ❏   . . . .

■ JOHN, Katherine [P]

Katherine John is the pseudonym of Karo Nadolny for her medical thrillers featuring police sergeant Trevor Joseph, introduced in *Without Trace* (1989), published in the U.S. in 1995. When a doctor disappears on an emergency call, Sgt. Joseph suspects a serial killer preying on local motorists. Suffering from clinical depression after injuries sustained in book 1, Sgt. Joseph is a temporary patient at Compton Castle Psychiatric Hospital in *Six Foot Under* (1993). An unexpected incentive for the sergeant to recover quickly comes in the guise of another serial killer. Compton Castle is "an enthralling palimpsest of architectures and rehabs just waiting for gothic lightning to strike," said *Kirkus*. The medical drama in book 3, *Murder of a Dead Man* (1994), involves facial transplants. John has also written the espionage thriller, *By Any Other Name* (1998). Born in Wales, John studied English and sociology at Swansea College. After spending time in the U.S. and Europe, she lives on the Gower Peninsula, near Swansea, in Wales.

Trevor Joseph...police sergeant...England
- ❏ ❏   1 - Without Trace (1989)
- ❏ ❏   2 - Six Foot Under (1993)
- ❏ ❏   3 - Murder of a Dead Man (1994)
- ❏ ❏   . . . .
- ❏ ❏   . . . .

■ JOHNSON, Barbara

Technical editor Barbara Johnson writes a lesbian mystery series featuring novice insurance investigator Colleen Fitzgerald, introduced in *The Beach Affair* (1995). Based in Washington, D.C., Colleen travels to Rehoboth Beach, Delaware in the series opener, where a former professional bodybuilder has been found dead in her gym. An apparent drug overdose needs investigating in book 2, *Bad Moon Rising* (1998), and Colleen will head for West Virginia in book 3, *Sanctuary*, as yet unscheduled. Johnson has also writ-ten a Regency romance, *Stonehurst* (1992). Born in Germany, she emigrated to the U.S. at the age of three and began the travels that have taken her to England, Egypt, Germany, Italy, Jamaica, Japan, Canada, Kenya, Korea and Panama. Johnson's favorite vacation destination is Disney World, but her most unusual trip involved several run-ins with male baboons at the Masai Game Preserve in Kenya, where she found a large baboon sitting on the cot in her tent one day, picking through her clothes.

Colleen Fitzgerald...lesbian insurance investigator...Washington, District of Columbia

❑ ❑   1 - The Beach Affair (1995)
❑ ❑   2 - Bad Moon Rising (1998)
❑ ❑   . . . .
❑ ❑   . . . .

■ JOHNSON, Dolores

As a field editor for *American Drycleaner* magazine, Dolores Johnson knows plenty about dry cleaning, so it's no surprise her amateur sleuth is the owner of a dry cleaning establishment. Introduced in *Taken to the Cleaners* (1997), 30-something Denver divorcee, Mandy Dyer, has inherited Dyer's Cleaners from her uncle, complete with a haughty in-store cat named Spot. After Betty the Bag Lady arrives with a man's suit slashed and stained with blood, Mandy's store is ransacked in the middle of the night, one of her customers is murdered and Betty is found half-dead in front of Dyer's Cleaners. After her good friend Kate is killed for a genuine 1920s Fortuny in *A Dress To Die For* (1998), Mandy and friends return in book 4, *Wash, Fold and Die* (1999). A bonus in this series is the cleaning tips and suggestions for stain removal that are scattered throughout the books. A freelance magazine writer and former newspaper reporter, Johnson lives in Aurora, Colorado, with a cat named Max who bears no resemblance to Spot.

Mandy Dyer...owner of Dyer's Cleaners...Denver, Colorado

❑ ❑   1 - Taken to the Cleaners (1997)
❑ ❑   2 - Hung Up To Die (1997)
❑ ❑   3 - A Dress To Die For (1998)
❑ ❑   . . . .
❑ ❑   . . . .

■ JONES, D.J.H. [P]

D.J.H. Jones is the pseudonymous author of two mysteries featuring Chaucer scholar Nancy Cook, an untenured professor at Yale with a taste for Bakelite jewelry, introduced in *Murder at the M.L.A.* (1993). With 6,000 literature professors and graduate students convened in Chicago for the annual meeting of the Modern Language Association, someone poisons the entire Wellesley hiring committee, killing one. Homicide cop Boaz Dixon recruits Cook for a crash course in academic politics, but not before an unpopular deconstructionist is pushed over the edge of a hotel atrium. When last seen in *Murder in the New Age* (1997), Nancy is on sabbatical in Santa Fe, New Mexico, where she is sharing the rent with a bunch of fuzzy-headed, channeling New Agers. When mysticism turns to murder, the professor turns to sleuthing. "Both Nancy and the author are wasting their talent for invective on these chowderheads, even if one of them does happen to be a killer," said Marilyn Stasio of The *New York Times Book Review*.

Nancy Cook...Chaucer scholar and professor...Chicago, Illinois

❑ ❑   1 - Murder at the MLA (1993)
❑ ❑   2 - Murder in the New Age (1997)
❑ ❑   . . . .
❑ ❑   . . . .

■ JORDAN, Jennifer

Jennifer Jordan is the author of two contemporary series, including three mysteries set in England and a pair of novels with a Denver, Colorado setting. Dee and Barry Vaughn are a sleuthing couple from the London suburb of Woodfield, introduced in *A Good Weekend for Murder* (1987). A former roving reporter for the magazine *Trends*, Dee works occasionally as a part-time office temp, while her husband Barry, a history lecturer at Woodfield Tech, has become a minor celebrity with his spoofy crime novels, *Proof of the Pudding* and *Penny for the Guy*. A third family member is their much-loved Schnauzer, Bella. They're having a lovely country Christmas in book 2, *Murder Under the Mistletoe* (1988), when one of the guests at the Grove Inn is murdered. In book 3, *Book Early for Murder* (1990), the couple are guests at a Cotswolds country manor for a weekend of make-believe murder. Jordan's American amateur sleuth is Kristin Ashe of Denver, Colorado, who makes her debut in *A Safe Place to Sleep* (1992).

Barry & Dee Vaughan...spoofy crime writer & office temp wife...Woodfield, England

❏ ❏	1 - A Good Weekend for Murder (1987)
❏ ❏	2 - Murder Under the Mistletoe (1988)
❏ ❏	3 - Book Early for Murder (1990)
❏ ❏	. . . .
❏ ❏	. . . .

Kristin Ashe...amateur sleuth...Denver, Colorado

❏ ❏	1 - A Safe Place To Sleep (1992)
❏ ❏	2 - Existing Solutions (1993)
❏ ❏	. . . .
❏ ❏	. . . .

■ JORGENSEN, Christine T.

Christine T. Jorgensen is the creator of Stella the Stargazer, astrologer and advice columnist to the lovelorn, introduced in *A Love To Die For* (1994). Stella is really the former Jane Smith, a Denver accountant with a penchant for handmade lingerie and a yen for change. Her cherished pet is an anole named Fluffy, later joined by Lips. In *You Bet Your Life* (1995), Stella and Fluffy head for Silverado and a weekend of bridge and slot machines. When last seen in book 5, *Dead on Her Feet* (1999), Stella has signed on as the community theater's assistant director, to help keep Fluffy and Lips in gourmet crickets. "Endearingly quirky characters" and "clever plot lightly laced with psychic phenomenon," said *Booklist*. Formerly a Denver social worker, Jorgensen owns two little Fluffies of her own and has first-hand experience traveling with anoles. Originally from Monmouth, Illinois, Jorgensen grew up in a funeral home, which she says gave her a special outlook on life and death, including the occasional absurdity of it all.

Stella the Stargazer...astrologer & lovelorn columnist...Denver, Colorado

❏ ❏	1 - A Love To Die For (1994)
❏ ❏	2 - You Bet Your Life (1995)
❏ ❏	3 - Curl Up and Die (1996)
❏ ❏	4 - Death of a Dustbunny (1998)
❏ ❏	. . . .
❏ ❏	. . . .

■ JOSEPH, Alison

While working as a partner in an independent production company, Alison Joseph produced a series about women and religion, which led to the creation of Sister Agnes Bourdillon. Once married to a violent and abusive man, Agnes has spent 15 years in a convent, but in the series opener, *Sacred Hearts* (1994), she is cast out for disobedience. Calling herself a "nun at large," Agnes takes a job in London with Father Julius, her spiritual confessor and closest friend. "One helluva nun," said the *Hampstead and Highgate Express*. In book 5, *The Dying Light* (1999), Agnes is sent to work in a women's prison in Southwark, while her mother deteriorates in a nursing home in France. With fellow mystery author Annie Ross, Joseph teaches a hilarious workshop titled "How To Write a Crime Novel in an Hour." Born in North London, Joseph was educated at Leeds University and has worked as a radio and television presenter and reader for BBC Radio Drama. The mother of three children, she lives in North London.

Agnes Bourdillon...ex-cloistered nun...London, England

❑ ❑ 1 - Sacred Hearts (1994)
❑ ❑ 2 - The Hour of Our Death (1995)
❑ ❑ 3 - The Quick and the Dead (1996)
❑ ❑ 4 - A Dark and Sinful Death (1997)
❑ ❑ . . . .
❑ ❑ . . . .

■ KAEWERT, Julie Wallin

After graduating from Dartmouth College, Julie Wallin Kaewert took a Radcliffe publishing course and signed on with a Boston fine books publisher. While working as a textbook editor for Addison-Wesley, she transferred to their London office in Bedford Square, the setting for her Booklovers' mysteries. When first seen in *Unsolicited* (1994), Alex Plumtree must locate a missing author whose unfinished novel can save Plumtree Press. In book 3, *Unprintable* (1998), the Prime Minister needs a favor from Alex. Completed in just six weeks from only a movie script, Kaewert rented plenty of videos before writing her novelization of *The Avengers* (1998). A former staff writer for a London computer magazine, she has worked in marketing for an artificial intelligence software developer and written *Developing Expert Systems for Manufacturing* (1990) for McGraw Hill. Armed with a Harvard master's degree in education, Kaewert has been involved with several adult literacy projects. She lives in Longmont, Colorado.

Alex Plumtree...head of family publishing firm...London, England

❑ ❑ 1 - Unsolicited (1994)
❑ ❑ 2 - Unbound (1997)
❑ ❑ 3 - Unprintable (1998)
❑ ❑ . . . .
❑ ❑ . . . .

■ KAHN, Sharon

A rabbi's wife for 31 years, Sharon Kahn writes mysteries featuring Ruby Rothman of Eternal, Texas, a lover of bagels and a rabbi's widow. In the series opener, *Fax Me a Bagel* (1998), a member of Ruby's congregation pushes in front of her at The Hot Bagel and promptly dies from eating a hot one laced with cyanide. Ruby had been considering the baker's offer to become a partner in The Hot Bagel, so she springs into action to prove her friend's innocence. Meanwhile she's fending off the temple yenta, who is trying to make a match between Ruby and the new rabbi. "Effectively combines humor with crime," said the *Booklist* reviewer. Kahn is the author of two children's books, *Kacy and the Space Shuttle Secret* (1995), and with Ruthe Winegarten, *Brave Black Women: From Slavery to the Space Shuttle* (1997). After graduating from Vassar College and the University of Arizona Law School, Kahn worked as an arbitrator, attorney and freelance writer. A lover of opera and model trains, she lives in Austin, Texas.

Ruby Rothman...rabbi's widow...Eternal, Texas

❑ ❑ 1 - Fax Me a Bagel (1998)
❑ ❑ 2 - Never Nosh a Matzo Ball (2000)
❑ ❑ . . . .
❑ ❑ . . . .

■ KALLEN, Lucille

Best known for her early work in television, Lucille Kallen (1922-1999) was the only woman in a raucous group of men who wrote comedy material for Sid Caesar and Imogene Coca on *Your Show of Shows*, broadcast live for 90 minutes every Saturday night from 1950 to 1954. At various times the group included Mel Brooks, Carl Reiner and Neil Simon. Working seven days a week, 39 weeks a year at NBC offices in midtown Manhattan, Sid Caesar once noted that Kallen was the only one who could write and talk at the same time. When the team moved to California, Kallen stayed in New York and began writing plays and television scripts. Her first novel was an early feminist comedy about the plight of working women, *Outside There, Somewhere* (1964), published in England as *Gentlemen Prefer Slaves*. Kallen's five mysteries feature small-town newspaper editor C.B. Greenfield and reporter Maggie Rome, who plays Archie to his Nero Wolfe. The series opener, *Introducing C.B. Greenfield* (1979), was an American Book Award nominee.

Maggie Rome & C.B. Greenfield...reporter & editor-publisher...Connecticut

- ❑ ❑ 1 - Introducing C.B. Greenfield (1979)
- ❑ ❑ 2 - The Tanglewood Murder (1980)
- ❑ ❑ 3 - No Lady in the House (1982)
- ❑ ❑ 4 - The Piano Bird (1984)
- ❑ ❑ 5 - A Little Madness (1986)
- ❑ ❑ ....
- ❑ ❑ ....

■ KELLERMAN, Faye

Best-selling author Faye Kellerman has written 13 novels, including 11 mysteries featuring L.A.P.D. detective Peter Decker, an ethnic Jew reared as a Protestant by adoptive parents, and Rina Lazarus, an Orthodox Jewish widow with two young sons. Decker and Lazarus meet in the Macavity award-winning series opener, *The Ritual Bath* (1986), when Rina serves as interpreter and liaison with the Orthodox Los Angeles community where she lives. Book 11, *Jupiter's Bones* (1999), features an astrophysicist turned cult leader. Kellerman's Elizabethan novel, *The Quality of Mercy* (1988), features a plot she charges (in a lawsuit filed in Federal court in early 1999) was stolen by Miramax for *Shakespeare in Love*. She has also written *Moon Music* (1998), a novel of Native American mysticism featuring a Las Vegas police detective. Born in St. Louis, Kellerman holds an B.A. in math and a D.D.S. degree from U.C.L.A., where she met husband Jonathan Kellerman, a clinical child psychologist and Edgar award-winning mystery writer.

Peter Decker & Rina Lazarus...LAPD detective & Orthodox Jewish wife...Los Angeles, California

- ❑ ❑ 1 - **The Ritual Bath (1986) Macavity winner ★**
- ❑ ❑ 2 - Sacred and Profane (1987)
- ❑ ❑ 3 - Milk and Honey (1990)
- ❑ ❑ 4 - Day of Atonement (1992)
- ❑ ❑ 5 - False Prophet (1992)
- ❑ ❑ 6 - Grievous Sin (1993)
- ❑ ❑ 7 - Sanctuary (1994)
- ❑ ❑ 8 - Justice (1995)
- ❑ ❑ 9 - Prayers for the Dead (1996)
- ❑ ❑ 10 - A Serpent's Tooth (1997)
- ❑ ❑ ....
- ❑ ❑ ....

■ KELLOGG, Marne Davis

Fifth-generation Westerner Marne (MAR-nee) Davis Kellogg is the creator of a former California chief of detectives who returns to Wyoming after an unfortunate incident in the series opener, *Bad Manners* (1995). With degrees in criminology and toxicology, Lilly Bennett starts her own security consulting firm and signs on as the U.S. Marshal for Bennett's Fort, a town owned by her cousin. "Miss Manners with a bad streak; wickedly on the mark," says *The Denver Post*. Lilly's love interest is ex-Morgan banker, Richard Jerome, opera impresario and professional team-roper. Educated in Paris and Rome, Kellogg has worked as a translator and consumer reporter for a Colorado radio station. Former Rocky Mountain assistant bureau chief for *People* magazine, she has served as regional sales manager for Frontier Airlines, and communications director for the Denver Center for the Performing Arts and San Francisco's American Conservatory Theatre. She and her husband live in Denver and Norfolk, Virginia, and on their Colorado ranch.

Lilly Bennett...US marshal and security firm owner...Roundup, Wyoming

- ❑ ❑ 1 - Bad Manners (1995)
- ❑ ❑ 2 - Curtsey (1996)
- ❑ ❑ 3 - Tramp (1997)
- ❑ ❑ 4 - Nothing But Gossip (1998)
- ❑ ❑ 5 - The Birthday Party (1999)
- ❑ ❑ ....
- ❑ ❑ ....

■ KELLY, Mary

Gold Dagger winner Mary (Coolican) Kelly wrote two short-lived mystery series during the late 1950s and early 1960s. Her first three novels featured Scottish Inspector Brett Nightingale, introduced in *A Cold Coming* (1956). The Nightingale trilogy was published in reverse order (books 3, 2 and 1) in the U.S. in the late '60s. It was *The Spoilt Kill* (1961), Kelly's first private eye novel featuring Hedley Nicholson, that earned her a Gold Dagger award from the British Crime Writers' Association for best crime novel of the

year. Her subsequent mysteries were all standalones, including *March to the Gallows* (1964), *Dead Corse* (1966), *Write on Both Sides of the Paper* (1969), *The Twenty-Fifth Hour* (1971) and *The Girl in the Alley* (1974). H.R.F. Keating once described Mary Kelly as "a never blinking eye" with the ability to meticulously observe, and exactly and economically describe her "incorrigibly human" characters. Born in London, she earned a master's degree at the University of Edinburgh and taught briefly in a private school.

Brett Nightingale...Scottish police inspector...Edinburgh, Scotland
- ❏ ❏   1 - A Cold Coming (1956)
- ❏ ❏   2 - Dead Man's Riddle (1957)
- ❏ ❏   3 - The Christmas Egg (1958)
- ❏ ❏   . . . .
- ❏ ❏   . . . .

Hedley Nicholson...private investigator...England
- ❏ ❏   1 - **The Spoilt Kill (1961) Gold Dagger winner ★**
- ❏ ❏   2 - Due to a Death (1962)
- ❏ ❏   - U.S.-The Dead of Summer
- ❏ ❏   . . . .
- ❏ ❏   . . . .

■ KELLY, Mary Anne

Former model and song lyricist Mary Anne Kelly has written four mysteries featuring ex-model turned photographer, Claire Breslinsky, introduced in *Park Lane South, Queens* (1990). Recently returned to her childhood neighborhood in Queens, Claire has been living in Europe and India for the past ten years. The zany cast includes Claire's two sisters, Zinnie the cop and Carmela the fashion columnist, their Polish father, Irish mother and one gay ex-brother-in-law. After marrying the investigating officer from book 1,

Claire is delighted to find a high school chum as her new neighbor in book 2, *Foxglove* (1992). When her friend is murdered, Claire suspects the woman's husband. Claire returns to Munich, where she once lived, for a friend's wedding and a search for diamonds in *Keeper of the Mill* (1995). When she travels to County Cork, Ireland to attend the funeral of her Aunt Dierdre in book 4, *Jenny Rose* (1999), the big surprise is her older sister's illegitimate child, now 17 and a talented artist. Kelly lives in Queens.

Claire Breslinsky...freelance photographer...New York, New York
- ❏ ❏   1 - Park Lane South, Queens (1990)
- ❏ ❏   2 - Foxglove (1992)
- ❏ ❏   3 - Keeper of the Mill (1995)
- ❏ ❏   . . . .
- ❏ ❏   . . . .

■ KELLY, Nora

Nora Kelly is the creator of history professor Gillian Adams, on sabbatical for a year in London in the series opener, *In the Shadow of King's* (1984). The professor has been invited to lecture at Cambridge University, where she earned her doctorate 15 years earlier. After witnessing the murder of a colleague, Adams assists the Scotland Yard detective who had come to hear her lecture. She returns to the university history department she chairs in Vancouver, British Columbia for book 2, *My Sister's Keeper* (1992),

but book 3, *Bad Chemistry* (1993), sends her back to England and another murder among academics. When last seen in book 4, *Old Wounds* (1998), Adams has returned to her childhood home to care for her elderly mother. Like her series protagonist, Kelly is a professor of history. Born in the United States, she grew up in New Jersey and New York City and spent summers on Cape Cod. She currently divides her time between Cambridge, England and Vancouver, British Columbia, where she teaches part time.

Gillian Adams...college history department chair...Vancouver, British Columbia, Canada

❑ ❑ 1 - In the Shadow of King's (1984)
❑ ❑ 2 - My Sister's Keeper (1992)
❑ ❑ 3 - Bad Chemistry (1993)
❑ ❑ 4 - Old Wounds (1998)
❑ ❑ . . . .
❑ ❑ . . . .

■ KELLY, Susan

American crime writer Susan Kelly has written six mysteries featuring Cambridge magazine writer and former English professor Liz Connors, introduced in *The Gemini Man* (1985), a best first novel Anthony nominee. When last seen in book 6, *Out of the Darkness* (1992), Liz has lost her major source of writing income and agreed to work as a research assistant for a handsome best-selling true-crime writer. Griffin Marcus is writing a book about the Merrimack Valley Killer, but Liz doubts the alledged killer's confession. Kelly is also the author of *The Boston Stranglers: The Wrongful Conviction of Albert DeSalvo and the True Story of Eleven Shocking Murders* (1995). A consultant to the Massachusetts Criminal Justice Training Council, Kelly has taught crime-report writing at the Cambridge Police Academy. Like the immensely likable Liz Connors, Kelly is a former English professor who lives and works in Cambridge, Massachusetts. She holds a doctorate in medieval literature from the University of Edinburgh.

Liz Connors...freelance crime writer...Cambridge, Massachusetts

❑ ❑ 1 - **The Gemini Man (1985) Anthony nominee** ☆
❑ ❑ 2 - The Summertime Soldiers (1986)
❑ ❑ 3 - Trail of the Dragon (1988)
❑ ❑ 4 - Until Proven Innocent (1990)
❑ ❑ 5 - And Soon I'll Come To Kill You (1991)
❑ ❑ 6 - Out of the Darkness (1992)
❑ ❑ . . . .
❑ ❑ . . . .

■ KELLY, Susan B.

British author Susan B. Kelly writes the genteel Hop Valley series featuring Detective Inspector Nick Trevellyan and Alison Hope, savvy and successful owner of a London software company that relocates to the Hop Valley in the series opener, *Hope Against Hope* (1990). Alison meets the handsome D.I. when she becomes a suspect in the murder of her cousin and former business partner, Aiden Hope. Newly-promoted to D.C.I., Nick takes center stage in search of a rapist in book 3, *Hope Will Answer* (1993). Kelly has also written a time travel novel, *The Ghosts of Albi* (1998), set in France at the site of an archaeological dig. Her nonseries mysteries include *The Seventh Victim* (1995) and *Quick Brown Fox* (1999), set in Suffolk. Born in the Thames Valley region of England, Kelly worked for twelve years as a computer programmer before writing fiction. When her mysteries crossed the Atlantic, her U.S. publisher added the middle initial 'B' to distinguish the British Susan Kelly from the American mystery writer of the same name.

Alison Hope & Nick Trevellyan...software designer & detective inspector...Hop Valley, England

❑ ❑ 1 - Hope Against Hope (1990)
❑ ❑ 2 - Time of Hope (1990)
❑ ❑ 3 - Hope Will Answer (1993)
❑ ❑ 4 - Kid's Stuff (1994)
❑ ❑ 5 - Death is Sweet (1996)
❑ ❑ . . . .
❑ ❑ . . . .

■ KELNER, Toni L.P.

Native Southerner Toni L.P. Kelner writes mysteries featuring M.I.T. graduate and computer programmer Laura Fleming, transplanted to Boston from her home-town of Byerly, North Carolina. In the series opener, *Down Home Murder* (1993), Laura returns home when her grandfather is seriously injured in a mill mishap that she discovers is no accident. She's back home again in book 2, *Dead Ringer* (1994), when Aunt Daphine must be rescued from a blackmailer. Book 4, *Country Comes to Town* (1996), is the only installment not set in the South. Laura's Shakespeare-quoting professor husband is away, and she ends up the prime suspect in the murder of an old boyfriend.

Kelner says the victim was inspired by an old boyfriend of hers. She took special pleasure in giving everyone who'd known him a motive for murder. Like Laura, Kelner grew up in North Carolina, moved to the Boston area, and has worked in the computer field. She lives with her husband and their two young daughters in Malden, Massachusetts.

Laura Fleming...small-town Southern sleuth...Byerly, North Carolina

- ❏ ❏ 1 - Down Home Murder (1993)
- ❏ ❏ 2 - Dead Ringer (1994)
- ❏ ❏ 3 - Trouble Looking for a Place To Happen (1995)
- ❏ ❏ 4 - Country Comes to Town (1996)
- ❏ ❏ 5 - Tight as a Tick (1998)
- ❏ ❏ 6 - Death of a Damn Yankee (1999)
- ❏ ❏ . . . .
- ❏ ❏ . . . .

■ KENNETT, Shirley

Involved with computers all her adult life, Shirley Kennett writes mysteries featuring computer expert P.J. Gray, hired by the St. Louis Police Department to re-create homicide cases in virtual reality (V.R.), starting with *Gray Matter* (1996). Kennett says crime scene analysis using V.R. techniques is beginning to take hold around the country, though it's still very much in its infancy. P.J.'s computer-phobic partner, Leo Schultz, gradually warms to P.J. and her expertise. A divorced single-mother, P.J. is especially concerned

with violence committed by children. Her third case, *Chameleon* (1998), involves a homicidal 12-year-old computer genius named Columbus. An engineering graduate of Washington University, Kennett has worked as an information systems manager and independent computer consultant. After 20 years of marriage (she was a teenage bride), Kennett and her husband adopted their first child from Peru. Kennett says she changed her first diaper and floated down the Amazon, all in one trip.

P.J. Gray...police dept. virtual reality expert...St. Louis, Missouri

- ❏ ❏ 1 - Gray Matter (1996)
- ❏ ❏ 2 - Fire Cracker (1997)
- ❏ ❏ 3 - Chameleon (1998)
- ❏ ❏ 4 - Cut Loose (1999)
- ❏ ❏ . . . .
- ❏ ❏ . . . .

■ KENNEY, Susan

Susan Kenney launched her fiction career with a grant from the National Endowment for the Arts, after winning the 1982 O Henry Prize for her short story, "Facing Front." Her three mysteries feature English professor, Roz Howard, and British artist and painter, Alan Stewart, introduced in Kenney's first novel, *Garden of Malice* (1983). A series of literature-based murders plague Howard's small college in book 2, *Graves in Academe* (1985). Sailors and locked-room mystery fans will enjoy book 3, *One Fell Sloop* (1990),

set on an island off the coast of Maine. A Roz Howard short story, "Aunt Agatha Leaving," appears in *Malice Domestic 8*. Kenney has also written *In Another Country* (1984) and *Sailing* (1988), the continuing story of a Vermont family told in first-person, complete with ghosts. An honors graduate of Northwestern University, Kenney earned M.A. and Ph.D. degrees at Cornell University. Born in New Jersey, she lives in Maine, where she has taught English and creative writing at Colby College since 1968.

Roz Howard & Alan Stewart...American professor & British painter...Maine

- ❏ ❏ 1 - Garden of Malice (1983)
- ❏ ❏ 2 - Graves in Academe (1985)
- ❏ ❏ 3 - One Fell Sloop (1990)
- ❏ ❏ . . . .
- ❏ ❏ . . . .

■ KERSHAW, Valerie

Valerie Kershaw is the creator of 50-year-old Mitch Mitchell, a freelance current affairs producer at Birmingham's Radio Brum, and partner with 70-year-old Tommy Hung in the detective agency, Mitchell and Orient Bureau. Ten years a widow, Mitch is short, plump and wiry-haired. She drives a red sports car and lives alone in the big house she shared with her husband Max. In the series opener, *Murder Is Too Expensive* (1993), Mitch has been in radio 30 years when she meets Tommy Hung, a former laundryman for the Royal Navy. After working together in their search for the killer of one of Mitch's radio colleagues, Tommy decides that he and Mitch should open an agency and he provides the initial funding. Kershaw has also written *Rosa* (1980), *The Snow Man* (1979), *The Bank Manager's Wife* (1981), adapted for Independent Television, and *Rockabye* (1990), winner of the Litchfield Prize. A former newspaper and radio journalist and broadcaster, Kershaw was born in Lancashire. She lives with her husband on Malta.

Mitch Mitchell & Tommy Hung...radio journalist P.I. & Chinese partner...Birmingham, England

- ❏ ❏ 1 - Murder Is Too Expensive (1993)
- ❏ ❏ 2 - Funny Money (1994)
- ❏ ❏ 3 - Late Knights (1995)
- ❏ ❏ 4 - Juicy Lucy (1996)
- ❏ ❏ . . . .
- ❏ ❏ . . . .

■ KIECOLT-GLASER, Janice

Psychologist Janice Kiecolt-Glaser has written two mysteries featuring Dr. Haley McAlister, a 41-year-old psychologist with special expertise in lie detection, who teaches in a Texas university medical center. A widow after eight years of marriage, the doctor enjoys reading historical novels and cruising around Houston in her 1960 Corvette with the top down, accompanied by her black Great Dane, Pavlov. After investigating the suspicious suicide of a patient in the series opener, *Detecting Lies* (1997), McAlister has another patient die under strange circumstances in book 2, *Unconscious Truths* (1998). Kiecolt-Glaser is the editor of the *Handbook of Human Stress and Immunity* (1994), which presents a current summary of the field of psychoneuroimmunology as it relates to stress and illness. Kiecolt-Glaser, who shares the profession and academic setting of her fictional creation, teaches in the Department of Psychiatry of the Ohio State University College of Medicine. She lives in Columbus.

Haley McAlister...psychologist and professor...Houston, Texas

- ❏ ❏ 1 - Detecting Lies (1997)
- ❏ ❏ 2 - Unconscious Truths (1998)
- ❏ ❏ . . . .
- ❏ ❏ . . . .

■ KIJEWSKI, Karen

Karen Kijewski (key-EFF-ski) writes a triple award-winning series featuring bar-tending Sacramento P.I., Kat Colorado, first seen in *Katwalk* (1988), winner of the St. Martin's Press PWA contest for best first private eye novel, and Shamus and Anthony award winner. "Much of the terse, breezy dialogue is downright hilarious," said *Washington Post Book World*. The supporting cast includes Kat's best friend, Charity Collins, a hotshot advice columnist and dessert maven; Kat's 80-something adopted grandmother, Alma; handsome Las Vegas cop, Hank, and his dog Mars, and Kat's dog Ranger, a blue and brown-eyed Australian sheepdog. The kitten who arrives at the conclusion of book 2 is still nameless at the end of book 3. Born in Berkeley, California, where her father was a university professor, Kijewski earned B.A. and M.A. degrees from the University of California. A former high school English teacher in Massachusetts, Kijewski tended bar at night for more than ten years. She lives in Sacramento, California.

Kat Colorado...bar-tending private investigator...Sacramento, California

- ❏ ❏ 1 - **Katwalk (1989) Anthony, Shamus & SMP/PWA winner ★★★**
- ❏ ❏ 2 - Katapult (1990)
- ❏ ❏ 3 - Kat's Cradle (1991)

❏ ❏ 4 - Copy Kat (1992)
❏ ❏ 5 - Wild Kat (1994)
❏ ❏ 6 - Alley Cat Blues (1995)
❏ ❏ 7 - Honky Tonk Kat (1996)
❏ ❏ 8 - Kat Scratch Fever (1997)
❏ ❏ 9 - Stray Kat Waltz (1998)
❏ ❏ . . . .
❏ ❏ . . . .

■ KING, Laurie R.

Edgar award winner Laurie R. King is a third-generation native of the San Francisco area. Since her marriage to an Anglo-Indian professor of religious studies 30 years her senior, she has lived in 20 countries on five continents. King's first novel with San Francisco homicide detectives Kate Martinelli and Alonzo Hawkin, *A Grave Talent* (1993), was an Edgar award winner and a Creasey and Anthony nominee. King is perhaps best known as the creator of Mary Russell, a teenage student of Sherlock Holmes, introduced in the Agatha-nominated *The Beekeeper's Apprentice* (1994). In the Nero Wolfe award-winning book 2, *A Monstrous Regiment of Women* (1995), Russell has come into her inheritance and sets out for London to visit Holmes. Out-of-sequence book 5, *O Jerusalem* (1999), takes Holmes and Russell to Palestine, just a few weeks after the conclusion of the series opener. King's standalone thriller, *A Darker Place* (1999), was published in the U.K. as *The Birth of a New Moon*. King holds a master's degree in theology.

Kate Martinelli & Alonzo Hawkin...SFPD homicide detectives...San Francisco, California
❏ ❏ 1 - **A Grave Talent (1993) Edgar winner ★ Anthony & Creasey nominee** ☆☆
❏ ❏ 2 - To Play the Fool (1995)
❏ ❏ 3 - **With Child (1996) Edgar nominee** ☆
❏ ❏ . . . .
❏ ❏ . . . .

Mary Russell...Sherlock Holmes' detecting partner...London, England
❏ ❏ 1 - **The Beekeeper's Apprentice (1994) Agatha nominee** ☆
❏ ❏ 2 - **A Monstrous Regiment of Women (1995) Nero Wolfe winner ★**
❏ ❏ 3 - A Letter of Mary (1996)
❏ ❏ 4 - The Moor (1998)
❏ ❏ . . . .
❏ ❏ . . . .

■ KINGSBURY, Kate [P]

London-born author Doreen Roberts has published more than 35 novels since 1987, including her 12-book Pennyfoot Hotel series written as Kate Kingsbury. Pennyfoot owner, Cecily Sinclair, runs a four-story seaside hotel, complete with rooftop garden, introduced in *Room with a Clue* (1993). Roberts' mother once owned a seaside English hotel, smaller than the Pennyfoot, but similar in many ways. The series begins in 1905, with each book advancing in time three months, changing the seasons as well as the fortunes and misfortunes of the characters. The series concludes with book 12, *Maid to Murder* (1999). Roberts wrote a dozen romance novels before venturing into mystery, but says all her romantic fiction contains elements of mystery and suspense. In 1991 she published one novel as Kim Blake and another as Roberta Kent. A U.S. resident for more than 30 years, Roberts has moved eight times in the last six years with her computer consultant husband. She currently lives in Tigard, Oregon, where she is working on a new mystery series.

Cecily Sinclair...Edwardian hotel owner...Badger's End, England
❏ ❏ 1 - Room With a Clue (1993)
❏ ❏ 2 - Do Not Disturb (1994)
❏ ❏ 3 - Service for Two (1994)
❏ ❏ 4 - Eat, Drink, and Be Buried (1994)
❏ ❏ 5 - Check-out Time (1995)
❏ ❏ 6 - Grounds for Murder (1995)

❏ ❏ 7 - Pay the Piper (1996)
❏ ❏ 8 - Chivalry Is Dead (1996)
❏ ❏ 9 - Ring for Tomb Service (1997)
❏ ❏ 10 - Death With Reservations (1998)
❏ ❏ 11 - Dying Room Only (1998)
❏ ❏ . . . .
❏ ❏ . . . .

■ KITTREDGE, Mary

A former respiratory therapist for a major Connecticut hospital, Mary Kittredge has written 15 nonfiction books for young adults, including ten titles for the Encyclopedia of Health series. She has also written two Connecticut mystery series. Freelance writer Charlotte Kent makes her first appearance in California with *Murder in Mendocino* (1987), but returns to Connecticut in book 2, accompanied by the young boy she later adopts. Charlotte's love interest is a surgeon. A longer-running series features independently wealthy Edwina Crusoe, a registered nurse who becomes a medical consultant, handling only those cases that intrigue her. The supporting cast includes Edwina's mother, a best-selling romance novelist, and police detective Martin McIntyre. By book 6, Edwina and Martin are parents of hell-raising twin boys. A Wisconsin native, Kittredge is a graduate of Connecticut's Trinity College. She lives in Maine, where she writes Maine mysteries as Sarah Graves, beginning with *The Dead Cat Bounce* (1998).

Charlotte Kent...freelance writer...Connecticut
❏ ❏ 1 - Murder in Mendocino (1987)
❏ ❏ 2 - Dead and Gone (1989)
❏ ❏ 3 - Poison Pen (1990)
❏ ❏ . . . .
❏ ❏ . . . .

Edwina Crusoe...RN and medical consultant...New Haven, Connecticut
❏ ❏ 1 - Fatal Diagnosis (1990)
❏ ❏ 2 - Rigor Mortis (1991)
❏ ❏ 3 - Cadaver (1992)
❏ ❏ 4 - Walking Dead Man (1992)
❏ ❏ 5 - Desperate Remedy (1993)
❏ ❏ 6 - Kill or Cure (1995)
❏ ❏ . . . .
❏ ❏ . . . .

■ KNIGHT, Alanna

Historical novelist and Robert Louis Stevenson scholar, Alanna Knight is the author of more than 40 books. Her first, *Legend of the Loch* (1970), won a first novel award from the Romantic Novelists Association. Knight published 18 novels, including four written as Margaret Hope, before introducing Victorian police inspector Jeremy Faro of Edinburgh, Scotland. The inspector is a widower whose two young daughters live with their grandmother in Orkney, but a grown stepson, Dr. Vincent Laurie, is frequently on hand to assist unofficially. Now in its 11th installment, the series begins with *Enter Second Murderer* (1988). Knight's work on Stevenson includes her two-act play, *The Private Life of Robert Louis Stevenson*, based on her novel, *The Passionate Kindness: The Love Story of Robert Louis Stevenson and Fanny Osborne* (1975); *The Robert Louis Stevenson Treasury* (1986) and *Robert Louis Stevenson in the South Seas* (1987). A writer for television and theatre, Knight lives in Edinburgh.

Jeremy Faro...Victorian detective inspector...Edinburgh, Scotland
❏ ❏ 1 - Enter Second Murderer (1988)
❏ ❏ 2 - Blood Line (1989)
❏ ❏ 3 - Deadly Beloved (1989)
❏ ❏ 4 - Killing Cousins (1990)
❏ ❏ 5 - A Quiet Death (1991)
❏ ❏ 6 - To Kill a Queen (1992)

❑ ❑ 7 - The Evil That Men Do (1993)
❑ ❑ 8 - The Missing Duchess (1994)
❑ ❑ 9 - The Bull Slayers (1995)
❑ ❑ 10 - Murder by Appointment (1996)
❑ ❑ 11 - The Coffin Lane Murders (1998)
❑ ❑ . . . .
❑ ❑ . . . .

■ KNIGHT, Kathryn Lasky

Award-winning children's author Kathryn Lasky has written a four-book mystery series as Kathryn Lasky Knight. Her first adult novel, *Trace Elements* (1986), introduces Calista Jacobs, an illustrator of children's books in Cambridge, Massachusetts. Calista starts her sleuthing career with a desperate search for her husband's killer. Other regulars in the series are Calista's new love interest, Archie Baldwin, a brilliant archaeologist from the Smithsonian Institute, and her computer-wizard teenage son Charley. When last seen in book 4, *Dark Swan* (1994), Calista is house-sitting and sketching bonsai trees on Beacon Hill, when she discovers the body of a friend, stabbed through the heart with garden shears. Writing as Kathryn Lasky, the author has published more than 50 books for children, some illustrated by her photographer-film-maker husband, Christopher Knight. Born in Indianapolis, she is a graduate of the University of Michigan and lives in Cambridge, Massachusetts.

Calista Jacobs...illustrator of children's books...Cambridge, Massachusetts
❑ ❑ 1 - Trace Elements (1986)
❑ ❑ 2 - Mortal Words (1990)
❑ ❑ 3 - Mumbo Jumbo (1991)
❑ ❑ 4 - Dark Swan (1994)
❑ ❑ . . . .
❑ ❑ . . . .

■ KNIGHT, Phyllis

Shamus nominee Phyllis Knight is the creator of ex-rocker, gay woman P.I. Lil Ritchie, who moves from the coast of Maine to the Virginia Blue Ridge in the series opener, *Switching the Odds* (1992). Throughout the series Lil travels to places the author knows well, including Downeast Maine; Austin, Texas; Charlottesville, Virginia; and Montreal, Quebec. Music is Lil's driving force, an inheritance from Knight, who is a direct descendent of Francis Scott Key on her mother's side, and country musicians aplenty on her father's. As children, Knight and her sister sang in the family dance band and appeared weekly on T.V. and radio programs broadcast to 26 states. Starting in high school she was a regular on the folk music and coffee house circuit, solo and with her various bands—Possum Delight, Violet Crown and Dulces Suenos (Sweet Dreams). After moving back home from Maine, Knight lives in Charlottesville, Virginia where she frequently plays her 12-string guitar on the front porch.

Lil Ritchie...ex-rocker and gay woman P.I....Charlottesville, Virginia
❑ ❑ 1 - **Switching the Odds (1992) Shamus nominee** ☆
❑ ❑ 2 - Shattered Rhythms (1994)
❑ ❑ . . . .
❑ ❑ . . . .

■ KRAFT, Gabrielle

After growing up in the Hollywood film industry, Gabrielle Kraft became a studio executive and worked as an executive story editor and story analyst for major film studios. She has written a four-book Hollywood series, appropriately titled with the names of cocktails, beginning with the Edgar award-nominated *Bullshot* (1987). Cigar-chomping Beverly Hills attorney and deal-maker, Jerry Zalman, is forever devising schemes to get his clients and friends out of trouble, often with murderous consequences. When last seen in book 4, *Bloody Mary* (1990), Jerry's 13-year-old nephew needs his uncle's help returning a Picasso medallion stolen by the teenager's girlfriend. No sooner has Jerry accomplished the medallion's return, when the jeweler-owner is shot and killed and the medallion is stolen again. Labeled "smart and snappy," Kraft's mysteries are full of sarcastic commentary on the "Looney Tunes of LaLa Land." She is the author of two Hollywood-insider novels, *Hollywood Hills* (1993) and *Hollywood's Child* (1994).

Jerry Zalman...Beverly Hills deal maker...Los Angeles, California

- ❏ ❏ 1 - **Bullshot (1987) Edgar nominee** ☆
- ❏ ❏ 2 - Screwdriver (1988)
- ❏ ❏ 3 - Let's Rob Roy (1989)
- ❏ ❏ 4 - Bloody Mary (1990)
- ❏ ❏ ....
- ❏ ❏ ....

■ KRICH, Rochelle Majer

Anthony award winner Rochelle Majer (rhymes with mayor) Krich is the creator of L.A.P.D. homicide detective Jessie Drake, whose first appearance, *Fair Game* (1993), was nominated for an Agatha award. Krich's first mystery, the Anthony award-winning *Where's Mommy Now?* was retitled *Perfect Alibi* for the Hollywood movie starring Teri Garr and Hector Elizondo. The daughter of Holocaust survivors, Krich has chosen a number of Holocaust survivors as lead characters in *Angel of Death* (1994), Jessie Drake's second case and another Agatha award nominee. Jessie returns with a case of kidnapping and murder in book 4, *Dead Air* (2000). With a master's degree from U.C.L.A., Krich chaired the English department at a private high school where she taught for 18 years. Former newsletter editor for Sisters in Crime, she also served on the M.W.A. national board. Born in Germany, Krich lived in New York and New Jersey before moving to Los Angeles, where she lives with her husband and their six children.

Debra Laslow...criminal defense attorney...Los Angeles, California

- ❏ ❏ 1 - Speak No Evil (1996)
- ❏ ❏ ....
- ❏ ❏ ....

Jessie Drake...LAPD homicide detective...Los Angeles, California

- ❏ ❏ 1 - **Fair Game (1993) Agatha nominee** ☆
- ❏ ❏ 2 - **Angel of Death (1994) Agatha nominee** ☆
- ❏ ❏ 3 - Blood Money (1999)
- ❏ ❏ ....
- ❏ ❏ ....

■ KRUGER, Mary

Mary Kruger has written three Gilded Age mysteries featuring society debutante Brooke Cassidy and police detective Matt Devlin, introduced in *Death on the Cliff Walk* (1994). Matt is thrown off the force after mistakenly arresting Brooke's uncle for the murder of five young women the summer of 1895. When the gardener is arrested, Matt and Brooke start their own investigation. The two lovebirds set sail on a honeymoon cruise aboard the *S.S. New York* in *No Honeymoon for Death* (1995), only to be enlisted in another murder inquiry. In their last outing, *Masterpiece of Murder* (1996), Matt is a New York City detective, personally selected for service by Teddy Roosevelt. When Brooke is asked to look into forgery, theft and murder at the Manhattan Museum of Art, the couple works together yet again. Writing as Mary Kingsley, Kruger is the author of ten romance novels, including her most recent title, *Beyond the Sea* (1999), as well as *Masquerade* (1997) and *In a Pirate's Arms* (1996). She lives in Massachusetts.

Brooke Cassidy & Matt Devlin...1890s debutante & detective husband...Newport, Rhode Island

- ❏ ❏ 1 - Death on the Cliff Walk (1994)
- ❏ ❏ 2 - No Honeymoon for Death (1995)
- ❏ ❏ 3 - Masterpiece of Murder (1996)
- ❏ ❏ ....
- ❏ ❏ ....

■ LACEY, Sarah [P]

Sarah Lacey is the pseudonym used by Kay Mitchell for her series featuring 25-year-old tax inspector Leah Hunter, introduced in *File Under: Deceased* (1992). Leah's favorite possession is her speedy, powerful car—a black Morris Minor shell hiding a BMW engine coupled with a close-ratio gearbox. Happily single and dating a newly-promoted D.I., Leah says she lives alone to keep household chores to a minimum. She describes Bramfield, the Yorkshire town where she lives and works, as the kind of place where pubs still sport dart boards and beer-bellied males are more common than litter bins. Under her own name, Mitchell writes a police series featuring Malminster Chief Inspector John Morrissey, a married father of two teenagers. After earning an honors degree in English at Leeds University, Mitchell trained as a nurse and midwife. Her assignments have included staff medicine, surgery, and emergency room duty. She has also worked as a visiting nurse. Mitchell lives near Wakefield, England, where she was born.

Leah Hunter...20-something tax inspector...Yorkshire, England

- ❑ ❑ 1 - File Under: Deceased (1992)
- ❑ ❑ 2 - File Under: Missing (1993)
- ❑ ❑ 3 - File Under: Arson (1994)
- ❑ ❑ 4 - File Under: Jeopardy (1995)
- ❑ ❑ . . . .
- ❑ ❑ . . . .

■ LACHNIT, Carroll

Former newspaper reporter Carroll Lachnit writes mysteries featuring Hannah Barlow, an ex-cop turned law student, accused of plagiarism along with her moot court partner in the series opener, *Murder in Brief* (1995). After joining her former study partner at his new firm, Hannah gets involved with an open adoption that goes hopelessly wrong in book 3, *Akin to Death* (1998). "The twists keep coming right to the final pages," said *Publishers Weekly*. Hannah returns in book 4, *Janie's Law* (1999). Although Lachnit's fictional Orange County law school is suspiciously similar to Orange County's real Chapman University, she says her first glimpse of law school's fierce competition came when her husband entered Southwestern University School of Law in 1985. During almost nine years at the *Orange County Register*, Lachnit covered a wide range of stories, including the 1984 Olympics and the trial in Yugoslavia of an Orange County resident charged with Nazi-era war crimes. She lives in Long Beach, California.

Hannah Barlow...ex-cop turned lawyer...Orange County, California

- ❑ ❑ 1 - Murder in Brief (1995)
- ❑ ❑ 2 - A Blessed Death (1996)
- ❑ ❑ 3 - Akin to Death (1998)
- ❑ ❑ . . . .
- ❑ ❑ . . . .

■ LACKEY, Mercedes

Fantasy and science fiction author Mercedes Lackey has written a cross-genre mystery series featuring Diana Tregarde, a freelance investigator of unnatural events, practicing witch and romance novelist in Hartford, Connecticut. Refusing compensation for her occult work, Diana earns a living writing romance novels, including the occasional Regency. In the series opener, *Burning Water* (1989), she heads for Dallas at the request of college friend turned police detective, Mark Valdez, to consult on a case involving a serial killer. Lackey's *Heralds of Valdemar* series, and *The Mage Wars* series written with Larry Dixon, have sold more than one million copies. She has written and recorded more than 50 songs for Off-Centaur, a small recording company specializing in science fiction folk music. A Chicago native and graduate of Purdue University, Lackey has worked as an artist's model, computer programmer, surveyor, layout designer and data processing analyst. An avid scuba diver, she lives in Oklahoma.

Diana Tregarde...investigator of unnatural events...Hartford, Connecticut

- ❑ ❑ 1 - Burning Water (1989)
- ❑ ❑ 2 - Children of the Night (1990)
- ❑ ❑ 3 - Jinx High (1991)
- ❑ ❑ . . . .
- ❑ ❑ . . . .

■ LAKE, Deryn [P]

Popular historical novelist Dinah Lampitt was hired by Canada Dry in 1983 to research the origins of their newest acquisition, H.D. Rawlings and Co., makers of tonic and soda waters. With only two weeks to complete her assignment, Lampitt was able to connect Victorian apothecary, John Rawlings, to H.D. Rawlings and Co. (founded 1754), enabling Canada Dry to supersede Schweppes' (founded 1783) claim as the oldest maker (still in operation) of carbonated water in Europe. Ten years later Lampitt dusted off her Rawlings file, reinvented herself as Deryn Lake, and wrote her first mystery featuring the 18th century apothecary and his magistrate friend, John Fielding, the legendary Blind Beak, introduced in *Death in the Dark Walk* (1994). Their fifth case, *Death in the Peerless Pool* (1999), takes the pair to Bath. Among the author's eight novels as Dinah Lampitt is *As Shadows Haunting* (1993), a book suggested to her by Prince Charles, dealing with the love affair of George III. She lives in England near Tunbridge Wells, Kent.

John Rawlings & the Blind Beak...18th century apothecary & blind magistrate...London, England

- ❏ ❏ 1 - Death in the Dark Walk (1994)
- ❏ ❏ 2 - Death at the Beggar's Opera (1995)
- ❏ ❏ 3 - Death at the Devil's Tavern (1996)
- ❏ ❏ 4 - Death on the Romney Marsh (1998)
- ❏ ❏ . . . .
- ❏ ❏ . . . .

■ LAMB, J. Dayne

Former C.P.A. J. Dayne Lamb has written three mysteries featuring 30-something Teal Stewart, a Certified Public Accountant from Boston's Beacon Hill. The savvy financial investigator is introduced in *Questionable Behavior* (1993), when she looks into the death of a journalist who had been writing about mob involvement in Boston banking. Combining business with pleasure in book 2, *A Question of Preference* (1994), Teal visits a trendy California spa after her former college roommate, now a celebrated artist, is killed in a hit-and-run accident on Cape Cod. After making partner at a prestigious Boston accounting firm in *Unquestioned Loyalty* (1995), Teal finds herself investigating a case of corporate espionage. Born in San Francisco but raised in Brookline, Massachusetts, Lamb is a former C.P.A. with Price Waterhouse. She holds a B.A. in philosophy from Michigan's Hope College and an M.S. in accounting from Northeastern University. Like her fictional sleuth, Lamb lives on Beacon Hill in Boston.

Teal Stewart...Certified Public Accountant...Boston, Massachusetts

- ❏ ❏ 1 - Questionable Behavior (1993)
- ❏ ❏ 2 - A Question of Preference (1994)
- ❏ ❏ 3 - Unquestioned Loyalty (1995)
- ❏ ❏ . . . .
- ❏ ❏ . . . .

■ LAMBERT, Mercedes [P]

Mercedes Lambert is the pseudonymous author of a pair of mysteries featuring "rough, tough, and likable" Los Angeles attorney, Whitney Logan, and her some-times partner, street-smart Chicana prostitute, Lupe Ramos. A recent law school graduate, in debt to her ex-criminal-attorney-landlord and desperate for income, Whitney accepts a thousand dollars from a well-dressed housewife to locate the woman's missing Guatemalan maid in *Dogtown* (1991). "Complex, suspenseful, socially conscious and riveting, it emanates eroticism and sensuality," said Les Roberts in *The Cleveland Plain Dealer*. "Put it at the top of your reading list." After serving a prison sentence for soliciting an undercover cop, Lupe is back in *Soultown* (1996), working with Whitney on a case that takes them to Koreatown. *Library Journal* liked Lambert's "in-your-face language, humor, and jaunty heroine," while *Publishers Weekly* noted her "sympathetic eye for troubled souls." The author, an attorney, lives in Los Angeles with her two children.

Whitney Logan & Lupe Ramos...20-something attorney & Chicana partner...Los Angeles, California

- ❏ ❏ 1 - Dogtown (1991)
- ❏ ❏ 2 - Soultown (1996)
- ❏ ❏ . . . .
- ❏ ❏ . . . .

■ LANDRETH, Marsha

Marsha Landreth has written three mysteries featuring Sheridan, Wyoming medical examiner, Dr. Samantha Turner, first seen in *The Holiday Murders* (1992). After narrowly escaping a plane crash on her return flight to Wyoming in *A Clinic for Murder* (1993), Sam determines smallpox was the cause of death in *Vial Murders* (1994). Since the disease was supposed to have been eradicated in 1977, no one believes her. Writing as Tyler Cortland, Landreth is the author of three medical sagas set in a large Texas medical center: *The* *Healers* (1993), *The Hospital* (1994), and *The Doctors* (1995). Author of *William T. Sherman* (1990), a biography of the famous Civil War general, she has also written a western, *French Creek* (1993). A Denver native with a degree in theatre arts from the University of Northern Colorado, Landreth taught school for 12 years. A former Sheridan, Wyoming resident, she now lives in Southern California, where she writes screenplays, including one for *The Holiday Murders*, optioned for a television movie.

Samantha Turner…medical examiner…Sheridan, Wyoming

- ❑ ❑   1 - The Holiday Murders (1992)
- ❑ ❑   2 - A Clinic for Murder (1993)
- ❑ ❑   3 - Vial Murders (1994)
- ❑ ❑   . . . .
- ❑ ❑   . . . .

■ LANGTON, Jane

Nero Wolfe award winner and Edgar nominee Jane Langton is the creator of retired police lieutenant Homer Kelly, a Thoreau scholar and American literature professor at Harvard, introduced in *The Transcendental Murder* (1964), later reissued as *The Minuteman Murder* (1976). Kelly's wife Mary, also a Harvard professor, accompanies him to Venice in book 14, *The Thief of Venice* (1999), for a rare book seminar. Both literate and literary, the series draws on Langton's rich background of academia, poetry, art, culture and natural history. Her many devoted fans look forward to her lovely pen and ink sketches (drawn for each book), almost as much as the stories themselves. Langton earned master's degrees from Radcliffe College and the University of Michigan, where she was Phi Beta Kappa. After studying at the Boston Museum School of Art, Langton taught children's literature and wrote a number of children's books. She once told an interviewer that her experience with the seamy side of life comes from teaching Sunday School.

Homer Kelly…ex-cop turned Harvard professor…Cambridge, Massachusetts

- ❑ ❑   1 - The Transcendental Murder (1964)
- ❑ ❑   - APA-The Minuteman Murder (1976)
- ❑ ❑   2 - Dark Nantucket Noon (1975)
- ❑ ❑   3 - The Memorial Hall Murder (1978)
- ❑ ❑   4 - Natural Enemy (1982)
- ❑ ❑   5 - **Emily Dickinson Is Dead (1984) Nero Wolfe winner ★ Edgar nominee ☆**
- ❑ ❑   6 - Good and Dead (1986)
- ❑ ❑   7 - Murder at the Gardner (1988)
- ❑ ❑   8 - The Dante Game (1991)
- ❑ ❑   9 - God in Concord (1992)
- ❑ ❑   10 - Divine Inspiration (1993)
- ❑ ❑   11 - The Shortest Day (1995)
- ❑ ❑   12 - Dead as a Dodo (1996)
- ❑ ❑   13 - The Face on the Wall (1998)
- ❑ ❑   . . . .
- ❑ ❑   . . . .

■ LANIER, Virginia

Something of a legend in mystery circles, Virginia Lanier was 64 when her Anthony-award winning first novel, *Death in Bloodhound Red* (1995), also nominated for Agatha and Macavity awards, was published by Pineapple Press. Living on Social Security, Lanier had written the first 300 pages longhand, while her husband saved $94.50 to buy her a typewriter at Wal-Mart. Purchased by HarperCollins for 1996 release in mass market paperback, the book introduced blood-hound trainer Jo Beth Sidden, a chain-smoking, good old Georgia gal with a special talent for search-and-rescue missions. After solving a 30-year-old crime in *Blind Bloodhound Justice* (1998), and surviving yet another confrontation with her "homicidally-frisky"

ex-husband Bubba, Jo Beth is hired to find an eccentric billionaire's lost cat in book 5, *Ten Little Bloodhounds* (1999). She's also attacked by an alligator, kidnapped, and put on trial for her life. Lanier and her husband live on the edge of the Okefenokee Swamp in Echols County, Georgia.

Jo Beth Sidden...search-and-rescue bloodhound trainer...Dunston County, Georgia

❏	❏	1 -	**Death in Bloodhound Red (1995) Anthony winner ★**
			Agatha & Macavity nominee ☆☆
❏	❏	2 -	The House on Bloodhound Lane (1996)
❏	❏	3 -	A Brace of Bloodhounds (1997)
❏	❏	4 -	Blind Bloodhound Justice (1998)
❏	❏		. . . .
❏	❏		. . . .

■ LaPIERRE, Janet

Former high school English teacher Janet LaPierre writes novels of mystery and suspense, set on the chilly, foggy, sparsely-populated coast of Northern California. The fictitious Port Silva is a university town perched on a dramatic headland overlooking a small harbor on the Mendocino coast. The population of 24,000 is a mix of old families, urban escapers, students, academics, and tourists in season. LaPierre's cast of characters is headed by single mother and teacher, Meg Halloran, and Port Silva's chief of

police, Vince Gutierrez, introduced in the Macavity-nominated *Unquiet Grave* (1987). "A razor-sharp debut novel; great atmosphere, quirkily believable charac-ters, and a satisfying romance," raved *Kirkus*. After a six-year absence, Vince and Meg return in book 6, *Baby Mine* (1999). Born in Iowa and educated at the University of Arizona, (Tucson), LaPierre once helped run a large co-op nursery school, where she says she learned small children have no conscience, much cunning, and will do anything.

Meg Halloran & Vince Gutierrez...single-mother school teacher & police chief...Port Silva, California

❏	❏	1 -	**Unquiet Grave (1987) Macavity nominee ☆**
❏	❏	2 -	Children's Games (1989)
❏	❏	3 -	Cruel Mother (1990)
❏	❏	4 -	Grandmother's House (1991)
❏	❏	5 -	**Old Enemies (1993) Anthony nominee ☆**
❏	❏		. . . .
❏	❏		. . . .

■ La PLANTE, Lynda

Former stage and television actress Lynda La Plante was the original writer for the award-winning television series featuring London's Detective Chief Inspector Jane Tennison, shown on PBS *Mystery!*, and later novelized as *Prime Suspect 1, 2, and 3*. Her original script for *Prime Suspect* won La Plante an Edgar award in 1993. Starting with *Prime Suspect 4*, a different writer scripted each episode. After training for the stage at the Royal Academy of Dramatic Arts, La Plante worked exten-sively with the National Theatre and Royal Shakespeare

Theatre. She once told the *New York Times* that because she was short, red-haired and very loud, she played more prostitutes than any other actress. Following the phenomenal success of her television series *Widows*, which sold in 26 countries, La Plante turned to writing full time. Her current series features ex-L.A.P.D. lieutenant, Lorraine Page, who lost everything after shooting a teenage suspect in a haze of alcohol. Born in Liverpool, La Plante divides her time between London and Los Angeles.

Dolly Rawlins...bank robber's widow...London, England

❏	❏	1 -	The Widows (1983)
❏	❏	2 -	The Widows II (1985)
❏	❏	3 -	She's Out (1995)
❏	❏	4 -	Trial and Retribution (1997)
❏	❏	5 -	Trial and Retribution II (1998)
❏	❏		. . . .
❏	❏		. . . .

Jane Tennison…detective chief inspector…London, England

- ❑ ❑ 1 - Prime Suspect (1993)
- ❑ ❑ 2 - Prime Suspect 2 (1993)
- ❑ ❑ 3 - Prime Suspect 3 (1994)
- ❑ ❑ . . . .
- ❑ ❑ . . . .

Lorraine Page…sober ex-cop turned private eye …Los Angeles, California

- ❑ ❑ 1 - Cold Shoulder (1994)
- ❑ ❑ 2 - Cold Blood (1996)
- ❑ ❑ 3 - Cold Heart (1998)
- ❑ ❑ . . . .
- ❑ ❑ . . . .

■ LATHEN, Emma [P]

Emma Lathen is the pseudonym of Harvard economist, Mary Jane Latsis (1927-1997), and Harvard attorney Martha Henissart, whose Gold and Silver Dagger award-winning mysteries feature John Putnam Thatcher. A reserved and dignified widower, the senior vice president of New York's Sloan Guaranty Trust is introduced in *Banking on Death* (1961). Thatcher is ably assisted throughout 24 books by stalwart secretary Miss Corsa, along with other banking colleagues, including fussy Everett Gabler, whose attention to detail extends even to dog shows (*A Place for Murder*). Different aspects of commerce and finance are central to each book, ranging from Russian wheat deals (*Murder Against the Grain*), to the garment industry (*The Longer the Thread*), and even the Lake Placid Winter Olympics (*Going for the Gold*). After agreeing on basic structure and major characters, the two authors wrote alternating chapters. Writing in ink on yellow legal pads, Latsis always penned the first chapter. Using a manual typewriter, Henissart always wrote the last. Their only serious disagreement came when Latsis killed off one of Henissart's favorite characters. A 25th manuscript set during the Persian Gulf War was 80% complete when Latsis died and will likely be finished by Henissart. Six months before Latsis' death in 1997, the pair was honored with a Lifetime Achievement Award at Malice Domestic, the first mystery convention ever attended by Emma Lathen.

John Putnam Thatcher…Wall Street financial whiz…New York, New York

- ❑ ❑ 1 - Banking on Death (1961)
- ❑ ❑ 2 - A Place for Murder (1963)
- ❑ ❑ 3 - **Accounting for Murder (1964) Silver Dagger winner ★**
- ❑ ❑ 4 - Murder Makes the Wheels Go 'Round (1966)
- ❑ ❑ 5 - Death Shall Overcome (1966)
- ❑ ❑ 6 - **Murder Against the Grain (1967) Gold Dagger winner ★**
- ❑ ❑ 7 - A Stitch in Time (1968)
- ❑ ❑ 8 - Come to Dust (1968)
- ❑ ❑ 9 - **When in Greece (1969) Edgar nominee ☆**
- ❑ ❑ 10 - Murder To Go (1969)
- ❑ ❑ 11 - Pick up Sticks (1970)
- ❑ ❑ 12 - Ashes to Ashes (1971)
- ❑ ❑ 13 - The Longer the Thread (1971)
- ❑ ❑ 14 - Murder Without Icing (1972)
- ❑ ❑ 15 - Sweet and Low (1974)
- ❑ ❑ 16 - By Hook or by Crook (1975)
- ❑ ❑ 17 - Double, Double, Oil and Trouble (1978)
- ❑ ❑ 18 - Going for the Gold (1981)
- ❑ ❑ 19 - Green Grow the Dollars (1982)
- ❑ ❑ 20 - Something in the Air (1988)
- ❑ ❑ 21 - East Is East (1991)
- ❑ ❑ 22 - Right on the Money (1993)
- ❑ ❑ 23 - Brewing Up a Storm (1996)
- ❑ ❑ 24 - A Shark Out of Water (1997)
- ❑ ❑ . . . .
- ❑ ❑ . . . .

■ LAURENCE, Janet

Former public relations executive Janet Laurence brings both cooking and writing experience to her mysteries featuring Cordon bleu cook, caterer and food writer, Darina Lisle, and her police detective boyfriend, William Pigram, introduced in *A Deepe Coffyn* (1989). The nine-book series offers a super-abundance of glorious food descriptions, but no actual recipes. With *Canaletto and the Case of the Westminster Bridge* (1998), Laurence has introduced amateur detective and real-life 18th century Venetian painter, Canaletto, who has traveled to London in search of commissions. "A tale to gladden the hearts of historical romance lovers, providing adequate fare for puzzle fans as well," proclaimed *Kirkus*. A former teacher of residential cookery courses, Laurence is the author of several cookbooks, including *A Little French Cookbook* (1989), *A Little Scandinavian Cookbook* (1990) and *A Little Coffee Cookbook* (1992). Once a weekly columnist for *The Daily Telegraph*, Laurence lives with her husband in Somerset, England.

Canaletto...18th century Italian painter...London, England
- ❏ ❏ 1 - Canaletto and the Case of the Westminster Bridge (1998)
- ❏ ❏ 2 - The Case of the Privvy Garden (1999)
- ❏ ❏ . . . .
- ❏ ❏ . . . .

Darina Lisle...caterer-chef and food writer...West Country, England
- ❏ ❏ 1 - A Deepe Coffyn (1989)
- ❏ ❏ 2 - A Tasty Way To Die (1990)
- ❏ ❏ 3 - Hotel Morgue (1991)
- ❏ ❏ 4 - Recipe for Death (1992)
- ❏ ❏ 5 - Death and the Epicure (1993)
- ❏ ❏ 6 - Death at the Table (1994)
- ❏ ❏ 7 - Death a la Provencale (1995)
- ❏ ❏ 8 - Diet for Death (1996)
- ❏ ❏ 9 - Appetite for Death (1998)
- ❏ ❏ . . . .
- ❏ ❏ . . . .

■ LAW, Janice

Janice Law is the creator of Anna Peters, a Washington, D.C. private eye skilled in corporate blackmail, first seen in *The Big Pay-off* (1976). Inspired by the Watergate investigation (then ongoing), the Edgar-nominated first mystery features business intrigue mixed with North Sea oil exploration. Long out of print, this book will not be easy to find, but you'll be richly rewarded for your effort. The enterprising and likable Anna is one tough cookie, and if you've ever dreamed of blackmailing a jerk of a boss, you'll cheer out loud as you tear through 179 pages. Golf enthusiasts will especially enjoy book 5, *Death Under Par* (1981), where Anna accompanies her sports illustrator husband Harry to the British Open. Set in the world of professional hockey, book 9, *Cross-Check* (1997), is "one of the dependable series' best," said *Booklist*. A Phi Beta Kappa graduate of Syracuse University, Law holds an M.A. from the University of Connecticut. Also published as Janice Law Trecker, she lives with her sportswriter husband in Connecticut.

Anna Peters...oil company executive turned P.I....Washington, District of Columbia
- ❏ ❏ 1 - **The Big Pay-off (1976) Edgar nominee** ☆
- ❏ ❏ 2 - Gemini Trip (1977)
- ❏ ❏ 3 - Under Orion (1978)
- ❏ ❏ 4 - The Shadow of the Palms (1980)
- ❏ ❏ 5 - Death Under Par (1981)
- ❏ ❏ 6 - Time Lapse (1992)
- ❏ ❏ 7 - A Safe Place To Die (1993)
- ❏ ❏ 8 - Backfire (1994)
- ❏ ❏ 9 - Cross-Check (1997)
- ❏ ❏ . . . .
- ❏ ❏ . . . .

■ LAWRENCE, Hilda

Hilda Lawrence wrote a three-book series during the 1940s featuring Manhattan private eye Mark East, and two spinster sleuths, Bessie Petty and Beulah Pond, introduced in *Blood Upon the Snow* (1944). According to Marcia Muller in *1001 Midnights* (1986), the series is "an interesting juxtaposition of the hard-boiled school versus little-old-lady sleuth, between the customs and mores of Manhattan and those of a small New England village." Michele Slung says Lawrence's masterpiece is *Death of a Doll* (1947),

which takes place in a New York boarding house for women. Miss Beulah and Miss Bessie go undercover at Hope House. Aided and abetted by Mark East, the ladies solve the crime. Lawrence also wrote a novel of suspense titled *The Deadly Pavilion* (1948) and two novellas published together as *Duet of Death* (1949). During her varied career, she graded papers at Johns Hopkins University, worked at *Publishers Weekly* and wrote radio scripts for *The Rudy Vallee Show*.

Mark East, Bessie Petty & Beulah Pond...Manhattan P.I. & little old ladies...New York, New York

- ❑ ❑   1 - Blood Upon the Snow (1944)
- ❑ ❑   2 - A Time To Die (1944)
- ❑ ❑   3 - Death of a Doll (1947)
- ❑ ❑   . . . .
- ❑ ❑   . . . .

■ LAWRENCE, Margaret [P]

Margaret Lawrence is a pseudonym of Margaret Keilstrup (KEEL-strup), who has also written mysteries as M.K. Lorens. Reinventing herself as Margaret Lawrence for *Hearts and Bones* (1996) netted the author four award nominations for best novel—Edgar, Anthony, Agatha and Macavity. "A murder mystery, a powerful historical novel of war and its aftermath, and a vivid love story," proclaimed *Kirkus*. The book introduces gifted 1780s midwife, Hannah Trevor, a Revolutionary War widow and unwed mother of a deaf

mute eight-year-old daughter in Rufford, Maine. "Stirring and revealing—a whole different picture of Revolutionary life," said the *San Jose Mercury-News*. "Lawrence paints the period as an era not of triumphant freedom, but of terrible injustice." Keilstrup has written for stage and film, including *Wonderland*, produced Off-Broadway in 1980, and "Riding the Elephant," an early episode of the *Equalizer* television series, also in 1980. She lives in Nebraska where she is working on a new novel.

Hannah Trevor...18th century widwife...Rufford, Maine

- ❑ ❑   1 - **Hearts and Bones (1996) Agatha, Anthony, Edgar &**
  Macavity nominee ☆☆☆☆
- ❑ ❑   2 - Blood Red Roses (1997)
- ❑ ❑   3 - The Burning Bride (1998)
- ❑ ❑   . . . .
- ❑ ❑   . . . .

■ LAWRENCE, Martha

A former editor for Simon & Schuster in New York, Martha Lawrence grew up in Rancho Santa Fe, California, where the family home included a ghost. Inspired by her own experiences with the paranormal, Lawrence chose a parapsychologist-private investigator to star in her first novel, *Murder in Scorpio* (1995). A Stanford-trained parapsychologist with a double-Ph.D. and a "gift," Dr. Elizabeth Chase takes on the skeptics, including San Diego police officer Tom McGowan, who asks for Elizabeth's help in the series opener. The

book was nominated for Edgar, Agatha and Anthony awards as best first mystery. Lawrence has chosen the last sign of the zodiac for book 4, *Pisces Rising* (2000), coming in the last year of the millennium. Book 5 will feature the first sign, Aries, for year one of the new millennium. In September 1999 Lawrence is leading a 15-day tour of Britain's haunted castles and monuments. She lives in Escondido, California, site of the 19th century Hooper House which is home to Elizabeth Chase.

Elizabeth Chase...parapsychologist turned P.I....San Diego, California

- ❑ ❑   1 - **Murder in Scorpio (1995) Agatha, Anthony & Edgar nominee** ☆☆☆
- ❑ ❑   2 - The Cold Heart of Capricorn (1997)
- ❑ ❑   3 - Aquarius Descending (1999)
- ❑ ❑   . . . .
- ❑ ❑   . . . .

■ LEE, Barbara

Barbara Lee's first mystery, *Death in Still Waters*, won the Malice Domestic Best First Mystery Contest in 1994 and was published by St. Martin's the following year. Divorced New York advertising executive, Eve Elliott, moves to Maryland to join her widowed Aunt Lillian's real estate business. When last seen in book 3, *Dead Man's Fingers* (1999), the murder of documentary film maker Lauren DeWitt escalates a growing conflict between environmentalists and developers in the Chesapeake Bay community of Pines on Magothy. Lee has also written four nonfiction books for young adults, including *Working With Music* (1996) and *Working With Animals* (1996). Born in the Adirondacks where her parents owned a summer resort, she grew up in Cooperstown, went to college in New York City and later worked at New York University. After moving to Maryland, Lee wrote relocation guides for realtors. One of the organizers of the Chesapeake Chapter of Sisters in Crime, she lives in Columbia, Maryland.

Eve Elliott...real estate agent...Anne Arundel Co., Maryland

- ❏ ❏ 1 - **Death in Still Waters (1995) SMP/MD winner ★**
- ❏ ❏ 2 - Final Closing (1997)
- ❏ ❏ 3 - Dead Man's Fingers (1999)
- ❏ ❏ ....
- ❏ ❏ ....

■ LEE, Marie

Former science teacher Marie Lee writes Cape Cod mysteries featuring retired science teacher Marguerite Smith, introduced in *The Curious Cape Cod Skull* (1995). After Marguerite discovers the body of an archaeologist in charge of a local Native American homesite excavation, her dog retrieves a mysterious skull from the murder site. The book reads like "a cross between an Agatha Christie Miss Marple novel and an episode of *Murder She Wrote*," said *The Boston Sunday Herald*. An unexpected body is found near a freshly dug grave in a local Indian cemetery in book 2, *The Fatal Cape Cod Funeral* (1996). Marguerite rushes home from a Florida vacation, when she receives word that she is a suspect in her ex-husband's murder in book 3, *The Mysterious Cape Cod Manuscript* (1997). After earning B.S. and M.S. degrees in science, Lee worked as a bacteriologist and later taught high school and college science courses. A native of New Jersey, Lee lives on Cape Cod where she coaxes an organic garden from the sandy soil.

Marguerite Smith...retired science teacher...Cape Cod, Massachusetts

- ❏ ❏ 1 - The Curious Cape Cod Skull (1995)
- ❏ ❏ 2 - The Fatal Cape Cod Funeral (1996)
- ❏ ❏ 3 - The Mysterious Cape Cod Manuscript (1997)
- ❏ ❏ ....
- ❏ ❏ ....

■ LEE, Wendi

As W.W. Lee, Wendi Lee has written six mysteries starring Jefferson Birch, a private eye in the Old West, introduced in *Rogue's Gold* (1989) as an agent for Tisdale Investigations. As Wendi Lee she writes a contemporary private eye series featuring Angela Matelli, a good Italian girl from East Boston who joined the Marines. After several short story appearances, the ex-Marine turned P.I. makes her novel-length debut in *The Good Daughter* (1994), with an ex-cop, who later turns up dead, as her first client. In book 4, *He Who Dies* (2000), Angela's wiseguy brother disappears, and a body is found in the trunk of his car. Lee has also written *The Overland Trail* (1996), a novel based on the actual diaries of women who crossed the country in 1846. With her husband, cartoonist Terry Beatty, Lee has co-authored short stories for children's fantasy anthologies. A one-time resident of Boston, Lee lives in Muscatine, Iowa, also home to award-winning author Max Allen Collins. Lee is associate editor of *Mystery Scene* magazine.

Angela Matelli...ex-Marine turned P.I....Boston, Massachusetts

- ❏ ❏ 1 - The Good Daughter (1994)
- ❏ ❏ 2 - Missing Eden (1996)
- ❏ ❏ 3 - Deadbeat (1999)
- ❏ ❏ ....
- ❏ ❏ ....

Jefferson Birch...P.I. in the Old West

- ❏ ❏   1 - Rogue's Gold [as W.W. Lee] (1989)
- ❏ ❏   2 - Rustler's Venom [as W.W. Lee] (1990)
- ❏ ❏   3 - Rancher's Blood [as W.W. Lee] (1991)
- ❏ ❏   4 - Robber's Trail [as W.W. Lee] (1992)
- ❏ ❏   5 - Outlaw's Fortune [as W.W. Lee] (1993)
- ❏ ❏   6 - Cannon's Revenge [as W.W. Lee] (1995)
- ❏ ❏   . . . .
- ❏ ❏   . . . .

■ LEMARCHAND, Elizabeth

From 1940 until 1960, Elizabeth Lemarchand was Deputy Headmistress of Godolphin School, the alma mater of Josephine Bell and Dorothy L. Sayers. Forced to retire early because of illness, she began writing as a hobby during convalescence and published her first mystery at the age of 61. She went on to complete 17 novels featuring Scotland Yard investigators Tom Pollard and Gregory Toye, first seen in *Death of an Old Girl* (1967). In each of her well-constructed and often ingenious books, readers are treated to maps, timetables, floor plans and printed casts of characters—standard fare during the early Golden Age of Detection. Lemarchand's detectives are old-fashioned family men. Pollard's wife Jane, a red-headed art teacher, presents her husband with twins in book 2, *The Affacombe Affair* (1968). Toye has a weakness for Western movies and a vast knowledge of automobiles. Born in Devon and educated at the Ursuline Convent, Lemarchand earned a master's degree in 1929 at the University of Exeter.

Tom Pollard & Gregory Toye...Scotland Yard detectives...London, England

- ❏ ❏   1 - Death of an Old Girl (1967)
- ❏ ❏   2 - The Affacombe Affair (1968)
- ❏ ❏   3 - Alibi for a Corpse (1969)
- ❏ ❏   4 - Death on Doomsday (1971)
- ❏ ❏   5 - Cyanide With Compliments (1972)
- ❏ ❏   6 - Let or Hindrance (1973)
- ❏ ❏   - U.S.-No Vacation from Murder
- ❏ ❏   7 - Buried in the Past (1974)
- ❏ ❏   8 - Step in the Dark (1976)
- ❏ ❏   9 - Unhappy Returns (1977)
- ❏ ❏ 10 - Suddenly While Gardening (1978)
- ❏ ❏ 11 - Change for the Worse (1980)
- ❏ ❏ 12 - Nothing To Do With the Case (1981)
- ❏ ❏ 13 - Troubled Waters (1982)
- ❏ ❏ 14 - The Wheel Turns (1983)
- ❏ ❏ 15 - Light through the Glass (1984)
- ❏ ❏ 16 - Who Goes Home? (1986)
- ❏ ❏ 17 - The Glade Manor Murder (1988)
- ❏ ❏   . . . .
- ❏ ❏   . . . .

■ LEON, Donna

International best-selling author Donna Leon is frequently stopped on the streets of Venice by German and Swiss tourists asking for her autograph. An American expatriate who has lived in Venice for almost 20 years, Leon spoke not a word of Italian when she sold her furniture and moved with her infant son to the city that has enthusiastically adopted her and Commissario Guido Brunetti, Leon's fictional Italian police officer based at the Petit Palace. Continuing characters include Brunetti's wife Paola, a professor of English literature, their two teenage children, and Paola's wealthy and influential parents. The series debut, *Death at La Fenice* (1992), winner of Japan's Suntory prize for best suspense novel, involves the murder of a German conductor at the famed Venice opera house. Last published in the U.S. with book 5, the Brunetti series finds Paola committing vandalism in book 8, *Fatal Remedies* (1999). Up next is *Structural Problems* (2000). Leon teaches English at the local University of Maryland extension.

Guido Brunetti...police commissario...Venice, Italy

- ❑ ❑ 1 - Death at La Fenice (1992)
- ❑ ❑ 2 - Death in a Strange Country (1993)
- ❑ ❑ 3 - Dressed for Death (1994)
- ❑ ❑   - Brit.-The Anonymous Venetian
- ❑ ❑ 4 - Death and Judgment (1995)
- ❑ ❑   - Brit.-A Venetian Reckoning
- ❑ ❑ 5 - Acqua Alta (1996)
- ❑ ❑ 6 - The Death of Faith (1997)
- ❑ ❑ 7 - A Noble Radiance (1998)
- ❑ ❑ 8 - Fatal Remedies (1999)
- ❑ ❑ . . . .
- ❑ ❑ . . . .

■ LEWIS, Sherry

Romance and mystery author Sherry Lewis is the creator of 73-year-old widowed Colorado retiree Fred Vickery, who finds himself investigating a supposed suicide in the series opener, *No Place for Secrets* (1995). Fred defends his dead wife's honor with his fists when the class bully speaks ill of Phoebe at their 55th high school reunion in book 6, *No Place for Memories* (1999). After the bully is found dead, Fred must prove his innocence. Lewis' romance novels include *Call Me Mom* (1995), *This Montana Home* (1996), *Keeping Her Safe* (1997), *Let It Snow* (1998), and *A Man for Mom* (1999). Her short story, "Send Me No Flowers," is included in *Secret Valentines* (1998). Lewis has worked in florist and garden shops, a convenience store, insurance agency and bank. While singing and playing keyboard with local bands, she spent 15 years working as a bankruptcy paralegal. After growing up in Billings, Montana, Lewis moved to Utah, where she has lived since age 12. When not writing, she enjoys gardening and taking long car drives.

Fred Vickery...70-something retiree...Cutler, Colorado

- ❑ ❑ 1 - No Place for Secrets (1995)
- ❑ ❑ 2 - No Place Like Home (1996)
- ❑ ❑ 3 - No Place for Death (1996)
- ❑ ❑ 4 - No Place for Tears (1997)
- ❑ ❑ 5 - No Place for Sin (1997)
- ❑ ❑ . . . .
- ❑ ❑ . . . .

■ LIN-CHANDLER, Irene

new

Born Lin Yu-chun in Taipei, Irene Lin-Chandler was educated in Japan, worked in London, and now lives in Taipei with her English husband. Her four mysteries feature Holly-Jean Ho, a bisexual Anglo-Chinese woman raised in Chinatown by her Hakka mother. A computer fraud consultant and private investigator, Holly-Jean is hired to find out who is raping Asian girls at an English boarding school in the series opener, *The Healing of Holly-Jean* (1995). The death of a fashion model leads Holly-Jean to an internet pornography ring in book 2, *Grievous Angel* (1996). When last seen in book 3, *Hour of the Tigress* (1999), a messy probate matter involves a vast inheritance and a Scottish earldom. Something of a black sheep, the Earl had been living in the Philippines. His only heir is a young woman television producer making an underground documentary about Chinese dissidents. Gun battles in China, attacks in the Philippines and assaults on Holly's friends in the U.K. are all part of the action.

Holly-Jean Ho...Anglo-Chinese bisexual investigator...London, England

- ❑ ❑ 1 - The Healing of Holly-Jean (1995)
- ❑ ❑ 2 - Grievous Angel (1996)
- ❑ ❑ 3 - Hour of the Tigress (1999)
- ❑ ❑ . . . .
- ❑ ❑ . . . .

■ LINSCOTT, Gillian

A former Parliamentary reporter for the BBC, Gillian Linscott writes Edwardian mysteries featuring radical suffragette Nell Bray, a follower of Emmeline Pankhurst and member of the Women's Social and Political Union. Nell first confronts murder in the high-fashion resort town of Biarritz in *Sister Beneath the Sheet* (1991), and then moves into a World War I military hospital for *Hanging on the Wire* (1992). In book 5, *Crown Witness* (1995), she is recruited to watch for trouble during a procession of suffragettes to honor the upcoming coronation of King George V. In book 8, *Absent Friends* (1999), Nell is thrilled to be part of the first woman's vote in 1918, and is looking for a district where she can run in the general election. Linscott has also written four mysteries featuring Birdie Linnet, an ex-cop working as a fitness trainer and involved with a younger woman who is a travel agent. On holiday in France, the well-meaning but not-too-smart Birdie finds himself the prime suspect in the murder of his ex-wife's lover.

Birdie Linnet...ex-cop fitness trainer...England
- ❑ ❑   1 - A Healthy Body (1984)
- ❑ ❑   2 - Murder Makes Tracks (1985)
- ❑ ❑   3 - Knightfall (1986)
- ❑ ❑   4 - A Whiff of Sulphur (1987)
- ❑ ❑   . . . .
- ❑ ❑   . . . .

Nell Bray...British suffragette...London, England
- ❑ ❑   1 - Sister Beneath the Sheet (1991)
- ❑ ❑   2 - Hanging on the Wire (1992)
- ❑ ❑   3 - Stage Fright (1993)
- ❑ ❑   4 - Widow's Peak (1994)
- ❑ ❑   - U.S.-An Easy Day for a Lady
- ❑ ❑   5 - Crown Witness (1995)
- ❑ ❑   6 - Dead Man's Sweetheart (1996)
- ❑ ❑   - U.S.-Dead Man's Music
- ❑ ❑   7 - Dance on Blood (1998)
- ❑ ❑   . . . .
- ❑ ❑   . . . .

■ LIPPMAN, Laura

Edgar and Shamus award winner Laura Lippman was genetically programmed to write. Her father was a long-time newspaper columnist and editorial writer and her mother, a children's librarian. During Lippman's journalism studies at Northwestern University, one of her professors was Edgar winner Stuart M. Kaminsky. During her ten years at the *Baltimore Sun*, where Lippman has been a feature writer since 1994, five *Sun* reporters have become published mystery authors—Stephen Hunter, David Simon, Dan Fesperman, Sujata Massey and Lippman.

Although Lippman borrows much of her own newspaper experience for fictional P.I. Tess Monaghan, the author has not lost her job, as Tess did. And despite her recent shooting lessons, Lippman does not expect to follow the somewhat-reluctant Tess into private investigating. In book 4, *In Big Trouble* (1999), she takes Tess to San Antonio, where Lippman spent five years as a reporter and once bloodied then-Mayor Henry Cisneros in a game of touch football. Tess returns in book 5, *The Sugar House* (2000).

Tess Monaghan...newspaper reporter turned P.I....Baltimore, Maryland
- ❑ ❑   1 - **Baltimore Blues (1997) Shamus nominee** ☆
- ❑ ❑   2 - **Charm City (1997) Edgar & Shamus winner ★★ Anthony nominee** ☆
- ❑ ❑   3 - Butchers Hill (1998)
- ❑ ❑   4 - In Big Trouble (1999)
- ❑ ❑   . . . .
- ❑ ❑   . . . .

■ LIVESAY, Ann [P]

Geologist and former Illinois State Museum curator Ann Livesay has written more than 25 books, including 22 nonfiction titles of biography, natural history, science and travel co-authored as Ann Sutton with husband Myron Sutton. As consultants to some 80 governments in the establishment of national parks and nature reserves, the Suttons have traveled to more than 75 countries where they have taken 100,000 photographs. Nearly 10,000 of these pictures are marketed by agents and published worldwide, including the images used for the covers of Livesay's Barry Ross mysteries, beginning with *The Isis Command* (1998). A private investigator funded by his super-rich Aunt Kelly, Ross focuses on environmental crime, including illegal animal trade, tomb-robbing and ecoterrorism. Skilled in criminal investigation, international law, languages, wildlife biology and ecology, he frequently travels to remote and dangerous places. Ross' assistants are Joe and Julie Muck, a wildlife biologist and his wife, a former park ranger.

Barry Ross...international investigator
- ❏ ❏ 1 - The Isis Command (1998)
- ❏ ❏ 2 - Death in the Amazon (1998)
- ❏ ❏ 3 - The Madman of Mt. Everest (1999)
- ❏ ❏ 4 - The Chala Project [Grand Canyon] (2000)
- ❏ ❏ 5 - The Dinkum Deaths [Great Barrier Reef] (2001)
- ❏ ❏ . . . .
- ❏ ❏ . . . .

■ LOGAN, Margaret

Margaret Logan is the creator of Boston interior decorator Olivia Chapman, introduced in *The End of an Altruist* (1994), where Olivia is suspected of involvement in the death of a woman whose Roxbury home was undergoing renovation. "The real pleasure here is watching Olivia—who's as tough-minded and resourceful a she needs to be—keep landing miraculously on her feet," said *Kirkus*. Logan has written a travel memoir, *Happy Ending* (1979), numerous travel articles and the nonseries mysteries, *A Killing in Venture Capital* (1989), and *C.A.T. Caper* (1990), a tale inspired by the author's experience grading essays on English composition achievement tests. Logan was born in China, where all four of her grandparents had been missionaries, as were her parents. A graduate of the University of Richmond, she holds an M.A. in creative writing from Boston University, and has taught travel writing at the Harvard Extension School. She lives in Southampton, New York.

Olivia Chapman...interior decorator...Boston, Massachusetts
- ❏ ❏ 1 - The End of an Altruist (1994)
- ❏ ❏ 2 - Never Let a Stranger in Your House (1995)
- ❏ ❏ . . . .
- ❏ ❏ . . . .

■ LORDON, Randye

Lambda award winner and two-time Shamus nominee Randye Lordon says her fictional private eye, Sydney Sloane, is baffled by family dynamics. "There is no question that [we] share some similar genetic coding, but we are as different as cantaloupes and scissors," says Sydney about her cousin Mark in book 5, *Say Uncle* (1999). Each of the lesbian detective's cases involves a family member, close friend, or relative of a client, beginning with the Shamus-nominated first novel, *Brotherly Love* (1993). Sydney and her best friend and partner, Max Cabe, work from an office on Manhattan's Upper West Side, but Max is away when Sydney gets the shock of her life in book 1. The brother she thought was dead might still be alive, wanted for a double homicide. Sydney's upcoming cases will include book 6, *East of Niece* (2000), followed by *Auntie Up*. Born and raised in Chicago, Lordon lives in Amagansett, New York, where she is a partner in BarkingFish Productions, a new media and website design firm.

Sydney Sloane...lesbian private investigator...New York, New York
- ❏ ❏ 1 - **Brotherly Love (1993) Shamus nominee** ☆
- ❏ ❏ 2 - Sister's Keeper (1994)

❑ ❑   3 - **Father Forgive Me (1997) Lambda winner ★ Shamus nominee ☆**
❑ ❑   4 - Mother May I (1998)
❑ ❑   5 - Say Uncle (1999)
❑ ❑   . . . .
❑ ❑   . . . .

■ LORENS, M.K.

M.K. Lorens is a pseudonym of Margaret Keilstrup (KEEL-strup), author of three historical mysteries as Margaret Lawrence. As Lorens she has created Shakespearean scholar and mystery writer Winston Marlowe Sherman, featured in five books beginning with *Sweet Narcissus* (1990). In addition to his college teaching, Sherman writes pseudonymous mysteries, as Henrietta Slocum, featuring amateur detective Winchester Hyde. The professor's lady-love is concert pianist Sarah Cromwell, whose younger brother (the

actor) lives with them. Joining the trio in Sarah's family mansion is the professor's retired colleague, Edward Merriman. In book 4, *Dreamland* (1992), Winston expects to lose the Edgar award for the ninth year in a row to his former lover, the queen of kinky crime fiction. When she is murdered at the Edgar dinner, Winston is the prime suspect. After earning her Ph.D. from the University of Nebraska, Keilstrup taught at several colleges and universities. She has also worked as a translator, singer, artist and designer.

Winston Marlowe Sherman...mystery-writing Shakespeare professor...New York, New York

❑ ❑   1 - Sweet Narcissus (1990)
❑ ❑   2 - Ropedancer's Fall (1990)
❑ ❑   3 - Deception Island (1991)
❑ ❑   4 - Dreamland (1992)
❑ ❑   5 - Sorrowheart (1993)
❑ ❑   . . . .
❑ ❑   . . . .

■ LOVETT, Sarah

Sarah Lovett writes forensic mysteries featuring Sante Fe psychologist Dr. Sylvia Strange, introduced in *Dangerous Attachments* (1995). Published in seven countries simultaneously, the book is under development for a television movie. Research for her debut novel included Lovett working as a legal researcher for more than four months inside the Penitentiary of New Mexico for the attorney general's office; completing three years of criminal justice courses, including a firearms training course and classes at the

Law Enforcement Academy; touring the forensic unit at Las Vegas State Hospital, and surveiling someone for an entire day without being detected. Dr. Strange's fourth case is *Dantes' Inferno* (2000). Lovett is the author of more than 20 science and travel titles, including the *Extremely Weird* series for kids, which had her raising tadpoles for *Extremely Weird Frogs* (1996). Raised in California, Lovett lives in a passive solar adobe house in Sante Fe, New Mexico, with her four-legged friends, Big Mac and Little Lulu.

Sylvia Strange...forensic psychologist...Sante Fe, New Mexico

❑ ❑   1 - Dangerous Attachments (1995)
❑ ❑   2 - Acquired Motives (1996)
❑ ❑   3 - A Desperate Silence (1998)
❑ ❑   . . . .
❑ ❑   . . . .

■ LYNDS, Gayle

Former newspaper reporter and magazine editor Gayle Lynds spent four years doing research for her first novel, *Masquerade* (1996), the best-selling international spy thriller picked as a Page-Turner of the Week by *People* magazine. "One of the oldest chestnuts in the thriller genre is given a lively and original roasting, said

the *Amazon.com* reviewer. "Gloriously paranoid, immensely satisfying," raved the *Los Angeles Times* about this tale of an amnesiac who discovers she is a crack shot and a C.I.A. employee. Lynds has also written *Mosaic* (1998), a spy thriller featuring a blind concert pianist who regains her sight just in time to witness her mother's murder. A journalism graduate of the University of Iowa, Lynds started her career as a reporter at *The Arizona Republic*. A former editor of *Santa Barbara Magazine*, she once held top secret securi- ty clearance as an editor at a classified think tank. Lynds lives with her Edgar award-winning husband, Dennis Lynds, a.k.a. Michael Collins et al, in Santa Barbara, California.

Sarah Walker & Liz Sansborough...CIA agents

❑ ❑ 1 - Masquerade (1996)
❑ ❑ 2 - "M" (2000)
❑ ❑ . . . .
❑ ❑ . . . .

■ LYONS, Nan & Ivan

When Nan and Ivan Lyons were looking for something fun to do one summer, they decided to collaborate on a mystery. A professional singer and amateur cook, Nan suggested a detective who liked to cook. Because Ivan was dieting, they chose a dieting character who wanted to murder each of his favorite chefs. Between July Fourth and Labor Day they produced the comedy classic *Someone is Killing the Great Chefs of Europe* (1976), adapted for film as *Who Is Killing the Great Chefs of Europe?* (1978), starring Jacqueline Bisset as dessert queen Natasha O'Brien. *Kirkus* pronounced the sequel, *Someone is Killing the Great Chefs of America* (1993), "déjà vu all over again, as leading chefs about Manhattan begin turning up deboned, roasted and glazed." Other fiction collaborations include *Sold!* (1982), a humorous suspense novel featuring a small-town auctioneer who discovers a trunkful of Faberge masterpieces valued at $20 million, and *The President is Coming to Lunch* (1988). The Lyons have written numerous travel guides.

Natasha O'Brien & Millie Ogden...pair of culinary artists...New York, New York

❑ ❑ 1 - Someone Is Killing the Great Chefs of Europe (1976)
❑ ❑ 2 - Someone Is Killing the Great Chefs of America (1993)
❑ ❑ . . . .
❑ ❑ . . . .

■ MACDONALD, Marianne

After 30 years of college teaching and three academic books on Ezra Pound and literary theory, Marianne Macdonald has turned her attention to literary crime, with a series of bibliomysteries featuring antiquarian bookseller Dido (rhymes with Fido) Hoare and her retired Oxford professor father, Barnabas. Introduced in *Death's Autograph* (1996), the 30-something Dido (named for a princess in Vergil's Aeneid) is a single mother who lives upstairs from her moderately suc- cessful London bookshop. "A charmingly off-beat heroine," pronounced *Kirkus*. After finding the eccen- tric Tom Ashe unconscious on her doorstep, Dido gets drawn into a trail of deceit that stretches back 50 years in *Ghost Walk* (1997). Born in Northern Ontario and educated in Montreal and Toronto, Macdonald went to Oxford for graduate study and has lived in England ever since. The author of two plays and half a dozen children's books, she makes her home in London's Muswell Hill, where she enjoys old movies and walk- ing her very large dogs.

Dido Hoare...single-mother antiquarian bookseller...London, England

❑ ❑ 1 - Death's Autograph (1996)
❑ ❑ 2 - Ghost Walk (1997)
❑ ❑ . . . .
❑ ❑ . . . .

■ MacDOUGAL, Bonnie

Trial attorney Bonnie MacDougal practiced law for 16 years in major firms across the country. Her career took her to Anchorage, Alaska, where she met her hus- band, and Little Rock, Arkansas, where she was one of the few lawyers ever to practice law with Bill Clinton. In Philadelphia she joined a firm of more than 200 attorneys, where she tried a number of high-profile lawsuits, including the cases which inspired her first two novels. *Breach of Trust* (1996) features Jennifer Lodge, a young Jackson, Rieders associate handling a case of fiduciary fraud. Partner Dana Svenssen takes center state in *Angle of Impact* (1998), when a freak helicopter-small plane crash above a popular amusement park results in mass tort litigation. Svenssen plays a supporting role in *Out of Order* (1999), which "finds the author in ripping form," according to *Kirkus*. Shortly after marrying into Wilmington society, divorce lawyer Campbell Smith gets involved with a case of kidnapping and murder that turns her neatly-arranged life upside down.

Jackson, Rieders...large law firm...Philadelphia, Pennsylvania
- ❏ ❏ 1 - Breach of Trust (1996)
- ❏ ❏ 2 - Angle of Impact (1998)
- ❏ ❏ 3 - Out of Order (1999)
- ❏ ❏ . . . .
- ❏ ❏ . . . .

■ MACGREGOR, T.J. [P]

Writing as T.J. MacGregor, Patricia Janeshutz (JANE-shoots) MacGregor is the author of an action-packed private eye series starring Quin St. James and Mike McCleary, husband and wife P.I.s and owners of a South Florida investigations firm. After their Shamus-nominated debut in *Dark Fields* (1986), Quin and Mike make nine more appearances, most recently in *Mistress of the Bones* (1995). "A mix of journal entries, hidden passages, unidentified rustlings and e-mail messages leads Quin and Mike to a breathtaking climax, and an unexpected denouement," said *Publishers Weekly*. In addition to *The Hanged Man* (1998) and *The Seventh Sense* (1999) as T.J. MacGregor, she has also published suspense thrillers as Trish Janeshutz. As Alison Drake she has written the Aline Scott series and the horror novel, *Lagoon* (1990). Born and raised in Caracas, Venezuela, she lives in South Florida with her husband, writer Rob MacGregor. A former social worker and Spanish teacher, MacGregor is a professional astrologer.

Quin St. James & Mike McCleary...wife & husband P.I. team...Florida
- ❏ ❏ 1 - **Dark Fields (1986) Shamus nominee** ☆
- ❏ ❏ 2 - Kill Flash (1987)
- ❏ ❏ 3 - Death Sweet (1988)
- ❏ ❏ 4 - On Ice (1989)
- ❏ ❏ 5 - Kin Dread (1990)
- ❏ ❏ 6 - Death Flats (1991)
- ❏ ❏ 7 - Spree (1992)
- ❏ ❏ 8 - Storm Surge (1993)
- ❏ ❏ 9 - Blue Pearl (1994)
- ❏ ❏ 10 - Mistress of the Bones (1995)
- ❏ ❏ . . . .
- ❏ ❏ . . . .

■ MACKAY, Amanda [P]

Writing as Amanda MacKay, Amanda Joan MacKay Smith is the author of two mysteries featuring college professor Hannah Land, a mild-mannered and slightly-bookish sleuth, who makes her first appearance in *Death Is Academic* (1976). Armed with a recent Ph.D. in political science, Hannah has left New York after a divorce, to take a job at Duke University where she meets charming Durham police lieutenant Bobby Gene Jenkins. Hannah's predicament in book 2, *Death on the Eno* (1981), gives new meaning to the term "armchair detective." After a suspicious boating accident, Hannah spends the major part of the book in a body cast to the waist. "Her role, as she recuperates, is as catalyst and observer," notes Kathleen L. Maio in *1001 Midnights* (1986). "The pace is slow and quiet." When *Death on the Eno* was published in the U.K. in 1983, it appeared as *Death on the River*. A native of Virginia, Mackay lives in Durham, North Carolina, according to Hubin's *Crime Fiction III*.

Hannah Land...divorced New York PhD...Durham, North Carolina
- ❏ ❏ 1 - Death Is Academic (1976)
- ❏ ❏ 2 - Death on the Eno (1981)
- ❏ ❏ - Brit.-Death on the River
- ❏ ❏ . . . .
- ❏ ❏ . . . .

■ MacLEOD, Charlotte

Author of more than 45 novels for adults and juveniles, Charlotte MacLeod has created two New England mystery series under her own name. Her Nero Wolfe award-winning Peter Shandy series stars the professor and his librarian wife, Helen, in ten books featuring Balaclava Agricultural College. The professor is world renowned for developing a hybrid rutabaga, the Balaclava Buster. Her 12-book Sarah Kelling series features blue-blooded Sarah and her quirky Boston family, along with Sarah's investigator husband Max. Writing as Alisa Craig, MacLeod produced two shorter series set in Canada. Her biography of Mary Roberts Rinehart, *Had She But Known*, was published in 1994. Born in New Brunswick, Canada, MacLeod lived for many years in the Boston area, where she spent 30 years in advertising. Sadly for her many fans, MacLeod has Alzheimer's disease and has retired to a nursing home in Maine. She was recognized with a lifetime achievement award from Malice Domestic in 1998.

Peter Shandy & Helen Marsh Shandy
…botany professor & librarian wife…Balaclava Co., Massachusetts

- ❏ ❏ 1 - Rest You Merry (1978)
- ❏ ❏ 2 - The Luck Runs Out (1979)
- ❏ ❏ 3 - Wrack and Rune (1982)
- ❏ ❏ 4 - Something the Cat Dragged In (1983)
- ❏ ❏ 5 - The Curse of the Giant Hogweed (1985)
- ❏ ❏ 6 - **The Corpse in Oozak's Pond (1986) Nero Wolfe winner ★ Edgar nominee ☆**
- ❏ ❏ 7 - Vane Pursuit (1989)
- ❏ ❏ 8 - **An Owl Too Many (1991) Agatha nominee ☆**
- ❏ ❏ 9 - Something in the Water (1994)
- ❏ ❏ 10 - Exit the Milkman (1996)
- ❏ ❏ . . . .
- ❏ ❏ . . . .

Sarah Kelling & Max Bittersohn…investigative couple…Boston, Massachusetts

- ❏ ❏ 1 - The Family Vault (1979)
- ❏ ❏ 2 - The Withdrawing Room (1980)
- ❏ ❏ 3 - The Palace Guard (1981)
- ❏ ❏ 4 - The Bilbao Looking Glass (1983)
- ❏ ❏ 5 - The Convivial Codfish (1984)
- ❏ ❏ 6 - The Plain Old Man (1985)
- ❏ ❏ 7 - The Recycled Citizen (1987)
- ❏ ❏ 8 - The Silver Ghost (1987)
- ❏ ❏ 9 - The Gladstone Bag (1989)
- ❏ ❏ 10 - The Resurrection Man (1992)
- ❏ ❏ 11 - The Odd Job (1995)
- ❏ ❏ 12 - The Balloon Man (1998)
- ❏ ❏ . . . .
- ❏ ❏ . . . .

■ MacPHERSON, Rett [P]

When Lauretta Allen needed a pseudonym for her genealogical mysteries, the choice of Rett MacPherson was an easy one. Nicknamed Rett, she had always liked the sound of MacPherson, one of the many names on her half-Scots, half-French family tree. Her three novels feature genealogist Victory (Torie) O'Shea, resident historian and tour guide in New Kassel, Missouri, a fictional blend of the Mississippi River towns of Kimmswick, Ste. Genevieve and Hermann. A 30-something wife and mother of two pre-schoolers, Torie is hired to research a local woman's family tree, only to have the client turn up dead in the series opener, *Family Skeletons* (1997). While planning for Christmas and the annual family reunion in book 3, *A Comedy of Heirs* (1999), Torie discovers something strange about her great-grandfather's death. An avid quilter and antique-hunter, Allen is a native St. Louisan addicted to genealogy. She works for a St. Louis wholesale book company and lives in the suburbs with her husband and two children.

Torie O'Shea...historian-genealogist-tour guide...New Kassel, Missouri

- ❏ ❏ 1 - Family Skeletons (1997)
- ❏ ❏ 2 - A Veiled Antiquity (1998)
- ❏ ❏ . . . .
- ❏ ❏ . . . .

■ MAIMAN, Jaye

Lambda award winner Jaye Maiman (MAY-man) writes mysteries featuring Robin Miller, a New York City travel writer and romance novelist turned private investigator. Introduced in *I Left My Heart* (1991), Robin travels to San Francisco to investigate the suspicious death of her estranged lover, investigative reporter Mary Oswell. Back in New York for book 2, Robin is being groomed to take over a detective agency in *Crazy for Loving* (1992), winner of the Lambda award for best lesbian mystery. She's hot on the trail of a sultry singer and con artist in book 4, *Someone To Watch* (1995), where "the writing is crisp, the action taut, and the denouement a near hysterical nail-biter," raved *Booklist*. Robin's seventh song-titled case is *Every Time We Say Goodbye* (1999). Born and raised in Brooklyn, Maiman holds a B.A. from Brooklyn College and has done graduate study at the University of Virginia. She shares her Halloween birthday with mystery authors Janet Dawson, Dick Francis, H.R.F. Keating and Don Winslow.

Robin Miller...lesbian travel & romance writer turned P.I....New York, New York

- ❏ ❏ 1 - I Left My Heart (1991)
- ❏ ❏ **2 - Crazy for Loving (1992) Lambda winner ★**
- ❏ ❏ 3 - Under My Skin (1993)
- ❏ ❏ 4 - Someone To Watch (1995)
- ❏ ❏ 5 - Baby It's Cold (1996)
- ❏ ❏ 6 - Old Black Magic (1997)
- ❏ ❏ . . . .
- ❏ ❏ . . . .

■ MALMONT, Valerie S.

Valerie S. Malmont is the author of two mysteries featuring New York novelist Tori Miracle, who gets involved with murder while visiting her friend Alice-Ann in Lickin Creek, Pennsylvania, light years away from The Big Apple, in *Death Pays the Rose Rent* (1994). Tori returns to Lickin Creek for a week's vacation in *Death, Lies, and Apple Pies* (1997), hoping to rekindle a romance with the town's good-looking police chief. A librarian like her mother, Malmont worked in Washington, Virginia, Pennsylvania and Taiwan, before settling in Chambersburg, Pennsylvania, an area much like the one Tori Miracle likes to visit. "My mother and I were on the first boatload of American families to arrive on Okinawa after World War II," says Malmont, whose father was in charge of reorganizing the Ryukuan Police Department. Malmont later lived in Vientianne, Laos. An anthropology graduate of the University of New Mexico, she earned her master's degree in library science from the University of Washington.

Tori Miracle...crime writer turned novelist...Lickin Creek, Pennsylvania

- ❏ ❏ 1 - Death Pays the Rose Rent (1994)
- ❏ ❏ 2 - Death, Lies and Apple Pies (1997)
- ❏ ❏ . . . .
- ❏ ❏ . . . .

■ MANEY, Mabel

Mixed-media artist Mabel Maney lampoons girls' fiction of the 1950s with her Nancy Clue series featuring "hapless, do-gooding detectives with keen sleuthing abilities, up-to-the-minute fashion sense and gracious finishing school manners." *The Case of the Not-So-Nice Nurse* (1993) is "shriekingly funny, wonderfully wry and a not-bad mystery," raved *Booklist*. Maney's installation art frequently takes the form of bookshelf books, some as large as 40 feet long, made of '50s linen and curtain fabric, and some as small as one-inch boxes. Her handmade books, self-published as World O'Girls Books, earned her several fellowships, including one from San Francisco State University where she earned her M.F.A. in 1991. Born into a working class Irish-Catholic family in Appleton, Wisconsin, Maney grew up in Ohio where she later earned a bachelor's degree from Ohio State University with a concentration in film. She has lived in San Francisco since the late 1980s, where she is working on a book project for a major publisher.

Nancy Clue...gay-lesbian Nancy Drew parody...River Depths, Illinois
- ❑ ❑ 1 - The Case of the Not-So-Nice Nurse (1993)
- ❑ ❑ 2 - The Case of the Good-for-Nothing Girlfriend (1994)
- ❑ ❑ 3 - The Ghost in the Closet (1995)
- ❑ ❑ . . . .
- ❑ ❑ . . . .

■ MANN, Jessica

Educated at Cambridge where she studied archaeology and Anglo-Saxon, Jessica Mann earned her law degreee at the University of Leicester. Among her 15 crime novels are at least eight featuring archaeologist sleuths, Professor Thea Crawford and her student Tamara Hoyland. Later recruited to work as a Department E spy, Hoyland uses her archaeological work as a cover for her intelligence work. In the bibliomystery *Grave Goods* (1984), Hoyland discovers that the East German national art collection, on its way to London for a ground-breaking cultural exchange, contains the fake Crown jewels of Charlemagne. Mann's nonfiction book, *Deadlier Than the Male: An Investigation into Feminine Crime Writing* (1981), analyzes the work of Agatha Christie, Dorothy L. Sayers and others. Mann's observations about the authors' lives and personalities include her assessment of why these writers continue to appeal to modern readers. A respected critic for the BBC, Mann was born in London and lives in Cornwall, England.

Tamara Hoyland...British secret agent archaeologist...England
- ❑ ❑ 1 - Funeral Sites (1982)
- ❑ ❑ 2 - No Man's Island (1983)
- ❑ ❑ 3 - Grave Goods (1984)
- ❑ ❑ 4 - A Kind of Healthy Grave (1986)
- ❑ ❑ 5 - Death Beyond the Nile (1988)
- ❑ ❑ 6 - Faith, Hope and Homicide (1991)
- ❑ ❑ . . . .
- ❑ ❑ . . . .

Thea Crawford...archaeology professor...England
- ❑ ❑ 1 - The Only Security (1972)
- ❑ ❑   - U.S.-Troublecross
- ❑ ❑ 2 - Captive Audience (1975)
- ❑ ❑ . . . .
- ❑ ❑ . . . .

■ MANTHORNE, Jackie

After writing five mysteries featuring a Montreal lesbian sleuth, Jackie Manthorne launches a Toronto series featuring lesbian P.I. Elizabeth Ellis, introduced in Phantom of *Queen Street* (2000). "Manthorne knows how to keep the action moving and she never lets the dialogue sink to polemic," said Canada's *Globe and Mail* about Harriet Hubbley's first Montreal adventure in *Ghost Motel* (1994). Known to her friends as Harry, the intrepid lesbian is en route to a Provincetown vacation when she seeks refuge from a storm in a deserted motel. The author of two short story collections, *Without Wings* (1993) and *Fascination and Other Bar Stories* (1991), Manthorne is the editor of *Canadian Women and A.I.D.S.: Beyond the Statistics* (1990). Raised in Nova Scotia, she lived in Montreal for almost 20 years before moving to Toronto, where she worked as an administrator for the Royal Canadian Academy of Arts. A former junior high school teacher and owner of a Montreal feminist press, Maney has recently moved to Ottawa.

Elizabeth Ellis...lesbian private eye...Toronto, Ontario, Canada
- ❑ ❑ 1 - Phantom of Queen Street (2000)
- ❑ ❑ . . . .
- ❑ ❑ . . . .

Harriet Hubbley...intrepid lesbian sleuth...Montreal, Quebec, Canada
- ❑ ❑ 1 - Ghost Motel (1994)
- ❑ ❑ 2 - Deadly Reunion (1995)

❑	❑	3 - Last Resort (1995)
❑	❑	4 - Final Take (1996)
❑	❑	5 - Sudden Death (1997)
❑	❑	. . . .
❑	❑	. . . .

■ MARACOTTA, Lindsay

Hollywood script doctor Lindsay Maracotta writes "delightfully sharp-clawed page-turners" narrated by Lucy Freers, an award-winning animator of children's films who has it all—the requisite mansion, a successful movie producer husband, a whip-smart nine-year-old daughter, and a hunky male nanny. After being suspected in the swimming pool death of a glamorous neighbor in *The Dead Hollywood Moms Society* (1996), Lucy knows her husband is among the suspects when his film's director is murdered in *The Dead Celeb* (1997).

Researching the world of child actors for book 3, *Playing Dead* (1999), Maracotta went undercover auditioning for commercials with several highly competitive tots. Her earlier novels include *Everything We Wanted* (1986) and *Hide-and-Seek* (1982). In addition to working as a screenwriter and television producer, she has written for such stars as Goldie Hawn, Jessica Lange and Robert Redford. Maracotta lives in Los Angeles with her film consultant husband.

Lucy Freers...children's film animator...Los Angeles, California

❑	❑	1 - The Dead Hollywood Moms Society (1996)
❑	❑	- Brit.-Turnaround...You're Dead
❑	❑	2 - The Dead Celeb (1997)
❑	❑	. . . .
❑	❑	. . . .

■ MARCY, Jean [P]

Jean Marcy is the joint pseudonym of Jean Hutchinson and Marcy Jacobs for their St. Louis series featuring lonely, single, working-class lesbian private investigator Meg Darcy, introduced in *Cemetery Murders* (1997). The dyke P.I. crosses paths with aloof police detective Sarah Lindstrom in a St. Louis cemetery where a serial killer has been leaving the bodies of homeless women propped up against tombstones. Conflict and competition dominate as Darcy and Lindstrom race to unmask the killer. "A rousing good read," pronounced *Midwest*

Book Review, calling Marcy's first novel "one of those mysteries spiced with tension and flavored with colorful characters." When detective Lindstrom finds her ex-lover bludgeoned to death in *Dead and Blonde* (1998), it turns out Lindstrom was the intended victim. P.I. Darcy rushes in to offer protection. A "promisingly grisly murder...lots of clue gathering, and a rousing chase—on foot through a crowded produce market at dawn," said *Booklist*. Hutchinson and Jacobs live near St. Louis.

Meg Darcy...blue-collar lesbian private eye...St. Louis, Missouri

❑	❑	1 - Cemetery Murders (1997)
❑	❑	2 - Dead and Blonde (1998)
❑	❑	. . . .
❑	❑	. . . .

■ MARIZ, Linda French

Linda French Mariz has written two mysteries featuring Laura Ireland, a former Olympic volleyball star working on a Ph.D. in anthropology in Washington state. The character of Laura is modeled after Mariz's six-foot-tall sister who played five college sports, women's professional basketball, and worked out for eight months with the Olympic volleyball team. After her brush with an Indian artifact smuggling ring in *Body English* (1992), Laura accompanies her police detective boyfriend to Louisiana in *Snake Dance*

(1992), where he is framed for the murder of the local sheriff. Mariz writes the Teddy Morelli mysteries under the name Linda French. A former Georgia state backstroke record-holder, Mariz works out daily with a local swim team and recently purchased a black rubber wetsuit for swimming in Puget Sound. Born in New Orleans and raised in Atlanta, she has lived in the Pacific Northwest for 20 years. Trained in American history, she has worked as a college instructor, grants administrator and creative writing teacher.

Laura Ireland...grad student volleyball player...Seattle, Washington

- ❑ ❑   1 - Body English (1992)
- ❑ ❑   2 - Snake Dance (1992)
- ❑ ❑   . . . .
- ❑ ❑   . . . .

■ MARON, Margaret

Margaret Maron's 14 series mysteries feature two very different lead characters—New York cop, Lt. Sigrid Harald, and North Carolina judge, Deborah Knott. After winning an Agatha award for best short story with "Deborah's Judgment," Maron swept the field the following year with *Bootlegger's Daughter* (1992), winning Agatha, Anthony, Edgar and Macavity awards for best novel. One year later, Maron picked up Agatha and Anthony best-novel nominations for *Southern Discomfort* (1993). After a four-year gap between books seven and eight, Maron's New York cop returned in *Fugitive Colors* (1995). Although the eight-book series spans 14 years in Maron's life, just one incredible year passes in the fictional life of Sigrid Harald. Twenty-two of Maron's short stories, including all the short cases of Lt. Harald and Judge Knott, are available in *Shoveling Smoke* (1997). A North Carolina native, Maron lived for many years in Brooklyn, New York. A past president of Sisters in Crime, she is back on the family homestead in North Carolina.

Deborah Knott...district judge...North Carolina

- ❑ ❑   1 - **Bootlegger's Daughter (1992) Agatha, Anthony, Edgar & Macavity winner ★★★★**
- ❑ ❑   2 - **Southern Discomfort (1993) Agatha & Anthony nominee ☆☆**
- ❑ ❑   3 - Shooting at Loons (1994)
- ❑ ❑   4 - **Up Jumps the Devil (1996) Agatha winner ★**
- ❑ ❑   5 - Killer Market (1997)
- ❑ ❑   6 - Home Fires (1998)
- ❑ ❑   . . . .
- ❑ ❑   . . . .

Sigrid Harald...police lieutenant...New York, New York

- ❑ ❑   1 - One Coffee With (1981)
- ❑ ❑   2 - Death of a Butterfly (1984)
- ❑ ❑   3 - Death in Blue Folders (1985)
- ❑ ❑   4 - The Right Jack (1987)
- ❑ ❑   5 - Baby Doll Games (1988)
- ❑ ❑   6 - **Corpus Christmas (1989) Agatha & Anthony nominee ☆☆**
- ❑ ❑   7 - Past Imperfect (1991)
- ❑ ❑   8 - Fugitive Colors (1995)
- ❑ ❑   . . . .
- ❑ ❑   . . . .

■ MARTIN, Allana

new

Allana Martin's first novel introduces trading-post owner Texana Jones, who lives on the Mexican border in El Polvo, Texas, with her veterinarian husband Clay. Winner of the Medicine Pipe Bearer's award from Western Writers of America for best first western novel, *Death of a Healing Woman* (1996) centers around the deaths of two of Texana's best friends and that of an old recluse and curandera, or healing woman. Authorities think the killings are random, but Texana thinks otherwise. "A persuasive portrait of bicultural life along a vibrant, violent border," said *Kirkus*. After discovering the body of a carver of wooden saints, Texana becomes embroiled in a murder investigation that involves traveling photographers, a passionate environmentalist and a Mexican arms dealer in book 2, *Death of a Saint Maker* (1997). An out of control brush fire in Mexico jumps the Rio Grande and threatens the tiny community of Polvo in book 4, *Death of a Mythmaker* (2000). A native Texan, Martin lives in Lipan, Texas.

Texana Jones...desert trading post owner...El Povo, Texas

- ❑ ❑   1 - Death of a Healing Woman (1996)
- ❑ ❑   2 - Death of a Saint Maker (1998)
- ❑ ❑   3 - Death of an Evangelista (1999)
- ❑ ❑   . . . .
- ❑ ❑   . . . .

■ MARTIN, Lee [P]

In a 1985 *New York Times Book Review* feature on women mystery writers, Marilyn Stasio singled out Lee Martin and Martha G. Webb as "two of the most promising new authors in the field who have produced crime novels out of their personal experience as police officers." Stasio added that while both women write persuasively, "they approach the character of the female police detective from dramatically different angles." Knowing that she was both Lee Martin and Martha G. Webb, Texas police officer Anne Wingate must have been delighted. Quick to note

that she did not base her plots on personal police experience, Wingate instead used incidents from her own life. "When you read about the reason Deb Ralston wears a shoulder holster, you're reading about why I wore a shoulder holster," says Wingate. During 13 series installments, Deb Ralston juggles police work with a trio of adopted children of differing ethnicity, and a husband who works full time while completing a graduate degree. Wingate lives in Salt Lake City, Utah.

Deb Ralston...police detective mom...Fort Worth, Texas
- ❏ ❏   1 - Too Sane a Murder (1984)
- ❏ ❏   2 - A Conspiracy of Strangers (1986)
- ❏ ❏   3 - Death Warmed Over (1988)
- ❏ ❏   4 - Murder at the Blue Owl (1988)
- ❏ ❏   5 - Hal's Own Murder Case (1989)
- ❏ ❏   6 - Deficit Ending (1990)
- ❏ ❏   7 - The Mensa Murders (1990)
- ❏ ❏   8 - Hacker (1992)
- ❏ ❏   9 - The Day That Dusty Died (1993)
- ❏ ❏ 10 - Inherited Murder (1994)
- ❏ ❏ 11 - Bird in a Cage (1995)
- ❏ ❏ 12 - Genealogy of Murder (1996)
- ❏ ❏ 13 - The Thursday Club (1997)
- ❏ ❏ ....
- ❏ ❏ ....

■ MASON, Sarah J.

Sarah J. Mason published 20 mysteries during the 1990s, including six featuring "the oddest partners ever to trample a country road," Detective Superintendent Trewley and his female detective sergeant, a former medical student with a black belt in judo. The newly-formed partnership cracks their first case in *Murder in the Maze* (1993), when Dr. Radlett's lovely young wife is found murdered in the center of a hedge maze during the village's annual summer festival. Mason has also written a nonseries mystery, *Let's Talk*

of Wills (1985). Writing as Hamilton Crane, she is the author of 14 installments (books 9-22) in the Miss Seeton series which began in 1968. While researching her final Miss Seeton mystery, set in 1940, Mason became fascinated with her father's wartime career in the Royal Navy. She is currently working with the son of her father's commanding officer, who has inherited his father's unpublished memoirs. Mason lives with her husband and their two Schipperke dogs outside London.

Trewley & Stone...village Det. Supt. & female sergeant...Plummergen, Kent, England
- ❏ ❏ 1 - Murder in the Maze (1993)
- ❏ ❏ 2 - Frozen Stiff (1993)
- ❏ ❏ 3 - Corpse in the Kitchen (1993)
- ❏ ❏ 4 - Dying Breath (1994)
- ❏ ❏ 5 - Sew Easy To Kill (1996)
- ❏ ❏ 6 - Seeing Is Deceiving (1997)
- ❏ ❏ ....
- ❏ ❏ ....

■ MASSEY, Sujata

Agatha award winner Sujata Massey was born in Sussex, England to an Indian father and German mother who emigrated to the United States when she

was five. Raised in Philadelphia, Berkeley and St. Paul, Massey lived for two years in Japan, where she taught English, studied Japanese, and took classes in cooking and flower-arranging. Her English-style mysteries, set in modern Japan, feature the first-person voice of 27-year-old Rei Shimura, a California-raised Japanese-American English teacher and antiques dealer, introduced in *The Salaryman's Wife* (1997). "A nearly pitch-perfect voice in modern-day Japan," raved the *Japan Times*. Winner of the Agatha award for best first novel and a *People* magazine Page-Turner of the Week, Massey's first novel was also nominated for Anthony and Macavity awards. After graduating from Johns Hopkins University, Massey spent five years as a features reporter for the now-defunct *Baltimore Evening Sun*. She lives in Baltimore with her physician husband and their two-year-old daughter Pia.

Rei Shimura...Japanese-American antiques dealer...Tokyo, Japan

- ❏ ❏ 1 - **The Salaryman's Wife (1997) Agatha winner ★**
  Anthony and Macavity nominee ☆☆
- ❏ ❏ 2 - Zen Attitude (1998)
- ❏ ❏ 3 - The Flower Master (1999)
- ❏ ❏ . . . .
- ❏ ❏ . . . .

■ MASTERS, Priscilla

Priscilla Masters writes contemporary police procedurals set in the real village of Leek, in the midst of the Staffordshire moorlands of northwest England. Her "cleverly-constructed and tight plots" feature Detective Inspector Joanna Piercy and her half-Polish body-builder sergeant, Mike Korpanski. An independent-thinking "feminine feminist" who enjoys cycling and her married pathologist boyfriend, D.I. Piercy is introduced in *Winding Up the Serpent* (1995). When last seen in book 5, *Scaring Crows* (1999), Joanna has a case of murder-suicide that is starting to look like a double murder. A farmer and his son are found dead in their stone farmhouse, with an abandoned shotgun by the front door. D.I. Piercy is confounded by the news that the farmer has a daughter who seems to have vanished. Masters' medical thriller, *Night Visit* (1998), features a woman doctor threatened and manipulated by her patients. Masters works part-time as a nurse and lives in Yorkshire with her physician husband and their two teenage sons.

Joanna Piercy...detective inspector...Leek, Staffordshire, England

- ❏ ❏ 1 - Winding Up the Serpent (1995)
- ❏ ❏ 2 - Catch the Fallen Sparrow (1996)
- ❏ ❏ 3 - A Wreath for My Sister (1997)
- ❏ ❏ 4 - And None Shall Sleep (1997)
- ❏ ❏ 5 - Scaring Crows (1999)
- ❏ ❏ . . . .
- ❏ ❏ . . . .

■ MATERA, Lia

Two-time Edgar nominee and former practicing attorney Lia Matera launched her mystery-writing career with the murder of a law review editor and a professor in *Where Lawyers Fear To Tread* (1987). Matera's first novel introduced then-law-student Willa Jansson, "among the most articulate and surely the wittiest of amateur sleuths," said the *New York Times Review of Books*. The daughter of aging-but-still-active Berkeley radicals, Willa was last seen in book 7, *Havana Twist* (1998), where she travels to Cuba in search of her missing grey-haired brigadista mother. Matera's second series featuring Laura Di Palma is darker by comparison. The dragon defense attorney with a paid-for Mercedes and a high-profile life was last seen in book 5, *Designer Crimes* (1995). A fellow lawyer dies in her arms and a bullet that strikes the D.A. was surely intended for Laura. Editor of the *Constitutional Law Review* at Hastings College of Law and a former teaching fellow at Stanford Law School, the Canadian-born Matera lives in Santa Cruz, California.

Laura Di Palma...high-profile attorney...San Francisco, California

- ❏ ❏ 1 - The Smart Money (1988)
- ❏ ❏ 2 - **The Good Fight (1990) Anthony & Macavity nominee ☆☆**
- ❏ ❏ 3 - A Hard Bargain (1992)

❏ ❏   4 - Face Value (1994)
❏ ❏   5 - Designer Crimes (1995)
❏ ❏   . . . .
❏ ❏   . . . .

Willa Jansson...Red diaper baby turned attorney...San Francisco, California
❏ ❏   1 - **Where Lawyers Fear To Tread (1987) Anthony & Macavity nominee** ☆☆
❏ ❏   2 - **A Radical Departure (1988) Anthony & Edgar nominee** ☆☆
❏ ❏   3 - Hidden Agenda (1989)
❏ ❏   4 - **Prior Convictions (1991) Edgar nominee** ☆
❏ ❏   5 - Last Chants (1996)
❏ ❏   6 - Star Witness (1997)
❏ ❏   7 - Havana Twist (1998)
❏ ❏   . . . .
❏ ❏   . . . .

■ MATHER, Linda [P]

Linda Mather is the pseudonym of Linda Ainsbury for her three-book zodiac series featuring professional astrologer Jo Hughes, who works part-time for an investigations agency in England. When Jo starts making connections between the horoscopes of murder victims in the series opener, *Blood of an Aries* (1993), she finds herself on the trail of a vicious serial killer. When last seen in book 3, *Gemini Doublecross* (1995), Jo has been hired to act as a minder for Antonia Carlyle, a woman deathly afraid of her boss, Oliver Sargent. The very jumpy Antonia is convinced that Sargent killed her sister many years ago and now intends to kill her. Jo is initially skeptical, but when Antonia's worst fears are realized, Jo is left with a heavy conscience and the task of proving that a calculating killer is on the loose. *Blood of an Aries* was published in both the U.K. and the U.S., but *Beware Taurus* was released only in England. A large print edition of *Gemini Doublecross* is available in the U.S.

Jo Hughes...astrologer-investigator...England
❏ ❏   1 - Blood of an Aries (1993)
❏ ❏   2 - Beware Taurus (1994)
❏ ❏   3 - Gemini Doublecross (1995)
❏ ❏   . . . .
❏ ❏   . . . .

■ MATHEWS, Francine

In the days when Francine Mathews was working as an intelligence analyst for the C.I.A., she would lose herself at night in the calm of Nantucket Island, disturbed only by the murders she plotted for Detective Meredith Folger to solve. The only woman on the force and daughter of the police chief, Merry spends much of her time proving to her father and herself that she has what it takes to do the job. Called home from a December vacation by Chief Folger in book 4, *Death in a Cold Hard Light* (1998), Merry wrestles with the death of a young Harvard scholar turned scalloper. While growing up in Washington, D.C., Mathews summered on Cape Cod and Nantucket and tries to get back every year. To stay current, she subscribes to a Nantucket newspaper. A graduate of Princeton and Stanford universities, Mathews lives in Colorado where she writes a Regency series as Stephanie (her middle name) Barron (her maiden name). Her espionage thriller featuring a female C.I.A. analyst is scheduled for 2000 publication.

Meredith Folger...police detective...Nantucket, Massachusetts
❏ ❏   1 - Death in the Off-Season (1994)
❏ ❏   2 - Death in Rough Water (1995)
❏ ❏   3 - Death in a Mood Indigo (1997)
❏ ❏   4 - Death in a Cold Hard Light (1998)
❏ ❏   . . . .
❏ ❏   . . . .

■ MATTESON, Stefanie

Stefanie Matteson is the author of eight mysteries starring Charlotte Graham, the Oscar-winning actress of film and stage introduced in *Murder at the Spa* (1990). "A cross between Elizabeth Taylor, Katharine Hepburn, and Miss Marple, Charlotte Graham is a charming heroine," said the *Baltimore Sun*. When last seen in *Murder Under the Palms* (1997), Charlotte is vacationing in Palm Beach, Florida, catching up with old friends and renewing a romance of 50 years past. When a prominent local jeweler is found murdered at a gala celebration aboard the famous French ocean liner *Normandie*, Charlotte's friends become suspects and she is quickly drawn into the case. "Charlotte is as acute and enchanting as ever in this intricate, deftly worked mystery," said *Publishers Weekly*. After earning a bachelor's degree from Skidmore College, Matteson did graduate study at Boston University. A former reporter and editor for a suburban New Jersey daily, she lives with her husband and two children in Mendham, New Jersey.

Charlotte Graham...Oscar-winning actress...New York, New York

- ❏ ❏ 1 - Murder at the Spa (1990)
- ❏ ❏ 2 - Murder on the Cliff (1991)
- ❏ ❏ 3 - Murder at Teatime (1991)
- ❏ ❏ 4 - Murder on the Silk Road (1992)
- ❏ ❏ 5 - Murder at the Falls (1993)
- ❏ ❏ 6 - Murder on High (1994)
- ❏ ❏ 7 - Murder Among the Angels (1996)
- ❏ ❏ 8 - Murder Under the Palms (1997)
- ❏ ❏ ....
- ❏ ❏ ....

■ MATTHEWS, Alex

Oak Park psychotherapist Alex Matthews writes mysteries featuring 37-year-old Oak Park therapist Cassidy McCabe, introduced in *Secret's Shadow* (1996), where Cassidy finds a calico cat and romance with a client's brother. When one of Cassidy's patients reveals a vision of satanic rituals in the woods, the therapist's investigative reporter boyfriend pushes her to help him look into the matter. "Matthews goes out of her way to create flaws in her heroine, whose interior observations are revealed," said *Publishers Weekly*.

When last seen in book 4, *Wanton's Web* (1999), Cassidy and reporter Zack Moran are about to be married, but not before his "ex-lover, a call-girl named Xandra calls and asks him to watch a teenage son he never knew existed." Like her protagonist, Matthews works from a home office in Oak Park, Illinois. Her therapy practice is a partnership with husband Allen Matthews, undoubtedly the world's largest non-retail purchaser of McCabe's signature candy, Reese's Peanut Butter Cups. The family includes four cats.

Cassidy McCabe...psychotherapist...Oak Park, Illinois

- ❏ ❏ 1 - Secret's Shadow (1996)
- ❏ ❏ 2 - Satan's Silence (1997)
- ❏ ❏ 3 - Vendetta's Victim (1998)
- ❏ ❏ ....
- ❏ ❏ ....

■ MATTHEWS, Patricia

Best known as an author of historical romance, Patricia Matthews made her first writing sale with two poems for the Portland *Oregonian* in 1957. But it wasn't until publication of her best-selling historical romance, *Love's Avenging Heart* (1977), 20 years later that Matthews was able to leave her job, as an office manager at California State University in Los Angeles, to write full time. Individually and with her husband Clayton Matthews, she is the author of 45 novels, including romance, gothic, suspense, horror, fantasy, juvenile mysteries and five adult mysteries featuring Casey Farrel. Introduced in *The Scent of Fear* (1992), Farrel is a member of the Arizona governor's task force on crime. When the bodies of five illegal aliens are found in the desert in *Vision of Death* (1993), Farrel investigates on the governor's behalf and uncovers resistance from people in high places Matthews has also written as P.A. Brisco, Patty Brisco, Patricia Anne Matthews, Laura Wylie and Laurie Wylie. She lives in Prescott, Arizona.

Casey Farrel...governor's crime task force member...Arizona

- ❏ ❏ 1 - The Scent of Fear (1992)
- ❏ ❏ 2 - Vision of Death (1993)
- ❏ ❏ 3 - Taste of Evil (1993)
- ❏ ❏ 4 - The Sound of Murder (1994)
- ❏ ❏ 5 - The Touch of Terror (1995)
- ❏ ❏ . . . .
- ❏ ❏ . . . .

■ MAXWELL, A.E. [P]

Writing together as A.E. Maxwell, Ann and Evan Maxwell have published eight books in their Fiddler and Fiora series, starting with *Just Another Day in Paradise* (1985). Thanks to Uncle Jake's ill-gotten gains and ex-wife Fiora's investment banking genius, Jake is independently wealthy. He is also something of a knight-errant, a throwback to the days when a knight traveled widely in search of adventure, to show off his military skills or engage in deeds of chivalry. In Fiddler's case, such opportunities always find him.

Individually and with her husband, Ann Maxwell has written over 50 novels, with 23 million copies in print in 21 languages. Writing as Elizabeth Lowell, she is a member of the Romance Writers Hall of Fame, with 11 novels on the *New York Times* Bestsellers list, including *Pearl Cove* (1999), her third "riveting mix of suspense and romance" featuring Seattle's powerful Donovan clan. Evan Lowell Maxwell is a former reporter for the *Los Angeles Times*. The Maxwells live in the San Juan Islands of Washington state.

Fiddler & Fiora Flynn...knight-errant & investment banker...Southern California

- ❏ ❏ 1 - Just Another Day in Paradise (1985)
- ❏ ❏ 2 - The Frog and the Scorpion (1986)
- ❏ ❏ 3 - Gatsby's Vineyard (1987)
- ❏ ❏ 4 - Just Enough Light To Kill (1988)
- ❏ ❏ 5 - The Art of Survival (1989)
- ❏ ❏ 6 - Money Burns (1991)
- ❏ ❏ 7 - The King of Nothing (1992)
- ❏ ❏ 8 - Murder Hurts (1993)
- ❏ ❏ . . . .
- ❏ ❏ . . . .

■ McALLESTER, Melanie

Melanie McAllester is the author of two California mysteries featuring half-black, half-Mexican homicide detective Elizabeth (Tenny) Mendoza, a lesbian cop first seen in *The Lessons* (1994). The case of a serial rapist assaulting Bay Area lesbians is linked with similar crimes in Southern California and Mendoza finds herself teamed with two detectives from another department. Rookie Ashley Johnson, a young lesbian, has only two years on the street, and homophobic sexual assault detective Steve Carlton has a serious

attitude problem. "A good inside look at how investigations are handled and how detectives deal with one another and department brass," said Don Kazak in *Criminal Intent*. "The voice that emerges most clearly is the author's and her deeply held conviction that communication and cooperation can triumph over fear and violence," said *Publishers Weekly*. At the time her first mystery was published, McAllester was an experienced officer with the Palo Alto Police Department, near San Francisco.

Elizabeth Mendoza...Hispanic-black lesbian homicide detective...San Francisco, California

- ❏ ❏ 1 - The Lessons (1994)
- ❏ ❏ 2 - The Search (1996)
- ❏ ❏ . . . .
- ❏ ❏ . . . .

■ McCAFFERTY, Barbara Taylor and Beverly Taylor Herald

Barbara Taylor McCafferty and Beverly Taylor Herald write mysteries about identical twin sisters, Bert and Nan Tatum, named for the Bobbsey Twins, introduced

in *Double Murder* (1996). Identical twins themselves, the sisters alternate chapters between straight-laced Bert, a recently-divorced mother of college kids, and her single sister Nan, a country and western disc jockey. "The real charm here is the exploration of the special bond between twins," said *Booklist*. Beverly typically writes the first draft and Barbara the last. If pressed, they will admit that Barbara is a lot like Bert, while Beverly favors Nan. After switching places with dire consequences in *Double Cross* (1998), the twins return in book 4, *Double Dealer* (2000). Barbara writes a second series as Taylor McCafferty and a third as Tierney McClellan. With degrees in journalism and biology, Beverly worked previously as a Louisville police department secretary, a radio news reporter and T.V. talk show host. She lives with her radio announcer husband in Slaughters, Kentucky.

Bert & Nan Tatum...identical twin sisters...Louisville, Kentucky

- ❑ ❑ 1 - Double Murder (1996)
- ❑ ❑ 2 - Double Exposure (1997)
- ❑ ❑ 3 - Double Cross (1998)
- ❑ ❑ . . . .
- ❑ ❑ . . . .

■ McCAFFERTY, Jeanne

Jeanne McCafferty is the author of three mysteries featuring criminal psychologist and police consultant Mackenzie Griffin, introduced in *Star Gazer* (1994). When a serial killer begins targeting victims who resemble popular singer Peter Rossellini, Griffin is hired to help figure out who among the star's friends, ex-friends and fanatical fans wants him dead. Murder scenes have never looked this good. The lighting and staging, the arrangement of the body, even the victims' clothing are recreations of Rossellini's hottest videos. When last seen in *Finales and Overtures* (1996), Dr. Griffin has been asked by new friend, Sylvie Morgan, to find a killer in her New York theatre company. Sylvie's about to open in a big musical, but she's the chief suspect in a cast member's murder. While the series opener was published in both the U.S. and the U.K., books 2 and 3 were released only in England. A music industry insider who has worked in New York and Los Angeles, McCafferty lives in North Hollywood, California.

Mackenzie Griffin...consulting criminal psychologist...New York, New York

- ❑ ❑ 1 - Star Gazer (1994)
- ❑ ❑ 2 - Artist Unknown (1995)
- ❑ ❑ 3 - Finales and Overtures (1996)
- ❑ ❑ . . . .
- ❑ ❑ . . . .

■ McCAFFERTY, Taylor [P]

Taylor McCafferty is Barbara Taylor McCafferty, who set her sights on a writing career at the age of eight, graduated magna cum laude with a degree in fine art from the University of Louisville, and worked as an art director and advertising copywriter before turning to mystery writing. McCafferty writes two series set in Kentucky, one with a male private eye, the other a middle-aged woman selling real estate. The only P.I. in Pigeon Fork, Howdy Doody look-alike Haskell Blevins is introduced in the "wickedly delightful" and "downright hilarious" *Pet Peeves* (1990). After a five-year absence, Blevins returns in book 6, *Funny Money* (2000). McCafferty's real estate series, written pseudonymously as Tierney McClellan, features 40-something Schuyler Ridgway of Louisville, Kentucky. As one half of mystery fiction's first twin-sister act, McCafferty collaborates with Beverly Taylor Herald on a series featuring twin sisters, Bert and Nan Tatum, introduced in *Double Murder* (1996). McCafferty lives in Lebanon Junction, Kentucky.

Haskell Blevins...small-town private eye...Pigeon Fork, Kentucky

- ❑ ❑ 1 - Pet Peeves (1990)
- ❑ ❑ 2 - Ruffled Feathers (1992)
- ❑ ❑ 3 - Bed Bugs (1992)
- ❑ ❑ 4 - Thin Skins (1994)
- ❑ ❑ 5 - Hanky Panky (1995)
- ❑ ❑ 6 - Funny Money (2000)
- ❑ ❑ . . . .
- ❑ ❑ . . . .

■ McCLELLAN, Janet

Janet McClellan started her criminal justice career as a 19-year-old undercover narcotics investigator, and over the past 20 years has worked as a homicide detective, corrections administrator, college professor and police chief. She writes mysteries featuring lesbian Kansas City police detective Tru North, introduced in *K.C. Bomber* (1997), where a serial bomber is sending beautifully-crafted exploding gift-boxes. When last seen in book 4, *Chimney Rock Blues* (1999), Tru has a case taken from the author's personal experience as a young officer in a Wyoming boom town. In book 5, *Spider on the Web* (2000), Tru enters the world of online chat rooms to catch a predator. Author of the lesbian romance, *Window Garden* (1998), McClellan is working on another, *Like Day and Knight*, set at Kansas City's Renaissance Festival. Raised on a farm near Leavenworth, Kansas, where her father worked in the prison system, McClellan once thought of becoming attorney, but her work as an undercover investigator changed all that.

Tru North...lesbian police detective...Kansas City, Missouri

- ❏ ❏ 1 - K.C. Bomber (1997)
- ❏ ❏ 2 - Penn Valley Phoenix (1997)
- ❏ ❏ 3 - River Quay (1998)
- ❏ ❏ . . . .
- ❏ ❏ . . . .

■ McCLELLAN, Tierney [P]

Tierney McClellan is the pseudonym of Barbara Taylor McCafferty for her series featuring Schuyler (SKY-ler) Ridgway, 40-something real estate agent in Louisville, Kentucky, and divorced mother of 20-something sons, Nathan and Daniel. In her debut adventure, *Heir Condition* (1995), Schuyler is suspected of having an affair with a rich old man who names her in his will, despite the fact Schuyler barely knew him. When last seen in book 4, *Two-Story Frame* (1997), she foolishly agrees to help her ex-husband Ed and his 27-year-old fiancée hunt for a house. Under the name Taylor McCafferty, McClellan writes the Haskell Blevins series, featuring Pigeon Fork, Kentucky's only hard-boiled private eye, who makes his sixth appearance in *Funny Money* (2000). The author lives on eleven wooded acres in Lebanon Junction, Kentucky, where she collaborates via e-mail, fax and phone with her sister and identical twin, Beverly Taylor Herald. Together they write the Bert and Nan Tatum mysteries, beginning with *Double Murder* (1996).

Schuyler Ridgway...40-something real estate agent...Louisville, Kentucky

- ❏ ❏ 1 - Heir Condition (1995)
- ❏ ❏ 2 - Closing Statement (1995)
- ❏ ❏ 3 - A Killing in Real Estate (1996)
- ❏ ❏ 4 - Two-Story Frame (1997)
- ❏ ❏ . . . .
- ❏ ❏ . . . .

■ McCLENDON, Lise

Lise (LEE-zuh) McClendon is the creator of art forgery expert Alix Thorssen, a "semi-prosperous art dealer, so-so kayaker, single girl, thirty-something," first seen in *The Bluejay Shaman* (1994), set in Montana. Alix returns home to the Jackson Hole, Wyoming art gallery she co-owns with Paolo Segundo in *Painted Truth* (1995). The gallery and her partnership are at a crossroads when her appraisal skills are sought in the investigation of a fire at a neighboring gallery where an artist has died. "This lightning-fast adventure has enough false trails to stock a national park," said *Publishers Weekly*. When Alix invites a Norwegian muralist to display his Viking myth paintings during carnival, the artist turns up dead and her stepfather is arrested in book 3, *Nordic Nights* (1999). A mysterious rune-caster who predicts the future is joined by hunky Nordic skiers and lots of naughty ice carvings. A former broadcasting instructor and public relations hack (her words), McClendon once owned a video production business. She lives in Montana.

Alix Thorssen...gallery owner and art forgery expert...Jackson Hole, Wyoming

- ❏ ❏ 1 - The Bluejay Shaman (1994)
- ❏ ❏ 2 - Painted Truth (1995)
- ❏ ❏ . . . .
- ❏ ❏ . . . .

■ McCONNELL, Vicki P.

Theatre major turned technical writer Vicki P. McConnell has written three lesbian mysteries featuring investigative journalist Nyla Wade, introduced in *Mrs. Porter's Letter* (1982). While *The Burnton Widows* (1984) takes Nyla to Oregon, she's back in Denver for *Double Daughter* (1988), which features a writing group reminiscent of one McConnell belonged to at Kansas State University. Her standalone crime novel, *Berrigan* (1978), was re-released by Madwoman Press in 1990. A contributing editor for *Design News*, McConnell writes

frequently for technology publications such as *Reinforced Plastics* and the *S.A.M.P.E. Journal* for the Society of Aerospace Material and Process Engineers. A former freelance editor for New Victoria and Rising Tide Press, McConnell edits *Scientific American* newsletters on transportation composites and the fuel cell industry. She has worked as a high school English teacher in Kansas, a technical administrator in Denver, and on a one-rig oil drilling operation in Oklahoma. She lives in Denver, Colorado.

Nyla Wade...lesbian journalist...Denver, Colorado

- ❏ ❏ 1 - Mrs. Porter's Letter (1982)
- ❏ ❏ 2 - The Burnton Widows (1984)
- ❏ ❏ 3 - Double Daughter (1988)
- ❏ ❏ ....
- ❏ ❏ ....

■ McCORMICK, Claire [P]

Writing as Claire McCormick, Marta Haake Labus is the author of three mysteries featuring executive recruiter John Waltz, introduced in *Resumé for Murder* (1982). After penning radio scripts in high school, including one published in *National Scholastic*, Labus stopped producing fiction when she got to college. The worst grade she received as an English major came from the creative writing instructor who disliked everything she wrote for his class. She told *Contemporary Authors* she tries to keep her ear keen by

reading French fiction and plans to learn Spanish. Her travels in France, French Polynesia and Mexico have provided settings and characters for her mysteries. A summa cum laude graduate of Ohio University where she was a Woodrow Wilson fellow, Labus earned her Ph.D. at the University of Illinois. She later taught at Westminster College in Pennsylvania. The daughter of a mining engineer and a teacher of French, Labus was born in Huntington, West Virginia. She and her husband live in Scottsdale, Arizona.

John Waltz...executive recruiter...Pennsylvania

- ❏ ❏ 1 - Resumé for Murder (1982)
- ❏ ❏ 2 - The Club Paradis Murders [Tahiti] (1983)
- ❏ ❏ 3 - Murder in Cowboy Bronze [Arizona] (1985)
- ❏ ❏ ....
- ❏ ❏ ....

■ McCRUMB, Sharyn

A recognized voice of Appalachian culture and mythology, Sharyn McCrumb has created award-winning characters in mystery, science fiction and folklore. In 1995 she became the first mystery writer to win an Anthony award in two categories the same night, when she took home honors for best novel and best short story. Her primary mystery character is Elizabeth MacPherson, forensic anthropologist and cousin of the disappearing bride in the series opener, *Sick of Shadows* (1984). Her award-winning science

fiction satire, *Bimbos of the Death Sun* (1988), has college professor James Owens Mega exploring the zany world of sci-fi fandom as author Jay Omega. Her critically-acclaimed and best-known Ballad series features Appalachian sheriff Spencer Arrowood, last seen in book 5, *The Ballad of Frankie Silver* (1998). McCrumb says her storytelling gifts and love of the Appalachian Mountains come from her great-grandfathers, who were circuit preachers in North Carolina 100 years ago. She lives in Virginia.

Elizabeth MacPherson...forensic anthropologist...Virginia

- ❏ ❏ 1 - Sick of Shadows (1984)
- ❏ ❏ 2 - Lovely in Her Bones (1985)
- ❏ ❏ 3 - Highland Laddie Gone (1986)

❑ ❑ 4 - **Paying the Piper (1988) Anthony & Agatha nominee** ☆☆
❑ ❑ 5 - The Windsor Knot (1990)
❑ ❑ 6 - Missing Susan (1991)
❑ ❑ 7 - MacPherson's Lament (1992)
❑ ❑ 8 - **If I'd Killed Him When I Met Him (1995) Agatha winner** ★
❑ ❑ . . . .
❑ ❑ . . . .

James Owens Mega...science fiction author professor...Tennessee
❑ ❑ 1 - **Bimbos of the Death Sun (1988) Edgar winner** ★ **Anthony nominee** ☆
❑ ❑ 2 - Zombies of the Gene Pool (1992)
❑ ❑ . . . .
❑ ❑ . . . .

Spencer Arrowood...Appalachian sheriff...Tennessee
❑ ❑ 1 - **If Ever I Return, Pretty Peggy-O (1990) Macavity winner** ★
       Anthony nominee ☆
❑ ❑ 2 - **The Hangman's Beautiful Daughter (1992) Anthony & Agatha nominee** ☆☆
❑ ❑ 3 - **She Walks These Hills (1994) Anthony, Agatha, Macavity &**
       Nero Wolfe winner ★★★★
❑ ❑ 4 - The Rosewood Casket (1996)
❑ ❑ 5 - The Ballad of Frankie Silver (1998)
❑ ❑ . . . .
❑ ❑ . . . .

■ McDERMID, Val

Gold Dagger winner Val McDermid is the author of 15 crime novels, including three mystery series and two standalone novels. Manchester P.I. Kate Brannigan, last seen in *Star Struck* (1998), lives next door to her rock music journalist boyfriend, whose house is connected to hers by a shared conservatory. Lindsay Gordon, appearing last in *Booked for Murder* (1996), is a self-described cynical socialist lesbian feminist. Clinical psychologist Tony Hill and D.I. Carol Jordan first work together in *The Mermaids Singing* (1995), a

Gold Dagger winner. McDermid's one-offs include *A Place of Execution* (1999) and *Killing the Shadows* (2000), where a serial killer eliminates thriller writers, starting in Edinburgh. After growing up in a Scottish mining community and reading English at Oxford, McDermid spent 15 years as a working journalist, including a three-year stint as Northern Bureau Chief of a national Sunday tabloid. Her nonfiction book about working P.I.s, *A Suitable Job for a Woman* (1995), was published in the U.S. in 1999.

Kate Brannigan...5' 3" redheaded private eye...Manchester, England
❑ ❑ 1 - Dead Beat (1992)
❑ ❑ 2 - Kick Back (1993)
❑ ❑ 3 - **Crack Down (1994) Anthony & Gold Dagger nominee** ☆☆
❑ ❑ 4 - Clean Break (1995)
❑ ❑ 5 - Blue Genes (1996)
❑ ❑ 6 - Star Struck (1998)
❑ ❑ . . . .
❑ ❑ . . . .

Lindsay Gordon...lesbian socialist journalist...Glasgow, Scotland
❑ ❑ 1 - Report for Murder (1987)
❑ ❑ 2 - Common Murder (1989)
❑ ❑ 3 - Final Edition (1991)
❑ ❑   - U.S.-Open and Shut
❑ ❑ 4 - Union Jack (1993)
❑ ❑   - U.S.-Conferences are Murder (1999)
❑ ❑ 5 - Booked for Murder (1996)
❑ ❑ . . . .
❑ ❑ . . . .

Tony Hill & Carol Jordan...clinical psychologist & D.I....Bradfield, England

❏ ❏   1 - **The Mermaids Singing (1995) Gold Dagger winner ★**

❏ ❏   2 - The Wire in the Blood (1998)

❏ ❏   . . . .

❏ ❏   . . . .

■ McGIFFIN, Janet

Janet McGiffin has written three medical mysteries featuring Dr. Maxene St. Clair, 38-year-old emergency room physician who works the night shift at an inner city Catholic hospital in Milwaukee, Wisconsin. The doc herself is the prime suspect in *Emergency Murder* (1992), when a surgeon's young wife dies from a rare fish poison that may have come from Maxene's research lab at Marquette University. Series regulars include a smart, well-dressed pimp named Rolondo, head nurse Shirley Fitzgerald, and homicide detective Joseph Grabowski, who has a romantic history with the doctor. The death of a hooker, a double drive-by shooting, and attacks on Dr. St. Clair may be related to the murder of a master sculptor, killed when his mobile of 15 yellow wooden chairs falls on him in *Prescription for Death* (1993). When she is appointed to interim office in the Wisconsin legislature in *Elective Murder* (1995), Maxene finds out firsthand that politics can be murder. The author, who knows Milwaukee well, lives in Tel Aviv, Israel.

Maxene St. Clair...emergency room physician...Milwaukee, Wisconsin

❏ ❏   1 - Emergency Murder (1992)

❏ ❏   2 - Prescription for Death (1993)

❏ ❏   3 - Elective Murder (1995)

❏ ❏   . . . .

❏ ❏   . . . .

■ McGOWN, Jill

Jill McGown is "one of the most seriously underrated crime novelists around," said *The Times* of London about *Plots and Errors* (1999), her tenth book featuring Chief Inspector Lloyd (whose first name is an ongoing mystery), and his partner Sergeant Judy Hill, later promoted to Inspector. There is "nothing cute or coy about the relationship" between Lloyd and Hill. After many years together, they still maintain separate residences. "She tolerates his smugness and flair for dramatic; he appreciates her cool logic and occasionally brilliant insights," said Dick Adler for *Amazon.com*. Telling her stories from multiple points of view, McGown frequently shifts back and forth between detectives and suspects. In addition to four nonseries novels under her own name, she has written a suspense novel, *A Hostage to Fortune* (1992), as Elizabeth Chaplin. Born in Argyll, Scotland, McGown worked as a secretary and administrative assistant for more than 15 years before writing mysteries. She has lived in Corby, England since she was ten.

Lloyd & Judy Hill...chief inspector & detective partner...East Anglia, England

❏ ❏   1 - A Perfect Match (1983)

❏ ❏   2 - Redemption (1988)

❏ ❏   - U.S.-Murder at the Old Vicarage

❏ ❏   3 - Death of a Dancer (1989)

❏ ❏   - U.S.-Gone to Her Death

❏ ❏   4 - The Murders of Mrs. Austin & Mrs. Beale (1991)

❏ ❏   5 - The Other Woman (1992)

❏ ❏   6 - Murder Now and Then (1993)

❏ ❏   7 - A Shred of Evidence (1995)

❏ ❏   8 - Verdict Unsafe (1996)

❏ ❏   9 - Picture of Innocence (1998)

❏ ❏   . . . .

❏ ❏   . . . .

■ McGUIRE, Christine

Criminal prosecutor Christine McGuire writes a series about her fictional alter ego, deputy district attorney Kathryn Mackay, first seen in *Until Proven Guilty* (1993). Struggling with the demands of single motherhood, Mackay becomes the target of a serial killer who has already killed three women. "McGuire's sharp, observant writing style makes for compulsive page turning," said the *San Francisco Chronicle*. After prosecuting a defendant charged with attempted murder by intentional infliction of H.I.V. in book 3, Mackay gets an arson murder case with a surprise defense of battered wife syndrome in book 4. The hard-working A.D.A. was last seen in book 5, *Until We Meet Again*

(1999). McGuire heads the Special Prosecutions Unit in a Northern California D.A.'s office and has taught at the F.B.I. academy in Quantico, Virginia. With Carla Norton she co-authored *Perfect Victim* (1989), the nonfiction account of a sexual enslavement case. A #1 *New York Times* bestseller, the book sold more than one million copies.

Kathryn Mackay...senior prosecuting attorney...Northern California
- ❏ ❏ 1 - Until Proven Guilty (1993)
- ❏ ❏ 2 - Until Justice is Done (1994)
- ❏ ❏ 3 - Until Death Do Us Part (1997)
- ❏ ❏ 4 - Until The Bough Breaks (1998)
- ❏ ❏ . . . .
- ❏ ❏ . . . .

■ McKENNA, Bridget

Shamus nominee Bridget McKenna is the author of three Caley Burke P.I. mysteries, beginning with *Murder Beach* (1993), where Caley gets involved in her first murder case when she returns to her hometown for a high school reunion. When last seen in *Caught Dead* (1995), Caley is on a forced sabbatical, but ends up helping a runaway boy whose mother has been arrested for murder. "Caley weeds out the innocent from the guilty and pegs the murderer in a shoot-out conclusion," said *Booklist*. An author of science fiction

and fantasy, McKenna was nominated for Nebula and Hugo awards in 1994. Writing as Melissa Cleary, she has taken over the Jackie Walsh and Jake series beginning with book 10. She is also the pseudonymous author of Melissa Cleary stories in *Canine Crimes* (1998) and *Canine Christmas* (1999). McKenna lives in Uptown Seattle with a view from her desk of the city skyline, Mt. Rainier and the Space Needle. Her day job, which she does at home, is writing computer games.

Caley Burke...30-something private eye...Northern California
- ❏ ❏ 1 - Murder Beach (1993)
- ❏ ❏ **2 - Dead Ahead (1994) Shamus nominee** ☆
- ❏ ❏ 3 - Caught Dead (1995)
- ❏ ❏ . . . .
- ❏ ❏ . . . .

■ McKERNAN, Victoria

Certified scuba instructor Victoria McKernan has written three mysteries featuring professional scuba diver Chicago Nordejoong. While preparing her boat for a two-year sail, Chicago crosses paths with ex-lover Alex Sanders, an island-hopping charter pilot and former government agent. He brings flowers as a peace offering for her and a guinea pig for her eight-foot boa constrictor Lassie. When last seen in *Crooked Island* (1994), they're on an expedition with an archaeologist and his 12-year-old daughter to raise a 250-year-old

coffin. Like her character, McKernan has crewed on yachts and dived around the world. She has skied St. Moritz, trekked Nepal, danced in an opera, and brought home the skulls of a beaver, goat, bison, cougar and caribou found on her paths in Ireland, North Dakota, Alaska, Belize and Montana. Read more of her story in Finney and Dasch's *Find Your Calling, Love Your Life* (1998). A graduate of George Washington University, she lives in Washington, D.C. with her pet boa constrictor Thornton.

Chicago Nordejoong...professional scuba diver...Florida
- ❏ ❏ 1 - Osprey Reef (1990)
- ❏ ❏ 2 - Point Deception (1992)
- ❏ ❏ 3 - Crooked Island (1994)
- ❏ ❏ . . . .
- ❏ ❏ . . . .

■ McKEVETT, G.A. [P]

G.A. McKevett is the pseudonym of Sonja Massie for a Southern California series featuring voluptuous Detective Sergeant Savannah Reid, dropped from the San Carmelita Police Department for being overweight. The Georgia-born karate expert promptly sets up the Moonlight Magnolia Detective Agency and takes a case involving adultery and dirty politics in *Just Desserts* (1995). After locating the long-lost sister of a local real estate broker in *Bitter Sweets* (1996), Savannah checks into the Royal Palms spa for a week-long stay, after promiscuous one-time disco queen, Kat Valentina, drowns in an herbal mudbath in book 3, *Killer Calories* (1997). An anonymous client promises $10,000 if Savannah can track down Kat's killer. Hired to catch a "Santa Rapist" attacking women in the shopping mall parking lot, Savannah mistakenly disables a legitimate store Santa and things go downhill from there in *Cooked Goose* (1998). The Moonlight Magnolia gang returns in book 5, *Sugar and Spite* (2000).

Savannah Reid...voluptuous ex-cop private eye...San Carmelita, California

- ❏ ❏ 1 - Just Desserts (1995)
- ❏ ❏ 2 - Bitter Sweets (1996)
- ❏ ❏ 3 - Killer Calories (1997)
- ❏ ❏ 4 - Cooked Goose (1998)
- ❏ ❏ . . . .
- ❏ ❏ . . . .

■ McKITTERICK, Molly

Former television anchor and reporter Molly McKitterick has written two St. Louis mysteries featuring self-absorbed, middle-aged television anchor William (Heck) Hecklepeck, introduced in *The Medium is Murder* (1992). When the station's consumer affairs reporter announces the first segment of her tell-all with mistresses of the city's most powerful men, she is strangled with a microphone cord. Hiding her incriminating tapes from the cops, Heck starts his own investigation. Much of the investigative work in *Murder in a Mayonnaise Jar* (1993), is done by young reporter Jennifer Burgess, while Heck plays mentor. "McKitterick's deft plotting and appealing characters keep readers interested and involved in this tale of greed, venality, and madness," said *Booklist*. An English graduate of Middlebury College, McKitterick spent ten years in television as an anchor and reporter in Louisville, Washington, D.C. and St. Louis. She lives in Washington, D.C. with her television meteorologist husband.

William Hecklepeck...egotistical television anchor...St. Louis, Missouri

- ❏ ❏ 1 - The Medium is Murder (1992)
- ❏ ❏ 2 - Murder in a Mayonnaise Jar (1993)
- ❏ ❏ . . . .
- ❏ ❏ . . . .

■ McNAB, Claire [P]

Writing as Claire McNab, Claire Carmichael is the author of more than 35 books, including her Australian police series featuring lesbian Detective Inspector Carol Ashton, introduced in *Lessons in Murder* (1988). Sydney's top cop tracks down a ruthless killer in book 11, *Set Up* (1999). With *Murder Undercover* (1999), McNab launches a new series starring Denise Cleever, an ambitious young agent with the Australian Security Intelligence Organization. In her debut appearance, Cleever is deep undercover at an exclusive family-owned resort off the Great Barrier Reef, where nothing looks out of the ordinary until the killing starts. McNab worked in television and taught psychology and communications for more than ten years before writing comedy plays and textbooks. In her native Australia, she is known for her adult crime fiction, science fiction and mysteries for children and young adults, and self-help books. She lives in Los Angeles, where she teaches fiction and crime writing at the U.C.L.A. Extension.

Carol Ashton...lesbian detective inspector...Sydney, Australia

- ❏ ❏ 1 - Lessons in Murder (1988)
- ❏ ❏ 2 - Fatal Reunion (1989)
- ❏ ❏ 3 - Death Down Under (1990)
- ❏ ❏ 4 - Cop Out (1991)

❑	❑	5 - Dead Certain (1992)
❑	❑	- APA-Off Key
❑	❑	6 - Body Guard (1994)
❑	❑	7 - Double Bluff (1995)
❑	❑	8 - Inner Circle (1996)
❑	❑	9 - Chain Letter (1997)
❑	❑	10 - Past Due (1998)
❑	❑	. . . .
❑	❑	. . . .

■ McQUILLAN, Karin

Karin McQuillan arrived in Senegal as a Peace Corps volunteer three weeks after graduation from Brandeis. Visiting remote villages by dugout canoe through crocodile-infested waters, she was often the first white woman natives had ever seen. She witnessed devil dancing and female circumcision, consulted a witch doctor and visited urban shantytowns and homes of the elite. Return trips to Kenya to study elephants, lions and cheetahs have given her an intimate knowledge of man and animal behavior. Jazz Jasper, introduced in *Deadly Safari* (1990), is an independent safari leader in Kenya, passionate about conservation and all things African. When last seen in *The Cheetah Chase* (1994), Jazz is "absolutely smashing," said the *Jackson Clarion-Ledger*. The daughter of a cinematographer and a painter, McQuillan is a psychotherapist and ardent conservationist with an M.S.W. from Boston University. She lives in Cambridge, Massachusetts, where she teaches mystery writing.

Jazz Jasper...American safari guide...Kenya

❑	❑	1 - Deadly Safari (1990)
❑	❑	2 - Elephants' Graveyard (1993)
❑	❑	3 - The Cheetah Chase (1994)
❑	❑	. . . .
❑	❑	. . . .

■ McSHEA, Susanna Hofmann

Susanna Hofmann McShea writes hard-boiled cozies set in Raven's Wing, Connecticut, a thinly-disguised version of her Ridgefield hometown. Aided by society divorcée Mildred Bennett, retired police chief Forrest Haggarty sets out to prove his 30-year-old claim about a serial killer in *Hometown Heroes* (1990). Joined again by nurse Irene Purdy and retired physician Trevor Bradford, Mildred and Forrest want to know how a staid Raven's Wing matron died in a sleazy New York City hotel, tarted up like a whore in *The Pumpkin-Shell Wife* (1992). In *Ladybug, Ladybug* (1994) the Hometown Heroes investigate the alleged suicide of a popular college freshman who leaves Yale to study for the priesthood. "A delicate balance between folksy humor and menacing mayhem," said *Booklist*. When friends mention her father's resemblance to Forrest Haggarty, McShea quickly notes his strong disapproval of Forrest's use of four-letter words. "We can't understand it, because Susanna never speaks that way in person," he says.

Mildred Bennett and friends...quartet of senior sleuths...Raven's Wing, Connecticut

❑	❑	1 - Hometown Heroes (1990)
❑	❑	2 - The Pumpkin-Shell Wife (1992)
❑	❑	3 - Ladybug, Ladybug (1994)
❑	❑	. . . .
❑	❑	. . . .

■ MEDAWAR, Mardi Oakley

Mardi Oakley Medawar's Native American ancestry lends authenticity to her historical mysteries featuring 1860s Kiowa healer, Tay-bodal, introduced in *Death at Rainy Mountain* (1996). A relative nobody among his tribe, Tay-bodal is a reluctant investigator when Coyote Walking is brutally murdered. Nobody trusts Tay-bodal with weapons and he's not good at tracking, but a primitive post-mortem on Coyote Walking holds the answer. Success in naming the killer earns Tay-bodal a respected place among his tribesman and wins him the love of a beautiful woman, a young son and many new friends. "A cunningly plotted story that is as devilishly funny as it is charmingly told," raved *Booklist*. Medawar's western fiction includes *The Misty Hills of Home* (1998), *Remembering the Osage Kid* (1997) and *People of the Whistling Waters* (1993), winner of a best first novel award from Western Writers of America. An Eastern Band Cherokee, Medawar lives in Lizard Lick, North Carolina.

Tay-bodal...19th century Kiowa healer...Oklahoma
- ❏ ❏ 1 - Death at Rainy Mountain (1996)
- ❏ ❏ 2 - Witch of the Palo Duro (1997)
- ❏ ❏ 3 - Murder at Medicine Lodge (1999)
- ❏ ❏ . . . .
- ❏ ❏ . . . .

■ MEEK, M.R.D.

M(argaret) R(eid) D(uncan) Meek began writing detective fiction in her early 60s, after a varied career as a wife, mother and solicitor. She earned a Law Degree with honors from London University at the age of 50, and worked as an articled clerk and solicitor in Hertfordshire and Cornwall for more than 15 years before retiring to write mysteries featuring solicitor-detective Lennox Kemp. Having run afoul of the Law Society, Kemp works as a private detective early in the series, but is practicing law again by book 5, and promoted to head of the Newtown office of Gillorns, Solicitors by book 8. "Practicing lawyers tend to see people at their most vulnerable," Meek once remarked, when commenting on the choice of Kemp as her central protagonist. Short, fat and 40, with a bald spot on top of his head and a soft spot for women, Kemp last appeared in book 12, *A House To Die For* (1999). As Alison Cairns, Meek has written *Strained Relations* (1983) and *New Year Resolution* (1984). Born in Scotland, she lives in London.

Lennox Kemp...solicitor detective...England
- ❏ ❏ 1 - With Flowers That Fell (1983)
- ❏ ❏ 2 - The Sitting Ducks (1984)
- ❏ ❏ 3 - Hang the Consequences (1984)
- ❏ ❏ 4 - The Split Second (1985)
- ❏ ❏ 5 - In Remembrance of Rose (1986)
- ❏ ❏ 6 - A Worm of Doubt (1987)
- ❏ ❏ 7 - A Mouthful of Sand (1988)
- ❏ ❏ 8 - A Loose Connection (1989)
- ❏ ❏ 9 - This Blessed Plot (1990)
- ❏ ❏ 10 - Touch and Go (1992)
- ❏ ❏ 11 - Postscript to Murder (1996)
- ❏ ❏ . . . .
- ❏ ❏ . . . .

■ MEIER, Leslie

Leslie Meier writes cozy mysteries featuring part-time sleuth Lucy Stone, wife of a building contractor, evening college student and mother of four in Tinker's Cove, Maine. While working the holiday night shift at Country Cousins, Lucy finds the company founder dead in the parking lot in the series opener, *Mail-Order Murder* (1991), re-released in 1998 as *Mistletoe Murder*. Supermom Lucy is a murder suspect in book 5, *Valentine Murder* (1999), when the Tinker's Cove children's librarian dies just before the start of story hour. Only two people had access to the librarian's office and the newest board member (Lucy) is one of them. "Strong opening, light humor, vivid Maine landscapes, and a cast of generally sympathetic characters, despite some slightly stereotyped librarians," said *Booklist* reviewer John Rowen of the American Library Association. Lucy's sixth adventure is *Christmas Cookie Murder* (2000). Meier lives in Harwich, Massachusetts, where she has never harmed a librarian.

Lucy Stone...sleuthing mother of four...Tinker's Cove, Maine
- ❏ ❏ 1 - Mail-Order Murder (1991)
- ❏ ❏ - APA-Mistletoe Murder (1998)
- ❏ ❏ 2 - Tippy-Toe Murder (1994)

❑ ❑   3 - Trick or Treat Murder (1996)
❑ ❑   4 - Back to School Murder (1997)
❑ ❑   . . . .
❑ ❑   . . . .

■ MELVILLE, Jennie [P]

Jennie Melville is the pseudonym of Silver Dagger winner Gwendoline Butler for her 19-book series featuring police detective Charmian Daniels, first seen in *Come Home and Be Killed* (1962). Butler started the series while living in St. Andrews, Scotland, a university town where women police officers were being trained. Missing England, she created the fictional town of Deerham Hills for a woman constable and chose her grandmother's name for a pseudonym. Book 8, *Murder Has a Pretty Face* (1981), was shortlisted for the Gold Dagger. Butler has also written more than 15 nonseries novels as Jennie Melville, primarily historical and romantic suspense. Author of more than 60 novels, she is best known for her 27-book Coffin series featuring the Chief Commander of the Second City of London. Her 1973 Silver Dagger winner, *A Coffin for Pandora*, not a Coffin book, is set in 1880s Oxford, a town where Butler earned her master's degree and later taught in two different colleges. A member of the Detection Club, she lives in Surrey, England.

Charmian Daniels...police detective...Deerham Hills, England
❑ ❑   1 - Come Home and Be Killed (1962)
❑ ❑   2 - Burning Is a Substitute for Loving (1963)
❑ ❑   3 - Murderers' Houses (1964)
❑ ❑   4 - There Lies Your Love (1965)
❑ ❑   5 - Nell Alone (1966)
❑ ❑   6 - A Different Kind of Summer (1967)
❑ ❑   7 - A New Kind of Killer, An Old Kind of Death (1970)
❑ ❑   - APA-A New Kind of Killer
❑ ❑   **8 - Murder Has a Pretty Face (1981) Gold Dagger nominee** ☆
❑ ❑   9 - Death in the Garden (1987)
❑ ❑   - U.S.-Murder in the Garden
❑ ❑ 10 - Windsor Red (1988)
❑ ❑ 11 - A Cure for Dying (1989)
❑ ❑ 12 - Witching Murder (1990)
❑ ❑ 13 - Making Good Blood (1990)
❑ ❑   - U.S.-Footsteps in the Blood
❑ ❑ 14 - Dead Set (1992)
❑ ❑ 15 - Whoever Has the Heart (1993)
❑ ❑ 16 - Baby Drop (1994)
❑ ❑   - U.S.-Death in the Family
❑ ❑ 17 - The Morbid Kitchen (1995)
❑ ❑ 18 - The Woman Who Was Not There (1996)
❑ ❑ 19 - Revengeful Death (1998)
❑ ❑   . . . .
❑ ❑   . . . .

■ MERCER, Judy

Judy Mercer's first novel "lives up to its title," said *Publishers Weekly* about *Fast Forward* (1995), the series opener featuring television newsmagazine producer Ariel Gold. When she wakes up bruised, bloodied and suffering from amnesia, Ariel assumes the life of the woman whose identification she finds strewn around the ransacked Los Angeles house she assumes is her own. While keeping her memory loss a secret, she has to re-learn her job in television and figure out who wants her dead. Each succeeding installment adds more pieces to the puzzle, including the discovery in book 3, *Split Image* (1998), that she may have a romantic history with Jack Spurling, an accused wife-killer. *Split Image* was a *People* magazine Page-Turner of the Week. Ariel's fourth adventure is *Blind Spot* (2000). After earning a degree in broadcast journalism from the University of Georgia, Mercer worked as a news reporter, disc jockey, advertising copywriter and advertising director. She lives with her husband in Marin County, California.

Ariel Gold...amnesiac TV newsmagazine producer...Los Angeles, California

❏ ❏ 1 - Fast Forward (1995)
❏ ❏ 2 - Double Take (1997)
❏ ❏ 3 - Split Image (1998)
❏ ❏ . . . .
❏ ❏ . . . .

■ MEREDITH, D.R.

Two-time Anthony nominee D(oris) R. Meredith is a former librarian and bookstore manager, and author of 11 mysteries set in the Texas Panhandle. Honest, courageous Sheriff Charles Matthews of fictional Crawford County is introduced in *The Sheriff and the Panhandle Murders* (1984). Meredith's second series features the actual town of Canadian, with its lovely Victorian homes, brick streets and giant cottonwood trees. Wise and good defense attorney, John Lloyd Branson, and his smart and lovely assistant, Dallas law student Lydia Fairchild, are introduced in *Murder by Impulse* (1988). She calls him John Lloyd and he calls her Miss Fairchild, as they struggle to keep their personal attraction under wraps. Starting with *Murder By Volume* (2000), Meredith launches a third series with aspiring paleopathologist Megan Clark and her museum curator sidekick, a widowed history professor 20 years her senior. The two join a mystery reading club that meets in a used bookstore on Old Route 66. Meredith lives in Amarillo, Texas.

Charles Matthews...honest county sheriff...Crawford Co., Texas

❏ ❏ 1 - The Sheriff & the Panhandle Murders (1984)
❏ ❏ 2 - The Sheriff & the Branding Iron Murders (1985)
❏ ❏ 3 - The Sheriff & the Folsom Man Murders (1987)
❏ ❏ 4 - The Sheriff & the Pheasant Hunt Murders (1993)
❏ ❏ 5 - The Homefront Murders (1995)
❏ ❏ . . . .
❏ ❏ . . . .

John Lloyd Branson & Lydia Fairchild...defense attorney & legal assistant...Canadian, Texas

❏ ❏ 1 - **Murder by Impulse (1988) Anthony nominee** ☆
❏ ❏ 2 - **Murder by Deception (1989) Anthony nominee** ☆
❏ ❏ 3 - Murder by Masquerade (1990)
❏ ❏ 4 - Murder by Reference (1991)
❏ ❏ 5 - Murder by Sacrilege (1993)
❏ ❏ . . . .
❏ ❏ . . . .

■ MEYERS, Annette

After 16 years on Wall Street as an executive search consultant and 16 years as assistant to Broadway director-producer Hal Prince, Annette Meyers has brought the two worlds together in her Smith & Wetzon series. Former Broadway dancer Leslie Wetzon and her pretentious head-hunting partner Xenia Smith are introduced in *The Big Killing* (1989), re-released in 1998. Wetzon occupies center stage in *The Groaning Board* (1997), with a murder case involving Manhattan's hottest caterers and some poison muffins. "Slick dialogue, snappy humor, and a dazzling cast of high-flying movers and shakers add up to a fun, stylish read," raved *Booklist*. Greenwich Village poet and private-eye-in-training Olivia Brown gets her own 1920s series starting with *Free Love* (1999) and *Cold Passion* (2000). The series mixes real people and places with fiction. Writing as Maan Meyers, Annette and her husband Martin co-author the Dutchman historical series. Past president of Sisters in Crime, she lives in New York City.

Olivia Brown...1920s Greenwich Village poet P.I....New York, New York

❏ ❏ 1 - Free Love (1999)
❏ ❏ . . . .
❏ ❏ . . . .

Xenia Smith & Leslie Wetzon...Wall Street headhunters...New York, New York

❏ ❏ 1 - The Big Killing (1989)
❏ ❏ 2 - Tender Death (1990)

❑ ❑ 3 - The Deadliest Option (1991)
❑ ❑ 4 - Blood on the Street (1992)
❑ ❑ 5 - Murder: The Musical (1993)
❑ ❑ 6 - These Bones Were Made for Dancin' (1995)
❑ ❑ 7 - The Groaning Board (1997)
❑ ❑ . . . .
❑ ❑ . . . .

■ MEYERS, Maan [P]

Maan Meyers is the joint pseudonym of Martin and Annette Meyers for their New Amsterdam historical series beginning with *The Dutchman* (1992). Spanning 200 years, the series traces the Tonneman family history, with each installment featuring a mystery from a different period in New York City history. A plot by Confederates to burn the city during the Civil War is the set-up for book 6, *The Lucifer Contract* (1998). New York comes alive with "a wealth of surprising and entertaining historical tidbits," said *Publishers Weekly*. Author of five books in the Patrick Hardy detective series, Martin is a stage and television actor whose credits include a role on the daytime drama *One Life to Live*. He novelized the Cher movie *Suspect* and once wrote television song lyrics for the Captain Kangaroo show. A former senior vice president of a Wall Street search firm, Annette writes Smith and Wetzon mysteries and a 1920s series set in Greenwich Village with poet and private eye Olivia Brown, first seen in *Free Love* (1999).

The Tonnemans…New Amsterdam family…New York, New York

❑ ❑ 1 - The Dutchman (1992)
❑ ❑ 2 - The Kingsbridge Plot (1993)
❑ ❑ 3 - The High Constable (1994)
❑ ❑ 4 - The Dutchman's Dilemma (1995)
❑ ❑ 5 - The House on Mulberry Street (1996)
❑ ❑ 6 - The Lucifer Contract (1998)
❑ ❑ . . . .
❑ ❑ . . . .

■ MICHAELS, Barbara [P]

Barbara Michaels is one of two pseudonyms of Dr. Barbara Mertz, who trained as an archaeologist and holds a Ph.D. from the University of Chicago's Oriental Institute. As Dr. Mertz she is the author of two popular nonfiction books on ancient Egypt. As Elizabeth Peters and Barbara Michaels she is the author of more than 60 novels of mystery and suspense, and holds Grand Master honors for lifetime achievement from Mystery Writers of America and the World Mystery Convention. Her three series as Elizabeth Peters include the Amelia Peabody series featuring a Victorian Egyptologist, the Vicky Bliss series starring a sexy art historian, and the Jacqueline Kirby series with a librarian turned romance writer. As Barbara Michaels she writes best-selling suspense novels, often with historical and supernatural aspects. The Barbara Michaels novel, *Stitches in Time* (1995), is the third installment of a trilogy featuring the historic Georgetown house introduced in *Ammie, Come Home* (1968) more than 30 years ago.

Georgetown house…historic home…Washington, District of Columbia

❑ ❑ 1 - Ammie, Come Home (1968)
❑ ❑ 2 - Shattered Silk (1986)
❑ ❑ 3 - Stitches in Time (1995)
❑ ❑ . . . .
❑ ❑ . . . .

■ MICHAELS, Melisa

Science fiction and fantasy author Melisa Michaels has written two cross-genre mysteries featuring California private investigator Rosie Lavine, hired to protect the charismatic lead singer of an elfrock band in *Cold Iron* (1997). Tired of their homeland, elves from Faerie travel to earth, become musicians and assemble a band they call Cold Iron. After tragically mishandling the Cold Iron case, Rosie tries to put her life back together in *Sister to the Rain* (1998), and agrees to investigate strange noises and petty disturbances at a secluded artists' community of elves and humans. Michaels has published six science fiction novels, including her Skyrider series, beginning with *Skirmish* (1985), her first novel. "Ingenious and perplexing," said *Publishers Weekly* about her San Francisco P.I. novel, *Through the Eyes of the Dead* (1988). Born in the Midwest, Michaels has lived in Hawaii since 1983, where she paints local landscapes, helps her husband remodel their fixer-upper, and maintains the official S.F.W.A. website which she designed.

Rosie Lavine...private eye to the elf world...California

❏ ❏	1 - Cold Iron (1997)
❏ ❏	2 - Sister to the Rain (1998)
❏ ❏	. . . .
❏ ❏	. . . .

■ MICKELBURY, Penny

Former *Washington Post* reporter Penny Mickelbury has chased stories in print, radio and television in Georgia, Washington and New York. After writing about government and politics for most of her 15 years in journalism, she has turned to detective fiction with two series featuring strong black women. Starting with *Keeping Secrets* (1994), Mickelbury introduces D.C. police detective and head of the Hate Crimes Unit, Gianna Maglione, and her lover Mimi Patterson, the black investigative reporter whose work often puts the two in conflict. Mickelbury's newer series introduces black criminal defense attorney Carole Ann Gibson, "one of the most appealing heroines to appear in crime fiction in years," according to *Booklist*. First seen in *One Must Wait* (1998), C.A. (as she's known in the trenches) is a woman with "a sharp mind, quick wit, and big heart." After going home to West Los Angeles in *Where To Choose* (1999), C.A. returns in book 3, *The Step Between* (2000). Mickelbury lives in Washington, D.C.

Carole Ann Gibson...black criminal defense attorney...Washington, District of Columbia

❏ ❏	1 - One Must Wait (1998)
❏ ❏	2 - Where To Choose (1999)
❏ ❏	. . . .
❏ ❏	. . . .

Gianna Maglione & Mimi Patterson...lesbian police lieutenant & reporter... Washington, District of Columbia

❏ ❏	1 - Keeping Secrets (1994)
❏ ❏	2 - Night Songs (1995)
❏ ❏	. . . .
❏ ❏	. . . .

■ MIKULSKI, Barbara and Marylouise Oates

U.S. Senator Barbara Mikulski and former *Los Angeles Times* columnist Marylouise Oates have written two political thrillers featuring feisty, Polish-American Senator Eleanor (Norie) Gorzack. On her first day in Washington, Gorzack witnesses a brutal murder on the Senate subway in *Capitol Offense* (1996). "Lively, juicy insider dish," said *Kirkus*. In *Capitol Venture* (1997) a colleague with confidential information to share with Norie is murdered in an apparent car-jacking. Elected in 1998 to her third Senate term, Mikulski previously served ten years in the House of Representatives. The first Democratic woman elected to both houses of Congress, Mikulski became the first woman ever to win a statewide election in Maryland in 1986. Currently the only woman member of the Senate Democratic leadership, Mikulski is serving her third term as Democratic Conference Secretary. A longtime political activist, Oates also wrote *Making Peace* (1991), a novel of the 1960s. She lives in Washington with her political consultant husband.

Norie Gorzack...Polish-American U.S. senator...Washington, District of Columbia

❏ ❏	1 - Capitol Offense (1996)
❏ ❏	2 - Capitol Venture (1997)
❏ ❏	. . . .
❏ ❏	. . . .

MILES, Margaret

Margaret Miles writes American historical mysteries set in the village of Bracebridge, Massachusetts, near Boston. Widowed Colonial farm owner Charlotte Willett and her neighbor, gentleman farmer and scientist Richard Longfellow, are introduced in *A Wicked Way to Burn* (1998). It's 1763 and a wealthy stranger bursts into flame by the side of the road and promptly disappears. While townsfolk gossip about witchcraft and spontaneous combustion, Charlotte and Richard speculate about elaborate murder plots.

When the detecting duo returns in *Too Soon for Flowers* (1999), it's 1764 and wealthy Bostonians are fleeing the city to escape a smallpox outbreak. Among the arrivals in Bracebridge is Richard's sister Diana, coerced by her brother to accept a state-of-the-art inoculation. Suicide and murder soon follow. Charlotte and Richard return in book 3, *No Rest for the Dove* (2000). Miles previously spent 20 years writing and producing short films and videos. She lives near Washington, D.C. with her husband and cat.

Charlotte Willett & Richard Longfellow...Colonial farm woman & scientist-farmer...Bracebridge, Massachusetts

- ❏ ❏ 1 - A Wicked Way To Burn (1998)
- ❏ ❏ 2 - Too Soon for Flowers (1999)
- ❏ ❏ . . . .
- ❏ ❏ . . . .

MILLHISER, Marlys

Marlys Millhiser writes the Charlie Greene mysteries featuring a Hollywood literary agent and single mother introduced in *Murder at Moot Point* (1992), where Charlie travels to the Oregon coast to deliver a reclusive author's contract and ends up a murder suspect. "Entertainingly oddball," said *Kirkus*. When a horror-film director gets the ax (literally) in book 3, *Murder in a Hot Flash* (1995), Charlie's menopausal mother is the prime suspect. When last seen in book 5, *Nobody Dies in a Casino* (1999), Charlie is in Las Vegas on a vacation

that is anything but restful. Among her fans, the favorite Millhiser novel is *The Mirror* (1978), re-released by Rue Morgue Press in 1997. It tells the story of a Boulder, Colorado woman drawn into her grandmother's life (and vice versa). After graduating from the University of Iowa, Millhiser earned an M.A. from the University of Colorado. At home in Boulder, she recently completed a sixth Charlie Green mystery, *Killer Commute*, and her first Lennora Poole mystery, *Discretion Guaranteed*.

Charlie Greene...literary agent and single mother...Hollywood, California

- ❏ ❏ 1 - Murder at Moot Point (1992)
- ❏ ❏ 2 - Death of the Office Witch (1993)
- ❏ ❏ 3 - Murder in a Hot Flash (1995)
- ❏ ❏ 4 - It's Murder Going Home (1996)
- ❏ ❏ 5 - Nobody Dies in a Casino (1999)
- ❏ ❏ . . . .
- ❏ ❏ . . . .

MINICHINO, Camille

Retired Physicist and former nun Camille Minichino (mih-nih-KEE-noh) writes mysteries based on the elements of the periodic table, featuring 50-something Italian-American physicist Gloria Lamerino, a former Berkeley professor who returns to her hometown roots where she rents an apartment above the local mortuary. In book 1, *The Hydrogen Murder* (1997), Gloria consults with the local police in Revere Beach, when a former colleague is murdered. Like her fictional alter ego, Minichino grew up in Massachusetts where she earned a Ph.D. in physics and started her

career in research and teaching. Gloria and police detective Matt Gennaro return in book 4, *The Beryllium Murder* (2000). Minichino teaches physics, logic and philosophy, and develops and teaches classes in science literacy. She is also writing her first Sister Francesca mystery, set in the Bronx in 1965. During a period of foment in the Catholic church, Sister Francesca enters grad school a conservative and finishes as something else. Minichino and her husband live in San Leandro, California.

Gloria Lamerino...50-something physicist...Revere Beach, Massachusetts
- ❏ ❏ 1 - The Hydrogen Murder (1997)
- ❏ ❏ 2 - The Helium Murder (1998)
- ❏ ❏ 3 - The Lithium Murder (1999)
- ❏ ❏ . . . .
- ❏ ❏ . . . .

■ MITCHELL, Kay

Kay Mitchell gave herself six months to sell her first short story in 1985. It sold in half that time and she completed her first novel four years later. *A Lively Form of Death* (1990) introduces Chief Inspector John Morrissey of Malminster C.I.D., a married father of two teenagers, who has since appeared in four additional installments. "Mitchell's sensitive treatment of her heroes and villains is as artful as her skill at weaving all the dangling threads of a complex puzzle into a compelling whole," said *Kirkus*. Malminster

seems under siege in book 5, *A Rage of Innocents*, "another winner from one of the genre's best," raved *Kirkus*. Writing as Sarah Lacey, she is the author of a four-book series featuring Yorkshire tax inspector Leah Hunter, first seen in *File Under: Deceased* (1992). Born in Wakefield, England, Mitchell earned an honors degree in English at Leeds University. She later trained as a nurse and midwife and worked in a hospital casualty department and as a health visitor. She lives with her husband near Wakefield, England.

John Morrissey...chief inspector and family man...Malminster, England
- ❏ ❏ 1 - A Lively Form of Death (1990)
- ❏ ❏ 2 - In Stony Places (1991)
- ❏ ❏ 3 - A Strange Desire (1994)
- ❏ ❏   - U.S.-Roots of Evil
- ❏ ❏ 4 - A Portion for Foxes (1995)
- ❏ ❏ 5 - A Rage of Innocents (1996)
- ❏ ❏ . . . .
- ❏ ❏ . . . .

■ MOEN, Ruth Raby

Two-time winner of the Washington Publishers Association award for best mystery, Ruth Raby Moen has written three novels featuring Pacific Northwest journalist Kathleen O'Shaughnessy, introduced in *Deadly Deceptions* (1993). When last seen in *Return to the Kill* (1996), O'Shaughnessy has joined forces with Native American Deputy Sheriff Benjamin Jack, the best tracker in the county. With the help of some Indian folklore learned from his grandfather and a

cedar board invested with spiritual powers, Sheriff Jack hunts down a killer with a mysterious past, while O'Shaughnessy takes on a local politician and a disgruntled logger. Moen has also written *Hayseeds in My Hair*, her memoir of growing up during the 1940s as the youngest of three children raised in an isolated logging town in Washington's Cascade Mountains. Moen lives in Sedro-Wooley, Washington, where she owns and operates Flying Swan Publications.

Kathleen O'Shaughnessy...newspaper reporter...Seattle, Washington
- ❏ ❏ 1 - Deadly Deceptions (1993)
- ❏ ❏ 2 - Only One Way Out (1994)
- ❏ ❏ 3 - Return to the Kill (1996)
- ❏ ❏ . . . .
- ❏ ❏ . . . .

■ MOFFAT, Gwen

Mountaineer Gwen Moffat, who served for 20 years as a member of rescue teams in Britain and the Swiss Alps, was the first woman to become a professional rock-climbing guide. Still going strong at 75, Moffat has given Melinda Pink many of her own proficiencies, including mountain climbing and novel writing.

A middle-aged Justice of the Peace with incipient arthritis and a weight problem, Miss Pink is a perceptive investigator, but not a particularly good climber. Set in Montana, book 15 is *Private Sins* (1999). While Moffat exploits personal interests in her mysteries (wildlife, food and wine, organic living, prehistory, the supernatural and cats), she gives Miss Pink enough flaws to retain superiority over an otherwise intimidating woman. Moffat's nonfiction book, *Hard Road West: Alone on the California Trail* (1981), is an account of her journey across America. Her historical novel, *The Buckskin Girl* (1982), is based on the same adventure. Author of 30 books, including four volumes of autobiography, Moffat lives in North Wales.

Melinda Pink...mountain climbing novelist...Utah
- ❑ ❑ 1 - Lady With a Cool Eye (1973)
- ❑ ❑ 2 - Miss Pink at the Edge of the World (1975)
- ❑ ❑ 3 - Over the Sea to Death (1976)
- ❑ ❑ 4 - A Short Time To Live (1976)
- ❑ ❑ 5 - Persons Unknown (1978)
- ❑ ❑ 6 - Die Like a Dog (1982)
- ❑ ❑ 7 - Last Chance Country (1983)
- ❑ ❑ 8 - Grizzly Trail (1984)
- ❑ ❑ 9 - Snare (1987)
- ❑ ❑ 10 - The Stone Hawk (1989)
- ❑ ❑ 11 - Rage (1990)
- ❑ ❑ 12 - The Raptor Zone (1990)
- ❑ ❑ 13 - Veronica's Sisters (1992)
- ❑ ❑ 14 - The Lost Girls (1998)
- ❑ ❑ . . . .
- ❑ ❑ . . . .

■ MONFREDO, Miriam Grace

Miriam Grace Monfredo is the creator of Glynis Tryon, town librarian and fiercely independent woman of Seneca Falls, New York, introduced in *Seneca Falls Inheritance* (1992), nominated for Agatha and Macavity awards. Outcast from her Rochester family for her staunch refusal to marry, Glynis meets Elizabeth Cady Stanton at a historic 1848 meeting on women's rights. By 1854 Glynis is involved with the Underground Railway and the town constable, Cullen Stuart, who wants to marry her. Continuing players include Deputy Jacques Sundown (part Seneca Indian), Jeremiah Merrycoyf, Esq., a good friend to Glynis and the constable, hardware store owner Abraham Levy, and Glynis's landlady Harriet Peartree. Director of a legal and historical research firm, Monfredo is a former newspaper columnist and feature writer specializing in women's history. With degrees in history and library and information science, she conducts writing workshops for New York State Council of the Arts.

Glynis Tryon...1860s librarian suffragette...Seneca Falls, New York
- ❑ ❑ 1 - **Seneca Falls Inheritance (1992) Agatha & Macavity nominee** ☆☆
- ❑ ❑ 2 - North Star Conspiracy (1993)
- ❑ ❑ 3 - Blackwater Spirits (1995)
- ❑ ❑ 4 - Through a Gold Eagle (1996)
- ❑ ❑ 5 - The Stalking Horse (1998)
- ❑ ❑ 6 - Must the Maiden Die (1999)
- ❑ ❑ . . . .
- ❑ ❑ . . . .

■ MONTGOMERY, Yvonne

Yvonne Montgomery is the creator of successful 36-year-old Denver stockbroker Finny Aletter, whose mother thinks of her as "my unmarried daughter the stockbroker." *Publishers Weekly* called Finny "a quick and likable sleuth—a Nancy Drew with an M.B.A. and a sex life." Despite ten years of success as an account executive at Lakin & Fulton, Finny thinks she'd be happier as a carpenter. While restoring her house on Capitol Hill, she gets more satisfaction refinishing an oak mantel than landing a big account at work. When her boss is murdered and Finny becomes the prime suspect in *Scavengers* (1987), her decision to quit comes easily. "Intriguing and well-crafted," said *Bloomsbury Review*. With fellow mystery writer, M.J. Adamson, Montgomery writes historical romance as Yvonne Adamson. Their Irish family saga, *Bridey's Mountain* (1993), features four generations of Gregory women, plenty of Colorado history and a dash of the supernatural. Montgomery lives in Denver.

Finny Aletter...stockbroker turned carpenter...Denver, Colorado

- ❏ ❏ 1 - Scavengers (1987)
- ❏ ❏ 2 - Obstacle Course (1990)
- ❏ ❏ ....
- ❏ ❏ ....

■ MOODY, Skye Kathleen

Playwright and photojournalist Skye Kathleen Moody has written four Pacific Northwest mysteries featuring U.S. Fish and Wildlife Agent, Venus Diamond, first seen in *Rain Dance* (1996). "An utterly captivating crime novel," raved *Publishers Weekly* in a starred review. The tiny, leather-clad, Harley-riding agent investigates rare-animal embryo-cloning in book 4, *Habitat* (1999). After studying photography and Russian in New York City, Moody worked for several years as a safari bush guide in Kenya and Tanzania and later served as a cultural exchange liaison for physicians throughout Asia, East Africa and Eastern Europe. Since 1995 she has conducted photography workshops at Chengdu University in China, and spoken at writers and artists conferences in Russia and Finland as a U.S.I.A. fellow. A former V.I.S.T.A. volunteer, she is the author of two award-winning nonfiction books as Kathy Kahn. Born and raised in Seattle, she divides her time between California and Washington State after a recent move from New Orleans.

Venus Diamond...U.S. Fish & Wildlife agent...Washington

- ❏ ❏ 1 - Rain Dance (1996)
- ❏ ❏ 2 - Blue Poppy (1997)
- ❏ ❏ 3 - Wildcrafters (1998)
- ❏ ❏ ....
- ❏ ❏ ....

■ MOODY, Susan

Past chairman of the British Crime Writers' Association, Susan Moody has created two mystery series with unusual women protagonists. Featured in seven books is Penny Wanawake, beautiful, black, six-foot daughter of an English noblewoman and an ambassador to the U.N. Educated in England, France, Switzerland and the U.S., Penny travels the globe as a freelance photographer, while her jewel-thief sweetheart steals from the rich to aid her fund-raising efforts for world famine relief. Moody's second series features bridge professional Cassandra Swann, last seen in book 6, *Dummy Hand* (1998), where Cassie is injured by a hit-and-run driver, allowing Moody to use her personal experience of being knocked off her bicycle by a bus. Author of *Falling Angel* (1998), *Playing with Fire* (1990), *The Italian Garden* (1994), *Mosaic* (1991) and *Misselthwaite* (1995), published in the U.S. in 1998 as *Return to the Secret Garden*, Moody has also written as Susannah James. A native of Oxford, Moody spent ten years in Tennessee during the '60s. She lives in Bedford, England.

Cassandra Swann...bridge professional...Cotswolds, England

- ❏ ❏ 1 - Death Takes a Hand (1993)
- ❏ ❏ - Brit.-Takeout Double
- ❏ ❏ 2 - Grand Slam (1994)
- ❏ ❏ 3 - King of Hearts (1995)
- ❏ ❏ 4 - Doubled in Spades (1996)
- ❏ ❏ 5 - Sacrifice Bid (1997)
- ❏ ❏ 6 - Dummy Hand (1998)
- ❏ ❏ ....
- ❏ ❏ ....

Penny Wanawake...photographer daughter of black diplomat...England

- ❏ ❏ 1 - Penny Black (1984)
- ❏ ❏ 2 - Penny Dreadful (1984)
- ❏ ❏ 3 - Penny Post (1985)
- ❏ ❏ 4 - Penny Royal (1986)
- ❏ ❏ 5 - Penny Wise (1988)

❑ ❑ 6 - Penny Pinching (1989)
❑ ❑ 7 - Penny Saving (1993)
❑ ❑ ....
❑ ❑ ....

■ MOORE, Barbara

Barbara Moore is the author of two mysteries featuring Dr. Gordon Christy, a New Mexico veterinarian introduced in *The Doberman Wore Black* (1983). Along with a chameleon and a couple of cockatoos, Dr. Christy is on his way to Vail, Colorado, to baby-sit the practice of a veterinary colleague when he is run off the road by a black MG. Next to the driver sits a grinning Doberman named Gala, who later joins forces with the doc. Lots of interesting animal lore is deftly woven into the mystery. Along with two other novels,

Moore has written *The Fever Called Living* (1976), a novel about Edgar Allan Poe, and with her husband John Lee, a nonfiction book, *Monsters Among Us* (1975). Moore earned B.A. and M.A. degrees from the University of Arizona, where she graduated magna cum laude and Phi Beta Kappa in 1971. The daughter of a petroleum journalist, she has worked as a newspaper reporter in Fort Worth and San Antonio, Texas and Denver, Colorado. An Oklahoma native, she lives in Texas.

Gordon Christy...veterinarian...New Mexico
❑ ❑ 1 - The Doberman Wore Black (1983)
❑ ❑ 2 - The Wolf Whispered Death (1986)
❑ ❑ ....
❑ ❑ ....

■ MOORE, Margaret

Margaret Moore has written a trio of mysteries featuring Chief Inspector Richard Baxter, introduced in *Forests of the Night* (1987), set in the world of child guidance clinics. Shortly after England's New Radical Party leader, Michael Giddings, is assassinated at a public speech in book 2, *Dangerous Conceits* (1988), a fellow panelist at the same event is found dead of an apparent heart attack. No sooner has Giddings' widow, a famous actress, disappeared than Baxter learns Giddings' mother has a scandalous secret in her

past. The Chief Inspector has a lot to investigate. While the first two installments were published in both England and the United States, book 3, *Murder in Good Measure* (1990), was released only in the U.K. Born and raised in Northern Ireland, Moore studied in Edinburgh and London and later worked as an educational psychologist and teacher. She lives in Cambridge, England, where she is an administrator at Trinity College.

Richard Baxter...police inspector...England
❑ ❑ 1 - Forests of the Night (1987)
❑ ❑ 2 - Dangerous Conceits (1988)
❑ ❑ 3 - Murder in Good Measure (1990)
❑ ❑ ....
❑ ❑ ....

■ MOORE, Miriam Ann

Miriam Ann Moore has written three mysteries featuring 1980s New Yorker Marti Hirsch, introduced in *Last Dance* (1997). A mass of contradictions, Marti is a strong woman perpetually on the verge of a nervous breakdown. A '60s radical who loves to disco, she is a nice Jewish girl who likes oysters. "A truly delightful and feisty heroine who would be good company no matter what the decade," said *Publishers Weekly*. Marti's third adventure, *I Will Survive* (1999), begins during the 1981 holiday season when she is

the prime suspect in the death of girlhood chum Jana Crowley. Born in New York City and raised in New Jersey, Moore works as a travel agent in San Francisco, where she has lived since 1986. She and her Shaigetz husband share their home with a snake named Tony Blair. If you don't know what Shaigetz means, Moore suggests picking up copy of *The Joy of Yiddish* before reading her mysteries. Her mother, Roberta Rogow, writes a mystery series featuring Charles Dodgson and Conan Doyle.

Marti Hirsch...would-be writer and disco lover...New York, New York

❏ ❏ 1 - Last Dance (1997)
❏ ❏ 2 - Stayin' Alive (1998)
❏ ❏ . . . .
❏ ❏ . . . .

■ MORELL, Mary

Mary Morell is the creator of crime fiction's first Chicana lesbian mysteries, starting with *Final Session* (1991), winner of a 1990 lesbian fiction contest sponsored by Spinsters Ink. San Antonio, Texas police detective Lucia Ramos is called in when psychotherapist Elizabeth Freeman is murdered. It seems the lesbian therapist had a history of sexual involvement with her clients. The book "gets off to a splendid start with a deliciously suspicious death and an engaging detective to sort things out," said *Publishers Weekly*. Ramos returns in *Final Rest* (1993), where she flies to Alabama to help her lover's aunt, accused of murdering a friend by lacing her cinnamon-sugar with digitalis. After several decades in Texas, Morell moved to New Mexico where her partner helped with her writing, but their two dogs, four cats and two horses did not. With Anne Frost, Morell previously co-owned Full Circle Books, a feminist bookstore in Albuquerque, which is now closed. She has worked as a counselor, an English teacher and a travel agency manager.

Lucia Ramos...Chicana lesbian police detective...San Antonio, Texas

❏ ❏ 1 - Final Session (1991)
❏ ❏ 2 - Final Rest (1993)
❏ ❏ . . . .
❏ ❏ . . . .

■ MORGAN, D Miller

Texas author D Miller Morgan has written two mysteries featuring San Diego private investigator Daisy Marlow and sheriff Sam Milo, introduced in *Money Leads to Murder* (1987), also published as *Rendezvous Kit Marlow*. Middle-aged, overweight and given to strong language, Daisy collects hand-made French silk lingerie and makes a different color choice every day from her extensive lingerie wardrobe. Hired to retrieve a kidnapped dog being held for ransom, Daisy travels to Las Vegas in book 2, *A Lovely Night To Kill* (1988). Named for Dolores Del Rio (her father was the proprietor of three movie theaters), Morgan frequently wore monogrammed apparel as a girl, thanks to her mother's embroidery expertise. As a consequence, her friends started calling her 'D' and she has used the initial (without a period) as her name ever since. Mother of three, grandmother of six and great-grandmother of two, Morgan lives in Plano, Texas, where she has completed books 3 and 4 in the Daisy Marlow series.

Daisy Marlow & Sam Milo...lingerie-addicted P.I. & sheriff...San Diego, California

❏ ❏ 1 - Money Leads to Murder (1987)
❏ ❏   - APA-Rendezvous Kit Marlow
❏ ❏ 2 - A Lovely Night To Kill (1988)
❏ ❏ . . . .
❏ ❏ . . . .

■ MORGAN, Kate [P]

Kate Morgan is the pseudonym of Ann Hamilton Whitman, author of seven mysteries featuring small-town librarian Dewey James, a Kentucky police chief's widow, introduced in *A Slay at the Races* (1990). A 60-something woman with sparkling blue eyes and unruly silver hair, Dewey is frequently given to quoting literary classics and solving local crimes. Hamilton's first-rate library has been her life's work and she is justifiably proud of her accomplishments. Dewey's black Labrador retriever Isaiah, her horse Starbuck, and old friend and would-be beau, George Farnham, are series regulars. In book 5, *Days of Crime and Roses* (1992), Dewey travels to New York City, where she is surprised to learn that her fabulously wealthy college roommate, Jane Duncan, is about to marry for the fifth time. Jane's intended, successful playwright Donald Brewster, is accused of plagiarizing the work for which he has just received a prestigious award. A "highly entertaining" series, says *Booklist*.

Dewey James...60-something small-town librarian...Hamilton, Kentucky

❏ ❏   1 - A Slay at the Races (1990)
❏ ❏   2 - Murder Most Fowl (1991)
❏ ❏   3 - Home Sweet Homicide (1992)
❏ ❏   4 - Mystery Loves Company (1992)
❏ ❏   5 - Days of Crime and Roses (1992)
❏ ❏   6 - Wanted Dude or Alive (1994)
❏ ❏   7 - Old School Dies (1996)
❏ ❏   . . . .
❏ ❏   . . . .

■ MORISON, B.J.

B.J. Morison is Betty Jane Morison, author of five books in the Little Maine Murder series set in 1970s Bar Harbor. Precocious eight-year-old Elizabeth Lamb Worthington is introduced in *Champagne and a Gardener* (1982). A twelve-year-old Elizabeth wangles passage from Boston to Mount Desert Island aboard a luxury Italian yacht in book 4, *The Voyage of the Chianti* (1987), where she solves a locked-room mystery. Daughter-in-law of the late historian Samuel Elliot Morrison, the author operates a famous art deco theater in Bar Harbor. She is the author of *Reality and Dream* (1985), a collection of Christmas stories, and *The Founding of the Bar Harbor Mouse Bakery*, a fable for children and adults. A special breed of mice who owe their super-intelligence and longevity to the experiments of a mad scientist, the Springs are clever mice who read Karl Marx, attend Ivy League colleges, fly little airplanes and make their fortune selling wonderful baked goods. Born in Kittery, Maine, Morison has traveled widely and lives in Bar Harbor.

Elizabeth Lamb Worthington...precocious adolescent girl...Bar Harbor, Maine

❏ ❏   1 - Champagne and a Gardener (1982)
❏ ❏   2 - Port and a Star Border (1984)
❏ ❏   3 - Beer and Skittles (1985)
❏ ❏   4 - The Voyage of the Chianti (1987)
❏ ❏   5 - The Martini Effect (1992)
❏ ❏   . . . .
❏ ❏   . . . .

■ MORRONE, Wenda Wardell

When Wenda Wardell Morrone (muh-RO-nee) was diagnosed with stage three ovarian cancer in 1989, she stopped putting off things she had always wanted to do. When her hair grew back after chemotherapy, she dyed it red and started writing her first mystery novel. Despite having two nonfiction books in print, it took seven years of writing and rewriting before finding a publisher for *No Time for an Everyday Woman* (1997). When Lorelei Muldoon flies to Montana for an illicit weekend, the plane crashes, her boss dies, and she meets John Goodman lookalike, Sheriff Claud Willetts. After surviving terrorism by computer in *The Year 2000 Killers* (1999), Lorelei gets involved in a smuggling case with Kosovo ties in *When Nightmares Grow Bones* (2000). Sheriff Willetts returns with *Freefall in Cutthroat Gorge* (2001). Former features editor for *Glamour* magazine, Morrone is a graduate of Bryn Mawr College. After living in New York for more than 25 years, she has recently returned to Montana. She and her husband live in Bozeman.

Claud Willetts...small-town sheriff...Merciful Valley, Montana

❏ ❏   1 - Freefall in Cutthroat Gorge (2001)
❏ ❏   . . . .
❏ ❏   . . . .

Lorelei Muldoon...high-profile numbers analyst...New York, New York

❏ ❏   1 - No Time For an Everyday Woman [incl Claud Willetts] (1997)
❏ ❏   2 - The Year 2000 Killers (1999)
❏ ❏   . . . .
❏ ❏   . . . .

■ MOYES, Patricia

Patricia Moyes has written 19 books featuring globe-trotting Scotland Yard Chief Superintendent Henry Tibbett and his wife Emmy, first seen in *Dead Men Don't Ski* (1959). Their ninth adventure, *Many Deadly Returns* (1970) was a best-novel Edgar nominee. The Tibbetts' travels reflect Moyes' varied residences—Switzerland, the Netherlands, Washington, D.C. and the British Virgin Islands, as well as her favorite sports—skiing and sailing. Born in Ireland and educated in England, she launched her writing career with a World War II documentary script on radar. Following war-time service in the Women's Auxiliary Air Force (background for *Johnny Underground*), she spent eight years as company secretary for Peter Ustinov Productions in London (background for *Falling Star*), followed by five years as assistant editor for *Vogue* magazine (background for *Murder a la Mode*). In addition to several plays, she is the author of *How To Talk to Your Cat* (1978). Known to friends as Penny Haszard, Moyes lives on Virgin Gorda in the Caribbean.

Henry & Emmy Tibbett...Scotland Yard inspector & wife...London, England

- ❑ ❑ 1 - Dead Men Don't Ski (1959)
- ❑ ❑ 2 - Down Among the Dead Men (1961)
- ❑ ❑   - Brit.-The Sunken Sailor
- ❑ ❑ 3 - Death on the Agenda (1962)
- ❑ ❑ 4 - Murder a la Mode (1963)
- ❑ ❑ 5 - Falling Star (1964)
- ❑ ❑ 6 - Johnny Underground (1965)
- ❑ ❑ 7 - Murder Fantastical (1967)
- ❑ ❑ 8 - Death and the Dutch Uncle (1968)
- ❑ ❑ 9 - **Many Deadly Returns (1970) Edgar nominee** ☆
- ❑ ❑   - Brit.-Who Saw Her Die?
- ❑ ❑ 10 - Season of Snows and Sins (1971)
- ❑ ❑ 11 - The Curious Affair of the Third Dog (1973)
- ❑ ❑ 12 - Black Widower (1975)
- ❑ ❑ 13 - The Coconut Killings (1977)
- ❑ ❑   - Brit.-To Kill a Coconut
- ❑ ❑ 14 - Who Is Simon Warwick? (1979)
- ❑ ❑ 15 - Angel Death (1980)
- ❑ ❑ 16 - A Six-Letter Word for Death (1983)
- ❑ ❑ 17 - Night Ferry to Death (1985)
- ❑ ❑ 18 - Black Girl, White Girl (1989)
- ❑ ❑ 19 - Twice in a Blue Moon (1993)
- ❑ ❑ . . . .
- ❑ ❑ . . . .

■ MULLER, Marcia

With *Edwin of the Iron Shoes* (1977), Marcia Muller became the first American woman to launch a hard-boiled P.I. series with a female detective. Introduced as the investigator for San Francisco's All Souls Legal Cooperative, Sharon McCone later forms her own agency and learns to fly, in a series that now numbers 20 books and a volume of short stories. In book 6, *Double* (1984), she teams up with husband Bill Pronzini and his Nameless Detective to solve a murder at a San Diego P.I. convention. The two have also collaborated on *1001 Midnights: The Aficionado's Guide to Mystery and Detective Fiction* (1986) and numerous anthologies. Muller's two other series characters, each intended to make only three appearances, are Hispanic museum curator Elena Oliverez, and international art investigator Joanna Stark. A Detroit native and University of Michigan graduate (B.A. in English, M.A. in journalism), Muller lives in the San Francisco Bay area. A Shamus and Anthony award-winner, she was honored with a Life Achievement award by Private Eye Writers of America in 1993.

Elena Oliverez...Mexican arts museum curator...Santa Barbara, California

- ❑ ❑ 1 - The Tree of Death (1983)
- ❑ ❑ 2 - The Legend of the Slain Soldiers (1985)
- ❑ ❑ 3 - Beyond the Grave (1986)
- ❑ ❑ . . . .
- ❑ ❑ . . . .

Joanna Stark…international art investigator…Napa Valley, California
- ❑ ❑ 1 - The Cavalier in White (1986)
- ❑ ❑ 2 - There Hangs the Knife (1988)
- ❑ ❑ 3 - Dark Star (1989)
- ❑ ❑ . . . .
- ❑ ❑ . . . .

Sharon McCone…legal investigator turned P.I….San Francisco, California
- ❑ ❑ 1 - Edwin of the Iron Shoes (1977)
- ❑ ❑ 2 - Ask the Cards a Question (1982)
- ❑ ❑ 3 - The Cheshire Cat's Eye (1983)
- ❑ ❑ 4 - Games To Keep the Dark Away (1984)
- ❑ ❑ 5 - Leave a Message for Willie (1984)
- ❑ ❑ 6 - Double [w/Bill Pronzini] (1984)
- ❑ ❑ 7 - There's Nothing To Be Afraid Of (1985)
- ❑ ❑ 8 - Eye of the Storm (1988)
- ❑ ❑ 9 - There's Something in a Sunday (1989)
- ❑ ❑ 10 - **The Shape of Dread (1989) Shamus nominee** ☆
- ❑ ❑ 11 - Trophies and Dead Things (1990)
- ❑ ❑ 12 - **Where Echoes Live (1991) Shamus nominee** ☆
- ❑ ❑ 13 - Pennies on a Dead Woman's Eyes (1992)
- ❑ ❑ 14 - **Wolf in the Shadows (1993) Anthony winner** ★
  Edgar & Shamus nominee ☆☆
- ❑ ❑ 15 - Till the Butchers Cut Him Down (1994)
- ❑ ❑ ss - The McCone Files (1995)
- ❑ ❑ 16 - **A Wild and Lonely Place (1995) Macavity nominee** ☆
- ❑ ❑ 17 - The Broken Promise Land (1996)
- ❑ ❑ 18 - Both Ends of the Night (1997)
- ❑ ❑ 19 - While Other People Sleep (1998)
- ❑ ❑ ss - McCone and Friends (1999)
- ❑ ❑ 20 - A Walk Through The Fire (1999)
- ❑ ❑ . . . .
- ❑ ❑ . . . .

■ MUNGER, Katy

Shamus nominee Katy Munger writes smart, comic mysteries featuring wise-cracking North Carolina investigator Casey Jones, an in-your-face woman of the New South, introduced in *Legwork* (1997). Owing to her time in a Florida jail, Casey works as an unlicensed P.I. for 360-pound Bobby D., who thinks of himself as a modern Nero Wolfe. After a favorite client gets killed on Casey's watch in book 3, *Money To Burn* (1999), she lives to fight another day in *Bad to the Bone* (2000). Munger's first four mysteries, written as Gallagher Gray, feature New Yorkers Theodore S. Hubbert and his irrepressible Auntie Lil. Born in Honolulu, Hawaii, Munger moved to North Carolina at an early age, took careful notes on her sociable parents and friends, and earned a degree in creative writing at the University of North Carolina, Chapel Hill, before heading to New York for 16 years where she worked for a private banking group. Munger lives in Durham, North Carolina, where she reviews mysteries for *Washington Post Book World*.

Casey Jones…unlicensed private eye…Durham, North Carolina
- ❑ ❑ 1 - **Legwork (1997) Shamus nominee** ☆
- ❑ ❑ 2 - Out of Time (1998)
- ❑ ❑ . . . .
- ❑ ❑ . . . .

■ MURPHY, Shirley Rousseau

Award-winning painter and sculptor Shirley Rousseau Murphy is the author of more than 30 books of fantasy, folklore and mystery for children and adults. She has written books with talking dragons and wolves, and a nation of otters who speak, so it's no surprise her P.I. Joe Grey is a cat. When a mysterious accident gives him the ability to read, talk and feel human emotions, Joe even finds himself planning his day. Introduced in *Cat on the Edge* (1996), Joe and girlfriend Dulcie find talking very useful for scaring dogs and solving crimes. Last seen in book 5, *Cat to the Dogs* (1999), Joe and Dulcie's sixth case is *Cat Out for Blood* (2000). Among Murphy's fantasy titles are *The Catswold Portal* (1992), about a race of shape-changing cats, and the *Dragonbards* trilogy for young adults. After graduating from the California School of Fine Arts, she worked as a packaging designer, department store decorator, museum documents assistant and college art teacher of mosaics. She lives with her husband in Carmel, California.

Joe Grey...talking-cat private eye...Molena Point, California

- ❑ ❑ 1 - Cat on the Edge (1996)
- ❑ ❑ 2 - Cat Under Fire (1997)
- ❑ ❑ 3 - Cat Raise the Dead (1997)
- ❑ ❑ 4 - Cat in the Dark (1999)
- ❑ ❑ . . . .
- ❑ ❑ . . . .

■ MURRAY, Donna Huston

Donna Huston Murray writes Main Line mysteries featuring Ginger Struve Barnes, a transplant from the other side of the Schuykill, married to the head of a fledgling private school. There is no shortage of pretentiousness, fictionally speaking, on Philadelphia's Main Line, that string of upscale real estate on the city's west side. Introduced in *The Main Line is Murder* (1995), Mrs. Fix-it Ginger was hailed by one reviewer as "Spenser as a housewife." When last seen in book 5, *A Score To Settle* (1999), Ginger is in Norfolk, Virginia to help her pregnant cousin, whose N.F.L. quarterback husband is suspected of murdering a teammate. She's back on the Main Line just in time for book 6, *Final Performance* (2000), when a movie star with local ties returns to Philadelphia. While Murray's husband was a private school headmaster for 14 years, he currently directs a boys' sports camp. They have two children and a disobedient dog, but Murray says her alter ego is much taller and braver. She lives with her family in Radnor, Pennsylvania.

Ginger Struve Barnes...headmaster's wife and suburban mother...Philadelphia, Pennsylvania

- ❑ ❑ 1 - The Main Line Is Murder (1995)
- ❑ ❑ 2 - Final Arrangements (1996)
- ❑ ❑ 3 - School of Hard Knocks (1997)
- ❑ ❑ 4 - No Bones About It (1998)
- ❑ ❑ 5 - A Score to Settle (1999)
- ❑ ❑ . . . .
- ❑ ❑ . . . .

■ MURRAY, Lynne

Lynne Murray is the creator of Josephine Fuller, a woman of size who doesn't apologize. Think Camryn Manheim meets Stephanie Plum. In the series opener, *Larger Than Death* (1997), Jo finds her dream job when she answers an ad in the *San Francisco Chronicle*— traveling the country investigating potential candidates for charitable gifts and doing the odd favor for feminist San Diego philanthropist Alicia Madrone. In book 2, *Large Target* (2000), Jo looks into a young woman's involvement with a strange band of do-gooders. Murray's first published mystery featured free-lance photographer Ingrid Hunter, reluctantly supporting herself as an office temp in *Termination Interview* (1988). Born in Decatur, Illinois, Murray has lived in Southern California, Alaska, Texas and Washington. A psychology graduate of San Francisco State University, she has been a practicing Buddhist for 30 years. Murray lives in San Francisco where she works part-time transcribing police surveillance tapes for criminal defense attorneys.

Josephine Fuller...Queen-sized private investigator...Seattle, Washington

- ❑ ❑ 1 - Larger Than Death (1997)
- ❑ ❑ 2 - Large Target (2000)
- ❑ ❑ 3 - Murder at Large (2001)
- ❑ ❑ 4 - A Ton of Trouble (2002)
- ❑ ❑ . . . .
- ❑ ❑ . . . .

■ MYERS, Amy

British author Amy Myers writes historical mysteries featuring Victorian master chef Auguste Didier, a man both British and French. In the series opener, *Murder in Pug's Parlor* (1986), the master chef is forced to investigate when accused of poisoning a man with mushrooms prepared on the night of the murder. When last seen in book 10, *Murder with Majesty* (1999), the year is 1905 and Didier has been summoned to Farthing Court by King Edward VII to cook for the wedding of Lord Arthur Montfoy and American heiress Gertrude Pennyfather. In addition to mystery short stories published in several anthologies, Myers writes historical and contemporary fiction as Alice Carr, Harriet Hudson and Laura Daniels. Previously a director and editor for a London publisher specializing in military history, Myers met her American husband at a book launch party. They lived in Paris for a number of years, where she first hit on the idea of a detecting chef. She and her husband live in a Kentish village by the North Downs.

Auguste Didier...British-French Victorian master chef...England
- ❏ ❏ 1 - Murder in Pug's Parlour (1986)
- ❏ ❏ 2 - Murder in the Limelight (1986)
- ❏ ❏ 3 - Murder at Plum's (1989)
- ❏ ❏ 4 - Murder at the Masque (1991)
- ❏ ❏ 5 - Murder Makes an Entree (1992)
- ❏ ❏ 6 - Murder Under the Kissing Bough (1992)
- ❏ ❏ 7 - Murder in the Smokehouse (1994)
- ❏ ❏ 8 - Murder at the Music Hall (1995)
- ❏ ❏ 9 - Murder in the Motor Stable (1996)
- ❏ ❏ ....
- ❏ ❏ ....

■ MYERS, Tamar

During the past five years, the indefatigable Tamar (ta-MAHR) Myers has published 13 mysteries in two light-hearted, cozy series. Her Pennsylvania Dutch mysteries (with recipes) feature Magdalena Yoder, owner and operator of a Mennonite inn, first seen in *Too Many Crooks Spoil the Broth* (1994). Abigail Timberlake, owner of The Den of Antiquity antique shop, introduced in *Larceny and Old Lace* (1996), makes her seventh appearance in *A Penny Urned* (2000). The daughter of Mennonite missionaries, Myers was born and raised in a remote region of the Belgian Congo (now Zaire), where her family lived with a tribe of headhunters. She wrote her first book at age ten, after reading everything her parents had brought with them to the jungle. After graduating from the American College in Jerusalem, Myers earned an M.A. from Eastern Kentucky University. The author of hundreds of articles on topics of horticultural interest, Myers lives with her family in South Carolina, where she enjoys oil painting and teaching piano.

Abigail Timberlake...antiques dealer...Charlotte, North Carolina
- ❏ ❏ 1 - Larceny and Old Lace (1996)
- ❏ ❏ 2 - Gilt by Association (1996)
- ❏ ❏ 3 - The Ming and I (1997)
- ❏ ❏ 4 - So Faux, So Good (1998)
- ❏ ❏ 5 - Baroque and Desperate (1999)
- ❏ ❏ 6 - Estate of Mind (1999)
- ❏ ❏ ....
- ❏ ❏ ....

Magdalena Yoder...Mennonite inn owner-operator...Hernia, Pennsylvania
- ❏ ❏ 1 - Too Many Crooks Spoil the Broth (1994)
- ❏ ❏ 2 - Parsley, Sage, Rosemary and Crime (1995)
- ❏ ❏ 3 - No Use Dying Over Spilled Milk (1996)
- ❏ ❏ 4 - Just Plain Pickled to Death (1997)
- ❏ ❏ 5 - Between a Wok and a Hard Place (1998)
- ❏ ❏ 6 - Eat, Drink and Be Wary (1998)
- ❏ ❏ 7 - Play It Again, Spam (1999)
- ❏ ❏ 8 - The Hand That Rocks the Ladle (2000)
- ❏ ❏ ....
- ❏ ❏ ....

■ NABB, Magdalen

Englishwoman Magdalen Nabb has lived in Florence since 1975, the setting for her mysteries featuring the "likable, slow-moving and on occasion taciturn" Marshal Salvatore Guarnaccia of the Carabinieri, "most Maigret-like of contemporary policemen." A man "who proceeds by feeling and intuition, rather than logic and deduction," the Marshal is featured in eleven installments beginning with *Death of an Englishman* (1981). Commander of the Palazzo Pitti station, he is a detective of cogent powers, "a solid believable character, buttressed by an equally believable marriage," according to Simon Brett. Originally a potter, Nabb paints exquisite portraits of the very secret city of Florence and the surrounding Tuscan countryside. She is "magnificent on the medieval pageantry and sinister facades," said the *Sunday Times*. Also an award-winning children's author, Nabb has written seven books set in her native Lancashire featuring Josie Smith, the subject of a successful British television series scripted by the author.

Salvatore Guarnaccia...Sicilian Carabinieri marshal...Florence, Italy

- ❏ ❏ 1 - Death of an Englishman (1981)
- ❏ ❏ 2 - Death of a Dutchman (1982)
- ❏ ❏ 3 - Death in Springtime (1983)
- ❏ ❏ 4 - Death in Autumn (1984)
- ❏ ❏ 5 - The Marshal and the Murderer (1987)
- ❏ ❏ 6 - The Marshal and the Madwoman (1988)
- ❏ ❏ 7 - The Marshal's Own Case (1990)
- ❏ ❏ 8 - The Marshal Makes His Report (1991)
- ❏ ❏ 9 - The Marshal at the Villa Torrini (1993)
- ❏ ❏ 10 - The Marshal and the Forgery (1995)
- ❏ ❏ 11 - The Monster of Florence (1996)
- ❏ ❏ . . . .
- ❏ ❏ . . . .

■ NADELSON, Reggie

American journalist and documentary film-maker Reggie Nadelson is the creator of Russian-born New York City cop Artie Cohen, introduced in *Red Mercury Blues* (1995), published first in England and later in the U.S. as *Red Hot Blues* (1998). "This series effectively combines the traditional hard-boiled formula (loner/knight errant walking the mean streets) with a savvy, '90s feel for the silk-suited nature of international crime," said Bill Ott in *Booklist*. Born Artemy Maximovich Otalsky, the N.Y.P.D. cop left Moscow at age 14. Twenty-five years later his father's best friend, an ex-K.G.B. general, is shot and killed on live television while in New York promoting his book. Artie's search for the killer takes him from the tight-lipped Russian community of Brighton Beach to the streets of Moscow. "A *Gorky Park* for the '90s, as Dashiell Hammett might have done it," said the *London Times*. Artie goes to Hong Kong in book 2 and London in book 3. A New York City native, Nadelson divides her time between London and New York.

Artie Cohen...39-year-old Russian-born cop...New York, New York

- ❏ ❏ 1 - Red Mercury Blues (1995)
- ❏ ❏ - U.S.-Red Hot Blues (1998)
- ❏ ❏ 2 - Hot Poppies (1997)
- ❏ ❏ 3 - Bloody London (1999)
- ❏ ❏ . . . .
- ❏ ❏ . . . .

■ NAVRATILOVA, Martina and Liz Nickles

World champion Martina Navratilova and marketing consultant Liz Nickles teamed up to write tennis mysteries featuring physical therapist Jordan Myles, a former tennis star turned trainer. Nickles approached Navratilova with the idea while she was still on tour and the publication of their series opener, *The Total Zone* (1994), was timed to coincide with Navratilova's retirement. In book 2, *Breaking Point* (1996), Jordan suspects foul play when a promoter's assistant falls to her death at a Paris reception. She's a partner and head physical therapist at a Desert Springs sports center in book 3, *Killer Instinct* (1997), when clients start suffering sudden, mysterious collapses. A former advertising executive, Nickles has written several novels, six nonfiction books and a trio of illustrated cat books, including *First Cat, Second Term: Socks Pussyfoots His Way Back into the White House* (1997). After winning more than 1,400 matches, including a streak of 74 wins in a row, Navratilova was still in the top five when she retired from singles play.

Jordan Myles...ex-tennis star physical therapist...Palm Springs,California
- ❑ ❑ 1 - The Total Zone (1994)
- ❑ ❑ 2 - Breaking Point (1996)
- ❑ ❑ 3 - Killer Instinct (1997)
- ❑ ❑ . . . .
- ❑ ❑ . . . .

■ NEEL, Janet [P]

Janet Neel is the pseudonym of Janet Cohen for her mysteries featuring John McLeish of New Scotland Yard and civil servant Francesca Wilson. Their series debut, *Death's Bright Angel* (1988), won the Creasey award for best first novel. Short-listed for CWA's best novel award, book 4 has Francesca studying fraud and murder at an all-women's college. When last seen in *To Die For* (1998), McLeish is investigating the death of a glamorous restaurant owner. A former administrator in the Department of Trade and Industry, Neel worked for 13 years in a merchant bank and is now a Governor of the BBC, vice-chairman of a building society and non-executive director of a bank and two public companies. She also founded and financed two successful London restaurants. After reading law at Cambridge and qualifying as a solicitor, she worked briefly as a war games designer in the U.S. and later in industrial relations in London's construction industry. As Janet Cohen she wrote a 1992 legal thriller, *The Highest Bidder*.

John McLeish & Francesca Wilson...DCI & businesswoman...London, England
- ❑ ❑ 1 - **Death's Bright Angel (1988) Creasey winner ★**
- ❑ ❑ 2 - Death on Site (1989)
- ❑ ❑ 3 - Death of a Partner (1991)
- ❑ ❑ 4 - **Death Among the Dons (1993) Gold Dagger nominee ☆**
- ❑ ❑ 5 - A Timely Death (1996)
- ❑ ❑ 6 - To Die For (1998)
- ❑ ❑ . . . .
- ❑ ❑ . . . .

■ NEELY, Barbara

Barbara Neely is the creator of Blanche White, a middle-aged black domestic whose debut appearance, *Blanche on the Lam* (1992), won Agatha, Anthony and Macavity awards for best first novel. Feisty, funny, feminist queen-sized Blanche has fled a North Carolina courthouse after being sentenced to 30 days in jail for writing $42.50 worth of bad checks when four of her employers left town without paying her. She ends up at the summer house of a wealthy family keeping secrets of their own, including a dead body. After adopting her niece and nephew in book 2, Blanche takes the family to an exclusive black resort in Maine, but they're back in Boston for book 3. Neely's short fiction has been published in *Essence* magazine and various anthologies. During the '60s she organized community housing for female felons, creating a program that still exists. In the '70s and '80s, Neely worked with homeless women, teenage mothers and women on welfare. A Pennsylvania native, she lives in Massachusetts.

Blanche White...black domestic worker...Boston, Massachusetts
- ❑ ❑ 1 - **Blanche on the Lam (1992) Anthony, Agatha, & Macavity winner ★★★**
- ❑ ❑ 2 - Blanche Among the Talented Tenth (1994)
- ❑ ❑ 3 - Blanche Cleans Up (1998)
- ❑ ❑ . . . .
- ❑ ❑ . . . .

NESSEN, Ron and Johanna Neuman

Husband-and-wife team Ron Nessen and Johanna Neuman (rhymes with Truman) are co-authors of three mysteries featuring Washington, D.C. odd couple, Jerry Knight and Jane Day. Knight is the 50-something, three-times-divorced, ultra-conservative host of America's most popular radio call-in show. Jane Day is 20 years younger, as liberal as Knight is conservative, and White House correspondent for the *Washington Post*. They're both after the scoop when a prominent environmentalist dies in *Knight & Day* (1995). Former NBC chief White House correspondent and presidential press secretary for Gerald R. Ford, Nessen is communications vice-president at the Brookings Institute. His other books include *The First Lady, The Hour,* and *It Sure Looks Different from the Inside.* Newman is a former *USA Today* White House correspondent and foreign editor. Author of *Lights, Camera, War: Is Media Technology Driving International Politics?*, she is a projects editor in the Washington Bureau of the *Los Angeles Times*. The couple lives in Bethesda, Maryland.

Jerry Knight & Jane Day...right-wing radio host & liberal reporter...Washington, D.C.

- ❏ ❏ 1 - Knight & Day (1995)
- ❏ ❏ 2 - Press Corpse (1996)
- ❏ ❏ 3 - Death With Honors (1998)
- ❏ ❏ . . . .
- ❏ ❏ . . . .

NEWMAN, Sharan

Medievalist Sharan Newman writes mysteries set in 12th century France featuring the daughter of a wealthy merchant who enters a convent to curb her willfulness (Catherine) and a Saxon nobleman (Edgar) and student of Peter Abelard. The Macavity award- winning series has collected four additional nominations for mystery awards. Catherine travels to Germany in book 6, *The Difficult Saint* (1999), when her sister is accused of murdering her husband, a German lord. With Miriam Grace Monfredo, Newman is co-editor of two historical mystery collections of original short stories, *Crime Through Time* (1997) and *Crime Through Time II* (1998). Recently reissued in paperback is Newman's Arthurian trilogy from the viewpoint of Guinevere– *Guinevere* (1981), *The Chessboard Queen* (1983), and *Guinevere Evermore* (1985). With a Ph.D. in history from the University of California at Santa Barbara, Newman has also written science fiction short stories and numerous academic papers. She lives in Portland, Oregon.

Catherine LeVendeur...12th-century merchant's daughter...France

- ❏ ❏ 1 - **Death Comes as Epiphany (1993) Macavity winner ★**
  Anthony & Agatha nominee ☆☆
- ❏ ❏ 2 - The Devil's Door (1994)
- ❏ ❏ 3 - **The Wandering Arm (1995) Agatha nominee ☆**
- ❏ ❏ 4 - **Strong as Death (1996) Agatha nominee ☆**
- ❏ ❏ 5 - Cursed in the Blood (1998)
- ❏ ❏ . . . .
- ❏ ❏ . . . .

NIELSEN, Helen

In the early 1950s Helen Nielsen was one of a few women to write for men's magazines such as *Manhunt*, and the influence of this early training shows in her "crisp prose and skillful handling of action scenes," says Marcia Muller (*1001 Midnights*). Nielsen's 18 crime novels include five featuring Chicago attorney Simon Drake, transplanted to Southern California after the series opener, *Gold Coast Nocturne* (1951), published in Britain as *Murder by Proxy*, and again as *Dead on the Level* (1954). Anthony Boucher particularly liked her cloak-and-dagger tale set in Denmark, *Stranger in the Dark* (1955). Nielsen published more than 50 short stories and wrote television scripts for *Alfred Hitchcock Presents, Perry Mason, Alcoa Theatre* and others. As a teenager she worked as a costumer for Old Globe Theatre Productions in Chicago. After attending Chicago Art Institute, she studied aeronautical drafting and worked as a draftsman for several California engineering firms. For more than 35 years, Nielsen owned and managed a Southern California apartment house.

Simon Drake...transplanted Chicago attorney...Southern California

☐ ☐ 1 - Gold Coast Nocturne (1951)
☐ ☐   - Brit.-Murder by Proxy -APA: Dead on the Level
☐ ☐ 2 - After Midnight (1966)
☐ ☐ 3 - The Darkest Hour (1969)
☐ ☐ 4 - The Severed Key (1973)
☐ ☐ 5 - The Brink of Murder (1976)
☐ ☐ . . . .
☐ ☐ . . . .

■ NILES, Chris

Television and radio journalist Chris Niles introduces City Radio reporter Sam Ridley in *Spike It* (1997), a "sharp and funny portrait of life in a low-rent radio station," says the *Daily Mail*. Sam is drunk in the series opener, but not so drunk he can't recognize a good story. But then he's demoted to the hard-news reporter's version of hell—FEMALE AM—his station's daily women's program. In book 2, *Run Time* (1998), Sam is in Sydney on holiday with a hangover "wilder than a kangaroo on a trampoline" when his new girlfriend is murdered in the next room. Sam is on the run in a town that thinks he killed her. Back in London for book 3, *Crossing Live* (1999), Sam agrees to work the overnight shift and just when he thinks his career-low can't get any lower, he's assigned to interview a builder who thinks the ghosts in his house are a warning from the cosmos to change his errant ways. Niles has worked in radio and television in her native New Zealand, Australia and Eastern Europe. She is currently with CNN in London.

Sam Ridley...radio news reporter...London, England

☐ ☐ 1 - Spike It (1997)
☐ ☐ 2 - Run Time (1998)
☐ ☐ . . . .
☐ ☐ . . . .

■ NORTH, Suzanne

Professional horse player Suzanne North is the author of three laugh-outloud crime novels written on a computer purchased with her racetrack winnings. Her nonfiction writing has been for CBC television, documentary films and various periodicals. She has also worked as a bibliographic researcher, waitress in a Soho vegetarian restaurant, and television announcer. North's fictional creation is Calgary T.V. video photographer, Phoebe Fairfax, introduced in *Healthy, Wealthy and Dead* (1994), Ellis award nominee for best first mystery. In her second outing, *Seeing Is Deceiving* (1996), Phoebe's crew is filming at a psychics' fair when the live-in lover of the reporter's friend drops dead. Phoebe's third adventure, *Unnatural Selection* (2000), is set partly in Drumheller, Alberta at the Royal Tyrrell Museum of Paleontology. A Calgary native and avid golfer, the author shares her Saskatoon, Saskatchewan home with Bess the dog and many thousands of dead spiders belonging to her arachnologist husband.

Phoebe Fairfax...TV video photographer...Calgary, Alberta, Canada

☐ ☐ 1 - **Healthy, Wealthy & Dead (1994) Ellis nominee** ☆
☐ ☐ 2 - Seeing is Deceiving (1996)
☐ ☐ 3 - Unnatural Selection (2000)
☐ ☐ . . . .
☐ ☐ . . . .

■ NUNNALLY, Tiina

Scandinavian translator Tiina Nunnally is the creator of Margit Andersson, a Seattle translator who makes her debut in *Runemaker* (1996). Summoned to a hospital to decipher the ravings of an 80-year-old Danish fisherman, Margit is later rewarded for her kindness by being the one to discover his corpse. During her investigation Margit solves a 200-year-old mystery surrounding one of Denmark's national treasures. "Not bad for a first case," said *Booklist*. Patterned after a Seattle professor who is an expert in runes, Margit has extensive knowledge of Scandinavian languages and lore. In book 2, she takes an interpreting assignment at Sea-Tac Airport, only to have an arriving passenger involve her in another murder investigation. Among Nunnally's translations are *Smilla's Sense of Snow*; the first volume of *Kristin Lavransdatter (The Wreath)*, a soap opera set in med-ieval Norway; and *Early Spring*, the autobiography of one of Denmark's favorite writers. Nunnally lives in Seattle with her publisher husband, the founder of Fjord Press.

Margit Andersson...freelance Danish translator ...Seattle, Washington

- ❑ ❑ 1 - Runemaker (1996)
- ❑ ❑ 2 - Fate of Ravens (1998)
- ❑ ❑ . . . .
- ❑ ❑ . . . .

■ O'BRIEN, Meg

Meg O'Brien has written five mysteries featuring smart-mouthed investigative reporter Jessica James, recovering alcoholic from Rochester, New York, first seen in *The Daphne Decisions* (1990). Jesse's love interest is Marcus Andrelli, part of the elite branch of the New York mob where everybody went to Harvard. Book 5, *A Bright Flamingo Shroud* (1997), published only in the U.K., is still available from The Women's Press. Concentrating these days on suspense thrillers, O'Brien has written six novels, including *Crashing Down* (1999). Begun in 1986 as a first novel, the story draws on the author's childhood experience of sexual abuse. Other novels include *Take My Breath Away* (1997), set in Hawaii; *A Deep and Dreamless Sleep* (1996), set on Whidbey Island; *I'll Love You Till I Die* (1995), set in Cornwall, England; *Thin Ice* (1993) and *The Keeper* (1992). A mother of five, O'Brien once leapt over the wall to escape a Rochester convent at age 15½. After a recent move from Carmel, California, she lives on an island in Puget Sound.

Jessica James...investigative reporter...Rochester, New York

- ❑ ❑ 1 - The Daphne Decisions (1990)
- ❑ ❑ 2 - Salmon in the Soup (1990)
- ❑ ❑ 3 - Hare Today, Gone Tomorrow (1991)
- ❑ ❑ 4 - Eagles Die Too (1992)
- ❑ ❑ 5 - A Bright Flamingo Shroud (1997)
- ❑ ❑ . . . .
- ❑ ❑ . . . .

■ O'CALLAGHAN, Maxine

Maxine O'Callaghan has written more than a dozen novels of mystery, horror, dark suspense and romance. Her six books about Delilah West feature "the toughest cookie in Orange County." Solo operator of the investigations business once co-owned with husband Jack, Delilah is on the trail of Jack's killer, consumed with revenge in *Death is Forever* (1980). The Shamus-nominated sixth book, *Down for the Count* (1997), is "as good a marriage of detective work and domestic problems as you're likely to see this season," said *Kirkus*. Independent, realistic and stubborn as a mule, characteristics O'Callaghan says she shares, Delilah is sometimes cited as the first modern American woman P.I., based on her debut in a 1974 *Alfred Hitchcock Mystery Magazine* short story, "A Change of Clients." O'Callaghan also wrote two mysteries featuring Phoenix child psychologist Dr. Anne Menlo and a romance novel as Marissa Owens. Her Hollywood mystery, "Murder South of Melrose," is featured in *Murder at the Movies* (1999). O'Callaghan lives in Orange County, California.

Anne Menlo...child psychologist...Phoenix, Arizona

- ❑ ❑ 1 - Shadow of a Child (1996)
- ❑ ❑ 2 - Only in the Ashes (1997)
- ❑ ❑ . . . .
- ❑ ❑ . . . .

Delilah West...private investigator...Orange County, California

- ❑ ❑ 1 - Death Is Forever (1980)
- ❑ ❑ 2 - Run From Nightmare (1981)
- ❑ ❑ 3 - Hit and Run (1989)

❏ ❏ 4 - Set-Up (1991)
❏ ❏ 5 - Trade-Off (1994)
❏ ❏ 6 - **Down for the Count (1997) Shamus nominee** ☆
❏ ❏ . . . .
❏ ❏ . . . .

■ O'CONNELL, Carol

Failed painter Carol O'Connell writes a "break-the-mold detective" series featuring Kathleen Mallory, an N.Y.P.D. sergeant raised by a police inspector and his wife after a youth of crime that lasted into her teens on the streets of Manhattan. Quirky, brilliant and beautiful, Mallory gives new meaning to the terms "borderline sociopath" and "lone-wolf investigator." One reviewer called her a "gun-packing Alice" in a "world of characters as clever and without conscience as she." Sold first to a U.K. publisher, the Edgar- and Anthony-nominated series opener, *Mallory's Oracle*

(1994), was praised by *Kirkus* for the "high level of intelligence and unpredictability" of the main characters. In her fifth case, *Shell Game* (1999), Mallory stakes out Macy's Thanksgiving Day parade when magicians turn up as her prime suspects. O'Connell's standalone *Judas Child* (1998) is a "violent murder mystery, heart-breaking love story, intricate allegory, tangled tale of redemption and forgiveness and more," says *Booklist*. O'Connell, who earned her B.F.A. at Arizona State University, lives in Manhattan.

Kathleen Mallory...lone-wolf police sergeant...New York, New York
❏ ❏ 1 - **Mallory's Oracle (1994) Anthony & Edgar nominee** ☆☆
❏ ❏ 2 - The Man Who Cast Two Shadows (1995)
❏ ❏ - Brit.-The Man Who Lied to Women
❏ ❏ 3 - Killing Critics (1996)
❏ ❏ 4 - Stone Angel (1997)
❏ ❏ - Brit.-Flight of the Stone Angel
❏ ❏ . . . .
❏ ❏ . . . .

■ O'DONNELL, Lillian

Lillian O'Donnell is the creator of Norah Mulcahaney, star of crime fiction's longest-running police series (more than 25 years) starring a woman officer. The 28-year-old N.Y.P.D. rookie makes her first appearance in *The Phone Calls* (1972), the basis for a French film, *The Night Caller*, starring Jean Paul Belmando. Several members of the continuing cast are featured in two pre-Norah books, *Death of a Player* (1964) and *The Face of the Crime* (1968). O'Donnell has written three books featuring Mici (MIT-zee) Anhalt, a Hungarian-American

(like O'Donnell) caseworker with the Crime Victim's Compensation Board. Her Gwenn Ramadge series features a young woman P.I. some think reminiscent of Cordelia Gray. After training at the American Academy of Dramatic Arts, O'Donnell appeared on Broadway in *Pal Joey* and was named stage manager for *Private Lives* in 1943, the first woman stage manager in New York theater history. She also worked as a director for the Schubert Organization and has performed in live television.

Gwenn Ramadge...corporate investigator...New York, New York
❏ ❏ 1 - A Wreath for the Bride (1990)
❏ ❏ 2 - Used To Kill (1993)
❏ ❏ 3 - Raggedy Man (1995)
❏ ❏ 4 - The Goddess Affair (1997)
❏ ❏ . . . .
❏ ❏ . . . .

Mici Anhalt...criminal justice investigator...New York, New York
❏ ❏ 1 - Aftershock (1977)
❏ ❏ 2 - Falling Star (1979)
❏ ❏ 3 - Wicked Designs (1980)
❏ ❏ . . . .
❏ ❏ . . . .

Norah Mulcahaney...police detective...New York, New York

- ❑ ❑ 1 - The Phone Calls (1972)
- ❑ ❑ 2 - Don't Wear Your Wedding Ring (1973)
- ❑ ❑ 3 - Dial 557 R-A-P-E (1974)
- ❑ ❑ 4 - The Baby Merchants (1975)
- ❑ ❑ 5 - Leisure Dying (1976)
- ❑ ❑ 6 - No Business Being a Cop (1979)
- ❑ ❑ 7 - The Children's Zoo (1981)
- ❑ ❑ 8 - Cop Without a Shield (1983)
- ❑ ❑ 9 - Ladykiller (1984)
- ❑ ❑ 10 - Casual Affairs (1985)
- ❑ ❑ 11 - The Other Side of the Door (1987)
- ❑ ❑ 12 - A Good Night To Kill (1989)
- ❑ ❑ 13 - A Private Crime (1991)
- ❑ ❑ 14 - Pushover (1992)
- ❑ ❑ 15 - Lockout (1994)
- ❑ ❑ 16 - Blue Death (1998)
- ❑ ❑ . . . .
- ❑ ❑ . . . .

■ O'KANE, Leslie

Leslie O'Kane got her humorous crime-writing start with a college journalism assignment about what she did over the weekend. As luck would have it, she'd been a hostage in the Friday-night robbery at a bar where she worked. When she laughed at the drunken gunman, he smacked her with his shotgun. O'Kane gave herself seven years to publish a book, after the birth of her second child. The first Molly Masters mystery, *Death and Faxes* (1996) sold six years and nine months later. The witty greeting-card entrepreneur (who is 90% O'Kane) and her two funny kids make their fourth appearance in *The Fax of Life* (1999). O'Kane's newer series stars Boulder, Colorado dog psychologist Allida Babcock, introduced in *Play Dead* (1998) with a depressed-collie client whose owner may have been murdered. O'Kane has worked as a computer repair technician and technical writer, but has never sold faxable greeting cards or counseled dogs for a fee. Raised in Upstate New York, she lives in Boulder with her husband and two children.

Allida Babcock...dog psychologist...Boulder, Colorado

- ❑ ❑ 1 - Play Dead (1998)
- ❑ ❑ 2 - Wee Paws at a Murder (1999)
- ❑ ❑ . . . .
- ❑ ❑ . . . .

Molly Masters...greeting card entrepreneur...Albany, New York

- ❑ ❑ 1 - Death and Faxes (1996)
- ❑ ❑ 2 - Just the Fax Ma'am (1996)
- ❑ ❑ 3 - The Cold Hard Fax (1997)
- ❑ ❑ . . . .
- ❑ ❑ . . . .

■ O'MARIE, Carol Anne, Sister

Sister Carol Anne O'Marie (Oh-MAIR-ee), C.S.J. has been a Sister of St. Joseph of Carondelet since the mid-1950s, having entered the convent right out of high school. She is the only Roman Catholic nun still in the convent writing fiction with glimpses of convent life. Her amateur sleuth, patterned after a former principal and superior of the same name, is Sister Mary Helen, a 70-something San Francisco nun first seen in *A Novena for Murder* (1984). The real Sister Mary Helen has not done any sleuthing says O'Marie, but would be very capable of it. Her supporting cast includes colleague Sister Eileen, Inspector Kate Murphy and Detective Sergeant Bob Little of the San Francisco P.D. A former Catholic school teacher and principal, O'Marie earned B.A. and M.A.T. degrees from Mount St. Mary's College. She ministers to homeless women in downtown Oakland at A Friendly Place, drop-in center turned shelter she co-founded in 1990. A San Francisco native, she won second place in the Cable Car Bell Ringing Contest in 1979.

Sister Mary Helen...70-something nun...San Francisco, California

- ❑ ❑ 1 - A Novena for Murder (1984)
- ❑ ❑ 2 - Advent of Dying (1986)
- ❑ ❑ 3 - The Missing Madonna (1988)
- ❑ ❑ 4 - Murder in Ordinary Time (1991)
- ❑ ❑ 5 - Murder Makes a Pilgrimage (1993)
- ❑ ❑ 6 - Death Goes on Retreat (1995)
- ❑ ❑ 7 - Death of an Angel (1997)
- ❑ ❑ 8 - Death Takes Up a Collection (1998)
- ❑ ❑ . . . .
- ❑ ❑ . . . .

■ O'SHAUGHNESSY, Perri [P]

Writing together as Perri O'Shaughnessy, sisters Pamela and Mary O'Shaughnessy are co-authors of five courtroom thrillers featuring Lake Tahoe defense attorney and single mother Nina Reilly, introduced in *Motion To Suppress* (1995). Nina has more than her share of problems, including a 13-year-old son, a high-pressure job that doesn't pay enough, a strong attraction to the prosecutor and an on-again, off-again romance with a private investigator. Things go awry on a grand scale in book 4, *Breach of Promise* (1998), when Nina loses a big-bucks palimony case into which she has sunk her last dollar. *Kirkus* says book 5, *Acts of Malice* (1999) is the best yet. A former trial lawyer and Harvard Law School graduate, Pamela O'Shaughnessy lives in California, 100 miles from her sister Mary who previously worked as a multimedia writer-editor. Starting with an outline, one writes a chapter and the other edits. They exchange computer files electronically, reverse roles and repeat the process, rewriting the entire manuscript at least twice.

Nina Reilly...single-mother attorney...Lake Tahoe, Nevada

- ❑ ❑ 1 - Motion To Suppress (1995)
- ❑ ❑ 2 - Invasion of Privacy (1996)
- ❑ ❑ 3 - Obstruction of Justice (1997)
- ❑ ❑ 4 - Breach of Promise (1998)
- ❑ ❑ . . . .
- ❑ ❑ . . . .

■ OCORK, Shannon

Shannon OCork is the author of a three-book series featuring 20-something sports photographer, Theresa Tracy "T.T." Baldwin, introduced in *Sports Freak* (1980), a *New York Times* Notable Book. Inspired by the author's experience as a *New York Daily News* freelancer, T.T.'s exploits also drew on her work as a novice photographer for a boxing magazine. In *The Murder of Muriel Lake* (1990), OCork has an unpopular best-selling author killed by an avalanche of falling books at a Writers of Mystery convention. Her nonfiction book, *How To Write Mysteries* (1989), includes an introduction by her then-husband, M.W.A. Grand Master Hillary Waugh. OCork's 1989 Titanic-inspired romance, *Icefall*, was rediscovered by Harlequin editors two days after the movie *Titanic* swept the 1998 Oscars. Promptly re-issued as *Titanic: A Love Story*, the ten-year-old book may turn out to be her best-selling novel. A Kentucky native, OCork lives in Connecticut where she is writing another disaster romance and a mystery inspired by her current job selling real estate.

Theresa Tracy Baldwin...sports news photographer...New York, New York

- ❑ ❑ 1 - Sports Freak (1980)
- ❑ ❑ 2 - End of the Line (1981)
- ❑ ❑ 3 - Hell Bent for Heaven (1983)
- ❑ ❑ . . . .
- ❑ ❑ . . . .

■ OLEKSIW, Susan

Susan Oleksiw (oh-LECK-see) writes a Massachusetts-seacoast series featuring Mellingham police chief Joe Silva, introduced in *Murder in Mellingham* (1993). When last seen in *Family Album* (1995), the "proud Yankee enclave" is awash in scandal and treasured antiques are disappearing from the historical society's showcase Arabella House. Oleksiw is the editor of *A Reader's Guide to the Classic British Mystery*, which includes short synopses of the works of 121 authors up to 1985. Within the almost 600 pages of this ambitious work, she also provides useful information about the British class system and structure of the metropolitan and local police forces. Oleksiw started the book as a guide for her husband's leisure reading, but ended up reading most of the 1,440 cited mysteries herself. She earned a Ph.D. in Sanskrit from the University of Pennsylvania and has lived and traveled extensively in India. Oleksiw currently teaches literature and writing at several colleges in the Boston area.

Joe Silva...small-town chief of police...Mellingham, Massachusetts

- ❏ ❏ 1 - Murder in Mellingham (1993)
- ❏ ❏ 2 - Double Take (1994)
- ❏ ❏ 3 - Family Album (1995)
- ❏ ❏ . . . .
- ❏ ❏ . . . .

■ OLIPHANT, B.J. [P]

B.J. Oliphant is the pseudonym of science fiction and fantasy author Sheri S. Tepper for a seven-book series featuring six-foot three-inch Washington, D.C. career woman Shirley McClintock, introduced in the Edgar- and Anthony-nominated *Dead in the Scrub* (1990). Fifty-something Shirley returns to Colorado to manage the family ranch after the death of her parents. After book 4, *Death and the Delinquent* (1992), she moves to New Mexico. Tepper has written more than 40 novels, including the Hugo-nominated science fiction work, *Grass* (1989). Her first published novels were the intricate fantasies of her *True Game* series, *King's Blood Four* (1983), *Necromancer Nine* (1983) and *Wizard's Eleven* (1984). Born near Littleton, Colorado, Tepper spent 24 years with Rocky Mountain Planned Parenthood, eventually becoming executive director. Today she runs a guest ranch in Santa Fe, New Mexico. Her mysteries as A.J. Orde feature Denver antiques dealer Jason Lynx. She has also written horror novels as E.E. Horlak.

Shirley McClintock...50-something rancher...Colorado

- ❏ ❏ 1 - **Dead in the Scrub (1990) Anthony & Edgar nominee** ☆☆
- ❏ ❏ 2 - The Unexpected Corpse (1990)
- ❏ ❏ 3 - Deservedly Dead (1992)
- ❏ ❏ 4 - Death and the Delinquent (1992)
- ❏ ❏ 5 - Death Served up Cold (1994)
- ❏ ❏ 6 - A Ceremonial Death (1996)
- ❏ ❏ 7 - Here's to the Newly Deads (1997)
- ❏ ❏ . . . .
- ❏ ❏ . . . .

■ OLIVER, Maria-Antònia

Maria-Antònia Oliver is a well-known translator of English and American classics into her native Catalan, a language spoken by more than ten million people in Spain, Andorra, Southern France and Sardinia. Her recent translations include *The Adventures of Tom Sawyer*, published in Barcelona in 1995. The first of Oliver's translated mysteries introduces fiercely-feminist Barcelona investigator Lònia Guiu in *A Study in Lilac* (1987). Well-received in Europe and North America, "the hard-boiled mystery pays tribute to Dashiell Hammett while turning the macho conventions of his work upside down," says Nina King in *Crimes of the Scene* (1997). The fictional detectives of two other Barcelona mystery writers appear as characters in *A Study in Lilac*, but "the city of Barcelona is not a vivid player in this violent tale," according to King. In *Antipodes* (1989) Guiu does her investigating in Australia and Majorca. A choreographer and dancer, Oliver lives in Barcelona. Like her fictional detective, she is a native of Majorca.

Lònia Guiu…Catalan investigator…Barcelona, Spain
- ❏ ❏ 1 - A Study in Lilac (1987)
- ❏ ❏ 2 - Antipodes (1989)
- ❏ ❏ . . . .
- ❏ ❏ . . . .

■ ORDE, A.J. [P]

A.J. Orde is one of the pseudonyms of best-selling science fiction author Sheri S. Tepper, who writes mysteries under two different names. As A.J. Orde she's the creator of Jason Lynx, Denver antiques dealer and compulsive puzzle solver last seen in book 6, *A Death of Innocents* (1997). His romantic interest, Grace Willis, is a Denver cop, making this series a charming reversal of the female amateur detective with a male-cop love-interest. Their supporting cast includes Grace's troubled brother Ron, Jason's partner Mark and their office manager Eugenia from Jason Lynx Interiors, and the delightful animal trio of Bela, Schnitz and Critter. Bela is Jason's 120-pound white Kuvasz dog. Schnitz is his 12-pound Maine Coon kitten, offspring of Grace's 29-pound tomcat Critter. Be sure to start this series at the beginning so you don't miss any of the continuing story about Jason's mysterious family origins. Tepper runs a Santa Fe, New Mexico guest ranch. As B.J. Oliphant, she writes the Edgar-nominated Shirley McClintock series.

Jason Lynx…antiques dealer and decorator…Denver, Colorado
- ❏ ❏ 1 - A Little Neighborhood Murder (1989)
- ❏ ❏ 2 - Death and the Dogwalker (1990)
- ❏ ❏ 3 - Death for Old Times' Sake (1992)
- ❏ ❏ 4 - Looking for the Aardvark (1993)
- ❏ ❏   - APA-Dead on Sunday
- ❏ ❏ 5 - A Long Time Dead (1995)
- ❏ ❏ 6 - A Death of Innocents (1997)
- ❏ ❏ . . . .
- ❏ ❏ . . . .

■ OSBORNE, Denise

California author Denise Osborne is the creator of struggling screenwriter Queenie Davilov, who moonlights doing security checks in the Hollywood film community. Part-time script supervisor on a horror film plagued by production problems, Queenie makes her fictional debut in *Murder Offscreen* (1994). The film's premiere turns disastrous when the producer-director is found hacked to death with an axe that was the film's main prop. *Booklist* raved about the "pumped-up, fast-paced, pell-mell action filled with bizarre plot twists, charmingly eccentric characters, oodles of Hollywood glamour, and wacky, wisecracking wit." In *Cut to: Murder* (1995) Queenie is hired to doctor the script of a Spanish Civil War drama being shot on location in Barcelona and the mountains of Catalonia. A brilliant, alcoholic scriptwriter has disappeared before completing the final scenes. Osborne, who earned a degree in motion picture production from the University of Oklahoma, has won awards for her screenplays and short films. She lives in Capitola.

Queenie Davilov…screenwriter-investigator…Hollywood, California
- ❏ ❏ 1 - Murder Offscreen (1994)
- ❏ ❏ 2 - Cut to: Murder (1995)
- ❏ ❏ . . . .
- ❏ ❏ . . . .

■ PADGETT, Abigail

With *Child of Silence* (1993) Abigail Padgett introduced the fiction world's first working professional who lives with bipolar disorder, San Diego child abuse investigator Barbara Joan "Bo" Bradley. This debut novel was nominated for Agatha, Anthony and Macavity awards. Padgett's avid interests in desert preservation, Native American culture and mental health issues are showcased brilliantly in her mysteries. The supporting cast includes Bo's friend Estrella, the wise Dr. Eva Broussard and the dashing Dr. Andrew LaMarche, pediatrician and international child abuse authority who falls for Bo in book 1. With *Blue* (1998) Padgett begins a new series featuring reclusive lesbian psychologist Blue McCarron. *Kirkus* called the opener a "suspenseful, boldly plotted tribute to the power of sisterhood." A former investigator for San Diego Child Protective Services, Padgett holds an M.S. in counseling from Washington University. She once taught English at an all-black St. Louis high school and served as director of the A.C.L.U. in Houston.

Barbara Joan "Bo" Bradley...child abuse investigator...San Diego, California

❑ ❑	1 -	**Child of Silence (1993) Agatha, Anthony & Macavity nominee** ☆☆☆
❑ ❑	2 -	Strawgirl (1994)
❑ ❑	3 -	Turtle Baby (1995)
❑ ❑	4 -	Moonbird Boy (1996)
❑ ❑	5 -	The Dollmaker's Daughters (1997)
❑ ❑		....
❑ ❑		....

Blue McCarron...lesbian social psychologist...San Diego, California

❑ ❑	1 -	Blue (1998)
❑ ❑	2 -	The Last Blue Plate Special (2000)
❑ ❑		....
❑ ❑		....

■ PAGE, Emma [P]

Emma Page is the pseudonym of Englishwoman Honoria Tirbutt, author of more than a dozen mysteries, including nine books in her series featuring Inspector Kelsey. Referred to simply as Kelsey or Chief, the inspector's first name is never mentioned. The setting for these village mysteries is loosely based on the Worcestershire and Hereford area, but actual place names have been changed. Introduced in *Missing Woman* (1980), Detective Chief Inspector Kelsey was last seen in book 9, *Intent To Kill* (1998). Constable will publish the U.K. edition of book 10 in 2000. Page also wrote four standalone mysteries in the early 1970s, including *A Fortnight by the Sea* (1973), renamed *Add a Pinch of Cyanide* for U.S. publication the same year. According to the London *Sunday Times*, "Emma Page stitches craftily with a pricking needle." Born Honoria O'Mahony in West Hartlepool, Durham, she may have first learned about police work at the family dinner table. Her father was a policeman and her mother a headmistress.

Inspector Kelsey...police inspector...England

❑ ❑	1 -	Missing Woman (1980)
❑ ❑	2 -	Every Second Thursday (1981)
❑ ❑	3 -	Last Walk Home (1982)
❑ ❑	4 -	Cold Light of Day (1983)
❑ ❑	5 -	Scent of Death (1985)
❑ ❑	6 -	Final Moments (1987)
❑ ❑	7 -	A Violent End (1988)
❑ ❑	8 -	Murder Comes Calling (1995)
❑ ❑	9 -	Intent To Kill (1998)
❑ ❑		....
❑ ❑		....

■ PAGE, Katherine Hall

Katherine Hall Page wrote her Agatha-award winning first novel, *The Body in the Belfry* (1990), while living in Lyons, France on sabbatical with her husband and young son. When New York gourmet caterer, Faith Sibley Fairchild, marries a minister and moves to tiny Aleford, Massachusetts, she adds detective work and motherhood to the business demands of Have Faith catering and the duties of a minister's wife. After surviving a burglary (based on a Page home invasion) in *The Body in the Book Case* (1998), Faith bounces back in *The Body in the Big Apple* (1999)—all the way back to 1989 Manhattan, before she was married. Page's Edgar-nominated Christie and Company mysteries feature three eighth grade girls last seen on vacation in Quebec City in book 4, *Bon Voyage* (1999). A Wellesley graduate with a Harvard Ph.D. in education, Page previously taught English and history and directed special education programs for adolescents. She lives with her M.I.T. professor husband and teenage son in Lexington, Massachusetts.

Faith Sibley Fairchild...caterer and minister's wife...Aleford, Massachusetts
- ❏ ❏ 1 - **The Body in the Belfry (1990) Agatha winner ★**
- ❏ ❏ 2 - The Body in the Kelp (1991)
- ❏ ❏ 3 - The Body in the Bouillon (1991)
- ❏ ❏ 4 - The Body in the Vestibule (1992)
- ❏ ❏ 5 - The Body in the Cast (1993)
- ❏ ❏ 6 - The Body in the Basement (1994)
- ❏ ❏ 7 - The Body in the Bog (1996)
- ❏ ❏ 8 - The Body in the Fjord (1997)
- ❏ ❏ 9 - The Body in the Bookcase (1998)
- ❏ ❏ ....
- ❏ ❏ ....

■ PAIGE, Robin [P]

Robin Paige is the joint pseudonym of Texas authors Susan Albert and her husband Bill for their late 1890s series featuring a pair of amateur detectives introduced in *Death at Bishop's Keep* (1994). American Kathryn Ardleigh, a 25-year-old self-supporting pseudonymous author of penny dreadfuls, is called to England to serve as secretary for her aunt. In book 1, she meets her future detecting partner, amateur forensic scientist Sir Charles Ardleigh. Each book features a different Victorian personality, such as Beatrix Potter, Jennie Churchill, the Prince of Wales, and Rudyard Kipling. Since 1986 the Alberts have co-authored more than 60 young adult novels, including books in the Nancy Drew and Hardy Boys series. Under her own name, Susan Albert writes the China Bayles mystery series featuring former practicing attorney turned herb shop owner. When he isn't writing, Bill collects antique tools and turns wooden vases for Texas gift shops and galleries. The Alberts live in the Texas Hill country near Austin.

Kathryn Ardleigh & Charles Sheridan...American author & British scientist...Dedham, England
- ❏ ❏ 1 - Death at Bishop's Keep (1994)
- ❏ ❏ 2 - Death at Gallows Green (1995)
- ❏ ❏ 3 - Death at Daisy's Folly (1997)
- ❏ ❏ 4 - Death at Devil's Bridge (1998)
- ❏ ❏ 5 - Death at Rottingdean (1999)
- ❏ ❏ ....
- ❏ ❏ ....

■ PAPAZOGLOU, Orania

Orania Papazoglou's first mystery featuring Patience Campbell McKenna, closet romance novelist turned true crime writer, was the Edgar-nominated *Sweet, Savage Death* (1984). A freelance magazine writer who pens romance novels to pay the rent, six-foot Pay McKenna was born rich but refused her trust fund and moved to Manhattan. A never-published magazine feature on the romance publishing business inspired Papazoglou's very funny five-book series. Former editor of *Greek Accent* magazine, she freelanced for *Glamour, Mademoiselle, Working Woman* and *First Things*. Although she wrote two psychological thrillers under her own name, *Sanctity* (1986) and *Charisma* (1992), she is best known for her Edgar- and Anthony-nominated mysteries as Jane Haddam (rhymes with Adam). As Ann Paris she is the author of *Graven Image* (1987) and *Arrowheart* (1988). A graduate of Vassar College, Papazoglou was married to three-time Edgar award-winning mystery writer and *Armchair Detective* columnist William DeAndrea (1952-1996).

Patience Campbell McKenna...6-ft. romance novelist turned crime writer...New York, New York
- ❏ ❏ 1 - **Sweet, Savage Death (1984) Edgar nominee ☆**
- ❏ ❏ 2 - Wicked, Loving Murder (1985)
- ❏ ❏ 3 - Death's Savage Passion (1986)
- ❏ ❏ 4 - Rich, Radiant Slaughter (1988)
- ❏ ❏ 5 - Once and Always Murder (1990)
- ❏ ❏ ....
- ❏ ❏ ....

■ PARETSKY, Sara

Silver Dagger winner Sara Paretsky has written nine novel-length mysteries and a short story collection featuring Chicago private eye V.I. Warshawski, introduced in *Indemnity Only* (1982). The daughter of a Polish cop and an Italian-Jewish opera singer, Victoria Iphegenia is a former public defender with a nose for white collar crime. Call her V.I., Victoria or Vic, but never Vicki. She has a fondness for silk shirts and the red Bruno Magli pumps that bring her luck. Five years after *Tunnel Vision*, V.I. and friends—Lotty, Mr. Contreras, Murray, Mitch and Peppy—return in the much-anticipated *Hard Time* (1999). Born in Ames, Iowa, Paretsky grew up in Kansas where she graduated summa cum laude from the University of Kansas. She holds a Ph.D. in medieval history and an M.B.A. from the University of Chicago. Founding president of Sisters in Crime, Paretsky once worked as a freelance business writer and marketing manager for a major insurance company. She shares with V.I. a special affection for the Chicago Cubs and Golden Labs.

V. I. Warshawski...attorney turned P.I....Chicago, Illinois

❑	❑	1 - Indemnity Only (1982)
❑	❑	2 - Deadlock (1984)
❑	❑	3 - Killing Orders (1985)
❑	❑	4 - Bitter Medicine (1987)
❑	❑	5 - **Blood Shot (1988) Anthony & Shamus nominee** ☆☆
❑	❑	- **Brit.-Toxic Shock – Silver Dagger winner** ★
❑	❑	6 - Burn Marks (1990)
❑	❑	7 - Guardian Angel (1991)
❑	❑	8 - **Tunnel Vision (1994) Gold Dagger nominee** ☆
❑	❑	ss - Windy City Blues [short stories] (1995)
❑	❑	....
❑	❑	....

■ PARKER, Barbara

Barbara Parker writes legal thrillers featuring Miami corporate attorney Gail Connor, introduced in the Edgar-nominated *Suspicion of Innocence* (1994). The supporting cast includes Gail's fiancé, Cuban-born criminal defense attorney Anthony Quintana, and her precocious 10-year-old daughter Karen. Book 4 in the series, *Suspicion of Betrayal* (1999), finds Gail dealing with progressively ugly threats to Karen in the midst of planning her own wedding. The series opener was adapted for a 1997 CBS-television movie, *Sisters and Other Strangers*, starring Joanna Kerns and Steven Bauer. Inexplicably, the action was moved from Miami to the desert Southwest. Parker's nonseries thrillers include *Blood Relations* (1996), set on South Beach, and *Criminal Justice* (1997). A former prosecutor in the Dade County State Attorney's Office and later an attorney in private practice, Parker earned an M.F.A. in creative writing from Florida International University in 1993. A South Floridian since 1974, she lives in Dade County.

Gail Connor...corporate attorney...Miami, Florida

❑	❑	1 - **Suspicion of Innocence (1994) Edgar nominee** ☆
❑	❑	2 - Suspicion of Guilt (1995)
❑	❑	3 - Suspicion of Deceit (1998)
❑	❑	....
❑	❑	....

■ PATON WALSH, Jill

Renowned children's author Jill Paton (PAY-ten) Walsh spent three years writing *The Emperor's Winding Sheet* (1974), her award-winning tale about the destruction of 15th century Byzantium. Much of that time was spent learning Greek so she could read the necessary background. It comes as no surprise that during her time at Oxford, where she earned an M.A. in English with honors, she attended lectures by C.S. Lewis and J.R.R. Tolkien, who was her tutor. Among her novels for adults are two mysteries featuring school nurse Imogen Quy (rhymes with WHY), who tends to Cambridge University students at St. Agatha's College. In 1996 Paton Walsh was commissioned by the literary trustees of Dorothy L. Sayers to complete the final mystery featuring Lord Peter Wimsey, based on six chapters and a plot diagram. The resulting *Thrones, Dominations* (1998) was "the most difficult and interesting job of my career, and also the most fun," said Paton Walsh. A visiting professor at Boston's Simmons College for eight years, she lives in Cambridge, England.

Imogen Quy...St. Agatha's College nurse...Cambridge, England
- ❑ ❑ 1 - The Wyndham Case (1993)
- ❑ ❑ 2 - **A Piece of Justice (1995) Gold Dagger nominee** ☆
- ❑ ❑ . . . .
- ❑ ❑ . . . .

■ PAUL, Barbara

Author of 22 novels and numerous short stories, Barbara Paul has written five works of science fiction and 17 mysteries, including 10 books in two series and seven standalone novels. Her early 20th century opera mysteries feature Enrico Caruso and Geraldine Farrar as amateur sleuths, beginning with *A Cadenzo for Caruso* (1984). Paul also writes a police series featuring no-nonsense N.Y.P.D. officer Marian Larch and her television actress friend Kelly Ingram, last seen in book 7, *Full Frontal Murder* (1997). The nonseries *Kill Fee* (1985) was adapted as *Murder C.O.D.*, a 1990 NBC-television movie. Among Paul's many short stories are those appearing in *New York Crime* (1999), *Future Crime* (1999) and *First Ladies* (1998). A former English and drama teacher with a working theatre background, Paul graduated from Bowling Green State University and went on to earn an M.A. from California's University of Redlands and a Ph.D. from the University of Pittsburgh. The Kentucky native lives in Pittsburgh, Pennsylvania.

Enrico Caruso & Geraldine Farrar...Italian tenor & American soprano...New York, New York
- ❑ ❑ 1 - A Cadenza for Caruso [1910] (1984)
- ❑ ❑ 2 - Prima Donna at Large [1915] (1985)
- ❑ ❑ 3 - A Chorus of Detectives [1920] (1987)
- ❑ ❑ . . . .
- ❑ ❑ . . . .

Marian Larch...no-nonsense NYPD officer...New York, New York
- ❑ ❑ 1 - The Renewable Virgin (1984)
- ❑ ❑ 2 - He Huffed and He Puffed (1989)
- ❑ ❑ 3 - Good King Sauerkraut (1989)
- ❑ ❑ 4 - You Have the Right To Remain Silent (1992)
- ❑ ❑ 5 - The Apostrophe Thief (1993)
- ❑ ❑ 6 - Fare Play (1995)
- ❑ ❑ 7 - Full Frontal Murder (1997)
- ❑ ❑ . . . .
- ❑ ❑ . . . .

■ PEART, Jane

"It is the threat of danger to an intelligent, courageous heroine that interests me," says Jane Peart, author of more than 45 novels since 1979. Restless young Victorian women are the central characters in Peart's Edgecliffe Manor mysteries, most recently Nell Winston in book 4, *Thread of Suspicion* (1998). Hired as the companion to a young woman in a wheelchair, Nell has suspicions about the carriage accident that injured the girl and killed her parents. Highly recommended by *Library Journal,* these mysteries have been likened to the writings of Victoria Holt. Book 5, *A Sinister Silence,* will be published in 2000. With book 15, *Montclair Homecoming* (2000), Peart will conclude her Brides of Montclair series. An Asheville, North Carolina native, Peart lives in Fortuna, California where she swims three to five times a week, but not in the ocean. An avid mystery reader, she finds beach walking perfect for setting a mysterious mood. Peart enjoys painting with acrylics and collecting miniature porcelain dolls crafted of her fictional heroines.

Edgecliffe Manor Series...young, restless Victorian women...England
- ❑ ❑ 1 - Web of Deception (1996)
- ❑ ❑ 2 - Shadow of Fear (1996)
- ❑ ❑ 3 - A Perilous Bargain (1997)
- ❑ ❑ 4 - Thread of Suspicion (1998)
- ❑ ❑ . . . .
- ❑ ❑ . . . .

■ PENCE, Joanne

Joanne Pence has written half a dozen wickedly-humorous food mysteries featuring freelance cooking writer Angelina Amalfi and San Francisco homicide detective Paavo Smith. Wealthy, pampered and bossy, Angie is a pint-sized whirlwind whose heart is bigger than her father's fortune. Paavo falls for her in the series opener "like a loser in cement shoes going off a pier." It's a toss-up who finds this more annoying— Angie's rich father or Paavo's disapproving colleagues. "Lucille Ball meets the Streets of San Francisco,"

suggested one reviewer. Book 1 of the paperback series, *Something's Cooking*, was nominated for Best Romantic Suspense of 1993 by Romance Writers of America. Angie and Paavo's seventh adventure, *A Cook in Time* (1999), ushers in the new millennium with UFOs, aliens, dead bodies and lots of wild fun. A San Francisco native, Pence lives north of the city in Marin County. A long-time manager with the Social Security Administration, she recently gave up the supervisory rat race to write full time.

Angelina Amalfi...freelance food writer...San Francisco, California

- ❑ ❑ 1 - Something's Cooking (1993)
- ❑ ❑ 2 - Too Many Cooks (1994)
- ❑ ❑ 3 - Cooking Up Trouble (1995)
- ❑ ❑ 4 - Cooking Most Deadly (1996)
- ❑ ❑ 5 - Cook's Night Out (1998)
- ❑ ❑ 6 - Cooks Overboard (1998)
- ❑ ❑ . . . .
- ❑ ❑ . . . .

■ PENMAN, Sharon Kay

For many years as a student and then a tax attorney, Sharon Kay Penman worked steadily on a novel about the life of Richard III. Shortly after it was finished, the only copy of the manuscript was stolen from her car. She promptly rewrote the entire book, published in 1982 as *The Sunne in Splendor*. Her 12th century Welsh trilogy includes *Here Be Dragons* (1985), *Falls the Shadow* (1988) and *The Reckoning* (1991). *When Christ and the Saints Slept* (1995) launches a new medieval trilogy. Penman's Edgar-nominated first mystery, *The*

Queen's Man (1996), introduces 20-something Justin de Quincy, special envoy, spy and confidant to Queen Elinor of Aquitaine. The illegitimate Justin has just discovered that his father is the Bishop of Chester. Although the Bishop has overseen Justin's excellent education and provided for his welfare, he refuses to acknowledge his son's paternity. Featuring real and fictional characters of the English royal court, the mystery series will continue with book 3 in late 2000 or early 2001.

Justin de Quincy...Queen Mother's investigator...England

- ❑ ❑ 1 - **The Queen's Man (1996) Edgar nominee** ☆
- ❑ ❑ 2 - Cruel as the Grave (1998)
- ❑ ❑ . . . .
- ❑ ❑ . . . .

■ PENN, John [P]

John Penn is a joint pseudonym of Palma Harcourt and her husband Jack H. Trotman for 18 Thames Valley police mysteries in two series. Although some characters are featured in both, the two series have different investigating officers who do not cross paths. Detective Superintendent George Thorne, first seen in *A Will to Kill* (1983), appears in six books. Detective Chief Inspector Richard Tansey is featured in 12 books, beginning with *Outrageous Exposures* (1988), a "taut and compelling tale" with a chilling conclusion," according to Ellen Nehr's *Doubleday*

Crime Club Compendium (1992). Author or more than 20 novels before she began writing with her husband, Harcourt was born in the Channel Islands. She earned an M.A. at St. Anne's College, Oxford. Born in London, Trotman earned a B.A. with honors from Oxford University. After wartime service with Army Intelligence, he served in the British Foreign Office and later worked for Canadian National Defense in Ottawa for over 25 years. Upon retirement, his wife's agent suggested he try his hand at crime writing.

George Thorne...detective superintendent...Oxfordshire, England

- ❑ ❑ 1 - A Will To Kill (1983)
- ❑ ❑ 2 - Mortal Term (1984)

❑ ❑ 3 - A Deadly Sickness (1985)
❑ ❑ 4 - Unto the Grave (1986)
❑ ❑ 5 - Barren Revenge (1986)
❑ ❑ 6 - Accident Prone (1987)
❑ ❑ . . . .
❑ ❑ . . . .

Richard Tansey...chief inspector...Oxfordshire, England
❑ ❑ 1 - Outragous Exposures (1988)
❑ ❑ 2 - A Feast of Death (1989)
❑ ❑ 3 - A Killing To Hide (1990)
❑ ❑ 4 - A Knife Ill-Used (1991)
❑ ❑ 5 - Death's Long Shadow (1991)
❑ ❑ 6 - A Legacy of Death (1992)
❑ ❑ 7 - A Haven of Danger (1993)
❑ ❑ 8 - Widow's End (1993)
❑ ❑ 9 - A Guilty Party (1994)
❑ ❑ 10 - So Many Steps to Death (1995)
❑ ❑ 11 - Bridal Shroud (1996)
❑ ❑ 12 - Sterner Stuff (1997)
❑ ❑ . . . .
❑ ❑ . . . .

■ PERRY, Anne

Two-time Agatha and Edgar nominee Anne Perry has written 29 Victorian-era mysteries in two critically-acclaimed series. Her longer-running series, set in the 1880s, features Inspector Thomas Pitt and his upper-middle-class wife, Charlotte, who marries the London policeman after assisting him in book 1, *The Cater Street Hangman* (1979), adapted for A&E television in 1999. *Bedford Square* (1999) is book 19. "If you ever wondered why women began to rebel against social constriction at the turn of the 20th century, these books will clear up that mystery," said one observer.

Perry's second series features Inspector William Monk who wakes up in a hospital during the mid-1850s with no memory. Monk and Nurse Latterly return in book 10, *A Twisted Root* (1999). During the 1994 film release of *Heavenly Creatures*, it was revealed that Perry had been involved in the 1954 murder of a teenage friend's mother. She told the *New York Times* that admitting her past to friends and associates was "one of the worse days of my life." In a departure from her mysteries, Perry has written a fantasy novel, *Tathea* (1999).

Thomas & Charlotte Pitt...Victorian police inspector & wife...London, England
❑ ❑ 1 - The Cater Street Hangman (1979)
❑ ❑ 2 - Callander Square (1980)
❑ ❑ 3 - Paragon Walk (1981)
❑ ❑ 4 - Resurrection Row (1981)
❑ ❑ 5 - Rutland Place (1983)
❑ ❑ 6 - Bluegate Fields (1984)
❑ ❑ 7 - Death in Devil's Acre (1985)
❑ ❑ 8 - Cardington Crescent (1987)
❑ ❑ 9 - Silence in Hanover Close (1988)
❑ ❑ 10 - Bethlehem Road (1990)
❑ ❑ 11 - Highgate Rise (1991)
❑ ❑ 12 - Belgrave Square (1992)
❑ ❑ 13 - Farriers' Lane (1993)
❑ ❑ 14 - The Hyde Park Headsman (1994)
❑ ❑ 15 - Traitor's Gate (1995)
❑ ❑ 16 - **Pentecost Alley (1996) Edgar nominee** ☆
❑ ❑ 17 - Ashworth Hall (1997)
❑ ❑ 18 - Brunswick Gardens (1998)
❑ ❑ . . . .
❑ ❑ . . . .

William Monk...amnesiac Victorian police inspector...London, England

❑ ❑ 1 - **The Face of a Stranger (1990) Agatha nominee** ☆
❑ ❑ 2 - A Dangerous Mourning (1991)
❑ ❑ 3 - **Defend and Betray (1992) Agatha nominee** ☆
❑ ❑ 4 - A Sudden, Fearful Death (1993)
❑ ❑ 5 - Sins of the Wolf (1994)
❑ ❑ 6 - Cain His Brother (1995)
❑ ❑ 7 - Weighed in the Balance (1996)
❑ ❑ 8 - The Silent Cry (1997)
❑ ❑ 9 - A Breach of Promise (1998)
❑ ❑ - Brit.-Whited Sepulchres

❑ ❑ . . . .
❑ ❑ . . . .

■ PETERS, Elizabeth [P]

Author of 60 novels of mystery and suspense, two-time Grand Master Elizabeth Peters, a.k.a. Barbara Michaels, is actually Barbara Mertz, Ph.D. in Egyptology from the University of Chicago. Her longest and best-known series features Victorian archaeologist Amelia Peabody, patterned after a real Egyptologist of the time, Amelia B. Edwards, a founder of the Egypt Exploration Fund. "Indiana Jones, Sherlock Holmes and Miss Marple all in one," said *The Washington Post* of Peters' creation. Since Amelia's 1975 debut, the cast has grown to include her Egyptologist-husband Radcliffe Emerson, their son Ramses and countless others, with younger characters taking the lead in books 9 through 12. Peters' other series characters are librarian-turned-romance-novelist Jacqueline Kirby, and art historian Vicky Bliss. As Barbara Michaels she has written 31 novels, many of them *New York Times* bestsellers. Twice recognized for lifetime achievement, the Maryland resident has been named Grand Master by Mystery Writers of America and the World Mystery Convention.

Amelia Peabody...Victorian feminist archaeologist...Kent, England

❑ ❑ 1 - Crocodile on the Sandbank (1975)
❑ ❑ 2 - The Curse of the Pharaohs (1981)
❑ ❑ 3 - The Mummy Case (1985)
❑ ❑ 4 - Lion in the Valley (1986)
❑ ❑ 5 - The Deeds of the Disturber (1988)
❑ ❑ 6 - **The Last Camel Died at Noon (1991) Agatha nominee** ☆
❑ ❑ 7 - **The Snake, the Crocodile and the Dog (1992) Agatha nominee** ☆
❑ ❑ 8 - The Hippopotamus Pool (1996)
❑ ❑ 9 - **Seeing a Large Cat (1997) Agatha nominee** ☆
❑ ❑ 10 - The Ape Who Guards the Balance (1998)
❑ ❑ 11 - The Falcon at the Portal (1999)
❑ ❑ 12 - He Shall Thunder in the Sky (2000)

❑ ❑ . . . .
❑ ❑ . . . .

Jacqueline Kirby...librarian turned romance novelist...New York, New York

❑ ❑ 1 - The Seventh Sinner (1972)
❑ ❑ 2 - The Murders of Richard III (1974)
❑ ❑ 3 - Die for Love (1984)
❑ ❑ 4 - **Naked Once More (1989) Agatha winner** ★

❑ ❑ . . . .
❑ ❑ . . . .

Vicky Bliss...art historian...Germany

❑ ❑ 1 - Borrower of the Night (1973)
❑ ❑ 2 - Street of the Five Moons (1978)
❑ ❑ 3 - Silhouette in Scarlet (1983)
❑ ❑ 4 - **Trojan Gold (1987) Anthony nominee** ☆
❑ ❑ 5 - **Night Train to Memphis (1994) Agatha nominee** ☆

❑ ❑ . . . .
❑ ❑ . . . .

■ PETERSON, Audrey [P]

Pseudonymous English professor Audrey Peterson has written two academic mystery series set primarily in England. Her six-book series featuring music professor, Andrew Quentin, and his former graduate student, Jane Winfield, begins with *The Nocturne Murder* (1988). The pair spends a lot of time in England and on the continent, places which Peterson often visits. She told *Contemporary Authors* that the music background allows her to incorporate a lifelong interest in opera and concert-going. Like her second series character, Claire Camden, Peterson has done academic research in England, but has yet to solve a murder. She has written a study of 19th century writers, *Victorian Masters of Mystery: From Wilkie Collins to Conan Doyle* (1984). A Los Angeles native, she earned a Ph.D. at the University of Southern California and taught English literature at California State University, Long Beach for 20 years. Peterson lives in Bellingham, Washington, home to mystery authors Jo Dereske, Linda French and Steve Martini.

Claire Camden...California English professor...London, England
- ❑ ❑ 1 - Dartmoor Burial (1992)
- ❑ ❑ 2 - Death Too Soon (1994)
- ❑ ❑ 3 - Shroud for a Scholar (1995)
- ❑ ❑ . . . .
- ❑ ❑ . . . .

Jane Winfield...British journalist and music writer...London, England
- ❑ ❑ 1 - The Nocturne Murder (1988)
- ❑ ❑ 2 - Death in Wessex (1989)
- ❑ ❑ 3 - Murder in Burgundy (1989)
- ❑ ❑ 4 - Deadly Rehearsal (1990)
- ❑ ❑ 5 - Elegy in a Country Graveyard (1990)
- ❑ ❑ 6 - Lament for Christabel (1991)
- ❑ ❑ . . . .
- ❑ ❑ . . . .

■ PETIT, Diane

new

Diane Petit has written three light-hearted mysteries featuring Kathryn Bogert, owner of an estate sale business aptly named Good Buys. In the series opener, *Goodbye, Charli* (1997), Kathryn is adopted by a Brittany spaniel named Charli, patterned after Petit's own Brittany named Charli. The fictional spaniel had belonged to practical joker Herb Pawlicki whose mysterious death prompts Kathryn to investigate. Petit also writes Avalon career romances, including *Heart of Gold* (1995). Borrowing from her husband's E.M.S. experience, Petit writes romantic suspense as D.B. Petit, including the first of a series, *Street Pizza* (1996), featuring paramedic Greg Marsh and the staff of the fictional St. Antony's emergency room. Firefighter Nick Zurowski returns in *A Savage Ecstasy* (1997) with another unsolved mystery from the past. With degrees in dance and elementary education, Petit has recently resumed teaching part-time. She lives in Chicago's south suburbs, where she also reviews romantic fiction for *Rendezvous* magazine.

Kathryn Bogert...owner of an estate sale business...Chicago, Illinois
- ❑ ❑ 1 - Goodbye, Charli (1997)
- ❑ ❑ 2 - Goodbye, Charli – Take Two (1998)
- ❑ ❑ 3 - Goodbye, Charli – Third TIme Lucky (1998)
- ❑ ❑ . . . .
- ❑ ❑ . . . .

■ PETRIE, Rhona [P]

Rhona Petrie is one of the pseudonyms of Eileen-Marie Duell Buchanan, author of more than 30 novels over the past 35 years. After launching her crime-writing career as Rhona Petrie with *Death in Deakins Wood* (1963), she "went straight" as Marie Buchanan (her words) and then returned to crime as Clare Curzon. Her five-book series from the 1960s features Inspector Marcus MacLurg in classic whodunnit police stories. Also published under the Petrie pseudonym are a pair of mysteries—*Foreign Bodies* (1967) and *Despatch of a Dove* (1969)—featuring the urbane Dr. Nassim Pride, an Anglo-Sudanese forensic scientist with a love for all things British. The pseudonymous Petrie is best known as Clare Curzon for her Thames Valley police procedurals. C.I.D. Superintendent Mike Yeadings will be seen next in book 14, *Cold Hands* (1999). Born in Sussex and educated at the University of London, the author has worked as an interpreter, translator, language teacher and social secretary in various European countries.

Marcus MacLurg...police inspector...England

❑	❑	1 - Death in Deakins Wood (1963)
❑	❑	2 - Murder by Precedent (1964)
❑	❑	3 - Running Deep (1965)
❑	❑	4 - Dead Loss (1966)
❑	❑	5 - MacLurg Goes West (1968)
❑	❑	....
❑	❑	....

Nassim Pride...Anglo-Sudanese forensic scientist...England

❑	❑	1 - Foreign Bodies (1967)
❑	❑	2 - Despatch of a Dove (1969)
❑	❑	....
❑	❑	....

■ PICKARD, Nancy

Nancy Pickard's light-hearted Jenny Cain mysteries have collected five awards and seven additional nominations for Agatha, Anthony, Edgar and Macavity honors. A Massachusetts foundation director in the seaport town of Port Frederick, Jenny is married to a handsome police lieutenant. During the ten-book series she solves enough crimes to qualify as a pro. Past president of Sisters in Crime, Pickard (pih-CARD) has also written *The 27-Ingredient Chili Con Carne Murders* (1993), based on an unfinished manuscript left by Virginia Rich. Pickard will write a third Eugenia Potter cooking mystery and launch a new series featuring South Florida true crime writer Marie Lightfoot. Seen first in *The Whole Truth* (2000), Lightfoot's Bahia Beach turf is reminiscent of Broward County. Winner of numerous short story awards, including a Shamus, Pickard is the editor of several recent anthologies, including *The First Lady Murders* (1999). A University of Missouri journalism graduate, she lives in a suburb of Kansas City, near mystery author Jill Churchill.

Eugenia Potter...60-something widowed chef...USA

❑	❑	1 - The Cooking School Murders [by Virginia Rich] (1982)
❑	❑	2 - The Baked Bean Supper Murders [by Virginia Rich] (1983)
❑	❑	3 - The Nantucket Diet Murders [by Virginia Rich] (1985)
❑	❑	4 - The 27-Ingredient Chile Con Carne Murders [with Virginia Rich] (1993)
❑	❑	5 - The Blue Corn Murders (1998)
❑	❑	....
❑	❑	....

Jenny Cain...New England foundation director...Port Frederick, Massachusetts

❑	❑	1 - Generous Death (1984)
❑	❑	2 - **Say No to Murder (1985) Anthony winner ★**
❑	❑	3 - **No Body (1986) Anthony nominee ☆**
❑	❑	4 - **Marriage Is Murder (1987) Macavity winner ★ Anthony nominee ☆**
❑	❑	5 - **Dead Crazy (1988) Agatha & Anthony nominee ☆☆**
❑	❑	6 - **Bum Steer (1989) Agatha winner ★**
❑	❑	7 - **I.O.U. (1991) Agatha & Macavity winner ★★ Anthony & Edgar nominee ☆☆**
❑	❑	8 - But I Wouldn't Want To Die There (1993)
❑	❑	9 - Confession (1994)
❑	❑	10 - **Twilight (1995) Agatha nominee ☆**
❑	❑	....
❑	❑	....

■ PIESMAN, Marissa

New York attorney Marissa Piesman (PIZE-man) launched her writing career with *The Yuppie Handbook* (1984), co-authored with Marilee Hartley. Five years later she published her first mystery featuring Nina Fischman, a neurotic, 35-year-old Jewish attorney who lives on the Upper West Side of Manhattan. Nina and her 70-something mother Ida, a retired school-teacher, debut in *Unorthodox Practices* (1989), where the two obsess about men, money, fashion, crime, religion and real estate. In book 5, *Alternate Sides* (1995), Nina's boyfriend is a murder suspect for the second time since she's known him. His doorman is blown away sitting behind the wheel of Jonathan's double-parked car. When last seen in book 6, *Survival Instincts* (1997), Nina is beau-less, unemployed and living with her mother. Oy vay! A *Booklist* reviewer found Piesman's humor and social insights suggestive of Nora Ephron, Fran Lebowitz and "even a touch of Jane Austen." Piesman is an assistant attorney general with the New York State Law Department.

Nina Fischman...legal services attorney...New York, New York

- ❏ ❏ 1 - Unorthodox Practices (1989)
- ❏ ❏ 2 - Personal Effects (1991)
- ❏ ❏ 3 - Heading Uptown (1993)
- ❏ ❏ 4 - Close Quarters (1994)
- ❏ ❏ 5 - Alternate Sides (1995)
- ❏ ❏ 6 - Survival Instincts (1997)
- ❏ ❏ . . . .
- ❏ ❏ . . . .

■ PINCUS, Elizabeth

Former private investigator Elizabeth Pincus has written three mysteries featuring San Francisco private eye Nell Fury, introduced in *The Two-Bit Tango* (1992), Lambda award winner for best lesbian mystery. "Such an engaging sleuth—part Philip Marlowe, part good buddy, and part politically savvy sexual outlaw," said *Publishers Weekly*. When last seen in *The Hangdog Hustle* (1995), Nell is investigating the unsolved murder of a young man who lived in the Castro district but worked at the Presidio as a civilian employee of the Army. "Ripping good action and a page-turning yarn," said *Midwest Book Review*. The entire series is available in trade paperback from Spinsters Ink. Pincus has worked as a film editor and reviewer and is currently assistant sports editor at the *Savannah Morning News*. Her writing has appeared in *The Village Voice*, *Harper's Bazaar*, the *San Francisco Chronicle* and the *San Francisco Review of Books*, while her short stories have been published in the WomanSleuth Anthologies.

Nell Fury...lesbian P.I....San Francisco, California

- ❏ ❏ **1 - The Two-Bit Tango (1992) Lambda winner ★**
- ❏ ❏ 2 - The Solitary Twist (1993)
- ❏ ❏ 3 - The Hangdog Hustle (1995)
- ❏ ❏ . . . .
- ❏ ❏ . . . .

■ PORTER, Anna

Hungarian-born Anna Porter has had a highly successful career in Canadian publishing as editor-in-chief of McClelland and Stewart, president and publisher of Key Porter Books, chairman of Doubleday Canada Ltd. and author of three mystery novels. Her first-hand publishing experience adds a special dimension to the protagonist Judith Hayes, freelance Toronto journalist and mother of two teenagers, introduced in *Hidden Agenda* (1985). Along with the cop boyfriend she met in book 1, Hayes returns in *Mortal Sins* (1987). Her life-long best friend, editor Marsha Hillier, featured in the earlier books, takes over in *The Bookfair Murders* (1997), set at the Frankfurt International Book Fair. Born in Budapest, Porter earned an M.A. with honors at the University of Canterbury in Christchurch, New Zealand. With Marjorie Harris she has written *Farewell to the '70s: A Canadian Salute to a Confusing Decade* (1979). A member of numerous boards of directors, including Imperial Life and York University, Porter lives in Toronto.

Judith Hayes...freelance journalist...Toronto, Ontario, Canada

- ❑ ❑ 1 - Hidden Agenda (1985)
- ❑ ❑ 2 - Mortal Sins (1987)
- ❑ ❑ 3 - The Bookfair Murders [Marsha Hillier] (1997)
- ❑ ❑ . . . .
- ❑ ❑ . . . .

■ POWELL, Deborah

Deborah Powell has written two Texas mysteries featuring Hollis Carpenter, a gay woman crime reporter in 1930s Houston. In the series opener, *Bayou City Secrets* (1991), it's 1936 and the veteran reporter has been yanked from her beat on the *Houston Times* to cover a no-news society item. She resigns in disgust, only to be invited for dinner at the home of the paper's owner. He seems genuinely interested in her story about guns missing from a police evidence room. When Hollis seeks the advice of cop-friend Joe Mahan after finding her apartment burgled, she discovers Joe's murdered body. After receiving a death threat, Hollis is nearly gunned down in public with Lily Delacroix, the beautiful wife of the *Times'* owner. A "promising debut," said *Publishers Weekly*, "with a fast-moving, entertaining mystery served up in the hard-boiled style." Although the reviewer found Hollis "more a smart aleck than a wit," Powell was credited with making the "lesbian relationship integral to the mystery." Hollis' second adventure is *Houston Town* (1992).

Hollis Carpenter...gay woman crime reporter...Houston, Texas

- ❑ ❑ 1 - Bayou City Secrets (1991)
- ❑ ❑ 2 - Houston Town (1992)
- ❑ ❑ . . . .
- ❑ ❑ . . . .

■ PROWELL, Sandra West

Two-time Shamus nominee Sandra West Prowell (rhymes with Powell) is a fourth-generation Montanan and great-granddaughter of early pioneers. Her fictional private eye is Montanan Phoebe Siegel, a former cop and F.B.I. dropout, introduced in the Hammett and Shamus-nominated *By Evil Means* (1993). Book 2 finds Phoebe trying to disprove murder charges against a local Native American accused of killing unpopular antiquities dealer Monday Brown. Phoebe's third case, *When Wallflowers Die* (1996), involves the long-unsolved murder of an heiress whose husband, a one-time suspect, is now a candidate for governor. Family problems and her budding romance with a police officer complicate Phoebe's investigation. A one-time radio traffic manager, photographer, pet groomer and nurse, Prowell is cofounder of the Montana Authors Coalition and co-producer of the literary heritage map of Montana. Born in Helena, Prowell lives in Billings. When not writing, she enjoys fishing, beading and researching herbal and medicinal plants native to Montana.

Phoebe Siegel...ex-cop P.I....Billings, Montana

- ❑ ❑ 1 - **By Evil Means (1993) Hammett & Shamus nominee** ☆☆
- ❑ ❑ 2 - **The Killing of Monday Brown (1994) Shamus nominee** ☆
- ❑ ❑ 3 - When Wallflowers Die (1996)
- ❑ ❑ . . . .
- ❑ ❑ . . . .

■ PUGH, Dianne G.

Los Angeles author Dianne G. Pugh is the creator of Oreo cookie-loving Iris Thorne, a 30-something investment counselor with blue collar roots, first seen in *Cold Call* (1993). "With her bold moral compass, her appealing in-your-face attitude and unsettled romantic life, Iris is a compelling heroine," said *Publishers Weekly*. Her raucous male co-workers at the Los Angeles firm of McKinney Alitzer call her the ice princess, but Dick Lochte found her "sleek, smart and refreshingly bitchy," in his *Los Angeles Times* review. After dealing with computer gamesmanship and securities fraud in book 4, *Foolproof* (1998), Iris travels to Moscow, at the request of an ex-fiancé she once left at the altar, in *Pushover* (1999), published first in the U.K. A former department store fashion buyer, Pugh has worked as a marketing director in both the packaging and software industries. Like Iris, she is wild about her red Triumph convertible, despite its tendency to leak oil. Pugh earned a B.A. in philosophy and an M.B.A. in marketing and finance from U.C.L.A.

Iris Thorne…investment counselor…Los Angeles, California
- ❏ ❏ 1 - Cold Call (1993)
- ❏ ❏ 2 - Slow Squeeze (1994)
- ❏ ❏ 3 - Fast Friends (1997)
- ❏ ❏ - Brit.-Body Blow
- ❏ ❏ 4 - Foolproof (1998)
- ❏ ❏ . . . .
- ❏ ❏ . . . .

■ PULVER, Mary Monica

Anthony nominee Mary Monica Pulver has written three mystery series under three different names. Her five-book series featuring Illinois police detective Peter Brichter and his horse-breeder wife, Kori Price, appears under the Pulver name, starting with the Anthony-nominated *Murder at the War* (1987), re-released in 1991 as *Knight Fall*. Horse-loving fans of police procedurals may want to begin this series with the second installment, a prequel to book 1. Writing as Margaret Frazer, Pulver co-authored with Gail Fraser the first six books in their medieval series featuring Sister Frevisse of the St. Frideswide convent. As Monica Ferris, she recently launched a needlework series featuring 50-something Betsy Devonshire, seen first in the paperback original *Crewel World* (1999). A Navy veteran and Arabian horse-lover, Pulver is a member of the Society for Creative Anachronism, as are her characters, Peter and Kori Brichter. Born in Terre Haute, Indiana, Pulver lives in St. Louis Park, Minnesota.

Peter & Kori Price Brichter…police detective & horse breeder…Illinois
- ❏ ❏ 1 - **Murder at the War (1987) Anthony nominee** ☆
- ❏ ❏ - APA-Knight Fall
- ❏ ❏ 2 - The Unforgiving Minutes [prequel] (1988)
- ❏ ❏ 3 - Ashes to Ashes (1988)
- ❏ ❏ 4 - Original Sin (1991)
- ❏ ❏ 5 - Show Stopper (1992)
- ❏ ❏ . . . .
- ❏ ❏ . . . .

■ QUEST, Erica [P]

Erica Quest is the joint pseudonym of British authors Nancy Buckingham Sawyer and her husband John Sawyer for at least six mysteries published by Doubleday Crime Club, including three featuring the first woman D.C.I. in Chipping Bassett. Newly-appointed Detective Chief Inspector Kate Maddox faces unhappy male subordinates and numerous likely suspects following a precision hit-and-run on quiet Cotswolds back roads in *Death Walk* (1988). After solving a double homicide in *Cold Coffin* (1990), Kate contends with a victim's bankrupt ex-husband, jealous spouse and jilted lover in *Model Murder* (1991). Alibis abound in this case of rape and murder. In addition to their pseudonymous work as Erica Quest, the Sawyers have written at least 15 novels of historical romance and romantic suspense as Christina Abbey, Nancy Buckingham, Nancy John and Hilary London. Before writing fiction full time, Nancy Buckingham Sawyer was a medical social worker and John Sawyer an advertising executive.

Kate Maddox…first woman DCI…Cotswolds, England
- ❏ ❏ 1 - Death Walk (1988)
- ❏ ❏ 2 - Cold Coffin (1990)
- ❏ ❏ 3 - Model Murder (1991)
- ❏ ❏ . . . .
- ❏ ❏ . . . .

■ QUINN, Elizabeth [P]

Elizabeth Quinn is the penname of Elizabeth Quinn Barnard for seven novels, including four paperback mysteries featuring Lauren Maxwell, Ph.D., Anchorage-based naturalist-investigator for the Wild American Society. The widowed mother of two young children is last seen in *Killer Whale* (1997), where Lauren clashes with a French biologist on Prince of Wales Island while trying to prevent the capture of wild orcas. A planned fifth book in the series was set aside when Quinn returned to daily journalism in 1997. After a short stint on a smaller paper, she is currently Southern Oregon correspondent for *The Oregonian*, writing as Beth Quinn. After earning an M.A. in journalism at Boston University, Quinn worked for several small dailies including the *Cape Cod Times*. She later taught journalism at the University of Rhode Island before moving to Oregon with her Associated Press correspondent husband. Her first novel, *Alliances* (1986), featuring a woman World War II correspondent, sold 100,000 copies worldwide.

Lauren Maxwell...wildlife investigator PhD...Anchorage, Alaska

❏	❏	1 -	Murder Most Grizzly (1993)
❏	❏	2 -	A Wolf in Death's Clothing (1995)
❏	❏	3 -	Lamb to the Slaughter (1996)
❏	❏	4 -	Killer Whale (1997)
❏	❏		. . . .
❏	❏		. . . .

■ QUINTON, Ann

Former librarian Ann Quinton has written at least six police novels set in rural Suffolk featuring 32-year-old D.I. James Roland and his 45-year-old partner, D.S. Patrick Mansfield, introduced in *To Mourn a Mischief* (1989). Book 2, *Death of a Dear Friend* (1990), is a case of double murder wrapped in an art mystery according to Carol Harper in *Deadly Pleasures* (Issue 12). The music world takes center stage in book 3, *A Fatal End* (1992), when a Russian cellist tries to defect. After a case of multiple child abductions in book 4, a potential serial killer known as "The Joker" is at work in book 5, *The Sleeping and the Dead* (1994). The series is well-written with complex plots and sympathetic characters, says Harper. A new Quinton series may be starting with *This Mortal Coil* (1998), as police detectives Michael Croft and Nick Holroyd investigate a contract killer who leaves a business card from the "Coil Shuffler" on his victims. "A fiendishly tough mystery" with "vivid characters and evocative English atmosphere," says *Booklist*.

James Roland & Patrick Mansfield...det. inspector & det. sergeant...Suffolk, England

❏	❏	1 -	To Mourn a Mischief (1989)
❏	❏	2 -	Death of a Dear Friend (1990)
❏	❏	3 -	A Fatal End (1992)
❏	❏	4 -	A Little Grave (1994)
❏	❏	5 -	The Sleeping and the Dead (1994)
❏	❏	6 -	Some Foul Play (1997)
❏	❏		. . . .
❏	❏		. . . .

■ RADLEY, Sheila [P]

Sheila Radley is the pseudonym of Sheila Robinson for a nine-book series with Inspector Douglas Quantrill, a plodding but likable detective and family man in rural Suffolk. His original partner is replaced by a woman sergeant in book 4. According to Robert Barnard *(20th Century Crime & Mystery Writers, 3rd edition)*, Radley's picture of village life is neither sentimentalized nor condescending. Her murderers are not psychopaths, nor are they particularly violent. Instead she favors ordinary people driven to murder by extraordinary stress. After earning a B.A. in history from the University of London, she served nine years in the Women's Royal Air Force and later worked as a teacher and college lecturer and in advertising. She moved to rural Norfolk in 1964 and spent 14 years running a village store and post office. As Hester Rowan she wrote three romantic thrillers before turning to mysteries, with the first Quantrill book reaching publication just before her 50th birthday. *New Blood From Old Bones* (1998) is Radley's historical novel set in 1530 Norfolk.

Douglas Quantrill & Hilary Lloyd...DCI & sergeant partner...Suffolk, England

❏	❏	1 -	Death and the Maiden (1978)
❏	❏	-	U.S.-Death in the Morning
❏	❏	2 -	The Chief Inspector's Daughter (1980)
❏	❏	3 -	A Talent for Destruction (1982)

❏ ❏	4 - Blood on the Happy Highway (1983)
❏ ❏	- U.S.-The Quiet Road to Death
❏ ❏	5 - Fate Worse Than Death (1985)
❏ ❏	6 - Who Saw Him Die? (1987)
❏ ❏	7 - This Way Out (1989)
❏ ❏	8 - Cross My Heart and Hope To Die (1992)
❏ ❏	9 - Fair Game (1994)
❏ ❏	. . . .
❏ ❏	. . . .

■ RAWLINGS, Ellen

Ellen Rawlings has written two mysteries featuring freelance investigative journalist Rachel Crowne, introduced in *The Murder Lover* (1997). Young, Jewish and twice-divorced, Rachel has strong feelings for her heritage, but is not particularly religious. She lives in the fictional planned community of Fairfield, a thinly-disguised Columbia, Maryland, outside Washington, D.C. In book 1, Rachel interviews two men with ties to a local murder—a cross-burning white supremacist and the charismatic founder of the Church of Unconditional Love. Rawlings has also written four Regency romance novels, *A Convenient Marriage* (1993), *A Perfect Arrangement* (1992), *A Larcenous Affair* (1991), and *A Serious Pursuit* (1991). A Yuletide romantic story by Rawlings, "The Baby Shoppe," is included in *A Christmas Treasure* (1992). A former writer and editor for a Washington area government agency, Rawlings has also taught college English. She lives in Columbia, Maryland with her mathematician husband and their Chihuahua Tommy.

Rachel Crowne...Jewish investigative reporter...Washington, District of Columbia

❏ ❏	1 - The Murder Lover (1997)
❏ ❏	2 - Deadly Harvest (1997)
❏ ❏	. . . .
❏ ❏	. . . .

■ RAYNER, Claire

Author of more than 90 books, Claire Rayner is Britain's best-known medical and advice columnist, having written for two women's magazines for 25 years until 1992. Beginning her career as a nurse and later studying midwifery, Rayner traded hospital duties for writing when her first child was born in 1960. In addition to her many books on medical subjects ranging from sex education to child care, she has written historical, gothic, contemporary and crime novels under her own name and as Sheila Brandon. Her medical detective character is Dr. George Barnabas, resident forensic and general pathologist at London's Royal Eastern Hospital. George is a woman who loves nothing more than a good puzzle over a death. When last seen in *Fifth Member* (1997), she sees something in the death of a member of Parliament that reminds her of Jack the Ripper. Awarded an O.B.E. in 1996 for services to women's and health issues, Rayner is active in numerous medical and welfare organizations. She lives in North London.

George Barnabas...hospital forensic pathologist...London, England

❏ ❏	1 - First Blood (1993)
❏ ❏	2 - Second Opinion (1994)
❏ ❏	3 - Third Degree (1995)
❏ ❏	4 - Fourth Attempt (1996)
❏ ❏	5 - Fifth Member (1997)
❏ ❏	. . . .
❏ ❏	. . . .

■ REDMANN, J.M.

Lambda award-winner Jean M. Redmann is the creator of Michelle "Micky" Knight, a gay-woman investigator in New Orleans. The Bayou-bred P.I. is "gutsy" and "fast-thinking" in the "Raymond Chandler tradition, a detective [that] fans both gay and straight will want to see again and again," said

Booklist. Redmann started *Death by the Riverside* (1990), as a short story and ended up writing the first novel of a series. In an online interview for Sisters in Crime's Internet Chapter, she talks about finding the title for her third book in a newspaper article about a fatal shooting at the intersection of Law and Desire. Only in New Orleans could a writer hope to find intersecting streets named Law and Desire. In book 4, *Lost Daughters* (1999), Micky searches for her own mother in the midst of murders at her lover's clinic. Redmann grew up in Ocean Springs, Mississippi, a small town on the Gulf of Mexico. After living in New York City for a number of years she returned to the South and, like Micky, lives in New Orleans.

Michelle 'Micky' Knight...gay woman private eye...New Orleans, Louisiana

- ❑ ❑   1 - Death by the Riverside (1990)
- ❑ ❑   2 - Deaths of Jocasta (1993)
- ❑ ❑   3 - **The Intersection of Law and Desire (1995) Lambda winner ★**
- ❑ ❑   . . . .
- ❑ ❑   . . . .

■ REICHS, Kathy

A specialist in skeletal biology, Kathy Reichs is one of fewer than 100 certified forensic anthropologists in the U.S. and Canada. After completing her Ph.D. at Northwestern University, she expected to teach and study ancient bones of North American cultures, but a police request to look at skeletal remains of a murder victim changed all that. Like her fictional heroine, Dr. Temperance Brennan, Reichs serves as forensic anthropologist for the province of Quebec and commutes between Montreal and Charlotte, where she teaches anthropology at the University of North Carolina. Reichs is even busier than her fictional counterpart, teaching courses for the F.B.I. and other law enforcement agencies and writing mysteries in her spare time. Her Ellis award-winning best first novel, *Déjà Dead* (1997), was a *New York Times* best-seller and *Death du Jour* (1999) "reads like a house afire," says *Kirkus*. As Kathleen J. Reichs, she wrote *Hominid Origins: Inquiries Past and Present* (1983) and edited *Forensic Osteology: Advances in the Identification of Human Remains* (1997).

Temperance Brennan...forensic anthropologist...Montreal, Quebec, Canada

- ❑ ❑   1 - **Déjà Dead (1997) Ellis winner ★**
- ❑ ❑   2 - Death du Jour (1999)
- ❑ ❑   . . . .
- ❑ ❑   . . . .

■ RENDELL, Ruth

International best-selling author of almost 50 books in more than 20 languages, Ruth Rendell (REN-dle) has won three Edgars, four Gold Daggers, and the Diamond Dagger and Grand Master awards for lifetime achievement. Baroness Rendell of Babergh, a Labor life peer since 1997, is the first member of the House of Lords to use polar bears (her favorite animal) in her coat of arms. Resisting the temptation to choose pistols or daggers, she included a yellow Brimstone butterfly, noting that butterflies or moths appear in all her books. Rendell alternates traditional detective stories featuring Chief Inspector Reginald Wexford with more psychological crime novels under her own name and as Barbara Vine. A witty detective with a keen understanding of people, Wexford has appeared in 17 books and a television series since his 1964 debut in *From Doon with Death*. Book 18, *Harm Done* is due in September 1999. Born in London, Rendell worked for several years as a newspaper reporter and editor. In addition to writing two books a year, she is a frequent author of articles, reviews and short stories.

Reginald Wexford...chief inspector...Sussex, England

- ❑ ❑   1 - From Doon With Death (1964)
- ❑ ❑   2 - A New Lease of Death (1967)
- ❑ ❑   - APA-Sins of the Fathers (1970)
- ❑ ❑   3 - Wolf to Slaughter (1967)
- ❑ ❑   4 - The Best Man To Die (1969)
- ❑ ❑   5 - A Guilty Thing Surprised (1970)
- ❑ ❑   6 - No More Dying Then (1971)

❑ ❑   7 - Murder Being Once Done (1972)
❑ ❑   8 - Some Lie and Some Die (1973)
❑ ❑   9 - Shake Hands Forever (1975)
❑ ❑ **10 - A Sleeping Life (1978) Edgar nominee ☆**
❑ ❑ 11 - Put on by Cunning (1981)
❑ ❑   - U.S.-Death Notes
❑ ❑ 12 - The Speaker of Mandarin (1983)
❑ ❑ **13 - An Unkindness of Ravens (1985) Edgar nominee ☆**
❑ ❑ 14 - The Veiled One (1988)
❑ ❑ 15 - Kissing the Gunner's Daughter (1992)
❑ ❑ 16 - Simisola (1994)
❑ ❑ 17 - Road Rage (1997)
❑ ❑ . . . .
❑ ❑ . . . .

■ REUBEN, Shelly

Former journalist Shelly Reuben was researching an article on suspicious fires when she met arson investigator Charles King of the New York Fire Division. She and King later married and started their own fire analysis business. While working alongside her husband, Reuben obtained her P.I. license and began using her technical knowledge to write mysteries featuring New York City insurance investigator and P.I. Wylie Nolan and his attorney friend Max Bramble. In the series opener, *Origin and Cause* (1994), Max is defending Courtland Motors' antique-restoring division in a product liability claim. His good friend Wylie Nolan is convinced that a media giant's death-by-fire inside a $2,000,000 1930 Duesenberg Arlington sedan was murder. In *Spent Matches* (1996), Wylie is hired to solve a locked-room mystery at the Zigfield Art Museum, where a painting exhibition is plagued by suspicious fires. Reuben's first mystery, *Julian Solo* (1988) was an Edgar nominee for best first novel. She and King live in New York.

Wylie Nolan & Max Bramble...arson investigator & attorney...New York, New York

❑ ❑ 1 - Origin and Cause (1994)
❑ ❑ 2 - Spent Matches (1996)
❑ ❑ . . . .
❑ ❑ . . . .

■ RICHARDSON, Tracey

Canadian newspaper editor Tracey Richardson has written three mysteries featuring Toronto homicide detective Stevie Houston. In the series opener, *Last Rites* (1997), the newly-promoted lesbian detective has a hunch about the death of a beloved parish priest, but her superiors want the case closed quickly. Stevie goes undercover in a small-town police department after two of its detectives are murdered in her second case, *Over the Line* (1998). Richardson is also the author of *Northern Blue* (1996), featuring ambitious Ontario policewoman Miranda McCauley, who plans to be chief by the time she's 40. Born in Windsor, Ontario, Richardson earned a communications degree from the University of Windsor and a journalism diploma from St. Clair College. Editor for a daily Ontario newspaper, she lives with a police sergeant who is part of the inspiration for Richardson's mysteries. When not working or writing, she enjoys riding around in her 1978 Corvette, playing golf, making wine and collecting fine cigars.

Stevie Houston...gay rookie homicide detective...Toronto, Ontario, Canada

❑ ❑ 1 - Last Rites (1997)
❑ ❑ 2 - Over the Line (1998)
❑ ❑ 3 - Double Takeout (1999)
❑ ❑ . . . .
❑ ❑ . . . .

■ RICHMAN, Phyllis

One of the most feared women in the nation's capital, Phyllis Richman has been writing about restaurants and food for *The Washington Post* for more than 20 years as food editor, restaurant critic, and food writer in every section from *Style* to *Business*. With the introduction of Chas Wheatly, former chef turned restaurant critic, Richman has added mystery-writing to her already-full plate. When Washington's toniest chef drops dead of a heart attack, Chas is pretty sure the butter didn't do it. Among the helpful tips in Richman's Agatha-nominated *The Butter Did It* (1997) are suggestions for handling a haughty waiter and making fat-free potato salad. Chas returns for more

restaurant chicanery in book 2, *Murder on the Gravy Train* (1999). Also new from Richman is the 1999-2000 edition of her best-selling *Washington Post Dining Guide.* Her food commentary has also been featured in national magazines from *Bon Appetit* to *Travel & Leisure.* A Brandeis University graduate, Richman started her career as a Philadelphia city planner.

Chas Wheatley...restaurant critic...Washington, District of Columbia

 ❑ ❑ 1 - **The Butter Did It (1997) Agatha nominee** ☆
 ❑ ❑ 2 - Murder on the Gravy Train (1999)
 ❑ ❑ . . . .
 ❑ ❑ . . . .

■ RIPLEY, Ann

Former journalist Ann Ripley is the creator of foreign service wife Louise Eldridge, organic gardener and PBS television host in suburban Washington, D.C. In the series opener, Louise finds a body in her neighborhood collection of grass clippings and leaves. First published in 1994, *Mulch* was re-released in 1998 in a paperback edition enriched with Louise's gardening essays. In book 2, *Death of a Garden Pest*, Louise joins the PBS program *Gardening with Nature*, a virtual "compost heap of lust, jealousy and sponsor pres-

sures" according to *Kirkus Reviews*. In her latest adventure, book 4, *The Garden Tour Affair* (1999), Louise is up to her garden gloves in houseguests and the murder of an old flame. Ripley has worked as a stringer for the *New York Times*, writer and editor for a suburban daily and placement coordinator for Northwestern University's Medill School of Journalism. She is working on book 5, *The Perennial Killer* (2000), where she'll send Louise to Ripley's home state of Colorado.

Louise Eldridge...organic gardener TV host...Northern Virginia

 ❑ ❑ 1 - Mulch (1994)
 ❑ ❑ 2 - Death of a Garden Pest (1996)
 ❑ ❑ 3 - Death of a Political Plant (1998)
 ❑ ❑ . . . .
 ❑ ❑ . . . .

■ RIPPON, Marion

Former psychiatric nurse Marion Rippon told her family she wanted to write so she could buy an electric dishwasher. She later confessed to *Contemporary Authors* her desire "to create a fictional character so real he would become immortal." After finally completing her novel about a café owner with a very disturbed mind, Rippon feared rejection and put the manuscript on a bedroom shelf underneath an old hatbox. Her husband sent it to the Doubleday Crime Club which accepted it immediately. Rippon's

detective, retired French police inspector Maurice Ygrec (ee-GREK) is introduced in *The Hand of Solange* (1969). The inspector, who seems to always be vacationing, visits a villa in a remote wine valley in book 2, travels to Moulins in book 3 and returns to his beloved Paris to visit his friend Inspector Michelin of St. Denis in book 4, *Lucien's Tomb* (1979). A native of Drumheller, Alberta, Rippon has lived in British Columbia for more than 25 years. She has taught creative writing at the University of Victoria.

Maurice Ygrec...retired French police inspector...Moselle, France

 ❑ ❑ 1 - The Hand of Solange (1969)
 ❑ ❑ 2 - Behold, the Druid Weeps (1970)
 ❑ ❑ 3 - The Ninth Tentacle (1974)
 ❑ ❑ 4 - Lucien's Tomb (1979)
 ❑ ❑ . . . .
 ❑ ❑ . . . .

■ ROBB, Candace M.

Candace M. Robb's medieval mysteries are set in York, England, where she has become a local celebrity. Although book 1 began as a short story about

apothecary-wife Lucie Wilton, it was suggested that Robb expand on the story's mystery thread. Enter Owen Archer, one-eyed Welsh marksman turned detective-spy for the Archbishop of York. *The Apothecary Rose* (1993) was hailed as "full of tension, incident, and emotion" in a starred *Kirkus* review. Owen is trying to leave Wales for home, but is blackmailed into investigating a murder in book 7, *A Spy for the Redeemer* (1999). Meanwhile Lucie is dealing with an attack on her father's manor and struggling with her resentment of Owen's prolonged absences. Robb

earned an M.A. in medieval literature at the University of Cincinnati, but left the program before completing her doctoral dissertation. A North Carolina native, she lives in Seattle where she teaches creative writing at the University of Washington and tends an herb garden. Her husband draws the maps for her Owen Archer books.

Owen Archer...one-eyed medieval Welsh spy...York, England
- ❑ ❑ 1 - The Apothecary Rose (1993)
- ❑ ❑ 2 - The Lady Chapel (1994)
- ❑ ❑ 3 - The Nun's Tale (1995)
- ❑ ❑ 4 - The King's Bishop (1996)
- ❑ ❑ 5 - The Riddle of St. Leonard's (1996)
- ❑ ❑ 6 - A Gift of Sanctuary (1998)
- ❑ ❑ ....
- ❑ ❑ ....

■ ROBB, J.D. [P]

J.D. Robb is the pseudonym of best-selling romance writer Nora Roberts for her futuristic police series set in 21st century New York City. Homicide detective Eve Dallas and the multi-billionaire Roarke are introduced in *Naked in Death* (1995). Eve's eighth and ninth adventures, *Conspiracy in Death* and *Loyalty in Death* will be published in 1999. Roberts says she chose writing over a nervous breakdown while marooned with two young sons during a fierce winter in rural Maryland. The first inductee of the Romance

Writers of America (R.W.A.) Hall of Fame, she has won every award for excellence in her field. A veritable one-woman publishing empire, Roberts claimed 11 titles (four at #1) on *New York Times* best-seller lists in 1998. With more than 85 million books in print in 25 languages, it is estimated she sells 12 books every minute around the clock, 365 days a year. Her 128th novel, the romance *River's End*, was published in March 1999, not quite 18 years after her first, *Irish Thoroughbred*, in May 1981.

Eve Dallas...21st century NYPD lieutenant...New York, New York
- ❑ ❑ 1 - Naked in Death (1995)
- ❑ ❑ 2 - Glory in Death (1996)
- ❑ ❑ 3 - Immortal in Death (1996)
- ❑ ❑ 4 - Rapture in Death (1996)
- ❑ ❑ 5 - Ceremony in Death (1997)
- ❑ ❑ 6 - Vengeance in Death (1997)
- ❑ ❑ 7 - Holiday in Death (1998)
- ❑ ❑ 8 - Conspiracy in Death (1999)
- ❑ ❑ ....
- ❑ ❑ ....

■ ROBERTS, Carey

Former marketing and public relations executive Carey Roberts has written two books featuring Washington, D.C. homicide detective Anne Fitzhugh, first seen in *Touch a Cold Door* (1989). In book 2, *Pray God To Die* (1993), a well-connected environmentalist turned congressional assistant is murdered. To find her killer, the D.C. police must eliminate more than the usual suspects, starting with a high-profile Congressman and a charismatic Washington Cathedral canon. A working writer and practicing psychotherapist in suburban Maryland, Roberts has

written about Washington for numerous national publications. A graduate of Emory University in Atlanta, she previously worked as director of marketing for a Bethesda bank and hospital. With Rebecca Seely she co-authored *Tidewater Dynasty: The Lees of Stratford Hall* (1983), a fictional account of the Robert E. Lee family of Virginia. The book is "solidly researched and illuminating," said *Publishers Weekly*, including revelations about the personal liberation of the Lee women.

Anne Fitzhugh...police detective...Washington, District of Columbia

❑ ❑ 1 - Touch a Cold Door (1989)
❑ ❑ 2 - Pray God To Die (1993)
❑ ❑ . . . .
❑ ❑ . . . .

■ ROBERTS, Gillian [P]

Gillian Roberts is the pseudonym of Judith Greber (GREE-ber), author of nine books in the Anthony award-winning Amanda Pepper series featuring a 30-something Philadelphia prep school English teacher. Amanda takes her students on a deadly field trip to the Free Library in book 9, *Adam and Evil* (1999), but lives to teach again in book 10, *Helen Hath Fury* (2000). Roberts introduced 50-year-old no-nonsense Marin County private investigator, Emma Howe, and her new associate, 28-year-old single-mother, Billie August, in *Time and Trouble* (1998). Their second case will be *Whatever Doesn't Kill You* (2000). *Kirkus* called this series "one to watch," finding it "darker and richer" than Roberts' Philadelphia series. New from Writer's Digest Books is *You Can Write a Mystery* (1999) by Gillian Roberts. Among her four mainstream novels as Judith Greber are *As Good As It Gets* (1992) and *Mendocino* (1988). A former high school English teacher, Greber earned B.S. and M.A. degrees from the University of Pennsylvania. She lives in Marin County, California.

Amanda Pepper...high school English teacher...Philadelphia, Pennsylvania

❑ ❑ 1 - **Caught Dead in Philadelphia (1987) Anthony winner ★**
❑ ❑ 2 - **Philly Stakes (1989) Agatha nominee ☆**
❑ ❑ 3 - I'd Rather Be in Philadelphia (1991)
❑ ❑ 4 - With Friends Like These (1993)
❑ ❑ 5 - How I Spent My Summer Vacation (1994)
❑ ❑ 6 - In the Dead of Summer (1995)
❑ ❑ 7 - The Mummers' Curse (1996)
❑ ❑ 8 - The Bluest Blood (1998)
❑ ❑ . . . .
❑ ❑ . . . .

Emma Howe & Billie August...50-yr-old P.I. & single-mom partner...San Raphael, California

❑ ❑ 1 - Time and Trouble (1998)
❑ ❑ . . . .
❑ ❑ . . . .

■ ROBERTS, Lillian M.

Veterinarian and equestrienne Lillian M. Roberts is the creator of amateur sleuth Andi Pauling, D.V.M., owner of a Palm Springs animal clinic. The fictional setup is somewhat like the author's, except that Roberts' Palm Desert daytime practice is the Country Club Animal Clinic, not Dr. Doolittle's. Horse-crazy since the age of twelve when she bought her first horse with baby-sitting money, Roberts focuses on the world of polo in her Agatha-nominated series opener, *Riding for a Fall* (1996). A graduate of the University of Missouri College of Veterinary Medicine and Arizona State University, she has worked at an Arabian racing stable in Kansas City, the Garden State Racetrack in New Jersey and groomed racing quarter horses in New Mexico. She is also the author of *Emergency Vets* (1998), a collection of more than 45 true stories about situations that occurred during eight years of working nights at the Animal Emergency Clinic of the Desert before opening her own practice.

new

Andi Pauling...veterinarian...Palm Springs, California

❑ ❑ 1 - **Riding for a Fall (1996) Agatha nominee ☆**
❑ ❑ 2 - The Hand That Feeds You (1997)
❑ ❑ 3 - Almost Human (1998)
❑ ❑ . . . .
❑ ❑ . . . .

■ ROBERTS, Lora

Born and raised in Missouri, Lora Roberts has lived in Palo Alto, California more than 20 years, the setting for her series featuring freelance writer Liz Sullivan. An earlier Palo Alto mystery, *Revolting Development* (1988), published under the name Lora Roberts Smith, features several continuing characters, including detective Paul Drake, Bridget, Claudia and Melanie Dixon. The vagabond Liz rolls into town in her '69 Volkswagen microbus in *Murder in a Nice Neighborhood* (1994). A true child of the '60s, Liz works a plot in the community organic garden, leads a writing workshop at the senior center and recycles religiously. Her black and white mutt, Barker, introduced in book 2, joins the rest of the cast for book 6, *Murder Follows Money* (2000). A member of Palo Alto's community organic garden for almost 20 years, Roberts has yet to encounter murderous behavior among her fellow vegetable growers. She once owned a 1978 passenger bus, but swears she never lived on board, except for endless hours as a carpool mom.

Liz Sullivan...freelance writer and organic gardener...Palo Alto, California

❑ ❑ 1 - Murder in a Nice Neighborhood (1994)
❑ ❑ 2 - Murder in the Marketplace (1995)
❑ ❑ 3 - Murder Mile-High (1996)
❑ ❑ 4 - Murder Bone by Bone (1997)
❑ ❑ 5 - Murder Crops Up (1998)
❑ ❑ 6 - Murder Follows Money (2000)
❑ ❑ . . . .
❑ ❑ . . . .

■ ROBINSON, Leah Ruth [P]

Emergency medical technician Leah Ruth Robinson has created "one of the most insightful and compelling doctors to come down the commercial fiction pike in a long time," said the *San Francisco Chronicle*. Dr. Evelyn Sutcliffe and her E.R. crew of "adrenaline junkies" made their original debut in 1988 in *Blood Run*, updated and re-released in 1999. In *First Cut* (1997) University Hospital is being stalked by a serial killer, while poison mushrooms become the murder weapon in book 3, *Unnatural Causes* (1999). Robinson has worked in the emergency rooms of two major New York City hospitals and also taught C.P.R. for several years. A one-time premed student at Columbia University, she earned a B.A. in philosophy and religion and later worked for 12 years as associate registrar at New York's Union Theological Seminary. One of her great-great-grandfathers was the tailor who made the uniforms for the first North Pole expedition. Robinson and writer-husband John Rousmaniere divide their time between Manhattan and Stamford, Connecticut.

Evelyn Sutcliffe...emergency medicine resident...New York, New York

❑ ❑ 1 - Blood Run [revised 1999] (1988)
❑ ❑ 2 - First Cut (1997)
❑ ❑ . . . .
❑ ❑ . . . .

■ ROBINSON, Lynda S.

Lynda S. Robinson's first four Lord Meren novels earned her starred reviews from *Publishers Weekly* and countless fans, including science fiction icon Harlan Ellison, who eagerly await each new installment. Set in ancient Egypt, the series features Tutankhamen's fictional chief investigator, Lord Meren, who serves as the "Eyes and Ears" of the Pharaoh. Although not based on a specific historical figure, Lord Meren is drawn from Robinson's studies of ancient Egypt, as part of her Ph.D. program in anthropology at the University of Texas. The sixth installment, *Slayer of Gods* (2000), will complete the Queen Nefertiti trilogy which began with *Eater of Souls* (1997). Writing as Suzanne (her middle name) Robinson, she is the author of 11 novels of historical romance, including her first book, set in ancient Egypt, *Heart of the Falcon* (1990). Her latest historical romance, *The Treasure* (1999), features London's most skilled female pickpocket, disguised as a debutante to steal an aristocrat's fortune. Robinson lives in Texas.

Lord Meren...Tutankhamen's chief investigator...Egypt

❏ ❏	1 -	Murder in the Place of Anubis (1994)
❏ ❏	2 -	Murder at the God's Gate (1995)
❏ ❏	3 -	Murder at the Feast of Rejoicing (1996)
❏ ❏	4 -	Eater of Souls (1997)
❏ ❏	5 -	Drinker of Blood (1998)
❏ ❏		. . . .
❏ ❏		. . . .

■ ROBITAILLE, Julie

Former Hollywood story analyst Julie Robitaille (ro-bi-tay) has written a pair of mysteries featuring television sports reporter and part-time San Diego sportscaster Kathleen 'Kit' Powell. When first seen in *Jinx* (1992), Kit watches one of the pro football team owners fall to his death from a skybox. Recently-moved to San Diego, the team seems to be jinxed, having suffered 13 accidents and/or scandals since relocating from Galveston, Texas. Robitaille is "quite disarming about TV, its stars, and its newswriters," said *Kirkus*. Anxious for an upbeat story after an all-bad-news season, Kit takes an assignment to cover a local figure-skating tournament. Two murders, an attempted hit-and-run, racial threats against several top skaters and anti-tobacco protesters picketing the tournament sponsors round out the mayhem on ice. Adding to Kit's frustration is the appearance of her cop-boyfriend's glamorous ex-wife. A native of Los Angeles, Robitaille has worked for several major motion picture studios. She lives in Southern California.

Kit Powell...TV sports reporter...San Diego, California

❏ ❏	1 -	Jinx (1992)
❏ ❏	2 -	Iced (1994)
❏ ❏		. . . .
❏ ❏		. . . .

■ ROE, Caroline [P]

Caroline Roe is the pseudonym of Medora Sale for her Chronicles of Isaac of Girona, historical mysteries set in 14th century Spain. Blind Jewish physician, Isaac, and his most prominent patient, the Bishop of Girona, are introduced in *Remedy for Treason* (1998). The date is 1353, shortly after the plague that devastated Europe, and Isaac is called to treat the ailing illegitimate daughter of King Don Pedro. After the sons of local merchants die mysteriously in *Cure for a Charlatan* (1999), Isaac returns in *Antidote for Avarice* (1999). The first Canadian to serve as president of Sisters in Crime, Roe is a past president of Crime Writers of Canada. With a B.A. in modern languages (majoring in Spanish) and a Ph.D. in medieval studies, she has worked as a teacher, welfare case worker, advertising freelancer, translator and typist. As Medora Sale, she is the Ellis award-winning author of six mysteries featuring architectural photographer Harriet Jeffries and Toronto homicide detective John Sanders. She lives in Toronto.

Isaac & Bishop Berenguer...1350s blind physician & bishop...Girona, Spain

❏ ❏	1 -	Remedy for Treason (1998)
❏ ❏	2 -	Cure for a Charlatan (1999)
❏ ❏	3 -	Antidote for Avarice (2000)
❏ ❏		. . . .
❏ ❏		. . . .

■ ROGERS, Chris

Houston native Chris Rogers is the creator of Texas prosecutor turned bounty hunter Dixie Flannigan, introduced in *Bitch Factor* (1998) which has been optioned for a television movie. After ten years in the Houston district attorney's office, Dixie is burned out from watching the guilty get off on technicalities. Already a legend in Houston jails and courtrooms, she is ready for a more hands-on style of justice. In book 3, *Chill Factor* (2000), she'll be dealing with bank robbers. A long-time student of astrology, Rogers has co-authored *The Complete Guide to Establishing a Professional Astrological Practice* (1996) and *Plain Talk*

About Money (1989). With a background in commercial art, advertising and marketing, she works in the internal auditing department of a Houston bank. She is currently working on a mystery series featuring

Booker Krane, retired bank examiner turned commercial photographer in rural Texas. Although she and Dixie are both Scorpios, Rogers says the similarity ends there.

Dixie Flannigan...prosecutor turned bounty hunter...Houston, Texas
- ❏ ❏ 1 - Bitch Factor (1998)
- ❏ ❏ 2 - Rage Factor (1999)
- ❏ ❏ . . . .
- ❏ ❏ . . . .

■ ROGOW, Roberta

Children's librarian Roberta Rogow writes historical mysteries featuring 19th century English physician and Sherlock Holmes creator, Arthur Conan Doyle, and Reverend Charles Dodgson, the mathematician-professor better known as Lewis Carroll, author of *Alice's Adventures in Wonderland*. The two join forces in *The Problem of the Missing Miss* (1998) to locate the kidnapped daughter of a liberal member of Parliament who had been sent to Brighton to vacation with the retired Dodgson. "A fresh, imaginative debut," said

Kirkus. Conan Doyle and Dodgson find themselves in Portsmouth at a seance for a dead sea captain in *The Problem of the Spiteful Spiritualist* (1999). "A cleverly plotted story with authentic historical details and engaging characters," said *Booklist*. Rogow got her start writing science fiction short stories and *Futurespeak: A Fan's Guide to the Language of Science Fiction* (1991). The mother of mystery author Miriam Ann Moore, she lives in New Jersey with her public relations and publicity writer husband.

Charles Dodgson & Conan Doyle...19th century professor & doctor...England
- ❏ ❏ 1 - The Problem of the Missing Miss (1998)
- ❏ ❏ - Brit.-The Problem of the Missing Hoyden
- ❏ ❏ 2 - The Problem of the Spiteful Spiritualist (1999)
- ❏ ❏ . . . .
- ❏ ❏ . . . .

■ ROMBERG, Nina [P]

Nina Romberg writes mysteries with supernatural elements featuring Caddo-Comanche medicine woman Marian Winchester, introduced in *The Spirit Stalker* (1989). Writing as Jane Archer, she is the author 13 historical romance novels, including *Maverick Moon* (1997) and *Out of the West* (1996). Optioned for a T.V. movie before it was sold for print, *Out of the West* features a pair of women bounty hunters (one white, the other black), a stolen Black Madonna (solid gold), a former Buffalo Soldier and a lawman. Romberg's first

nonfiction (published as Jane Archer), *Texas Indian Myths and Legends* (1999), led to some discoveries she plans to fictionalize in future Marian Winchester mysteries. With C. Dean Andersson, Romberg has written two horror novels as Asa Drake. After earning a degree in advertising design, Romberg worked as an advertising art director. A descendent of Native Americans (she's part Comanche), Indian Territory settlers and Republic of Texas pioneers, she lives in Richardson, Texas.

Marian Winchester...Caddo-Comanche medicine woman...Texas
- ❏ ❏ 1 - The Spirit Stalker (1989)
- ❏ ❏ 2 - Shadow Walkers (1993)
- ❏ ❏ . . . .
- ❏ ❏ . . . .

■ ROOME, Annette

Creasey award-winner Annette Roome introduced 40-year-old cub reporter Christine Martin in *A Real Shot in the Arm*, Britain's best first crime novel of 1989. Against the objections of her husband Keith, Chris takes a job at the *Tipping Herald* where she becomes

involved in a murder investigation and falls in love with co-worker Pete Schiavo. "Enough plot shenanigans to keep the story moving at a fast pace," said *Washington Post Book World*. In book 2, *A Second Shot in the Dark* (1990), Chris moves in with Pete, just as his ex-wife's new husband is arrested for murder. "Roome juggles suspects, clues, and domestic subplots with dexterity," said *Kirkus Reviews*. After a long gap, Chris returns in book 3, *Bad Monday* (1998), where she investigates the death of an aging rock star. The possible road-rage killing of a woman whose husband is missing features in book 4, *Deceptive Relations* (1999). While the first two books have been published in the U.S., there is no sight yet of installments 3 and 4. Roome lives in Guilford, England.

Christine Martin...40-something cub reporter...England

❏ ❏	1 -	**A Real Shot in the Arm (1989) Creasey winner ★**
❏ ❏	2 -	A Second Shot in the Dark (1990)
❏ ❏	3 -	Bad Monday (1998)
❏ ❏		....
❏ ❏		....

■ ROSS, Annie [P]

British network television producer and director Annie Ross is the creator of television director and private investigator Bel Carson, introduced in *Moving Image* (1995). All of the books in this series are set in the world of television and film with plots that have a "cinematic sting in the tail." In her third and most recent appearance in *Double Vision* (1997), Bel is sent to the United States to document the Kansas City trial of Malcolm Laurie, an Englishman accused of the violent murder of his wife, a beautiful American heiress, during a visit to her home state. Not convinced of her countryman's guilt, Bel is annoyed that her assigned researcher has no television experience and perplexed by the repeated night-time disappearances of her cameraman. Born and raised in the north of Scotland, the pseudonymous Ross earned a degree in television production from the University of Kansas in Lawrence. An experienced producer of documentaries, both in the U.K. and abroad, she lives in London.

Bel Carson...TV director and investigator...London, England

❏ ❏	1 -	Moving Image (1995)
❏ ❏	2 -	Shot in the Dark (1996)
❏ ❏	3 -	Double Vision (1997)
❏ ❏		....
❏ ❏		....

■ ROSS, Kate

Agatha and Gargoyle award-winner Kate Ross (1956-1998) was a corporate trial attorney for a large Boston law firm. While studying legal history at Yale Law School, she realized the lack of professional police in early 19th century England made it the perfect setting for an amateur sleuth. Her series detective, the charming and elegant Julian Kestrel, is introduced in *Cut to the Quick* (1993), along with his manservant Dipper, a former pickpocket. While earning a degree in ancient Greek at Wellesley College, Ross aspired to read Euripedes in the original. By her senior year she had succeeded, and translated herself the dramatist's lines that close book 3, *Whom the Gods Love* (1995). Ross once said she had virtually no life outside 19th century England because even though she walked fast and talked fast, she researched very slowly. Her favorite library was the Boston Athenaeum; her favorite museum, the Victoria and Albert. Her favorite costume, in which she made several appearances, was an authentic 1820s wide-skirted turquoise taffeta complete with ruff, maroon-plumed hat and matching umbrella.

Julian Kestrel...1820s dandy-about-town...London, England

❏ ❏	1 -	Cut to the Quick (1993)
❏ ❏	2 -	**A Broken Vessel (1994) Gargoyle winner ★**
❏ ❏	3 -	Whom the Gods Love (1995)
❏ ❏	4 -	**The Devil in Music (1997) Agatha winner ★**
❏ ❏		....
❏ ❏		....

■ ROTHENBERG, Rebecca

Amateur botanist Rebecca Rothenberg (1948-1998) wrote three botanical mysteries featuring sharp-witted M.I.T. microbiologist Claire Sharples, who leaves her Boston research post for a new job in California's San Joaquin Valley. Named one of the ten best books of the year by the *Los Angeles Times*, *The Bulrush Murders* (1991) was nominated for Agatha and Anthony awards. An unfinished fourth mystery, *The Tumbleweed Murders* (2001), will be completed by Rothenberg's friend Taffy Cannon. A data analysis consultant in epidemiology and editor of her chapter's newsletter for the California Native Plant Society, Rothenberg worked in public relations at Caltech. Raised in Upstate New York, she attended Swarthmore College and earned degrees in epidemiology and the sociology of medicine at U.C.L.A. Before moving to Los Angeles, she lived in Nashville where hoped to break into country music as a singer-songwriter. In recognition of her devotion to preserving native plant species, a wildflower garden in the Eaton Canyon Nature Center in Pasadena was dedicated to Rothenberg's memory in early 1999.

Claire Sharples...microbiologist...Central California
- ❑ ❑ 1 - **The Bulrush Murders (1991) Agatha & Anthony nominee** ☆☆
- ❑ ❑ 2 - The Dandelion Murders (1994)
- ❑ ❑ 3 - The Shy Tulip Murders (1996)
- ❑ ❑ . . . .
- ❑ ❑ . . . .

■ ROWE, Jennifer

Award-winning publisher, editor and children's author Jennifer Rowe has written five mysteries and a short-story collection featuring Australian television researcher Verity "Birdie" Birdwood, starting with *Grim Pickings* (1987). Rowe's second series introduces homicide detective Tessa Vance in *Suspect* (1999), first published in Australia as *Deadline* (1997). In response to a request from Australian T.V. producer Hal McElroy, a fan of the Birdwood series, Rowe developed characters and wrote storylines for the first 22 episodes of *Murder Call*. The plot for a double episode became the novel *Suspect*. Tessa's crew includes partner Steve Hayden, their boss Inspector Thorne, pathologist Tootsie Soames, forensic expert Lance Fisk and photographer Dee Suzeraine. Former publisher at Angus and Robertson, Rowe had previously served as editor of *The Australian Women's Weekly* magazine for 14 years. Writing as Emily Rodda, she is a five-time winner of Australia's Children's Book of the Year. A mother of four (including twins), Rowe lives in the Blue Mountains west of Sydney.

Tessa Vance...senior homicide detective...Sydney, Australia
- ❑ ❑ 1 - Deadline (1997)
- ❑ ❑   - U.S.-Suspect (1999)
- ❑ ❑ 2 - Something Wicked (1998)
- ❑ ❑ . . . .
- ❑ ❑ . . . .

Verity "Birdie" Birdwood...TV researcher...Australia
- ❑ ❑ 1 - Grim Pickings (1987)
- ❑ ❑ 2 - Murder by the Book (1989)
- ❑ ❑ ss - Death in Store [short stories] (1992)
- ❑ ❑ 3 - The Makeover Murders (1993)
- ❑ ❑ 4 - Stranglehold (1994)
- ❑ ❑ 5 - Lamb to the Slaughter (1995)
- ❑ ❑ . . . .
- ❑ ❑ . . . .

■ ROWLAND, Laura Joh

Laura Joh Rowland is the creator of Sano Ichiro, samurai and reluctant police officer in the feudal Japanese capital of Edo. Introduced in *Shinju* (1994), the 17th century detective faces a routine investigation of the ritual double-suicide (shinju) of star-crossed lovers. The Hammett-nominated first novel is "an eerie

Japanese echo of *Presumed Innocent,"* said *Kirkus.* Sano is appointed Most Honorable Investigator for the shogun in *Bundori* (1996). The wedding ceremony for Sano's arranged marriage to a local magistrate's daughter in *The Concubine's Tattoo* (1998) is interrupted by the death of the shogun's favorite concubine. To Sano's horror, the sweet, submissive wife he had been expecting turns out to be a head-

strong, intelligent, aspiring detective, eager to help with his new case. A granddaughter of Chinese and Korean immigrants, Rowland earned degrees in microbiology and public health from the University of Michigan. She has worked as a chemist, microbiologist, sanitary inspector, freelance artist and quality engineer. A Michigan native, she lives in New Orleans.

Sano Ichiro...investigator for the shogun...Edo, Japan
- ❏ ❏ 1 - **Shinju (1994) Hammett nominee** ☆
- ❏ ❏ 2 - Bundori (1996)
- ❏ ❏ 3 - The Way of the Traitor (1997)
- ❏ ❏   - Brit.-Irizumi
- ❏ ❏ 4 - The Concubine's Tattoo (1998)
- ❏ ❏ . . . .
- ❏ ❏ . . . .

ROWLANDS, Betty

Winning a short-story competition in 1988 launched Betty Rowlands on an unexpected new career as a crime writer. She has since written eight mysteries featuring Melissa Craig, a successful British crime novelist who leaves London to write from a quiet cottage in the Cotswolds. Several of these old-fashioned whodunits include an insider's look at the writing life. When Melissa Craig spends a week at a writer's retreat she lands in a hotbed of hostility in *Malice Poetic* (1995). While completing the unfinished

novel of a local author, Melissa finds clues about the woman's death during an apparent burglary in *Deadly Legacy* (1996). A second series from Rowlands introduces police photographer and scene-of-the-crime officer, Sukey Reynolds, first seen in *A Hive of Bees* (1996). After a varied career as a secretary, language teacher and writer of educational materials for students of English as a foreign language, Rowlands writes full time. The mother of three and grandmother of four lives in the heart of the Cotswolds.

Melissa Craig...British crime novelist...Cotswolds, England
- ❏ ❏ 1 - A Little Gentle Sleuthing (1990)
- ❏ ❏ 2 - Finishing Touch (1993)
- ❏ ❏ 3 - Over the Edge (1993)
- ❏ ❏ 4 - Exhaustive Inquiries (1994)
- ❏ ❏ 5 - Malice Poetic (1995)
- ❏ ❏ 6 - Smiling at Death (1995)
- ❏ ❏ 7 - Deadly Legacy (1996)
- ❏ ❏ 8 - The Cherry Pickers (1997)
- ❏ ❏ . . . .
- ❏ ❏ . . . .

Sukey Reynolds...police photographer...England
- ❏ ❏ 1 - A Hive of Bees (1996)
- ❏ ❏ 2 - An Inconsiderate Death (1997)
- ❏ ❏ 3 - Death at Dearley Manor (1998)
- ❏ ❏ . . . .
- ❏ ❏ . . . .

ROZAN, S. J.

When Shamus and Anthony award-winner S.J. Rozan (rose-ANN) went to China in 1998, a CBS film crew took some of her best vacation (i.e., research trip) photos and included their footage in her *CBS Sunday Morning* interview later that year. Rozan's mysteries feature New York City private eyes Lydia Chin and Bill

Smith. The 30-something Chinese American and her 40-something Army brat partner are introduced in *China Trade* (1994), narrated by Lydia. The second installment is told from Bill's point of view, while Lydia retakes center stage in book 3. With each book they alternate points of view. Bill is hired to recover stolen paintings in Upstate New York in book 6, *Stone Quarry* (1999), and Lydia travels to Hong Kong in book 7, *Reflecting the Sky* (2000). An Oberlin College graduate, Rozan has worked as a self-defense instructor, jewelry saleswoman, photographer and janitor. During her days as a practicing architect, her specialties included police stations, firehouses and zoo buildings, especially aviaries. Her first name, Shira, is Hebrew for song.

Lydia Chin & Bill Smith...Chinese-American & Army-brat P.I. duo...New York, New York

❑ ❑	1 - China Trade (1994)
❑ ❑	2 - **Concourse (1995) Shamus winner ★**
❑ ❑	3 - Mandarin Plaid (1996)
❑ ❑	4 - **No Colder Place (1997) Anthony winner ★ Shamus nominee ☆**
❑ ❑	5 - A Bitter Feast (1998)
❑ ❑	6 - Stone Quarry (1999)
❑ ❑	. . . .
❑ ❑	. . . .

■ RUBINO, Jane

Former film columnist Jane Rubino is the creator of single mother and cop's widow, Cat Austen, and Puerto Rican homicide lieutenant, Victor Cardenas, introduced in *Death of a DJ* (1996). "A fast-moving first novel," said *Publishers Weekly*. A novice reporter and good Italian girl, Cat was born Allegrezza Caterina Fortunati, the only girl in a family of six brothers. Other supporting cast members are Cat's two children, Mats and Jane, and her mother Ellice. According to *Booklist*, "the multifaceted New Jersey setting is as central to the story as the characters themselves." Along with Cat, Rubino shares a passion for Jane Austen and rollicking family dinners with plenty of Italian food. Rubino has worked as a newspaper stringer, feature-writer and free-lancer. She wrote the film column, "Reel Estate," for 14 years. Rubino lives with her family on the barrier island of Ocean City, New Jersey where she is at work on the fourth Cat Austen mystery, a standalone novel and a volume of Sherlock Holmes pastiches.

Cat Austen & Victor Cardenas...single-mom reporter & police detective...Atlantic City, New Jersey

❑ ❑	1 - Death of a DJ (1996)
❑ ❑	2 - Fruitcake (1997)
❑ ❑	3 - Cheat the Devil (1998)
❑ ❑	. . . .
❑ ❑	. . . .

■ RURYK, Jean

Montreal advertising executive Jean Shepherd, writing under her Ukrainian birth name, Jean Ruryk (RRR-rik), published three light-hearted mysteries featuring Catherine "Cat" Wilde, 60-something advertising executive turned antiques restorer. In *Chicken Little Was Right* (1994) Cat uses a toy knife to rob a bank (she's facing foreclosure on her home) and ends up befriending the young mother of her hostage. A former Y&R creative director, Shepherd was a painter and antiques restorer. Her Holocaust love story, *My Darling Elia* (1999), was published under the name Eugenie Melnyk in June 1999, four months after the author's death. According to Shepherd's daughter Jenny, the novel (first written during the '70s) was her mother's life's work. Shepherd mortgaged her home and took a two-year leave to complete her research. The story involves a Ukrainian Jew separated from his pregnant wife in 1941. More than 40 years later he finds her locket at a Montreal flea market and his search begins anew. The first award nomination of Shepherd's mystery-writing career (a 1999 best novel Ellis nomination for *Next Week Will Be Better*) was announced just eight weeks after her death.

Catherine Wilde...ad exec turned antiques restorer...Montreal, Quebec, Canada

❑ ❑	1 - Chicken Little Was Right (1994)
❑ ❑	2 - Whatever Happened to Jennifer Steele? (1996)
❑ ❑	3 - **Next Week Will Be Better (1998) Ellis nominee ☆**
❑ ❑	. . . .
❑ ❑	. . . .

■ RUSHFORD, Patricia H.

Author of more than 25 books, Patricia Rushford has been writing for almost 20 years, with her first book, *Have You Hugged Your Teenager Today?* (1982), updated and re-released in 1996. Her young adult series featuring Oregon teenager Jennie McGrady now numbers 12 titles, including the Edgar-nominated book 2, *Silent Witness* (1993). Rushford's adult mysteries feature grandmother Helen Bradley, an ex-cop turned travel writer in her late 50s, who does occasional jobs for Uncle Sam. With new husband J.B.,

Helen lives on the Oregon coast near Lincoln City, but goes undercover in a Portland convalescent home for the series opener. In book 2, she's off to Washington State for a guide-book assignment on Long Beach Peninsula. An elderly uncle asks for help with a crisis at his luxurious San Juan island resort in book 3. A registered nurse with a master's degree in Christian counseling, Rushford is a mother of two and grandmother of nine. Associate editor of *Murderous Intent* magazine, she lives in Vancouver, Washington.

Helen Bradley...ex-cop travel-writer grandmother...Lincoln City, Oregon

- ❏ ❏ 1 - Now I Lay Me Down To Sleep (1997)
- ❏ ❏ 2 - Red Sky in Mourning (1997)
- ❏ ❏ 3 - A Haunting Refrain (1998)
- ❏ ❏ . . . .
- ❏ ❏ . . . .

■ RUST, Megan Mallory

Former commercial pilot Megan (MEE-gun) Mallory Rust writes an Alaskan mystery series where each book's title features a different flying maneuver. Introduced in *Dead Stick* (1998), a 35-year-old single woman named Taylor Morgan flies medical evacuations for LifeLine Air Ambulance Service. After certifying their newest pilot, Taylor suspects foul play when the young hire is blamed for a crash that killed her entire crew. In book 2, *Red Line* (1999), Taylor checks out illegal booze smuggling when police refuse to investigate. Walking away from her Cessna 402 one

day in 1984, Rust was run over by a forklift that crushed her skull and put her in a month-long coma. After a year of rehabilitation (re-learning everything, including walking and talking), she went back to college and earned a degree in journalism. The severe head injury that had put an end to her flying career became the start of her life as a writer. A life-long Alaskan (arriving at age one), Rust also has a degree in aeronautical science. She lives just north of Anchorage.

Taylor Morgan...air ambulance pilot...Anchorage, Alaska

- ❏ ❏ 1 - Dead Stick (1998)
- ❏ ❏ 2 - Red Line (1999)
- ❏ ❏ 3 - Coffin Corner (1999)
- ❏ ❏ 4 - Graveyard Spiral (2000)
- ❏ ❏ . . . .
- ❏ ❏ . . . .

■ SALE, Medora

Born in Windsor, Ontario where her father was an official in the court system, Medora Sale has a B.A. in modern languages and a Ph.D. in medieval studies. Her Ellis award-winning mystery series features Toronto homicide detective John Sanders, introduced in *Murder on the Run* (1986), named best first novel by a Canadian author. In book 2, Sanders goes to Ottawa for a seminar, where he runs (quite literally) into architectural photographer Harriet Jeffries. Past president of Crime Writers of Canada, Sale was the 1998-

99 president of Sisters in Crime. She has worked as a teacher, welfare case worker, advertising freelancer, translator and typist, while living in England, Switzerland, France, the United States and Canada. She lives in Toronto with her photographer husband, a professor of medieval studies originally from Boston. Writing as Caroline Roe, she has recently launched a 14th century historical series set in Spain, featuring a blind Jewish physician and his most prominent patient, the Bishop of Girona.

John Sanders & Harriet Jeffries...police detective & photographer...Toronto, Ontario, Canada

- ❑ ❑   1 - **Murder on the Run (1986) Ellis winner** ★
- ❑ ❑   2 - Murder in Focus (1989)
- ❑ ❑   3 - Murder in a Good Cause (1990)
- ❑ ❑   4 - Sleep of the Innocent (1991)
- ❑ ❑   5 - Pursued by Shadows (1992)
- ❑ ❑   6 - Short Cut to Santa Fe (1994)
- ❑ ❑   . . . .
- ❑ ❑   . . . .

■ SALTER, Anna

Top forensic psychologist Anna Salter specializes in treating sex offenders and their victims, as does her fictional alter ego, Dr. Michael Stone, introduced in *Shiny Water* (1997). A transplanted Southerner working in Vermont, Stone testifies as an expert witness in a child-custody case involving a prominent surgeon accused of sexual abuse. In *Fault Lines* (1998), Stone's life is threatened when a sadistic pedophile she was instrumental in jailing is unexpectedly released. "Steadily gripping in its psychology," said *Kirkus Reviews*. Salter has also written *Transforming Trauma: A Guide to Understanding and Treating Adult Survivors of Child Sexual Abuse* (1995). Calling the book "excellent overall," one clinical reviewer particularly praised the book's final chapter, describing it as a "poetic, metaphoric and beautifully-written essay that conveys the author's belief in the strength of survivors." A former professor of clinical psychiatry and pediatrics at Dartmouth Medical School, Salter currently works in Madison, Wisconsin.

Michael Stone...female forensic psychologist...Vermont

- ❑ ❑   1 - Shiny Water (1997)
- ❑ ❑   2 - Fault Lines (1998)
- ❑ ❑   . . . .
- ❑ ❑   . . . .

■ SANDSTROM, Eve K.

Wire editor Eve K. Sandstrom previously worked as a reporter and columnist for *The Lawton Constitution* in Oklahoma, the home state for her series characters Sam and Nicky Titus, abruptly relocated from Germany soon after their marriage. Introduced in *Death Down Home* (1990), Sam is an Army criminal investigations officer turned hometown county sheriff, and Nicky an artistic photographer and daughter of an Army general. Sandstrom's newer series features *Grantham Gazette* reporter Nell Matthews and her cop boyfriend Mike Svenson, a specialist in hostage negotiations, first seen in *The Violence Beat* (1997). A former big city detective, Mike has returned to his boyhood home in this fictional southwestern city where his father was once chief of police. In book 2, *The Homicide Report* (1998), Nell and Mike discover a dying copy editor whose last words provide a clue to the whereabouts of Nell's long-absent father. Book 3, *The Smoking Gun* is scheduled for Spring 2000 publication. Sandstrom lives in Lawton, Oklahoma.

Nell Matthews & Mike Svenson...reporter & homicide detective...Southwest USA

- ❑ ❑   1 - The Violence Beat (1997)
- ❑ ❑   2 - The Homicide Report (1998)
- ❑ ❑   . . . .
- ❑ ❑   . . . .

Sam & Nicky Titus...ex-CID sheriff & photographer wife...Holton, Oklahoma

- ❑ ❑   1 - Death Down Home (1990)
- ❑ ❑   2 - The Devil down Home (1991)
- ❑ ❑   3 - The Down Home Heifer Heist (1993)
- ❑ ❑   . . . .
- ❑ ❑   . . . .

■ SANTINI, Rosemarie

American-born author Rosemarie Santini has published soap opera novelizations, newspaper and magazine features, nonfiction, short stories and at least six novels, including two mysteries featuring Rick and Rosie Caesare Ramsey, first seen in *A Swell Style of Murder* (1986). Rick, a Connecticut WASP, and Rosie, his Italian-American princess wife, live in the artsy community of SoHo, once known as the Italian section of Greenwich Village. Santini's short fiction featuring the romantic twosome, "The Music Lesson,"

was named best short story of 1996 by *New Mystery* magazine and nominated for a Macavity award. Her nonfiction books include *The Sex Doctors* (1975) and *The Secret Fire: A New View of Women and Passion* (1976), reprinted as *The Santini Report*. She also wrote *Agnes Nixon's All My Children: Tara and Phillip, Volume I* (1981) and *The Lovers, Volume 3*. Her first novel, *Forty-One Grove Street* (1973), was followed by *Abracadabra* (1978), *Private Lies* (1989), *Ask Me What I Want* (1989) and *Blood Sisters* (1990).

Rick & Rosie Caesare Ramsey...husband & wife sleuths...New York, New York
- ❑ ❑ 1 - A Swell Style of Murder (1986)
- ❑ ❑ 2 - The Disenchanted Diva (1987)
- ❑ ❑ . . . .
- ❑ ❑ . . . .

■ SAUM, Karen

Karen Saum has written a three-book series featuring lesbian Brigid Donovan, a 50-something ex-nun, whose first adventure, *Murder is Relative* (1990), takes place in Maine. In the third installment, the action moves to Nova Scotia. Saum is also the author of *I Never Read Thoreau* (1996), featuring community activist and Jill-of-all Trades, Alex Adler, who finds herself marooned during a fierce Nor'easter on Monte Cassino, an island retreat off the coast of Maine, known for harboring South American refugees. A native of

Panama, Saum earned a B.A. from Stanford University and an M.A. from Johns Hopkins Univer-sity, where she was also a doctoral student in history. After a 10-year teaching career, she was fired from the University of Maine at Augusta, for her activist role in the community. She has since served as organizer, coordinator, director and board member for numerous community development programs for low-income families in Maine, where she still lives.

Brigid Donovan...50-something lesbian ex-nun...Maine
- ❑ ❑ 1 - Murder Is Relative (1990)
- ❑ ❑ 2 - Murder Is Germane (1992)
- ❑ ❑ 3 - Murder Is Material (1994)
- ❑ ❑ . . . .
- ❑ ❑ . . . .

■ SAWYER, Corinne Holt

Former college professor Corinne Holt Sawyer is the creator of Angela Benbow and Caledonia Wingate, 70-something widows of Navy admirals and residents of a posh California retirement community near San Diego. Their first adventure, *The J. Alfred Prufrock Murders* (1988), was nominated for a best-first-novel Agatha award. After some eventful trips to Tijuana in *Murder Ole!* (1997), the feisty pair make their ninth appearance in *Bed, Breakfast and Bodies* (1999). *Booklist* has called this series "fun, light-hearted, cleverly-

plotted entertainment." A Phi Beta Kappa graduate of the University of Minnesota, Sawyer earned her Ph.D. at the University of Birmingham. She has taught English, speech and broadcasting at universities in Minnesota, Florida and North and South Carolina, and has worked as an actress, announcer, writer and editor for radio and television. Past director of academic special projects at Clemson University, Sawyer lives in South Carolina where she enjoys duplicate bridge and French cooking.

Angela Benbow & Caledonia Wingate...70-something admirals' widows...Southern California
- ❑ ❑ 1 - **The J. Alfred Prufrock Murders (1988) Agatha nominee** ☆
- ❑ ❑ 2 - Murder in Gray & White (1989)
- ❑ ❑ 3 - Murder by Owl Light (1992)

❑ ❑ 4 - The Peanut Butter Murders (1993)
❑ ❑ 5 - Murder Has No Calories (1994)
❑ ❑ 6 - Ho-Ho Homicide (1995)
❑ ❑ 7 - The Geezer Factory Murders (1996)
❑ ❑ 8 - Murder Olé! (1997)
❑ ❑ . . . .
❑ ❑ . . . .

■ SCHIER, Norma

Colorado native Norma Schier (1930-1995) is best known for *The Anagram Detectives* (1979), a collection of 14 pastiche-parodies, ten of which first appeared in *Ellery Queen's Mystery Magazine.* Beginning with "If Hangman Treads" by Norma Haigs (Aug. 1965), Schier created elaborate anagrammatic puzzles, where the story's author, title and detective's name were scrambled, along with every proper name in the story itself. Norma Haigs was, of course, Ngaio Marsh and Cathie Haig Star ("The Teccomeshire Mystery," Nov.

1965), was Agatha Christie. Less obvious were character names like Kit Heller (the killer) or Spence Cuttinson (innocent suspect) from "Dying Message" by Leyne Requel (Jul. 1966). Schier also wrote a four-book series featuring Aspen, Colorado district attorney Kay Barth, introduced in *Death on the Slopes* (1978). Under her married name, Norma Schier Hitch, she wrote and contributed to language skills textbooks. She is also credited with founding the Rocky Mountain Chapter of Mystery Writers of America.

Kay Barth...district attorney...Aspen, Colorado
❑ ❑ 1 - Death on the Slopes (1978)
❑ ❑ 2 - Murder by the Book (1979)
❑ ❑ 3 - Death Goes Skiing (1979)
❑ ❑ 4 - Demon at the Opera (1980)
❑ ❑ . . . .
❑ ❑ . . . .

■ SCHMIDT, Carol

Carol Schmidt writes lesbian mysteries featuring reluctant sleuth Laney Samms, a Los Angeles bar owner in the series opener, *Silverlake Heat* (1993). Samms starts a new life in book 2, as the assistant to an executive in a women's music corporation. "Schmidt can tell a good story and has a firm grasp of the suspense and violence," said *Booklist* of *Sweet Cherry Wine* (1994). Samms gets a plum assignment in book 3, *Cabin Fever* (1995), when she heads to Michigan's Upper Peninsula as events coordinator for

a new women's music and arts center. An actual luxury hunting lodge, once frequented by Henry Ford, Firestone, DuPont and others, inspired Schmidt's setting for her latest title. When *Cabin Fever* was released, just two weeks after the Oklahoma City bombing, very few people had heard of the Michigan Militia, featured in Schmidt's latest mystery. Schmidt once lived down the road from the Nichols farmhouse in Dexter, Michigan, where Terry McVeigh and others practiced their bomb-making skills.

Laney Samms...lesbian bar owner...Los Angeles, California
❑ ❑ 1 - Silverlake Heat (1993)
❑ ❑ 2 - Sweet Cherry Wine (1994)
❑ ❑ 3 - Cabin Fever (1995)
❑ ❑ . . . .
❑ ❑ . . . .

■ SCHUMACHER, Aileen

Registered professional engineer Aileen Schumacher (SHEW-mock-er) set her first mystery, *Engineered for Murder* (1996), at New Mexico State University, where she earned degrees in biology and civil engineering. Her fictional sleuth is Tory Travers, a young, widowed structural engineer living with her son on the edge of

campus, while overseeing the construction of a new football stadium. When a quality control technician is found dead and Tory's life is threatened, El Paso police detective David Alvarez comes to town with a Texas-size chip on his shoulder. Schumacher's debut was the first work of fiction ever selected by McGraw-Hill

Technical Book Clubs. President of Blum, Schumacher & Associates, Inc. in Gainesville, Florida, the author has been the firm's co-owner, along with her structural engineer husband, since 1982. A Texas native transplanted to Florida by way of New Mexico and Washington State, Shumacher also owns a Florida export firm dealing in technical materials and supplies.

Tory Travers...structural engineer...Las Cruces, New Mexico

❏ ❏	1 -	Engineered for Murder (1996)
❏ ❏	2 -	Framework for Death (1998)
❏ ❏	3 -	Affirmative Reaction (1999)
❏ ❏		. . . .
❏ ❏		. . . .

■ SCOPPETTONE, Sandra

Shamus award-winner Sandra (SOHN-dra) Scoppettone is the creator of lesbian private eye Lauren Laurano of Greenwich Village and her psychotherapist lover Kip, introduced in *Everything You Have Is Mine*. When the short, Italian chocoholic feminist came on the scene in 1991, she was the first lesbian P.I. published by a mainstream house (Little, Brown). Scoppettone's first mysteries were published under the name Jack Early, including *A Creative Kind of Killer* (1984), Shamus winner for best first private eye novel in 1985. The book was an Edgar nominee, as was her fifth young adult novel, *Playing Murder* (1985). Scoppettone says she used a male pseudonym simply because the voice speaking to her was a man's voice. When Jack Early started winning awards, she decided to use the name for two more books. In 1995 the three original Early titles, all non-series mysteries, were re-released with Scoppettone's name on the cover. One of the founding members of Sisters in Crime, she lives on Long Island.

Lauren Laurano...lesbian private investigator...New York, New York

❏ ❏	1 -	Everything You Have Is Mine (1991)
❏ ❏	2 -	I'll Be Leaving You Always (1993)
❏ ❏	3 -	My Sweet Untraceable You (1994)
❏ ❏	4 -	Let's Face the Music and Die (1996)
❏ ❏	5 -	Gonna Take a Homicidal Journey (1998)
❏ ❏		. . . .
❏ ❏		. . . .

■ SCOTT, Barbara A.

Barbara A. Scott writes foreign intrigue mysteries featuring international team leader Brad Rollins and his wife Mary, introduced in *Always in a Foreign Land* (1993). Brad's ties are to the British Foreign Service, while his second in command is a Thai-American chemist. Their colleagues include a Greek-Swiss banker, a wealthy Roman society widow and an ex-Marine pilot from Kansas. In addition to kidnap-rescue, their investigative specialties include money-laundering and other illegal activities, but these experts are not spies. Scott once spent eight years overhauling, sailing and living aboard a 65-foot Bahamian Ketch on the Chesapeake Bay. Her extensive travels include five years in an international community in Saudi Arabia. Born and raised in Upstate New York, Scott is a graduate of Union University. She has also studied German, Arabic, Italian, judo, photography, watercolor painting and belly dancing. She currently lives near Sacramento, California where she spends time on the bike trails and at the shooting range.

Brad Rollins et al...international kidnap-rescue team

❏ ❏	1 -	Always in a Foreign Land (1993)
❏ ❏	2 -	Caught in the Web (1996)
❏ ❏	3 -	Pay Out & Pay Back (1999)
❏ ❏		. . . .
❏ ❏		. . . .

■ SCOTTOLINE, Lisa

Edgar award-winner Lisa Scottoline was once a Philadelphia lawyer and like her first protagonist, is a good Italian girl who went to the University of Pennsylvania and started her legal career at a large corporate firm. Scottoline later worked part-time for a federal appeals court judge, a background used for *Final Appeal*, 1995 Edgar winner for best paperback original. With book 4, *Legal Tender* (1996), she introduced Bennie Rosato, whose all-women firm unites the previous main characters. In late 1998, a terrific media buzz resulted from Scottoline's decision to post Chapter 1 of *Mistaken Identity* (1999) at www.scottoline.com, the website her husband created as a wedding gift. Along with Bennie, Scottoline shares a passion for M&Ms, as well as a new-found half sister, whose discovery inspired the creation of a possible twin in *Mistaken Identity*. While *People* magazine anointed her the "female John Grisham," *Kirkus* credits her with "the best hooks in the legal intrigue trade." She lives in suburban Philadelphia.

Rosato & Associates...all-women law firm...Philadelphia, Pennsylvania
- ❏ ❏ **1 - Everywhere That Mary Went [Mary DiNunzio] (1993) Edgar nominee** ☆
- ❏ ❏ **2 - Final Appeal [Grace Rossi] (1994) Edgar winner** ★
- ❏ ❏ 3 - Running From the Law [Rita Morrone] (1995)
- ❏ ❏ 4 - Legal Tender [Bennie Rosato] (1996)
- ❏ ❏ 5 - Rough Justice [Marta Richter] (1997)
- ❏ ❏ 6 - Mistaken Identity [Rosato et al] (1999)
- ❏ ❏ . . . .
- ❏ ❏ . . . .

■ SEDLEY, Kate [P]

Kate Sedley is the pseudonym of British author Brenda (Honeyman) Clarke for her mysteries featuring Roger the Chapman, a 15th century peddler traveling the English countryside solving crimes during the last years of the Wars of the Roses (1455-1485). A lapsed Benedictine monk, Roger answers the call of the outside world and makes the acquaintance of the Duke of Gloucester and future king Richard III. "Sedley skillfully interweaves romance, intrigue, and authentic period detail," says *Booklist*. Book 6, *The Wicked Winter* (1996), is scheduled for American publication in late 1999. Meanwhile, U.K. editions of books 7 and 8 appeared in 1997 and 1998. The author began her fiction-writing career with 16 historical novels written as Brenda Honeyman, before switching to historical romance in the late '70s under her married name. Since then she has written more than a dozen titles as Brenda Clarke. A native of Bristol, where she still lives, she once worked as a clerical officer in The Ministry of Labour for 13 years.

Roger the Chapman...medieval peddler...England
- ❏ ❏ 1 - Death and the Chapman (1991)
- ❏ ❏ 2 - The Plymouth Cloak (1992)
- ❏ ❏ 3 - The Hanged Man (1993)
- ❏ ❏ - APA-The Weaver's Tale
- ❏ ❏ 4 - The Holy Innocents (1994)
- ❏ ❏ 5 - The Eve of St. Hyacinth (1995)
- ❏ ❏ 6 - The Wicked Winter (1996)
- ❏ ❏ 7 - The Brothers of Glastonbury (1997)
- ❏ ❏ 8 - The Weaver's Inheritance (1998)
- ❏ ❏ . . . .
- ❏ ❏ . . . .

■ SHABER, Sarah R.

In 1996 Sarah R. Shaber won the annual St. Martin's Press Malice Domestic contest for best traditional mystery by a new author, resulting in the 1997 publication of *Simon Said*. Kenan College history professor Simon Shaw finds himself working with Raleigh police when a 70-year-old skeleton is unearthed on campus. "A perceptive take on academic rivalries," pronounced *Kirkus Reviews*, praising Shaber's dialogue as "bright" and "brisk." "A good example of the murder mystery on its best behavior," said *The New York Times Review of Books*. An "abundance of wry humor" and "strong atmosphere of small-town life in the South," concluded *Booklist*. Professor Shaw is scheduled to return in *Snipe Hunt* (2000). Shaber earned a B.A. in history from Duke University and an M.A. in communications from University of North Carolina at Chapel Hill. She has worked in advertising and public relations, winning several local and national awards for radio copy-writing and production. She lives in Raleigh.

Simon Shaw...young history professor...Raleigh, North Carolina
- ❑ ❑ 1 - **Simon Said (1997) SMP/MD winner ★**
- ❑ ❑ 2 - Snipe Hunt (2000)
- ❑ ❑ ....
- ❑ ❑ ....

■ SHAFFER, Louise

An Emmy award-winning actress for her role as Rae Woodard on *Ryan's Hope*, Louise Shaffer is the creator of amateur sleuth Angie DaVito, Brooklyn-born-and-bred producer of the fictional daytime drama *Bright Tomorrow*. When the unpopular president of daytime programming turns up naked and dead in the star's dressing room, Angie investigates in *All My Suspects* (1994). "Snappy pacing, intricate plot, and recognizable characters are likely to enchant even those who don't watch soaps," said *Publishers Weekly*. Angie returns in *Talked to Death* (1995), where she becomes the chief suspect in the murder of one of her staff shortly after being hired as the show's new producer. Shaffer's daytime writing credits include *General Hospital* and *Ryan's Hope*. She also played dramatic roles on *All My Children, Search for Tomorrow* and *Edge of Night*. Shaffer divides her time between New York and a farm in Georgia, where she operates Home Sweet Home, an amateur animal shelter.

Angie DaVito...daytime television producer...New York, New York
- ❑ ❑ 1 - All My Suspects (1994)
- ❑ ❑ 2 - Talked to Death (1995)
- ❑ ❑ ....
- ❑ ❑ ....

■ SHAH, Diane K.

Former *Newsweek* magazine associate editor Diane K. Shah has re-created Hollywood in the late 1940s for two paperback mysteries featuring Paris Chandler, an enterprising young widow who inherits a fortune when her newspaper-heir husband is killed in World War II. Starting with *As Crime Goes By* (1990), Paris wangles a job as assistant to the queen-of-gossip at the fictional Los Angeles *Examiner* and writes some block-busting stories of her own. More recently Shah has written *High Heel Blue* (1997) where a gung-ho woman cop hunts a knife-wielding serial killer whose victims are all A.T.M. customers in skirts and high heels. Shah is co-author with former Los Angeles police chief Daryl F. Gates of his autobiography, *Chief: My Life in the L.A.P.D.* A graduate of Indiana University, Shah has worked as a wire service reporter, radio writer and staff writer for several newspapers including the *National Observer* and the *Los Angeles Times*. A Chicago native, she lives in Los Angeles.

Paris Chandler...1940s private eye...Hollywood, California
- ❑ ❑ 1 - As Crime Goes By (1990)
- ❑ ❑ 2 - Dying Cheek to Cheek (1992)
- ❑ ❑ ....
- ❑ ❑ ....

■ SHANKMAN, Sarah

Sarah Shankman's fictional alter ego is smart-talking Atlanta journalist Samantha Adams, featured in seven rollicking Southern mysteries starting with *First Kill All the Lawyers* (1988). At her editor's insistence, Shankman used the pseudonym Alice Storey for the first two, but reverted to her own name for the third installment. Books 1 and 2 were later reprinted with Shankman's name on the cover. In *I Still Miss My Man But My Aim is Getting Better* (1996), she introduced aspiring Nashville songwriter Shelby Kay Tate. "A sizzling bull's-eye," raved *Kirkus*, "packed with vividly alive characters, ribald dialogue, and suspenseful incident." Shankman says her first novel, *Impersonal Attractions* (1985), is the scariest book she's ever written. It features San Francisco crime reporter Samantha Storey (the precursor of Sam Adams) on the trail of a serial killer. Shankman's personal account of growing up in the no-drinking, no-fun part of Louisiana is told in her semi-fictional non-mystery *Keeping Secrets* (1988). She lives in Northern California where she is working on a new project.

Samantha Adams...investigative reporter...Atlanta, Georgia

- ❏ ❏ 1 - First Kill All the Lawyers (1988)
- ❏ ❏ 2 - Then Hang All the Liars (1989)
- ❏ ❏ 3 - Now Let's Talk of Graves (1990)
- ❏ ❏ 4 - She Walks in Beauty (1991)
- ❏ ❏ 5 - The King Is Dead (1992)
- ❏ ❏ 6 - He Was Her Man (1993)
- ❏ ❏ 7 - Digging Up Momma (1998)
- ❏ ❏ . . . .
- ❏ ❏ . . . .

■ SHELTON, Connie

Author, publisher and bookseller Connie Shelton writes the Charlie Parker mysteries, featuring a New Mexico C.P.A. in partnership with her brother Ron, first seen in *Deadly Gamble* (1995). In *Vacations Can Be Murder* (1995) Charlie meets a handsome helicopter pilot in Hawaii. Never one to pass up a research opportunity, Shelton later married the helicopter pilot she met on her Hawaiian vacation. Like her earlier recorded titles, the audio edition of Charlie's fifth case, *Memories Can Be Murder* (1999), is narrated by Lynda Evans. As founder of Intrigue Press, Shelton publishes mysteries by Steve Brewer, Sophie Dunbar, Linda Grant and Alex Matthews, as well as her own. She has also written *How To Publish Your Own Novel* (1997). A commercial hot air balloon pilot, Shelton currently holds the woman's world altitude record for a size AX-4 balloon, and can sometimes be found flight-following on the radio for Angel Fire, New Mexico's Helicopters. She and a partner are co-owners of Angel Fire's first bookstore, opened in 1998.

Charlie Parker...CPA turned investigator...Albuquerque, New Mexico

- ❏ ❏ 1 - Deadly Gamble (1995)
- ❏ ❏ 2 - Vacations Can Be Murder (1995)
- ❏ ❏ 3 - Partnerships Can Kill (1997)
- ❏ ❏ 4 - Small Towns Can Be Murder (1998)
- ❏ ❏ . . . .
- ❏ ❏ . . . .

■ SHEPHERD, Stella

Former hospital physician Stella Shepherd puts her expert's knowledge of forensics to clever use in her police novels featuring Detective Inspector Richard Montgomery and Sergeant Bird of the Nottingham P.D., introduced in *Black Justice* (1989). *Kirkus* called this series "a treat for Anglophiles," while praising book 3, *Thinner Than Blood* (1992), as an "archetypal cozy thriller, replete with family eccentrics, village gossips, and a determined constabulary." A pyromaniac becomes a murderer in Montgomery's seventh and latest case, *Embers of Death* (1996). Shepherd's newest mystery, available thus far only in the U.K., is *Twilight Curtain* (1998), the series debut of journalist Rowena Kemp, whose cousin Ellie goes missing in Cornwall while transcribing the memoirs of a famous medium. Shepherd earned her medical degree at the University of Nottingham and specialized in radiotherapy during her years in hospital practice. Married to a pharmacist, she now writes full time.

Richard Montgomery...CID Inspector...Nottingham, England

- ❏ ❏ 1 - Black Justice (1989)
- ❏ ❏ 2 - Murderous Remedy (1990)
- ❏ ❏ 3 - Thinner Than Blood (1992)
- ❏ ❏ 4 - A Lethal Fixation (1993)
- ❏ ❏ 5 - Nurse Dawes Is Dead (1994)

❏ ❏   6 - Something in the Cellar (1995)
❏ ❏   7 - Embers of Death (1996)
❏ ❏   ....
❏ ❏   ....

■ SHERIDAN, Juanita

Juanita Sheridan (1917-1996) created the first Asian woman sleuth, Lily Wu, introduced with her novelist-roommate, Janice Cameron, in *The Chinese Chop* (1949). When Janice helps clear Lily of murder charges in Greenwich Village, she is adopted by the grateful Wu family. The plucky duo returns to Janice's native Hawaii and discover that someone has stolen her father's precious file cases in *Kahuna Killer* (1951). Their third adventure, *The Mamo Murders* (1952), finds them on an island ranch, sweltering under oppressive heat believed to be an omen of disaster. A friend's husband is missing, a native houseboy dies mysteriously in the stables and two more murders follow. In their fourth and final adventure, *The Waikiki Widow* (1953), a dying man's final words—tea, tiger, dragon—hold the key to a link between two widows and a stolen fortune. As co-author with Dorothy Dudley, Sheridan also wrote *What Dark Secret* (1943), featuring Chinese-Hawaiian reporter Angie Tudor, a precursor of Lily Wu.

Lily Wu & Janice Cameron...Asian sleuth & novelist roommate...Hawaii
❏ ❏   1 - The Chinese Chop (1949)
❏ ❏   2 - The Kahuna Killer (1951)
❏ ❏   3 - The Mamo Murders (1952)
❏ ❏   - Brit.-While the Coffin Waited
❏ ❏   4 - The Waikiki Widow (1953)
❏ ❏   ....
❏ ❏   ....

■ SHERMAN, Beth

Journalist Beth Sherman writes mysteries featuring New Jersey ghostwriter Anne Hardaway, starting with *Dead Man's Float* (1998). An expert in making how-to writers look good in print, 36-year-old Anne is known in Oceanside Heights, population 703, as the Crazy Lady's daughter, even though her mother has been dead for seven years. Seasonal visitors come to the "Christian seaside paradise" for the beautiful, clean beach and old-time preaching, but a local sexpot turned movie star comes home to shoot her latest movie in book 2, *Death at High Tide* (1999). While writing the prima donna's tell-all autobiography, Anne naturally suspects murder when her unpopular subject dies in an accident. In addition to her bi-weekly *Newsday* column, "Design and Decor," Sherman's how-to features have appeared in many national magazines, but she has yet to ghostwrite any books. A graduate of the University of Pennsylvania, she lives in New York City where she enjoys running and collecting teacups (nearly 100 at last count).

Anne Hardaway...ghostwriter...Oceanside Hts, New Jersey
❏ ❏   1 - Dead Man's Float (1998)
❏ ❏   2 - Death at High Tide (1999)
❏ ❏   ....
❏ ❏   ....

■ SHONE, Anna [P]

Anna Shone is the pseudonym used by London-born author Bridget Ann Shone for her mysteries featuring Shakespeare-spouting private investigator Ulysses Finnegan Donaghue, introduced in *Come Away Death* (1994), retitled *Mr. Donaghue Investigates* for U.S. publication the following year. The London-based private eye is vacationing in Provence when a notorious Hollywood film director is found dead during the opening weekend of a spiritual retreat at the abbey in St. Pierre la Croix. Although the death is made to look like suicide, the director's dying words— a quote from *Twelfth Night*—lead Ulysses to believe it was murder. Donaghue's second case takes him to a valley lodge in the French Alps where a handsome, arrogant archaeologist, who has recently discovered Bronze Age inscriptions at a site nearby, is found dead in a pool while a storm rages on the mountain, thereby delaying the police. Brought up in a large Irish family of storytellers, Shone is a former English teacher who lives in the South of France.

Ulysses Finnegan Donaghue...Shakespeare scholar private eye...Provence, France

❑ ❑   1 - Come Away Death (1994)

❑ ❑   - U.S. - Mr. Donaghue Investigates

❑ ❑   2 - Secrets in Stones (1996)

❑ ❑   . . . .

❑ ❑   . . . .

■ SHORT, Sharon Gwyn

Ohio native Sharon Gwyn Short is an experienced technical and business writer in the computer industry. Her fictional alter ego is suburban Cincinnati's five-foot 11-inch computer-whiz, investigative consultant Patricia Delaney, who uses computer data bases instead of shoe leather to search for answers. In the series opener, *Angel's Bidding* (1994), a valued representative of Kauffman Real Estate and Auctioneering disappears with $100,000, and the company's owner is receiving threatening notes skewered with antique hatpins that belonged to his mother. In book 2, *Past Pretense* (1994), Delaney learns the subject of her investigation is an old friend who once worked as a stripper at an Ohio River club. When last seen in *Death We Share* (1995), Delaney is hired to find out who's threatening to expose a retired opera superstar who may have abandoned a child in her past. Short earned a B.A. from Wright State University and an M.A. in Technical Communication from Bowling Green State University. She lives near Dayton, Ohio.

Patricia Delaney...computer-whiz investigator...Cincinnati, Ohio

❑ ❑   1 - Angel's Bidding (1994)

❑ ❑   2 - Past Pretense (1994)

❑ ❑   3 - The Death We Share (1995)

❑ ❑   . . . .

❑ ❑   . . . .

■ SIBLEY, Celestine

During her 55 years as a columnist for the *Atlanta Journal-Constitution*, Celestine Sibley (1914-1999) "captured everyday life in the changing South in more than 10,000 columns." Her long-running love affair with Atlanta was also evident in her six mysteries featuring Kathryn Kincaid, first seen in *The Malignant Heart* (1957). More than 30 years later, a not-so-young Katy Kincaid returns in *Ah, Sweet Mystery* (1991), where the widowed Kate Mulcay is still working as a reporter. Stuck with freeloading houseguests claiming to be her late husband's cousins in *A Plague of Kinfolks* (1995), Kate ends up a suspect in the murder of a neighbor. In *A Spider in the Sink* (1997) Kate investigates the Christmastime murder of an eccentric Iris Moon. A star court reporter who also covered the Georgia legislature, Sibley became the second woman ever to receive a Lifetime Achievement Award from the National Society of Newspaper Columnists in June 1999. Among her 19 nonfiction books is a collection of her favorite writings and photographs, *The Celestine Sibley Sampler* (1997).

Kate Kincaid Mulcay...veteran newspaperwoman...Atlanta, Georgia

❑ ❑   1 - The Malignant Heart (1957)

❑ ❑   2 - Ah, Sweet Mystery (1991)

❑ ❑   3 - Straight as an Arrow (1992)

❑ ❑   4 - Dire Happenings at Scratch Ankle (1993)

❑ ❑   5 - A Plague of Kinfolks (1995)

❑ ❑   6 - Spider in the Sink (1997)

❑ ❑   . . . .

❑ ❑   . . . .

■ SILVA, Linda Kay

Ex-cop and Harley enthusiast Linda Kay Silva is the creator of Delta Stevens, a gay woman police officer in California, introduced in *Taken by Storm* (1991). When last seen in *Tropical Storm* (1997), Delta is searching the rainforest of Costa Rica for a friend in trouble. The mystery continues in book 6, *Storm Rising*. Silva is also the author of *Tory Tuesday* (1992), written during two weeks in Greece after hearing the story of an Auschwitz survivor who spoke to her history students. An avid naturalist and beginning gardener, Silva built her own pond at the Oregon home she shares with her macaw and beagle Milo. She holds a master's degree in English with an emphasis in 18th century British literature. After writing the first draft with a Pentel mechanical pencil (she handwrites all first drafts), Silva is revising her past-lives novel set in medieval England and modern America. Her latest brain-child is Out of Bounds Books, the electronic publisher of her Storm Series, also available in traditional print editions.

Delta Stevens...gay woman police officer...Southern California

❑	❑	1 - Taken by Storm (1991)
❑	❑	2 - Storm Shelter (1993)
❑	❑	3 - Weathering the Storm (1994)
❑	❑	4 - Storm Front (1995)
❑	❑	5 - Tropical Storm (1997)
❑	❑	....
❑	❑	....

■ SIMONSON, Sheila

College professor Sheila Simonson has written five mysteries featuring six-foot San Francisco bookstore owner Lark Dailey, who marries homicide detective Jay Dodge in the series opener, *Larkspur* (1990). Book 2, *Skylark* (1992), takes place in London five years later, and Lark and Jay move to the rustic beaches of Shoalwater Peninsula (Washington State's thinly-disguised Olympic Peninsula) in book 3, *Mudlark* (1993). Ex-cop Jay has turned to teaching in book 4, *Meadowlark* (1996) and Lark has opened Larkspur Books, when the apartment tenant living above the bookshop is found dead, packed in ice meant for the local broccoli harvest. Lark takes off for Ireland to care for her convalescing father and reevaluate her strained marriage in book 5, *Malarkey* (1997). Before turning to mysteries, Simonson wrote historical romance novels, including *A Cousinly Connexion* (1984), *Lady Elizabeth's Comet* (1985), *The Bar Sinister* (1986) and *Love and Folly* (1988). She teaches history and English at Clark College in Vancouver, Washington.

Lark Dailey Dodge...6-ft. bookstore owner...Shoalwater, Washington

❑	❑	1 - Larkspur (1990)
❑	❑	2 - Skylark (1992)
❑	❑	3 - Mudlark (1993)
❑	❑	4 - Meadowlark (1996)
❑	❑	5 - Malarkey (1997)
❑	❑	....
❑	❑	....

■ SIMPSON, Dorothy

Silver Dagger winner Dorothy Simpson launched her Luke Thanet series in 1981 with *The Night She Died*. The congenial family-man police inspector with a good marriage but a chronic bad back solves crimes in the fictional Kentish town of Sturrenden, ably assisted by loyal Sergeant Lineham. The duo returns in book 15, *Dead and Gone* (2000). "Because she keeps murder to a minimum, and mayhem generally occurs offstage, the impact of Simpson's neatly-crafted mysteries is more of an aftershock than an initial jolt," observes Jane S. Bakerman in *St. James Guide to Crime & Mystery Writers* (4th edition). A former teacher of English and French, Simpson spent 13 years as a marriage guidance counselor, experience put to good use in her whydunit mysteries. Her first novel, *Harbingers of Fear* (1977), was published after a long illness had allowed Simpson to reassess her desire to write. Born in Wales, where her father was a civil servant and her mother a teacher of elocution, Simpson earned a B.A. with honors from the University of Bristol. She lives in Kent.

Luke Thanet...family-man police inspector...Kent, England

❑	❑	1 - The Night She Died (1981)
❑	❑	2 - Six Feet Under (1982)
❑	❑	3 - Puppet for a Corpse (1983)
❑	❑	4 - Close Her Eyes (1984)
❑	❑	**5 - Last Seen Alive (1985) Silver Dagger winner ★**
❑	❑	6 - Dead on Arrival (1986)

❑ ❑ 7 - Element of Doubt (1987)
❑ ❑ 8 - Suspicious Death (1988)
❑ ❑ 9 - Dead by Morning (1989)
❑ ❑ 10 - Doomed To Die (1991)
❑ ❑ 11 - Wake the Dead (1992)
❑ ❑ 12 - No Laughing Matter (1993)
❑ ❑ 13 - A Day for Dying (1995)
❑ ❑ 14 - Once Too Often (1998)
❑ ❑ . . . .
❑ ❑ . . . .

■ SIMS, L.V.

High-tech crimes, 20th century outlaws, and venture-capital shoot-'em-ups during the early days of Silicon Valley (late 1980s) provide a realistic and intriguing backdrop for L.V. Sims' three-book paperback series featuring police Sergeant Dixie T. Struthers, introduced in *Murder Is Only Skin Deep* (1987). The daughter and granddaughter of Irish cops, Dixie is one of the first women to join the San Jose, California police department. She plans to meet the challenges of sexism and discrimination by proving her competence, first with her partner and then with fellow officers. The grisly murder of a fellow detective's 17-year-old niece is the story in book 2, *Death Is a Family Affair* (1987). When a computer tycoon is gassed with halon in his lab, the only witness to the murder is Igor the computer in book 3, *To Sleep, Perchance to Kill* (1988). The case is complicated by the involvement of Dixie's attorney-stepfather. At the time her first book was published, Sims' police-officer-husband was an 18-year veteran of the San Jose Police Department.

Dixie T. Struthers...police sergeant...San Jose, California
❑ ❑ 1 - Murder Is Only Skin Deep (1987)
❑ ❑ 2 - Death Is a Family Affair (1987)
❑ ❑ 3 - To Sleep, Perchance To Kill (1988)
❑ ❑ . . . .
❑ ❑ . . . .

■ SINGER, Shelley

Shamus nominee Shelley Singer grew up in Minneapolis, Minnesota and began her career as a U.P.I. reporter in Chicago, where she met such notables as Jimmy Hoffa, Nikita Krushchev, Xavier Cugat and Martin Luther King, Jr. She currently lives in the San Francisco area, the setting for both her mystery series. Introduced in *Samson's Deal* (1983), ex-Chicago cop Jake Samson settles in Oakland after leaving the Midwest. Using press credentials provided by a magazine-editor buddy, Jake solves a series of crimes with the help of Rosie the carpenter, who rents a small cottage on Jake's property. To the delight of their many fans, Jake and Rosie return in *Royal Flush* (1999) after an 11-year hiatus. This time Jake's working for Rosie and they've moved to Marin County. Singer's second series stars high school history teacher Barrett Lake, who'd rather be a private eye. One-time owner of a Chicago boutique, Singer has worked as a carpenter, landscaper and antiques restorer. These days she teaches mystery writing and reviews books for Public Radio in Berkeley.

Barrett Lake...history teacher turned P.I....Berkeley, California
❑ ❑ 1 - Following Jane (1993)
❑ ❑ 2 - Picture of David (1993)
❑ ❑ 3 - Searching for Sara (1994)
❑ ❑ 4 - **Interview With Mattie (1995) Shamus nominee** ☆
❑ ❑ . . . .
❑ ❑ . . . .

Jake Samson & Rosie Vicente...ex-cop & carpenter...Berkeley, California
❑ ❑ 1 - Samson's Deal (1983)
❑ ❑ 2 - Free Draw (1984)

❏ ❏   3 - Full House (1986)
❏ ❏   4 - Spit in the Ocean (1987)
❏ ❏   5 - Suicide King (1988)
❏ ❏   . . . .
❏ ❏   . . . .

■ SJÖWALL, Maj & Per Wahlöö

Sweden's premier mystery writers, Maj Sjöwall and Per Wahlöö (1926-1975), created chess-playing Stockholm cop Martin Beck, featured in ten Swedish-edition procedurals over a ten-year period starting in 1965. The wife and husband wrote alternate chapters late at night after their children were asleep. Book 4 in the popular and critically-acclaimed series, *The Laughing Policeman*, won a 1971 Edgar for best novel. Published in Sweden in 1968, the book did not appear in the U.S. until 1970. Three years later it hit the big screen with the same title, but inexplicably the movie was set in San Francisco, featuring Walter Matthau and Bruce Dern. Subplots in the Martin Beck series involve the lives of Stockholm's Homicide Squad—a bit like 87th Precinct without the levity. A search for the killer in the series opener, *Roseanna*, is complicated by the victim's unknown identity. The case gets stranger yet, when it is learned that the young woman is a librarian from Lincoln, Nebraska, found dead in a canal south of Stockholm.

Martin Beck...Swedish police officer...Stockholm, Sweden
❏ ❏   1 - Roseanna (1967)
❏ ❏   2 - The Man Who Went Up in Smoke (1969)
❏ ❏   3 - The Man on the Balcony (1968)
❏ ❏   **4 - The Laughing Policeman (1970) Edgar winner ★**
❏ ❏   5 - The Fire Engine That Disappeared (1971)
❏ ❏   6 - Murder at the Savoy (1971)
❏ ❏   7 - The Abominable Man (1972)
❏ ❏   8 - The Locked Room (1973)
❏ ❏   9 - Cop Killer (1975)
❏ ❏ 10 - The Terrorists (1976)
❏ ❏   . . . .
❏ ❏   . . . .

■ SKOM, Edith

Northwestern University professor Edith Skom has created a fictional Midwestern University for English professor Elizabeth Austin, introduced in *The Mark Twain Murders* (1989), an Edgar, Anthony and Macavity award nominee for best first mystery. An expert in 19th century novels, the professor becomes involved with stolen books, plagiarism and a handsome, well-read F.B.I. agent who knows rare books. In book 2, *The George Eliot Murders* (1995), Austin is on the beach in Hawaii for a two-week semester break, preparing for her upcoming seminar on *Middlemarch*. When guests start dying at the Royal Aloha hotel, the professor teams with a retired lawyer and a famous writer to solve the crimes. In book 3, *The Charles Dickens Murders* (1998), Austin is preparing for a class on *Edwin Drood* when her mother confesses involvement in a similar love triangle, complete with an unsolved murder, at the University of Chicago when she was a student in the 1940s. Skom lives in Winnetka, Illinois.

Elizabeth Austin...English professor...Chicago, Illinois
❏ ❏   1 - **The Mark Twain Murders (1989) Agatha, Anthony &**
                                        Macavity nominees ☆☆☆
❏ ❏   2 - The George Eliot Murders (1995)
❏ ❏   3 - The Charles Dickens Murders (1998)
❏ ❏   . . . .
❏ ❏   . . . .

■ SLEEM, Patty

Independent publisher Patty Sleem has launched a mystery series featuring Harvard M.B.A. Maggie Dillitz, a divorced and remarried baby boomer who chucks her lucrative business career in favor of Yale Divinity School and an interim minister position at a Southern church. In her debut appearance, *Back in Time* (1997), Maggie returns to Boston for the 15th reunion of her Harvard Business School class. While planning funeral services for a friend with terminal cancer, Maggie ends up in a literal and metaphorical West Indies hurricane during a visit to a Jamaican mission with her clergy supervisor. Sleem has also written *Second Time Around* (1995), equal parts mystery, romance and spiritual fiction. With a B.A. in English from the University of North Carolina at Chapel Hill, she later earned an M.B.A. from Harvard Business School. Sleem lives in North Carolina where she owns and manages a company that has been providing writing services and employment agency services for almost 20 years.

Maggie Dillitz...Methodist woman clergy...Greenfield, North Carolina
- ❏ ❏ 1 - Back in Time (1997)
- ❏ ❏ 2 - Fall From Grace (1999)
- ❏ ❏ ....
- ❏ ❏ ....

■ SLOVO, Gillian

Gillian Slovo grew up in South Africa where her father, Joe Slovo, was head of the South African Communist Party and later a senior official with the African National Congress and cabinet minister. Her mother, Ruth First, was a pioneering anti-apartheid journalist killed in 1982 by a letter bomb mailed from South Africa by government agents. Slovo's memoir, *Every Secret Thing* (1997), tells the story of what it meant to her to be the child of parents totally committed to a cause at whatever cost. Slovo has published five mysteries featuring freelance, left-wing Portuguese journalist Kate Baeier, a saxophone-playing detective agency owner, whose milieu is a London of street politics and activist ferment, beginning with *Morbid Symptoms* (1984). Following a seven-year gap after book 3, Baeier returns to London to cat-sit for an expatriate friend when her life is threatened in *Catnap* (1994). Slovo, who lives in London, has worked as a journalist and film producer.

Kate Baeier...journalist turned P.I....London, England
- ❏ ❏ 1 - Morbid Symptoms (1984)
- ❏ ❏ 2 - Death by Analysis (1986)
- ❏ ❏ 3 - Death Comes Staccato (1987)
- ❏ ❏ 4 - Catnap (1994)
- ❏ ❏ 5 - Close Call (1995)
- ❏ ❏ ....
- ❏ ❏ ....

■ SMITH, Alison

Children's author Alison Smith has written two novels featuring Police Chief Judd Springfield of Coolridge Corners, Vermont, introduced in *Someone Else's Grave* (1984). Described as a middle-aged introspective man, Springfield is satisfied with his lot in life, but devoted to self-education. He takes up a new subject every year. In his first case, the Vermont detective has three murder victims with no apparent relationship to each other and no discernible motive. According to Ellen Nehr, writing in *1001 Midnights* (1986), Smith's crisp conversational style and low-key characterizations are definite assets. Dateline headings similar to those on a police blotter add to the tension, suggested Nehr, who concluded, "small-town cop stories abound, but this one stands out." Born in the Boston suburbs, Smith has worked as a newspaper columnist and lives in Rhode Island, according to *Hubin's Crime Fiction II*. Among her books for children are *The Kids' Nature Almanac* (1995) and *Come Away Home* (1991).

Judd Springfield...small town police chief...Coolridge Corners, Vermont
- ❏ ❏ 1 - **Someone Else's Grave (1984) Edgar nominee** ☆
- ❏ ❏ 2 - Rising (1987)
- ❏ ❏ ....
- ❏ ❏ ....

■ SMITH, Barbara Burnett

Barbara Burnett Smith has written four mysteries starring amateur sleuth and aspiring novelist Jolie Wyatt, introduced in *Writers of the Purple Sage* (1994). In this Agatha-nominated best first mystery, Jolie finds herself accused of murder after someone dies by the same method featured in her unpublished manuscript. Following book 4, *Mistletoe From Purple Sage* (1997), Jolie was last seen in "Writers Revenge," a *Malice Domestic 7* (1998) short story. After 16 years in radio, on the air as well as in sales and management, Smith works as a training consultant for corporations and state agencies, teaching leadership and presentation skills. She also voices radio and television commercials and reviews mysteries for *Mostly Murder*. Smith recently traveled to Costa Rica for a trek through the rainforest and an up-close look at an erupting volcano. An earlier trip to Egypt provided opportunities to bribe museum guards and change money on the black market—strictly for research purposes, of course. She lives in Austin, Texas.

Jolie Wyatt...aspiring novelist...Purple Sage, Texas

- ❑ ❑ 1 - **Writers of the Purple Sage (1994) Agatha nominee** ☆
- ❑ ❑ 2 - Dust Devils of the Purple Sage (1995)
- ❑ ❑ 3 - Celebration in Purple Sage (1996)
- ❑ ❑ 4 - Mistletoe From Purple Sage (1997)
- ❑ ❑ . . . .
- ❑ ❑ . . . .

■ SMITH, Cynthia

Former advertising director and magazine publisher Cynthia S. Smith has written five paperback mysteries featuring New York-born Emma Rhodes, Private Resolver for the rich. She works only to subsidize her high style of living and the minimum gratuity for her services (she hates the word "fee") is $20,000. But if Emma cannot resolve the problem in two weeks' time, the client owes nothing. She's beautiful, smart (I.Q. 165), rich (with homes in Manhattan, London and Vila do Mar, Portugal) and well-connected (her friend Abba is with Israeli Intelligence). The tales of her exploits are "fast," "clever" and "charming" says *Publishers Weekly*. Speedy resolution of a problem for the Belgian royal family nets her 608,000 Belgian francs and a small Picasso sketch in the series opener. She's off to Portugal for book 2 and Prague for book 3. Among Smith's nonfiction work are several business how-to books and *Doctors' Wives: The Truth About Medical Marriage*. Former editor and publisher of *Medical/Mrs.*, this Hunter College graduate lives in Rye, New York.

Emma Rhodes...private resolver for the rich...London, England

- ❑ ❑ 1 - Noblesse Oblige (1996)
- ❑ ❑ 2 - Impolite Society (1997)
- ❑ ❑ 3 - Misleading Ladies (1997)
- ❑ ❑ 4 - Silver and Guilt (1998)
- ❑ ❑ 5 - Royals and Rogues (1998)
- ❑ ❑ . . . .
- ❑ ❑ . . . .

■ SMITH, Evelyn E.

Evelyn E. Smith has written four zany mysteries featuring art teacher and painter Susan Melville, who inadvertently becomes a freelance assassin when, intending to kill herself, she shoots the speaker at a charity function in *Miss Melville Regrets* (1986). Although her trust fund has run dry, the 50-ish Miss Melville has high standards and will not take a contract unless the victim deserves to die. Scrupulous about paying her income tax, she always produces a painting to match the payment for her contract hits. A fifth book in the series, *Miss Melville Runs for Cover*, scheduled for publication in 1993, was never published. Under the name Delphine C. Lyons, Smith wrote five science fiction novels between 1965 and 1970, including *Phantom at Lost Lake* (1970), according to *Hawk's Authors' Pseudonyms*. Early in her writing career Smith published more than three dozen science fiction short stories and later wrote several science fiction novels, including *The Copy Shop* (1985), where aliens land in New York and nobody notices.

Susan Melville…freelance assassin-painter…New York, New York
- ❑ ❑   1 - Miss Melville Regrets (1986)
- ❑ ❑   2 - Miss Melville Returns (1987)
- ❑ ❑   3 - Miss Melville's Revenge (1989)
- ❑ ❑   4 - Miss Melville Rides a Tiger (1991)
- ❑ ❑   . . . .
- ❑ ❑   . . . .

■ SMITH, J.C.S. [P]

J.C.S. Smith is the name used by Jane S. Smith for two mysteries featuring retired New York City transit cop, Quentin Jacoby, introduced in *Jacoby's First Case* (1980). Bored with retirement, Jacoby agrees to hunt for a missing prostitute and ends up in a tangle of race-fixing and murder. In his *New York Times* review, Evan Hunter (Ed McBain) found Jacoby "difficult to dislike." Working as a night watchman for a fancy restaurant, Jacoby becomes a suspect in the owner's murder in *Nightcap* (1984). A *Washington Post* reviewer liked Smith's "sense of place, rich in the sights, sounds and smells of Manhattan." Her 1990 nonfiction book about polio and the Salk vaccine, *Patenting the Sun*, earned a Pulitzer prize nomination, and her 1982 biography of Elsie de Wolfe was nominated for a National Book Critics Circle award. Smith is adjunct professor of history and visiting scholar at Northwestern University's Institute for Health Services Research and Policy Studies. Born in New York City, she holds a Ph.D. from Yale University.

Quentin Jacoby…retired transit cop…New York, New York
- ❑ ❑   1 - Jacoby's First Case (1980)
- ❑ ❑   2 - Nightcap (1984)
- ❑ ❑   . . . .
- ❑ ❑   . . . .

■ SMITH, Janet L.

Seattle attorney Janet L. Smith is the creator of an amateur detective named Annie MacPherson who is similarly employed, starting with *Sea of Troubles* (1990). If you enjoy law firm politics, this series delivers with latte. Nominated for an Agatha award as best first traditional mystery, the opener finds Annie holding power of attorney for the ailing owner of an elegant island resort in the Pacific Northwest. Creepy guests, kidnapping and murder all figure into the story. Annie is asked to investigate when a top partner's secretary at a high-power firm kills herself in book 2, *Practice to Deceive* (1992). Annie is "an efficient, agreeable, no-nonsense sort—and so is this mystery," said *Kirkus Reviews*. When last seen in book 3, *A Vintage Murder* (1994), Annie rushes off to a Yakima Valley winery owned by a high school friend in trouble. A fourth-generation Californian who has worked as a trial attorney in a large regional firm, Smith is now a part-time litigator for a much smaller practice. She is also a partner with her husband in an elder-care management firm.

Annie MacPherson…attorney…Seattle, Washington
- ❑ ❑   **1 - Sea of Troubles (1990) Agatha nominee** ☆
- ❑ ❑   2 - Practice To Deceive (1992)
- ❑ ❑   3 - A Vintage Murder (1994)
- ❑ ❑   . . . .
- ❑ ❑   . . . .

■ SMITH, Joan

British author Joan Smith wrote about the Yorkshire Ripper murders while working as a radio and print journalist in Manchester during the late 1970s and her nonfiction book *Misogynies: Reflections on Myths and Malice* (1989) includes several essays resulting from this experience. According to Margaret Kinsman in *St. James Guide to Crime & Mystery Writers* (4th edition), Smith's motivation to write crime fiction was also a by-product of her experience with the gruesome murders. She has since written five mysteries featuring Loretta Lawson, English professor and active feminist scholar, starting at the University of London and moving to Oxford. The first two books in the series were filmed for BBC television. Born in London,

Smith has worked as a journalist and theatre critic for the *Sunday Times*. She currently lives in Oxfordshire where she writes for the *Guardian*, the *Observer*, and the *Independent on Sunday*. The work of this British author is often confused with that of the prolific Canadian novelist, Joan (G.) Smith, who writes primarily Regency romance. Both women are published under the name Joan Smith.

Loretta Lawson...British feminist professor...London, England

❑ ❑ 1 - A Masculine Ending (1987)
❑ ❑ 2 - Why Aren't They Screaming? (1988)
❑ ❑ 3 - Don't Leave Me This Way (1990)
❑ ❑ 4 - What Men Say (1993)
❑ ❑ 5 - Full Stop (1995)
❑ ❑ ....
❑ ❑ ....

■ SMITH, Joan G.

Canadian novelist Joan Smith is Joan Gerarda Smith, author of more than 100 romance novels, primarily Regency, published since 1977. Her romantic suspense includes two titles featuring amateur sleuth Cassie Newton, a French major at McGill University in Montreal, introduced in *Capriccio* (1989). In a 1993 *Contemporary Authors* interview, Smith commented on her love of mysteries and explained that she often includes an element of mystery in her plots. *Midnight Masquerade* (1984), *Royal Revels* (1985) and *The Devious Duchess* (1985) feature Baron Belami as the detective. More recently Smith has written several titles in the Berkeley Brigade series featuring four young aristocrats-turned-sleuths. First seen in *Murder Will Speak* (1996), the foursome also appears in *Murder and Misdeeds* (1997), *Murder While I Smile* (1998) and *Murder Comes to Mind* (1998). Smith has also written historical novels under the name Jennie Gallant. Before launching her writing career, she taught English and French to high school and college students.

Cassie Newton...college French major...Montreal, Quebec, Canada

❑ ❑ 1 - Capriccio (1989)
❑ ❑ 2 - A Brush With Death (1990)
❑ ❑ ....
❑ ❑ ....

■ SMITH, Julie

Edgar award-winner Julie Smith has written 15 mysteries in three different series since 1982. Freelance writer Paul MacDonald (two books) solves real crimes so that he can afford to write the fictional ones. Attorney Rebecca Schwartz (5 books), a nice Jewish girl from Marin County, opens her first adventure playing the piano in a feminist bordello and later finds murder at the Monterey Aquarium in book 4, *Dead in the Water* (1991). Smith's longest series features Skip Langdon, "the too-big, too-tall and too-straightforward" daughter of New Orleans high society who becomes a police detective. "Skip doesn't miss much as she probes the victim's tangled relationships, remaining all the while a consistently convincing character herself," said *Publishers Weekly*. Born in Annapolis, Maryland, raised in Savannah, Georgia, and educated at the University of Mississippi, Smith is a former reporter for the New Orleans *Times-Picayune* and San Fransisco *Chronicle*. She lives in Northern California.

Paul MacDonald...ex-reporter mystery writer...San Francisco, California

❑ ❑ 1 - True-Life Adventure (1985)
❑ ❑ 2 - Huckleberry Fiend (1987)
❑ ❑ ....
❑ ❑ ....

Rebecca Schwartz...defense attorney...San Francisco, California

❑ ❑ 1 - Death Turns a Trick (1982)
❑ ❑ 2 - The Sourdough Wars (1984)
❑ ❑ 3 - Tourist Trap (1986)
❑ ❑ 4 - Dead in the Water (1991)
❑ ❑ 5 - Other People's Skeletons (1993)
❑ ❑ ....
❑ ❑ ....

Skip Langdon...6-ft. police detective...New Orleans, Louisiana

- ❏ ❏ 1 - **New Orleans Mourning (1990) Edgar winner ★ Anthony nominee ☆**
- ❏ ❏ 2 - The Axeman's Jazz (1991)
- ❏ ❏ 3 - Jazz Funeral (1993)
- ❏ ❏ 4 - New Orleans Beat (1994)
- ❏ ❏ 5 - House of Blues (1995)
- ❏ ❏ 6 - The Kindness of Strangers (1996)
- ❏ ❏ 7 - Crescent City Kill (1997)
- ❏ ❏ 8 - 82 Desire (1998)
- ❏ ❏ . . . .
- ❏ ❏ . . . .

■ SMITH, Sarah

Sarah Smith is the author of two *New York Times* Notable Books—her first two Victorian-era mysteries featuring Alexander von Reisden and Perdita Halley. Introduced in *The Vanished Child* (1992), von Reisden is a 27-year-old Austrian biochemist and Perdita a 17-year-old American and aspiring concert pianist. They meet in 1906 Boston when he poses as an amnesia victim to solve a murder. *The Knowledge of Water* (1996) takes place in Paris three years later, just before the great flood of 1910. Smith's mystery involving art theft and forgery is "a rain-drenched portrait of Edwardian Paris that could hang in the Louvre," raved the *New York Times Book Review*. She has also written a science fiction novel, *King of Space* (1991). A Fulbright fellow with a Harvard Ph.D., Smith has lived in London, Paris and Japan. Among her ancestors are Robert Calef, the only voice of reason in the Salem witch trials, and the horse-stealing Doane brothers, hung during the American Revolution. A multimedia consultant, Smith lives in Brookline, Massachusetts.

Alexander von Reisden & Perdita Halley...biochemist & concert pianist...Paris, France

- ❏ ❏ 1 - The Vanished Child [Boston] (1992)
- ❏ ❏ 2 - The Knowledge of Water [Paris] (1996)
- ❏ ❏ . . . .
- ❏ ❏ . . . .

■ SMITH-LEVIN, Judith

Former police officer Judith Smith-Levin says black homicide lieutenant Starletta DuVall is taller (six feet), funnier, better-looking and nicer than her creator. First seen in *Do Not Go Gently* (1996), Star has been on the job 15 years, ten in homicide, when she risks it all to catch a serial killer. Supporting players include her partner, Dominic Paresi; love-interest, handsome six-foot seven-inch Chief Medical Examiner, Dr. Grant Mitchell; best friend, Vee; and cat Jake, a fat 10-year-old black-and-gray-striped tabby. The cast returns in *The Hoodoo Man* (1998) with a case of voodoo, magic and murder. The first uniformed female officer in Worcester, Massachusetts (fourth-highest score on her statewide qualifying exam), Smith-Levin earned two commendations for bravery during her five years on patrol. She previously worked as a police reporter, T.V. news line-producer, playwright, mystery bookstore owner, disc jockey, secretary and model. A Chicago native, she lives on an island in Puget Sound, Washington.

Starletta DuVall...6-ft. black homicide lieutenant...Brookport, Massachusetts

- ❏ ❏ 1 - Do Not Go Gently (1996)
- ❏ ❏ 2 - The Hoodoo Man (1998)
- ❏ ❏ 3 - Green Money (1999)
- ❏ ❏ . . . .
- ❏ ❏ . . . .

■ SONGER, C.J.

A former civilian employee of the Glendale police department, Christine J. Songer knows guns. She has taken courses at Arizona's Gunsite, the Harvard of shooting schools, Thunder Ranch in Texas and FrontSight in California. She has trained with Navy SEALS and has shot, by invitation, at tactical matches designed to measure street survival skills. Armed with her government model Colt 1911, Songer is taking aim on the cover of *Bait* (1998), the series debut featuring cop's widow, Meg Gillis. An ex-cop herself, Meg runs a security business with ex-cop Mike Johnson. Their first thrill-ride takes off like a rocket when Meg intercepts a strange phone call and Mike goes missing. In *Hook* (1999), Meg serves divorce papers in a domestic violence case. Songer and her husband, a former robbery-homicide investigator, live in Southern California with their two baseball-nut kids. A library-volunteer mom (she doesn't do cookies) Songer is currently studying knife-fighting and Krav Magna, the Israeli branch of martial arts.

Meg Gillis...ex-cop turned security consultant ...Beverly Hills, California

- ❑ ❑ 1 - Bait (1998)
- ❑ ❑ 2 - Hook (1999)
- ❑ ❑ ....
- ❑ ❑ ....

■ SPEART, Jessica

Environmental journalist and former television actress Jessica Speart is the creator of Rachel Porter, actress-turned-agent of the U.S. Fish and Wildlife Service, first seen in New Orleans in *Gator Aide* (1997). Rachel heads to Nevada in book 2, *Tortoise Soup* (1998), to investigate the theft of rare tortoise hatchlings. She's off to Miami, the smuggling capital of the nation, in book 3, *Bird Brained* (1999), for a case involving exotic parrots and cockatoos. After her bitchy head-nurse character was killed by a mad sci-entist in *One Life to Live*, Speart worked temporarily as a bartender, caterer and Lincoln Center tour guide before cashing in her life savings to spend a month in Kenya and Tanzania, where she caught the endangered species fever. Her first magazine feature involved Cincinnati Zoo efforts to save the black rhino through frozen embryo transfer. The walls of Speart's Connecticut home are decorated with folk-art masks (18 at last count) collected on her travels to Mexico, South America, Africa and Southeast Asia.

Rachel Porter...Fish & Wildlife agent...United States

- ❑ ❑ 1 - Gator Aide (1997)
- ❑ ❑ 2 - Tortoise Soup (1998)
- ❑ ❑ 3 - Bird Brained (1999)
- ❑ ❑ ....
- ❑ ❑ ....

■ SPRAGUE, Gretchen

Gretchen Sprague won an Edgar award in 1968 for her juvenile mystery *Signpost to Terror*. Thirty years later she launched an adult mystery series with *Death in Good Company* (1997), featuring pro bono attorney Martha Patterson. In the series debut, a former colleague offers the previously-retired Martha a job at West Brooklyn Legal Services. Starting from day one, she has to contend with a mugged and bleeding paralegal, stolen rent-strike money, an unhappy tenants' association, a crazy woman stalker, and a possible strangler. "A mazelike tale that features an unobtrusively gifted detective and a virtual handbook of rarely fictionalized pro bono legal maneuvers," said *Kirkus Reviews*. Martha Patterson returns in *Maquette for Murder* (1999). Sprague's other young adult novels include *A Question of Harmony* (1965) and *White in the Moon* (1968). After earning a B.A. degree at the University of Nebraska, she worked briefly as an English instructor. A native of Lincoln, Nebraska, Sprague lives in Cold Spring, New York.

Martha Patterson...retired attorney turned pro bono...Brooklyn, New York

- ❑ ❑ 1 - Death in Good Company (1997)
- ❑ ❑ 2 - Maquette for Murder (1999)
- ❑ ❑ ....
- ❑ ❑ ....

■ SPRING, Michelle

Former sociology professor Michelle Spring is the creator of Cambridge private investigator Laura Principal, introduced in *Every Breath You Take*, Ellis award nominee for best first mystery of 1994. Laura first came to Cambridge to read history at Newnham College and stayed to do graduate research. She found a best friend, survived a failed marriage and forged a business and personal partnership with the oh-so-appealing Sonny Mendlowitz. Their fourth and most recent song-title case is *Nights in White Satin* (1999). Spring chose Cambridge as the venue for her mysteries because she sees it as the captivating conjuncture of real life with a fairy tale English setting. After 25 years in academia, where she taught

at Cambridge and Anglia Universities and published four academic books as Michelle Stanworth, she recently committed to writing fiction full-time. Born and raised on beautiful Vancouver Island, British Columbia, Spring lives in Cambridge with her political theorist partner and their son and daughter.

Laura Principal...British academic turned P.I....Cambridge, England

- ❑ ❑   **1 - Every Breath You Take (1994) Ellis nominee** ☆
- ❑ ❑   2 - Running for Shelter (1995)
- ❑ ❑   3 - Standing in the Shadows (1998)
- ❑ ❑   4 - Nights in White Satin (1999)
- ❑ ❑   . . . .
- ❑ ❑   . . . .

■ SPRINKLE, Patricia H.

Vassar College graduate Patricia H(ouck) Sprinkle has written nine mysteries and more than half a dozen inspirational books. Her first mystery, *Murder at Markham* (1988), introduced embassy wife Sheila Travis, who returns to her native Atlanta as an executive for a Japanese firm. Last seen in book 7, *Deadly Secrets on the St. Johns* (1995), Sheila finds murder at an elegant party while visiting Jacksonville, Florida. Sprinkle's second series features small-town Georgia business-owner-turned-magistrate, MacLaren Yarbrough, and her hus-

band of 45 years in *When Did We Lose Harriet?* (1997) and *But Why Shoot the Magistrate?* (1998). Sprinkle begins a third series in 2000 with her first Job's Corner mystery, featuring a fictional North Carolina town much like the one where her minister father served a 200-year-old Presbyterian church in the late 1940s. Author of *Women Who Do Too Much* (1996) and *Children Who Do Too Little* (1996), Sprinkle was born in Bluefield, West Virginia. She and her minister husband live in Miami, Florida.

MacLaren Yarbrough...business-owner turned magistrate...Hopemore, Georgia

- ❑ ❑   1 - When Did We Lose Harriet? (1997)
- ❑ ❑   2 - But Why Shoot the Magistrate? (1998)
- ❑ ❑   . . . .
- ❑ ❑   . . . .

Sheila Travis...embassy wife turned executive...Atlanta, Georgia

- ❑ ❑   1 - Murder at Markham (1988)
- ❑ ❑   2 - Murder in the Charleston Manner (1990)
- ❑ ❑   3 - Murder on Peachtree Street (1991)
- ❑ ❑   4 - Somebody's Dead in Snellville (1992)
- ❑ ❑   5 - Death of a Dunwoody Matron (1993)
- ❑ ❑   6 - A Mystery Bred in Buckhead (1994)
- ❑ ❑   7 - Deadly Secrets on the St. Johns (1995)
- ❑ ❑   . . . .
- ❑ ❑   . . . .

■ SQUIRE, Elizabeth Daniels

Elizabeth Daniels Squire wrote two nonfiction books and another mystery before launching her six-book series about forgetful senior sleuth Peaches Dann, introduced in *Who Killed What's-Her-Name?* (1994). Squire's fans have turned her into a collector of jokes, anecdotes, coping devices and personal experiences about memory techniques. As a result, Squire has turned Peaches into the author of *How To Survive Without a Memory*. Born into a newspaper publishing family where both her father and grandfather were

controversial editors of *The News and Observer* in Raleigh, North Carolina, Squire has worked as a columnist in Beirut, a police reporter in Connecticut and once wrote the nationally-syndicated column "How To Read Your Own Hand." The idea for her first mystery, *Kill the Messenger* (1990), was inspired by death threats received by her editor grandfather. Squire and her writer husband live on a working organic farm near Asheville, North Carolina. She is a frequent speaker to library groups and writing workshops.

Peaches Dann...absent-minded widow...North Carolina

- ❑ ❑   1 - Who Killed What's-Her-Name? (1994)
- ❑ ❑   2 - Remember the Alibi (1994)
- ❑ ❑   3 - Memory Can Be Murder (1995)
- ❑ ❑   4 - Whose Death Is It Anyway? (1997)
- ❑ ❑   5 - Is There a Dead Man in the House? (1998)
- ❑ ❑   6 - Where There's a Will (1999)
- ❑ ❑   ....
- ❑ ❑   ....

■ STABENOW, Dana

Alaska native Dana Stabenow has published 14 novels since 1991, including nine mysteries featuring Aleut investigator Kate Shugak, first seen in the Edgar award-winning *A Cold Day for Murder* (1992). Stabenow's second Alaska series opens with disgraced state trooper Liam Campbell arriving at a remote post to find lost-love bush-pilot Wyanet (wy-ah-NET) Chouinard (shwee-NARD) crouched over a body. "Happily, this much mayhem has rarely been in surer hands," raved *Publishers Weekly* about Liam's debut in *Fire and Ice* (1998). Stabenow has also written a science fiction trilogy featuring a woman project leader on space colony Ellfive. Raised on a 75-foot fish tender where her mother was a deckhand, Stabenow earned a B.A. in journalism and an M.F.A. from the University of Alaska. A former pipeline worker, egg grader and seafood expediter, Stabenow lives in Anchorage, where her grandfather flew the first DC-3 for Alaska Airlines. She is currently finishing a sweeping historical novel about the travels of Marco Polo's granddaughter along the Silk Road from China to Europe.

Kate Shugak...Alaskan ex-D.A. investigator...Alaska

- ❑ ❑   **1 - A Cold Day for Murder (1992) Edgar winner ★**
- ❑ ❑   2 - A Fatal Thaw (1993)
- ❑ ❑   3 - Dead in the Water (1993)
- ❑ ❑   4 - A Cold-Blooded Business (1994)
- ❑ ❑   5 - Play With Fire (1995)
- ❑ ❑   6 - Blood Will Tell (1996)
- ❑ ❑   7 - Breakup (1997)
- ❑ ❑   8 - Killing Grounds (1998)
- ❑ ❑   9 - Hunter's Moon (1999)
- ❑ ❑ 10 - Tailspin (2000)
- ❑ ❑   ....
- ❑ ❑   ....

Liam Campbell & Wyanet Chouinard...state trooper & bush pilot...Alaska

- ❑ ❑   1 - Fire and Ice (1998)
- ❑ ❑   2 - So Sure of Death (1999)
- ❑ ❑   3 - Nothing Gold Can Say (2000)
- ❑ ❑   ....
- ❑ ❑   ....

■ STACEY, Susannah [P]

Susannah Stacey is one of the pseudonyms of London-born authors Jill Staynes and Margaret Storey, writing partners for two mystery series. As Susannah Stacey they have written eight Inspector Bone mysteries featuring a wise and quiet Englishman raising a daughter alone after the death of his wife. Bone's first appearance in *Goodbye Nanny Gray* (1987) was nominated for an Agatha award as best first traditional mystery after its U.S. publication in 1988. British editions of this series are published under the names of Staynes and Storey. As Elizabeth Eyre, the pair has written six historical mysteries set in Renaissance Italy featuring Sigismondo, agent for the Duke of Rocca. After their days together at St. Paul's School in London, Staynes earned a B.A. at St. Anne's, Oxford, while Storey went on to Girton College, Cambridge, where she earned B.A. and M.A. degrees. In addition to teaching language and literature, Storey has written 14 children's books including *The Double Wizard* (1978). Staynes lives in London and Storey in Kent.

Robert Bone...widowed British police inspector...England

- ❑ ❑ 1 - **Goodbye Nanny Gray (1987) Agatha nominee** ☆
- ❑ ❑ 2 - A Knife at the Opera (1988)
- ❑ ❑ 3 - Body of Opinion (1988)
- ❑ ❑ 4 - Grave Responsibility (1990)
- ❑ ❑ 5 - The Late Lady (1992)
- ❑ ❑ 6 - Bone Idle (1993)
- ❑ ❑ 7 - Dead Serious (1995)
- ❑ ❑ 8 - Hunter's Quarry (1997)
- ❑ ❑ ....
- ❑ ❑ ....

■ STAINCLIFFE, Cath

Cath Staincliffe has written three mysteries featuring Manchester single-mother private investigator Sal Kilkenny, introduced in *Looking for Trouble* (1994). The series opener, first published when it won a writing competition, was later short-listed for CWA's Creasey award for best first crime novel and serialized on *Woman's Hour* for BBC Radio. Sal and her young daughter Maddie share their home with another single parent, Ray Costello, and his son Tom and a variety of lodgers rent the attic flat. Investigating alongside the washing, shopping, cooking and school runs, Sal often gets emotionally involved in her cases and dislikes some of the compromises she has to make. She abhors violence, carries no weapons and has no martial arts skills. Raised in Bradford with a few years' interlude in Torquay, Staincliffe earned a degree in drama and theatre arts from Birmingham University. An aspiring gardener, she lives in Manchester, where she combines freelance community arts projects with raising three children and writing.

Sal Kilkenny...single-mother private eye...Manchester, England

- ❑ ❑ 1 - **Looking for Trouble (1994) Creasey nominee** ☆
- ❑ ❑ 2 - Go Not Gently (1997)
- ❑ ❑ 3 - Dead Wrong (1998)
- ❑ ❑ ....
- ❑ ❑ ....

■ STALLWOOD, Veronica

Veronica Stallwood has written six Oxford mysteries featuring historical romance novelist Kate Ivory, first seen in *Death and the Oxford Box* (1993) when she helps a woman from her running group reclaim heirloom boxes stolen by an estranged husband. In book 2, *Oxford Exit* (1994), Kate unmasks a book thief in the Bodleian, and later clashes with a college don tied to a Dickens scandal in book 3, *Oxford Mourning* (1995). *The Oxford Knot* (1998) finds Kate on an unplanned book tour, while a dead gardener intrudes on her writing in book 6, *Oxford Blue* (1998). In book 7, *The Oxford Shift* (1999), Kate tracks down a missing grandmother with the help of her mad mum Roz. Stallwood's nonseries novels include *Deathspell* (1992) and a psychological tale, *The Rainbow Sign* (1999). Born in London, Stallwood was educated abroad and now lives in the Oxfordshire countryside. She previously worked at Oxford's Lincoln College Library and the Bodleian Library, one of Europe's oldest, second in size only to the British Library.

Kate Ivory...historical romance novelist...Oxford, England

- ❑ ❑ 1 - Death and the Oxford Box (1993)
- ❑ ❑ 2 - Oxford Exit (1994)
- ❑ ❑ 3 - Oxford Mourning (1995)
- ❑ ❑ 4 - Oxford Fall (1996)
- ❑ ❑ 5 - Oxford Knot (1998)
- ❑ ❑ 6 - Oxford Blue (1998)
- ❑ ❑ ....
- ❑ ❑ ....

STAR, Nancy

Former Hollywood story editor Nancy Star developed script ideas for several movie companies, including the Samuel Goldwyn Company where she was responsible for such films as *Mystic Pizza*. During her time at the Ladd Company, Star was involved with successes such as *Body Heat* and *Blade Runner*. Her nonfiction book, *The International Guide to Tipping* (1988) almost led to an appearance on *Oprah*, but instead gave her the idea for a mystery series featuring a daytime talk show producer. Single-mother senior producer May Morrison debuts in *Up Next* (1998). "If you've ever wanted to kill someone responsible for a T.V. talk show, this book's for you," said *Publishers Weekly*. In May's next adventure, she visits a famous Southwest spa resort where guests are dying mysteriously, including May's best friend Stacie. Star's first novel, *Buried Lives* (1993), features a woman with buried memories of her brother's kidnapping. Along with her husband, two children and a pair of lovebirds, she lives in Northern New Jersey.

May Morrison...TV talk show producer...New York, New York

- ❏ ❏ 1 - Up Next (1998)
- ❏ ❏ 2 - Now This (1999)
- ❏ ❏ ....
- ❏ ❏ ....

STEIN, Triss

Triss Stein is the creator of Kay Engles, a nationally-known reporter who finds murder and a family mystery at her class reunion in the opening installment, *Murder at the Class Reunion* (1993). In book 2, *Digging Up Death* (1998), archaeologist Dr. Vera Contas leads her first dig on the site of a future Manhattan office building, only 50 feet from Wall Street. She is looking for 300-year-old pirate treasure belonging to Captain Kidd, and her good friend Kay, involved with the impatient builder, smells a dynamite magazine feature. Kay's next adventure will take place under the long shadow of the 1960s. Raised in a rural community near the Canadian border in Upstate New York, Stein used the setting for her first mystery. A graduate of Brandeis University, where she studied history and classics, Stein went to graduate school at Columbia University. A long-time children's librarian, she currently works in research for a major management consulting firm. She lives in Brooklyn, New York.

Kay Engles...nationally-known reporter...Brooklyn, New York

- ❏ ❏ 1 - Murder at the Class Reunion (1993)
- ❏ ❏ 2 - Digging Up Death (1998)
- ❏ ❏ ....
- ❏ ❏ ....

STEINBERG, Janice

Three years as promotion director for San Diego's National Public Radio station inspired Janice Steinberg to create 38-year-old public radio reporter Margo Simon, first seen in *Death of a Postmodernist* (1995). Steinberg says Margo is younger, thinner and taller than her creator, but they often share experiences, such as their visit to an American Indian sweat lodge for book 3, *Death-Fires Dance* (1996) and a trip to Israel for book 5, *Death in a City of Mystics* (1998). In addition to her work in urban planning, Steinberg covered dance and performance art as a freelancer for the *Los Angeles Times* and other publications. She also co-authored *Petite Style: The Ultimate Fashion Guide for Women 5' 4" and Under* (1988). After growing up in the Milwaukee suburb of Whitefish Bay, Wisconsin, Steinberg attended the University of California-Irvine where she earned her B.A. and an M.A. in social ecology. She is the founder of the San Diego chapter of Sisters In Crime and served two years on the national board.

Margo Simon...Public Radio reporter...San Diego, California

- ❏ ❏ 1 - Death of a Postmodernist (1995)
- ❏ ❏ 2 - Death Crosses the Border (1995)
- ❏ ❏ 3 - Death-Fires Dance (1996)
- ❏ ❏ 4 - The Dead Man and the Sea (1997)
- ❏ ❏ 5 - Death in a City of Mystics (1998)
- ❏ ❏ ....
- ❏ ❏ ....

■ STEINER, Susan

California author Susan Steiner is the creator of a tall, red-haired, green-eyed investigator named Alexandra Winter, from the California firm of Abromowitz & Stewart, the agency with a heart. First seen in *Murder on Her Mind* (1985), reprinted in paperback in 1991, divorcée Alex is the owner of a clever, one-eyed black cat named Ms. Watson. Vanished books, family feuds, a stabbing and death by overdose are just the beginning in book 2, *Library: No Murder Aloud* (1993), set at a famous, albeit fictional, old California library. A powerful right-wing politician and leader of the campaign to eliminate public funding is brutally murdered on the library premises with a pair of scissors, and the gentle chief librarian, implicated by strong circumstantial evidence, is arrested. Alex must pick her way through a minefield of old money, drug dealing, horticulture (Rainbow Irises created for Judy Garland), blackmail and bibliomania.

Alexandra Winter...red-haired investigator...Southern California
- ❏ ❏ 1 - Murder on Her Mind (1985)
- ❏ ❏ 2 - Library: No Murder Aloud (1993)
- ❏ ❏ ....
- ❏ ❏ ....

■ STEVENS, Serita

Forensic nurse Serita (suh-REE-tuh) Stevens is the author of the Anthony and Macavity-nominated *Deadly Doses: A Writer's Guide to Poisons* (1990). "It's enough to give anyone that Agatha Christie urge," said *School Library Journal*. Her nonfiction forensic nursing book, *Silent Language*, is expected in 2000 and a study on abusive relationships will follow. With Rayanne Moore she wrote two mysteries featuring Brooklyn Jewish grandmother Fanny Zindel, introduced in *Red Sea, Dead Sea* (1991). In addition to a number of historical romance novels, Stevens wrote a 1985 Cagney and Lacey novelization, *A Dream Forever* (1984) as Megan MacDonnell, *Deceptive Desires* (1987) as Shira Stevens, and *The Nurses* (1996) as Tyler Cortland. Born in Chicago, Stevens earned B.S.N. and M.A. degrees from the University of Illinois and Antioch University and later taught creative writing and worked as a film development assistant. She lives in Southern California, where she enjoys horseback riding and flying a Cessna 172.

Fanny Zindel...Jewish grandmother...Brooklyn, New York
- ❏ ❏ 1 - Red Sea, Dead Sea (1991)
- ❏ ❏ 2 - Bagels for Tea (1993)
- ❏ ❏ ....
- ❏ ❏ ....

■ STRUTHERS, Betsy

Canadian poet Betsy Struthers has written three mysteries featuring Rosalie "Rosie" Cairns, a Peterborough bookstore clerk turned academic, introduced in *Found: A Body* (1992). A body found in the river is the first of several mysterious deaths. Although Rosie never knew her father's family, she inherits her grandfather's cottage in book 2, *Grave Deeds* (1993). A subsequent reunion with her great aunt leads to murder in this Toronto and Halliburton setting. While acting as a student advisor in book 3, *A Studied Death* (1995), Rosie investigates the stabbing of one of her charges, found in an alley on campus. Struthers' four volumes of poetry include her first published work, *Censored Letters* (1984), as well as *Saying So Out Loud* (1988), *Running Out of Time* (1993), and *Virgin Territory* (1996). She earned a B.A. in English from Waterloo Lutheran, now the University of Waterloo. Born in Toronto, she lived for a time in Ottawa, before settling in Peterborough, Ontario.

Rosalie Cairns...bookstore clerk turned academic...Peterborough, Ontario, Canada
- ❏ ❏ 1 - Found: A Body (1992)
- ❏ ❏ 2 - Grave Deeds (1993)
- ❏ ❏ 3 - A Studied Death (1995)
- ❏ ❏ ....
- ❏ ❏ ....

■ STUBBS, Jean

Jean Stubbs wrote her first crime novel, *My Grand Enemy* (1967), after finding an old library book called *Famous Trials of History* (1926), which included the case of Mary Bandy, hanged for poisoning her father in 1752. Convinced Mary had been poorly treated, Stubbs researched the case in the British Museum and documented the crime in novel form. She did the same with another 18th century murder, *The Case of Kitty Ogilvie* (1970). Stubbs' third historical mystery, *Dear Laura* (1973), was nominated for a best-novel

Edgar award. The book introduced retired Scotland Yard Inspector John Joseph Lintott, a mutton-chop-whiskered guardian of Victorian values. During a U.S. publicity tour, Stubbs fell in love with San Francisco and returned to complete her research for Lintott's third case. In *The Golden Crucible* (1976), the inspector's feminist daughter Lizzie joins him in San Francisco in 1906. Stubbs has written 15 other novels, including the four-volume Howarth Chronicles. She lives in a 200-year-old cottage in Cornwall, England.

John Joseph Lintott...retired Scotland Yard inspector...London, England

- ❑ ❑ 1 - **Dear Laura [1890s London] (1973) Edgar nominee** ☆
- ❑ ❑ 2 - The Painted Face [1902 Paris] (1974)
- ❑ ❑ 3 - The Golden Crucible [1906 SF] (1976)
- ❑ ❑ . . . .
- ❑ ❑ . . . .

■ STUYCK, Karen Hanson

Karen Hanson Stuyck (rhymes with strike) is the author of a three-book paperback series featuring Liz James, journalist turned public relations officer for the Houston Mental Health Center, introduced in *Cry for Help* (1995). Fourteen years after their college graduation, Liz's former roommate, the oh-so-perfect, crackerjack investigative reporter, Caroline Marshall, tries to re-establish their battered friendship. But Liz rebuffs her and Caroline is found dead the following day. Feeling guilty, Liz steps in to help her old friend's

partner complete an exposé of psychiatrists who sleep with their patients, and she starts to wonder if Caroline really killed herself. When last seen in *Lethal Lessons* (1997), Liz is being pressured by a pushy colleague for help with the therapist's book about her Powerful Woman workshops. A media frenzy erupts when some newly-empowered women begin taking their motivational lessons to violent extremes and the workshop leader's unfaithful husband is one of the casualties. Stuyck lives in Houston, Texas.

Liz James...journalist turned PR rep...Houston, Texas

- ❑ ❑ 1 - Cry for Help (1995)
- ❑ ❑ 2 - Held Accountable (1996)
- ❑ ❑ 3 - Lethal Lessons (1997)
- ❑ ❑ . . . .
- ❑ ❑ . . . .

■ SUCHER, Dorothy

Psychotherapist Dorothy Sucher (rhymes with suture) has written two mysteries featuring Washington, D.C. private investigator, Sabina Swift, and her young sidekick, Vic Newman. Their first outing, *Dead Men Don't Give Seminars* (1988), was nominated for an Agatha award as best first traditional mystery. The pair returns in *Dead Men Don't Marry* (1989). Sucher's non-fiction account of gardening in Vermont, *The Invisible Garden* (1999), will include her experience with building a pond, the tale of an elderly widow

who practices "evil eye" gardening, and other stories. Former editor of a small-town Maryland weekly newspaper, Sucher spent twelve years as a practicing psychotherapist. Like Sabina, she is married to a physicist. A magna cum laude graduate of Brooklyn College, Sucher did graduate work at Columbia University and earned a master's degree in mental health from Johns Hopkins. She and her husband divide their time between suburban Washington, D.C. and their Vermont farmhouse.

Sabina Swift...detective agency owner...Washington, District of Columbia

- ❑ ❑ 1 - **Dead Men Don't Give Seminars (1988) Agatha nominee** ☆
- ❑ ❑ 2 - Dead Men Don't Marry (1989)
- ❑ ❑ . . . .
- ❑ ❑ . . . .

■ SULLIVAN, Winona

Winona Sullivan's first mystery, *A Sudden Death at the Norfolk Café* (1993), was named best unpublished P.I. novel of 1991 in a contest sponsored by St. Martin's Press and Private Eye Writers of America. Her licensed private eye is Sister Cecile Buddenbrooks, a beautiful heiress-nun, whose father had strongly disapproved of her vocation. Because his fortune was left with the stipulation that it not be spent for religious purposes, Sister Cecile finances investigations work with her inheritance and later donates the fees to her Boston convent, the only order in America with its own stockbroker. In *Dead South* (1996), Sister Cecile is on the streets of Miami in her red Ferrari, searching for a missing C.I.A. agent. Still in Miami for book 3, *Death's a Beach* (1998), she investigates the brutal slaying of a wealthy banker with underworld connections. A former teacher and C.I.A. analyst, Sullivan is the mother of seven. She and her husband live with their four youngest children in Miami, Florida, following their recent move from Massachusetts.

Cecile Buddenbrooks...licensed P.I. heiress-nun...Boston, Massachusetts

❏ ❏ **1 - A Sudden Death at the Norfolk Café (1993) SMP/PWA winner ★**
❏ ❏ 2 - Dead South (1996)
❏ ❏ 3 - Death's a Beach (1998)
❏ ❏ . . . .
❏ ❏ . . . .

SUMNER, Penny

Australian Penny Sumner has written two mysteries featuring British archivist turned private eye, Victoria Cross, introduced in *The End of April* (1992). At the request of her aunt, a professor at Oxford, Tor agrees to assist in transcribing some 19th century illicit sexual writings and secretly investigate threats on a lesbian activist law student. In *Crosswords* (1994), Tor takes a 25-year-old missing persons case with ties to London's gangland days of the 1960s. Sumner is also the editor of *Brought to Book* (1998), a collection of murderous stories from the literary world, where authors such as Barbara Paul, Joan M. Drury, Mary Wings, Susan Dunlap and others take revenge on editors and plot murder at award dinners and conferences. Sumner's story "Dead Head" was shortlisted for a C.W.A. Dagger award. After moving to England as a postgraduate student and earning a D.Phil. at Oxford, she currently teaches contemporary literature and creative writing at the University of Northumbria. Sumner lives in Newcastle-upon-Tyne.

Victoria Cross...archivist turned P.I....London, England

❏ ❏ 1 - The End of April (1992)
❏ ❏ 2 - Crosswords (1994)
❏ ❏ . . . .
❏ ❏ . . . .

SZYMANSKI, Therese

Michigan author Therese (ta-REECE) Szymanski (shuh-MAN-ski) is the creator of lesbian sleuth Brett Higgins, first seen in *When the Dancing Stops* (1997). While managing adult theaters and bookstores in Detroit, Brett is a prime suspect when her porn-king boss is murdered. On the lam in Alma, Michigan during book 2, Brett works for a Lansing advertising agency in book 3, and returns to Detroit in book 4, *When Evil Changes Face* (2000). Having managed adult bookstores and theaters in some pretty tough Detroit neighborhoods, Szymanski created Brett Higgins as her fictional evil twin. After a brief stint in the Army and private security, Szymanski managed fast food restaurants and later worked for a Michigan advertising agency. Active in Detroit theater troupes, where she has acted, directed, stage managed, constructed sets and handled publicity, Szymanski has won several awards for playwriting. A graduate of Michigan State University, she lives in Ann Arbor where she works for an accounting software company.

Brett Higgins...lesbian adult bookstore manager...Detroit, Michigan

❏ ❏ 1 - When the Dancing Stops (1997)
❏ ❏ 2 - When the Dead Speak (1998)
❏ ❏ 3 - When Some Body Disappears (1999)
❏ ❏ 4 - When Evil Changes Face (2000)
❏ ❏ . . . .
❏ ❏ . . . .

TAN, Maureen

Maureen Tan writes action-adventure spy thrillers starring Jane Nichols, British secret agent turned best-selling mystery author, introduced in *aka Jane* (1997). After a fellow agent she loved is killed protecting her from a contract killing ordered by an American-based I.R.A. terrorist, Jane quits M.I.-5 and retires to a Savannah, Georgia bed-and-breakfast to write. Who knew her I.R.A. adversary was a pillar of the local community? Jane is called back by M.I.-5 in *Run, Jane, Run* (1999), only to discover the father of a kidnap victim may be connected to her parents' murder. "Plenty of romance and derring-do," said *Booklist*, adding that "Jane is a far more rounded character than Bond." Growing up in a large Marine family, always on the move, Tan loved reading spy novels. Annoyed that the secret agents were always men, she vowed to write one with a woman as the hero. Currently assistant director of the Engineering Publications office at the University of Illinois at Urbana-Champaign, she lives in Champaign.

Jane Nichols...secret agent turned mystery writer...Savannah, Georgia

❏ ❏ 1 - aka Jane (1997)
❏ ❏ 2 - Run, Jane, Run (1999)
❏ ❏ ....
❏ ❏ ....

TAYLOR, Alison G. [P]

The pseudonymous Alison G. Taylor grew up in rural England, but has lived for many years in North Wales, the setting for her extremely dark psychological mysteries. Continuing characters include Detective Chief Inspector Michael McKenna, whose marriage is falling apart; senior detective Jack Tuttle, following in his boss's discontented footsteps; handsome, jealous, sarcastic Dewi Prys who lives with his mother; and bright, ambitious newcomer Janet Evans, whose minister father strongly disapproves of her occupational choice. In book 1, *Simeon's Bride* (1995), a woman's body, found hanging from a tree, signals a 200-year-old puzzle. A children's home runaway is murdered in book 2, *In Guilty Night* (1996), while a man dies mysteriously from an allergy in *The House of Women* (1998). Book 4, *An Unsafe Conviction*, is scheduled for U.K. publication in 1999. Taylor studied architecture before entering the field of social work and probation, and won an award in 1996 for her work exposing institutional child abuse. Her interests include baroque music, art and riding.

Michael McKenna...detective chief inspector...Wales

❏ ❏ 1 - Simeon's Bride (1995)
❏ ❏ 2 - In Guilty Night (1996)
❏ ❏ 3 - The House of Women (1998)
❏ ❏ ....
❏ ❏ ....

TAYLOR, Elizabeth Atwood

Elizabeth Atwood Taylor worked as a film editor, television news reporter, social worker and art therapist before writing her first mystery, *The Cable Car Murder* (1981), introducing ex-socialite Maggie Elliott. A |former film maker turned apprentice private investigator, Maggie is recently sober after the death of her husband five years earlier. When her estranged half-sister mysteriously disappears just before Christmas, Maggie enlists the help of Richard Patrick O'Reagan, a 50-something ex-cop who'd rather be painting, but still wears a police whistle around his neck. *Murder at Vassar* (1987), takes Maggie to her 15th college reunion, where the wealthy aunt of a classmate is killed by a masked gunman during a campus robbery. Recovering from a serious illness in *The Northwest Murders* (1992), Maggie is living in O'Reagan's Northern California cabin when a hiker is killed and his girlfriend left comatose. The story is full of Indian and gold-mining lore. A native of San Antonio, Texas, Taylor studied art history at Vassar and social work at Bryn Mawr.

Maggie Elliott...ex-film maker turned P.I....San Francisco, California

❏ ❏ 1 - The Cable Car Murder (1981)
❏ ❏ 2 - Murder at Vassar (1987)
❏ ❏ 3 - The Northwest Murders (1992)
❏ ❏ ....
❏ ❏ ....

TAYLOR, Jean

Jean Taylor's first novel, *We Know Where You Live* (1996), introduces red-haired lesbian investigator Maggie Garrett, sole proprietor of Windsor and Garrett Investigations in San Francisco. Along with her assistant, teenage computer hacker Ricardo Galvez, the supporting cast includes Maggie's best friends, health activists Liam and Jesse. Their first case involves alleged improprieties by a political organization with close ties to the city's mayor. In book 2, Maggie is hired by the parents of a therapist who disappears after being accused of sexual abuse. Fellow crime writer and former private investigator Elizabeth Pincus calls Maggie Garrett "a P.I.'s P.I.—witty and resourceful, reckless and wild." A proofreader at a major San Francisco law firm, Taylor has worked as a kitchen helper, secretary, volunteer coordinator, seamstress and emergency room clerk. She lives in the Mission District with Tigey and Fearless, models for her overindulged fictional cats, and sings soprano in the Metropolitan Community Church Choir.

Maggie Garrett...young lesbian P.I....San Francisco, California

❑ ❑ 1 - We Know Where You Live (1995)
❑ ❑ 2 - The Last of Her Lies (1996)
❑ ❑ . . . .
❑ ❑ . . . .

TAYLOR, Kathleen

Needlework expert, paper doll designer and Barbie collector Kathleen Taylor was born in the Pacific Northwest but has lived in the same South Dakota town for 25 years. Her 40-something Rubenesque waitress-with-attitude is Delphi's own Tory Bauer, first seen in a small-press limited edition titled *The Missionary Position* (1993). Later re-released as *Funeral Food* (1997), book 1 appeared after book 2, *Sex and Salmonella* (1996), for most readers. While there are laughs aplenty in these books, they are not small-town cozies. Occasionally explicit sex and liberal use of four-letter words are part of real life in Delphi, according to Taylor, who thinks of her series as "prairie noir." Coming next is book 5, *Cold Front* (1999). Before launching her mystery career, she was a contributing editor for as many as seven magazines at one time and sold over 500 craft and needlework articles to 66 different publications. Taylor and her building contractor husband live in a restored Victorian home where she is writing another Delphi mystery.

Tory Bauer...small-town diner waitress...Delphi, South Dakota

❑ ❑ 1 - The Missionary Position (1993)
❑ ❑ - APA-Funeral Food (1997)
❑ ❑ 2 - Sex and Salmonella (1996)
❑ ❑ 3 - The Hotel South Dakota (1997)
❑ ❑ 4 - Mourning Shift (1998)
❑ ❑ . . . .
❑ ❑ . . . .

TAYLOR, L.A.

L.A. Taylor is Laurie Aylma Taylor, whose published work includes a prize-winning poetry collection, *Changing the Past* (1981), and nine novels, including her first mystery, *Footnote to Murder* (1983), featuring Minneapolis library researcher Marge Brock. Taylor's four-book detective series features Minneapolis computer engineer J.J. Jamison, an investigator for C.A.T.C.H.—the Committee for Analysis of Tropospheric and Celestial Happenings. Jamison's first case was *Only Half a Hoax* (1983). When last seen in *A Murder Waiting to Happen* (1989), J.J.'s at a science fiction convention where fans are dying. A Phi Beta Kappa graduate of Ohio Wesleyan University, Taylor previously worked as a medical research technician at Harvard University Medical School, an educational researcher for the Pittsburgh Board of Education, and a community school instructor in Minneapolis. She has written a science fiction novel, *The Blossom of Edna* (1986), two other mysteries, *Love of Money* (1987) and *Poetic Justice* (1988), and the mystery-fantasy, *Cat's Paw* (1995).

J.J. Jamison...computer engineer...Minneapolis, Minnesota

❑ ❑ 1 - Only Half a Hoax (1983)
❑ ❑ 2 - Deadly Objectives (1984)

❑ ❑   3 - Shed Light on Death (1985)
❑ ❑   4 - A Murder Waiting To Happen (1989)
❑ ❑   . . . .
❑ ❑   . . . .

TELL, Dorothy

Dorothy Tell is the creator of 60-something Texan and lesbian amateur sleuth Poppy Dillworth, seen in *Murder at Red Rook Ranch* (1990) and *The Hallelujah Murders* (1991). Tell says her decision to write a mystery stemmed from her need to supply herself with an aging lesbian role model, "crusty but open to change and humorous in her approach to life." Writing in *Mystery Readers Journal* (Volume 9, Number 4), Tell added that mystery is her favorite genre because "it feels good to identify with the sleuth who sets the fictional universe of the story-world back to rights again". She likes watching Poppy successfully deal with problems she faces growing older. Tell's non-mystery, *Wilderness Trek* (1990), takes a diverse group of eight women on a two-week hike into the Ozark mountains. Her collection of erotic lesbian stories, *Certain Smiles*, was published in 1994. Tell lives in Grand Prairie, Texas.

Poppy Dillworth...60-something lesbian sleuth...Texas
❑ ❑   1 - Murder at Red Rook Ranch (1990)
❑ ❑   2 - The Hallelujah Murders (1991)
❑ ❑   . . . .
❑ ❑   . . . .

TEMPLE, Lou Jane

new

During her rock-concert catering days, Lou Jane Temple fed roadies, groupies, stagehands and stars backstage. For Pink Floyd she once served fried rice and egg rolls for a crew of 200 and a perfect English trifle for the band. When Temple hosted a 1997 brunch at New York's legendary James Beard House (a high honor for an American chef), she prepared scrambled eggs with truffles inspired by Nero Wolfe. Her culinary mysteries, complete with knock-out recipes, feature saucy red-headed chef and Kansas City café owner, Heaven Lee, introduced in *Death by Rhubarb* (1996). Starting with book 4, *Bread on Arrival* (1998), the series moved to hardcover, and Heaven will be up to her clever nose in soul food for book 5, *The Cornbread Killer* (1999). Married and pregnant at 13 and divorced at 22, Temple worked as a bridal consultant, radio host, artist's model, vintage clothing retailer and film script supervisor before opening her successful Kansas City restaurant, Café Lulu. A former food editor and restaurant critic she lives in Kansas City, Missouri.

Heaven Lee...trendy restaurant owner-chef...Kansas City, Missouri
❑ ❑   1 - Death by Rhubarb (1996)
❑ ❑   2 - Revenge of the Barbecue Queens (1997)
❑ ❑   3 - A Stiff Risotto (1997)
❑ ❑   4 - Bread on Arrival (1998)
❑ ❑   . . . .
❑ ❑   . . . .

■ TESLER, Nancy

new

Nancy Tesler is the creator of biofeedback clinician Carrie Carlin, a divorced single mother accused of murdering her ex-husband's gorgeous young fiancée in the series opener, *Pink Balloons and Other Deadly Things* (1997). While struggling with her new career, Carrie has two kids, three cats, a dog and one suspicious detective to contend with. In book 2, *Sharks, Jellyfish and Other Deadly Things* (1998), she's off to Key West when her best friend's husband disappears. When her elderly neighbor is the only witness to the murder of a local philanthropist, Carrie can't resist throwing herself into yet another case in book 3, *Shooting Stars and Other Deadly Things* (1999). Born and raised in Massachusetts, Tesler earned a B.F.A. in drama from Carnegie Mellon University. She has worked as a stage, film and television actor and has written for television and movies. Tesler's specialties as a biofeedback clinician include pain and stress-related conditions, and children with attention deficit disorder. She lives in New Jersey.

Carrie Carlin...single-mother biofeedback clinician...New Jersey
- ❏ ❏   1 - Pink Balloons and Other Deadly Things (1997)
- ❏ ❏   2 - Sharks, Jellyfish and Other Deadly Things (1998)
- ❏ ❏   3 - Shooting Stars and Other Deadly Things (1999)
- ❏ ❏   . . . .
- ❏ ❏   . . . .

■ THOMAS-GRAHAM, Pamela

Phi Beta Kappa Ivy Leaguer Pamela Thomas-Graham collected three degrees from Harvard (B.A. in economics, J.D., M.B.A.) before starting her climb at the international consulting firm, McKinsey & Company, where she became the first black woman partner. Still working 80-hour weeks, she serves on three charitable boards, plans to help her husband run for Congress, tends to their young child and writes mysteries, which she says relaxes her. Her fictional alter ego, introduced in *A Darker Shade of Crimson* (1998), is a young and flirty economics professor named Nikki Chase, who wields her black-bourgeoisie entitlement with "refreshing honesty," according to *Time* magazine. Nikki is on the case when her friend Ella, the black dean of students, dies in an apparent fall. With applause from both *Booklist* and *Kirkus* for her first adventure, the number-crunching professor moves to Yale for book 2, *Blue Blood* (1999). Thomas-Graham expects that Nikki will take on the entire Ivy League eventually. A Detroit native, she lives in New York.

Nikki Chase...black economics professor...Cambridge, Massachusetts
- ❏ ❏   1 - A Darker Shade of Crimson [Harvard] (1998)
- ❏ ❏   2 - Blue Blood [Yale] (1999)
- ❏ ❏   . . . .
- ❏ ❏   . . . .

■ THOMSON, June

June Thomson is second only to P.D. James "in the art of combining the puzzle story and the novel of character," said H.R.F. Keating in *Whodunnit? A Guide to Crime, Suspense, and Spy Fiction* (1982). As Thomson told *Contemporary Authors*, she is "interested in people, especially the outsider, in a closed community such as an English village and their behavior when faced with the ultimate crime." Her almost 20 novels feature deceptively mild-mannered Inspector Finch, who lives with his unmarried sister in Essex. For U.S. publication, the detective's name was changed to Inspector Rudd starting with book 2. Thomson has also written a number of books about Sherlock Holmes, including *Holmes and Watson: A Study in Friendship* (1995), and short story collections *The Secret Files of Sherlock Holmes* (1990), *The Secret Chronicles of Sherlock Holmes* (1992) and *The Secret Journals of Sherlock Holmes* (1993). Born in Kent, she earned a B.A. with honors from Bedford College, University of London, and taught English for 20 years before turning to mystery writing.

Inspector Finch (Inspector Rudd in the U.S.)...police inspector...Essex, England
- ❏ ❏   1 - Not One of Us (1971)
- ❏ ❏   2 - Death Cap (1973)
- ❏ ❏   3 - The Long Revenge (1974)
- ❏ ❏   4 - Case Closed (1977)
- ❏ ❏   5 - A Question of Identity (1977)
- ❏ ❏   6 - Deadly Relations (1979)
- ❏ ❏   - U.S.-The Habit of Loving
- ❏ ❏   7 - Alibi in Time (1980)
- ❏ ❏   8 - Shadow of a Doubt (1981)
- ❏ ❏   9 - To Make a Killing (1982)
- ❏ ❏   - U.S.-Portrait of Lilith
- ❏ ❏   10 - Sound Evidence (1984)
- ❏ ❏   11 - A Dying Fall (1985)
- ❏ ❏   12 - The Dark Stream (1986)

❑ ❑ 13 - No Flowers, By Request (1987)
❑ ❑ 14 - Rosemary for Remembrance (1988)
❑ ❑ 15 - The Spoils of Time (1989)
❑ ❑ 16 - Past Reckoning (1990)
❑ ❑ 17 - Foul Play (1991)
❑ ❑ 18 - Burden of Innocence (1996)
❑ ❑ . . . .
❑ ❑ . . . .

■ THRASHER, L.L. [P]

Written as L.L. Thrasher, Linda Baty's first novel, *Cat's-Paw, Inc.* (1991), features Oregon ex-cop private eye, Zachariah Smith, in search of a runaway teen in Portland. "A charming gumshoe" according to *Publishers Weekly*, Zack returns in *Dogsbody, Inc.* (1999), where he and a women doctor are hit by sniper-fire during an anti-abortion rally. Although Thrasher completed *Dogsbody, Inc.* in 1992, the book went unpublished for seven years. About the same time she sold *Charlie's Bones* (1998), introducing ex-truckstop wait-ress Lizbet Lange, whose rich, older husband dies, leaving her a fortune. Workers hired to build a swimming pool unearth the bones of a missing undercover cop, whose ghost asks Lizbet to solve his 30-year-old murder. *Booklist* liked the "intriguing juxtaposition of contemporary and 1960s society." Lizbet returns in *Charlie's Web* (2000). A librarian in Canby, Oregon, Thrasher once bagged an eight-point buck with her seven-year-old Nissan on a trip to Wal-Mart to buy her daughter a pink umbrella.

Lizbet Lange...millionaire ex-waitress...Oak Valley, California
❑ ❑ 1 - Charlie's Bones (1998)
❑ ❑ . . . .
❑ ❑ . . . .

Zachariah Smith...ex-cop private eye...Mackie, Oregon
❑ ❑ 1 - Cat's-Paw, Inc. (1991)
❑ ❑ 2 - Dogsbody, Inc. (1999)
❑ ❑ . . . .
❑ ❑ . . . .

■ THURLO, Aimée & David

Married over 20 years, Aimée and David Thurlo have been writing together for nearly that long, beginning with articles for a variety of publications. Together they have published 40 novels in more than 20 countries since 1981, primarily romance under Aimée's name, as well as the pseudonyms Aimée Martel and Aimée Duvall. Their mystery series, appearing under both their names, features Navajo F.B.I. agent Ella Clah, introduced in *Blackening Song* (1995) when Ella returns to the Navajo Nation after the murder of her minister father to find her brother the medicine man as the prime suspect. Book 5, *Shooting Chant*, is scheduled for 1999, with 6 and 7 coming in 2000 and 2001. While Aimée is a native of Cuba, David spent his first 17 years in Shiprock on the Navajo Indian Nation before leaving for the University of New Mexico. They live and write in Corrales, New Mexico. Recent romance titles include the "Four Winds" Trilogy: *Her Destiny*, *Her Hope* and *Her Shadow* (1997), *Redhawk's Heart* (1999) and *Redhawk's Return* (1999).

Ella Clah...Navajo FBI agent...Shiprock, New Mexico
❑ ❑ 1 - Blackening Song (1995)
❑ ❑ 2 - Death Walker (1996)
❑ ❑ 3 - Bad Medicine (1997)
❑ ❑ 4 - Enemy Way (1998)
❑ ❑ 5 - Shooting Chant (1999)
❑ ❑ . . . .
❑ ❑ . . . .

■ **TISHY, Cecelia [P]**

Vanderbilt University professor Cecelia Tichi writes mysteries as Cecelia Tishy, beginning with *Jealous Heart* (1997), introducing single mother Kate Banning. The former investigative reporter leaves Boston for Nashville and takes a staff writing job at a music company. In book 2, *Cryin' Time* (1998), a record-company executive asks her to check out rumors about a promising Cherokee singer. Along with teenage daughter Kelly and long-distance love interest, pilot Sam Powers, Kate returns in book 3, *Fall to Pieces* (2000). Published first by a small Nashville press, the three books are being re-released by Signet in 1999 and 2000. Among the author's numerous non-fiction titles as Cecelia Tichi are *Electronic Hearth* (1991), a study of American perceptions on television, *High Lonesome: The American Culture of Country Music* (1994), and *Reading Country Music* (1998). A native of Pittsburgh, Pennsylvania, she taught previously at Boston University before moving to Nashville, Tennessee in 1987. She teaches English and American studies at Vanderbilt.

Kate Banning...music company staff writer...Nashville, Tennessee

- ❑ ❑ 1 - Jealous Heart (1997)
- ❑ ❑ 2 - Cryin' Time (1998)
- ❑ ❑ . . . .
- ❑ ❑ . . . .

■ **TODD, Marilyn**

British author Marilyn Todd is the creator of a Roman mystery series featuring Claudia Seferius, hailed by the *Sunday Express* as "an arrogant superbitch who keeps us all on the edge where she loves to live." In the series opener, *I, Claudia* (1995), our heroine is trying to cover her gambling debts by offering 'personal services' to high-ranking Citizens. When her clients start turning up dead, the handsome investigating officer suspects Claudia. Upon the death of her much-older husband, Claudia inherits a wine business, instead of the gold she had hoped for in *Virgin Territory* (1996). To help pay her debts she agrees to chaperone a Vestal Virgin to Sicily. In book 3, *Man Eater* (1997), poor Claudia is being framed for murder and her vineyards threatened with arson. Book 4, *Wolf Whistle* (1998) will be followed by *Jail Bait* (1999). Born in Middlesex, Todd ran a secretarial business from her West Sussex home for ten years before turning to fiction. Thus far, her books are published only in Great Britain.

Claudia Seferius...13 B.C. superbitch...Rome, Italy

- ❑ ❑ 1 - I, Claudia (1995)
- ❑ ❑ 2 - Virgin Territory (1996)
- ❑ ❑ 3 - Man Eater (1997)
- ❑ ❑ 4 - Wolf Whistle (1998)
- ❑ ❑ . . . .
- ❑ ❑ . . . .

■ **TONE, Teona**

Former private investigator Teona (Tee-AH-na) Tone has written a pair of historical mysteries set at the turn-of-the-century, featuring Kyra Keaton, heir to one of America's great industrial fortunes. The aristocratic lady detective, who runs her own business in Washington, D.C., debuts in *Lady on the Line* (1983), a tale of murder and intrigue in the telephone industry. The sequel, *Full Cry* (1985), involves a Virginia fox hunting club, where a huntsman is killed in a strange accident just before the annual Race Day celebration. A native of Abilene, Texas, Tone earned a Ph.D. in 19th century literature from the University of California, where she also taught English. For eight years she was employed as a Los Angeles private investigator for Nick Harris Detectives and California Attorneys Investigators. A member of the Santa Ynez Valley Hunt Club, Tone is the author, with Deanna Sclar, of the non-fiction book *Housemates: How to Live with Other People*.

Kyra Keaton...turn-of-the-century P.I....Washington, District of Columbia

- ❑ ❑ 1 - Lady on the Line (1983)
- ❑ ❑ 2 - Full Cry (1985)
- ❑ ❑ . . . .
- ❑ ❑ . . . .

■ TRAVIS, Elizabeth

Former Reader's Digest book editor Elizabeth Travis is the creator of a pair of novels featuring amateur sleuths and mystery book publishers, Ben and Carrie Porter. Their quiet, genteel lifestyle in the artist's haven of Riverdale, Connecticut, is violently interrupted by a murder on Ben and Carrie's doorstep in *Under the Influence* (1989). When last seen in *Finders Keepers* (1990), the final manuscript of a dead literary agent has been divided into sections and bequeathed separately to different heirs. When someone starts eliminating the manuscript's new owners, Ben and Carrie must uncover a hidden plot. Travis has also written the non-series mystery *Deadlines* (1987). A former fashion coordinator for Burlington Industries, she served as editor of condensed books for Reader's Digest for almost 20 years. A native of Chicago, Illinois, Travis divides her time between Rowayton, Connecticut and Vero Beach, Florida.

Ben & Carrie Porter...husband & wife book publishers...Riverdale, Connecticut
- ❑ ❑ 1 - Under the Influence (1989)
- ❑ ❑ 2 - Finders Keepers (1990)
- ❑ ❑ ....
- ❑ ❑ ....

■ TROCHECK, Kathy Hogan

Five-time award nominee, Kathy Hogan Trocheck writes two Southern mystery series, beginning with her Anthony- and Macavity-nominated first novel, *Every Crooked Nanny* (1992). Burned-out ex-cop and part-time P.I., Julia Callahan Garrity, owns and operates the House Mouse cleaning service with her mother, Edna Mae. Among their mice are Baby and Sister, who together see and hear almost everything, even though one is almost blind and the other nearly deaf. Callahan and her crew take on their eighth case in *Irish Eyes* (2000). Trocheck's second series features retired wire-service reporter Truman Kicklighter, introduced in *Lickety-Split* (1996). An award-winning journalist, Trocheck spent 14 years as a newspaper reporter, primarily with the *Atlanta Journal-Constitution*. A journalism graduate of the University of Georgia, she also wrote for newspapers in her home state of Florida. Her suburban Atlanta backyard writing studio, featured in *Better Homes & Gardens* (September 1998), was constructed by her husband from a hut salvaged from the 1996 Olympics.

Callahan Garrity...ex-cop cleaning service operator...Atlanta, Georgia
- ❑ ❑ 1 - **Every Crooked Nanny (1992) Anthony & Macavity nominee** ☆☆
- ❑ ❑ 2 - **To Live and Die in Dixie (1993) Agatha, Anthony & Macavity nominee** ☆☆☆
- ❑ ❑ 3 - Homemade Sin (1994)
- ❑ ❑ 4 - Happy Never After (1995)
- ❑ ❑ 5 - Heart Trouble (1996)
- ❑ ❑ 6 - Strange Brew (1997)
- ❑ ❑ 7 - Midnight Clear (1998)
- ❑ ❑ ....
- ❑ ❑ ....

Truman Kicklighter...retired wire service reporter...St. Petersburg, Florida
- ❑ ❑ 1 - Lickety-Split (1996)
- ❑ ❑ 2 - Crash Course (1997)
- ❑ ❑ ....
- ❑ ❑ ....

■ TRUMAN, Margaret

Opera singer, radio and television host, and presidential daughter Margaret Truman published her first Capital Crimes mystery, *Murder in the White House*, in 1980. *Murder at the Library of Congress* (1999) is likely to become her 16th best-seller featuring a Washington, D.C. landmark, yet Truman did not introduce continuing protagonists until Mackenzie Smith and Annabel Reed appeared in book 9, *Murder at the Kennedy Center* (1989). Middle-aged law professor Mac Smith has plenty of friends among Washington's power elite, as does his love interest, attorney-turned-gallery-owner Annabel Reed. Their seventh and most recent case is

Murder at the Watergate (1998). Although *Contemporary Authors* credits Truman as sole author of the Capital Crimes mysteries, there are some who believe the books are the work of ghostwriter Donald Bain, co-author with the fictional Jessica Fletcher of close to a dozen "Murder, She Wrote" titles since 1994. Truman has also written biographies of father, *Harry S. Truman* (1972), and mother, *Bess W. Truman* (1986).

Mackenzie Smith & Annabel Reed...law professor & gallery owner...Washington, DC

- ❑ ❑ 1 - Murder at the Kennedy Center (1989)
- ❑ ❑ 2 - Murder at the National Cathedral (1990)
- ❑ ❑ 3 - Murder at the Pentagon (1992)
- ❑ ❑ 4 - Murder on the Potomac (1994)
- ❑ ❑ 5 - Murder at the National Gallery (1996)
- ❑ ❑ 6 - Murder in the House (1997)
- ❑ ❑ 7 - Murder at the Watergate (1998)
- ❑ ❑ ....
- ❑ ❑ ....

■ TUCKER, Kerry

Kerry Tucker is the creator of New York City photojournalist Libby Kincaid, lured back to her redneck Ohio hometown after the alleged suicide of her brother in the series opener, *Still Waters* (1991). When Libby is hired to photograph a legendary group of jazz tap dancers in *Cold Feet* (1992), she is arrested for stealing the victim's dancing shoes and assisting in his snakebite murder. The sleuthing photographer is back in Ohio, visiting her long-distance boyfriend in *Death Echo* (1993), when his old girlfriend's stepmother is fatally shot with an arrow. When last seen, Libby's in Boston, caught in the blizzard of the century, in what *Booklist* called "a honey of a book." The reviewer touted *Drift Away* (1994) as "chock-full of high-octane action, unexpected twists, and laugh-aloud humor." Tucker has also written *Greetings from New York—A Visit to Manhattan in Postcards* (1981) and *Greetings from Los Angeles* (1982). With husband Hal Morgan, she is the author of *Rumor!* (1984), *More Rumor!* and *Companies That Care* (1991).

Libby Kincaid...magazine photographer...New York, New York

- ❑ ❑ 1 - Still Waters (1991)
- ❑ ❑ 2 - Cold Feet (1992)
- ❑ ❑ 3 - Death Echo (1993)
- ❑ ❑ 4 - Drift Away (1994)
- ❑ ❑ ....
- ❑ ❑ ....

■ TYRE, Peg

Pulitzer Prize-winning journalist Peg Tyre has written two mysteries featuring novice crime reporter Kate Murray, first seen in *Strangers in the Night* (1994). When a Brooklyn nurse is murdered, Kate is on the killer's trail, along with homicide detective John Finn and a psychopathic informer. Book 2, *In the Midnight Hour* (1995), finds Detective Finn drunk and disgraced after a drug bust gone wrong. Tyre worked at *New York* magazine for five years before moving to Long Island's *Newsday*, where she covered the police beat and federal-level crime. For their coverage of the World Trade Center bombing, Tyre and three *Newsday* colleagues won a Pulitzer Prize and later wrote *Two Seconds Under the World* (1994), a detailed account of the 1993 event and its aftermath. She later covered criminal justice issues as a CNN correspondent, where she still consults. A graduate of Brown University, Tyre lives in New York where she is writing a historical suspense novel. She is married to Edgar-award-winning thriller writer Peter Blauner.

Kate Murray...novice crime reporter...Brooklyn, New York

- ❑ ❑ 1 - Strangers in the Night (1994)
- ❑ ❑ 2 - In the Midnight Hour (1995)
- ❑ ❑ ....
- ❑ ❑ ....

■ UHNAK, Dorothy

Edgar award-winner Dorothy Uhnak was a New York City transit cop for 14 years, 12 of them spent as detective second grade, before quitting the force in 1967 as a result of sex discrimination. Her first book was the semi-autobiographical *Policewoman: A Young Woman's Initiation into the Realities of Justice* (1964). Her second introduced Detective Second Grade Christie Opara in *The Bait* (1968), Edgar award winner for best first novel and inspiration for the 1974-75 T.V. series *Get Christie Love.* The final Opara title, *The Ledger* (1970), was awarded Le Grand Prix de Littérature Policière. But Uhnak's most compelling heroine, according to Marcia Muller (*1001 Midnights*), is 38-year-old Assistant District Attorney Lynne Jacobi, bureau chief of the Violent Sex Crimes Division and star of *False Witness* (1981). Uhnak's other best-selling police thrillers include *Law and Order* (1973), which became a 1975 television movie, and *The Investigation* (1987), filmed for television in 1987 as *Kojak: The Price of Justice.* Her most recent is *Codes of Betrayal* (1997).

Christine Opara...20-something police detective...New York, New York
- ❑ ❑ 1 - **The Bait (1968) Edgar winner ★**
- ❑ ❑ 2 - The Witness (1969)
- ❑ ❑ 3 - **The Ledger (1970) Le Grand Prix de Littérature Policière ★**
- ❑ ❑ . . . .
- ❑ ❑ . . . .

■ VALENTINE, Deborah

Two-time Edgar nominee Deborah Valentine is the creator of Lake Tahoe sheriff's-deputy-turned-novelist, Kevin Bryce, and artist Katharine Craig, who first meet in *Unorthodox Methods* (1989), when she is suspected of using a piece of sculpture as a murder weapon. Their second outing, *A Collector of Photographs* (1989), earned Valentine a trio of award nominations, including Edgar, Anthony and Shamus for best paperback original. Book 3, another Edgar nominee, takes the couple to a cosmopolitan Irish village outside Cork City, where Bryce's writing partner, James Parnismus, had docked his 33-foot Hans Christian cutter. A friend to Katharine since childhood, James is the link between Kevin and the moody sculptress. Despite a rumor that he's the head of the C.I.A. in Ireland, the ex-deputy finds himself working with Special Branch when Katharine disappears. American-born Valentine, who previously pursued wine and gardening interests in a small port town between San Francisco and the Napa Valley, lives in London.

Katharine Craig & Kevin Bryce...sculptor & ex-sheriff's detective...Lake Tahoe, California
- ❑ ❑ 1 - Unorthodox Methods (1989)
- ❑ ❑ 2 - **A Collector of Photographs (1989) Anthony, Edgar & Shamus nominee ☆☆☆**
- ❑ ❑ 3 - **Fine Distinctions (1991) Edgar nominee☆**
- ❑ ❑ . . . .
- ❑ ❑ . . . .

■ VAN GIESON, Judith

Shamus nominee Judith Van Gieson has written eight novels featuring hard-boiled attorney-investigator Neil Hamel, a women passionate about the environment, red-hot salsa and Cuervo Gold. Neil's accordion-playing auto mechanic (and lover) calls her Chiquita. She calls him the Kid. Their fifth adventure, *The Lies That Bind* (1993), was a best-novel Shamus nominee. In their final appearance, *Ditch Rider* (1998), Neil defends a 13-year-old girl who claims to have shot a teenage gang member. Van Gieson launches a new paperback series in 2000, featuring 50-something Claire Reynier (ray-NEER), a librarian at the University of New Mexico's Center for Southwest Research. The plots revolve around rare books, stolen artifacts, forgeries and New Mexico history. In addition to her mysteries, Van Gieson has published a collection of short stories and poetry and ghost-written a *Choose Your Own Adventure* book. A graduate of Northwestern University, she lives in Albuquerque's North Valley.

Neil Hamel...attorney & investigator...Albuquerque, New Mexico
- ❑ ❑ 1 - North of the Border (1988)
- ❑ ❑ 2 - Raptor (1990)

❏	❏	3 - The Other Side of Death (1991)
❏	❏	4 - The Wolf Path (1992)
❏	❏	**5 - The Lies That Bind (1993) Shamus nominee** ☆
❏	❏	6 - Parrot Blues (1995)
❏	❏	7 - Hotshots (1996)
❏	❏	8 - Ditch Rider (1998)
❏	❏	. . . .
❏	❏	. . . .

■ VAN HOOK, Beverly

Beverly Van Hook cleverly weaves history, geography and math into her Supergranny children's mysteries, set in a fictional Mississippi River community much like Quad-Cities, Illinois, where she lived for many years. Her septuagenarian crime-fighter, Sadie Geraldine Oglepop, drives a red Ferrari, and is ably assisted by the Poindexter kids; Shackleford, the old-English Sheepdog; and Chesterton, the spoiled mini-robot. Their most recent case, *The Villainous Vicar* (1996), takes the gang to England for a hilarious punt boat chase in Cambridge and daring rescue at an abbey on the Yorkshire Moors. Van Hook's first adult mystery, *Fiction, Fact & Murder* (1995), introduces Liza and Dutch Randolph, married, middle-aged amateur detectives in Van Hook's home state of West Virginia. Coincidentally, Liza Randolph writes Supergramps mysteries featuring a gray-haired sleuth in a yellow Lamborghini. Van Hook recently completed the screenplay for book 2, *Juliet's Ghost* (1999). She and her husband live in Charlottesville, Virginia, with the real Shackleford.

Liza & Dutch Randolph...married amateur sleuths...West Virginia

❏	❏	1 - Fiction, Fact, & Murder (1995)
❏	❏	2 - Juliet's Ghost (1999)
❏	❏	. . . .
❏	❏	. . . .

■ VIETS, Elaine

Syndicated newspaper columnist Elaine Viets (VEETS) is one of the few outsiders who has attended the annual St. Louis biker society ball, where 1000 Harley owners party hearty at the Casa Loma ballroom. Viets puts her experience judging "best in leather" and "best in lace" to good use in *Rubout* (1998), the second Francesca Vierling mystery. The 6-foot-tall St. Louis newspaper columnist is named for Viets' 5-foot, 200-pound grandmother who always wanted to be tall and thin. A former reporter for the *St. Louis Post-Dispatch*, Viets has hosted the nationally-syndicated radio show, "The Travel Holiday Magazine" and a local television program for which she won two regional Emmy awards. She is the author of *How to Commit Monogamy* (1997), *Images of St. Louis* (1996) and *St. Louis: Home on the River*. When Viets lived on Capitol Hill, her dishwasher was repaired by the same man who fixed Al Gore's washing machine. She and her author husband, Don Crinklaw, currently live on Florida's Hollywood Beach.

Francesca Vierling...6-ft. newspaper columnist...St. Louis, Missouri

❏	❏	1 - Backstab (1997)
❏	❏	2 - Rubout (1998)
❏	❏	3 - The Pink Flamingo Murders (1999)
❏	❏	4 - Home Wrecker (2000)
❏	❏	. . . .
❏	❏	. . . .

■ WAKEFIELD, Hannah [P]

Hannah Wakefield is the shared pseudonym of Sarah Burton and Judith Holland, American women who visited London in the early 1970s and decided to stay. One is a former editor who divides her time between writing and teaching, the other a practicing attorney who collaborates on story lines and characters. Their crime thrillers, beginning with *The Price You Pay* (1987), feature American lawyer Dee Street, partner in the all-women London firm of Aspinall Street. When her expert witness in another case is suspected of murdering his well-known journalist-wife and a young Chilean exile, Dee works to prove the man's innocence. "Lively, entertaining and legally accurate," said a *Guardian* reviewer. When last seen in book 3, *Cruel April* (1996), the London solicitor is being framed for the murder of a long-time friend who owes the financially-strapped law firm a lot of money and has refused to pay. "Witty, thrilling and compulsive," said the *Tribune*. "Riveting," proclaimed the *London Review of Books*.

Dee Street...solicitor in an all-women firm...London, England

❑ ❑	1 -	The Price You Pay (1987)
❑ ❑	2 -	A February Mourning (1990)
❑ ❑	-	U.S.-A Woman's Own Mystery
❑ ❑	3 -	Cruel April (1996)
❑ ❑		. . . .
❑ ❑		. . . .

■ WALKER, Mary Willis

Mary Willis Walker's award-winning first mystery featured Texas dog trainer Kate Driscoll in *Zero at the Bone* (1991). This first novel was an Agatha and Macavity award-winner and an Edgar nominee for best first mystery. Expecting a reunion with her long-estranged father, Kate arrives at the Austin Zoo where he is senior keeper of large cats, only to find he has been mauled to death by a tiger. Although Walker had planned to make Kate a series character, the debut of true-crime magazine reporter Molly Cates in the Edgar award-winning *The Red Scream* (1994) changed all that. Molly's second appearance, in the triple award-winning *Under the Beetle's Cellar* (1995), finds her negotiating the release of 11 Texas school children and a bus driver, held hostage by a crazed cult leader. The "superbly orchestrated final act will leave readers cheering, weeping, and gasping for breath," said *Publishers Weekly*. A graduate of Duke University, Walker taught high school for more than ten years. She lives in Austin, Texas.

Molly Cates...true crime writer-reporter...Austin, Texas

❑ ❑	1 -	**The Red Scream (1994) Edgar winner ★ Macavity nominee ☆**
❑ ❑	2 -	**Under the Beetle's Cellar (1995) Anthony, Hammett & Macavity winner ★★★**
❑ ❑	3 -	All the Dead Lie Down (1998)
❑ ❑		. . . .
❑ ❑		. . . .

■ WALLACE, Marilyn

Best known as an author of suspense thrillers, Marilyn Wallace launched her fiction-writing career with a Macavity award-winning police series featuring Oakland, California homicide detectives, Jay Goldstein and Carlos Cruz, introduced in *A Case of Loyalties* (1986). Twice-nominated for Anthony awards, the books in this series offer three points of view—those of the two detectives and that of a woman whose life is suddenly disrupted by criminal events beyond her control. A female police detective named Teresa Gallagher, who appears briefly in *Lost Angel* (1996) and *Current Danger* (1998), was engaged to marry Jay Goldstein from Wallace's earlier books. Editor of the five-volume *Sisters in Crime* anthologies, Wallace is co-editor with Robert J. Randisi of *Deadly Allies* (1992), a collaborative anthology of Private Eye Writers of America and Sisters in Crime. Daughter of a New York City police officer, Wallace was born in Brooklyn. A resident of New York City, she has also lived in Northern California and Upstate New York.

Jay Goldstein & Carlos Cruz...homicide detectives...Oakland, California

❑ ❑	1 -	**A Case of Loyalties (1986) Macavity winner ★**
❑ ❑	2 -	**Primary Target (1988) Anthony nominee ☆**
❑ ❑	3 -	**A Single Stone (1991) Anthony nominee ☆**
❑ ❑		. . . .
❑ ❑		. . . .

■ WALLACE, Patricia

A former freelance story analyst for NBC, Patricia Wallace has written 17 novels, including four featuring San Diego P.I. Sydney Bryant, who takes a baffling missing persons case in *Small Favors* (1988). When a friend's daughter finds the body of a murdered classmate at her private school, Sydney investigates in *Deadly Grounds* (1989). She puzzles over why an heiress is working at a small-town newspaper when a routine background check leads to murder in *Blood Lies* (1991). In her Shamus-nominated last appearance, Sydney finds a crucial piece of evidence overlooked by police in their haste to arrest a philandering husband for his wife's murder in *Deadly Devotion* (1994). Among Wallace's suspense thrillers are *Dark Intent* (1995) and *Fatal Outcome* (1992). After earning degrees in police science and film, Wallace is studying law at the University of Idaho in Moscow. She told her contracts professor that with so many attorneys invading the book world, it seemed only fair that at least one writer infiltrate the legal community.

Sydney Bryant...private investigator...San Diego, California
- ❑ ❑ 1 - Small Favors (1988)
- ❑ ❑ 2 - Deadly Grounds (1989)
- ❑ ❑ 3 - Blood Lies (1991)
- ❑ ❑ **4 - Deadly Devotion (1994) Shamus nominee** ☆
- ❑ ❑ . . . .
- ❑ ❑ . . . .

■ WALLINGFORD, Lee

Lee Wallingford has written two mysteries featuring U.S. Forest Service security officer, Frank Carver, and fire-dispatch ranger and young widow, Ginny Trask, working in the Neskanie National Forest on the central Oregon coast. Introduced in *Cold Tracks* (1991), Carver and Trask are investigating the death of a Christmas-tree plantation worker, while contending with fires, blackmail and office politics. "A promising debut, with interesting scenic detail and an engaging pair of sleuths," said *Kirkus Reviews*. In book 2, *Clear-Cut Murder* (1993), Ginny and Frank are up against radical environmentalists, local developers and Washington lawmakers, while their May-December romance heats up. With Carol Deppe, Wallingford co-authored the science fiction novel, *Special Delivery* (1989). Currently a school librarian and media specialist, Wallingford worked for six years as a forestry technician in Oregon's Siuslaw National Forest. Born in Montreal, Quebec, she lives in Milton-Freewater, Oregon.

Ginny Trask & Frank Carver...U.S. Forest Service officers...Oregon
- ❑ ❑ 1 - Cold Tracks (1991)
- ❑ ❑ 2 - Clear-Cut Murder (1993)
- ❑ ❑ . . . .
- ❑ ❑ . . . .

■ WALTCH, Lilla M.

Lilla M. Waltch is the creator of Braeton, Massachusetts newspaper reporter, Lisa Davis, featured in a pair of mysteries published during the late 1980s, *The Third Victim* (1987) and *Fearful Symmetry* (1988). Waltch is also the author of two books for young adults, *Miss Starr's Secret* (1957) and *Cave of the Incas* (1968). She earned a B.A. from Radcliffe College, an M.A. from Boston College and a Ph.D. from Brandeis University, where her doctoral dissertation was a study of the contemporaneity of the past and present in James Joyce's *Ulysses*. Born in Boston, she lives in Cambridge, Massachusetts.

Lisa Davis...newspaper reporter...Braeton, Massachusetts
- ❑ ❑ 1 - The Third Victim (1987)
- ❑ ❑ 2 - Fearful Symmetry (1988)
- ❑ ❑ . . . .
- ❑ ❑ . . . .

■ WARMBOLD, Jean

Jean Warmbold has written three San Francisco mysteries featuring magazine journalist Sarah Calloway, beginning with *June Mail* (1986) and *The White Hand* (1988). When last seen in *The Third Way* (1989), Sarah has flown to Paris with the hope of buying an important journal at auction. A mysterious Arab bidder named Assam offers his help but dies the next morning, an apparent suicide. Sarah is accused of collusion with Assam, who turns out to be a noted terrorist. The rapidly escalating intrigue involves her with the French police and secret service, the P.L.O., the Abu Nidal and the Mossad. "Ambushes, kidnapping, and political commentary culminate in a realistically described cave confrontation," according to the *Library Journal* reviewer, who concluded the book is "deftly concocted, mostly interesting, and well written." Warmbold has also written *Dead Man Running* (1989).

Sarah Calloway...magazine journalist...San Francisco, California
- ❑ ❑ 1 - June Mail (1986)
- ❑ ❑ 2 - The White Hand (1988)
- ❑ ❑ 3 - The Third Way (1989)
- ❑ ❑ . . . .
- ❑ ❑ . . . .

■ WARNER, Mignon

Mignon Warner has written seven books featuring British clairvoyant Edwina Charles. The series debut, published first in England as *A Nice Way To Die* (1976), appeared in the U.S. as *A Medium for Murder* (1977). Beginning with book 3, *The Girl Who Was Clairvoyant* (1982), the series was published first in the U.S. by Doubleday Crime Club. After travelling to Cornwall in book 3 to consult with a client whose cards she had read 25 years earlier, Mrs. Charles goes to Wales to assist an old friend, insurance investigator David Sayer, in book 4, *Death in Time* (1982). When last seen in book 7, *Speak No Evil* (1985), Mrs. Charles is investigating the death of a young female private detective who had consulted a prominent spiritualist in search of a cure for her migraine headaches. Mrs. Charles sees a possible connection to convicted murderer Rendell Pym, who supposedly died years ago. A native of Australia, Warner lives in England where she has worked with her husband in the design and manufacture of apparatus for magic.

Edwina Charles...British clairvoyant...England
- ❑ ❑ 1 - A Nice Way To Die (1976)
- ❑ ❑   - U.S.-A Medium for Murder
- ❑ ❑ 2 - The Tarot Murders (1978)
- ❑ ❑ 3 - The Girl Who Was Clairvoyant (1982)
- ❑ ❑ 4 - Death in Time (1982)
- ❑ ❑ 5 - Devil's Knell (1983)
- ❑ ❑ 6 - Illusion (1984)
- ❑ ❑ 7 - Speak No Evil (1985)
- ❑ ❑ . . . .
- ❑ ❑ . . . .

■ WARNER, Penny

Author of more than 25 books, Penny Warner writes mysteries featuring deaf reporter Connor Westphal, introduced in the Macavity award-winning, Agatha-nominated *Dead Body Language* (1997). An ex-*Chronicle* reporter from San Francisco, Connor moves to California Gold Country and launches her weekly newspaper in the tourist town of Flat Skunk. *Publishers Weekly* especially liked "Connor's spunky first-person narrative," and pronounced book 2, *Sign of Foul Play*, "delicious." Connor is scheduled to return in *Quiet Undertaking* (2000) and *Blind Spot* (2001). With a B.A. in child development and an M.A. in special education, Warner published the first of her 20 books on feeding and entertaining children, *Healthy Snacks for Kids* (1983), available in a new 1999 edition. She teaches child development, sign language and creative writing at California colleges and universities and has written for numerous publications, including a weekly newspaper column for 11 years. With husband Tom she writes and produces mystery entertainment events.

Connor Westphal...deaf reporter and newspaper owner...Flat Skunk, California

- ❏ ❏ 1 - **Dead Body Language (1997) Macavity winner ★ Agatha nominee ☆**
- ❏ ❏ 2 - Sign of Foul Play (1998)
- ❏ ❏ 3 - Right To Remain Silent (1998)
- ❏ ❏ ....
- ❏ ❏ ....

■ WATERHOUSE, Jane

Former theatrical agent Jane Waterhouse wrote award-winning plays and television scripts before starting a career developing industrial shows and multi-media presentations for major corporations. For more than ten years she was the most sought-after corporate writer on the East Coast, with clients ranging from American Express to Volvo. With the publication of her first novel, the standalone mystery *Playing for Keeps* (1988), Waterhouse traded corporate assignments for novel writing. She has since published three mysteries featuring best-selling true-crime writer Garner Quin, introduced in *Graven Images* (1995). When last seen in *Dead Letter* (1998), Garner is being inundated with mail from an obsessed fan, sent to the remote, unlisted Jersey-shore estate she shares with her daughter and housekeeper. Next from Waterhouse is a non-Quinn thriller, *Running Gear*. A communications graduate of Seton Hall University, she earned an M.F.A. in theatre at Rutgers University. Waterhouse lives in Fair Haven, New Jersey.

Garner Quin...best-selling true crime writer...Spring Lake, New Jersey

- ❏ ❏ 1 - Graven Images (1995)
- ❏ ❏ 2 - Shadow Walk (1997)
- ❏ ❏ 3 - Dead Letter (1998)
- ❏ ❏ ....
- ❏ ❏ ....

■ WATSON, Clarissa

Art expert Clarissa Watson has written five mysteries featuring 36-year-old art curator and gallery assistant, Persis Willum, whose adventures involve Long Island high society and the international art world. "Watson's writing, like her heroine, is witty and stylish, and her plot is full of surprises," said Marcia Muller of the series opener, *The Fourth Stage of Gainsborough Brown* (1977). A flamboyant painter drowns in the swimming pool during a birthday party for Persis' Aunt Lydie. Armed with a sketch pad, Persis travels to Manhattan and Paris during her investigation of the man's suspicious death. Co-founder and director of a Long Island gallery, Watson has founded and directed an art school, arranged film festivals and served as Adelphi University's art consultant for several years. She also edited a collection of gourmet recipes from artists around the world, *The Sensuous Carrot* (1972). An honors graduate of Milwaukee Downer College, she attended Layton Art School. Born in Ashland, Wisconsin, she lives on Long Island.

Persis Willum...artist and gallery assistant...Long Island, New York

- ❏ ❏ 1 - The Fourth Stage of Gainsborough Brown (1977)
- ❏ ❏ 2 - The Bishop in the Back Seat (1980)
- ❏ ❏ 3 - Runaway (1985)
- ❏ ❏ 4 - Last Plane From Nice (1988)
- ❏ ❏ 5 - Somebody Killed the Messenger (1988)
- ❏ ❏ ....
- ❏ ❏ ....

■ WEBB, Martha G. [P]

Martha G. Webb is a byline of Anne Wingate, former law enforcement officer and fingerprint expert, who writes fiction as Lee Martin and both fiction and nonfiction under her own name. As Martha G. Webb she published three mysteries during the mid '80s, including two small-town police procedurals with narcotics officer Smoky O'Donnell. The action takes place in north central Texas, in a fictional community called Farmer's Mound, where O'Donnell recruits Tommy Inman as his assistant. Wingate wrote three books in the series but only the second and third were published. Her standalone Webb mystery, *Darling*

Corey's Dead (1984), was intended to be a series but her publisher declined. Eventually she overhauled the plot and reused it in her Deb Ralston series, featuring a Ft. Worth police officer and mother. A former intelligence specialist with the Naval Reserve, Wingate was born in Savannah, Georgia. She lives in Salt Lake City, where she teaches writing at the University of Utah and the Writer's Digest School.

Smoky O'Donnell...small-town PD narcotics officer...Farmer's Mound, Texas

- ❏ ❏ 1 - A White Male Running (1985)
- ❏ ❏ 2 - Even Cops' Daughters (1986)
- ❏ ❏ ....
- ❏ ❏ ....

■ WEBER, Janice

Concert pianist Janice Weber first played Carnegie Hall at age nine. A summa cum laude graduate of the Eastman School of Music, she has performed with the Boston Pops and New York Philharmonic, and is one of only two living pianists included in a compendium of historic performances by 19 legendary artists. While in Beijing on tour in 1997, she ate fried scorpion and drank turtle's blood, so it's no surprise she has created secret agent and concert violinist Leslie Frost (code name: Smith), first seen in *Frost the Fiddler* (1992). "A virtuoso manipulation of superspy elements; very, very funny indeed," said *Kirkus*. Frost plays for the President in *Hot Ticket* (1998) and then finds one of her spy sisters (code name: Barnard) dead in a sumptuous suite at the Watergate. Weber has also written *The Secret Life of Eve Hathaway* (1985), *Customs Violation* (1987) and *Devil's Food* (1995). A member of the piano faculty at the Boston Conservatory, she shops for fabric on Seventh Avenue and reads dictionaries for relaxation.

Leslie Frost...secret agent and concert violinist...Washington, District of Columbia

- ❏ ❏ 1 - Frost the Fiddler (1992)
- ❏ ❏ 2 - Hot Ticket (1998)
- ❏ ❏ ....
- ❏ ❏ ....

■ WEIR, Charlene

Kansas native Charlene Weir (rhymes with cheer) worked and studied in the public health field in Oklahoma before moving to Northern California. Her detective, small-town police chief Susan Wren, has moved in the opposite direction, from California to Kansas, where she is suddenly widowed in the Agatha award-winning, Anthony-nominated series opener, *The Winter Widow* (1992). This first novel was published after winning the St. Martin's Press/Malice Domestic contest for best first traditional mystery in 1991. When last seen in book 4, *Murder Takes Two* (1998), Chief Wren and her department are suffering the disruptions of a Hollywood crew filming *Lethal Promise*. "Two diversionary subplots (one involving a mystery artist who draws erotic graffiti on trash), which are woven in with the murder, make the book's climax a surprise," said *Booklist*. The paperback reprint of *Murder Takes Two* is part of a three-piece collection titled *Murder at the Movies* (1999). Weir lives in Northern California.

Susan Wren...ex-cop turned police chief...Hampstead, Kansas

- ❏ ❏ 1 - **The Winter Widow (1992) SMP/MD & Agatha winner** ★★
  Anthony nominee ☆
- ❏ ❏ 2 - **Consider the Crows (1993) Anthony nominee** ☆
- ❏ ❏ 3 - Family Practice (1995)
- ❏ ❏ 4 - Murder Takes Two (1998)
- ❏ ❏ ....
- ❏ ❏ ....

■ WELCH, Pat

Pat Welch has written seven mysteries featuring Berkeley private eye, Helen Black, a lesbian ex-cop, introduced in *Murder by the Book* (1990). It's Christmas in Berkeley and Helen has her first homicide case—a bank employee is found dead in the vault with only $200 missing. Helen returns to her Mississippi roots to claim an inheritance and confront the father who disowned her in *Open House* (1995). A downsized corporate executive and closeted lesbian dies in a fall and Helen is hired to prove it was not an accident in *Fall from Grace* (1998). When last seen in book 7, *Snake Eyes* (1999), Helen has closed her office and is planning a casino weekend to help her forget. "A captivating writer who builds a convincing story to an exciting climax," says *Booklist*. Born in Japan, Welch grew up in several small Southern towns and later moved to Florida. After graduating from college in Southern California with a degree in English, she moved to the East Bay region of San Francisco where she currently lives and works.

Helen Black...ex-cop lesbian private eye...Berkeley, California

❏	❏	1 - Murder by the Book (1990)
❏	❏	2 - Still Waters (1992)
❏	❏	3 - A Proper Burial (1993)
❏	❏	4 - Open House (1995)
❏	❏	5 - Smoke and Mirrors (1996)
❏	❏	6 - Fallen From Grace (1998)
❏	❏	. . . .
❏	❏	. . . .

■ WELLS, Tobias [P]

Tobias Wells is one of the pseudonyms of DeLoris Florine Stanton Forbes who also wrote as Stanton Forbes and Forbes Rydell. Her series detective, Massachusetts cop Knute Severson, starred in 16 cases from 1966 to 1988, including his trip to the Caribbean island of St. Martin in *Hark, Hark, The Watchdogs Bark* (1975). Knute helps out his next-door neighbor, mystery writer Mercy Bird, after she moves to the estate of a Countess and finds trouble in *Have Mercy Upon Us* (1974). He cracks the case over the phone. "Good humor, fine characterization, and careful attention to detail make even the more improbable of Wells' novels readable," said Ellen Nehr in *1001 Midnights* (1986). As Stanton Forbes, the author's 22 nonseries novels include *If Laurel Shot Hardy the World Would End* (1970). Thirteen sad-faced Laurels adorn the wonderful orange dust jacket. A native of Kansas City, Forbes spent 15 years as assistant editor of the *Wellesley Townsman*. Since 1974 she has lived on St. Martin, where she and her husband own Pierre Lapin clothing shop.

Knute Severson...police officer...Boston, Massachusetts

❏	❏	1 - A Matter of Love and Death (1966)
❏	❏	2 - What Should You Know of Dying? (1967)
❏	❏	3 - Dead by the Light of the Moon (1967)
❏	❏	4 - Murder Most Fouled Up (1968)
❏	❏	5 - Die Quickly, Dear Mother (1969)
❏	❏	6 - The Young Can Die Protesting (1969)
❏	❏	7 - Dinky Died (1970)
❏	❏	8 - The Foo Dog (1971)
❏	❏	- Brit.-The Lotus Affair
❏	❏	9 - What To Do Until the Undertaker Comes (1971)
❏	❏	10 - How To Kill a Man (1972)
❏	❏	11 - A Die in the Country (1972)
❏	❏	12 - Brenda's Murder (1973)
❏	❏	13 - Have Mercy Upon Us (1974)
❏	❏	14 - Hark, Hark, the Watchdogs Bark (1975)
❏	❏	15 - A Creature Was Stirring (1977)
❏	❏	16 - Of Graves, Worms and Epitaphs (1988)
❏	❏	. . . .
❏	❏	. . . .

■ WENDER, Theodora

Classics professor Theodora Wender wrote "punny" stories while relearning to speak following a stroke and published two paperback mysteries as a result. With *Knight Must Fall* (1985) she introduced witty, pretty and wise English professor, Glad Gold, and smart, sexy and single Chief of Police, Alden Chase. It's springtime at Turnbull College in Massachusetts and college president Henderson N. Knight has made a number of people mad enough to kill. When one of them does, Gold and Chase join forces to track a killer. In *Murder*

Gets a Degree (1986) eccentric, old, rich alumnus, Adah Storm, dies in a suspicious Halloween fire that destroys her historic, run-down house just off campus. Chief Chase suspects arson and he and Gold have more than the usual suspects—a coven of witches led by a pretty coed, a visiting professor with a chilling interest in horror writer H.P. Lovecraft, and an archaeologist who digs erotic encounters. Wender has taught Latin, Greek and ancient history at Wheaton College in Norton, Massachusetts.

Glad Gold & Alden Chase...English professor & police chief...Wading River, Massachusetts

- ❑ ❑ 1 - Knight Must Fall (1985)
- ❑ ❑ 2 - Murder Gets a Degree (1986)
- ❑ ❑ ....
- ❑ ❑ ....

■ WESLEY, Valerie Wilson

Former *Essence* magazine executive editor Valerie Wilson Wesley is the creator of black private eye Tamara Hayle, a single parent and ex-cop in Newark, New Jersey, introduced in the Shamus-nominated *When Death Comes Stealing* (1994). The *Denver Post* called Wesley's P.I. "a wonderfully believable and independent sleuth who combines intellect and intuition, sexiness, and self-control, tenderness and toughness." Wesley's latest, the nonmystery *Ain't Nobody's Business If I Do* (1999), has a "consistently sharp, honest voice,"

said *Publishers Weekly*. A former associate editor at *Scholastic News*, Wesley has also written books for children and young adults, including *Freedom's Gifts: A Juneteenth Story* (1997), "a sprinter of a tale that takes off running and never slows," said *The New York Times*. A graduate of Howard University, she holds master's degrees in journalism and education from Columbia University and Bank Street College of Education. Wesley and her screenwriter-playwright husband are the parents of two grown daughters.

Tamara Hayle...black ex-cop single-mother P.I....Newark, New Jersey

- ❑ ❑ 1 - **When Death Comes Stealing (1994) Shamus nominee** ☆
- ❑ ❑ 2 - Devil's Gonna Get Him (1995)
- ❑ ❑ 3 - Where Evil Sleeps (1996)
- ❑ ❑ 4 - No Hiding Place (1997)
- ❑ ❑ 5 - Easier To Kill (1998)
- ❑ ❑ ....
- ❑ ❑ ....

■ WESTFALL, Patricia Tichenor

While recovering from a 1994 back injury, Patricia Tichenor Westfall read so many mysteries she decided to write one. The result was *Fowl Play* (1996), introducing 52-year-old mother-of-two Molly West, associate director of a hot-meals delivery program in rural southeastern Ohio. Her detecting sidekick is Louella Chalmers Benton, a coal miner's widow and former county commissioner in her mid-70s. When Molly's daughter announces her intention to marry during a Civil War enactment, a second murder investigation is not on her to-do list in *Mother of the*

Bride (1998). Westfall's nonfiction books include a 1994 guide to magazine feature-writing, and *Real Farm* (1989), an essay collection chosen for *500 Great Books by Women*. She teaches magazine editing and production, information gathering and feature writing at Ohio University, where she is professor of journalism. A former contributing editor and columnist for *Savvy* magazine, Westfall earned her master's degree in journalism from Columbia University. She lives in Athens, Ohio.

Molly West...50-something rural activist...Southern Ohio

- ❑ ❑ 1 - Fowl Play (1996)
- ❑ ❑ 2 - Mother of the Bride (1998)
- ❑ ❑ ....
- ❑ ❑ ....

■ WESTON, Carolyn

Hollywood native Carolyn Weston wrote three novels featuring Santa Monica police detectives Casey Kellog and Al Krug, an ex-surfer college-grad and his hard-bitten, street-wise veteran partner. Book 1, *Poor, Poor Ophelia* (1972), inspired the 1975 pilot film for the long-running television series, *The Streets of San Francisco*, starring Michael Douglas and Karl Malden. Still in syndication more than 20 years later, the hour-long episodes continue to run, with credits to Carolyn Weston as the characters' creator. When last seen in book 3, *Rouse the Demon* (1976), Casey Kellog is tempted to trade his badge for a surfboard when their second homicide in two weeks turns up a dead hypnotist. Her nonseries novel set in West Africa, *Danju Gig* (1969), was published in England as *Spy in Black* (1972). After working in an aircraft plant during World War II, Weston gypsied around the country, working at a Reno gambling club, a New Orleans nightclub, and Prentice-Hall and Lord & Taylor in New York City. She lives in California.

Casey Kellog & Al Krug...college-grad cop & hard-bitten partner...Santa Monica, California

- ❑ ❑   1 - Poor, Poor Ophelia (1972)
- ❑ ❑   2 - Susannah Screaming (1975)
- ❑ ❑   3 - Rouse the Demon (1976)
- ❑ ❑   . . . .
- ❑ ❑   . . . .

■ WHEAT, Carolyn

A former N.Y.P.D. staff attorney and public defender, two-time Edgar nominee Carolyn Wheat is the creator of Brooklyn Legal Aid defense attorney Cass Jameson, introduced in *Dead Man's Thoughts* (1983), a best-first Edgar nominee. Cass successfully defends a client who turns out to be a stalker in book 6, *Sworn To Defend* (1998). "Of all the legal eagles nesting in the thriller trees these days, Carolyn Wheat is definitely the one with the brightest feathers," said Dick Adler for *Amazon.com*. A four-time award winner for best short story, Wheat has earned Agatha, Anthony, Shamus and Macavity awards in this category. Her "Too Many Midnights" appears in *Murder on Route 66* (1999), an anthology Wheat conceived and edited. A native of Green Bay, Wisconsin, she earned B.A. and J.D. degrees at the University of Toledo. She has taught novel-writing as artist-in-residence at the University of Central Oklahoma, mystery writing at New York City's New School and legal writing at Brooklyn Law School. She lives in Southern California.

Cass Jameson...Legal Aid defense attorney...Brooklyn, New York

- ❑ ❑   1 - **Dead Man's Thoughts (1983) Edgar nominee** ☆
- ❑ ❑   2 - Where Nobody Dies (1986)
- ❑ ❑   3 - Fresh Kills (1995)
- ❑ ❑   4 - **Mean Streak (1996) Edgar nominee** ☆
- ❑ ❑   5 - Troubled Waters (1997)
- ❑ ❑   6 - Sworn To Defend (1998)
- ❑ ❑   . . . .
- ❑ ❑   . . . .

■ WHITE, Gloria

Six-time award nominee Gloria White is the creator of bi-cultural (Mexican-Anglo) San Francisco P.I. and security expert Ronnie (Veronica) Ventana, introduced in the Anthony award-nominated *Murder on the Run* (1991). The daughter of famed cat burglars, Ronnie is a pro at compromising alarm systems. In the triple-nominated third installment, she agrees to test the alarm system of a house in Presidio Heights, only to be accused of murder when a U.S. senator is found dead upstairs. When last seen in the Edgar and Shamus award-nominated *Sunset and Santiago* (1997), she is keeping a midnight vigil on the 20th anniversary of her parents' fatal car crash at the corner of Sunset and Santiago. After witnessing a body being dumped, she's up to her ears in a new case with ties to the past. Armed with a degree in economics, White has conducted computer background searches, worked in an equine veterinary clinic and investigated employment discrimination complaints for the government. Like her fictional creation, she lives in San Francisco.

Veronica 'Ronnie' Ventana...Anglo-Mexican private eye...San Francisco, California

❏ ❏ 1 - **Murder on the Run (1991) Anthony nominee** ☆
❏ ❏ 2 - Money To Burn (1993)
❏ ❏ 3 - **Charged With Guilt (1995) Anthony, Edgar & Shamus nominee** ☆☆☆
❏ ❏ 4 - **Sunset and Santiago (1997) Edgar & Shamus nominee** ☆☆
❏ ❏ . . . .
❏ ❏ . . . .

■ WHITE, Teri

Teri White won an Edgar for best paperback with her first novel, *Triangle* (1982). Her second, *Bleeding Hearts* (1984), introduced quirky Vietnam-veteran cops, earthy Spaceman Kowalski and his morose millionaire partner, Blue Maguire. Both the killers and their victims in this case are young male homosexuals. The tale is "brutal, bloody and so compelling the book will stick to your fingers and hold you in a horrified trance," said Julie Smith. An attempted diamond heist by a disturbed Vietnam vet and his buddies leads to plenty of killings and even more gunfire in *Tightrope* (1986). A recently-retired hit-man teams up with an aspiring criminal hired by the mob to kill him, and the two become targets of the mob and the police, in *Max Trueblood and the Jersey Desperado* (1987). Ex-cons and ex-lovers are robbing liquor stores to finance a Mexican vacation in *Fault Lines* (1987). White has also written *Thursday's Child* (1991), and as Stephen Lewis, *Cowboy Blues* (1985). Born in Kansas, she lives in Shaker Heights, Ohio.

Spaceman Kowalski & Blue Maguire...prickly cop partners...Los Angeles, California

❏ ❏ 1 - Bleeding Hearts (1984)
❏ ❏ 2 - Tightrope (1986)
❏ ❏ . . . .
❏ ❏ . . . .

■ WHITEHEAD, Barbara

British novelist Barbara Whitehead has written romance and historical fiction, children's books, literary biography and mysteries. Her eight-book York Cycle features Detective Chief Inspector Robert Southwell, introduced in *Playing God* (1988). According to *Kirkus Reviews*, Whitehead writes about "a lifestyle in transition—the old, genteel ways of York giving way to the influx of tourists, automation, and the less personal methods of doing business." In book 4, *Sweet Death Come Softly* (1992), an industrial spy is afoot in the family-owned Benn chocolate factory and a visiting French chocolatier is found dead among the confections. In her 1993 literary biography, *Charlotte Bronte and Her 'Dearest Nell'*, Whitehead has included maps and a genealogical table. Former chairperson of the York Family History Society, Whitehead is a member of the Society of Genealogists and has served as newsletter editor for the Yorkshire Archaeological Society. Born in Sheffield, she lives in York with her horticulturist husband.

Robert Southwell...detective chief inspector...York, England

❏ ❏ 1 - Playing God (1988)
❏ ❏ 2 - The Girl With Red Suspenders (1990)
❏ ❏ 3 - The Dean It Was That Died (1991)
❏ ❏ 4 - Sweet Death Come Softly (1992)
❏ ❏ 5 - The Killings at Barley Hall (1995)
❏ ❏ 6 - Secrets of the Dead (1995)
❏ ❏ 7 - Death at the Dutch House (1995)
❏ ❏ 8 - Dolls Don't Choose (1998)
❏ ❏ . . . .
❏ ❏ . . . .

■ WHITNEY, Polly

Polly Whitney's first novel, the Agatha award-nominated *Until Death* (1994), introduced Ike Tygart and her rollerblading ex-husband Abby Abagnarro, network producer and director, respectively, of a morning T.V. news show in New York City. *Until the Twelfth of Never* (2000) is the fourth entry in this wacky series. As Hialeah Jackson she writes mysteries featuring a pair of Florida security specialists. Writing as P.L. Whitney, she is the author of *This Is Graceanne's Book* (1999), a story set in 1960, narrated by nine-year-old Charlie Farrand about his beloved older sister, the most creative misbehaving genius in Cranepool's Landing, Missouri. After earning an M.A. in English from Yale University, Whitney worked as a crime reporter and photographer for the *New Haven Register*. Before turning to fulltime novel-writing she taught English for four years at a Miami prep school. Married to a network television producer, Whitney is a native of St. Louis and divides her time among Midtown Manhattan, Northern New Jersey and Florida.

Ike Tygart & Abby Abagnarro...network producer & TV news director...New York, New York

- ❑ ❑   1 - **Until Death (1994) Agatha nominee** ☆
- ❑ ❑   2 - Until the End of Time (1995)
- ❑ ❑   3 - Until It Hurts (1997)
- ❑ ❑   4 - Until the Twelfth of Never (2000)
- ❑ ❑   . . . .
- ❑ ❑   . . . .

■ WILCOX, Valerie

Sailing enthusiast Valerie Wilcox writes the Eliot Bay mysteries featuring 40-year-old Seattle widow Kellie Montgomery, a live-aboard sailing instructor introduced in *Sins of Silence* (1998). When a luxury yacht is found drifting outside Larstad's Marina with the dead owners on board, Kellie knows the marina's reputation and her job are at stake if the crime is not solved. She also knows the dead yacht owner. He's the attorney who handled the private adoption of her daughter Cassie 20 years earlier. The author's personal experience assisting her three adopted daughters in locating their birth mothers later became the subject of a Seattle television feature. A lifelong resident of the Pacific Northwest, Wilcox is a graduate of the University of Oregon with a master's degree in education. She worked for more than 25 years as a teacher and management training consultant. Although Wilcox and her husband lived on board their 40-foot sloop while she wrote her first mystery, they now live in Snohomish, Washington.

Kellie Montgomery...widowed sailing instructor ...Seattle, Washington

- ❑ ❑   1 - Sins of Silence (1998)
- ❑ ❑   2 - Sins of Betrayal (1999)
- ❑ ❑   3 - Sins of Deception (2000)
- ❑ ❑   . . . .
- ❑ ❑   . . . .

■ WILHELM, Kate

Hugo and Nebula award-winner Kate Wilhelm has published more than 40 books and short story collections since the early 1960s, including everything from science fiction to courtroom thrillers. Her first novel was a mystery, *More Bitter than Death* (1962), but it wasn't until 25 years later that she introduced her first series detectives—ex-arson investigator P.I., Charlie Meiklejohn, and psychologist Constance Leidl—in *The Hamlet Trap* (1987). Among Wilhelm's legal mysteries are those starring Oregon defense attorney Barbara Holloway who, after a five-year estrangement from the law and her lawyer-father Frank, returns to handle a death-penalty case in *Death Qualified* (1991). "Wilhelm's skill in spinning out endless complications while keeping every subplot perfectly clear makes this legal thriller her best in years," said *Kirkus Reviews* about Barbara's fourth case, *Defense for the Devil* (1999). A native of Toledo, Ohio, Wilhelm lives in Eugene, Oregon with her husband, author and editor Damon Knight.

Barbara Holloway...defense attorney...Eugene, Oregon

- ❑ ❑   1 - Death Qualified (1991)
- ❑ ❑   2 - The Best Defense (1994)
- ❑ ❑   3 - Malice Prepense (1996)
- ❑ ❑   - APA-For the Defense
- ❑ ❑   4 - Defense for the Devil (1999)
- ❑ ❑   . . . .
- ❑ ❑   . . . .

Charlie Meiklejohn & Constance Leidl...P.I. & psychologist...New York, New York
- ❏ ❏ 1 - The Hamlet Trap (1987)
- ❏ ❏ 2 - The Dark Door (1988)
- ❏ ❏ 3 - Smart House (1989)
- ❏ ❏ 4 - Sweet, Sweet Poison (1990)
- ❏ ❏ 5 - Seven Kinds of Death (1992)
- ❏ ❏ 6 - A Flush of Shadows [5 novellas] (1995)
- ❏ ❏ . . . .
- ❏ ❏ . . . .

■ WILLIAMS, Amanda Kyle

Amanda Kyle Williams has written the first espionage thrillers to feature a lesbian agent of the United States government, starting with *Club Twelve* (1990). The year is 1978 and deep-cover agent Madison McGuire is in pursuit of a multi-national terrorist group across the capitals of Europe. The C.I.A. lures Madison out of retirement in book 2, *The Providence File* (1991), for a daring covert operation designed to penetrate the Providence Liberation Army. Madison must locate their training camp for a lightning strike by American commandos. The assignment takes her to Frankfurt, Beirut and the Bekaa Valley. In an interview with *Contemporary Authors*, Williams stated she is not trying to change the world with her books, nor does she expect to raise social or political consciousness, but simply to entertain. Before writing fiction, she was vice president of manufacturing for Sovereign Carpet Mills in Dalton, Georgia. Born in Norfolk, Virginia, she lives in Marietta, Georgia where she enjoys Tae kwon do and karate.

Madison McGuire...deep cover intelligence agent
- ❏ ❏ 1 - Club Twelve (1990)
- ❏ ❏ 2 - The Providence File (1991)
- ❏ ❏ 3 - A Singular Spy (1992)
- ❏ ❏ 4 - The Spy in Question (1993)
- ❏ ❏ . . . .
- ❏ ❏ . . . .

■ WILSON, Anne

Anne Wilson has written two mysteries featuring community counselor and single-mother Sara Kingsley, introduced in *Truth or Dare* (1995). Overworked and underpaid, Sara balances the pressures of her job with the demands of daughter Hannah, who attends the local primary school, and young Jacob at the state nursery. When a successful woman journalist asks Sara's advice "for a friend" and is later found dead by apparent drug overdose in the series opener, Sara feels partly to blame and is compelled to investigate. "A credible and interestingly drawn cast of characters," said Val McDermid in the *Manchester Evening News*. "The story unfolds briskly," reported the *Sunday Telegraph*. Original paperbacks from The Women's Press in London, these mysteries have not yet been published in the United States. After completing a Ph.D. in sociology at the London School of Economics, Wilson worked as a freelance journalist. A corporate video scriptwriter, she is married with three children and lives in London.

Sara Kingsley...single-mother community counselor...London, England
- ❏ ❏ 1 - Truth or Dare (1995)
- ❏ ❏ 2 - Governing Body (1997)
- ❏ ❏ . . . .
- ❏ ❏ . . . .

■ WILSON, Barbara

Award-winning Norwegian translator Barbara Wilson writes mysteries featuring feminist lesbian detectives. Globe-trotting Spanish translator Cassandra Reilly is introduced in the Lambda award-winning comic mystery, *Gaudi Afternoon* (1991), winner of a C.W.A. award for best crime novel with a European setting. The book is set in Barcelona. After a Romanian adventure in book 2, Cassandra returns in *The Death of a Much-Travelled Woman* (1998), a collection of short stories set in Helsinki, Hawaii, Vladivostok and the English countryside. Wilson's earlier series features Seattle lesbian sleuth Pam Nilsen, first seen in *Murder in the Collective* (1984), "a paragon whodunnit," according to the *London Times*. Wilson has also written *Blue Windows, A Christian Science Childhood* (1997), "a memoir of exceptional sensitivity and intelligence," said *The New Yorker*. A native of Long Beach, California, she spent many years abroad before settling in Seattle. Co-founder of Seal Press and Women in Translation, Wilson is an avid traveler.

Cassandra Reilly...Spanish translator...London, England
- ❑ ❑   **1 - Gaudi Afternoon (1990) CWA '92 & Lambda winner ★★**
- ❑ ❑   2 - Trouble in Transylvania (1993)
- ❑ ❑   ss - The Death of a Much-Travelled Woman [9 stories] (1998)
- ❑ ❑   . . . .
- ❑ ❑   . . . .

Pam Nilsen...lesbian printing company owner...Seattle, Washington
- ❑ ❑   1 - Murder in the Collective (1984)
- ❑ ❑   2 - Sisters of the Road (1986)
- ❑ ❑   3 - The Dog Collar Murders (1989)
- ❑ ❑   . . . .
- ❑ ❑   . . . .

■ WILSON, Barbara Jaye

Barbara Jaye Wilson is the creator of New York City milliner Brenda Midnight, who constructs gravity-defying hats for her Midnight Millinery shop in Greenwich Village. In the Agatha-nominated series opener, *Death Brims Over* (1997), Brenda's hats for a society wedding are stolen at gunpoint and the friend who asked her to make them is murdered. When last seen in book 4, *Capped Off* (1999), Brenda is teaching a pony-tailed motorcycle-riding lady cop the tricks of the hat trade. Wilson has worked as a potter, fringe cutter, painter, graphic designer, back-up singer and milliner, whose own gravity-defying hats have sold in stores and boutiques in New York and Los Angeles. After majoring in ceramics at the Kansas City Art Institute, she took millinery courses at New York's Fashion Institute of Technology and graduated from the New School for Social Research. She still makes hats in the Greenwich Village apartment where her collections of typography memorabilia and toy cement trucks are artfully displayed.

Brenda Midnight...Greenwich Village milliner...New York, New York
- ❑ ❑   **1 - Death Brims Over (1997) Agatha nominee ☆**
- ❑ ❑   2 - Accessory to Murder (1998)
- ❑ ❑   3 - Death Flips Its Lid (1998)
- ❑ ❑   . . . .
- ❑ ❑   . . . .

■ WILSON, Karen Ann

Karen Ann Wilson has written four mysteries featuring 30-something veterinary technician Samantha Holt, assistant to Louis Augustin, D.V.M. in Paradise Cay, Florida. In the series opener, *Eight Dogs Flying* (1994), greyhounds are inexplicably turning vicious, including a champion racer belonging to Augustin's ex-wife Rachel, who trains and races greyhounds. The often-surly, but unnervingly attractive, Dr. Augustin is no James Herriott, but there's plenty of canine lore for dog lovers. A basket of malnourished kittens and $300 in counterfeit bills are left on Samantha's doorstep the same day one of her clients is murdered in *Copy Cat Crimes* (1995). She and Dr. Augustin are in serious danger when Samantha discovers a link between sick stray dogs, high-voltage power lines and a mysterious fire in *Beware Sleeping Dogs* (1996). When last seen in *Circle of Wolves* (1997), Samantha has volunteered to provide pet therapy at a pricey retirement facility, where she stumbles on a suspicious pattern involving drugs, deception and murder.

Samantha Holt...veterinary technician...Paradise Cay, Florida
- ❑ ❑   1 - Eight Dogs Flying (1994)
- ❑ ❑   2 - Copy Cat Crimes (1995)
- ❑ ❑   3 - Beware Sleeping Dogs (1996)
- ❑ ❑   4 - Circle of Wolves (1997)
- ❑ ❑   . . . .
- ❑ ❑   . . . .

■ WILTZ, Chris

Chris(tine) Wiltz has written three New Orleans mysteries featuring Neal Rafferty, a third generation cop turned private eye, introduced in *The Killing Circle* (1981). Although her first detective story, written at the age of eight, featured a girl detective, Wiltz chose a male private eye because she enjoys writing a point of view different from her own. When last seen in book 3, *The Emerald Lizard* (1991), Rafferty answers a distress call from Jackie Silva, a former girlfriend who owns a cocktail lounge near New Orleans. Jackie is in debt to a shady operator and her life and property have been threatened. When her bar is destroyed and she is murdered, Rafferty's investigation is complicated by the involvement of his best friend's fiancée. "An exciting mixture of romance and action," said *Booklist*. Wiltz has worked as an advertising proofreader, medical school secretary, grant researcher, bookstore clerk and staff writer for an electronics trade journal. A graduate of San Francisco State College, she lives in her native New Orleans.

Neal Rafferty...3rd-generation cop turned P.I....New Orleans, Louisiana

- ❏ ❏ 1 - The Killing Circle (1981)
- ❏ ❏ 2 - A Diamond Before You Die (1987)
- ❏ ❏ 3 - The Emerald Lizard (1991)
- ❏ ❏ . . . .
- ❏ ❏ . . . .

■ WINGATE, Anne

Fingerprint expert Anne Wingate, a former Georgia and Texas police officer with a Ph.D. in English, has written fiction and nonfiction under three names. As Anne Wingate she has written five books in the Mark Shigata series featuring a Japanese-American ex-F.B.I. agent turned chief of police in Bayport, Texas, last seen in *Yakuza, Go Home!* (1993). For Writer's Digest Books she has written *Scene of the Crime: A Writer's Guide to Crime-Scene Investigations* (1992) and, with Elaine Raco Chase, the Agatha-nominated *Amateur Detectives: A Writer's Guide to How Private Citizens Solve Criminal Cases* (1996). As Lee Martin she has written 13 mysteries in the Deb Ralston series featuring a police detective and working mother in Texas. Early in her writing career Wingate wrote mysteries as Martha G. Webb. A former intelligence specialist with the Naval Reserve, Wingate was born in Savannah, Georgia. She makes her home in Salt Lake City, where she teaches writing at the University of Utah and the Writer's Digest School.

Mark Shigata...ex-FBI agent turned sheriff...Bayport, Texas

- ❏ ❏ 1 - Death by Deception (1988)
- ❏ ❏ 2 - The Eye of Anna (1989)
- ❏ ❏ 3 - The Buzzards Must Also Be Fed (1991)
- ❏ ❏ 4 - Exception to Murder (1992)
- ❏ ❏ 5 - Yakuza, Go Home! (1993)
- ❏ ❏ . . . .
- ❏ ❏ . . . .

■ WINGS, Mary

Chicago native Mary Wings lived for eight years in the Netherlands where she wrote the first two titles of a hard-boiled lesbian series featuring private investigator Emma Victor. In the series opener, Emma is working as a counselor for a women's crisis hotline in Boston. She moves to San Francisco to handle publicity for a women's benefit concert in book 2 and subsequently turns to private investigating the third time out. Most recently, in book 5, Emma has been hired to protect a recently-outed rock diva in a Halloween parade of drag-queen lookalikes in *She Came in Drag* (1999). Wing's nonmysteries include the Lambda award-winning gothic thriller, *Divine Victim* (1993), three comic books and a film, *Greta Garbo: A Woman of Affairs*, which she co-wrote and produced with Eric Garber. She has also worked as a graphic designer, book illustrator, bus driver, freelance writer, sculptor, and banjo player in a feminist musical group. A 1993 nominee for the Raymond Chandler Fulbright award, she lives in San Francisco.

Emma Victor...lesbian activist private eye...San Francisco, California

- ❏ ❏ 1 - She Came Too Late [Boston] (1986)
- ❏ ❏ 2 - She Came in a Flash (1988)

■ WINSLOW, Pauline Glen

American author Pauline Glen Winslow is the creator of Scotland Yard Superintendent Merle Capricorn, first seen in *Death of an Angel* (1975). Capricorn is the conventional offspring of a flamboyant show business family headed by his father, the Great Capricornus, who taught his son all the tricks of the illusionist's trade. The detective's aunts, The Magic Merlinos, are music hall veterans turned television stars who provide their nephew with plenty of useful gossip. Among Winslow's ten non-Capricorn novels are three historical romance titles written as Jane Sheridan. Born in London, where her father was a professional boxer and her mother a trombonist, Winslow grew up in England. She later attended Hunter College, Columbia University and the New School for Social Research in New York City. As a freelance court reporter in New York, she worked for city, state and federal governments. Her court reporting for the United Nations inspired her sixth and final Capricorn book, *The Rockefeller Gift* (1982).

Merle Capricorn...magician turned police superintendent...England

❑ ❑ 1 - Death of an Angel (1975)
❑ ❑ 2 - The Brandenburg Hotel (1976) [prequel]
❑ ❑ 3 - The Witch Hill Murder (1977)
❑ ❑ 4 - Copper Gold (1978)
❑ ❑ - Brit.-Coppergold
❑ ❑ 5 - The Counsellor Heart (1980)
❑ ❑ - APA-Sister Death
❑ ❑ 6 - The Rockefeller Gift (1982)
❑ ❑ . . . .
❑ ❑ . . . .

■ WOLZIEN, Valerie

Valerie Wolzien (WOOL [as in sheep] zeen) has written 15 suburban mysteries since her first novel featuring upscale Connecticut housewife Susan Henshaw, *Murder at the PTA Luncheon* (1987), adapted for a 1990 CBS television movie. The neighborhood seems to have a crime for every holiday and social occasion, so it's a good thing Susan's friend Kathleen has police and security experience. Along with husbands, dogs and kids, Susan and Kathleen return in book 12, *The Student Body* (1999), when Susan goes back to college. With *Shore To Die* (1996), Wolzien launched a second series featuring Josie Pigeon, owner of an all-women construction crew, first seen in Susan's ninth adventure, *Remodeled to Death* (1995). Josie's next project, *This Old Murder* (2000), is book 4 in the series. Born in Ohio and raised in New Jersey, Wolzien went to college in Colorado and Alaska. After living in Pennsylvania, Oklahoma, Wisconsin and Washington, D.C., she has settled in Nyack, New York, where she and Josie are remodeling a charming 135-year-old house.

Josie Pigeon...all-women construction firm owner...Northeast USA

❑ ❑ 1 - Shore To Die (1996)
❑ ❑ 2 - Permit for Murder (1997)
❑ ❑ 3 - Deck the Halls With Murder (1998)
❑ ❑ . . . .
❑ ❑ . . . .

Susan Henshaw...upscale suburban housewife...Connecticut

❑ ❑ 1 - Murder at the PTA Luncheon (1987)
❑ ❑ 2 - The Fortieth Birthday Body (1989)
❑ ❑ 3 - We Wish You a Merry Murder (1991)
❑ ❑ 4 - All Hallow's Evil (1992)
❑ ❑ 5 - An Old Faithful Murder (1992)
❑ ❑ 6 - A Star-Spangled Murder (1993)
❑ ❑ 7 - A Good Year for a Corpse (1994)

❏ ❏   8 - Tis the Season To Be Murdered (1994)
❏ ❏   9 - Remodeled to Death (1995)
❏ ❏   10 - Elected to Death (1996)
❏ ❏   11 - Weddings Are Murder (1998)
❏ ❏   ....
❏ ❏   ....

■ WOODS, Paula L.

Los Angeles native Paula L. Woods is the creator of homicide detective Charlotte Justice, L.A.P.D.'s first black woman in Robbery-Homicide. Introduced in the musically-inspired title, *Inner City Blues* (1999), Charlotte still suffers the effects of the drive-by shooting deaths of her husband and daughter 14 years earlier. The year is 1992 and the city is aflame. Charlotte's next case, *Hollywood Swingers* (2000), involves the suspicious death of an elderly black actor-filmmaker. Among Woods' several nonfiction books is the Anthony and Macavity award-nominated *Spooks, Spies and Private Eyes: Black Mystery, Crime and Suspense Fiction of the 20th Century* (1996). A graduate of U.S.C., she holds a master's degree in public health from U.C.L.A. With her husband she owns and operates the consulting firm Woods/Lydell Group, and a book packaging and marketing company. She reviews books for major newspapers and magazines, and hosts the monthly "Book Doctor" radio program on KPCC 89.3 FM (Ebony 98) in Los Angeles.

Charlotte Justice...black woman homicide detective...Los Angeles, California
❏ ❏   1 - Inner City Blues (1999)
❏ ❏   2 - Hollywood Swingers (2000)
❏ ❏   ....
❏ ❏   ....

■ WOODS, Sherryl

The award-winning author of more than 70 novels, many of which are best-selling romances translated into more than a dozen languages, Sherryl Woods writes four books a year. Her mysteries include a nine-book series featuring investigative reporter Amanda Roberts, transplanted from New York to Georgia. Her four-book Molly DeWitt series recounts the adventures of a Miami film promoter and single mother last seen in *Hot Schemes* (1994). Woods' first four novels were published under the names Suzanne Sherrill and Alexandra Kitt. After graduating from Ohio State University, she spent 14 years as a working journalist in Ohio and Florida. Her various assignments included general reporting for the Columbus *Citizen-Journal* and editorial positions at the *Palm Beach Post* and *Miami News*, where she was radio and T.V. editor for six years. Daughter of an I.R.S. agent, Woods was born in Washington, D.C. She lives in Colonial Beach, Virginia, where she owns the Potomac Sunrise bookstore.

Amanda Roberts...ex-NYC investigative reporter...Atlanta, Georgia
❏ ❏   1 - Reckless (1989)
❏ ❏   2 - Body and Soul (1989)
❏ ❏   3 - Stolen Moments (1990)
❏ ❏   4 - Ties That Bind (1991)
❏ ❏   5 - Bank on It (1993)
❏ ❏   6 - Hide and Seek (1993)
❏ ❏   7 - Wages of Sin (1994)
❏ ❏   8 - Deadly Obsession (1995)
❏ ❏   9 - White Lightning (1995)
❏ ❏   ....
❏ ❏   ....

Molly DeWitt...film promoter and single mother...Miami, Florida
❏ ❏   1 - Hot Property (1991)
❏ ❏   2 - Hot Secret (1992)
❏ ❏   3 - Hot Money (1993)
❏ ❏   4 - Hot Schemes (1994)
❏ ❏   ....
❏ ❏   ....

■ WOODWARD, Ann

While raising seven children, Ann Woodward taught herself Japanese at night and later studied Japanese history and culture at the University of Michigan. During the 1980s she became a frequent contributor to *Alfred Hitchcock Mystery Magazine* after publishing her first Lady Aoi (ah-oh-ee) story, "The Girl from Ishikawa", in October 1980. Set in Japan's Imperial Palace in the late Heian period (early 11th century), *The Exile Way* (1996) is the first novel-length mystery featuring the lady-in-waiting. Named for her fondness of morning glories (Aoi means blue), she is widowed, in her early 30s. Educated against custom by a father who had no sons, Aoi is trained in the Chinese healing arts and has extensive knowledge of herbs and medicine. Observant by nature, she shows intense interest in human affairs. When a noble minister is accused of murder, she must flee the court to prevent his conviction. *Of Death and Black Rivers* (1998) returns Aoi to the palace where she must rescue Lady Saisho from the Dark Warrior of the North.

Lady Aoi...11th century Japanese healer...Kyoto, Japan
- ❑ ❑ 1 - The Exile Way (1996)
- ❑ ❑ 2 - Of Death and Black Rivers (1998)
- ❑ ❑ ....
- ❑ ❑ ....

■ WOODWORTH, Deborah

Deborah Woodworth has written three mysteries featuring Shaker Sister Rose Callahan, the only remaining trustee of the North Homage (Kentucky) United Society of Believers. In the series opener, *Death of a Winter Shaker* (1997), the year is 1936 and Sister Rose is 35 years old. A trustee for the past ten years, she is responsible for the community's financial health, as well as relations between Believers and the outside world. When last seen in book 3, *Sins of a Shaker Summer* (1999), Sister Rose is the newly-appointed eldress. Woodworth grew up near the abandoned sites of several Shaker villages in Southern Ohio and was fascinated by Shaker memorabilia. After earning a Ph.D. in the sociology of religion from the University of Minnesota she spent ten years teaching and conducting research before turning to writing full time. She also writes the Values Biographies series, including *Compassion: The Story of Clara Barton* (1997), *Faith: The Story of Mother Teresa* (1999) and *Adventure: The Story of Amelia Earhart* (1999).

Rose Callahan...1930s Shaker sister...North Homage, Kentucky
- ❑ ❑ 1 - Death of a Winter Shaker (1997)
- ❑ ❑ 2 - A Deadly Shaker Spring (1998)
- ❑ ❑ ....
- ❑ ❑ ....

■ WREN, M.K. [P]

M.K. Wren is the pseudonym of Martha Kay Renfroe, who once told *Contemporary Authors* she thinks of herself as an artist whose writing hobby got out of hand. Her first novel, *Curiosity Didn't Kill the Cat* (1973), introduced wealthy Oregon bookshop owner and art collector, Conan Flagg, a former intelligence agent, half Nez Perce Indian, turned reluctant private eye. With *Neely Jones: The Medusa Pool* (1999), Wren introduces sheriff-elect Cornelia Jones, the only woman in the Taft County Sheriff's office. The bi-racial daughter of '60s civil rights activists, Neely was a minor character in book 7, *Dead Matter* (1993), of the Conan Flagg series. Wren is the author of a 500,000-word science fiction trilogy titled *The Phoenix Legacy* (1991) and a mainstream novel set in the near future, *A Gift Upon the Shore* (1990). With a fine arts degree in painting and sculpture from the University of Oklahoma, she once designed greeting cards for Hallmark. A native of Amarillo, Texas, she lives in Lincoln City, Oregon where she continues to paint.

Conan Flagg...secret agent turned bookstore owner...Coastal Oregon
- ❑ ❑ 1 - Curiosity Didn't Kill the Cat (1973)
- ❑ ❑ 2 - A Multitude of Sins (1975)
- ❑ ❑ 3 - Oh Bury Me Not (1977)
- ❑ ❑ 4 - Nothing's Certain but Death (1978)
- ❑ ❑ 5 - Seasons of Death (1981)

❑ ❑ 6 - Wake Up, Darlin' Corey (1984)
❑ ❑ 7 - Dead Matter (1993)
❑ ❑ 8 - King of the Mountain (1995)
❑ ❑ . . . .
❑ ❑ . . . .

Neely Jones...black woman sheriff-elect...Taft County, Oregon
❑ ❑ 1 - Neely Jones: The Medusa Pool (1999)
❑ ❑ . . . .
❑ ❑ . . . .

■ WRIGHT, L.R.

Two-time Ellis award winner L(aurali) R. Wright gave up her journalism career at the *Calgary Herald* to write fiction. Three mainstream novels preceded her first mystery, the opening title in the Karl Alberg series, winner of the 1986 best-novel Edgar award. The series is set in the seaside town of Sechelt, on the Sunshine coast of British Columbia, where Alberg is a Royal Canadian Mounted Police officer in his late 40s, divorced, in a developing relationship with the town librarian, Cassandra Mitchell. The culprit is known at the outset of book 1, *The Suspect* (1985), but the mystery lies in discovering the motive behind the murder. Wright consistently provides "solid character studies neatly integrated with genuine suspense." With *Kidnap* (1999), she introduces a spin-off series featuring policewoman Eddie Henderson, who made an appearance in Alberg's ninth case, *Acts of Murder* (1998). Born in Saskatoon, Saskatchewan, Wright lives in British Columbia. She is a past president of Crime Writers of Canada.

Eddie Henderson...woman police officer...Vancouver, British Columbia, Canada
❑ ❑ 1 - Kidnap (1999)
❑ ❑ . . . .
❑ ❑ . . . .

Martin Karl Alberg...RCMP staff sergeant...Sechelt, British Columbia, Canada
❑ ❑ 1 - **The Suspect (1985) Edgar winner ★**
❑ ❑ 2 - Sleep While I Sing (1986)
❑ ❑ 3 - **A Chill Rain in January (1990) Ellis winner ★**
❑ ❑ 4 - Fall From Grace (1991)
❑ ❑ 5 - Prized Possessions (1993)
❑ ❑ 6 - **A Touch of Panic (1994) Ellis nominee ☆**
❑ ❑ 7 - **Mother Love (1995) Ellis winner ★**
❑ ❑ 8 - Strangers Among Us (1996)
❑ ❑ 9 - Acts of Murder (1998)
❑ ❑ . . . .
❑ ❑ . . . .

■ WRIGHT, Nancy Means

Nancy Means Wright wrote her first novel in the 4th grade—about the kidnapping of an obnoxious older brother. Her mother pronounced it "foolishness" and tore it up. Wright remained unpublished until the 1972 sale of her first adult novel, *The Losing*, written 10 years earlier while she was a Bread Loaf Writers Conference Scholar. During the 1980s, while completing an M.A. in French at Middlebury College, she published two nonfiction books—*Make Your Own Change* (1985) and *Vermonters and Their Craft* (1987)—inspired by her family craft business operated from their barn. While writing poetry and teaching in the early '90s, she read a newspaper account of two elderly farmers, robbed, beaten and left for dead, which sparked the idea for *Mad Season* (1996), her first mystery featuring farmwoman Ruth Willmarth. A Vermont single mother who names her cows after favorite literary characters, Willmarth makes her third appearance in *Poison Apples* (2000). A Vassar College graduate, Wright teaches at the Writer's Digest School.

Ruth Willmarth...single-mother farmer...Branbury, Vermont
❑ ❑ 1 - Mad Season (1996)
❑ ❑ 2 - Harvest of Bones (1998)
❑ ❑ . . . .
❑ ❑ . . . .

WRIGHT, Sally S.

Sally S. Wright is the creator of former intelligence agent and World War II commando, Ben Reese, introduced in *Publish and Perish* (1997), set during the 1960s. Archivist and historian at a private college in Ohio, Ben is an expert in rare books, coins, paintings and ancient documents. While doing research in Oxford, he receives a strange call from the English department chairman who promptly dies under mysterious circumstances. Ben returns home to investigate. In *Pride and Predator* (1997), a respected parish clergy dies in Scotland and Lord Alexander Chisholm wants Ben's help. A trail of clues takes the ex-commando through old family estates and rustic farms of the Scottish countryside. The third Ben Reese mystery is *Pursuit and Persuasion* (2000). Originally published by Multnomah Press, the series is available in paperback reprint from Ballantine. A graduate of Northwestern University, Wright holds a degree in oral interpretation of literature and has done graduate study at the University of Washington. She lives in Bowling Green, Ohio.

Ben Reese...1960s university archivist...Ohio
- ❏ ❏ 1 - Publish and Perish (1997)
- ❏ ❏ 2 - Pride and Predator (1997)
- ❏ ❏ ....
- ❏ ❏ ....

YARBRO, Chelsea Quinn

Past president of Horror Writers of America, Chelsea Quinn Yarbro, is best known for her historical horror novels, including a female vampire trilogy, and the critically-acclaimed Saint-Germain series. The compassionate and artistic Count Ragoczy Saint-Germain, introduced in *Hotel Transylvania* (1978), was praised by *Booklist* as "one of modern fantasy's more notable personages." Yarbro has also written musical works, science fiction, westerns, other historicals, books for children, nonfiction and a mystery series— more than 50 titles in all. Her mystery series protagonist is Charles Spotted Moon, a San Francisco attorney and Ojibway tribal shaman, first seen in *Ogilvie, Tallant and Moon* (1976). A two-time Edgar nominee, Yarbro describes herself as a composer, fortune teller and lifetime student of history. The Berkeley, California native attended San Francisco State and once worked as a cartographer in the family map-making business. Writing as Quinn Fawcett, she co-authors two historical mystery series with Bill Fawcett.

Charles Spotted Moon...attorney-Ojibway tribal shaman...San Francisco, California
- ❏ ❏ 1 - Ogilvie, Tallant and Moon (1976)
- ❏ ❏ - APA-Bad Medicine (1990)
- ❏ ❏ 2 - Music When Sweet Voices Die (1979)
- ❏ ❏ - APA-False Notes (1990)
- ❏ ❏ 3 - Poison Fruit (1991)
- ❏ ❏ 4 - Cat's Claw (1992)
- ❏ ❏ ....
- ❏ ❏ ....

YEAGER, Dorian

New Hampshire native Dorian Yeager is the author of two mystery series. She is also a working actor, director and freelance magazine humor writer living in New York City. No small surprise that her six-foot, red-headed working actress-sleuth, Victoria Bowering, bears a striking resemblance to Yeager herself. In her fourth Manhattan adventure, *Libation by Death* (1998), the chronically-unemployed actress takes a job as a daytime bartender after the mysterious death of her predecessor. While Yeager admits to tending bar, she has yet to find a dead colleague in the walk-in refrigerator. Last seen in *Summer Will End* (1996), watercolorist and gallery owner Elizabeth Will has to contend with a serial mischief-maker killing tourists in peaceful Dovekey Beach, New Hampshire. Elizabeth's cranky lobster fisherman father makes a return appearance after she saved him from a murder charge in the series opener.

Elizabeth Will...watercolorist-gallery owner...Dovekey, New Hampshire
- ❏ ❏ 1 - Murder Will Out (1994)
- ❏ ❏ 2 - Summer Will End (1995)
- ❏ ❏ ....
- ❏ ❏ ....

Victoria Bowering...6 ft-redhead sometime-actress...New York, New York

- ❏ ❏   1 - Cancellation by Death (1992)
- ❏ ❏   2 - Eviction by Death (1993)
- ❏ ❏   3 - Ovation by Death (1996)
- ❏ ❏   4 - Libation by Death (1998)
- ❏ ❏   . . . .
- ❏ ❏   . . . .

■ YORK, Kieran

A collector of antique typewriters, Kieran York is the creator of Timber City, Colorado deputy sheriff Royce Madison, "soft-spoken dyke-about-town," whose father's unsolved murder 10 years earlier had inspired his daughter's career choice. Royce vowed no other murder would go unsolved on her watch, and after three years with the Denver Police Department returned home to Timber City. York recently completed the first in an anticipated series featuring successful Palm Beach, Florida defense attorney, Beryl Trevar, who launches a detective agency aboard her yacht *The Radclyffe Hull*. Beryl and two unlikely partners—an ex-cop and an ex-con—soon become known as The Radclyffe Hull Trio. With degrees in art and journalism from the University of Kansas and Mexico's University of the Americas, York has worked as a reporter, reviewer, and magazine publisher, written and performed songs with a women's band and taught poetry and creative writing. She lives in Colorado.

Royce Madison...lesbian deputy sheriff...Timber City, Colorado

- ❏ ❏   1 - Timber City Masks (1993)
- ❏ ❏   2 - Crystal Mountain Veils (1995)
- ❏ ❏   . . . .
- ❏ ❏   . . . .

■ YORKE, Margaret [P]

Widely-recognized as one of Britain's finest writers of psychological suspense, Margaret Yorke is the pseudonym of Margaret Beda Larminie Nicholson, former librarian at St. Hilda's College and Christ Church, Oxford, and wartime veteran of the Women's Royal Naval Service. After writing 11 of what she called "family problem novels," Yorke launched her mystery-writing career with a five-book series featuring Oxford don Patrick Grant. Since then she has published more than two dozen suspense novels, most recently *False Pretences* (1999), *Act of Violence* (1998) and *A Question of Belief* (1997). In 1999, this former chair of the Crime Writers' Association becomes only the fourth woman to win the C.W.A. Cartier Diamond Dagger for her significant contribution to crime writing. In 1982 the Swedish Academy of Detection honored her for the best translated crime novel (*The Scent of Fear*). As noted by Karl G. Fredriksson in *St. James Guide to Crime & Mystery*, the people in Yorke's novels "commit small, seemingly insignificant mistakes with disastrous consequences."

Patrick Grant...Oxford don...Oxford, England

- ❏ ❏   1 - Dead in the Morning (1970)
- ❏ ❏   2 - Silent Witness (1972)
- ❏ ❏   3 - Grave Matters (1973)
- ❏ ❏   4 - Mortal Remains (1974)
- ❏ ❏   5 - Cast for Death (1976)
- ❏ ❏   . . . .
- ❏ ❏   . . . .

■ YOUMANS, Claire

Seattle native and former litigator Claire Youmans is an avid and expert sailor who lives and writes aboard her 43-foot ketch. In 1998, armed with computer, printer, fax, e-mail and Internet access, she sailed to Alaska, Japan, Taiwan, Mexico and Central America while completing the first title in her Sandy Whitacre series. *The First Death* (2000) introduces the widow of a U.S. Treasury agent, working as a sole practitioner and tort law specialist in Seattle, although the action takes place in the San Juan Islands, including a violent confrontation with an international gang of criminals in the storm-tossed Straits of Juan de Fuca. Youmans is currently writing her second Janet Schilling mystery starring a Washington State prosecutor in the fiction-al coastal town of Salmon Bay. A Nichiren Shoshu Buddhist and author of *How to Live Aboard and Like It* (1994), Youmans is also an expert skier.

Janet Schilling...county chief deputy prosecutor...Coastal Washington
- ❑ ❑ 1 - Rough Justice (1996)
- ❑ ❑ 2 - Rough Trip (2000)
- ❑ ❑ . . . .
- ❑ ❑ . . . .

Sandy Whitacre...attorney in sole practice tort law...Seattle, Washington
- ❑ ❑ 1 - The First Death (2000)
- ❑ ❑ . . . .
- ❑ ❑ . . . .

■ ZACHARY, Fay

Arizona writer and web entrepreneur Fay Zachary is the creator of Dr. Liz Broward, family practice physi-cian, and Zack James, single father and computer graphic artist, who uses his genealogy expertise to help solve a medical mystery when he becomes Liz's patient after the leukemia death of his wife. The series opens with *Blood Work* (1994) in Philadelphia where the author lived for eight years, but moves to Phoenix with the second installment. A former public health R.N., Zachary studied nursing at the University of Pittsburgh and the University of Pennsylvania. She now lives in Scottsdale, Arizona where she operates The Free Gallery of Authors' Voices, home of the vir-tual book tour at <http://fregalry.interspeed.net>. After a recent short-story sale to *WIN Magazine*, she is exploring e-book publishing opportunities for Liz and Zack's return. Her other crime fiction includes *Fertility Rights* (1987) and *Cradle and All* (1989).

Liz Broward & Zack James...family physician & computer artist...Phoenix, Arizona
- ❑ ❑ 1 - Blood Work (1994)
- ❑ ❑ 2 - A Poison in the Blood (1994)
- ❑ ❑ . . . .
- ❑ ❑ . . . .

■ ZAREMBA, Eve

Canadian author and long-time feminist activist, Eve Zaremba has written six novels featuring 40-some-thing lesbian private investigator Helen Keremos, once described by Margaret Atwood as a "cross between Lily Tomlin and Philip Marlowe." First seen in *A Reason to Kill* (1978), Helen is a former employee of the U.S. Naval Security Division with a vast net-work of professional resources across Canada and around the world. While book 3 is set in Vancouver's Chinatown with a long-lost '60s revolutionary who is the daughter of an American right-wing presidential candidate, book 5 takes Helen to Tokyo on a missing person's assignment that turns into a case of interna-tional art smuggling. A native of Poland and long-time resident of Toronto, Zaremba was one of the founders of *Broadside, A Feminist Review*. She has worked as a writer, publisher, and marketing consul-tant, and previously owned a used-book store.

Helen Keremos...40-something lesbian private eye...Toronto, Ontario, Canada
- ❑ ❑ 1 - A Reason to Kill (1978)
- ❑ ❑ 2 - Work for a Million (1987)
- ❑ ❑ 3 - Beyond Hope (1988)
- ❑ ❑ 4 - Uneasy Lies (1990)
- ❑ ❑ 5 - The Butterfly Effect (1994)
- ❑ ❑ 6 - White Noise (1997)
- ❑ ❑ . . . .
- ❑ ❑ . . . .

■ ZUKOWSKI, Sharon

Inveterate traveler Sharon Zukowski has written five books featuring Manhattan private eye Blaine Stewart, in business with her attorney sister Eileen. Their clients are typically Fortune 500 and Wall Street firms with concerns too sensitive for in-house legal staffs. Before starting their very profitable investigations business, Blaine did a cop tour with the N.Y.P.D., while Eileen worked for the Manhattan District Attorney. A former stockbroker, financial planner and housing coordinator, Zukowski is currently senior publications editor for a major New York financial services firm. By night from her New Jersey home, she is writing a big scary book (thriller), which she intends to follow with a big funny book before returning to the mystery genre. In 1998 she fed her travel addiction with trips to Scotland, Iceland, France (two visits), California and the Grand Canyon. Her 1999 travel plans included rafting the Grand Canyon and visiting Italy.

Blaine Stewart...ex-cop turned corporate P.I....New York, New York

- ❏ ❏ 1 - The Hour of the Knife (1991)
- ❏ ❏ 2 - Dancing in the Dark (1992)
- ❏ ❏ 3 - Leap of Faith (1994)
- ❏ ❏ 4 - Prelude to Death (1996)
- ❏ ❏ 5 - Jungleland (1997)
- ❏ ❏ . . . .
- ❏ ❏ . . . .

Mystery Types 2

Author	1 - #	Series Character	Occupation	Setting
Police				
Adams, Jane	'95 - 3	Mike Croft	detective inspector	Norwich, England
Adamson, M.J.	'87 - 5	Balthazar Marten & Sixto Cardenas	NYPD homicide detective & Puerto Rican cop	Puerto Rico
Aird, Catherine	'66 - 16	Christopher Dennis "Seedy" Sloan	CID department head	West Calleshire, England
Allen, Kate	'93 - 4	Alison Kaine	lesbian leather cop	Denver, CO
Amato, Angela	'98 - 2	Gerry Conte	undercover cop turned defense attorney	New York, NY
Ayres, Noreen	'92 - 2	Samantha "Smokey" Brandon	sheriff's forensic expert	Orange County, CA
Bannister, Jo	'84 - 3	Clio Rees & Harry Marsh	physician novelist & chief inspector	England
Bannister, Jo	'93 - 6	Shapiro, Donovan & Graham	police officers	Castlemere, England
Barr, Nevada	'93 - 7	Anna Pigeon	park ranger	National Parks
Barrett, Margaret	'98 - 2	Susan Given	asset forfeiture prosecutor	New York, NY
Beaton, M.C.	'85 - 14	Hamish Macbeth	Scottish police constable	Lochdubh, Scotland
Beecham, Rose	'92 - 3	Amanda Valentine	lesbian detective inspector	Wellington, New Zealand
Bell, Pauline	'90 - 8	Benny Mitchell	brash detective constable	Yorkshire, England
Benke, Patricia D.	'95 - 3	Judith Thornton	chief assistant district attorney	San Diego, CA
Blanc, Suzanne	'61 - 3	Miguel Menendez	Aztec police inspector	San Luis Potosi, Mexico
Bland, Eleanor Taylor	'92 - 7	Marti MacAlister	widowed black police detective	Lincoln Prairie, IL
Bolitho, Janie	'93 - 8	Ian Roper	detective chief inspector	Rickenham Green, Eng.
Bowen, Rhys	'97 - 3	Evan Evans	village constable	Llanfair, N Wales
Burden, Pat	'90 - 4	Henry Bassett	retired cop	Herefordshire, England
Butler, Gwendoline	'57 - 26	John Coffin	Scotland Yard commander	London, England
Carlson, P.M.	'92 - 2	Marty LaForte Hopkins	deputy sheriff mom	Southern IN
Cercone, Karen Rose	'97 - 3	Helen Sorby & Milo Kachigan	social worker & policeman in 1905	Pittsburgh, PA
Clayton, Mary	'95 - 5	John Reynolds	ex-inspector turned crime writer	Cornwall, England
Cleeves, Ann	'90 - 6	Stephen Ramsay	impulsive police inspector	Northumberland, Eng.
Coburn, Laura	'95 - 4	Kate Harrod	single-mother police detective	San Madera, CA
Cooper, Susan R.	'88 - 6	Milton Kovak	chief deputy	Prophesy County, OK
Cornwell, Patricia	'97 - 2	Andy Brazil	reporter and volunteer cop	Charlotte, NC
Cornwell, Patricia	'90 - 9	Kay Scarpetta	chief medical examiner	Richmond, VA
Craig, Alisa	'80 - 5	Madoc & Janet Rhys	RCMP inspector & wife	New Brunswick, Canada
Crombie, Deborah	'93 - 5	Duncan Kincaid & Gemma James	Scotland Yard detective partners	London, England
Curzon, Clare	'83 - 13	Mike Yeadings	Serious Crime Squad superintendent	Thames Valley, England
D'Amato, Barbara	'96 - 2	Suze Figueroa & Norm Bennis	pair of cops	Chicago, IL
Davis, Dorothy S.	'57 - 3	Jasper Tully & Mrs. Norris	DA's investigator & Scottish housekeeper	New York, NY
Davis, Kaye	'97 - 3	Maris Middleton	lesbian forensic chemist	Texas
Dengler, Sandy	'93 - 4	Jack Prester	U.S. park ranger	National Parks
Dengler, Sandy	'93 - 4	Joe Rodriguez	police sergeant	Phoenix, AZ
Dewhurst, Eileen	'77 - 5	Neil Carter	Scotland Yard detective	London, England
Dewhurst, Eileen	'92 - 2	Tim Le Page	local detective inspector	Guernsey, England
Dixon, Louisa	'98 - 3	Laura Owen	state public safety commissioner	Jackson, MS
Drake, Alison	'88 - 4	Aline Scott	homicide detective	Tango Key, FL
Dreyer, Eileen	'95 - 2	Molly Burke	death investigator	St. Louis, MO
Duffy, Margaret	'94 - 4	Joanna MacKenzie & James Carrick	ex-CID detective & Det. Chief Insp.	Bath, England
Dunlap, Susan	'81 - 10	Jill Smith	homicide detective	Berkeley, CA
Dymmoch, Michael	'93 - 3	John Thinnes & Jack Caleb	cop & gay psychiatrist	Chicago, IL

Author	1 - #	Series Character	Occupation	Setting
Police				
Eccles, Marjorie	'88 - 10	Gil Mayo	detective chief inspector	Midlands, England
Ennis, Catherine	'91 - 2	Bernadette Hebert	lesbian crime lab expert	Louisiana
Evans, Geraldine	'93 - 3	Joseph Rafferty & Dafyd Llewellyn	D.I.& his Welsh sergeant	Yorkshire, England
Fairstein, Linda	'96 - 3	Alexandra Cooper	chief sex crimes prosecutor	New York, NY
Ferguson, Frances	'93 - 4	Jane Perry	French-speaking detective sergeant	Canterbury, Kent, Eng.
Forrest, Katherine V.	'84 - 6	Kate Delafield	LAPD lesbian homicide detective	Los Angeles, CA
Fraser, Anthea	'84 - 14	David Webb	detective chief inspector	Wiltshire, England
Fyfield, Frances	'88 - 6	Helen West	London Crown prosecutor	London, England
George, Elizabeth	'88 - 9	Thomas Lynley & Barbara Havers	Scotland Yard inspector & detective sergeant	London, England
Gill, B.M.	'81 - 3	Tom Maybridge	detective chief inspector	England
Gilpatrick, Noreen	'93 - 2	Kate MacLean	police detective	Seattle, WA
Glass, Leslie	'93 - 4	April Woo	Chinese-American police detective	New York, NY
Gosling, Paula	'85 - 2	Jack Stryker & Kate Trevorne	homicide cop & English professor	Michigan
Gosling, Paula	'86 - 2	Luke Abbott	English cop	England
Gosling, Paula	'92 - 4	Matt Gabriel	sheriff	Blackwater Bay, MI
Graham, Caroline	'87 - 5	Tom Barnaby	chief inspector	Causton, England
Granger, Ann	'91 - 11	Alan Markby & Meredith Mitchell	D.I. & Foreign Service officer	Cotswolds, England
Gray, Dulcie	'60 - 2	Insp. Supt. Cardiff	inspector superintendent	England
Green, Christine	'93 - 3	Connor O'Neill & Fran Wilson	village chief insp. & detective sgt.	Fowchester, England
Green, Kate	'86 - 3	Theresa Fortunato & Oliver Jardine	professional psychic & LAPD detective	Los Angeles, CA
Grimes, Martha	'81 - 15	Richard Jury	Scotland Yard inspector	London, England
Grindle, Lucretia	'93 - 2	H.W. Ross	detective superintendent	England
Gunn, Elizabeth	'97 - 2	Jake Hines	small town police detective	Rutherford, MN
Gur, Batya	'92 - 4	Michael Ohayon	Moroccan-born chief inspector	Jerusalem, Israel
Haddam, Jane	'90 - 15	Gregor Demarkian	former FBI department head	Philadelphia, PA
Hager, Jean	'89 - 5	Mitch Bushyhead	police chief of Cherokee descent	Buckskin, OK
Hall, Linda	'95 - 3	Roger Sheppard	RCMP officer and family man	Alberta, Canada
Hall, Patricia	'93 - 5	Laura Ackroyd & Michael Thackeray	investigative reporter & police inspector	Bradfield, Yorkshire, Eng.
Haney, Lauren	'97 - 2	Lt. Bak	ex-charioteer turned Medjay police head	Buhen, Egypt
Harrison, Jamie	'95 - 3	Jules Clement	30-something archaeologist turned sheriff	Blue Deer, MT
Harrod-Eagles, C.	'91 - 7	Bill Slider	Shepherd's Bush CID inspector	London, England
Haymon, S.T.	'80 - 8	Benjamin Jurnet	Angleby CID detective inspector	Norwich, England
Hebden, Juliet	'79 - 22	Clovis Pel	curmudgeonly police inspector	Burgundy, France
Herndon, Nancy	'95 - 6	Elena Jarvis	wise-cracking police detective	Los Santos, TX
Hess, Joan	'87 - 11	Arly Hanks	small-town police chief	Maggody, AR
Hightower, Lynn S.	'92 - 4	David Silver & String	homicide cop & alien partner	USA
Hightower, Lynn S.	'95 - 3	Sonora Blair	homicide detective	Cincinnati, OH
Horansky, Ruby	'90 - 2	Nikki Trakos	6-ft. NYPD homicide detective	Brooklyn, NY
Hornsby, Wendy	'87 - 2	Kate Teague & Roger Tejeda	college professor & homicide detective	Los Angeles, CA
Jackson, Marian J.A.	'90 - 5	Abigail Patience Danforth	19th century American heiress detective	International
James, P.D.	'62 - 10	Adam Dalgleish	published poet of Scotland Yard	London, England
Jance, J.A.	'85 - 14	J.P. Beaumont	homicide detective	Seattle, WA
Jance, J.A.	'93 - 7	Joanna Brady	single-mother sheriff	Cochise County, AZ
Jennings, Maureen	'97 - 2	William Murdoch	Victorian police inspector	Toronto, ON, Canada
John, Katherine	'89 - 3	Trevor Joseph	police sergeant	England
Kellerman, Faye	'86 - 10	Peter Decker & Rina Lazarus	LAPD detective & Orthodox Jewish wife	Los Angeles, CA
Kelly, Mary	'56 - 3	Brett Nightingale	Scottish police inspector	Edinburgh, Scotland
Kelly, Susan B.	'90 - 5	Alison Hope & Nick Trevellyan	software designer & detective inspector	Hop Valley, England
Kennett, Shirley	'96 - 4	P.J. Gray	police dept. virtual reality expert	St. Louis, MO
King, Laurie R.	'93 - 3	Kate Martinelli & Alonzo Hawkin	SFPD homicide detectives	San Francisco, CA
Knight, Alanna	'88 - 11	Jeremy Faro	Victorian detective inspector	Edinburgh, Scotland
Krich, Rochelle Majer	'93 - 3	Jessie Drake	LAPD homicide detective	Los Angeles, CA
La Plante, Lynda	'93 - 3	Jane Tennison	detective chief inspector	London, England
LaPierre, Janet	'87 - 5	Meg Halloran & Vince Gutierrez	single-mother school teacher & police chief	Port Silva, CA
Lemarchand, Elizabeth	'67 - 17	Tom Pollard & Gregory Toye	Scotland Yard detectives	London, England
Leon, Donna	'92 - 9	Guido Brunetti	police commissario	Venice, Italy
Maron, Margaret	'81 - 8	Sigrid Harald	police lieutenant	New York, NY
Martin, Lee	'84 - 13	Deb Ralston	police detective mom	Fort Worth, TX
Mason, Sarah J.	'93 - 6	Trewley & Stone	village Det. Supt. & female sergeant	Plummergen, Kent, Eng.
Masters, Priscilla	'95 - 5	Joanna Piercy	detective inspector	Leek, Staffordshire, Eng.
Mathews, Francine	'94 - 4	Meredith Folger	police detective	Nantucket, MA
McAllester, Melanie	'94 - 2	Elizabeth Mendoza	Hispanic-black lesbian homicide detective	San Francisco, CA
McCafferty, Jeanne	'94 - 3	Mackenzie Griffin	consulting criminal psychologist	New York, NY
McClellan, Janet	'97 - 3	Tru North	lesbian police detective	Kansas City, MO
McCrumb, Sharyn	'90 - 5	Spencer Arrowood	Appalachian sheriff	Tennessee

Author	1 - #	Series Character	Occupation	Setting

Police

McDermid, Val	'95 - 2	Tony Hill & Carol Jordan	clinical psychologist & D.I.	Bradfield, England
McGown, Jill	'83 - 9	Lloyd & Judy Hill	chief inspector & detective partner	East Anglia, England
McGuire, Christine	'93 - 4	Kathryn Mackay	senior prosecuting attorney	Northern CA
McNab, Claire	'88 - 10	Carol Ashton	lesbian detective inspector	Sydney, Australia
Melville, Jennie	'62 - '	Charmian Daniels	police detective	Deerham Hills, England
Meredith, D.R.	'84 - 5	Charles Matthews	honest county sheriff	Crawford Co., TX
Mickelbury, Penny	'94 - 2	Gianna Maglione & Mimi Patterson	lesbian police lieutenant & reporter	Washington, DC
Mitchell, Kay	'90 - 5	John Morrissey	chief inspector and family man	Malminster, England
Moody, Skye K.	'96 - 3	Venus Diamond	U.S. Fish & Wildlife agent	Washington
Moore, Margaret	'87 - 3	Richard Baxter	police inspector	England
Morell, Mary	'91 - 2	Lucia Ramos	Chicana lesbian police detective	San Antonio, TX
Morrone, Wenda W.	'01 - 1	Claud Willetts	small-town sheriff	Merciful Valley, MT
Moyes, Patricia	'59 - '	Henry & Emmy Tibbett	Scotland Yard inspector & wife	London, England
Nabb, Magdalen	'81 - 11	Salvatore Guarnaccia	Sicilian Carabinieri marshal	Florence, Italy
Nadelson, Reggie	'95 - 3	Artie Cohen	39-year-old Russian-born cop	New York, NY
Neel, Janet	'88 - 6	John McLeish & Francesca Wilson	DCI & businesswoman	London, England
O'Connell, Carol	'94 - 4	Kathleen Mallory	lone-wolf police sergeant	New York, NY
O'Donnell, Lillian	'77 - 3	Mici Anhalt	criminal justice investigator	New York, NY
O'Donnell, Lillian	'72 - 16	Norah Mulcahaney	police detective	New York, NY
Oleksiw, Susan	'93 - 3	Joe Silva	small-town chief of police	Mellingham, MA
Padgett, Abigail	'93 - 5	Barbara Joan "Bo" Bradley	child abuse investigator	San Diego, CA
Page, Emma	'80 - 9	Kelsey, Inspector	police inspector	England
Paul, Barbara	'84 - 7	Marian Larch	no-nonsense NYPD officer	New York, NY
Penn, John	'83 - 6	George Thorne	detective superintendent	Oxfordshire, England
Penn, John	'88 - 12	Richard Tansey	chief inspector	Oxfordshire, England
Perry, Anne	'79 - 18	Thomas & Charlotte Pitt	Victorian police inspector & wife	London, England
Perry, Anne	'90 - 9	William Monk	amnesiac Victorian police inspector	London, England
Petrie, Rhona	'63 - 5	Marcus MacLurg	police inspector	England
Petrie, Rhona	'67 - 2	Nassim Pride	Anglo-Sudanese forensic scientist	England
Pulver, Mary Monica	'87 - 5	Peter & Kori Price Brichter	police detective & horse breeder	Illinois
Quest, Erica	'88 - 3	Kate Maddox	first woman DCI	Cotswolds, England
Quinton, Ann	'89 - 6	James Roland & Patrick Mansfield	det. inspector & det. sergeant	Suffolk, England
Radley, Sheila	'78 - 9	Douglas Quantrill & Hilary Lloyd	DCI & sergeant partner	Suffolk, England
Reichs, Kathy	'97 - 2	Temperance Brennan	forensic anthropologist	Montreal, QB, Canada
Rendell, Ruth	'64 - 17	Reginald Wexford	chief inspector	Sussex, England
Richardson, Tracey	'97 - 3	Stevie Houston	gay rookie homicide detective	Toronto, ON, Canada
Rippon, Marion	'69 - 4	Maurice Ygrec	retired French police inspector	Moselle, France
Robb, J.D.	'95 - 8	Eve Dallas	21st century NYPD lieutenant	New York, NY
Roberts, Carey	'89 - 2	Anne Fitzhugh	police detective	Washington, DC
Rowe, Jennifer	'97 - 2	Tessa Vance	senior homicide detective	Sydney, Australia
Rowlands, Betty	'96 - 3	Sukey Reynolds	police photographer	England
Sale, Medora	'86 - 6	John Sanders & Harriet Jeffries	police detective & photographer	Toronto, ON, Canada
Sandstrom, Eve K.	'90 - 3	Sam & Nicky Titus	ex-CID sheriff & photographer wife	Holton, OK
Schier, Norma	'78 - 4	Kay Barth	district attorney	Aspen, CO
Shepherd, Stella	'89 - 7	Richard Montgomery	CID Inspector	Nottingham, England
Silva, Linda Kay	'91 - 5	Delta Stevens	gay woman police officer	Southern CA
Simpson, Dorothy	'81 - 14	Luke Thanet	family-man police inspector	Kent, England
Sims, L.V.	'87 - 3	Dixie T. Struthers	police sergeant	San Jose, CA
Sjöwall, Maj & Per Wahlöö	'67 - 10	Martin Beck	Swedish police officer	Stockholm, Sweden
Smith, Alison	'84 - 2	Judd Springfield	small town police chief	Coolridge Corners, VT
Smith, Julie	'90 - 8	Skip Langdon	6-ft. police detective	New Orleans, LA
Smith-Levin, Judith	'96 - 3	Starletta DuVall	6-ft. black homicide lieutenant	Brookport, MA
Speart, Jessica	'97 - 3	Rachel Porter	Fish & Wildlife agent	USA
Stacey, Susannah	'87 - 8	Robert Bone	widowed British police inspector	England
Stubbs, Jean	'73 - 3	John Joseph Lintott	retired Scotland Yard inspector	London, England
Taylor, Alison G.	'95 - 3	Michael McKenna	detective chief inspector	Wales
Thomson, June	'71 - 18	Inspector Finch	police inspector	Essex, England
Thurlo, Aimée & David	'95 - 5	Ella Clah	Navajo FBI agent	Shiprock, NM
Uhnak, Dorothy	'68 - 3	Christine Opara	20-something police detective	New York, NY
Wallace, Marilyn	'86 - 3	Jay Goldstein & Carlos Cruz	homicide detectives	Oakland, CA
Wallingford, Lee	'91 - 2	Ginny Trask & Frank Carver	U.S. Forest Service officers	Oregon
Webb, Martha G.	'85 - 2	Smoky O'Donnell	small-town PD narcotics officer	Farmer's Mound, TX
Weir, Charlene	'92 - 4	Susan Wren	ex-cop turned police chief	Hampstead, KS

Author	1 - #	Series Character	Occupation	Setting

Police

Author	1 - #	Series Character	Occupation	Setting
Wells, Tobias	'66 - 16	Knute Severson	police officer	Boston, MA
Wender, Theodora	'85 - 2	Glad Gold & Alden Chase	English professor & police chief	Wading River, MA
Weston, Carolyn	'72 - 3	Casey Kellog & Al Krug	college-grad cop & hard-bitten partner	Santa Monica, CA
White, Teri	'84 - 2	Spaceman Kowalski & Blue Maguire	prickly cop partners	Los Angeles, CA
Whitehead, Barbara	'88 - 8	Robert Southwell	detective chief inspector	York, England
Wingate, Anne	'88 - 5	Mark Shigata	ex-FBI agent turned sheriff	Bayport, TX
Winslow, Pauline Glen	'75 - 6	Merle Capricorn	magician turned police superintendent	England
Woods, Paula L.	'99 - 2	Charlotte Justice	black woman homicide detective	Los Angeles, CA
Wren, M.K.	'99 - 1	Neely Jones	black woman sheriff-elect	Taft County, OR
Wright, L.R.	'99 - 1	Eddie Henderson	woman police officer	Vancouver, BC, Canada
Wright, L.R.	'85 - 9	Martin Karl Alberg	RCMP staff sergeant	Sechelt, BC, Canada
York, Kieran	'93 - 2	Royce Madison	lesbian deputy sheriff	Timber City, CO
Youmans, Claire	'96 - 2	Janet Schilling	county chief deputy prosecutor	Coastal WA

Private Investigators

Author	1 - #	Series Character	Occupation	Setting
Babbin, Jacqueline	'72 - 2	Clovis Kelly	homicide cop turned crime consultant	New York, NY
Bacon-Smith, Camille	'96 - 2	Kevin Bradley	daemon art recovery specialist	Philadelphia, PA
Barnes, Linda	'87 - 7	Carlotta Carlyle	6'1" cab-driving ex-cop P.I.	Boston, MA
Beck, K.K.	'92 - 4	Jane da Silva	former lounge singer	Seattle, WA
Bedford, Jean	'90 - 3	Anna Southwood	private enquiry agent	Sydney, Australia
Benjamin, Carole Lea	'96 - 3	Rachel Alexander & Dash	dog trainer turned P.I. & pitbull sidekick	New York, NY
Black, Cara	'99 - 2	Aimée Leduc	French-American private eye	Paris, France
Borton, D.B.	'93 - 6	Cat Caliban	60-something P.I.-in-training	Cincinnati, OH
Bowers, Elisabeth	'88 - 2	Meg Lacey	single-mother private eye	Vancouver, BC, Canada
Brod, D.C.	'89 - 4	Quint McCauley	ex-cop turned private eye	Chicago suburb, IL
Bryan, Kate	'98 - 2	Maggie Maguire	ex-Pinkerton agent	San Francisco, CA
Buggé, Carole	'98 - 1	Sherlock Holmes	consulting detective	London, England
Bushell, Agnes	'89 - 2	Wilson & Wilder	lesbian private eye duo	Portland, ME
Calloway, Kate	'96 - 7	Cassidy James	rookie lesbian private eye	Cedar Hills, OR
Cannon, Taffy	'93 - 3	Nan Robinson	state bar investigator	Los Angeles, CA
Chapman, Sally	'91 - 4	Juliet Blake	computer fraud investigator	Silicon Valley, CA
Chase, Elaine Raco	'87 - 2	Nikki Holden & Roman Cantrell	investigative reporter & private eye	Miami, FL
Clark, Carol Higgins	'92 - 4	Regan Reilly	P.I. and novelist's daughter	Los Angeles, CA
Cody, Liza	'80 - 6	Anna Lee	investigator for security firm	London, England
Cody, Liza	'92 - 3	Eva Wylie	wrestler and security guard	London, England
Dain, Catherine	'92 - 7	Freddie O'Neal	plane-flying keno-playing P.I.	Reno, NV
Davis, Lindsey	'89 - 11	Marcus Didius Falco	1st century Roman private eye	Rome, Italy
Dawson, Janet	'90 - 8	Jeri Howard	private eye	Oakland, CA
Day, Marele	'88 - 4	Claudia Valentine	private investigator	Sydney, Australia
Donald, Anabel	'93 - 5	Alex Tanner	TV researcher and part-time P.I.	London, England
Douglas, Lauren W.	'87 - 6	Caitlin Reece	lesbian private eye	Victoria, BC, Canada
Duffy, Stella	'94 - 3	Saz Martin	lesbian private eye	London, England
Dunant, Sarah	'92 - 3	Hannah Wolfe	contract private investigator	London, England
Dunlap, Susan	'89 - 4	Kiernan O'Shaughnessy	medical examiner turned P.I.	La Jolla, CA
Edwards, Grace F.	'97 - 2	Mali Anderson	black ex-cop in Harlem	New York, NY
Eichler, Selma	'94 - 6	Desiree Shapiro	5'2" queen-size P.I.	New York, NY
Elrod, P.N.	'90 - 7	Jack Fleming	'30s reporter turned vampire	Chicago, IL
Evanovich, Janet	'94 - 4	Stephanie Plum	lingerie buyer turned bounty hunter	Trenton, NJ
Eyre, Elizabeth	'92 - 6	Sigismondo	agent of a Renaissance duke	Venice, Italy
Farrell, Gillian B.	'92 - 2	Annie McGrogan	actor-P.I. returned from LA	New York, NY
Femling, Jean	'89 - 2	Martha Brant	insurance claims investigator	Orange County, CA
Fickling, G.G.	'62 - 3	Erik March	macho private eye	Los Angeles, CA
Fickling, G.G.	'57 - 11	Honey West	sexiest P.I. ever to pull a trigger	Los Angeles, CA
Frankel, Valerie	'91 - 4	Wanda Mallory	detective agency owner	New York, NY
Furie, Ruthe	'95 - 3	Fran Kirk	ex-battered wife turned fledgling P.I.	Buffalo, NY
Gallison, Kate	'86 - 3	Nick Magaracz	private investigator	Trenton, NJ
Garcia-Aguilera, C.	'96 - 3	Lupe Solano	Cuban-American princess P.I.	Miami, FL
Geason, Susan	'90 - 3	Syd Fish	politically incorrect P.I.	Sydney, Australia
Grafton, Sue	'82 - 14	Kinsey Millhone	blue-collar ex-cop P.I.	Santa Teresa, CA
Granger, Ann	'97 - 3	Fran Varaday	unlicensed young investigator	London, England
Grant, Linda	'88 - 6	Catherine Sayler	single-mother corporate P.I.	San Francisco, CA
Green, Christine	'91 - 4	Kate Kinsella	nurse and medical investigator	Longborough, England
Haddad, C.A.	'92 - 2	Becky Belski	computer investigator	Chicago, IL
Hager, Jean	'92 - 4	Molly Bearpaw	Cherokee civil rights investigator	Tahlequah, OK

Author	1 - #	Series Character	Occupation	Setting
Private Investigators				
Hamilton, Laurell K.	'93 - 8	Anita Blake	reanimator and vampire hunter	St. Louis, MO
Hightower, Lynn S.	'93 - 1	Lena Padget	private investigator	Lexington, KY
Hooper, Kay	'91 - 2	Lane Montana & Trey Fortier	finder of lost things & homicide detective	Atlanta, GA
Howe, Melodie J.	'89 - 2	Claire Conrad & Maggie Hill	elegant P.I. & assistant	Los Angeles, CA
Huff, Tanya	'92 - 5	Vicki Nelson	ex-cop turned P.I. with vampire lover	Toronto, ON, Canada
Jackson, Hialeah	'98 - 2	Annabelle Hardy-Maratos & Dave the Monkeyman	security specialists	Miami, FL
Jacobs, Nancy Baker	'91 - 3	Devon MacDonald	ex-teacher private eye	Minneapolis, MN
James, P.D.	'72 - 2	Cordelia Gray	fledgling P.I.	London, England
Johnson, Barbara	'95 - 2	Colleen Fitzgerald	lesbian insurance investigator	Washington, DC
Kellogg, Marne Davis	'95 - 5	Lilly Bennett	US marshal and security firm owner	Roundup, WY
Kelly, Mary	'61 - 2	Hedley Nicholson	private investigator	England
Kershaw, Valerie	'93 - 4	Mitch Mitchell & Tommy Hung	radio journalist P.I. & Chinese partner	Birmingham, England
Kijewski, Karen	'89 - 9	Kat Colorado	bar-tending private investigator	Sacramento, CA
King, Laurie R.	'94 - 4	Mary Russell	Sherlock Holmes' detecting partner	London, England
Kittredge, Mary	'90 - 6	Edwina Crusoe	RN and medical consultant	New Haven, CT
Knight, Phyllis	'92 - 2	Lil Ritchie	ex-rocker and gay woman P.I.	Charlottesville, VA
La Plante, Lynda	'94 - 3	Lorraine Page	sober ex-cop turned private eye	Los Angeles, CA
Lackey, Mercedes	'89 - 3	Diana Tregarde	investigator of unnatural events	Hartford, CT
Lanier, Virginia	'95 - 4	Jo Beth Sidden	search-and-rescue bloodhound trainer	Dunston County, GA
Law, Janice	'76 - 9	Anna Peters	oil company executive turned P.I.	Washington, DC
Lawrence, Hilda	'44 - 3	Mark East, Bessie Petty & Beulah Pond	Manhattan P.I. & little old ladies	New York, New York
Lawrence, Martha	'95 - 3	Elizabeth Chase	parapsychologist turned P.I.	San Diego, CA
Lee, Wendi	'94 - 3	Angela Matelli	ex-Marine turned P.I.	Boston, MA
Lee, Wendi	'89 - 6	Jefferson Birch	P.I. in the Old West	Western
Lin-Chandler, Irene	'95 - 3	Holly-Jean Ho	Anglo-Chinese bisexual investigator	London, England
Lippman, Laura	'97 - 4	Tess Monaghan	newspaper reporter turned P.I.	Baltimore, MD
Livesay, Ann	'98 - 5	Barry Ross	international investigator	International
Lordon, Randye	'93 - 5	Sydney Sloane	lesbian private investigator	New York, NY
MacGregor, T.J.	'86 - 10	Quin St. James & Mike McCleary	wife & husband P.I. team	Florida
Maiman, Jaye	'91 - 6	Robin Miller	lesbian travel & romance writer turned P.I.	New York, NY
Manthorne, Jackie	'00 - 1	Elizabeth Ellis	lesbian private eye	Toronto, ON, Canada
Marcy, Jean	'97 - 2	Meg Darcy	blue-collar lesbian private eye	St. Louis, MO
Mather, Linda	'94 - 2	Jo Hughes	astrologer-investigator	England
McCafferty, Taylor	'90 - 6	Haskell Blevins	small-town private eye	Pigeon Fork, KY
McDermid, Val	'92 - 6	Kate Brannigan	5' 3" redheaded private eye	Manchester, England
McKenna, Bridget	'93 - 3	Caley Burke	30-something private eye	Northern CA
McKevett, G.A.	'95 - 4	Savannah Reid	voluptuous ex-cop private eye	San Carmelita, CA
Meek, M.R.D.	'82 - 11	Lennox Kemp	solicitor detective	England
Meyers, Annette	'99 - 1	Olivia Brown	20s Greenwich Village poet P.I.	New York, NY
Michaels, Melisa	'97 - 2	Rosie Lavine	private eye to the elf world	California
Morgan, D Miller	'87 - 2	Daisy Marlow & Sam Milo	lingerie-addicted P.I. & sheriff	San Diego, CA
Muller, Marcia	'86 - 3	Joanna Stark	international art investigator	Napa Valley, CA
Muller, Marcia	'77 - '	Sharon McCone	legal investigator turned P.I.	San Francisco, CA
Munger, Katy	'97 - 2	Casey Jones	unlicensed private eye	Durham, NC
Murphy, Shirley R.	'96 - 4	Joe Grey	talking-cat private eye	Molena Point, CA
Murray, Lynne	'97 - 4	Josephine Fuller	Queen-sized private investigator	Seattle, WA
O'Callaghan, Maxine	'80 - 6	Delilah West	private investigator	Orange County, CA
O'Donnell, Lillian	'90 - 4	Gwenn Ramadge	corporate investigator	New York, NY
Oliver, Maria-Antonia	'87 - 2	Lonia Guiu	Catalan investigator	Barcelona, Spain
Osborne, Denise	'94 - 2	Queenie Davilov	screenwriter-investigator	Hollywood, CA
Paretsky, Sara	'82 - 8	V. I. Warshawski	attorney turned P.I.	Chicago, IL
Penman, Sharon Kay	'96 - 2	Justin de Quincy	Queen Mother's investigator	England
Pincus, Elizabeth	'92 - 3	Nell Fury	lesbian P.I.	San Francisco, CA
Prowell, Sandra West	'93 - 3	Phoebe Siegel	ex-cop P.I.	Billings, MT
Redmann, J.M.	'90 - 3	Michelle 'Micky' Knight	gay woman private eye	New Orleans, LA
Reuben, Shelly	'94 - 2	Wylie Nolan & Max Bramble	arson investigator & attorney	New York, NY
Robb, Candace M.	'93 - 6	Owen Archer	one-eyed medieval Welsh spy	York, England
Roberts, Gillian	'98 - 1	Emma Howe & Billie August	50-yr-old P.I. & single-mom partner	San Raphael, CA
Robinson, Lynda S.	'94 - 5	Lord Meren	Tutankhamen's chief investigator	Egypt
Rogers, Chris	'98 - 2	Dixie Flannigan	prosecutor turned bounty hunter	Houston, TX
Ross, Annie	'95 - 3	Bel Carson	TV director and investigator	London, England
Rowland, Laura Joh	'94 - 4	Sano Ichiro	investigator for the shogun	Edo, Japan
Rozan, S.J.	'94 - 6	Lydia Chin & Bill Smith	Chinese-American & Army-brat P.I. duo	New York, NY
Scoppettone, Sandra	'91 - 5	Lauren Laurano	lesbian private investigator	New York, NY

Author	1 - #	Series Character	Occupation	Setting

Private Investigators

Author	1 - #	Series Character	Occupation	Setting
Shone, Anna	'94 - 2	Ulysses Finnegan Donaghue	Shakespeare scholar private eye	Provence, France
Short, Sharon Gwyn	'94 - 3	Patricia Delaney	computer-whiz investigator	Cincinnati, OH
Singer, Shelley	'93 - 4	Barrett Lake	history teacher turned P.I.	Berkeley, CA
Singer, Shelley	'83 - 5	Jake Samson & Rosie Vicente	ex-cop & carpenter	Berkeley, CA
Slovo, Gillian	'84 - 5	Kate Baeier	journalist turned P.I.	London, England
Smith, Cynthia	'96 - 5	Emma Rhodes	private resolver for the rich	London, England
Smith, J.C.S.	'80 - 2	Quentin Jacoby	retired transit cop	New York, NY
Songer, C.J.	'98 - 2	Meg Gillis	ex-cop turned security consultant	Beverly Hills, CA
Spring, Michelle	'94 - 4	Laura Principal	British academic turned P.I.	Cambridge, England
Stabenow, Dana	'92 - 10	Kate Shugak	Alaskan ex-D.A. investigator	Arkansas
Stabenow, Dana	'98 - 3	L. Campbell & W. Chouinard	state trooper & bush pilot	Arkansas
Staincliffe, Cath	'94 - 3	Sal Kilkenny	single-mother private eye	Manchester, England
Sucher, Dorothy	'88 - 2	Sabina Swift	detective agency owner	Washington, DC
Sullivan, Winona	'93 - 3	Cecile Buddenbrooks	licensed P.I. heiress-nun	Boston, MA
Sumner, Penny	'92 - 2	Victoria Cross	archivist turned P.I.	London, England
Taylor, Elizabeth A.	'81 - 3	Maggie Elliott	ex-film maker turned P.I.	San Francisco, CA
Taylor, Jean	'95 - 2	Maggie Garrett	young lesbian P.I.	San Francisco, CA
Thrasher, L.L.	'91 - 2	Zachariah Smith	ex-cop private eye	Mackie, OR
Tone, Teona	'83 - 2	Kyra Keaton	turn-of-the-century P.I.	Washington, DC
Trocheck, Kathy H.	'92 - 7	Callahan Garrity	ex-cop cleaning service operator	Atlanta, GA
Van Gieson, Judith	'88 - 8	Neil Hamel	attorney & investigator	Albuquerque, NM
Wallace, Patricia	'88 - 4	Sydney Bryant	private investigator	San Diego, CA
Welch, Pat	'90 - 6	Helen Black	ex-cop lesbian private eye	Berkeley, CA
Wesley, Valerie Wilson	'94 - 5	Tamara Hayle	black ex-cop single-mother P.I.	Newark, NJ
White, Gloria	'91 - 4	Veronica 'Ronnie' Ventana	Anglo-Mexican private eye	San Francisco, CA
Wilhelm, Kate	'87 - 6	C. Meiklejohn & C. Leidl	P.I. & psychologist	New York, NY
Wiltz, Chris	'81 - 3	Neal Rafferty	3rd-generation cop turned P.I.	New Orleans, LA
Wings, Mary	'86 - 4	Emma Victor	lesbian activist private eye	San Francisco, CA
Wren, M.K.	'73 - 8	Conan Flagg	secret agent turned bookstore owner	Coastal OR
Zaremba, Eve	'78 - 6	Helen Keremos	40-something lesbian private eye	Toronto, ON, Canada
Zukowski, Sharon	'91 - 5	Blaine Stewart	ex-cop turned corporate P.I.	New York, NY

Espionage

Author	1 - #	Series Character	Occupation	Setting
Dewhurst, Eileen	'82 - 2	Helen Markham Johnson	actress recruited by Secret Service	London, England
Duffy, Margaret	'87 - 6	Ingrid Langley & Patrick Gillard	novelist secret agent & army major	England
Dunnett, Dorothy	'68 - 7	Johnson Johnson	British agent and yachtsman	International
Gilman, Dorothy	'66 - 13	Emily Pollifax	grandmother CIA agent	International
Haddad, C.A.	'76 - 2	David Haham	government agent	Middle East
Hooper, Kay	'87 - 11	Hagen	government agent	USA
Lynds, Gayle	'96 - 2	Sarah Walker & Liz Sansborough	CIA agents	International
Mann, Jessica	'82 - 6	Tamara Hoyland	British secret agent archaeologist	England
Scott, Barbara A.	'93 - 3	Brad Rollins et al	international kidnap-rescue team	International
Tan, Maureen	'97 - 2	Jane Nichols	secret agent turned mystery writer	Savannah, Georgia
Weber, Janice	'92 - 2	Leslie Frost	secret agent and concert violinist	Washington, DC
Williams, Amanda K.	'90 - 4	Madison McGuire	deep cover intelligence agent	International

Background Type

Academic

Author	1 - #	Series Character	Occupation	Setting
Belfort, Sophie	'86 - 3	Molly Rafferty	college history professor	Boston, MA
Berenson, Laurien	'95 - 6	Melanie Travis	special ed teacher and dog lover	Connecticut
Borthwick, J.S.	'82 - 9	Sarah Deane & Alex McKenzie	English professor & internist	Boston, MA
Bowen, Gail	'90 - 6	Joanne Kilbourn	political science professor	Regina, SK, Canada
Carlson, P.M.	'85 - 8	Maggie Ryan	coed turned statistician mom	New York, NY
Clarke, Anna	'85 - 9	Paula Glenning	British professor & writer	London, England
Cleary, Melissa	'92 - 10	Jackie Walsh & Jake	film instructor & ex-police dog	Palmer, OH
Cross, Amanda	'64 - 12	Kate Fansler	feminist English professor	New York, NY
Cutler, Judith	'95 - 5	Sophie Rivers	college lecturer and amateur singer	Birmingham, England
Dobson, Joanne	'97 - 3	Karen Pelletier	single-mother English professor	Enfield, MA
Farrelly, Gail E.	'95 - 2	Lisa King	finance professor and CPA	Boston, MA
Flora, Kate Clark	'94 - 5	Thea Kozak	educational consultant	Boston, MA
French, Linda	'98 - 3	Teddy Morelli	college history professor	Seattle, WA
Gosling, Paula	'85 - 2	Jack Stryker & Kate Trevorne	homicide cop & English professor	Michigan
Hornsby, Wendy	'87 - 2	Kate Teague & Roger Tejeda	college professor & homicide detective	Los Angeles, CA

Author	1 - #	Series Character	Occupation	Setting

Background Type

Academic

Author	1 - #	Series Character	Occupation	Setting
Jones, D.J.H.	'93 - 2	Nancy Cook	Chaucer scholar and professor	Chicago, IL
Kelly, Nora	'84 - 4	Gillian Adams	college history department chair	Vancouver, BC, Canada
Kenney, Susan	'83 - 3	Roz Howard & Alan Stewart	American professor & British painter	Maine
Kiecolt-Glaser, Janice	'97 - 2	Haley McAlister	psychologist and professor	Houston, TX
Langton, Jane	'64 - 13	Homer Kelly	ex-cop turned Harvard professor	Cambridge, MA
LaPierre, Janet	'87 - 5	Meg Halloran & Vince Gutierrez	single-mother school teacher & police chief	Port Silva, CA
Lee, Marie	'95 - 3	Marguerite Smith	retired science teacher	Cape Cod, MA
Lorens, M.K.	'90 - 5	Winston Marlowe Sherman	mystery-writing Shakespeare professor	New York, NY
Mackay, Amanda	'76 - 2	Hannah Land	divorced New York PhD	Durham, NC
MacLeod, Charlotte	'78 - 10	Peter Shandy & Helen M. Shandy	botany professor & librarian wife	Balaclava Co., MA
Mann, Jessica	'72 - 2	Thea Crawford	archaeology professor	England
Mariz, Linda French	'92 - 2	Laura Ireland	grad student volleyball player	Seattle, WA
McCrumb, Sharyn	'88 - 2	James Owens Mega	science fiction author professor	Tennessee
Paton Walsh, Jill	'93 - 2	Imogen Quy	St. Agatha's College nurse	Cambridge, England
Peterson, Audrey	'92 - 3	Claire Camden	California English professor	London, England
Roberts, Gillian	'87 - 8	Amanda Pepper	high school English teacher	Philadelphia, PA
Shaber, Sarah R.	'97 - 2	Simon Shaw	young history professor	Raleigh, NC
Singer, Shelley	'93 - 4	Barrett Lake	history teacher turned P.I.	Berkeley, CA
Skom, Edith	'89 - 3	Elizabeth Austin	English professor	Chicago, IL
Smith, Joan	'87 - 5	Loretta Lawson	British feminist professor	London, England
Smith, Joan G.	'89 - 2	Cassie Newton	college French major	Montreal, QB, Canada
Thomas-Graham, P.	'98 - 2	Nikki Chase	black economics professor	Cambridge, MA
Wender, Theodora	'85 - 2	Glad Gold & Alden Chase	English professor & police chief	Wading River, MA
Wright, Sally S.	'97 - 2	Ben Reese	'60s university archivist	Ohio
Yorke, Margaret	'70 - 5	Patrick Grant	Oxford don	Oxford, England

Advertising & Public Relations

Author	1 - #	Series Character	Occupation	Setting
Babson, Marian	'71 - 4	Douglas Perkins	public relations agent	London, England
Bennett, Liza	'89 - 2	Peg Goodenough	ad agency creative director	New York, NY
Brennan, Carol	'91 - 2	Liz Wareham	40-ish public relations consultant	New York, NY
Claire, Edie	'99 - 3	Leigh Koslow	advertising copywriter	Pittsburgh, PA
Crespi, Camilla	'91 - 7	Simona Griffo	gourmet cook ad executive	New York, NY
Douglas, Carole N.	'92 - 9	Temple Barr & Midnight Louie	PR freelancer & tomcat sleuth	Las Vegas, NV
Grant, Anne U.	'98 - 3	Sydney Teague	single-mother ad agency owner	Charlotte, NC
Stuyck, Karen Hanson	'95 - 3	Liz James	journalist turned PR rep	Houston, TX
Woods, Sherryl	'91 - 4	Molly DeWitt	film promoter and single mother	Miami, FL

Animals, cats

Author	1 - #	Series Character	Occupation	Setting
Braun, Lilian Jackson	'66 - 21	Jim Qwilleran, Koko & Yum Yum	ex-police reporter & cats	Upper Peninsula, MI
Brown, Rita Mae	'90 - 6	Mary Minor Haristeen	small-town postmistress	Crozet, VA
Douglas, Carole N.	'92 - 9	Temple Barr & Midnight Louie	PR freelancer & tomcat sleuth	Las Vegas, NV
Matthews, Alex	'96 - 3	Cassidy McCabe	psychotherapist	Oak Park, IL
Murphy, Shirley R.	'96 - 4	Joe Grey	talking-cat private eye	Molena Point, CA

Animals, dogs

Author	1 - #	Series Character	Occupation	Setting
Benjamin, Carole Lea	'96 - 3	Rachel Alexander & Dash	dog trainer turned P.I. & pitbull sidekick	New York, NY
Berenson, Laurien	'95 - 6	Melanie Travis	special ed teacher and dog lover	Connecticut
Cleary, Melissa	'92 - 10	Jackie Walsh & Jake	film instructor & ex-police dog	Palmer, OH
Conant, Susan	'89 - 11	Holly Winter	dog trainer & magazine columnist	Cambridge, MA
Henry, Sue	'91 - 5	Jessie Arnold & Alex Jensen	sled dog racer & Alaska state trooper	Anchorage, AK
Lanier, Virginia	'95 - 4	Jo Beth Sidden	search-and-rescue bloodhound trainer	Dunston County, GA
Moore, Barbara	'83 - 2	Gordon Christy	veterinarian	New Mexico
Petit, Diane	'97 - 3	Kathryn Bogert	owner of an estate sale business	Chicago, IL

Animals, horses

Author	1 - #	Series Character	Occupation	Setting
Banks, Carolyn	'93 - 5	Robin Vaughan	equestrienne sleuth	Texas
Crum, Laura	'94 - 4	Gail McCarthy	horse veterinarian	Santa Cruz, CA
Jaffe, Jody	'95 - 3	Natalie Gold	reporter on horse show circuit	Charlotte, NC

Animals, other

Author	1 - #	Series Character	Occupation	Setting
Block, Barbara	'94 - 5	Robin Light	pet store owner	Syracuse, NY
Claire, Edie	'99 - 3	Leigh Koslow	advertising copywriter	Pittsburgh, PA
Cleeves, Ann	'86 - 8	George & Molly Palmer-Jones	ex-Home Office bird-watcher & wife	Surrey, England

Author	1 - #	Series Character	Occupation	Setting

Background Type

Animals, other

Author	1 - #	Series Character	Occupation	Setting
Fiedler, Jacqueline	'98 - 2	Caroline Canfield	wildlife artist	River Ridge, IL
Fritchley, Alma	'97 - 3	Letty Campbell	lesbian chicken farmer	Manchester, England
Roberts, Lillian M.	'96 - 3	Andi Pauling	veterinarian	Palm Springs, CA
Wilson, Karen Ann	'94 - 4	Samantha Holt	veterinary technician	Paradise Cay, FL

new Archaeology & Anthropology

Author	1 - #	Series Character	Occupation	Setting
Arnold, Margot	'79 - 12	Penny Spring & Toby Glendower	anthropologist & archaeologist	World Travelers
Connor, Beverly	'96 - 3	Lindsay Chamberlain	forensic archaeologist	Athens, GA
Cramer, Rebecca	'98 - 2	Linda Bluenight	anthropologist turned teacher	Tucson, AZ
Davis, Val	'96 - 3	Nicolette Scott	UC-Berkeley archaeologist	New Mexico
Godfrey, Ellen	'76 - 2	Rebecca Rosenthal	80-year-old Polish-born anthropologist	Toronto, ON, Canada
Hamilton, Lyn	'97 - 4	Lara McClintock	antiquities dealer and shop owner	Toronto, ON, Canada
Livesay, Ann	'98 - 5	Barry Ross	international investigator	International
Mann, Jessica	'82 - 6	Tamara Hoyland	British secret agent archaeologist	England
Mann, Jessica	'72 - 2	Thea Crawford	archaeology professor	England
McCrumb, Sharyn	'84 - 8	Elizabeth MacPherson	forensic anthropologist	Virginia
Reichs, Kathy	'97 - 2	Temperance Brennan	forensic anthropologist	Montreal, QB, Canada

new Architecture & Engineering

Author	1 - #	Series Character	Occupation	Setting
Schumacher, Aileen	'96 - 3	Tory Travers	structural engineer	Las Cruces, NM
Wolzien, Valerie	'96 - 3	Josie Pigeon	all-women construction firm owner	Northeast

Art & Antiques

Author	1 - #	Series Character	Occupation	Setting
Bacon-Smith, Camille	'96 - 2	Kevin Bradley	daemon art recovery specialist	Philadelphia, PA
Bolitho, Janie	'97 - 2	Rose Trevelyan	widowed painter and photographer	Cornwall, England
Brown, Lizbie	'92 - 2	Elizabeth Blair	American widow quilt shop owner	Bath, England
Coker, Carolyn	'84 - 5	Andrea Perkins	art historian & restorer	Boston, MA
Comfort, Barbara	'86 - 5	Tish McWhinny	70-something artist-painter	Lofton, VT
Crane, Hamilton	'68 - 22	Emily D. Seeton	retired British art teacher	Kent, England
Dawkins, Cecil	'93 - 2	Ginevra Prettifield	art museum assistant director	Santa Fe, NM
Dunnett, Dorothy	'68 - 7	Johnson Johnson	British agent and yachtsman	International
Ferris, Monica	'99 - 2	Betsy Devonshire	needlework shop owner	Excelsior, MN
Fiedler, Jacqueline	'98 - 2	Caroline Canfield	wildlife artist	River Ridge, IL
Fowler, Earlene	'94 - 7	Benni Harper	folk art museum curator	San Celina, CA
Hamilton, Lyn	'97 - 4	Lara McClintock	antiquities dealer and shop owner	Toronto, ON, Canada
Hardwick, Mollie	'86 - 7	Doran Fairweather	British antiques dealer	Kent, England
Henderson, Lauren	'95 - 4	Sam Jones	20-something sculptress	London, England
Kenney, Susan	'83 - 3	Roz Howard & Alan Stewart	American professor & British painter	Maine
Knight, Kathryn Lasky	'86 - 4	Calista Jacobs	illustrator of children's books	Cambridge, MA
Laurence, Janet	'98 - 2	Canaletto	18th century Italian painter	London, England
Logan, Margaret	'94 - 2	Olivia Chapman	interior decorator	Boston, MA
MacLeod, Charlotte	'79 - 12	Sarah Kelling & Max Bittersohn	investigative couple	Boston, MA
Massey, Sujata	'97 - 3	Rei Shimura	Japanese-American antiques dealer	Tokyo, Japan
McClendon, Lise	'94 - 2	Alix Thorssen	gallery owner and art forgery expert	Jackson Hole, WY
Montgomery, Yvonne	'87 - 2	Finny Aletter	stockbroker turned carpenter	Denver, CO
Muller, Marcia	'83 - 3	Elena Oliverez	Mexican arts museum curator	Santa Barbara, CA
Muller, Marcia	'86 - 3	Joanna Stark	international art investigator	Napa Valley, CA
Myers, Tamar	'96 - 6	Abigail Timberlake	antiques dealer	Charlotte, NC
Orde, A.J.	'89 - 6	Jason Lynx	antiques dealer and decorator	Denver, CO
Peters, Elizabeth	'75 - 12	Amelia Peabody	Victorian feminist archaeologist	Kent, England
Peters, Elizabeth	'73 - 5	Vicky Bliss	art historian	Germany
Ruryk, Jean	'94 - 3	Catherine Wilde	ad exec turned antiques restorer	Montreal, QB, Canada
Smith, Evelyn E.	'86 - 4	Susan Melville	freelance assassin-painter	New York, NY
Valentine, Deborah	'89 - 3	Katharine Craig & Kevin Bryce	sculptor & ex-sheriff's detective	Lake Tahoe, CA
Watson, Clarissa	'77 - 5	Persis Willum	artist and gallery assistant	Long Island, NY
Yeager, Dorian	'94 - 2	Elizabeth Will	watercolorist-gallery owner	Dovekey, NH

Astrology [see Paranormal]

Author	1 - #	Series Character	Occupation	Setting

Background Type

Authors & Writers

Author	1 - #	Series Character	Occupation	Setting
Bannister, Jo	'84 - 3	Clio Rees & Harry Marsh	physician novelist & chief inspector	England
Barron, Stephanie	'96 - 3	Jane Austen	19th century British novelist	Bath, England
Brill, Toni	'91 - 2	Midge Cohen	children's author fluent in Russian	Brooklyn, NY
Clarke, Anna	'85 - 9	Paula Glenning	British professor & writer	London, England
Clayton, Mary	'95 - 5	John Reynolds	ex-inspector turned crime writer	Cornwall, England
Cooper, Natasha	'90 - 7	Willow King	civil-servant romance-novelist	London, England
Cooper, Susan Rogers	'92 - 5	E.J. Pugh	housewife-mom romance writer	Black Cat Ridge, TX
Dank, Gloria	'89 - 4	B. Woodruff & S. Randolph	children's author & his brother-in-law	Connecticut
Duffy, Margaret	'87 - 6	Ingrid Langley & Patrick Gillard	novelist secret agent & army major	England
Fitzwater, Judy	'98 - 2	Jennifer Marsh	aspiring mystery novelist	Atlanta, GA
Fletcher, Jessica	'89 - 11	Jessica Fletcher	60-something mystery writer	Cabot Cove, ME
Friedman, Mickey	'88 - 2	Georgia Lee Maxwell	freelance writer	Paris, France
Glen, Alison	'92 - 2	Charlotte Sams	freelance writer	Columbus, OH
Goldstone, Nancy	'95 - 2	Elizabeth Halperin	single-mother mystery writer	Berkshires, MA
Holbrook, Teri	'95 - 3	Gale Grayson	American expatriate historian	England
James, P.D.	'62 - 10	Adam Dalgleish	published poet of Scotland Yard	London, England
Jordan, Jennifer	'87 - 3	Barry & Dee Vaughan	spoofy crime writer & office temp wife	Woodfield, England
Kittredge, Mary	'87 - 3	Charlotte Kent	freelance writer	Connecticut
Laurence, Janet	'89 - 9	Darina Lisle	caterer-chef and food writer	West Country, England
Lorens, M.K.	'90 - 5	Winston Marlowe Sherman	mystery-writing Shakespeare professor	New York, NY
Maiman, Jaye	'91 - 6	Robin Miller	lesbian travel & romance writer turned P.I.	New York, NY
Malmont, Valerie S.	'94 - 2	Tori Miracle	crime writer turned novelist	Lickin Creek, PA
McCrumb, Sharyn	'88 - 2	James Owens Mega	science fiction author professor	Tennessee
Meyers, Annette	'99 - 1	Olivia Brown	'20s Greenwich Village poet P.I.	New York, NY
Moffat, Gwen	'73 - 14	Melinda Pink	mountain climbing novelist	Utah
Paige, Robin	'94 - 5	K. Ardleigh & C. Sheridan	American author & British scientist	Dedham, England
Papazoglou, Orania	'84 - 5	Patience Campbell McKenna	6-ft. romance novelist turned crime writer	New York, NY
Peters, Elizabeth	'72 - 4	Jacqueline Kirby	librarian turned romance novelist	New York, NY
Rowlands, Betty	'90 - 8	Melissa Craig	British crime novelist	Cotswolds, England
Rushford, Patricia H.	'97 - 3	Helen Bradley	ex-cop travel-writer grandmother	Lincoln City, OR
Saum, Karen	'90 - 3	Brigid Donovan	50-something lesbian ex-nun	Maine
Sherman, Beth	'98 - 2	Anne Hardaway	ghostwriter	Oceanside Hts, NJ
Smith, Barbara B.	'94 - 4	Jolie Wyatt	aspiring novelist	Purple Sage, TX
Smith, Julie	'85 - 2	Paul MacDonald	ex-reporter mystery writer	San Francisco, CA
Stallwood, Veronica	'93 - 6	Kate Ivory	historical romance novelist	Oxford, England
Tan, Maureen	'97 - 2	Jane Nichols	secret agent turned mystery writer	Savannah, Georgia
Waterhouse, Jane	'95 - 3	Garner Quin	best-selling true crime writer	Spring Lake, NJ

Baseball [see Sports]

Bed & Breakfast [see Hotels & Inns]

Black

Author	1 - #	Series Character	Occupation	Setting
Baker, Nikki	'91 - 3	Virginia Kelly	black lesbian stockbroker	Chicago, IL
Banks, Jacqueline T.	'98 - 2	Ruby Gordon	college-educated black cleaning woman	Oakland, CA
Bland, Eleanor Taylor	'92 - 7	Marti MacAlister	widowed black police detective	Lincoln Prairie, IL
Carter, Charlotte	'97 - 2	Nanette Hayes	young black tenor sax player	New York, NY
Coleman, Evelyn	'98 - 2	Pat Conley	black woman journalist	Atlanta, GA
Deloach, Nora	'94 - 6	Candi & Simone Covington	black social worker & paralegal daughter	Otis, SC
Edwards, Grace F.	'97 - 2	Mali Anderson	black ex-cop in Harlem	New York, NY
Grimes, Terris M.	'96 - 3	Theresa Galloway	black married-mother civil servant	Sacramento, CA
Hambly, Barbara	'97 - 2	Benjamin January	1830s Paris-trained black doctor	New Orleans, LA
McAllester, Melanie	'94 - 2	Elizabeth Mendoza	Hispanic-black lesbian homicide detective	San Francisco, CA
Mickelbury, Penny	'98 - 2	Carole Ann Gibson	black criminal defense attorney	Washington, DC
Mickelbury, Penny	'94 - 2	Gianna Maglione & Mimi Patterson	lesbian police lieutenant & reporter	Washington, DC
Moody, Susan	'84 - 7	Penny Wanawake	photographer daughter of black diplomat	England
Neely, Barbara	'92 - 3	Blanche White	black domestic worker	Boston, Massachusetts
Petrie, Rhona	'67 - 2	Nassim Pride	Anglo-Sudanese forensic scientist	England
Smith-Levin, Judith	'96 - 3	Starletta DuVall	6-ft. black homicide lieutenant	Brookport, MA
Thomas-Graham, P.	'98 - 2	Nikki Chase	black economics professor	Cambridge, MA
Wesley, Valerie Wilson	'94 - 5	Tamara Hayle	black ex-cop single-mother P.I.	Newark, NJ
Woods, Paula L.	'99 - 2	Charlotte Justice	black woman homicide detective	Los Angeles, CA
Wren, M.K.	'99 - 1	Neely Jones	black woman sheriff-elect	Taft County, OR

Author	1 - #	Series Character	Occupation	Setting

Background Type

Books & Libraries

Buggé, Carole	'99 - 3	Claire Rawlings	book editor with 12-year-old ward	New York, NY
Dereske, Jo	'94 - 6	Helma Zukas	public librarian	Bellehaven, WA
Harris, Charlaine	'90 - 6	Aurora Teagarden	librarian turned real estate agent	Lawrenceton, GA
Hart, Carolyn G.	'87 - 10	Annie Laurance & Max Darling	bookstore owner & investigator	Broward's Rock, SC
Hess, Joan	'86 - 12	Claire Malloy	small-town bookstore owner	Farberville, AR
Kaewert, Julie Wallin	'94 - 3	Alex Plumtree	head of family publishing firm	London, England
Knight, Kathryn Lasky	'86 - 4	Calista Jacobs	illustrator of children's books	Cambridge, MA
Macdonald, Marianne	'96 - 2	Dido Hoare	single-mother antiquarian bookseller	London, England
Millhiser, Marlys	'92 - 5	Charlie Greene	literary agent and single mother	Hollywood, CA
Monfredo, Miriam G.	'92 - 6	Glynis Tryon	1860s librarian suffragette	Seneca Falls, NY
Morgan, Kate	'90 - 7	Dewey James	60-something small-town librarian	Hamilton, KY
Shone, Anna	'94 - 2	Ulysses Finnegan Donaghue	Shakespeare scholar private eye	Provence, France
Simonson, Sheila	'90 - 5	Lark Dailey Dodge	6-ft. bookstore owner	Shoalwater, WA
Struthers, Betsy	'92 - 3	Rosalie Cairns	bookstore clerk turned academic	Ontario, Canada
Sumner, Penny	'92 - 2	Victoria Cross	archivist turned P.I.	London, England
Travis, Elizabeth	'89 - 2	Ben & Carrie Porter	husband & wife book publishers	Riverdale, CT
Wilson, Barbara	'90 - 2	Cassandra Reilly	Spanish translator	London, England
Wren, M.K.	'73 - 8	Conan Flagg	secret agent turned bookstore owner	Coastal OR

Botanical

Albert, Susan Wittig	'92 - 7	China Bayles	herb shop owner & former attorney	Pecan Springs, TX
Craig, Alisa	'81 - 5	Dittany Monk & Osbert Monk	garden club member & author of westerns	Ontario, Canada
Hadley, Joan	'86 - 2	Theo Bloomer	retired florist and former spy	USA
MacLeod, Charlotte	'78 - 10	Peter Shandy & Helen M. Shandy	botany professor & librarian wife	Balaclava Co., MA
Miles, Margaret	'98 - 2	C. Willett & R. Longfellow	Colonial farm woman & scientist-farmer	Bracebridge, MA
Ripley, Ann	'94 - 3	Louise Eldridge	organic gardener TV host	Northern VA
Roberts, Lora	'94 - 6	Liz Sullivan	freelance writer and organic gardener	Palo Alto, CA
Rothenberg, Rebecca	'91 - 3	Claire Sharples	microbiologist	Central CA
Wright, Nancy Means	'96 - 2	Ruth Willmarth	single-mother farmer	Branbury, VT

Business & Finance

Amey, Linda	'92 - 2	Blair Emerson	funeral director	Austin, TX
Bailey, Michele	'94 - 3	Matilda Haycastle	30-something office temp	Brussels, Belgium
Baker, Nikki	'91 - 3	Virginia Kelly	black lesbian stockbroker	Chicago, IL
Berne, Karin	'85 - 3	Ellie Gordon	law firm office manager	Orange County, CA
Berry, Carole	'87 - 7	Bonnie Indermill	tap-dancing Manhattan office temp	New York, NY
Castle, Jayne	'86 - 4	Guinevere Jones	office-temps business owner	Seattle, WA
Christmas, Joyce	'93 - 3	Betty Trenka	retired office manager	Connecticut
Day, Dianne	'95 - 6	Fremont Jones	1900s typewriting-business owner	San Francisco, CA
Epstein, Carole	'96 - 2	Barbara Simons	downsized business executive	Montreal, QB, Canada
Farrelly, Gail E.	'95 - 2	Lisa King	finance professor and CPA	Boston, MA
Feddersen, Connie	'93 - 6	Amanda Hazard	sexy small-town CPA	Vamoose, OK
Ferris, Monica	'99 - 2	Betsy Devonshire	needlework shop owner	Excelsior, MN
Flora, Kate Clark	'94 - 5	Thea Kozak	educational consultant	Boston, MA
Girdner, Jaqueline	'91 - 11	Kate Jasper	gag gift wholesaler	Marin County, CA
Godfrey, Ellen	'88 - 2	Jane Tregar	corporate headhunter	Toronto, ON, Canada
Grant, Linda	'88 - 6	Catherine Sayler	single-mother corporate P.I.	San Francisco, CA
Graves, Sarah	'98 - 3	Jacobia Triptree	ex-investment banker	Eastport, ME
Gunning, Sally	'90 - 10	Peter Bartholomew	odd-jobs company owner	Cape Cod, MA
Hartzmark, Gini	'92 - 5	Katherine Prescott Milholland	blueblood corporate attorney	Chicago, IL
Johnson, Barbara	'95 - 2	Colleen Fitzgerald	lesbian insurance investigator	Washington, DC
Johnson, Dolores	'97 - 3	Mandy Dyer	owner of Dyer's Cleaners	Denver, CO
Lacey, Sarah	'92 - 4	Leah Hunter	20-something tax inspector	Yorkshire, England
Lamb, J. Dayne	'93 - 3	Teal Stewart	Certified Public Accountant	Boston, MA
Lathen, Emma	'61 - 24	John Putnam Thatcher	Wall Street financial whiz	New York, NY
Law, Janice	'76 - 9	Anna Peters	oil company executive turned P.I.	Washington, DC
Maxwell, A.E.	'85 - 8	Fiddler & Fiora Flynn	knight-errant & investment banker	Southern CA
McCormick, Claire	'82 - 3	John Waltz	executive recruiter	Pennsylvania
Meyers, Annette	'89 - 7	Xenia Smith & Leslie Wetzon	Wall Street headhunters	New York, NY
Montgomery, Yvonne	'87 - 2	Finny Aletter	stockbroker turned carpenter	Denver, CO
Neel, Janet	'88 - 6	John McLeish & Francesca Wilson	DCI & businesswoman	London, England
Nunnally, Tiina	'96 - 2	Margit Andersson	freelance Danish translator	Seattle, WA
O'Donnell, Lillian	'90 - 4	Gwenn Ramadge	corporate investigator	New York, NY

Author	1 - #	Series Character	Occupation	Setting

Background Type

Business & Finance

Author	1 - #	Series Character	Occupation	Setting
O'Kane, Leslie	'96 - 3	Molly Masters	greeting card entrepreneur	Albany, NY
Petit, Diane	'97 - 3	Kathryn Bogert	owner of an estate sale business	Chicago, IL
Pickard, Nancy	'84 - 10	Jenny Cain	New England foundation director	Port Frederick, MA
Pugh, Dianne G.	'93 - 4	Iris Thorne	investment counselor	Los Angeles, CA
Shelton, Connie	'95 - 4	Charlie Parker	CPA turned investigator	Albuquerque, NM
Sprinkle, Patricia H.	'88 - 7	Sheila Travis	embassy wife turned executive	Atlanta, GA
Yeager, Dorian	'94 - 2	Elizabeth Will	watercolorist-gallery owner	Dovekey, NH
Zukowski, Sharon	'91 - 5	Blaine Stewart	ex-cop turned corporate P.I.	New York, NY

Comic Mysteries [see Humor]

Computers & Technology

Author	1 - #	Series Character	Occupation	Setting
Chapman, Sally	'91 - 4	Juliet Blake	computer fraud investigator	Silicon Valley, CA
D'Amato, Barbara	'96 - 2	Suze Figueroa & Norm Bennis	pair of cops	Chicago, IL
Danks, Denise	'89 - 4	Georgina Powers	British computer journalist	London, England
Godfrey, Ellen	'88 - 2	Jane Tregar	corporate headhunter	Toronto, ON, Canada
Haddad, C.A.	'92 - 2	Becky Belski	computer investigator	Chicago, IL
Holtzer, Susan	'94 - 5	Anneke Haagen	computer consultant	Ann Arbor, MI
Kelly, Susan B.	'90 - 5	Alison Hope & Nick Trevellyan	software designer & detective inspector	Hop Valley, England
Kennett, Shirley	'96 - 4	P.J. Gray	police dept. virtual reality expert	St. Louis, MO
Lin-Chandler, Irene	'95 - 3	Holly-Jean Ho	Anglo-Chinese bisexual investigator	London, England
Morrone, Wenda W.	'97 - 2	Lorelei Muldoon	high-profile numbers analyst	New York, NY
Short, Sharon Gwyn	'94 - 3	Patricia Delaney	computer-whiz investigator	Cincinnati, OH
Taylor, L.A.	'83 - 4	J.J. Jamison	computer engineer	Minneapolis, MN
Zachary, Fay	'94 - 2	Liz Broward & Zack James	family physician & computer artist	Phoenix, AZ

Cooking [see Gourmet & Food]

Criminals

Author	1 - #	Series Character	Occupation	Setting
Grant-Adamson, L.	'92 - 2	Jim Rush	American on the run from British police	England
La Plante, Lynda	'83 - 5	Dolly Rawlins	bank robber's widow	London, England
Smith, Evelyn E.	'86 - 4	Susan Melville	freelance assassin-painter	New York, NY

Cross Genre

Author	1 - #	Series Character	Occupation	Setting
Bacon-Smith, Camille	'96 - 2	Kevin Bradley	daemon art recovery specialist	Philadelphia, PA
Douglas, Carole N.	'85 - 2	Kevin Blake	psychiatrist	Minnesota
Elrod, P.N.	'90 - 7	Jack Fleming	'30s reporter turned vampire	Chicago, IL
Hambly, Barbara	'88 - 2	James Asher	professor and part-time spy	London, England
Hamilton, Laurell K.	'93 - 8	Anita Blake	reanimator and vampire hunter	St. Louis, MO
Hightower, Lynn S.	'92 - 4	David Silver & String	homicide cop & alien partner	USA
Huff, Tanya	'92 - 5	Vicki Nelson	ex-cop turned P.I. with vampire lover	Toronto, ON, Canada
Lackey, Mercedes	'89 - 3	Diana Tregarde	investigator of unnatural events	Hartford, CT
Martin, Allana	'96 - 3	Texana Jones	desert trading post owner	El Povo, TX
Michaels, Melisa	'97 - 2	Rosie Lavine	private eye to the elf world	California
Robb, J.D.	'95 - 8	Eve Dallas	21st century NYPD lieutenant	New York, NY

Detectives with Disabilities

Author	1 - #	Series Character	Occupation	Setting
Fennelly, Tony	'85 - 3	Matthew Arthur Sinclair	gay epileptic D.A. turned store owner	New Orleans, LA
Hoff, B.J.	'86 - 5	Daniel & Jennifer Kaine	Christian radio station owner & exec asst	West Virginia
Jackson, Hialeah	'98 - 2	Annabelle Hardy-Maratos & Dave the Monkeyman	security specialists	Miami, FL
Mercer, Judy	'96 - 3	Ariel Gold	amnesiac TV newsmagazine producer	Los Angeles, CA
Padgett, Abigail	'93 - 5	Barbara Joan "Bo" Bradley	child abuse investigator	San Diego, CA
Robb, Candace M.	'93 - 6	Owen Archer	one-eyed medieval Welsh spy	York, England
Roe, Caroline	'98 - 3	Isaac & Bishop Berenguer	1350s blind physician & bishop	Girona, Spain
Warner, Penny	'97 - 3	Connor Westphal	deaf reporter and newspaper owner	Flat Skunk, CA

Domestic

Author	1 - #	Series Character	Occupation	Setting
Banks, Jacqueline T.	'98 - 2	Ruby Gordon	college-educated black cleaning woman	Oakland, CA
Brightwell, Emily	'93 - 13	G. Witherspoon & H. Jeffries	Victorian inspector & his housekeeper	London, England
Dams, Jeanne M.	'99 - 2	Hilda Johansson	turn-of-the-century Swedish housemaid	South Bend, IN
Davis, Dorothy S.	'57 - 3	Jasper Tully & Mrs. Norris	DA's investigator & Scottish housekeeper	New York, NY
Harris, Charlaine	'96 - 3	Lily Bard	30-something cleaning woman	Shakespeare, AR

Author	1 - #	Series Character	Occupation	Setting

Background Type

Domestic

Author	1 - #	Series Character	Occupation	Setting
Neely, Barbara	'92 - 3	Blanche White	black domestic worker	Boston, MA
Trocheck, Kathy H.	'92 - 7	Callahan Garrity	ex-cop cleaning service operator	Atlanta, GA

Ecclesiastical & Religious [see also Jewish]

Author	1 - #	Series Character	Occupation	Setting
Allen, Irene	'92 - 4	Elizabeth Elliot	widowed Quaker meeting clerk	Cambridge, MA
Black, Veronica	'90 - 10	Joan, Sister	British investigative nun	Cornwall, England
Byfield, Barbara N.	'75 - 4	Simon Bede & Helen Bullock	Episcopal priest & photographer	New York, NY
Charles, Kate	'91 - 5	L. Kingsley & D. Middleton-Brown	artist & solicitor	London, England
Coel, Margaret	'95 - 4	J. Aloysius O'Malley & V. Holden	Jesuit missionary & Arapaho attorney	Wind River, WY
Frazer, Margaret	'92 - 8	Dame Frevisse	15th century Benedictine nun	Oxfordshire, England
Gallison, Kate	'95 - 5	Lavinia Grey	Episcopal vicar	Fishersville, NJ
Greenwood, D.M.	'91 - 8	Theodora Braithwaite	British woman clergy	London, England
Highsmith, Domini	'94 - 3	Father Simeon & Elvira	medieval priest & nurse	East Yorkshire, England
Holland, Isabelle	'83 - 6	Claire Aldington	Episcopal priest	New York, NY
Joseph, Alison	'94 - 4	Agnes Bourdillon	ex-cloistered nun	London, England
Kahn, Sharon	'98 - 2	Ruby Rothman	rabbi's widow	Eternal, TX
Kellerman, Faye	'86 - 10	Peter Decker & Rina Lazarus	LAPD detective & Orthodox Jewish wife	Los Angeles, CA
Newman, Sharan	'93 - 5	Catherine LeVendeur	12th-century merchant's daughter	France
O'Marie, Carol A., Sr.	'84 - 8	Mary Helen, Sister	70-something nun	San Francisco, CA
Page, Katherine Hall	'90 - 9	Faith Sibley Fairchild	caterer and minister's wife	Aleford, MA
Robb, Candace M.	'93 - 6	Owen Archer	one-eyed medieval Welsh spy	York, England
Sleem, Patty	'97 - 2	Maggie Dillitz	Methodist woman clergy	Greenfield, NC
Woodworth, Deborah	'97 - 2	Rose Callahan	'30s Shaker sister	North Homage, KY

Environment & Wilderness

Author	1 - #	Series Character	Occupation	Setting
Andreae, Christine	'92 - 3	Lee Squires	camp cook & poet	Montana
Andrews, Sarah	'94 - 4	Em Hansen	oil company geologist	Wyoming
Barr, Nevada	'93 - 7	Anna Pigeon	park ranger	National Parks
Cleeves, Ann	'86 - 8	George & Molly Palmer-Jones	ex-Home Office bird-watcher & wife	Surrey, England
Cramer, Rebecca	'98 - 2	Linda Bluenight	anthropologist turned teacher	Tucson, AZ
Dengler, Sandy	'98 - 2	Gar	Neanderthal shaman	Germany
Dengler, Sandy	'93 - 4	Jack Prester	U.S. park ranger	National Parks
Dunlap, Susan	'83 - 3	Vejay Haskell	utility meter reader	Northern, CA
Henry, Sue	'91 - 5	Jessie Arnold & Alex Jensen	sled dog racer & Alaska state trooper	Anchorage, AK
Livesay, Ann	'98 - 5	Barry Ross	international investigator	International
Martin, Allana	'96 - 3	Texana Jones	desert trading post owner	El Povo, TX
McQuillan, Karin	'90 - 3	Jazz Jasper	American safari guide	Kenya
Moffat, Gwen	'73 - 14	Melinda Pink	mountain climbing novelist	Utah
Moody, Skye Kathleen	'96 - 3	Venus Diamond	U.S. Fish & Wildlife agent	Washington
Oliphant, B.J.	'90 - 7	Shirley McClintock	50-something rancher	Colorado
Quinn, Elizabeth	'93 - 4	Lauren Maxwell	wildlife investigator PhD	Anchorage, AK
Rust, Megan Mallory	'98 - 4	Taylor Morgan	air ambulance pilot	Anchorage, AK
Speart, Jessica	'97 - 3	Rachel Porter	Fish & Wildlife agent	USA
Stabenow, Dana	'92 - 10	Kate Shugak	Alaskan ex-D.A. investigator	Arkansas
Stabenow, Dana	'98 - 3	L. Campbell & W. Chouinard	state trooper & bush pilot	Arkansas
Wallingford, Lee	'91 - 2	Ginny Trask & Frank Carver	U.S. Forest Service officers	Oregon

Ethnic [see also Jewish] [see also Native American]

Author	1 - #	Series Character	Occupation	Setting
Black, Cara	'99 - 2	Aimée Leduc	French-American private eye	Paris, France
Garcia-Aguilera, C.	'96 - 3	Lupe Solano	Cuban-American princess P.I.	Miami, FL
Glass, Leslie	'93 - 4	April Woo	Chinese-American police detective	New York, NY
Gur, Batya	'92 - 4	Michael Ohayon	Moroccan-born chief inspector	Jerusalem, Israel
Haddam, Jane	'90 - 15	Gregor Demarkian	former FBI department head	Philadelphia, PA
Kershaw, Valerie	'93 - 4	Mitch Mitchell & Tommy Hung	radio journalist P.I. & Chinese partner	Birmingham, England
Lambert, Mercedes	'91 - 2	Whitney Logan & Lupe Ramos	20-something attorney & Chicana partner	Los Angeles, CA
Lin-Chandler, Irene	'95 - 3	Holly-Jean Ho	Anglo-Chinese bisexual investigator	London, England
Massey, Sujata	'97 - 3	Rei Shimura	Japanese-American antiques dealer	Tokyo, Japan
McAllester, Melanie	'94 - 2	Elizabeth Mendoza	Hispanic-black lesbian homicide detective	San Francisco, CA
Morell, Mary	'91 - 2	Lucia Ramos	Chicana lesbian police detective	San Antonio, TX
Muller, Marcia	'83 - 3	Elena Oliverez	Mexican arts museum curator	Santa Barbara, CA
Myers, Tamar	'94 - 8	Magdalena Yoder	Mennonite inn owner-operator	Hernia, PA
Rowland, Laura Joh	'94 - 4	Sano Ichiro	investigator for the shogun	Edo, Japan
Rozan, S.J.	'94 - 6	Lydia Chin & Bill Smith	Chinese-American & Army-brat P.I. duo	New York, NY
White, Gloria	'91 - 4	Veronica 'Ronnie' Ventana	Anglo-Mexican private eye	San Francisco, CA

Author	1 - #	Series Character	Occupation	Setting

Background Type

F.B.I. [see Police Procedurals]

Fantasy [see Cross Genre]

Fashion

Author	1 - #	Series Character	Occupation	Setting
Dunbar, Sophie	'93 - 5	Claire Claiborne	beauty salon owner	New Orleans, LA
Hyde, Eleanor	'95 - 2	Lydia Miller	30-something fashion editor	New York, NY
Johnson, Dolores	'97 - 3	Mandy Dyer	owner of Dyer's Cleaners	Denver, CO
Logan, Margaret	'94 - 2	Olivia Chapman	interior decorator	Boston, MA
Morgan, D Miller	'87 - 2	Daisy Marlow & Sam Milo	lingerie-addicted P.I. & sheriff	San Diego, CA
Wilson, Barbara Jaye	'97 - 3	Brenda Midnight	Greenwich Village milliner	New York, NY

Filmmaking [see Movies & Filmmaking]

Food [see Gourmet & Food]

Forensic

Author	1 - #	Series Character	Occupation	Setting
Ayres, Noreen	'92 - 2	Samantha "Smokey" Brandon	sheriff's forensic expert	Orange County, CA
Connor, Beverly	'96 - 3	Lindsay Chamberlain	forensic archaeologist	Athens, GA
Cornwell, Patricia	'90 - 9	Kay Scarpetta	chief medical examiner	Richmond, VA
D'Amato, Barbara	'80 - 2	Gerritt DeGraaf	forensic pathologist	Chicago, IL
Davis, Kaye	'97 - 3	Maris Middleton	lesbian forensic chemist	Texas
Dunlap, Susan	'89 - 4	Kiernan O'Shaughnessy	medical examiner turned P.I.	La Jolla, CA
Ennis, Catherine	'91 - 2	Bernadette Hebert	lesbian crime lab expert	Louisiana
Hendricksen, Louise	'93 - 3	Amy Prescott	crime lab physician	Seattle, WA
Landreth, Marsha	'92 - 3	Samantha Turner	medical examiner	Sheridan, WY
Lovett, Sarah	'95 - 3	Sylvia Strange	forensic psychologist	Sante Fe, NM
McCrumb, Sharyn	'84 - 8	Elizabeth MacPherson	forensic anthropologist	Virginia
Petrie, Rhona	'67 - 2	Nassim Pride	Anglo-Sudanese forensic scientist	England
Rayner, Claire	'93 - 5	George Barnabas	hospital forensic pathologist	London, England
Reichs, Kathy	'97 - 2	Temperance Brennan	forensic anthropologist	Montreal, QB, Canada
Reuben, Shelly	'94 - 2	Wylie Nolan & Max Bramble	arson investigator & attorney	New York, NY
Salter, Anna	'97 - 2	Michael Stone	female forensic psychologist	Vermont

Gardening [see Botanical]

Gay and Lesbian

Author	1 - #	Series Character	Occupation	Setting
Allen, Kate	'93 - 4	Alison Kaine	lesbian leather cop	Denver, CO
Baker, Nikki	'91 - 3	Virginia Kelly	black lesbian stockbroker	Chicago, IL
Beecham, Rose	'92 - 3	Amanda Valentine	lesbian detective inspector	Wellington, New Zealand
Bushell, Agnes	'89 - 2	Wilson & Wilder	lesbian private eye duo	Portland, ME
Calloway, Kate	'96 - 7	Cassidy James	rookie lesbian private eye	Cedar Hills, OR
Davis, Kaye	'97 - 3	Maris Middleton	lesbian forensic chemist	Texas
Douglas, Lauren W.	'96 - 2	Allison O'Neil	lesbian B & B owner	Lavner Bay, OR
Douglas, Lauren W.	'87 - 6	Caitlin Reece	lesbian private eye	Victoria, BC, Canada
Dreher, Sarah	'85 - 7	Stoner McTavish	lesbian travel agent	Boston, MA
Drury, Joan M.	'93 - 3	Tyler Jones	lesbian activist newspaper columnist	San Francisco, CA
Duffy, Stella	'94 - 3	Saz Martin	lesbian private eye	London, England
Dymmoch, Michael A.	'93 - 3	John Thinnes & Jack Caleb	cop & gay psychiatrist	Chicago, IL
Ennis, Catherine	'91 - 2	Bernadette Hebert	lesbian crime lab expert	Louisiana
Fennelly, Tony	'85 - 3	Matthew Arthur Sinclair	gay epileptic D.A. turned store owner	New Orleans, LA
Forrest, Katherine V.	'84 - 6	Kate Delafield	LAPD lesbian homicide detective	Los Angeles, CA
Fritchley, Alma	'97 - 3	Letty Campbell	lesbian chicken farmer	Manchester, England
Haddock, Lisa	'94 - 2	Carmen Ramirez	lesbian newspaper copy editor	Frontier City, OK
Hart, Ellen	'89 - 8	Jane Lawless	lesbian restaurateur	Minneapolis, MN
Johnson, Barbara	'95 - 2	Colleen Fitzgerald	lesbian insurance investigator	Washington, DC
King, Laurie R.	'93 - 3	Kate Martinelli & Alonzo Hawkin	SFPD homicide detectives	San Francisco, CA
Knight, Phyllis	'92 - 2	Lil Ritchie	ex-rocker and gay woman P.I.	Charlottesville, VA
Lin-Chandler, Irene	'95 - 3	Holly-Jean Ho	Anglo-Chinese bisexual investigator	London, England
Lordon, Randye	'93 - 5	Sydney Sloane	lesbian private investigator	New York, NY
Maiman, Jaye	'91 - 6	Robin Miller	lesbian travel & romance writer turned P.I.	New York, NY
Maney, Mabel	'93 - 3	Nancy Clue	gay-lesbian Nancy Drew parody	River Depths, IL

Author	1 - #	Series Character	Occupation	Setting

Background Type

Gay and Lesbian

Manthorne, Jackie	'00 - 1	Elizabeth Ellis	lesbian private eye	Toronto, ON, Canada
Manthorne, Jackie	'94 - 5	Harriet Hubbley	intrepid lesbian sleuth	Montreal, QB, Canada
McAllester, Melanie	'94 - 2	Elizabeth Mendoza	Hispanic-black lesbian homicide detective	San Francisco, CA
McClellan, Janet	'97 - 3	Tru North	lesbian police detective	Kansas City, MO
McConnell, Vicki P.	'82 - 3	Nyla Wade	lesbian journalist	Denver, CO
McDermid, Val	'87 - 5	Lindsay Gordon	lesbian socialist journalist	Glasgow, Scotland
McNab, Claire	'88 - 10	Carol Ashton	lesbian detective inspector	Sydney, Australia
Mickelbury, Penny	'94 - 2	Gianna Maglione & Mimi Patterson	lesbian police lieutenant & reporter	Washington, DC
Morell, Mary	'91 - 2	Lucia Ramos	Chicana lesbian police detective	San Antonio, TX
Padgett, Abigail	'98 - 2	Blue McCarron	lesbian social psychologist	San Diego, CA
Pincus, Elizabeth	'92 - 3	Nell Fury	lesbian P.I.	San Francisco, CA
Powell, Deborah	'91 - 2	Hollis Carpenter	gay woman crime reporter	Houston, TX
Redmann, J.M.	'90 - 3	Michelle 'Micky' Knight	gay woman private eye	New Orleans, LA
Richardson, Tracey	'97 - 3	Stevie Houston	gay rookie homicide detective	Toronto, ON, Canada
Saum, Karen	'90 - 3	Brigid Donovan	50-something lesbian ex-nun	Maine
Schmidt, Carol	'93 - 3	Laney Samms	lesbian bar owner	Los Angeles, CA
Scoppettone, Sandra	'91 - 5	Lauren Laurano	lesbian private investigator	New York, NY
Silva, Linda Kay	'91 - 5	Delta Stevens	gay woman police officer	Southern CA
Szymanski, Therese	'97 - 4	Brett Higgins	lesbian adult bookstore manager	Detroit, MI
Taylor, Jean	'95 - 2	Maggie Garrett	young lesbian P.I.	San Francisco, CA
Tell, Dorothy	'90 - 2	Poppy Dillworth	60-something lesbian sleuth	Texas
Welch, Pat	'90 - 6	Helen Black	ex-cop lesbian private eye	Berkeley, CA
Williams, Amanda K.	'90 - 4	Madison McGuire	deep cover intelligence agent	International
Wilson, Barbara	'84 - 3	Pam Nilsen	lesbian printing company owner	Seattle, WA
Wings, Mary	'86 - 4	Emma Victor	lesbian activist private eye	San Francisco, CA
York, Kieran	'93 - 2	Royce Madison	lesbian deputy sheriff	Timber City, CO
Zaremba, Eve	'78 - 6	Helen Keremos	40-something lesbian private eye	Toronto, ON, Canada

Genealogy [see Historical, other]

Ghosts [see Paranormal]

Gourmet & Food

Bishop, Claudia	'94 - 6	Sarah & Meg Quilliam	inn owner & chef sisters	Hemlock Falls, NY
Cannell, Dorothy	'84 - 8	Ellie & Ben Haskell	interior decorator & writer-chef	Chitterton Fells, England
Crespi, Camilla	'91 - 7	Simona Griffo	gourmet cook ad executive	New York, NY
Davidson, Diane Mott	'90 - 8	Goldy Bear Schultz	detecting caterer Aspen	Meadow, CO
Dietz, Denise	'92 - 2	Ellie Bernstein	diet group leader	Colorado Springs, CO
Farmer, Jerrilyn	'98 - 2	Madeline Bean	Hollywood party planner	Los Angeles, CA
Hart, Ellen	'89 - 8	Jane Lawless	lesbian restaurateur	Minneapolis, MN
Hart, Ellen	'94 - 4	Sophie Greenway	food critic and magazine editor	Minneapolis, MN
Iakovou, Takis & Judy	'96 - 2	Nick & Julia Lambros	college-town cafe owners	Delphi, GA
John, Cathie	'97 - 4	Kate Cavanaugh	gourmet caterer	Cincinnati, OH
Kahn, Sharon	'98 - 2	Ruby Rothman	rabbi's widow	Eternal, TX
Laurence, Janet	'89 - 9	Darina Lisle	caterer-chef and food writer	West Country, England
Lyons, Nan & Ivan	'76 - 2	Natasha O'Brien & Millie Ogden	pair of culinary artists	New York, NY
Myers, Amy	'86 - 9	Auguste Didier	British-French Victorian master chef	England
Page, Katherine Hall	'90 - 9	Faith Sibley Fairchild	caterer and minister's wife	Aleford, MA
Pence, Joanne	'93 - 6	Angelina Amalfi	freelance food writer	San Francisco, CA
Pickard, Nancy	'82 - 5	Eugenia Potter	60-something widowed chef	USA
Richman, Phyllis	'97 - 2	Chas Wheatley	restaurant critic	Washington, DC
Taylor, Kathleen	'93 - 4	Tory Bauer	small-town diner waitress	Delphi, SD
Temple, Lou Jane	'96 - 4	Heaven Lee	trendy restaurant owner-chef	Kansas City, MO

Government & Politics

Cooper, Natasha	'90 - 7	Willow King	civil-servant romance-novelist	London, England
Dixon, Louisa	'98 - 3	Laura Owen	state public safety commissioner	Jackson, MS
Dominic, R.B.	'68 - 7	Ben Safford	Democratic Congressman from Ohio	Washington, DC
Edwards, Ruth Dudley	'81 - 8	James Milton & Robert Amiss	police superintendent & ex-civil servant	London, England
Granger, Ann	'91 - 11	Alan Markby & Meredith Mitchell	D.I. & Foreign Service officer	Cotswolds, England
Grimes, Terris M.	'96 - 3	Theresa Galloway	black married-mother civil servant	Sacramento, CA
Lacey, Sarah	'92 - 4	Leah Hunter	20-something tax inspector	Yorkshire, England
Linscott, Gillian	'91 - 7	Nell Bray	British suffragette	London, England

Author	1 - #	Series Character	Occupation	Setting

Background Type

Government & Politics

Author	1 - #	Series Character	Occupation	Setting
Matera, Lia	'87 - 7	Willa Jansson	Red diaper baby turned attorney	San Francisco, CA
Matthews, Patricia	'92 - 5	Casey Farrel	governor's crime task force member	Arizona
Mikulski, Barbara	'96 - 2	Norie Gorzack	Polish-American U.S. senator	Washington, DC
Monfredo, Miriam G.	'92 - 6	Glynis Tryon	1860s librarian suffragette	Seneca Falls, NY
Nessen, Ron	'95 - 3	Jerry Knight & Jane Day	right-wing radio host & liberal reporter	Washington, DC
Sprinkle, Patricia H.	'97 - 2	MacLaren Yarbrough	business-owner turned magistrate	Hopemore, GA
Truman, Margaret	'89 - 7	Mackenzie Smith & Annabel Reed	law professor & gallery owner	Washington, DC

Historical, prehistoric

Author	1 - #	Series Character	Occupation	Setting
Dengler, Sandy	'98 - 2	Gar	Neanderthal shaman	Germany

Historical, ancient

Author	1 - #	Series Character	Occupation	Setting
Davis, Lindsey	'89 - 11	Marcus Didius Falco	1st century Roman private eye	Rome, Italy
Haney, Lauren	'97 - 2	Lt. Bak	ex-charioteer turned Medjay police head	Buhen, Egypt
Robinson, Lynda S.	'94 - 5	Lord Meren	Tutankhamen's chief investigator	Egypt
Todd, Marilyn	'95 - 4	Claudia Seferius	13 B.C. superbitch	Rome, Italy

Historical, 11th century

Author	1 - #	Series Character	Occupation	Setting
Woodward, Ann	'96 - 2	Lady Aoi	11th century Japanese healer	Kyoto, Japan

Historical, 12th century

Author	1 - #	Series Character	Occupation	Setting
Beaufort, Simon	'98 - 2	Geoffrey de Mappestone	brave knight of the Crusades	England
Penman, Sharon Kay	'96 - 2	Justin de Quincy	Queen Mother's investigator	England

Historical, 14th century

Author	1 - #	Series Character	Occupation	Setting
Robb, Candace M.	'93 - 6	Owen Archer	one-eyed medieval Welsh spy	York, England
Roe, Caroline	'98 - 3	Isaac & Bishop Berenguer	1350s blind physician & bishop	Girona, Spain

Historical, 15th century

Author	1 - #	Series Character	Occupation	Setting
Frazer, Margaret	'92 - 8	Dame Frevisse	15th century Benedictine nun	Oxfordshire, England

Historical, 16th century

Author	1 - #	Series Character	Occupation	Setting
Buckley, Fiona	'97 - 2	Ursula Blanchard	lady-in-waiting to Elizabeth I	London, England
Chisholm, P.F.	'94 - 4	Robert Carey	Elizabethan nobleman	England
Cook, Judith	'97 - 2	Simon Forman	Elizabethan physician-astrologer	London, England
Emerson, Kathy Lynn	'97 - 4	Susanna Appleton	Elizabethan herbalist noblewoman	England

Historical, 17th century

Author	1 - #	Series Character	Occupation	Setting
Brown, Molly	'97 - 2	Aphra Behn	17th century spy turned playwright	London, England
Rowland, Laura Joh	'94 - 4	Sano Ichiro	investigator for the shogun	Edo, Japan

Historical, 18th century

Author	1 - #	Series Character	Occupation	Setting
Lake, Deryn	'94 - 4	John Rawlings & the Blind Beak	18th century apothecary & blind magistrate	London, England
Laurence, Janet	'98 - 2	Canaletto	18th century Italian painter	London, England
Lawrence, Margaret	'96 - 3	Hannah Trevor	18th century widwife	Rufford, ME
Miles, Margaret	'98 - 2	C. Willett & R. Longfellow	Colonial farm woman & scientist-farmer	Bracebridge, MA

Historical, 19th century

Author	1 - #	Series Character	Occupation	Setting
Barron, Stephanie	'96 - 3	Jane Austen	19th century British novelist	Bath, England
Brightwell, Emily	'93 - 13	G. Witherspoon & H. Jeffries	Victorian inspector & his housekeeper	London, England
Bryan, Kate	'98 - 2	Maggie Maguire	ex-Pinkerton agent	San Francisco, CA
Buggé, Carole	'98 - 1	Sherlock Holmes	consulting detective	London, England
Crowleigh, Ann	'93 - 2	Mirinda & Clare Clively	Victorian twin sisters	London, England
Douglas, Carole N.	'90 - 4	Irene Adler	19th century American diva	Paris, France
Fawcett, Quinn	'94 - 3	Mycroft Holmes	Sherlock Holmes' older brother	London, England
Fawcett, Quinn	'93 - 2	Victoire Vernet	wife of Napoleonic gendarme	Paris, France
Hambly, Barbara	'97 - 2	Benjamin January	1830s Paris-trained black doctor	New Orleans, LA
Hambly, Barbara	'88 - 2	James Asher	professor and part-time spy	London, England
Jackson, Marian J.A.	'90 - 5	Abigail Patience Danforth	19th century American heiress detective	International
Jakeman, Jane	'97 - 3	Ambrose Malfine	lord and heir to a decaying estate	West Country, England
Kingsbury, Kate	'93 - 11	Cecily Sinclair	Edwardian hotel owner	Badger's End, England

Author	1 - #	Series Character	Occupation	Setting

Background Type

Historical, 19th Century

Author	1 - #	Series Character	Occupation	Setting
Knight, Alanna	'88 - 11	Jeremy Faro	Victorian detective inspector	Edinburgh, Scotland
Kruger, Mary	'94 - 3	Brooke Cassidy & Matt Devlin	1890s debutante & detective husband	Newport, RI
Lee, Wendi	'89 - 6	Jefferson Birch	P.I. in the Old West	Western
Linscott, Gillian	'91 - 7	Nell Bray	British suffragette	London, England
Medawar, Mardi O.	'96 - 3	Tay-bodal	19th century Kiowa healer	Oklahoma
Monfredo, Miriam G.	'92 - 6	Glynis Tryon	1860s librarian suffragette	Seneca Falls, NY
Myers, Amy	'86 - 9	Auguste Didier	British-French Victorian master chef	England
Paige, Robin	'94 - 5	K. Ardleigh & C. Sheridan	American author & British scientist	Dedham, England
Peart, Jane	'96 - 4	Edgecliffe Manor Series	young, restless Victorian women	England
Perry, Anne	'79 - 18	Thomas & Charlotte Pitt	Victorian police inspector & wife	London, England
Perry, Anne	'90 - 9	William Monk	amnesiac Victorian police inspector	London, England
Peters, Elizabeth	'75 - 12	Amelia Peabody	Victorian feminist archaeologist	Kent, England
Rogow, Roberta	'98 - 2	Charles Dodgson & Conan Doyle	19th century professor & doctor	England
Ross, Kate	'93 - 4	Julian Kestrel	1820s dandy-about-town	London, England
Tone, Teona	'83 - 2	Kyra Keaton	turn-of-the-century P.I.	Washington, DC

Historical, 1900s

Author	1 - #	Series Character	Occupation	Setting
Cercone, Karen Rose	'97 - 3	Helen Sorby & Milo Kachigan	social worker & policeman in 1905	Pittsburgh, PA
Dams, Jeanne M.	'99 - 2	Hilda Johansson	turn-of-the-century Swedish housemaid	South Bend, IN
Day, Dianne	'95 - 6	Fremont Jones	1900s typewriting-business owner	San Francisco, CA
Jennings, Maureen	'97 - 2	William Murdoch	Victorian police inspector	Toronto, ON, Canada
Smith, Sarah	'92 - 2	A. von Reisden & Perdita Halley	biochemist & concert pianist	Paris, France

Historical, 1910s

Author	1 - #	Series Character	Occupation	Setting
Paul, Barbara	'84 - 3	Enrico Caruso & Geraldine Farrar	Italian tenor & American soprano	New York, NY

Historical, 1920s

Author	1 - #	Series Character	Occupation	Setting
Beck, K.K.	'84 - 3	Iris Cooper	'20s Stanford University co-ed	Palo Alto, CA
Dunn, Carola	'94 - 6	Daisy Dalrymple	'20s aristocratic feature writer	Hampshire, England
Greenwood, Kerry	'89 - 9	Phryne Fisher	'20s Londoner	Melbourne, Australia
King, Laurie R.	'94 - 4	Mary Russell	Sherlock Holmes' detecting partner	London, England
Meyers, Annette	'99 - 1	Olivia Brown	'20s Greenwich Village poet P.I.	New York, NY

Historical, 1930s

Author	1 - #	Series Character	Occupation	Setting
Churchill, Jill	'99 - 1	Lily & Robert Brewster	sister & brother inn owners in 1930	Voorburg-on-Hudson, NY
Elrod, P.N.	'90 - 7	Jack Fleming	'30s reporter turned vampire	Chicago, IL
Powell, Deborah	'91 - 2	Hollis Carpenter	gay woman crime reporter	Houston, TX
Woodworth, Deborah	'97 - 2	Rose Callahan	'30s Shaker sister	North Homage, KY

Historical, 1960s

Author	1 - #	Series Character	Occupation	Setting
Wright, Sally S.	'97 - 2	Ben Reese	'60s university archivist	Ohio

Historical, other

Author	1 - #	Series Character	Occupation	Setting
MacPherson, Rett	'97 - 2	Torie O'Shea	historian-genealogist-tour guide	New Kassel, MO
Meyers, Maan	'92 - 6	The Tonnemans	New Amsterdam family	New York, NY

new Historical Figures

Author	1 - #	Series Character	Occupation	Setting
Barron, Stephanie	'96 - 3	Jane Austen	19th century British novelist	Bath, England
Douglas, Carole N.	'90 - 4	Irene Adler	19th century American diva	Paris, France
Lake, Deryn	'94 - 4	John Rawlings & the Blind Beak	18th century apothecary & blind magistrate	London, England
Paige, Robin	'94 - 5	K. Ardleigh & C. Sheridan	American author & British scientist	Dedham, England
Rogow, Roberta	'98 - 2	Charles Dodgson & Conan Doyle	19th century professor & doctor	England

Hollywood [see Movies & Filmmaking]

Horror [see Cross Genre]

Hotels & Inns

Author	1 - #	Series Character	Occupation	Setting
Bishop, Claudia	'94 - 6	Sarah & Meg Quilliam	inn owner & chef sisters	Hemlock Falls, NY
Churchill, Jill	'99 - 1	Lily & Robert Brewster	sister & brother inn owners in 1930	Voorburg-on-Hudson, NY
Daheim, Mary	'91 - 13	Judith McMonigle Flynn	bed & breakfast owner	Seattle, WA
Douglas, Lauren W.	'96 - 2	Allison O'Neil	lesbian B & B owner	Lavner Bay, OR

TYPES

Author	1 - #	Series Character	Occupation	Setting

Background Type

Hotels & Inns

Author	1 - #	Series Character	Occupation	Setting
Hager, Jean	'94 - 5	Tess Darcy	Ozarks bed & breakfast owner	Victoria Springs, MO
Kingsbury, Kate	'93 - 11	Cecily Sinclair	Edwardian hotel owner	Badger's End, England
Myers, Tamar	'94 - 8	Magdalena Yoder	Mennonite inn owner-operator	Hernia, PA

Humor

Author	1 - #	Series Character	Occupation	Setting
Bartholomew, Nancy	'98 - 2	Sierra Lavotini	exotic dancer	Panama City, FL
Bell, Nancy	'96 - 3	Biggie Weatherford & J.R.	grandmother & nephew sidekick	Job's Crossing, TX
Borton, D.B.	'99 - 1	Gilda Liberty	small-town movie theater proprietor	Eden, OH
Brill, Toni	'91 - 2	Midge Cohen	children's author fluent in Russian	Brooklyn, NY
Cannell, Dorothy	'84 - 8	Ellie & Ben Haskell	interior decorator & writer-chef	Chitterton Fells, England
Caudwell, Sarah	'81 - 4	Hilary Tamar	medieval law specialist	London, England
Chappell, Helen	'96 - 3	Hollis Ball & Sam Wescott	reporter & her ex-husband's ghost	Santimoke County, MD
Churchill, Jill	'89 - 11	Jane Jeffry	suburban single mother	Chicago, IL
Churchill, Jill	'99 - 1	Lily & Robert Brewster	sister & brother inn owners in 1930	Voorburg-on-Hudson, NY
Cooper, Susan Rogers	'92 - 5	E.J. Pugh	housewife-mom romance writer	Black Cat Ridge, TX
Craig, Alisa	'81 - 5	Dittany H. Monk & Osbert Monk	garden club member & author of westerns	Lobelia Falls, ON, Canada
Dunbar, Sophie	'93 - 5	Claire Claiborne	beauty salon owner	New Orleans, LA
Edwards, Ruth Dudley	'81 - 8	James Milton & Robert Amiss	police superintendent & ex-civil servant	London, England
Eichler, Selma	'94 - 6	Desiree Shapiro	5'2" queen-size P.I.	New York, NY
Evanovich, Janet	'94 - 4	Stephanie Plum	lingerie buyer turned bounty hunter	Trenton, NJ
Fitzwater, Judy	'98 - 2	Jennifer Marsh	aspiring mystery novelist	Atlanta, GA
Frankel, Valerie	'91 - 4	Wanda Mallory	detective agency owner	New York, NY
Fritchley, Alma	'97 - 3	Letty Campbell	lesbian chicken farmer	Manchester, England
George, Anne	'96 - 5	Mary Alice Crane & Patricia Anne Hollowell	60-something sister sleuths	Birmingham, AL
Girdner, Jaqueline	'91 - 11	Kate Jasper	gag gift wholesaler	Marin County, CA
Griffin, Annie	'98 - 2	Hannah Malloy & Kiki Goldstein	unlikely pair of 60-something sisters	Marin County, CA
Hayter, Sparkle	'94 - 4	Robin Hudson	cable news reporter	New York, NY
Hess, Joan	'87 - 11	Arly Hanks	small-town police chief	Maggody, AR
Kellogg, Marne Davis	'95 - 5	Lilly Bennett	US marshal and security firm owner	Roundup, WY
Maney, Mabel	'93 - 3	Nancy Clue	gay-lesbian Nancy Drew parody	River Depths, IL
Maracotta, Lindsay	'96 - 2	Lucy Freers	children's film animator	Los Angeles, CA
McCafferty, Barbara T.	'96 - 3	Bert & Nan Tatum	identical twin sisters	Louisville, KY
McCafferty, Taylor	'90 - 6	Haskell Blevins	small-town private eye	Pigeon Fork, KY
McKevett, G.A.	'95 - 4	Savannah Reid	voluptuous ex-cop private eye	San Carmelita, CA
Munger, Katy	'97 - 2	Casey Jones	unlicensed private eye	Durham, NC
Murray, Lynne	'97 - 4	Josephine Fuller	Queen-sized private investigator	Seattle, WA
Myers, Tamar	'96 - 6	Abigail Timberlake	antiques dealer	Charlotte, NC
North, Suzanne	'94 - 3	Phoebe Fairfax	TV video photographer	Calgary, AB, Canada
O'Kane, Leslie	'96 - 3	Molly Masters	greeting card entrepreneur	Albany, NY
Pence, Joanne	'93 - 6	Angelina Amalfi	freelance food writer	San Francisco, CA
Piesman, Marissa	'89 - 6	Nina Fischman	legal services attorney	New York, NY
Sawyer, Corinne Holt	'88 - 8	A. Benbow & C. Wingate	70-something admirals' widows	Southern CA
Shankman, Sarah	'88 - 7	Samantha Adams	investigative reporter	Atlanta, GA
Smith, Cynthia	'96 - 5	Emma Rhodes	private resolver for the rich	London, England
Smith, Evelyn E.	'86 - 4	Susan Melville	freelance assassin-painter	New York, NY
Squire, Elizabeth D.	'94 - 6	Peaches Dann	absent-minded widow	North Carolina
Taylor, Kathleen	'93 - 4	Tory Bauer	small-town diner waitress	Delphi, SD
Todd, Marilyn	'95 - 4	Claudia Seferius	13 B.C. superbitch	Rome, Italy
Whitney, Polly	'94 - 4	Ike Tygart & Abby Abagnarro	network producer & TV news director	New York, NY

Jewish

Author	1 - #	Series Character	Occupation	Setting
Brill, Toni	'91 - 2	Midge Cohen	children's author fluent in Russian	Brooklyn, NY
Gur, Batya	'92 - 4	Michael Ohayon	Moroccan-born chief inspector	Jerusalem, Israel
Haymon, S.T.	'80 - 8	Benjamin Jurnet	Angleby CID detective inspector	Norwich, England
Kahn, Sharon	'98 - 2	Ruby Rothman	rabbi's widow	Eternal, TX
Kellerman, Faye	'86 - 10	Peter Decker & Rina Lazarus	LAPD detective & Orthodox Jewish wife	Los Angeles, CA
Kelly, Mary Anne	'90 - 3	Claire Breslinsky	freelance photographer	New York, NY
Krich, Rochelle Majer	'96 - 1	Debra Laslow	criminal defense attorney	Los Angeles, CA
Krich, Rochelle Majer	'93 - 3	Jessie Drake	LAPD homicide detective	Los Angeles, CA
Lordon, Randye	'93 - 5	Sydney Sloane	lesbian private investigator	New York, NY
Piesman, Marissa	'89 - 6	Nina Fischman	legal services attorney	New York, NY
Rawlings, Ellen	'97 - 2	Rachel Crowne	Jewish investigative reporter	Washington, DC
Stevens, Serita	'91 - 2	Fanny Zindel	Jewish grandmother	Brooklyn, NY

Author	1 - #	Series Character	Occupation	Setting

Background Type

Journalism, magazine

Author	1 - #	Series Character	Occupation	Setting
Buckstaff, Kathryn	'94 - 2	Emily Stone	Florida-based travel writer	Branson, MO
Caverly, Carol	'94 - 2	Thea Barlow	Western magazine editor	Wyoming
Conant, Susan	'89 - 11	Holly Winter	dog trainer & magazine columnist	Cambridge, MA
D'Amato, Barbara	'90 - 7	Cat Marsala	freelance investigative journalist	Chicago, IL
Dunn, Carola	'94 - 6	Daisy Dalrymple	'20s aristocratic feature writer	Hampshire, England
Hart, Ellen	'94 - 4	Sophie Greenway	food critic and magazine editor	Minneapolis, MN
Holt, Hazel	'89 - 8	Sheila Malory	British literary magazine writer	Devon, England
Hyde, Eleanor	'95 - 2	Lydia Miller	30-something fashion editor	New York, NY
Kelly, Susan	'85 - 6	Liz Connors	freelance crime writer	Cambridge, MA
Roberts, Lora	'94 - 6	Liz Sullivan	freelance writer and organic gardener	Palo Alto, CA
Warmbold, Jean	'86 - 3	Sarah Calloway	magazine journalist	San Francisco, CA
Woods, Sherryl	'89 - 9	Amanda Roberts	ex-NYC investigative reporter	Atlanta, GA

Journalism, newspaper

Author	1 - #	Series Character	Occupation	Setting
Bannister, Jo	'90 - 2	Mickey Flynn	American photojournalist	London, England
Bannister, Jo	'98 - 1	Primrose Holland	newspaper advice columnist	Skipley, England
Braun, Lilian Jackson	'66 - 21	Jim Qwilleran, Koko & Yum Yum	ex-police reporter & cats	Upper Peninsula, MI
Buchanan, Edna	'92 - 5	Britt Montero	Cuban-American crime reporter	Miami, FL
Burke, Jan	'93 - 6	Irene Kelly	newspaper reporter	Las Piernas, CA
Cail, Carol	'93 - 3	Maxey Burnell	investigative reporter	Boulder, CO
Chappell, Helen	'96 - 3	Hollis Ball & Sam Wescott	reporter & her ex-husband's ghost	Santimoke County, MD
Chase, Elaine Raco	'87 - 2	Nikki Holden & Roman Cantrell	investigative reporter & private eye	Miami, FL
Coleman, Evelyn	'98 - 2	Pat Conley	black woman journalist	Atlanta, GA
Cornwell, Patricia	'97 - 2	Andy Brazil	reporter and volunteer cop	Charlotte, NC
Daheim, Mary	'92 - 11	Emma Lord	small-town newspaper owner-editor	Alpine, WA
Danks, Denise	'89 - 4	Georgina Powers	British computer journalist	London, England
Davis, Dorothy S.	'76 - 4	Julie Hayes	actress turned columnist and fortuneteller	New York, NY
Drury, Joan M.	'93 - 3	Tyler Jones	lesbian activist newspaper columnist	San Francisco, CA
Elrod, P.N.	'90 - 7	Jack Fleming	'30s reporter turned vampire	Chicago, IL
English, Brenda	'97 - 2	Sutton McPhee	police reporter	Fairfax County, VA
Fennelly, Tony	'94 - 2	Margo Fortier	ex-stripper turned columnist	New Orleans, LA
Gordon, Alison	'89 - 6	Kate Henry	baseball newswriter	Toronto, ON, Canada
Grant-Adamson, L.	'85 - 5	Rain Morgan	Fleet Street gossip columnist	London, England
Haddock, Lisa	'94 - 2	Carmen Ramirez	lesbian newspaper copy editor	Frontier City, OK
Hall, Patricia	'93 - 5	Laura Ackroyd & Michael Thackeray	investigative reporter & police inspector	Yorkshire, England
Hart, Carolyn G.	'93 - 4	Henrietta O'Dwyer Collins	70-something reporter	Oklahoma
Jaffe, Jody	'95 - 3	Natalie Gold	reporter on horse show circuit	Charlotte, NC
Kallen, Lucille	'79 - 5	Maggie Rome & C.B. Greenfield	reporter & editor-publisher	Connecticut
Lippman, Laura	'97 - 4	Tess Monaghan	newspaper reporter turned P.I.	Baltimore, MD
McConnell, Vicki P.	'82 - 3	Nyla Wade	lesbian journalist	Denver, CO
McDermid, Val	'87 - 5	Lindsay Gordon	lesbian socialist journalist	Glasgow, Scotland
Mickelbury, Penny	'94 - 2	Gianna Maglione & Mimi Patterson	lesbian police lieutenant & reporter	Washington, DC
Moen, Ruth Raby	'93 - 3	Kathleen O'Shaughnessy	newspaper reporter	Seattle, WA
Nessen, Ron	'95 - 3	Jerry Knight & Jane Day	right-wing radio host & liberal reporter	Washington, DC
O'Brien, Meg	'90 - 5	Jessica James	investigative reporter	Rochester, NY
Peterson, Audrey	'88 - 6	Jane Winfield	British journalist and music writer	London, England
Porter, Anna	'85 - 3	Judith Hayes	freelance journalist	Toronto, ON, Canada
Powell, Deborah	'91 - 2	Hollis Carpenter	gay woman crime reporter	Houston, TX
Rawlings, Ellen	'97 - 2	Rachel Crowne	Jewish investigative reporter	Washington, DC
Richman, Phyllis	'97 - 2	Chas Wheatley	restaurant critic	Washington, DC
Roome, Annette	'89 - 3	Christine Martin	40-something cub reporter	England
Rubino, Jane	'96 - 3	Cat Austen & Victor Cardenas	single-mom reporter & police detective	Atlantic City, NJ
Sandstrom, Eve K.	'97 - 2	Nell Matthews & Mike Svenson	reporter & homicide detective	Southwest
Shankman, Sarah	'88 - 7	Samantha Adams	investigative reporter	Atlanta, GA
Sibley, Celestine	'57 - 6	Kate Kincaid Mulcay	veteran newspaperwoman	Atlanta, GA
Stein, Triss	'93 - 2	Kay Engles	nationally-known reporter	Brooklyn, NY
Trocheck, Kathy H.	'96 - 2	Truman Kicklighter	retired wire service reporter	St. Petersburg, FL
Tyre, Peg	'94 - 2	Kate Murray	novice crime reporter	Brooklyn, NY
Viets, Elaine	'97 - 4	Francesca Vierling	6-ft. newspaper columnist	St. Louis, MO
Walker, Mary Willis	'94 - 3	Molly Cates	true crime writer-reporter	Austin, TX
Waltch, Lilla M.	'87 - 2	Lisa Davis	newspaper reporter	Braeton, MA
Warner, Penny	'97 - 3	Connor Westphal	deaf reporter and newspaper owner	Flat Skunk, CA

Author	1 - #	Series Character	Occupation	Setting

Background Type

Journalism, photography

Author	1 - #	Series Character	Occupation	Setting
Bolitho, Janie	'97 - 2	Rose Trevelyan	widowed painter and photographer	Cornwall, England
Byfield, Barbara N.	'75 - 4	Simon Bede & Helen Bullock	Episcopal priest & phototographer	New York, NY
Kelly, Mary Anne	'90 - 3	Claire Breslinsky	freelance photographer	New York, NY
Moody, Susan	'84 - 7	Penny Wanawake	photographer daughter of black diplomat	England
North, Suzanne	'94 - 3	Phoebe Fairfax	TV video photographer	Calgary, AB, Canada
OCork, Shannon	'80 - 3	Theresa Tracy Baldwin	sports news photographer	New York, NY
Rowlands, Betty	'96 - 3	Sukey Reynolds	police photographer	England
Sale, Medora	'86 - 6	John Sanders & Harriet Jeffries	police detective & photographer	Toronto, ON, Canada
Tucker, Kerry	'91 - 4	Libby Kincaid	magazine photographer	New York, NY

Journalism, radio & television

Author	1 - #	Series Character	Occupation	Setting
Babbin, Jacqueline	'72 - 2	Clovis Kelly	homicide cop turned crime consultant	New York, NY
Donald, Anabel	'93 - 5	Alex Tanner	TV researcher and part-time P.I.	London, England
Fraser, Antonia	'77 - 8	Jemima Shore	British TV interviewer	London, England
Hayter, Sparkle	'94 - 4	Robin Hudson	cable news reporter	New York, NY
Hoff, B.J.	'86 - 5	Daniel & Jennifer Kaine	Christian radio station owner & exec asst	West Virginia
Howell, Lis	'95 - 3	Kate Wilkinson	television producer	London, England
Kershaw, Valerie	'93 - 4	Mitch Mitchell & Tommy Hung	radio journalist P.I. & Chinese partner	Birmingham, England
McKitterick, Molly	'92 - 2	William Hecklepeck	egotistical television anchor	St. Louis, MO
Mercer, Judy	'96 - 3	Ariel Gold	amnesiac TV newsmagazine producer	Los Angeles, CA
Nessen, Ron	'95 - 3	Jerry Knight & Jane Day	right-wing radio host & liberal reporter	Washington, DC
Niles, Chris	'97 - 2	Sam Ridley	radio news reporter	London, England
Ripley, Ann	'94 - 3	Louise Eldridge	organic gardener TV host	Northern VA
Robitaille, Julie	'92 - 2	Kit Powell	TV sports reporter	San Diego, CA
Ross, Annie	'95 - 3	Bel Carson	TV director and investigator	London, England
Rowe, Jennifer	'87 - 5	Verity Birdwood	TV researcher	Australia
Shaffer, Louise	'94 - 2	Angie DaVito	daytime television producer	New York, NY
Star, Nancy	'98 - 2	May Morrison	TV talk show producer	New York, NY
Steinberg, Janice	'95 - 5	Margo Simon	Public Radio reporter	San Diego, CA
Whitney, Polly	'94 - 4	Ike Tygart & Abby Abagnarro	network producer & TV news director	New York, NY

Legal, attorney

Author	1 - #	Series Character	Occupation	Setting
Amato, Angela	'98 - 2	Gerry Conte	undercover cop turned defense attorney	New York, NY
Arnold, Catherine	'96 - 3	Karen Perry-Mondori	criminal defense attorney	Tampa, FL
Barrett, Kathleen A.	'96 - 3	Beth Hartley	attorney turned legal researcher	Milwaukee, WI
Berne, Karin	'85 - 3	Ellie Gordon	law firm office manager	Orange County, CA
Cannon, Taffy	'93 - 3	Nan Robinson	state bar investigator	Los Angeles, CA
Caudwell, Sarah	'81 - 4	Hilary Tamar	medieval law specialist	London, England
Cooper, Natasha	'98 - 1	Trish Maguire	family law barrister	London, England
Dominic, R.B.	'68 - 7	Ben Safford	Democratic Congressman from Ohio	Washington, DC
Fallon, Ann C.	'90 - 5	James Fleming	train-loving solicitor	Dublin, Ireland
Fyfield, Frances	'89 - 2	Sarah Fortune	lawyer in prestigious British firm	London, England
Giroux, E.X.	'84 - 10	R. Forsythe & A. Sanderson	barrister & his secretary	London, England
Hartzmark, Gini	'92 - 5	Katherine Prescott Milholland	blueblood corporate attorney	Chicago, IL
Holms, Joyce	'96 - 3	Tam Buchanan & Fizz	older Scottish attorney & law student	Edinburgh, Scotland
Jacobs, Jonnie	'96 - 3	Kali O'Brien	attorney	Gold Country, CA
Kraft, Gabrielle	'87 - 4	Jerry Zalman	Beverly Hills deal maker	Los Angeles, CA
Krich, Rochelle Majer	'96 - 1	Debra Laslow	criminal defense attorney	Los Angeles, CA
Lachnit, Carroll	'95 - 3	Hannah Barlow	ex-cop turned lawyer	Orange County, CA
Lambert, Mercedes	'91 - 2	Whitney Logan & Lupe Ramos	20-something attorney & Chicana partner	Los Angeles, CA
MacDougal, Bonnie	'96 - 3	Jackson, Rieders	large law firm	Philadelphia, PA
Matera, Lia	'88 - 5	Laura Di Palma	high-profile attorney	San Francisco, CA
Matera, Lia	'87 - 7	Willa Jansson	Red diaper baby turned attorney	San Francisco, CA
Meek, M.R.D.	'82 - 11	Lennox Kemp	solicitor detective	England
Meredith, D.R.	'88 - 5	John L. Branson & Lydia Fairchild	defense attorney & legal assistant	Canadian, TX
Mickelbury, Penny	'98 - 2	Carole Ann Gibson	black criminal defense attorney	Washington, DC
Nielsen, Helen	'51 - 5	Simon Drake	transplanted Chicago attorney	Southern CA
O'Shaughnessy, Perri	'95 - 4	Nina Reilly	single-mother attorney	Lake Tahoe, NV
Parker, Barbara	'94 - 3	Gail Connor	corporate attorney	Miami, FL
Piesman, Marissa	'89 - 6	Nina Fischman	legal services attorney	New York, NY
Reuben, Shelly	'94 - 2	Wylie Nolan & Max Bramble	arson investigator & attorney	New York, NY
Rogers, Chris	'98 - 2	Dixie Flannigan	prosecutor turned bounty hunter	Houston, TX

Author	1 - #	Series Character	Occupation	Setting
Background Type				
Legal, attorney				
Scottoline, Lisa	'93 - 6	Rosato & Associates	all-women law firm	Philadelphia, PA
Smith, Janet L.	'90 - 3	Annie MacPherson	attorney	Seattle, WA
Smith, Julie	'82 - 5	Rebecca Schwartz	defense attorney	San Francisco, CA
Sprague, Gretchen	'97 - 4	Martha Patterson	retired attorney turned pro bono	Brooklyn, NY
Truman, Margaret	'89 - 7	Mackenzie Smith & Annabel Reed	law professor & gallery owner	Washington, DC
Van Gieson, Judith	'88 - 8	Neil Hamel	attorney & investigator	Albuquerque, NM
Wakefield, Hannah	'87 - 3	Dee Street	solicitor in an all-women firm	London, England
Wheat, Carolyn	'83 - 6	Cass Jameson	Legal Aid defense attorney	Brooklyn, NY
Wilhelm, Kate	'91 - 4	Barbara Holloway	defense attorney	Eugene, OR
Yarbro, Chelsea Q.	'76 - 4	Charles Spotted Moon	attorney-Ojibway tribal shaman	San Francisco, CA
Youmans, Claire	'00 - 1	Sandy Whitacre	attorney in sole practice tort law	Seattle, WA
Legal, judge				
Maron, Margaret	'92 - 6	Deborah Knott	district judge	North Carolina
Legal, prosecutor				
Barrett, Margaret	'98 - 2	Susan Given	asset forfeiture prosecutor	New York, NY
Benke, Patricia D.	'95 - 3	Judith Thornton	chief assistant district attorney	San Diego, CA
Fairstein, Linda	'96 - 3	Alexandra Cooper	chief sex crimes prosecutor	New York, NY
Fyfield, Frances	'88 - 6	Helen West	London Crown prosecutor	London, England
McGuire, Christine	'93 - 4	Kathryn Mackay	senior prosecuting attorney	Northern CA
Schier, Norma	'78 - 4	Kay Barth	district attorney	Aspen, CO
Youmans, Claire	'96 - 2	Janet Schilling	county chief deputy prosecutor	Coastal WA
Medical				
Bannister, Jo	'84 - 3	Clio Rees & Harry Marsh	physician novelist & chief inspector	England
Borthwick, J.S.	'82 - 9	Sarah Deane & Alex McKenzie	English professor & internist	Boston, MA
Cohen, Anthea	'82 - 15	Agnes Carmichael	hospital staff nurse	England
Cook, Judith	'97 - 2	Simon Forman	Elizabethan physician-astrologer	London, England
Cornwell, Patricia	'90 - 9	Kay Scarpetta	chief medical examiner	Richmond, VA
Crum, Laura	'94 - 4	Gail McCarthy	horse veterinarian	Santa Cruz, CA
D'Amato, Barbara	'80 - 2	Gerritt DeGraaf	forensic pathologist	Chicago, IL
Dreyer, Eileen	'95 - 2	Molly Burke	death investigator	St. Louis, MO
Dunlap, Susan	'89 - 4	Kiernan O'Shaughnessy	medical examiner turned P.I.	La Jolla, CA
Fromer, Margot J.	'91 - 2	Amanda Knight	hospital director of nursing	Washington, DC
Green, Christine	'91 - 4	Kate Kinsella	nurse and medical investigator	Longborough, England
Gregory, Susanna	'96 - 4	Matthew Bartholomew	14th century physician and teacher	Cambridge, England
Hambly, Barbara	'97 - 2	Benjamin January	1830s Paris-trained black doctor	New Orleans, LA
Hathaway, Robin	'98 - 2	Andrew Fenimore	old-fashioned cardiologist	Philadelphia, PA
Hendricksen, Louise	'93 - 3	Amy Prescott	crime lab physician	Seattle, WA
Heron, Echo	'98 - 3	Adele Monsarrat	hospital registered nurse	Marin County, CA
Horowitz, Renee B.	'97 - 2	Ruthie Kantor Morris	widowed pharmacist	Scottsdale, AZ
Kittredge, Mary	'90 - 6	Edwina Crusoe	RN and medical consultant	New Haven, CT
Lake, Deryn	'94 - 4	John Rawlings & the Blind Beak	18th century apothecary & blind magistrate	London, England
Landreth, Marsha	'92 - 3	Samantha Turner	medical examiner	Sheridan, WY
McGiffin, Janet	'92 - 3	Maxene St. Clair	emergency room physician	Milwaukee, WI
Moore, Barbara	'83 - 2	Gordon Christy	veterinarian	New Mexico
Paton Walsh, Jill	'93 - 2	Imogen Quy	St. Agatha's College nurse	Cambridge, England
Rayner, Claire	'93 - 5	George Barnabas	hospital forensic pathologist	London, England
Roberts, Lillian M.	'96 - 3	Andi Pauling	veterinarian	Palm Springs, CA
Robinson, Leah Ruth	'88 - 2	Evelyn Sutcliffe	emergency medicine resident	New York, NY
Roe, Caroline	'98 - 3	Isaac & Bishop Berenguer	1350s blind physician & bishop	Girona, Spain
Romberg, Nina	'89 - 2	Marian Winchester	Caddo-Comanche medicine woman	Texas
Rust, Megan Mallory	'98 - 4	Taylor Morgan	air ambulance pilot	Anchorage, AK
Tesler, Nancy	'97 - 3	Carrie Carlin	single-mother biofeedback clinician	New Jersey
Wilson, Karen Ann	'94 - 4	Samantha Holt	veterinary technician	Paradise Cay, FL
Zachary, Fay	'94 - 2	Liz Broward & Zack James	family physician & computer artist	Phoenix, AZ

Medieval *[see Historical]*

Author	1 - #	Series Character	Occupation	Setting
Background Type				
Military				
Duffy, Margaret	'87 - 6	Ingrid Langley & Patrick Gillard	novelist secret agent & army major	England
Gom, Leona	'96 - 2	Vicky Bauer	Army wife of mixed Indian heritage	Canada
Miscellaneous				
Jordan, Jennifer	'92 - 2	Kristin Ashe	amateur sleuth	Denver, CO
Michaels, Barbara	'68 - 3	Georgetown house	historic home	Washington, DC
Moody, Susan	'93 - 6	Cassandra Swann	bridge professional	Cotswolds, England
Morison, B.J.	'82 - 5	Elizabeth Lamb Worthington	precocious adolescent girl	Bar Harbor, ME
new *Movies & Filmmaking*				
Borton, D.B.	'99 - 1	Gilda Liberty	small-town movie theater proprietor	Eden, OH
Farmer, Jerrilyn	'98 - 2	Madeline Bean	Hollywood party planner	Los Angeles, CA
Hornsby, Wendy	'92 - 5	Maggie MacGowen	documentary filmmaker	Los Angeles, CA
Kraft, Gabrielle	'87 - 4	Jerry Zalman	Beverly Hills deal maker	Los Angeles, CA
Maracotta, Lindsay	'96 - 2	Lucy Freers	children's film animator	Los Angeles, CA
Osborne, Denise	'94 - 2	Queenie Davilov	screenwriter-investigator	Hollywood, CA
Woods, Sherryl	'91 - 4	Molly DeWitt	film promoter and single mother	Miami, FL
new *Music*				
Carter, Charlotte	'97 - 2	Nanette Hayes	young black tenor sax player	New York, NY
Chittenden, Margaret	'96 - 4	Charlie Plato & Zack Hunter	country-western tavern owners	San Francisco, CA
Douglas, Carole N.	'90 - 4	Irene Adler	19th century American diva	Paris, France
Frommer, Sara H.	'86 - 3	Joan Spencer	symphony orchestra manager	Oliver, IN
Knight, Phyllis	'92 - 2	Lil Ritchie	ex-rocker and gay woman P.I.	Charlottesville, VA
Moore, Miriam Ann	'97 - 2	Marti Hirsch	would-be writer and disco lover	New York, NY
Peterson, Audrey	'88 - 6	Jane Winfield	British journalist and music writer	London, England
Smith, Sarah	'92 - 2	A. von Reisden & Perdita Halley	biochemist & concert pianist	Paris, France
Tishy, Cecelia	'97 - 2	Kate Banning	music company staff writer	Nashville, TN
Weber, Janice	'92 - 2	Leslie Frost	secret agent and concert violinist	Washington, DC
Native American				
Blanc, Suzanne	'61 - 3	Miguel Menendez	Aztec police inspector	San Luis Potosi, Mexico
Coel, Margaret	'95 - 4	John A. O'Malley & Vicky Holden	Jesuit missionary & Arapaho attorney	Wind River, WY
Cogan, Priscilla	'97 - 2	Meggie O'Connor	practicing psychologist	Leelanau Peninsula, MI
Corpi, Lucha	'92 - 2	Gloria Damasco	Chicana activist with ESP	Oakland, CA
Dawkins, Cecil	'93 - 2	Ginevra Prettifield	art museum assistant director	Santa Fe, NM
Gom, Leona	'96 - 2	Vicky Bauer	Army wife of mixed Indian heritage	Canada
Hager, Jean	'89 - 5	Mitch Bushyhead	police chief of Cherokee descent	Buckskin, OK
Hager, Jean	'92 - 4	Molly Bearpaw	Cherokee civil rights investigator	Tahlequah, OK
Medawar, Mardi O.	'96 - 3	Tay-bodal	19th century Kiowa healer	Oklahoma
Romberg, Nina	'89 - 2	Marian Winchester	Caddo-Comanche medicine woman	Texas
Thurlo, Aimée & David	'95 - 5	Ella Clah	Navajo FBI agent	Shiprock, NM
Yarbro, Chelsea Q.	'76 - 4	Charles Spotted Moon	attorney-Ojibway tribal shaman	San Francisco, CA
Occult [see Paranormal]				
Paranormal				
Alexander, Skye	'97 - 3	Charlotte McCrae	Boston astrologer	Clearwater, NC
Atherton, Nancy	'92 - 4	Aunt Dimity	romantic ghost	England
Chappell, Helen	'96 - 3	Hollis Ball & Sam Wescott	reporter & her ex-husband's ghost	Santimoke County, MD
Cook, Judith	'97 - 2	Simon Forman	Elizabethan physician-astrologer	London, England
Corpi, Lucha	'92 - 2	Gloria Damasco	Chicana activist with ESP	Oakland, CA
Davis, Dorothy S.	'76 - 4	Julie Hayes	actress turned columnist and fortuneteller	New York, NY
Edghill, Rosemary	'94 - 3	Karen Hightower aka Bast	white witch graphic designer	New York, NY
Green, Kate	'86 - 3	Theresa Fortunato & Oliver Jardine	professional psychic & LAPD detective	Los Angeles, CA
Jorgensen, Christine T.	'94 - 4	Stella the Stargazer	astrologer & lovelorn columnist	Denver, CO
Lackey, Mercedes	'89 - 3	Diana Tregarde	investigator of unnatural events	Hartford, CT
Lawrence, Martha	'95 - 3	Elizabeth Chase	parapsychologist turned P.I.	San Diego, CA
Mather, Linda	'94 - 2	Jo Hughes	astrologer-investigator	England
Thrasher, L.L.	'98 - 1	Lizbet Lange	millionaire ex-waitress	Oak Valley, CA
Warner, Mignon	'76 - 7	Edwina Charles	British clairvoyant	England

Author	1 - #	Series Character	Occupation	Setting

Background Type

Photography [see Journalism, Photography]

new Psychology & Psychiatry

Author	1 - #	Series Character	Occupation	Setting
Cogan, Priscilla	'97 - 2	Meggie O'Connor	practicing psychologist	Leelanau Peninsula, MI
Douglas, Carole N.	'85 - 2	Kevin Blake	psychiatrist	New Mexico
Dymmoch, Michael A.	'93 - 3	John Thinnes & Jack Caleb	cop & gay psychiatrist	Chicago, IL
Kiecolt-Glaser, Janice	'97 - 2	Haley McAlister	psychologist and professor	Houston, TX
Lawrence, Martha	'95 - 3	Elizabeth Chase	parapsychologist turned P.I.	San Diego, CA
Lovett, Sarah	'95 - 3	Sylvia Strange	forensic psychologist	Sante Fe, NM
Matthews, Alex	'96 - 3	Cassidy McCabe	psychotherapist	Oak Park, IL
McCafferty, Jeanne	'94 - 3	Mackenzie Griffin	consulting criminal psychologist	New York, NY
McDermid, Val	'95 - 2	Tony Hill & Carol Jordan	clinical psychologist & D.I.	Bradfield, England
O'Callaghan, Maxine	'96 - 2	Anne Menlo	child psychologist	Phoenix, AZ
O'Kane, Leslie	'98 - 2	Allida Babcock	dog psychologist	Boulder, CO
Padgett, Abigail	'98 - 2	Blue McCarron	lesbian social psychologist	San Diego, CA
Salter, Anna	'97 - 2	Michael Stone	female forensic psychologist	Vermont
Wilhelm, Kate	'87 - 6	C. Meiklejohn & C. Leidl	P.I. & psychologist	New York, NY

new Real Estate

Author	1 - #	Series Character	Occupation	Setting
Harris, Charlaine	'90 - 6	Aurora Teagarden	librarian turned real estate agent	Lawrenceton, GA
Lee, Barbara	'95 - 3	Eve Elliott	real estate agent	Anne Arundel Co., MD
McClellan, Tierney	'95 - 4	Schuyler Ridgway	40-something real estate agent	Louisville, KY

Renaissance [see Historical]

Romantic

Author	1 - #	Series Character	Occupation	Setting
Atherton, Nancy	'92 - 4	Aunt Dimity	romantic ghost	England
Cannell, Dorothy	'84 - 8	Ellie & Ben Haskell	interior decorator & writer-chef	Chitterton Fells, England
Chapman, Sally	'91 - 4	Juliet Blake	computer fraud investigator	Silicon Valley, CA
Chittenden, Margaret	'96 - 4	Charlie Plato & Zack Hunter	country-western tavern owners	San Francisco, CA
Dunbar, Sophie	'93 - 5	Claire Claiborne	beauty salon owner	New Orleans, LA
Feddersen, Connie	'93 - 6	Amanda Hazard	sexy small-town CPA	Vamoose, OK
Fulton, Eileen	'88 - 6	Nina McFall & Dino Rossi	TV soap star & NYPD lieutenant	New York, NY
Jorgensen, Christine T.	'94 - 4	Stella the Stargazer	astrologer & lovelorn columnist	Denver, CO
Peart, Jane	'96 - 4	Edgecliffe Manor Series	young, restless Victorian women	England
Pence, Joanne	'93 - 6	Angelina Amalfi	freelance food writer	San Francisco, CA
Robb, J.D.	'95 - 8	Eve Dallas	21st century NYPD lieutenant	New York, NY
Shaffer, Louise	'94 - 2	Angie DaVito	daytime television producer	New York, NY

new Royals & Aristocrats

Author	1 - #	Series Character	Occupation	Setting
Beaufort, Simon	'98 - 2	Geoffrey de Mappestone	brave knight of the Crusades	England
Buckley, Fiona	'97 - 2	Ursula Blanchard	lady-in-waiting to Elizabeth I	London, England
Chisholm, P.F.	'94 - 4	Robert Carey	Elizabethan nobleman	England
Christmas, Joyce	'88 - 9	Margaret Priam	English noblewoman	New York, NY
Crowleigh, Ann	'93 - 2	Mirinda & Clare Clively	Victorian twin sisters	London, England
Dunn, Carola	'94 - 6	Daisy Dalrymple	'20s aristocratic feature writer	Hampshire, England
Emerson, Kathy Lynn	'97 - 4	Susanna Appleton	Elizabethan herbalist noblewoman	England
Eyre, Elizabeth	'92 - 6	Sigismondo	agent of a Renaissance duke	Venice, Italy
George, Elizabeth	'88 - 9	Thomas Lynley & Barbara Havers	Scotland Yard inspector & detective sergeant	London, England
Greenwood, Kerry	'89 - 9	Phryne Fisher	'20s Londoner	Melbourne, Australia
Greth, Roma	'88 - 2	Hana Shaner	40-something heiress	Conover, PA
Jakeman, Jane	'97 - 3	Ambrose Malfine	lord and heir to a decaying estate	West Country, England
Penman, Sharon Kay	'96 - 2	Justin de Quincy	Queen Mother's investigator	England
Robinson, Lynda S.	'94 - 5	Lord Meren	Tutankhamen's chief investigator	Egypt
Ross, Kate	'93 - 4	Julian Kestrel	1820s dandy-about-town	London, England
Rowland, Laura Joh	'94 - 4	Sano Ichiro	investigator for the shogun	Edo, Japan
Woodward, Ann	'96 - 2	Lady Aoi	11th century Japanese healer	Kyoto, Japan

new Science

Author	1 - #	Series Character	Occupation	Setting
Davis, Kaye	'97 - 3	Maris Middleton	lesbian forensic chemist	Texas
Miles, Margaret	'98 - 2	C. Willett & R. Longfellow	Colonial farm woman & scientist-farmer	Bracebridge, MA
Petrie, Rhona	'67 - 2	Nassim Pride	Anglo-Sudanese forensic scientist	England
Rothenberg, Rebecca	'91 - 3	Claire Sharples	microbiologist	Central CA
Smith, Sarah	'92 - 2	A. von Reisden & Perdita Halley	biochemist & concert pianist	Paris, France

Author	1 - #	Series Character	Occupation	Setting
Background Type				
Science Fiction [see Cross Genre]				
Secret Agents [see Espionage]				
Senior Sleuths				
Allen, Irene	'92 - 4	Elizabeth Elliot	widowed Quaker meeting clerk	Cambridge, MA
Arnold, Margot	'79 - 12	Penny Spring & Toby Glendower	anthropologist & archaeologist	World Travelers
Babson, Marian	'86 - 5	Evangeline Sinclair & Trixie Dolan	aging American ex-movie queens	London, England
Beaton, M.C.	'92 - 8	Agatha Raisin	cranky London retiree	Carsely, England
Bell, Nancy	'96 - 3	Biggie Weatherford & J.R.	grandmother & nephew sidekick	Job's Crossing, TX
Borton, D.B.	'93 - 6	Cat Caliban	60-something P.I.-in-training	Cincinnati, OH
Boylan, Eleanor	'89 - 5	Clara Gamadge	widow of Henry the forgery expert	New York, NY
Brightwell, Emily	'93 - 13	G. Witherspoon & H. Jeffries	Victorian inspector & his housekeeper	London, England
Brown, Lizbie	'92 - 2	Elizabeth Blair	American widow quilt shop owner	Bath, England
Burden, Pat	'90 - 4	Henry Bassett	retired cop	Herefordshire, England
Christmas, Joyce	'93 - 3	Betty Trenka	retired office manager	Connecticut
Clayton, Mary	'95 - 5	John Reynolds	ex-inspector turned crime writer	Cornwall, England
Cleeves, Ann	'86 - 8	George & Molly Palmer-Jones	ex-Home Office bird-watcher & wife	Surrey, England
Comfort, Barbara	'86 - 5	Tish McWhinny	70-something artist-painter	Lofton, VT
Crane, Hamilton	'68 - 22	Emily D. Seeton	retired British art teacher	Kent, England
Dams, Jeanne M.	'95 - 4	Dorothy Martin	60-something American widow	Sherebury, England
Deloach, Nora	'94 - 6	Candi & Simone Covington	black social worker & paralegal daughter	Otis, SC
Ferris, Monica	'99 - 2	Betsy Devonshire	needlework shop owner	Excelsior, MN
Fletcher, Jessica	'89 - 11	Jessica Fletcher	60-something mystery writer	Cabot Cove, ME
Frommer, Sara H.	'86 - 3	Joan Spencer	symphony orchestra manager	Oliver, IN
George, Anne	'96 - 5	Mary Alice Crane & Patricia Anne Hollowell	60-something sister sleuths	Birmingham, AL
Gilman, Dorothy	'66 - 13	Emily Pollifax	grandmother CIA agent	International
Godfrey, Ellen	'76 - 2	Rebecca Rosenthal	80-year-old Polish-born anthropologist	Toronto, ON, Canada
Gray, Gallagher	'91 - 4	Theodore S. Hubbert & Auntie Lil	retired personnel manager & dress designer	New York, NY
Green, Edith Pinero	'77 - 3	Dearborn V. Pinch	70-something ladies man	New York, NY
Griffin, Annie	'98 - 2	Hannah Malloy & Kiki Goldstein	unlikely pair of 60-something sisters	Marin County, CA
Guiver, Patricia	'97 - 3	Delilah Doolittle	British widow pet detective	Surf City, CA
Haddam, Jane	'90 - 15	Gregor Demarkian	former FBI department head	Philadelphia, PA
Hadley, Joan	'86 - 2	Theo Bloomer	retired florist and former spy	USA
Hart, Carolyn G.	'93 - 4	Henrietta O'Dwyer Collins	70-something reporter	Oklahoma
Holt, Hazel	'89 - 8	Sheila Malory	British literary magazine writer	Devon, England
Horowitz, Renee B.	'97 - 2	Ruthie Kantor Morris	widowed pharmacist	Scottsdale, AZ
Kershaw, Valerie	'93 - 4	Mitch Mitchell & Tommy Hung	radio journalist P.I. & Chinese partner	Birmingham, England
Langton, Jane	'64 - 13	Homer Kelly	ex-cop turned Harvard professor	Cambridge, MA
Lawrence, Hilda	'44 - 3	M. East, B. Petty & B. Pond	Manhattan P.I. & little old ladies	New York, New York
Lee, Marie	'95 - 3	Marguerite Smith	retired science teacher	Cape Cod, MA
Lewis, Sherry	'95 - 5	Fred Vickery	70-something retiree	Cutler, CO
Matteson, Stefanie	'90 - 8	Charlotte Graham	Oscar-winning actress	New York, NY
McShea, Susanna H.	'90 - 3	Mildred Bennett & friends	quartet of senior sleuths	Raven's Wing, CT
Minichino, Camille	'97 - 3	Gloria Lamerino	50-something physicist	Revere Beach, MA
Morgan, Kate	'90 - 7	Dewey James	60-something small-town librarian	Hamilton, KY
O'Marie, Carol A., Sr.	'84 - 8	Mary Helen, Sister	70-something nun	San Francisco, CA
Pickard, Nancy	'82 - 5	Eugenia Potter	60-something widowed chef	USA
Rippon, Marion	'69 - 4	Maurice Ygrec	retired French police inspector	Moselle, France
Ruryk, Jean	'94 - 3	Catherine Wilde	ad exec turned antiques restorer	Montreal, QB, Canada
Rushford, Patricia H.	'97 - 3	Helen Bradley	ex-cop travel-writer grandmother	Lincoln City, OR
Sawyer, Corinne Holt	'88 - 8	A. Benbow & C. Wingate	70-something admirals' widows	Southern CA
Sprague, Gretchen	'97 - 4	Martha Patterson	retired attorney turned pro bono	Brooklyn, NY
Squire, Elizabeth D.	'94 - 6	Peaches Dann	absent-minded widow	North Carolina
Stevens, Serita	'91 - 2	Fanny Zindel	Jewish grandmother	Brooklyn, NY
Stubbs, Jean	'73 - 3	John Joseph Lintott	retired Scotland Yard inspector	London, England
Tell, Dorothy	'90 - 2	Poppy Dillworth	60-something lesbian sleuth	Texas
Trocheck, Kathy H.	'96 - 2	Truman Kicklighter	retired wire service reporter	St. Petersburg, FL
Van Hook, Beverly	'95 - 2	Liza & Dutch Randolph	married amateur sleuths	West Virginia
Warner, Mignon	'76 - 7	Edwina Charles	British clairvoyant	England
Westfall, Patricia T.	'96 - 2	Molly West	50-something rural activist	Southern OH

Author	1 - #	Series Character	Occupation	Setting

Background Type

new Sherlockian

Author	1 - #	Series Character	Occupation	Setting
Buggé, Carole	'98 - 1	Sherlock Holmes	consulting detective	London, England
Fawcett, Quinn	'94 - 3	Mycroft Holmes	Sherlock Holmes' older brother	London, England
King, Laurie R.	'94 - 4	Mary Russell	Sherlock Holmes' detecting partner	London, England
Rogow, Roberta	'98 - 2	Charles Dodgson & Conan Doyle	19th century professor & doctor	England

new Single Parent

Author	1 - #	Series Character	Occupation	Setting
Bowen, Gail	'90 - 6	Joanne Kilbourn	political science professor	Regina, SK, Canada
Bowers, Elisabeth	'88 - 2	Meg Lacey	single-mother private eye	Vancouver, BC, Canada
Buggé, Carole	'99 - 3	Claire Rawlings	book editor with 12-year-old ward	New York, NY
Carlson, P.M.	'92 - 2	Marty LaForte Hopkins	deputy sheriff mom	Southern IN
Churchill, Jill	'89 - 11	Jane Jeffry	suburban single mother	Chicago, IL
Coburn, Laura	'95 - 4	Kate Harrod	single-mother police detective	San Madera, CA
Cramer, Rebecca	'98 - 2	Linda Bluenight	anthropologist turned teacher	Tucson, AZ
Dereske, Jo	'96 - 3	Ruby Crane	questioned-documents expert	Western MI
Dixon, Louisa	'98 - 3	Laura Owen	state public safety commissioner	Jackson, MS
Dobson, Joanne	'97 - 3	Karen Pelletier	single-mother English professor	Enfield, MA
Goldstone, Nancy	'95 - 2	Elizabeth Halperin	single-mother mystery writer	Berkshires, MA
Grant, Anne U.	'98 - 3	Sydney Teague	single-mother ad agency owner	Charlotte, NC
Grant, Linda	'88 - 6	Catherine Sayler	single-mother corporate P.I.	San Francisco, CA
Haffner, Margaret	'92 - 2	Catherine Edison	scientist and single mother	Kingsport, ON, Canada
Hess, Joan	'86 - 12	Claire Malloy	small-town bookstore owner	Farberville, AR
Holbrook, Teri	'95 - 3	Gale Grayson	American expatriate historian	England
Jacobs, Jonnie	'94 - 3	Kate Austen	suburban single mother	Walnut Hills, CA
Jance, J.A.	'93 - 7	Joanna Brady	single-mother sheriff	Cochise County, AZ
Kennett, Shirley	'96 - 4	P.J. Gray	police dept. virtual reality expert	St. Louis, MO
LaPierre, Janet	'87 - 5	Meg Halloran & Vince Gutierrez	single-mother school teacher & police chief	Port Silva, CA
Macdonald, Marianne	'96 - 2	Dido Hoare	single-mother antiquarian bookseller	London, England
McClellan, Tierney	'95 - 4	Schuyler Ridgway	40-something real estate agent	Louisville, KY
McGuire, Christine	'93 - 4	Kathryn Mackay	senior prosecuting attorney	Northern CA
Millhiser, Marlys	'92 - 5	Charlie Greene	literary agent and single mother	Hollywood, CA
Neely, Barbara	'92 - 3	Blanche White	black domestic worker	Boston, Massachusetts
O'Shaughnessy, Perri	'95 - 4	Nina Reilly	single-mother attorney	Lake Tahoe, NV
Quinn, Elizabeth	'93 - 4	Lauren Maxwell	wildlife investigator PhD	Anchorage, AK
Roberts, Gillian	'98 - 1	Emma Howe & Billie August	50-yr-old P.I. & single-mom partner	San Raphael, CA
Rubino, Jane	'96 - 3	Cat Austen & Victor Cardenas	single-mom reporter & police detective	Atlantic City, NJ
Spring, Michelle	'94 - 4	Laura Principal	British academic turned P.I.	Cambridge, England
Staincliffe, Cath	'94 - 3	Sal Kilkenny	single-mother private eye	Manchester, England
Star, Nancy	'98 - 2	May Morrison	TV talk show producer	New York, NY
Tesler, Nancy	'97 - 3	Carrie Carlin	single-mother biofeedback clinician	New Jersey
Tishy, Cecelia	'97 - 2	Kate Banning	music company staff writer	Nashville, TN
Waterhouse, Jane	'95 - 3	Garner Quin	best-selling true crime writer	Spring Lake, NJ
Wesley, Valerie W.	'94 - 5	Tamara Hayle	black ex-cop single-mother P.I.	Newark, NJ
Wilson, Anne	'95 - 2	Sara Kingsley	single-mother community counselor	London, England
Woods, Sherryl	'91 - 4	Molly DeWitt	film promoter and single mother	Miami, FL
Wright, Nancy M.	'96 - 2	Ruth Willmarth	single-mother farmer	Branbury, VT

Small Town

Author	1 - #	Series Character	Occupation	Setting
Adams, Deborah	'92 - 6	Jesus Creek TN	eccentric small town	Jesus Creek, TN
Bell, Nancy	'96 - 3	Biggie Weatherford & J.R.	grandmother & nephew sidekick	Job's Crossing, TX
Borton, D.B.	'99 - 1	Gilda Liberty	small-town movie theater proprietor	Eden, OH
Brown, Rita Mae	'90 - 6	Mary Minor Haristeen	small-town postmistress	Crozet, VA
Dereske, Jo	'96 - 3	Ruby Crane	questioned-documents expert	Western, MI
Feddersen, Connie	'93 - 6	Amanda Hazard	sexy small-town CPA	Vamoose, OK
Gunn, Elizabeth	'97 - 3	Jake Hines	small town police detective	Rutherford, MN
Harris, Charlaine	'96 - 3	Lily Bard	30-something cleaning woman	Shakespeare, AR
Hayden, G. Miki	'98 - 2	Dennis Astin	psychopharmacologist	Center City, MI
Hess, Joan	'87 - 11	Arly Hanks	small-town police chief	Maggody, AR
Hess, Joan	'86 - 12	Claire Malloy	small-town bookstore owner	Farberville, AR
Iakovou, Takis & Judy	'96 - 2	Nick & Julia Lambros	college-town cafe owners	Delphi, GA
Kelner, Toni L.P.	'93 - 6	Laura Fleming	small-town Southern sleuth	Byerly, NC
Malmont, Valerie S.	'94 - 2	Tori Miracle	crime writer turned novelist	Lickin Creek, PA

Author	1 - #	Series Character	Occupation	Setting

Background Type

Small Town

Author	1 - #	Series Character	Occupation	Setting
McCafferty, Taylor	'90 - 6	Haskell Blevins	small-town private eye	Pigeon Fork, KY
Morgan, Kate	'90 - 7	Dewey James	60-something small-town librarian	Hamilton, KY
Oleksiw, Susan	'93 - 3	Joe Silva	small-town chief of police	Mellingham, MA
Smith, Alison	'84 - 2	Judd Springfield	small town police chief	Coolridge Corners, VT
Taylor, Kathleen	'93 - 4	Tory Bauer	small-town diner waitress	Delphi, SD

new Social Services

Author	1 - #	Series Character	Occupation	Setting
Cercone, Karen Rose	'97 - 3	Helen Sorby & Milo Kachigan	social worker & policeman in 1905	Pittsburgh, PA
Cooper, Natasha	'98 - 1	Trish Maguire	family law barrister	London, England
Deloach, Nora	'94 - 6	Candi & Simone Covington	black social worker & paralegal daughter	Otis, SC
Godfrey, Ellen	'99 - 3	Janet Barkin	high school dropout	Evanston, IL
Joseph, Alison	'94 - 4	Agnes Bourdillon	ex-cloistered nun	London, England
O'Donnell, Lillian	'77 - 3	Mici Anhalt	criminal justice investigator	New York, NY
Padgett, Abigail	'93 - 5	Barbara Joan "Bo" Bradley	child abuse investigator	San Diego, CA
Padgett, Abigail	'98 - 2	Blue McCarron	lesbian social psychologist	San Diego, CA
Westfall, Patricia T.	'96 - 2	Molly West	50-something rural activist	Southern OH
Wheat, Carolyn	'83 - 6	Cass Jameson	Legal Aid defense attorney	Brooklyn, NY
Wilson, Anne	'95 - 2	Sara Kingsley	single-mother community counselor	London, England

Sports

Author	1 - #	Series Character	Occupation	Setting
Cody, Liza	'92 - 3	Eva Wylie	wrestler and security guard	London, England
Dunnett, Dorothy	'68 - 7	Johnson Johnson	British agent and yachtsman	International
Elkins, C. & A.	'89 - 3	Lee Ofsted & Graham Sheldon	woman golf pro & homicide detective	Washington
Gordon, Alison	'89 - 6	Kate Henry	baseball newswriter	Toronto, ON, CA
Kenney, Susan	'83 - 3	Roz Howard & Alan Stewart	American professor & British painter	Maine
McKernan, Victoria	'90 - 3	Chicago Nordejoong	professional scuba diver	Florida
Moffat, Gwen	'73 - 14	Melinda Pink	mountain climbing novelist	Utah
Navratilova, Martina	'94 - 3	Jordan Myles	ex-tennis star physical therapist	Palm Springs, CA
OCork, Shannon	'80 - 3	Theresa Tracy Baldwin	sports news photographer	New York, NY
Robitaille, Julie	'92 - 2	Kit Powell	TV sports reporter	San Diego, CA
Wilcox, Valerie	'98 - 3	Kellie Montgomery	widowed sailing instructor	Seattle, WA

Suburban

Author	1 - #	Series Character	Occupation	Setting
Churchill, Jill	'89 - 11	Jane Jeffry	suburban single mother	Chicago, IL
Harris, Lee	'92 - 11	Christine Bennett	former nun	Oakwood, NY
Jacobs, Jonnie	'94 - 3	Kate Austen	suburban single mother	Walnut Hills, CA
Meier, Leslie	'93 - 4	Lucy Stone	sleuthing mother of four	Tinker's Cove, ME
Murray, Donna H.	'95 - 5	Ginger Struve Barnes	headmaster's wife and suburban mother	Philadelphia, PA
Wolzien, Valerie	'96 - 3	Josie Pigeon	all-women construction firm owner	Northeast
Wolzien, Valerie	'87 - 12	Susan Henshaw	upscale suburban housewife	Connecticut

Theatre & Performing Arts

Author	1 - #	Series Character	Occupation	Setting
Babson, Marian	'86 - 5	Evangeline Sinclair & Trixie Dolan	aging American ex-movie queens	London, England
Barnes, Linda	'82 - 4	Michael Spraggue	wealthy actor ex-private eye	Boston, MA
Bartholomew, Nancy	'98 - 2	Sierra Lavotini	exotic dancer	Panama City, FL
Beck, K.K.	'92 - 4	Jane da Silva	former lounge singer	Seattle, WA
Brennan, Carol	'94 - 2	Emily Silver	New York actress	New York, NY
Brown, Molly	'97 - 2	Aphra Behn	17th century spy turned playwright	London, England
Cooper, Susan R.	'93 - 2	Kimmey Kruse	stand-up comic	Austin, TX
Dentinger, Jane	'83 - 6	Jocelyn O'Roarke	Broadway actor and director	New York, NY
Dewhurst, Eileen	'82 - 2	Helen Markham Johnson	actress recruited by Secret Service	London, England
Dewhurst, Eileen	'95 - 3	Phyllida Moon	television private eye	London, England
Farrell, Gillian B.	'92 - 2	Annie McGrogan	actor-P.I. returned from LA	New York, NY
Fulton, Eileen	'88 - 6	Nina McFall & Dino Rossi	TV soap star & NYPD lieutenant	New York, NY
Matteson, Stefanie	'90 - 8	Charlotte Graham	Oscar-winning actress	New York, NY
Meyers, Annette	'89 - 7	Xenia Smith & Leslie Wetzon	Wall Street headhunters	New York, NY
Paul, Barbara	'84 - 3	Enrico Caruso & Geraldine Farrar	Italian tenor & American soprano	New York, NY
Yeager, Dorian	'92 - 4	Victoria Bowering	6 ft-redhead sometime-actress	New York, NY

Author	1 - #	Series Character	Occupation	Setting

Background Type

Travel

Author	1 - #	Series Character	Occupation	Setting
Dreher, Sarah	'85 - 7	Stoner McTavish	lesbian travel agent	Boston, MA
Gilman, Dorothy	'66 - 13	Emily Pollifax	grandmother CIA agent	International
Jackson, Marian J.A.	'90 - 5	Abigail Patience Danforth	19th century American heiress detective	International
Linscott, Gillian	'84 - 4	Birdie Linnet	ex-cop fitness trainer	England

Series 3 Characters

Series Character	Author	1 - #	Occupation	Setting

Character's First Name

A

Series Character	Author	1 - #	Occupation	Setting
Abby Abagnarro & Ike Tygart	Whitney, Polly	'94 - 4	network producer & TV news director	New York, NY
Abigail Patience Danforth	Jackson, Marian J.A.	'90 - 5	19th century American heiress detective	International
Abigail Sanderson & Robert Forsythe	Giroux, E.X.	'84 -10	barrister & his secretary	London, England
Abigail Timberlake	Myers, Tamar	'96 - 6	antiques dealer	Charlotte, NC
Adam Dalgleish	James, P.D.	'62 -10	published poet of Scotland Yard	London, England
Adele Monsarrat	Heron, Echo	'98 - 3	hospital registered nurse	Marin County, CA
Agatha Raisin	Beaton, M.C.	'92 - 8	cranky London retiree	Carsely, England
Agnes Bourdillon	Joseph, Alison	'94 - 4	ex-cloistered nun	London, England
Agnes Carmichael	Cohen, Anthea	'82 -15	hospital staff nurse	England
Aimée Leduc	Black, Cara	'99 - 2	French-American private eye	Paris, France
Alan Markby & M. Mitchell	Granger, Ann	'91 - 11	D.I. & Foreign Service officer	Cotswolds, England
Alex Jensen & Jessie Arnold	Henry, Sue	'91 - 5	sled dog racer & Alaska state trooper	Anchorage, AK
Alex McKenzie & Sarah Deane	Borthwick, J.S.	'82 - 9	English professor & internist	Boston, MA
Alex Plumtree	Kaewert, Julie Wallin	'94 - 3	head of family publishing firm	London, England
Alex Tanner	Donald, Anabel	'93 - 5	TV researcher and part-time P.I.	London, England
Alexander von Reisden & Perdlta Halley	Smith, Sarah	'92 - 2	biochemist & concert pianist	Paris, France
Alexandra Cooper	Fairstein, Linda	'96 - 3	chief sex crimes prosecutor	New York, NY
Alexandra Winter	Steiner, Susan	'91 - 2	red-haired investigator	Southern CA
Aline Scott	Drake, Alison	'88 - 4	homicide detective	Tango Key, FL
Alison Hope & N. Trevellyan	Kelly, Susan B.	'90 - 5	software designer & detective inspector	Hop Valley, England
Alison Kaine	Allen, Kate	'93 - 4	lesbian leather cop	Denver, CO
Alix Thorssen	McClendon, Lise	'94 - 2	gallery owner and art forgery expert	Jackson Hole, WY
Alan Stewart & Roz Howard	Kenney, Susan	'83 - 3	American professor & British painter	Maine
Allida Babcock	O'Kane, Leslie	'98 - 2	dog psychologist	Boulder, CO
Allison O'Neil	Douglas, Lauren Wright	'96 - 2	lesbian B & B owner	Lavner Bay, OR
Alonzo Hawkin & K. Martinelli	King, Laurie R.	'93 - 3	SFPD homicide detectives	San Francisco, CA
Amanda Hazard	Feddersen, Connie	'93 - 6	sexy small-town CPA	Vamoose, OK
Amanda Knight	Fromer, Margot J.	'91 - 2	hospital director of nursing	Washington, DC
Amanda Pepper	Roberts, Gillian	'87 - 8	high school English teacher	Philadelphia, PA
Amanda Roberts	Woods, Sherryl	'89 - 9	ex-NYC investigative reporter	Atlanta, GA
Amanda Valentine	Beecham, Rose	'92 - 3	lesbian detective inspector	Wellington, New Zealand
Ambrose Malfine	Jakeman, Jane	'97 - 3	lord and heir to a decaying estate	West Country, England
Amelia Peabody	Peters, Elizabeth	'75 -12	Victorian feminist archaeologist	Kent, England
Amy Prescott	Hendricksen, Louise	'93 - 3	crime lab physician	Seattle, WA
Andi Pauling	Roberts, Lillian M.	'96 - 3	veterinarian	Palm Springs, CA
Andrea Perkins	Coker, Carolyn	'84 - 5	art historian & restorer	Boston, MA
Andrew Fenimore	Hathaway, Robin	'98 - 2	old-fashioned cardiologist	Philadelphia, PA
Andy Brazil	Cornwell, Patricia	'97 - 2	reporter and volunteer cop	Charlotte, NC
Angela Benbow & C. Wingate	Sawyer, Corinne Holt	'88 - 8	70-something admirals' widows	Southern CA

Series Character	Author	1 - #	Occupation	Setting

Character's First Name

A...B

Angela Matelli	Lee, Wendi	'94 - 3	ex-Marine turned P.I.	Boston, MA
Angelina Amalfi	Pence, Joanne	'93 - 6	freelance food writer	San Francisco, CA
Angie DaVito	Shaffer, Louise	'94 - 2	daytime television producer	New York, NY
Anita Blake	Hamilton, Laurell K.	'93 - 8	reanimator and vampire hunter	St. Louis, MO
Anna Lee	Cody, Liza	'80 - 6	investigator for security firm	London, England
Anna Peters	Law, Janice	'76 - 9	oil company executive turned P.I.	Washington, DC
Anna Pigeon	Barr, Nevada	'93 - 7	park ranger	National Parks
Anna Southwood	Bedford, Jean	'90 - 3	private enquiry agent	Sydney, Australia
Annabelle Hardy-Maratos & Dave the Monkeyman	Jackson, Hialeah	'98 - 2	security specialists	Miami, FL,
Annabel Reed & M. Smith	Truman, Margaret	'89 - 7	law professor & gallery owner	Washington, DC
Anne Fitzhugh	Roberts, Carey	'89 - 2	police detective	Washington, DC
Anne Hardaway	Sherman, Beth	'98 - 2	ghostwriter	Oceanside Hts, NJ
Anne Menlo	O'Callaghan, Maxine	'96 - 2	child psychologist	Phoenix, AZ
Anneke Haagen	Holtzer, Susan	'94 - 5	computer consultant	Ann Arbor, MI
Annie Laurance & M. Darling	Hart, Carolyn G.	'87 - 10	bookstore owner & investigator	Broward's Rock, SC
Annie MacPherson	Smith, Janet L.	'90 - 3	attorney	Seattle, WA
Annie McGrogan	Farrell, Gillian B.	'92 - 2	actor-P.I. returned from LA	New York, NY
Aphra Behn	Brown, Molly	'97 - 2	17th century spy turned playwright	London, England
April Woo	Glass, Leslie	'93 - 4	Chinese-American police detective	New York, NY
Ariel Gold	Mercer, Judy	'96 - 3	amnesiac TV newsmagazine producer	Los Angeles, CA
Arly Hanks	Hess, Joan	'87 - 11	small-town police chief	Maggody, AR
Artie Cohen	Nadelson, Reggie	'95 - 3	39-year-old Russian-born cop	New York, NY
Auguste Didier	Myers, Amy	'86 - 9	British-French Victorian master chef	England
Aunt Dimity	Atherton, Nancy	'92 - 4	romantic ghost	England
Auntie Lil & Theodore S. Hubbert	Gray, Gallagher	'91 - 4	retired personnel manager & dress designer	New York, NY
Aurora Teagarden	Harris, Charlaine	'90 - 6	librarian turned real estate agent	Lawrenceton, GA

B

Balthazar Marten & Sixto Cardenas	Adamson, M.J.	'87 - 5	NYPD homicide detective & Puerto Rican cop	Puerto Rico
Barbara Havers & T. Lynley	George, Elizabeth	'88 - 9	Scotland Yard inspector & detective sergeant	London, England
Barbara Holloway	Wilhelm, Kate	'91 - 4	defense attorney	Eugene, OR
Barbara Joan "Bo" Bradley	Padgett, Abigail	'93 - 5	child abuse investigator	San Diego, CA
Barbara Simons	Epstein, Carole	'96 - 2	downsized business executive	Montreal, QB, Canada
Barrett Lake	Singer, Shelley	'93 - 4	history teacher turned P.I.	Berkeley, CA
Barry Vaughan & Dee Vaughan	Jordan, Jennifer	'87 - 3	spoofy crime writer & office temp wife	Woodfield, England
Barry Ross	Livesay, Ann	'98 - 5	international investigator	International
Becky Belski	Haddad, C.A.	'92 - 2	computer investigator	Chicago, IL
Bel Carson	Ross, Annie	'95 - 3	TV director and investigator	London, England
Ben Porter & Carrie Porter	Travis, Elizabeth	'89 - 2	husband & wife book publishers	Riverdale, CT
Ben Haskell & Ellie Haskell	Cannell, Dorothy	'84 - 8	interior decorator & writer-chef	Chitterton Fells, England
Ben Reese	Wright, Sally S.	'97 - 2	'60s university archivist	Ohio
Ben Safford	Dominic, R.B.	'68 - 7	Democratic Congressman from Ohio	Washington, DC
Benjamin January	Hambly, Barbara	'97 - 2	1830s Paris-trained black doctor	New Orleans, LA
Benjamin Jurnet	Haymon, S.T.	'80 - 8	Angleby CID detective inspector	Norwich, England
Benni Harper	Fowler, Earlene	'94 - 7	folk art museum curator	San Celina, CA
Benny Mitchell	Bell, Pauline	'90 - 8	brash detective constable	Yorkshire, England
Bernadette Hebert	Ennis, Catherine	'91 - 2	lesbian crime lab expert	Louisiana
Bernard Woodruff & Snooky Randolph	Dank, Gloria	'89 - 4	children's author & his brother-in-law	Connecticut
Bert & Nan Tatum	McCafferty, Barbara T.	'96 - 3	identical twin sisters	Louisville, KY
Beulah Pond, B. Petty, M. East	Lawrence, Hilda	'44 - 3	Manhattan P.I. & little old ladies	New York, New York
Beth Hartley	Barrett, Kathleen Anne	'96 - 3	attorney turned legal researcher	Milwaukee, WI
Betsy Devonshire	Ferris, Monica	'99 - 2	needlework shop owner	Excelsior, MN
Betty Trenka	Christmas, Joyce	'93 - 3	retired office manager	Connecticut
Bessie Petty, M. East, B. Pond	Lawrence, Hilda	'44 - 3	Manhattan P.I. & little old ladies	New York, New York
Biggie Weatherford & J.R.	Bell, Nancy	'96 - 3	grandmother & nephew sidekick	Job's Crossing, TX
Bill Slider	Harrod-Eagles, Cynthia	'91 - 7	Shepherd's Bush CID inspector	London, England
Bill Smith & Lydia Chin	Rozan, S.J.	'94 - 6	Chinese-American & Army-brat P.I. duo	New York, NY
Billie August & Emma Howe	Roberts, Gillian	'98 - 1	50-yr-old P.I. & single-mom partner	San Raphael, CA

Series Character	Author	1 - #	Occupation	Setting

Character's First Name

B...C

Series Character	Author	1 - #	Occupation	Setting
Birdie Linnet	Linscott, Gillian	'84 - 4	ex-cop fitness trainer	England
Bishop Berenguer & Isaac	Roe, Caroline	'98 - 3	1350s blind physician & bishop	Girona, Spain
Blaine Stewart	Zukowski, Sharon	'91 - 5	ex-cop turned corporate P.I.	New York, NY
Blair Emerson	Amey, Linda	'92 - 2	funeral director	Austin, TX
Blanche White	Neely, Barbara	'92 - 3	black domestic worker	Boston, Massachusetts
Blind Beak, the & J. Rawlings	Lake, Deryn	'94 - 4	18th century apothecary & blind magistrate	London, England
Blue Maguire & Spaceman Kowalski	White, Teri	'84 - 2	prickly cop partners	Los Angeles, CA
Blue McCarron	Padgett, Abigail	'98 - 2	lesbian social psychologist	San Diego, CA
Bonnie Indermill	Berry, Carole	'87 - 7	tap-dancing Manhattan office temp	New York, NY
Brad Rollins et al	Scott, Barbara A.	'93 - 3	international kidnap-rescue team	International
Brenda Midnight	Wilson, Barbara Jaye	'97 - 3	Greenwich Village milliner	New York, NY
Brett Higgins	Szymanski, Therese	'97 - 4	lesbian adult bookstore manager	Detroit, MI
Brett Nightingale	Kelly, Mary	'56 - 3	Scottish police inspector	Edinburgh, Scotland
Brigid Donovan	Saum, Karen	'90 - 3	50-something lesbian ex-nun	Maine
Britt Montero	Buchanan, Edna	'92 - 5	Cuban-American crime reporter	Miami, FL
Brooke Cassidy & M. Devlin	Kruger, Mary	'94 - 3	1890s debutante & detective husband	Newport, RI

C

Series Character	Author	1 - #	Occupation	Setting
Caitlin Reece	Douglas, Lauren W.	'87 - 6	lesbian private eye	Victoria, BC, Canada
Caledonia Wingate & Angela Benbow	Sawyer, Corinne Holt	'88 - 8	70-something admirals' widows	Southern CA
Caley Burke	McKenna, Bridget	'93 - 3	30-something private eye	Northern CA
Calista Jacobs	Knight, Kathryn Lasky	'86 - 4	illustrator of children's books	Cambridge, MA
Callahan Garrity	Trocheck, Kathy Hogan	'92 - 7	ex-cop cleaning service operator	Atlanta, GA
Canaletto	Laurence, Janet	'98 - 2	18th century Italian painter	London, England
Candi & Simone Covington	Deloach, Nora	'94 - 6	black social worker & paralegal daughter	Otis, SC
Carlos Cruz & Jay Goldstein	Wallace, Marilyn	'86 - 3	homicide detectives	Oakland, CA
Carlotta Carlyle	Barnes, Linda	'87 - 7	6'1" cab-driving ex-cop P.I.	Boston, MA
Carmen Ramirez	Haddock, Lisa	'94 - 2	lesbian newspaper copy editor	Frontier City, OK
Carol Ashton	McNab, Claire	'88 -10	lesbian detective inspector	Sydney, Australia
Carole Ann Gibson	Mickelbury, Penny	'98 - 2	black criminal defense attorney	Washington, DC
Caroline Canfield	Fiedler, Jacqueline	'98 - 2	wildlife artist	River Ridge, IL
Carrie Carlin	Tesler, Nancy	'97 - 3	single-mother biofeedback clinician	New Jersey
Frank Carver & Ginny Trask	Wallingford, Lee	'91 - 2	U.S. Forest Service officers	Oregon
Casey Farrel	Matthews, Patricia	'92 - 5	governor's crime task force member	Arizona
Casey Jones	Munger, Katy	'97 - 2	unlicensed private eye	Durham, NC
Casey Kellog & Al Krug	Weston, Carolyn	'72 - 3	college-grad cop & hard-bitten partner	Santa Monica, CA
Cass Jameson	Wheat, Carolyn	'83 - 6	Legal Aid defense attorney	Brooklyn, NY
Cassandra Reilly	Wilson, Barbara	'90 - 2	Spanish translator	London, England
Cassandra Swann	Moody, Susan	'93 - 6	bridge professional	Cotswolds, England
Cassidy James	Calloway, Kate	'96 - 7	rookie lesbian private eye	Cedar Hills, OR
Cassidy McCabe	Matthews, Alex	'96 - 3	psychotherapist	Oak Park, IL
Cassie Newton	Smith, Joan G.	'89 - 2	college French major	Montreal, QB, Canada
Cat Austen & Victor Cardenas	Rubino, Jane	'96 - 3	single-mom reporter & police detective	Atlantic City, NJ
Cat Caliban	Borton, D.B.	'93 - 6	60-something P.I.-in-training	Cincinnati, OH
Cat Marsala	D'Amato, Barbara	'90 - 7	freelance investigative journalist	Chicago, IL
Catherine Edison	Haffner, Margaret	'92 - 2	scientist and single mother	Kingsport, ON, Canada
Catherine LeVendeur	Newman, Sharan	'93 - 5	12th-century merchant's daughter	France
Catherine Sayler	Grant, Linda	'88 - 6	single-mother corporate P.I.	San Francisco, CA
Catherine Wilde	Ruryk, Jean	'94 - 3	ad exec turned antiques restorer	Montreal, QB, Canada
Cecile Buddenbrooks	Sullivan, Winona	'93 - 3	licensed P.I. heiress-nun	Boston, MA
Cecily Sinclair	Kingsbury, Kate	'93 -11	Edwardian hotel owner	Badger's End, England
Charles Dodgson & C. Doyle	Rogow, Roberta	'98 - 2	19th century professor & doctor	England
Charles Matthews	Meredith, D.R.	'84 - 5	honest county sheriff	Crawford Co., TX
Charles Sheridan & Kathryn Ardleigh	Paige, Robin	'94 - 5	American author & British scientist	Dedham, England
Charles Spotted Moon	Yarbro, Chelsea Quinn	'76 - 4	attorney-Ojibway tribal shaman	San Francisco, CA
Charlie Greene	Millhiser, Marlys	'92 - 5	literary agent and single mother	Hollywood, CA
Charlie Meiklejohn & C. Leidl	Wilhelm, Kate	'87 - 6	P.I. & psychologist	New York, NY
Charlie Parker	Shelton, Connie	'95 - 4	CPA turned investigator	Albuquerque, NM

Series Character	Author	1 - #	Occupation	Setting

Character's First Name

C...D

Series Character	Author	1 - #	Occupation	Setting
Charlie Plato & Zack Hunter	Chittenden, Margaret	'96 - 4	country-western tavern owners	San Francisco, CA
Charlotte Graham	Matteson, Stefanie	'90 - 8	Oscar-winning actress	New York, NY
Charlotte Justice	Woods, Paula L.	'99 - 3	black woman homicide detective	Los Angeles, CA
Charlotte Kent	Kittredge, Mary	'87 - 3	freelance writer	Connecticut
Charlotte McCrae	Alexander, Skye	'97 - 3	Boston astrologer	Clearwater, NC
Charlotte & Thomas Pitt	Perry, Anne	'79 -18	Victorian police inspector & wife	London, England
Charlotte Sams	Glen, Alison	'92 - 2	freelance writer	Columbus, OH
Charlotte Willett & R. Longfellow	Miles, Margaret	'98 - 2	Colonial farm woman & scientist-farmer	Bracebridge, MA
Charmian Daniels	Melville, Jennie	'62 -19	police detective	Deerham Hills, England
Chas Wheatley	Richman, Phyllis	'97 - 2	restaurant critic	Washington, DC
Chicago Nordejoong	McKernan, Victoria	'90 - 3	professional scuba diver	Florida
China Bayles	Albert, Susan Wittig	'92 - 7	herb shop owner & former attorney	Pecan Springs, TX
Christine Bennett	Harris, Lee	'92 -11	former nun	Oakwood, NY
Christine Martin	Roome, Annette	'89 - 3	40-something cub reporter	England
Christine Opara	Uhnak, Dorothy	'68 - 3	20-something police detective	New York, NY
Christopher Dennis "Seedy" Sloan	Aird, Catherine	'66 -16	CID department head	W. Calleshire, England
Claire Aldington	Holland, Isabelle	'83 - 6	Episcopal priest	New York, NY
Claire Breslinsky	Kelly, Mary Anne	'90 - 3	freelance photographer	New York, NY
Claire Camden	Peterson, Audrey	'92 - 3	California English professor	London, England
Claire Claiborne	Dunbar, Sophie	'93 - 5	beauty salon owner	New Orleans, LA
Clare & Mirinda Clively	Crowleigh, Ann	'93 - 2	Victorian twin sisters	London, England
Claire Conrad & Maggie Hill	Howe, Melodie J.	'89 - 2	elegant P.I. & assistant	Los Angeles, CA
Claire Malloy	Hess, Joan	'86 -12	small-town bookstore owner	Farberville, AR
Claire Rawlings	Buggé, Carole	'99 - 3	book editor with 12-year-old ward	New York, NY
Claire Sharples	Rothenberg, Rebecca	'91 - 3	microbiologist	Central CA
Clara Gamadge	Boylan, Eleanor	'89 - 5	widow of Henry the forgery expert	New York, NY
Claud Willetts	Morrone, Wenda W.	'01 - 1	small-town sheriff	Merciful Valley, MT
Claudia Seferius	Todd, Marilyn	'95 - 4	13 B.C. superbitch	Rome, Italy
Claudia Valentine	Day, Marele	'88 - 4	private investigator	Sydney, Australia
Clio Rees & Harry Marsh	Bannister, Jo	'84 - 3	physician novelist & chief inspector	England
Clovis Kelly	Babbin, Jacqueline	'72 - 2	homicide cop turned crime consultant	New York, NY
Clovis Pel	Hebden, Juliet	'79 -22	curmudgeonly police inspector	Burgundy, France
Colleen Fitzgerald	Johnson, Barbara	'95 - 2	lesbian insurance investigator	Washington, DC
Conan Doyle & C. Dodgson	Rogow, Roberta	'98 - 2	19th century professor & doctor	England
Conan Flagg	Wren, M.K.	'73 - 8	secret agent turned bookstore owner	Coastal OR
Connor O'Neill & Fran Wilson	Green, Christine	'93 - 3	village chief insp. & detective sgt.	Fowchester, England
Connor Westphal	Warner, Penny	'97 - 3	deaf reporter and newspaper owner	Flat Skunk, CA
Constance Leidl & C. Meiklejohn	Wilhelm, Kate	'87 - 6	P.I. & psychologist	New York, NY
Cordelia Gray	James, P.D.	'72 - 2	fledgling P.I.	London, England

D

Series Character	Author	1 - #	Occupation	Setting
Dafyd Llewellyn & J. Rafferty	Evans, Geraldine	'93 - 3	D.I. & his Welsh sergeant	Yorkshire, England
Daisy Dalrymple	Dunn, Carola	'94 - 6	'20s aristocratic feature writer	Hampshire, England
Daisy Marlow & Sam Milo	Morgan, D Miller	'87 - 2	lingerie-addicted P.I. & sheriff	San Diego, CA
Dame Frevisse	Frazer, Margaret	'92 - 8	15th century Benedictine nun	Oxfordshire, England
Daniel & Jennifer Kaine	Hoff, B.J.	'86 - 5	Christian radio station owner & exec asst	West Virginia
Darina Lisle	Laurence, Janet	'89 - 9	caterer-chef and food writer	West Country, England
Dave the Monkeyman & Annabelle Hardy-Maratos	Jackson, Hialeah	'98 - 2	security specialists	Miami, FL,
David Middleton-Brown & L. Kingsley	Charles, Kate	'91 - 5	artist & solicitor	London, England
David Haham	Haddad, C.A.	'76 - 2	government agent	Middle East
David Silver & String	Hightower, Lynn S.	'92 - 4	homicide cop & alien partner	USA
David Webb	Fraser, Anthea	'84 -14	detective chief inspector	Wiltshire, England
Dearborn V. Pinch	Green, Edith Pinero	'77 - 3	70-something ladies man	New York, NY
Deb Ralston	Martin, Lee	'84 -13	police detective mom	Fort Worth, TX
Deborah Knott	Maron, Margaret	'92 - 6	district judge	North Carolina
Debra Laslow	Krich, Rochelle Majer	'96 - 1	criminal defense attorney	Los Angeles, CA

Series Character	Author	1 - #	Occupation	Setting

Character's First Name

D...E

Series Character	Author	1 - #	Occupation	Setting
Dee Street	Wakefield, Hannah	'87 - 3	solicitor in an all-women firm	London, England
Dee & Berry Vaughan	Jordan, Jennifer	'87 - 3	spoofy crime writer & office temp wife	Woodfield, England
Delilah Doolittle	Guiver, Patricia	'97 - 3	British widow pet detective	Surf City, CA
Delilah West	O'Callaghan, Maxine	'80 - 6	private investigator	Orange County, CA
Delta Stevens	Silva, Linda Kay	'91 - 5	gay woman police officer	Southern CA
Dennis Astin	Hayden, G. Miki	'98 - 2	psychopharmacologist	Center City, MI
Desiree Shapiro	Eichler, Selma	'94 - 6	5'2" queen-size P.I.	New York, NY
Devon MacDonald	Jacobs, Nancy Baker	'91 - 3	ex-teacher private eye	Minneapolis, MN
Dewey James	Morgan, Kate	'90 - 7	60-something small-town librarian	Hamilton, KY
Diana Tregarde	Lackey, Mercedes	'89 - 3	investigator of unnatural events	Hartford, CT
Dido Hoare	Macdonald, Marianne	'96 - 2	single-mother antiquarian bookseller	London, England
Dino Rossi & Nina McFall	Fulton, Eileen	'88 - 6	TV soap star & NYPD lieutenant	New York, NY
Dittany Henbit Monk & Osbert Monk	Craig, Alisa	'81 - 5	garden club member & author of western	Lobelia Falls, ON, Canada
Dixie Flannigan	Rogers, Chris	'98 - 2	prosecutor turned bounty hunter	Houston, TX
Dixie T. Struthers	Sims, L.V.	'87 - 3	police sergeant	San Jose, CA
Dolly Rawlins	La Plante, Lynda	'83 - 5	bank robber's widow	London, England
Cal Donovan, Frank Shapiro, & Liz Graham	Bannister, Jo	'93 - 6	police officers	Castlemere, England
Doran Fairweather	Hardwick, Mollie	'86 - 7	British antiques dealer	Kent, England
Dorothy Martin	Dams, Jeanne M.	'95 - 4	60-something American widow	Sherebury, England
Douglas Perkins	Babson, Marian	'71 - 4	public relations agent	London, England
Douglas Quantrill & H. Lloyd	Radley, Sheila	'78 - 9	DCI & sergeant partner	Suffolk, England
Duncan Kincaid & G. James	Crombie, Deborah	'93 - 5	Scotland Yard detective partners	London, England
Dutch & Liza Randolph	Van Hook, Beverly	'95 - 2	married amateur sleuths	West Virginia

E

Series Character	Author	1 - #	Occupation	Setting
E.J. Pugh	Cooper, Susan Rogers	'92 - 5	housewife-mom romance writer	Black Cat Ridge, TX
Eddie Henderson	Wright, L.R.	'99 - 1	woman police officer	Vancouver, BC, Canada
Edgecliffe Manor Series	Peart, Jane	'96 - 4	young, restless Victorian women	England
Edwina Charles	Warner, Mignon	'76 - 7	British clairvoyant	England
Edwina Crusoe	Kittredge, Mary	'90 - 6	RN and medical consultant	New Haven, CT
Elena Jarvis	Herndon, Nancy	'95 - 6	wise-cracking police detective	Los Santos, TX
Elena Oliverez	Muller, Marcia	'83 - 3	Mexican arts museum curator	Santa Barbara, CA
Elizabeth Austin	Skom, Edith	'89 - 3	English professor	Chicago, IL
Elizabeth Blair	Brown, Lizbie	'92 - 2	American widow quilt shop owner	Bath, England
Elizabeth Chase	Lawrence, Martha	'95 - 3	parapsychologist turned P.I.	San Diego, CA
Elizabeth Elliot	Allen, Irene	'92 - 4	widowed Quaker meeting clerk	Cambridge, MA
Elizabeth Ellis	Manthorne, Jackie	'00 - 1	lesbian private eye	Toronto, ON, Canada
Elizabeth Halperin	Goldstone, Nancy	'95 - 2	single-mother mystery writer	Berkshires, MA
Elizabeth Lamb Worthington	Morison, B.J.	'82 - 5	precocious adolescent girl	Bar Harbor, ME
Elizabeth MacPherson	McCrumb, Sharyn	'84 - 8	forensic anthropologist	Virginia
Elizabeth Mendoza	McAllester, Melanie	'94 - 2	Hispanic-black lesbian homicide detective	San Francisco, CA
Elizabeth Will	Yeager, Dorian	'94 - 2	watercolorist-gallery owner	Dovekey, NH
Ella Clah	Thurlo, Aimée & David	'95 - 5	Navajo FBI agent	Shiprock, NM
Ellie & Ben Haskell	Cannell, Dorothy	'84 - 8	interior decorator & writer-chef	Chitterton Fells, Eng.
Ellie Bernstein	Dietz, Denise	'92 - 2	diet group leader	Colorado Springs, CO
Ellie Gordon	Berne, Karin	'85 - 3	law firm office manager	Orange County, CA
Em Hansen	Andrews, Sarah	'94 - 4	oil company geologist	Wyoming
Emily D. Seeton	Crane, Hamilton	'68 -22	retired British art teacher	Kent, England
Emily Pollifax	Gilman, Dorothy	'66 -13	grandmother CIA agent	International
Emily Silver	Brennan, Carol	'94 - 2	New York actress	New York, NY
Emily Stone	Buckstaff, Kathryn	'94 - 2	Florida-based travel writer	Branson, MO
Emmy & Henry Tibbett	Moyes, Patricia	'59 - '	Scotland Yard inspector & wife	London, England
Emma Howe & Billie August	Roberts, Gillian	'98 - 1	50-yr-old P.I. & single-mom partner	San Raphael, CA
Emma Lord	Daheim, Mary	'92 -11	small-town newspaper owner-editor	Alpine, WA
Emma Rhodes	Smith, Cynthia	'96 - 5	private resolver for the rich	London, England
Emma Victor	Wings, Mary	'86 - 4	lesbian activist private eye	San Francisco, CA
Enrico Caruso & G. Farrar	Paul, Barbara	'84 - 3	Italian tenor & American soprano	New York, NY
Erik March	Fickling, G.G.	'62 - 3	macho private eye	Los Angeles, CA
Eugenia Potter	Pickard, Nancy	'82 - 5	60-something widowed chef	USA
Eva Wylie	Cody, Liza	'92 - 3	wrestler and security guard	London, England

Series Character	Author	1 - #	Occupation	Setting

Character's First Name

E...G

Series Character	Author	1 - #	Occupation	Setting
Evan Evans	Bowen, Rhys	'97 - 3	village constable	Llanfair, N Wales
Evangeline Sinclair & Trixie Dolan	Babson, Marian	'86 - 5	aging American ex-movie queens	London, England
Eve Dallas	Robb, J.D.	'95 - 8	21st century NYPD lieutenant	New York, NY
Eve Elliott	Lee, Barbara	'95 - 3	real estate agent	Anne Arundel Co., MD
Evelyn Sutcliffe	Robinson, Leah Ruth	'88 - 2	emergency medicine resident	New York, NY

F

Series Character	Author	1 - #	Occupation	Setting
Faith Sibley Fairchild	Page, Katherine Hall	'90 - 9	caterer and minister's wife	Aleford, MA
Fanny Zindel	Stevens, Serita	'91 - 2	Jewish grandmother	Brooklyn, NY
Father Simeon & Elvira	Highsmith, Domini	'94 - 3	medieval priest & nurse	East Yorkshire, England
Fiddler & Fiora Flynn	Maxwell, A.E.	'85 - 8	knight-errant & investment banker	Southern CA
Finny Aletter	Montgomery, Yvonne	'87 - 2	stockbroker turned carpenter	Denver, CO
Fizz & Tam Buchanan	Holms, Joyce	'96 - 3	older Scottish attorney & law student	Edinburgh, Scotland
Fran Kirk	Furie, Ruthe	'95 - 3	ex-battered wife turned fledgling P.I.	Buffalo, NY
Fran Varaday	Granger, Ann	'97 - 3	unlicensed young investigator	London, England
Francesca Vierling	Viets, Elaine	'97 - 4	6-ft. newspaper columnist	St. Louis, MO
Frank Shapiro, Cal Donovan & Liz Graham	Bannister, Jo	'93 - 6	police officers	Castlemere, England
Fred Vickery	Lewis, Sherry	'95 - 5	70-something retiree	Cutler, CO
Freddie O'Neal	Dain, Catherine	'92 - 7	plane-flying keno-playing P.I.	Reno, NV
Fremont Jones	Day, Dianne	'95 - 6	'00s typewriting-business owner	San Francisco, CA

G

Series Character	Author	1 - #	Occupation	Setting
Gail Connor	Parker, Barbara	'94 - 3	corporate attorney	Miami, FL
Gail McCarthy	Crum, Laura	'94 - 4	horse veterinarian	Santa Cruz, CA
Gale Grayson	Holbrook, Teri	'95 - 3	American expatriate historian	England
Gar	Dengler, Sandy	'98 - 2	Neanderthal shaman	Germany
Garner Quin	Waterhouse, Jane	'95 - 3	best-selling true crime writer	Spring Lake, NJ
Gemma James & D Kincaid	Crombie, Deborah	'93 - 5	Scotland Yard detective partners	London, England
Geoffrey de Mappestone	Beaufort, Simon	'98 - 2	brave knight of the Crusades	England
George Barnabas	Rayner, Claire	'93 - 5	hospital forensic pathologist	London, England
George & Molly Palmer-Jones	Cleeves, Ann	'86 - 8	ex-Home Office bird-watcher & wife	Surrey, England
George Thorne	Penn, John	'83 - 6	detective superintendent	Oxfordshire, England
Georgetown house	Michaels, Barbara	'68 - 3	historic home	Washington, DC
Georgia Lee Maxwell	Friedman, Mickey	'88 - 2	freelance writer	Paris, France
Georgina Powers	Danks, Denise	'89 - 4	British computer journalist	London, England
Gerald Witherspoon & H. Jeffries	Brightwell, Emily	'93 -13	Victorian inspector & his housekeeper	London, England
Geraldine Farrar & E. Caruso	Paul, Barbara	'84 - 3	Italian tenor & American soprano	New York, NY
Gerritt DeGraaf	D'Amato, Barbara	'80 - 2	forensic pathologist	Chicago, IL
Gerry Conte	Amato, Angela	'98 - 2	undercover cop turned defense atty.	New York, NY
Gianna Maglione & Mimi Patterson	Mickelbury, Penny	'94 - 2	lesbian police lieutenant & reporter	Washington, DC
Gil Mayo	Eccles, Marjorie	'88 -10	detective chief inspector	Midlands, England
Gilda Liberty	Borton, D.B.	'99 - 1	small-town movie theater proprietor	Eden, OH
Gillian Adams	Kelly, Nora	'84 - 4	college history department chair	Vancouver, BC, Canada
Ginevra Prettifield	Dawkins, Cecil	'93 - 2	art museum assistant director	Santa Fe, NM
Ginger Struve Barnes	Murray, Donna Huston	'95 - 5	headmaster's wife & suburban mother	Philadelphia, PA
Ginny Trask & Frank Carver	Wallingford, Lee	'91 - 2	U.S. Forest Service officers	Oregon
Glad Gold & Alden Chase	Wender, Theodora	'85 - 2	English professor & police chief	Wading River, MA
Gloria Damasco	Corpi, Lucha	'92 - 2	Chicana activist with ESP	Oakland, CA
Gloria Lamerino	Minichino, Camille	'97 - 3	50-something physicist	Revere Beach, MA
Glynis Tryon	Monfredo, Miriam G.	'92 - 6	1860s librarian suffragette	Seneca Falls, NY
Goldy Bear Schultz	Davidson, Diane Mott	'90 - 8	detecting caterer	Aspen Meadow, CO
Gordon Christy	Moore, Barbara	'83 - 2	veterinarian	New Mexico
Graham Sheldon & Lee Ofsted	Elkins, Charlotte & Aaron	'89 - 3	woman golf pro & homicide detective	Washington
Gregor Demarkian	Haddam, Jane	'90 -15	former FBI department head	Philadelphia, PA
Gregory Toye & Tom Pollard	Lemarchand, Elizabeth	'67 -17	Scotland Yard detectives	London, England
Guido Brunetti	Leon, Donna	'92 - 9	police commissario	Venice, Italy
Guinevere Jones	Castle, Jayne	'86 - 4	office-temps business owner	Seattle, WA
Gwenn Ramadge	O'Donnell, Lillian	'90 - 4	corporate investigator	New York, NY

Series Character	Author	1 - #	Occupation	Setting

Character's First Name

H...J

H.W. Ross	Grindle, Lucretia	'93 - 2	detective superintendent	England
Hagen	Hooper, Kay	'87 - 11	government agent	USA
Haley McAlister	Kiecolt-Glaser, Janice	'97 - 2	psychologist and professor	Houston, TX
Hamish Macbeth	Beaton, M.C.	'85 - 14	Scottish police constable	Lochdubh, Scotland
Hana Shaner	Greth, Roma	'88 - 2	40-something heiress	Conover, PA
Hannah Barlow	Lachnit, Carroll	'95 - 3	ex-cop turned lawyer	Orange County, CA
Hannah Land	Mackay, Amanda	'76 - 2	divorced New York PhD	Durham, NC
Hannah Malloy & K. Goldstein	Griffin, Annie	'98 - 2	unlikely pair of 60-something sisters	Marin County, CA
Hannah Trevor	Lawrence, Margaret	'96 - 3	18th century widwife	Rufford, ME
Hannah Wolfe	Dunant, Sarah	'92 - 3	contract private investigator	London, England
Harriet Hubbley	Manthorne, Jackie	'94 - 5	intrepid lesbian sleuth	Montreal, QB, Canada
Harriet Jeffries & J. Sanders	Sale, Medora	'86 - 6	police detective & photographer	Toronto, ON, Canada
Haskell Blevins	McCafferty, Taylor	'90 - 6	small-town private eye	Pigeon Fork, KY
Heaven Lee	Temple, Lou Jane	'96 - 4	trendy restaurant owner-chef	Kansas City, MO
Hedley Nicholson	Kelly, Mary	'61 - 2	private investigator	England
Helen Black	Welch, Pat	'90 - 6	ex-cop lesbian private eye	Berkeley, CA
Helen Bradley	Rushford, Patricia H.	'97 - 3	ex-cop travel-writer grandmother	Lincoln City, OR
Helen Bullock & Simon Bede	Byfield, Barbara Ninde	'75 - 4	Episcopal priest & phototographer	New York, NY
Helen Keremos	Zaremba, Eve	'78 - 6	40-something lesbian private eye	Toronto, ON, Canada
Helen Markham Johnson	Dewhurst, Eileen	'82 - 2	actress recruited by Secret Service	London, England
Helen M. Shandy & P. Shandy	MacLeod, Charlotte	'78 - 10	botany professor & librarian wife	Balaclava Co., MA
Helen Sorby & Milo Kachigan	Cercone, Karen Rose	'97 - 3	social worker & policeman in 1905	Pittsburgh, PA
Helen West	Fyfield, Frances	'88 - 6	London Crown prosecutor	London, England
Helma Zukas	Dereske, Jo	'94 - 6	public librarian	Bellehaven, WA
Henrietta O'Dwyer Collins	Hart, Carolyn G.	'93 - 4	70-something reporter	Oklahoma
Henry Bassett	Burden, Pat	'90 - 4	retired cop	Herefordshire, England
Henry & Emmy Tibbett	Moyes, Patricia	'59 - 19	Scotland Yard inspector & wife	London, England
Hepzibah Jeffries & G. Witherspoon	Brightwell, Emily	'93 - 13	Victorian inspector & his housekeeper	London, England
Hilary Lloyd & D. Quantrill	Radley, Sheila	'78 - 9	DCI & sergeant partner	Suffolk, England
Hilary Tamar	Caudwell, Sarah	'81 - 4	medieval law specialist	London, England
Hilda Johansson	Dams, Jeanne M.	'99 - 2	turn-of-the-century Swedish housemaid	South Bend, IN
Hollis Ball & Sam Wescott	Chappell, Helen	'96 - 3	reporter & her ex-husband's ghost	Santimoke County, MD
Hollis Carpenter	Powell, Deborah	'91 - 2	gay woman crime reporter	Houston, TX
Holly Winter	Conant, Susan	'89 - 11	dog trainer & magazine columnist	Cambridge, MA
Holly-Jean Ho	Lin-Chandler, Irene	'95 - 3	Anglo-Chinese bisexual investigator	London, England
Homer Kelly	Langton, Jane	'64 - 13	ex-cop turned Harvard professor	Cambridge, MA
Honey West	Fickling, G.G.	'57 - 11	sexiest P.I. ever to pull a trigger	Los Angeles, CA

I

Ian Roper	Bolitho, Janie	'93 - 8	detective chief inspector	Rickenham Green, Eng.
Ike Tygart & Abby Abagnarro	Whitney, Polly	'94 - 4	network producer & TV news director	New York, NY
Imogen Quy	Paton Walsh, Jill	'93 - 2	St. Agatha's College nurse	Cambridge, England
Ingrid Langley & P. Gillard	Duffy, Margaret	'87 - 6	novelist secret agent & army major	England
Insp. Supt. Cardiff	Gray, Dulcie	'60 - 2	inspector superintendent	England
Inspector Finch	Thomson, June	'71 - 18	police inspector	Essex, England
Irene Adler	Douglas, Carole N.	'90 - 4	19th century American diva	Paris, France
Irene Kelly	Burke, Jan	'93 - 6	newspaper reporter	Las Piernas, CA
Iris Cooper	Beck, K.K.	'84 - 3	1920s Stanford University co-ed	Palo Alto, CA
Iris Thorne	Pugh, Dianne G.	'93 - 4	investment counselor	Los Angeles, CA
Isaac & Bishop Berenguer	Roe, Caroline	'98 - 3	1350s blind physician & bishop	Girona, Spain

J

J.J. Jamison	Taylor, L.A.	'83 - 4	computer engineer	Minneapolis, MN
J.P. Beaumont	Jance, J.A.	'85 - 14	homicide detective	Seattle, WA
J.R. & Biggie Weatherford	Bell, Nancy	'96 - 3	grandmother & nephew sidekick	Job's Crossing, TX
Jack Caleb & John Thinnes	Dymmoch, Michael A.	'93 - 3	cop & gay psychiatrist	Chicago, IL
Jack Fleming	Elrod, P.N.	'90 - 7	'30s reporter turned vampire	Chicago, IL
Jack Prester	Dengler, Sandy	'93 - 4	U.S. park ranger	National Parks
Jack Stryker & Kate Trevorne	Gosling, Paula	'85 - 2	homicide cop & English professor	Michigan
Jackie Walsh & Jake	Cleary, Melissa	'92 - 10	film instructor & ex-police dog	Palmer, OH
Jackson, Rieders	MacDougal, Bonnie	'96 - 3	large law firm	Philadelphia, PA
Jacobia Triptree	Graves, Sarah	'98 - 3	ex-investment banker	Eastport, ME

Series Character	Author	1 - #	Occupation	Setting
Character's First Name				
J				
Jacqueline Kirby	Peters, Elizabeth	'72 - 4	librarian turned romance novelist	New York, NY
Jake & Jackie Walsh	Cleary, Melissa	'92 -10	film instructor & ex-police dog	Palmer, OH
Jake Hines	Gunn, Elizabeth	'97 - 2	small town police detective	Rutherford, MN
Jake Samson & Rosie Vicente	Singer, Shelley	'83 - 5	ex-cop & carpenter	Berkeley, CA
James Asher	Hambly, Barbara	'88 - 2	professor and part-time spy	London, England
James Carrick & J. MacKenzie	Duffy, Margaret	'94 - 4	ex-CID detective & Det. Chief Insp.	Bath, England
James Fleming	Fallon, Ann C.	'90 - 5	train-loving solicitor	Dublin, Ireland
James Milton & Robert Amiss	Edwards, Ruth Dudley	'81 - 8	police superintendent & ex-civil servant	London, England
James Owens Mega	McCrumb, Sharyn	'88 - 2	science fiction author professor	Tennessee
James Roland & P. Mansfield	Quinton, Ann	'89 - 6	det. inspector & det. sergeant	Suffolk, England
Jane Austen	Barron, Stephanie	'96 - 3	19th century British novelist	Bath, England
Jane da Silva	Beck, K.K.	'92 - 4	former lounge singer	Seattle, WA
Jane Day & Jerry Knight	Nessen, Ron	'95 - 3	right-wing radio host & liberal reporter	Washington, DC
Jane Jeffry	Churchill, Jill	'89 -11	suburban single mother	Chicago, IL
Jane Lawless	Hart, Ellen	'89 - 8	lesbian restaurateur	Minneapolis, MN
Jane Nichols	Tan, Maureen	'97 - 2	secret agent turned mystery writer	Savannah, Georgia
Jane Perry	Ferguson, Frances	'93 - 4	French-speaking detective sergeant	Kent, England
Janet & Madoc Rhys	Craig, Alisa	'80 - 5	RCMP inspector & wife	New Brunswick, Can.
Jane Tennison	La Plante, Lynda	'93 - 3	detective chief inspector	London, England
Jane Tregar	Godfrey, Ellen	'88 - 2	corporate headhunter	Toronto, ON, Canada
Jane Winfield	Peterson, Audrey	'88 - 6	British journalist and music writer	London, England
Janet Barkin	Godfrey, Ellen	'99 - 3	high school dropout	Evanston, IL
Janet Schilling	Youmans, Claire	'96 - 2	county chief deputy prosecutor	coastal, WA
Janice Cameron & Lily Wu	Sheridan, Juanita	'49 - 4	Asian sleuth & novelist roommate	Hawaii
Jason Lynx	Orde, A.J.	'89 - 6	antiques dealer and decorator	Denver, CO
Jasper Tully & Mrs. Norris	Davis, Dorothy S.	'57 - 3	DA's investigator & Scottish housekeeper	New York, NY
Jay Goldstein & Carlos Cruz	Wallace, Marilyn	'86 - 3	homicide detectives	Oakland, CA
Jazz Jasper	McQuillan, Karin	'90 - 3	American safari guide	Kenya
Jefferson Birch	Lee, Wendi	'89 - 6	P.I. in the Old West	Western
Jemima Shore	Fraser, Antonia	'77 - 8	British TV interviewer	London, England
Jennifer Marsh	Fitzwater, Judy	'98 - 2	aspiring mystery novelist	Atlanta, GA
Jenny Cain	Pickard, Nancy	'84 -10	New England foundation director	Port Frederick, MA
Jeremy Faro	Knight, Alanna	'88 -11	Victorian detective inspector	Edinburgh, Scotland
Jeri Howard	Dawson, Janet	'90 - 8	private eye	Oakland, CA
Jerry Knight & Jane Day	Nessen, Ron	'95 - 3	right-wing radio host & liberal reporter	Washington, DC
Jerry Zalman	Kraft, Gabrielle	'87 - 4	Beverly Hills deal maker	Los Angeles, CA
Jessica Fletcher	Fletcher, Jessica	'89 -11	60-something mystery writer	Cabot Cove, ME
Jessica James	O'Brien, Meg	'90 - 5	investigative reporter	Rochester, NY
Jessie Arnold & Alex Jensen	Henry, Sue	'91 - 5	sled dog racer & Alaska state trooper	Anchorage, AK
Jessie Drake	Krich, Rochelle Majer	'93 - 3	LAPD homicide detective	Los Angeles, CA
Jesus Creek TN	Adams, Deborah	'92 - 6	eccentric small town	Jesus Creek, TN
Jill Smith	Dunlap, Susan	'81 -10	homicide detective	Berkeley, CA
Jim Qwilleran, Koko & Yum Yum	Braun, Lilian Jackson	'66 -21	ex-police reporter & cats	Upper Peninsula, MI
Jim Rush	Grant-Adamson, Lesley	'92 - 2	American on the run from British police	England
Jo Beth Sidden	Lanier, Virginia	'95 - 4	search-and-rescue bloodhound trainer	Dunston County, GA
Jo Hughes	Mather, Linda	'94 - 2	astrologer-investigator	England
Joan, Sister	Black, Veronica	'90 -10	British investigative nun	Cornwall, England
Joan Spencer	Frommer, Sara H.	'86 - 3	symphony orchestra manager	Oliver, IN
Joanna Brady	Jance, J.A.	'93 - 7	single-mother sheriff	Cochise County, AZ
Joanna MacKenzie & James Carrick	Duffy, Margaret	'94 - 4	ex-CID detective & Det. Chief Insp.	Bath, England
Joanna Piercy	Masters, Priscilla	'95 - 5	detective inspector	Staffordshire, England
Joanna Stark	Muller, Marcia	'86 - 3	international art investigator	Napa Valley, CA
Joanne Kilbourn	Bowen, Gail	'90 - 6	political science professor	Regina, SK, Canada
Jocelyn O'Roarke	Dentinger, Jane	'83 - 6	Broadway actor and director	New York, NY
Joe Grey	Murphy, Shirley R	'96 - 4	talking-cat private eye	Molena Point, CA
Joe Rodriguez	Dengler, Sandy	'93 - 4	police sergeant	Phoenix, AZ
Joe Silva	Oleksiw, Susan	'93 - 3	small-town chief of police	Mellingham, MA
John Aloysius O'Malley	Coel, Margaret	'95 - 4	Jesuit missionary & Arapaho attorney	Wind River, WY
John Coffin	Butler, Gwendoline	'57 -26	Scotland Yard commander	London, England

Series Character	Author	1 - #	Occupation	Setting

Character's First Name

J...K

John Joseph Lintott	Stubbs, Jean	'73 - 3	retired Scotland Yard inspector	London, England
John Lloyd Branson & Lydia Fairchild	Meredith, D.R.	'88 - 5	defense attorney & legal assistant	Canadian, TX
John McLeish & F. Wilson	Neel, Janet	'88 - 6	DCI & businesswoman	London, England
John Morrissey	Mitchell, Kay	'90 - 5	chief inspector and family man	Malminster, England
John Putnam Thatcher	Lathen, Emma	'61 -24	Wall Street financial whiz	New York, NY
John Rawlings & the Blind Beak	Lake, Deryn	'94 - 4	18th century apothecary & blind magistrate	London, England
John Reynolds	Clayton, Mary	'95 - 5	ex-inspector turned crime writer	Cornwall, England
John Sanders & H. Jeffries	Sale, Medora	'86 - 6	police detective & photographer	Toronto, ON, Canada
John Thinnes & Jack Caleb	Dymmoch, Michael A.	'93 - 3	cop & gay psychiatrist	Chicago, IL
John Waltz	McCormick, Claire	'82 - 3	executive recruiter	Pennsylvania
Johnson Johnson	Dunnett, Dorothy	'68 - 7	British agent and yachtsman	International
Jolie Wyatt	Smith, Barbara Burnett	'94 - 4	aspiring novelist	Purple Sage, TX
Jordan Myles	Navratilova, Martina	'94 - 3	ex-tennis star physical therapist	Palm Springs, CA
Joseph Rafferty & D. Llewellyn	Evans, Geraldine	'93 - 3	D.I.& his Welsh sergeant	Yorkshire, England
Josephine Fuller	Murray, Lynne	'97 - 4	Queen-sized private investigator	Seattle, WA
Josie Pigeon	Wolzien, Valerie	'96 - 3	all-women construction firm owner	Northeast
Judd Springfield	Smith, Alison	'84 - 2	small town police chief	Coolridge Corners, VT
Judith Hayes	Porter, Anna	'85 - 3	freelance journalist	Toronto, ON, Canada
Judith McMonigle Flynn	Daheim, Mary	'91 -13	bed & breakfast owner	Seattle, WA
Judith Thornton	Benke, Patricia D.	'95 - 3	chief assistant district attorney	San Diego, CA
Judy & Lloyd Hill	McGown, Jill	'83 - 9	chief inspector & detective partner	East Anglia, England
Jules Clement	Harrison, Jamie	'95 - 3	30-something archaeologist turned sheriff	Blue Deer, MT
Julia & Nick Lambros	Iakovou, Takis & Judy	'96 - 2	college-town cafe owners	Delphi, GA
Julian Kestrel	Ross, Kate	'93 - 4	1820s dandy-about-town	London, England
Julie Hayes	Davis, Dorothy S.	'76 - 4	actress turned columnist & fortuneteller	New York, NY
Juliet Blake	Chapman, Sally	'91 - 4	computer fraud investigator	Silicon Valley, CA
Justin de Quincy	Penman, Sharon Kay	'96 - 2	Queen Mother's investigator	England

K

Kali O'Brien	Jacobs, Jonnie	'96 - 3	attorney	Gold Country, CA
Karen Hightower aka Bast	Edghill, Rosemary	'94 - 3	white witch graphic designer	New York, NY
Karen Pelletier	Dobson, Joanne	'97 - 3	single-mother English professor	Enfield, MA
Karen Perry-Mondori	Arnold, Catherine	'96 - 3	criminal defense attorney	Tampa, FL
Kat Colorado	Kijewski, Karen	'89 - 9	bar-tending private investigator	Sacramento, CA
Kate Austen	Jacobs, Jonnie	'94 - 3	suburban single mother	Walnut Hills, CA
Kate Baeier	Slovo, Gillian	'84 - 5	journalist turned P.I.	London, England
Kate Banning	Tishy, Cecelia	'97 - 2	music company staff writer	Nashville, TN
Kate Brannigan	McDermid, Val	'92 - 6	5' 3" redheaded private eye	Manchester, England
Kate Cavanaugh	John, Cathie	'97 - 4	gourmet caterer	Cincinnati, OH
Kate Delafield	Forrest, Katherine V.	'84 - 6	LAPD lesbian homicide detective	Los Angeles, CA
Kate Fansler	Cross, Amanda	'64 -12	feminist English professor	New York, NY
Kate Harrod	Coburn, Laura	'95 - 4	single-mother police detective	San Madera, CA
Kate Henry	Gordon, Alison	'89 - 6	baseball newswriter	Toronto, ON, Canada
Kate Ivory	Stallwood, Veronica	'93 - 6	historical romance novelist	Oxford, England
Kate Jasper	Girdner, Jaqueline	'91 - 11	gag gift wholesaler	Marin County, CA
Kate Kincaid Mulcay	Sibley, Celestine	'57 - 6	veteran newspaperwoman	Atlanta, GA
Kate Kinsella	Green, Christine	'91 - 4	nurse and medical investigator	Longborough, England
Kate MacLean	Gilpatrick, Noreen	'93 - 2	police detective	Seattle, WA
Kate Maddox	Quest, Erica	'88 - 3	first woman DCI	Cotswolds, England
Kate Martinelli & A. Hawkin	King, Laurie R.	'93 - 3	SFPD homicide detectives	San Francisco, CA
Kate Murray	Tyre, Peg	'94 - 2	novice crime reporter	Brooklyn, NY
Kate Shugak	Stabenow, Dana	'92 -10	Alaskan ex-D.A. investigator	Alaska
Kate Teague & Roger Tejeda	Hornsby, Wendy	'87 - 2	college professor & homicide detective	Los Angeles, CA
Kate Trevorne & Jack Stryker	Gosling, Paula	'85 - 2	homicide cop & English professor	Michigan
Kate Wilkinson	Howell, Lis	'95 - 3	television producer	London, England
Katharine Craig & Kevin Bryce	Valentine, Deborah	'89 - 3	sculptor & ex-sheriff's detective	Lake Tahoe, CA
Katherine Prescott Milholland	Hartzmark, Gini	'92 - 5	blueblood corporate attorney	Chicago, IL
Kathleen Mallory	O'Connell, Carol	'94 - 4	lone-wolf police sergeant	New York, NY
Kathleen O'Shaughnessy	Moen, Ruth Raby	'93 - 3	newspaper reporter	Seattle, WA

Series Character	Author	1 - #	Occupation	Setting
Character's First Name				

K...L

Kathryn Ardleigh & Charles Sheridan	Paige, Robin	'94 - 5	American author & British scientist	Dedham, England
Kathryn Bogert	Petit, Diane	'97 - 3	owner of an estate sale business	Chicago, IL
Kathryn Mackay	McGuire, Christine	'93 - 4	senior prosecuting attorney	Northern CA
Kay Barth	Schier, Norma	'78 - 4	district attorney	Aspen, CO
Kay Engles	Stein, Triss	'93 - 2	nationally-known reporter	Brooklyn, NY
Kay Scarpetta	Cornwell, Patricia	'90 - 9	chief medical examiner	Richmond, VA
Kellie Montgomery	Wilcox, Valerie	'98 - 3	widowed sailing instructor	Seattle, WA
Kelsey, Inspector	Page, Emma	'80 - 9	police inspector	England
Kevin Blake	Douglas, Carole N.	'85 - 2	psychiatrist	Minnesota
Kevin Bradley	Bacon-Smith, Camille	'96 - 2	daemon art recovery specialist	Philadelphia, PA
Kevin Bryce & K. Craig	Valentine, Deborah	'89 - 3	sculptor & ex-sheriff's detective	Lake Tahoe, CA
Kiernan O'Shaughnessy	Dunlap, Susan	'89 - 4	medical examiner turned P.I.	La Jolla, CA
Kiki Goldstein & H. Malloy	Griffin, Annie	'98 - 2	unlikely pair of 60-something sisters	Marin County, CA
Kimmey Kruse	Cooper, Susan Rogers	'93 - 2	stand-up comic	Austin, TX
Kinsey Millhone	Grafton, Sue	'82 -14	blue-collar ex-cop P.I.	Santa Teresa, CA
Kit Powell	Robitaille, Julie	'92 - 2	TV sports reporter	San Diego, CA
Knute Severson	Wells, Tobias	'66 -16	police officer	Boston, MA
Koko, Yum Yum & J. Qwilleran	Braun, Lilian Jackson	'66 -21	ex-police reporter & cats	Upper Peninsula, MI
Kristin Ashe	Jordan, Jennifer	'92 - 2	amateur sleuth	Denver, CO
Kyra Keaton	Tone, Teona	'83 - 2	turn-of-the-century P.I.	Washington, DC

L

Lady Aoi	Woodward, Ann	'96 - 2	11th century Japanese healer	Kyoto, Japan
Lane Montana & Trey Fortier	Hooper, Kay	'91 - 2	finder of lost things & homicide detective	Atlanta, GA
Laney Samms	Schmidt, Carol	'93 - 3	lesbian bar owner	Los Angeles, CA
Lara McClintock	Hamilton, Lyn	'97 - 4	antiquities dealer and shop owner	Toronto, ON, Canada
Lark Dailey Dodge	Simonson, Sheila	'90 - 5	6-ft. bookstore owner	Shoalwater, WA
Laura Ackroyd & M. Thackeray	Hall, Patricia	'93 - 5	investigative reporter & police inspector	Yorkshire, England
Laura Di Palma	Matera, Lia	'88 - 5	high-profile attorney	San Francisco, CA
Laura Fleming	Kelner, Toni L.P.	'93 - 6	small-town Southern sleuth	Byerly, NC
Laura Ireland	Mariz, Linda French	'92 - 2	grad student volleyball player	Seattle, WA
Laura Owen	Dixon, Louisa	'98 - 3	state public safety commissioner	Jackson, MS
Laura Principal	Spring, Michelle	'94 - 4	British academic turned P.I.	Cambridge, England
Lauren Laurano	Scoppettone, Sandra	'91 - 5	lesbian private investigator	New York, NY
Lauren Maxwell	Quinn, Elizabeth	'93 - 4	wildlife investigator PhD	Anchorage, AK
Lavinia Grey	Gallison, Kate	'95 - 5	Episcopal vicar	Fishersville, NJ
Leah Hunter	Lacey, Sarah	'92 - 4	20-something tax inspector	Yorkshire, England
Lee Ofsted & Graham Sheldon	Elkins, Charlotte & Aaron	'89 - 3	woman golf pro & homicide detective	Washington
Lee Squires	Andreae, Christine	'92 - 3	camp cook & poet	Montana
Leigh Koslow	Claire, Edie	'99 - 3	advertising copywriter	Pittsburgh, PA
Lena Padget	Hightower, Lynn S.	'93 - 1	private investigator	Lexington, KY
Lennox Kemp	Meek, M.R.D.	'82 -11	solicitor detective	England
Leslie Frost	Weber, Janice	'92 - 2	secret agent and concert violinist	Washington, DC
Leslie Wetzon & Xenia Smith	Meyers, Annette	'89 - 7	Wall Street headhunters	New York, NY
Letty Campbell	Fritchley, Alma	'97 - 3	lesbian chicken farmer	Manchester, England
Liam Campbell & W. Chouinard	Stabenow, Dana	'98 - 3	state trooper & bush pilot	Alaska
Libby Kincaid	Tucker, Kerry	'91 - 4	magazine photographer	New York, NY
Lydia Fairchild & J. L. Branson	Meredith, D.R.	'88 - 5	defense attorney & legal assistant	Canadian, TX
Lil Ritchie	Knight, Phyllis	'92 - 2	ex-rocker and gay woman P.I.	Charlottesville, VA
Lilly Bennett	Kellogg, Marne Davis	'95 - 5	US marshal and security firm owner	Roundup, WY
Lily Bard	Harris, Charlaine	'96 - 3	30-something cleaning woman	Shakespeare, Arkansas
Lily & Robert Brewster	Churchill, Jill	'99 - 1	sister & brother inn owners in 1930	Voorburg-on-Hudson, New York
Lily Wu & Janice Cameron	Sheridan, Juanita	'49 - 4	Asian sleuth & novelist roommate	Hawaii
Linda Bluenight	Cramer, Rebecca	'98 - 2	anthropologist turned teacher	Tucson, AZ
Lindsay Chamberlain	Connor, Beverly	'96 - 3	forensic archaeologist	Athens, GA
Lindsay Gordon	McDermid, Val	'87 - 5	lesbian socialist journalist	Glasgow, Scotland
Lisa Davis	Waltch, Lilla M.	'87 - 2	newspaper reporter	Braeton, MA

Series Character	Author	1 - #	Occupation	Setting

Character's First Name

L...M

Series Character	Author	1 - #	Occupation	Setting
Lisa King	Farrelly, Gail E.	'95 - 2	finance professor and CPA	Boston, MA
Liz Broward & Zack James	Zachary, Fay	'94 - 2	family physician & computer artist	Phoenix, AZ
Liz Connors	Kelly, Susan	'85 - 6	freelance crime writer	Cambridge, MA
Liz Graham, Frank Shapiro, & Cal Donovan	Bannister, Jo	'93 - 6	police officers	Castlemere, England
Liz James	Stuyck, Karen Hanson	'95 - 3	journalist turned PR rep	Houston, TX
Liz Sansborough & S. Walker	Lynds, Gayle	'96 - 2	CIA agents	International
Liz Sullivan	Roberts, Lora	'94 - 6	freelance writer and organic gardener	Palo Alto, CA
Liz Wareham	Brennan, Carol	'91 - 2	40-ish public relations consultant	New York, NY
Liza & Dutch Randolph	Van Hook, Beverly	'95 - 2	married amateur sleuths	West Virginia
Lizbet Lange	Thrasher, L.L.	'98 - 1	millionaire ex-waitress	Oak Valley, CA
Lloyd & Judy Hill	McGown, Jill	'83 - 9	chief inspector & detective partner	East Anglia, England
Lonia Guiu	Oliver, Maria-Antonia	'87 - 2	Catalan investigator	Barcelona, Spain
Lord Meren	Robinson, Lynda S.	'94 - 5	Tutankhamen's chief investigator	Egypt
Lorelei Muldoon	Morrone, Wenda W.	'97 - 2	high-profile numbers analyst	New York, NY
Loretta Lawson	Smith, Joan	'87 - 5	British feminist professor	London, England
Lorraine Page	La Plante, Lynda	'94 - 3	sober ex-cop turned private eye	Los Angeles, CA
Louise Eldridge	Ripley, Ann	'94 - 3	organic gardener TV host	Northern VA
Lt. Bak	Haney, Lauren	'97 - 2	ex-charioteer turned Medjay police head	Buhen, Egypt
Lucia Ramos	Morell, Mary	'91 - 2	Chicana lesbian police detective	San Antonio, TX
Lucy Freers	Maracotta, Lindsay	'96 - 2	children's film animator	Los Angeles, CA
Lucy Kingsley & D. Middleton-Brown	Charles, Kate	'91 - 5	artist & solicitor	London, England
Lucy Stone	Meier, Leslie	'93 - 4	sleuthing mother of four	Tinker's Cove, ME
Luke Abbott	Gosling, Paula	'86 - 2	English cop	England
Luke Thanet	Simpson, Dorothy	'81 -14	family-man police inspector	Kent, England
Lupe Ramos & Whitney Logan	Lambert, Mercedes	'91 - 2	20-something attorney & Chicana partner	Los Angeles, CA
Lupe Solano	Garcia-Aguilera, Carolina	'96 - 3	Cuban-American princess P.I.	Miami, FL
Lydia Chin & Bill Smith	Rozan, S.J.	'94 - 6	Chinese-American & Army-brat P.I. duo	New York, NY
Lydia Fairchild & J. L. Branson	Meredith, D.R.	'88 - 5	defense attorney & legal assistant	Canadian, TX
Lydia Miller	Hyde, Eleanor	'95 - 2	30-something fashion editor	New York, NY

M

Series Character	Author	1 - #	Occupation	Setting
Mackenzie Griffin	McCafferty, Jeanne	'94 - 3	consulting criminal psychologist	New York, NY
Mackenzie Smith & A. Reed	Truman, Margaret	'89 - 7	law professor & gallery owner	Washington, DC
MacLaren Yarbrough	Sprinkle, Patricia H.	'97 - 2	business-owner turned magistrate	Hopemore, GA
Madeline Bean	Farmer, Jerrilyn	'98 - 2	Hollywood party planner	Los Angeles, CA
Madison McGuire	Williams, Amanda Kyle	'90 - 4	deep cover intelligence agent	International
Madoc & Janet Rhys	Craig, Alisa	'80 - 5	RCMP inspector & wife	New Brunswick, Can.
Magdalena Yoder	Myers, Tamar	'94 - 8	Mennonite inn owner-operator	Hernia, PA
Maggie Dillitz	Sleem, Patty	'97 - 2	Methodist woman clergy	Greenfield, NC
Maggie Elliott	Taylor, Elizabeth Atwood	'81 - 3	ex-film maker turned P.I.	San Francisco, CA
Maggie Garrett	Taylor, Jean	'95 - 2	young lesbian P.I.	San Francisco, CA
Maggie MacGowen	Hornsby, Wendy	'92 - 5	documentary filmmaker	Los Angeles, CA
Maggie Maguire	Bryan, Kate	'98 - 2	ex-Pinkerton agent	San Francisco, CA
Maggie Rome & C.B. Greenfield	Kallen, Lucille	'79 - 5	reporter & editor-publisher	Connecticut
Maggie Ryan	Carlson, P.M.	'85 - 8	coed turned statistician mom	New York, NY
Mali Anderson	Edwards, Grace F.	'97 - 2	black ex-cop in Harlem	New York, NY
Mandy Dyer	Johnson, Dolores	'97 - 3	owner of Dyer's Cleaners	Denver, CO
Marcus Didius Falco	Davis, Lindsey	'89 - 11	1st century Roman private eye	Rome, Italy
Marcus MacLurg	Petrie, Rhona	'63 - 5	police inspector	England
Margaret Priam	Christmas, Joyce	'88 - 9	English noblewoman	New York, NY
Margit Andersson	Nunnally, Tiina	'96 - 2	freelance Danish translator	Seattle, WA
Margo Fortier	Fennelly, Tony	'94 - 2	ex-stripper turned columnist	New Orleans, LA
Margo Simon	Steinberg, Janice	'95 - 5	Public Radio reporter	San Diego, CA
Marguerite Smith	Lee, Marie	'95 - 3	retired science teacher	Cape Cod, MA
Marian Larch	Paul, Barbara	'84 - 7	no-nonsense NYPD officer	New York, NY
Marian Winchester	Romberg, Nina	'89 - 2	Caddo-Comanche medicine woman	Texas

Series Character	Author	1 - #	Occupation	Setting

Character's First Name

M

Series Character	Author	1 - #	Occupation	Setting
Maris Middleton	Davis, Kaye	'97 - 3	lesbian forensic chemist	Texas
Mark East, B. Petty & B. Pond	Lawrence, Hilda	'44 - 3	Manhattan P.I. & little old ladies	New York, New York
Mark Shigata	Wingate, Anne	'88 - 5	ex-FBI agent turned sheriff	Bayport, TX
Martha Brant	Femling, Jean	'89 - 2	insurance claims investigator	Orange County, CA
Martha Patterson	Sprague, Gretchen	'97 - 4	retired attorney turned pro bono	Brooklyn, NY
Marti Hirsch	Moore, Miriam Ann	'97 - 2	would-be writer and disco lover	New York, NY
Marti MacAlister	Bland, Eleanor Taylor	'92 - 7	widowed black police detective	Lincoln Prairie, IL
Martin Beck	Sjöwall, Maj & Per Wahlöö	'67 -10	Swedish police officer	Stockholm, Sweden
Martin Karl Alberg	Wright, L.R.	'85 - 9	RCMP staff sergeant	Sechelt, BC, Canada
Marty LaForte Hopkins	Carlson, P.M.	'92 - 2	deputy sheriff mom	Southern IN
Mary A. Crane & Patricia A. Hollowell	George, Anne	'96 - 5	60-something sister sleuths	Birmingham, AL
Mary Helen, Sister	O'Marie, Carol A., Sr.	'84 - 8	70-something nun	San Francisco, CA
Mary Minor Haristeen	Brown, Rita Mae	'90 - 6	small-town postmistress	Crozet, VA
Mary Russell	King, Laurie R.	'94 - 4	Sherlock Holmes' detecting partner	London, England
Matilda Haycastle	Bailey, Michele	'94 - 3	30-something office temp	Brussels, Belgium
Matt Devlin & Brooke Cassidy	Kruger, Mary	'94 - 3	1890s debutante & detective husband	Newport, RI
Matt Gabriel	Gosling, Paula	'92 - 4	sheriff	Blackwater Bay, MI
Matthew Arthur Sinclair	Fennelly, Tony	'85 - 3	gay epileptic D.A. turned store owner	New Orleans, LA
Matthew Bartholomew	Gregory, Susanna	'96 - 4	14th century physician and teacher	Cambridge, England
Maurice Ygrec	Rippon, Marion	'69 - 4	retired French police inspector	Moselle, France
Max Bittersohn & S. Kelling	MacLeod, Charlotte	'79 -12	investigative couple	Boston, MA
Max Bramble & Wylie Nolan	Reuben, Shelly	'94 - 2	arson investigator & attorney	New York, NY
Max Darling & A. Laurance	Hart, Carolyn G.	'87 -10	bookstore owner & investigator	Broward's Rock, SC
Maxene St. Clair	McGiffin, Janet	'92 - 3	emergency room physician	Milwaukee, WI
Maxey Burnell	Cail, Carol	'93 - 3	investigative reporter	Boulder, CO
May Morrison	Star, Nancy	'98 - 2	TV talk show producer	New York, NY
Meg Darcy	Marcy, Jean	'97 - 2	blue-collar lesbian private eye	St. Louis, MO
Meg Gillis	Songer, C.J.	'98 - 2	ex-cop turned security consultant	Beverly Hills, CA
Meg Halloran & V. Gutierrez	LaPierre, Janet	'87 - 5	single-mother school teacher & police chief	Port Silva, CA
Meg Lacey	Bowers, Elisabeth	'88 - 2	single-mother private eye	Vancouver, BC, Canada
Meg & Sarah Quilliam	Bishop, Claudia	'94 - 6	inn owner & chef sisters	Hemlock Falls, NY
Meggie O'Connor	Cogan, Priscilla	'97 - 2	practicing psychologist	Leelanau Peninsula, MI
Melanie Travis	Berenson, Laurien	'95 - 6	special ed teacher and dog lover	Connecticut
Melinda Pink	Moffat, Gwen	'73 -14	mountain climbing novelist	Utah
Melissa Craig	Rowlands, Betty	'90 - 8	British crime novelist	Cotswolds, England
Meredith Folger	Mathews, Francine	'94 - 4	police detective	Nantucket, MA
Meredith Mitchell & A. Markby	Granger, Ann	'91 -11	D.I. & Foreign Service officer	Cotswolds, England
Merle Capricorn	Winslow, Pauline Glen	'75 - 6	magician turned police superintendent	England
Mimi Patterson & G. Maglione	Mickelbury, Penny	'94 - 2	lesbian police lieutenant & reporter	Washington, DC
Michael McKenna	Taylor, Alison G.	'95 - 3	detective chief inspector	Wales
Michael Ohayon	Gur, Batya	'92 - 4	Moroccan-born chief inspector	Jerusalem, Israel
Michael Spraggue	Barnes, Linda	'82 - 4	wealthy actor ex-private eye	Boston, MA
Michael Stone	Salter, Anna	'97 - 2	female forensic psychologist	Vermont
Michael Thackeray & Laura Ackroyd	Hall, Patricia	'93 - 5	investigative reporter & police inspector	Yorkshire, England
Michelle 'Micky' Knight	Redmann, J.M.	'90 - 3	gay woman private eye	New Orleans, LA
Mici Anhalt	O'Donnell, Lillian	'77 - 3	criminal justice investigator	New York, NY
Mickey Flynn	Bannister, Jo	'90 - 2	American photojournalist	London, England
Midge Cohen	Brill, Toni	'91 - 2	children's author fluent in Russian	Brooklyn, NY
Midnight Louie & Temple Barr	Douglas, Carole Nelson	'92 - 9	PR freelancer & tomcat sleuth	Las Vegas, NV
Miguel Menendez	Blanc, Suzanne	'61 - 3	Aztec police inspector	San Luis Potosi, Mexico
Mike Croft	Adams, Jane	'95 - 3	detective inspector	Norwich, England
Mike McCleary & Quin St. James	MacGregor, T.J.	'86 -10	wife & husband P.I. team	Florida
Mike Svenson & N. Matthews	Sandstrom, Eve K.	'97 - 2	reporter & homicide detective	Southwest
Mike Yeadings	Curzon, Clare	'83 -13	Serious Crime Squad superintendent	Thames Valley, Eng.
Mildred Bennett & friends	McShea, Susanna H.	'90 - 3	quartet of senior sleuths	Raven's Wing, CT

Series Character	Author	1 - #	Occupation	Setting

Character's First Name

M...P

Millie Ogden & N. O'Brien	Lyons, Nan & Ivan	'76 - 2	pair of culinary artists	New York, NY
Milo Kachigan & Helen Sorby	Cercone, Karen Rose	'97 - 3	social worker & policeman in 1905	Pittsburgh, PA
Milton Kovak	Cooper, Susan Rogers	'88 - 6	chief deputy	Prophesy County, OK
Mirinda & Clare Clively	Crowleigh, Ann	'93 - 2	Victorian twin sisters	London, England
Mitch Bushyhead	Hager, Jean	'89 - 5	police chief of Cherokee descent	Buckskin, OK
Mitch Mitchell & Tommy Hung	Kershaw, Valerie	'93 - 4	radio journalist P.I. & Chinese partner	Birmingham, England
Molly Bearpaw	Hager, Jean	'92 - 4	Cherokee civil rights investigator	Tahlequah, OK
Molly Burke	Dreyer, Eileen	'95 - 2	death investigator	St. Louis, MO
Molly Cates	Walker, Mary Willis	'94 - 3	true crime writer-reporter	Austin, TX
Molly DeWitt	Woods, Sherryl	'91 - 4	film promoter and single mother	Miami, FL
Molly Masters	O'Kane, Leslie	'96 - 3	greeting card entrepreneur	Albany, NY
Molly & George Palmer-Jones	Cleeves, Ann	'86 - 8	ex-Home Office bird-watcher & wife	Surrey, England
Molly Rafferty	Belfort, Sophie	'86 - 3	college history professor	Boston, MA
Molly West	Westfall, Patricia T.	'96 - 2	50-something rural activist	Southern OH
Mrs. Norris & Jasper Tully	Davis, Dorothy Salisbury	'57 - 3	DA's investigator & Scottish housekeeper	New York, NY
Mycroft Holmes	Fawcett, Quinn	'94 - 3	Sherlock Holmes' older brother	London, England

N

Nan Robinson	Cannon, Taffy	'93 - 3	state bar investigator	Los Angeles, CA
Nan & Bert Tatum	McCafferty, Barbara T.	'96 - 3	identical twin sisters	Louisville, KY
Nancy Clue	Maney, Mabel	'93 - 3	gay-lesbian Nancy Drew parody	River Depths, IL
Nancy Cook	Jones, D.J.H.	'93 - 2	Chaucer scholar and professor	Chicago, IL
Nanette Hayes	Carter, Charlotte	'97 - 2	young black tenor sax player	New York, NY
Nassim Pride	Petrie, Rhona	'67 - 2	Anglo-Sudanese forensic scientist	England
Natalie Gold	Jaffe, Jody	'95 - 3	reporter on horse show circuit	Charlotte, NC
Natasha O'Brien & M. Ogden	Lyons, Nan & Ivan	'76 - 2	pair of culinary artists	New York, NY
Neal Rafferty	Wiltz, Chris	'81 - 3	3rd-generation cop turned P.I.	New Orleans, LA
Neely Jones	Wren, M.K.	'99 - 1	black woman sheriff-elect	Taft County, OR
Neil Carter	Dewhurst, Eileen	'77 - 5	Scotland Yard detective	London, England
Neil Hamel	Van Gieson, Judith	'88 - 8	attorney & investigator	Albuquerque, NM
Nell Bray	Linscott, Gillian	'91 - 7	British suffragette	London, England
Nell Fury	Pincus, Elizabeth	'92 - 3	lesbian P.I.	San Francisco, CA
Nell Matthews & M. Svenson	Sandstrom, Eve K.	'97 - 2	reporter & homicide detective	Southwest
Nick & Julia Lambros	Iakovou, Takis and Judy	'96 - 2	college-town cafe owners	Delphi, GA
Nick Magaracz	Gallison, Kate	'86 - 3	private investigator	Trenton, NJ
Nick Trevellyan & Alison Hope	Kelly, Susan B.	'90 - 5	software designer & detective inspector	Hop Valley, England
Nicolette Scott	Davis, Val	'96 - 3	UC-Berkeley archaeologist	New Mexico
Nikki Chase	Thomas-Graham, P.	'98 - 2	black economics professor	Cambridge, MA
Nikki Holden & R. Cantrell	Chase, Elaine Raco	'87 - 2	investigative reporter & private eye	Miami, FL
Nikki Trakos	Horansky, Ruby	'90 - 2	6-ft. NYPD homicide detective	Brooklyn, NY
Nina Fischman	Piesman, Marissa	'89 - 6	legal services attorney	New York, NY
Nina McFall & Dino Rossi	Fulton, Eileen	'88 - 6	TV soap star & NYPD lieutenant	New York, NY
Nina Reilly	O'Shaughnessy, Perri	'95 - 4	single-mother attorney	Lake Tahoe, NV
Norah Mulcahaney	O'Donnell, Lillian	'72 -16	police detective	New York, NY
Norie Gorzack	Mikulski, Barbara	'96 - 2	Polish-American U.S. senator	Washington, DC
Norm Bennis & Suze Figueroa	D'Amato, Barbara	'96 - 2	pair of cops	Chicago, IL
Nyla Wade	McConnell, Vicki P.	'82 - 3	lesbian journalist	Denver, CO

O

Oliver Jardine & T. Fortunato	Green, Kate	'86 - 3	professional psychic & LAPD detective	Los Angeles, CA
Olivia Brown	Meyers, Annette	'99 - 1	'20s Greenwich Village poet P.I.	New York, NY
Olivia Chapman	Logan, Margaret	'94 - 2	interior decorator	Boston, MA
Osbert Monk & Dittany Henbit Monk	Craig, Alisa	'81 - 5	garden club member & author of westerns	Lobelia Falls, ON, Canada
Owen Archer	Robb, Candace M.	'93 - 6	one-eyed medieval Welsh spy	York, England

P

P.J. Gray	Kennett, Shirley	'96 - 4	police dept. virtual reality expert	St. Louis, MO
Pam Nilsen	Wilson, Barbara	'84 - 3	lesbian printing company owner	Seattle, WA
Paris Chandler	Shah, Diane K.	'90 - 2	'40s private eye	Hollywood, CA
Pat Conley	Coleman, Evelyn	'98 - 2	black woman journalist	Atlanta, GA
Patience Campbell McKenna	Papazoglou, Orania	'84 - 5	6-ft. romance novelist turned crime writer	New York, NY

Series Character	Author	1 - #	Occupation	Setting

Character's First Name

P...R

Series Character	Author	1 - #	Occupation	Setting
Patricia Delaney	Short, Sharon Gwyn	'94 - 3	computer-whiz investigator	Cincinnati, OH
Patrick Gillard & Ingrid Langley	Duffy, Margaret	'87 - 6	novelist secret agent & army major	England
Patricia A. Hollowell & Mary A. Crane	George, Anne	'96 - 5	60-something sister sleuths	Birmingham, AL
Patrick Grant	Yorke, Margaret	'70 - 5	Oxford don	Oxford, England
Paul MacDonald	Smith, Julie	'85 - 2	ex-reporter mystery writer	San Francisco, CA
Patrick Mansfield & J. Roland	Quinton, Ann	'89 - 6	det. inspector & det. sergeant	Suffolk, England
Paula Glenning	Clarke, Anna	'85 - 9	British professor & writer	London, England
Peaches Dann	Squire, Elizabeth Daniels	'94 - 6	absent-minded widow	North Carolina
Peg Goodenough	Bennett, Liza	'89 - 2	ad agency creative director	New York, NY
Penny Spring & T. Glendower	Arnold, Margot	'79 -12	anthropologist & archaeologist	World Travelers
Penny Wanawake	Moody, Susan	'84 - 7	photographer daughter of black diplomat	England
Perdita Halley & A. von Reisden	Smith, Sarah	'92 - 2	biochemist & concert pianist	Paris, France
Persis Willum	Watson, Clarissa	'77 - 5	artist and gallery assistant	Long Island, NY
Peter Bartholomew	Gunning, Sally	'90 -10	odd-jobs company owner	Cape Cod, MA
Peter Brichter & Kori Price	Pulver, Mary Monica	'87 - 5	police detective & horse breeder	Illinois
Peter Decker & Rina Lazarus	Kellerman, Faye	'86 -10	LAPD detective & Orthodox Jewish wife	Los Angeles, CA
Peter & Kori Price Brichter	Pulver, Mary Monica	'87 - 5	police detective & horse breeder	Illinois
Peter Shandy & Helen Marsh Shandy	MacLeod, Charlotte	'78 -10	botany professor & librarian wife	Balaclava Co., MA
Phoebe Fairfax	North, Suzanne	'94 - 3	TV video photographer	Alberta, Canada
Phoebe Siegel	Prowell, Sandra West	'93 - 3	ex-cop P.I.	Billings, MT
Phryne Fisher	Greenwood, Kerry	'89 - 9	'20s Londoner Melbourne, Australia	
Phyllida Moon	Dewhurst, Eileen	'95 - 3	television private eye	London, England
Poppy Dillworth	Tell, Dorothy	'90 - 2	60-something lesbian sleuth	Texas
Primrose Holland	Bannister, Jo	'98 - 1	newspaper advice columnist	Skipley, England
Queenie Davilov	Osborne, Denise	'94 - 2	screenwriter-investigator	Hollywood, CA
Quentin Jacoby	Smith, J.C.S.	'80 - 2	retired transit cop	New York, NY
Quin St. James & M. McCleary	MacGregor, T.J.	'86 -10	wife & husband P.I. team	Florida
Quint McCauley	Brod, D.C.	'89 - 4	ex-cop turned private eye	Chicago suburb, IL

R

Series Character	Author	1 - #	Occupation	Setting
Rachel Alexander & Dash	Benjamin, Carole Lea	'96 - 3	dog trainer turned P.I. & pitbull sidekick	New York, NY
Rachel Crowne	Rawlings, Ellen	'97 - 2	Jewish investigative reporter	Washington, DC
Rachel Porter	Speart, Jessica	'97 - 3	Fish & Wildlife agent	USA
Rain Morgan	Grant-Adamson, Lesley	'85 - 5	Fleet Street gossip columnist	London, England
Rebecca Rosenthal	Godfrey, Ellen	'76 - 2	80-year-old Polish-born anthropologist	Toronto, ON, Canada
Rebecca Schwartz	Smith, Julie	'82 - 5	defense attorney	San Francisco, CA
Regan Reilly	Clark, Carol Higgins	'92 - 4	P.I. and novelist's daughter	Los Angeles, CA
Reginald Wexford	Rendell, Ruth	'64 -17	chief inspector	Sussex, England
Rei Shimura	Massey, Sujata	'97 - 3	Japanese-American antiques dealer	Tokyo, Japan
Richard Baxter	Moore, Margaret	'87 - 3	police inspector	England
Richard Jury	Grimes, Martha	'81 -15	Scotland Yard inspector	London, England
Richard Longfellow & C. Willett	Miles, Margaret	'98 - 2	Colonial farm woman & scientist-farmer	Bracebridge, MA,
Richard Montgomery	Shepherd, Stella	'89 - 7	CID Inspector	Nottingham, England
Richard Tansey	Penn, John	'88 -12	chief inspector	Oxfordshire, England
Rick & Rosie Caesare Ramsey	Santini, Rosemarie	'86 - 2	husband & wife sleuths	New York, NY
Rina Lazarus & Peter Decker	Kellerman, Faye	'86 -10	LAPD detective & Orthodox Jewish wife	Los Angeles, CA
Robert Amiss & James Milton	Edwards, Ruth Dudley	'81 - 8	police superintendent & ex-civil servant	London, England
Robert Bone	Stacey, Susannah	'87 - 8	widowed British police inspector	England
Robert & Lily Brewster	Churchill, Jill	'99 - 1	sister & brother inn owners in 1930	Voorburg-on-Hudson, New York
Robert Carey	Chisholm, P.F.	'94 - 4	Elizabethan nobleman	England
Robert Forsythe & Abigail Sanderson	Giroux, E.X.	'84 -10	barrister & his secretary	London, England
Robert Southwell	Whitehead, Barbara	'88 - 8	detective chief inspector	York, England
Robin Hudson	Hayter, Sparkle	'94 - 4	cable news reporter	New York, NY
Robin Light	Block, Barbara	'94 - 5	pet store owner	Syracuse, NY
Robin Miller	Maiman, Jaye	'91 - 6	lesbian travel & romance writer turned P.I.	New York, NY

Series Character	Author	1 - #	Occupation	Setting

Character's First Name

R...S

Robin Vaughan	Banks, Carolyn	'93 - 5	equestrienne sleuth	Texas
Roger Sheppard	Hall, Linda	'95 - 3	RCMP officer and family man	Alberta, Canada
Roger Tejeda & Kate Teague	Hornsby, Wendy	'87 - 2	college professor & homicide detective	Los Angeles, CA
Roger the Chapman	Sedley, Kate	'91 - 8	medieval peddler	England
Roman Cantrell & N. Holden	Chase, Elaine Raco	'87 - 2	investigative reporter & private eye	Miami, FL
Rosalie Cairns	Struthers, Betsy	'92 - 3	bookstore clerk turned academic	Ontario, Canada
Rosato & Associates	Scottoline, Lisa	'93 - 6	all-women law firm	Philadelphia, PA
Rose Callahan	Woodworth, Deborah	'97 - 2	'30s Shaker sister	North Homage, KY
Rose Trevelyan	Bolitho, Janie	'97 - 2	widowed painter and photographer	Cornwall, England
Rosie Caesare Ramsey & Rick	Santini, Rosemarie	'86 - 2	husband & wife sleuths	New York, NY
Rosie Lavine	Michaels, Melisa	'97 - 2	private eye to the elf world	California
Rosie Vicente & Jake Samson	Singer, Shelley	'83 - 5	ex-cop & carpenter	Berkeley, CA
Royce Madison	York, Kieran	'93 - 2	lesbian deputy sheriff	Timber City, CO
Roz Howard & Alan Stewart	Kenney, Susan	'83 - 3	American professor & British painter	Maine
Ruby Crane	Dereske, Jo	'96 - 3	questioned-documents expert	Western MI
Ruby Gordon	Banks, Jacqueline Turner	'98 - 2	college-educated black cleaning woman	Oakland, CA
Ruby Rothman	Kahn, Sharon	'98 - 2	rabbi's widow	Eternal, TX
Ruth Willmarth	Wright, Nancy Means	'96 - 2	single-mother farmer	Branbury, VT
Ruthie Kantor Morris	Horowitz, Renee B.	'97 - 2	widowed pharmacist	Scottsdale, AZ

S

Sabina Swift	Sucher, Dorothy	'88 - 2	detective agency owner	Washington, DC
Sal Kilkenny	Staincliffe, Cath	'94 - 3	single-mother private eye	Manchester, England
Salvatore Guarnaccia	Nabb, Magdalen	'81 - 11	Sicilian Carabinieri marshal	Florence, Italy
Sam Jones	Henderson, Lauren	'95 - 4	20-something sculptress	London, England
Sam & Nicky Titus	Sandstrom, Eve K.	'90 - 3	ex-CID sheriff & photographer wife	Holton, OK
Sam Ridley	Niles, Chris	'97 - 2	radio news reporter	London, England
Sam Wescott & Hollis Ball	Chappell, Helen	'96 - 3	reporter & her ex-husband's ghost	Santimoke County, MD
Samantha Adams	Shankman, Sarah	'88 - 7	investigative reporter	Atlanta, GA
Samantha Holt	Wilson, Karen Ann	'94 - 4	veterinary technician	Paradise Cay, FL
Samantha "Smokey" Brandon	Ayres, Noreen	'92 - 2	sheriff's forensic expert	Orange County, CA
Samantha Turner	Landreth, Marsha	'92 - 3	medical examiner	Sheridan, WY
Sandy Whitacre	Youmans, Claire	'00 - 1	attorney in sole practice tort law	Seattle, WA
Sano Ichiro	Rowland, Laura Joh	'94 - 4	investigator for the shogun	Edo, Japan
Sara Kingsley	Wilson, Anne	'95 - 2	single-mother community counselor	London, England
Sarah Calloway	Warmbold, Jean	'86 - 3	magazine journalist	San Francisco, CA
Sarah Deane & A. McKenzie	Borthwick, J.S.	'82 - 9	English professor & internist	Boston, MA
Sarah Fortune	Fyfield, Frances	'89 - 2	lawyer in prestigious British firm	London, England
Sarah Kelling & M. Bittersohn	MacLeod, Charlotte	'79 - 12	investigative couple	Boston, MA
Sarah & Meg Quilliam	Bishop, Claudia	'94 - 6	inn owner & chef sisters	Hemlock Falls, NY
Sarah Walker & Liz Sansborough	Lynds, Gayle	'96 - 2	CIA agents	International
Savannah Reid	McKevett, G.A.	'95 - 4	voluptuous ex-cop private eye	San Carmelita, CA
Saz Martin	Duffy, Stella	'94 - 3	lesbian private eye	London, England
Schuyler Ridgway	McClellan, Tierney	'95 - 4	40-something real estate agent	Louisville, KY
Sharon McCone	Muller, Marcia	'77 - 20	legal investigator turned P.I.	San Francisco, CA
Sheila Malory	Holt, Hazel	'89 - 8	British literary magazine writer	Devon, England
Sheila Travis	Sprinkle, Patricia H.	'88 - 7	embassy wife turned executive	Atlanta, GA
Sherlock Holmes	Buggé, Carole	'98 - 1	consulting detective	London, England
Shirley McClintock	Oliphant, B.J.	'90 - 7	50-something rancher	Colorado
Sierra Lavotini	Bartholomew, Nancy	'98 - 2	exotic dancer	Panama City, FL
Sigismondo	Eyre, Elizabeth	'92 - 6	agent of a Renaissance duke	Venice, Italy
Sigrid Harald	Maron, Margaret	'81 - 8	police lieutenant	New York, NY
Simone & Candi Covington	Deloach, Nora	'94 - 6	black social worker & paralegal daughter	Otis, SC
Simon Bede & Helen Bullock	Byfield, Barbara Ninde	'75 - 4	Episcopal priest & photographer	New York, NY
Simon Drake	Nielsen, Helen	'51 - 5	transplanted Chicago attorney	Southern CA
Simon Forman	Cook, Judith	'97 - 2	Elizabethan physician-astrologer	London, England
Simon Shaw	Shaber, Sarah R.	'97 - 2	young history professor	Raleigh, NC
Simona Griffo	Crespi, Camilla	'91 - 7	gourmet cook ad executive	New York, NY
Sixto Cardenas & B. Marten	Adamson, M.J.	'87 - 5	NYPD homicide detective & Puerto Rican cop	Puerto Rico
Skip Langdon	Smith, Julie	'90 - 8	6-ft. police detective	New Orleans, LA
Smoky O'Donnell	Webb, Martha G.	'85 - 2	small-town PD narcotics officer	Farmer's Mound, TX

Series Character	Author	1 - #	Occupation	Setting

Character's First Name

S...T

Series Character	Author	1 - #	Occupation	Setting
Snooky Randolph & Bernard Woodruff	Dank, Gloria	'89 - 4	children's author & his brother-in-law	Connecticut
Sonora Blair	Hightower, Lynn S.	'95 - 3	homicide detective	Cincinnati, OH
Sophie Greenway	Hart, Ellen	'94 - 4	food critic and magazine editor	Minneapolis, MN
Sophie Rivers	Cutler, Judith	'95 - 5	college lecturer and amateur singer	Birmingham, England
Spaceman Kowalski & Blue Maguire	White, Teri	'84 - 2	prickly cop partners	Los Angeles, CA
Spencer Arrowood	McCrumb, Sharyn	'90 - 5	Appalachian sheriff	Tennessee
Starletta DuVall	Smith-Levin, Judith	'96 - 3	6-ft. black homicide lieutenant	Brookport, MA
Stella the Stargazer	Jorgensen, Christine T.	'94 - 4	astrologer & lovelorn columnist	Denver, CO
Stephanie Plum	Evanovich, Janet	'94 - 4	lingerie buyer turned bounty hunter	Trenton, NJ
Stephen Ramsay	Cleeves, Ann	'90 - 6	impulsive police inspector	Northumberland, Eng.
Stevie Houston	Richardson, Tracey	'97 - 3	gay rookie homicide detective	Toronto, ON, Canada
Stoner McTavish	Dreher, Sarah	'85 - 7	lesbian travel agent	Boston, MA
Sukey Reynolds	Rowlands, Betty	'96 - 3	police photographer	England
Susan Given	Barrett, Margaret	'98 - 2	asset forfeiture prosecutor	New York, NY
Susan Henshaw	Wolzien, Valerie	'87 -12	upscale suburban housewife	Connecticut
Susan Melville	Smith, Evelyn E.	'86 - 4	freelance assassin-painter	New York, NY
Susan Wren	Weir, Charlene	'92 - 4	ex-cop turned police chief	Hampstead, KS
Susanna Appleton	Emerson, Kathy Lynn	'97 - 4	Elizabethan herbalist noblewoman	England
Sutton McPhee	English, Brenda	'97 - 2	police reporter	Fairfax County, VA
Suze Figueroa & Norm Bennis	D'Amato, Barbara	'96 - 2	pair of cops	Chicago, IL
Syd Fish	Geason, Susan	'90 - 3	politically incorrect P.I.	Sydney, Australia
Sydney Bryant	Wallace, Patricia	'88 - 4	private investigator	San Diego, CA
Sydney Sloane	Lordon, Randye	'93 - 5	lesbian private investigator	New York, NY
Sydney Teague	Grant, Anne Underwood	'98 - 3	single-mother ad agency owner	Charlotte, NC
Sylvia Strange	Lovett, Sarah	'95 - 3	forensic psychologist	Sante Fe, NM

T

Series Character	Author	1 - #	Occupation	Setting
Tam Buchanan & Fizz	Holms, Joyce	'96 - 3	older Scottish attorney & law student	Edinburgh, Scotland
Tamara Hayle	Wesley, Valerie Wilson	'94 - 5	black ex-cop single-mother P.I.	Newark, NJ
Tamara Hoyland	Mann, Jessica	'82 - 6	British secret agent archaeologist	England
Tay-bodal	Medawar, Mardi Oakley	'96 - 3	19th century Kiowa healer	Oklahoma
Taylor Morgan	Rust, Megan Mallory	'98 - 4	air ambulance pilot	Anchorage, AK
Teal Stewart	Lamb, J. Dayne	'93 - 3	Certified Public Accountant	Boston, MA
Teddy Morelli	French, Linda	'98 - 3	college history professor	Seattle, WA
Temperance Brennan	Reichs, Kathy	'97 - 2	forensic anthropologist	Montreal, QB, Canada
Temple Barr & M. Louie	Douglas, Carole Nelson	'92 - 9	PR freelancer & tomcat sleuth	Las Vegas, NV
Tess Darcy	Hager, Jean	'94 - 5	Ozarks bed & breakfast owner	Victoria Springs, MO
Tess Monaghan	Lippman, Laura	'97 - 4	newspaper reporter turned P.I.	Baltimore, MD
Tessa Vance	Rowe, Jennifer	'97 - 2	senior homicide detective	Sydney, Australia
Texana Jones	Martin, Allana	'96 - 3	desert trading post owner	El Povo, TX
The Tonnemans	Meyers, Maan	'92 - 6	New Amsterdam family	New York, NY
Thea Barlow	Caverly, Carol	'94 - 2	Western magazine editor	Wyoming
Thea Crawford	Mann, Jessica	'72 - 2	archaeology professor	England
Thea Kozak	Flora, Kate Clark	'94 - 5	educational consultant	Boston, MA
Theo Bloomer	Hadley, Joan	'86 - 2	retired florist and former spy	
Theodora Braithwaite	Greenwood, D.M.	'91 - 8	British woman clergy	London, England
Theodore S. Hubbert & Auntie Lil	Gray, Gallagher	'91 - 4	retired personnel manager & dress designer	New York, NY
Theresa Fortunato & Oliver Jardine	Green, Kate	'86 - 3	professional psychic & LAPD detective	Los Angeles, CA
Theresa Galloway	Grimes, Terris McMahan	'96 - 3	black married-mother civil servant	Sacramento, CA
Theresa Tracy Baldwin	OCork, Shannon	'80 - 3	sports news photographer	New York, NY
Thomas & Charlotte Pitt	Perry, Anne	'79 -18	Victorian police inspector & wife	London, England
Thomas Lynley & B. Havers	George, Elizabeth	'88 - 9	Scotland Yard inspector & det. sgt.	London, England
Tim Le Page	Dewhurst, Eileen	'92 - 2	local detective inspector	Guernsey, England
Tish McWhinny	Comfort, Barbara	'86 - 5	70-something artist-painter	Lofton, VT
Toby Glendower & P. Spring	Arnold, Margot	'79 -12	anthropologist & archaeologist	World Travelers
Tom Barnaby	Graham, Caroline	'87 - 5	chief inspector	Causton, England
Tom Maybridge	Gill, B.M.	'81 - 3	detective chief inspector	England

Series Character	Author	1 - #	Occupation	Setting

Character's First Name

T...Z

Series Character	Author	1 - #	Occupation	Setting
Tom Pollard & Gregory Toye	Lemarchand, Elizabeth	'67 -17	Scotland Yard detectives	London, England
Tommy Hung & Mitch Mitchell	Kershaw, Valerie	'93 - 4	radio journalist P.I. & Chinese partner	Birmingham, England
Tony Hill & Carol Jordan	McDermid, Val	'95 - 2	clinical psychologist & D.I.	Bradfield, England
Tori Miracle	Malmont, Valerie S.	'94 - 2	crime writer turned novelist	Lickin Creek, PA
Torie O'Shea	MacPherson, Rett	'97 - 2	historian-genealogist-tour guide	New Kassel, MO
Tory Bauer	Taylor, Kathleen	'93 - 4	small-town diner waitress	Delphi, SD
Tory Travers	Schumacher, Aileen	'96 - 3	structural engineer	Las Cruces, NM
Trevor Joseph	John, Katherine	'89 - 3	police sergeant	England
Trewley & Stone	Mason, Sarah J.	'93 - 6	village Det. Supt. & female sergeant	Kent, England
Trey Fortier & Lane Montana	Hooper, Kay	'91 - 2	finder of lost things & homicide detective	Atlanta, GA
Trish Maguire	Cooper, Natasha	'98 - 1	family law barrister	London, England
Trixie Dolan & E. Sinclair	Babson, Marian	'86 - 5	aging American ex-movie queens	London, England
Tru North	McClellan, Janet	'97 - 3	lesbian police detective	Kansas City, MO
Truman Kicklighter	Trocheck, Kathy Hogan	'96 - 2	retired wire service reporter	St. Petersburg, FL
Tyler Jones	Drury, Joan M.	'93 - 3	lesbian activist newspaper columnist	San Francisco, CA

U

Series Character	Author	1 - #	Occupation	Setting
Ulysses Finnegan Donaghue	Shone, Anna	'94 - 2	Shakespeare scholar private eye	Provence, France
Ursula Blanchard	Buckley, Fiona	'97 - 2	lady-in-waiting to Elizabeth I	London, England

V

Series Character	Author	1 - #	Occupation	Setting
V. I. Warshawski	Paretsky, Sara	'82 - 8	attorney turned P.I.	Chicago, IL
Vejay Haskell	Dunlap, Susan	'83 - 3	utility meter reader	Northern CA
Venus Diamond	Moody, Skye Kathleen	'96 - 3	U.S. Fish & Wildlife agent	Washington
Verity Birdwood	Rowe, Jennifer	'87 - 5	TV researcher	Australia
Veronica 'Ronnie' Ventana	White, Gloria	'91 - 4	Anglo-Mexican private eye	San Francisco, CA
Vicki Nelson	Huff, Tanya	'92 - 5	ex-cop turned P.I. with vampire lover	Toronto, ON, Canada
Vicky Bauer	Gom, Leona	'96 - 2	Army wife of mixed Indian heritage	Canada
Vicky Bliss	Peters, Elizabeth	'73 - 5	art historian	Germany
Vicky Holden & J. A. O'Malley	Coel, Margaret	'95 - 4	Jesuit missionary & Arapaho attorney	Wind River, WY
Victoire Vernet	Fawcett, Quinn	'93 - 2	wife of Napoleonic gendarme	Paris, France
Victor Cardenas & C. Austen	Rubino, Jane	'96 - 3	single-mom reporter & police detective	Atlantic City, NJ
Victoria Bowering	Yeager, Dorian	'92 - 4	6 ft-redhead sometime-actress	New York, NY
Victoria Cross	Sumner, Penny	'92 - 2	archivist turned P.I.	London, England
Vince Gutierrez & M. Halloran	LaPierre, Janet	'87 - 5	single-mother school teacher & police chief	Port Silva, CA
Virginia Kelly	Baker, Nikki	'91 - 3	black lesbian stockbroker	Chicago, IL

W

Series Character	Author	1 - #	Occupation	Setting
Wanda Mallory	Frankel, Valerie	'91 - 4	detective agency owner	New York, NY
Whitney Logan & L. Ramos	Lambert, Mercedes	'91 - 2	20-something attorney & Chicana partner	Los Angeles, CA
Wilder & Wilson	Bushell, Agnes	'89 - 2	lesbian private eye duo	Portland, ME
Willa Jansson	Matera, Lia	'87 - 7	Red diaper baby turned attorney	San Francisco, CA
William Hecklepeck	McKitterick, Molly	'92 - 2	egotistical television anchor	St. Louis, MO
William Monk	Perry, Anne	'90 - 9	amnesiac Victorian police inspector	London, England
William Murdoch	Jennings, Maureen	'97 - 2	Victorian police inspector	Toronto, ON, Canada
Willow King	Cooper, Natasha	'90 - 7	civil-servant romance-novelist	London, England
Wilson & Wilder	Bushell, Agnes	'89 - 2	lesbian private eye duo	Portland, ME
Winston Marlowe Sherman	Lorens, M.K.	'90 - 5	mystery-writing Shakespeare professor	New York, NY
Wyanet Chouinard & Liam Campbell	Stabenow, Dana	'98 - 3	state trooper & bush pilot	Alaska
Wylie Nolan & Max Bramble	Reuben, Shelly	'94 - 2	arson investigator & attorney	New York, NY

X

Series Character	Author	1 - #	Occupation	Setting
Xenia Smith & L. Wetzon	Meyers, Annette	'89 - 7	Wall Street headhunters	New York, NY

Y

Series Character	Author	1 - #	Occupation	Setting
Yum Yum, Koko & Jim Qwilleran	Braun, Lilian Jackson	'66 -21	ex-police reporter & cats	Upper Peninsula, MI

Series Character	Author	1 - #	Occupation	Setting

Character's First Name

Z

Series Character	Author	1 - #	Occupation	Setting
Zack James & Liz Broward	Zachary, Fay	'94 - 2	family physician & computer artist	Phoenix, AZ
Zachariah Smith	Thrasher, L.L.	'91 - 2	ex-cop private eye	Mackie, OR

Settings 4

Setting	Author	1 - #	Series Character	Occupation
Australia				
	Rowe, Jennifer	'87 - 5	Verity Birdwood	TV researcher
Melbourne	Greenwood, Kerry	'89 - 9	Phryne Fisher	1920s Londoner
Sydney	Bedford, Jean	'90 - 3	Anna Southwood	private enquiry agent
Sydney	Day, Marele	'88 - 4	Claudia Valentine	private investigator
Sydney	Geason, Susan	'90 - 3	Syd Fish	politically incorrect P.I.
Sydney	McNab, Claire	'88 -10	Carol Ashton	lesbian detective inspector
Sydney	Rowe, Jennifer	'97 - 2	Tessa Vance	senior homicide detective
Belgium				
Brussels	Bailey, Michele	'94 - 3	Matilda Haycastle	30-something office temp
Canada				
	Gom, Leona	'96 - 2	Vicky Bauer	Army wife of mixed Indian heritage
Alberta	Hall, Linda	'95 - 3	Roger Sheppard	RCMP officer and family man
Calgary, AB	North, Suzanne	'94 - 3	Phoebe Fairfax	TV video photographer
Sechelt, BC	Wright, L.R.	'85 - 9	Martin Karl Alberg	RCMP staff sergeant
Vancouver, BC	Bowers, Elisabeth	'88 - 2	Meg Lacey	single-mother private eye
Vancouver, BC	Kelly, Nora	'84 - 4	Gillian Adams	college history department chair
Vancouver, BC	Wright, L.R.	'99 - 1	Eddie Henderson	woman police officer
Victoria, BC	Douglas, Lauren W.	'87 - 6	Caitlin Reece	lesbian private eye
New Brunswick	Craig, Alisa	'80 - 5	Madoc & Janet Rhys	RCMP inspector & wife
ON, Kingsport	Haffner, Margaret	'92 - 2	Catherine Edison	scientist and single mother
Lobelia Falls, ON	Craig, Alisa	'81 - 5	Dittany Henbit Monk & Osbert Monk	garden club member & author of westerns
Peterborough, ON	Struthers, Betsy	'92 - 3	Rosalie Cairns	bookstore clerk turned academic
Toronto, ON	Godfrey, Ellen	'88 - 2	Jane Tregar	corporate headhunter
Toronto, ON	Godfrey, Ellen	'76 - 2	Rebecca Rosenthal	80-year-old Polish-born anthropologist
Toronto, ON	Gordon, Alison	'89 - 6	Kate Henry	baseball newswriter
Toronto, ON	Hamilton, Lyn	'97 - 4	Lara McClintock	antiquities dealer and shop owner
Toronto, ON	Huff, Tanya	'92 - 5	Vicki Nelson	ex-cop turned P.I. with vampire lover
Toronto, ON	Jennings, Maureen	'97 - 2	William Murdoch	Victorian police inspector
Toronto, ON	Manthorne, Jackie	'00 - 1	Elizabeth Ellis	lesbian private eye
Toronto, ON	Porter, Anna	'85 - 3	Judith Hayes	freelance journalist
Toronto, ON	Richardson, Tracey	'97 - 3	Stevie Houston	gay rookie homicide detective
Toronto, ON	Sale, Medora	'86 - 6	John Sanders & Harriet Jeffries	police detective & photographer
Toronto, ON	Zaremba, Eve	'78 - 6	Helen Keremos	40-something lesbian private eye
Montreal, QC	Epstein, Carole	'96 - 2	Barbara Simons	downsized business executive
Montreal, QC	Manthorne, Jackie	'94 - 5	Harriet Hubbley	intrepid lesbian sleuth
Montreal, QC	Reichs, Kathy	'97 - 2	Temperance Brennan	forensic anthropologist
Montreal, QC	Ruryk, Jean	'94 - 3	Catherine Wilde	ad exec turned antiques restorer
Montreal, QC	Smith, Joan G.	'89 - 2	Cassie Newton	college French major
Regina, SK	Bowen, Gail	'90 - 6	Joanne Kilbourn	political science professor

Setting	Author	1 - #	Series Character	Occupation
Egypt				
Buhen	Robinson, Lynda S.	'94 - 5	Lord Meren	Tutankhamen's chief investigator
	Haney, Lauren	'97 - 2	Lt. Bak	ex-charioteer turned Medjay police head
England				
	Atherton, Nancy	'92 - 4	Aunt Dimity	romantic ghost
	Bannister, Jo	'84 - 3	Clio Rees & Harry Marsh	physician novelist & chief inspector
	Beaufort, Simon	'98 - 2	Geoffrey de Mappestone	brave knight of the Crusades
	Chisholm, P.F.	'94 - 4	Robert Carey	Elizabethan nobleman
	Cohen, Anthea	'82 -15	Agnes Carmichael	hospital staff nurse
	Duffy, Margaret	'87 - 6	Ingrid Langley & Patrick Gillard	novelist secret agent & army major
	Emerson, Kathy Lynn	'97 - 4	Susanna Appleton	Elizabethan herbalist noblewoman
	Gill, B.M.	'81 - 3	Tom Maybridge	detective chief inspector
	Gosling, Paula	'86 - 2	Luke Abbott	English cop
	Grant-Adamson, L.	'92 - 2	Jim Rush	American on the run from British police
	Gray, Dulcie	'60 - 2	Insp. Supt. Cardiff	inspector superintendent
	Grindle, Lucretia	'93 - 2	H.W. Ross	detective superintendent
	Holbrook, Teri	'95 - 3	Gale Grayson	American expatriate historian
	John, Katherine	'89 - 3	Trevor Joseph	police sergeant
	Kelly, Mary	'61 - 2	Hedley Nicholson	private investigator
	Linscott, Gillian	'84 - 4	Birdie Linnet	ex-cop fitness trainer
	Mann, Jessica	'82 - 6	Tamara Hoyland	British secret agent archaeologist
	Mann, Jessica	'72 - 2	Thea Crawford	archaeology professor
	Mather, Linda	'94 - 2	Jo Hughes	astrologer-investigator
	Meek, M.R.D.	'82 - 11	Lennox Kemp	solicitor detective
	Moody, Susan	'84 - 7	Penny Wanawake	photographer daughter of black diplomat
	Moore, Margaret	'87 - 3	Richard Baxter	police inspector
	Myers, Amy	'86 - 9	Auguste Didier	British-French Victorian master chef
	Page, Emma	'80 - 9	Kelsey, Inspector	police inspector
	Peart, Jane	'96 - 4	Edgecliffe Manor Series	young, restless Victorian women
	Penman, Sharon Kay	'96 - 2	Justin de Quincy	Queen Mother's investigator
	Petrie, Rhona	'63 - 5	Marcus MacLurg	police inspector
	Petrie, Rhona	'67 - 2	Nassim Pride	Anglo-Sudanese forensic scientist
	Rogow, Roberta	'98 - 2	Charles Dodgson & Conan Doyle	19th century professor & doctor
	Roome, Annette	'89 - 3	Christine Martin	40-something cub reporter
	Rowlands, Betty	'96 - 3	Sukey Reynolds	police photographer
	Sedley, Kate	'91 - 8	Roger the Chapman	medieval peddler
	Stacey, Susannah	'87 - 8	Robert Bone	widowed British police inspector
	Warner, Mignon	'76 - 7	Edwina Charles	British clairvoyant
	Winslow, Pauline Glen	'75 - 6	Merle Capricorn	magician turned police superintendent
Badger's End	Kingsbury, Kate	'93 - 11	Cecily Sinclair	Edwardian hotel owner
Bath	Barron, Stephanie	'96 - 3	Jane Austen	19th century British novelist
Bath	Brown, Lizbie	'92 - 2	Elizabeth Blair	American widow quilt shop owner
Bath	Duffy, Margaret	'94 - 4	Joanna MacKenzie & J. Carrick	ex-CID detective & Det. Chief Insp.
Birmingham	Cutler, Judith	'95 - 5	Sophie Rivers	college lecturer and amateur singer
Birmingham	Kershaw, Valerie	'93 - 4	Mitch Mitchell & Tommy Hung	radio journalist P.I. & Chinese partner
Bradfield	McDermid, Val	'95 - 2	Tony Hill & Carol Jordan	clinical psychologist & D.I.
Cambridge	Gregory, Susanna	'96 - 4	Matthew Bartholomew	14th century physician and teacher
Cambridge	Paton Walsh, Jill	'93 - 2	Imogen Quy	St. Agatha's College nurse
Cambridge	Spring, Michelle	'94 - 4	Laura Principal	British academic turned P.I.
Canterbury, Kent	Ferguson, Frances	'93 - 4	Jane Perry	French-speaking detective sergeant
Carsely	Beaton, M.C.	'92 - 8	Agatha Raisin	cranky London retiree
Castlemere	Bannister, Jo	'93 - 6	Frank Shapiro, Cal Donovan & Liz Graham	police officers
Causton	Graham, Caroline	'87 - 5	Tom Barnaby	chief inspector
Chitterton Fells	Cannell, Dorothy	'84 - 8	Ellie & Ben Haskell	interior decorator & writer-chef
Cornwall	Bolitho, Janie	'97 - 2	Rose Trevelyan	widowed painter and photographer
Cornwall	Black, Veronica	'90 -10	Joan, Sister	British investigative nun
Cornwall	Clayton, Mary	'95 - 5	John Reynolds	ex-inspector turned crime writer
Cotswolds	Granger, Ann	'91 - 11	Alan Markby & Meredith Mitchell	D.I. & Foreign Service officer
Cotswolds	Moody, Susan	'93 - 6	Cassandra Swann	bridge professional
Cotswolds	Quest, Erica	'88 - 3	Kate Maddox	first woman DCI
Cotswolds	Rowlands, Betty	'90 - 8	Melissa Craig	British crime novelist
Dedham	Paige, Robin	'94 - 5	Kathryn Ardleigh & C. Sheridan	American author & British scientist
Deerham Hills	Melville, Jennie	'62 -19	Charmian Daniels	police detective
Devon	Holt, Hazel	'89 - 8	Sheila Malory	British literary magazine writer
East Anglia	McGown, Jill	'83 - 9	Lloyd & Judy Hill	chief inspector & detective partner
East Yorkshire	Highsmith, Domini	'94 - 3	Father Simeon & Elvira	medieval priest & nurse

Setting	Author	1 - #	Series Character	Occupation
England				
Essex	Thomson, June	'71 -18	Inspector Finch	police inspector
Fowchester	Green, Christine	'93 - 3	Connor O'Neill & Fran Wilson	village chief insp. & detective sgt.
Guernsey	Dewhurst, Eileen	'92 - 2	Tim Le Page	local detective inspector
Hampshire	Dunn, Carola	'94 - 6	Daisy Dalrymple	1920s aristocratic feature writer
Herefordshire	Burden, Pat	'90 - 4	Henry Bassett	retired cop
Hop Valley	Kelly, Susan B.	'90 - 5	Alison Hope & Nick Trevellyan	software designer & detective inspector
Kent	Crane, Hamilton	'68 -22	Emily D. Seeton	retired British art teacher
Kent	Hardwick, Mollie	'86 - 7	Doran Fairweather	British antiques dealer
Kent	Peters, Elizabeth	'75 -12	Amelia Peabody	Victorian feminist archaeologist
Kent	Simpson, Dorothy	'81 -14	Luke Thanet	family-man police inspector
London	Babson, Marian	'71 - 4	Douglas Perkins	public relations agent
London	Babson, Marian	'86 - 5	Evangeline Sinclair & Trixie Dolan	aging American ex-movie queens
London	Bannister, Jo	'90 - 2	Mickey Flynn	American photojournalist
London	Brightwell, Emily	'93 -13	Gerald Witherspoon & Hepzibah Jeffries	Victorian inspector & his housekeeper
London	Brown, Molly	'97 - 2	Aphra Behn	17th century spy turned playwright
London	Buckley, Fiona	'97 - 2	Ursula Blanchard	lady-in-waiting to Elizabeth I
London	Buggé, Carole	'98 - 1	Sherlock Holmes	consulting detective
London	Butler, Gwendoline	'57 -26	John Coffin	Scotland Yard commander
London	Caudwell, Sarah	'81 - 4	Hilary Tamar	medieval law specialist
London	Charles, Kate	'91 - 5	Lucy Kingsley & David Middleton-Brown	artist & solicitor
London	Clarke, Anna	'85 - 9	Paula Glenning	British professor & writer
London	Cody, Liza	'80 - 6	Anna Lee	investigator for security firm
London	Cody, Liza	'92 - 3	Eva Wylie	wrestler and security guard
London	Cook, Judith	'97 - 2	Simon Forman	Elizabethan physician-astrologer
London	Cooper, Natasha	'98 - 1	Trish Maguire	family law barrister
London	Cooper, Natasha	'90 - 7	Willow King	civil-servant romance-novelist
London	Crombie, Deborah	'93 - 3	Duncan Kincaid & Gemma James	Scotland Yard detective partners
London	Crowleigh, Ann	'93 - 2	Mirinda & Clare Clively	Victorian twin sisters
London	Danks, Denise	'89 - 4	Georgina Powers	British computer journalist
London	Dewhurst, Eileen	'82 - 2	Helen Markham Johnson	actress recruited by Secret Service
London	Dewhurst, Eileen	'77 - 5	Neil Carter	Scotland Yard detective
London	Dewhurst, Eileen	'95 - 3	Phyllida Moon	television private eye
London	Donald, Anabel	'93 - 5	Alex Tanner	TV researcher and part-time P.I.
London	Duffy, Stella	'94 - 3	Saz Martin	lesbian private eye
London	Dunant, Sarah	'92 - 3	Hannah Wolfe	contract private investigator
London	Edwards, Ruth D.	'81 - 8	James Milton & Robert Amiss	police superintendent & ex-civil servant
London	Fawcett, Quinn	'94 - 3	Mycroft Holmes	Sherlock Holmes' older brother
London	Fraser, Antonia	'77 - 8	Jemima Shore	British TV interviewer
London	Fyfield, Frances	'88 - 6	Helen West	London Crown prosecutor
London	Fyfield, Frances	'89 - 2	Sarah Fortune	lawyer in prestigious British firm
London	George, Elizabeth	'88 - 9	Thomas Lynley & Barbara Havers	Scotland Yard inspector & detective sergeant
London	Giroux, E.X.	'84 -10	Robert Forsythe & Abigail Sanderson	barrister & his secretary
London	Granger, Ann	'97 - 3	Fran Varaday	unlicensed young investigator
London	Grant-Adamson, L.	'85 - 5	Rain Morgan	Fleet Street gossip columnist
London	Greenwood, D.M.	'91 - 8	Theodora Braithwaite	British woman clergy
London	Grimes, Martha	'81 -15	Richard Jury	Scotland Yard inspector
London	Hambly, Barbara	'88 - 2	James Asher	professor and part-time spy
London	Harrod-Eagles, C.	'91 - 7	Bill Slider	Shepherd's Bush CID inspector
London	Henderson, Lauren	'95 - 4	Sam Jones	20-something sculptress
London	Howell, Lis	'95 - 3	Kate Wilkinson	television producer
London	James, P.D.	'62 -10	Adam Dalgleish	published poet of Scotland Yard
London	James, P.D.	'72 - 2	Cordelia Gray	fledgling P.I.
London	Joseph, Alison	'94 - 4	Agnes Bourdillon	ex-cloistered nun
London	Kaewert, Julie Wallin	'94 - 3	Alex Plumtree	head of family publishing firm
London	King, Laurie R.	'94 - 4	Mary Russell	Sherlock Holmes' detecting partner
London	La Plante, Lynda	'83 - 5	Dolly Rawlins	bank robber's widow
London	La Plante, Lynda	'93 - 3	Jane Tennison	detective chief inspector
London	Lake, Deryn	'94 - 4	John Rawlings & the Blind Beak	18th century apothecary & blind magistrate
London	Laurence, Janet	'98 - 2	Canaletto	18th century Italian painter
London	Lemarchand, Elizabeth	'67 -17	Tom Pollard & Gregory Toye	Scotland Yard detectives

Setting	Author	1 - #	Series Character	Occupation

England

Setting	Author	1 - #	Series Character	Occupation
London	Lin-Chandler, Irene	'95 - 3	Holly-Jean Ho	Anglo-Chinese bisexual investigator
London	Linscott, Gillian	'91 - 7	Nell Bray	British suffragette
London	Macdonald, Marianne	'96 - 2	Dido Hoare	single-mother antiquarian bookseller
London	Moyes, Patricia	'59 -19	Henry & Emmy Tibbett	Scotland Yard inspector & wife
London	Neel, Janet	'88 - 6	John McLeish & F. Wilson	DCI & businesswoman
London	Niles, Chris	'97 - 2	Sam Ridley	radio news reporter
London	Perry, Anne	'79 -18	Thomas & Charlotte Pitt	Victorian police inspector & wife
London	Perry, Anne	'90 - 9	William Monk	amnesiac Victorian police inspector
London	Peterson, Audrey	'92 - 3	Claire Camden	California English professor
London	Peterson, Audrey	'88 - 6	Jane Winfield	British journalist and music writer
London	Rayner, Claire	'93 - 5	George Barnabas	hospital forensic pathologist
London	Ross, Annie	'95 - 3	Bel Carson	TV director and investigator
London	Ross, Kate	'93 - 4	Julian Kestrel	1820s dandy-about-town
London	Slovo, Gillian	'84 - 5	Kate Baeier	journalist turned P.I.
London	Smith, Cynthia	'96 - 5	Emma Rhodes	private resolver for the rich
London	Smith, Joan	'87 - 5	Loretta Lawson	British feminist professor
London	Stubbs, Jean	'73 - 3	John Joseph Lintott	retired Scotland Yard inspector
London	Sumner, Penny	'92 - 2	Victoria Cross	archivist turned P.I.
London	Wakefield, Hannah	'87 - 3	Dee Street	solicitor in an all-women firm
London	Wilson, Anne	'95 - 2	Sara Kingsley	single-mother community counselor
London	Wilson, Barbara	'90 - 2	Cassandra Reilly	Spanish translator
Longborough	Green, Christine	'91 - 4	Kate Kinsella	nurse and medical investigator
Malminster	Mitchell, Kay	'90 - 5	John Morrissey	chief inspector and family man
Manchester	Fritchley, Alma	'97 - 3	Letty Campbell	lesbian chicken farmer
Manchester	McDermid, Val	'92 - 6	Kate Brannigan	5' 3" redheaded private eye
Manchester	Staincliffe, Cath	'94 - 3	Sal Kilkenny	single-mother private eye
Midlands	Eccles, Marjorie	'88 -10	Gil Mayo	detective chief inspector
Northumberland	Cleeves, Ann	'90 - 6	Stephen Ramsay	impulsive police inspector
Norwich	Adams, Jane	'95 - 3	Mike Croft	detective inspector
Norwich	Haymon, S.T.	'80 - 8	Benjamin Jurnet	Angleby CID detective inspector
Nottingham	Shepherd, Stella	'89 - 7	Richard Montgomery	CID Inspector
Oxford	Stallwood, Veronica	'93 - 4	Kate Ivory	historical romance novelist
Oxford	Yorke, Margaret	'70 - 5	Patrick Grant	Oxford don
Oxfordshire	Frazer, Margaret	'92 - 8	Dame Frevisse	15th century Benedictine nun
Oxfordshire	Penn, John	'83 - 6	George Thorne	detective superintendent
Oxfordshire	Penn, John	'88 -12	Richard Tansey	chief inspector
Plummergen	Mason, Sarah J.	'93 - 6	Trewley & Stone	village Det. Supt. & female sergeant
Rickenham Green	Bolitho, Janie	'93 - 8	Ian Roper	detective chief inspector
Sherebury	Dams, Jeanne M.	'95 - 4	Dorothy Martin	60-something American widow
Skipley	Bannister, Jo	'98 - 1	Primrose Holland	newspaper advice columnist
Staffordshire	Masters, Priscilla	'95 - 5	Joanna Piercy	detective inspector
Suffolk	Quinton, Ann	'89 - 6	James Roland & Patrick Mansfield	det. inspector & det. sergeant
Suffolk	Radley, Sheila	'78 - 9	Douglas Quantrill & Hilary Lloyd	DCI & sergeant partner
Surrey	Cleeves, Ann	'86 - 8	George & Molly Palmer-Jones	ex-Home Office bird-watcher & wife
Sussex	Rendell, Ruth	'64 -17	Reginald Wexford	chief inspector
Thames Valley	Curzon, Clare	'83 -13	Mike Yeadings	Serious Crime Squad superintendent
West Calleshire	Aird, Catherine	'66 -16	Christopher Dennis "Seedy" Sloan	CID department head
West Country	Jakeman, Jane	'97 - 3	Ambrose Malfine	lord and heir to a decaying estate
West Country	Laurence, Janet	'89 - 9	Darina Lisle	caterer-chef and food writer
Wiltshire	Fraser, Anthea	'84 -14	David Webb	detective chief inspector
Woodfield	Jordan, Jennifer	'87 - 3	Barry & Dee Vaughan	spoofy crime writer & office temp wife
York	Robb, Candace M.	'93 - 6	Owen Archer	one-eyed medieval Welsh spy
York	Whitehead, Barbara	'88 - 8	Robert Southwell	detective chief inspector
Yorkshire	Bell, Pauline	'90 - 8	Benny Mitchell	brash detective constable
Yorkshire	Evans, Geraldine	'93 - 3	Joseph Rafferty & Dafyd Llewellyn	D.I.& his Welsh sergeant
Yorkshire	Hall, Patricia	'93 - 5	Laura Ackroyd & M. Thackeray	investigative reporter & police inspector
Yorkshire	Lacey, Sarah	'92 - 4	Leah Hunter	20-something tax inspector

France

Setting	Author	1 - #	Series Character	Occupation
	Newman, Sharan	'93 - 5	Catherine LeVendeur	12th-century merchant's daughter
Burgundy	Hebden, Juliet	'79 -22	Clovis Pel	curmudgeonly police inspector
Moselle	Rippon, Marion	'69 - 4	Maurice Ygrec	retired French police inspector
Paris	Black, Cara	'99 - 2	Aimée Leduc	French-American private eye
Paris	Douglas, Carole Nelson	'90 - 4	Irene Adler	19th century American diva

Setting	Author	1 - #	Series Character	Occupation
France				
Paris	Fawcett, Quinn	'93 - 2	Victoire Vernet	wife of Napoleonic gendarme
Paris	Friedman, Mickey	'88 - 2	Georgia Lee Maxwell	freelance writer
Paris	Smith, Sarah	'92 - 2	Alexander von Reisden & P. Halley	biochemist & concert pianist
Provence	Shone, Anna	'94 - 2	Ulysses Finnegan Donaghue	Shakespeare scholar private eye
Germany				
	Dengler, Sandy	'98 - 2	Gar	Neanderthal shaman
	Peters, Elizabeth	'73 - 5	Vicky Bliss	art historian
Ireland				
Dublin	Fallon, Ann C.	'90 - 5	James Fleming	train-loving solicitor
Israel				
Jerusalem	Gur, Batya	'92 - 4	Michael Ohayon	Moroccan-born chief inspector
Italy				
Florence	Nabb, Magdalen	'81 - 11	Salvatore Guarnaccia	Sicilian Carabinieri marshal
Rome	Davis, Lindsey	'89 - 11	Marcus Didius Falco	1st century Roman private eye
Rome	Todd, Marilyn	'95 - 4	Claudia Seferius	13 B.C. superbitch
Venice	Eyre, Elizabeth	'92 - 6	Sigismondo	agent of a Renaissance duke
Venice	Leon, Donna	'92 - 9	Guido Brunetti	police commissario
Japan				
Edo	Rowland, Laura Joh	'94 - 4	Sano Ichiro	investigator for the shogun
Kyoto	Woodward, Ann	'96 - 2	Lady Aoi	11th century Japanese healer
Tokyo	Massey, Sujata	'97 - 3	Rei Shimura	Japanese-American antiques dealer
Kenya				
	McQuillan, Karin	'90 - 3	Jazz Jasper	American safari guide
Mexico				
San Luis Potosi	Blanc, Suzanne	'61 - 3	Miguel Menendez	Aztec police inspector
Middle East				
	Haddad, C.A.	'76 - 2	David Haham	government agent
New Zealand				
Wellington	Beecham, Rose	'92 - 3	Amanda Valentine	lesbian detective inspector
Puerto Rico				
	Adamson, M.J.	'87 - 5	Balthazar Marten & Sixto Cardenas	NYPD homicide detective & Puerto Rican cop
Scotland				
Edinburgh	Holms, Joyce	'96 - 3	Tam Buchanan & Fizz	older Scottish attorney & law student
Edinburgh	Kelly, Mary	'56 - 3	Brett Nightingale	Scottish police inspector
Edinburgh	Knight, Alanna	'88 - 11	Jeremy Faro	Victorian detective inspector
Glasgow	McDermid, Val	'87 - 5	Lindsay Gordon	lesbian socialist journalist
Lochdubh	Beaton, M.C.	'85 - 14	Hamish Macbeth	Scottish police constable
Spain				
Barcelona	Oliver, Maria-Antonia	'87 - 2	Lonia Guiu	Catalan investigator
Girona	Roe, Caroline	'98 - 3	Isaac & Bishop Berenguer	1350s blind physician & bishop
Sweden				
Stockholm	Sjöwall, Maj & Per Wahlöö	'67 - 10	Martin Beck	Swedish police officer

Setting	Author	1 - #	Series Character	Occupation
United States				
Alabama (AL)				
Birmingham	George, Anne	'96 - 5	Mary Alice Crane & Patricia Ann Howell	60-something sister sleuths
Alaska (AK)				
	Stabenow, Dana	'92 -10	Kate Shugak	Alaskan ex-D.A. investigator
	Stabenow, Dana	'98 - 3	Liam Campbell & Wyanet Chouinard	state trooper & bush pilot
Anchorage	Henry, Sue	'91 - 5	Jessie Arnold & Alex Jensen	sled dog racer & Alaska state trooper
Anchorage	Quinn, Elizabeth	'93 - 4	Lauren Maxwell	wildlife investigator PhD
Anchorage	Rust, Megan Mallory	'98 - 4	Taylor Morgan	air ambulance pilot
Farberville	Hess, Joan	'86 -12	Claire Malloy	small-town bookstore owner
Maggody	Hess, Joan	'87 - 11	Arly Hanks	small-town police chief
Arizona (AZ)				
	Matthews, Patricia	'92 - 5	Casey Farrel	governor's crime task force member
Cochise County	Jance, J.A.	'93 - 7	Joanna Brady	single-mother sheriff
Phoenix	Dengler, Sandy	'93 - 4	Joe Rodriguez	police sergeant
Phoenix	O'Callaghan, Maxine	'96 - 2	Anne Menlo	child psychologist
Phoenix	Zachary, Fay	'94 - 2	Liz Broward & Zack James	family physician & computer artist
Scottsdale	Horowitz, Renee B.	'97 - 2	Ruthie Kantor Morris	widowed pharmacist
Tucson	Cramer, Rebecca	'98 - 2	Linda Bluenight	anthropologist turned teacher
Arkansas (AR)				
Shakespeare	Harris, Charlaine	'96 - 3	Lily Bard	30-something cleaning woman
California (CA)				
	Michaels, Melisa	'97 - 2	Rosie Lavine	private eye to the elf world
Berkeley	Dunlap, Susan	'81 -10	Jill Smith	homicide detective
Berkeley	Singer, Shelley	'93 - 4	Barrett Lake	history teacher turned P.I.
Berkeley	Singer, Shelley	'83 - 5	Jake Samson & Rosie Vicente	ex-cop & carpenter
Berkeley	Welch, Pat	'90 - 6	Helen Black	ex-cop lesbian private eye
Beverly Hills	Songer, C.J.	'98 - 2	Meg Gillis	ex-cop turned security consultant
Central	Rothenberg, Rebecca	'91 - 3	Claire Sharples	microbiologist
Flat Skunk	Warner, Penny	'97 - 3	Connor Westphal	deaf reporter and newspaper owner
Gold Country	Jacobs, Jonnie	'96 - 3	Kali O'Brien	attorney
Hollywood	Millhiser, Marlys	'92 - 5	Charlie Greene	literary agent and single mother
Hollywood	Osborne, Denise	'94 - 2	Queenie Davilov	screenwriter-investigator
Hollywood	Shah, Diane K.	'90 - 2	Paris Chandler	1940s private eye
La Jolla	Dunlap, Susan	'89 - 4	Kiernan O'Shaughnessy	medical examiner turned P.I.
Lake Tahoe	Valentine, Deborah	'89 - 3	Katharine Craig & Kevin Bryce	sculptor & ex-sheriff's detective
Las Piernas	Burke, Jan	'93 - 6	Irene Kelly	newspaper reporter
Los Angeles	Cannon, Taffy	'93 - 3	Nan Robinson	state bar investigator
Los Angeles	Clark, Carol Higgins	'92 - 4	Regan Reilly	P.I. and novelist's daughter
Los Angeles	Farmer, Jerrilyn	'98 - 2	Madeline Bean	Hollywood party planner
Los Angeles	Fickling, G.G.	'62 - 3	Erik March	macho private eye
Los Angeles	Fickling, G.G.	'57 - 11	Honey West	sexiest P.I. ever to pull a trigger
Los Angeles	Forrest, Katherine V.	'84 - 6	Kate Delafield	LAPD lesbian homicide detective
Los Angeles	Green, Kate	'86 - 3	Theresa Fortunato & Oliver Jardine	professional psychic & LAPD detective
Los Angeles	Hornsby, Wendy	'87 - 2	Kate Teague & Roger Tejeda	college professor & homicide detective
Los Angeles	Hornsby, Wendy	'92 - 5	Maggie MacGowen	documentary filmmaker
Los Angeles	Howe, Melodie J.	'89 - 2	Claire Conrad & Maggie Hill	elegant P.I. & assistant
Los Angeles	Kellerman, Faye	'86 -10	Peter Decker & Rina Lazarus	LAPD detective & Orthodox Jewish wife
Los Angeles	Kraft, Gabrielle	'87 - 4	Jerry Zalman	Beverly Hills deal maker
Los Angeles	Krich, Rochelle Majer	'96 - 1	Debra Laslow	criminal defense attorney
Los Angeles	Krich, Rochelle Majer	'93 - 3	Jessie Drake	LAPD homicide detective
Los Angeles	La Plante, Lynda	'94 - 3	Lorraine Page	sober ex-cop turned private eye
Los Angeles	Lambert, Mercedes	'91 - 2	Whitney Logan & Lupe Ramos	20-something attorney & Chicana partner
Los Angeles	Maracotta, Lindsay	'96 - 2	Lucy Freers	children's film animator
Los Angeles	Mercer, Judy	'96 - 3	Ariel Gold	amnesiac TV newsmagazine producer
Los Angeles	Pugh, Dianne G.	'93 - 4	Iris Thorne	investment counselor
Los Angeles	Schmidt, Carol	'93 - 3	Laney Samms	lesbian bar owner
Los Angeles	White, Teri	'84 - 2	Spaceman Kowalski & Blue Maguire	prickly cop partners
Los Angeles	Woods, Paula L.	'99 - 2	Charlotte Justice	black woman homicide detective

Setting	Author	1 - #	Series Character	Occupation

United States

California (CA)

Setting	Author	1 - #	Series Character	Occupation
Marin County	Girdner, Jaqueline	'91 - 11	Kate Jasper	gag gift wholesaler
Marin County	Griffin, Annie	'98 - 2	Hannah Malloy & Kiki Goldstein	unlikely pair of 60-something sisters
Marin County	Heron, Echo	'98 - 3	Adele Monsarrat	hospital registered nurse
Molena Point	Murphy, Shirley R.	'96 - 4	Joe Grey	talking-cat private eye
Napa Valley	Muller, Marcia	'86 - 3	Joanna Stark	international art investigator
Northern	Dunlap, Susan	'83 - 3	Vejay Haskell	utility meter reader
Northern	McGuire, Christine	'93 - 4	Kathryn Mackay	senior prosecuting attorney
Northern	McKenna, Bridget	'93 - 3	Caley Burke	30-something private eye
Oak Valley	Thrasher, L.L.	'98 - 1	Lizbet Lange	millionaire ex-waitress
Oakland	Banks, Jacqueline T.	'98 - 2	Ruby Gordon	college-educated black cleaning woman
Oakland	Corpi, Lucha	'92 - 2	Gloria Damasco	Chicana activist with ESP
Oakland	Dawson, Janet	'90 - 8	Jeri Howard	private eye
Oakland	Wallace, Marilyn	'86 - 3	Jay Goldstein & Carlos Cruz	homicide detectives
Orange County	Ayres, Noreen	'92 - 2	Samantha "Smokey" Brandon	sheriff's forensic expert
Orange County	Berne, Karin	'85 - 3	Ellie Gordon	law firm office manager
Orange County	Femling, Jean	'89 - 2	Martha Brant	insurance claims investigator
Orange County	Lachnit, Carroll	'95 - 3	Hannah Barlow	ex-cop turned lawyer
Orange County	O'Callaghan, Maxine	'80 - 6	Delilah West	private investigator
Palm Springs	Navratilova, Martina	'94 - 3	Jordan Myles	ex-tennis star physical therapist
Palm Springs	Roberts, Lillian M.	'96 - 3	Andi Pauling	veterinarian
Palo Alto	Beck, K.K.	'84 - 3	Iris Cooper	1920s Stanford University co-ed
Palo Alto	Roberts, Lora	'94 - 6	Liz Sullivan	freelance writer and organic gardener
Port Silva	LaPierre, Janet	'87 - 5	Meg Halloran & Vince Gutierrez	single-mother school teacher & police chief
Sacramento	Grimes, Terris McMahan	'96 - 3	Theresa Galloway	black married-mother civil servant
Sacramento	Kijewski, Karen	'89 - 9	Kat Colorado	bar-tending private investigator
San Carmelita	McKevett, G.A.	'95 - 4	Savannah Reid	voluptuous ex-cop private eye
San Celina	Fowler, Earlene	'94 - 7	Benni Harper	folk art museum curator
San Diego	Benke, Patricia D.	'95 - 3	Judith Thornton	chief assistant district attorney
San Diego	Lawrence, Martha	'95 - 3	Elizabeth Chase	parapsychologist turned P.I.
San Diego	Morgan, D Miller	'87 - 2	Daisy Marlow & Sam Milo	lingerie-addicted P.I. & sheriff
San Diego	Padgett, Abigail	'93 - 5	Barbara Joan "Bo" Bradley	child abuse investigator
San Diego	Padgett, Abigail	'98 - 2	Blue McCarron	lesbian social psychologist
San Diego	Robitaille, Julie	'92 - 2	Kit Powell	TV sports reporter
San Diego	Steinberg, Janice	'95 - 5	Margo Simon	Public Radio reporter
San Diego	Wallace, Patricia	'88 - 4	Sydney Bryant	private investigator
San Francisco	Bryan, Kate	'98 - 2	Maggie Maguire	ex-Pinkerton agent
San Francisco	Chittenden, Margaret	'96 - 4	Charlie Plato & Zack Hunter	country-western tavern owners
San Francisco	Day, Dianne	'95 - 6	Fremont Jones	1900s typewriting-business owner
San Francisco	Drury, Joan M.	'93 - 3	Tyler Jones	lesbian activist newspaper columnist
San Francisco	Grant, Linda	'88 - 6	Catherine Sayler	single-mother corporate P.I.
San Francisco	King, Laurie R.	'93 - 3	Kate Martinelli & Alonzo Hawkin	SFPD homicide detectives
San Francisco	Matera, Lia	'88 - 5	Laura Di Palma	high-profile attorney
San Francisco	Matera, Lia	'87 - 7	Willa Jansson	Red diaper baby turned attorney
San Francisco	McAllester, Melanie	'94 - 2	Elizabeth Mendoza	Hispanic-black lesbian homicide detective
San Francisco	Muller, Marcia	'77 -20	Sharon McCone	legal investigator turned P.I.
San Francisco	O'Marie, Carol A., Sr.	'84 - 8	Mary Helen, Sister	70-something nun
San Francisco	Pence, Joanne	'93 - 6	Angelina Amalfi	freelance food writer
San Francisco	Pincus, Elizabeth	'92 - 3	Nell Fury	lesbian P.I.
San Francisco	Smith, Julie	'85 - 2	Paul MacDonald	ex-reporter mystery writer
San Francisco	Smith, Julie	'82 - 5	Rebecca Schwartz	defense attorney
San Francisco	Taylor, Elizabeth A.	'81 - 3	Maggie Elliott	ex-film maker turned P.I.
San Francisco	Taylor, Jean	'95 - 2	Maggie Garrett	young lesbian P.I.
San Francisco	Warmbold, Jean	'86 - 3	Sarah Calloway	magazine journalist
San Francisco	White, Gloria	'91 - 4	Veronica 'Ronnie' Ventana	Anglo-Mexican private eye
San Francisco	Wings, Mary	'86 - 4	Emma Victor	lesbian activist private eye
San Francisco	Yarbro, Chelsea Quinn	'76 - 4	Charles Spotted Moon	attorney-Ojibway tribal shaman
San Jose	Sims, L.V.	'87 - 3	Dixie T. Struthers	police sergeant
San Madera	Coburn, Laura	'95 - 4	Kate Harrod	single-mother police detective
San Raphael	Roberts, Gillian	'98 - 1	Emma Howe & Billie August	50-yr-old P.I. & single-mom partner
Santa Barbara	Muller, Marcia	'83 - 3	Elena Oliverez	Mexican arts museum curator
Santa Cruz	Crum, Laura	'94 - 4	Gail McCarthy	horse veterinarian
Santa Monica	Weston, Carolyn	'72 - 3	Casey Kellog & Al Krug	college-grad cop & hard-bitten partner
Santa Teresa	Grafton, Sue	'82 -14	Kinsey Millhone	blue-collar ex-cop P.I.

Setting	Author	1 - #	Series Character	Occupation

United States

California (CA)

Setting	Author	1 - #	Series Character	Occupation
Silicon Valley	Chapman, Sally	'91 - 4	Juliet Blake	computer fraud investigator
Southern	Maxwell, A.E.	'85 - 8	Fiddler & Fiora Flynn	knight-errant & investment banker
Southern	Nielsen, Helen	'51 - 5	Simon Drake	transplanted Chicago attorney
Southern	Sawyer, Corinne Holt	'88 - 8	Angela Benbow & Caledonia Wingate	70-something admirals' widows
Southern	Silva, Linda Kay	'91 - 5	Delta Stevens	gay woman police officer
Southern	Steiner, Susan	'91 - 2	Alexandra Winter	red-haired investigator
Surf City	Guiver, Patricia	'97 - 3	Delilah Doolittle	British widow pet detective
Walnut Hills	Jacobs, Jonnie	'94 - 3	Kate Austen	suburban single mother

Colorado (CO)

Setting	Author	1 - #	Series Character	Occupation
	Oliphant, B.J.	'90 - 7	Shirley McClintock	50-something rancher
Aspen	Schier, Norma	'78 - 4	Kay Barth	district attorney
Aspen Meadow	Davidson, Diane Mott	'90 - 8	Goldy Bear Schultz	detecting caterer
Boulder	Cail, Carol	'93 - 3	Maxey Burnell	investigative reporter
Boulder	O'Kane, Leslie	'98 - 2	Allida Babcock	dog psychologist
Colorado Springs	Dietz, Denise	'92 - 2	Ellie Bernstein	diet group leader
Cutler	Lewis, Sherry	'95 - 5	Fred Vickery	70-something retiree
Denver	Allen, Kate	'93 - 4	Alison Kaine	lesbian leather cop
Denver	Johnson, Dolores	'97 - 3	Mandy Dyer	owner of Dyer's Cleaners
Denver	Jordan, Jennifer	'92 - 2	Kristin Ashe	amateur sleuth
Denver	Jorgensen, Christine T.	'94 - 4	Stella the Stargazer	astrologer & lovelorn columnist
Denver	McConnell, Vicki P.	'82 - 3	Nyla Wade	lesbian journalist
Denver	Montgomery, Yvonne	'87 - 2	Finny Aletter	stockbroker turned carpenter
Denver	Orde, A.J.	'89 - 6	Jason Lynx	antiques dealer and decorator
Timber City	York, Kieran	'93 - 2	Royce Madison	lesbian deputy sheriff

Connecticut (CT)

Setting	Author	1 - #	Series Character	Occupation
	Berenson, Laurien	'95 - 6	Melanie Travis	special ed teacher and dog lover
	Christmas, Joyce	'93 - 3	Betty Trenka	retired office manager
	Dank, Gloria	'89 - 4	Bernard Woodruff & Snooky Randolph	children's author & his brother-in-law
	Kallen, Lucille	'79 - 5	Maggie Rome & C.B. Greenfield	reporter & editor-publisher
	Kittredge, Mary	'87 - 3	Charlotte Kent	freelance writer
	Wolzien, Valerie	'87 -12	Susan Henshaw	upscale suburban housewife
Hartford	Lackey, Mercedes	'89 - 3	Diana Tregarde	investigator of unnatural events
New Haven	Kittredge, Mary	'90 - 6	Edwina Crusoe	RN and medical consultant
Raven's Wing	McShea, Susanna Hofmann	'90 - 3	Mildred Bennett & friends	quartet of senior sleuths
Riverdale	Travis, Elizabeth	'89 - 2	Ben & Carrie Porter	husband & wife book publishers

District of Columia (DC)

Setting	Author	1 - #	Series Character	Occupation
Washington	Dominic, R.B.	'68 - 7	Ben Safford	Democratic Congressman from Ohio
Washington	Fromer, Margot J.	'91 - 2	Amanda Knight	hospital director of nursing
Washington	Johnson, Barbara	'95 - 2	Colleen Fitzgerald	lesbian insurance investigator
Washington	Law, Janice	'76 - 9	Anna Peters	oil company executive turned P.I.
Washington	Michaels, Barbara	'68 - 3	Georgetown house	historic home
Washington	Mickelbury, Penny	'98 - 2	Carole Ann Gibson	black criminal defense attorney
Washington	Mickelbury, Penny	'94 - 2	Gianna Maglione & Mimi Patterson	lesbian police lieutenant & reporter
Washington	Mikulski, Barbara	'96 - 2	Norie Gorzack	Polish-American U.S. senator
Washington	Nessen, Ron	'95 - 3	Jerry Knight & Jane Day	right-wing radio host & liberal reporter
Washington	Rawlings, Ellen	'97 - 2	Rachel Crowne	Jewish investigative reporter
Washington	Richman, Phyllis	'97 - 2	Chas Wheatley	restaurant critic
Washington	Roberts, Carey	'89 - 2	Anne Fitzhugh	police detective
Washington	Sucher, Dorothy	'88 - 2	Sabina Swift	detective agency owner
Washington	Tone, Teona	'83 - 2	Kyra Keaton	turn-of-the-century P.I.
Washington	Truman, Margaret	'89 - 7	Mackenzie Smith & Annabel Reed	law professor & gallery owner
Washington	Weber, Janice	'92 - 2	Leslie Frost	secret agent and concert violinist

Florida (FL)

Setting	Author	1 - #	Series Character	Occupation
	MacGregor, T.J.	'86 -10	Quin St. James & Mike McCleary	wife & husband P.I. team
	McKernan, Victoria	'90 - 3	Chicago Nordejoong	professional scuba diver
Miami	Buchanan, Edna	'92 - 5	Britt Montero	Cuban-American crime reporter
Miami	Chase, Elaine Raco	'87 - 2	Nikki Holden & Roman Cantrell	investigative reporter & private eye
Miami	Garcia-Aguilera, C.	'96 - 3	Lupe Solano	Cuban-American princess P.I.

Setting	Author	1 - #	Series Character	Occupation
United States				
Florida (FL)				
Miami	Jackson, Hialeah	'98 - 2	Annabelle Hardy-Maratos & Dave the Monkeyman	security specialists
Miami	Parker, Barbara	'94 - 3	Gail Connor	corporate attorney
Miami	Woods, Sherryl	'91 - 4	Molly DeWitt	film promoter and single mother
Panama City	Bartholomew, Nancy	'98 - 2	Sierra Lavotini	exotic dancer
Paradise Cay	Wilson, Karen Ann	'94 - 4	Samantha Holt	veterinary technician
St. Petersburg	Trocheck, Kathy H.	'96 - 2	Truman Kicklighter	retired wire service reporter
Tampa	Arnold, Catherine	'96 - 3	Karen Perry-Mondori	criminal defense attorney
Tango Key	Drake, Alison	'88 - 4	Aline Scott	homicide detective
Georgia (GA)				
Athens	Connor, Beverly	'96 - 3	Lindsay Chamberlain	forensic archaeologist
Atlanta	Coleman, Evelyn	'98 - 2	Pat Conley	black woman journalist
Atlanta	Fitzwater, Judy	'98 - 2	Jennifer Marsh	aspiring mystery novelist
Atlanta	Hooper, Kay	'91 - 2	Lane Montana & Trey Fortier	finder of lost things & homicide detective
Atlanta	Shankman, Sarah	'88 - 7	Samantha Adams	investigative reporter
Atlanta	Sibley, Celestine	'57 - 6	Kate Kincaid Mulcay	veteran newspaperwoman
Atlanta	Sprinkle, Patricia H.	'88 - 7	Sheila Travis	embassy wife turned executive
Atlanta	Trocheck, Kathy H.	'92 - 7	Callahan Garrity	ex-cop cleaning service operator
Atlanta	Woods, Sherryl	'89 - 9	Amanda Roberts	ex-NYC investigative reporter
Delphi	Iakovou, Takis & Judy	'96 - 2	Nick & Julia Lambros	college-town cafe owners
Dunston County	Lanier, Virginia	'95 - 4	Jo Beth Sidden	search-and-rescue bloodhound trainer
Hopemore	Sprinkle, Patricia H.	'97 - 2	MacLaren Yarbrough	business-owner turned magistrate
Lawrenceton	Harris, Charlaine	'90 - 6	Aurora Teagarden	librarian turned real estate agent
Savannah	Tan, Maureen	'97 - 2	Jane Nichols	secret agent turned mystery writer
Hawaii (HI)				
	Sheridan, Juanita	'49 - 4	Lily Wu & Janice Cameron	Asian sleuth & novelist roommate
Illinois (IL)				
	Pulver, Mary Monica	'87 - 5	Peter & Kori Price Brichter	police detective & horse breeder
Chicago	Baker, Nikki	'91 - 3	Virginia Kelly	black lesbian stockbroker
Chicago	Churchill, Jill	'89 - 11	Jane Jeffry	suburban single mother
Chicago	D'Amato, Barbara	'90 - 7	Cat Marsala	freelance investigative journalist
Chicago	D'Amato, Barbara	'80 - 2	Gerritt DeGraaf	forensic pathologist
Chicago	D'Amato, Barbara	'96 - 2	Suze Figueroa & Norm Bennis	pair of cops
Chicago	Dymmoch, Michael A.	'93 - 3	John Thinnes & Jack Caleb	cop & gay psychiatrist
Chicago	Elrod, P.N.	'90 - 7	Jack Fleming	1930s reporter turned vampire
Chicago	Haddad, C.A.	'92 - 2	Becky Belski	computer investigator
Chicago	Hartzmark, Gini	'92 - 5	Katherine Prescott Milholland	blueblood corporate attorney
Chicago	Jones, D.J.H.	'93 - 2	Nancy Cook	Chaucer scholar and professor
Chicago	Paretsky, Sara	'82 - 8	V. I. Warshawski	attorney turned P.I.
Chicago	Petit, Diane	'97 - 3	Kathryn Bogert	owner of an estate sale business
Chicago	Skom, Edith	'89 - 3	Elizabeth Austin	English professor
Chicago suburb	Brod, D.C.	'89 - 4	Quint McCauley	ex-cop turned private eye
Evanston	Godfrey, Ellen	'99 - 3	Janet Barkin	high school dropout
Lincoln Prairie	Bland, Eleanor Taylor	'92 - 7	Marti MacAlister	widowed black police detective
Oak Park	Matthews, Alex	'96 - 3	Cassidy McCabe	psychotherapist
River Depths	Maney, Mabel	'93 - 3	Nancy Clue	gay-lesbian Nancy Drew parody
River Ridge	Fiedler, Jacqueline	'98 - 2	Caroline Canfield	wildlife artist
Indiana (IN)				
Oliver	Frommer, Sara H.	'86 - 3	Joan Spencer	symphony orchestra manager
South Bend	Dams, Jeanne M.	'99 - 2	Hilda Johansson	turn-of-the-century Swedish housemaid
Southern	Carlson, P.M.	'92 - 2	Marty LaForte Hopkins	deputy sheriff mom
Kansas (KS)				
Hampstead	Weir, Charlene	'92 - 4	Susan Wren	ex-cop turned police chief
Kentucky (KY)				
Hamilton	Morgan, Kate	'90 - 7	Dewey James	60-something small-town librarian
Lexington	Hightower, Lynn S.	'93 - 1	Lena Padget	private investigator
Louisville	McCafferty, Barbara T.	'96 - 3	Bert & Nan Tatum	identical twin sisters
Louisville	McClellan, Tierney	'95 - 4	Schuyler Ridgway	40-something real estate agent
North Homage	Woodworth, Deborah	'97 - 2	Rose Callahan	1930s Shaker sister
Pigeon Fork	McCafferty, Taylor	'90 - 6	Haskell Blevins	small-town private eye

Setting	Author	1 - #	Series Character	Occupation

United States

Louisiana (LA)

Setting	Author	1 - #	Series Character	Occupation
	Ennis, Catherine	'91 - 2	Bernadette Hebert	lesbian crime lab expert
New Orleans	Dunbar, Sophie	'93 - 5	Claire Claiborne	beauty salon owner
New Orleans	Fennelly, Tony	'94 - 2	Margo Fortier	ex-stripper turned columnist
New Orleans	Fennelly, Tony	'85 - 3	Matthew Arthur Sinclair	gay epileptic D.A. turned store owner
New Orleans	Hambly, Barbara	'97 - 2	Benjamin January	1830s Paris-trained black doctor
New Orleans	Redmann, J.M.	'90 - 3	Michelle 'Micky' Knight	gay woman private eye
New Orleans	Smith, Julie	'90 - 8	Skip Langdon	6-ft. police detective
New Orleans	Wiltz, Chris	'81 - 3	Neal Rafferty	3rd-generation cop turned P.I.

Maine (ME)

Setting	Author	1 - #	Series Character	Occupation
	Kenney, Susan	'83 - 3	Roz Howard & Alan Stewart	American professor & British painter
	Saum, Karen	'90 - 3	Brigid Donovan	50-something lesbian ex-nun
Bar Harbor	Morison, B.J.	'82 - 5	Elizabeth Lamb Worthington	precocious adolescent girl
Cabot Cove	Fletcher, Jessica	'89 - 11	Jessica Fletcher	60-something mystery writer
Eastport	Graves, Sarah	'98 - 3	Jacobia Triptree	ex-investment banker
Portland	Bushell, Agnes	'89 - 2	Wilson & Wilder	lesbian private eye duo
Rufford	Lawrence, Margaret	'96 - 3	Hannah Trevor	18th century widwife
Tinker's Cove	Meier, Leslie	'93 - 4	Lucy Stone	sleuthing mother of four

Maryland (MD)

Setting	Author	1 - #	Series Character	Occupation
Anne Arundel Co.	Lee, Barbara	'95 - 3	Eve Elliott	real estate agent
Baltimore	Lippman, Laura	'97 - 4	Tess Monaghan	newspaper reporter turned P.I.
Santimoke Co.	Chappell, Helen	'96 - 3	Hollis Ball & Sam Wescott	reporter & her ex-husband's ghost

Massachusetts (MA)

Setting	Author	1 - #	Series Character	Occupation
Aleford	Page, Katherine Hall	'90 - 9	Faith Sibley Fairchild	caterer and minister's wife
Balaclava Co.	MacLeod, Charlotte	'78 - 10	Peter Shandy & Helen Marsh Shandy	botany professor & librarian wife
Berkshires	Goldstone, Nancy	'95 - 2	Elizabeth Halperin	single-mother mystery writer
Boston	Barnes, Linda	'87 - 7	Carlotta Carlyle	6'1" cab-driving ex-cop P.I.
Boston	Barnes, Linda	'82 - 4	Michael Spraggue	wealthy actor ex-private eye
Boston	Belfort, Sophie	'86 - 3	Molly Rafferty	college history professor
Boston	Borthwick, J.S.	'82 - 9	Sarah Deane & Alex McKenzie	English professor & internist
Boston	Coker, Carolyn	'84 - 5	Andrea Perkins	art historian & restorer
Boston	Dreher, Sarah	'85 - 7	Stoner McTavish	lesbian travel agent
Boston	Farrelly, Gail E.	'95 - 2	Lisa King	finance professor and CPA
Boston	Flora, Kate Clark	'94 - 5	Thea Kozak	educational consultant
Boston	Lamb, J. Dayne	'93 - 3	Teal Stewart	Certified Public Accountant
Boston	Lee, Wendi	'94 - 3	Angela Matelli	ex-Marine turned P.I.
Boston	Logan, Margaret	'94 - 2	Olivia Chapman	interior decorator
Boston	MacLeod, Charlotte	'79 - 12	Sarah Kelling & Max Bittersohn	investigative couple
Boston	Neely, Barbara	'92 - 3	Blanche White	black domestic worker
Boston	Sullivan, Winona	'93 - 3	Cecile Buddenbrooks	licensed P.I. heiress-nun
Boston	Wells, Tobias	'66 - 16	Knute Severson	police officer
Bracebridge	Miles, Margaret	'98 - 2	Charlotte Willett & Richard Longfellow	Colonial farm woman & scientist-farmer
Braeton	Waltch, Lilla M.	'87 - 2	Lisa Davis	newspaper reporter
Brookport	Smith-Levin, Judith	'96 - 3	Starletta DuVall	6-ft. black homicide lieutenant
Cambridge	Allen, Irene	'92 - 4	Elizabeth Elliot	widowed Quaker meeting clerk
Cambridge	Conant, Susan	'89 - 11	Holly Winter	dog trainer & magazine columnist
Cambridge	Kelly, Susan	'85 - 6	Liz Connors	freelance crime writer
Cambridge	Knight, Kathryn Lasky	'86 - 4	Calista Jacobs	illustrator of children's books
Cambridge	Langton, Jane	'64 - 13	Homer Kelly	ex-cop turned Harvard professor
Cambridge	Thomas-Graham, Pamela	'98 - 2	Nikki Chase	black economics professor
Cape Cod	Gunning, Sally	'90 - 10	Peter Bartholomew	odd-jobs company owner
Cape Cod	Lee, Marie	'95 - 3	Marguerite Smith	retired science teacher
Enfield	Dobson, Joanne	'97 - 3	Karen Pelletier	single-mother English professor
Mellingham	Oleksiw, Susan	'93 - 3	Joe Silva	small-town chief of police
Nantucket	Mathews, Francine	'94 - 4	Meredith Folger	police detective
Port Frederick	Pickard, Nancy	'84 - 10	Jenny Cain	New England foundation director
Revere Beach	Minichino, Camille	'97 - 3	Gloria Lamerino	50-something physicist
Wading River	Wender, Theodora	'85 - 2	Glad Gold & Alden Chase	English professor & police chief

Setting	Author	1 - #	Series Character	Occupation

United States

Michigan (MI)

Setting	Author	1 - #	Series Character	Occupation
Ann Arbor	Gosling, Paula	'85 - 2	Jack Stryker & Kate Trevorne	homicide cop & English professor
Blackwater Bay	Holtzer, Susan	'94 - 5	Anneke Haagen	computer consultant
Center City	Gosling, Paula	'92 - 4	Matt Gabriel	sheriff
Detroit	Hayden, G. Miki	'98 - 2	Dennis Astin	psychopharmacologist
Leelanau Penin.	Szymanski, Therese	'97 - 4	Brett Higgins	lesbian adult bookstore manager
Upper Penin.	Cogan, Priscilla	'97 - 2	Meggie O'Connor	practicing psychologist
Western	Braun, Lilian Jackson	'66 -21	Jim Qwilleran, Koko & Yum Yum	ex-police reporter & cats
	Dereske, Jo	'96 - 3	Ruby Crane	questioned-documents expert

Minnesota (MN)

Setting	Author	1 - #	Series Character	Occupation
Excelsior	Douglas, Carole Nelson	'85 - 2	Kevin Blake	psychiatrist
Minneapolis	Ferris, Monica	'99 - 2	Betsy Devonshire	needlework shop owner
Minneapolis	Hart, Ellen	'89 - 8	Jane Lawless	lesbian restaurateur
Minneapolis	Hart, Ellen	'94 - 4	Sophie Greenway	food critic and magazine editor
Minneapolis	Jacobs, Nancy Baker	'91 - 3	Devon MacDonald	ex-teacher private eye
Rutherford	Taylor, L.A.	'83 - 4	J.J. Jamison	computer engineer
	Gunn, Elizabeth	'97 - 2	Jake Hines	small town police detective

Missouri (MO)

Setting	Author	1 - #	Series Character	Occupation
Branson	Buckstaff, Kathryn	'94 - 2	Emily Stone	Florida-based travel writer
Kansas City	McClellan, Janet	'97 - 3	Tru North	lesbian police detective
Kansas City	Temple, Lou Jane	'96 - 4	Heaven Lee	trendy restaurant owner-chef
New Kassel	MacPherson, Rett	'97 - 2	Torie O'Shea	historian-genealogist-tour guide
St. Louis	Dreyer, Eileen	'95 - 2	Molly Burke	death investigator
St. Louis	Hamilton, Laurell K.	'93 - 8	Anita Blake	reanimator and vampire hunter
St. Louis	Kennett, Shirley	'96 - 4	P.J. Gray	police dept. virtual reality expert
St. Louis	Marcy, Jean	'97 - 2	Meg Darcy	blue-collar lesbian private eye
St. Louis	McKitterick, Molly	'92 - 2	William Hecklepeck	egotistical television anchor
St. Louis	Viets, Elaine	'97 - 4	Francesca Vierling	6-ft. newspaper columnist
Victoria Springs	Hager, Jean	'94 - 5	Tess Darcy	Ozarks bed & breakfast owner

Mississippi (MS)

Setting	Author	1 - #	Series Character	Occupation
Jackson	Dixon, Louisa	'98 - 3	Laura Owen	state public safety commissioner

Montana (MT)

Setting	Author	1 - #	Series Character	Occupation
Billings	Andreae, Christine	'92 - 3	Lee Squires	camp cook & poet
Blue Deer	Prowell, Sandra West	'93 - 3	Phoebe Siegel	ex-cop P.I.
Merciful Valley	Harrison, Jamie	'95 - 3	Jules Clement	30-something archaeologist turned sheriff
	Morrone, Wenda W.	'01 - 1	Claud Willetts	small-town sheriff

Nevada (NV)

Setting	Author	1 - #	Series Character	Occupation
Lake Tahoe	O'Shaughnessy, P.	'95 - 4	Nina Reilly	single-mother attorney
Las Vegas	Douglas, Carole N.	'92 - 9	Temple Barr & Midnight Louie	PR freelancer & tomcat sleuth
Reno	Dain, Catherine	'92 - 7	Freddie O'Neal	plane-flying keno-playing P.I.

New Hampshire (NH)

Setting	Author	1 - #	Series Character	Occupation
Dovekey	Yeager, Dorian	'94 - 2	Elizabeth Will	watercolorist-gallery owner

New Jersey (NJ)

Setting	Author	1 - #	Series Character	Occupation
Atlantic City	Tesler, Nancy	'97 - 3	Carrie Carlin	single-mother biofeedback clinician
Fishersville	Rubino, Jane	'96 - 3	Cat Austen & Victor Cardenas	single-mom reporter & police detective
Newark	Gallison, Kate	'95 - 5	Lavinia Grey	Episcopal vicar
Oceanside Hts	Wesley, Valerie W.	'94 - 5	Tamara Hayle	black ex-cop single-mother P.I.
Spring Lake	Sherman, Beth	'98 - 2	Anne Hardaway	ghostwriter
Trenton	Waterhouse, Jane	'95 - 3	Garner Quin	best-selling true crime writer
Trenton	Evanovich, Janet	'94 - 4	Stephanie Plum	lingerie buyer turned bounty hunter
	Gallison, Kate	'86 - 3	Nick Magaracz	private investigator

New Mexico (NM)

Setting	Author	1 - #	Series Character	Occupation
Albuquerque	Davis, Val	'96 - 3	Nicolette Scott	UC-Berkeley archaeologist
Albuquerque	Moore, Barbara	'83 - 2	Gordon Christy	veterinarian
Las Cruces	Shelton, Connie	'95 - 4	Charlie Parker	CPA turned investigator
Santa Fe	Van Gieson, Judith	'88 - 8	Neil Hamel	attorney & investigator
Sante Fe	Schumacher, Aileen	'96 - 3	Tory Travers	structural engineer
Shiprock	Dawkins, Cecil	'93 - 2	Ginevra Prettifield	art museum assistant director
	Lovett, Sarah	'95 - 3	Sylvia Strange	forensic psychologist
	Thurlo, Aimee & D.	'95 - 5	Ella Clah	Navajo FBI agent

Setting	Author	1 - #	Series Character	Occupation

United States

New York (NY)

Setting	Author	1 - #	Series Character	Occupation
	Lawrence, Hilda	'44 - 3	Mark East, B. Petty & B. Pond	Manhattan P.I. & little old ladies
Albany	O'Kane, Leslie	'96 - 3	Molly Masters	greeting card entrepreneur
Brooklyn	Brill, Toni	'91 - 2	Midge Cohen	children's author fluent in Russian
Brooklyn	Horansky, Ruby	'90 - 2	Nikki Trakos	6-ft. NYPD homicide detective
Brooklyn	Sprague, Gretchen	'97 - 4	Martha Patterson	retired attorney turned pro bono
Brooklyn	Stein, Triss	'93 - 2	Kay Engles	nationally-known reporter
Brooklyn	Stevens, Serita	'91 - 2	Fanny Zindel	Jewish grandmother
Brooklyn	Tyre, Peg	'94 - 2	Kate Murray	novice crime reporter
Brooklyn	Wheat, Carolyn	'83 - 6	Cass Jameson	Legal Aid defense attorney
Buffalo	Furie, Ruthe	'95 - 3	Fran Kirk	ex-battered wife turned fledgling P.I.
Hemlock Falls	Bishop, Claudia	'94 - 6	Sarah & Meg Quilliam	inn owner & chef sisters
Long Island	Watson, Clarissa	'77 - 5	Persis Willum	artist and gallery assistant
New York	Amato, Angela	'98 - 2	Gerry Conte	undercover cop turned defense attorney
New York	Babbin, Jacqueline	'72 - 2	Clovis Kelly	homicide cop turned crime consultant
New York	Barrett, Margaret	'98 - 2	Susan Given	asset forfeiture prosecutor
New York	Benjamin, Carole Lea	'96 - 3	Rachel Alexander & Dash	dog trainer turned P.I. & pitbull sidekick
New York	Bennett, Liza	'89 - 2	Peg Goodenough	ad agency creative director
New York	Berry, Carole	'87 - 7	Bonnie Indermill	tap-dancing Manhattan office temp
New York	Boylan, Eleanor	'89 - 5	Clara Gamadge	widow of Henry the forgery expert
New York	Brennan, Carol	'94 - 2	Emily Silver	New York actress
New York	Brennan, Carol	'91 - 2	Liz Wareham	40-ish public relations consultant
New York	Bugg, Carole	'99 - 3	Claire Rawlings	book editor with 12-year-old ward
New York	Byfield, Barbara N.	'75 - 4	Simon Bede & Helen Bullock	Episcopal priest & photographer
New York	Carlson, P.M.	'85 - 8	Maggie Ryan	coed turned statistician mom
New York	Carter, Charlotte	'97 - 2	Nanette Hayes	young black tenor sax player
New York	Christmas, Joyce	'88 - 9	Margaret Priam	English noblewoman
New York	Crespi, Camilla	'91 - 7	Simona Griffo	gourmet cook ad executive
New York	Cross, Amanda	'64 -12	Kate Fansler	feminist English professor
New York	Davis, Dorothy S.	'57 - 3	Jasper Tully & Mrs. Norris	DA's investigator & Scottish housekeeper
New York	Davis, Dorothy S.	'76 - 4	Julie Hayes	actress turned columnist and fortuneteller
New York	Dentinger, Jane	'83 - 6	Jocelyn O'Roarke	Broadway actor and director
New York	Edghill, Rosemary	'94 - 3	Karen Hightower aka Bast	white witch graphic designer
New York	Edwards, Grace F.	'97 - 2	Mali Anderson	black ex-cop in Harlem
New York	Eichler, Selma	'94 - 6	Desiree Shapiro	5'2" queen-size P.I.
New York	Fairstein, Linda	'96 - 3	Alexandra Cooper	chief sex crimes prosecutor
New York	Farrell, Gillian B.	'92 - 2	Annie McGrogan	actor-P.I. returned from LA
New York	Frankel, Valerie	'91 - 4	Wanda Mallory	detective agency owner
New York	Fulton, Eileen	'88 - 6	Nina McFall & Dino Rossi	TV soap star & NYPD lieutenant
New York	Glass, Leslie	'93 - 4	April Woo	Chinese-American police detective
New York	Gray, Gallagher	'91 - 4	Theodore S. Hubbert & Auntie Lil	retired personnel manager & dress designer
New York	Green, Edith Pinero	'77 - 3	Dearborn V. Pinch	70-something ladies man
New York	Hayter, Sparkle	'94 - 4	Robin Hudson	cable news reporter
New York	Holland, Isabelle	'83 - 6	Claire Aldington	Episcopal priest
New York	Hyde, Eleanor	'95 - 2	Lydia Miller	30-something fashion editor
New York	Kelly, Mary Anne	'90 - 3	Claire Breslinsky	freelance photographer
New York	Lathen, Emma	'61 -24	John Putnam Thatcher	Wall Street financial whiz
New York	Lordon, Randye	'93 - 5	Sydney Sloane	lesbian private investigator
New York	Lorens, M.K.	'90 - 5	Winston Marlowe Sherman	mystery-writing Shakespeare professor
New York	Lyons, Nan & Ivan	'76 - 2	Natasha O'Brien & Millie Ogden	pair of culinary artists
New York	Maiman, Jaye	'91 - 6	Robin Miller	lesbian travel & romance writer turned P.I.
New York	Maron, Margaret	'81 - 8	Sigrid Harald	police lieutenant
New York	Matteson, Stefanie	'90 - 8	Charlotte Graham	Oscar-winning actress
New York	McCafferty, Jeanne	'94 - 3	Mackenzie Griffin	consulting criminal psychologist
New York	Meyers, Annette	'99 - 1	Olivia Brown	1920s Greenwich Village poet P.I.
New York	Meyers, Annette	'89 - 7	Xenia Smith & Leslie Wetzon	Wall Street headhunters
New York	Meyers, Maan	'92 - 6	The Tonnemans	New Amsterdam family
New York	Moore, Miriam Ann	'97 - 2	Marti Hirsch	would-be writer and disco lover
New York	Morrone, Wenda W.	'97 - 2	Lorelei Muldoon	high-profile numbers analyst
New York	Nadelson, Reggie	'95 - 3	Artie Cohen	39-year-old Russian-born cop
New York	O'Connell, Carol	'94 - 4	Kathleen Mallory	lone-wolf police sergeant
New York	O'Donnell, Lillian	'90 - 4	Gwenn Ramadge	corporate investigator
New York	O'Donnell, Lillian	'77 - 3	Mici Anhalt	criminal justice investigator
New York	O'Donnell, Lillian	'72 -16	Norah Mulcahaney	police detective
New York	OCork, Shannon	'80 - 3	Theresa Tracy Baldwin	sports news photographer

Setting	Author	1 - #	Series Character	Occupation

United States

New York (NY)

Setting	Author	1 - #	Series Character	Occupation
New York	Papazoglou, Orania	'84 - 5	Patience Campbell McKenna	6-ft. romance novelist turned crime writer
New York	Paul, Barbara	'84 - 3	Enrico Caruso & Geraldine Farrar	Italian tenor & American soprano
New York	Paul, Barbara	'84 - 7	Marian Larch	no-nonsense NYPD officer
New York	Peters, Elizabeth	'72 - 4	Jacqueline Kirby	librarian turned romance novelist
New York	Piesman, Marissa	'89 - 6	Nina Fischman	legal services attorney
New York	Reuben, Shelly	'94 - 2	Wylie Nolan & Max Bramble	arson investigator & attorney
New York	Robb, J.D.	'95 - 8	Eve Dallas	21st century NYPD lieutenant
New York	Robinson, Leah Ruth	'88 - 2	Evelyn Sutcliffe	emergency medicine resident
New York	Rozan, S.J.	'94 - 6	Lydia Chin & Bill Smith	Chinese-American & Army-brat P.I. duo
New York	Santini, Rosemarie	'86 - 2	Rick & Rosie Caesare Ramsey	husband & wife sleuths
New York	Scoppettone, Sandra	'91 - 5	Lauren Laurano	lesbian private investigator
New York	Shaffer, Louise	'94 - 2	Angie DaVito	daytime television producer
New York	Smith, Evelyn E.	'86 - 4	Susan Melville	freelance assassin-painter
New York	Smith, J.C.S.	'80 - 2	Quentin Jacoby	retired transit cop
New York	Star, Nancy	'98 - 2	May Morrison	TV talk show producer
New York	Tucker, Kerry	'91 - 4	Libby Kincaid	magazine photographer
New York	Uhnak, Dorothy	'68 - 3	Christine Opara	20-something police detective
New York	Whitney, Polly	'94 - 4	Ike Tygart & Abby Abagnarro	network producer & TV news director
New York	Wilhelm, Kate	'87 - 6	Charlie Meiklejohn & Constance Leidl	P.I. & psychologist
New York	Wilson, Barbara Jaye	'97 - 3	Brenda Midnight	Greenwich Village milliner
New York	Yeager, Dorian	'92 - 4	Victoria Bowering	6 ft-redhead sometime-actress
New York	Zukowski, Sharon	'91 - 5	Blaine Stewart	ex-cop turned corporate P.I.
Oakwood	Harris, Lee	'92 -11	Christine Bennett	former nun
Rochester	O'Brien, Meg	'90 - 5	Jessica James	investigative reporter
Seneca Falls	Monfredo, Miriam G.	'92 - 6	Glynis Tryon	1860s librarian suffragette
Syracuse	Block, Barbara	'94 - 5	Robin Light	pet store owner
Voorburg-on-Hudson	Churchill, Jill	'99 - 1	Lily & Robert Brewster	sister & brother inn owners in 1930

North Carolina (NC)

Setting	Author	1 - #	Series Character	Occupation
	Maron, Margaret	'92 - 6	Deborah Knott	district judge
	Squire, Elizabeth D..	'94 - 6	Peaches Dann	absent-minded widow
Byerly	Kelner, Toni L.P.	'93 - 6	Laura Fleming	small-town Southern sleuth
Charlotte	Cornwell, Patricia	'97 - 2	Andy Brazil	reporter and volunteer cop
Charlotte	Grant, Anne U.	'98 - 3	Sydney Teague	single-mother ad agency owner
Charlotte	Jaffe, Jody	'95 - 3	Natalie Gold	reporter on horse show circuit
Charlotte	Myers, Tamar	'96 - 6	Abigail Timberlake	antiques dealer
Clearwater	Alexander, Skye	'97 - 3	Charlotte McCrae	Boston astrologer
Durham	Mackay, Amanda	'76 - 2	Hannah Land	divorced New York PhD
Durham	Munger, Katy	'97 - 2	Casey Jones	unlicensed private eye
Greenfield	Sleem, Patty	'97 - 2	Maggie Dillitz	Methodist woman clergy
Raleigh	Shaber, Sarah R.	'97 - 2	Simon Shaw	young history professor

Ohio (OH)

Setting	Author	1 - #	Series Character	Occupation
	Wright, Sally S.	'97 - 2	Ben Reese	1960s university archivist
Cincinnati	Borton, D.B.	'93 - 6	Cat Caliban	60-something P.I.-in-training
Cincinnati	Hightower, Lynn S.	'95 - 3	Sonora Blair	homicide detective
Cincinnati	John, Cathie	'97 - 4	Kate Cavanaugh	gourmet caterer
Cincinnati	Short, Sharon Gwyn	'94 - 3	Patricia Delaney	computer-whiz investigator
Columbus	Glen, Alison	'92 - 2	Charlotte Sams	freelance writer
Eden	Borton, Della	'99 - 1	Gilda Liberty	small-town movie theater proprietor
Palmer	Cleary, Melissa	'92 -10	Jackie Walsh & Jake	film instructor & ex-police dog
Southern	Westfall, Patricia T.	'96 - 2	Molly West	50-something rural activist

Oklahoma (OK)

Setting	Author	1 - #	Series Character	Occupation
	Hart, Carolyn G.	'93 - 4	Henrietta O'Dwyer Collins	70-something reporter
	Medawar, Mardi Oakley	'96 - 3	Tay-bodal	19th century Kiowa healer
Buckskin	Hager, Jean	'89 - 5	Mitch Bushyhead	police chief of Cherokee descent
Frontier City	Haddock, Lisa	'94 - 2	Carmen Ramirez	lesbian newspaper copy editor
Holton	Sandstrom, Eve K.	'90 - 3	Sam & Nicky Titus	ex-CID sheriff & photographer wife
Prophesy County	Cooper, Susan Rogers	'88 - 6	Milton Kovak	chief deputy
Tahlequah	Hager, Jean	'92 - 4	Molly Bearpaw	Cherokee civil rights investigator
Vamoose	Feddersen, Connie	'93 - 6	Amanda Hazard	sexy small-town CPA

Setting	Author	1 - #	Series Character	Occupation

United States

Oregon (OR)

Setting	Author	1 - #	Series Character	Occupation
	Wallingford, Lee	'91 - 2	Ginny Trask & Frank Carver	U.S. Forest Service officers
Cedar Hills	Calloway, Kate	'96 - 7	Cassidy James	rookie lesbian private eye
Coastal	Wren, M.K.	'73 - 8	Conan Flagg	secret agent turned bookstore owner
Eugene	Wilhelm, Kate	'91 - 4	Barbara Holloway	defense attorney
Lavner Bay	Douglas, Lauren W.	'96 - 2	Allison O'Neil	lesbian B & B owner
Lincoln City	Rushford, Patricia H.	'97 - 3	Helen Bradley	ex-cop travel-writer grandmother
Mackie	Thrasher, L.L.	'91 - 2	Zachariah Smith	ex-cop private eye
Taft County	Wren, M.K.	'99 - 1	Neely Jones	black woman sheriff-elect

Pennsylvania (PA)

Setting	Author	1 - #	Series Character	Occupation
	McCormick, Claire	'82 - 3	John Waltz	executive recruiter
Conover	Greth, Roma	'88 - 2	Hana Shaner	40-something heiress
Hernia	Myers, Tamar	'94 - 8	Magdalena Yoder	Mennonite inn owner-operator
Lickin Creek	Malmont, Valerie S.	'94 - 2	Tori Miracle	crime writer turned novelist
Philadelphia	Bacon-Smith, Camille	'96 - 2	Kevin Bradley	daemon art recovery specialist
Philadelphia	Haddam, Jane	'90 -15	Gregor Demarkian	former FBI department head
Philadelphia	Hathaway, Robin	'98 - 2	Andrew Fenimore	old-fashioned cardiologist
Philadelphia	MacDougal, Bonnie	'96 - 3	Jackson, Rieders	large law firm
Philadelphia	Murray, Donna H.	'95 - 5	Ginger Struve Barnes	headmaster's wife and suburban mother
Philadelphia	Roberts, Gillian	'87 - 8	Amanda Pepper	high school English teacher
Philadelphia	Scottoline, Lisa	'93 - 6	Rosato & Associates	all-women law firm
Pittsburgh	Cercone, Karen Rose	'97 - 3	Helen Sorby & Milo Kachigan	social worker & policeman in 1905
Pittsburgh	Claire, Edie	'99 - 3	Leigh Koslow	advertising copywriter

Rhode Island (RI)

Setting	Author	1 - #	Series Character	Occupation
Newport	Kruger, Mary	'94 - 3	Brooke Cassidy & Matt Devlin	1890s debutante & detective husband

South Carolina (SC)

Setting	Author	1 - #	Series Character	Occupation
Broward's Rock	Hart, Carolyn G.	'87 -10	Annie Laurance & Max Darling	bookstore owner & investigator
Otis	Deloach, Nora	'94 - 6	Candi & Simone Covington	black social worker & paralegal daughter

South Dakota (SD)

Setting	Author	1 - #	Series Character	Occupation
Delphi	Taylor, Kathleen	'93 - 4	Tory Bauer	small-town diner waitress

Tennessee (TN)

Setting	Author	1 - #	Series Character	Occupation
	McCrumb, Sharyn	'88 - 2	James Owens Mega	science fiction author professor
	McCrumb, Sharyn	'90 - 5	Spencer Arrowood	Appalachian sheriff
Jesus Creek	Adams, Deborah	'92 - 6	Jesus Creek TN	eccentric small town
Nashville	Tishy, Cecelia	'97 - 2	Kate Banning	music company staff writer

Texas (TX)

Setting	Author	1 - #	Series Character	Occupation
	Banks, Carolyn	'93 - 5	Robin Vaughan	equestrienne sleuth
	Davis, Kaye	'97 - 3	Maris Middleton	lesbian forensic chemist
	Romberg, Nina	'89 - 2	Marian Winchester	Caddo-Comanche medicine woman
	Tell, Dorothy	'90 - 2	Poppy Dillworth	60-something lesbian sleuth
Austin	Amey, Linda	'92 - 2	Blair Emerson	funeral director
Austin	Cooper, Susan R.	'93 - 2	Kimmey Kruse	stand-up comic
Austin	Walker, Mary Willis	'94 - 3	Molly Cates	true crime writer-reporter
Bayport	Wingate, Anne	'88 - 5	Mark Shigata	ex-FBI agent turned sheriff
Black Cat Ridge	Cooper, Susan R.	'92 - 5	E.J. Pugh	housewife-mom romance writer
Canadian	Meredith, D.R.	'88 - 5	John Lloyd Branson & Lydia Fairchild	defense attorney & legal assistant
Crawford Co.	Meredith, D.R.	'84 - 5	Charles Matthews	honest county sheriff
El Povo	Martin, Allana	'96 - 3	Texana Jones	desert trading post owner
Eternal	Kahn, Sharon	'98 - 2	Ruby Rothman	rabbi's widow
Farmer's Mound	Webb, Martha G.	'85 - 2	Smoky O'Donnell	small-town PD narcotics officer
Fort Worth	Martin, Lee	'84 -13	Deb Ralston	police detective mom
Houston	Kiecolt-Glaser, Janice	'97 - 2	Haley McAlister	psychologist and professor
Houston	Powell, Deborah	'91 - 2	Hollis Carpenter	gay woman crime reporter
Houston	Rogers, Chris	'98 - 2	Dixie Flannigan	prosecutor turned bounty hunter
Houston	Stuyck, Karen Hanson	'95 - 3	Liz James	journalist turned PR rep
Job's Crossing	Bell, Nancy	'96 - 2	Biggie Weatherford & J.R.	grandmother & nephew sidekick
Los Santos	Herndon, Nancy	'95 - 6	Elena Jarvis	wise-cracking police detective
Pecan Springs	Albert, Susan Wittig	'92 - 7	China Bayles	herb shop owner & former attorney
Purple Sage	Smith, Barbara B.	'94 - 4	Jolie Wyatt	aspiring novelist
San Antonio	Morell, Mary	'91 - 2	Lucia Ramos	Chicana lesbian police detective

Setting	Author	1 - #	Series Character	Occupation

United States

Utah (UT)

	Moffat, Gwen	'73 -14	Melinda Pink	mountain climbing novelist

Vermont (VT)

	Salter, Anna	'97 - 2	Michael Stone	female forensic psychologist
Branbury	Wright, Nancy Means	'96 - 2	Ruth Willmarth	single-mother farmer
Coolridge Corners	Smith, Alison	'84 - 2	Judd Springfield	small town police chief
Lofton	Comfort, Barbara	'86 - 5	Tish McWhinny	70-something artist-painter

Virginia (VA)

	McCrumb, Sharyn	'84 - 8	Elizabeth MacPherson	forensic anthropologist
Charlottesville	Knight, Phyllis	'92 - 2	Lil Ritchie	ex-rocker and gay woman P.I.
Crozet	Brown, Rita Mae	'90 - 6	Mary Minor Haristeen	small-town postmistress
Fairfax County	English, Brenda	'97 - 2	Sutton McPhee	police reporter
Northern	Ripley, Ann	'94 - 3	Louise Eldridge	organic gardener TV host
Richmond	Cornwell, Patricia	'90 - 9	Kay Scarpetta	chief medical examiner

Washington (WA)

	Elkins, Charlotte & A.	'89 - 3	Lee Ofsted & Graham Sheldon	woman golf pro & homicide detective
	Moody, Skye K.	'96 - 3	Venus Diamond	U.S. Fish & Wildlife agent
Alpine	Daheim, Mary	'92 -11	Emma Lord	small-town newspaper owner-editor
Bellehaven	Dereske, Jo	'94 - 6	Helma Zukas	public librarian
coastal	Youmans, Claire	'96 - 2	Janet Schilling	county chief deputy prosecutor
Seattle	Beck, K.K.	'92 - 4	Jane da Silva	former lounge singer
Seattle	Castle, Jayne	'86 - 4	Guinevere Jones	office-temps business owner
Seattle	Daheim, Mary	'91 -13	Judith McMonigle Flynn	bed & breakfast owner
Seattle	French, Linda	'98 - 3	Teddy Morelli	college history professor
Seattle	Gilpatrick, Noreen	'93 - 2	Kate MacLean	police detective
Seattle	Hendricksen, Louise	'93 - 3	Amy Prescott	crime lab physician
Seattle	Jance, J.A.	'85 -14	J.P. Beaumont	homicide detective
Seattle	Mariz, Linda French	'92 - 2	Laura Ireland	grad student volleyball player
Seattle	Moen, Ruth Raby	'93 - 3	Kathleen O'Shaughnessy	newspaper reporter
Seattle	Murray, Lynne	'97 - 4	Josephine Fuller	Queen-sized private investigator
Seattle	Nunnally, Tiina	'96 - 2	Margit Andersson	freelance Danish translator
Seattle	Smith, Janet L.	'90 - 3	Annie MacPherson	attorney
Seattle	Wilcox, Valerie	'98 - 3	Kellie Montgomery	widowed sailing instructor
Seattle	Wilson, Barbara	'84 - 3	Pam Nilsen	lesbian printing company owner
Seattle	Youmans, Claire	'00 - 1	Sandy Whitacre	attorney in sole practice tort law
Shoalwater	Simonson, Sheila	'90 - 5	Lark Dailey Dodge	6-ft. bookstore owner

West Virginia (WV)

	Hoff, B.J.	'86 - 5	Daniel & Jennifer Kaine	Christian radio station owner & exec asst
	Van Hook, Beverly	'95 - 2	Liza & Dutch Randolph	married amateur sleuths

Wisconsin (WI)

Milwaukee	Barrett, Kathleen A.	'96 - 3	Beth Hartley	attorney turned legal researcher
Milwaukee	McGiffin, Janet	'92 - 3	Maxene St. Clair	emergency room physician

Wyoming (WY)

	Andrews, Sarah	'94 - 4	Em Hansen	oil company geologist
	Caverly, Carol	'94 - 2	Thea Barlow	Western magazine editor
Jackson Hole	McClendon, Lise	'94 - 2	Alix Thorssen	gallery owner and art forgery expert
Roundup	Kellogg, Marne Davis	'95 - 5	Lilly Bennett	US marshal and security firm owner
Sheridan	Landreth, Marsha	'92 - 3	Samantha Turner	medical examiner
Wind River	Coel, Margaret	'95 - 4	John Aloysius O'Malley & Vicky Holden	Jesuit missionary & Arapaho attorney

Other U.S.

	Hightower, Lynn S.	'92 - 4	David Silver & String	homicide cop & alien partner
	Hightower, Lynn S.	'92 - 4	David Silver & String	homicide cop & alien partner
	Pickard, Nancy	'82 - 5	Eugenia Potter	60-something widowed chef
	Hooper, Kay	'87 - 11	Hagen	government agent
	Speart, Jessica	'97 - 3	Rachel Porter	Fish & Wildlife agent
National Parks	Barr, Nevada	'93 - 7	Anna Pigeon	park ranger
National Parks	Dengler, Sandy	'93 - 4	Jack Prester	U.S. park ranger
Northeast	Wolzien, Valerie	'96 - 3	Josie Pigeon	all-women construction firm owner
Southwest	Sandstrom, Eve K.	'97 - 2	Nell Matthews & Mike Svenson	reporter & homicide detective
Western	Lee, Wendi	'89 - 6	Jefferson Birch	P.I. in the Old West

Setting	Author	1 - #	Series Character	Occupation
Wales				
	Taylor, Alison G.	'95 - 3	Michael McKenna	detective chief inspector
Llanfair	Bowen, Rhys	'97 - 3	Evan Evans	village constable
International				
	Arnold, Margot	'79 -12	Penny Spring & Toby Glendower	anthropologist & archaeologist
	Dunnett, Dorothy	'68 - 7	Johnson Johnson	British agent and yachtsman
	Gilman, Dorothy	'66 -13	Emily Pollifax	grandmother CIA agent
	Jackson, Marian J.A.	'90 - 5	Abigail Patience Danforth	19th century American heiress detective
	Livesay, Ann	'98 - 5	Barry Ross	international investigator
	Lynds, Gayle	'96 - 2	Sarah Walker & Liz Sansborough	CIA agents
	Scott, Barbara A.	'93 - 3	Brad Rollins et al	international kidnap-rescue team
	Williams, Amanda Kyle	'90 - 4	Madison McGuire	deep cover intelligence agent

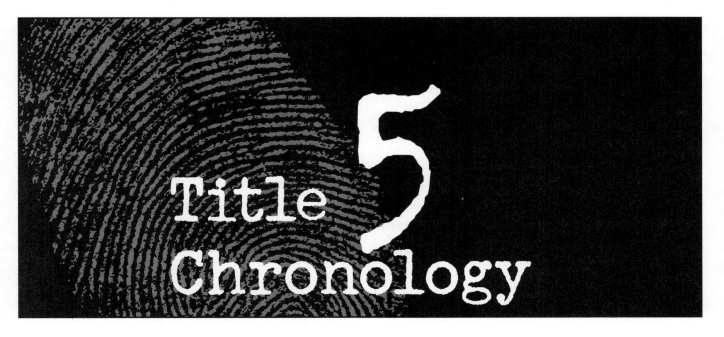

Title 5 Chronology

1967 ◼ Death of an Old Girl (Lemarchand, Elizabeth)
1967 A Different Kind of Summer (Melville, Jennie)
1967 Murder Fantastical (Moyes, Patricia)
1967 Wolf to Slaughter (Rendell, Ruth)
1967 A New Lease of Death [APA- Sins of the Fathers (1970)] (Rendell, Ruth)
1967 Dead by the Light of the Moon (Wells, Tobias)
1967 What Should You Know of Dying? (Wells, Tobias)
1967 The Rose Window (Blanc, Suzanne)
1967 ◼ Foreign Bodies (Petrie, Rhona)
1967 ◼ Roseanna (Sjöwall, Maj & Per Wahlöö)

1968 Henrietta Who? (Aird, Catherine)
1968 The Cat Who Turned On and Off (Braun, Lilian Jackson)
1968 Coffin Following (Butler, Gwendoline)
1968 ◼ Picture Miss Seeton (Crane, Hamilton) ☆
1968 ◼ Murder Sunny Side Up (Dominic, R.B.)
1968 ◼ The Photogenic Soprano [Brit- Dolly and the Singing Bird] (Dunnett, Dorothy)
1968 A Stitch in Time (Lathen, Emma)
1968 Come to Dust (Lathen, Emma)
1968 The Affacombe Affair (Lemarchand, Elizabeth)
1968 ◼ Ammie, Come Home (Michaels, Barbara)
1968 Death and the Dutch Uncle (Moyes, Patricia)
1968 MacLurg Goes West (Petrie, Rhona)
1968 The Man on the Balcony (Sjöwall, Maj & Per Wahlöö)
1968 ◼ The Bait (Uhnak, Dorothy) ★
1968 Murder Most Fouled Up (Wells, Tobias)

1969 The Complete Steel [U.S.- The Stately Home Murder] (Aird, Catherine)
1969 Coffin's Dark Number (Butler, Gwendoline)
1969 Miss Seeton Draws the Line (Crane, Hamilton)
1969 When in Greece (Lathen, Emma) ☆
1969 Murder To Go (Lathen, Emma)
1969 Alibi for a Corpse (Lemarchand, Elizabeth)
1969 The Darkest Hour (Nielsen, Helen)
1969 Despatch of a Dove (Petrie, Rhona)
1969 The Best Man To Die (Rendell, Ruth)
1969 ◼ The Hand of Solange (Rippon, Marion)
1969 The Man Who Went Up in Smoke (Sjöwall, Maj & Per Wahlöö)
1969 The Witness (Uhnak, Dorothy)
1969 The Young Can Die Protesting (Wells, Tobias)
1969 Die Quickly, Dear Mother (Wells, Tobias)

1970s

1970 A Late Phoenix (Aird, Catherine)
1970 A Coffin From the Past (Butler, Gwendoline)
1970 Poetic Justice (Cross, Amanda)
1970 Murder in High Place (Dominic, R.B.)
1970 Murder in the Round [Brit- Dolly and the Cookie Bird] (Dunnett, Dorothy)
1970 The Amazing Mrs. Pollifax (Gilman, Dorothy)
1970 Pick up Sticks (Lathen, Emma)
1970 A New Kind of Killer, An Old Kind of Death [APA- A New Kind of Killer] (Melville, Jennie)
1970 Many Deadly Returns [Brit- Who Saw Her Die?] (Moyes, Patricia) ☆
1970 A Guilty Thing Surprised (Rendell, Ruth)
1970 Behold, the Druid Weeps (Rippon, Marion)
1970 The Laughing Policeman (Sjöwall, Maj & Per Wahlöö) ★
1970 The Ledger (Uhnak, Dorothy) ★
1970 Dinky Died (Wells, Tobias)
1970 ◼ Dead in the Morning (Yorke, Margaret)

1971 ◼ Cover-up Story (Babson, Marian)
1971 Witch Miss Seeton [Brit- Miss Seeton, Bewitched] (Crane, Hamilton)
1971 There is No Justice [Brit- Murder Out of Court] (Dominic, R.B.)
1971 Match for a Murderer [Brit- Dolly and the Doctor Bird] (Dunnett, Dorothy)
1971 Honey on Her Tail (Fickling, G.G.)
1971 The Elusive Mrs. Pollifax (Gilman, Dorothy)

1971 Shroud for a Nightingale (James, P.D.) ★
1971 Ashes to Ashes (Lathen, Emma)
1971 The Longer the Thread (Lathen, Emma)
1971 Death on Doomsday (Lemarchand, Elizabeth)
1971 Season of Snows and Sins (Moyes, Patricia)
1971 No More Dying Then (Rendell, Ruth)
1971 Murder at the Savoy (Sjöwall, Maj & Per Wahlöö)
1971 The Fire Engine That Disappeared (Sjöwall, Maj & Per Wahlöö)
1971 ◼ Not One of Us (Thomson, June)
1971 The Foo Dog [Brit- The Lotus Affair] (Wells, Tobias)
1971 What To Do Until the Undertaker Comes (Wells, Tobias)

1972 ◼ Prime Time Corpse [APA- Bloody Special (1989)] (Babbin, Jacqueline)
1972 Murder on Show [U.S.- Murder at the Cat Show (1989)] (Babson, Marian)
1972 The Theban Mysteries (Cross, Amanda)
1972 Murder in Focus [Brit- Dolly and the Starry Bird] (Dunnett, Dorothy)
1972 Stiff as a Broad [includes Erik March] (Fickling, G.G.)
1972 ◼ An Unsuitable Job for a Woman (James, P.D.) ☆
1972 Murder Without Icing (Lathen, Emma)
1972 Cyanide With Compliments (Lemarchand, Elizabeth)
1972 ◼ The Only Security [U.S.-Troublecross] (Mann, Jessica)
1972 ◼ The Phone Calls (O'Donnell, Lillian)
1972 ◼ The Seventh Sinner (Peters, Elizabeth)
1972 Murder Being Once Done (Rendell, Ruth)
1972 The Abominable Man (Sjöwall, Maj & Per Wahlöö)
1972 A Die in the Country (Wells, Tobias)
1972 How To Kill a Man (Wells, Tobias)
1972 ◼ Poor, Poor Ophelia (Weston, Carolyn)
1972 Silent Witness (Yorke, Margaret)

1973 His Burial Too (Aird, Catherine)
1973 Miss Seeton Sings (Crane, Hamilton)
1973 A Palm for Mrs. Pollifax (Gilman, Dorothy)
1973 Let or Hindrance [U.S.- No Vacation from Murder] (Lemarchand, Elizabeth)
1973 ◼ Lady With a Cool Eye (Moffat, Gwen)
1973 The Curious Affair of the Third Dog (Moyes, Patricia)
1973 The Severed Key (Nielsen, Helen)
1973 Don't Wear Your Wedding Ring (O'Donnell, Lillian)
1973 ◼ Borrower of the Night (Peters, Elizabeth)
1973 Some Lie and Some Die (Rendell, Ruth)
1973 The Locked Room (Sjöwall, Maj & Per Wahlöö)
1973 ◼ Dear Laura [1890s London] (Stubbs, Jean) ☆
1973 Death Cap (Thomson, June)
1973 Brenda's Murder (Wells, Tobias)
1973 ◼ Curiosity Didn't Kill the Cat (Wren, M.K.)
1973 Grave Matters (Yorke, Margaret)

1974 A Coffin for the Canary [U.S.- Sarsen Place] (Butler, Gwendoline)
1974 Epitaph for a Lobbyist (Dominic, R.B.)
1974 Sweet and Low (Lathen, Emma)
1974 Buried in the Past (Lemarchand, Elizabeth)
1974 Dial 557 R-A-P-E (O'Donnell, Lillian)
1974 The Murders of Richard III (Peters, Elizabeth)
1974 The Ninth Tentacle (Rippon, Marion)
1974 The Painted Face [1902 Paris] (Stubbs, Jean)
1974 The Long Revenge (Thomson, June)
1974 Have Mercy Upon Us (Wells, Tobias)
1974 Mortal Remains (Yorke, Margaret)

1975 Slight Mourning (Aird, Catherine)
1975 Odds on Miss Seeton (Crane, Hamilton)
1975 The Black Tower (James, P.D.) ★
1975 Dark Nantucket Noon (Langton, Jane)
1975 By Hook or by Crook (Lathen, Emma)
1975 Captive Audience (Mann, Jessica)
1975 Miss Pink at the Edge of the World (Moffat, Gwen)
1975 Black Widower (Moyes, Patricia)
1975 The Baby Merchants (O'Donnell, Lillian)
1975 ◼ Crocodile on the Sandbank (Peters, Elizabeth)
1975 Shake Hands Forever (Rendell, Ruth)

1975		Cop Killer (Sjöwall, Maj & Per Wahlöö)
1975		Hark, Hark, the Watchdogs Bark (Wells, Tobias)
1975		Susannah Screaming (Weston, Carolyn)
1975	▯	Death of an Angel (Winslow, Pauline Glen)
1975		A Multitude of Sins (Wren, M.K.)
1975	▯	Solemn High Murder [with Frank L. Tedeschi] (Byfield, Barbara Ninde)

1976		Forever Wilt Thou Die [MI] (Byfield, Barbara Ninde)
1976		The Question of Max (Cross, Amanda)
1976	▯	A Death in the Life (Davis, Dorothy Salisbury)
1976		Murder Out of Commission (Dominic, R.B.)
1976		Split Code [Brit- Dolly and the Nanny Bird] (Dunnett, Dorothy)
1976		Mrs. Pollifax on Safari (Gilman, Dorothy)
1976	▯	The Case of the Cold Murderer (Godfrey, Ellen)
1976	▯	Bloody September (Haddad, C.A.)
1976	▯	The Big Pay-off (Law, Janice) ☆
1976		Step in the Dark (Lemarchand, Elizabeth)
1976	▯	Someone Is Killing the Great Chefs of Europe (Lyons, Nan & Ivan)
1976	▯	Death Is Academic (Mackay, Amanda)
1976		Over the Sea to Death (Moffat, Gwen)
1976		A Short Time To Live (Moffat, Gwen)
1976		The Brink of Murder (Nielsen, Helen)
1976		Leisure Dying (O'Donnell, Lillian)
1976		The Terrorists (Sjöwall, Maj & Per Wahlöö)
1976		The Golden Crucible [1906 SF] (Stubbs, Jean)
1976	▯	A Nice Way to Die [U.S.- A Medium for Murder] (Warner, Mignon)
1976		Rouse the Demon (Weston, Carolyn)
1976		The Brandenburg Hotel [prequel] (Winslow, Pauline Glen)
1976	▯	Ogilvie, Tallant and Moon [APA- Bad Medicine (1990)] (Yarbro, Chelsea Quinn)
1976		Cast for Death (Yorke, Margaret)

1977		Parting Breath (Aird, Catherine)
1977		A Harder Thing Than Triumph [MA] (Byfield, Barbara Ninde)
1977	▯	Curtain Fall (Dewhurst, Eileen)
1977	▯	Quiet as a Nun (Fraser, Antonia)
1977	▯	Rotten Apples (Green, Edith Pinero)
1977		Murder Among the Well-to-do (Godfrey, Ellen)
1977		Death of an Expert Witness (James, P. D.)
1977		Gemini Trip (Law, Janice)
1977		Unhappy Returns (Lemarchand, Elizabeth)
1977		The Coconut Killings [Brit- To Kill a Coconut] (Moyes, Patricia)
1977	▯	Edwin of the Iron Shoes (Muller, Marcia)
1977	▯	Aftershock (O'Donnell, Lillian)
1977		Case Closed (Thomson, June)
1977		A Question of Identity (Thomson, June)
1977	▯	The Fourth Stage of Gainsborough Brown (Watson, Clarissa)
1977		A Creature Was Stirring (Wells, Tobias)
1977		The Witch Hill Murder (Winslow, Pauline Glen)
1977		Oh Bury Me Not (Wren, M.K.)

1978		The Wild Island (Fraser, Antonia)
1978		Operation Apricot (Haddad, C.A.)
1978		The Memorial Hall Murder (Langton, Jane)
1978		Double, Double, Oil and Trouble (Lathen, Emma)
1978		Under Orion (Law, Janice)
1978		Suddenly While Gardening (Lemarchand, Elizabeth)
1978	▯	Rest You Merry (MacLeod, Charlotte)
1978		Persons Unknown (Moffat, Gwen)
1978		Street of the Five Moons (Peters, Elizabeth)
1978	▯	Death and the Maiden [U.S.- Death in the Morning] (Radley, Sheila)
1978		A Sleeping Life (Rendell, Ruth) ☆
1978	▯	Death on the Slopes (Schier, Norma)
1978		The Tarot Murders (Warner, Mignon)
1978		Copper Gold [Brit- Coppergold] (Winslow, Pauline Glen)

1978		Nothing's Certain but Death (Wren, M.K.)
1978	▯	A Reason To Kill (Zaremba, Eve)

1979		Some Die Eloquent (Aird, Catherine)
1979		Zadock's Treasure (Arnold, Margot)
1979	▯	Exit Actors, Dying (Arnold, Margot)
1979		A Parcel of Their Fortunes [Morocco] (Byfield, Barbara Ninde)
1979		Sneaks (Green, Edith Pinero)
1979	▯	Death Set to Music [by Mark Hebden] [APA- Pel and the Parked Car (1995)] (Hebden, Juliet)
1979		Pel and Faceless Corpse [by Mark Hebden] (Hebden, Juliet)
1979	▯	Introducing C.B. Greenfield (Kallen, Lucille)
1979		The Luck Runs Out (MacLeod, Charlotte)
1979	▯	The Family Vault (MacLeod, Charlotte)
1979		Who Is Simon Warwick? (Moyes, Patricia)
1979		Falling Star (O'Donnell, Lillian)
1979		No Business Being a Cop (O'Donnell, Lillian)
1979	▯	The Cater Street Hangman (Perry, Anne)
1979		Lucien's Tomb (Rippon, Marion)
1979		Murder by the Book (Schier, Norma)
1979		Death Goes Skiing (Schier, Norma)
1979		Deadly Relations [U.S.-The Habit of Loving] (Thomson, June)
1979		Music When Sweet Voices Die [APA- False Notes (1990)] (Yarbro, Chelsea Quinn)

1980s

1980		Passing Strange (Aird, Catherine)
1980		The Cape Cod Caper (Arnold, Margot)
1980	▯	Dupe (Cody, Liza) ★
1980	▯	A Pint of Murder (Craig, Alisa)
1980	▯	The Hands of Healing Murder (D'Amato, Barbara)
1980		Drink This (Dewhurst, Eileen)
1980		Scarlet Night (Davis, Dorothy Salisbury)
1980		The Attending Physician (Dominic, R.B.)
1980	▯	Death and the Pregnant Virgin (Haymon, S. T.)
1980		Pel Under Pressure [by Mark Hebden] (Hebden, Juliet)
1980		The Tanglewood Murder (Kallen, Lucille)
1980		The Shadow of the Palms (Law, Janice)
1980		Change for the Worse (Lemarchand, Elizabeth)
1980		The Withdrawing Room (MacLeod, Charlotte)
1980		Angel Death (Moyes, Patricia)
1980	▯	Death Is Forever (O'Callaghan, Maxine)
1980		Wicked Designs (O'Donnell, Lillian)
1980	▯	Sports Freak (OCork, Shannon)
1980	▯	Missing Woman (Page, Emma)
1980		Callander Square (Perry, Anne)
1980		The Chief Inspector's Daughter (Radley, Sheila)
1980		Demon at the Opera (Schier, Norma)
1980	▯	Jacoby's First Case (Smith, J. C. S.)
1980		Alibi in Time (Thomson, June)
1980		The Bishop in the Back Seat (Watson, Clarissa)
1980		The Counsellor Heart [APA- Sister Death] (Winslow, Pauline Glen)

1981	▯	Thus Was Adonis Murdered (Caudwell, Sarah)
1981	▯	The Grub-and-Stakers Move a Mountain (Craig, Alisa)
1981		Murder Goes Mumming (Craig, Alisa)
1981		Death in a Tenured Position [Brit- A Death in the Faculty] (Cross, Amanda) ★
1981		The Eyes on Utopia Murders (D'Amato, Barbara)
1981		Trio in Three Flats (Dewhurst, Eileen)
1981	▯	Karma (Dunlap, Susan)
1981	▯	Corridors of Death (Edwards, Ruth Dudley) ☆
1981		A Splash of Red (Fraser, Antonia)
1981	▯	Victims [U.S.- Suspect] (Gill, B.M.)
1981	▯	The Man With a Load of Mischief (Grimes, Martha)
1981		Pel Is Puzzled [by Mark Hebden] (Hebden, Juliet)
1981		Going for the Gold (Lathen, Emma)
1981		Death Under Par (Law, Janice)
1981		Nothing To Do With the Case (Lemarchand, Elizabeth)

1981   Death on the Eno (Mackay, Amanda)
1981   The Palace Guard (MacLeod, Charlotte)
1981 ∎ One Coffee With (Maron, Margaret)
1981   Murder Has a Pretty Face (Melville, Jennie) ☆
1981 ∎ Death of an Englishman (Nabb, Magdalen)
1981   Run From Nightmare (O'Callaghan, Maxine)
1981   The Children's Zoo (O'Donnell, Lillian)
1981   End of the Line (OCork, Shannon)
1981   Every Second Thursday (Page, Emma)
1981   Paragon Walk (Perry, Anne)
1981   Resurrection Row (Perry, Anne)
1981   The Curse of the Pharaohs (Peters, Elizabeth)
1981   Put on by Cunning [U.S.- Death Notes] (Rendell, Ruth)
1981 ∎ The Night She Died (Simpson, Dorothy)
1981 ∎ The Cable Car Murder (Taylor, Elizabeth Atwood)
1981   Shadow of a Doubt (Thomson, June)
1981 ∎ The Killing Circle (Wiltz, Chris)
1981   Seasons of Death (Wren, M.K.)

1982   Last Respects (Aird, Catherine)
1982   Death of a Voodoo Doll (Arnold, Margot)
1982   Lament for a Lady Laird (Arnold, Margot)
1982   Death on a Dragon's Tongue (Arnold, Margot)
1982 ∎ Blood Will Have Blood (Barnes, Linda)
1982 ∎ The Case of the Hook-Billed Kites (Borthwick, J. S.)
1982   Bad Company (Cody, Liza)
1982   Angel Without Mercy (Cohen, Anthea)
1982 ∎ Angel of Vengeance (Cohen, Anthea)
1982 ∎ Whoever I Am (Dewhurst, Eileen)
1982   Cool Repentance (Fraser, Antonia)
1982 ∎ "A" is for Alibi (Grafton, Sue) ★☆
1982   Perfect Fools (Green, Edith Pinero)
1982   The Old Fox Deceived (Grimes, Martha)
1982   Ritual Murder (Haymon, S.T.) ★
1982   Pel and the Bombers [by Mark Hebden]
        (Hebden, Juliet)
1982   Pel and the Staghound [by Mark Hebden]
        (Hebden, Juliet)
1982   The Skull Beneath the Skin (James, P. D.)
1982   No Lady in the House (Kallen, Lucille)
1982   Natural Enemy (Langton, Jane)
1982   Green Grow the Dollars (Lathen, Emma)
1982   Troubled Waters (Lemarchand, Elizabeth)
1982   Wrack and Rune (MacLeod, Charlotte)
1982 ∎ Funeral Sites (Mann, Jessica)
1982 ∎ Mrs. Porter's Letter (McConnell, Vicki P.)
1982 ∎ Resumé for Murder (McCormick, Claire)
1982 ∎ With Flowers That Fell (Meek, M.R.D.)
1982   Die Like a Dog (Moffat, Gwen)
1982 ∎ Champagne and a Gardener (Morison, B.J.)
1982   Ask the Cards a Question (Muller, Marcia)
1982   Death of a Dutchman (Nabb, Magdalen)
1982   Last Walk Home (Page, Emma)
1982 ∎ Indemnity Only (Paretsky, Sara)
1982 ∎ The Cooking School Murders [by Virginia Rich]
        (Pickard, Nancy)
1982   A Talent for Destruction (Radley, Sheila)
1982   Six Feet Under (Simpson, Dorothy)
1982 ∎ Death Turns a Trick (Smith, Julie)
1982   To Make a Killing [U.S.- Portrait of Lilith]
        (Thomson, June)
1982   Death in Time (Warner, Mignon)
1982   The Girl Who Was Clairvoyant (Warner, Mignon)
1982   The Rockefeller Gift (Winslow, Pauline Glen)

1983   Bitter Finish (Barnes, Linda)
1983 ∎ I Give You Five Days (Curzon, Clare)
1983 ∎ Murder on Cue (Dentinger, Jane)
1983 ∎ An Equal Opportunity Death (Dunlap, Susan)
1983   Tropical Issue [Brit- Dolly and the Bird of Paradise]
        (Dunnett, Dorothy)
1983   Mrs. Pollifax on the China Station (Gilman, Dorothy)

1983   The Anodyne Necklace (Grimes, Martha) ★
1983 ∎ The Lost Madonna (Holland, Isabelle)
1983 ∎ Garden of Malice (Kenney, Susan)
1983 ∎ The Widows (La Plante, Lynda)
1983   The Wheel Turns (Lemarchand, Elizabeth)
1983   Something the Cat Dragged In (MacLeod, Charlotte)
1983   The Bilbao Looking Glass (MacLeod, Charlotte)
1983   No Man's Island (Mann, Jessica)
1983   The Club Paradis Murders [Tahiti] (McCormick, Claire)
1983 ∎ A Perfect Match (McGown, Jill)
1983   The Sitting Ducks (Meek, M.R.D.)
1983   Last Chance Country (Moffat, Gwen)
1983 ∎ The Doberman Wore Black (Moore, Barbara)
1983   A Six-Letter Word for Death (Moyes, Patricia)
1983 ∎ The Tree of Death (Muller, Marcia)
1983   The Cheshire Cat's Eye (Muller, Marcia)
1983   Death in Springtime (Nabb, Magdalen)
1983   Cop Without a Shield (O'Donnell, Lillian)
1983   Hell Bent for Heaven (OCork, Shannon)
1983   Cold Light of Day (Page, Emma)
1983 ∎ A Will To Kill (Penn, John)
1983   Rutland Place (Perry, Anne)
1983   Silhouette in Scarlet (Peters, Elizabeth)
1983   The Baked Bean Supper Murders [by Virginia Rich]
        (Pickard, Nancy)
1983   Blood on the Happy Highway [U.S.- The Quiet
        Road to Death] (Radley, Sheila)
1983   The Speaker of Mandarin (Rendell, Ruth)
1983   Puppet for a Corpse (Simpson, Dorothy)
1983 ∎ Samson's Deal (Singer, Shelley)
1983 ∎ Only Half a Hoax (Taylor, L. A.)
1983 ∎ Lady on the Line (Tone, Teona)
1983   Devil's Knell (Warner, Mignon)
1983 ∎ Dead Man's Thoughts (Wheat, Carolyn) ☆

1984   Harm's Way (Aird, Catherine)
1984 ∎ Striving With Gods (Bannister, Jo)
1984   Dead Heat (Barnes, Linda)
1984 ∎ Death in a Deck Chair (Beck, K. K.)
1984 ∎ The Thin Woman (Cannell, Dorothy)
1984   Stalker (Cody, Liza)
1984   Angel of Death (Cohen, Anthea)
1984   Fallen Angel (Cohen, Anthea)
1984 ∎ The Other David (Coker, Carolyn)
1984   Sweet Death, Kind Death (Cross, Amanda)
1984   Masks and Faces (Curzon, Clare)
1984   Lullaby of Murder (Davis, Dorothy Salisbury)
1984   First Hit of the Season (Dentinger, Jane)
1984   There Was a Little Girl (Dewhurst, Eileen)
1984   Unexpected Developments [Brit- A Flaw in the System]
        (Dominic, R.B.)
1984   As a Favor (Dunlap, Susan)
1984   The St. Valentine's Day Murders (Edwards, Ruth
        Dudley)
1984 ∎ Amateur City (Forrest, Katherine V.)
1984 ∎ A Shroud for Delilah (Fraser, Anthea)
1984 ∎ A Death for Adonis (Giroux, E.X.)
1984   The Dirty Duck (Grimes, Martha)
1984   Jerusalem Inn (Grimes, Martha)
1984   Stately Homicide (Haymon, S. T.)
1984   Pel and the Pirates [by Mark Hebden] (Hebden, Juliet)
1984   Pel and the Predators [by Mark Hebden]
        (Hebden, Juliet)
1984   A Death at St. Anselm's (Holland, Isabelle)
1984   The Piano Bird (Kallen, Lucille)
1984 ∎ In the Shadow of King's (Kelly, Nora)
1984   Emily Dickinson Is Dead (Langton, Jane) ★☆
1984   Light through the Glass (Lemarchand, Elizabeth)
1984 ∎ A Healthy Body (Linscott, Gillian)
1984   The Convivial Codfish (MacLeod, Charlotte)
1984   Grave Goods (Mann, Jessica)
1984   Death of a Butterfly (Maron, Margaret)

1984 ∎ Too Sane a Murder (Martin, Lee)
1984 The Burnton Widows (McConnell, Vicki P.)
1984 ∎ Sick of Shadows (McCrumb, Sharyn)
1984 Hang the Consequences (Meek, M.R.D.)
1984 ∎ The Sheriff & the Panhandle Murders (Meredith, D. R.)
1984 Grizzly Trail (Moffat, Gwen)
1984 ∎ Penny Black (Moody, Susan)
1984 Penny Dreadful (Moody, Susan)
1984 Port and a Star Border (Morison, B.J.)
1984 Games To Keep the Dark Away (Muller, Marcia)
1984 Leave a Message for Willie (Muller, Marcia)
1984 Double [w/Bill Pronzini] (Muller, Marcia)
1984 Death in Autumn (Nabb, Magdalen)
1984 Ladykiller (O'Donnell, Lillian)
1984 ∎ A Novena for Murder (O'Marie, Carol Anne, Sister)
1984 ∎ Sweet, Savage Death (Papazoglou, Orania) ☆
1984 Deadlock (Paretsky, Sara)
1984 ∎ A Cadenza for Caruso [1910] (Paul, Barbara)
1984 ∎ The Renewable Virgin (Paul, Barbara)
1984 Mortal Term (Penn, John)
1984 Bluegate Fields (Perry, Anne)
1984 Die for Love (Peters, Elizabeth)
1984 ∎ Generous Death (Pickard, Nancy)
1984 Close Her Eyes (Simpson, Dorothy)
1984 Free Draw (Singer, Shelley)
1984 ∎ Morbid Symptoms (Slovo, Gillian)
1984 ∎ Someone Else's Grave (Smith, Alison) ☆
1984 Nightcap (Smith, J. C. S.)
1984 The Sourdough Wars (Smith, Julie)
1984 Deadly Objectives (Taylor, L. A.)
1984 Sound Evidence (Thomson, June)
1984 Illusion (Warner, Mignon)
1984 ∎ Bleeding Hearts (White, Teri)
1984 ∎ Murder in the Collective (Wilson, Barbara)
1984 Wake Up, Darlin' Corey (Wren, M.K.)

1985 ∎ Death of a Gossip (Beaton, M.C.)
1985 Murder in a Mummy Case (Beck, K. K.)
1985 Shock Value (Berne, Karin)
1985 ∎ Bare Acquaintances (Berne, Karin)
1985 The Down East Murders (Borthwick, J. S.)
1985 Down the Garden Path (Cannell, Dorothy)
1985 ∎ Audition for Murder (Carlson, P.M.)
1985 Murder Is Academic (Carlson, P.M.) ☆
1985 The Shortest Way to Hades (Caudwell, Sarah)
1985 ∎ Last Judgment (Clarke, Anna)
1985 Head Case (Cody, Liza)
1985 Guardian Angel (Cohen, Anthea)
1985 The Grub-and-Stakers Quilt a Bee (Craig, Alisa)
1985 The Trojan Hearse (Curzon, Clare)
1985 ∎ Probe (Douglas, Carole Nelson)
1985 Playing Safe (Dewhurst, Eileen)
1985 ∎ Stoner McTavish (Dreher, Sarah)
1985 Not Exactly a Brahmin (Dunlap, Susan)
1985 The Bohemian Connection (Dunlap, Susan)
1985 ∎ The Glory Hole Murders (Fennelly, Tony) ☆
1985 A Necessary End (Fraser, Anthea)
1985 Oxford Blood (Fraser, Antonia)
1985 Seminar for Murder (Gill, B.M.)
1985 Mrs. Pollifax and the Hong Kong Buddha
        (Gilman, Dorothy)
1985 A Death for a Darling (Giroux, E.X.)
1985 ∎ Monkey Puzzle (Gosling, Paula) ★
1985 "B" is for Burglar (Grafton, Sue) ★★
1985 ∎ Patterns in the Dust [U.S.- Death on Widow's Walk]
        (Grant-Adamson, Lesley)
1985 The Face of Death (Grant-Adamson, Lesley)
1985 Help the Poor Struggler (Grimes, Martha)
1985 The Deer Leap (Grimes, Martha)
1985 Pel and the Prowler[by Mark Hebden] (Hebden, Juliet)
1985 Flight of the Archangel (Holland, Isabelle)
1985 ∎ Until Proven Guilty (Jance, J.A.)

1985 ∎ The Gemini Man (Kelly, Susan) ☆
1985 Graves in Academe (Kenney, Susan)
1985 The Widows II (La Plante, Lynda)
1985 Murder Makes Tracks (Linscott, Gillian)
1985 The Curse of the Giant Hogweed (MacLeod, Charlotte)
1985 The Plain Old Man (MacLeod, Charlotte)
1985 Death in Blue Folders (Maron, Margaret)
1985 ∎ Just Another Day in Paradise (Maxwell, A.E.)
1985 Murder in Cowboy Bronze [Arizona]
        (McCormick, Claire)
1985 Lovely in Her Bones (McCrumb, Sharyn)
1985 The Split Second (Meek, M.R.D.)
1985 The Sheriff & the Branding Iron Murders
        (Meredith, D. R.)
1985 Penny Post (Moody, Susan)
1985 Beer and Skittles (Morison, B.J.)
1985 Night Ferry to Death (Moyes, Patricia)
1985 The Legend of the Slain Soldiers (Muller, Marcia)
1985 There's Nothing To Be Afraid Of (Muller, Marcia)
1985 Casual Affairs (O'Donnell, Lillian)
1985 Scent of Death (Page, Emma)
1985 Wicked, Loving Murder (Papazoglou, Orania)
1985 Killing Orders (Paretsky, Sara)
1985 Prima Donna at Large [1915] (Paul, Barbara)
1985 A Deadly Sickness (Penn, John)
1985 Death in Devil's Acre (Perry, Anne)
1985 The Mummy Case (Peters, Elizabeth)
1985 The Nantucket Diet Murders [by Virginia Rich]
        (Pickard, Nancy)
1985 Say No to Murder (Pickard, Nancy) ★
1985 ∎ Hidden Agenda (Porter, Anna)
1985 Fate Worse Than Death (Radley, Sheila)
1985 An Unkindness of Ravens (Rendell, Ruth) ☆
1985 Last Seen Alive (Simpson, Dorothy) ★
1985 ∎ True-Life Adventure (Smith, Julie)
1985 Shed Light on Death (Taylor, L. A.)
1985 A Dying Fall (Thomson, June)
1985 Full Cry (Tone, Teona)
1985 Speak No Evil (Warner, Mignon)
1985 Runaway (Watson, Clarissa)
1985 ∎ A White Male Running (Webb, Martha G.)
1985 ∎ Knight Must Fall (Wender, Theodora)
1985 ∎ The Suspect (Wright, L.R.) ★

1986 A Dead Liberty (Aird, Catherine)
1986 ∎ Reel Murder (Babson, Marian)
1986 Cities of the Dead (Barnes, Linda)
1986 ∎ The Lace Curtain Murders (Belfort, Sophie)
1986 False Impressions (Berne, Karin)
1986 The Student Body (Borthwick, J. S.)
1986 The Cat Who Saw Red (Braun, Lilian Jackson) ☆
1986 Coffin on the Water (Butler, Gwendoline)
1986 Murder Is Pathological (Carlson, P.M.)
1986 ∎ The Desperate Game (Castle, Jayne)
1986 The Chilling Deception (Castle, Jayne)
1986 The Sinister Touch (Castle, Jayne)
1986 The Fatal Fortune (Castle, Jayne)
1986 Cabin 3033 (Clarke, Anna)
1986 The Mystery Lady (Clarke, Anna)
1986 ∎ A Bird in the Hand (Cleeves, Ann)
1986 Under Contract (Cody, Liza) ☆
1986 Hell's Angel (Cohen, Anthea)
1986 Ministering Angel (Cohen, Anthea)
1986 The Vines of Ferrara (Coker, Carolyn)
1986 ∎ Phoebe's Knee (Comfort, Barbara)
1986 A Dismal Thing To Do (Craig, Alisa)
1986 No Word From Winifred (Cross, Amanda)
1986 The Quest for K (Curzon, Clare)
1986 Something Shady (Dreher, Sarah)
1986 The Last Annual Slugfest (Dunlap, Susan)
1986 Murder at the Nightwood Bar (Forrest, Katherine V.)
1986 Pretty Maids All in a Row (Fraser, Anthea)

1986 Jemima Shore's First Case & Other Stories (Fraser, Antonia)
1986 ◆ Murder in C Major (Frommer, Sara Hoskinson)
1986 ◆ Unbalanced Accounts (Gallison, Kate)
1986 A Death for a Dancer (Giroux, E.X.)
1986 A Death for a Doctor (Giroux, E.X.)
1986 ◆ The Wychford Murders (Gosling, Paula)
1986 "C" is for Corpse (Grafton, Sue) ★☆
1986 Guilty Knowledge (Grant-Adamson, Lesley)
1986 ◆ Shattered Moon (Green, Kate) ☆
1986 ◆ I Am the Only Running Footman (Grimes, Martha)
1986 ◆ Night-Blooming Cereus [Israel] (Hadley, Joan)
1986 ◆ Malice Domestic (Hardwick, Mollie)
1986 Pel and the Paris Mob [by Mark Hebden] (Hebden, Juliet)
1986 ◆ Strangled Prose (Hess, Joan) ☆
1986 The Murder at the Murder at the Mimosa Inn (Hess, Joan)
1986 ◆ Storm at Daybreak (Hoff, B.J.)
1986 A Lover Scorned (Holland, Isabelle)
1986 A Taste for Death (James, P. D.) ★★
1986 Injustice for All (Jance, J.A.)
1986 Trial by Fury (Jance, J.A.)
1986 A Little Madness (Kallen, Lucille)
1986 ◆ The Ritual Bath (Kellerman, Faye) ★
1986 The Summertime Soldiers (Kelly, Susan)
1986 ◆ Trace Elements (Knight, Kathryn Lasky)
1986 Good and Dead (Langton, Jane)
1986 Who Goes Home? (Lemarchand, Elizabeth)
1986 Knightfall (Linscott, Gillian)
1986 ◆ Dark Fields (MacGregor, T.J.) ☆
1986 The Corpse in Oozak's Pond (MacLeod, Charlotte) ★☆
1986 A Kind of Healthy Grave (Mann, Jessica)
1986 A Conspiracy of Strangers (Martin, Lee)
1986 The Frog and the Scorpion (Maxwell, A.E.)
1986 Highland Laddie Gone (McCrumb, Sharyn)
1986 In Remembrance of Rose (Meek, M.R.D.)
1986 Shattered Silk (Michaels, Barbara)
1986 Penny Royal (Moody, Susan)
1986 The Wolf Whispered Death (Moore, Barbara)
1986 Beyond the Grave (Muller, Marcia)
1986 ◆ The Cavalier in White (Muller, Marcia)
1986 ◆ Murder in Pug's Parlour (Myers, Amy)
1986 Murder in the Limelight (Myers, Amy)
1986 Advent of Dying (O'Marie, Carol Anne, Sister)
1986 Death's Savage Passion (Papazoglou, Orania)
1986 Barren Revenge (Penn, John)
1986 Unto the Grave (Penn, John)
1986 Lion in the Valley (Peters, Elizabeth)
1986 No Body (Pickard, Nancy) ☆
1986 ◆ Murder on the Run (Sale, Medora) ★
1986 ◆ A Swell Style of Murder (Santini, Rosemarie)
1986 Dead on Arrival (Simpson, Dorothy)
1986 Full House (Singer, Shelley)
1986 Death by Analysis (Slovo, Gillian)
1986 ◆ Miss Melville Regrets (Smith, Evelyn E.)
1986 Tourist Trap (Smith, Julie)
1986 The Dark Stream (Thomson, June)
1986 ◆ A Case of Loyalties (Wallace, Marilyn) ★
1986 ◆ June Mail (Warmbold, Jean)
1986 Even Cops' Daughters (Webb, Martha G.)
1986 Murder Gets a Degree (Wender, Theodora)
1986 Where Nobody Dies (Wheat, Carolyn)
1986 Tightrope (White, Teri)
1986 Sisters of the Road (Wilson, Barbara)
1986 ◆ She Came Too Late (Wings, Mary)
1986 Sleep While I Sing (Wright, L.R.)

1987 ◆ Not Till a Hot January (Adamson, M. J.)
1987 A February Face (Adamson, M. J.)
1987 ◆ A Trouble of Fools (Barnes, Linda) ☆☆☆
1987 Death of a Cad (Beaton, M.C.)

1987 ◆ The Letter of the Law (Berry, Carole)
1987 ◆ The Cat Who Played Brahms (Braun, Lilian Jackson) ☆
1987 The Cat Who Played Post Office (Braun, Lilian Jackson)
1987 Coffin in Fashion (Butler, Gwendoline)
1987 ◆ Dangerous Places (Chase, Elaine Raco)
1987 Last Seen in London (Clarke, Anna)
1987 Come Death and High Water (Cleeves, Ann)
1987 The Hand of the Lion (Coker, Carolyn)
1987 The Habit of Fear (Davis, Dorothy Salisbury)
1987 A Nice Little Business (Dewhurst, Eileen)
1987 ◆ The Always Anonymous Beast (Douglas, Lauren Wright)
1987 Gray Magic (Dreher, Sarah)
1987 ◆ A Murder of Crows (Duffy, Margaret)
1987 Too Close to the Edge (Dunlap, Susan)
1987 A Dinner To Die For (Dunlap, Susan)
1987 The Closet Hanging (Fennelly, Tony)
1987 Death Speaks Softly (Fraser, Anthea)
1987 The Nine Bright Shiners (Fraser, Anthea)
1987 Your Royal Hostage (Fraser, Antonia)
1987 The Death Tape (Gallison, Kate)
1987 A Death for a Dilettante (Giroux, E.X.)
1987 "D" is for Deadbeat (Grafton, Sue)
1987 ◆ The Killings at Badger's Drift (Graham, Caroline) ★☆☆
1987 Wild Justice (Grant-Adamson, Lesley)
1987 The Five Bells and Bladebone (Grimes, Martha)
1987 Parson's Pleasure (Hardwick, Mollie)
1987 ◆ Death on Demand (Hart, Carolyn G.) ☆☆
1987 Design for Murder (Hart, Carolyn G.)
1987 Death of a God (Haymon, S. T.)
1987 Pel Among the Pueblos [by Mark Hebden] (Hebden, Juliet)
1987 Pel and the Touch of Pitch [by Mark Hebden] (Hebden, Juliet)
1987 ◆ Malice in Maggody (Hess, Joan)
1987 Dear Miss Demeanor (Hess, Joan)
1987 The Domino Image [APA- The Captive Voice (1995)] (Hoff, B.J.)
1987 ◆ In Serena's Web (Hooper, Kay)
1987 Raven on the Wing (Hooper, Kay)
1987 Rafferty's Wife (Hooper, Kay)
1987 Zach's Law (Hooper, Kay)
1987 ◆ No Harm (Hornsby, Wendy)
1987 Taking the Fifth (Jance, J.A.)
1987 ◆ A Good Weekend for Murder (Jordan, Jennifer)
1987 Sacred and Profane (Kellerman, Faye)
1987 ◆ Murder in Mendocino (Kittredge, Mary)
1987 ◆ Bullshot (Kraft, Gabrielle) ☆
1987 ◆ Unquiet Grave (LaPierre, Janet) ☆
1987 A Whiff of Sulphur (Linscott, Gillian)
1987 Kill Flash (MacGregor, T.J.)
1987 The Silver Ghost (MacLeod, Charlotte)
1987 The Recycled Citizen (MacLeod, Charlotte)
1987 The Right Jack (Maron, Margaret)
1987 ◆ Where Lawyers Fear To Tread (Matera, Lia) ☆☆
1987 Gatsby's Vineyard (Maxwell, A.E.)
1987 ◆ Report for Murder (McDermid, Val)
1987 A Worm of Doubt (Meek, M.R.D.)
1987 Death in the Garden [U.S.- Murder in the Garden] (Melville, Jennie)
1987 The Sheriff & the Folsom Man Murders (Meredith, D. R.)
1987 Snare (Moffat, Gwen)
1987 ◆ Scavengers (Montgomery, Yvonne)
1987 ◆ Forests of the Night (Moore, Margaret)
1987 ◆ Money Leads to Murder [APA- Rendezvous Kit Marlow] (Morgan, D Miller)
1987 The Voyage of the Chianti (Morison, B.J.)
1987 The Marshal and the Murderer (Nabb, Magdalen)
1987 The Other Side of the Door (O'Donnell, Lillian)
1987 ◆ A Study in Lilac (Oliver, Maria-Antonia)

1987		Final Moments (Page, Emma)
1987		Bitter Medicine (Paretsky, Sara)
1987		A Chorus of Detectives [1920] (Paul, Barbara)
1987		Accident Prone (Penn, John)
1987		Cardington Crescent (Perry, Anne)
1987		Trojan Gold (Peters, Elizabeth) ☆
1987		Marriage Is Murder (Pickard, Nancy) ★☆
1987		Mortal Sins (Porter, Anna)
1987	🔳	Murder at the War [APA- Knight Fall] (Pulver, Mary Monica) ☆
1987		Who Saw Him Die? (Radley, Sheila)
1987	🔳	Caught Dead in Philadelphia (Roberts, Gillian) ★
1987	🔳	Grim Pickings (Rowe, Jennifer)
1987		The Disenchanted Diva (Santini, Rosemarie)
1987		Element of Doubt (Simpson, Dorothy)
1987	🔳	Murder Is Only Skin Deep (Sims, L. V.)
1987		Death Is a Family Affair (Sims, L. V.)
1987		Spit in the Ocean (Singer, Shelley)
1987		Death Comes Staccato (Slovo, Gillian)
1987		Rising (Smith, Alison)
1987		Miss Melville Returns (Smith, Evelyn E.)
1987	🔳	A Masculine Ending (Smith, Joan)
1987		Huckleberry Fiend (Smith, Julie)
1987	🔳	Goodbye Nanny Gray (Stacey, Susannah) ☆
1987		Murder at Vassar (Taylor, Elizabeth Atwood)
1987		No Flowers, By Request (Thomson, June)
1987	🔳	The Price You Pay (Wakefield, Hannah)
1987	🔳	The Third Victim (Waltch, Lilla M.)
1987	🔳	The Hamlet Trap (Wilhelm, Kate)
1987		A Diamond Before You Die (Wiltz, Chris)
1987	🔳	Murder at the PTA Luncheon (Wolzien, Valerie)
1987		Work for a Million (Zaremba, Eve)
1988		Remember March (Adamson, M. J.)
1988		April When They Woo (Adamson, M. J.)
1988		Death of an Outsider (Beaton, M.C.)
1988		The Year of the Monkey (Berry, Carole)
1988	🔳	Ladies' Night (Bowers, Elisabeth)
1988		The Cat Who Knew Shakespeare (Braun, Lilian Jackson)
1988		The Cat Who Sniffed Glue (Braun, Lilian Jackson)
1988		Coffin Underground (Butler, Gwendoline)
1988		The Widow's Club (Cannell, Dorothy) ☆☆
1988		Murder Unrenovated (Carlson, P.M.) ☆☆
1988		Rehearsal for Murder (Carlson, P.M.)
1988		Dark Corners (Chase, Elaine Raco)
1988	🔳	Suddenly in Her Sorbet (Christmas, Joyce)
1988		Murder in Writing (Clarke, Anna)
1988		Destroying Angel (Cohen, Anthea)
1988	🔳	The Man in the Green Chevy (Cooper, Susan Rogers)
1988		The Grub-and-Stakers Pinch a Poke (Craig, Alisa)
1988		Three-Core Lead (Curzon, Clare)
1988	🔳	The Life and Crimes of Harry Lavender (Day, Marele)
1988		Death Mask (Dentinger, Jane)
1988	🔳	Tango Key (Drake, Alison)
1988		Fevered (Drake, Alison)
1988		Death of a Raven (Duffy, Margaret)
1988	🔳	Cast a Cold Eye (Eccles, Marjorie)
1988		Six Proud Walkers (Fraser, Anthea)
1988	🔳	Magic Mirror [Brit- Deadly Reflections] (Friedman, Mickey)
1988	🔳	Take One for Murder (Fulton, Eileen)
1988		Death of a Golden Girl (Fulton, Eileen)
1988		Dying for Stardom (Fulton, Eileen)
1988		Lights, Camera, Death (Fulton, Eileen)
1988		A Setting for Murder (Fulton, Eileen)
1988	🔳	A Question of Guilt (Fyfield, Frances) ☆☆☆
1988	🔳	A Great Deliverance (George, Elizabeth) ★★☆☆
1988	🔳	Murder Behind Locked Doors (Godfrey, Ellen)
1988		Mrs. Pollifax and the Golden Triangle (Gilman, Dorothy)
1988		A Death for a Dietician (Giroux, E.X.)

1988		"E" is for Evidence (Grafton, Sue) ☆
1988	🔳	Random Access Murder (Grant, Linda) ☆
1988	🔳	Now You Don't (Greth, Roma)
1988		Deadly Ackee [Jamaica] (Hadley, Joan)
1988	🔳	Those Who Hunt the Night (Hambly, Barbara)
1988		Uneaseful Death (Hardwick, Mollie)
1988		Something Wicked (Hart, Carolyn G.) ★★
1988		Honeymoon With Murder (Hart, Carolyn G.) ★
1988		Mischief in Maggody (Hess, Joan) ☆☆
1988		A Really Cute Corpse (Hess, Joan)
1988		The Tangled Web (Hoff, B.J.)
1988		Vow of Silence (Hoff, B.J.)
1988		Captain's Paradise (Hooper, Kay)
1988		Outlaw Derek (Hooper, Kay)
1988		Shades of Gray (Hooper, Kay)
1988		The Fall of Lucas Kendrick (Hooper, Kay)
1988		Unmasking Kelsey (Hooper, Kay)
1988		Improbable Cause (Jance, J.A.)
1988		A More Perfect Union (Jance, J.A.)
1988		Murder Under the Mistletoe (Jordan, Jennifer)
1988		Trail of the Dragon (Kelly, Susan)
1988	🔳	Enter Second Murderer (Knight, Alanna)
1988		Screwdriver (Kraft, Gabrielle)
1988		Murder at the Gardner (Langton, Jane)
1988		Something in the Air (Lathen, Emma)
1988		The Glade Manor Murder (Lemarchand, Elizabeth)
1988		Death Sweet (MacGregor, T.J.)
1988		Death Beyond the Nile (Mann, Jessica)
1988		Baby Doll Games (Maron, Margaret)
1988		Death Warmed Over (Martin, Lee)
1988		Murder at the Blue Owl (Martin, Lee)
1988	🔳	The Smart Money (Matera, Lia)
1988		A Radical Departure (Matera, Lia) ☆☆
1988		Hidden Agenda (Matera, Lia)
1988		Just Enough Light To Kill (Maxwell, A.E.)
1988		Double Daughter (McConnell, Vicki P.)
1988		Paying the Piper (McCrumb, Sharyn) ☆☆
1988	🔳	Bimbos of the Death Sun (McCrumb, Sharyn) ★☆
1988		Redemption [U.S.-Murder at the Old Vicarage] (McGown, Jill)
1988	🔳	Lessons in Murder (McNab, Claire)
1988		A Mouthful of Sand (Meek, M.R.D.)
1988		Windsor Red (Melville, Jennie)
1988	🔳	Murder by Impulse (Meredith, D. R.) ☆
1988		Penny Wise (Moody, Susan)
1988		Dangerous Conceits (Moore, Margaret)
1988		A Lovely Night To Kill (Morgan, D Miller)
1988		There Hangs the Knife (Muller, Marcia)
1988		Eye of the Storm (Muller, Marcia)
1988		The Marshal and the Madwoman (Nabb, Magdalen)
1988	🔳	Death's Bright Angel (Neel, Janet) ★
1988		The Missing Madonna (O'Marie, Carol Anne, Sister)
1988		A Violent End (Page, Emma)
1988		Rich, Radiant Slaughter (Papazoglou, Orania)
1988		Blood Shot [Brit- Toxic Shock] (Paretsky, Sara) ★☆☆
1988	🔳	Outrageous Exposures (Penn, John)
1988		Silence in Hanover Close (Perry, Anne)
1988		The Deeds of the Disturber (Peters, Elizabeth)
1988	🔳	The Nocturne Murder (Peterson, Audrey)
1988		Dead Crazy (Pickard, Nancy) ☆☆
1988		The Unforgiving Minutes [prequel] (Pulver, Mary Monica)
1988		Ashes to Ashes (Pulver, Mary Monica)
1988	🔳	Death Walk (Quest, Erica)
1988		The Veiled One (Rendell, Ruth)
1988	🔳	Blood Run [revised 1999] (Robinson, Leah Ruth)
1988	🔳	The J. Alfred Prufrock Murders (Sawyer, Corinne Holt) ☆
1988	🔳	First Kill All the Lawyers (Shankman, Sarah)
1988		Suspicious Death (Simpson, Dorothy)
1988		To Sleep, Perchance To Kill (Sims, L. V.)

1988		Suicide King (Singer, Shelley)
1988		Why Aren't They Screaming? (Smith, Joan)
1988	∎	Murder at Markham (Sprinkle, Patricia H.)
1988		A Knife at the Opera (Stacey, Susannah)
1988		Body of Opinion (Stacey, Susannah)
1988	∎	Dead Men Don't Give Seminars (Sucher, Dorothy) ☆
1988		Rosemary for Remembrance (Thomson, June)
1988	∎	North of the Border (Van Gieson, Judith)
1988		Primary Target (Wallace, Marilyn) ☆
1988	∎	Small Favors (Wallace, Patricia)
1988		Fearful Symmetry (Waltch, Lilla M.)
1988		The White Hand (Warmbold, Jean)
1988		Last Plane From Nice (Watson, Clarissa)
1988		Somebody Killed the Messenger (Watson, Clarissa)
1988		Of Graves, Worms and Epitaphs (Wells, Tobias)
1988		The Dark Door (Wilhelm, Kate)
1988	∎	Death by Deception (Wingate, Anne)
1988		She Came in a Flash (Wings, Mary)
1988	∎	Playing God (Whitehead, Barbara)
1988		Beyond Hope (Zaremba, Eve)
1989		May's Newfangled Mirth (Adamson, M. J.)
1989		The Menehune Murders (Arnold, Margot)
1989		Bloody Soaps (Babbin, Jacqueline)
1989		Encore Murder (Babson, Marian)
1989		Tourists are for Trapping (Babson, Marian)
1989		Gilgamesh (Bannister, Jo)
1989		The Snake Tattoo (Barnes, Linda)
1989		Death of a Perfect Wife (Beaton, M.C.)
1989		Peril Under the Palms (Beck, K. K.)
1989	∎	Madison Avenue Murder (Bennett, Liza)
1989	∎	Working Murder (Boylan, Eleanor) ☆
1989		The Cat Who Went Underground (Braun, Lilian Jackson)
1989	∎	Murder in Store (Brod, D. C.)
1989	∎	Shadowdance (Bushell, Agnes)
1989		Coffin in the Black Museum (Butler, Gwendoline)
1989		Coffin in the Museum of Crime (Butler, Gwendoline)
1989		The Sirens Sang of Murder (Caudwell, Sarah) ★☆
1989		Simply To Die For (Christmas, Joyce)
1989	∎	Grime & Punishment (Churchill, Jill) ★★☆
1989		The Whitelands Affair (Clarke, Anna)
1989		Murder in Paradise (Cleeves, Ann)
1989		A Prey To Murder (Cleeves, Ann)
1989		Angel Dust (Cohen, Anthea)
1989		Grave Consequences (Comfort, Barbara)
1989	∎	A New Leash on Death (Conant, Susan)
1989		Trouble in the Brasses (Craig, Alisa)
1989		A Trap for Fools (Cross, Amanda)
1989	∎	Friends Till the End (Dank, Gloria)
1989	∎	The Pizza House Crash [U.S.- User Deadly] (Danks, Denise)
1989	∎	The Silver Pigs (Davis, Lindsey)
1989		Ninth Life (Douglas, Lauren Wright) ★
1989		Black Moon (Drake, Alison)
1989		Brass Eagle (Duffy, Margaret)
1989	∎	Pious Deception (Dunlap, Susan) ☆
1989		Death of a Good Woman (Eccles, Marjorie)
1989	∎	A Wicked Slice (Elkins, Charlotte & Aaron)
1989	∎	Hush, Money (Femling, Jean)
1989		Kiss Yourself Goodbye (Fennelly, Tony)
1989	∎	Gin & Daggers (Fletcher, Jessica)
1989		The Beverly Malibu (Forrest, Katherine V.) ★
1989		The April Rainers (Fraser, Anthea)
1989		A Temporary Ghost (Friedman, Mickey)
1989		Fatal Flashback (Fulton, Eileen)
1989	∎	Shadows on the Mirror (Fyfield, Frances)
1989		Payment in Blood (George, Elizabeth)
1989		A Death for a Dreamer (Giroux, E.X.)
1989	∎	The Dead Pull Hitter (Gordon, Alison)
1989		Backlash (Gosling, Paula)
1989		"F" is for Fugitive (Grafton, Sue)

1989		Death of a Hollow Man (Graham, Caroline)
1989	∎	Cocaine Blues [U.S.- Death by Misadventure] (Greenwood, Kerry)
1989		Plain Murder (Greth, Roma)
1989		The Old Silent (Grimes, Martha)
1989	∎	The Grandfather Medicine (Hager, Jean)
1989		The Bandersnatch (Hardwick, Mollie)
1989		Perish in July (Hardwick, Mollie)
1989		A Little Class on Murder (Hart, Carolyn G.) ★☆☆
1989	∎	Hallowed Murder (Hart, Ellen)
1989		A Very Particular Murder (Haymon, S. T.)
1989		Pel and the Party Spirit [by Mark Hebden] (Hebden, Juliet)
1989		Pel and the Picture of Innocence[by Mark Hebden] (Hebden, Juliet)
1989		Much Ado in Maggody (Hess, Joan)
1989		A Diet To Die For (Hess, Joan)
1989		A Fatal Advent (Holland, Isabelle)
1989	∎	Mrs. Malory Investigates [Brit- Gone Away] (Holt, Hazel)
1989		Aces High (Hooper, Kay)
1989		It Takes a Thief (Hooper, Kay)
1989	∎	The Mother Shadow (Howe, Melodie Johnson) ☆☆☆
1989		Devices and Desires (James, P. D.)
1989		Dismissed With Prejudice (Jance, J.A.)
1989	∎	Without Trace (John, Katherine)
1989	∎	Katwalk (Kijewski, Karen) ★★★
1989		Dead and Gone (Kittredge, Mary)
1989		Blood Line (Knight, Alanna)
1989		Deadly Beloved (Knight, Alanna)
1989		Let's Rob Roy (Kraft, Gabrielle)
1989	∎	Burning Water (Lackey, Mercedes)
1989		Children's Games (LaPierre, Janet)
1989	∎	A Deepe Coffyn (Laurence, Janet)
1989	∎	Rogue's Gold [as W.W. Lee] (Lee, Wendi)
1989		On Ice (MacGregor, T.J.)
1989		Vane Pursuit (MacLeod, Charlotte)
1989		The Gladstone Bag (MacLeod, Charlotte)
1989		Corpus Christmas (Maron, Margaret) ☆☆
1989		Hal's Own Murder Case (Martin, Lee)
1989		The Art of Survival (Maxwell, A.E.)
1989		Common Murder (McDermid, Val)
1989		Death of a Dancer [U.S.- Gone to Her Death] (McGown, Jill)
1989		Fatal Reunion (McNab, Claire)
1989		A Loose Connection (Meek, M.R.D.)
1989		A Cure for Dying (Melville, Jennie)
1989		Murder by Deception (Meredith, D. R.) ☆
1989	∎	The Big Killing (Meyers, Annette)
1989		The Stone Hawk (Moffat, Gwen)
1989		Penny Pinching (Moody, Susan)
1989		Black Girl, White Girl (Moyes, Patricia)
1989		Dark Star (Muller, Marcia)
1989		There's Something in a Sunday (Muller, Marcia)
1989		The Shape of Dread (Muller, Marcia) ☆
1989		Murder at Plum's (Myers, Amy)
1989		Death on Site (Neel, Janet)
1989		Hit and Run (O'Callaghan, Maxine)
1989		A Good Night To Kill (O'Donnell, Lillian)
1989		Antipodes (Oliver, Maria-Antonia)
1989	∎	A Little Neighborhood Murder (Orde, A. J.)
1989		He Huffed and He Puffed (Paul, Barbara)
1989		Good King Sauerkraut (Paul, Barbara)
1989		A Feast of Death (Penn, John)
1989		Naked Once More (Peters, Elizabeth) ★
1989		Death in Wessex (Peterson, Audrey)
1989		Murder in Burgundy (Peterson, Audrey)
1989		Bum Steer (Pickard, Nancy) ★
1989	∎	Unorthodox Practices (Piesman, Marissa)
1989	∎	To Mourn a Mischief (Quinton, Ann)
1989		This Way Out (Radley, Sheila)

1989	▌ Touch a Cold Door (Roberts, Carey)
1989	Philly Stakes (Roberts, Gillian) ☆
1989	▌ The Spirit Stalker (Romberg, Nina)
1989	▌ A Real Shot in the Arm (Roome, Annette) ★
1989	Murder by the Book (Rowe, Jennifer)
1989	Murder in Focus (Sale, Medora)
1989	Murder in Gray & White (Sawyer, Corinne Holt)
1989	Then Hang All the Liars (Shankman, Sarah)
1989	▌ Black Justice (Shepherd, Stella)
1989	Dead by Morning (Simpson, Dorothy)
1989	▌ The Mark Twain Murders (Skom, Edith) ☆☆☆
1989	Miss Melville's Revenge (Smith, Evelyn E.)
1989	▌ Capriccio (Smith, Joan G.)
1989	Dead Men Don't Marry (Sucher, Dorothy)
1989	A Murder Waiting To Happen (Taylor, L. A.)
1989	The Spoils of Time (Thomson, June)
1989	▌ Under the Influence (Travis, Elizabeth)
1989	▌ Murder at the Kennedy Center (Truman, Margaret)
1989	▌ Unorthodox Methods (Valentine, Deborah)
1989	A Collector of Photographs (Valentine, Deborah) ☆☆☆
1989	Deadly Grounds (Wallace, Patricia)
1989	The Third Way (Warmbold, Jean)
1989	Smart House (Wilhelm, Kate)
1989	The Dog Collar Murders (Wilson, Barbara)
1989	The Eye of Anna (Wingate, Anne)
1989	The Fortieth Birthday Body (Wolzien, Valerie)
1989	▌ Reckless (Woods, Sherryl)
1989	Body and Soul (Woods, Sherryl

1990

1990	The Body Politic (Aird, Catherine)
1990	Toby's Folly (Arnold, Margot)
1990	In the Teeth of Adversity (Babson, Marian)
1990	▌ Shards (Bannister, Jo)
1990	The Going Down of the Sun (Bannister, Jo)
1990	Coyote (Barnes, Linda)
1990	Death of a Hussy (Beaton, M.C.)
1990	▌ To Make a Killing (Bedford, Jean)
1990	▌ The Dead Do Not Praise (Bell, Pauline)
1990	Seventh Avenue Murder (Bennett, Liza)
1990	Good Night, Sweet Prince (Berry, Carole)
1990	▌ A Vow of Silence (Black, Veronica)
1990	Bodies of Water (Borthwick, J. S.)
1990	▌ Deadly Appearances (Bowen, Gail)
1990	Murder Observed (Boylan, Eleanor)
1990	The Cat Who Talked to Ghosts (Braun, Lilian Jackson)
1990	The Cat Who Lived High (Braun, Lilian Jackson)
1990	Error In Judgment (Brod, D. C.)
1990	▌ Wish You Were Here (Brown, Rita Mae)
1990	▌ Screaming Bones (Burden, Pat) ☆
1990	Wreath of Honesty (Burden, Pat)
1990	Advantage Miss Seeton [Hampton Charles] (Crane, Hamilton)
1990	Mum's the Word (Cannell, Dorothy)
1990	Murder Misread (Carlson, P.M.)
1990	A Fete Worse than Death (Christmas, Joyce)
1990	▌ A Lesson in Dying (Cleeves, Ann)
1990	The Balmoral Nude (Coker, Carolyn)
1990	Dead and Doggone (Conant, Susan)
1990	▌ Festering Lilies [U.S.- A Common Death] (Cooper, Natasha)
1990	Houston in the Rear View Mirror (Cooper, Susan Rogers)
1990	Other People's Houses (Cooper, Susan Rogers)
1990	▌ Postmortem (Cornwell, Patricia) ★★★★
1990	The Grub-and-Stakers Spin a Yarn (Craig, Alisa)
1990	Miss Seeton, by Appointment [Hampton Charles] (Crane, Hamilton)
1990	The Players Come Again (Cross, Amanda)
1990	The Blue-Eyed Boy (Curzon, Clare)
1990	▌ Hardball (D'Amato, Barbara)
1990	Going Out in Style (Dank, Gloria)
1990	▌ Catering to Nobody (Davidson, Diane Mott) ☆☆☆
1990	Shadows in Bronze (Davis, Lindsey)
1990	▌ Kindred Crimes (Dawson, Janet) ★☆☆☆
1990	The Case of the Chinese Boxes (Day, Marele)
1990	▌ Good Night, Mr. Holmes (Douglas, Carole Nelson)
1990	Good Morning, Irene (Douglas, Carole Nelson)
1990	Counterprobe (Douglas, Carole Nelson)
1990	A Captive in Time (Dreher, Sarah)
1990	Diamond in the Buff (Dunlap, Susan)
1990	Requiem for a Dove (Eccles, Marjorie)
1990	More Deaths Than One (Eccles, Marjorie)
1990	The English School of Murder [APA- The School of English Murder] (Edwards, Ruth Dudley)
1990	▌ Bloodlist (Elrod, P.N.)
1990	Lifeblood (Elrod, P.N.)
1990	Bloodcircle (Elrod, P.N.)
1990	▌ Blood Is Thicker (Fallon, Ann C.)
1990	Symbols at Your Door (Fraser, Anthea)
1990	Trial by Fire [U.S.- Not That Kind of Place] (Fyfield, Frances)
1990	▌ Shaved Fish (Geason, Susan)
1990	Well-Schooled in Murder (George, Elizabeth)
1990	Mrs. Pollifax and the Whirling Dervish (Gilman, Dorothy)
1990	A Death for a Double (Giroux, E.X.)
1990	"G" is for Gumshoe (Grafton, Sue) ★★
1990	Blind Trust (Grant, Linda)
1990	Curse the Darkness (Grant-Adamson, Lesley)
1990	Flying Too High (Greenwood, Kerry)
1990	The Old Contemptibles (Grimes, Martha)
1990	▌ Hot Water (Gunning, Sally)
1990	▌ Not a Creature Was Stirring (Haddam, Jane) ☆☆
1990	Night Walker (Hager, Jean)
1990	The Dreaming Damozel (Hardwick, Mollie)
1990	▌ Real Murders (Harris, Charlaine)
1990	Deadly Valentine (Hart, Carolyn G.) ☆☆
1990	Pel and the Missing Persons [by Mark Hebden] (Hebden, Juliet)
1990	Dark River Legacy (Hoff, B.J.)
1990	The Long Search (Holland, Isabelle)
1990	▌ Dead Ahead (Horansky, Ruby)
1990	Half a Mind (Hornsby, Wendy)
1990	▌ The Punjat's Ruby (Jackson, Marian J. A.)
1990	The Arabian Pearl (Jackson, Marian J. A.)
1990	Minor in Possession (Jance, J.A.)
1990	Book Early for Murder (Jordan, Jennifer)
1990	Milk and Honey (Kellerman, Faye)
1990	▌ Parklane South, Queens (Kelly, Mary Anne)
1990	Until Proven Innocent (Kelly, Susan)
1990	▌ Hope Against Hope (Kelly, Susan B.)
1990	Time of Hope (Kelly, Susan B.)
1990	One Fell Sloop (Kenney, Susan)
1990	Katapult (Kijewski, Karen)
1990	Poison Pen (Kittredge, Mary)
1990	▌ Fatal Diagnosis (Kittredge, Mary)
1990	Killing Cousins (Knight, Alanna)
1990	Mortal Words (Knight, Kathryn Lasky)
1990	Bloody Mary (Kraft, Gabrielle)
1990	Children of the Night (Lackey, Mercedes)
1990	Cruel Mother (LaPierre, Janet)
1990	A Tasty Way To Die (Laurence, Janet)
1990	Rustler's Venom [as W.W. Lee] (Lee, Wendi)
1990	▌ Sweet Narcissus (Lorens, M.K.)
1990	Ropedancer's Fall (Lorens, M.K.)
1990	Kin Dread (MacGregor, T.J.)

1990		Deficit Ending (Martin, Lee)
1990		The Mensa Murders (Martin, Lee)
1990		The Good Fight (Matera, Lia) ☆☆
1990	∎	Murder at the Spa (Matteson, Stefanie)
1990	∎	Pet Peeves (McCafferty, Taylor)
1990		The Windsor Knot (McCrumb, Sharyn)
1990	∎	Ever I Return, Pretty Peggy-O (McCrumb, Sharyn) ★☆
1990	∎	Osprey Reef (McKernan, Victoria)
1990		Death Down Under (McNab, Claire)
1990	∎	Deadly Safari (McQuillan, Karin)
1990	∎	Hometown Heroes (McShea, Susanna Hofmann)
1990		This Blessed Plot (Meek, M.R.D.)
1990		Witching Murder (Melville, Jennie)
1990		Making Good Blood [U.S.- Footsteps in the Blood] (Melville, Jennie)
1990		Murder by Masquerade (Meredith, D. R.)
1990		Tender Death (Meyers, Annette)
1990	∎	A Lively Form of Death (Mitchell, Kay)
1990		The Raptor Zone (Moffat, Gwen)
1990		Rage (Moffat, Gwen)
1990		Obstacle Course (Montgomery, Yvonne)
1990		Murder in Good Measure (Moore, Margaret)
1990	∎	A Slay at the Races (Morgan, Kate)
1990		Trophies and Dead Things (Muller, Marcia)
1990		The Marshal's Own Case (Nabb, Magdalen)
1990	∎	The Daphne Decisions (O'Brien, Meg)
1990		Salmon in the Soup (O'Brien, Meg)
1990	∎	A Wreath for the Bride (O'Donnell, Lillian)
1990	∎	Dead in the Scrub (Oliphant, B. J.) ☆☆
1990		The Unexpected Corpse (Oliphant, B. J.)
1990		Death and the Dogwalker (Orde, A. J.)
1990	∎	The Body in the Belfry (Page, Katherine Hall) ★
1990		Once and Always Murder (Papazoglou, Orania)
1990		Burn Marks (Paretsky, Sara)
1990		A Killing To Hide (Penn, John)
1990		Bethlehem Road (Perry, Anne)
1990	∎	The Face of a Stranger (Perry, Anne) ☆
1990		Deadly Rehearsal (Peterson, Audrey)
1990		Elegy in a Country Graveyard (Peterson, Audrey)
1990		Cold Coffin (Quest, Erica)
1990		Death of a Dear Friend (Quinton, Ann)
1990	∎	Death by the Riverside (Redmann, J. M.)
1990		A Second Shot in the Dark (Roome, Annette)
1990	∎	A Little Gentle Sleuthing (Rowlands, Betty)
1990		Murder in a Good Cause (Sale, Medora)
1990	∎	Death Down Home (Sandstrom, Eve K.)
1990	∎	Murder Is Relative (Saum, Karen)
1990	∎	As Crime Goes By (Shah, Diane K.)
1990		Now Let's Talk of Graves (Shankman, Sarah)
1990		Murderous Remedy (Shepherd, Stella)
1990	∎	Larkspur (Simonson, Sheila)
1990	∎	Sea of Troubles (Smith, Janet L.) ☆
1990		Don't Leave Me This Way (Smith, Joan)
1990		A Brush With Death (Smith, Joan G.)
1990	∎	New Orleans Mourning (Smith, Julie) ★☆
1990		Murder in the Charleston Manner (Sprinkle, Patricia H.)
1990		Grave Responsibility (Stacey, Susannah)
1990	∎	Murder at Red Rook Ranch (Tell, Dorothy)
1990		Past Reckoning (Thomson, June)
1990		Finders Keepers (Travis, Elizabeth)
1990		Murder at the National Cathedral (Truman, Margaret)
1990		Raptor (Van Gieson, Judith)
1990		A February Mourning [U.S.- A Woman's Own Mystery] (Wakefield, Hannah)
1990	∎	Murder by the Book (Welch, Pat)
1990		The Girl With Red Suspenders (Whitehead, Barbara)
1990		Sweet, Sweet Poison (Wilhelm, Kate)
1990	∎	Club Twelve (Williams, Amanda Kyle)

1990	∎	Gaudi Afternoon (Wilson, Barbara) ★★
1990		Stolen Moments (Woods, Sherryl)
1990		A Chill Rain in January (Wright, L.R.) ★
1990		Uneasy Lies (Zaremba, Eve)

1991

1991		The Catacomb Conspiracy (Arnold, Margot)
1991	∎	In the Game (Baker, Nikki)
1991		Death and Other Lovers (Bannister, Jo)
1991		Steel Guitar (Barnes, Linda)
1991		Death of a Snob (Beaton, M.C.)
1991		The Marvell College Murders (Belfort, Sophie)
1991		Feast into Mourning (Bell, Pauline)
1991		Island Girl (Berry, Carole)
1991		Love and Murder [APA- Murder at the Mendel] (Bowen, Gail)
1991		No Forwarding Address (Bowers, Elisabeth)
1991		The Cat Who Knew a Cardinal (Braun, Lilian Jackson)
1991	∎	Headhunt (Brennan, Carol)
1991	∎	Date With a Dead Doctor (Brill, Toni)
1991		Masquerade in Blue [APA- Framed in Blue] (Brod, D. C.)
1991		Coffin and the Paper Man (Butler, Gwendoline)
1991		Murder in the Dog Days (Carlson, P.M.) ☆
1991		Bad Blood (Carlson, P.M.)
1991	∎	Raw Data (Chapman, Sally)
1991	∎	A Drink of Deadly Wine (Charles, Kate)
1991		A Stunning Way To Die (Christmas, Joyce)
1991		Friend or Faux (Christmas, Joyce)
1991		A Farewell to Yarns (Churchill, Jill)
1991		The Case of the Paranoid Patient (Clarke, Anna)
1991		Sea Fever (Cleeves, Ann)
1991		Murder in My Backyard (Cleeves, Ann)
1991		Backhand (Cody, Liza) ☆
1991		Recording Angel (Cohen, Anthea)
1991		A Bite of Death (Conant, Susan)
1991		Poison Flowers (Cooper, Natasha)
1991		Chasing Away the Devil (Cooper, Susan Rogers)
1991		Body of Evidence (Cornwell, Patricia)
1991		Miss Seeton Cracks the Case (Crane, Hamilton)
1991		Miss Seeton Paints the Town (Crane, Hamilton)
1991	∎	The Trouble With a Small Raise (Crespi, Camilla)
1991		The Trouble With Moonlighting (Crespi, Camilla)
1991		Hard Tack (D'Amato, Barbara)
1991	∎	Just Desserts (Daheim, Mary) ☆
1991		Fowl Prey (Daheim, Mary)
1991		Better Off Dead (Danks, Denise)
1991		Venus in Copper (Davis, Lindsey)
1991		The Daughters of Artemis (Douglas, Lauren Wright)
1991		Rook-Shoot (Duffy, Margaret)
1991		Rogue Wave (Dunlap, Susan) ☆
1991		Art in the Blood (Elrod, P.N.)
1991		Fire in the Blood (Elrod, P.N.)
1991	∎	Clearwater (Ennis, Catherine)
1991		Where Death Lies (Fallon, Ann C.)
1991		Getting Mine (Femling, Jean)
1991		Murder by Tradition (Forrest, Katherine V.) ★
1991	∎	A Deadline for Murder (Frankel, Valerie)
1991		The Lily-White Boys [U.S.- I'll Sing You Two-O (1996)] (Fraser, Anthea)
1991		The Cavalier Case (Fraser, Antonia)
1991	∎	Scalpel's Edge (Fromer, Margot J.)
1991		Deep Sleep (Fyfield, Frances) ★
1991		Dogfish (Geason, Susan)
1991		A Suitable Vengeance (George, Elizabeth)
1991		The Fifth Rapunzel (Gill, B.M.)
1991	∎	Adjusted to Death (Girdner, Jaqueline)
1991		The Last Resort (Girdner, Jaqueline)
1991		A Death for a Dancing Doll (Giroux, E.X.)
1991		Georgia Disappeared (Godfrey, Ellen)

1991   Safe at Home (Gordon, Alison)
1991   Death Penalties (Gosling, Paula)
1991   "H" is for Homicide (Grafton, Sue)
1991 ■ Say It With Poison (Granger, Ann)
1991   Love nor Money (Grant, Linda) ☆
1991 ■ Partners in Crime (Gray, Gallagher)
1991 ■ Deadly Errand (Green, Christine) ☆
1991 ■ Clerical Errors (Greenwood, D.M.)
1991   Murder on the Ballarat Train (Greenwood, Kerry)

1991   Precious Blood (Haddam, Jane)
1991   Act of Darkness (Haddam, Jane)
1991   Quoth the Raven (Haddam, Jane)
1991 ■ Orchestrated Death (Harrod-Eagles, Cynthia)
1991   The Christie Caper (Hart, Carolyn G.) ☆☆☆
1991   Vital Lies (Hart, Ellen)
1991   Death of a Warrior Queen (Haymon, S. T.)
1991   Pel and the Promised Land [by Mark Hebden] (Hebden, Juliet)
1991 ■ Murder on the Iditarod Trail (Henry, Sue) ★★
1991   Mortal Remains in Maggody (Hess, Joan)
1991   Madness in Maggody (Hess, Joan)
1991   Roll Over and Play Dead (Hess, Joan)
1991   The Cruellest Month (Holt, Hazel)
1991 ■ Crime of Passion (Hooper, Kay)
1991   House of Cards (Hooper, Kay) ☆

1991   The Cat's Eye (Jackson, Marian J. A.)
1991 ■ The Turquoise Tattoo (Jacobs, Nancy Baker)
1991   Payment in Kind (Jance, J.A.)

1991   And Soon I'll Come To Kill You (Kelly, Susan)
1991   Kat's Cradle (Kijewski, Karen)
1991   Rigor Mortis (Kittredge, Mary)
1991   A Quiet Death (Knight, Alanna)
1991   Mumbo Jumbo (Knight, Kathryn Lasky)

1991   Jinx High (Lackey, Mercedes)
1991 ■ Dogtown (Lambert, Mercedes)
1991   The Dante Game (Langton, Jane)
1991   Grandmother's House (LaPierre, Janet)
1991   East Is East (Lathen, Emma)
1991   Hotel Morgue (Laurence, Janet)
1991   Rancher's Blood [as W.W. Lee] (Lee, Wendi)
1991 ■ Sister Beneath the Sheet (Linscott, Gillian)
1991   Deception Island (Lorens, M.K.)

1991   Death Flats (MacGregor, T.J.)
1991   An Owl Too Many (MacLeod, Charlotte) ☆
1991 ■ I Left My Heart (Maiman, Jaye)
1991   Faith, Hope and Homicide (Mann, Jessica)
1991   Past Imperfect (Maron, Margaret)
1991   Prior Convictions (Matera, Lia) ☆
1991   Murder on the Cliff (Matteson, Stefanie)
1991   Murder at Teatime (Matteson, Stefanie)
1991   Money Burns (Maxwell, A.E.)
1991   Missing Susan (McCrumb, Sharyn)
1991   Final Edition [U.S.- Open and Shut] (McDermid, Val)
1991   The Murders of Mrs. Austin & Mrs. Beale (McGown, Jill)
1991   Cop Out (McNab, Claire)
1991   Murder by Reference (Meredith, D. R.)
1991   The Deadliest Option (Meyers, Annette)
1991   In Stony Places (Mitchell, Kay)
1991 ■ Final Session (Morell, Mary)
1991   Murder Most Fowl (Morgan, Kate)
1991   Where Echoes Live (Muller, Marcia) ☆
1991   Murder at the Masque (Myers, Amy)

1991   The Marshal Makes His Report (Nabb, Magdalen)
1991   Death of a Partner (Neel, Janet)

1991   Hare Today, Gone Tomorrow (O'Brien, Meg)
1991   Set-Up (O'Callaghan, Maxine)

1991   A Private Crime (O'Donnell, Lillian)
1991   Murder in Ordinary Time (O'Marie, Carol Anne, Sister)

1991   The Body in the Kelp (Page, Katherine Hall)
1991   The Body in the Bouillon (Page, Katherine Hall)
1991   Guardian Angel (Paretsky, Sara)
1991   A Knife Ill-Used (Penn, John)
1991   Death's Long Shadow (Penn, John)
1991   Highgate Rise (Perry, Anne)
1991   A Dangerous Mourning (Perry, Anne)
1991   The Last Camel Died at Noon (Peters, Elizabeth) ☆
1991   Lament for Christabel (Peterson, Audrey)
1991   I. O. U. (Pickard, Nancy) ★★☆☆
1991   Personal Effects (Piesman, Marissa)
1991 ■ Bayou City Streets (Powell, Deborah)
1991   Original Sin (Pulver, Mary Monica)

1991   Model Murder (Quest, Erica)

1991   I'd Rather Be in Philadelphia (Roberts, Gillian)
1991 ■ The Bulrush Murders (Rothenberg, Rebecca) ☆☆

1991   Sleep of the Innocent (Sale, Medora)
1991   The Devil down Home (Sandstrom, Eve K.)
1991 ■ Everything You Have Is Mine (Scoppettone, Sandra)
1991 ■ Death and the Chapman (Sedley, Kate)
1991   She Walks in Beauty (Shankman, Sarah)
1991   Ah, Sweet Mystery (Sibley, Celestine)
1991 ■ Taken by Storm (Silva, Linda Kay)
1991   Doomed To Die (Simpson, Dorothy)
1991   Miss Melville Rides a Tiger (Smith, Evelyn E.)
1991   Dead in the Water (Smith, Julie)
1991   The Axeman's Jazz (Smith, Julie)
1991   Murder on Peachtree Street (Sprinkle, Patricia H.)
1991 ■ Murder on Her Mind (Steiner, Susan)
1991 ■ Red Sea, Dead Sea (Stevens, Serita)

1991   The Hallelujah Murders (Tell, Dorothy)
1991 ■ Cat's-Paw, Inc. (Thrasher, L. L.)
1991   Foul Play (Thomson, June)
1991 ■ Still Waters (Tucker, Kerry)

1991   Fine Distinctions (Valentine, Deborah) ☆
1991   The Other Side of Death (Van Gieson, Judith)

1991   A Single Stone (Wallace, Marilyn) ☆
1991   Blood Lies (Wallace, Patricia)
1991 ■ Cold Tracks (Wallingford, Lee)
1991 ■ Murder on the Run (White, Gloria) ☆
1991   The Dean It Was That Died (Whitehead, Barbara)
1991 ■ Death Qualified (Wilhelm, Kate)
1991   The Providence File (Williams, Amanda Kyle)
1991   The Emerald Lizard (Wiltz, Chris)
1991   The Buzzards Must Also Be Fed (Wingate, Anne)
1991   We Wish You a Merry Murder (Wolzien, Valerie)
1991   Ties That Bind (Woods, Sherryl)
1991 ■ Hot Property (Woods, Sherryl)
1991   Fall From Grace (Wright, L.R.)

1991   Poison Fruit (Yarbro, Chelsea Quinn)

1991 ■ The Hour of the Knife (Zukowski, Sharon)

1992

1992 ■ All the Great Pretenders (Adams, Deborah) ☆
1992   All the Crazy Winters (Adams, Deborah)
1992 ■ Thyme of Death (Albert, Susan Wittig) ☆☆
1992 ■ Quaker Silence (Allen, Irene)
1992 ■ Bury Her Sweetly (Amey, Linda)
1992 ■ Trail of Murder (Andreae, Christine) ☆
1992   Cape Cod Conundrum (Arnold, Margot)
1992 ■ Aunt Dimity's Death (Atherton, Nancy)
1992 ■ A World the Color of Salt (Ayres, Noreen)

1992   The Lavender House Murder (Baker, Nikki)
1992 ■ Agatha Raisin and the Quiche of Death (Beaton, M.C.)
1992   Death of a Prankster (Beaton, M.C.)

1992	▮ A Hopeless Case (Beck, K. K.)
1992	Worse Than Death (Bedford, Jean)
1992	Eyewitness to Murder (Belfort, Sophie)
1992	No Pleasure in Death (Bell, Pauline)
1992	A Vow of Chastity (Black, Veronica)
1992	▮ Dead Time (Bland, Eleanor Taylor)
1992	Dude on Arrival (Borthwick, J. S.)
1992	Murder Machree (Boylan, Eleanor)
1992	The Cat Who Moved a Mountain (Braun, Lilian Jackson)
1992	Full Commission (Brennan, Carol)
1992	▮ Broken Star (Brown, Lizbie)
1992	Rest in Pieces (Brown, Rita Mae)
1992	▮ Contents Under Pressure (Buchanan, Edna)
1992	Bury Him Kindly (Burden, Pat)
1992	Coffin on Murder Street (Butler, Gwendoline)

1992	Femmes Fatal (Cannell, Dorothy)
1992	▮ Gravestone (Carlson, P.M.)
1992	It's Her Funeral (Christmas, Joyce)
1992	▮ Decked (Clark, Carol Higgins) ☆☆
1992	▮ A Tail of Two Murders (Cleary, Melissa)
1992	Another Man's Poison (Cleeves, Ann)
1992	A Day in the Death of Dorothea Cassidy (Cleeves, Ann)
1992	▮ Bucket Nut (Cody, Liza) ★
1992	Angel in Action (Cohen, Anthea)
1992	Paws Before Dying (Conant, Susan)
1992	Gone to the Dogs (Conant, Susan)
1992	Bloodlines (Conant, Susan)
1992	Bloody Roses (Cooper, Natasha)
1992	One, Two, What Did Daddy Do? (Cooper, Susan Rogers)
1992	All That Remains (Cornwell, Patricia)
1992	▮ Eulogy for a Brown Angel (Corpi, Lucha)
1992	The Wrong Rite (Craig, Alisa)
1992	Miss Seeton Rocks the Cradle (Crane, Hamilton)
1992	Hands up, Miss Seeton (Crane, Hamilton)
1992	Miss Seeton by Moonlight (Crane, Hamilton)
1992	The Trouble With Too Much Sun (Crespi, Camilla)
1992	Cat's Cradle (Curzon, Clare)

1992	Hard Luck (D'Amato, Barbara)
1992	▮ The Alpine Advocate (Daheim, Mary) ☆
1992	Holy Terrors (Daheim, Mary)
1992	▮ Lay It on the Line (Dain, Catherine) ☆
1992	As the Sparks Fly Upward (Dank, Gloria)
1992	Frame Grabber (Danks, Denise)
1992	Dying for Chocolate (Davidson, Diane Mott)
1992	The Iron Hand of Mars (Davis, Lindsey)
1992	The Last Tango of Delores Delgado (Day, Marele) ★
1992	Dead Pan (Dentinger, Jane)
1992	▮ Death in Candie Gardens (Dewhurst, Eileen)
1992	▮ Throw Darts at a Cheesecake (Dietz, Denise)
1992	Irene at Large (Douglas, Carole Nelson)
1992	▮ Catnap (Douglas, Carole Nelson)
1992	A Tiger's Heart (Douglas, Lauren Wright)
1992	High Strangeness (Drake, Alison)
1992	▮ Birth Marks (Dunant, Sarah)
1992	Death and Taxes (Dunlap, Susan)
1992	Moroccan Traffic [Brit- Send a Fax to the Kasbah] (Dunnett, Dorothy)

1992	Late of This Parish (Eccles, Marjorie)
1992	Clubbed to Death (Edwards, Ruth Dudley) ☆
1992	Blood on the Water (Elrod, P.N.)
1992	▮ Death of a Duchess (Eyre, Elizabeth)

1992	Dead Ends (Fallon, Ann C.)
1992	▮ Alibi for an Actress (Farrell, Gillian B.)
1992	Murder on Wheels (Frankel, Valerie)
1992	Three, Three the Rivals (Fraser, Anthea)
1992	▮ The Novice's Tale (Frazer, Margaret)

1992	The Jersey Monkey (Gallison, Kate)
1992	For the Sake of Elena (George, Elizabeth)
1992	Murder Most Mellow (Girdner, Jaqueline)
1992	▮ Showcase (Glen, Alison)
1992	▮ The Body in Blackwater Bay [incl Stryker & Trevorne] (Gosling, Paula)
1992	"I" is for Innocent (Grafton, Sue)
1992	Death in Disguise (Graham, Caroline)
1992	A Season for Murder (Granger, Ann)
1992	▮ A Life of Adventure (Grant-Adamson, Lesley)
1992	A Cast of Killers (Gray, Gallagher)
1992	Deadly Admirer (Green, Christine)
1992	Unholy Ghosts (Greenwood, D.M.)
1992	Death at Victoria Dock (Greenwood, Kerry)
1992	Under Water (Gunning, Sally)
1992	▮ The Saturday Morning Murder (Gur, Batya)

1992	▮ Caught in the Shadows (Haddad, C.A.)
1992	A Great Day for the Deadly (Haddam, Jane)
1992	Feast of Murder (Haddam, Jane)
1992	A Stillness in Bethlehem (Haddam, Jane)
1992	Ghostland (Hager, Jean)
1992	▮ Ravenmocker (Hager, Jean)
1992	A Bone To Pick (Harris, Charlaine)
1992	▮ The Good Friday Murder (Harris, Lee) ☆
1992	The Yom Kippur Murder (Harris, Lee)
1992	Death Watch (Harrod-Eagles, Cynthia)
1992	Southern Ghost (Hart, Carolyn G.) ☆☆
1992	Stage Fright (Hart, Ellen)
1992	▮ Principal Defense (Hartzmark, Gini) ☆
1992	▮ A Murder of Crows (Haffner, Margaret)
1992	Pel and the Sepulchre [by Mark Hebden] (Hebden, Juliet)
1992	Maggody in Manhattan (Hess, Joan)
1992	Death by the Light of the Moon (Hess, Joan)
1992	▮ Alien Blues (Hightower, Lynn S.)
1992	The Shortest Journey (Holt, Hazel)
1992	▮ Telling Lies (Hornsby, Wendy)
1992	▮ Blood Price (Huff, Tanya)
1992	Blood Trail (Huff, Tanya)

1992	Diamond Head (Jackson, Marian J. A.)
1992	A Slash of Scarlet (Jacobs, Nancy Baker)
1992	Without Due Process (Jance, J.A.)
1992	▮ A Safe Place To Sleep (Jordan, Jennifer)

1992	Day of Atonement (Kellerman, Faye)
1992	False Prophet (Kellerman, Faye)
1992	Foxglove (Kelly, Mary Anne)
1992	My Sister's Keeper (Kelly, Nora)
1992	Out of the Darkness (Kelly, Susan)
1992	Copy Kat (Kijewski, Karen)
1992	Cadaver (Kittredge, Mary)
1992	Walking Dead Man (Kittredge, Mary)
1992	To Kill a Queen (Knight, Alanna)
1992	▮ Switching the Odds (Knight, Phyllis) ☆

1992	▮ File Under: Deceased (Lacey, Sarah)
1992	▮ The Holiday Murders (Landreth, Marsha)
1992	God in Concord (Langton, Jane)
1992	Recipe for Death (Laurence, Janet)
1992	Time Lapse (Law, Janice)
1992	Robber's Trail [as W.W. Lee] (Lee, Wendi)
1992	▮ Death at La Fenice (Leon, Donna)
1992	Hanging on the Wire (Linscott, Gillian)
1992	Dreamland (Lorens, M.K.)

1992	Spree (MacGregor, T.J.)
1992	The Resurrection Man (MacLeod, Charlotte)
1992	Crazy for Loving (Maiman, Jaye) ★
1992	▮ Body English (Mariz, Linda French)
1992	Snake Dance (Mariz, Linda French)
1992	▮ Bootlegger's Daughter (Maron, Margaret) ★★★★
1992	Hacker (Martin, Lee)

1992 A Hard Bargain (Matera, Lia)
1992 Murder on the Silk Road (Matteson, Stefanie)
1992 ❶ The Scent of Fear (Matthews, Patricia)
1992 The King of Nothing (Maxwell, A.E.)
1992 Ruffled Feathers (McCafferty, Taylor)
1992 Bed Bugs (McCafferty, Taylor)
1992 MacPherson's Lament (McCrumb, Sharyn)
1992 Zombies of the Gene Pool (McCrumb, Sharyn)
1992 The Hangman's Beautiful Daughter
        (McCrumb, Sharyn) ☆☆
1992 ❶ Dead Beat (McDermid, Val)
1992 ❶ Emergency Murder (McGiffin, Janet)
1992 The Other Woman (McGown, Jill)
1992 Point Deception (McKernan, Victoria)
1992 ❶ The Medium is Murder (McKitterick, Molly)
1992 Dead Certain [APA- Off Key] (McNab, Claire)
1992 The Pumpkin-Shell Wife (McShea, Susanna Hofmann)
1992 Touch and Go (Meek, M.R.D.)
1992 Dead Set (Melville, Jennie)
1992 Blood on the Street (Meyers, Annette)
1992 ❶ The Dutchman (Meyers, Maan)
1992 ❶ Murder at Moot Point (Millhiser, Marlys)
1992 Veronica's Sisters (Moffat, Gwen)
1992 ❶ Seneca Falls Inheritance (Monfredo, Miriam Grace) ☆ ☆
1992 Home Sweet Homicide (Morgan, Kate)
1992 Mystery Loves Company (Morgan, Kate)
1992 Days of Crime and Roses (Morgan, Kate)
1992 The Martini Effect (Morison, B.J.)
1992 Pennies on a Dead Woman's Eyes (Muller, Marcia)
1992 Murder Makes an Entree (Myers, Amy)
1992 Murder Under the Kissing Bough (Myers, Amy)

1992 ❶ Blanche on the Lam (Neely, Barbara) ★★★

1992 Eagles Die Too (O'Brien, Meg)
1992 Pushover (O'Donnell, Lillian)
1992 Deservedly Dead (Oliphant, B. J.)
1992 Death and the Delinquent (Oliphant, B. J.)
1992 Death for Old Times' Sake (Orde, A. J.)

1992 The Body in the Vestibule (Page, Katherine Hall)
1992 You Have the Right To Remain Silent (Paul, Barbara)
1992 A Legacy of Death (Penn, John)
1992 Belgrave Square (Perry, Anne)
1992 Defend and Betray (Perry, Anne) ☆
1992 The Snake, the Crocodile and the Dog
        (Peters, Elizabeth) ☆
1992 ❶ Dartmoor Burial (Peterson, Audrey)
1992 ❶ The Two-Bit Tango (Pincus, Elizabeth) ★
1992 Houston Town (Powell, Deborah)
1992 Show Stopper (Pulver, Mary Monica)

1992 A Fatal End (Quinton, Ann)

1992 Cross My Heart and Hope To Die (Radley, Sheila)
1992 Kissing the Gunner's Daughter (Rendell, Ruth)
1992 ❶ Jinx (Robitaille, Julie)
1992 Death in Store [short stories] (Rowe, Jennifer)

1992 Pursued by Shadows (Sale, Medora)
1992 Murder Is Germane (Saum, Karen)
1992 Murder by Owl Light (Sawyer, Corinne Holt)
1992 The Plymouth Cloak (Sedley, Kate)
1992 Dying Cheek to Cheek (Shah, Diane K.)
1992 The King Is Dead (Shankman, Sarah)
1992 Thinner Than Blood (Shepherd, Stella)
1992 Straight as an Arrow (Sibley, Celestine)
1992 Skylark (Simonson, Sheila)
1992 Wake the Dead (Simpson, Dorothy)
1992 Practice To Deceive (Smith, Janet L.)
1992 ❶ The Vanished Child [Boston] (Smith, Sarah)
1992 Somebody's Dead in Snellville (Sprinkle, Patricia H.)
1992 ❶ A Cold Day for Murder (Stabenow, Dana) ★
1992 ❶ Found: A Body (Struthers, Betsy)
1992 The Late Lady (Stacey, Susannah)

1992 ❶ The End of April (Sumner, Penny)

1992 The Northwest Murders (Taylor, Elizabeth Atwood)
1992 ❶ Every Crooked Nanny (Trocheck, Kathy Hogan) ☆☆
1992 Murder at the Pentagon (Truman, Margaret)
1992 Cold Feet (Tucker, Kerry)

1992 The Wolf Path (Van Gieson, Judith)

1992 ❶ The Winter Widow (Weir, Charlene) ★★☆
1992 ❶ Frost the Fiddler (Weber, Janice)
1992 Still Waters (Welch, Pat)
1992 Sweet Death Come Softly (Whitehead, Barbara)
1992 A Singular Spy (Williams, Amanda Kyle)
1992 Seven Kinds of Death (Wilhelm, Kate)
1992 Exception to Murder (Wingate, Anne)
1992 All Hallow's Evil (Wolzien, Valerie)
1992 An Old Faithful Murder (Wolzien, Valerie)
1992 Hot Secret (Woods, Sherryl)

1992 Cat's Claw (Yarbro, Chelsea Quinn)
1992 ❶ Cancellation by Death (Yeager, Dorian)

1992 Dancing in the Dark (Zukowski, Sharon)

1993

1993 All the Dark Disguises (Adams, Deborah)
1993 All the Hungry Mothers (Adams, Deborah)
1993 A Going Concern (Aird, Catherine)
1993 Witches' Bane (Albert, Susan Wittig)
1993 Quaker Witness (Allen, Irene)
1993 ❶ Tell Me What You Like (Allen, Kate)

1993 Shadows in Their Blood (Babson, Marian)
1993 Even Yuppies Die (Babson, Marian)
1993 Long Goodbyes (Baker, Nikki)
1993 ❶ Death by Dressage (Banks, Carolyn)
1993 ❶ A Bleeding of Innocents (Bannister, Jo)
1993 Snapshot (Barnes, Linda)
1993 ❶ Track of the Cat (Barr, Nevada) ★★
1993 Agatha Raisin and the Vicious Vet (Beaton, M.C.)
1993 Death of a Glutton (Beaton, M.C.)
1993 Death of a Travelling Man (Beaton, M.C.)
1993 Amateur Night (Beck, K. K.)
1993 Signs of Murder (Bedford, Jean)
1993 ❶ The Garbage Dump Murders [U.S.- Introducing
        Amanda Valentine] (Beecham, Rose)
1993 The Way of a Serpent (Bell, Pauline)
1993 A Vow of Sanctity (Black, Veronica)
1993 A Vow of Obedience (Black, Veronica)
1993 Slow Burn (Bland, Eleanor Taylor)
1993 ❶ Kindness Can Kill (Bolitho, Janie)
1993 ❶ One for the Money (Borton, D.B.)
1993 Two Points for Murder (Borton, D.B.)
1993 The Wandering Soul Murders (Bowen, Gail)
1993 Pushing Murder (Boylan, Eleanor)
1993 The Cat Who Wasn't There (Braun, Lilian Jackson)
1993 ❶ The Inspector and Mrs. Jeffries (Brightwell, Emily)
1993 Mrs. Jeffries Dusts for Clues (Brightwell, Emily)
1993 The Ghost and Mrs. Jeffries (Brightwell, Emily)
1993 Date With a Plummeting Publisher (Brill, Toni)
1993 Brothers in Blood (Brod, D. C.)
1993 Father, Forgive Me (Burden, Pat)
1993 ❶ Goodnight, Irene (Burke, Jan) ☆☆
1993 Death by Crystal (Bushell, Agnes)
1993 Cracking Open a Coffin (Butler, Gwendoline)

1993 ❶ Private Lies (Cail, Carol)
1993 ❶ A Pocketful of Karma (Cannon, Taffy)
1993 The Snares of Death (Charles, Kate)
1993 ❶ This Business Is Murder (Christmas, Joyce)
1993 A Quiche Before Dying (Churchill, Jill)
1993 The Class Menagerie (Churchill, Jill)
1993 Snagged (Clark, Carol Higgins)
1993 Dog Collar Crime (Cleary, Melissa)
1993 Hounded to Death (Cleary, Melissa)

1993		Angel in Love (Cohen, Anthea)
1993		Appearance of Evil (Coker, Carolyn)
1993		The Cashmere Kid (Comfort, Barbara)
1993		Ruffly Speaking (Conant, Susan)
1993		Bitter Herbs (Cooper, Natasha)
1993	❶	Funny as a Dead Comic (Cooper, Susan Rogers)
1993		Cruel and Unusual (Cornwell, Patricia) ★
1993		The Grub-and-Stakers House a Haunt (Craig, Alisa)
1993		Miss Seeton Plants Suspicion (Crane, Hamilton)
1993		Miss Seeton Goes to Bat (Crane, Hamilton)
1993		The Trouble With Thin Ice (Crespi, Camilla)
1993	❶	A Share in Death (Crombie, Deborah) ☆☆
1993	❶	Dead as Dead Can Be (Crowleigh, Ann)
1993		Wait for the Dark (Crowleigh, Ann)
1993		First Wife, Twice Removed (Curzon, Clare)

1993		Hard Women (D'Amato, Barbara) ☆
1993		The Alpine Betrayal (Daheim, Mary)
1993		The Alpine Christmas (Daheim, Mary)
1993		Dune to Death (Daheim, Mary)
1993		Bantam of the Opera (Daheim, Mary)
1993		Sing a Song of Death (Dain, Catherine)
1993		The Misfortune of Others (Dank, Gloria)
1993		Wink a Hopeful Eye (Danks, Denise)
1993		Cereal Murders (Davidson, Diane Mott)
1993		Poseidon's Gold (Davis, Lindsey) ☆
1993	❶	The Santa Fe Rembrandt (Dawkins, Cecil)
1993		Till the Old Men Die (Dawson, Janet)
1993		Take a Number (Dawson, Janet)
1993		Death Valley (Dengler, Sandy)
1993		A Model Murder (Dengler, Sandy)
1993	❶	Cat Killer (Dengler, Sandy)
1993		Mouse Trapped (Dengler, Sandy)
1993	❶	An Uncommon Murder (Donald, Anabel)
1993		Pussyfoot (Douglas, Carole Nelson)
1993		Goblin Market (Douglas, Lauren Wright)
1993		Otherworld (Dreher, Sarah)
1993	❶	The Other Side of Silence (Drury, Joan M.)
1993		Gallows Bird (Duffy, Margaret)
1993		Fat Lands (Dunant, Sarah) ★
1993	❶	Behind Eclaire's Doors (Dunbar, Sophie)
1993		Time Expired (Dunlap, Susan)
1993	❶	The Man Who Understood Cats (Dymmoch, Michael Allen) ★

1993		The Company She Kept (Eccles, Marjorie)
1993		Chatauqua (Ennis, Catherine)
1993	❶	Dead Before Morning (Evans, Geraldine)
1993		Curtains for the Cardinal (Eyre, Elizabeth)

1993		Potter's Field (Fallon, Ann C.)
1993		Death Wears a Crown (Fawcett, Quinn)
1993	❶	Napoleon Must Die (Fawcett, Quinn)
1993	❶	Dead in the Water (Feddersen, Connie)
1993	❶	Missing Person (Ferguson, Frances)
1993		Jemima Shore at the Sunny Grave [9 stories] (Fraser, Antonia)
1993		The Servant's Tale (Frazer, Margaret) ☆
1993		Night Shift (Fromer, Margot J.)
1993		Shadow Play (Fyfield, Frances)

1993		Sharkbait (Geason, Susan)
1993		Missing Joseph (George, Elizabeth)
1993		Mrs. Pollifax and the Second Thief (Gilman, Dorothy)
1993	❶	Final Design (Gilpatrick, Noreen)
1993		Fat-Free and Fatal (Girdner, Jaqueline)
1993		A Death for a Dodo (Giroux, E.X.)
1993	❶	Burning Time (Glass, Leslie)
1993		Night Game (Gordon, Alison)
1993		"J" is for Judgment (Grafton, Sue)
1993		Cold in the Earth (Granger, Ann)
1993		Murder Among Us (Granger, Ann)
1993		Where Old Bones Lie (Granger, Ann)
1993	❶	Death in the Country (Green, Christine)

1993		Black Dreams (Green, Kate)
1993		Idol Bones (Greenwood, D.M.)
1993		The Green Mill Murder (Greenwood, Kerry)
1993		The Horse You Came in On (Grimes, Martha)
1993	❶	The Killing of Ellis Martin (Grindle, Lucretia)
1993		Ice Water (Gunning, Sally)
1993		Troubled Water (Gunning, Sally)
1993		Literary Murder (Gur, Batya)

1993		Murder Superior (Haddam, Jane)
1993	❶	Death by Election (Hall, Patricia)
1993	❶	Guilty Pleasures (Hamilton, Laurell K.)
1993		The Christening Day Murder (Harris, Lee)
1993		Death To Go [APA- Necrochip] (Harrod-Eagles, Cynthia)
1993	❶	Dead Man's Island (Hart, Carolyn G.) ★
1993		A Killing Cure (Hart, Ellen)
1993		A Beautiful Death (Haymon, S. T.)
993		Pel Picks up the Pieces (Hebden, Juliet)
1993	❶	With Deadly Intent (Hendricksen, Louise)
1993		O Little Town of Maggody (Hess, Joan) ☆☆
1993		Poisoned Pins (Hess, Joan)
1993		Alien Eyes (Hightower, Lynn S.)
1993	❶	Satan's Lambs (Hightower, Lynn S.) ★
1993		Mrs. Malory and the Festival Murders [Brit- Uncertain Death] (Holt, Hazel)
1993		Midnight Baby (Hornsby, Wendy)
1993		Blood Lines (Huff, Tanya)
1993		Blood Pact (Huff, Tanya)

1993		The Silver Scalpel (Jacobs, Nancy Baker)
1993		Failure To Appear (Jance, J.A.)
1993	❶	Desert Heat (Jance, J.A.)
1993		Six Foot Under (John, Katherine)
1993	❶	Murder at the MLA (Jones, D. J. H.)
1993		Existing Solutions (Jordan, Jennifer)

1993		Grievous Sin (Kellerman, Faye)
1993		Bad Chemistry (Kelly, Nora)
1993		Hope Will Answer (Kelly, Susan B.)
1993	❶	Down Home Murder (Kelner, Toni L.P.)
1993	❶	Murder Is Too Expensive (Kershaw, Valerie)
1993	❶	A Grave Talent (King, Laurie R.) ★☆☆
1993	❶	Room With a Clue (Kingsbury, Kate)
1993		Desperate Remedy (Kittredge, Mary)
1993		The Evil That Men Do (Knight, Alanna)
1993	❶	Fair Game (Krich, Rochelle Majer) ☆

1993		File Under: Missing (Lacey, Sarah)
1993	❶	Questionable Behavior (Lamb, J. Dayne)
1993		A Clinic for Murder (Landreth, Marsha)
1993		Divine Inspiration (Langton, Jane)
1993		Old Enemies (LaPierre, Janet) ☆
1993	❶	Prime Suspect (La Plante, Lynda)
1993		Prime Suspect 2 (La Plante, Lynda)
1993		Right on the Money (Lathen, Emma)
1993		Death and the Epicure (Laurence, Janet)
1993		A Safe Place To Die (Law, Janice)
1993		Outlaw's Fortune [as W.W. Lee] (Lee, Wendi)
1993		Death in a Strange Country (Leon, Donna)
1993		Stage Fright (Linscott, Gillian)
1993	❶	Brotherly Love (Lordon, Randye) ☆
1993		Sorrowheart (Lorens, M.K.)
1993		Someone Is Killing the Great Chefs of America (Lyons, Nan & Ivan)

1993		Storm Surge (MacGregor, T.J.)
1993		Under My Skin (Maiman, Jaye)
1993	❶	The Case of the Not-So-Nice Nurse (Maney, Mabel)
1993		Southern Discomfort (Maron, Margaret) ☆☆
1993		The Day That Dusty Died (Martin, Lee)
1993	❶	Murder in the Maze (Mason, Sarah J.)
1993		Frozen Stiff (Mason, Sarah J.)
1993		Corpse in the Kitchen (Mason, Sarah J.)
1993		Murder at the Falls (Matteson, Stefanie)

1993		Taste of Evil (Matthews, Patricia)
1993		Vision of Death (Matthews, Patricia)
1993		Murder Hurts (Maxwell, A.E.)
1993		Kick Back (McDermid, Val)
1993		Union Jack [U.S.- Conferences are Murder (1999)] (McDermid, Val)
1993		Prescription for Death (McGiffin, Janet)
1993		Murder Now and Then (McGown, Jill)
1993	❶	Until Proven Guilty (McGuire, Christine)
1993	❶	Murder Beach (McKenna, Bridget)
1993		Murder in a Mayonnaise Jar (McKitterick, Molly)
1993		Elephants' Graveyard (McQuillan, Karin)
1993	❶	Mail-Order Murder [APA- Mistletoe Murder (1998)] (Meier, Leslie)
1993		Whoever Has the Heart (Melville, Jennie)
1993		The Sheriff & the Pheasant Hunt Murders (Meredith, D. R.)
1993		Murder by Sacrilege (Meredith, D. R.)
1993		Murder: The Musical (Meyers, Annette)
1993		The Kingsbridge Plot (Meyers, Maan)
1993		Death of the Office Witch (Millhiser, Marlys)
1993	❶	Deadly Deceptions (Moen, Ruth Raby)
1993		North Star Conspiracy (Monfredo, Miriam Grace)
1993	❶	Death Takes a Hand [Brit- Takeout Double] (Moody, Susan)
1993		Penny Saving (Moody, Susan)
1993		Final Rest (Morell, Mary)
1993		Twice in a Blue Moon (Moyes, Patricia)
1993		Wolf in the Shadows (Muller, Marcia) ★☆☆
1993		The Marshal at the Villa Torrini (Nabb, Magdalen)
1993		Death Among the Dons (Neel, Janet) ☆
1993	❶	Death Comes as Epiphany (Newman, Sharan) ★☆☆
1993		Used To Kill (O'Donnell, Lillian)
1993		Murder Makes a Pilgrimage (O'Marie, Carol Anne, Sister)
1993	❶	Murder in Mellingham (Oleksiw, Susan)
1993		Looking for the Aardvark [APA- Dead on Sunday] (Orde, A. J.)
1993	❶	Child of Silence (Padgett, Abigail) ☆☆☆
1993		The Body in the Cast (Page, Katherine Hall)
1993		The Apostrophe Thief (Paul, Barbara)
1993	❶	Something's Cooking (Pence, Joanne)
1993		A Haven of Danger (Penn, John)
1993		Widow's End (Penn, John)
1993		Farriers' Lane (Perry, Anne)
1993		A Sudden, Fearful Death (Perry, Anne)
1993		But I Wouldn't Want To Die There (Pickard, Nancy)
1993		The 27-Ingredient Chile Con Carne Murders [with Virginia Rich] (Pickard, Nancy)
1993		Heading Uptown (Piesman, Marissa)
1993		The Solitary Twist (Pincus, Elizabeth)
1993	❶	By Evil Means (Prowell, Sandra West) ☆
1993	❶	Cold Call (Pugh, Dianne G.)
1993	❶	Murder Most Grizzly (Quinn, Elizabeth)
1993	❶	First Blood (Rayner, Claire)
1993		Deaths of Jocasta (Redmann, J. M.)
1993	❶	The Apothecary Rose (Robb, Candace M.)
1993		Pray God To Die (Roberts, Carey)
1993		With Friends Like These (Roberts, Gillian)
1993		Shadow Walkers (Romberg, Nina)
1993	❶	Cut to the Quick (Ross, Kate)
1993		The Makeover Murders (Rowe, Jennifer)
1993		Finishing Touch (Rowlands, Betty)
1993		Over the Edge (Rowlands, Betty)
1993		The Down Home Heifer Heist (Sandstrom, Eve K.)
1993		The Peanut Butter Murders (Sawyer, Corinne Holt)
1993	❶	Silverlake Heat (Schmidt, Carol)
1993		I'll Be Leaving You Always (Scoppettone, Sandra)
1993	❶	Always in a Foreign Land (Scott, Barbara A.)

1993	❶	Everywhere That Mary Went [Mary DiNunzio] (Scottoline, Lisa) ☆
1993		The Hanged Man [APA- The Weaver's Tale] (Sedley, Kate)
1993		He Was Her Man (Shankman, Sarah)
1993		A Lethal Fixation (Shepherd, Stella)
1993		Dire Happenings at Scratch Ankle (Sibley, Celestine)
1993		Storm Shelter (Silva, Linda Kay)
1993		Mudlark (Simonson, Sheila)
1993		No Laughing Matter (Simpson, Dorothy)
1993	❶	Following Jane (Singer, Shelley)
1993		Picture of David (Singer, Shelley)
1993		What Men Say (Smith, Joan)
1993		Other People's Skeletons (Smith, Julie)
1993		Jazz Funeral (Smith, Julie)
1993		Death of a Dunwoody Matron (Sprinkle, Patricia H.)
1993		A Fatal Thaw (Stabenow, Dana)
1993		Dead in the Water (Stabenow, Dana)
1993		Bone Idle (Stacey, Susannah)
1993	❶	Death and the Oxford Box (Stallwood, Veronica)
1993	❶	Murder at the Class Reunion (Stein, Triss)
1993		Library: No Murder Aloud (Steiner, Susan)
1993		Bagels for Tea (Stevens, Serita)
1993	❶	A Sudden Death at the Norfolk Café (Sullivan, Winona) ★
1993	❶	The Missionary Position [APA- Funeral Food (1997)] (Taylor, Kathleen)
1993		To Live and Die in Dixie (Trocheck, Kathy Hogan) ☆☆☆
1993		Death Echo (Tucker, Kerry)
1993		The Lies That Bind (Van Gieson, Judith) ☆
1993		Clear Cut Murder (Wallingford, Lee)
1993	❶	The Wyndham Case (Paton Walsh, Jill)
1993		Consider the Crows (Weir, Charlene) ☆
1993		A Proper Burial (Welch, Pat)
1993		Money To Burn (White, Gloria)
1993		The Spy in Question (Williams, Amanda Kyle)
1993		Trouble in Transylvania (Wilson, Barbara)
1993		Yakuza, Go Home! (Wingate, Anne)
1993		A Star-Spangled Murder (Wolzien, Valerie)
1993		Bank on It (Woods, Sherryl)
1993		Hide and Seek (Woods, Sherryl)
1993		Hot Money (Woods, Sherryl)
1993		Dead Matter (Wren, M.K.)
1993		Prized Possessions (Wright, L.R.)
1993		Eviction by Death (Yeager, Dorian)
1993	❶	Timber City Masks (York, Kieran)

1994

1994		Hangman's Root (Albert, Susan Wittig)
1994		Grizzly, A Murder (Andreae, Christine)
1994	❶	Tensleep (Andrews, Sarah)
1994		Dirge for a Dorset Druid (Arnold, Margot)
1994		Aunt Dimity and the Duke (Atherton, Nancy)
1994		Carcass Trade (Ayres, Noreen)
1994	❶	Dreadful Lies (Bailey, Michele)
1994		Groomed for Death (Banks, Carolyn)
1994		Sins of the Heart [U.S.- Charisma] (Bannister, Jo)
1994		A Superior Death (Barr, Nevada)
1994		Agatha Raisin and the Potted Gardener (Beaton, M.C.)
1994		Death of a Charming Man (Beaton, M.C.)
1994		Electric City (Beck, K. K.)
1994		Second Guess (Beecham, Rose)
1994		Downhill to Death (Bell, Pauline)
1994		The Death of a Difficult Woman (Berry, Carole)
1994		Motive for Murder (Bolitho, Janie)
1994	❶	A Taste for Murder (Bishop, Claudia)
1994		A Vow of Penance (Black, Veronica)
1994		A Vow of Devotion (Black, Veronica)
1994		Gone Quiet (Bland, Eleanor Taylor)

1994 🔳 Chutes and Adders (Block, Barbara)
1994   Twister (Block, Barbara)
1994   Ripe for Revenge (Bolitho, Janie)
1994   The Bridled Groom (Borthwick, J. S.)
1994   Three Is a Crowd (Borton, D.B.)
1994   A Colder Kind of Death (Bowen, Gail) ★
1994   The Cat Who Came to Breakfast (Braun, Lilian Jackson)
1994   The Cat Who Went into the Closet (Braun, Lilian Jackson)
1994 🔳 In the Dark (Brennan, Carol)
1994   Mrs. Jeffries Takes Stock (Brightwell, Emily)
1994   Mrs. Jeffries on the Ball (Brightwell, Emily)
1994   Murder at Monticello (Brown, Rita Mae)
1994   Miami, It's Murder (Buchanan, Edna) ☆
1994 🔳 No One Dies in Branson (Buckstaff, Kathryn)
1994   Sweet Dreams, Irene (Burke, Jan)
1994   A Coffin for Charley (Butler, Gwendoline)
1994   The Coffin Tree (Butler, Gwendoline)

1994   How To Murder Your Mother-in-law (Cannell, Dorothy)
1994 🔳 All the Old Lions (Caverly, Carol)
1994   Love Bytes (Chapman, Sally)
1994   Appointed To Die (Charles, Kate)
1994 🔳 A Famine of Horses (Chisholm, P. F.)
1994   A Perfect Day for Dying (Christmas, Joyce)
1994   A Knife to Remember (Churchill, Jill)
1994   The Case of the Ludicrous Letters (Clarke, Anna)
1994   Skull and Dog Bones (Cleary, Melissa)
1994   First Pedigree Murder (Cleary, Melissa)
1994   Dead and Buried (Cleary, Melissa)
1994   The Mill on the Shore (Cleeves, Ann)
1994   Monkey Wrench (Cody, Liza)
1994   Funny as a Dead Relative (Cooper, Susan Rogers)
1994   Dead Moon on the Rise (Cooper, Susan Rogers)
1994   The Body Farm (Cornwell, Patricia)
1994   Starring Miss Seeton (Crane, Hamilton)
1994   Miss Seeton Undercover (Crane, Hamilton)
1994   Miss Seeton Rules (Crane, Hamilton)
1994   All Shall Be Well (Crombie, Deborah)
1994 🔳 Cutter (Crum, Laura)
1994   Death Prone (Curzon, Clare)

1994   Hard Case (D'Amato, Barbara)
1994   The Alpine Decoy (Daheim, Mary)
1994   Fit of Tempera (Daheim, Mary)
1994   Walk a Crooked Mile (Dain, Catherine)
1994   Lament for a Dead Cowboy (Dain, Catherine) ☆
1994   The Last Suppers (Davidson, Diane Mott)
1994   Last Act in Palmyra (Davis, Lindsey)
1994   Don't Turn Your Back on the Ocean (Dawson, Janet)
1994   The Disappearance of Madalena Grimaldi (Day, Marele)
1994 🔳 Mama Solves a Murder (Deloach, Nora)
1994   Murder on the Mount (Dengler, Sandy)
1994   The Last Dinosaur (Dengler, Sandy)
1994   Gila Monster (Dengler, Sandy)
1994   The Queen Is Dead (Dentinger, Jane)
1994 🔳 Miss Zukas and the Library Murders (Dereske, Jo)
1994   Beat up a Cookie (Dietz, Denise)
1994   In at the Deep End (Donald, Anabel)
1994   Irene's Last Waltz (Douglas, Carole Nelson)
1994   Cat on a Blue Monday (Douglas, Carole Nelson)
1994   A Rage of Maidens (Douglas, Lauren Wright)
1994 🔳 Dressed To Kill (Duffy, Margaret)
1994 🔳 Calendar Girl (Duffy, Stella)
1994   High Fall (Dunlap, Susan)
1994 🔳 Death at Wentwater Court (Dunn, Carola)

1994   An Accidental Shroud (Eccles, Marjorie)
1994 🔳 Speak Daggers to Her (Edghill, Rosemary)
1994   Matricide at St. Martha's (Edwards, Ruth Dudley)
1994 🔳 Murder Can Kill Your Social Life (Eichler, Selma)
1994 🔳 One for the Money (Evanovich, Janet) ★☆☆☆☆

1994   Down Among the Dead Men (Evans, Geraldine)
1994   Poison for the Prince (Eyre, Elizabeth)
1994   Bravo for the Bride (Eyre, Elizabeth)

1994   Murder and a Muse (Farrell, Gillian B.)
1994 🔳 The Adventures of Mycroft Holmes (Fawcett, Quinn)
1994   Dead in the Cellar (Feddersen, Connie)
1994 🔳 The Hippie in the Wall (Fennelly, Tony)
1994   No Fixed Abode (Ferguson, Frances)
1994   Manhattans & Murder (Fletcher, Jessica)
1994 🔳 Chosen for Death (Flora, Kate Clark)
1994 🔳 Fool's Puzzle (Fowler, Earlene) ☆
1994   Prime Time for Murder (Frankel, Valerie)
1994   The Gospel Makers (Fraser, Anthea)
1994   Political Death (Fraser, Antonia)
1994   The Outlaw's Tale (Frazer, Margaret)
1994   The Bishop's Tale (Frazer, Margaret)
1994   Buried in Quilts (Frommer, Sara Hoskinson)
1994   A Clear Conscience (Fyfield, Frances)
1994   Perfectly Pure and Good (Fyfield, Frances)

1994   Playing for the Ashes (George, Elizabeth)
1994   Tea-Totally Dead (Girdner, Jaqueline)
1994   A Few Dying Words (Gosling, Paula)
1994   "K" is for Killer (Grafton, Sue) ★☆☆
1994   Written in Blood (Graham, Caroline) ☆
1994   Flowers for His Funeral (Granger, Ann)
1994   A Fine Place for Death (Granger, Ann)
1994   A Woman's Place (Grant, Linda)
1994   Dangerous Games (Grant-Adamson, Lesley)
1994   Deadly Practice (Green, Christine)
1994   Holy Terrors (Greenwood, D.M.)
1994   Blood and Circuses (Greenwood, Kerry)
1994   So Little To Die For (Grindle, Lucretia)
1994   Rough Water (Gunning, Sally)
1994   Murder on a Kibbutz: A Communal Case (Gur, Batya) ☆

1994   Bleeding Hearts (Haddam, Jane)
1994   Dear Old Dead (Haddam, Jane)
1994   Festival of Deaths (Haddam, Jane)
1994   Root Canal (Haddad, C.A.)
1994 🔳 Edited Out (Haddock, Lisa)
1994   A Killing Frost (Haffner, Margaret)
1994   The Redbird's Cry (Hager, Jean)
1994 🔳 Blooming Murder (Hager, Jean)
1994   Dying Fall (Hall, Patricia)
1994   The Laughing Corpse (Hamilton, Laurell K.)
1994   Three Bedrooms, One Corpse (Harris, Charlaine)
1994   The St. Patrick's Day Murder (Harris, Lee)
1994   The Christmas Night Murder (Harris, Lee)
1994   Grave Music [Brit- Dead End] (Harrod-Eagles, Cynthia)
1994   Scandal in Fair Haven (Hart, Carolyn G.) ☆
1994   A Small Sacrifice (Hart, Ellen) ★
1994 🔳 This Little Piggy Went To Murder (Hart, Ellen)
1994   Final Option (Hartzmark, Gini)
1994 🔳 What's a Girl Gotta Do? (Hayter, Sparkle) ★
1994   Pel and the Perfect Partner (Hebden, Juliet)
1994   Grave Secrets (Hendricksen, Louise)
1994   Martians in Maggody (Hess, Joan)
1994   Tickled to Death (Hess, Joan)
1994 🔳 Keeper at the Shrine (Highsmith, Domini)
1994   Alien Heat (Hightower, Lynn S.)
1994   Mrs. Malory: Detective in Residence [Brit- Murder on Campus] (Holt, Hazel)
1994 🔳 Something To Kill For (Holtzer, Susan) ★
1994   Dead Center (Horansky, Ruby)
1994   Bad Intent (Hornsby, Wendy)
1994   Beauty Dies (Howe, Melodie Johnson)

1994   The Sunken Treasure (Jackson, Marian J. A.)
1994 🔳 Murder Among Neighbors (Jacobs, Jonnie)
1994   Original Sin (James, P. D.)
1994   Lying in Wait ()
1994   Tombstone Courage (Jance, J.A.)

1994		Murder of a Dead Man (John, Katherine)
1994	■	A Love To Die For (Jorgensen, Christine T.)
1994	■	Sacred Hearts (Joseph, Alison)

1994	■	Unsolicited (Kaewert, Julie Wallin)
1994		Sanctuary (Kellerman, Faye)
1994		Kid's Stuff (Kelly, Susan B.)
1994		Dead Ringer (Kelner, Toni L.P.)
1994		Funny Money (Kershaw, Valerie)
1994		Wild Kat (Kijewski, Karen)
1994	■	The Beekeeper's Apprentice (King, Laurie R.) ☆
1994		Do Not Disturb (Kingsbury, Kate)
1994		Service for Two (Kingsbury, Kate)
1994		Eat, Drink, and Be Buried (Kingsbury, Kate)
1994		The Missing Duchess (Knight, Alanna)
1994		Dark Swain (Knight, Kathryn Lasky)
1994		Shattered Rhythms (Knight, Phyllis)
1994		Angel of Death (Krich, Rochelle Majer) ☆
1994	■	Death on the Cliff Walk (Kruger, Mary)

1994		File Under: Arson (Lacey, Sarah)
1994	■	Death in the Dark Walk (Lake, Deryn)
1994		A Question of Preference (Lamb, J. Dayne)
1994		Vial Murders (Landreth, Marsha)
1994	■	Cold Shoulder (La Plante, Lynda)
1994		Prime Suspect 3 (La Plante, Lynda)
1994		Death at the Table (Laurence, Janet)
1994		Backfire (Law, Janice)
1994	■	The Good Daughter (Lee, Wendi)
1994		Dressed for Death [Brit- The Anonymous Venetian] (Leon, Donna)
1994		Widow's Peak [U.S.- An Easy Day for a Lady] (Linscott, Gillian)
1994	■	The End of an Altruist (Logan, Margaret)
1994		Sister's Keeper (Lordon, Randye)

1994		Blue Pearl (MacGregor, T.J.)
1994		Something in the Water (MacLeod, Charlotte)
1994	■	Death Pays the Rose Rent (Malmont, Valerie S.)
1994		The Case of the Good-for-Nothing Girlfriend (Maney, Mabel)
1994	■	Ghost Motel (Manthorne, Jackie)
1994		Shooting at Loons (Maron, Margaret)
1994		Inherited Murder (Martin, Lee)
1994		Dying Breath (Mason, Sarah J.)
1994		Face Value (Matera, Lia)
1994	■	Blood of an Aries (Mather, Linda)
1994		Beware Taurus (Mather, Linda)
1994	■	Death in the Off-Season (Mathews, Francine)
1994		Murder on High (Matteson, Stefanie)
1994		The Sound of Murder (Matthews, Patricia)
1994	■	The Lessons (McAllester, Melanie)
1994	■	Star Gazer (McCafferty, Jeanne)
1994		Thin Skins (McCafferty, Taylor)
1994	■	The Bluejay Shaman (McClendon, Lise)
1994		She Walks These Hills (McCrumb, Sharyn) ★★★★
1994		Crack Down (McDermid, Val) ☆☆
1994		Until Justice is Done (McGuire, Christine)
1994		Dead Ahead (McKenna, Bridget) ☆
1994		Crooked Island (McKernan, Victoria)
1994		Body Guard (McNab, Claire)
1994		The Cheetah Chase (McQuillan, Karin)
1994		Ladybug, Ladybug (McShea, Susanna Hofmann)
1994		Tippy-Toe Murder (Meier, Leslie)
1994		Baby Drop [U.S.-Death in the Family] (Melville, Jennie)
1994		The High Constable (Meyers, Maan)
1994	■	Keeping Secrets (Mickelbury, Penny)
1994		A Strange Desire [U.S.- Roots of Evil] (Mitchell, Kay)
1994		Only One Way Out (Moen, Ruth Raby)
1994		Grand Slam (Moody, Susan)
1994		Wanted Dude or Alive (Morgan, Kate)
1994		Till the Butchers Cut Him Down (Muller, Marcia)

1994		Murder in the Smokehouse (Myers, Amy)
1994	■	Too Many Crooks Spoil the Broth (Myers, Tamar)

1994	■	The Total Zone (Navratilova, Martina)
1994		Blanche Among the Talented Tenth (Neely, Barbara)
1994		The Devil's Door (Newman, Sharan)
1994	■	Healthy, Wealthy & Dead (North, Suzanne) ☆

1994		Trade-Off (O'Callaghan, Maxine)
1994	■	Mallory's Oracle (O'Connell, Carol) ☆☆
1994		Lockout (O'Donnell, Lillian)
1994		Double Take (Oleksiw, Susan)
1994		Death Served up Cold (Oliphant, B. J.)
1994	■	Murder Offscreen (Osborne, Denise)

1994		Strawgirl (Padgett, Abigail)
1994		The Body in the Basement (Page, Katherine Hall)
1994	■	Death at Bishop's Keep (Paige, Robin)
1994		Tunnel Vision (Paretsky, Sara) ☆
1994	■	Suspicion of Innocence (Parker, Barbara) ☆
1994		Too Many Cooks (Pence, Joanne)
1994		A Guilty Party (Penn, John)
1994		The Hyde Park Headsman (Perry, Anne)
1994		Sins of the Wolf (Perry, Anne)
1994		Night Train to Memphis (Peters, Elizabeth) ☆
1994		Death Too Soon (Peterson, Audrey)
1994		Confession (Pickard, Nancy)
1994		Close Quarters (Piesman, Marissa)
1994		The Killing of Monday Brown (Prowell, Sandra West) ☆
1994		Slow Squeeze (Pugh, Dianne G.)

1994		A Little Grave (Quinton, Ann)
1994		The Sleeping and the Dead (Quinton, Ann)

1994		Fair Game (Radley, Sheila)
1994		Second Opinion (Rayner, Claire)
1994		Simisola (Rendell, Ruth)
1994	■	Origin and Cause (Reuben, Shelly)
1994	■	Mulch (Ripley, Ann)
1994		The Lady Chapel (Robb, Candace M.)
1994		How I Spent My Summer Vacation (Roberts, Gillian)
1994	■	Murder in a Nice Neighborhood (Roberts, Lora)
1994	■	Murder in the Place of Anubis (Robinson, Lynda S.)
1994		Iced (Robitaille, Julie)
1994		A Broken Vessel (Ross, Kate) ★
1994		The Dandelion Murders (Rothenberg, Rebecca)
1994		Stranglehold (Rowe, Jennifer)
1994	■	Shinju (Rowland, Laura Joh) ☆
1994		Exhaustive Inquiries (Rowlands, Betty)
1994	■	China Trade (Rozan, S.J.)
1994	■	Chicken Little Was Right (Ruryk, Jean)

1994		Short Cut to Santa Fe (Sale, Medora)
1994		Murder Is Material (Saum, Karen)
1994		Murder Has No Calories (Sawyer, Corinne Holt)
1994		Sweet Cherry Wine (Schmidt, Carol)
1994		My Sweet Untraceable You (Scoppettone, Sandra)
1994		Final Appeal [Grace Rossi] (Scottoline, Lisa) ★
1994		The Holy Innocents (Sedley, Kate)
1994	■	All My Suspects (Shaffer, Louise)
1994		Nurse Dawes Is Dead (Shepherd, Stella)
1994	■	Come Away Death [U.S.- Mr. Donaghue Investigates] (Shone, Anna)
1994	■	Angel's Bidding (Short, Sharon Gwyn)
1994		Past Pretense (Short, Sharon Gwyn)
1994		Weathering the Storm (Silva, Linda Kay)
1994		Searching for Sara (Singer, Shelley)
1994		Catnap (Slovo, Gillian)
1994	■	Writers of the Purple Sage (Smith, Barbara Burnett) ☆
1994		A Vintage Murder (Smith, Janet L.)
1994		New Orleans Beat (Smith, Julie)
1994	■	Every Breath You Take (Spring, Michelle) ☆
1994		A Mystery Bred in Buckhead (Sprinkle, Patricia H.)
1994	■	Who Killed What's-Her-Name? (Squire, Elizabeth Daniels)

1994 Remember the Alibi (Squire, Elizabeth Daniels)
1994 A Cold-Blooded Business (Stabenow, Dana)
1994 ◫ Looking for Trouble (Staincliffe, Cath) ☆
1994 Oxford Exit (Stallwood, Veronica)
1994 Grave Deeds (Struthers, Betsy)
1994 Crosswords (Sumner, Penny)

1994 Homemade Sin (Trocheck, Kathy Hogan)
1994 Murder on the Potomac (Truman, Margaret)
1994 Drift Away (Tucker, Kerry)
1994 ◫ Strangers in the Night (Tyre, Peg)

1994 ◫ The Red Scream (Walker, Mary Willis) ★☆
1994 Deadly Devotion (Wallace, Patricia) ☆
1994 ◫ When Death Comes Stealing (Wesley, Valerie Wilson) ☆
1994 ◫ Until Death (Whitney, Polly) ☆
1994 The Best Defense (Wilhelm, Kate)
1994 ◫ Eight Dogs Flying (Wilson, Karen Ann)
1994 A Good Year for a Corpse (Wolzien, Valerie)
1994 Tis the Season To Be Murdered (Wolzien, Valerie)
1994 Wages of Sin (Woods, Sherryl)
1994 Hot Schemes (Woods, Sherryl)
1994 A Touch of Panic (Wright, L.R.) ☆

1994 ◫ Murder Will Out (Yeager, Dorian)

1994 ◫ Blood Work (Zachary, Fay)
1994 A Poison in the Blood (Zachary, Fay)
1994 The Butterfly Effect (Zaremba, Eve)
1994 Leap of Faith (Zukowski, Sharon)

1995

1995 All the Deadly Beloved (Adams, Deborah)
1995 ◫ The Greenway (Adams, Jane) ☆
1995 Rosemary Remembered (Albert, Susan Wittig)
1995 Give My Secrets Back (Allen, Kate)
1995 At Dead of Night (Amey, Linda)
1995 A Fall in Denver (Andrews, Sarah)
1995 The Midas Murders (Arnold, Margot)

1995 Break a Leg Darlings (Babson, Marian)
1995 The Cuckoo Case (Bailey, Michele)
1995 Murder Well-Bred (Banks, Carolyn)
1995 Burning Desires [U.S.-A Taste for Burning]
      (Bannister, Jo)
1995 Hardware (Barnes, Linda)
1995 Ill Wind (Barr, Nevada)
1995 Agatha Raisin and the Walkers of Dembley
      (Beaton, M.C.)
1995 Death of a Nag (Beaton, M.C.)
1995 Cold Smoked (Beck, K. K.)
1995 Fair Play (Beecham, Rose)
1995 Sleeping Partners (Bell, Pauline)
1995 ◫ Guilty By Choice (Benke, Patricia D.)
1995 ◫ A Pedigree To Die For (Berenson, Laurien)
1995 A Dash of Death (Bishop, Claudia)
1995 A Pinch of Poison (Bishop, Claudia)
1995 A Vow of Fidelity (Black, Veronica)
1995 Done Wrong (Bland, Eleanor Taylor)
1995 Dangerous Deceit (Bolitho, Janie)
1995 Dolly Is Dead (Borthwick, J. S.)
1995 Four Elements of Murder (Borton, D.B.)
1995 The Cat Who Blew the Whistle (Braun, Lilian Jackson)
1995 Chill of Summer (Brennan, Carol)
1995 Mrs. Jeffries on the Trail (Brightwell, Emily)
1995 Mrs. Jeffries Plays the Cook (Brightwell, Emily)
1995 Turkey Tracks (Brown, Lizbie)
1995 Pay Dirt (Brown, Rita Mae)
1995 Suitable for Framing (Buchanan, Edna)
1995 Dear Irene, (Burke, Jan)
1995 A Dark Coffin (Butler, Gwendoline)

1995 Unsafe Keeping (Cail, Carol)
1995 How To Murder the Man of Your Dreams
      (Cannell, Dorothy)

1995 Tangled Roots (Cannon, Taffy)
1995 Bloodstream (Carlson, P.M.)
1995 A Dead Man Out of Mind (Charles, Kate)
1995 Evil Angels Among Them (Charles, Kate)
1995 A Season of Knives (Chisholm, P. F.)
1995 Death at Face Value (Christmas, Joyce)
1995 From Here to Paternity (Churchill, Jill)
1995 Iced (Clark, Carol Higgins)
1995 ◫ Pearls Before Swine (Clayton, Mary)
1995 The Maltese Puppy (Cleary, Melissa)
1995 Killjoy (Cleeves, Ann)
1995 The Healers (Cleeves, Ann)
1995 ◫ A Desperate Call (Coburn, Laura)
1995 ◫ The Eagle Catcher (Coel, Margaret)
1995 Angel in Autumn (Cohen, Anthea)
1995 Elusive Quarry (Comfort, Barbara)
1995 Black Ribbon (Conant, Susan)
1995 Rotten Apples (Cooper, Natasha)
1995 Doctors and Lawyers and Such
      (Cooper, Susan Rogers)
1995 From Potter's Field (Cornwell, Patricia)
1995 Cactus Blood (Corpi, Lucha)
1995 Sold to Miss Seeton (Crane, Hamilton)
1995 The Trouble With Going Home (Crespi, Camilla)
1995 Leave the Grave Green (Crombie, Deborah)
1995 An Imperfect Spy (Cross, Amanda)
1995 Nice People (Curzon, Clare)
1995 ◫ Dying Fall (Cutler, Judith)

1995 Hard Christmas (D'Amato, Barbara) ☆☆
1995 Major Vices (Daheim, Mary)
1995 Murder, My Suite (Daheim, Mary)
1995 The Alpine Escape (Daheim, Mary)
1995 The Alpine Fury (Daheim, Mary)
1995 Bet Against the House (Dain, Catherine)
1995 ◫ The Body in the Transept (Dams, Jeanne M.) ★☆
1995 Killer Pancake (Davidson, Diane Mott)
1995 Time To Depart (Davis, Lindsey)
1995 Rare Earth (Dawkins, Cecil)
1995 Nobody's Child (Dawson, Janet)
1995 ◫ The Strange Files of Fremont Jones (Day, Dianne)
1995 Mama Traps a Killer (Deloach, Nora)
1995 The Quick and the Dead (Dengler, Sandy)
1995 Who Dropped Peter Pan? (Dentinger, Jane)
1995 Miss Zukas and the Island Murders (Dereske, Jo)
1995 ◫ Now You See Her (Dewhurst, Eileen)
1995 The Glass Ceiling (Donald, Anabel)
1995 Cat in a Crimson Haze (Douglas, Carole Nelson)
1995 Bad Company (Dreher, Sarah)
1995 ◫ Bad Medicine (Dreyer, Eileen) ☆
1995 Prospect of Death [incl Patrick Gillard] (Duffy,
      Margaret)
1995 Under My Skin (Dunant, Sarah)
1995 The Winter Garden Mystery (Dunn, Carola)
1995 The Death of Blue Mountain Cat
      (Dymmoch, Michael Allen)

1995 A Death of Distinction (Eccles, Marjorie)
1995 Book of Moons (Edghill, Rosemary)
1995 Murder Can Ruin Your Looks (Eichler, Selma)
1995 Rotten Lies (Elkins, Charlotte & Aaron)
1995 Death Line (Evans, Geraldine)

1995 Hour of Our Death (Fallon, Ann C.)
1995 ◫ Beaned in Boston (Farrelly, Gail)
1995 Dead in the Melon Patch (Feddersen, Connie)
1995 Identity Unknown (Ferguson, Frances)
1995 Martinis & Mayhem (Fletcher, Jessica)
1995 Rum & Razors (Fletcher, Jessica)
1995 Death in a Funhouse Mirror (Flora, Kate Clark)
1995 Irish Chain (Fowler, Earlene)
1995 A Body To Die For (Frankel, Valerie)
1995 The Seven Stars (Fraser, Anthea)

1995 The Boy's Tale (Frazer, Margaret)
1995 🔳 If Looks Could Kill (Furie, Ruthe) ☆

1995 🔳 Bury the Bishop (Gallison, Kate)
1995 Mrs. Pollifax Pursued (Gilman, Dorothy)
1995 Shadow of Death (Gilpatrick, Noreen)
1995 A Stiff Critique (Girdner, Jaqueline)
1995 Hanging Time (Glass, Leslie)
1995 Trunk Show (Glen, Alison)
1995 🔳 Mommy and the Murder (Goldstone, Nancy)
1995 Striking Out (Gordon, Alison)
1995 The Dead of Winter (Gosling, Paula)
1995 "L" is for Lawless (Grafton, Sue)
1995 A Candle for a Corpse (Granger, Ann)
1995 Death of a Dream Maker (Gray, Gallagher)
1995 Die in My Dreams (Green, Christine)
1995 Every Deadly Sin (Greenwood, D.M.)
1995 Ruddy Gore (Greenwood, Kerry)
1995 Rainbow's End (Grimes, Martha)
1995 Still Water (Gunning, Sally)

1995 Fountain of Death (Haddam, Jane)
1995 Final Cut (Haddock, Lisa)
1995 Dead and Buried (Hager, Jean)
1995 Seven Black Stones (Hager, Jean)
1995 🔳 August Gamble (Hall, Linda)
1995 In the Bleak Midwinter [U.S.-Dead of Winter]
   (Hall, Patricia)
1995 Traveling With the Dead (Hambly, Barbara)
1995 Circus of the Damned (Hamilton, Laurell K.)
1995 The Julius House (Harris, Charlaine)
1995 The Thanksgiving Day Murder (Harris, Lee)
1995 🔳 The Edge of the Crazies (Harrison, Jamie)
1995 The Mint Julep Murder (Hart, Carolyn G.)
1995 Faint Praise (Hart, Ellen)
1995 For Every Evil (Hart, Ellen)
1995 Bitter Business (Hartzmark, Gini)
1995 🔳 Dead White Female (Henderson, Lauren)
1995 Lethal Legacy (Hendricksen, Louise)
1995 Termination Dust (Henry, Sue)
1995 🔳 Acid Bath (Herndon, Nancy)
1995 Widows' Watch (Herndon, Nancy)
1995 Busy Bodies (Hess, Joan)
1995 Miracles in Maggody (Hess, Joan) ☆
1995 Guardian at the Gate (Highsmith, Domini)
1995 Alien Rites (Hightower, Lynn S.)
1995 Eyeshot (Hightower, Lynn S.)
1995 🔳 Flashpoint (Hightower, Lynn S.)
1995 🔳 A Far and Deadly Cry (Holbrook, Teri) ☆☆☆
1995 Mrs. Malory Wonders Why [Brit.-Superfluous Death]
   (Holt, Hazel)
1995 Curly Smoke (Holtzer, Susan)
1995 77th Street Requiem (Hornsby, Wendy)
1995 🔳 After the Break (Howell, Lis)
1995 🔳 In Murder We Trust (Hyde, Eleanor)

1995 Murder Among Friends (Jacobs, Jonnie)
1995 🔳 Horse of a Different Killer (Jaffe, Jody) ☆☆
1995 Name Withheld (Jance, J.A.)
1995 Shoot, Don't Shoot (Jance, J.A.)
1995 🔳 The Beach Affair (Johnson, Barbara)
1995 You Bet Your Life (Jorgensen, Christine T.)

1995 The Hour of Our Death (Joseph, Alison)
1995 Justice (Kellerman, Faye)
1995 🔳 Bad Manners (Kellogg, Marne Davis)
1995 Keeper of the Mill (Kelly, Mary Anne)
1995 Trouble Looking for a Place To Happen
   (Kelner, Toni L.P.)
1995 Late Knights (Kershaw, Valerie)
1995 Alley Cat Blues (Kijewski, Karen)
1995 A Monstrous Regiment of Women (King, Laurie R.) ★
1995 To Play the Fool (King, Laurie R.)
1995 Check-out Time (Kingsbury, Kate)

1995 Grounds for Murder (Kingsbury, Kate)
1995 Kill or Cure (Kittredge, Mary)
1995 The Bull Slayers (Knight, Alanna)
1995 No Honeymoon for Death (Kruger, Mary)

1995 She's Out (La Plante, Lynda)
1995 File Under: Jeopardy (Lacey, Sarah)
1995 🔳 Murder in Brief (Lachnit, Carroll)
1995 Death at the Beggar's Opera (Lake, Deryn)
1995 Unquestioned Loyalty (Lamb, J. Dayne)
1995 The Shortest Day (Langton, Jane)
1995 🔳 Death in Bloodhound Red (Lanier, Virginia) ★☆☆
1995 Death a la Provencale (Laurence, Janet)
1995 🔳 Murder in Scorpio (Lawrence, Martha) ☆☆☆
1995 🔳 Death in Still Waters (Lee, Barbara) ★
1995 🔳 The Curious Cape Cod Skull (Lee, Marie)
1995 Cannon's Revenge [as W.W. Lee] (Lee, Wendi)
1995 Death and Judgment [Brit.-A Venetian Reckoning]
   (Leon, Donna)
1995 🔳 No Place for Secrets (Lewis, Sherry)
1995 🔳 The Healing of Holly-Jean (Lin-Chandler, Irene)
1995 Crown Witness (Linscott, Gillian)
1995 Never Let a Stranger in Your House (Logan, Margaret)
1995 🔳 Dangerous Attachments (Lovett, Sarah)

1995 Mistress of the Bones (MacGregor, T.J.)
1995 The Odd Job (MacLeod, Charlotte)
1995 Someone To Watch (Maiman, Jaye)
1995 The Ghost in the Closet (Maney, Mabel)
1995 Deadly Reunion (Manthorne, Jackie)
1995 Last Resort (Manthorne, Jackie)
1995 Fugitive Colors (Maron, Margaret)
1995 Bird in a Cage (Martin, Lee)
1995 🔳 Winding up the Serpent (Masters, Priscilla)
1995 Designer Crimes (Matera, Lia)
1995 Gemini Doublecross (Mather, Linda)
1995 Death in Rough Water (Mathews, Francine)
1995 The Touch of Terror (Matthews, Patricia)
1995 Artist Unknown (McCafferty, Jeanne)
1995 Hanky Panky (McCafferty, Taylor)
1995 Closing Statement (McClellan, Tierney)
1995 🔳 Heir Condition (McClellan, Tierney)
1995 Painted Truth (McClendon, Lise)
1995 If I'd Killed Him When I Met Him (McCrumb, Sharyn) ★
1995 Clean Break (McDermid, Val)
1995 🔳 The Mermaids Singing (McDermid, Val) ★
1995 Elective Murder (McGiffin, Janet)
1995 A Shred of Evidence (McGown, Jill)
1995 Caught Dead (McKenna, Bridget)
1995 🔳 Just Desserts (McKevett, G.A.)
1995 Double Bluff (McNab, Claire)
1995 The Morbid Kitchen (Melville, Jennie)
1995 The Homefront Murders (Meredith, D. R.)
1995 These Bones Were Made for Dancin' (Meyers, Annette)
1995 The Dutchman's Dilemma (Meyers, Maan)
1995 Stitches in Time (Michaels, Barbara)
1995 Night Songs (Mickelbury, Penny)
1995 Murder in a Hot Flash (Millhiser, Marlys)
1995 A Portion for Foxes (Mitchell, Kay)
1995 Blackwater Spirits (Monfredo, Miriam Grace)
1995 King of Hearts (Moody, Susan)
1995 A Wild and Lonely Place (Muller, Marcia) ☆
1995 The McCone Files (Muller, Marcia)
1995 🔳 The Main Line Is Murder (Murray, Donna Huston)
1995 Murder at the Music Hall (Myers, Amy)
1995 Parsley, Sage, Rosemary and Crime (Myers, Tamar)

1995 The Marshal and the Forgery (Nabb, Magdalen)
1995 🔳 Red Mercury Blues [U.S.-Red Hot Blues (1998)]
   (Nadelson, Reggie)
1995 🔳 Knight & Day (Nessen, Ron)
1995 The Wandering Arm (Newman, Sharan) ☆

1995		The Man Who Cast Two Shadows [Brit.-The Man Who Lied to Women] (O'Connell, Carol)
1995		Raggedy Man (O'Donnell, Lillian)
1995		Death Goes on Retreat (O'Marie, Carol Anne, Sister)
1995	🔢	Motion To Suppress (O'Shaughnessy, Perri)
1995		Family Album (Oleksiw, Susan)
1995		A Long Time Dead (Orde, A. J.)
1995		Cut to: Murder (Osborne, Denise)

1995		Turtle Baby (Padgett, Abigail)
1995		Murder Comes Calling (Page, Emma)
1995		Death at Gallows Green (Paige, Robin)
1995		Windy City Blues [short stories] (Paretsky, Sara)
1995		Suspicion of Guilt (Parker, Barbara)
1995		A Piece of Justice (Paton Walsh, Jill) ☆
1995		Fare Play (Paul, Barbara)
1995		Cooking Up Trouble (Pence, Joanne)
1995		So Many Steps to Death (Penn, John)
1995		Cain His Brother (Perry, Anne)
1995		Traitor's Gate (Perry, Anne)
1995		Shroud for a Scholar (Peterson, Audrey)
1995		Twilight (Pickard, Nancy) ☆
1995		Alternate Sides (Piesman, Marissa)
1995		The Hangdog Hustle (Pincus, Elizabeth)

1995		A Wolf in Death's Clothing (Quinn, Elizabeth)

1995		Third Degree (Rayner, Claire)
1995		The Intersection of Law and Desire (Redmann, J. M.) ★
1995		The Nun's Tale (Robb, Candace M.)
1995	🔢	Naked in Death (Robb, J.D.)
1995		In the Dead of Summer (Roberts, Gillian)
1995		Murder in the Marketplace (Roberts, Lora)
1995		Murder at the God's Gate (Robinson, Lynda S.)
1995	🔢	Moving Image (Ross, Annie)
1995		Whom the Gods Love (Ross, Kate)
1995		Lamb to the Slaughter (Rowe, Jennifer)
1995		Malice Poetic (Rowlands, Betty)
1995		Smiling at Death (Rowlands, Betty)
1995		Concourse (Rozan, S.J.) ★

1995		Ho-Ho Homicide (Sawyer, Corinne Holt)
1995		Cabin Fever (Schmidt, Carol)
1995		Running From the Law [Rita Morrone] (Scottoline, Lisa)
1995		The Eve of St. Hyacinth (Sedley, Kate)
1995		Talked to Death (Shaffer, Louise)
1995	🔢	Deadly Gamble (Shelton, Connie)
1995		Vacations Can Be Murder (Shelton, Connie)
1995		Something in the Cellar (Shepherd, Stella)
1995		Secrets in Stones (Shone, Anna)
1995		The Death We Share (Short, Sharon Gwyn)
1995		A Plague of Kinfolks (Sibley, Celestine)
1995		Storm Front (Silva, Linda Kay)
1995		A Day for Dying (Simpson, Dorothy)
1995		Interview With Mattie (Singer, Shelley) ☆
1995		The George Eliot Murders (Skom, Edith)
1995		Close Call (Slovo, Gillian)
1995		Dust Devils of the Purple Sage (Smith, Barbara Burnett)
1995		Full Stop (Smith, Joan)
1995		House of Blues (Smith, Julie)
1995		Running for Shelter (Spring, Michelle)
1995		Deadly Secrets on the St. Johns (Sprinkle, Patricia H.)
1995		Memory Can Be Murder (Squire, Elizabeth Daniels)
1995		Play With Fire (Stabenow, Dana)
1995		Dead Serious (Stacey, Susannah)
1995		Death Crosses the Border (Steinberg, Janice)
1995	🔢	Death of a Postmodernist (Steinberg, Janice)
1995		A Studied Death (Struthers, Betsy)
1995	🔢	Cry for Help (Stuyck, Karen Hanson)

1995	🔢	Simeon's Bride (Taylor, Alison G.)
1995	🔢	We Know Where You Live (Taylor, Jean)

1995	🔢	Blackening Song (Thurlo, Aimée & David)
1995	🔢	I, Claudia (Todd, Marilyn)
1995		Happy Never After (Trocheck, Kathy Hogan)
1995		In the Midnight Hour (Tyre, Peg)

1995		Parrot Blues (Van Gieson, Judith)
1995	🔢	Fiction, Fact, & Murder (Van Hook, Beverly)

1995		Under the Beetle's Cellar (Walker, Mary Willis) ★★★
1995	🔢	Graven Images (Waterhouse, Jane)
1995		Family Practice (Weir, Charlene)
1995		Open House (Welch, Pat)
1995		Devil's Gonna Get Him (Wesley, Valerie Wilson)
1995		Fresh Kills (Wheat, Carolyn)
1995		Charged With Guilt (White, Gloria) ☆☆☆
1995		Death at the Dutch House (Whitehead, Barbara)
1995		Secrets of the Dead (Whitehead, Barbara)
1995		The Killings at Barley Hall (Whitehead, Barbara)
1995		Until the End of Time (Whitney, Polly)
1995		A Flush of Shadows [5 novellas] (Wilhelm, Kate)
1995	🔢	Truth or Dare (Wilson, Anne)
1995		Copy Cat Crimes (Wilson, Karen Ann)
1995		She Came by the Book (Wings, Mary)
1995		Remodeled to Death (Wolzien, Valerie)
1995		Deadly Obsession (Woods, Sherryl)
1995		White Lightning (Woods, Sherryl)
1995		King of the Mountain (Wren, M.K.)
1995		Mother Love (Wright, L.R.) ★

1995		Summer Will End (Yeager, Dorian)
1995		Crystal Mountain Veils (York, Kieran)

1996

1996		Cast the First Stone (Adams, Jane)
1996		After Effects (Aird, Catherine)
1996		Rueful Death (Albert, Susan Wittig)
1996		Quaker Testimony (Allen, Irene)
1996		Takes One To Know One (Allen, Kate)
1996		A Small Target (Andreae, Christine)
1996	🔢	Due Process (Arnold, Catherine)
1996		Aunt Dimity's Good Deed (Atherton, Nancy)

1996	🔢	Eye of the Daemon (Bacon-Smith, Camille)
1996		Haycastle's Cricket (Bailey, Michele)
1996		A Horse To Die For (Banks, Carolyn)
1996		Death on the Diagonal (Banks, Carolyn)
1996		No Birds Sing (Bannister, Jo)
1996		Firestorm (Barr, Nevada)
1996	🔢	Milwaukee Winters Can Be Murder (Barrett, Kathleen Anne)
1996		Jane and the Unpleasantness at Scargrave Manor (Barron, Stephanie)
1996		Agatha Raisin and the Murderous Marriage (Beaton, M.C.)
1996		Death of a Macho Man (Beaton, M.C.)
1996	🔢	Biggie and the Poisoned Politician (Bell, Nancy) ☆
1996	🔢	This Dog for Hire (Benjamin, Carole Lea) ★
1996		False Witness (Benke, Patricia D.)
1996		Dog Eat Dog (Berenson, Laurien)
1996		Underdog (Berenson, Laurien)
1996		The Death of a Dancing Fool (Berry, Carole)
1996		Murder Well-Done (Bishop, Claudia)
1996		A Vow of Poverty (Black, Veronica)
1996		Keep Still (Bland, Eleanor Taylor)
1996		In Plain Sight (Block, Barbara)
1996		Finger of Fate (Bolitho, Janie)
1996		Sequence of Shame (Bolitho, Janie)
1996		Five Alarm Fire (Borton, D.B.)
1996		A Killing Spring (Bowen, Gail)
1996		Murder Crossed (Boylan, Eleanor)
1996		The Cat Who Said Cheese (Braun, Lilian Jackson)
1996		Mrs. Jeffries and the Missing Alibi (Brightwell, Emily)
1996		Mrs. Jeffries Stands Corrected (Brightwell, Emily)
1996		Murder, She Meowed (Brown, Rita Mae)

1996	Act of Betrayal (Buchanan, Edna)
1996	Evil Harmony (Buckstaff, Kathryn)
1996	Remember Me, Irene (Burke, Jan)
1996	A Double Coffin (Butler, Gwendoline)

1996	If Two of Them Are Dead (Cail, Carol)
1996	❶ First Impressions (Calloway, Kate)
1996	Second Fiddle (Calloway, Kate)
1996	Class Reunions are Murder (Cannon, Taffy)
1996	Frogskin and Muttonfat (Caverly, Carol)
1996	Cyberkiss (Chapman, Sally)
1996	❶ Slow Dancing With the Angel of Death (Chappell, Helen)
1996	A Surfeit of Guns (Chisholm, P. F.)
1996	❶ Dying To Sing (Chittenden, Margaret)
1996	Mourning Gloria (Christmas, Joyce)
1996	Silence of the Hams (Churchill, Jill)
1996	War and Peas (Churchill, Jill)
1996	The Case of the Anxious Aunt (Clarke, Anna)
1996	Dead Men's Bones (Clayton, Mary)
1996	Murder Most Beastly (Cleary, Melissa)
1996	High Island Blues (Cleeves, Ann)
1996	An Uncertain Death (Coburn, Laura)
1996	The Ghost Walker (Coel, Margaret)
1996	Stud Rites (Conant, Susan)
1996	❶ A Rumor of Bones (Connor, Beverly)
1996	Fruiting Bodies (Cooper, Natasha)
1996	Hickory, Dickory Stalk (Cooper, Susan Rogers)
1996	Cause of Death (Cornwell, Patricia)
1996	Sweet Miss Seeton (Crane, Hamilton)
1996	The Trouble With a Bad Fit (Crespi, Camilla)
1996	Mourn Not Your Dead (Crombie, Deborah)
1996	Hoofprints (Crum, Laura)
1996	Past Mischief (Curzon, Clare)
1996	Dying on Principle (Cutler, Judith)
1996	Dying To Write (Cutler, Judith)

1996	❶ KILLER.app (D'Amato, Barbara)
1996	Auntie Mayhem (Daheim, Mary)
1996	Nutty as a Fruitcake (Daheim, Mary)
1996	The Alpine Gamble (Daheim, Mary)
1996	The Luck of the Draw (Dain, Catherine)
1996	Trouble in the Town Hall (Dams, Jeanne M.)
1996	The Main Corpse (Davidson, Diane Mott)
1996	A Dying Light in Corduba (Davis, Lindsey)
1996	❶ Track of the Scorpion (Davis, Val)
1996	A Credible Threat (Dawson, Janet)
1996	Fire and Fog (Day, Dianne)
1996	Miss Zukas and the Raven's Dance (Dereske, Jo)
1996	Miss Zukas and the Stroke of Death (Dereske, Jo)
1996	❶ Savage Cut (Dereske, Jo)
1996	The Verdict on Winter (Dewhurst, Eileen)
1996	The Loop (Donald, Anabel)
1996	Cat in a Diamond Dazzle (Douglas, Carole Nelson)
1996	Cat With an Emerald Eye (Douglas, Carole Nelson)
1996	❶ Death at Lavender Bay (Douglas, Lauren Wright)
1996	Silent Words (Drury, Joan M.) ☆
1996	Wavewalker (Duffy, Stella)
1996	A Bad Hair Day (Dunbar, Sophie)
1996	Sudden Exposure (Dunlap, Susan)
1996	Requiem for a Mezzo (Dunn, Carola)

1996	A Species of Revenge (Eccles, Marjorie)
1996	The Bowl of Night (Edghill, Rosemary)
1996	Murder in a Cathedral (Edwards, Ruth Dudley)
1996	Ten Lords A-Leaping (Edwards, Ruth Dudley) ☆
1996	Murder Can Stunt Your Growth (Eichler, Selma)
1996	❶ Perilous Friends (Epstein, Carole)
1996	Two for the Dough (Evanovich, Janet) ★
1996	Axe for an Abbot (Eyre, Elizabeth)

1996	❶ Final Jeopardy (Fairstein, Linda) ☆
1996	Dead in the Dirt (Feddersen, Connie)
1996	With Intent To Kill (Ferguson, Frances)

1996	A Deadly Judgment (Fletcher, Jessica)
1996	A Palette for Murder (Fletcher, Jessica)
1996	Death at the Wheel (Flora, Kate Clark)
1996	Liberty Square (Forrest, Katherine V.)
1996	Kansas Troubles (Fowler, Earlene) ☆
1996	One Is One and All Alone (Fraser, Anthea)
1996	The Murderer's Tale (Frazer, Margaret)
1996	A Deadly Paté (Furie, Ruthe)
1996	Natural Death (Furie, Ruthe) ☆
1996	Without Consent (Fyfield, Frances)

1996	Devil's Workshop (Gallison, Kate)
1996	Unholy Angels (Gallison, Kate)
1996	❶ Bloody Waters (Garcia-Aguilera, Carolina)
1996	Murder on a Bad Hair Day (George, Anne)
1996	❶ Murder on a Girls' Night Out (George, Anne) ★
1996	In the Presence of the Enemy (George, Elizabeth)
1996	Mrs. Pollifax and the Lion Killer (Gilman, Dorothy)
1996	Most Likely To Die (Girdner, Jaqueline)
1996	Loving Time (Glass, Leslie)
1996	❶ After-Image [Germany] (Gom, Leona)
1996	"M" is for Malice (Grafton, Sue)
1996	Faithful Unto Death (Graham, Caroline)
1996	A Touch of Mortality (Granger, Ann)
1996	A Word After Dying (Granger, Ann)
1996	Lethal Genes (Grant, Linda) ☆
1996	A Motive for Murder (Gray, Gallagher)
1996	Deadly Partners (Green, Christine)
1996	Mortal Spoils (Greenwood, D.M.)
1996	Urn Burial (Greenwood, Kerry)
1996	❶ A Plague on Both Your Houses (Gregory, Susanna)
1996	An Unholy Alliance (Gregory, Susanna)
1996	❶ Somebody Else's Child (Grimes, Terris McMahan) ★★☆
1996	Deep Water (Gunning, Sally)

1996	And One To Die On (Haddam, Jane)
1996	Baptism in Blood (Haddam, Jane)
1996	Death on the Drunkard's Path (Hager, Jean)
1996	The Fire Carrier (Hager, Jean)
1996	November Veil (Hall, Linda)
1996	Bloody Bones (Hamilton, Laurell K.)
1996	The Lunatic Cafe (Hamilton, Laurell K.)
1996	Dead Over Heels (Harris, Charlaine)
1996	❶ Shakespeare's Landlord (Harris, Charlaine)
1996	The Passover Murder (Harris, Lee)
1996	Going Local (Harrison, Jamie)
1996	Blood Lines (Harrod-Eagles, Cynthia)
1996	Killing Time (Harrod-Eagles, Cynthia)
1996	Robber's Wine (Hart, Ellen) ★
1996	The Oldest Sin (Hart, Ellen)
1996	Death of a Hero (Haymon, S. T.)
1996	Nice Girls Finish Last (Hayter, Sparkle) ☆
1996	Pel and the Patriarch (Hebden, Juliet)
1996	Too Many Blondes (Henderson, Lauren)
1996	Sleeping Lady (Henry, Sue)
1996	Hunting Game (Herndon, Nancy)
1996	Lethal Statues (Herndon, Nancy)
1996	Closely Akin to Murder (Hess, Joan)
1996	Master of the Keys (Highsmith, Domini)
1996	The Grass Widow (Holbrook, Teri) ☆☆☆☆
1996	❶ Payment Deferred (Holms, Joyce)
1996	Mrs. Malory: Death of a Dean (Holt, Hazel)
1996	Bleeding Maize and Blue (Holtzer, Susan)
1996	The Director's Cut (Howell, Lis)
1996	Animal Instincts (Hyde, Eleanor)

| 1996 | ❶ So Dear to Wicked Men (Iakovou, Takis and Judy) |

1996	❶ Shadow of Doubt (Jacobs, Jonnie)
1996	Chestnut Mare, Beware (Jaffe, Jody)
1996	Dead to Rights (Jance, J.A.)
1996	Curl Up and Die (Jorgensen, Christine T.)
1996	The Quick and the Dead (Joseph, Alison)

1996　Prayers for the Dead (Kellerman, Faye)
1996　Curtsey (Kellogg, Marne Davis)
1996　Death is Sweet (Kelly, Susan B.)
1996　Country Comes to Town (Kelner, Toni L.P.)
1996　🔳 Gray Matter (Kennett, Shirley)
1996　Juicy Lucy (Kershaw, Valerie)
1996　Honky Tonk Kat (Kijewski, Karen)
1996　A Letter of Mary (King, Laurie R.)
1996　With Child (King, Laurie R.) ☆
1996　Chivalry Is Dead (Kingsbury, Kate)
1996　Pay the Piper (Kingsbury, Kate)
1996　Murder by Appointment (Knight, Alanna)
1996　🔳 Speak No Evil (Krich, Rochelle Majer)
1996　Masterpiece of Murder (Kruger, Mary)

1996　Cold Blood (La Plante, Lynda)
1996　A Blessed Death (Lachnit, Carroll)
1996　Death at the Devil's Tavern (Lake, Deryn)
1996　Soultown (Lambert, Mercedes)
1996　Dead as a Dodo (Langton, Jane)
1996　The House on Bloodhound Lane (Lanier, Virginia)
1996　Brewing Up a Storm (Lathen, Emma)
1996　Diet for Death (Laurence, Janet)
1996　🔳 Hearts and Bones (Lawrence, Margaret) ☆☆☆☆
1996　The Fatal Cape Cod Funeral (Lee, Marie)
1996　Missing Eden (Lee, Wendi)
1996　Acqua Alta [U.S.-Death in High Water] (Leon, Donna)
1996　No Place for Death (Lewis, Sherry)
1996　No Place Like Home (Lewis, Sherry)
1996　Grievous Angel (Lin-Chandler, Irene)
1996　Dead Man's Sweetheart [U.S.- Dead Man's Music] (Linscott, Gillian)
1996　Acquired Motives (Lovett, Sarah)
1996　🔳 Masquerade (Lynds, Gayle)

1996　🔳 Death's Autograph (Macdonald, Marianne)
1996　🔳 Breach of Trust (MacDougal, Bonnie)
1996　Exit the Milkman (MacLeod, Charlotte)
1996　Baby It's Cold (Maiman, Jaye)
1996　Final Take (Manthorne, Jackie)
1996　🔳 The Dead Hollywood Moms Society (Maracotta, Lindsay)
1996　Up Jumps the Devil (Maron, Margaret) ★
1996　🔳 Death of a Healing Woman (Martin, Allana)
1996　Genealogy of Murder (Martin, Lee)
1996　Sew Easy To Kill (Mason, Sarah J.)
1996　Catch the Fallen Sparrow (Masters, Priscilla)
1996　Last Chants (Matera, Lia)
1996　Murder Among the Angels (Matteson, Stefanie)
1996　🔳 Secret's Shadow (Matthews, Alex)
1996　The Search (McAllester, Melanie)
1996　🔳 Double Murder (McCafferty, Barbara Taylor)
1996　Finales & Overtures (McCafferty, Jeanne)
1996　A Killing in Real Estate (McClellan, Tierney)
1996　The Rosewood Casket (McCrumb, Sharyn)
1996　Blue Genes (McDermid, Val)
1996　Booked for Murder (McDermid, Val)
1996　Verdict Unsafe (McGown, Jill)
1996　Bitter Sweets (McKevett, G.A.)
1996　Inner Circle (McNab, Claire)
1996　🔳 Death at Rainy Mountain (Medawar, Mardi Oakley)
1996　Postscript to Murder (Meek, M.R.D.)
1996　Trick or Treat Murder (Meier, Leslie)
1996　The Woman Who Was Not There (Melville, Jennie)
1996　🔳 Fast Forward (Mercer, Judy)
1996　The House on Mulberry Street (Meyers, Maan)
1996　🔳 Capitol Offense (Mikulski, Barbara)
1996　It's Murder Going Home (Millhiser, Marlys)
1996　A Rage of Innocents (Mitchell, Kay)
1996　Return to the Kill (Moen, Ruth Raby)
1996　Through a Gold Eagle (Monfredo, Miriam Grace)
1996　🔳 Rain Dance (Moody, Skye Kathleen)

1996　Doubled in Spades (Moody, Susan)
1996　Old School Dies (Morgan, Kate)
1996　The Broken Promise Land (Muller, Marcia)
1996　🔳 Cat on the Edge (Murphy, Shirley Rousseau)
1996　Final Arrangements (Murray, Donna Huston)
1996　Murder in the Motor Stable (Myers, Amy)
1996　Gilt by Association (Myers, Tamar)
1996　🔳 Larceny and Old Lace (Myers, Tamar)
1996　No Use Dying Over Spilled Milk (Myers, Tamar)

1996　The Monster of Florence (Nabb, Magdalen)
1996　Breaking Point (Navratilova, Martina)
1996　A Timely Death (Neel, Janet)
1996　Press Corpse (Nessen, Ron)
1996　Strong as Death (Newman, Sharan) ☆
1996　Seeing is Deceiving (North, Suzanne)
1996　🔳 Runemaker (Nunnally, Tiina)

1996　🔳 Shadow of a Child (O'Callaghan, Maxine)
1996　Killing Critics (O'Connell, Carol)
1996　🔳 Death and Faxes (O'Kane, Leslie)
1996　Just the Fax, Ma'am (O'Kane, Leslie)
1996　Invasion of Privacy (O'Shaughnessy, Perri)
1996　A Ceremonial Death (Oliphant, B. J.)

1996　Moonbird Boy (Padgett, Abigail)
1996　The Body in the Bog (Page, Katherine Hall)
1996　Shadow of Fear (Peart, Jane)
1996　🔳 Web of Deception (Peart, Jane)
1996　Cooking Most Deadly (Pence, Joanne)
1996　🔳 The Queen's Man (Penman, Sharon Kay) ☆
1996　Bridal Shroud (Penn, John)
1996　Pentecost Alley (Perry, Anne) ☆
1996　Weighed in the Balance (Perry, Anne)
1996　The Hippopotamus Pool (Peters, Elizabeth)
1996　When Wallflowers Die (Prowell, Sandra West)

1996　Lamb to the Slaughter (Quinn, Elizabeth)

1996　Fourth Attempt (Rayner, Claire)
1996　Spent Matches (Reuben, Shelly)
1996　Death of a Garden Pest (Ripley, Ann)
1996　The King's Bishop (Robb, Candace M.)
1996　The Riddle of St. Leonard's (Robb, Candace M.)
1996　Glory in Death (Robb, J.D.)
1996　Immortal in Death (Robb, J.D.)
1996　Rapture in Death (Robb, J.D.)
1996　The Mummers' Curse (Roberts, Gillian)
1996　🔳 Riding for a Fall (Roberts, Lillian M.) ☆
1996　Murder Mile-High (Roberts, Lora)
1996　Murder at the Feast of Rejoicing (Robinson, Lynda S.)
1996　Shot in the Dark (Ross, Annie)
1996　The Shy Tulip Murders (Rothenberg, Rebecca)
1996　Bundori (Rowland, Laura Joh)
1996　🔳 A Hive of Bees (Rowlands, Betty)
1996　Deadly Legacy (Rowlands, Betty)
1996　Mandarin Plaid (Rozan, S.J.)
1996　🔳 Death of a DJ (Rubino, Jane)
1996　Whatever Happened to Jennifer Steele? (Ruryk, Jean)

1996　The Geezer Factory Murders (Sawyer, Corinne Holt)
1996　🔳 Engineered for Murder (Schumacher, Aileen)
1996　Let's Face the Music and Die (Scoppettone, Sandra)
1996　Caught in the Web (Scott, Barbara A.)
1996　Legal Tender [Bennie Rosato] (Scottoline, Lisa)
1996　The Wicked Winter (Sedley, Kate)
1996　Embers of Death (Shepherd, Stella)
1996　Meadowlark (Simonson, Sheila)
1996　Celebration in Purple Sage (Smith, Barbara Burnett)
1996　🔳 Noblesse Oblige (Smith, Cynthia)
1996　The Kindness of Strangers (Smith, Julie)
1996　The Knowledge of Water [Paris] (Smith, Sarah)
1996　🔳 Do Not Go Gently (Smith-Levin, Judith)
1996　Blood Will Tell (Stabenow, Dana)
1996　Oxford Fall (Stallwood, Veronica)

1996	Oxford Mourning (Stallwood, Veronica)
1996	Death-Fires Dance (Steinberg, Janice)
1996	Held Accountable (Stuyck, Karen Hanson)
1996	Dead South (Sullivan, Winona)

1996 In Guilty Night (Taylor, Alison G.)
1996 The Last of Her Lies (Taylor, Jean)
1996 Sex and Salmonella (Taylor, Kathleen)
1996 ❶ Death by Rhubarb (Temple, Lou Jane)
1996 Burden of Innocence (Thomson, June)
1996 Death Walker (Thurlo, Aimée & David)
1996 Virgin Territory (Todd, Marilyn)
1996 Heart Trouble (Trocheck, Kathy Hogan)
1996 ❶ Lickety-Split (Trocheck, Kathy Hogan)
1996 Murder at the National Gallery (Truman, Margaret)

1996 Hotshots (Van Gieson, Judith)

1996 Smoke and Mirrors (Welch, Pat)
1996 Where Evil Sleeps (Wesley, Valerie Wilson)
1996 ❶ Fowl Play (Westfall, Patricia Tichenor)
1996 Mean Streak (Wheat, Carolyn) ☆
1996 Malice Prepense [APA-For the Defense] (Wilhelm, Kate)
1996 Beware Sleeping Dogs (Wilson, Karen Ann)

1996 Elected to Death (Wolzien, Valerie)
1996 ❶ Shore To Die (Wolzien, Valerie)
1996 ❶ The Exile Way (Woodward, Ann)
1996 Strangers Among Us (Wright, L.R.)
1996 ❶ Mad Season (Wright, Nancy Means)

1996 Ovation by Death (Yeager, Dorian)
1996 ❶ Rough Justice (Youmans, Claire)

1996 Prelude to Death (Zukowski, Sharon)

1997

1997 All the Blood Relations (Adams, Deborah)
1997 Injury Time [16 stories] (Aird, Catherine)
1997 Love Lies Bleeding (Albert, Susan Wittig)
1997 ❶ Hidden Agenda (Alexander, Skye) ★
1997 Mother Nature (Andrews, Sarah)
1997 Imperfect Justice (Arnold, Catherine)

1997 Cold Case (Barnes, Linda)
1997 Endangered Species (Barr, Nevada)
1997 Milwaukee Summers Can Be Deadly (Barrett, Kathleen Anne)
1997 Jane and the Man of the Cloth (Barron, Stephanie)
1997 Agatha Raisin and the Terrible Tourist (Beaton, M.C.)
1997 Death of a Dentist (Beaton, M.C.)
1997 Biggie and the Mangled Mortician (Bell, Nancy)
1997 A Multitude of Sins (Bell, Pauline)
1997 The Dog Who Knew Too Much (Benjamin, Carole Lea)
1997 Above the Law (Benke, Patricia D.)
1997 Hair of the Dog (Berenson, Laurien)
1997 Death of a Dimpled Darling (Berry, Carole)
1997 Death Dines Out (Bishop, Claudia)
1997 A Vow of Adoration (Black, Veronica)
1997 The Scent of Murder (Block, Barbara)
1997 Absence of Angels (Bolitho, Janie)
1997 ❶ Snapped in Cornwall (Bolitho, Janie)
1997 The Garden Plot (Borthwick, J. S.)
1997 Six Feet Under (Borton, D.B.)
1997 ❶ Evans Above (Bowen, Rhys)
1997 The Cat Who Tailed a Thief (Braun, Lilian Jackson)
1997 Mrs. Jeffries Questions the Answer (Brightwell, Emily)
1997 Mrs. Jeffries Takes the Stage (Brightwell, Emily)
1997 ❶ Invitation to a Funeral (Brown, Molly)
1997 Margin of Error (Buchanan, Edna)
1997 ❶ The Robsart Mystery [U.S.-To Shield the Queen] (Buckley, Fiona)
1997 Hocus (Burke, Jan) ☆☆

1997 Third Degree (Calloway, Kate)
1997 ❶ Rhode Island Red (Carter, Charlotte)

1997 ❶ Steel Ashes (Cercone, Karen Rose)
1997 Hardwired (Chapman, Sally)
1997 Dead Duck (Chappell, Helen)
1997 Dead Men Don't Dance (Chittenden, Margaret)
1997 Downsized to Death (Christmas, Joyce)
1997 Fear of Frying (Churchill, Jill)
1997 The Prodigal's Return (Clayton, Mary)
1997 The Word Is Death (Clayton, Mary)
1997 Old Dogs (Cleary, Melissa)
1997 The Baby Snatcher (Cleeves, Ann)
1997 A Lying Silence (Coburn, Laura)
1997 Musclebound (Cody, Liza)
1997 The Dream Stalker (Coel, Margaret)
1997 ❶ Winona's Web (Cogan, Priscilla)
1997 Dedicated Angel (Cohen, Anthea)
1997 Animal Appetite (Conant, Susan)
1997 Questionable Remains (Connor, Beverly)
1997 ❶ Death of a Lady's Maid (Cook, Judith)
1997 Sour Grapes (Cooper, Natasha)
1997 Home Again, Home Again (Cooper, Susan Rogers) ☆
1997 ❶ Hornet's Nest (Cornwell, Patricia)
1997 Unnatural Exposure (Cornwell, Patricia)
1997 Bonjour, Miss Seeton (Crane, Hamilton)
1997 The Trouble With a Hot Summer (Crespi, Camilla)
1997 Dreaming of the Bones (Crombie, Deborah) ★☆☆
1997 The Collected Stories [10 stories] (Cross, Amanda)
1997 Roughstock (Crum, Laura)
1997 Close Quarters (Curzon, Clare)
1997 Dying for Millions (Cutler, Judith)

1997 Hard Bargain (D'Amato, Barbara)
1997 September Mourn (Daheim, Mary)
1997 The Alpine Hero (Daheim, Mary)
1997 The Alpine Icon (Daheim, Mary)
1997 Dead Man's Hand (Dain, Catherine)
1997 Holy Terror in the Hebrides (Dams, Jeanne M.)
1997 The Grilling Season (Davidson, Diane Mott)
1997 ❶ Devil's Leg Crossing (Davis, Kaye)
1997 Three Hands in the Fountain (Davis, Lindsey)
1997 Witness to Evil (Dawson, Janet)
1997 The Bohemian Murders (Day, Dianne)
1997 Mama Saves a Victim (Deloach, Nora)
1997 Mama Stalks the Past (Deloach, Nora)
1997 Mama Stands Accused (Deloach, Nora)
1997 Cut and Dry (Dereske, Jo)
1997 Out of Circulation (Dereske, Jo)
1997 Alias the Enemy (Dewhurst, Eileen)
1997 ❶ Quieter Than Sleep (Dobson, Joanne) ☆
1997 Cat in a Flamingo Fedora (Douglas, Carole Nelson)
1997 Cat in a Golden Garland (Douglas, Carole Nelson)
1997 Swimming at Cat Cove (Douglas, Lauren Wright)
1997 Music in the Blood (Duffy, Margaret)
1997 Beneath the Blonde (Duffy, Stella)
1997 Cop Out (Dunlap, Susan)
1997 Damsel in Distress (Dunn, Carola)
1997 Murder on the Flying Scotsman (Dunn, Carola)

1997 ❶ If I Should Die (Edwards, Grace F.) ☆
1997 Murder Can Wreck Your Reunion (Eichler, Selma)
1997 Nasty Breaks (Elkins, Charlotte & Aaron)
1997 ❶ Face Down in the Marrow-Bone Pie (Emerson, Kathy Lynn)
1997 ❶ Corruption of Faith (English, Brenda)
1997 Perilous Relations (Epstein, Carole)
1997 Three To Get Deadly (Evanovich, Janet) ★
1997 Dirge for a Doge (Eyre, Elizabeth)

1997 Likely To Die (Fairstein, Linda)
1997 Against the Brotherhood (Fawcett, Quinn)
1997 Dead in the Mud (Feddersen, Connie)
1997 1-900-DEAD (Fennelly, Tony)
1997 Brandy & Bullets (Fletcher, Jessica)
1997 Murder on the QE2 (Fletcher, Jessica)

1997		The Highland Fling Murders (Fletcher, Jessica)
1997		An Educated Death (Flora, Kate Clark)
1997		Apparition Alley (Forrest, Katherine V.)
1997		Goose in the Pond (Fowler, Earlene) ☆
1997		The Ten Commandments (Fraser, Anthea)
1997		The Prioress' Tale (Frazer, Margaret) ☆
1997	▮	Chicken Run (Fritchley, Alma)
1997		Murder & Sullivan (Frommer, Sara Hoskinson)

1997		Hasty Retreat (Gallison, Kate)
1997		Bloody Shame (Garcia-Aguilera, Carolina)
1997		Murder Makes Waves (George, Anne)
1997		Murder Runs in the Family (George, Anne)
1997		Deception on His Mind (George, Elizabeth)
1997		Mrs. Pollifax, Innocent Tourist (Gilman, Dorothy)
1997		A Cry for Self Help (Girdner, Jaqueline)
1997		Mommy and the Money (Goldstone, Nancy)
1997		Prairie Hardball (Gordon, Alison)
1997	▮	Asking for Trouble (Granger, Ann)
1997		Keeping Bad Company (Granger, Ann)
1997		Angel Falls (Green, Kate)
1997		Heavenly Vices (Greenwood, D.M.)
1997		Raisins and Almonds (Greenwood, Kerry)
1997		A Bone of Contention (Gregory, Susanna)
1997		The Case Has Altered (Grimes, Martha)
1997		Blood Will Tell (Grimes, Terris McMahan)
1997	▮	Delilah Doolittle and the Purloined Pooch (Guiver, Patricia)
1997	▮	Triple Play (Gunn, Elizabeth)
1997		Muddy Water (Gunning, Sally)

1997		Deadly Beloved (Haddam, Jane)
1997		The Last Noel (Hager, Jean)
1997		The Spirit Caller (Hager, Jean)
1997		April Operation (Hall, Linda)
1997		Perils of the Night (Hall, Patricia)
1997	▮	A Free Man of Color (Hambly, Barbara)
1997		The Killing Dance (Hamilton, Laurell K.)
1997	▮	The Xibalba Murders [Mexico] (Hamilton, Lyn) ☆
1997	▮	The Right Hand of Amon (Haney, Lauren)
1997		Come Away, Death (Hardwick, Mollie)
1997		Shakespeare's Champion (Harris, Charlaine)
1997		The New Year's Eve Murder (Harris, Lee)
1997		The Valentine's Day Murder (Harris, Lee)
1997		Death in Lovers' Lane (Hart, Carolyn G.)
1997		Murder in the Air (Hart, Ellen)
1997		Fatal Reaction (Hartzmark, Gini)
1997		Revenge of the Cootie Girls (Hayter, Sparkle)
1997		Pel and the Precious Parcel (Hebden, Juliet)
1997		Black Rubber Dress (Henderson, Lauren)
1997		Death Takes Passage (Henry, Sue)
1997		Time Bombs (Herndon, Nancy)
1997		A Holly, Jolly Murder (Hess, Joan)
1997		The Maggody Militia (Hess, Joan)
1997		Foreign Body (Holms, Joyce)
1997		Mrs. Malory and the Only Good Lawyer (Holt, Hazel)
1997		Black Diamond (Holtzer, Susan)
1997		A Hard Light (Hornsby, Wendy)
1997		Deadly Rx (Horowitz, Renee B.)
1997	▮	Rx for Murder (Horowitz, Renee B.)
1997		A Job To Die For (Howell, Lis)
1997		Blood Debt (Huff, Tanya)

1997		Evidence of Guilt (Jacobs, Jonnie)
1997	▮	Let There Be Blood (Jakeman, Jane)
1997		Skeleton Canyon (Jance, J.A.)
1997	▮	Except the Dying (Jennings, Maureen) ☆☆
1997	▮	Add One Dead Critic (John, Cathie)
1997		Hung Up To Die (Johnson, Dolores)
1997	▮	Taken to the Cleaners (Johnson, Dolores)
1997		Murder in the New Age (Jones, D. J. H.)
1997		A Dark and Sinful Death (Joseph, Alison)

1997		Unbound (Kaewert, Julie Wallin)

1997		A Serpent's Tooth (Kellerman, Faye)
1997		Tramp (Kellogg, Marne Davis)
1997		Fire Cracker (Kennett, Shirley)
1997	▮	Detecting Lies (Kiecolt-Glaser, Janice)
1997		Kat Scratch Fever (Kijewski, Karen)
1997		Ring for Tomb Service (Kingsbury, Kate)

1997		Trial and Retribution (La Plante, Lynda)
1997		A Brace of Bloodhounds (Lanier, Virginia)
1997		A Shark Out of Water (Lathen, Emma)
1997		Cross-Check (Law, Janice)
1997		Blood Red Roses (Lawrence, Margaret)
1997		The Cold Heart of Capricorn (Lawrence, Martha)
1997		Final Closing (Lee, Barbara)
1997		The Mysterious Cape Cod Manuscript (Lee, Marie)
1997		The Death of Faith (Leon, Donna)
1997		No Place for Sin (Lewis, Sherry)
1997		No Place for Tears (Lewis, Sherry)
1997	▮	Baltimore Blues (Lippman, Laura) ☆
1997		Charm City (Lippman, Laura) ★★☆
1997		Father Forgive Me (Lordon, Randye) ★☆

1997		Ghost Walk (Macdonald, Marianne)
1997	▮	Family Skeletons (MacPherson, Rett)
1997		Old Black Magic (Maiman, Jaye)
1997		Death, Lies and Apple Pies (Malmont, Valerie S.)
1997		Sudden Death (Manthorne, Jackie)
1997		The Dead Celeb (Maracotta, Lindsay)
1997	▮	Cemetery Murders (Marcy, Jean)
1997		Killer Market (Maron, Margaret)
1997		The Thursday Club (Martin, Lee)
1997		Seeing Is Deceiving (Mason, Sarah J.)
1997	▮	The Salaryman's Wife (Massey, Sujata) ★☆☆
1997		A Wreath for My Sister (Masters, Priscilla)
1997		And None Shall Sleep (Masters, Priscilla)
1997		Star Witness (Matera, Lia)
1997		Death in a Mood Indigo (Mathews, Francine)
1997		Murder Under the Palms (Matteson, Stefanie)
1997		Satan's Silence (Matthews, Alex)
1997		Double Exposure (McCafferty, Barbara Taylor)
1997	▮	K.C. Bomber (McClellan, Janet)
1997		Penn Valley Phoenix (McClellan, Janet)
1997		Two-Story Frame (McClellan, Tierney)
1997		Until Death Do Us Part (McGuire, Christine)
1997		Killer Calories (McKevett, G.A.)
1997		Chain Letter (McNab, Claire)
1997		Witch of the Palo Duro (Medawar, Mardi Oakley)
1997		Back to School Murder (Meier, Leslie)
1997		Double Take (Mercer, Judy)
1997		The Groaning Board (Meyers, Annette)
1997	▮	Cold Iron (Michaels, Melisa)
1997		Capitol Venture (Mikulski, Barbara)
1997	▮	The Hydrogen Murder (Minichino, Camille)
1997		Blue Poppy (Moody, Skye Kathleen)
1997		Sacrifice Bid (Moody, Susan)
1997	▮	Last Dance (Moore, Miriam Ann)
1997	▮	No Time For an Everyday Woman [incl Claud Willetts] (Morrone, Wenda Wardell)
1997		Both Ends of the Night (Muller, Marcia)
1997	▮	Legwork (Munger, Katy) ☆
1997		Cat Raise the Dead (Murphy, Shirley Rousseau)
1997		Cat Under Fire (Murphy, Shirley Rousseau)
1997		School of Hard Knocks (Murray, Donna Huston)
1997	▮	Larger Than Death (Murray, Lynne)
1997		Just Plain Pickled to Death (Myers, Tamar)
1997		The Ming and I (Myers, Tamar)

1997		Hot Poppies (Nadelson, Reggie)
1997		Killer Instinct (Navratilova, Martina)
1997	▮	Spike It (Niles, Chris)

1997		A Bright Flamingo Shroud (O'Brien, Meg)
1997		Down for the Count (O'Callaghan, Maxine) ☆
1997		Only in the Ashes (O'Callaghan, Maxine)

1997 Stone Angel [Brit.-Flight of the Stone Angel]
     (O'Connell, Carol)
1997 The Goddess Affair (O'Donnell, Lillian)
1997 The Cold Hard Fax (O'Kane, Leslie)
1997 Death of an Angel (O'Marie, Carol Anne, Sister)
1997 Obstruction of Justice (O'Shaughnessy, Perri)
1997 Here's to the Newly Deads (Oliphant, B. J.)
1997 A Death of Innocents (Orde, A. J.)

1997 The Dollmaker's Daughters (Padgett, Abigail)
1997 The Body in the Fjord (Page, Katherine Hall)
1997 Death at Daisy's Folly (Paige, Robin)
1997 Full Frontal Murder (Paul, Barbara)
1997 A Perilous Bargain (Peart, Jane)
1997 Sterner Stuff (Penn, John)
1997 Ashworth Hall (Perry, Anne)
1997 The Silent Cry (Perry, Anne)
1997 Seeing a Large Cat (Peters, Elizabeth) ☆
1997 ❶ Goodbye, Charli (Petit, Diane)
1997 Survival Instincts (Piesman, Marissa)
1997 The Bookfair Murders [Marsha Hillier] (Porter, Anna)
1997 Fast Friends [Brit.-Body Blow] (Pugh, Dianne G.)

1997 Killer Whale (Quinn, Elizabeth)
1997 Some Foul Play (Quinton, Ann)

1997 Deadly Harvest (Rawlings, Ellen)
1997 ❶ The Murder Lover (Rawlings, Ellen)
1997 Fifth Member (Rayner, Claire)
1997 ❶ Déjà Dead (Reichs, Kathy) ★
1997 Road Rage (Rendell, Ruth)
1997 ❶ Last Rites (Richardson, Tracey)
1997 ❶ The Butter Did It (Richman, Phyllis) ☆
1997 Ceremony in Death (Robb, J.D.)
1997 Vengeance in Death (Robb, J.D.)
1997 The Hand That Feeds You (Roberts, Lillian M.)
1997 Murder Bone by Bone (Roberts, Lora)
1997 First Cut (Robinson, Leah Ruth)
1997 Eater of Souls (Robinson, Lynda S.)
1997 Double Vision (Ross, Annie)
1997 The Devil in Music (Ross, Kate) ★
1997 ❶ Deadline [U.S.-Suspect (1999)] (Rowe, Jennifer)
1997 The Way of the Traitor [Brit.-Irizumi] (Rowland,
     Laura Joh)
1997 An Inconsiderate Death (Rowlands, Betty)
1997 The Cherry Pickers (Rowlands, Betty)
1997 No Colder Place (Rozan, S.J.) ★☆
1997 Fruitcake (Rubino, Jane)
1997 ❶ Now I Lay Me Down To Sleep (Rushford, Patricia H.)
1997 Red Sky in Mourning (Rushford, Patricia H.)

1997 ❶ Shiny Water (Salter, Anna)
1997 ❶ The Violence Beat (Sandstrom, Eve K.)
1997 Murder Ole! (Sawyer, Corinne Holt)
1997 Rough Justice [Marta Richter] (Scottoline, Lisa)
1997 The Brothers of Glastonbury (Sedley, Kate)
1997 ❶ Simon Said (Shaber, Sarah R.) ★
1997 Partnerships Can Kill (Shelton, Connie)
1997 Spider in the Sink (Sibley, Celestine)
1997 Tropical Storm (Silva, Linda Kay)
1997 Malarkey (Simonson, Sheila)
1997 ❶ Back in Time (Sleem, Patty)
1997 Mistletoe From Purple Sage (Smith, Barbara Burnett)
1997 Impolite Society (Smith, Cynthia)
1997 Misleading Ladies (Smith, Cynthia)
1997 Crescent City Kill (Smith, Julie)
1997 ❶ Gator Aide (Speart, Jessica)
1997 ❶ Death in Good Company (Sprague, Gretchen)
1997 ❶ When Did We Lose Harriet? (Sprinkle, Patricia H.)
1997 Whose Death Is It Anyway? (Squire, Elizabeth Daniels)
1997 Breakup (Stabenow, Dana)
1997 Go Not Gently (Staincliffe, Cath)
1997 The Dead Man and the Sea (Steinberg, Janice)

1997 Lethal Lessons (Stuyck, Karen Hanson)
1997 ❶ When the Dancing Stops (Szymanski, Therese)

1997 ❶ aka Jane (Tan, Maureen)
1997 The Hotel South Dakota (Taylor, Kathleen)
1997 A Stiff Risotto (Temple, Lou Jane)
1997 Revenge of the Barbecue Queens (Temple, Lou Jane)
1997 ❶ Pink Balloons and Other Deadly Things (Tesler, Nancy)
1997 Bad Medicine (Thurlo, Aimée & David)
1997 ❶ Jealous Heart (Tishy, Cecelia)
1997 Man Eater (Todd, Marilyn)
1997 Crash Course (Trocheck, Kathy Hogan)
1997 Strange Brew (Trocheck, Kathy Hogan)
1997 Murder in the House (Truman, Margaret)

1997 ❶ Backstab (Viets, Elaine)

1997 Cruel April (Wakefield, Hannah)
1997 ❶ Dead Body Language (Warner, Penny) ★☆
1997 Shadow Walk (Waterhouse, Jane)
1997 No Hiding Place (Wesley, Valerie Wilson)
1997 Troubled Waters (Wheat, Carolyn)
1997 Sunset and Santiago (White, Gloria) ☆☆
1997 Until It Hurts (Whitney, Polly)
1997 Governing Body (Wilson, Anne)
1997 ❶ Death Brims Over (Wilson, Barbara Jaye) ☆
1997 Circle of Wolves (Wilson, Karen Ann)
1997 She Came to the Castro (Wings, Mary)
1997 Permit for Murder (Wolzien, Valerie)
1997 ❶ Death of a Winter Shaker (Woodworth, Deborah)
1997 Pride and Predator (Wright, Sally S.)
1997 ❶ Publish and Perish (Wright, Sally S.)

1997 White Noise (Zaremba, Eve)
1997 Jungleland (Zukowski, Sharon)

1998

1998 Fade to Grey (Adams, Jane)
1998 Stiff News (Aird, Catherine)
1998 Chile Death (Albert, Susan Wittig)
1998 Quaker Indictment (Allen, Irene)
1998 Just a Little Lie (Allen, Kate)
1998 ❶ LadyGold (Amato, Angela)
1998 Only Flesh and Bones (Andrews, Sarah)
1998 Aunt Dimity Digs In (Atherton, Nancy)

1998 Eyes of the Empress (Bacon-Smith, Camille)
1998 ❶ Maid in the Shade (Banks, Jacqueline Turner)
1998 Broken Lines (Bannister, Jo)
1998 ❶ The Primrose Convention (Bannister, Jo)
1998 Blind Descent (Barr, Nevada)
1998 Milwaukee Autumns Can Be Lethal (Barrett,
     Kathleen Anne)
1998 ❶ Given the Crime (Barrett, Margaret)
1998 Given the Evidence (Barrett, Margaret)
1998 Jane and the Wandering Eye (Barron, Stephanie)
1998 ❶ The Miracle Strip (Bartholomew, Nancy)
1998 Agatha Raisin and the Wellspring of Death
     (Beaton, M.C.)
1998 Death of a Scriptwriter (Beaton, M.C.)
1998 ❶ Murder in the Holy City (Beaufort, Simon)
1998 Biggie and the Fricasseed Fat Man (Bell, Nancy)
1998 Blood Ties (Bell, Pauline)
1998 A Hell of a Dog (Benjamin, Carole Lea)
1998 Watchdog (Berenson, Laurien)
1998 A Touch of the Grape (Bishop, Claudia)
1998 A Vow of Compassion (Black, Veronica)
1998 See No Evil (Bland, Eleanor Taylor)
1998 Vanishing Act (Block, Barbara)
1998 Exposure of Evil (Bolitho, Janie)
1998 Framed in Cornwall (Bolitho, Janie)
1998 A Verdict in Blood (Bowen, Gail)
1998 Evan Help Us (Bowen, Rhys)
1998 The Cat Who Sang for the Birds (Braun, Lilian Jackson)

1998   Mrs. Jeffries Reveals Her Art (Brightwell, Emily)
1998   Mrs. Jeffries Takes the Cake (Brightwell, Emily)
1998   Murder on the Prowl (Brown, Rita Mae)
1998   A Record of Death (Bryan, Kate)
1998 ❶ Murder at Bent Elbow (Bryan, Kate)
1998   The Doublet Affair (Buckley, Fiona)
1998 ❶ The Star of India (Buggé, Carole)
1998   Liar (Burke, Jan)
1998   Coffin's Game [U.S.-Coffin's Games] (Butler, Gwendoline)

1998   Fifth Wheel (Calloway, Kate)
1998   Fourth Down (Calloway, Kate)
1998   The Spring Cleaning Murders (Cannell, Dorothy)
1998   Renowned Be Thy Grave (Carlson, P.M.)
1998   Blood Tracks (Cercone, Karen Rose)
1998   Ghost of a Chance (Chappell, Helen)
1998   A Plague of Angels (Chisholm, P. F.)
1998   Dead Beat and Deadly (Chittenden, Margaret)
1998   Going Out in Style (Christmas, Joyce)
1998   The Merchant of Menace (Churchill, Jill)
1998   Twanged (Clark, Carol Higgins)
1998   Death Is the Inheritance (Clayton, Mary)
1998   And Your Little Dog, Too (Cleary, Melissa)
1998   A Missing Suspect (Coburn, Laura)
1998   The Story Teller (Coel, Margaret)
1998   Compass of the Heart (Cogan, Priscilla)
1998   Angel of Retribution (Cohen, Anthea)
1998 ❶ What's a Woman Gotta Do? (Coleman, Evelyn)
1998   A Pair for the Queen (Comfort, Barbara)
1998   The Barker Street Regulars (Conant, Susan)
1998   Dressed To Die (Connor, Beverly)
1998   Murder at the Rose (Cook, Judith)
1998 ❶ Creeping Ivy (Cooper, Natasha)
1998   There Was a Little Girl (Cooper, Susan Rogers)
1998   Point of Origin (Cornwell, Patricia)
1998 ❶ Mission to Sonora (Cramer, Rebecca)
1998   The Puzzled Heart (Cross, Amanda)
1998   Roped (Crum, Laura)
1998   All Unwary (Curzon, Clare)
1998   Dying for Power (Cutler, Judith)

1998   Good Cop, Bad Cop (D'Amato, Barbara)
1998   Snow Place To Die (Daheim, Mary)
1998   The Alpine Journey (Daheim, Mary)
1998   The Alpine Kindred (Daheim, Mary)
1998   Wed and Buried (Daheim, Mary)
1998   Malice in Miniature (Dams, Jeanne M.)
1998   Prime Cut (Davidson, Diane Mott)
1998   Possessions (Davis, Kaye)
1998   Until the End (Davis, Kaye)
1998   Two for the Lions (Davis, Lindsey)
1998   Flight of the Serpent (Davis, Val)
1998   Where the Bodies Are Buried (Dawson, Janet)
1998   Emperor Norton's Ghost (Day, Dianne)
1998   Mama Rocks the Empty Cradle (Deloach, Nora)
1998 ❶ Hyaenas (Dengler, Sandy)
1998   Final Notice (Dereske, Jo)
1998   Short Cut (Dereske, Jo)
1998   Roundabout (Dewhurst, Eileen)
1998 ❶ Next to Last Chance (Dixon, Louisa)
1998   The Northbury Papers (Dobson, Joanne)
1998   Cat on a Hyacinth Hunt (Douglas, Carole Nelson)
1998   Shaman's Moon (Dreher, Sarah)
1998   Closed in Silence (Drury, Joan M.)
1998   A Fine Target (Duffy, Margaret)
1998   Redneck Riviera (Dunbar, Sophie)
1998   No Immunity (Dunlap, Susan)
1998   Dead in the Water (Dunn, Carola)
1998   Incendiary Designs (Dymmoch, Michael Allen)

1998   Killing Me Softly (Eccles, Marjorie)
1998   A Toast Before Dying (Edwards, Grace F.)

1998   Publish and Be Murdered (Edwards, Ruth Dudley)
1998   Murder Can Spook Your Cat (Eichler, Selma)
1998   A Chill in the Blood (Elrod, P.N.)
1998   Face Down Upon an Herbal (Emerson, Kathy Lynn)
1998   Corruption of Power (English, Brenda)
1998   Four To Score (Evanovich, Janet)

1998 ❶ Sympathy for the Devil (Farmer, Jerrilyn)
1998   Embassy Row (Fawcett, Quinn)
1998   Dead in the Driver's Seat (Feddersen, Connie)
1998 ❶ Tiger's Palette (Fiedler, Jacqueline)
1998 ❶ Dying To Get Published (Fitzwater, Judy)
1998   A Little Yuletide Murder (Fletcher, Jessica)
1998   Murder in Moscow (Fletcher, Jessica)
1998   Death in Paradise (Flora, Kate Clark)
1998   Dove in the Window (Fowler, Earlene)
1998   The Maiden's Tale (Frazer, Margaret)
1998   Coffee To Die For (French, Linda)
1998 ❶ Talking Rain (French, Linda)
1998   Chicken Feed (Fritchley, Alma)

1998   Grave Misgivings (Gallison, Kate)
1998   Bloody Secrets (Garcia-Aguilera, Carolina)
1998   Murder Gets a Life (George, Anne)
1998   Death Hits the Fan (Girdner, Jaqueline)
1998   Judging Time (Glass, Leslie)
1998   Double Negative (Gom, Leona)
1998   "N" is for Noose (Grafton, Sue)
1998   Call the Dead Again (Granger, Ann)
1998   Running Scared (Granger, Ann)
1998 ❶ Multiple Listing (Grant, Anne Underwood)
1998   Smoke Screen (Grant, Anne Underwood)
1998   Vampire Bytes (Grant, Linda)
1998 ❶ The Dead Cat Bounce (Graves, Sarah)
1998   A Grave Disturbance (Greenwood, D.M.)
1998   A Deadly Brew (Gregory, Susanna)
1998 ❶ A Very Eligible Corpse (Griffin, Annie)
1998   The Stargazey (Grimes, Martha)
1998   Delilah Doolittle and the Careless Coyote (Guiver, Patricia)
1998   Delilah Doolittle and the Motley Mutts (Guiver, Patricia)
1998   Par Four (Gunn, Elizabeth)
1998   Dirty Water (Gunning, Sally)

1998   Masked Dancers (Hager, Jean)
1998   Sew Deadly (Hager, Jean)
1998   The Italian Girl (Hall, Patricia)
1998   Fever Season (Hambly, Barbara)
1998   Blue Moon (Hamilton, Laurell K.)
1998   Burnt Offerings (Hamilton, Laurell K.)
1998   The Maltese Goddess [Malta] (Hamilton, Lyn)
1998   A Face Turned Backward (Haney, Lauren)
1998   Shakespeare's Christmas (Harris, Charlaine)
1998   The Labor Day Murder (Harris, Lee)
1998   An Unfortunate Prairie Occurance (Harrison, Jamie)
1998   Shallow Grave (Harrod-Eagles, Cynthia)
1998   Death in Paradise (Hart, Carolyn G.)
1998   Yankee Doodle Dead (Hart, Carolyn G.)
1998   Wicked Games (Hart, Ellen)
1998 ❶ The Doctor Digs a Grave (Hathaway, Robin) ★
1998 ❶ By Reason of Insanity (Hayden, G. Miki)
1998   The Last Manly Man (Hayter, Sparkle)
1998   Freeze My Margarita (Henderson, Lauren)
1998   Deadfall (Henry, Sue)
1998   C.O.P. Out (Herndon, Nancy)
1998   Panic (Heron, Echo)
1998 ❶ Pulse (Heron, Echo)
1998   No Good Deed (Hightower, Lynn S.)
1998   Bad Vibes (Holms, Joyce)

1998   Go Close Against the Enemy (Iakovou, Takis and Judy)

1998 ❶ The Alligator's Farewell (Jackson, Hialeah)

1998		Murder Among Us (Jacobs, Jonnie)
1998		In Colt Blood (Jaffe, Jody)
1998		Fool's Gold (Jakeman, Jane)
1998		The Egyptian Coffin (Jakeman, Jane)
1998		A Certain Justice (James, P. D.)
1998		Rattlesnake Crossing (Jance, J.A.)
1998		Under the Dragon's Tail (Jennings, Maureen)
1998		Beat a Rotten Egg to the Punch (John, Cathie)
1998		Bad Moon Rising (Johnson, Barbara)
1998		A Dress To Die For (Johnson, Dolores)
1998		Death of a Dustbunny (Jorgensen, Christine T.)
1998		Unprintable (Kaewert, Julie Wallin)
1998	❶	Fax Me a Bagel (Kahn, Sharon)
1998		Nothing But Gossip (Kellogg, Marne Davis)
1998		Old Wounds (Kelly, Nora)
1998		Tight as a Tick (Kelner, Toni L.P.)
1998		Chameleon (Kennett, Shirley)
1998		Unconscious Truths (Kiecolt-Glaser, Janice)
1998		Stray Kat Waltz (Kijewski, Karen)
1998		The Moor (King, Laurie R.)
1998		Death With Reservations (Kingsbury, Kate)
1998		Dying Room Only (Kingsbury, Kate)
1998		The Coffin Lane Murders (Knight, Alanna)
1998		Cold Heart (La Plante, Lynda)
1998		Trial and Retribution II (La Plante, Lynda)
1998		Akin to Death (Lachnit, Carroll)
1998		Death on the Romney Marsh (Lake, Deryn)
1998		The Face on the Wall (Langton, Jane)
1998		Blind Bloodhound Justice (Lanier, Virginia)
1998		Appetite for Death (Laurence, Janet)
1998	❶	Canaletto and the Case of the Westminster Bridge (Laurence, Janet)
1998		The Burning Bride (Lawrence, Margaret)
1998		Deadbeat (Lee, Wendi)
1998		A Noble Radiance (Leon, Donna)
1998		Dance on Blood (Linscott, Gillian)
1998		Butchers Hill (Lippman, Laura)
1998		Death in the Amazon (Livesay, Ann)
1998	❶	The Isis Command (Livesay, Ann)
1998		Mother May I (Lordon, Randye)
1998		A Desperate Silence (Lovett, Sarah)
1998		Angle of Impact (MacDougal, Bonnie)
1998		The Balloon Man (MacLeod, Charlotte)
1998		A Veiled Antiquity (MacPherson, Rett)
1998		Dead and Blonde (Marcy, Jean)
1998		Home Fires (Maron, Margaret)
1998		Death of a Saint Maker (Martin, Allana)
1998		Zen Attitude (Massey, Sujata)
1998		Havana Twist (Matera, Lia)
1998		Death in a Cold Hard Light (Mathews, Francine)
1998		Vendetta's Victim (Matthews, Alex)
1998		Double Cross (McCafferty, Barbara Taylor)
1998		River Quay (McClellan, Janet)
1998		The Ballad of Frankie Silver (McCrumb, Sharyn)
1998		Star Struck (McDermid, Val)
1998		The Wire in the Blood (McDermid, Val)
1998		Picture of Innocence (McGown, Jill)
1998		Until The Bough Breaks (McGuire, Christine)
1998		Cooked Goose (McKevett, G.A.)
1998		Past Due (McNab, Claire)
1998		Revengeful Death (Melville, Jennie)
1998		Split Image (Mercer, Judy)
1998		The Lucifer Contract (Meyers, Maan)
1998		Sister to the Rain (Michaels, Melisa)
1998	❶	One Must Wait (Mickelbury, Penny)
1998	❶	A Wicked Way To Burn (Miles, Margaret)
1998		The Helium Murder (Minichino, Camille)
1998		The Lost Girls (Moffat, Gwen)
1998		The Stalking Horse (Monfredo, Miriam Grace)
1998		Wildcrafters (Moody, Skye Kathleen)
1998		Dummy Hand (Moody, Susan)
1998		Stayin' Alive (Moore, Miriam Ann)
1998		While Other People Sleep (Muller, Marcia)
1998		Out of Time (Munger, Katy)
1998		No Bones About It (Murray, Donna Huston)
1998		Between a Wok and a Hard Place (Myers, Tamar)
1998		Eat, Drink and Be Wary (Myers, Tamar)
1998		So Faux, So Good (Myers, Tamar)
1998		To Die For (Neel, Janet)
1998		Blanche Cleans Up (Neely, Barbara)
1998		Death With Honors (Nessen, Ron)
1998		Cursed in the Blood (Newman, Sharan)
1998		Run Time (Niles, Chris)
1998		Fate of Ravens (Nunnally, Tiina)
1998		Blue Death (O'Donnell, Lillian)
1998	❶	Play Dead (O'Kane, Leslie)
1998		Death Takes Up a Collection (O'Marie, Carol Anne, Sister)
1998		Breach of Promise (O'Shaughnessy, Perri)
1998	❶	Blue (Padgett, Abigail)
1998		Intent To Kill (Page, Emma)
1998		The Body in the Bookcase (Page, Katherine Hall)
1998		Death at Devil's Bridge (Paige, Robin)
1998		Suspicion of Deceit (Parker, Barbara)
1998		Thread of Suspicion (Peart, Jane)
1998		Cook's Night Out (Pence, Joanne)
1998		Cooks Overboard (Pence, Joanne)
1998		Cruel as the Grave (Penman, Sharon Kay)
1998		A Breach of Promise [Brit.-Whited Sepulchres] (Perry, Anne)
1998		Brunswick Gardens (Perry, Anne)
1998		The Ape Who Guards the Balance (Peters, Elizabeth)
1998		Goodbye, Charli—Take Two (Petit, Diane)
1998		Goodbye, Charli—Third Time Lucky (Petit, Diane)
1998		The Blue Corn Murders (Pickard, Nancy)
1998		Foolproof (Pugh, Dianne G.)
1998		Over the Line (Richardson, Tracey)
1998		Death of a Political Plant (Ripley, Ann)
1998		A Gift of Sanctuary (Robb, Candace M.)
1998		Holiday in Death (Robb, J.D.)
1998		The Bluest Blood (Roberts, Gillian)
1998	❶	Time and Trouble (Roberts, Gillian)
1998		Almost Human (Roberts, Lillian M.)
1998		Murder Crops Up (Roberts, Lora)
1998		Drinker of Blood (Robinson, Lynda S.)
1998	❶	Remedy for Treason (Roe, Caroline)
1998	❶	Bitch Factor (Rogers, Chris)
1998	❶	The Problem of the Missing Miss [Brit.-The Problem of the Missing Hoyden] (Rogow, Roberta)
1998		Bad Monday (Roome, Annette)
1998		Something Wicked (Rowe, Jennifer)
1998		The Concubine's Tattoo (Rowland, Laura Joh)
1998		Death at Dearley Manor (Rowlands, Betty)
1998		A Bitter Feast (Rozan, S.J.)
1998		Cheat the Devil (Rubino, Jane)
1998		Next Week Will Be Better (Ruryk, Jean) ☆
1998		A Haunting Refrain (Rushford, Patricia H.)
1998	❶	Dead Stick (Rust, Megan Mallory)
1998		Fault Lines (Salter, Anna)
1998		The Homicide Report (Sandstrom, Eve K.)
1998		Framework for Death (Schumacher, Aileen)
1998		Gonna Take a Homicidal Journey (Scoppettone, Sandra)
1998		The Weaver's Inheritance (Sedley, Kate)
1998		Digging Up Momma (Shankman, Sarah)
1998		Small Towns Can Be Murder (Shelton, Connie)
1998	❶	Dead Man's Float (Sherman, Beth)
1998		Once Too Often (Simpson, Dorothy)
1998		The Charles Dickens Murders (Skom, Edith)

1998	Royals and Rogues (Smith, Cynthia)
1998	Silver and Guilt (Smith, Cynthia)
1998	82 Desire (Smith, Julie)
1998	The Hoodoo Man (Smith-Levin, Judith)
1998 ❶	Bait (Songer, C. J.)
1998	Tortoise Soup (Speart, Jessica)
1998	Standing in the Shadows (Spring, Michelle)
1998	But Why Shoot the Magistrate? (Sprinkle, Patricia H.)
1998	Is There a Dead Man in the House? (Squire, Elizabeth Daniels)
1998 ❶	Fire and Ice (Stabenow, Dana)
1998	Killing Grounds (Stabenow, Dana)
1998	Hunter's Quarry (Stacey, Susannah)
1998	Dead Wrong (Staincliffe, Cath)
1998	Oxford Blue (Stallwood, Veronica)
1998	Oxford Knot (Stallwood, Veronica)
1998 ❶	Up Next (Star, Nancy)
1998	Digging Up Death (Stein, Triss)
1998	Death in a City of Mystics (Steinberg, Janice)
1998	Death's a Beach (Sullivan, Winona)
1998	When the Dead Speak (Szymanski, Therese)

1998	The House of Women (Taylor, Alison G.)
1998	Mourning Shift (Taylor, Kathleen)
1998	Bread on Arrival (Temple, Lou Jane)
1998	Sharks, Jellyfish and Other Deadly Things (Tesler, Nancy)
1998 ❶	A Darker Shade of Crimson [Harvard] (Thomas-Graham, Pamela)
1998 ❶	Charlie's Bones (Thrasher, L. L.)
1998	Enemy Way (Thurlo, Aimée & David)
1998	Cryin' Time (Tishy, Cecelia)
1998	Wolf Whistle (Todd, Marilyn)
1998	Midnight Clear (Trocheck, Kathy Hogan)
1998	Murder at the Watergate (Truman, Margaret)

1998	Ditch Rider (Van Gieson, Judith)
1998	Rubout (Viets, Elaine)

1998	All the Dead Lie Down (Walker, Mary Willis)
1998	Right To Remain Silent (Warner, Penny)
1998	Sign of Foul Play (Warner, Penny)
1998	Dead Letter (Waterhouse, Jane)
1998	Hot Ticket (Weber, Janice)
1998	Murder Takes Two (Weir, Charlene)
1998	Fallen From Grace (Welch, Pat)
1998	Easier To Kill (Wesley, Valerie Wilson)
1998	Mother of the Bride (Westfall, Patricia Tichenor)
1998	Sworn To Defend (Wheat, Carolyn)
1998	Dolls Don't Choose (Whitehead, Barbara)
1998 ❶	Sins of Silence (Wilcox, Valerie)
1998	The Death of a Much-Travelled Woman [9 stories] (Wilson, Barbara)
1998	Accessory to Murder (Wilson, Barbara Jaye)
1998	Death Flips Its Lid (Wilson, Barbara Jaye)
1998	Deck the Halls With Murder (Wolzien, Valerie)
1998	Weddings Are Murder (Wolzien, Valerie)
1998	Of Death and Black Rivers (Woodward, Ann)
1998	A Deadly Shaker Spring (Woodworth, Deborah)
1998	Acts of Murder (Wright, L.R.)
1998	Harvest of Bones (Wright, Nancy Means)

1998	Libation by Death (Yeager, Dorian)

1999

1999	Hide in Plain Sight (Alexander, Skye)
1999	Jackpot (Amato, Angela)
1999	Wrongful Death (Arnold, Catherine)

1999	Barely Maid (Banks, Jacqueline Turner)
1999	The Hireling's Tale (Bannister, Jo)
1999	Liberty Falling (Barr, Nevada)
1999	Dragstrip (Bartholomew, Nancy)

1999	Agatha Raisin and the Wizard of Evesham (Beaton, M.C.)
1999	A Head for Poisoning (Beaufort, Simon)
1999	Hush Puppy (Berenson, Laurien)
1999 ❶	Murder in the Marais (Black, Cara)
1999	Tell No Tales (Bland, Eleanor Taylor)
1999	My Body Lies Over the Ocean (Borthwick, J. S.)
1999 ❶	Fade to Black [as Della Borton] (Borton, D.B.)
1999	Evanly Choirs (Bowen, Rhys)
1999	The Cat Who Saw Stars (Braun, Lilian Jackson)
1999	Murder at Ravenscroft (Buggé, Carole)
1999 ❶	Who Killed Blanche Dubois (Buggé, Carole)

1999	Seventh Heaven (Calloway, Kate)
1999	Sixth Sense (Calloway, Kate)
1999	Coq au Vin (Carter, Charlotte)
1999	The Sibyl in Her Grave (Caudwell, Sarah)
1999	Coal Bones (Cercone, Karen Rose)
1999	Don't Forget To Die (Chittenden, Margaret)
1999	A Groom with a View (Churchill, Jill)
1999 ❶	Anything Goes (Churchill, Jill)
1999 ❶	Never Buried (Claire, Edie)
1999	Never Sorry (Claire, Edie)
1999	When the Gods Take a Wife (Coleman, Evelyn)
1999	A Crooked Little House (Cooper, Susan Rogers)
1999	Southern Cross (Cornwell, Patricia)
1999	Miss Seeton's Finest Hour (Crane, Hamilton)

1999 ❶	Death in Lacquer Red (Dams, Jeanne M.)
1999	One Dead Virgin (Davis, Lindsey)
1999	Death Train to Boston (Day, Dianne)
1999	Outside Chance (Dixon, Louisa)
1999	The Raven and the Nightingale (Dobson, Joanne)
1999	Destroy Unopened (Donald, Anabel)
1999	Shiveree (Dunbar, Sophie)

1999	Murder Can Singe Your Old Flame (Eichler, Selma)
1999	Face Down Among the Winchester Geese (Emerson, Kathy Lynn)

1999	Cold Hit (Fairstein, Linda)
1999	Immaculate Reception (Farmer, Jerrilyn)
1999	Duped by Derivatives (Farrelly, Gail)
1999 ❶	Crewel World (Ferris, Monica)
1999	Framed in Lace (Ferris, Monica)
1999	Dying To Get Even (Fitzwater, Judy)
1999	Mariner's Compass (Fowler, Earlene)
1999	Steeped in Murder (French, Linda)
1999	Chicken Out (Fritchley, Alma)

1999	Murder on the Astral Plane (Girdner, Jaqueline)
1999	Murder in the Shadows (Godfrey, Ellen)
1999 ❶	Murder on the Loose (Godfrey, Ellen)
1999	Murder on the Lover's Bridge (Godfrey, Ellen)
1999	Death and Shadows (Gosling, Paula)
1999	Cuttings (Grant, Anne Underwood)
1999	A Blonde for a Shilling (Graves, Sarah)
1999	Triple Witch (Graves, Sarah)
1999	Fatal Cut (Green, Christine)
1999	Date With the Perfect Dead Man (Griffin, Annie)
1999	Fire Water (Gunning, Sally)
1999	Murder Duet (Gur, Batya)

1999	The Moche Warrior [Peru] (Hamilton, Lyn)
1999	A Fool and His Honey (Harris, Charlaine)
1999	The Father's Day Murder (Harris, Lee)
1999	Rough Trade (Hartzmark, Gini)
1999	Too Old for Murder (Hayden, G. Miki)
1999	Pel is Provoked (Hebden, Juliet)
1999	Paradox (Heron, Echo)
1999	Misery in Maggody (Hess, Joan)
1999	Sad Water (Holbrook, Teri)
1999	The Silly Season (Holtzer, Susan)

1999	Farewell, Conch Republic (Jackson, Hialeah)

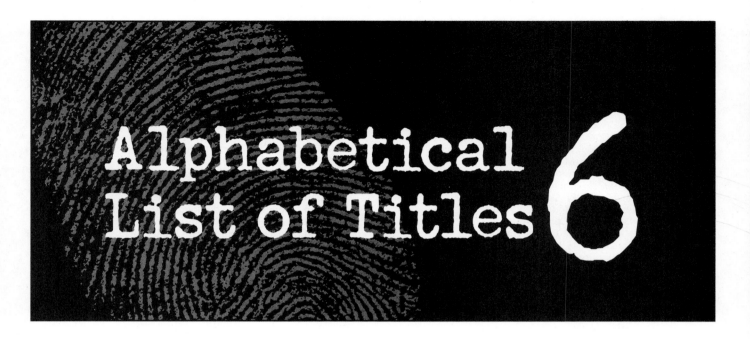

Alphabetical List of Titles 6

1-900-DEAD [1997] (Fennelly, Tony)
27-Ingredient Chile Con Carne Murders [with Virginia Rich] [1993] (Pickard, Nancy)
77th Street Requiem [1995] (Hornsby, Wendy)
82 Desire [1998] (Smith, Julie)

A

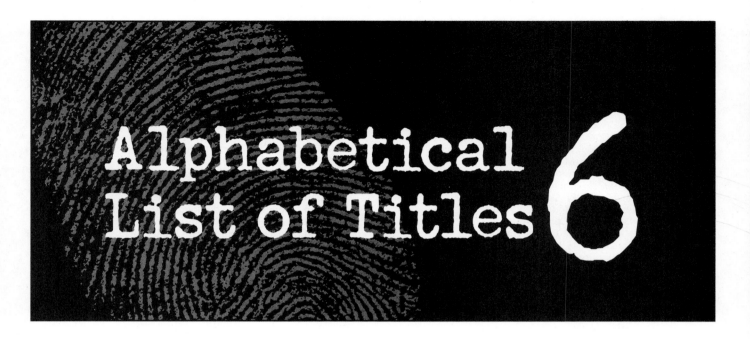 "A" is for Alibi [1982] (Grafton, Sue) ★☆
Abominable Man [1972] (Sjöwall, Maj & Per Wahlöö)
Above the Law [1997] (Benke, Patricia D.)
Absence of Angels [1997] (Bolitho, Janie)
Accessory to Murder [1998] (Wilson, Barbara Jaye)
Accident Prone [1987] (Penn, John)
Accidental Shroud [1994] (Eccles, Marjorie)
Accounting for Murder [1964] (Lathen, Emma) ★
Aces High [1989] (Hooper, Kay)
Acid Bath [1995] (Herndon, Nancy)
Acqua Alta [1996] (Leon, Donna)
Acquired Motives [1996] (Lovett, Sarah)
Act of Betrayal [1996] (Buchanan, Edna)
Act of Darkness [1991] (Haddam, Jane)
Acts of Murder [1998] (Wright, L.R.)
Add One Dead Critic [1997] (John, Cathie)
Adjusted to Death [1991] (Girdner, Jaqueline)
Advantage Miss Seeton [Hampton Charles] [1990] (Crane, Hamilton)
Advent of Dying [1986] (O'Marie, Carol Anne, Sister)
Adventures of Mycroft Holmes [1994] (Fawcett, Quinn)
Affacombe Affair [1968] (Lemarchand, Elizabeth)
Affirmative Reaction [1999] (Schumacher, Aileen)
After Effects [1996] (Aird, Catherine)
After Midnight [1966] (Nielsen, Helen)
After the Break [1995] (Howell, Lis)
After-Image [Germany] [1996] (Gom, Leona)
Aftershock [1977] (O'Donnell, Lillian)
Against the Brotherhood [1997] (Fawcett, Quinn)
Agatha Raisin and the Murderous Marriage [1996] (Beaton, M.C.)
Agatha Raisin and the Potted Gardener [1994] (Beaton, M.C.)
Agatha Raisin and the Quiche of Death [1992] (Beaton, M.C.)
Agatha Raisin and the Terrible Tourist [1997] (Beaton, M.C.)
Agatha Raisin and the Vicious Vet [1993] (Beaton, M.C.)
Agatha Raisin and the Walkers of Dembley [1995] (Beaton, M.C.)

Agatha Raisin and the Wellspring of Death [1998] (Beaton, M.C.)
Agatha Raisin and the Wizard of Evesham [1999] (Beaton, M.C.)
Ah, Sweet Mystery [1991] (Sibley, Celestine)
aka Jane [1997] (Tan, Maureen)
Akin to Death [1998] (Lachnit, Carroll)
Alias the Enemy [1997] (Dewhurst, Eileen)
Alibi for a Corpse [1969] (Lemarchand, Elizabeth)
Alibi for an Actress [1992] (Farrell, Gillian B.)
Alibi in Time [1980] (Thomson, June)
Alien Blues [1992] (Hightower, Lynn S.)
Alien Eyes [1993] (Hightower, Lynn S.)
Alien Heat [1994] (Hightower, Lynn S.)
Alien Rites [1995] (Hightower, Lynn S.)
All Hallow's Evil [1992] (Wolzien, Valerie)
All My Suspects [1994] (Shaffer, Louise)
All Shall Be Well [1994] (Crombie, Deborah)
All That Remains [1992] (Cornwell, Patricia)
All the Blood Relations [1997] (Adams, Deborah)
All the Crazy Winters [1992] (Adams, Deborah)
All the Dark Disguises [1993] (Adams, Deborah)
All the Dead Lie Down [1998] (Walker, Mary Willis)
All the Deadly Beloved [1995] (Adams, Deborah)
All the Great Pretenders [1992] (Adams, Deborah) ☆
All the Hungry Mothers [1993] (Adams, Deborah)
All the Old Lions [1994] (Caverly, Carol)
All Unwary [1998] (Curzon, Clare)
Alley Cat Blues [1995] (Kijewski, Karen)
Alligator's Farewell [1998] (Jackson, Hialeah)
Almost Human [1998] (Roberts, Lillian M.)
Alpine Advocate [1992] (Daheim, Mary) ☆
Alpine Betrayal [1993] (Daheim, Mary)
Alpine Christmas [1993] (Daheim, Mary)
Alpine Decoy [1994] (Daheim, Mary)
Alpine Escape [1995] (Daheim, Mary)
Alpine Fury [1995] (Daheim, Mary)
Alpine Gamble [1996] (Daheim, Mary)
Alpine Hero [1997] (Daheim, Mary)
Alpine Icon [1997] (Daheim, Mary)
Alpine Journey [1998] (Daheim, Mary)
Alpine Kindred [1998] (Daheim, Mary)
Alternate Sides [1995] (Piesman, Marissa)
Always Anonymous Beast [1987] (Douglas, Lauren Wright)
Always in a Foreign Land [1993] (Scott, Barbara A.)
Amateur City [1984] (Forrest, Katherine V.)

Bird Brained [1999] (Speart, Jessica)
Bird in a Cage [1995] (Martin, Lee)
∎ Bird in the Hand [1986] (Cleeves, Ann)
∎ Birth Marks [1992] (Dunant, Sarah)
Birthday Party [1999] (Kellogg, Marne Davis)
Bishop in the Back Seat [1980] (Watson, Clarissa)
Bishop's Tale [1994] (Frazer, Margaret)
∎ Bitch Factor [1998] (Rogers, Chris)
Bite of Death [1991] (Conant, Susan)
Bitter Business [1995] (Hartzmark, Gini)
Bitter Feast [1998] (Rozan, S.J.)
Bitter Finish [1983] (Barnes, Linda)
Bitter Herbs [1993] (Cooper, Natasha)
Bitter Medicine [1987] (Paretsky, Sara)
Bitter Sweets [1996] (McKevett, G.A.)
Black Diamond [1997] (Holtzer, Susan)
Black Dreams [1993] (Green, Kate)
∎ Black Girl, White Girl [1989] (Moyes, Patricia)
∎ Black Justice [1989] (Shepherd, Stella)
Black Moon [1989] (Drake, Alison)
Black Ribbon [1995] (Conant, Susan)
Black Rubber Dress [1997] (Henderson, Lauren)
Black Tower [1975] (James, P. D.) ★
∎ Black Widower [1975] (Moyes, Patricia)
∎ Blackening Song [1995] (Thurlo, Aimée & David)
Blackwater Spirits [1995] (Monfredo, Miriam Grace)
Blanche Among the Talented Tenth [1994] (Neely, Barbara)
Blanche Cleans Up [1998] (Neely, Barbara
∎ Blanche on the Lam [1992] (Neely, Barbara)) ★★★
Bleeding Hearts [1994] (Haddam, Jane)
∎ Bleeding Hearts [1984] (White, Teri)
Bleeding Maize and Blue [1996] (Holtzer, Susan)
∎ Bleeding of Innocents [1993] (Bannister, Jo)
Blessed Death [1996] (Lachnit, Carroll)
Blind Bloodhound Justice [1998] (Lanier, Virginia)
Blind Descent [1998] (Barr, Nevada)
Blind Trust [1990] (Grant, Linda)
Blonde for a Shilling [1999] (Graves, Sarah)
Blood and Circuses [1994] (Greenwood, Kerry)
Blood and Honey [1961] (Fickling, G.G.)
Blood Debt [1997] (Huff, Tanya)
∎ Blood Is Thicker [1990] (Fallon, Ann C.)
Blood Lies [1991] (Wallace, Patricia)
Blood Line [1989] (Knight, Alanna)
Blood Lines [1996] (Harrod-Eagles, Cynthia)
Blood Lines [1993] (Huff, Tanya)
Blood Money [1999] (Krich, Rochelle Majer)
∎ Blood of an Aries [1994] (Mather, Linda)
Blood on the Happy Highway [1983] (Radley, Sheila)
Blood on the Street [1992] (Meyers, Annette)
Blood on the Water [1992] (Elrod, P.N.)
Blood Pact [1993] (Huff, Tanya)
∎ Blood Price [1992] (Huff, Tanya)
Blood Red Roses [1997] (Lawrence, Margaret)
∎ Blood Run [revised 1999] [1988] (Robinson, Leah Ruth)
Blood Shot [1988] (Paretsky, Sara) ☆☆
Blood Ties [1998] (Bell, Pauline)
Blood Tracks [1998] (Cercone, Karen Rose)
Blood Trail [1992] (Huff, Tanya)
∎ Blood Upon the Snow [1944] (Lawrence, Hilda)
∎ Blood Will Have Blood [1982] (Barnes, Linda)
Blood Will Tell [1996] (Stabenow, Dana)
Blood Will Tell [1997] (Grimes, Terris McMahan)
∎ Blood Work [1994] (Zachary, Fay)
Bloodcircle [1990] (Elrod, P.N.)
Bloodlines [1992] (Conant, Susan)
∎ Bloodlist [1990] (Elrod, P.N.)
Bloodstream [1995] (Carlson, P.M.)
Bloody Bones [1996] (Hamilton, Laurell K.)
Bloody London [1999] (Nadelson, Reggie)
Bloody Mary [1990] (Kraft, Gabrielle)

Bloody Roses [1992] (Cooper, Natasha)
Bloody Secrets [1998] (Garcia-Aguilera, Carolina)
∎ Bloody September [1976] (Haddad, C.A.)
Bloody Shame [1997] (Garcia-Aguilera, Carolina)
Bloody Soaps [1989] (Babbin, Jacqueline)
∎ Bloody Special [1989] (Babbin, Jacqueline)
∎ Bloody Waters [1996] (Garcia-Aguilera, Carolina)
∎ Blooming Murder [1994] (Hager, Jean)
∎ Blue [1998] (Padgett, Abigail)
Blue Blood [Yale] [1999] (Thomas-Graham, Pamela)
Blue Corn Murders [1998] (Pickard, Nancy)
∎ Blue Death [1998] (O'Donnell, Lillian)
Blue Genes [1996] (McDermid, Val)
Blue Moon [1998] (Hamilton, Laurell K.)
Blue Pearl [1994] (MacGregor, T.J.)
Blue Poppy [1997] (Moody, Skye Kathleen)
Blue-Eyed Boy [1990] (Curzon, Clare)
Bluegate Fields [1984] (Perry, Anne)
∎ Bluejay Shaman [1994] (McClendon, Lise)
Bluest Blood [1998] (Roberts, Gillian)
Bodies of Water [1990] (Borthwick, J. S.)
Body and Soul [1989] (Woods, Sherryl)
Body Blow [Pugh, Dianne G.)
∎ Body English [1992] (Mariz, Linda French)
Body Farm [1994] (Cornwell, Patricia)
Body Guard [1994] (McNab, Claire)
∎ Body in Blackwater Bay [incl Stryker & Trevorne] [1992] (Gosling, Paula)
Body in the Basement [1994] (Page, Katherine Hall)
∎ Body in the Belfry [1990] (Page, Katherine Hall) ★
Body in the Bog [1996] (Page, Katherine Hall)
Body in the Bookcase [1998] (Page, Katherine Hall)
Body in the Bouillon [1991] (Page, Katherine Hall)
Body in the Cast [1993] (Page, Katherine Hall)
Body in the Fjord [1997] (Page, Katherine Hall)
Body in the Kelp [1991] (Page, Katherine Hall)
∎ Body in the Transept [1995] (Dams, Jeanne M.) ★☆
Body in the Vestibule [1992] (Page, Katherine Hall)
Body of Evidence [1991] (Cornwell, Patricia)
Body of Opinion [1988] (Stacey, Susannah)
∎ Body Politic [1990] (Aird, Catherine)
Body To Die For [1995] (Frankel, Valerie)
Bohemian Connection [1985] (Dunlap, Susan)
Bohemian Murders [1997] (Day, Dianne)
Bombshell [1964] (Fickling, G.G.)
Bone Idle [1993] (Stacey, Susannah)
Bone of Contention [1997] (Gregory, Susanna)
Bone To Pick [1992] (Harris, Charlaine)
Bonjour, Miss Seeton [1997] (Crane, Hamilton)
Book Early for Murder [1990] (Jordan, Jennifer)
Book of Moons [1995] (Edghill, Rosemary)
Booked for Murder [1996] (McDermid, Val)
Bookfair Murders [Marsha Hillier] [1997] (Porter, Anna)
∎ Bootlegger's Daughter [1992] (Maron, Margaret) ★★★★
∎ Borrower of the Night [1973] (Peters, Elizabeth)
∎ Both Ends of the Night [1997] (Muller, Marcia)
Bowl of Night [1996] (Edghill, Rosemary)
Boy's Tale [1995] (Frazer, Margaret)
Brace of Bloodhounds [1997] (Lanier, Virginia)
Brandenburg Hotel [prequel] [1976] (Winslow, Pauline Glen)
Brandy & Bullets [1997] (Fletcher, Jessica)
Brass Eagle [1989] (Duffy, Margaret)
Bravo for the Bride [1994] (Eyre, Elizabeth)
∎ Breach of Duty [1999] (Jance, J.A.)
Breach of Promise [1998] (Perry, Anne)
Breach of Promise [1998] (O'Shaughnessy, Perri)
∎ Breach of Trust [1996] (MacDougal, Bonnie)
Bread on Arrival [1998] (Temple, Lou Jane)
Break a Leg Darlings [1995] (Babson, Marian)
Breaking Point [1996] (Navratilova, Martina)

Breakup [1997] (Stabenow, Dana)
∎ Brenda's Murder [1973] (Wells, Tobias)
Brewing Up a Storm [1996] (Lathen, Emma)
Bridal Shroud [1996] (Penn, John)
Bridled Groom [1994] (Borthwick, J. S.)
Bright Flamingo Shroud [1997] (O'Brien, Meg)
Brink of Murder [1976] (Nielsen, Helen)
Broken Lines [1998] (Bannister, Jo)
∎ Broken Promise Land [1996] (Muller, Marcia)
∎ Broken Star [1992] (Brown, Lizbie)
Broken Vessel [1994] (Ross, Kate) ★
∎ Brotherly Love [1993] (Lordon, Randye) ☆
Brothers in Blood [1993] (Brod, D. C.)
Brothers of Glastonbury [1997] (Sedley, Kate)
∎ Brunswick Gardens [1998] (Perry, Anne)
Brush With Death [1990] (Smith, Joan G.)
∎ Bucket Nut [1992] (Cody, Liza) ★
Bull Slayers [1995] (Knight, Alanna)
∎ Bullshot [1987] (Kraft, Gabrielle) ☆
∎ Bulrush Murders [1991] (Rothenberg, Rebecca) ☆☆
Bum Steer [1989] (Pickard, Nancy) ★
Bundori [1996] (Rowland, Laura Joh)
∎ Burden of Innocence [1996] (Thomson, June)
Buried in Quilts [1994] (Frommer, Sara Hoskinson)
Buried in the Past [1974] (Lemarchand, Elizabeth)
Burn Marks [1990] (Paretsky, Sara)
Burning Bride [1998] (Lawrence, Margaret)
Burning Desires [1995] (Bannister, Jo)
Burning Is a Substitute for Loving [1963] (Melville, Jennie)
∎ Burning Time [1993] (Glass, Leslie)
∎ Burning Water [1989] (Lackey, Mercedes)
Burnt Offerings [1998] (Hamilton, Laurell K.)
Burnton Widows [1984] (McConnell, Vicki P.)
∎ Bury Her Sweetly [1992] (Amey, Linda)
Bury Him Kindly [1992] (Burden, Pat)
∎ Bury the Bishop [1995] (Gallison, Kate)
Busy Bodies [1995] (Hess, Joan)
But I Wouldn't Want To Die There [1993] (Pickard, Nancy)
But Why Shoot the Magistrate? [1998] (Sprinkle, Patricia H.)
Butchers Hill [1998] (Lippman, Laura)
∎ Butter Did It [1997] (Richman, Phyllis) ☆
Butterfly Effect [1994] (Zaremba, Eve)
Buzzards Must Also Be Fed [1991] (Wingate, Anne)
∎ By Evil Means [1993] (Prowell, Sandra West) ☆☆
∎ By Hook or by Crook [1975] (Lathen, Emma)
∎ By Reason of Insanity [1998] (Hayden, G. Miki)

C

"C" is for Corpse [1986] (Grafton, Sue) ★☆
C.O.P. Out [1998] (Herndon, Nancy)
Cabin 3033 [1986] (Clarke, Anna)
Cabin Fever [1995] (Schmidt, Carol)
∎ Cable Car Murder [1981] (Taylor, Elizabeth Atwood)
Cactus Blood [1995] (Corpi, Lucha)
Cadaver [1992] (Kittredge, Mary)
∎ Cadenza for Caruso [1910] [1984] (Paul, Barbara)
Cain His Brother [1995] (Perry, Anne)
∎ Calendar Girl [1994] (Duffy, Stella)
Call the Dead Again [1998] (Granger, Ann)
Callander Square [1980] (Perry, Anne)
∎ Canaletto and the Case of the Westminster Bridge [1998] (Laurence, Janet)
∎ Cancellation by Death [1992] (Yeager, Dorian)
Candle for a Corpse [1995] (Granger, Ann)
Cannon's Revenge [as W.W. Lee] [1995] (Lee, Wendi)
Cape Cod Caper [1980] (Arnold, Margot)
Cape Cod Conundrum [1992] (Arnold, Margot)
∎ Capitol Offense [1996] (Mikulski, Barbara)
Capitol Venture [1997] (Mikulski, Barbara)
∎ Capriccio [1989] (Smith, Joan G.)

Captain's Paradise [1988] (Hooper, Kay)
Captive Audience [1975] (Mann, Jessica)
Captive in Time [1990] (Dreher, Sarah)
Captive Voice (1995) (Hoff, B.J.)
Carcass Trade [1994] (Ayres, Noreen)
Cardington Crescent [1987] (Perry, Anne)
Carve a Witness to Shreds [1999] (John, Cathie)
Case Closed [1977] (Thomson, June)
∎ Case Has Altered [1997] (Grimes, Martha)
∎ Case of Loyalties [1986] (Wallace, Marilyn) ★
Case of the Anxious Aunt [1996] (Clarke, Anna)
Case of the Chinese Boxes [1990] (Day, Marele)
∎ Case of the Cold Murderer [1976] (Godfrey, Ellen)
Case of the Good-for-Nothing Girlfriend [1994] (Maney, Mabel)
∎ Case of the Hook-Billed Kites [1982] (Borthwick, J. S.)
Case of the Ludicrous Letters [1994] (Clarke, Anna)
∎ Case of the Not-So-Nice Nurse [1993] (Maney, Mabel)
Case of the Paranoid Patient [1991] (Clarke, Anna)
Case of the Privvy Garden [1999] (Laurence, Janet)
Case of the Radioactive Redhead [1963] (Fickling, G.G.)
Cashmere Kid [1993] (Comfort, Barbara)
∎ Cast a Cold Eye [1988] (Eccles, Marjorie)
Cast for Death [1976] (Yorke, Margaret)
Cast of Killers [1992] (Gray, Gallagher)
Cast the First Stone [1996] (Adams, Jane)
Casual Affairs [1985] (O'Donnell, Lillian)
Cat in a Crimson Haze [1995] (Douglas, Carole Nelson)
Cat in a Diamond Dazzle [1996] (Douglas, Carole Nelson)
Cat in a Flamingo Fedora [1997] (Douglas, Carole Nelson)
Cat in a Golden Garland [1997] (Douglas, Carole Nelson)
Cat in the Dark [1999] (Murphy, Shirley Rousseau)
∎ Cat Killer [1993] (Dengler, Sandy)
Cat on a Blue Monday [1994] (Douglas, Carole Nelson)
Cat on a Hyacinth Hunt [1998] (Douglas, Carole Nelson)
∎ Cat on the Edge [1996] (Murphy, Shirley Rousseau)
Cat Raise the Dead [1997] (Murphy, Shirley Rousseau)
Cat Under Fire [1997] (Murphy, Shirley Rousseau)
Cat Who Ate Danish Modern [1967] (Braun, Lilian Jackson)
∎ Cat Who Blew the Whistle [1995] (Braun, Lilian Jackson)
∎ Cat Who Came to Breakfast [1994] (Braun, Lilian Jackson)
∎ Cat Who Could Read Backwards [1966] (Braun, Lilian Jackson)
∎ Cat Who Knew a Cardinal [1991] (Braun, Lilian Jackson)
Cat Who Knew Shakespeare [1988] (Braun, Lilian Jackson)
Cat Who Lived High [1990] (Braun, Lilian Jackson)
∎ Cat Who Moved a Mountain [1992] (Braun, Lilian Jackson)
Cat Who Played Brahms [1987] (Braun, Lilian Jackson) ☆
Cat Who Played Post Office [1987] (Braun, Lilian Jackson)
∎ Cat Who Said Cheese [1996] (Braun, Lilian Jackson)
Cat Who Sang for the Birds [1998] (Braun, Lilian Jackson)
Cat Who Saw Red [1986] (Braun, Lilian Jackson) ☆
∎ Cat Who Saw Stars [1999] (Braun, Lilian Jackson)
Cat Who Sniffed Glue [1988] (Braun, Lilian Jackson)
∎ Cat Who Tailed a Thief [1997] (Braun, Lilian Jackson)
Cat Who Talked to Ghosts [1990] (Braun, Lilian Jackson)
∎ Cat Who Turned On and Off [1968] (Braun, Lilian Jackson)
∎ Cat Who Wasn't There [1993] (Braun, Lilian Jackson)
∎ Cat Who Went into the Closet [1994] (Braun, Lilian Jackson)
Cat Who Went Underground [1989] (Braun, Lilian Jackson)
Cat With an Emerald Eye [1996] (Douglas, Carole Nelson)
Cat's Claw [1992] (Yarbro, Chelsea Quinn)
Cat's Cradle [1992] (Curzon, Clare)
Cat's Eye [1991] (Jackson, Marian J. A.)
∎ Cat's-Paw, Inc. [1991] (Thrasher, L. L.)
Catacomb Conspiracy [1991] (Arnold, Margot)
Catch the Fallen Sparrow [1996] (Masters, Priscilla)
∎ Cater Street Hangman [1979] (Perry, Anne)
∎ Catering to Nobody [1990] (Davidson, Diane Mott) ☆☆☆

■ Catnap [1992] (Douglas, Carole Nelson)
Catnap [1994] (Slovo, Gillian)
Caught Dead [1995] (McKenna, Bridget)
■ Caught Dead in Philadelphia [1987] (Roberts, Gillian) ★
■ Caught in the Shadows [1992] (Haddad, C.A.)
Caught in the Web [1996] (Scott, Barbara A.)
Cause of Death [1996] (Cornwell, Patricia)
Cavalier Case [1991] (Fraser, Antonia)
■ Cavalier in White [1986] (Muller, Marcia)
Celebration in Purple Sage [1996] (Smith, Barbara Burnett)
Celtic Riddle [Ireland] [2000] (Hamilton, Lyn)
■ Cemetery Murders [1997] (Marcy, Jean)
Cereal Murders [1993] (Davidson, Diane Mott)
Ceremonial Death [1996] (Oliphant, B. J.)
Ceremony in Death [1997] (Robb, J.D.)
Certain Justice [1998] (James, P. D.)
Chain Letter [1997] (McNab, Claire)
Chala Project [Grand Canyon] [2000] (Livesay, Ann)
Chameleon [1998] (Kennett, Shirley)
■ Champagne and a Gardener [1982] (Morison, B.J.)
Change for the Worse [1980] (Lemarchand, Elizabeth)
Charged With Guilt [1995] (White, Gloria) ☆☆☆
Charisma (Bannister, Jo)
Charles Dickens Murders [1998] (Skom, Edith)
■ Charlie's Bones [1998] (Thrasher, L. L.)
Charm City [1997] (Lippman, Laura) ★★☆
Chasing Away the Devil [1991] (Cooper, Susan Rogers)
Chatauqua [1993] (Ennis, Catherine)
Cheat the Devil [1998] (Rubino, Jane)
Check-out Time [1995] (Kingsbury, Kate)
Cheetah Chase [1994] (McQuillan, Karin)
Cherry Pickers [1997] (Rowlands, Betty)
Cheshire Cat's Eye [1983] (Muller, Marcia)
Chestnut Mare, Beware [1996] (Jaffe, Jody)
Chicken Feed [1998] (Fritchley, Alma)
■ Chicken Little Was Right [1994] (Ruryk, Jean)
Chicken Out [1999] (Fritchley, Alma)
■ Chicken Run [1997] (Fritchley, Alma)
Chief Inspector's Daughter [1980] (Radley, Sheila)
■ Child of Silence [1993] (Padgett, Abigail) ☆☆☆
Children of the Night [1990] (Lackey, Mercedes)
Children's Games [1989] (LaPierre, Janet)
Children's Zoo [1981] (O'Donnell, Lillian)
Chile Death [1998] (Albert, Susan Wittig)
Chill in the Blood [1998] (Elrod, P.N.)
Chill of Summer [1995] (Brennan, Carol)
Chill Rain in January [1990] (Wright, L.R.) ★
Chilling Deception [1986] (Castle, Jayne)
■ China Trade [1994] (Rozan, S.J.)
■ Chinese Chop [1949] (Sheridan, Juanita)
Chivalry Is Dead [1996] (Kingsbury, Kate)
Chorus of Detectives [1920] [1987] (Paul, Barbara)
■ Chosen for Death [1994] (Flora, Kate Clark)
Christening Day Murder [1993] (Harris, Lee)
Christie Caper [1991] (Hart, Carolyn G.) ☆☆☆
Christmas Egg [1958] (Kelly, Mary)
Christmas Night Murder [1994] (Harris, Lee)
■ Chutes and Adders [1994] (Block, Barbara)
Circle of Wolves [1997] (Wilson, Karen Ann)
Circus of the Damned [1995] (Hamilton, Laurell K.)
Cities of the Dead [1986] (Barnes, Linda)
Class Menagerie [1993] (Churchill, Jill)
Class Reunions are Murder [1996] (Cannon, Taffy)
Clean Break [1995] (McDermid, Val)
Clear Conscience [1994] (Fyfield, Frances)
Clear Cut Murder [1993] (Wallingford, Lee)
■ Clearwater [1991] (Ennis, Catherine)
■ Clerical Errors [1991] (Greenwood, D.M.)
Clinic for Murder [1993] (Landreth, Marsha)
Close Call [1995] (Slovo, Gillian)

Close Her Eyes [1984] (Simpson, Dorothy)
Close Quarters [1994] (Piesman, Marissa)
■ Close Quarters [1997] (Curzon, Clare)
Closed in Silence [1998] (Drury, Joan M.)
Closely Akin to Murder [1996] (Hess, Joan)
Closet Hanging [1987] (Fennelly, Tony)
Closing Statement [1995] (McClellan, Tierney)
Club Paradis Murders [Tahiti] [1983] (McCormick, Claire)
■ Club Twelve [1990] (Williams, Amanda Kyle)
Clubbed to Death [1992] (Edwards, Ruth Dudley) ☆
Coal Bones [1999] (Cercone, Karen Rose)
■ Cocaine Blues [1989] (Greenwood, Kerry)
■ Coconut Killings [1977] (Moyes, Patricia)
Coffee To Die For [1998] (French, Linda)
■ Coffin and the Paper Man [1991] (Butler, Gwendoline)
Coffin Corner [1999] (Rust, Megan Mallory)
Coffin Following [1968] (Butler, Gwendoline)
Coffin for Baby [1963] (Butler, Gwendoline)
Coffin for Charley [1994] (Butler, Gwendoline)
■ Coffin for the Canary [1974] (Butler, Gwendoline)
■ Coffin From the Past [1970] (Butler, Gwendoline)
Coffin's Games (Butler, Gwendoline)
■ Coffin in Fashion [1987] (Butler, Gwendoline)
Coffin in Oxford [1962] (Butler, Gwendoline)
■ Coffin in the Black Museum [1989] (Butler, Gwendoline)
■ Coffin in the Museum of Crime [1989] (Butler, Gwendoline)
Coffin Lane Murders [1998] (Knight, Alanna)
Coffin on Murder Street [1992] (Butler, Gwendoline)
■ Coffin on the Water [1986] (Butler, Gwendoline)
Coffin Tree [1994] (Butler, Gwendoline)
■ Coffin Underground [1988] (Butler, Gwendoline)
Coffin Waiting [1964] (Butler, Gwendoline)
Coffin's Dark Number [1969] (Butler, Gwendoline)
Coffin's Game [1998] (Butler, Gwendoline)
Cold Blood [1996] (La Plante, Lynda)
■ Cold Call [1993] (Pugh, Dianne G.)
Cold Case [1997] (Barnes, Linda)
Cold Coffin [1990] (Quest, Erica)
■ Cold Coming [1956] (Kelly, Mary)
■ Cold Day for Murder [1992] (Stabenow, Dana) ★
Cold Feet [1992] (Tucker, Kerry)
Cold Hard Fax [1997] (O'Kane, Leslie)
Cold Heart [1998] (La Plante, Lynda)
Cold Heart of Capricorn [1997] (Lawrence, Martha)
Cold Hit [1999] (Fairstein, Linda)
Cold in the Earth [1993] (Granger, Ann)
■ Cold Iron [1997] (Michaels, Melisa)
Cold Light of Day [1983] (Page, Emma)
■ Cold Shoulder [1994] (La Plante, Lynda)
Cold Smoked [1995] (Beck, K. K.)
■ Cold Tracks [1991] (Wallingford, Lee)
Cold-Blooded Business [1994] (Stabenow, Dana)
Colder Kind of Death [1994] (Bowen, Gail) ★
Collected Stories [10 stories] [1997] (Cross, Amanda)
Collector of Photographs [1989] (Valentine, Deborah) ☆☆☆
■ Come Away Death [1994] (Shone, Anna)
Come Away, Death [1997] (Hardwick, Mollie)
Come Death and High Water [1987] (Cleeves, Ann)
■ Come Home and Be Killed [1962] (Melville, Jennie)
Come to Dust [1968] (Lathen, Emma)
■ Common Death (Cooper, Natasha)
Common Murder [1989] (McDermid, Val)
Company She Kept [1993] (Eccles, Marjorie)
Compass of the Heart [1998] (Cogan, Priscilla)
Complete Steel [1969] (Aird, Catherine)
Concourse [1995] (Rozan, S.J.) ★
Concubine's Tattoo [1998] (Rowland, Laura Joh)
Confession [1994] (Pickard, Nancy)
Conferences are Murder (1999) (McDermid, Val)
Consider the Crows [1993] (Weir, Charlen) ☆

Conspiracy in Death [1999] (Robb, J.D.)
Conspiracy of Strangers [1986] (Martin, Lee)
∎ Contents Under Pressure [1992] (Buchanan, Edna)
Convivial Codfish [1984] (MacLeod, Charlotte)
Cook's Night Out [1998] (Pence, Joanne)
Cooked Goose [1998] (McKevett, G.A.)
Cooking Most Deadly [1996] (Pence, Joanne)
∎ Cooking School Murders [by Virginia Rich] [1982]
   (Pickard, Nancy)
Cooking Up Trouble [1995] (Pence, Joanne)
Cooks Overboard [1998] (Pence, Joanne)
Cool Repentance [1982] (Fraser, Antonia)
Cop Killer [1975] (Sjöwall, Maj & Per Wahlöö)
Cop Out [1991] (McNab, Claire)
Cop Out [1997] (Dunlap, Susan)
Cop Without a Shield [1983] (O'Donnell, Lillian)
Copper Gold [1978] (Winslow, Pauline Glen)
Coppergold (Winslow, Pauline Glen)
Copy Cat Crimes [1995] (Wilson, Karen Ann)
Copy Kat [1992] (Kijewski, Karen)
Coq au Vin [1999] (Carter, Charlotte)
Corpse in Oozak's Pond [1986] (MacLeod, Charlotte) ★☆
Corpse in the Kitchen [1993] (Mason, Sarah J.)
Corpus Christmas [1989] (Maron, Margaret) ☆☆
∎ Corridors of Death [1981] (Edwards, Ruth Dudley) ☆
∎ Corruption of Faith [1997] (English, Brenda)
Corruption of Power [1998] (English, Brenda)
Counsellor Heart [1980] (Winslow, Pauline Glen)
Counterprobe [1990] (Douglas, Carole Nelson)
Country Comes to Town [1996] (Kelner, Toni L.P.)
∎ Cover Her Face [1962] (James, P. D.)
∎ Cover-up Story [1971] (Babson, Marian)
Coyote [1990] (Barnes, Linda)
Crack Down [1994] (McDermid, Val) ☆☆
∎ Cracking Open a Coffin [1993] (Butler, Gwendoline)
Crash Course [1997] (Trocheck, Kathy Hogan)
Crazy for Loving [1992] (Maiman, Jaye) ★
Crazy Mixed-Up Nude [1964] (Fickling, G.G.)
∎ Creature Was Stirring [1977] (Wells, Tobias)
Credible Threat [1996] (Dawson, Janet)
∎ Creeping Ivy [1998] (Cooper, Natasha)
Crescent City Kill [1997] (Smith, Julie)
∎ Crewel World [1999] (Ferris, Monica)
∎ Crime of Passion [1991] (Hooper, Kay)
∎ Crocodile on the Sandbank [1975] (Peters, Elizabeth)
Crooked Island [1994] (McKernan, Victoria)
Crooked Little House [1999] (Cooper, Susan Rogers)
Cross My Heart and Hope To Die [1992] (Radley, Sheila)
Cross-Check [1997] (Law, Janice)
Crosswords [1994] (Sumner, Penny)
Crown Witness [1995] (Linscott, Gillian)
Cruel and Unusual [1993] (Cornwell, Patricia) ★
Cruel April [1997] (Wakefield, Hannah)
Cruel as the Grave [1998] (Penman, Sharon Kay)
Cruel Mother [1990] (LaPierre, Janet)
Cruellest Month [1991] (Holt, Hazel)
∎ Cry for Help [1995] (Stuyck, Karen Hanson)
Cry for Self Help [1997] (Girdner, Jaqueline)
Cryin' Time [1998] (Tishy, Cecelia)
Crystal Mountain Veils [1995] (York, Kieran)
Cuckoo Case [1995] (Bailey, Michele)
Cure for a Charlatan [1999] (Roe, Caroline)
Cure for Dying [1989] (Melville, Jennie)
∎ Curiosity Didn't Kill the Cat [1973] (Wren, M.K.)
Curious Affair of the Third Dog [1973] (Moyes, Patricia)
∎ Curious Cape Cod Skull [1995] (Lee, Marie)
Curl Up and Die [1996] (Jorgensen, Christine T.)
Curly Smoke [1995] (Holtzer, Susan)
Curse of the Giant Hogweed [1985] (MacLeod, Charlotte)
Curse of the Pharaohs [1981] (Peters, Elizabeth)
Curse the Darkness [1990] (Grant-Adamson, Lesley)

Cursed in the Blood [1998] (Newman, Sharan)
∎ Curtain Fall [1977] (Dewhurst, Eileen)
Curtains for the Cardinal [1993] (Eyre, Elizabeth)
Curtsey [1996] (Kellogg, Marne Davis)
Cut and Dry [1997] (Dereske, Jo)
Cut Loose [1999] (Kennett, Shirley)
Cut to: Murder [1995] (Osborne, Denise)
∎ Cut to the Quick [1993] (Ross, Kate)
∎ Cutter [1994] (Crum, Laura)
Cuttings [1999] (Grant, Anne Underwood)
Cyanide With Compliments [1972] (Lemarchand,
   Elizabeth)
Cyberkiss [1996] (Chapman, Sally)

D

"D" is for Deadbeat [1987] (Grafton, Sue)
Damsel in Distress [1997] (Dunn, Carola)
Dance on Blood [1998] (Linscott, Gillian)
Dancing in the Dark [1992] (Zukowski, Sharon)
Dandelion Murders [1994] (Rothenberg, Rebecca)
∎ Dangerous Attachments [1995] (Lovett, Sarah)
Dangerous Conceits [1988] (Moore, Margaret)
Dangerous Deceit [1995] (Bolitho, Janie)
Dangerous Games [1994] (Grant-Adamson, Lesley)
Dangerous Mourning [1991] (Perry, Anne)
∎ Dangerous Places [1987] (Chase, Elaine Raco)
Dante Game [1991] (Langton, Jane)
∎ Daphne Decisions [1990] (O'Brien, Meg)
Dark and Sinful Death [1997] (Joseph, Alison)
Dark Coffin [1995] (Butler, Gwendoline)
Dark Corners [1988] (Chase, Elaine Raco)
Dark Door [1988] (Wilhelm, Kate)
∎ Dark Fields [1986] (MacGregor, T.J.) ☆
Dark Nantucket Noon [1975] (Langton, Jane)
Dark River Legacy [1990] (Hoff, B.J.)
Dark Star [1989] (Muller, Marcia)
∎ Dark Stream [1986] (Thomson, June)
Dark Swain [1994] (Knight, Kathryn Lasky)
∎ Darker Shade of Crimson [Harvard] [1998] (Thomas-
   Graham, Pamela)
Darkest Hour [1969] (Nielsen, Helen)
∎ Dartmoor Burial [1992] (Peterson, Audrey)
Dash of Death [1995] (Bishop, Claudia)
∎ Date With a Dead Doctor [1991] (Brill, Toni)
Date With a Plummeting Publisher [1993] (Brill, Toni)
Date With the Perfect Dead Man [1999] (Griffin, Annie)
Daughters of Artemis [1991] (Douglas, Lauren Wright)
∎ Day for Dying [1995] (Simpson, Dorothy)
Day in the Death of Dorothea Cassidy [1992]
   (Cleeves, Ann)
Day of Atonement [1992] (Kellerman, Faye)
Day That Dusty Died [1993] (Martin, Lee)
Days of Crime and Roses [1992] (Morgan, Kate)
∎ Dead Ahead [1990] (Horansky, Ruby)
Dead Ahead [1994] (McKenna, Bridget) ☆
Dead and Blonde [1998] (Marcy, Jean)
Dead and Buried [1994] (Cleary, Melissa)
Dead and Buried [1995] (Hager, Jean)
Dead and Doggone [1990] (Conant, Susan)
Dead and Gone [1989] (Kittredge, Mary)
∎ Dead as a Dodo [1996] (Langton, Jane)
∎ Dead as Dead Can Be [1993] (Crowleigh, Ann)
∎ Dead Beat [1992] (McDermid, Val)
Dead Beat and Deadly [1998] (Chittenden, Margaret)
∎ Dead Before Morning [1993] (Evans, Geraldine)
∎ Dead Body Language [1997] (Warner, Penny) ★☆
Dead by Morning [1989] (Simpson, Dorothy)
Dead by the Light of the Moon [1967] (Wells, Tobias)
∎ Dead Cat Bounce [1998] (Graves, Sarah)
Dead Celeb [1997] (Maracotta, Lindsay)
Dead Center [1994] (Horansky, Ruby)

Dead Certain [1992] (McNab, Claire)
Dead Crazy [1988] (Pickard, Nancy) ☆☆
∎ Dead Do Not Praise [1990] (Bell, Pauline)
Dead Duck [1997] (Chappell, Helen)
Dead End (Harrod-Eagles, Cynthia)
Dead Ends [1992] (Fallon, Ann C.)
Dead Heat [1984] (Barnes, Linda)
∎ Dead Hollywood Moms Society [1996]
   (Maracotta, Lindsay)
∎ Dead in a Row [1957] (Butler, Gwendoline)
Dead in the Cellar [1994] (Feddersen, Connie)
Dead in the Dirt [1996] (Feddersen, Connie)
Dead in the Driver's Seat [1998] (Feddersen, Connie)
Dead in the Melon Patch [1995] (Feddersen, Connie)
∎ Dead in the Morning [1970] (Yorke, Margaret)
Dead in the Mud [1997] (Feddersen, Connie)
∎ Dead in the Scrub [1990] (Oliphant, B. J.) ☆☆
∎ Dead in the Water [1993] (Feddersen, Connie)
Dead in the Water [1991] (Smith, Julie)
Dead in the Water [1993] (Stabenow, Dana)
Dead in the Water [1998] (Dunn, Carola)
Dead Letter [1998] (Waterhouse, Jane)
∎ Dead Liberty [1986] (Aird, Catherine)
Dead Loss [1966] (Petrie, Rhona)
Dead Man and the Sea [1997] (Steinberg, Janice)
Dead Man Out of Mind [1995] (Charles, Kate)
Dead Man's Fingers [1999] (Lee, Barbara)
∎ Dead Man's Float [1998] (Sherman, Beth)
Dead Man's Hand [1997] (Dain, Catherine)
∎ Dead Man's Island [1993] (Hart, Carolyn G.) ★
Dead Man's Music (Linscott, Gillian)
Dead Man's Riddle [1957] (Kelly, Mary)
Dead Man's Sweetheart [1996] (Linscott, Gillian)
∎ Dead Man's Thoughts [1983] (Wheat, Carolyn) ☆
Dead Matter [1993] (Wren, M.K.)
Dead Men Don't Dance [1997] (Chittenden, Margaret)
∎ Dead Men Don't Give Seminars [1988] (Sucher, Dorothy) ☆
Dead Men Don't Marry [1989] (Sucher, Dorothy)
∎ Dead Men Don't Ski [1959] (Moyes, Patricia)
Dead Men's Bones [1996] (Clayton, Mary)
Dead Moon on the Rise [1994] (Cooper, Susan Rogers)
Dead of Summer (Kelly, Mary)
Dead of Winter [1995] (Gosling, Paula)
Dead of Winter (Hall, Patricia)
Dead on Arrival [1986] (Simpson, Dorothy)
Dead on Sunday (Orde, A. J.)
Dead Over Heels [1996] (Harris, Charlaine)
Dead Pan [1992] (Dentinger, Jane)
∎ Dead Pull Hitter [1989] (Gordon, Alison)
Dead Ringer [1994] (Kelner, Toni L.P.)
Dead Serious [1995] (Stacey, Susannah)
∎ Dead Set [1992] (Melville, Jennie)
Dead South [1996] (Sullivan, Winona)
∎ Dead Stick [1998] (Rust, Megan Mallory)
∎ Dead Time [1992] (Bland, Eleanor Taylor)
Dead to Rights [1996] (Jance, J.A.)
∎ Dead White Female [1995] (Henderson, Lauren)
Dead Wrong [1998] (Staincliffe, Cath)
Deadbeat [1998] (Lee, Wendi)
Deadfall [1998] (Henry, Sue)
Deadliest Option [1991] (Meyers, Annette)
∎ Deadline [1997] (Rowe, Jennifer)
∎ Deadline for Murder [1991] (Frankel, Valerie)
Deadlock [1984] (Paretsky, Sara)
Deadly Ackee [Jamaica] [1988] (Hadley, Joan)
Deadly Admirer [1992] (Green, Christine)
∎ Deadly Appearances [1990] (Bowen, Gail)
Deadly Beloved [1989] (Knight, Alanna)
∎ Deadly Beloved [1997] (Haddam, Jane)
Deadly Brew [1998] (Gregory, Susanna)
∎ Deadly Deceptions [1993] (Moen, Ruth Raby)

Deadly Devotion [1994] (Wallace, Patricia) ☆
∎ Deadly Errand [1991] (Green, Christine) ☆
∎ Deadly Gamble [1995] (Shelton, Connie)
Deadly Grounds [1989] (Wallace, Patricia)
Deadly Harvest [1997] (Rawlings, Ellen)
Deadly Judgment [1996] (Fletcher, Jessica)
Deadly Legacy [1996] (Rowlands, Betty)
Deadly Objectives [1984] (Taylor, L. A.)
Deadly Obsession [1995] (Woods, Sherryl)
Deadly Partners [1996] (Green, Christine)
Deadly Paté [1996] (Furie, Ruthe)
Deadly Practice [1994] (Green, Christine)
∎ Deadly Reflections (Friedman, Mickey)
Deadly Rehearsal [1990] (Peterson, Audrey)
Deadly Relations [1979] (Thomson, June)
Deadly Reunion [1995] (Manthorne, Jackie)
Deadly Rx [1997] (Horowitz, Renee B.)
∎ Deadly Safari [1990] (McQuillan, Karin)
Deadly Secrets on the St. Johns [1995]
   (Sprinkle, Patricia H.)
Deadly Shaker Spring [1998] (Woodworth, Deborah)
Deadly Sickness [1985] (Penn, John)
Deadly Valentine [1990] (Hart, Carolyn G.) ☆☆
Dean It Was That Died [1991] (Whitehead, Barbara)
Dear Irene, [1995] (Burke, Jan)
∎ Dear Laura [1890s London] [1973] (Stubbs, Jean) ☆
Dear Miss Demeanor [1987] (Hess, Joan)
Dear Old Dead [1994] (Haddam, Jane)
Death a la Provencale [1995] (Laurence, Janet)
Death Among the Dons [1993] (Neel, Janet) ☆
∎ Death and Faxes [1996] (O'Kane, Leslie)
Death and Judgment [1995] (Leon, Donna)
Death and Other Lovers [1991] (Bannister, Jo)
Death and Shadows [1999] (Gosling, Paula)
Death and Taxes [1992] (Dunlap, Susan)
∎ Death and the Chapman [1991] (Sedley, Kate)
Death and the Delinquent [1992] (Oliphant, B. J.)
Death and the Dogwalker [1990] (Orde, A. J.)
Death and the Dutch Uncle [1968] (Moyes, Patricia)
Death and the Epicure [1993] (Laurence, Janet)
∎ Death and the Maiden [1978] (Radley, Sheila)
∎ Death and the Oxford Box [1993] (Stallwood, Veronica)
∎ Death and the Pregnant Virgin [1980] (Haymon, S. T.)
∎ Death at Bishop's Keep [1994] (Paige, Robin)
Death at Daisy's Folly [1997] (Paige, Robin)
Death at Dearley Manor [1998] (Rowlands, Betty)
Death at Devil's Bridge [1998] (Paige, Robin)
Death at Face Value [1995] (Christmas, Joyce)
Death at Gallows Green [1995] (Paige, Robin)
Death at High Tide [1999] (Sherman, Beth)
∎ Death at La Fenice [1992] (Leon, Donna)
∎ Death at Lavender Bay [1996] (Douglas, Lauren Wright)
∎ Death at Rainy Mountain [1996] (Medawar, Mardi Oakley)
Death at Rottingdean [1999] (Paige, Robin)
Death at St. Anselm's [1984] (Holland, Isabelle)
Death at the Beggar's Opera [1995] (Lake, Deryn)
Death at the Devil's Tavern [1996] (Lake, Deryn)
Death at the Dutch House [1995] (Whitehead, Barbara)
Death at the Table [1994] (Laurence, Janet)
Death at the Wheel [1996] (Flora, Kate Clark)
Death at Victoria Dock [1992] (Greenwood, Kerry)
∎ Death at Wentwater Court [1994] (Dunn, Carola)
Death Beyond the Nile [1988] (Mann, Jessica)
∎ Death Brims Over [1997] (Wilson, Barbara Jaye) ☆
Death by Analysis [1986] (Slovo, Gillian)
Death by Crystal [1993] (Bushell, Agnes)
∎ Death by Deception [1988] (Wingate, Anne)
∎ Death by Dressage [1993] (Banks, Carolyn)
∎ Death by Election [1993] (Hall, Patricia)
∎ Death by Misadventure (Greenwood, Kerry)
∎ Death by Rhubarb [1996] (Temple, Lou Jane)

Death by the Light of the Moon [1992] (Hess, Joan)
∎ Death by the Riverside [1990] (Redmann, J. M.)
Death Cap [1973] (Thomson, June)
∎ Death Comes as Epiphany [1993] (Newman, Sharan) ★☆☆
Death Comes Staccato [1987] (Slovo, Gillian)
Death Crosses the Border [1995] (Steinberg, Janice)
Death Dines Out [1997] (Bishop, Claudia)
∎ Death Down Home [1990] (Sandstrom, Eve K.)
Death Down Under [1990] (McNab, Claire)
Death du Jour [1999] (Reichs, Kathy)
Death Echo [1993] (Tucker, Kerry)
Death Flats [1991] (MacGregor, T.J.)
Death Flips Its Lid [1998] (Wilson, Barbara Jaye)
Death for a Dancer [1986] (Giroux, E.X.)
Death for a Dancing Doll [1991] (Giroux, E.X.)
Death for a Darling [1985] (Giroux, E.X.)
Death for a Dietician [1988] (Giroux, E.X.)
Death for a Dilletante [1987] (Giroux, E.X.)
Death for a Doctor [1986] (Giroux, E.X.)
Death for a Dodo [1993] (Giroux, E.X.)
Death for a Double [1990] (Giroux, E.X.)
Death for a Dreamer [1989] (Giroux, E.X.)
∎ Death for Adonis [1984] (Giroux, E.X.)
Death for Old Times' Sake [1992] (Orde, A. J.)
Death Goes on Retreat [1995] (O'Marie,
    Carol Anne, Sister)
Death Goes Skiing [1979] (Schier, Norma)
Death Hits the Fan [1998] (Girdner, Jaqueline)
Death in a City of Mystics [1998] (Steinberg, Janice)
Death in a Cold Hard Light [1998] (Mathews, Francine)
∎ Death in a Deck Chair [1984] (Beck, K. K.)
Death in a Funhouse Mirror [1995] (Flora, Kate Clark)
Death in a Mood Indigo [1997] (Mathews, Francine)
Death in a Strange Country [1993] (Leon, Donna)
Death in a Tenured Position [1981] (Cross, Amanda) ★
Death in Autumn [1984] (Nabb, Magdalen)
∎ Death in Bloodhound Red [1995] (Lanier, Virginia) ★☆☆
Death in Blue Folders [1985] (Maron, Margaret)
∎ Death in Candie Gardens [1992] (Dewhurst, Eileen)
∎ Death in Deakins Wood [1963] (Petrie, Rhona)
Death in Devil's Acre [1985] (Perry, Anne)
Death in Disguise [1992] (Graham, Caroline)
∎ Death in Good Company [1997] (Sprague, Gretchen)
Death in High Water (Leon, Donna)
∎ Death in Lacquer Red [1999] (Dams, Jeanne M.)
Death in Lovers' Lane [1997] (Hart, Carolyn G.)
Death in Paradise [1998] (Hart, Carolyn G.)
Death in Paradise [1998] (Flora, Kate Clark)
Death in Rough Water [1995] (Mathews, Francine)
Death in Springtime [1983] (Nabb, Magdalen)
∎ Death in Still Waters [1995] (Lee, Barbara) ★
Death in Store [short stories] [1992] (Rowe, Jennifer)
Death in the Amazon [1998] (Livesay, Ann)
∎ Death in the Country [1993] (Green, Christine)
∎ Death in the Dark Walk [1994] (Lake, Deryn)
∎ Death in the Faculty (Cross, Amanda)
∎ Death in the Family (Melville, Jennie)
Death in the Garden [1987] (Melville, Jennie)
∎ Death in the Life [1976] (Davis, Dorothy Salisbury)
∎ Death in the Morning (Radley, Sheila)
∎ Death in the Off-Season [1994] (Mathews, Francine)
Death in Time [1982] (Warner, Mignon)
Death in Wessex [1989] (Peterson, Audrey)
Death Is a Family Affair [1987] (Sims, L. V.)
∎ Death Is Academic [1976] (Mackay, Amanda)
∎ Death Is Forever [1980] (O'Callaghan, Maxine)
Death is Sweet [1996] (Kelly, Susan B.)
Death Is the Inheritance [1998] (Clayton, Mary)
Death, Lies and Apple Pies [1997] (Malmont, Valerie S.)
Death Line [1995] (Evans, Geraldine)
Death Lives Next Door [1960] (Butler, Gwendoline)

Death Mask [1988] (Dentinger, Jane)
Death Notes (Rendell, Ruth)
Death of a Butterfly [1984] (Maron, Margaret)
Death of a Cad [1987] (Beaton, M.C.)
Death of a Charming Man [1994] (Beaton, M.C.)
Death of a Damn Yankee [1999] (Kelner, Toni L.P.)
Death of a Dancer [1989] (McGown, Jill)
Death of a Dancing Fool [1996] (Berry, Carole)
Death of a Dear Friend [1990] (Quinton, Ann)
∎ Death of a Dentist [1997] (Beaton, M.C.)
Death of a Difficult Woman [1994] (Berry, Carole)
Death of a Dimpled Darling [1997] (Berry, Carole)
∎ Death of a DJ [1996] (Rubino, Jane)
Death of a Doll [1947] (Lawrence, Hilda)
Death of a Dream Maker [1995] (Gray, Gallagher)
∎ Death of a Duchess [1992] (Eyre, Elizabeth)
Death of a Dunwoody Matron [1993] (Sprinkle, Patricia H.)
Death of a Dustbunny [1998] (Jorgensen, Christine T.)
Death of a Dutchman [1982] (Nabb, Magdalen)
Death of a Garden Pest [1996] (Ripley, Ann)
Death of a Glutton [1993] (Beaton, M.C.)
Death of a God [1987] (Haymon, S. T.)
Death of a Golden Girl [1988] (Fulton, Eileen)
Death of a Good Woman [1989] (Eccles, Marjorie)
∎ Death of a Gossip [1985] (Beaton, M.C.)
∎ Death of a Healing Woman [1996] (Martin, Allana)
Death of a Hero [1996] (Haymon, S. T.)
Death of a Hollow Man [1989] (Graham, Caroline)
Death of a Hussy [1990] (Beaton, M.C.)
∎ Death of a Lady's Maid [1997] (Cook, Judith)
∎ Death of a Macho Man [1996] (Beaton, M.C.)
Death of a Much-Travelled Woman [9 stories] [1998]
    (Wilson, Barbara)
Death of a Nag [1995] (Beaton, M.C.)
Death of a Partner [1991] (Neel, Janet)
Death of a Perfect Wife [1989] (Beaton, M.C.)
Death of a Political Plant [1998] (Ripley, Ann)
∎ Death of a Postmodernist [1995] (Steinberg, Janice)
Death of a Prankster [1992] (Beaton, M.C.)
Death of a Raven [1988] (Duffy, Margaret)
Death of a Saint Maker [1998] (Martin, Allana)
∎ Death of a Scriptwriter [1998] (Beaton, M.C.)
Death of a Snob [1991] (Beaton, M.C.)
Death of a Travelling Man [1993] (Beaton, M.C.)
Death of a Voodoo Doll [1982] (Arnold, Margot)
Death of a Warrior Queen [1991] (Haymon, S. T.)
∎ Death of a Winter Shaker [1997] (Woodworth, Deborah)
∎ Death of an Angel [1975] (Winslow, Pauline Glen)
Death of an Angel [1997] (O'Marie, Carol Anne, Sister)
∎ Death of an Englishman [1981] (Nabb, Magdalen)
Death of an Evangelista [1999] (Martin, Allana)
Death of an Expert Witness [1977] (James, P. D.)
∎ Death of an Old Girl [1967] (Lemarchand, Elizabeth)
∎ Death of an Old Sinner [1957] (Davis, Dorothy Salisbury)
Death of an Outsider [1988] (Beaton, M.C.)
Death of Blue Mountain Cat [1995] (Dymmoch,
    Michael Allen)
Death of Distinction [1995] (Eccles, Marjorie)
Death of Faith [1997] (Leon, Donna)
Death of Innocents [1997] (Orde, A. J.)
Death of the Office Witch [1993] (Millhiser, Marlys)
Death on a Dragon's Tongue [1982] (Arnold, Margot)
∎ Death on Demand [1987] (Hart, Carolyn G.) ☆☆
Death on Doomsday [1971] (Lemarchand, Elizabeth)
Death on Site [1989] (Neel, Janet)
Death on the Agenda [1962] (Moyes, Patricia)
∎ Death on the Cliff Walk [1994] (Kruger, Mary)
Death on the Diagonal [1996] (Banks, Carolyn)
Death on the Drunkard's Path [1996] (Hager, Jean)
Death on the Eno [1981] (Mackay, Amanda)
Death on the Romney Marsh [1998] (Lake, Deryn)

🔳 Death on the Slopes [1978] (Schier, Norma)
🔳 Death on Widow's Walk (Grant-Adamson, Lesley)
🔳 Death Pays the Rose Rent [1994] (Malmont, Valerie S.)
Death Penalties [1991] (Gosling, Paula)
Death Prone [1994] (Curzon, Clare)
🔳 Death Qualified [1991] (Wilhelm, Kate)
Death Served up Cold [1994] (Oliphant, B. J.)
🔳 Death Set to Music [by Mark Hebden] [1979] (Hebden, Juliet)
Death Shall Overcome [1966] (Lathen, Emma)
Death Speaks Softly [1987] (Fraser, Anthea)
Death Sweet [1988] (MacGregor, T.J.)
🔳 Death Takes a Hand [1993] (Moody, Susan)
Death Takes Passage [1997] (Henry, Sue)
Death Takes Up a Collection [1998] (O'Marie, Carol Anne, Sister)
Death Tape [1987] (Gallison, Kate)
Death To Go [1993] (Harrod-Eagles, Cynthia)
Death Too Soon [1994] (Peterson, Audrey)
Death Train to Boston [1999] (Day, Dianne)
🔳 Death Turns a Trick [1982] (Smith, Julie)
Death Under Par [1981] (Law, Janice)
🔳 Death Valley [1993] (Dengler, Sandy)
🔳 Death Walk [1988] (Quest, Erica)
Death Walker [1996] (Thurlo, Aimée & David)
Death Warmed Over [1988] (Martin, Lee)
Death Watch [1992] (Harrod-Eagles, Cynthia)
Death We Share [1995] (Short, Sharon Gwyn)
Death Wears a Crown [1993] (Fawcett, Quinn)
Death With Honors [1998] (Nessen, Ron)
Death With Reservations [1998] (Kingsbury, Kate)
Death's a Beach [1998] (Sullivan, Winona)
🔳 Death's Autograph [1996] (Macdonald, Marianne)
🔳 Death's Bright Angel [1988] (Neel, Janet) ★
Death's Long Shadow [1991] (Penn, John)
Death's Savage Passion [1986] (Papazoglou, Orania)
Death-Fires Dance [1996] (Steinberg, Janice)
Deaths of Jocasta [1993] (Redmann, J. M.)
Debone a Killer's Alibi [2000] (John, Cathie)
Deception Island [1991] (Lorens, M.K.)
Deception on His Mind [1997] (George, Elizabeth)
Deck the Halls With Murder [1998] (Wolzien, Valerie)
🔳 Decked [1992] (Clark, Carol Higgins) ☆☆
🔳 Dedicated Angel [1997] (Cohen, Anthea)
Deeds of the Disturber [1988] (Peters, Elizabeth)
Deep Sleep [1991] (Fyfield, Frances) ★
Deep Water [1996] (Gunning, Sally)
🔳 Deepe Coffyn [1989] (Laurence, Janet)
Deer Leap [1985] (Grimes, Martha)
Defend and Betray [1992] (Perry, Anne) ☆
Defense for the Devil [1999] (Wilhelm, Kate)
Deficit Ending [1990] (Martin, Lee)
🔳 Déjà Dead [1997] (Reichs, Kathy) ★
Delilah Doolittle and the Careless Coyote [1998] (Guiver, Patricia)
Delilah Doolittle and the Motley Mutts [1998] (Guiver, Patricia)
🔳 Delilah Doolittle and the Purloined Pooch [1997] (Guiver, Patricia)
Demon at the Opera [1980] (Schier, Norma)
🔳 Desert Heat [1993] (Jance, J.A.)
Deservedly Dead [1992] (Oliphant, B. J.)
Design for Murder [1987] (Hart, Carolyn G.)
Designer Crimes [1995] (Matera, Lia)
Despatch of a Dove [1969] (Petrie, Rhona)
🔳 Desperate Call [1995] (Coburn, Laura)
🔳 Desperate Game [1986] (Castle, Jayne)
Desperate Remedy [1993] (Kittredge, Mary)
Desperate Silence [1998] (Lovett, Sarah)
Destroy Unopened [1999] (Donald, Anabel)
Destroying Angel [1988] (Cohen, Anthea)
🔳 Detecting Lies [1997] (Kiecolt-Glaser, Janice)

Devices and Desires [1989] (James, P. D.)
Devil down Home [1991] (Sandstrom, Eve K.)
Devil in Music [1997] (Ross, Kate) ★
Devil's Door [1994] (Newman, Sharan)
Devil's Gonna Get Him [1995] (Wesley, Valerie Wilson)
Devil's Knell [1983] (Warner, Mignon)
🔳 Devil's Leg Crossing [1997] (Davis, Kaye)
Devil's Workshop [1996] (Gallison, Kate)
Dial 557 R-A-P-E [1974] (O'Donnell, Lillian)
Diamond Before You Die [1987] (Wiltz, Chris)
Diamond Head [1992] (Jackson, Marian J. A.)
Diamond in the Buff [1990] (Dunlap, Susan)
Die for Love [1984] (Peters, Elizabeth)
Die in My Dreams [1995] (Green, Christine)
Die in the Country [1972] (Wells, Tobias)
Die Like a Dog [1982] (Moffat, Gwen)
Die Quickly, Dear Mother [1969] (Wells, Tobias)
Died in the Red [1967] (Gray, Dulcie)
Diet for Death [1996] (Laurence, Janet)
Diet To Die For [1989] (Hess, Joan)
Different Kind of Summer [1967] (Melville, Jennie)
Dig a Dead Doll [1960] (Fickling, G.G.)
Digging Up Death [1998] (Stein, Triss)
Digging Up Momma [1998] (Shankman, Sarah)
Dinkum Deaths [Great Barrier Reef] [2001] (Livesay, Ann)
Dinky Died [1970] (Wells, Tobias)
Dinner To Die For [1987] (Dunlap, Susan)
Dire Happenings at Scratch Ankle [1993] (Sibley, Celestine)
Director's Cut [1996] (Howell, Lis)
Dirge for a Doge [1997] (Eyre, Elizabeth)
Dirge for a Dorset Druid [1994] (Arnold, Margot)
Dirty Duck [1984] (Grimes, Martha)
Dirty Water [1998] (Gunning, Sally)
Disappearance of Madalena Grimaldi [1994] (Day, Marele)
Disenchanted Diva [1987] (Santini, Rosemarie)
Dismal Thing To Do [1986] (Craig, Alisa)
Dismissed With Prejudice [1989] (Jance, J.A.)
Ditch Rider [1998] (Van Gieson, Judith)
Divine Inspiration [1993] (Langton, Jane)
Do Not Disturb [1994] (Kingsbury, Kate)
🔳 Do Not Go Gently [1996] (Smith-Levin, Judith)
🔳 Doberman Wore Black [1983] (Moore, Barbara)
🔳 Doctor Digs a Grave [1998] (Hathaway, Robin) ★
Doctor Makes a Dollhouse Call [2000] (Hathaway, Robin)
Doctors and Lawyers and Such [1995] (Cooper, Susan Rogers)
Dog Collar Crime [1993] (Cleary, Melissa)
Dog Collar Murders [1989] (Wilson, Barbara)
Dog Eat Dog [1996] (Berenson, Laurien)
Dog Who Knew Too Much [1997] (Benjamin, Carole Lea)
Dogfish [1991] (Geason, Susan)
Dogsbody, Inc. [1999] (Thrasher, L. L.)
🔳 Dogtown [1991] (Lambert, Mercedes)
Dollmaker's Daughters [1997] (Padgett, Abigail)
Dolls Don't Choose [1998] (Whitehead, Barbara)
Dolly and the Bird of Paradise (Dunnett, Dorothy)
Dolly and the Cookie Bird (Dunnett, Dorothy)
Dolly and the Doctor Bird (Dunnett, Dorothy)
Dolly and the Nanny Bird (Dunnett, Dorothy)
🔳 Dolly and the Singing Bird (Dunnett, Dorothy)
Dolly and the Starry Bird (Dunnett, Dorothy)
Dolly Is Dead [1995] (Borthwick, J. S.)
Domino Image [1987] (Hoff, B.J.)
Don't Forget To Die [1999] (Chittenden, Margaret)
Don't Leave Me This Way [1990] (Smith, Joan)
Don't Turn Your Back on the Ocean [1994] (Dawson, Janet)
Don't Wear Your Wedding Ring [1973] (O'Donnell, Lillian)
Done Wrong [1995] (Bland, Eleanor Taylor)
Doomed To Die [1991] (Simpson, Dorothy)
Double Bluff [1995] (McNab, Claire)
Double Coffin [1996] (Butler, Gwendoline)

Double Cross [1998] (McCafferty, Barbara Taylor)
Double Daughter [1988] (McConnell, Vicki P.)
❶ Double, Double, Oil and Trouble [1978] (Lathen, Emma)
Double Exposure [1997] (McCafferty, Barbara Taylor)
❶ Double Murder [1996] (McCafferty, Barbara Taylor)
Double Negative [1998] (Gom, Leona)
Double Take [1994] (Oleksiw, Susan)
Double Take [1997] (Mercer, Judy)
Double Takeout [1999] (Richardson, Tracey)
Double Vision [1997] (Ross, Annie)
Double [w/Bill Pronzini] [1984] (Muller, Marcia)
Doubled in Spades [1996] (Moody, Susan)
Doublet Affair [1998] (Buckley, Fiona)
Dove in the Window [1998] (Fowler, Earlene)
Down Among the Dead Men [1961] (Moyes, Patricia)
Down Among the Dead Men [1994] (Evans, Geraldine)
Down East Murders [1985] (Borthwick, J. S.)
Down for the Count [1997] (O'Callaghan, Maxine) ☆
Down Home Heifer Heist [1993] (Sandstrom, Eve K.)
❶ Down Home Murder [1993] (Kelner, Toni L.P.)
Down the Garden Path [1985] (Cannell, Dorothy)
Downhill to Death [1994] (Bell, Pauline)
Downsized to Death [1997] (Christmas, Joyce)
Dragstrip [1999] (Bartholomew, Nancy)
❶ Dreadful Lies [1994] (Bailey, Michele)
Dream Stalker [1997] (Coel, Margaret)
Dreaming Damozel [1990] (Hardwick, Mollie)
Dreaming of the Bones [1997] (Crombie, Deborah) ★☆☆
Dreamland [1992] (Lorens, M.K.)
Dress To Die For [1998] (Johnson, Dolores)
Dressed for Death [1994] (Leon, Donna)
Dressed To Die [1998] (Connor, Beverly)
❶ Dressed To Kill [1994] (Duffy, Margaret)
Drift Away [1994] (Tucker, Kerry)
❶ Drink of Deadly Wine [1991] (Charles, Kate)
Drink This [1980] (Dewhurst, Eileen)
Drinker of Blood [1998] (Robinson, Lynda S.)
Dude on Arrival [1992] (Borthwick, J. S.)
❶ Due Process [1996] (Arnold, Catherine)
Due to a Death [1962] (Kelly, Mary)
Dull Dead [1958] (Butler, Gwendoline)
Dummy Hand [1998] (Moody, Susan)
Dune to Death [1993] (Daheim, Mary)
❶ Dupe [1980] (Cody, Liza) ★☆
Duped by Derivatives [1999] (Farrelly, Gail)
Dust Devils of the Purple Sage [1995] (Smith, Barbara Burnett)
❶ Dutchman [1992] (Meyers, Maan)
Dutchman's Dilemma [1995] (Meyers, Maan)
Dying Breath [1994] (Mason, Sarah J.)
Dying Cheek to Cheek [1992] (Shah, Diane K.)
Dying Fall [1994] (Hall, Patricia)
Dying Fall [1985] (Thomson, June)
❶ Dying Fall [1995] (Cutler, Judith)
Dying for Chocolate [1992] (Davidson, Diane Mott)
Dying for Millions [1997] (Cutler, Judith)
Dying for Power [1998] (Cutler, Judith)
Dying for Stardom [1988] (Fulton, Eileen)
Dying Light in Corduba [1996] (Davis, Lindsey)
Dying on Principle [1996] (Cutler, Judith)
Dying Room Only [1998] (Kingsbury, Kate)
Dying To Get Even [1999] (Fitzwater, Judy)
❶ Dying To Get Published [1998] (Fitzwater, Judy)
❶ Dying To Sing [1996] (Chittenden, Margaret)
Dying To Write [1996] (Cutler, Judith)

E

"E" is for Evidence [1988] (Grafton, Sue) ☆
❶ Eagle Catcher [1995] (Coel, Margaret)
Eagles Die Too [1992] (O'Brien, Meg)
Easier To Kill [1998] (Wesley, Valerie Wilson)
East Is East [1991] (Lathen, Emma)

Easy Day for a Lady (Linscott, Gillian)
Eat, Drink, and Be Buried [1994] (Kingsbury, Kate)
Eat, Drink and Be Wary [1998] (Myers, Tamar)
Eater of Souls [1997] (Robinson, Lynda S.)
❶ Edge of the Crazies [1995] (Harrison, Jamie)
❶ Edited Out [1994] (Haddock, Lisa)
Educated Death [1997] (Flora, Kate Clark)
❶ Edwin of the Iron Shoes [1977] (Muller, Marcia)
Egyptian Coffin [1998] (Jakeman, Jane)
❶ Eight Dogs Flying [1994] (Wilson, Karen Ann)
Elected to Death [1996] (Wolzien, Valerie)
Elective Murder [1995] (McGiffin, Janet)
Electric City [1994] (Beck, K. K.)
Elegy in a Country Graveyard [1990] (Peterson, Audrey)
Element of Doubt [1987] (Simpson, Dorothy)
Elephants' Graveyard [1993] (McQuillan, Karin)
Elusive Mrs. Pollifax [1971] (Gilman, Dorothy)
Elusive Quarry [1995] (Comfort, Barbara)
Embassy Row [1998] (Fawcett, Quinn)
Embers of Death [1996] (Shepherd, Stella)
Emerald Lizard [1991] (Wiltz, Chris)
❶ Emergency Murder [1992] (McGiffin, Janet)
Emily Dickinson Is Dead [1984] (Langton, Jane) ★☆
Emperor Norton's Ghost [1998] (Day, Dianne)
Encore Murder [1989] (Babson, Marian)
❶ End of an Altruist [1994] (Logan, Margaret)
❶ End of April [1992] (Sumner, Penny)
End of the Line [1981] (OCork, Shannon)
Endangered Species [1997] (Barr, Nevada)
Enemy Way [1998] (Thurlo, Aimée & David)
❶ Engineered for Murder [1996] (Schumacher, Aileen)
English School of Murder [1990] (Edwards, Ruth Dudley)
❶ Enter Second Murderer [1988] (Knight, Alanna)
❶ Epitaph for a Dead Actor [1960] (Gray, Dulcie)
Epitaph for a Lobbyist [1974] (Dominic, R.B.)
❶ Equal Opportunity Death [1983] (Dunlap, Susan)
Error In Judgment [1990] (Brod, D. C.)
Estate of Mind [1999] (Myers, Tamar)
❶ Eulogy for a Brown Angel [1992] (Corpi, Lucha)
Evan Help Us [1998] (Bowen, Rhys)
Evanly Choirs [1999] (Bowen, Rhys)
❶ Evans Above [1997] (Bowen, Rhys)
Eve of St. Hyacinth [1995] (Sedley, Kate)
Even Cops' Daughters [1986] (Webb, Martha G.)
Even Yuppies Die [1993] (Babson, Marian)
❶ Every Breath You Take [1994] (Spring, Michelle) ☆
❶ Every Crooked Nanny [1992] (Trocheck, Kathy Hogan) ☆☆
Every Deadly Sin [1995] (Greenwood, D.M.)
Every Second Thursday [1981] (Page, Emma)
❶ Everything You Have Is Mine [1991] (Scoppettone, Sandra)
❶ Everywhere That Mary Went [Mary DiNunzio] [1993] (Scottoline, Lisa) ☆
Eviction by Death [1993] (Yeager, Dorian)
Evidence of Guilt [1997] (Jacobs, Jonnie)
Evil Angels Among Them [1995] (Charles, Kate)
Evil Harmony [1996] (Buckstaff, Kathryn)
Evil That Men Do [1993] (Knight, Alanna)
❶ Except the Dying [1997] (Jennings, Maureen) ☆☆
Exception to Murder [1992] (Wingate, Anne)
Exhaustive Inquiries [1994] (Rowlands, Betty)
❶ Exile Way [1996] (Woodward, Ann)
Existing Solutions [1993] (Jordan, Jennifer)
❶ Exit Actors, Dying [1979] (Arnold, Margot)
Exit the Milkman [1996] (MacLeod, Charlotte)
Exposure of Evil [1998] (Bolitho, Janie)
Eye of Anna [1989] (Wingate, Anne)
❶ Eye of the Daemon [1996] (Bacon-Smith, Camille)
Eye of the Storm [1988] (Muller, Marcia)
Eyes of the Empress [1998] (Bacon-Smith, Camille)
Eyes on Utopia Murders [1981] (D'Amato, Barbara)
Eyeshot [1995] (Hightower, Lynn S.)
Eyewitness to Murder [1992] (Belfort, Sophie)

F

"F" is for Fugitive [1989] (Grafton, Sue)
Face Down Among the Winchester Geese [1999] (Emerson, Kathy Lynn)
Face Down Beneath the Eleanor Cross [2000] (Emerson, Kathy Lynn)
■ Face Down in the Marrow-Bone Pie [1997] (Emerson, Kathy Lynn)
Face Down Upon an Herbal [1998] (Emerson, Kathy Lynn)
■ Face of a Stranger [1990] (Perry, Anne) ☆
Face of Death [1985] (Grant-Adamson, Lesley)
■ Face on the Wall [1998] (Langton, Jane)
Face Turned Backward [1998] (Haney, Lauren)
Face Value [1994] (Matera, Lia)
■ Fade to Black [as Della Borton] [1999] (Borton, D.B.)
Fade to Grey [1998] (Adams, Jane)
Failure To Appear [1993] (Jance, J.A.)
Faint Praise [1995] (Hart, Ellen)
■ Fair Game [1993] (Krich, Rochelle Majer) ☆
Fair Game [1994] (Radley, Sheila)
Fair Play [1995] (Beecham, Rose)
Faith, Hope and Homicide [1991] (Mann, Jessica)
Faithful Unto Death [1996] (Graham, Caroline)
Falcon at the Portal [1999] (Peters, Elizabeth)
Fall From Grace [1991] (Wright, L.R.)
Fall From Grace [1999] (Sleem, Patty)
Fall in Denver [1995] (Andrews, Sarah)
Fall of Lucas Kendrick [1988] (Hooper, Kay)
Fallen Angel [1984] (Cohen, Anthea)
Fallen From Grace [1998] (Welch, Pat)
Falling Star [1964] (Moyes, Patricia)
Falling Star [1979] (O'Donnell, Lillian)
False Impressions [1986] (Berne, Karin)
False Notes (1990) (Yarbro, Chelsea Quinn)
False Prophet [1992] (Kellerman, Faye)
False Witness [1996] (Benke, Patricia D.)
Family Album [1995] (Oleksiw, Susan)
Family Practice [1995] (Weir, Charlene)
■ Family Skeletons [1997] (MacPherson, Rett)
■ Family Vault [1979] (MacLeod, Charlotte)
■ Famine of Horses [1994] (Chisholm, P. F.)
■ Far and Deadly Cry [1995] (Holbrook, Teri) ☆☆☆
Fare Play [1995] (Paul, Barbara)
Farewell, Conch Republic [1999] (Jackson, Hialeah)
Farewell to Yarns [1991] (Churchill, Jill)
■ Farriers' Lane [1993] (Perry, Anne)
■ Fast Forward [1996] (Mercer, Judy)
Fast Friends [1997] (Pugh, Dianne G.)
Fat Lands [1993] (Dunant, Sarah) ★
Fat-Free and Fatal [1993] (Girdner, Jaqueline)
Fatal Advent [1989] (Holland, Isabelle)
Fatal Cape Cod Funeral [1996] (Lee, Marie)
Fatal Cut [1999] (Green, Christine)
■ Fatal Diagnosis [1990] (Kittredge, Mary)
Fatal End [1992] (Quinton, Ann)
Fatal Flashback [1989] (Fulton, Eileen)
Fatal Fortune [1986] (Castle, Jayne)
Fatal Reaction [1997] (Hartzmark, Gini)
Fatal Remedies [1999] (Leon, Donna)
Fatal Reunion [1989] (McNab, Claire)
Fatal Thaw [1993] (Stabenow, Dana)
Fate of Ravens [1998] (Nunnally, Tiina)
Fate Worse Than Death [1985] (Radley, Sheila)
Father, Forgive Me [1993] (Burden, Pat)
Father Forgive Me [1997] (Lordon, Randye) ★☆
Father's Day Murder [1999] (Harris, Lee)
Fault Lines [1998] (Salter, Anna)
■ Fax Me a Bagel [1998] (Kahn, Sharon)
Fear of Frying [1997] (Churchill, Jill)
Fearful Symmetry [1988] (Waltch, Lilla M.)

Feast into Mourning [1991] (Bell, Pauline)
Feast of Death [1989] (Penn, John)
Feast of Murder [1992] (Haddam, Jane)
February Face [1987] (Adamson, M. J.)
February Mourning [1990] (Wakefield, Hannah)
Femmes Fatal [1992] (Cannell, Dorothy)
■ Festering Lilies [1990] (Cooper, Natasha)
Festival of Deaths [1994] (Haddam, Jane)
Fete Worse than Death [1990] (Christmas, Joyce)
Fever Season [1998] (Hambly, Barbara)
Fevered [1988] (Drake, Alison)
Few Dying Words [1994] (Gosling, Paula)
■ Fiction, Fact, & Murder [1995] (Van Hook, Beverly)
Fifth Member [1997] (Rayner, Claire)
Fifth Rapunzel [1991] (Gill, B.M.)
Fifth Wheel [1998] (Calloway, Kate)
File Under: Arson [1994] (Lacey, Sarah)
■ File Under: Deceased [1992] (Lacey, Sarah)
File Under: Jeopardy [1995] (Lacey, Sarah)
File Under: Missing [1993] (Lacey, Sarah)
Final Appeal [Grace Rossi] [1994] (Scottoline, Lisa) ★
Final Arrangements [1996] (Murray, Donna Huston)
Final Closing [1997] (Lee, Barbara)
Final Cut [1995] (Haddock, Lisa)
■ Final Design [1993] (Gilpatrick, Noreen)
Final Edition [1991] (McDermid, Val)
■ Final Jeopardy [1996] (Fairstein, Linda) ☆
Final Moments [1987] (Page, Emma)
Final Notice [1998] (Dereske, Jo)
Final Option [1994] (Hartzmark, Gini)
Final Rest [1993] (Morell, Mary)
■ Final Session [1991] (Morell, Mary)
Final Take [1996] (Manthorne, Jackie)
Finales & Overtures [1996] (McCafferty, Jeanne)
Finders Keepers [1990] (Travis, Elizabeth)
Fine Distinctions [1991] (Valentine, Deborah) ☆
Fine Place for Death [1994] (Granger, Ann)
Fine Target [1998] (Duffy, Margaret)
Finger of Fate [1996] (Bolitho, Janie)
Finishing Touch [1993] (Rowlands, Betty)
Fire and Fog [1996] (Day, Dianne)
■ Fire and Ice [1998] (Stabenow, Dana)
Fire Carrier [1996] (Hager, Jean)
Fire Cracker [1997] (Kennett, Shirley)
Fire Engine That Disappeared [1971] (Sjöwall, Maj & Per Wahlöö)
Fire in the Blood [1991] (Elrod, P.N.)
Fire Water [1999] (Gunning, Sally)
Firestorm [1996] (Barr, Nevada)
■ First Blood [1993] (Rayner, Claire)
First Cut [1997] (Robinson, Leah Ruth)
■ First Death [2000] (Youmans, Claire)
First Hit of the Season [1984] (Dentinger, Jane)
■ First Impressions [1996] (Calloway, Kate)
■ First Kill All the Lawyers [1988] (Shankman, Sarah)
First Pedigree Murder [1994] (Cleary, Melissa)
First Wife, Twice Removed [1993] (Curzon, Clare)
Fit of Tempera [1994] (Daheim, Mary)
Five Alarm Fire [1996] (Borton, D.B.)
Five Bells and Bladebone [1987] (Grimes, Martha)
■ Flashpoint [1995] (Hightower, Lynn S.)
Flaw in the System (Dominic, R.B.)
Flight of the Stone Angel (O'Connell, Carol)
Flight of the Archangel [1985] (Holland, Isabelle)
Flight of the Serpent [1998] (Davis, Val)
Flower Master [1999] (Massey, Sujata)
Flowers for His Funeral [1994] (Granger, Ann)
Flush of Shadows [5 novellas] [1995] (Wilhelm, Kate)
Flying Too High [1990] (Greenwood, Kerry)
■ Following Jane [1993] (Singer, Shelley)
Foo Dog [1971] (Wells, Tobias)

Fool and His Honey [1999] (Harris, Charlaine)
Fool's Gold [1998] (Jakeman, Jane)
∎ Fool's Puzzle [1994] (Fowler, Earlene) ☆
Foolproof [1998] (Pugh, Dianne G.)
∎ Footsteps in the Blood (Melville, Jennie)
For Every Evil [1995] (Hart, Ellen)
For the Sake of Elena [1992] (George, Elizabeth)
∎ Foreign Bodies [1967] (Petrie, Rhona)
Foreign Body [1997] (Holms, Joyce)
∎ Forests of the Night [1987] (Moore, Margaret)
Forever Wilt Thou Die [MI] [1976] (Byfield, Barbara Ninde)
Fortieth Birthday Body [1989] (Wolzien, Valerie)
∎ Foul Play [1991] (Thomson, June)
∎ Found: A Body [1992] (Struthers, Betsy)
∎ Fountain of Death [1995] (Haddam, Jane)
For the Defense (Wilhelm, Kate)
Four Elements of Murder [1995] (Borton, D.B.)
Four To Score [1998] (Evanovich, Janet)
Fourth Attempt [1996] (Rayner, Claire)
Fourth Down [1998] (Calloway, Kate)
∎ Fourth Stage of Gainsborough Brown [1977]
   (Watson, Clarissa)
∎ Fowl Play [1996] (Westfall, Patricia Tichenor)
Fowl Prey [1991] (Daheim, Mary)
Foxglove [1992] (Kelly, Mary Anne)
Frame Grabber [1992] (Danks, Denise)
Framed in Blue (Brod, D. C.)
Framed in Cornwall [1998] (Bolitho, Janie)
Framed in Lace [1999] (Ferris, Monica)
Framework for Death [1998] (Schumacher, Aileen)
Free Draw [1984] (Singer, Shelley)
∎ Free Love [1999] (Meyers, Annette)
∎ Free Man of Color [1997] (Hambly, Barbara)
∎ Freefall in Cutthroat Gorge [2001] (Morrone,
   Wenda Wardell)
Freeze My Margarita [1998] (Henderson, Lauren)
Fresh Kills [1995] (Wheat, Carolyn)
Friend or Faux [1991] (Christmas, Joyce)
∎ Friends Till the End [1989] (Dank, Gloria)
Frog and the Scorpion [1986] (Maxwell, A.E.)
Frogskin and Muttonfat [1996] (Caverly, Carol)
∎ From Doon With Death [1964] (Rendell, Ruth)
From Here to Paternity [1995] (Churchill, Jill)
From Potter's Field [1995] (Cornwell, Patricia)
∎ Frost the Fiddler [1992] (Weber, Janice)
Frozen Stiff [1993] (Mason, Sarah J.)
Fruitcake [1997] (Rubino, Jane)
Fruiting Bodies [1996] (Cooper, Natasha)
Fugitive Colors [1995] (Maron, Margaret)
Full Commission [1992] (Brennan, Carol)
Full Cry [1985] (Tone, Teona)
Full Frontal Murder [1997] (Paul, Barbara)
Full House [1986] (Singer, Shelley)
Full Stop [1995] (Smith, Joan)
∎ Funeral Food (1997) (Taylor, Kathleen)
∎ Funeral Sites [1982] (Mann, Jessica)
∎ Funny as a Dead Comic [1993] (Cooper, Susan Rogers)
Funny as a Dead Relative [1994] (Cooper, Susan Rogers)
Funny Money [1994] (Kershaw, Valerie)
Funny Money [2000] (McCafferty, Taylor)

G

"G" is for Gumshoe [1990] (Grafton, Sue) ★★
Gallows Bird [1993] (Duffy, Margaret)
Games To Keep the Dark Away [1984] (Muller, Marcia)
∎ Garbage Dump Murders [1993] (Beecham, Rose)
∎ Garden of Malice [1983] (Kenney, Susan)
Garden Plot [1997] (Borthwick, J. S.)
∎ Gator Aide [1997] (Speart, Jessica)
Gatsby's Vineyard [1987] (Maxwell, A.E.)
∎ Gaudi Afternoon [1990] (Wilson, Barbara) ★★

Geezer Factory Murders [1996] (Sawyer, Corinne Holt)
Gemini Doublecross [1995] (Mather, Linda)
∎ Gemini Man [1985] (Kelly, Susan) ☆
Gemini Trip [1977] (Law, Janice)
∎ Genealogy of Murder [1996] (Martin, Lee)
∎ Generous Death [1984] (Pickard, Nancy)
Gentleman Called [1958] (Davis, Dorothy Salisbury)
George Eliot Murders [1995] (Skom, Edith)
Georgia Disappeared [1991] (Godfrey, Ellen)
Getting Mine [1991] (Femling, Jean)
Ghost and Mrs. Jeffries [1993] (Brightwell, Emily)
Ghost in the Closet [1995] (Maney, Mabel)
∎ Ghost Motel [1994] (Manthorne, Jackie)
Ghost of a Chance [1998] (Chappell, Helen)
Ghost Walk [1997] (Macdonald, Marianne)
Ghost Walker [1996] (Coel, Margaret)
Ghostland [1992] (Hager, Jean)
Gift of Sanctuary [1998] (Robb, Candace M.)
Gila Monster [1994] (Dengler, Sandy)
Gilgamesh [1989] (Bannister, Jo)
Gilt by Association [1996] (Myers, Tamar)
∎ Gin & Daggers [1989] (Fletcher, Jessica)
Girl on the Loose [1958] (Fickling, G.G.)
Girl on the Prowl [1959] (Fickling, G.G.)
Girl Who Was Clairvoyant [1982] (Warner, Mignon)
Girl With Red Suspenders [1990] (Whitehead, Barbara)
Give My Secrets Back [1995] (Allen, Kate)
∎ Given the Crime [1998] (Barrett, Margaret)
Given the Evidence [1998] (Barrett, Margaret)
∎ Glade Manor Murder [1988] (Lemarchand, Elizabeth)
Gladstone Bag [1989] (MacLeod, Charlotte)
Glass Ceiling [1995] (Donald, Anabel)
∎ Glory Hole Murders [1985] (Fennelly, Tony) ☆
Glory in Death [1996] (Robb, J.D.)
Go Close Against the Enemy [1998] (Iakovou, Takis
   and Judy)
Go Not Gently [1997] (Staincliffe, Cath)
Goblin Market [1993] (Douglas, Lauren Wright)
God in Concord [1992] (Langton, Jane)
Goddess Affair [1997] (O'Donnell, Lillian)
∎ Going Concern [1993] (Aird, Catherine)
Going Down of the Sun [1990] (Bannister, Jo)
∎ Going for the Gold [1981] (Lathen, Emma)
Going Local [1996] (Harrison, Jamie)
Going Out in Style [1990] (Dank, Gloria)
Going Out in Style [1998] (Christmas, Joyce)
∎ Gold Coast Nocturne [1951] (Nielsen, Helen)
Golden Crucible [1906 SF] [1976] (Stubbs, Jean)
∎ Gone Away (Holt, Hazel)
Gone Quiet [1994] (Bland, Eleanor Taylor)
Gone to Her Death [1990] (McGown, Jill)
Gone to the Dogs [1992] (Conant, Susan)
Gonna Take a Homicidal Journey [1998]
   (Scoppettone, Sandra)
Good and Dead [1986] (Langton, Jane)
∎ Good Cop, Bad Cop [1998] (D'Amato, Barbara)
∎ Good Daughter [1994] (Lee, Wendi)
Good Fight [1990] (Matera, Lia) ☆☆
∎ Good Friday Murder [1992] (Harris, Lee) ☆
Good King Sauerkraut [1989] (Paul, Barbara)
Good Morning, Irene [1990] (Douglas, Carole Nelson)
∎ Good Night, Mr. Holmes [1990] (Douglas, Carole Nelson)
Good Night, Sweet Prince [1990] (Berry, Carole)
∎ Good Night To Kill [1989] (O'Donnell, Lillian)
∎ Good Weekend for Murder [1987] (Jordan, Jennifer)
Good Year for a Corpse [1994] (Wolzien, Valerie)
∎ Goodbye, Charli [1997] (Petit, Diane)
Goodbye, Charli—Take Two [1998] (Petit, Diane)
Goodbye, Charli—Third Time Lucky [1998] (Petit, Diane)
∎ Goodbye Nanny Gray [1987] (Stacey, Susannah) ☆
∎ Goodnight, Irene [1993] (Burke, Jan) ☆☆

Goose in the Pond [1997] (Fowler, Earlene) ☆
Gospel Makers [1994] (Fraser, Anthea)
Governing Body [1997] (Wilson, Anne)
Grand Slam [1994] (Moody, Susan)
■ Grandfather Medicine [1989] (Hager, Jean)
Grandmother's House [1991] (LaPierre, Janet)
Grass Widow [1996] (Holbrook, Teri) ☆☆☆☆
Grave Consequences [1989] (Comfort, Barbara)
Grave Deeds [1994] (Struthers, Betsy)
Grave Disturbance [1998] (Greenwood, D.M.)
Grave Goods [1984] (Mann, Jessica)
Grave Matters [1973] (Yorke, Margaret)
Grave Misgivings [1998] (Gallison, Kate)
Grave Music [1994] (Harrod-Eagles, Cynthia)
Grave Responsibility [1990] (Stacey, Susannah)
Grave Secrets [1994] (Hendricksen, Louise)
■ Grave Talent [1993] (King, Laurie R.) ★☆☆
■ Graven Images [1995] (Waterhouse, Jane)
Graves in Academe [1985] (Kenney, Susan)
■ Gravestone [1992] (Carlson, P.M.)
Graveyard Spiral [2000] (Rust, Megan Mallory)
Gray Magic [1987] (Dreher, Sarah)
■ Gray Matter [1996] (Kennett, Shirley)
Great Day for the Deadly [1992] (Haddam, Jane)
■ Great Deliverance [1988] (George, Elizabeth) ★★☆☆
■ Green Grow the Dollars [1982] (Lathen, Emma)
Green Mill Murder [1993] (Greenwood, Kerry)
Green Money [1999] (Smith-Levin, Judith)
■ Green Stone [1961] (Blanc, Suzanne) ★
■ Greenway [1995] (Adams, Jane) ☆
Grievous Angel [1996] (Lin-Chandler, Irene)
Grievous Sin [1993] (Kellerman, Faye)
Grilling Season [1997] (Davidson, Diane Mott)
■ Grim Pickings [1987] (Rowe, Jennifer)
■ Grime & Punishment [1989] (Churchill, Jill) ★★☆
Grizzly, A Murder [1994] (Andreae, Christine)
Grizzly Trail [1984] (Moffat, Gwen)
Groaning Board [1997] (Meyers, Annette)
Groom with a View [1999] (Churchill, Jill)
Groomed for Death [1994] (Banks, Carolyn)
Grounds for Murder [1995] (Kingsbury, Kate)
Grub-and-Stakers House a Haunt [1993] (Craig, Alisa)
■ Grub-and-Stakers Move a Mountain [1981] (Craig, Alisa)
Grub-and-Stakers Pinch a Poke [1988] (Craig, Alisa)
Grub-and-Stakers Quilt a Bee [1985] (Craig, Alisa)
Grub-and-Stakers Spin a Yarn [1990] (Craig, Alisa)
Guardian Angel [1985] (Cohen, Anthea)
Guardian Angel [1991] (Paretsky, Sara)
Guardian at the Gate [1995] (Highsmith, Domini)
■ Guilty By Choice [1995] (Benke, Patricia D.)
Guilty Knowledge [1986] (Grant-Adamson, Lesley)
Guilty Party [1994] (Penn, John)
■ Guilty Pleasures [1993] (Hamilton, Laurell K.)
Guilty Thing Surprised [1970] (Rendell, Ruth)
Gun for Honey [1958] (Fickling, G.G.)

H

"H" is for Homicide [1991] (Grafton, Sue)
Habit of Fear [1987] (Davis, Dorothy Salisbury)
Habit of Loving (Thomson, June)
Hacker [1992] (Martin, Lee)
Hair of the Dog [1997] (Berenson, Laurien)
Hal's Own Murder Case [1989] (Martin, Lee)
Half a Mind [1990] (Hornsby, Wendy)
Hallelujah Murders [1991] (Tell, Dorothy)
■ Hallowed Murder [1989] (Hart, Ellen)
■ Hamlet Trap [1987] (Wilhelm, Kate)
■ Hand of Solange [1969] (Rippon, Marion)
Hand of the Lion [1987] (Coker, Carolyn)
Hand That Feeds You [1997] (Roberts, Lillian M.)
Hand That Rocks the Ladle [2000] (Myers, Tamar)
■ Hands of Healing Murder [1980] (D'Amato, Barbara)

■ Hands up, Miss Seeton [1992] (Crane, Hamilton)
Hang the Consequences [1984] (Meek, M.R.D.)
Hangdog Hustle [1995] (Pincus, Elizabeth)
Hanged Man [1993] (Sedley, Kate)
Hanging on the Wire [1992] (Linscott, Gillian)
Hanging Time [1995] (Glass, Leslie)
Hangman's Beautiful Daughter [1992] (McCrumb, Sharyn) ☆☆
Hangman's Root [1994] (Albert, Susan Wittig)
Hanky Panky [1995] (McCafferty, Taylor)
Happy Never After [1995] (Trocheck, Kathy Hogan)
Hard Bargain [1992] (Matera, Lia)
Hard Bargain [1997] (D'Amato, Barbara)
Hard Case [1994] (D'Amato, Barbara)
Hard Christmas [1995] (D'Amato, Barbara) ☆☆
Hard Light [1997] (Hornsby, Wendy)
Hard Luck [1992] (D'Amato, Barbara)
Hard Tack [1991] (D'Amato, Barbara)
Hard Women [1993] (D'Amato, Barbara) ☆
■ Hardball [1990] (D'Amato, Barbara)
Harder Thing Than Triumph [MA] [1977] (Byfield, Barbara Ninde)
Hardware [1995] (Barnes, Linda)
Hardwired [1997] (Chapman, Sally)
Hare Today, Gone Tomorrow [1991] (O'Brien, Meg)
■ Hark, Hark, the Watchdogs Bark [1975] (Wells, Tobias)
Harm's Way [1984] (Aird, Catherine)
Harvest of Bones [1998] (Wright, Nancy Means)
Hasty Retreat [1997] (Gallison, Kate)
Haunting Refrain [1998] (Rushford, Patricia H.)
Havana Twist [1998] (Matera, Lia)
■ Have Mercy Upon Us [1974] (Wells, Tobias)
Haven of Danger [1993] (Penn, John)
Haycastle's Cricket [1996] (Bailey, Michele)
He Huffed and He Puffed [1989] (Paul, Barbara)
■ He Shall Thunder in the Sky [2000] (Peters, Elizabeth)
He Was Her Man [1993] (Shankman, Sarah)
Head Case [1985] (Cody, Liza)
Head for Poisoning [1999] (Beaufort, Simon)
■ Headhunt [1991] (Brennan, Carol)
Heading Uptown [1993] (Piesman, Marissa)
Healers [1995] (Cleeves, Ann)
■ Healing of Holly-Jean [1995] (Lin-Chandler, Irene)
■ Healthy Body [1984] (Linscott, Gillian)
■ Healthy, Wealthy & Dead [1994] (North, Suzanne) ☆
Heart Trouble [1996] (Trocheck, Kathy Hogan)
■ Hearts and Bones [1996] (Lawrence, Margaret) ☆☆☆☆
Heavenly Vices [1997] (Greenwood, D.M.)
■ Heir Condition [1995] (McClellan, Tierney)
Held Accountable [1996] (Stuyck, Karen Hanson)
Helium Murder [1998] (Minichino, Camille)
Hell Bent for Heaven [1983] (OCork, Shannon)
Hell of a Dog [1998] (Benjamin, Carole Lea)
Hell's Angel [1986] (Cohen, Anthea)
Help the Poor Struggler [1985] (Grimes, Martha)
Henrietta Who? [1968] (Aird, Catherine)
Here's to the Newly Deads [1997] (Oliphant, B. J.)
Hickory, Dickory Stalk [1996] (Cooper, Susan Rogers)
Hidden Agenda [1988] (Matera, Lia)
■ Hidden Agenda [1985] (Porter, Anna)
■ Hidden Agenda [1997] (Alexander, Skye) ★
Hide and Seek [1993] (Woods, Sherryl)
Hide in Plain Sight [1999] (Alexander, Skye)
High Constable [1994] (Meyers, Maan)
High Fall [1994] (Dunlap, Susan)
High Island Blues [1996] (Cleeves, Ann)
High Strangeness [1992] (Drake, Alison)
Highgate Rise [1991] (Perry, Anne)
Highland Fling Murders [1997] (Fletcher, Jessica)
Highland Laddie Gone [1986] (McCrumb, Sharyn)
■ Hippie in the Wall [1994] (Fennelly, Tony)
Hippopotamus Pool [1996] (Peters, Elizabeth)
Hireling's Tale [1999] (Bannister, Jo)

His Burial Too [1973] (Aird, Catherine)
Hit and Run [1989] (O'Callaghan, Maxine)
▨ Hive of Bees [1996] (Rowlands, Betty)
Ho-Ho Homicide [1995] (Sawyer, Corinne Holt)
Hocus [1997] (Burke, Jan) ☆☆
Holiday in Death [1998] (Robb, J.D.)
▨ Holiday Murders [1992] (Landreth, Marsha)
▨ Holly, Jolly Murder [1997] (Hess, Joan)
Hollywood Swingers [2000] (Woods, Paula L.)
Holy Innocents [1994] (Sedley, Kate)
Holy Terror in the Hebrides [1997] (Dams, Jeanne M.)
Holy Terrors [1992] (Daheim, Mary)
Holy Terrors [1994] (Greenwood, D.M.)
Home Again, Home Again [1997] (Cooper, Susan Rogers) ☆
Home Fires [1998] (Maron, Margaret)
Home Sweet Homicide [1992] (Morgan, Kate)
Home Wrecker [2000] (Viets, Elaine)
Homefront Murders [1995] (Meredith, D. R.)
Homemade Sin [1994] (Trocheck, Kathy Hogan)
▨ Hometown Heroes [1990] (McShea, Susanna Hofmann)
Homicide Report [1998] (Sandstrom, Eve K.)
Honey in the Flesh [1959] (Fickling, G.G.)
Honey on Her Tail [1971] (Fickling, G.G.)
Honeymoon With Murder [1988] (Hart, Carolyn G.) ★
Honky Tonk Kat [1996] (Kijewski, Karen)
Hoodoo Man [1998] (Smith-Levin, Judith)
Hoofprints [1996] (Crum, Laura)
Hook [1999] (Songer, C. J.)
▨ Hope Against Hope [1990] (Kelly, Susan B.)
Hope Will Answer [1993] (Kelly, Susan B.)
▨ Hopeless Case [1992] (Beck, K. K.)
▨ Hornet's Nest [1997] (Cornwell, Patricia)
▨ Horse of a Different Killer [1995] (Jaffe, Jody) ☆☆
Horse To Die For [1996] (Banks, Carolyn)
▨ Horse You Came in On [1993] (Grimes, Martha)
Hot Money [1993] (Woods, Sherryl)
Hot Poppies [1997] (Nadelson, Reggie)
▨ Hot Property [1991] (Woods, Sherryl)
Hot Schemes [1994] (Woods, Sherryl)
Hot Secret [1992] (Woods, Sherryl)
Hot Ticket [1998] (Weber, Janice)
▨ Hot Water [1990] (Gunning, Sally)
Hotel Morgue [1991] (Laurence, Janet)
Hotel South Dakota [1997] (Taylor, Kathleen)
Hotshots [1996] (Van Gieson, Judith)
Hounded to Death [1993] (Cleary, Melissa)
Hour of Our Death [1995] (Fallon, Ann C.)
Hour of Our Death [1995] (Joseph, Alison)
▨ Hour of the Knife [1991] (Zukowski, Sharon)
Hour of the Tigress [1999] (Lin-Chandler, Irene)
House of Blues [1995] (Smith, Julie)
House of Cards [1991] (Hooper, Kay) ☆
House of Women [1998] (Taylor, Alison G.)
House on Bloodhound Lane [1996] (Lanier, Virginia)
House on Mulberry Street [1996] (Meyers, Maan)
Houston in the Rear View Mirror [1990] (Cooper, Susan Rogers)
Houston Town [1992] (Powell, Deborah)
How I Spent My Summer Vacation [1994] (Roberts, Gillian)
How To Kill a Man [1972] (Wells, Tobias)
How To Murder the Man of Your Dreams [1995] (Cannell, Dorothy)
How To Murder Your Mother-in-law [1994] (Cannell, Dorothy)
Huckleberry Fiend [1987] (Smith, Julie)
Hung Up To Die [1997] (Johnson, Dolores)
Hunter's Moon [1999] (Stabenow, Dana)
Hunter's Quarry [1998] (Stacey, Susannah)
Hunting Game [1996] (Herndon, Nancy)
▨ Hush, Money [1989] (Femling, Jean)

Hush Puppy [1999] (Berenson, Laurien)
▨ Hyaenas [1998] (Dengler, Sandy)
▨ Hyde Park Headsman [1994] (Perry, Anne)
▨ Hydrogen Murder [1997] (Minichino, Camille)

I

I Am the Only Running Footman [1986] (Grimes, Martha)
▨ I, Claudia [1995] (Todd, Marilyn)
▨ I Give You Five Days [1983] (Curzon, Clare)
"I" is for Innocent [1992] (Grafton, Sue)
▨ I Left My Heart [1991] (Maiman, Jaye)
I. O. U. [1991] (Pickard, Nancy) ★★☆☆
I'd Rather Be in Philadelphia [1991] (Roberts, Gillian)
I'll Be Leaving You Always [1993] (Scoppettone, Sandra)
I'll Sing You Two-O (1996) (Fraser, Anthea)
Ice Water [1993] (Gunning, Sally)
Iced [1995] (Clark, Carol Higgins)
Iced [1994] (Robitaille, Julie)
Identity Unknown [1995] (Ferguson, Frances)
Idol Bones [1993] (Greenwood, D.M.)
▨ If Ever I Return, Pretty Peggy-O [1990] (McCrumb, Sharyn) ★☆
▨ If I Should Die [1997] (Edwards, Grace F.) ☆
If I'd Killed Him When I Met Him [1995] (McCrumb, Sharyn) ★
▨ If Looks Could Kill [1995] (Furie, Ruthe) ☆
If Two of Them Are Dead [1996] (Cail, Carol)
Ill Wind [1995] (Barr, Nevada)
Illusion [1984] (Warner, Mignon)
Immaculate Reception [1999] (Farmer, Jerrilyn)
Immortal in Death [1996] (Robb, J.D.)
Imperfect Justice [1997] (Arnold, Catherine)
Imperfect Spy [1995] (Cross, Amanda)
Impolite Society [1997] (Smith, Cynthia)
Improbable Cause [1988] (Jance, J.A.)
In at the Deep End [1994] (Donald, Anabel)
In Big Trouble [1999] (Lippman, Laura)
In Colt Blood [1998] (Jaffe, Jody)
In Guilty Night [1996] (Taylor, Alison G.)
▨ In Murder We Trust [1995] (Hyde, Eleanor)
In Plain Sight [1996] (Block, Barbara)
In Remembrance of Rose [1986] (Meek, M.R.D.)
▨ In Serena's Web [1987] (Hooper, Kay)
In Stony Places [1991] (Mitchell, Kay)
In the Bleak Midwinter [1995] (Hall, Patricia)
▨ In the Dark [1994] (Brennan, Carol)
In the Dead of Summer [1995] (Roberts, Gillian)
▨ In the Game [1991] (Baker, Nikki)
▨ In the Last Analysis [1964] (Cross, Amanda) ☆
In the Midnight Hour [1995] (Tyre, Peg)
In the Presence of the Enemy [1996] (George, Elizabeth)
▨ In the Shadow of King's [1984] (Kelly, Nora)
In the Teeth of Adversity [1990] (Babson, Marian)
Incendiary Designs [1998] (Dymmoch, Michael Allen)
Inconsiderate Death [1997] (Rowlands, Betty)
▨ Indemnity Only [1982] (Paretsky, Sara)
Inherited Murder [1994] (Martin, Lee)
Injury Time [16 stories] [1997] (Aird, Catherine)
Injustice for All [1986] (Jance, J.A.)
Inner Circle [1996] (McNab, Claire)
▨ Inner City Blues [1999] (Woods, Paula L.)
▨ Inspector and Mrs. Jeffries [1993] (Brightwell, Emily)
Intent To Kill [1998] (Page, Emma)
Intersection of Law and Desire [1995] (Redmann, J. M.) ★
Interview With Mattie [1995] (Singer, Shelley) ☆
▨ Introducing Amanda Valentine [1992] (Beecham, Rose)
▨ Introducing C.B. Greenfield [1979] (Kallen, Lucille)
Invasion of Privacy [1996] (O'Shaughnessy, Perri)
▨ Invitation to a Funeral [1997] (Brown, Molly)
Irene at Large [1992] (Douglas, Carole Nelson)
Irene's Last Waltz [1994] (Douglas, Carole Nelson)

Irish Chain [1995] (Fowler, Earlene)
Irizumi (Rowland, Laura Joh)
Iron Hand of Mars [1992] (Davis, Lindsey)
Is There a Dead Man in the House? [1998] (Squire, Elizabeth Daniels)
∎ Isis Command [1998] (Livesay, Ann)
Island Girl [1991] (Berry, Carole)
It Takes a Thief [1989] (Hooper, Kay)
It's Her Funeral [1992] (Christmas, Joyce)
It's Murder Going Home [1996] (Millhiser, Marlys)
Italian Girl [1998] (Hall, Patricia)

J

∎ J. Alfred Prufrock Murders [1988] (Sawyer, Corinne Holt) ☆
"J" is for Judgment [1993] (Grafton, Sue)
Jackpot [1999] (Amato, Angela)
∎ Jacoby's First Case [1980] (Smith, J. C. S.)
James Joyce Murder [1967] (Cross, Amanda)
Jane and the Man of the Cloth [1997] (Barron, Stephanie)
∎ Jane and the Unpleasantness at Scargrave Manor [1996] (Barron, Stephanie)
Jane and the Wandering Eye [1998] (Barron, Stephanie)
Jazz Funeral [1993] (Smith, Julie)
∎ Jealous Heart [1997] (Tishy, Cecelia)
Jemima Shore at the Sunny Grave [9 stories] [1993] (Fraser, Antonia)
Jemima Shore's First Case & Other Stories [1986] (Fraser, Antonia)
Jersey Monkey [1992] (Gallison, Kate)
Jerusalem Inn [1984] (Grimes, Martha)
∎ Jinx [1992] (Robitaille, Julie)
Jinx High [1991] (Lackey, Mercedes)
Job To Die For [1997] (Howell, Lis)
Johnny Underground [1965] (Moyes, Patricia)
Judging Time [1998] (Glass, Leslie)
Juicy Lucy [1996] (Kershaw, Valerie)
Juliet's Ghost [1999] (Van Hook, Beverly)
Julius House [1995] (Harris, Charlaine)
∎ June Mail [1986] (Warmbold, Jean)
Jungleland [1997] (Zukowski, Sharon)
Just a Little Lie [1998] (Allen, Kate)
∎ Just Another Day in Paradise [1985] (Maxwell, A.E.)
∎ Just Desserts [1991] (Daheim, Mary) ☆
∎ Just Desserts [1995] (McKevett, G.A.)
Just Enough Light To Kill [1988] (Maxwell, A.E.)
Just Plain Pickled to Death [1997] (Myers, Tamar)
Just the Fax, Ma'am [1996] (O'Kane, Leslie)
Justice [1995] (Kellerman, Faye)

K

∎ K.C. Bomber [1997] (McClellan, Janet)
"K" is for Killer [1994] (Grafton, Sue) ★☆☆
Kahuna Killer [1951] (Sheridan, Juanita)
Kansas Troubles [1996] (Fowler, Earlene) ☆
∎ Karma [1981] (Dunlap, Susan)
Kat Scratch Fever [1997] (Kijewski, Karen)
Kat's Cradle [1991] (Kijewski, Karen)
Katapult [1990] (Kijewski, Karen)
∎ Katwalk [1989] (Kijewski, Karen) ★★★
Keep Still [1996] (Bland, Eleanor Taylor)
∎ Keeper at the Shrine [1994] (Highsmith, Domini)
Keeper of the Mill [1995] (Kelly, Mary Anne)
Keeping Bad Company [1997] (Granger, Ann)
∎ Keeping Secrets [1994] (Mickelbury, Penny)
Kick Back [1993] (McDermid, Val)
Kid's Stuff [1994] (Kelly, Susan B.)
∎ Kidnap [1999] (Wright, L.R.)
Kill Flash [1987] (MacGregor, T.J.)
Kill or Cure [1995] (Kittredge, Mary)
∎ KILLER.app [1996] (D'Amato, Barbara)
Killer Calories [1997] (McKevett, G.A.)

Killer Instinct [1997] (Navratilova, Martina)
Killer Market [1997] (Maron, Margaret)
Killer Pancake [1995] (Davidson, Diane Mott)
Killer Whale [1997] (Quinn, Elizabeth)
∎ Killing Circle [1981] (Wiltz, Chris)
Killing Cousins [1990] (Knight, Alanna)
Killing Critics [1996] (O'Connell, Carol)
Killing Cure [1993] (Hart, Ellen)
Killing Dance [1997] (Hamilton, Laurell K.)
Killing Frost [1994] (Haffner, Margaret)
Killing Grounds [1998] (Stabenow, Dana)
Killing in Real Estate [1996] (McClellan, Tierney)
Killing Me Softly [1998] (Eccles, Marjorie)
∎ Killing of Ellis Martin [1993] (Grindle, Lucretia)
Killing of Monday Brown [1994] (Prowell, Sandra West) ☆
Killing Orders [1985] (Paretsky, Sara)
Killing Spring [1996] (Bowen, Gail)
Killing Time [1996] (Harrod-Eagles, Cynthia)
Killing To Hide [1990] (Penn, John)
∎ Killings at Badger's Drift [1987] (Graham, Caroline) ★☆☆
Killings at Barley Hall [1995] (Whitehead, Barbara)
Killjoy [1995] (Cleeves, Ann)
Kin Dread [1990] (MacGregor, T.J.)
Kind of Healthy Grave [1986] (Mann, Jessica)
∎ Kindness Can Kill [1993] (Bolitho, Janie)
Kindness of Strangers [1996] (Smith, Julie)
∎ Kindred Crimes [1990] (Dawson, Janet) ★☆☆☆
King Is Dead [1992] (Shankman, Sarah)
King of Hearts [1995] (Moody, Susan)
King of Nothing [1992] (Maxwell, A.E.)
King of the Mountain [1995] (Wren, M.K.)
King's Bishop [1996] (Robb, Candace M.)
Kingsbridge Plot [1993] (Meyers, Maan)
Kiss for a Killer [1960] (Fickling, G.G.)
Kiss Yourself Goodbye [1989] (Fennelly, Tony)
∎ Kissing the Gunner's Daughter [1992] (Rendell, Ruth)
Knife at the Opera [1988] (Stacey, Susannah)
Knife III-Used [1991] (Penn, John)
Knife to Remember [1994] (Churchill, Jill)
∎ Knight & Day [1995] (Nessen, Ron)
∎ Knight Fall (Pulver, Mary Monica)
∎ Knight Must Fall [1985] (Wender, Theodora)
Knightfall [1986] (Linscott, Gillian)
Knowledge of Water [Paris] [1996] (Smith, Sarah)

L

∎ "L" is for Lawless [1995] (Grafton, Sue)
Labor Day Murder [1998] (Harris, Lee)
∎ Lace Curtain Murders [1986] (Belfort, Sophie)
∎ Ladies' Night [1988] (Bowers, Elisabeth)
Lady Chapel [1994] (Robb, Candace M.)
∎ Lady on the Line [1983] (Tone, Teona)
∎ Lady With a Cool Eye [1973] (Moffat, Gwen)
Ladybug, Ladybug [1994] (McShea, Susanna Hofmann)
∎ LadyGold [1998] (Amato, Angela)
Ladykiller [1984] (O'Donnell, Lillian)
Lamb to the Slaughter [1996] (Quinn, Elizabeth)
Lamb to the Slaughter [1995] (Rowe, Jennifer)
Lament for a Dead Cowboy [1994] (Dain, Catherine) ☆
Lament for a Lady Laird [1982] (Arnold, Margot)
Lament for Christabel [1991] (Peterson, Audrey)
∎ Larceny and Old Lace [1996] (Myers, Tamar)
Large Target [2000] (Murray, Lynne)
∎ Larger Than Death [1997] (Murray, Lynne)
∎ Larkspur [1990] (Simonson, Sheila)
Last Act in Palmyra [1994] (Davis, Lindsey)
Last Annual Slugfest [1986] (Dunlap, Susan)
Last Blue Plate Special [2000] (Padgett, Abigail)
Last Camel Died at Noon [1991] (Peters, Elizabeth) ☆
Last Chance Country [1983] (Moffat, Gwen)
Last Chants [1996] (Matera, Lia)

▣ Man in the Green Chevy [1988] (Cooper, Susan Rogers)
Man on the Balcony [1968] (Sjöwall, Maj & Per Wahlöö)
Man Who Cast Two Shadows [1995] (O'Connell, Carol)
▣ Man Who Understood Cats [1993] (Dymmoch, Michael Allen) ★
Man Who Went Up in Smoke [1969] (Sjöwall, Maj & Per Wahlöö)
▣ Man With a Load of Mischief [1981] (Grimes, Martha)
Mandarin Plaid [1996] (Rozan, S.J.)
Manhattans & Murder [1994] (Fletcher, Jessica)
Many Deadly Returns [1970] (Moyes, Patricia) ☆
Maquette for Murder [1999] (Sprague, Gretchen)
Margin of Error [1997] (Buchanan, Edna)
Mariner's Compass [1999] (Fowler, Earlene)
▣ Mark Twain Murders [1989] (Skom, Edith) ☆☆☆
Marriage Is Murder [1987] (Pickard, Nancy) ★☆
Marshal and the Forgery [1995] (Nabb, Magdalen)
Marshal and the Madwoman [1988] (Nabb, Magdalen)
Marshal and the Murderer [1987] (Nabb, Magdalen)
Marshal at the Villa Torrini [1993] (Nabb, Magdalen)
Marshal Makes His Report [1991] (Nabb, Magdalen)
Marshal's Own Case [1990] (Nabb, Magdalen)
Martians in Maggody [1994] (Hess, Joan)
Martini Effect [1992] (Morison, B.J.)
Martinis & Mayhem [1995] (Fletcher, Jessica)
Marvell College Murders [1991] (Belfort, Sophie)
▣ Masculine Ending [1987] (Smith, Joan)
Masked Dancers [1998] (Hager, Jean)
Masks and Faces [1984] (Curzon, Clare)
▣ Masquerade [1996] (Lynds, Gayle)
Masquerade in Blue [1991] (Brod, D. C.)
Master of the Keys [1996] (Highsmith, Domini)
Masterpiece of Murder [1996] (Kruger, Mary)
Match for a Murderer [1971] (Dunnett, Dorothy)
Matricide at St. Martha's [1994] (Edwards, Ruth Dudley)
▣ Matter of Love and Death [1966] (Wells, Tobias)
May's Newfangled Mirth [1989] (Adamson, M. J.)
McCone and Friends [1999] (Muller, Marcia)
McCone Files [1995] (Muller, Marcia)
Meadowlark [1996] (Simonson, Sheila)
Mean Streak [1996] (Wheat, Carolyn) ☆
▣ Medium for Murder (Warner, Mignon)
▣ Medium is Murder [1992] (McKitterick, Molly)
Memorial Hall Murder [1978] (Langton, Jane)
Memory Can Be Murder [1995] (Squire, Elizabeth Daniels)
Menehune Murders [1989] (Arnold, Margot)
Mensa Murders [1990] (Martin, Lee)
Merchant of Menace [1998] (Churchill, Jill)
▣ Mermaids Singing [1995] (McDermid, Val) ★
Miami, It's Murder [1994] (Buchanan, Edna) ☆
▣ Midas Murders [1995] (Arnold, Margot)
Midnight Baby [1993] (Hornsby, Wendy)
Midnight Clear [1998] (Trocheck, Kathy Hogan)
Milk and Honey [1990] (Kellerman, Faye)
Mill on the Shore [1994] (Cleeves, Ann)
Milwaukee Autumns Can Be Lethal [1998] (Barrett, Kathleen Anne)
Milwaukee Summers Can Be Deadly [1997] (Barrett, Kathleen Anne)
▣ Milwaukee Winters Can Be Murder [1996] (Barrett, Kathleen Anne)
Mind To Murder [1963] (James, P. D.)
Ming and I [1997] (Myers, Tamar)
Ministering Angel [1986] (Cohen, Anthea)
▣ Minuteman Murder [1976] (Langton, Jane)
Minor in Possession [1990] (Jance, J.A.)
Mint Julep Murder [1995] (Hart, Carolyn G.)
▣ Miracle Strip [1998] (Bartholomew, Nancy)
Miracles in Maggody [1995] (Hess, Joan) ☆
Mischief in Maggody [1988] (Hess, Joan) ☆☆
Misery in Maggody [1999] (Hess, Joan)
Misfortune of Others [1993] (Dank, Gloria)

Misleading Ladies [1997] (Smith, Cynthia)
▣ Miss Melville Regrets [1986] (Smith, Evelyn E.)
Miss Melville Returns [1987] (Smith, Evelyn E.)
Miss Melville Rides a Tiger [1991] (Smith, Evelyn E.)
Miss Melville's Revenge [1989] (Smith, Evelyn E.)
Miss Pink at the Edge of the World [1975] (Moffat, Gwen)
Miss Seeton at the Helm [Hampton Charles] [1990] (Crane, Hamilton)
Miss Seeton, Bewitched (Crane, Hamilton)
Miss Seeton, by Appointment [Hampton Charles] [1990] (Crane, Hamilton)
▣ Miss Seeton by Moonlight [1992] (Crane, Hamilton)
Miss Seeton Cracks the Case [1991] (Crane, Hamilton)
Miss Seeton Draws the Line [1969] (Crane, Hamilton)
▣ Miss Seeton Goes to Bat [1993] (Crane, Hamilton)
Miss Seeton Paints the Town [1991] (Crane, Hamilton)
▣ Miss Seeton Plants Suspicion [1993] (Crane, Hamilton)
Miss Seeton Rocks the Cradle [1992] (Crane, Hamilton)
▣ Miss Seeton Rules [1994] (Crane, Hamilton)
Miss Seeton Sings [1973] (Crane, Hamilton)
▣ Miss Seeton Undercover [1994] (Crane, Hamilton)
Miss Seeton's Finest Hour [1999] (Crane, Hamilton)
Miss Zukas and the Island Murders [1995] (Dereske, Jo)
▣ Miss Zukas and the Library Murders [1994] (Dereske, Jo)
Miss Zukas and the Raven's Dance [1996] (Dereske, Jo)
Miss Zukas and the Stroke of Death [1996] (Dereske, Jo)
Missing Duchess [1994] (Knight, Alanna)
Missing Eden [1996] (Lee, Wendi)
Missing Joseph [1993] (George, Elizabeth)
Missing Madonna [1988] (O'Marie, Carol Anne, Sister)
▣ Missing Person [1993] (Ferguson, Frances)
Missing Susan [1991] (McCrumb, Sharyn)
Missing Suspect [1998] (Coburn, Laura)
▣ Missing Woman [1980] (Page, Emma)
▣ Mission to Sonora [1998] (Cramer, Rebecca)
▣ Missionary Position [1993] (Taylor, Kathleen)
Mistaken Identity [Rosato et al] [1999] (Scottoline, Lisa)
Mistletoe From Purple Sage [1997] (Smith, Barbara Burnett)
▣ Mistletoe Murder (1998) (Meier, Leslie)
Mistress of the Bones [1995] (MacGregor, T.J.)
Moche Warrior [Peru] [1999] (Hamilton, Lyn)
Model Murder [1993] (Dengler, Sandy)
Model Murder [1991] (Quest, Erica)
Mommy and the Money [1997] (Goldstone, Nancy)
▣ Mommy and the Murder [1995] (Goldstone, Nancy)
Money Burns [1991] (Maxwell, A.E.)
▣ Money Leads to Murder [1987] (Morgan, D Miller)
Money To Burn [1993] (White, Gloria)
▣ Monkey Puzzle [1985] (Gosling, Paula) ★
Monkey Wrench [1994] (Cody, Liza)
Monster of Florence [1996] (Nabb, Magdalen)
Monstrous Regiment of Women [1995] (King, Laurie R.) ★
Moonbird Boy [1996] (Padgett, Abigail)
Moor [1998] (King, Laurie R.)
▣ Morbid Kitchen [1995] (Melville, Jennie)
▣ Morbid Symptoms [1984] (Slovo, Gillian)
More Deaths Than One [1990] (Eccles, Marjorie)
More Perfect Union [1988] (Jance, J.A.)
Moroccan Traffic [1992] (Dunnett, Dorothy)
Mortal Remains [1974] (Yorke, Margaret)
Mortal Remains in Maggody [1991] (Hess, Joan)
Mortal Sins [1987] (Porter, Anna)
Mortal Spoils [1996] (Greenwood, D.M.)
Mortal Term [1984] (Penn, John)
Mortal Words [1990] (Knight, Kathryn Lasky)
Most Likely To Die [1996] (Girdner, Jaqueline)
Mother Love [1995] (Wright, L.R.) ★
Mother May I [1998] (Lordon, Randye)
Mother Nature [1997] (Andrews, Sarah)
Mother of the Bride [1998] (Westfall, Patricia Tichenor)
▣ Mother Shadow [1989] (Howe, Melodie Johnson) ☆☆☆

Motion To Dismiss [1999] (Jacobs, Jonnie)
▯ Motion To Suppress [1995] (O'Shaughnessy, Perri)
Motive for Murder [1996] (Gray, Gallagher)
Motive for Murder [1994] (Bolitho, Janie)
Mourn Not Your Dead [1996] (Crombie, Deborah)
Mourning Gloria [1996] (Christmas, Joyce)
Mourning Shift [1998] (Taylor, Kathleen)
Mouse Trapped [1993] (Dengler, Sandy)
Mouthful of Sand [1988] (Meek, M.R.D.)
▯ Moving Image [1995] (Ross, Annie)
▯ Mr. Donaghue Investigates (Shone, Anna)
Mrs. Jeffries and the Missing Alibi [1996]
   (Brightwell, Emily)
Mrs. Jeffries Dusts for Clues [1993] (Brightwell, Emily)
Mrs. Jeffries on the Ball [1994] (Brightwell, Emily)
Mrs. Jeffries on the Trail [1995] (Brightwell, Emily)
Mrs. Jeffries Plays the Cook [1995] (Brightwell, Emily)
Mrs. Jeffries Questions the Answer [1997]
   (Brightwell, Emily)
▯ Mrs. Jeffries Reveals Her Art [1998] (Brightwell, Emily)
Mrs. Jeffries Stands Corrected [1996] (Brightwell, Emily)
Mrs. Jeffries Takes Stock [1994] (Brightwell, Emily)
▯ Mrs. Jeffries Takes the Cake [1998] (Brightwell, Emily)
Mrs. Jeffries Takes the Stage [1997] (Brightwell, Emily)
Mrs. Malory and the Festival Murders [1993] (Holt, Hazel)
Mrs. Malory and the Only Good Lawyer [1997]
   (Holt, Hazel)
Mrs. Malory: Death of a Dean [1996] (Holt, Hazel)
Mrs. Malory: Detective in Residence [1994] (Holt, Hazel)
▯ Mrs. Malory Investigates [1989] (Holt, Hazel)
Mrs. Malory Wonders Why [1995] (Holt, Hazel)
Mrs. Pollifax and the Golden Triangle [1988]
   (Gilman, Dorothy)
Mrs. Pollifax and the Hong Kong Buddha [1985]
   (Gilman, Dorothy)
▯ Mrs. Pollifax and the Lion Killer [1996] (Gilman, Dorothy)
Mrs. Pollifax and the Second Thief [1993]
   (Gilman, Dorothy)
Mrs. Pollifax and the Whirling Dervish [1990]
   (Gilman, Dorothy)
▯ Mrs. Pollifax, Innocent Tourist [1997] (Gilman, Dorothy)
Mrs. Pollifax on Safari [1976] (Gilman, Dorothy)
Mrs. Pollifax on the China Station [1983]
   (Gilman, Dorothy)
Mrs. Pollifax Pursued [1995] (Gilman, Dorothy)
▯ Mrs. Porter's Letter [1982] (McConnell, Vicki P.)
Much Ado in Maggody [1989] (Hess, Joan)
Muddy Water [1997] (Gunning, Sally)
Mudlark [1993] (Simonson, Sheila)
▯ Mulch [1994] (Ripley, Ann)
▯ Multiple Listing [1998] (Grant, Anne Underwood)
Multitude of Sins [1975] (Wren, M.K.)
Multitude of Sins [1997] (Bell, Pauline)
Mum's the Word [1990] (Cannell, Dorothy)
Mumbo Jumbo [1991] (Knight, Kathryn Lasky)
Mummers' Curse [1996] (Roberts, Gillian)
Mummy Case [1985] (Peters, Elizabeth)
Murder a la Mode [1963] (Moyes, Patricia)
Murder Against the Grain [1967] (Lathen, Emma) ★
Murder Among Friends [1995] (Jacobs, Jonnie)
▯ Murder Among Neighbors [1994] (Jacobs, Jonnie)
Murder Among the Angels [1996] (Matteson, Stefanie)
Murder Among the Well-to-do [1977] (Godfrey, Ellen)
Murder Among Us [1993] (Granger, Ann)
Murder Among Us [1998] (Jacobs, Jonnie)
Murder and a Muse [1994] (Farrell, Gillian B.)
▯ Murder at Bent Elbow [1998] (Bryan, Kate)
Murder at the Cat Show [1989] (Babson, Marian)
Murder at Large [2001] (Murray, Lynne)
▯ Murder at Markham [1988] (Sprinkle, Patricia H.)
Murder at Medicine Lodge [1999] (Medawar,
   Mardi Oakley)

Murder at the Mendel (Bowen, Gail)
Murder at Monticello [1994] (Brown, Rita Mae)
▯ Murder at Moot Point [1992] (Millhiser, Marlys)
Murder at Plum's [1989] (Myers, Amy)
Murder at Ravenscroft [1999] (Buggé, Carole)
▯ Murder at Red Rook Ranch [1990] (Tell, Dorothy)
Murder at Teatime [1991] (Matteson, Stefanie)
Murder at the Blue Owl [1988] (Martin, Lee)
▯ Murder at the Class Reunion [1993] (Stein, Triss)
Murder at the Falls [1993] (Matteson, Stefanie)
Murder at the Feast of Rejoicing [1996] (Robinson,
   Lynda S.)
Murder at the Gardner [1988] (Langton, Jane)
Murder at the God's Gate [1995] (Robinson, Lynda S.)
▯ Murder at the Kennedy Center [1989] (Truman, Margaret)
Murder at the Masque [1991] (Myers, Amy)
▯ Murder at the MLA [1993] (Jones, D. J. H.)
Murder at the Murder at the Mimosa Inn [1986]
   (Hess, Joan)
Murder at the Music Hall [1995] (Myers, Amy)
Murder at the National Cathedral [1990]
   (Truman, Margaret)
Murder at the National Gallery [1996] (Truman, Margaret)
Murder at the Nightwood Bar [1986] (Forrest,
   Katherine V.)
Murder at the Old Vicarage (1989) (McGown, Jill)
Murder at the Pentagon [1992] (Truman, Margaret)
▯ Murder at the PTA Luncheon [1987] (Wolzien, Valerie)
Murder at the Rose [1998] (Cook, Judith)
Murder at the Savoy [1971] (Sjöwall, Maj & Per Wahlöö)
▯ Murder at the Spa [1990] (Matteson, Stefanie)
▯ Murder at the War [1987] (Pulver, Mary Monica) ☆
Murder at the Watergate [1998] (Truman, Margaret)
Murder at Vassar [1987] (Taylor, Elizabeth Atwood)
▯ Murder Beach [1993] (McKenna, Bridget)
▯ Murder Behind Locked Doors [1988] (Godfrey, Ellen)
Murder Being Once Done [1972] (Rendell, Ruth)
Murder Bone by Bone [1997] (Roberts, Lora)
Murder by Appointment [1996] (Knight, Alanna)
Murder by Deception [1989] (Meredith, D. R.) ☆
▯ Murder by Impulse [1988] (Meredith, D. R.) ☆
Murder by Masquerade [1990] (Meredith, D. R.)
Murder by Owl Light [1992] (Sawyer, Corinne Holt)
Murder by Precedent [1964] (Petrie, Rhona)
▯ Murder by Proxy (Nielsen, Helen)
Murder by Reference [1991] (Meredith, D. R.)
Murder by Sacrilege [1993] (Meredith, D. R.)
Murder by the Book [1989] (Rowe, Jennifer)
Murder by the Book [1979] (Schier, Norma)
▯ Murder by the Book [1990] (Welch, Pat)
Murder by Tradition [1991] (Forrest, Katherine V.) ★
▯ Murder Can Kill Your Social Life [1994] (Eichler, Selma)
Murder Can Ruin Your Looks [1995] (Eichler, Selma)
Murder Can Singe Your Old Flame [1999] (Eichler, Selma)
Murder Can Spook Your Cat [1998] (Eichler, Selma)
Murder Can Stunt Your Growth [1996] (Eichler, Selma)
Murder Can Wreck Your Reunion [1997] (Eichler, Selma)
Murder Comes Calling [1995] (Page, Emma)
Murder Crops Up [1998] (Roberts, Lora)
Murder Crossed [1996] (Boylan, Eleanor)
Murder Duet [1999] (Gur, Batya)
Murder Fantastical [1967] (Moyes, Patricia)
Murder Follows Money [2000] (Roberts, Lora)
Murder Gets a Degree [1986] (Wender, Theodora)
Murder Gets a Life [1998] (George, Anne)
Murder Goes Mumming [1981] (Craig, Alisa)
Murder Has a Pretty Face [1981] (Melville, Jennie) ☆
Murder Has No Calories [1994] (Sawyer, Corinne Holt)
Murder Hurts [1993] (Maxwell, A.E.)
Murder in a Cathedral [1996] (Edwards, Ruth Dudley)
Murder in a Good Cause [1990] (Sale, Medora)
Murder in a Hot Flash [1995] (Millhiser, Marlys)

Murder in a Mayonnaise Jar [1993] (McKitterick, Molly)
Murder in a Mummy Case [1985] (Beck, K. K.)
🔳 Murder in a Nice Neighborhood [1994] (Roberts, Lora)
🔳 Murder in Brief [1995] (Lachnit, Carroll)
Murder in Burgundy [1989] (Peterson, Audrey)
🔳 Murder in C Major [1986] (Frommer, Sara Hoskinson)
Murder in Cowboy Bronze [Arizona] [1985]
    (McCormick, Claire)
Murder in Focus [1972] (Dunnett, Dorothy)
Murder in Focus [1989] (Sale, Medora)
Murder in Good Measure [1990] (Moore, Margaret)
Murder in Gray & White [1989] (Sawyer, Corinne Holt)
Murder in High Place [1970] (Dominic, R.B.)
🔳 Murder in Mellingham [1993] (Oleksiw, Susan)
🔳 Murder in Mendocino [1987] (Kittredge, Mary)
Murder in Moscow [1998] (Fletcher, Jessica)
Murder in My Backyard [1991] (Cleeves, Ann)
Murder in Ordinary Time [1991] (O'Marie,
    Carol Anne, Sister)
Murder in Paradise [1989] (Cleeves, Ann)
🔳 Murder in Pug's Parlour [1986] (Myers, Amy)
🔳 Murder in Scorpio [1995] (Lawrence, Martha) ☆☆☆
🔳 Murder in Store [1989] (Brod, D. C.)
Murder in the Air [1997] (Hart, Ellen)
Murder in the Chabris [2000] (Black, Cara)
Murder in the Charleston Manner [1990]
    (Sprinkle, Patricia H.)
🔳 Murder in the Collective [1984] (Wilson, Barbara)
Murder in the Dog Days [1991] (Carlson, P.M.) ☆
Murder in the Garden (Melville, Jennie)
🔳 Murder in the Holy City [1998] (Beaufort, Simon)
Murder in the House [1997] (Truman, Margaret)
Murder in the Limelight [1986] (Myers, Amy)
🔳 Murder in the Marais [1999] (Black, Cara)
Murder in the Marketplace [1995] (Roberts, Lora)
🔳 Murder in the Maze [1993] (Mason, Sarah J.)
Murder in the Motor Stable [1996] (Myers, Amy)
Murder in the New Age [1997] (Jones, D. J. H.)
🔳 Murder in the Place of Anubis [1994] (Robinson, Lynda S.)
Murder in the Round [1970] (Dunnett, Dorothy)
Murder in the Shadows [1999] (Godfrey, Ellen)
Murder in the Smokehouse [1994] (Myers, Amy)
Murder in Writing [1988] (Clarke, Anna)
Murder Is Academic [1985] (Carlson, P.M.) ☆
Murder Is Germane [1992] (Saum, Karen)
Murder Is Material [1994] (Saum, Karen)
🔳 Murder Is Only Skin Deep [1987] (Sims, L. V.)
Murder Is Pathological [1986] (Carlson, P.M.)
🔳 Murder Is Relative [1990] (Saum, Karen)
🔳 Murder Is Too Expensive [1993] (Kershaw, Valerie)
🔳 Murder Lover [1997] (Rawlings, Ellen)
Murder Machree [1992] (Boylan, Eleanor)
Murder Makes a Pilgrimage [1993] (O'Marie,
    Carol Anne, Sister)
Murder Makes an Entree [1992] (Myers, Amy)
Murder Makes the Wheels Go 'Round [1966]
    (Lathen, Emma)
Murder Makes Tracks [1985] (Linscott, Gillian)
Murder Makes Waves [1997] (George, Anne)
Murder Mile-High [1996] (Roberts, Lora)
Murder Misread [1990] (Carlson, P.M.)
Murder Most Beastly [1996] (Cleary, Melissa)
Murder Most Fouled Up [1968] (Wells, Tobias)
Murder Most Fowl [1991] (Morgan, Kate)
🔳 Murder Most Grizzly [1993] (Quinn, Elizabeth)
Murder Most Mellow [1992] (Girdner, Jaqueline)
Murder, My Deer [2000] (Girdner, Jaqueline)
Murder, My Suite [1995] (Daheim, Mary)
Murder Now and Then [1993] (McGown, Jill)
Murder Observed [1990] (Boylan, Eleanor)

Murder of a Dead Man [1994] (John, Katherine)
🔳 Murder of Crows [1987] (Duffy, Margaret)
🔳 Murder of Crows [1992] (Haffner, Margaret)
🔳 Murder Offscreen [1994] (Osborne, Denise)
Murder Ole! [1997] (Sawyer, Corinne Holt)
Murder on a Bad Hair Day [1996] (George, Anne)
🔳 Murder on a Girls' Night Out [1996] (George, Anne) ★
Murder on a Kibbutz: A Communal Case [1994]
    (Gur, Batya) ☆
Murder on Campus (Holt, Hazel)
🔳 Murder on Cue [1983] (Dentinger, Jane)
🔳 Murder on Her Mind [1991] (Steiner, Susan)
Murder on High [1994] (Matteson, Stefanie)
Murder on Peachtree Street [1991] (Sprinkle, Patricia H.)
Murder on Show [1972] (Babson, Marian)
Murder on the Astral Plane [1999] (Girdner, Jaqueline)
Murder on the Ballarat Train [1991] (Greenwood, Kerry)
Murder on the Cliff [1991] (Matteson, Stefanie)
Murder on the Flying Scotsman [1997] (Dunn, Carola)
Murder on the Gravy Train [1999] (Richman, Phyllis)
🔳 Murder on the Iditarod Trail [1991] (Henry, Sue) ★★
🔳 Murder on the Loose [1999] (Godfrey, Ellen)
Murder on the Lover's Bridge [1999] (Godfrey, Ellen)
Murder on the Mount [1994] (Dengler, Sandy)
Murder on the Potomac [1994] (Truman, Margaret)
Murder on the Prowl [1998] (Brown, Rita Mae)
Murder on the QE2 [1997] (Fletcher, Jessica)
🔳 Murder on the Run [1986] (Sale, Medora) ★
🔳 Murder on the Run [1991] (White, Gloria) ☆
Murder on the Silk Road [1992] (Matteson, Stefanie)
Murder on Wheels [1992] (Frankel, Valerie)
Murder Out of Commission [1976] (Dominic, R.B.)
Murder Out of Court (Dominic, R.B.)
Murder Runs in the Family [1997] (George, Anne)
Murder, She Meowed [1996] (Brown, Rita Mae)
Murder & Sullivan [1997] (Frommer, Sara Hoskinson)
🔳 Murder Sunny Side Up [1968] (Dominic, R.B.)
Murder Superior [1993] (Haddam, Jane)
Murder Takes Two [1998] (Weir, Charlene)
Murder: The Musical [1993] (Meyers, Annette)
Murder To Go [1969] (Lathen, Emma)
Murder Under the Kissing Bough [1992] (Myers, Amy)
Murder Under the Mistletoe [1988] (Jordan, Jennifer)
Murder Under the Palms [1997] (Matteson, Stefanie)
Murder Unrenovated [1988] (Carlson, P.M.) ☆☆
Murder Waiting To Happen [1989] (Taylor, L. A.)
Murder Well-Bred [1995] (Banks, Carolyn)
Murder Well-Done [1996] (Bishop, Claudia)
🔳 Murder Will Out [1994] (Yeager, Dorian)
🔳 Murder Without Icing [1972] (Lathen, Emma)
Murderer's Tale [1996] (Frazer, Margaret)
Murderers' Houses [1964] (Melville, Jennie)
Murdering Kind [1958] (Butler, Gwendoline)
Murderous Remedy [1990] (Shepherd, Stella)
Murders of Mrs. Austin & Mrs. Beale [1991]
    (McGown, Jill)
Murders of Richard III [1974] (Peters, Elizabeth)
Musclebound [1997] (Cody, Liza)
Music in the Blood [1997] (Duffy, Margaret)
Music When Sweet Voices Die [1979] (Yarbro,
    Chelsea Quinn)
Must the Maiden Die [1999] (Monfredo, Miriam Grace)
My Body Lies Over the Ocean [1999] (Borthwick, J. S.)
My Sister's Keeper [1992] (Kelly, Nora)
My Sweet Untraceable You [1994] (Scoppettone, Sandra)
Mysterious Cape Cod Manuscript [1997] (Lee, Marie)
Mystery Bred in Buckhead [1994] (Sprinkle, Patricia H.)
Mystery Lady [1986] (Clarke, Anna)
Mystery Loves Company [1992] (Morgan, Kate)

N

- ▌ "N" is for Noose [1998] (Grafton, Sue)
- ▌ Naked in Death [1995] (Robb, J.D.)
- Naked Once More [1989] (Peters, Elizabeth) ★
- ▌ Name Withheld [1995] (Jance, J.A.)
- Nameless Coffin [1966] (Butler, Gwendoline)
- Nantucket Diet Murders [by Virginia Rich] [1985] (Pickard, Nancy)
- ▌ Napoleon Must Die [1993] (Fawcett, Quinn)
- Nasty Breaks [1997] (Elkins, Charlotte & Aaron)
- Natural Death [1996] (Furie, Ruthe) ☆
- Natural Enemy [1982] (Langton, Jane)
- ▌ Naughty But Dead [1962] (Fickling, G.G.)
- Necessary End [1985] (Fraser, Anthea)
- Necrochip (Harrod-Eagles, Cynthia)
- ▌ Neely Jones: The Medusa Pool [1999] (Wren, M.K.)
- Nell Alone [1966] (Melville, Jennie)
- ▌ Never Buried [1999] (Claire, Edie)
- Never Let a Stranger in Your House [1995] (Logan, Margaret)
- Never Nosh a Matzo Ball [2000] (Kahn, Sharon)
- Never Preach Past Noon [2000] (Claire, Edie)
- Never Sorry [1999] (Claire, Edie)
- New Kind of Killer (Melville, Jennie)
- New Kind of Killer, An Old Kind of Death [1970] (Melville, Jennie)
- New Lease of Death [1967] (Rendell, Ruth)
- ▌ New Leash on Death [1989] (Conant, Susan)
- New Orleans Beat [1994] (Smith, Julie)
- ▌ New Orleans Mourning [1990] (Smith, Julie) ★☆
- New Year's Eve Murder [1997] (Harris, Lee)
- ▌ Next to Last Chance [1998] (Dixon, Louisa)
- Next Week Will Be Better [1998] (Ruryk, Jean) ☆
- Nice Girls Finish Last [1996] (Hayter, Sparkle) ☆
- Nice Little Business [1987] (Dewhurst, Eileen)
- Nice People [1995] (Curzon, Clare)
- ▌ Nice Way to Die [1976] (Warner, Mignon)
- ▌ Night Ferry to Death [1985] (Moyes, Patricia)
- Night Game [1993] (Gordon, Alison)
- ▌ Night She Died [1981] (Simpson, Dorothy)
- Night Shift [1993] (Fromer, Margot J.)
- Night Songs [1995] (Mickelbury, Penny)
- Night Train to Memphis [1994] (Peters, Elizabeth) ☆
- Night Walker [1990] (Hager, Jean)
- ▌ Night-Blooming Cereus [Israel] [1986] (Hadley, Joan)
- Nightcap [1984] (Smith, J. C. S.)
- Nights in White Satin [1999] (Spring, Michelle)
- Nine Bright Shiners [1987] (Fraser, Anthea)
- Ninth Life [1989] (Douglas, Lauren Wright) ★
- Ninth Tentacle [1974] (Rippon, Marion)
- No Birds Sing [1996] (Bannister, Jo)
- No Body [1986] (Pickard, Nancy) ☆
- No Bones About It [1998] (Murray, Donna Huston)
- No Business Being a Cop [1979] (O'Donnell, Lillian)
- No Chance [2000] (Dixon, Louisa)
- No Colder Place [1997] (Rozan, S.J.) ★☆
- No Fixed Abode [1994] (Ferguson, Frances)
- ▌ No Flowers, By Request [1987] (Thomson, June)
- No Forwarding Address [1991] (Bowers, Elisabeth)
- No Good Deed [1998] (Hightower, Lynn S.)
- ▌ No Harm [1987] (Hornsby, Wendy)
- No Hiding Place [1997] (Wesley, Valerie Wilson)
- No Honeymoon for Death [1995] (Kruger, Mary)
- No Immunity [1998] (Dunlap, Susan)
- No Lady in the House [1982] (Kallen, Lucille)
- ▌ No Laughing Matter [1993] (Simpson, Dorothy)
- No Man's Island [1983] (Mann, Jessica)
- No More Dying Then [1971] (Rendell, Ruth)
- ▌ No One Dies in Branson [1994] (Buckstaff, Kathryn)
- No Place for Death [1996] (Lewis, Sherry)
- ▌ No Place for Secrets [1995] (Lewis, Sherry)

- No Place for Sin [1997] (Lewis, Sherry)
- No Place for Tears [1997] (Lewis, Sherry)
- No Place Like Home [1996] (Lewis, Sherry)
- No Pleasure in Death [1992] (Bell, Pauline)
- ▌ No Time For an Everyday Woman [incl Claud Willetts] [1997] (Morrone, Wenda Wardell)
- No Use Dying Over Spilled Milk [1996] (Myers, Tamar)
- No Vacation from Murder (Lemarchand, Elizabeth)
- No Word From Winifred [1986] (Cross, Amanda)
- Noble Radiance [1998] (Leon, Donna)
- ▌ Noblesse Oblige [1996] (Smith, Cynthia)
- Nobody Dies in a Casino [1999] (Millhiser, Marlys)
- Nobody's Child [1995] (Dawson, Janet)
- ▌ Nocturne Murder [1988] (Peterson, Audrey)
- ▌ North of the Border [1988] (Van Gieson, Judith)
- North Star Conspiracy [1993] (Monfredo, Miriam Grace)
- Northbury Papers [1998] (Dobson, Joanne)
- Northwest Murders [1992] (Taylor, Elizabeth Atwood)
- ▌ Not a Creature Was Stirring [1990] (Haddam, Jane) ☆☆
- Not Exactly a Brahmin [1985] (Dunlap, Susan)
- ▌ Not One of Us [1971] (Thomson, June)
- Not That Kind of Place (Fyfield, Frances)
- ▌ Not Till a Hot January [1987] (Adamson, M. J.)
- Nothing But Gossip [1998] (Kellogg, Marne Davis)
- Nothing Gold Can Say [2000] (Stabenow, Dana)
- ▌ Nothing To Do With the Case [1981] (Lemarchand, Elizabeth)
- Nothing's Certain but Death [1978] (Wren, M.K.)
- November Veil [1996] (Hall, Linda)
- ▌ Novena for Murder [1984] (O'Marie, Carol Anne, Sister)
- ▌ Novice's Tale [1992] (Frazer, Margaret)
- ▌ Now I Lay Me Down To Sleep [1997] (Rushford, Patricia H.)
- Now Let's Talk of Graves [1990] (Shankman, Sarah)
- Now This [1999] (Star, Nancy)
- ▌ Now You Don't [1988] (Greth, Roma)
- ▌ Now You See Her [1995] (Dewhurst, Eileen)
- Nun's Tale [1995] (Robb, Candace M.)
- Nurse Dawes Is Dead [1994] (Shepherd, Stella)
- Nutty as a Fruitcake [1996] (Daheim, Mary)

O

- O Little Town of Maggody [1993] (Hess, Joan) ☆☆
- Obstacle Course [1990] (Montgomery, Yvonne)
- Obstruction of Justice [1997] (O'Shaughnessy, Perri)
- Odd Job [1995] (MacLeod, Charlotte)
- Odds on Miss Seeton [1975] (Crane, Hamilton)
- Of Death and Black Rivers [1998] (Woodward, Ann)
- ▌ Of Graves, Worms and Epitaphs [1988] (Wells, Tobias)
- Off Key (McNab, Claire)
- ▌ Ogilvie, Tallant and Moon [1976] (Yarbro, Chelsea Quinn)
- Oh Bury Me Not [1977] (Wren, M.K.)
- Old Black Magic [1997] (Maiman, Jaye)
- Old Contemptibles [1990] (Grimes, Martha)
- Old Dogs [1997] (Cleary, Melissa)
- Old Enemies [1993] (LaPierre, Janet) ☆
- Old Faithful Murder [1992] (Wolzien, Valerie)
- Old Fox Deceiv'd [1982] (Grimes, Martha)
- Old School Dies [1996] (Morgan, Kate)
- Old Silent [1989] (Grimes, Martha)
- Old Sinners Never Die [1959] (Davis, Dorothy Salisbury)
- Old Wounds [1998] (Kelly, Nora)
- Oldest Sin [1996] (Hart, Ellen)
- On Ice [1989] (MacGregor, T.J.)
- Once and Always Murder [1990] (Papazoglou, Orania)
- ▌ Once Too Often [1998] (Simpson, Dorothy)
- ▌ One Coffee With [1981] (Maron, Margaret)
- One Dead Virgin [1999] (Davis, Lindsey)
- One Fell Sloop [1990] (Kenney, Susan)
- ▌ One for the Money [1993] (Borton, D.B.)
- ▌ One for the Money [1994] (Evanovich, Janet) ★☆☆☆☆

One Is One and All Alone [1996] (Fraser, Anthea)
One Must Wait [1998] (Mickelbury, Penny)
One, Two, What Did Daddy Do? [1992] (Cooper, Susan Rogers)
Only Flesh and Bones [1998] (Andrews, Sarah)
Only Half a Hoax [1983] (Taylor, L. A.)
Only in the Ashes [1997] (O'Callaghan, Maxine)
Only One Way Out [1994] (Moen, Ruth Raby)
Only Security [1972] (Mann, Jessica)
Open and Shut (McDermid, Val)
Open House [1995] (Welch, Pat)
Operation Apricot [1978] (Haddad, C.A.)
Orchestrated Death [1991] (Harrod-Eagles, Cynthia)
Origin and Cause [1994] (Reuben, Shelly)
Original Sin [1994] (James, P. D.)
Original Sin [1991] (Pulver, Mary Monica)
Osprey Reef [1990] (McKernan, Victoria)
Other David [1984] (Coker, Carolyn)
Other Duties As Required [2000] (Grimes, Terris McMahan)
Other People's Houses [1990] (Cooper, Susan Rogers)
Other People's Skeletons [1993] (Smith, Julie)
Other Side of Death [1991] (Van Gieson, Judith)
Other Side of Silence [1993] (Drury, Joan M.)
Other Side of the Door [1987] (O'Donnell, Lillian)
Other Woman [1992] (McGown, Jill)
Otherworld [1993] (Dreher, Sarah)
Out of Circulation [1997] (Dereske, Jo)
Out of Order [1999] (MacDougal, Bonnie)
Out of the Darkness [1992] (Kelly, Susan)
Out of Time [1998] (Munger, Katy)
Outlaw Derek [1988] (Hooper, Kay)
Outlaw Mountain [1999] (Jance, J.A.)
Outlaw's Fortune [as W.W. Lee] [1993] (Lee, Wendi)
Outlaw's Tale [1994] (Frazer, Margaret)
Outrageous Exposures [1988] (Penn, John)
Outside Chance [1999] (Dixon, Louisa)
Ovation by Death [1996] (Yeager, Dorian)
Over the Edge [1993] (Rowlands, Betty)
Over the Line [1998] (Richardson, Tracey)
Over the Sea to Death [1976] (Moffat, Gwen)
Owl Too Many [1991] (MacLeod, Charlotte) ☆
Oxford Blood [1985] (Fraser, Antonia)
Oxford Blue [1998] (Stallwood, Veronica)
Oxford Exit [1994] (Stallwood, Veronica)
Oxford Fall [1996] (Stallwood, Veronica)
Oxford Knot [1998] (Stallwood, Veronica)
Oxford Mourning [1996] (Stallwood, Veronica)

P

Painted Face [1902 Paris] [1974] (Stubbs, Jean)
Painted Truth [1995] (McClendon, Lise)
Pair for the Queen [1998] (Comfort, Barbara)
Palace Guard [1981] (MacLeod, Charlotte)
Palette for Murder [1996] (Fletcher, Jessica)
Palm for Mrs. Pollifax [1973] (Gilman, Dorothy)
Panic [1998] (Heron, Echo)
Par Four [1998] (Gunn, Elizabeth)
Paradox [1999] (Heron, Echo)
Paragon Walk [1981] (Perry, Anne)
Parcel of Their Fortunes [Morocco] [1979] (Byfield, Barbara Ninde)
Parklane South, Queens [1990] (Kelly, Mary Anne)
Parrot Blues [1995] (Van Gieson, Judith)
Parsley, Sage, Rosemary and Crime [1995] (Myers, Tamar)
Parson's Pleasure [1987] (Hardwick, Mollie)
Parting Breath [1977] (Aird, Catherine)
Partners in Crime [1991] (Gray, Gallagher)
Partnerships Can Kill [1997] (Shelton, Connie)
Passing Strange [1980] (Aird, Catherine)
Passover Murder [1996] (Harris, Lee)

Past Due [1998] (McNab, Claire)
Past Imperfect [1991] (Maron, Margaret)
Past Mischief [1996] (Curzon, Clare)
Past Pretense [1994] (Short, Sharon Gwyn)
Past Reckoning [1990] (Thomson, June)
Patterns in the Dust [1985] (Grant-Adamson, Lesley)
Paws Before Dying [1992] (Conant, Susan)
Pay Dirt [1995] (Brown, Rita Mae)
Pay Out & Pay Back [1999] (Scott, Barbara A.)
Pay the Piper [1996] (Kingsbury, Kate)
Paying the Piper [1988] (McCrumb, Sharyn) ☆☆
Payment Deferred [1996] (Holms, Joyce)
Payment in Blood [1989] (George, Elizabeth)
Payment in Kind [1991] (Jance, J.A.)
Peanut Butter Murders [1993] (Sawyer, Corinne Holt)
Pearls Before Swine [1995] (Clayton, Mary)
Pedigree To Die For [1995] (Berenson, Laurien)
Pel Among the Pueblos [by Mark Hebden] [1987] (Hebden, Juliet)
Pel and Faceless Corpse [by Mark Hebden] [1979] (Hebden, Juliet)
Pel and the Parked Car (1995) (Hebden, Juliet)
Pel and the Bombers [by Mark Hebden] [1982] (Hebden, Juliet)
Pel and the Missing Persons [by Mark Hebden] [1990] (Hebden, Juliet)
Pel and the Paris Mob [by Mark Hebden] [1986] (Hebden, Juliet)
Pel and the Party Spirit [by Mark Hebden] [1989] (Hebden, Juliet)
Pel and the Patriarch [1996] (Hebden, Juliet)
Pel and the Perfect Partner [1994] (Hebden, Juliet)
Pel and the Picture of Innocence[by Mark Hebden] [1989] (Hebden, Juliet)
Pel and the Pirates [by Mark Hebden] [1984] (Hebden, Juliet)
Pel and the Precious Parcel [1997] (Hebden, Juliet)
Pel and the Predators [by Mark Hebden] [1984] (Hebden, Juliet)
Pel and the Promised Land [by Mark Hebden] [1991] (Hebden, Juliet)
Pel and the Prowler[by Mark Hebden] [1985] (Hebden, Juliet)
Pel and the Sepulchre [by Mark Hebden] [1992] (Hebden, Juliet)
Pel and the Staghound [by Mark Hebden] [1982] (Hebden, Juliet)
Pel and the Touch of Pitch [by Mark Hebden] [1987] (Hebden, Juliet)
Pel is Provoked [1999] (Hebden, Juliet)
Pel Is Puzzled [by Mark Hebden] [1981] (Hebden, Juliet)
Pel Picks up the Pieces [1993] (Hebden, Juliet)
Pel Under Pressure [by Mark Hebden] [1980] (Hebden, Juliet)
Penn Valley Phoenix [1997] (McClellan, Janet)
Pennies on a Dead Woman's Eyes [1992] (Muller, Marcia)
Penny Black [1984] (Moody, Susan)
Penny Dreadful [1984] (Moody, Susan)
Penny Pinching [1989] (Moody, Susan)
Penny Post [1985] (Moody, Susan)
Penny Royal [1986] (Moody, Susan)
Penny Saving [1993] (Moody, Susan)
Penny Wise [1988] (Moody, Susan)
Pentecost Alley [1996] (Perry, Anne) ☆
Perfect Day for Dying [1994] (Christmas, Joyce)
Perfect Fools [1982] (Green, Edith Pinero)
Perfect Match [1983] (McGown, Jill)
Perfectly Pure and Good [1994] (Fyfield, Frances)
Peril Under the Palms [1989] (Beck, K. K.)
Perilous Bargain [1997] (Peart, Jane)
Perilous Friends [1996] (Epstein, Carole)

Perilous Relations [1997] (Epstein, Carole)
Perils of the Night [1997] (Hall, Patricia)
Perish in July [1989] (Hardwick, Mollie)
Permit for Murder [1997] (Wolzien, Valerie)
Personal Effects [1991] (Piesman, Marissa)
Persons Unknown [1978] (Moffat, Gwen)
▮ Pet Peeves [1990] (McCafferty, Taylor)
▮ Phantom of Queen Street [2000] (Manthorne, Jackie)
▮ Philly Stakes [1989] (Roberts, Gillian) ☆
▮ Phoebe's Knee [1986] (Comfort, Barbara)
▮ Phone Calls [1972] (O'Donnell, Lillian)
▮ Photogenic Soprano [1968] (Dunnett, Dorothy)
Piano Bird [1984] (Kallen, Lucille)
Pick up Sticks [1970] (Lathen, Emma)
▮ Picture Miss Seeton [1968] (Crane, Hamilton) ☆
Picture of David [1993] (Singer, Shelley)
Picture of Innocence [1998] (McGown, Jill)
Piece of Justice [1995] (Paton Walsh, Jill) ☆
Pinch of Poison [1995] (Bishop, Claudia)
▮ Pink Balloons and Other Deadly Things [1997]
    (Tesler, Nancy)
Pink Flamingo Murders [1999] (Viets, Elaine)
▮ Pint of Murder [1980] (Craig, Alisa)
▮ Pious Deception [1989] (Dunlap, Susan) ☆
▮ Pizza House Crash [1989] (Danks, Denise)
Place for Murder [1963] (Lathen, Emma)
Plague of Angels [1998] (Chisholm, P. F.)
Plague of Kinfolks [1995] (Sibley, Celestine)
▮ Plague on Both Your Houses [1996] (Gregory, Susanna)
Plain Murder [1989] (Greth, Roma)
Plain Old Man [1985] (MacLeod, Charlotte)
▮ Play Dead [1998] (O'Kane, Leslie)
Play It Again, Spam [1999] (Myers, Tamar)
Play With Fire [1995] (Stabenow, Dana)
Players Come Again [1990] (Cross, Amanda)
Playing for the Ashes [1994] (George, Elizabeth)
▮ Playing God [1988] (Whitehead, Barbara)
Playing Safe [1985] (Dewhurst, Eileen)
Plymouth Cloak [1992] (Sedley, Kate)
▮ Pocketful of Karma [1993] (Cannon, Taffy)
Poetic Justice [1970] (Cross, Amanda)
Point Deception [1992] (McKernan, Victoria)
Point of Origin [1998] (Cornwell, Patricia)
Poison Flowers [1991] (Cooper, Natasha)
Poison for the Prince [1994] (Eyre, Elizabeth)
Poison Fruit [1991] (Yarbro, Chelsea Quinn)
Poison in the Blood [1994] (Zachary, Fay)
Poison Pen [1990] (Kittredge, Mary)
Poisoned Pins [1993] (Hess, Joan)
Political Death [1994] (Fraser, Antonia)
▮ Poor, Poor Ophelia [1972] (Weston, Carolyn)
Port and a Star Border [1984] (Morison, B.J.)
Portion for Foxes [1995] (Mitchell, Kay)
Portrait of Lilith (Thomson, June)
Poseidon's Gold [1993] (Davis, Lindsey) ☆
Possessions [1998] (Davis, Kaye)
▮ Postmortem [1990] (Cornwell, Patricia) ★★★★
Postscript to Murder [1996] (Meek, M.R.D.)
Potter's Field [1993] (Fallon, Ann C.)
Practice To Deceive [1992] (Smith, Janet L.)
Prairie Hardball [1997] (Gordon, Alison)
Pray God To Die [1993] (Roberts, Carey)
Prayers for the Dead [1996] (Kellerman, Faye)
Precious Blood [1991] (Haddam, Jane)
Prelude to Death [1996] (Zukowski, Sharon)
Prescription for Death [1993] (McGiffin, Janet)
Press Corpse [1996] (Nessen, Ron)
Pretty Maids All in a Row [1986] (Fraser, Anthea)
Prey To Murder [1989] (Cleeves, Ann)
▮ Price You Pay [1987] (Wakefield, Hannah)
Pride and Predator [1997] (Wright, Sally S.)

Prima Donna at Large [1915] [1985] (Paul, Barbara)
Primary Target [1988] (Wallace, Marilyn) ☆
Prime Cut [1998] (Davidson, Diane Mott)
▮ Prime Suspect [1993] (La Plante, Lynda)
Prime Suspect 2 [1993] (La Plante, Lynda)
Prime Suspect 3 [1994] (La Plante, Lynda)
▮ Prime Time Corpse [1972] (Babbin, Jacqueline)
Prime Time for Murder [1994] (Frankel, Valerie)
▮ Primrose Convention [1998] (Bannister, Jo)
▮ Principal Defense [1992] (Hartzmark, Gini) ☆
Prior Convictions [1991] (Matera, Lia) ☆
Prioress' Tale [1997] (Frazer, Margaret) ☆
▮ Private Crime [1991] (O'Donnell, Lillian)
▮ Private Lies [1993] (Cail, Carol)
Prized Possessions [1993] (Wright, L.R.)
▮ Probe [1985] (Douglas, Carole Nelson)
▮ Problem of the Missing Hoyden (Rogow, Roberta)
▮ Problem of the Missing Miss [1998] (Rogow, Roberta)
Problem of the Spiteful Spiritualist [1999]
    (Rogow, Roberta)
Prodigal's Return [1997] (Clayton, Mary)
Proper Burial [1993] (Welch, Pat)
Prospect of Death [incl Patrick Gillard] [1995]
    (Duffy, Margaret)
Providence File [1991] (Williams, Amanda Kyle)
Publish and Be Murdered [1998] (Edwards, Ruth Dudley)
▮ Publish and Perish [1997] (Wright, Sally S.)
▮ Pulse [1998] (Heron, Echo)
Pumpkin-Shell Wife [1992] (McShea, Susanna Hofmann)
▮ Punjat's Ruby [1990] (Jackson, Marian J. A.)
Puppet for a Corpse [1983] (Simpson, Dorothy)
Pursued by Shadows [1992] (Sale, Medora)
Pushing Murder [1993] (Boylan, Eleanor)
▮ Pushover [1992] (O'Donnell, Lillian)
Pussyfoot [1993] (Douglas, Carole Nelson)
Put on by Cunning [1981] (Rendell, Ruth)
▮ Puzzled Heart [1998] (Cross, Amanda)

Q

Quaker Indictment [1998] (Allen, Irene)
▮ Quaker Silence [1992] (Allen, Irene)
Quaker Testimony [1996] (Allen, Irene)
Quaker Witness [1993] (Allen, Irene)
Queen Is Dead [1994] (Dentinger, Jane)
▮ Queen's Man [1996] (Penman, Sharon Kay) ☆
Quest for K [1986] (Curzon, Clare)
▮ Question of Guilt [1988] (Fyfield, Frances) ☆☆☆
Question of Identity [1977] (Thomson, June)
Question of Max [1976] (Cross, Amanda)
Question of Preference [1994] (Lamb, J. Dayne)
▮ Questionable Behavior [1993] (Lamb, J. Dayne)
Questionable Remains [1997] (Connor, Beverly)
Quiche Before Dying [1993] (Churchill, Jill)
Quick and the Dead [1995] (Dengler, Sandy)
Quick and the Dead [1996] (Joseph, Alison)
▮ Quiet as a Nun [1977] (Fraser, Antonia)
Quiet Death [1991] (Knight, Alanna)
Quiet Road to Death (Radley, Sheila)
▮ Quieter Than Sleep [1997] (Dobson, Joanne) ☆
Quoth the Raven [1991] (Haddam, Jane)

R

Radical Departure [1988] (Matera, Lia) ☆☆
Rafferty's Wife [1987] (Hooper, Kay)
Rage [1990] (Moffat, Gwen)
Rage Factor [1999] (Rogers, Chris)
Rage of Innocents [1996] (Mitchell, Kay)
Rage of Maidens [1994] (Douglas, Lauren Wright)
Raggedy Man [1995] (O'Donnell, Lillian)
▮ Rain Dance [1996] (Moody, Skye Kathleen)
▮ Rainbow's End [1995] (Grimes, Martha)

Raisins and Almonds [1997] (Greenwood, Kerry)
Rancher's Blood [as W.W. Lee] [1991] (Lee, Wendi)
∎ Random Access Murder [1988] (Grant, Linda) ☆
Raptor [1990] (Van Gieson, Judith)
∎ Raptor Zone [1990] (Moffat, Gwen)
Rapture in Death [1996] (Robb, J.D.)
Rare Earth [1995] (Dawkins, Cecil)
Rattlesnake Crossing [1998] (Jance, J.A.)
Raven and the Nightingale [1999] (Dobson, Joanne)
Raven on the Wing [1987] (Hooper, Kay)
∎ Ravenmocker [1992] (Hager, Jean)
∎ Raw Data [1991] (Chapman, Sally)
∎ Real Murders [1990] (Harris, Charlaine) ☆
∎ Real Shot in the Arm [1989] (Roome, Annette) ★
Really Cute Corpse [1988] (Hess, Joan)
∎ Reason To Kill [1978] (Zaremba, Eve)
Recipe for Death [1992] (Laurence, Janet)
∎ Reckless [1989] (Woods, Sherryl)
Record of Death [1998] (Bryan, Kate)
Recording Angel [1991] (Cohen, Anthea)
Recycled Citizen [1987] (MacLeod, Charlotte)
∎ Red Hot Blues (1998) (Nadelson, Reggie)
Red Line [1999] (Rust, Megan Mallory)
∎ Red Mercury Blues [1995] (Nadelson, Reggie)
∎ Red Scream [1994] (Walker, Mary Willis) ★☆
∎ Red Sea, Dead Sea [1991] (Stevens, Serita)
Red Sky in Mourning [1997] (Rushford, Patricia H.)
Red, White and Blue Murder [2000] (Dams, Jeanne M.)
Redbird's Cry [1994] (Hager, Jean)
Redemption [1988] (McGown, Jill)
Redneck Riviera [1998] (Dunbar, Sophie)
∎ Reel Murder [1986] (Babson, Marian)
Rehearsal for Murder [1988] (Carlson, P.M.)
∎ Religious Body [1966] (Aird, Catherine)
∎ Remedy for Treason [1998] (Roe, Caroline)
Remember March [1988] (Adamson, M. J.)
Remember Me, Irene [1996] (Burke, Jan)
Remember the Alibi [1994] (Squire, Elizabeth Daniels)
Remodeled to Death [1995] (Wolzien, Valerie)
∎ Rendezvous Kit Marlow (Morgan, D Miller)
∎ Renewable Virgin [1984] (Paul, Barbara)
Renowned Be Thy Grave [1998] (Carlson, P.M.)
∎ Report for Murder [1987] (McDermid, Val)
Requiem for a Dove [1990] (Eccles, Marjorie)
Requiem for a Mezzo [1996] (Dunn, Carola)
Rest in Pieces [1992] (Brown, Rita Mae)
∎ Rest You Merry [1978] (MacLeod, Charlotte)
∎ Resumé for Murder [1982] (McCormick, Claire)
Resurrection Man [1992] (MacLeod, Charlotte)
Resurrection Row [1981] (Perry, Anne)
Return to the Kill [1996] (Moen, Ruth Raby)
Revenge of the Barbecue Queens [1997] (Temple, Lou Jane)
Revenge of the Cootie Girls [1997] (Hayter, Sparkle)
∎ Revengeful Death [1998] (Melville, Jennie)
∎ Rhode Island Red [1997] (Carter, Charlotte)
Rich, Radiant Slaughter [1988] (Papazoglou, Orania)
Riddle of St. Leonard's [1996] (Robb, Candace M.)
∎ Riding for a Fall [1996] (Roberts, Lillian M.) ☆
∎ Right Hand of Amon [1997] (Haney, Lauren)
Right Jack [1987] (Maron, Margaret)
Right on the Money [1993] (Lathen, Emma)
Right To Remain Silent [1998] (Warner, Penny)
Rigor Mortis [1991] (Kittredge, Mary)
Ring for Tomb Service [1997] (Kingsbury, Kate)
Ripe for Revenge [1994] (Bolitho, Janie)
Rising [1987] (Smith, Alison)
∎ Ritual Bath [1986] (Kellerman, Faye) ★
Ritual Murder [1982] (Haymon, S.T.) ★
River Quay [1998] (McClellan, Janet)
∎ Road Rage [1997] (Rendell, Ruth)

Robber's Trail [as W.W. Lee] [1992] (Lee, Wendi)
∎ Robber's Wine [1996] (Hart, Ellen) ★
∎ Robsart Mystery [1997] (Buckley, Fiona)
Rockefeller Gift [1982] (Winslow, Pauline Glen)
Rogue Wave [1991] (Dunlap, Susan) ☆
∎ Rogue's Gold [as W.W. Lee] [1989] (Lee, Wendi)
Roll Over and Play Dead [1991] (Hess, Joan)
Rook-Shoot [1991] (Duffy, Margaret)
∎ Room With a Clue [1993] (Kingsbury, Kate)
Root Canal [1994] (Haddad, C.A.)
Roots of Evil (Mitchell, Kay)
Roped [1998] (Crum, Laura)
Ropedancer's Fall [1990] (Lorens, M.K.)
Rose Window [1967] (Blanc, Suzanne)
Rose-Colored Glasses [2000] (Alexander, Skye)
∎ Roseanna [1967] (Sjöwall, Maj & Per Wahlöö)
∎ Rosemary for Remembrance [1988] (Thomson, June)
Rosemary Remembered [1995] (Albert, Susan Wittig)
Rosewood Casket [1996] (McCrumb, Sharyn)
∎ Rotten Apples [1995] (Cooper, Natasha)
Rotten Apples [1977] (Green, Edith Pinero)
Rotten Lies [1995] (Elkins, Charlotte & Aaron)
∎ Rough Justice [1996] (Youmans, Claire)
Rough Justice [Marta Richter] [1997] (Scottoline, Lisa)
Rough Trade [1999] (Hartzmark, Gini)
Rough Trip [2000] (Youmans, Claire)
Rough Water [1994] (Gunning, Sally)
Roughstock [1997] (Crum, Laura)
Roundabout [1998] (Dewhurst, Eileen)
Rouse the Demon [1976] (Weston, Carolyn)
Royals and Rogues [1998] (Smith, Cynthia)
Rubout [1998] (Viets, Elaine)
Ruddy Gore [1995] (Greenwood, Kerry)
Rueful Death [1996] (Albert, Susan Wittig)
Ruffled Feathers [1992] (McCafferty, Taylor)
Ruffly Speaking [1993] (Conant, Susan)
Rum & Razors [1995] (Fletcher, Jessica)
∎ Rumor of Bones [1996] (Connor, Beverly)
Run From Nightmare [1981] (O'Callaghan, Maxine)
Run, Jane, Run [1999] (Tan, Maureen)
Run Time [1998] (Niles, Chris)
Runaway [1985] (Watson, Clarissa)
∎ Runemaker [1996] (Nunnally, Tiina)
Running Deep [1965] (Petrie, Rhona)
Running for Shelter [1995] (Spring, Michelle)
Running From the Law [Rita Morrone] [1995] (Scottoline, Lisa)
Running Scared [1998] (Granger, Ann)
Rustler's Venom [as W.W. Lee] [1990] (Lee, Wendi)
Rutland Place [1983] (Perry, Anne)
∎ Rx for Murder [1997] (Horowitz, Renee B.)

S

Sacred and Profane [1987] (Kellerman, Faye)
∎ Sacred Hearts [1994] (Joseph, Alison)
Sacrifice Bid [1997] (Moody, Susan)
Sad Water [1999] (Holbrook, Teri)
Safe at Home [1991] (Gordon, Alison)
Safe Place To Die [1993] (Law, Janice)
∎ Safe Place To Sleep [1992] (Jordan, Jennifer)
∎ Salaryman's Wife [1997] (Massey, Sujata) ★☆☆
Salmon in the Soup [1990] (O'Brien, Meg)
∎ Samson's Deal [1983] (Singer, Shelley)
Sanctuary [1994] (Kellerman, Faye)
∎ Santa Fe Rembrandt [1993] (Dawkins, Cecil)
∎ Sarsen Place (Butler, Gwendoline)
∎ Satan's Lambs [1993] (Hightower, Lynn S.) ★
Satan's Silence [1997] (Matthews, Alex)
∎ Saturday Morning Murder [1992] (Gur, Batya)
∎ Savage Cut [1996] (Dereske, Jo)
∎ Say It With Poison [1991] (Granger, Ann)

Say No to Murder [1985] (Pickard, Nancy) ★
Say Uncle [1999] (Lordon, Randye)
🔳 Scalpel's Edge [1991] (Fromer, Margot J.)
Scandal in Fair Haven [1994] (Hart, Carolyn G.) ☆
Scaring Crows [1999] (Masters, Priscilla)
Scarlet Night [1980] (Davis, Dorothy Salisbury)
🔳 Scavengers [1987] (Montgomery, Yvonne)
Scent of Death [1985] (Page, Emma)
🔳 Scent of Fear [1992] (Matthews, Patricia)
Scent of Murder [1997] (Block, Barbara)
School of English Murder (Edwards, Ruth Dudley)
School of Hard Knocks [1997] (Murray, Donna Huston)
Score To Settle [1999] (Murray, Donna Huston)
🔳 Screaming Bones [1990] (Burden, Pat) ☆
Screwdriver [1988] (Kraft, Gabrielle)
Sea Fever [1991] (Cleeves, Ann)
🔳 Sea of Troubles [1990] (Smith, Janet L.) ☆
Search [1996] (McAllester, Melanie)
Searching for Sara [1994] (Singer, Shelley)
Season for Murder [1992] (Granger, Ann)
Season of Knives [1995] (Chisholm, P. F.)
Season of Snows and Sins [1971] (Moyes, Patricia)
Seasons of Death [1981] (Wren, M.K.)
Second Fiddle [1996] (Calloway, Kate)
Second Guess [1994] (Beecham, Rose)
Second Opinion [1994] (Rayner, Claire)
Second Shot in the Dark [1990] (Roome, Annette)
Secret Drawer Society [2000] (Buggé, Carole)
🔳 Secret's Shadow [1996] (Matthews, Alex)
Secrets in Stones [1995] (Shone, Anna)
Secrets of the Dead [1995] (Whitehead, Barbara)
See No Evil [1998] (Bland, Eleanor Taylor)
Seeing a Large Cat [1997] (Peters, Elizabeth) ☆
Seeing is Deceiving [1996] (North, Suzanne)
Seeing Is Deceiving [1997] (Mason, Sarah J.)
Seminar for Murder [1985] (Gill, B.M.)
🔳 Seneca Falls Inheritance [1992] (Monfredo,
　　Miriam Grace) ☆☆
Send a Fax to the Kasbah (Dunnett, Dorothy)
Senseless Ax of Beauty [2000] (Dunbar, Sophie)
September Mourn [1997] (Daheim, Mary)
Sequence of Shame [1996] (Bolitho, Janie)
Serpent's Tooth [1997] (Kellerman, Faye)
Servant's Tale [1993] (Frazer, Margaret) ☆
Service for Two [1994] (Kingsbury, Kate)
Set-Up [1991] (O'Callaghan, Maxine)
Setting for Murder [1988] (Fulton, Eileen)
Seven Black Stones [1995] (Hager, Jean)
Seven Kinds of Death [1992] (Wilhelm, Kate)
Seven Sisters [2000] (Fowler, Earlene)
🔳 Seven Stars [1995] (Fraser, Anthea)
Seventh Avenue Murder [1990] (Bennett, Liza)
Seventh Heaven [1999] (Calloway, Kate)
🔳 Seventh Sinner [1972] (Peters, Elizabeth)
Severed Key [1973] (Nielsen, Helen)
Sew Deadly [1998] (Hager, Jean)
Sew Easy To Kill [1996] (Mason, Sarah J.)
Sex and Salmonella [1996] (Taylor, Kathleen)
Shades of Gray [1988] (Hooper, Kay)
🔳 Shadow of a Child [1996] (O'Callaghan, Maxine)
Shadow of a Doubt [1981] (Thomson, June)
Shadow of Death [1995] (Gilpatrick, Noreen)
🔳 Shadow of Doubt [1996] (Jacobs, Jonnie)
Shadow of Fear [1996] (Peart, Jane)
Shadow of the Palms [1980] (Law, Janice)
Shadow Play [1993] (Fyfield, Frances)
Shadow Walk [1997] (Waterhouse, Jane)
Shadow Walkers [1993] (Romberg, Nina)
🔳 Shadowdance [1989] (Bushell, Agnes)
Shadows in Bronze [1990] (Davis, Lindsey)
Shadows in Their Blood [1993] (Babson, Marian)

🔳 Shadows on the Mirror [1989] (Fyfield, Frances)
Shake Hands Forever [1975] (Rendell, Ruth)
Shakespeare's Champion [1997] (Harris, Charlaine)
Shakespeare's Christmas [1998] (Harris, Charlaine)
🔳 Shakespeare's Landlord [1996] (Harris, Charlaine)
Shallow Grave [1998] (Harrod-Eagles, Cynthia)
Shaman's Moon [1998] (Dreher, Sarah)
Shape of Dread [1989] (Muller, Marcia) ☆
🔳 Shards [1990] (Bannister, Jo)
🔳 Share in Death [1993] (Crombie, Deborah) ☆☆
Shark Out of Water [1997] (Lathen, Emma)
Sharkbait [1993] (Geason, Susan)
Sharks, Jellyfish and Other Deadly Things [1998]
　　(Tesler, Nancy)
🔳 Shattered Moon [1986] (Green, Kate) ☆
Shattered Rhythms [1994] (Knight, Phyllis)
Shattered Silk [1986] (Michaels, Barbara)
🔳 Shaved Fish [1990] (Geason, Susan)
She Came by the Book [1995] (Wings, Mary)
She Came in a Flash [1988] (Wings, Mary)
She Came to the Castro [1997] (Wings, Mary)
🔳 She Came Too Late [1986] (Wings, Mary)
She Walks in Beauty [1991] (Shankman, Sarah) ★★★★
She Walks These Hills [1994] (McCrumb, Sharyn)
She's Out [1995] (La Plante, Lynda)
Shed Light on Death [1985] (Taylor, L. A.)
Sheriff & the Branding Iron Murders [1985]
　　(Meredith, D. R.)
Sheriff & the Folsom Man Murders [1987]
　　(Meredith, D. R.)
🔳 Sheriff & the Panhandle Murders [1984] (Meredith, D. R.)
Sheriff & the Pheasant Hunt Murders [1993]
　　(Meredith, D. R.)
🔳 Shinju [1994] (Rowland, Laura Joh) ☆
🔳 Shiny Water [1997] (Salter, Anna)
Shiveree [1999] (Dunbar, Sophie)
Shock Value [1985] (Berne, Karin)
Shoot, Don't Shoot [1995] (Jance, J.A.)
Shooting at Loons [1994] (Maron, Margaret)
Shooting Chant [1999] (Thurlo, Aimée & David)
Shooting Stars and Other Deadly Things [1999]
　　(Tesler, Nancy)
🔳 Shore To Die [1996] (Wolzien, Valerie)
Short Cut [1998] (Dereske, Jo)
Short Cut to Santa Fe [1994] (Sale, Medora)
Short Time To Live [1976] (Moffat, Gwen)
Shortest Day [1995] (Langton, Jane)
Shortest Journey [1992] (Holt, Hazel)
Shortest Way to Hades [1985] (Caudwell, Sarah)
Shot in the Dark [1996] (Ross, Annie)
Show Stopper [1992] (Pulver, Mary Monica)
🔳 Showcase [1992] (Glen, Alison)
Shred of Evidence [1995] (McGown, Jill)
Shroud for a Nightingale [1971] (James, P. D.) ★☆
Shroud for a Scholar [1995] (Peterson, Audrey)
🔳 Shroud for Delilah [1984] (Fraser, Anthea)
Shy Tulip Murders [1996] (Rothenberg, Rebecca)
Sibyl in Her Grave [1999] (Caudwell, Sarah)
🔳 Sick of Shadows [1984] (McCrumb, Sharyn)
Sign of Foul Play [1998] (Warner, Penny)
Signs of Murder [1993] (Bedford, Jean)
Silence in Hanover Close [1988] (Perry, Anne)
Silence of the Hams [1996] (Churchill, Jill)
Silent Cry [1997] (Perry, Anne)
Silent Witness [1972] (Yorke, Margaret)
Silent Words [1996] (Drury, Joan M.) ☆
Silhouette in Scarlet [1983] (Peters, Elizabeth)
Silly Season [1999] (Holtzer, Susan)
Silver and Guilt [1998] (Smith, Cynthia)
Silver Ghost [1987] (MacLeod, Charlotte)
🔳 Silver Pigs [1989] (Davis, Lindsey)

■ Silver Scalpel [1993] (Jacobs, Nancy Baker)
■ Silverlake Heat [1993] (Schmidt, Carol)
■ Simeon's Bride [1995] (Taylor, Alison G.)
■ Simisola [1994] (Rendell, Ruth)
■ Simon Said [1997] (Shaber, Sarah R.) ★
Simply To Die For [1989] (Christmas, Joyce)
Sing a Song of Death [1993] (Dain, Catherine)
Single Stone [1991] (Wallace, Marilyn) ☆
Singular Spy [1992] (Williams, Amanda Kyle)
Sinister Touch [1986] (Castle, Jayne)
Sins of Betrayal [1999] (Wilcox, Valerie)
Sins of Deception [2000] (Wilcox, Valerie)
■ Sins of Silence [1998] (Wilcox, Valerie)
Sins of the Fathers (1970) (Rendell, Ruth)
Sins of the Heart [1994] (Bannister, Jo)
Sins of the Wolf [1994] (Perry, Anne)
Sirens Sang of Murder [1989] (Caudwell, Sarah) ★☆
■ Sister Beneath the Sheet [1991] (Linscott, Gillian)
Sister Death (Winslow, Pauline Glen)
Sister to the Rain [1998] (Michaels, Melisa)
Sister's Keeper [1994] (Lordon, Randye)
Sisters of the Road [1986] (Wilson, Barbara)
Sitting Ducks [1983] (Meek, M.R.D.)
Six Feet Under [1982] (Simpson, Dorothy)
Six Feet Under [1997] (Borton, D.B.)
Six Foot Under [1993] (John, Katherine)
Six Proud Walkers [1988] (Fraser, Anthea)
■ Six-Letter Word for Death [1983] (Moyes, Patricia)
Sixth Sense [1999] (Calloway, Kate)
Skeleton Canyon [1997] (Jance, J.A.)
Sketches With Wolves [2000] (Fiedler, Jacqueline)
Skull and Dog Bones [1994] (Cleary, Melissa)
Skull Beneath the Skin [1982] (James, P. D.)
Skylark [1992] (Simonson, Sheila)
Slash of Scarlet [1992] (Jacobs, Nancy Baker)
■ Slay at the Races [1990] (Morgan, Kate)
Sleep of the Innocent [1991] (Sale, Medora)
Sleep While I Sing [1986] (Wright, L.R.)
Sleeping and the Dead [1994] (Quinton, Ann)
Sleeping Lady [1996] (Henry, Sue)
Sleeping Life [1978] (Rendell, Ruth) ☆
Sleeping Partners [1995] (Bell, Pauline)
Slight Mourning [1975] (Aird, Catherine)
Slow Burn [1993] (Bland, Eleanor Taylor)
■ Slow Dancing With the Angel of Death [1996]
    (Chappell, Helen)
Slow Squeeze [1994] (Pugh, Dianne G.)
■ Small Favors [1988] (Wallace, Patricia)
■ Small Sacrifice [1994] (Hart, Ellen) ★
Small Target [1996] (Andreae, Christine)
Small Towns Can Be Murder [1998] (Shelton, Connie)
Smart House [1989] (Wilhelm, Kate)
■ Smart Money [1988] (Matera, Lia)
Smiling at Death [1995] (Rowlands, Betty)
Smoke and Mirrors [1996] (Welch, Pat)
Smoke Screen [1998] (Grant, Anne Underwood)
Snagged [1993] (Clark, Carol Higgins)
Snake Dance [1992] (Mariz, Linda French)
Snake Tattoo [1989] (Barnes, Linda)
Snake, the Crocodile and the Dog [1992]
    (Peters, Elizabeth) ☆
■ Snapped in Cornwall [1997] (Bolitho, Janie)
Snapshot [1993] (Barnes, Linda)
Snare [1987] (Moffat, Gwen)
Snares of Death [1993] (Charles, Kate)
Sneaks [1979] (Green, Edith Pinero)
Snipe Hunt [2000] (Shaber, Sarah R.)
■ Snow Place To Die [1998] (Daheim, Mary)
■ So Dear to Wicked Men [1996] (Iakovou, Takis and Judy)
So Faux, So Good [1998] (Myers, Tamar)
So Little To Die For [1994] (Grindle, Lucretia)

So Many Steps to Death [1995] (Penn, John)
So Sure of Death [1999] (Stabenow, Dana)
■ Sold to Miss Seeton [1995] (Crane, Hamilton)
■ Solemn High Murder [with Frank L. Tedeschi] [1975]
    (Byfield, Barbara Ninde)
Solitary Twist [1993] (Pincus, Elizabeth)
Some Die Eloquent [1979] (Aird, Catherine)
Some Foul Play [1997] (Quinton, Ann)
Some Lie and Some Die [1973] (Rendell, Ruth)
■ Somebody Else's Child [1996] (Grimes,
    Terris McMahan) ★★☆
Somebody Killed the Messenger [1988] (Watson, Clarissa)
Somebody's Dead in Snellville [1992]
    (Sprinkle, Patricia H.)
■ Someone Else's Grave [1984] (Smith, Alison) ☆
Someone Is Killing the Great Chefs of America
    [1993] (Lyons, Nan & Ivan)
■ Someone Is Killing the Great Chefs of Europe
    [1976] (Lyons, Nan & Ivan)
Someone To Watch [1995] (Maiman, Jaye)
Something in the Air [1988] (Lathen, Emma)
Something in the Cellar [1995] (Shepherd, Stella)
Something in the Water [1994] (MacLeod, Charlotte)
Something Shady [1986] (Dreher, Sarah)
Something the Cat Dragged In [1983]
    (MacLeod, Charlotte)
■ Something To Kill For [1994] (Holtzer, Susan) ★
Something Wicked [1988] (Hart, Carolyn G.) ★★
Something Wicked [1998] (Rowe, Jennifer)
■ Something's Cooking [1993] (Pence, Joanne)
Sorrowheart [1993] (Lorens, M.K.)
Soultown [1996] (Lambert, Mercedes)
Sound Evidence [1984] (Thomson, June)
Sound of Murder [1994] (Matthews, Patricia)
Sour Grapes [1997] (Cooper, Natasha)
Sourdough Wars [1984] (Smith, Julie)
Southern Cross [1999] (Cornwell, Patricia)
Southern Discomfort [1993] (Maron, Margaret) ☆☆
Southern Ghost [1992] (Hart, Carolyn G.) ☆☆
■ Speak Daggers to Her [1994] (Edghill, Rosemary)
Speak No Evil [1985] (Warner, Mignon)
■ Speak No Evil [1996] (Krich, Rochelle Majer)
■ Speaker of Mandarin [1983] (Rendell, Ruth)
Species of Revenge [1996] (Eccles, Marjorie)
Spent Matches [1996] (Reuben, Shelly)
Spider in the Sink [1997] (Sibley, Celestine)
■ Spike It [1997] (Niles, Chris)
Spirit Caller [1997] (Hager, Jean)
■ Spirit Stalker [1989] (Romberg, Nina)
Spit in the Ocean [1987] (Singer, Shelley)
Splash of Red [1981] (Fraser, Antonia)
Split Code [1976] (Dunnett, Dorothy)
Split Image [1998] (Mercer, Judy)
Split Second [1985] (Meek, M.R.D.)
■ Spoils of Time [1989] (Thomson, June)
■ Spoilt Kill [1961] (Kelly, Mary) ★
■ Sports Freak [1980] (OCork, Shannon)
Spree [1992] (MacGregor, T.J.)
Spring Cleaning Murders [1998] (Cannell, Dorothy)
Spy in Question [1993] (Williams, Amanda Kyle)
St. Patrick's Day Murder [1994] (Harris, Lee)
St. Valentine's Day Murders [1984] (Edwards,
    Ruth Dudley)
Stage Fright [1992] (Hart, Ellen)
Stage Fright [1993] (Linscott, Gillian)
Stalker [1984] (Cody, Liza)
Stalking Horse [1998] (Monfredo, Miriam Grace)
Standing in the Shadows [1998] (Spring, Michelle)
■ Star Gazer [1994] (McCafferty, Jeanne)
■ Star of India [1998] (Buggé, Carole)
Star Struck [1998] (McDermid, Val)

Star Witness [1997] (Matera, Lia)
Star-Spangled Murder [1993] (Wolzien, Valerie)
🔳 Stargazey [1998] (Grimes, Martha)
🔳 Starring Miss Seeton [1994] (Crane, Hamilton)
Stately Home Murder (Aird, Catherine)
Stately Homicide [1984] (Haymon, S. T.)
Stayin' Alive [1998] (Moore, Miriam Ann)
🔳 Steel Ashes [1997] (Cercone, Karen Rose)
Steel Guitar [1991] (Barnes, Linda)
Steeped in Murder [1999] (French, Linda)
Step in the Dark [1976] (Lemarchand, Elizabeth)
🔳 Sterner Stuff [1997] (Penn, John)
Stiff as a Broad [includes Erik March] [1972]
    (Fickling, G.G.)
Stiff Critique [1995] (Girdner, Jaqueline)
🔳 Stiff News [1998] (Aird, Catherine)
Stiff Risotto [1997] (Temple, Lou Jane)
Still Water [1995] (Gunning, Sally)
🔳 Still Waters [1991] (Tucker, Kerry)
Still Waters [1992] (Welch, Pat)
Stillness in Bethlehem [1992] (Haddam, Jane)
Stitch in Time [1968] (Lathen, Emma)
Stitches in Time [1995] (Michaels, Barbara)
Stolen Moments [1990] (Woods, Sherryl)
Stone Angel [1997] (O'Connell, Carol)
Stone Hawk [1989] (Moffat, Gwen)
Stone Quarry [1999] (Rozan, S.J.)
🔳 Stoner McTavish [1985] (Dreher, Sarah)
🔳 Storm at Daybreak [1986] (Hoff, B.J.)
Storm Front [1995] (Silva, Linda Kay)
Storm Shelter [1993] (Silva, Linda Kay)
Storm Surge [1993] (MacGregor, T.J.)
Story Teller [1998] (Coel, Margaret)
Straight as an Arrow [1992] (Sibley, Celestine)
Strange Brew [1997] (Trocheck, Kathy Hogan)
Strange Desire [1994] (Mitchell, Kay)
🔳 Strange Files of Fremont Jones [1995] (Day, Dianne) ★
🔳 Strangers Among Us [1996] (Wright, L.R.)
🔳 Strangers in the Night [1994] (Tyre, Peg)
🔳 Strangled Prose [1986] (Hess, Joan) ☆
Stranglehold [1994] (Rowe, Jennifer)
Strawgirl [1994] (Padgett, Abigail)
Stray Kat Waltz [1998] (Kijewski, Karen)
Street of the Five Moons [1978] (Peters, Elizabeth)
Striking Out [1995] (Gordon, Alison)
🔳 Striving With Gods [1984] (Bannister, Jo)
Strong as Death [1996] (Newman, Sharan) ☆
Stud Rites [1996] (Conant, Susan)
Student Body [1986] (Borthwick, J. S.)
Studied Death [1995] (Struthers, Betsy)
🔳 Study in Lilac [1987] (Oliver, Maria-Antonia)
Stunning Way To Die [1991] (Christmas, Joyce)
Sudden Death [1997] (Manthorne, Jackie)
🔳 Sudden Death at the Norfolk Café [1993]
    (Sullivan, Winona) ★
Sudden Exposure [1996] (Dunlap, Susan)
Sudden, Fearful Death [1993] (Perry, Anne)
🔳 Suddenly in Her Sorbet [1988] (Christmas, Joyce)
Suddenly While Gardening [1978] (Lemarchand, Elizabeth)
Suicide King [1988] (Singer, Shelley)
Suicide Squeeze [2000] (Gordon, Alison)
Suitable for Framing [1995] (Buchanan, Edna)
Suitable Vengeance [1991] (George, Elizabeth)
Summer Will End [1995] (Yeager, Dorian)
Summertime Soldiers [1986] (Kelly, Susan)
Sunken Sailor (Moyes, Patricia)
Sunken Treasure [1994] (Jackson, Marian J. A.)
Sunset and Santiago [1997] (White, Gloria) ☆☆
Superior Death [1994] (Barr, Nevada)
Surfeit of Guns [1996] (Chisholm, P. F.)
Survival Instincts [1997] (Piesman, Marissa)

Susannah Screaming [1975] (Weston, Carolyn)
🔳 Suspect [1985] (Wright, L.R.) ★
Superfluous Death (Holt, Hazel)
🔳 Suspect (Gill, B.M.)
🔳 Suspect (1999) (Rowe, Jennifer)
Suspicion of Deceit [1998] (Parker, Barbara)
Suspicion of Guilt [1995] (Parker, Barbara)
🔳 Suspicion of Innocence [1994] (Parker, Barbara) ☆
Suspicious Death [1988] (Simpson, Dorothy)
🔳 Sweet and Low [1974] (Lathen, Emma)
Sweet Cherry Wine [1994] (Schmidt, Carol)
Sweet Death Come Softly [1992] (Whitehead, Barbara)
Sweet Death, Kind Death [1984] (Cross, Amanda)
Sweet Dreams, Irene [1994] (Burke, Jan)
Sweet Miss Seeton [1996] (Crane, Hamilton)
🔳 Sweet Narcissus [1990] (Lorens, M.K.)
🔳 Sweet, Savage Death [1984] (Papazoglou, Orania) ☆
Sweet, Sweet Poison [1990] (Wilhelm, Kate)
🔳 Swell Style of Murder [1986] (Santini, Rosemarie)
Swimming at Cat Cove [1997] (Douglas, Lauren Wright)
🔳 Switching the Odds [1992] (Knight, Phyllis) ☆
Sworn To Defend [1998] (Wheat, Carolyn)
Symbols at Your Door [1990] (Fraser, Anthea)
🔳 Sympathy for the Devil [1998] (Farmer, Jerrilyn)

T

🔳 Tail of Two Murders [1992] (Cleary, Melissa)
Tailspin [2000] (Stabenow, Dana)
Take a Number [1993] (Dawson, Janet)
🔳 Take One for Murder [1988] (Fulton, Eileen)
🔳 Taken by Storm [1991] (Silva, Linda Kay)
🔳 Taken to the Cleaners [1997] (Johnson, Dolores)
🔳 Takeout Double (Moody, Susan)
Takes One To Know One [1996] (Allen, Kate)
Taking the Fifth [1987] (Jance, J.A.)
Talent for Destruction [1982] (Radley, Sheila)
Talked to Death [1995] (Shaffer, Louise)
🔳 Talking Rain [1998] (French, Linda)
Tangled Roots [1995] (Cannon, Taffy)
Tangled Web [1988] (Hoff, B.J.)
Tanglewood Murder [1980] (Kallen, Lucille)
🔳 Tango Key [1988] (Drake, Alison)
Tarot Murders [1978] (Warner, Mignon)
Taste for Burning (Bannister, Jo)
Taste for Death [1986] (James, P. D.) ★★
🔳 Taste for Murder [1994] (Bishop, Claudia)
Taste of Evil [1993] (Matthews, Patricia)
Tasty Way To Die [1990] (Laurence, Janet)
Tea-Totally Dead [1994] (Girdner, Jaqueline)
Tell Me What You Like [1993] (Allen, Kate)
Tell No Tales [1999] (Bland, Eleanor Taylor)
🔳 Telling Lies [1992] (Hornsby, Wendy)
Temporary Ghost [1989] (Friedman, Mickey)
🔳 Ten Commandments [1997] (Fraser, Anthea)
Ten Lords A-Leaping [1996] (Edwards, Ruth Dudley) ☆
Tender Death [1990] (Meyers, Annette)
🔳 Tensleep [1994] (Andrews, Sarah)
Termination Dust [1995] (Henry, Sue)
Terrorists [1976] (Sjöwall, Maj & Per Wahlöö)
Thanksgiving Day Murder [1995] (Harris, Lee)
Theban Mysteries [1972] (Cross, Amanda)
Then Hang All the Liars [1989] (Shankman, Sarah)
There Hangs the Knife [1988] (Muller, Marcia)
There is No Justice [1971] (Dominic, R.B.)
There Lies Your Love [1965] (Melville, Jennie)
There Was a Little Girl [1984] (Dewhurst, Eileen)
There Was a Little Girl [1998] (Cooper, Susan Rogers)
There's Nothing To Be Afraid Of [1985] (Muller, Marcia)
There's Something in a Sunday [1989] (Muller, Marcia)
These Bones Were Made for Dancin' [1995]
    (Meyers, Annette)

1 Thin Skins [1994] (McCafferty, Taylor)
Thin Woman [1984] (Cannell, Dorothy)
Thinner Than Blood [1992] (Shepherd, Stella)
Third Degree [1995] (Rayner, Claire)
Third Degree [1997] (Calloway, Kate)
1 Third Victim [1987] (Waltch, Lilla M.)
Third Way [1989] (Warmbold, Jean)
This Blessed Plot [1990] (Meek, M.R.D.)
1 This Business Is Murder [1993] (Christmas, Joyce)
1 This Dog for Hire [1996] (Benjamin, Carole Lea) ★
1 This Girl for Hire [includes Erik March] [1957]
   (Fickling, G.G.)
1 This Little Piggy Went To Murder [1994] (Hart, Ellen)
This Way Out [1989] (Radley, Sheila)
1 Those Who Hunt the Night [1988] (Hambly, Barbara)
Thread of Suspicion [1998] (Peart, Jane)
Three Bedrooms, One Corpse [1994] (Harris, Charlaine)
Three Hands in the Fountain [1997] (Davis, Lindsey)
Three Is a Crowd [1994] (Borton, D.B.)
Three, Three the Rivals [1992] (Fraser, Anthea)
Three To Get Deadly [1997] (Evanovich, Janet) ★
Three-Core Lead [1988] (Curzon, Clare)
Through a Gold Eagle [1996] (Monfredo, Miriam Grace)
1 Throw Darts at a Cheesecake [1992] (Dietz, Denise)
1 Thursday Club [1997] (Martin, Lee)
1 Thus Was Adonis Murdered [1981] (Caudwell, Sarah)
1 Thyme of Death [1992] (Albert, Susan Wittig) ☆☆
Tickled to Death [1994] (Hess, Joan)
Ties That Bind [1991] (Woods, Sherryl)
Tiger's Heart [1992] (Douglas, Lauren Wright)
1 Tiger's Palette [1998] (Fiedler, Jacqueline)
Tight as a Tick [1998] (Kelner, Toni L.P.)
Tightrope [1986] (White, Teri)
1 Till the Butchers Cut Him Down [1994] (Muller, Marcia)
Till the Old Men Die [1993] (Dawson, Janet)
1 Timber City Masks [1993] (York, Kieran)
1 Time and Trouble [1998] (Roberts, Gillian)
Time Bombs [1997] (Herndon, Nancy)
Time Expired [1993] (Dunlap, Susan)
Time Lapse [1992] (Law, Janice)
Time of Hope [1990] (Kelly, Susan B.)
Time To Depart [1995] (Davis, Lindsey)
Time To Die [1944] (Lawrence, Hilda)
Timely Death [1996] (Neel, Janet)
Tippy-Toe Murder [1994] (Meier, Leslie)
Tis the Season To Be Murdered [1994] (Wolzien, Valerie)
To Die For [1998] (Neel, Janet)
1 To Kill a Coconut (Moyes, Patricia)
To Kill a Queen [1992] (Knight, Alanna)
To Live and Die in Dixie [1993] (Trocheck,
   Kathy Hogan) ☆☆☆
1 To Make a Killing [1990] (Bedford, Jean)
To Make a Killing [1982] (Thomson, June)
1 To Mourn a Mischief [1989] (Quinton, Ann)
To Play the Fool [1995] (King, Laurie R.)
1 To Shield the Queen (Buckley, Fiona)
To Sleep, Perchance To Kill [1988] (Sims, L. V.)
Toast Before Dying [1998] (Edwards, Grace F.)
Toby's Folly [1990] (Arnold, Margot)
Tombstone Courage [1994] (Jance, J.A.)
Ton of Trouble [2002] (Murray, Lynne)
Too Close to the Edge [1987] (Dunlap, Susan)
Too Many Blondes [1996] (Henderson, Lauren)
Too Many Cooks [1994] (Pence, Joanne)
1 Too Many Crooks Spoil the Broth [1994] (Myers, Tamar)
Too Old for Murder [1999] (Hayden, G. Miki)
1 Too Sane a Murder [1984] (Martin, Lee)
Too Soon for Flowers [1999] (Miles, Margaret)
Tortoise Soup [1998] (Speart, Jessica)
1 Total Zone [1994] (Navratilova, Martina)
1 Touch a Cold Door [1989] (Roberts, Carey)

Touch and Go [1992] (Meek, M.R.D.)
Touch of Mortality [1996] (Granger, Ann)
Touch of Panic [1994] (Wright, L.R.) ☆
Touch of Terror [1995] (Matthews, Patricia)
Touch of the Grape [1998] (Bishop, Claudia)
Tourist Trap [1986] (Smith, Julie)
Tourists are for Trapping [1989] (Babson, Marian)
Toxic Shock (Paretsky, Sara) ★
1 Trace Elements [1986] (Knight, Kathryn Lasky)
1 Track of the Cat [1993] (Barr, Nevada) ★★
1 Track of the Scorpion [1996] (Davis, Val)
Trade-Off [1994] (O'Callaghan, Maxine)
1 Trail of Murder [1992] (Andreae, Christine) ☆
Trail of the Dragon [1988] (Kelly, Susan)
1 Traitor's Gate [1995] (Perry, Anne)
Tramp [1997] (Kellogg, Marne Davis)
1 Transcendental Murder [1964] (Langton, Jane)
Trap for Fools [1989] (Cross, Amanda)
Traveling With the Dead [1995] (Hambly, Barbara)
1 Tree of Death [1983] (Muller, Marcia)
Trial and Retribution [1997] (La Plante, Lynda)
Trial and Retribution II [1998] (La Plante, Lynda)
Trial by Fire [1990] (Fyfield, Frances)
Trial by Fury [1986] (Jance, J.A.)
Trick or Treat Murder [1996] (Meier, Leslie)
Trio in Three Flats [1981] (Dewhurst, Eileen)
1 Triple Play [1997] (Gunn, Elizabeth)
Triple Witch [1999] (Graves, Sarah)
Trojan Gold [1987] (Peters, Elizabeth) ☆
Trojan Hearse [1985] (Curzon, Clare)
Trophies and Dead Things [1990] (Muller, Marcia)
Tropical Issue [1983] (Dunnett, Dorothy)
Tropical Storm [1997] (Silva, Linda Kay)
Trouble in the Brasses [1989] (Craig, Alisa)
Trouble in the Town Hall [1996] (Dams, Jeanne M.)
Trouble in Transylvania [1993] (Wilson, Barbara)
Trouble Looking for a Place To Happen [1995] (Kelner,
   Toni L.P.)
1 Trouble of Fools [1987] (Barnes, Linda) ☆☆☆
Trouble With a Bad Fit [1996] (Crespi, Camilla)
Trouble With a Hot Summer [1997] (Crespi, Camilla)
1 Trouble With a Small Raise [1991] (Crespi, Camilla)
Trouble With Going Home [1995] (Crespi, Camilla)
Trouble With Moonlighting [1991] (Crespi, Camilla)
Trouble With Thin Ice [1993] (Crespi, Camilla)
Trouble With Too Much Sun [1992] (Crespi, Camilla)
1 Troublecross (Mann, Jessica)
Troubled Water [1993] (Gunning, Sally)
1 Troubled Waters [1982] (Lemarchand, Elizabeth)
Troubled Waters [1997] (Wheat, Carolyn)
1 True-Life Adventure [1985] (Smith, Julie)
Trunk Show [1995] (Glen, Alison)
1 Truth or Dare [1995] (Wilson, Anne)
Tunnel Vision [1994] (Paretsky, Sara) ☆
Turkey Tracks [1995] (Brown, Lizbie)
1 Turquoise Tattoo [1991] (Jacobs, Nancy Baker)
Turtle Baby [1995] (Padgett, Abigail)
Twanged [1998] (Clark, Carol Higgins)
1 Twice in a Blue Moon [1993] (Moyes, Patricia)
Twilight [1995] (Pickard, Nancy) ☆
Twister [1994] (Block, Barbara)
Two for the Dough [1996] (Evanovich, Janet) ★
Two for the Lions [1998] (Davis, Lindsey)
Two Points for Murder [1993] (Borton, D.B.)
1 Two-Bit Tango [1992] (Pincus, Elizabeth) ★
Two-Story Frame [1997] (McClellan, Tierney)

U

1 Unbalanced Accounts [1986] (Gallison, Kate)
Unbound [1997] (Kaewert, Julie Wallin)
Uncertain Death (Holt, Hazel)

Uncertain Death [1996] (Coburn, Laura)
▪ Uncommon Murder [1993] (Donald, Anabel)
Unconscious Truths [1998] (Kiecolt-Glaser, Janice)
Under Contract [1986] (Cody, Liza) ☆
Under My Skin [1995] (Dunant, Sarah)
Under My Skin [1993] (Maiman, Jaye)
Under Orion [1978] (Law, Janice)
Under the Beetle's Cellar [1995] (Walker,
    Mary Willis) ★★★
Under the Dragon's Tail [1998] (Jennings, Maureen)
▪ Under the Influence [1989] (Travis, Elizabeth)
Under Water [1992] (Gunning, Sally)
Underdog [1996] (Berenson, Laurien)
Uneaseful Death [1988] (Hardwick, Mollie)
Uneasy Lies [1990] (Zaremba, Eve)
Unexpected Corpse [1990] (Oliphant, B. J.)
Unexpected Developments [1984] (Dominic, R.B.)
▪ Unexpected Mrs. Pollifax [1966] (Gilman, Dorothy)
Unforgiving Minutes [prequel] [1988] (Pulver,
    Mary Monica)
Unfortunate Prairie Occurance [1998]
    (Harrison, Jamie)
Unhappy Returns [1977] (Lemarchand, Elizabeth)
Unholy Alliance [1996] (Gregory, Susanna)
Unholy Angels [1996] (Gallison, Kate)
Unholy Ghosts [1992] (Greenwood, D.M.)
Union Jack [1993] (McDermid, Val)
▪ Unkindness of Ravens [1985] (Rendell, Ruth) ☆
Unmasking Kelsey [1988] (Hooper, Kay)
Unnatural Causes [1967] (James, P. D.)
Unnatural Exposure [1997] (Cornwell, Patricia)
Unnatural Selection [2000] (North, Suzanne)
▪ Unorthodox Methods [1989] (Valentine, Deborah)
▪ Unorthodox Practices [1989] (Piesman, Marissa)
Unprintable [1998] (Kaewert, Julie Wallin)
Unquestioned Loyalty [1995] (Lamb, J. Dayne)
▪ Unquiet Grave [1987] (LaPierre, Janet) ☆
Unsafe Keeping [1995] (Cail, Carol)
▪ Unsolicited [1994] (Kaewert, Julie Wallin)
▪ Unsuitable Job for a Woman [1972] (James, P. D.) ☆
▪ Until Death [1994] (Whitney, Polly) ☆
Until Death Do Us Part [1997] (McGuire, Christine)
Until It Hurts [1997] (Whitney, Polly)
Until Justice is Done [1994] (McGuire, Christine)
▪ Until Proven Guilty [1985] (Jance, J.A.)
▪ Until Proven Guilty [1993] (McGuire, Christine)
Until Proven Innocent [1990] (Kelly, Susan)
Until The Bough Breaks [1998] (McGuire, Christine)
Until the End [1998] (Davis, Kaye)
Until the End of Time [1995] (Whitney, Polly)
Until the Twelfth of Never [2000] (Whitney, Polly)
Unto the Grave [1986] (Penn, John)
Up Jumps the Devil [1996] (Maron, Margaret) ★
▪ Up Next [1998] (Star, Nancy)
Urn Burial [1996] (Greenwood, Kerry)
▪ User Deadly (Danks, Denise)
Used To Kill [1993] (O'Donnell, Lillian)

V

Vacations Can Be Murder [1995] (Shelton, Connie)
Valentine's Day Murder [1997] (Harris, Lee)
Vampire Bytes [1998] (Grant, Linda)
Vane Pursuit [1989] (MacLeod, Charlotte)
▪ Vanished Child [Boston] [1992] (Smith, Sarah)
Vanishing Act [1998] (Block, Barbara)
Veiled Antiquity [1998] (MacPherson, Rett)
▪ Veiled One [1988] (Rendell, Ruth)
Vendetta's Victim [1998] (Matthews, Alex)
Venetian Reckoning (Leon, Donna)
Vengeance in Death [1997] (Robb, J.D.)
Venus in Copper [1991] (Davis, Lindsey)

Verdict in Blood [1998] (Bowen, Gail)
Verdict on Winter [1996] (Dewhurst, Eileen)
Verdict Unsafe [1996] (McGown, Jill)
▪ Veronica's Sisters [1992] (Moffat, Gwen)
▪ Very Eligible Corpse [1998] (Griffin, Annie)
Very Particular Murder [1989] (Haymon, S. T.)
Vial Murders [1994] (Landreth, Marsha)
▪ Victims [1981] (Gill, B.M.)
View From Frog Mountain [2000] (Cramer, Rebecca)
Vines of Ferrara [1986] (Coker, Carolyn)
Vintage Murder [1994] (Smith, Janet L.)
▪ Violence Beat [1997] (Sandstrom, Eve K.)
Violent End [1988] (Page, Emma)
Virgin Territory [1996] (Todd, Marilyn)
Vision of Death [1993] (Matthews, Patricia)
Vital Lies [1991] (Hart, Ellen)
Vow of Adoration [1997] (Black, Veronica)
Vow of Chastity [1992] (Black, Veronica)
Vow of Compassion [1998] (Black, Veronica)
Vow of Devotion [1994] (Black, Veronica)
Vow of Fidelity [1995] (Black, Veronica)
Vow of Obedience [1993] (Black, Veronica)
Vow of Penance [1994] (Black, Veronica)
Vow of Poverty [1996] (Black, Veronica)
Vow of Sanctity [1993] (Black, Veronica)
▪ Vow of Silence [1990] (Black, Veronica)
Vow of Silence [1988] (Hoff, B.J.)
Voyage of the Chianti [1987] (Morison, B.J.)

W

Wages of Sin [1994] (Woods, Sherryl)
Waikiki Widow [1953] (Sheridan, Juanita)
Wait for the Dark [1993] (Crowleigh, Ann)
Wake of the Hornet [2000] (Davis, Val)
Wake the Dead [1992] (Simpson, Dorothy)
Wake Up, Darlin' Corey [1984] (Wren, M.K.)
Walk a Crooked Mile [1994] (Dain, Catherine)
Walk Through the Fire [1999] (Muller, Marcia)
Walking Dead Man [1992] (Kittredge, Mary)
Wandering Arm [1995] (Newman, Sharan) ☆
Wandering Soul Murders [1993] (Bowen, Gail)
Wanted Dude or Alive [1994] (Morgan, Kate)
War and Peas [1996] (Churchill, Jill)
Watchdog [1998] (Berenson, Laurien)
Wavewalker [1996] (Duffy, Stella)
Way of a Serpent [1993] (Bell, Pauline)
Way of the Traitor [1997] (Rowland, Laura Joh)
▪ We Know Where You Live [1995] (Taylor, Jean)
We Wish You a Merry Murder [1991] (Wolzien, Valerie)
Weathering the Storm [1994] (Silva, Linda Kay)
Weaver's Inheritance [1998] (Sedley, Kate)
Weaver's Tale (Sedley, Kate)
▪ Web of Deception [1996] (Peart, Jane)
▪ Wed and Buried [1998] (Daheim, Mary)
Weddings Are Murder [1998] (Wolzien, Valerie)
Wee Paws at a Murder [1999] (O'Kane, Leslie)
Weighed in the Balance [1996] (Perry, Anne)
Well-Schooled in Murder [1990] (George, Elizabeth)
What Men Say [1993] (Smith, Joan)
What Should You Know of Dying? [1967] (Wells, Tobias)
What To Do Until the Undertaker Comes [1971]
    (Wells, Tobias)
▪ What's a Girl Gotta Do? [1994] (Hayter, Sparkle) ★
▪ What's a Woman Gotta Do? [1998] (Coleman, Evelyn)
Whatever Happened to Jennifer Steele? [1996]
    (Ruryk, Jean)
▪ Wheel Turns [1983] (Lemarchand, Elizabeth)
▪ When Death Comes Stealing [1994] (Wesley,
    Valerie Wilson) ☆
▪ When Did We Lose Harriet? [1997] (Sprinkle, Patricia H.)
When First We Practice [1999] (Szymanski, Therese)

When in Greece [1969] (Lathen, Emma) ☆
When Some Body Disappears [1999] (Szymanski, Therese)
∎ When the Dancing Stops [1997] (Szymanski, Therese)
When the Dead Speak [1998] (Szymanski, Therese)
When the Gods Take a Wife [1999] (Coleman, Evelyn)
When Wallflowers Die [1996] (Prowell, Sandra West)
Where Death Lies [1991] (Fallon, Ann C.)
∎ Where Echoes Live [1991] (Muller, Marcia) ☆
Where Evil Sleeps [1996] (Wesley, Valerie Wilson)
∎ Where Lawyers Fear To Tread [1987] (Matera, Lia) ☆☆
Where Nobody Dies [1986] (Wheat, Carolyn)
Where Old Bones Lie [1993] (Granger, Ann)
Where the Bodies Are Buried [1998] (Dawson, Janet)
Where There's a Will [1999] (Squire, Elizabeth Daniels)
Where To Choose [1999] (Mickelbury, Penny)
Whiff of Sulphur [1987] (Linscott, Gillian)
∎ While Other People Sleep [1998] (Muller, Marcia)
While the Coffin Waited (Sheridan, Juanita)
White Hand [1988] (Warmbold, Jean)
White Lightning [1995] (Woods, Sherryl)
∎ White Male Running [1985] (Webb, Martha G.)
White Noise [1997] (Zaremba, Eve)
Whited Sepulchres (Perry, Anne)
Whitelands Affair [1989] (Clarke, Anna)
Who Dropped Peter Pan? [1995] (Dentinger, Jane)
∎ Who Goes Home? [1986] (Lemarchand, Elizabeth)
∎ Who Is Simon Warwick? [1979] (Moyes, Patricia)
∎ Who Killed Blanche Dubois [1999] (Buggé, Carole)
∎ Who Killed Cock Robin? [1990] (Duffy, Margaret)
∎ Who Killed What's-Her-Name? [1994] (Squire, Elizabeth Daniels)
Who Saw Her Die? (Moyes, Patricia)
Who Saw Him Die? [1987] (Radley, Sheila)
∎ Whoever Has the Heart [1993] (Melville, Jennie)
∎ Whoever I Am [1982] (Dewhurst, Eileen)
Whom the Gods Love [1995] (Ross, Kate)
Whose Death Is It Anyway? [1997] (Squire, Elizabeth Daniels)
Why Aren't They Screaming? [1988] (Smith, Joan)
Wicked Designs [1980] (O'Donnell, Lillian)
Wicked Games [1998] (Hart, Ellen)
Wicked, Loving Murder [1985] (Papazoglou, Orania)
∎ Wicked Slice [1989] (Elkins, Charlotte & Aaron)
∎ Wicked Way To Burn [1998] (Miles, Margaret)
Wicked Winter [1996] (Sedley, Kate)
Widow's Club [1988] (Cannell, Dorothy) ☆☆
Widow's End [1993] (Penn, John)
Widow's Peak [1994] (Linscott, Gillian)
∎ Widows [1983] (La Plante, Lynda)
Widows II [1985] (La Plante, Lynda)
Widows' Watch [1995] (Herndon, Nancy)
∎ Wild and Lonely Place [1995] (Muller, Marcia) ☆
Wild Island [1978] (Fraser, Antonia)
Wild Justice [1987] (Grant-Adamson, Lesley)
Wild Kat [1994] (Kijewski, Karen)
Wildcrafters [1998] (Moody, Skye Kathleen)
∎ Will To Kill [1983] (Penn, John)
∎ Winding up the Serpent [1995] (Masters, Priscilla)
Windsor Knot [1990] (McCrumb, Sharyn)
Windsor Red [1988] (Melville, Jennie)
Windy City Blues [short stories] [1995] (Paretsky, Sara)
Wink a Hopeful Eye [1993] (Danks, Denise)
∎ Winona's Web [1997] (Cogan, Priscilla)
Winter Garden Mystery [1995] (Dunn, Carola)
∎ Winter Widow [1992] (Weir, Charlene) ★★☆
Wire in the Blood [1998] (McDermid, Val)
∎ Wish You Were Here [1990] (Brown, Rita Mae)
Witch Hill Murder [1977] (Winslow, Pauline Glen)
Witch Miss Seeton [1971] (Crane, Hamilton)
Witch of the Palo Duro [1997] (Medawar, Mardi Oakley)
Witches' Bane [1993] (Albert, Susan Wittig)

∎ Witching Murder [1990] (Melville, Jennie)
∎ With Child [1996] (King, Laurie R.) ☆
∎ With Deadly Intent [1993] (Hendricksen, Louise)
∎ With Flowers That Fell [1982] (Meek, M.R.D.)
With Friends Like These [1993] (Roberts, Gillian)
With Intent To Kill [1996] (Ferguson, Frances)
Withdrawing Room [1980] (MacLeod, Charlotte)
Without Consent [1996] (Fyfield, Frances)
Without Due Process [1992] (Jance, J.A.)
∎ Without Trace [1989] (John, Katherine)
Witness [1969] (Uhnak, Dorothy)
Witness to Evil [1997] (Dawson, Janet)
Wolf in Death's Clothing [1995] (Quinn, Elizabeth)
∎ Wolf in the Shadows [1993] (Muller, Marcia) ★☆☆
Wolf Path [1992] (Van Gieson, Judith)
Wolf to Slaughter [1967] (Rendell, Ruth)
Wolf Whispered Death [1986] (Moore, Barbara)
Wolf Whistle [1998] (Todd, Marilyn)
Wolves [2000] (Dengler, Sandy)
∎ Woman Who Was Not There [1996] (Melville, Jennie)
Woman's Own Mystery (Wakefield, Hannah)
Woman's Place [1994] (Grant, Linda)
Word After Dying [1996] (Granger, Ann)
Word Is Death [1997] (Clayton, Mary)
Work for a Million [1987] (Zaremba, Eve)
∎ Working Murder [1989] (Boylan, Eleanor) ☆
∎ World the Color of Salt [1992] (Ayres, Noreen)
Worm of Doubt [1987] (Meek, M.R.D.)
Worse Than Death [1992] (Bedford, Jean)
Wrack and Rune [1982] (MacLeod, Charlotte)
Wreath for My Sister [1997] (Masters, Priscilla)
∎ Wreath for the Bride [1990] (O'Donnell, Lillian)
Wreath of Honesty [1990] (Burden, Pat)
∎ Writers of the Purple Sage [1994] (Smith, Barbara Burnett) ☆
Written in Blood [1994] (Graham, Caroline) ☆
Wrong Rite [1992] (Craig, Alisa)
Wrongful Death [1999] (Arnold, Catherine)
∎ Wychford Murders [1986] (Gosling, Paula)
∎ Wyndham Case [1993] (Paton Walsh, Jill)

X

∎ Xibalba Murders [Mexico] [1997] (Hamilton, Lyn) ☆

Y

Yakuza, Go Home! [1993] (Wingate, Anne)
Yankee Doodle Dead [1998] (Hart, Carolyn G.)
Year 2000 Killers [1999] (Morrone, Wenda Wardell)
Year of the Monkey [1988] (Berry, Carole)
Yellow Villa [1964] (Blanc, Suzanne)
Yom Kippur Murder [1992] (Harris, Lee)
You Bet Your Life [1995] (Jorgensen, Christine T.)
You Have the Right To Remain Silent [1992] (Paul, Barbara)
Young Can Die Protesting [1969] (Wells, Tobias)
Your Royal Hostage [1987] (Fraser, Antonia)

Z

Zach's Law [1987] (Hooper, Kay)
Zadock's Treasure [1979] (Arnold, Margot)
Zen Attitude [1998] (Massey, Sujata)
Zombies of the Gene Pool [1992] (McCrumb, Sharyn)

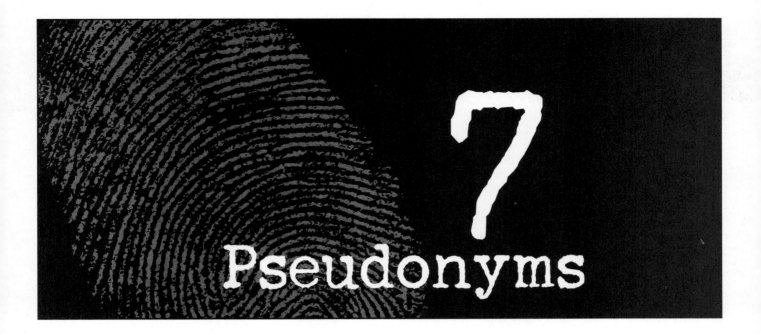

7 Pseudonyms

Pseudonym literally means 'false name,' from the Greek pseudo meaning false, pretended, or unreal, and -*nym*, the root for name, as in synonym and homonym. The term for an author's own name, or autonym, also derives from the Greek autos, or self. In the publishing world, pseudonyms are used to hide or protect an author's identity, often at the insistence of the publisher. Throughout Detecting Women and Detecting Women Pocket Guide, [P] is used to designate a pseudonymous author.

The primary sources for author pseudonyms and autonyms identified in Detecting Women are Hawk's Authors' Pseudonyms by Pat Hawk, Contemporary Authors, mystery convention programs, and in some cases, the authors themselves. Detecting Women is not in the business of 'outing' authors who prefer to remain anonymous. However, when information regarding an author's identity has been published in more than one source, we have included that information in our pseudonym listings.

At one time, the most common reason for the use of a pseudonym was to hide the author's identity for professional reasons. When Carolyn G. Heilbrun published her first Kate Fansler mystery in 1964, her colleagues in the English department at Columbia University, where she was an assistant professor, would have been horrified (and hugely disapproving) if the novel had appeared under her own name. Heilbrun kept her mystery-writing identity a secret until after she had been granted tenure. English professor Lynette Carpenter faced a similar situation with her D.B. Borton mysteries, although in Carpenter's case, the pseudonymously-written mysteries later worked to her advantage. During her battle for tenure, Carpenter elected to tell the University about her fiction writing. To her great surprise, the University was delighted to have a published mystery author in its ranks and she was granted tenure.

Pseudonyms are frequently used when a pair of authors collaborate on a work of fiction, particularly if a man and woman are writing together. A single author name fits more neatly on the book's cover, and a female (or androgynous) name is thought to have greater appeal to a largely female audience. For their Victorian mysteries featuring Kathryn Ardleigh and Sir Charles Sheridan, Susan Wittig Albert and her husband Bill Albert write together as Robin Paige (named for Susan's daughter Robin). Husband and wife, Robert and Angela Irvine, write the Nicolette Sheridan series as Val Davis. She chose Val because she likes Val Kilmer; he chose Davis because it is his father's middle name. For their 12th century Crusader series, the already-pseudonymous Susanna Gregory and her husband Beau Riffenburgh write together as Simon Beaufort, a pseudonym chosen by their publisher, St. Martin's Press.

Writers who work in multiple genres frequently use pseudonyms at the insistence of their publishers. While Patricia Finney writes sweeping historical fiction under her own name, her Robert Carey mysteries are published under the name P.F. Chisholm. Ellen Recknor writes western fiction under her own name and mysteries featuring ex-Pinkerton agent Maggie Maguire as Kate Bryan. When a well-known author is especially prolific, publishers often insist on pseudonyms for work in different genres. With more than 40 novels to her credit, Sheri S. Tepper writes science fiction and horror under her own name and mysteries as A.J. Orde and B.J. Oliphant. She has also written horror as E.E. Horlak.

Sometimes a mystery series is written as a work for hire, with the publishing house owing the pseudonym, hence the term 'house name.' The best known house name in mysteries is Carolyn Keene, author of the Nancy Drew series. Many authors, including Susan and Bill Albert, have written Nancy Drew mysteries, all of which appear under the name Carolyn Keene. Sometimes a single author writes all of the mysteries appearing under a house name. Such is the case with Cheryl Arguile, who writes the Mrs. Jeffries series as Emily Brightwell, and Doreen Roberts, whose Pennyfoot Hotel mysteries are written as Kate Kingsbury. In the case of Melissa Cleary, three authors in succession have written about Jackie Walsh and her ex-police dog Jake. Beginning with book 10, the series is written by Shamus-nominated author Bridget McKenna.

Where it was once commonplace for publishers to use initials or androgynous names to hide a woman author's gender (J.A. Jance, for example), initials and female pseudonyms are now used by some male writers. When Father Dowling's creator Ralph McInerny wrote about Sister Mary Teresa Dempsey, he became Monica Quill (a literal translation of pen name). The first novel of Canadian journalist Douglas Whiteway (Death at Buckingham Palace) was published in early 1996 under the name C.C. Benison. With a series featuring a young Canadian housemaid in the service of the Queen, an author who was presumed to be female seemed a prudent choice.

Another use of pseudonyms involves celebrity or fictional authors, such as Margaret Truman or Jessica Fletcher. It is strongly suspected that ghostwriter Donald Bain is the author-for-hire behind Margaret Truman's Capital Area mysteries and the exploits of the fictional Jessica Fletcher of Murder, She Wrote fame.

Lydia Adamson's light-hearted animal mysteries currently number more than two dozen titles in three series. When the Alice Nestleton series, featuring a New York actress and cat owner, was launched in 1990, it was thought the books would have a larger audience if the author was thought to be a woman. In this case, the choice of Adamson also put the books at the beginning of the mystery section, assuming standard alphabetical shelving by author's last name. The Adamson debut was so successful that her publisher commissioned two more series, and now releases six Adamson books each year (two titles per series). Unfortunately, more than a few female readers have been disappointed to learn that the charming Mrs. Adamson is, in fact, Frank King.

The presentation of pseudonyms and pen names in this chapter takes two formats. Entries in List 1 are sorted by pseudonym, whenever a pseudonym has been used for a mystery series written by a woman who is part of the Detecting Women data base. List 2 (a re-sorting of List 1) starts with the author's autonym and links it to pseudonyms used for her mystery series. Both lists include the name of the series character written pseudonymously, date of the first book and number of books in the series, as well as additional pseudonyms used by the author. Other Pseudonyms include work in other genres such as science fiction, westerns, fantasy, horror, mainstream fiction and books for children.

If you know the pseudonym for a mystery series and are looking for the author's identity, start with List 1. If you are looking for pseudonyms a particular author may have used, List 2 will be more helpful. Because this information is tied to mystery series written by women using pseudonyms, you will not find an author listed unless series mysteries are part of the pseudonym equation. For example, Kathryn Lasky Knight writes children's books as Kathryn Lasky, but her children's books are not part of the Detecting Women data base. Hence, there is no listing in this chapter for Kathryn Lasky Knight writing as Kathryn Lasky.

Pseudonym	Series Character	1- #	Autonym	Other Pseudonyms

List 1 - Pseudonyms Used for Mystery Series Written by Women

Pseudonym	Series Character	1- #	Autonym	Other Pseudonyms
Aird, Catherine	Christopher Dennis "Seedy" Sloan	'66 - 16	McIntosh, Kinn Hamilton	
Allen, Irene	Elizabeth Elliot	'92 - 4	Peters, Elsa Kirsten	
Allen, Kate	Alison Kaine	'93 - 4	undisclosed	
Arnold, Catherine	Karen Perry-Mondori	'96 - 3	Sandberg, Theresa	
Arnold, Margot	Penny Spring & Toby Glendower	'79 - 12	Cook, Petronelle	
Baker, Nikki	Virginia Kelly	'91 - 3	undisclosed	
Barrett, Margaret	Susan Given	'98 - 2	Rudman, Anne & Charles Dennis	
Barron, Stephanie	Jane Austen	'96 - 3	Mathews, Francine	
Bartholomew, Nancy	Sierra Lavotini	'98 - 2	undisclosed	
Beaton, M.C.	Agatha Raisin	'92 - 8	Chesney, Marion	Sarah Chester Helen Crampton Ann Fairfax Jennie Tremaine Charlotte Ward
Beaton, M.C.	Hamish Macbeth	'85 - 14	Chesney, Marion	Sarah Chester Helen Crampton Ann Fairfax Jennie Tremaine Charlotte Ward
Beaufort, Simon	Geoffrey de Mappestone	'98 - 2		
Beecham, Rose	Amanda Valentine	'92 - 3	Fulton, Jennifer	
Belfort, Sophie	Molly Rafferty	'86 - 3	Auspitz, Kate	
Berne, Karin	Ellie Gordon	'85 - 3	Bernell, Sue & Michaela Karni	
Bishop, Claudia	Sarah & Meg Quilliam	'94 - 6	Stanton, Mary	
Black, Veronica	Joan, Sister	'90 - 10	Peters, Maureen	Catherine Darby Elizabeth Law Judith Rothman
Borthwick, J.S.	Sarah Deane & Alex McKenzie	'82 - 9	Creighton, Joan Scott	
Borton, D.B.	Cat Caliban	'93 - 6	Carpenter, Lynette	Della Borton
Borton, Della	Gilda Liberty	'99 - 1	Carpenter, Lynette	
Bowen, Rhys	Evan Evans	'97 - 3	Quin-Harkin, Janet	
Brightwell, Emily	Gerald Witherspoon & Hepzibah Jeffries	'93 - 13	Arguile, Cheryl	
Brill, Toni	Midge Cohen	'91 - 2	Olcott, Anthony & Martha	
Brown, Lizbie	Elizabeth Blair	'92 - 2	Marriott, Mary	
Bryan, Kate	Maggie Maguire	'98 - 2	Recknor, Ellen	
Buckley, Fiona	Ursula Blanchard	'97 - 2	Anand, Valerie	
Castle, Jayne	Guinevere Jones	'86 - 4	Krentz, Jayne Ann	Jayne Bentley Amanda Glass Stephanie James Amanda Quick Jayne Taylor
Caudwell, Sarah	Hilary Tamar	'81 - 4	Cockburn, Sarah	
Charles, Kate	Lucy Kingsley & David Middleton-Brown	'91 - 5	Chase, Carol	
Chisholm, P.F.	Robert Carey	'94 - 4	Finney, Patricia	
Churchill, Jill	Jane Jeffry	'89 - 11	Brooks, Janice Young	
Churchill, Jill	Lily & Robert Brewster	'99 - 1	Brooks, Janice Young	
Cleary, Melissa	Jackie Walsh & Jake [10-]	'92 - 10	McKenna, Bridget	
Cody, Liza	Anna Lee	'80 - 6	Nassim, Liza	
Cody, Liza	Eva Wylie	'92 - 3	Nassim, Liza	
Cohen, Anthea	Agnes Carmichael	'82 - 15	Simpson, Doris	
Cooper, Natasha	Trish Maguire	'98 - 1	Wright, Daphne	
Cooper, Natasha	Willow King	'90 - 7	Wright, Daphne	

Pseudonym	Series Character	1 - #	Autonym	Other Pseudonyms
List 1 - Pseudonyms Used for Mystery Series Written by Women				
Craig, Alisa	Dittany Henbit Monk & Osbert Monk	'81 - 5	MacLeod, Charlotte	
Craig, Alisa	Madoc & Janet Rhys	'80 - 5	MacLeod, Charlotte	
Crane, Hamilton	Emily D. Seeton	'68 -22	Mason, Sarah J.	
Crespi, Camilla	Simona Griffo	'91 - 7	Trinchieri, Camilla	
Cross, Amanda	Kate Fansler	'64 -12	Heilbrun, Carolyn G.	
Crowleigh, Ann	Mirinda & Clare Clively	'93 - 2	Cummings, Barbara & Jo-Ann Power	
Curzon, Clare	Mike Yeadings	'83 -13	Buchanan, Eileen-Marie Duell	Marie Buchanan Rhona Petrie
Davis, Val	Nicolette Scott	'96 - 3	Irvine, Angela & Robert	
Dominic, R.B.	Ben Safford	'68 - 7	Latsis, Mary Jane & Martha Henissart	Emma Lathen
Drake, Alison	Aline Scott	'88 - 4	MacGregor, Patricia Janeshutz	Trish Janeshutz T.J. MacGregor
Dymmoch, Michael Allen	John Thinnes & Jack Caleb	'93 - 3	undisclosed	
Edghill, Rosemary	Karen Hightower aka Bast	'94 - 3	Bes-Shahar, Eluki	
Eyre, Elizabeth	Sigismondo	'92 - 6	Staynes, Jill & Margaret Storey	Susannah Stacey
Fawcett, Quinn	Mycroft Holmes	'94 - 3	Yarbro, Chelsea Quinn & Bill Fawcett	
Fawcett, Quinn	Victoire Vernet	'93 - 2	Yarbro, Chelsea Quinn & Bill Fawcett	
Ferguson, Frances	Jane Perry	'93 - 4	Perkins, Barbara-Serene	
Ferris, Monica	Betsy Devonshire	'99 - 2	Kuhfeld, Mary Pulver	Mary Monica Pulver
Fickling, G.G.	Erik March	'62 - 3	Fickling, Gloria & Forrest E.	
Fickling, G.G.	Honey West	'57 - 11	Fickling, Gloria & Forrest E.	
Frazer, Margaret	Dame Frevisse [7-10]	'92 - 8	Frazer, Gail	
Frazer, Margaret	Dame Frevisse [1-6]	'92 - 8	Kuhfeld, Mary Pulver & Gail Frazer	Monica Ferris
French, Linda	Teddy Morelli	'98 - 3	Mariz, Linda French	
Fyfield, Frances	Helen West	'88 - 6	Hegarty, Frances	
Fyfield, Frances	Sarah Fortune	'89 - 2	Hegarty, Frances	
Gill, B.M.	Tom Maybridge	'81 - 3	Trimble, Barbara Margaret	Margaret Blake Barbara Gilmour
Giroux, E.X.	Robert Forsythe & Abigail Sanderson	'84 - 10	Shannon, Doris	
Glen, Alison	Charlotte Sams	'92 - 2	Lowry, Cheryl Meredith & Louise Vetter	
Grant, Linda	Catherine Sayler	'88 - 6	Williams, Linda V.	
Graves, Sarah	Jacobia Triptree	'98 - 3	Kittredge, Mary	
Gray, Dulcie	Insp. Supt. Cardiff	'60 - 2	Dennison, Dulcie Winifred Catherine	
Gray, Gallagher	Theodore S. Hubbert & Auntie Lil	'91 - 4	Munger, Katy	
Gregory, Susanna	Matthew Bartholomew	'96 - 4	undisclosed	Simon Beaufort
Griffin, Annie	Hannah Malloy & Kiki Goldstein	'98 - 2	Chapman, Sally	
Haddam, Jane	Gregor Demarkian	'90 -15	Papazoglou, Orania	
Hadley, Joan	Theo Bloomer	'86 - 2	Hess, Joan	
Hall, Patricia	Laura Ackroyd & Michael Thackeray	'93 - 5	O'Connor, Maureen	
Haney, Lauren	Lt. Bak	'97 - 2	Winkelman, Betty	
Harris, Lee	Christine Bennett	'92 - 11	Leahy, Syrell Rogovin	
Hart, Ellen	Jane Lawless	'89 - 8	Boenhardt, Patricia	
Hart, Ellen	Sophie Greenway	'94 - 4	Boenhardt, Patricia	
Hebden, Juliet	Clovis Pel	'79 -22	Harris, Juliet	
Horansky, Ruby	Nikki Trakos	'90 - 2	Holland, Rebecca	
Jackson, Hialeah	Annabelle Hardy-Maratos & Dave the Monkeyman	'98 - 2	Whitney, Polly	P.L. Whitney

List 1 - Pseudonyms Used for Mystery Series Written by Women

Jackson, Marian J.A.	Abigail Patience Danforth	'90 - 5	Rogers, Marian	
John, Cathie	Kate Cavanaugh	'97 - 4	Celestri, Cathie & John	
John, Katherine	Trevor Joseph	'89 - 3	Nadolny, Karo	
Jones, D.J.H.	Nancy Cook	'93 - 2	unknown	
Kingsbury, Kate	Cecily Sinclair	'93 - 11	Roberts, Doreen	
Lacey, Sarah	Leah Hunter	'92 - 4	Mitchell, Kay	
Lake, Deryn	John Rawlings & the Blind Beak	'94 - 4	Lampitt, Dinah	
Lambert, Mercedes	Whitney Logan & Lupe Ramos	'91 - 2	unknown	
Lathen, Emma	John Putnam Thatcher	'61 -24	Latsis, Mary Jane & Martha Henissart	R.B. Dominc
Lawrence, Margaret	Hannah Trevor	'96 - 3	Lorens, Margaret Keilstrup	M.K. Lorens
Livesay, Ann	Barry Ross	'98 - 5	Sutton, Ann	
Lorens, M.K.	Winston Marlowe Sherman	'90 - 5	Lorens, Margaret Keilstrup	
MacGregor, T.J.	Quin St. James & Mike McCleary	'86 - 10	MacGregor, Patricia Janeshutz	Alison Drake Trish Janeshutz
Mackay, Amanda	Hannah Land	'76 - 2	Smith, Amanda Mackay	
MacPherson, Rett	Torie O'Shea	'97 - 2	Allen, Lauretta	
Marcy, Jean	Meg Darcy	'97 - 2	Hutchinson, Jean & Marcy Jacobs	
Martin, Lee	Deb Ralston	'84 -13	Wingate, Anne	Martha G. Webb
Mather, Linda	Jo Hughes	'94 - 2	Ainsbury, Linda	
Maxwell, A.E.	Fiddler & Fiora Flynn	'85 - 8	Maxwell, Ann & Evan	Elizabeth Lowell
McCafferty, Taylor	Haskell Blevins	'90 - 6	McCafferty, Barbara Taylor	Tierney McClellan
McClellan, Tierney	Schuyler Ridgway	'95 - 4	McCafferty, Barbara Taylor	Taylor McCafferty
McCormick, Claire	John Waltz	'82 - 3	Labus, Marta Haake	
McKevett, G.A.	Savannah Reid	'95 - 4	Massie, Sonja	
McNab, Claire	Carol Ashton	'88 - 10	Carmichael, Claire	
Melville, Jennie	Charmian Daniels	'62 - '	Butler, Gwendoline	
Meyers, Maan	The Tonnemans	'92 - 6	Meyers, Annette & Martin	
Michaels, Barbara	Georgetown house	'68 - 3	Mertz, Barbara	Elizabeth Peters
Morgan, Kate	Dewey James	'90 - 7	Whitman, Ann Hamilton	
Neel, Janet	John McLeish & Francesca Wilson	'88 - 6	Cohen, Janet	
O'Shaughnessy, Perri	Nina Reilly	'95 - 4	O'Shaughnessy, Pamela & Mary	
Oliphant, B.J.	Shirley McClintock	'90 - 7	Tepper, Sheri S.	A.J. Orde E.E. Horlak
Orde, A.J.	Jason Lynx	'89 - 6	Tepper, Sheri S.	B.J. Oliphant E.E. Horlak
Page, Emma	Kelsey, Inspector	'80 - 9	Tirbutt, Honoria	
Paige, Robin	Kathryn Ardleigh & Charles Sheridan	'94 - 5	Albert, Susan & Bill Albert	Nicholas Adams Franklin W. Dixon Carolyn Keene
Penn, John	George Thorne	'83 - 6	Harcourt, Palma & Jack H. Trotman	
Penn, John	Richard Tansey	'88 -12	Harcourt, Palma & Jack H. Trotman	
Peters, Elizabeth	Amelia Peabody	'75 - 12	Mertz, Barbara	Barbara Michaels
Peters, Elizabeth	Jacqueline Kirby	'72 - 4	Mertz, Barbara	Barbara Michaels
Peters, Elizabeth	Vicky Bliss	'73 - 5	Mertz, Barbara	Barbara Michaels
Peterson, Audrey	Claire Camden	'92 - 3	Buckland, Audrey Nelson	
Peterson, Audrey	Jane Winfield	'88 - 6	Buckland, Audrey Nelson	
Petrie, Rhona	Marcus MacLurg	'63 - 5	Buchanan, Eileen-Marie Duell	Marie Buchanan Claire Curzon
Petrie, Rhona	Nassim Pride	'67 - 2	Buchanan, Eileen-Marie Duell	Marie Buchanan Claire Curzon
Quest, Erica	Kate Maddox	'88 - 3	Sawyer, John & Nancy Buckingham Sawyer	Christina Abbey Nancy Buckingham Nancy John Hilary London

Pseudonym	Series Character	1 - #	Autonym	Other Pseudonyms
List 1 - Pseudonyms Used for Mystery Series Written by Wommen				
Quinn, Elizabeth	Lauren Maxwell	'93 - 4	Barnard, Elizabeth Quinn	
Radley, Sheila	Douglas Quantrill & Hilary Lloyd	'78 - 9	Robinson, Sheila	
Robb, J.D.	Eve Dallas	'95 - 8	Roberts, Nora	
Roberts, Gillian	Amanda Pepper	'87 - 8	Greber, Judith	
Roberts, Gillian	Emma Howe & Billie August	'98 - 1	Greber, Judith	
Robinson, Leah Ruth	Evelyn Sutcliffe	'88 - 2	Rousmaniere, Leah	
Roe, Caroline	Isaac & Bishop Berenguer	'98 - 3	Sale, Medora	
Romberg, Nina	Marian Winchester	'89 - 2	undisclosed	Jane Archer Asa Drake
Ross, Annie	Bel Carson	'95 - 3	unknown	
Ruryk, Jean	Catherine Wilde	'94 - 3	Shepherd, Jean	Eugenie Melnyk
Sedley, Kate	Roger the Chapman	'91 - 8	Clarke, Brenda Honeyman	
Shone, Anna	Ulysses Finnegan Donaghue	'94 - 2	Shone, Bridget Ann	
Smith, J.C.S.	Quentin Jacoby	'80 - 2	Smith, Jane S.	
Stacey, Susannah	Robert Bone	'87 - 8	Staynes, Jill & Margaret Storey	Elizabeth Eyre
Taylor, Alison G.	Michael McKenna	'95 - 3	unknown	
Thrasher, L.L.	Lizbet Lange	'98 - 1	Baty, Linda Thrasher	
Thrasher, L.L.	Zachariah Smith	'91 - 2	Baty, Linda Thrasher	
Tishy, Cecelia	Kate Banning	'97 - 2	Tichi, Cecelia	
Wakefield, Hannah	Dee Street	'87 - 3	Burton, Sarah & Judith Holland	
Webb, Martha G.	Smoky O'Donnell	'85 - 2	Wingate, Anne	Lee Martin
Wells, Tobias	Knute Severson	'66 -16	Forbes, DeLoris Florine Stanton	
Wren, M.K.	Conan Flagg	'73 - 8	Renfroe, Martha Kay	
Wren, M.K.	Neely Jones	'99 - 1	Renfroe, Martha Kay	
Yorke, Margaret	Patrick Grant	'70 - 5	Nicholson, Margaret Beda Larminie	

PSEUDONYMS

Autonym	Pseudonym	Series Character	1 - #	Other Pseudonyms
List 2 - Women Authors Who Write Pseudonymous Mystery Series				
Ainsbury, Linda	Mather, Linda	Jo Hughes	'94 - 2	
Albert, Susan & Bill	Paige, Robin	Kathryn Ardleigh & Charles Sheridan	'94 - 5	
Allen, Lauretta	MacPherson, Rett	Torie O'Shea	'97 - 2	
Anand, Valerie	Buckley, Fiona	Ursula Blanchard	'97 - 2	
Arguile, Cheryl	Brightwell, Emily	Gerald Witherspoon & Hepzibah Jeffries	'93 - 13	
Auspitz, Kate	Belfort, Sophie	Molly Rafferty	'86 - 3	
Barnard, Elizabeth Quinn	Quinn, Elizabeth	Lauren Maxwell	'93 - 4	
Baty, Linda Thrasher	Thrasher, L.L.	Lizbet Lange	'98 - 1	
Baty, Linda Thrasher	Thrasher, L.L.	Zachariah Smith	'91 - 2	
Bernell, Sue & Michaela Karni	Berne, Karin	Ellie Gordon	'85 - 3	
Bes-Shahar, Eluki	Edghill, Rosemary	Karen Hightower aka Bast	'94 - 3	
Boenhardt, Patricia	Hart, Ellen	Jane Lawless	'89 - 8	
Boenhardt, Patricia	Hart, Ellen	Sophie Greenway	'94 - 4	
Brooks, Janice Young	Churchill, Jill	Jane Jeffry	'89 - 11	
Brooks, Janice Young	Churchill, Jill	Lily & Robert Brewster	'99 - 1	
Buchanan, Eileen-Marie Duell	Petrie, Rhona	Marcus MacLurg	'63 - 5	Marie Buchanan Claire Curzon
Buchanan, Eileen-Marie Duell	Curzon, Clare	Mike Yeadings	'83 - 13	Marie Buchanan Rhona Petrie
Buchanan, Eileen-Marie Duell	Petrie, Rhona	Nassim Pride	'67 - 2	Marie Buchanan Claire Curzon
Buckland, Audrey Nelson	Peterson, Audrey	Claire Camden	'92 - 3	
Buckland, Audrey Nelson	Peterson, Audrey	Jane Winfield	'88 - 6	
Burton, Sarah & Judith Holland	Wakefield, Hannah	Dee Street	'87 - 3	
Butler, Gwendoline	Melville, Jennie	Charmian Daniels	'62 - '	
Carmichael, Claire	McNab, Claire	Carol Ashton	'88 - 10	
Carpenter, Lynette	Borton, D.B.	Cat Caliban	'93 - 6	Della Borton
Carpenter, Lynette	Borton, Della	Gilda Liberty	'99 - 1	
Celestri, Cathie & John	John, Cathie	Kate Cavanaugh	'97 - 4	
Chapman, Sally	Griffin, Annie	Hannah Malloy & Kiki Goldstein	'98 - 2	
Chase, Carol	Charles, Kate	Lucy Kingsley & David Middleton-Brown	'91 - 5	
Chesney, Marion	Beaton, M.C.	Agatha Raisin	'92 - 8	Sarah Chester Helen Crampton Ann Fairfax Jennie Tremaine Charlotte Ward
Chesney, Marion	Beaton, M.C.	Hamish Macbeth	'85 - 14	Sarah Chester Helen Crampton Ann Fairfax Jennie Tremaine Charlotte Ward
Clarke, Brenda Honeyman	Sedley, Kate	Roger the Chapman	'91 - 8	
Cockburn, Sarah	Caudwell, Sarah	Hilary Tamar	'81 - 4	
Cohen, Janet	Neel, Janet	John McLeish & Francesca Wilson	'88 - 6	
Cook, Petronelle	Arnold, Margot	Penny Spring & Toby Glendower	'79 - 12	
Creighton, Joan Scott	Borthwick, J.S.	Sarah Deane & Alex McKenzie	'82 - 9	
Cummings, Barbara & Jo-Ann Power	Crowleigh, Ann	Mirinda & Clare Clively	'93 - 2	
Dennison, Dulcie Winifred Catherine	Gray, Dulcie	Insp. Supt. Cardiff	'60 - 2	

Autonym	Pseudonym	Series Character	1 - #	Other Pseudonyms
List 2 - Women Authors Who Write Pseudonymous Mystery Series				
Fickling, Gloria & Forrest E.	Fickling, G.G.	Erik March	'62 - 3	
Fickling, Gloria & Forrest E.	Fickling, G.G.	Honey West	'57 - 11	
Finney, Patricia	Chisholm, P.F.	Robert Carey	'94 - 4	
Forbes, DeLoris Florine Stanton	Wells, Tobias	Knute Severson	'66 - 16	
Frazer, Gail	Frazer, Margaret	Dame Frevisse [7-10]	'92 - 8	
Fulton, Jennifer	Beecham, Rose	Amanda Valentine	'92 - 3	
Greber, Judith	Roberts, Gillian	Amanda Pepper	'87 - 8	
Greber, Judith	Roberts, Gillian	Emma Howe & Billie August	'98 - 1	
Gregory, Susanna & Beau Riffenburgh	Beaufort, Simon	Geoffrey de Mappestone	'98 - 2	
Harcourt, Palma & Jack H. Trotman	Penn, John	George Thorne	'83 - 6	
Harcourt, Palma & Jack H. Trotman	Penn, John	Richard Tansey	'88 - 12	
Harris, Juliet	Hebden, Juliet	Clovis Pel	'79 - 22	
Hegarty, Frances	Fyfield, Frances	Helen West	'88 - 6	
Hegarty, Frances	Fyfield, Frances	Sarah Fortune	'89 - 2	
Heilbrun, Carolyn G.	Cross, Amanda	Kate Fansler	'64 - 12	
Hess, Joan	Hadley, Joan	Theo Bloomer	'86 - 2	
Holland, Rebecca	Horansky, Ruby	Nikki Trakos	'90 - 2	
Hutchinson, Jean & Marcy Jacobs	Marcy, Jean	Meg Darcy	'97 - 2	
Irvine, Angela & Robert	Davis, Val	Nicolette Scott	'96 - 3	
Kittredge, Mary	Graves, Sarah	Jacobia Triptree	'98 - 3	
Krentz, Jayne Ann	Castle, Jayne	Guinevere Jones	'86 - 4	Jayne Bentley Amanda Glass Stephanie James Amanda Quick Jayne Taylor
Kuhfeld, Mary Pulver	Ferris, Monica	Betsy Devonshire	'99 - 2	Mary Monica Pulver
Kuhfeld, Mary Pulver & Gail Frazer	Frazer, Margaret	Dame Frevisse [1-6]	'92 - 8	Monica Ferris
Labus, Marta Haake	McCormick, Claire	John Waltz	'82 - 3	
Lampitt, Dinah	Lake, Deryn	John Rawlings & the Blind Beak	'94 - 4	
Latsis, Mary Jane & Martha Henissart	Dominic, R.B.	Ben Safford	'68 - 7	Emma Lathen
Latsis, Mary Jane & Martha Henissart	Lathen, Emma	John Putnam Thatcher	'61 - 24	R.B. Dominc
Leahy, Syrell Rogovin	Harris, Lee	Christine Bennett	'92 - 11	
Lorens, Margaret Keilstrup	Lawrence, Margaret	Hannah Trevor	'96 - 3	M.K. Lorens
Lorens, Margaret Keilstrup	Lorens, M.K.	Winston Marlowe Sherman	'90 - 5	
Lowry, Cheryl Meredith & Louise Vetter	Glen, Alison	Charlotte Sams	'92 - 2	
MacGregor, Patricia Janeshutz	Drake, Alison	Aline Scott	'88 - 4	Trish Janeshutz T.J. MacGregor
MacGregor, Patricia Janeshutz	MacGregor, T.J.	Quin St. James & Mike McCleary	'86 - 10	Alison Drake Trish Janeshutz
MacLeod, Charlotte	Craig, Alisa	Dittany Henbit Monk & Osbert Monk	'81 - 5	
MacLeod, Charlotte	Craig, Alisa	Madoc & Janet Rhys	'80 - 5	
Mariz, Linda French	French, Linda	Teddy Morelli	'98 - 3	
Marriott, Mary	Brown, Lizbie	Elizabeth Blair	'92 - 2	
Mason, Sarah J.	Crane, Hamilton	Emily D. Seeton	'68 - 22	
Massie, Sonja	McKevett, G.A.	Savannah Reid	'95 - 4	
Mathews, Francine	Barron, Stephanie	Jane Austen	'96 - 3	
Maxwell, Ann & Evan	Maxwell, A.E.	Fiddler & Fiora Flynn	'85 - 8	Elizabeth Lowell

Autonym	Pseudonym	Series Character	1 - #	Other Pseudonyms
List 2 - Women Authors Who Write Pseudonymous Mystery Series				
McCafferty, Barbara Taylor	McCafferty, Taylor	Haskell Blevins	'90 - 6	Tierney McClellan
McCafferty, Barbara Taylor	McClellan, Tierney	Schuyler Ridgway	'95 - 4	Taylor McCafferty
McIntosh, Kinn Hamilton	Aird, Catherine	Christopher Dennis "Seedy" Sloan	'66 - 16	
McKenna, Bridget	Cleary, Melissa	Jackie Walsh & Jake [10-]	'92 - 10	
Mertz, Barbara	Peters, Elizabeth	Amelia Peabody	'75 - 12	Barbara Michaels
Mertz, Barbara	Michaels, Barbara	Georgetown house	'68 - 3	Elizabeth Peters
Mertz, Barbara	Peters, Elizabeth	Jacqueline Kirby	'72 - 4	Barbara Michaels
Mertz, Barbara	Peters, Elizabeth	Vicky Bliss	'73 - 5	Barbara Michaels
Meyers, Annette & Martin	Meyers, Maan	The Tonnemans	'92 - 6	
Mitchell, Kay	Lacey, Sarah	Leah Hunter	'92 - 4	
Munger, Katy	Gray, Gallagher	Theodore S. Hubbert & Auntie Lil	'91 - 4	
Nadolny, Karo	John, Katherine	Trevor Joseph	'89 - 3	
Nassim, Liza	Cody, Liza	Anna Lee	'80 - 6	
Nassim, Liza	Cody, Liza	Eva Wylie	'92 - 3	
Nicholson, Margaret Beda Larminie	Yorke, Margaret	Patrick Grant	'70 - 5	
O'Connor, Maureen	Hall, Patricia	Laura Ackroyd & Michael Thackeray	'93 - 5	
O'Shaughnessy, Pamela & Mary	O'Shaughnessy, Perri	Nina Reilly	'95 - 4	
Olcott, Anthony & Martha	Brill, Toni	Midge Cohen	'91 - 2	
Papazoglou, Orania	Haddam, Jane	Gregor Demarkian	'90 - 15	
Perkins, Barbara-Serene	Ferguson, Frances	Jane Perry	'93 - 4	
Peters, Elsa Kirsten	Allen, Irene	Elizabeth Elliot	'92 - 4	
Peters, Maureen	Black, Veronica	Joan, Sister	'90 - 10	Catherine Darby Elizabeth Law Judith Rothman
Quin-Harkin, Janet	Bowen, Rhys	Evan Evans	'97 - 3	
Recknor, Ellen	Bryan, Kate	Maggie Maguire	'98 - 2	
Renfroe, Martha Kay	Wren, M.K.	Conan Flagg	'73 - 8	
Renfroe, Martha Kay	Wren, M.K.	Neely Jones	'99 - 1	
Roberts, Doreen	Kingsbury, Kate	Cecily Sinclair	'93 - 11	
Roberts, Nora	Robb, J.D.	Eve Dallas	'95 - 8	
Robinson, Sheila	Radley, Sheila	Douglas Quantrill & Hilary Lloyd	'78 - 9	
Rogers, Marian	Jackson, Marian J.A.	Abigail Patience Danforth	'90 - 5	
Rousmaniere, Leah	Robinson, Leah Ruth	Evelyn Sutcliffe	'88 - 2	
Rudman, Anne & Charles Dennis	Barrett, Margaret	Susan Given	'98 - 2	
Sale, Medora	Roe, Caroline	Isaac & Bishop Berenguer	'98 - 3	
Sandberg, Theresa	Arnold, Catherine	Karen Perry-Mondori	'96 - 3	
Sawyer, John & Nancy Buckingham Sawyer	Quest, Erica	Kate Maddox	'88 - 3	Christina Abbey Nancy Buckingham Nancy John Hilary London
Shannon, Doris	Giroux, E.X.	Robert Forsythe & Abigail Sanderson	'84 - 10	
Shepherd, Jean	Ruryk, Jean	Catherine Wilde	'94 - 3	Eugenie Melnyk
Shone, Bridget Ann	Shone, Anna	Ulysses Finnegan Donaghue	'94 - 2	
Simpson, Doris	Cohen, Anthea	Agnes Carmichael	'82 - 15	
Smith, Amanda Mackay	Mackay, Amanda	Hannah Land	'76 - 2	
Smith, Jane S.	Smith, J.C.S.	Quentin Jacoby	'80 - 2	
Stanton, Mary	Bishop, Claudia	Sarah & Meg Quilliam	'94 - 6	
Staynes, Jill & Margaret Storey	Stacey, Susannah	Robert Bone	'87 - 8	Elizabeth Eyre
Staynes, Jill & Margaret Storey	Eyre, Elizabeth	Sigismondo	'92 - 6	Susannah Stacey

Autonym	Pseudonym	Series Character	1 - #	Other Pseudonyms
List 2 - Women Authors Who Write Pseudonymous Mystery Series				
Sutton, Ann	Livesay, Ann	Barry Ross	'98 - 5	
Tepper, Sheri S.	Orde, A.J.	Jason Lynx	'89 - 6	B.J. Oliphant E.E. Horlak
Tepper, Sheri S.	Oliphant, B.J.	Shirley McClintock	'90 - 7	A.J. Orde E.E. Horlak
Tichi, Cecelia	Tishy, Cecelia	Kate Banning	'97 - 2	
Tirbutt, Honoria	Page, Emma	Kelsey, Inspector	'80 - 9	
Trimble, Barbara Margaret	Gill, B.M.	Tom Maybridge	'81 - 3	Margaret Blake Barbara Gilmour
Trinchieri, Camilla	Crespi, Camilla	Simona Griffo	'91 - 7	
Whitman, Ann Hamilton	Morgan, Kate	Dewey James	'90 - 7	
Whitney, Polly	Jackson, Hialeah	Annabelle Hardy-Maratos & Dave the Monkeyman	'98 - 2	P.L. Whitney
Williams, Linda V.	Grant, Linda	Catherine Sayler	'88 - 6	
Wingate, Anne	Martin, Lee	Deb Ralston	'84 - 13	Martha G. Webb
Wingate, Anne	Webb, Martha G.	Smoky O'Donnell	'85 - 2	Lee Martin
Winkelman, Betty	Haney, Lauren	Lt. Bak	'97 - 2	
Wright, Daphne	Cooper, Natasha	Trish Maguire	'98 - 1	
Wright, Daphne	Cooper, Natasha	Willow King	'90 - 7	
Yarbro, Chelsea Quinn & Bill Fawcett	Fawcett, Quinn	Mycroft Holmes	'94 - 3	
Yarbro, Chelsea Quinn & Bill Fawcett	Fawcett, Quinn	Victoire Vernet	'93 - 2	

Mystery 8 Book Awards

	AWARD			YEAR			AUTHOR NAME
Conf'd by	Name	Status	Category	Award	Pub	BOOK TITLE	Last, First
Acad Fran	Grand Prix	Winner	Police Novel	1971	1970	The Ledger	Uhnak, Dorothy
B'con	Anthony	Nominee	First Novel	1998	1997	If I Should Die	Edwards, Grace F.
B'con	Anthony	Nominee	First Novel	1998	1997	Except the Dying	Jennings, Maureen
B'con	Anthony	Nominee	First Novel	1998	1997	The Salaryman's Wife	Massey, Sujata
B'con	Anthony	Winner (tie)	First Novel	1997	1996	Somebody Else's Child	Grimes, Terris McMahan
B'con	Anthony	Winner	First Novel	1996	1995	Death in Bloodhound Red	Lanier, Virginia
B'con	Anthony	Nominee	First Novel	1996	1995	Murder in Scorpio	Lawrence, Martha
B'con	Anthony	Nominee	First Novel	1995	1994	Mallory's Oracle	O'Connell, Carol
B'con	Anthony	Winner	First Novel	1994	1993	Track of the Cat	Barr, Nevada
B'con	Anthony	Nominee	First Novel	1994	1993	Goodnight, Irene	Burke, Jan
B'con	Anthony	Nominee	First Novel	1994	1993	A Grave Talent	King, Laurie R.
B'con	Anthony	Nominee	First Novel	1994	1993	Death Comes as Epiphany	Newman, Sharan
B'con	Anthony	Nominee	First Novel	1994	1993	Child of Silence	Padgett, Abigail
B'con	Anthony	Nominee	First Novel	1993	1992	Thyme of Death	Albert, Susan Wittig
B'con	Anthony	Nominee	First Novel	1993	1992	Decked	Clark, Carol Higgins
B'con	Anthony	Winner	First Novel	1993	1992	Blanche on the Lam	Neely, Barbara
B'con	Anthony	Nominee	First Novel	1993	1992	Every Crooked Nanny	Trocheck, Kathy Hogan
B'con	Anthony	Nominee	First Novel	1993	1992	Winter Widow	Weir, Charlene
B'con	Anthony	Winner	First Novel	1992	1991	Murder on the Iditarod Trail	Henry, Sue
B'con	Anthony	Nominee	First Novel	1992	1991	The Bulrush Murders	Rothenberg, Rebecca
B'con	Anthony	Nominee	First Novel	1992	1991	Murder on the Run	White, Gloria
B'con	Anthony	Winner	First Novel	1991	1990	Postmortem	Cornwell, Patricia
B'con	Anthony	Nominee	First Novel	1991	1990	Catering to Nobody	Davidson, Diane Mott
B'con	Anthony	Nominee	First Novel	1991	1990	Kindred Crimes	Dawson, Janet
B'con	Anthony	Nominee	First Novel	1990	1989	Grime and Punishment	Churchill, Jill
B'con	Anthony	Nominee	First Novel	1990	1989	The Mother Shadow	Howe, Melodie Johnson
B'con	Anthony	Winner	First Novel	1990	1989	Katwalk	Kijewski, Karen
B'con	Anthony	Nominee	First Novel	1990	1989	The Mark Twain Murders	Skom, Edith
B'con	Anthony	Winner	First Novel	1989	1988	A Great Deliverance	George, Elizabeth
B'con	Anthony	Nominee	First Novel	1989	1988	The Killings at Badger's Drift	Graham, Caroline
B'con	Anthony	Nominee	First Novel	1989	1988	Random Access Murder	Grant, Linda
B'con	Anthony	Nominee	First Novel	1988	1987	Murder at the War	Pulver, Mary Monica
B'con	Anthony	Winner	First Novel	1988	1987	Caught Dead in Philadelphia	Roberts, Gillian
B'con	Anthony	Nominee	First Novel	1985	1984	The Gemini Man	Kelly, Susan
B'con	Grand Master	Winner	Lifetime	1986	1986	Lifetime Achievement	Peters, Elizabeth
B'con	Anthony	Winner	Novel	1998	1997	No Colder Place	Rozan, S.J.
B'con	Anthony	Nominee	Novel	1997	1996	Lethal Genes	Grant, Linda
B'con	Anthony	Nominee	Novel	1997	1996	Hearts and Bones	Lawrence, Margaret
B'con	Anthony	Nominee	Novel	1996	1995	Hard Christmas	D'Amato, Barbara
B'con	Anthony	Winner	Novel	1996	1995	Under the Beetle's Cellar	Walker, Mary Willis
B'con	Anthony	Nominee	Novel	1995	1994	"K" is for Killer	Grafton, Sue
B'con	Anthony	Winner	Novel	1995	1994	She Walks These Hills	McCrumb, Sharyn
B'con	Anthony	Nominee	Novel	1995	1994	Crack Down	McDermid, Val

Awards List 1 – Winners and Nominees by Award Name

Includes awards through 1998 for series novels only

Conf'd by	Name	Status	Category	Award	Pub	BOOK TITLE	Last, First
B'con	Anthony	Nominee	Novel	1994	1993	Murder on a Kibbutz	Gur, Batya
B'con	Anthony	Nominee	Novel	1994	1993	O Little Town of Maggody	Hess, Joan
B'con	Anthony	Nominee	Novel	1994	1993	Old Enemies	LaPierre, Janet
B'con	Anthony	Nominee	Novel	1994	1993	Southern Discomfort	Maron, Margaret
B'con	Anthony	Winner	Novel	1994	1993	Wolf in the Shadows	Muller, Marcia
B'con	Anthony	Nominee	Novel	1994	1993	To Live and Die in Dixie	Trocheck, Kathy Hogan
B'con	Anthony	Nominee	Novel	1994	1993	Consider the Crows	Weir, Charlene
B'con	Anthony	Nominee	Novel	1993	1992	Southern Ghost	Hart, Carolyn G.
B'con	Anthony	Winner	Novel	1993	1992	Bootlegger's Daughter	Maron, Margaret
B'con	Anthony	Nominee	Novel	1993	1992	The Hangman's Beautiful Daughter	McCrumb, Sharyn
B'con	Anthony	Nominee	Novel	1992	1991	Rogue Wave	Dunlap, Susan
B'con	Anthony	Nominee	Novel	1992	1991	Love Nor Money	Grant, Linda
B'con	Anthony	Nominee	Novel	1992	1991	The Christie Caper	Hart, Carolyn G.
B'con	Anthony	Nominee	Novel	1992	1991	I.O.U.	Pickard, Nancy
B'con	Anthony	Nominee	Novel	1992	1991	A Single Stone	Wallace, Marilyn
B'con	Anthony	Winner	Novel	1991	1990	"G" is for Gumshoe	Grafton, Sue
B'con	Anthony	Nominee	Novel	1991	1990	The Good Fight	Matera, Lia
B'con	Anthony	Nominee	Novel	1991	1990	If Ever I Return Pretty Peggy-O	McCrumb, Sharyn
B'con	Anthony	Nominee	Novel	1991	1990	New Orleans Mourning	Smith, Julie
B'con	Anthony	Winner	Novel	1990	1989	The Sirens Sang of Murder	Caudwell, Sarah
B'con	Anthony	Nominee	Novel	1990	1989	Pious Deception	Dunlap, Susan
B'con	Anthony	Nominee	Novel	1990	1989	A Question of Guilt [U.S. edition]	Fyfield, Frances
B'con	Anthony	Nominee	Novel	1990	1989	A Little Class on Murder	Hart, Carolyn G.
B'con	Anthony	Nominee	Novel	1990	1989	Corpus Christmas	Maron, Margaret
B'con	Anthony	Nominee	Novel	1989	1988	The Widow's Club	Cannell, Dorothy
B'con	Anthony	Nominee	Novel	1989	1988	"E" is for Evidence	Grafton, Sue
B'con	Anthony	Nominee	Novel	1989	1988	Mischief in Maggody	Hess, Joan
B'con	Anthony	Nominee	Novel	1989	1988	Blood Shot	Paretsky, Sara
B'con	Anthony	Nominee	Novel	1989	1988	Dead Crazy	Pickard, Nancy
B'con	Anthony	Nominee	Novel	1988	1987	A Trouble of Fools	Barnes, Linda
B'con	Anthony	Nominee	Novel	1988	1987	Trojan Gold	Peters, Elizabeth
B'con	Anthony	Nominee	Novel	1988	1987	Marriage is Murder	Pickard, Nancy
B'con	Anthony	Winner	Novel	1987	1986	"C" is for Corpse	Grafton, Sue
B'con	Anthony	Winner	Novel	1986	1985	"B" is for Burglar	Grafton, Sue
B'con	Anthony	Nominee	Novel	1986	1985	Strangled Prose	Hess, Joan
B'con	Anthony	Nominee	Novel	1986	1985	No Body	Pickard, Nancy
B'con	Anthony	Winner	Novel	1983	1982	"A" is for Alibi	Grafton, Sue
B'con	Anthony	Nominee	PB Original	1998	1997	Charm City	Lippman, Laura
B'con	Anthony	Winner	PB Original	1997	1996	Somebody Else's Child	Grimes, Terris McMahan
B'con	Anthony	Nominee	PB Original	1997	1996	The Grass Widow	Holbrook, Teri
B'con	Anthony	Nominee	PB Original	1996	1995	Bad Medicine	Dreyer, Eileen
B'con	Anthony	Nominee	PB Original	1996	1995	A Far and Deadly Cry	Holbrook, Teri
B'con	Anthony	Nominee	PB Original	1996	1995	Charged With Guilt	White, Gloria
B'con	Anthony	Nominee	PB Original	1991	1990	Not a Creature Was Stirring	Haddam, Jane
B'con	Anthony	Nominee	PB Original	1991	1990	Dead in the Scrub	Oliphant, B.J.
B'con	Anthony	Winner	PB Original	1990	1989	Honeymoon with Murder	Hart, Carolyn G.
B'con	Anthony	Nominee	PB Original	1990	1989	Murder by Deception	Meredith, D.R.
B'con	Anthony	Nominee	PB Original	1990	1989	A Collector of Photographs	Valentine, Deborah
B'con	Anthony	Nominee	PB Original	1989	1988	Murder Unrenovated	Carlson, P.M.
B'con	Anthony	Winner	PB Original	1989	1988	Something Wicked	Hart, Carolyn G.
B'con	Anthony	Nominee	PB Original	1989	1988	A Radical Departure	Matera, Lia
B'con	Anthony	Nominee	PB Original	1989	1988	Paying the Piper	McCrumb, Sharyn
B'con	Anthony	Nominee	PB Original	1989	1988	Murder by Impulse	Meredith, D.R.
B'con	Anthony	Nominee	PB Original	1989	1988	Primary Target	Wallace, Marilyn
B'con	Anthony	Nominee	PB Original	1988	1987	The Cat Who Played Brahms	Braun, Lilian Jackson
B'con	Anthony	Nominee	PB Original	1988	1987	Death on Demand	Hart, Carolyn G.
B'con	Anthony	Nominee	PB Original	1988	1987	Where Lawyers Fear to Tread	Matera, Lia
B'con	Anthony	Nominee	PB Original	1988	1987	Bimbos of the Death Sun	McCrumb, Sharyn
B'con	Anthony	Nominee	PB Original	1986	1985	Murder Is Academic	Carlson, P.M.
B'con	Anthony	Winner	PB Original	1986	1985	Say No To Murder	Pickard, Nancy
CWA	Creasey	Nominee	First Novel	1995	1995	The Greenway	Adams, Jane
CWA	Creasey	Winner	First Novel	1995	1995	One For The Money	Evanovich, Janet
CWA	Creasey	Nominee	First Novel	1995	1995	A Grave Talent	King, Laurie R.
CWA	Creasey	Nominee	First Novel	1994	1994	Looking for Trouble	Staincliffe, Cath
CWA	Creasey	Nominee	First Novel	1991	1991	Deadly Errand	Green, Christine
CWA	Creasey	Winner	First Novel	1990	1990	Postmortem	Cornwell, Patricia
CWA	Creasey	Winner	First Novel	1989	1989	A Real Shot in the Arm	Roome, Annette

Awards List 1 – Winners and Nominees by Award Name

Includes awards through 1998 for series novels only

Conf'd by	Name	Status	Category	Award	Pub	BOOK TITLE	Last, First
				YEAR			AUTHOR NAME
CWA	Creasey	Winner	First Novel	1988	1988	Death's Bright Angel	Neel, Janet
CWA	Creasey	Nominee	First Novel	1981	1981	Corridors of Death	Edwards, Ruth Dudley
CWA	Creasey	Winner	First Novel	1980	1980	Dupe	Cody, Liza
CWA	Diamond Dagger	Winner	Lifetime	1991	1991	Lifetime Achievement	Rendell, Ruth
CWA	Diamond Dagger	Winner	Lifetime	1987	1987	Lifetime Achievement	James, P.D.
CWA	Silver Dagger	Winner	Novel	1997	1997	Three To Get Deadly	Evanovich, Janet
CWA	Gold Dagger	Winner	Novel	1995	1995	The Mermaids Singing	McDermid, Val
CWA	Gold Dagger	Nominee	Novel	1995	1995	A Piece of Justice	Paton Walsh, Jill
CWA	Gold Dagger	Nominee	Novel	1994	1994	"K" is for Killer	Grafton, Sue
CWA	Gold Dagger	Nominee	Novel	1994	1994	Crack Down	McDermid, Val
CWA	Gold Dagger	Nominee	Novel	1994	1994	Tunnel Vision	Paretsky, Sara
CWA	Gold Dagger	Winner	Novel	1993	1993	Cruel and Unusual	Cornwell, Patricia
CWA	Silver Dagger	Winner	Novel	1993	1993	Fat Lands	Dunant, Sarah
CWA	Gold Dagger	Nominee	Novel	1993	1993	Death Among the Dons	Neel, Janet
CWA	Silver Dagger	Winner	Novel	1992	1992	Bucket Nut	Cody, Liza
CWA	Silver Dagger	Winner	Novel	1991	1991	Deep Sleep	Fyfield, Frances
CWA	Silver Dagger	Winner	Novel	1988	1988	Toxic Shock [U.S.-Blood Shot]	Paretsky, Sara
CWA	Gold Dagger	Nominee	Novel	1986	1986	Under Contract	Cody, Liza
CWA	Silver Dagger	Winner	Novel	1986	1986	A Taste for Death	James, P.D.
CWA	Gold Dagger	Winner	Novel	1985	1985	Monkey Puzzle	Gosling, Paula
CWA	Silver Dagger	Winner	Novel	1985	1985	Last Seen Alive	Simpson, Dorothy
CWA	Silver Dagger	Winner	Novel	1982	1982	Ritual Murder	Haymon, S.T.
CWA	Gold Dagger	Nominee	Novel	1981	1981	Murder Has a Pretty Face	Melville, Jennie
CWA	Silver Dagger	Winner	Novel	1975	1975	The Black Tower	James, P.D.
CWA	Silver Dagger	Winner	Novel	1971	1971	Shroud for a Nightingale	James, P.D.
CWA	Gold Dagger	Winner	Novel	1967	1967	Murder Against the Grain	Lathen, Emma
CWA	Silver Dagger	Winner	Novel	1965	1965	Accounting For Murder	Lathen, Emma
CWA	Gold Dagger	Winner	Novel	1961	1961	The Spoilt Kill	Kelly, Mary
CWA	CWA '92	Winner	Novel-Europe	1991	1991	Gaudi Afternoon [U.K. ed.]	Wilson, Barbara
CWA	Last Laugh	Winner	Novel-Funniest	1996	1996	Two for the Dough	Evanovich, Janet
CWA	Last Laugh	Nominee	Novel-Funniest	1995	1995	Ten Lords A-Leaping	Edwards, Ruth Dudley
CWA	Last Laugh	Nominee	Novel-Funniest	1995	1995	One For The Money	Evanovich, Janet
CWA	Last Laugh	Nominee	Novel-Funniest	1994	1994	Written in Blood	Graham, Caroline
CWA	Last Laugh	Nominee	Novel-Funniest	1993	1993	Poseidon's Gold	Davis, Lindsey
CWA	Last Laugh	Nominee	Novel-Funniest	1992	1992	Clubbed to Death	Edwards, Ruth Dudley
CWC	Ellis	Nominee	First Novel	1998	1997	The Xibalba Murders	Hamilton, Lyn
CWC	Ellis	Nominee	First Novel	1998	1997	Except the Dying	Jennings, Maureen
CWC	Ellis	Winner	First Novel	1998	1997	Déjà Dead	Reichs, Kathy
CWC	Ellis	Winner	First Novel	1995	1994	What's A Girl Gotta Do?	Hayter, Sparkle
CWC	Ellis	Nominee	First Novel	1994	1993	Healthy, Wealthy & Dead	North, Suzanne
CWC	Ellis	Nominee	First Novel	1994	1993	Every Breath You Take	Spring, Michelle
CWC	Ellis	Winner	First Novel	1986	1985	Murder on the Run	Sale, Medora
CWC	Ellis	Nominee	Novel	1999	1998	Next Week Will Be Better	Ruryk, Jean
CWC	Ellis	Nominee	Novel	1997	1996	Nice Girls Finish Last	Hayter, Sparkle
CWC	Ellis	Winner	Novel	1996	1995	Mother Love	Wright, L.R.
CWC	Ellis	Winner	Novel	1995	1994	A Colder Kind Of Death	Bowen, Gail
CWC	Ellis	Nominee	Novel	1994	1993	A Touch of Panic	Wright, L.R.
CWC	Ellis	Winner	Novel	1990	1989	A Chill Rain in January	Wright, L.R.
Historicon	Gargoyle	Winner	Novel-Historical	1994	1993	A Broken Vessel	Ross, Kate
IACW	Hammett	Winner	Novel	1996	1995	Under the Beetle's Cellar	Walker, Mary Willis
IACW	Hammett	Nominee	Novel	1995	1994	Shinju	Rowland, Laura Joh
IACW	Hammett	Nominee	Novel	1993	1992	By Evil Means	Prowell, Sandra West
LBR	Lambda	Winner	Lesbian Mystery	1998	1997	Father Forgive Me	Lordon, Randye
LBR	Lambda	Winner	Lesbian Mystery	1997	1996	Robber's Wine	Hart, Ellen
LBR	Lambda	Winner	Lesbian Mystery	1996	1995	The Intersection of Law and Desire	Redmann, J.M.
LBR	Lambda	Winner	Lesbian Mystery	1994	1993	A Small Sacrifice	Hart, Ellen
LBR	Lambda	Winner [tie]	Lesbian Mystery	1993	1992	Crazy for Loving	Maiman, Jaye
LBR	Lambda	Winner [tie]	Lesbian Mystery	1993	1992	The Two-Bit Tango	Pincus, Elizabeth
LBR	Lambda	Winner	Lesbian Mystery	1992	1991	Murder by Tradition	Forrest, Katherine V.
LBR	Lambda	Winner	Lesbian Mystery	1991	1990	Gaudi Afternoon	Wilson, Barbara
LBR	Lambda	Winner [tie]	Lesbian Mystery	1990	1989	Ninth Life	Douglas, Lauren Wright
LBR	Lambda	Winner	Lesbian Mystery	1990	1989	The Beverly Malibu	Forrest, Katherine V.
Malice	Agatha	Nominee	First Novel	1998	1997	Quieter Than Sleep	Dobson, Joanne
Malice	Agatha	Winner	First Novel	1998	1997	The Salaryman's Wife	Massey, Sujata

Awards List 1 – Winners and Nominees by Award Name

Includes awards through 1998 for series novels only

Conf'd by	A W A R D Name	Status	Category	Y E A R Award	Pub	B O O K T I T L E	AUTHOR NAME Last, First
Malice	Agatha	Nominee	First Novel	1998	1997	The Butter Did It	Richman, Phyllis
Malice	Agatha	Nominee	First Novel	1998	1997	Dead Body Language	Warner, Penny
Malice	Agatha	Nominee	First Novel	1998	1997	Death Brims Over	Wilson, Barbara Jaye
Malice	Agatha	Nominee	First Novel	1997	1996	Biggie and the Poisoned Politician	Bell, Nancy
Malice	Agatha	Winner	First Novel	1997	1996	Murder on a Girl's Night Out	George, Anne
Malice	Agatha	Nominee	First Novel	1997	1996	Somebody Else's Child	Grimes, Terris McMahan
Malice	Agatha	Nominee	First Novel	1997	1996	Riding for a Fall	Roberts, Lillian M.
Malice	Agatha	Winner	First Novel	1996	1995	The Body in the Transept	Dams, Jeanne M.
Malice	Agatha	Nominee	First Novel	1996	1995	A Far and Deadly Cry	Holbrook, Teri
Malice	Agatha	Nominee	First Novel	1996	1995	Horse of a Different Killer	Jaffe, Jody
Malice	Agatha	Nominee	First Novel	1996	1995	Death in Bloodhound Red	Lanier, Virginia
Malice	Agatha	Nominee	First Novel	1996	1995	Murder in Scorpio	Lawrence, Martha
Malice	Agatha	Nominee	First Novel	1995	1994	One For The Money	Evanovich, Janet
Malice	Agatha	Nominee	First Novel	1995	1994	Fool's Puzzle	Fowler, Earlene
Malice	Agatha	Nominee	First Novel	1995	1994	Writers of the Purple Sage	Smith, Barbara Burnett
Malice	Agatha	Nominee	First Novel	1995	1994	Until Death	Whitney, Polly
Malice	Agatha	Winner	First Novel	1994	1993	Track of the Cat	Barr, Nevada
Malice	Agatha	Nominee	First Novel	1994	1993	Goodnight, Irene	Burke, Jan
Malice	Agatha	Nominee	First Novel	1994	1993	A Share in Death	Crombie, Deborah
Malice	Agatha	Nominee	First Novel	1994	1993	Death Comes as Epiphany	Newman, Sharan
Malice	Agatha	Nominee	First Novel	1994	1993	Child of Silence	Padgett, Abigail
Malice	Agatha	Nominee	First Novel	1993	1992	All the Great Pretenders	Adams, Deborah
Malice	Agatha	Nominee	First Novel	1993	1992	Thyme of Death	Albert, Susan Wittig
Malice	Agatha	Nominee	First Novel	1993	1992	Decked	Clark, Carol Higgins
Malice	Agatha	Nominee	First Novel	1993	1992	Seneca Falls Inheritance	Monfredo, Miriam Grace
Malice	Agatha	Winner	First Novel	1993	1992	Blanche on the Lam	Neely, Barbara
Malice	Agatha	Winner	First Novel	1993	1992	Winter Widow	Weir, Charlene
Malice	Agatha	Nominee	First Novel	1992	1991	Just Desserts	Daheim, Mary
Malice	Agatha	Nominee	First Novel	1992	1991	The Bulrush Murders	Rothenberg, Rebecca
Malice	Agatha	Nominee	First Novel	1991	1990	Screaming Bones	Burden, Pat
Malice	Agatha	Nominee	First Novel	1991	1990	Catering to Nobody	Davidson, Diane Mott
Malice	Agatha	Winner	First Novel	1991	1990	The Body in the Belfry	Page, Katherine Hall
Malice	Agatha	Nominee	First Novel	1991	1990	Sea of Troubles	Smith, Janet L.
Malice	Agatha	Nominee	First Novel	1990	1989	Working Murder	Boylan, Eleanor
Malice	Agatha	Winner	First Novel	1990	1989	Grime and Punishment	Churchill, Jill
Malice	Agatha	Nominee	First Novel	1990	1989	A Question of Guilt [U.S. edition]	Fyfield, Frances
Malice	Agatha	Nominee	First Novel	1990	1989	The Mother Shadow	Howe, Melodie Johnson
Malice	Agatha	Nominee	First Novel	1990	1989	The Mark Twain Murders	Skom, Edith
Malice	Agatha	Winner	First Novel	1989	1988	A Great Deliverance	George, Elizabeth
Malice	Agatha	Nominee	First Novel	1989	1988	The Killings at Badger's Drift	Graham, Caroline
Malice	Agatha	Nominee	First Novel	1989	1988	The J. Alfred Prufrock Murders	Sawyer, Corinne Holt
Malice	Agatha	Nominee	First Novel	1989	1988	Goodbye Nanny Gray	Stacey, Susannah
Malice	Agatha	Nominee	First Novel	1989	1988	Dead Men Don't Give Seminars	Sucher, Dorothy
Malice	Lifetime	Winner	Lifetime	1997	1997	Lifetime Achievement	Lathen, Emma
Malice	Agatha	Nominee	Novel	1998	1997	Hocus	Burke, Jan
Malice	Agatha	Nominee	Novel	1998	1997	Dreaming of the Bones	Crombie, Deborah
Malice	Agatha	Nominee	Novel	1998	1997	Goose in the Pond	Fowler, Earlene
Malice	Agatha	Nominee	Novel	1998	1997	Seeing a Large Cat	Peters, Elizabeth
Malice	Agatha	Winner	Novel	1998	1997	The Devil in Music	Ross, Kate
Malice	Agatha	Nominee	Novel	1997	1996	Kansas Troubles	Fowler, Earlene
Malice	Agatha	Nominee	Novel	1997	1996	The Grass Widow	Holbrook, Teri
Malice	Agatha	Nominee	Novel	1997	1996	Hearts and Bones	Lawrence, Margaret
Malice	Agatha	Winner	Novel	1997	1996	Up Jumps the Devil	Maron, Margaret
Malice	Agatha	Nominee	Novel	1997	1996	Strong as Death	Newman, Sharan
Malice	Agatha	Nominee	Novel	1996	1995	Miracles in Maggody	Hess, Joan
Malice	Agatha	Winner	Novel	1996	1995	If I'd Killed Him When I Met Him	McCrumb, Sharyn
Malice	Agatha	Nominee	Novel	1996	1995	The Wandering Arm	Newman, Sharan
Malice	Agatha	Nominee	Novel	1996	1995	Twilight	Pickard, Nancy
Malice	Agatha	Nominee	Novel	1995	1994	Scandal in Fair Haven	Hart, Carolyn G.
Malice	Agatha	Nominee	Novel	1995	1994	The Beekeeper's Apprentice	King, Laurie R.
Malice	Agatha	Nominee	Novel	1995	1994	Angel of Death	Krich, Rochelle Majer
Malice	Agatha	Winner	Novel	1995	1994	She Walks These Hills	McCrumb, Sharyn
Malice	Agatha	Nominee	Novel	1995	1994	Night Train to Memphis	Peters, Elizabeth
Malice	Agatha	Winner	Novel	1994	1993	Dead Man's Island	Hart, Carolyn G.
Malice	Agatha	Nominee	Novel	1994	1993	O Little Town of Maggody	Hess, Joan
Malice	Agatha	Nominee	Novel	1994	1993	Fair Game	Krich, Rochelle Majer
Malice	Agatha	Nominee	Novel	1994	1993	Southern Discomfort	Maron, Margaret
Malice	Agatha	Nominee	Novel	1994	1993	To Live and Die in Dixie	Trocheck, Kathy Hogan

Awards List 1 – Winners and Nominees by Award Name

Includes awards through 1998 for series novels only

Conf'd by	Name	Status	Category	Award	Pub	BOOK TITLE	Last, First
							AUTHOR NAME
Malice	Agatha	Nominee	Novel	1993	1992	The Alpine Advocate	Daheim, Mary
Malice	Agatha	Nominee	Novel	1993	1992	Southern Ghost	Hart, Carolyn G.
Malice	Agatha	Winner	Novel	1993	1992	Bootlegger's Daughter	Maron, Margaret
Malice	Agatha	Nominee	Novel	1993	1992	The Hangman's Beautiful Daughter	McCrumb, Sharyn
Malice	Agatha	Nominee	Novel	1993	1992	Defend and Betray	Perry, Anne
Malice	Agatha	Nominee	Novel	1993	1992	The Snake, the Crocodile and the Dog	Peters, Elizabeth
Malice	Agatha	Nominee	Novel	1992	1991	The Christie Caper	Hart, Carolyn G.
Malice	Agatha	Nominee	Novel	1992	1991	An Owl Too Many	MacLeod, Charlotte
Malice	Agatha	Nominee	Novel	1992	1991	The Last Camel Died at Noon	Peters, Elizabeth
Malice	Agatha	Winner	Novel	1992	1991	I.O.U.	Pickard, Nancy
Malice	Agatha	Nominee	Novel	1991	1990	Real Murders	Harris, Charlaine
Malice	Agatha	Nominee	Novel	1991	1990	Deadly Valentine	Hart, Carolyn G.
Malice	Agatha	Nominee	Novel	1991	1990	The Face of a Stranger	Perry, Anne
Malice	Agatha	Winner	Novel	1991	1990	Bum Steer	Pickard, Nancy
Malice	Agatha	Nominee	Novel	1990	1989	The Sirens Sang of Murder	Caudwell, Sarah
Malice	Agatha	Nominee	Novel	1990	1989	A Little Class on Murder	Hart, Carolyn G.
Malice	Agatha	Nominee	Novel	1990	1989	Corpus Christmas	Maron, Margaret
Malice	Agatha	Winner	Novel	1990	1989	Naked Once More	Peters, Elizabeth
Malice	Agatha	Nominee	Novel	1990	1989	Philly Stakes	Roberts, Gillian
Malice	Agatha	Nominee	Novel	1989	1988	The Widow's Club	Cannell, Dorothy
Malice	Agatha	Winner	Novel	1989	1988	Something Wicked	Hart, Carolyn G.
Malice	Agatha	Nominee	Novel	1989	1988	Mischief in Maggody	Hess, Joan
Malice	Agatha	Nominee	Novel	1989	1988	Paying the Piper	McCrumb, Sharyn
Malice	Agatha	Nominee	Novel	1989	1988	Dead Crazy	Pickard, Nancy
MRI	Macavity	Nominee	First Novel	1998	1997	The Salaryman's Wife	Massey, Sujata
MRI	Macavity	Winner	First Novel	1998	1997	Dead Body Language	Warner, Penny
MRI	Macavity	Nominee	First Novel	1997	1996	Final Jeopardy	Fairstein, Linda
MRI	Macavity	Nominee	First Novel	1996	1995	The Body in the Transept	Dams, Jeanne M.
MRI	Macavity	Winner	First Novel	1996	1995	The Strange Files of Fremont Jones	Day, Dianne
MRI	Macavity	Nominee	First Novel	1996	1995	A Far and Deadly Cry	Holbrook, Teri
MRI	Macavity	Nominee	First Novel	1996	1995	Horse of a Different Killer	Jaffe, Jody
MRI	Macavity	Nominee	First Novel	1996	1995	Death in Bloodhound Red	Lanier, Virginia
MRI	Macavity	Nominee	First Novel	1994	1993	A Share in Death	Crombie, Deborah
MRI	Macavity	Winner	First Novel	1994	1993	Death Comes as Epiphany	Newman, Sharan
MRI	Macavity	Nominee	First Novel	1994	1993	Child of Silence	Padgett, Abigail
MRI	Macavity	Nominee	First Novel	1993	1992	Seneca Falls Inheritance	Monfredo, Miriam Grace
MRI	Macavity	Winner	First Novel	1993	1992	Blanche on the Lam	Neely, Barbara
MRI	Macavity	Nominee	First Novel	1993	1992	Every Crooked Nanny	Trocheck, Kathy Hogan
MRI	Macavity	Winner	First Novel	1992	1991	Murder on the Iditarod Trail	Henry, Sue
MRI	Macavity	Winner	First Novel	1991	1990	Postmortem	Cornwell, Patricia
MRI	Macavity	Nominee	First Novel	1991	1990	Catering to Nobody	Davidson, Diane Mott
MRI	Macavity	Nominee	First Novel	1991	1990	Kindred Crimes	Dawson, Janet
MRI	Macavity	Winner	First Novel	1990	1989	Grime and Punishment	Churchill, Jill
MRI	Macavity	Nominee	First Novel	1990	1989	The Mark Twain Murders	Skom, Edith
MRI	Macavity	Nominee	First Novel	1989	1988	A Great Deliverance	George, Elizabeth
MRI	Macavity	Winner	First Novel	1989	1988	The Killings at Badger's Drift	Graham, Caroline
MRI	Macavity	Nominee	First Novel	1988	1987	Where Lawyers Fear to Tread	Matera, Lia
MRI	Macavity	Winner	First Novel	1987	1986	A Ritual Bath	Kellerman, Faye
MRI	Macavity	Nominee	First Novel	1987	1986	Unquiet Grave	LaPierre, Janet
MRI	Macavity	Winner	First Novel	1987	1986	A Case of Loyalties	Wallace, Marilyn
MRI	Macavity	Nominee	Novel	1998	1997	Hocus	Burke, Jan
MRI	Macavity	Winner	Novel	1998	1997	Dreaming of the Bones	Crombie, Deborah
MRI	Macavity	Nominee	Novel	1997	1996	The Grass Widow	Holbrook, Teri
MRI	Macavity	Nominee	Novel	1997	1996	Hearts and Bones	Lawrence, Margaret
MRI	Macavity	Nominee	Novel	1996	1995	Hard Christmas	D'Amato, Barbara
MRI	Macavity	Nominee	Novel	1996	1995	A Wild and Lonely Place	Muller, Marcia
MRI	Macavity	Winner	Novel	1996	1995	Under the Beetle's Cellar	Walker, Mary Willis
MRI	Macavity	Winner	Novel	1995	1994	She Walks These Hills	McCrumb, Sharyn
MRI	Macavity	Nominee	Novel	1995	1994	The Red Scream	Walker, Mary Willis
MRI	Macavity	Nominee	Novel	1994	1993	To Live and Die in Dixie	Trocheck, Kathy Hogan
MRI	Macavity	Winner	Novel	1993	1992	Bootlegger's Daughter	Maron, Margaret
MRI	Macavity	Nominee	Novel	1992	1991	The Christie Caper	Hart, Carolyn G.
MRI	Macavity	Winner	Novel	1992	1991	I.O.U.	Pickard, Nancy
MRI	Macavity	Nominee	Novel	1991	1990	Deadly Valentine	Hart, Carolyn G.
MRI	Macavity	Nominee	Novel	1991	1990	The Good Fight	Matera, Lia
MRI	Macavity	Winner	Novel	1991	1990	If Ever I Return Pretty Peggy-O	McCrumb, Sharyn
MRI	Macavity	Winner	Novel	1990	1989	A Little Class on Murder	Hart, Carolyn G.

Awards List 1 – Winners and Nominees by Award Name
Includes awards through 1998 for series novels only

Conf'd by	Name	Status	Category	Award	Pub	BOOK TITLE	Last, First
MRI	Macavity	Nominee	Novel	1989	1988	Murder Unrenovated	Carlson, P.M.
MRI	Macavity	Nominee	Novel	1988	1987	Death on Demand	Hart, Carolyn G.
MRI	Macavity	Winner	Novel	1988	1987	Marriage is Murder	Pickard, Nancy
MRI	Macavity	Winner	Novel	1987	1986	A Taste for Death	James, P.D.
MWA	Edgar	Nominee	First Novel	1997	1996	The Queen's Man	Penman, Sharon Kay
MWA	Edgar	Nominee	First Novel	1996	1995	Murder in Scorpio	Lawrence, Martha
MWA	Edgar	Nominee	First Novel	1995	1994	One For The Money	Evanovich, Janet
MWA	Edgar	Nominee	First Novel	1995	1994	Mallory's Oracle	O'Connell, Carol
MWA	Edgar	Nominee	First Novel	1995	1994	Suspicion of Innocence	Parker, Barbara
MWA	Edgar	Winner	First Novel	1994	1993	A Grave Talent	King, Laurie R.
MWA	Edgar	Nominee	First Novel	1993	1992	Trail of Murder	Andreae, Christine
MWA	Edgar	Winner	First Novel	1991	1990	Postmortem	Cornwell, Patricia
MWA	Edgar	Nominee	First Novel	1990	1989	The Mother Shadow	Howe, Melodie Johnson
MWA	Edgar	Nominee	First Novel	1989	1988	A Great Deliverance	George, Elizabeth
MWA	Edgar	Nominee	First Novel	1986	1985	The Glory Hole Murders	Fennelly, Tony
MWA	Edgar	Nominee	First Novel	1985	1984	Sweet, Savage Death	Papazoglou, Orania
MWA	Edgar	Nominee	First Novel	1985	1984	Someone Else's Grave	Smith, Alison
MWA	Edgar	Nominee	First Novel	1984	1983	Dead Man's Thoughts	Wheat, Carolyn
MWA	Edgar	Nominee	First Novel	1977	1976	The Big Pay-Off	Law, Janice
MWA	Edgar	Winner [tie]	First Novel	1969	1968	The Bait	Uhnak, Dorothy
MWA	Edgar	Nominee	First Novel	1965	1964	In the Last Analysis	Cross, Amanda
MWA	Edgar	Winner	First Novel	1962	1961	The Green Stone	Blanc, Suzanne
MWA	Grand Master	Winner	Lifetime	1998	1998	Lifetime Achievement	Peters, Elizabeth
MWA	Grand Master	Winner	Lifetime	1997	1997	Lifetime Achievement	Rendell, Ruth
MWA	Grand Master	Winner	Lifetime	1985	1985	Lifetime Achievement	Davis, Dorothy Salisbury
MWA	Edgar	Nominee	Novel	1998	1997	Dreaming of the Bones	Crombie, Deborah
MWA	Edgar	Nominee	Novel	1997	1996	With Child	King, Laurie R.
MWA	Edgar	Nominee	Novel	1997	1996	Hearts and Bones	Lawrence, Margaret
MWA	Edgar	Nominee	Novel	1997	1996	Pentecost Alley	Perry, Anne
MWA	Edgar	Nominee	Novel	1997	1996	Mean Streak	Wheat, Carolyn
MWA	Edgar	Nominee	Novel	1995	1994	Miami, It's Murder	Buchanan, Edna
MWA	Edgar	Winner	Novel	1995	1994	The Red Scream	Walker, Mary Willis
MWA	Edgar	Nominee	Novel	1994	1993	Wolf in the Shadows	Muller, Marcia
MWA	Edgar	Nominee	Novel	1993	1992	Backhand	Cody, Liza
MWA	Edgar	Winner	Novel	1993	1992	Bootlegger's Daughter	Maron, Margaret
MWA	Edgar	Nominee	Novel	1992	1991	Prior Convictions	Matera, Lia
MWA	Edgar	Nominee	Novel	1992	1991	I.O.U.	Pickard, Nancy
MWA	Edgar	Winner	Novel	1991	1990	New Orleans Mourning	Smith, Julie
MWA	Edgar	Nominee	Novel	1990	1989	A Question of Guilt [U.S. edition]	Fyfield, Frances
MWA	Edgar	Nominee	Novel	1988	1987	A Trouble of Fools	Barnes, Linda
MWA	Edgar	Nominee	Novel	1987	1986	The Corpse in Oozak's Pond	MacLeod, Charlotte
MWA	Edgar	Nominee	Novel	1986	1985	An Unkindness of Ravens	Rendell, Ruth
MWA	Edgar	Winner	Novel	1986	1985	The Suspect	Wright, L.R.
MWA	Edgar	Nominee	Novel	1985	1984	Emily Dickinson Is Dead	Langton, Jane
MWA	Edgar	Nominee	Novel	1982	1981	Dupe	Cody, Liza
MWA	Edgar	Nominee	Novel	1979	1978	A Sleeping Life	Rendell, Ruth
MWA	Edgar	Nominee	Novel	1974	1973	An Unsuitable Job for a Woman	James, P.D.
MWA	Edgar	Nominee	Novel	1974	1973	Dear Laura	Stubbs, Jean
MWA	Edgar	Nominee	Novel	1972	1971	Shroud for a Nightingale	James, P.D.
MWA	Edgar	Nominee	Novel	1971	1970	Many Deadly Returns [Brit.-Who Saw Her Die]	Moyes, Patricia
MWA	Edgar	Winner	Novel	1971	1970	The Laughing Policeman	Sjöwall, Maj & Per Wahlöö
MWA	Edgar	Nominee	Novel	1970	1969	When in Greece	Lathen, Emma
MWA	Edgar	Nominee	Novel	1969	1968	Picture Miss Seeton	Crane , Hamilton
MWA	Edgar	Nominee	PB Original	1998	1997	Home Again, Home Again	Cooper, Susan Rogers
MWA	Edgar	Nominee	PB Original	1998	1997	The Prioress' Tale	Frazer, Margaret
MWA	Edgar	Winner	PB Original	1998	1997	Charm City	Lippman, Laura
MWA	Edgar	Nominee	PB Original	1998	1997	Sunset and Santiago	White, Gloria
MWA	Edgar	Nominee	PB Original	1997	1996	Silent Words	Drury, Joan M.
MWA	Edgar	Nominee	PB Original	1997	1996	The Grass Widow	Holbrook, Teri
MWA	Edgar	Nominee	PB Original	1996	1995	Charged With Guilt	White, Gloria
MWA	Edgar	Winner	PB Original	1995	1994	Final Appeal	Scottoline, Lisa
MWA	Edgar	Nominee	PB Original	1994	1993	The Servant's Tale	Frazer, Margaret
MWA	Edgar	Nominee	PB Original	1994	1993	Everywhere That Mary Went	Scottoline, Lisa
MWA	Edgar	Nominee	PB Original	1993	1992	The Good Friday Murder	Harris, Lee
MWA	Edgar	Nominee	PB Original	1993	1992	Principal Defense	Hartzmark, Gini

Awards List 1 – Winners and Nominees by Award Name

Includes awards through 1998 for series novels only

Conf'd by	Name	Status	Category	Award	Pub	BOOK TITLE	Last, First
MWA	Edgar	Winner	PB Original	1993	1992	A Cold Day for Murder	Stabenow, Dana
MWA	Edgar	Nominee	PB Original	1992	1991	Murder in the Dog Days	Carlson, P.M.
MWA	Edgar	Nominee	PB Original	1992	1991	Fine Distinctions	Valentine, Deborah
MWA	Edgar	Nominee	PB Original	1991	1990	Not a Creature Was Stirring	Haddam, Jane
MWA	Edgar	Nominee	PB Original	1991	1990	Dead in the Scrub	Oliphant, B.J.
MWA	Edgar	Nominee	PB Original	1990	1989	A Collector of Photographs	Valentine, Deborah
MWA	Edgar	Nominee	PB Original	1989	1988	A Radical Departure	Matera, Lia
MWA	Edgar	Nominee	PB Original	1988	1987	Bullshot	Kraft, Gabrielle
MWA	Edgar	Winner	PB Original	1988	1987	Bimbos of the Death Sun	McCrumb, Sharyn
MWA	Edgar	Nominee	PB Original	1987	1986	The Cat Who Saw Red	Braun, Lilian Jackson
MWA	Edgar	Nominee	PB Original	1987	1986	Shattered Moon	Green, Kate
PWA	Shamus	Nominee	First Novel	1998	1997	Baltimore Blues	Lippman, Laura
PWA	Shamus	Nominee	First Novel	1998	1997	Legwork	Munger, Katy
PWA	Shamus	Winner	First Novel	1997	1996	This Dog for Hire	Benjamin, Carol Lea
PWA	Shamus	Nominee	First Novel	1996	1995	If Looks Could Kill	Furie, Ruthe
PWA	Shamus	Nominee	First Novel	1995	1994	One For The Money	Evanovich, Janet
PWA	Shamus	Nominee	First Novel	1995	1994	When Death Comes Stealing	Wesley, Valerie Wilson
PWA	Shamus	Winner	First Novel	1994	1993	Satan's Lambs	Hightower, Lynn S.
PWA	Shamus	Nominee	First Novel	1994	1993	Brotherly Love	Lordon, Randye
PWA	Shamus	Nominee	First Novel	1994	1993	By Evil Means	Prowell, Sandra West
PWA	Shamus	Nominee	First Novel	1993	1992	Switching the Odds	Knight, Phyllis
PWA	Shamus	Nominee	First Novel	1991	1990	Kindred Crimes	Dawson, Janet
PWA	Shamus	Winner	First Novel	1990	1989	Katwalk	Kijewski, Karen
PWA	The Eye	Winner	Lifetime	1993	1993	Lifetime Achievement	Muller, Marcia
PWA	Shamus	Nominee	Novel	1998	1997	Down For the Count	O'Callaghan, Maxine
PWA	Shamus	Nominee	Novel	1998	1997	No Colder Place	Rozan, S.J.
PWA	Shamus	Winner	Novel	1996	1995	Concourse	Rozan, S.J.
PWA	Shamus	Winner	Novel	1995	1994	"K" is for Killer	Grafton, Sue
PWA	Shamus	Nominee	Novel	1995	1994	The Killing of Monday Brown	Prowell, Sandra West
PWA	Shamus	Nominee	Novel	1994	1993	Wolf in the Shadows	Muller, Marcia
PWA	Shamus	Nominee	Novel	1994	1993	The Lies That Bind	Van Gieson, Judith
PWA	Shamus	Nominee	Novel	1992	1991	Where Echoes Live	Muller, Marcia
PWA	Shamus	Winner	Novel	1991	1990	"G" is for Gumshoe	Grafton, Sue
PWA	Shamus	Nominee	Novel	1990	1989	The Shape of Dread	Muller, Marcia
PWA	Shamus	Nominee	Novel	1989	1988	Blood Shot	Paretsky, Sara
PWA	Shamus	Nominee	Novel	1988	1987	A Trouble of Fools	Barnes, Linda
PWA	Shamus	Nominee	Novel	1987	1986	"C" is for Corpse	Grafton, Sue
PWA	Shamus	Winner	Novel	1986	1985	"B" is for Burglar	Grafton, Sue
PWA	Shamus	Nominee	Novel	1983	1982	"A" is for Alibi	Grafton, Sue
PWA	Shamus	Winner	PB Original	1998	1997	Charm City	Lippman, Laura
PWA	Shamus	Nominee	PB Original	1998	1997	Father Forgive Me	Lordon, Randye
PWA	Shamus	Nominee	PB Original	1998	1997	Sunset and Santiago	White, Gloria
PWA	Shamus	Nominee	PB Original	1997	1996	Natural Death	Furie, Ruthe
PWA	Shamus	Nominee	PB Original	1996	1995	Interview With Mattie	Singer, Shelley
PWA	Shamus	Nominee	PB Original	1996	1995	Charged With Guilt	White, Gloria
PWA	Shamus	Nominee	PB Original	1995	1994	Lament for a Dead Cowboy	Dain, Catherine
PWA	Shamus	Nominee	PB Original	1995	1994	Dead Ahead	McKenna, Bridget
PWA	Shamus	Nominee	PB Original	1995	1994	Deadly Devotion	Wallace, Patricia
PWA	Shamus	Nominee	PB Original	1993	1992	Lay it on the Line	Dain, Catherine
PWA	Shamus	Winner	PB Original	1993	1992	The Last Tango of Delores Delgado	Day, Marele
PWA	Shamus	Nominee	PB Original	1992	1991	House of Cards	Hooper, Kay
PWA	Shamus	Nominee	PB Original	1990	1989	A Collector of Photographs	Valentine, Deborah
PWA	Shamus	Nominee	PB Original	1987	1986	Dark Fields	MacGregor, T.J.
RWA	Kiss of Death	Winner	Novel-Romantic	1998	1997	Hidden Agenda	Alexander, Skye
SMP/MD	SMP/MD	Winner	First Novel	1997	1998	The Doctor Digs a Grave	Hathaway, Robin
SMP/MD	SMP/MD	Winner	First Novel	1996	1997	Simon Said	Shaber, Sarah R.
SMP/MD	SMP/MD	Winner	First Novel	1994	1995	Death in Still Waters	Lee, Barbara
SMP/MD	SMP/MD	Winner	First Novel	1993	1994	Something To Kill For	Holtzer, Susan
SMP/MD	SMP/MD	Winner	First Novel	1992	1993	The Man Who Understood Cats	Dymmoch, Michael Allen
SMP/MD	SMP/MD	Winner	First Novel	1991	1992	Winter Widow	Weir, Charlene
SMP/PWA	SMP/PWA	Winner	First P.I. Novel	1991	1993	A Sudden Death at the Norfolk Cafè	Sullivan, Winona
SMP/PWA	SMP/PWA	Winner	First P.I. Novel	1989	1990	Kindred Crimes	Dawson, Janet
SMP/PWA	SMP/PWA	Winner	First P.I. Novel	1988	1989	Katwalk	Kijewski, Karen
Wolfe Pack	Nero Wolfe	Winner	Novel	1996	1995	A Monstrous Regiment of Women	King, Laurie R.
Wolfe Pack	Nero Wolfe	Winner	Novel	1995	1994	She Walks These Hills	McCrumb, Sharyn

Awards List 1 – Winners and Nominees by Award Name

Includes awards through 1998 for series novels only

Conf'd by	Name	Status	Category	Award	Pub	BOOK TITLE	Last, First
Wolfe Pack	Nero Wolfe	Winner	Novel	1987	1986	The Corpse in Oozak's Pond	MacLeod, Charlotte
Wolfe Pack	Nero Wolfe	Winner	Novel	1984	1984	Emily Dickinson Is Dead	Langton, Jane
Wolfe Pack	Nero Wolfe	Winner	Novel	1983	1983	The Anondyne Necklace	Grimes, Martha
Wolfe Pack	Nero Wolfe	Nominee	Novel	1994	1993	Hard Women	D'Amato, Barbara
Wolfe Pack	Nero Wolfe	Winner	Novel	1981	1981	Death in a Tenured Position	Cross, Amanda

Awards List 2 – Winners and Nominees by Award Category

Includes awards through 1998 for series novels only

Category	Status	Name	Conf'd by	Award	Pub	BOOK TITLE	Last, First
First Novel	Nominee	Anthony	B'con	1998	1997	If I Should Die	Edwards, Grace F.
First Novel	Nominee	Anthony	B'con	1998	1997	Except the Dying	Jennings, Maureen
First Novel	Nominee	Anthony	B'con	1998	1997	The Salaryman's Wife	Massey, Sujata
First Novel	Nominee	Ellis	CWC	1998	1997	The Xibalba Murders	Hamilton, Lyn
First Novel	Nominee	Ellis	CWC	1998	1997	Except the Dying	Jennings, Maureen
First Novel	Winner	Ellis	CWC	1998	1997	Déjà Dead	Reichs, Kathy
First Novel	Nominee	Agatha	Malice	1998	1997	Quieter Than Sleep	Dobson, Joanne
First Novel	Winner	Agatha	Malice	1998	1997	The Salaryman's Wife	Massey, Sujata
First Novel	Nominee	Agatha	Malice	1998	1997	The Butter Did It	Richman, Phyllis
First Novel	Nominee	Agatha	Malice	1998	1997	Dead Body Language	Warner, Penny
First Novel	Nominee	Agatha	Malice	1998	1997	Death Brims Over	Wilson, Barbara Jaye
First Novel	Nominee	Macavity	MRI	1998	1997	The Salaryman's Wife	Massey, Sujata
First Novel	Winner	Macavity	MRI	1998	1997	Dead Body Language	Warner, Penny
First Novel	Nominee	Shamus	PWA	1998	1997	Baltimore Blues	Lippman, Laura
First Novel	Nominee	Shamus	PWA	1998	1997	Legwork	Munger, Katy
First Novel	Winner [tie]	Anthony	B'con	1997	1996	Somebody Else's Child	Grimes, Terris McMahan
First Novel	Nominee	Agatha	Malice	1997	1996	Biggie and the Poisoned Politician	Bell, Nancy
First Novel	Winner	Agatha	Malice	1997	1996	Murder on a Girl's Night Out	George, Anne
First Novel	Nominee	Agatha	Malice	1997	1996	Somebody Else's Child	Grimes, Terris McMahan
First Novel	Nominee	Agatha	Malice	1997	1996	Riding for a Fall	Roberts, Lillian M.
First Novel	Nominee	Macavity	MRI	1997	1996	Final Jeopardy	Fairstein, Linda
First Novel	Nominee	Edgar	MWA	1997	1996	The Queen's Man	Penman, Sharon Kay
First Novel	Winner	Shamus	PWA	1997	1996	This Dog for Hire	Benjamin, Carol Lea
First Novel	Winner	SMP/MD	SMP/MD	1997	1998	The Doctor Digs a Grave	Hathaway, Robin
First Novel	Winner	Anthony	B'con	1996	1995	Death in Bloodhound Red	Lanier, Virginia
First Novel	Nominee	Anthony	B'con	1996	1995	Murder in Scorpio	Lawrence, Martha
First Novel	Winner	Agatha	Malice	1996	1995	The Body in the Transept	Dams, Jeanne M.
First Novel	Nominee	Agatha	Malice	1996	1995	A Far and Deadly Cry	Holbrook, Teri
First Novel	Nominee	Agatha	Malice	1996	1995	Horse of a Different Killer	Jaffe, Jody
First Novel	Nominee	Agatha	Malice	1996	1995	Death in Bloodhound Red	Lanier, Virginia
First Novel	Nominee	Agatha	Malice	1996	1995	Murder in Scorpio	Lawrence, Martha
First Novel	Nominee	Macavity	MRI	1996	1995	The Body in the Transept	Dams, Jeanne M.
First Novel	Winner	Macavity	MRI	1996	1995	The Strange Files of Fremont Jones	Day, Dianne
First Novel	Nominee	Macavity	MRI	1996	1995	A Far and Deadly Cry	Holbrook, Teri
First Novel	Nominee	Macavity	MRI	1996	1995	Horse of a Different Killer	Jaffe, Jody
First Novel	Nominee	Macavity	MRI	1996	1995	Death in Bloodhound Red	Lanier, Virginia
First Novel	Nominee	Edgar	MWA	1996	1995	Murder in Scorpio	Lawrence, Martha
First Novel	Nominee	Shamus	PWA	1996	1995	If Looks Could Kill	Furie, Ruthe
First Novel	Winner	SMP/MD	SMP/MD	1996	1997	Simon Said	Shaber, Sarah R.
First Novel	Nominee	Anthony	B'con	1995	1994	Mallory's Oracle	O'Connell, Carol
First Novel	Nominee	Creasey	CWA	1995	1995	The Greenway	Adams, Jane
First Novel	Winner	Creasey	CWA	1995	1995	One For The Money	Evanovich, Janet
First Novel	Nominee	Creasey	CWA	1995	1995	A Grave Talent	King, Laurie R.
First Novel	Winner	Ellis	CWC	1995	1994	What's A Girl Gotta Do?	Hayter, Sparkle
First Novel	Nominee	Agatha	Malice	1995	1994	One For The Money	Evanovich, Janet
First Novel	Nominee	Agatha	Malice	1995	1994	Fool's Puzzle	Fowler, Earlene
First Novel	Nominee	Agatha	Malice	1995	1994	Writers of the Purple Sage	Smith, Barbara Burnett
First Novel	Nominee	Agatha	Malice	1995	1994	Until Death	Whitney, Polly
First Novel	Nominee	Edgar	MWA	1995	1994	One For The Money	Evanovich, Janet
First Novel	Nominee	Edgar	MWA	1995	1994	Mallory's Oracle	O'Connell, Carol
First Novel	Nominee	Edgar	MWA	1995	1994	Suspicion of Innocence	Parker, Barbara
First Novel	Nominee	Shamus	PWA	1995	1994	One For The Money	Evanovich, Janet

Awards List 2 – Winners and Nominees by Award Category

Includes awards through 1998 for series novels only

Category	Status	Name	Conf'd by	Award	Pub	BOOK TITLE	Last, First
First Novel	Nominee	Shamus	PWA	1995	1994	When Death Comes Stealing	Wesley, Valerie Wilson
First Novel	Winner	Anthony	B'con	1994	1993	Track of the Cat	Barr, Nevada
First Novel	Nominee	Anthony	B'con	1994	1993	Goodnight, Irene	Burke, Jan
First Novel	Nominee	Anthony	B'con	1994	1993	A Grave Talent	King, Laurie R.
First Novel	Nominee	Anthony	B'con	1994	1993	Death Comes as Epiphany	Newman, Sharan
First Novel	Nominee	Anthony	B'con	1994	1993	Child of Silence	Padgett, Abigail
First Novel	Nominee	Creasey	CWA	1994	1994	Looking for Trouble	Staincliffe, Cath
First Novel	Nominee	Ellis	CWC	1994	1993	Healthy, Wealthy & Dead	North, Suzanne
First Novel	Nominee	Ellis	CWC	1994	1993	Every Breath You Take	Spring, Michelle
First Novel	Winner	Agatha	Malice	1994	1993	Track of the Cat	Barr, Nevada
First Novel	Nominee	Agatha	Malice	1994	1993	Goodnight, Irene	Burke, Jan
First Novel	Nominee	Agatha	Malice	1994	1993	A Share in Death	Crombie, Deborah
First Novel	Nominee	Agatha	Malice	1994	1993	Death Comes as Epiphany	Newman, Sharan
First Novel	Nominee	Agatha	Malice	1994	1993	Child of Silence	Padgett, Abigail
First Novel	Nominee	Macavity	MRI	1994	1993	A Share in Death	Crombie, Deborah
First Novel	Winner	Macavity	MRI	1994	1993	Death Comes as Epiphany	Newman, Sharan
First Novel	Nominee	Macavity	MRI	1994	1993	Child of Silence	Padgett, Abigail
First Novel	Winner	Edgar	MWA	1994	1993	A Grave Talent	King, Laurie R.
First Novel	Winner	Shamus	PWA	1994	1993	Satan's Lambs	Hightower, Lynn S.
First Novel	Nominee	Shamus	PWA	1994	1993	Brotherly Love	Lordon, Randye
First Novel	Nominee	Shamus	PWA	1994	1993	By Evil Means	Prowell, Sandra West
First Novel	Winner	SMP/MD	SMP/MD	1994	1995	Death in Still Waters	Lee, Barbara
First Novel	Nominee	Anthony	B'con	1993	1992	Thyme of Death	Albert, Susan Wittig
First Novel	Nominee	Anthony	B'con	1993	1992	Decked	Clark, Carol Higgins
First Novel	Winner	Anthony	B'con	1993	1992	Blanche on the Lam	Neely, Barbara
First Novel	Nominee	Anthony	B'con	1993	1992	Every Crooked Nanny	Trocheck, Kathy Hogan
First Novel	Nominee	Anthony	B'con	1993	1992	Winter Widow	Weir, Charlene
First Novel	Nominee	Agatha	Malice	1993	1992	All the Great Pretenders	Adams, Deborah
First Novel	Nominee	Agatha	Malice	1993	1992	Thyme of Death	Albert, Susan Wittig
First Novel	Nominee	Agatha	Malice	1993	1992	Decked	Clark, Carol Higgins
First Novel	Nominee	Agatha	Malice	1993	1992	Seneca Falls Inheritance	Monfredo, Miriam Grace
First Novel	Winner	Agatha	Malice	1993	1992	Blanche on the Lam	Neely, Barbara
First Novel	Winner	Agatha	Malice	1993	1992	Winter Widow	Weir, Charlene
First Novel	Nominee	Macavity	MRI	1993	1992	Seneca Falls Inheritance	Monfredo, Miriam Grace
First Novel	Winner	Macavity	MRI	1993	1992	Blanche on the Lam	Neely, Barbara
First Novel	Nominee	Macavity	MRI	1993	1992	Every Crooked Nanny	Trocheck, Kathy Hogan
First Novel	Nominee	Edgar	MWA	1993	1992	Trail of Murder	Andreae, Christine
First Novel	Nominee	Shamus	PWA	1993	1992	Switching the Odds	Knight, Phyllis
First Novel	Winner	SMP/MD	SMP/MD	1993	1994	Something To Kill For	Holtzer, Susan
First Novel	Winner	Anthony	B'con	1992	1991	Murder on the Iditarod Trail	Henry, Sue
First Novel	Nominee	Anthony	B'con	1992	1991	The Bulrush Murders	Rothenberg, Rebecca
First Novel	Nominee	Anthony	B'con	1992	1991	Murder on the Run	White, Gloria
First Novel	Nominee	Agatha	Malice	1992	1991	Just Desserts	Daheim, Mary
First Novel	Nominee	Agatha	Malice	1992	1991	The Bulrush Murders	Rothenberg, Rebecca
First Novel	Winner	Macavity	MRI	1992	1991	Murder on the Iditarod Trail	Henry, Sue
First Novel	Winner	SMP/MD	SMP/MD	1992	1993	The Man Who Understood Cats	Dymmoch, Michael Allen
First Novel	Winner	Anthony	B'con	1991	1990	Postmortem	Cornwell, Patricia
First Novel	Nominee	Anthony	B'con	1991	1990	Catering to Nobody	Davidson, Diane Mott
First Novel	Nominee	Anthony	B'con	1991	1990	Kindred Crimes	Dawson, Janet
First Novel	Nominee	Creasey	CWA	1991	1991	Deadly Errand	Green, Christine
First Novel	Nominee	Agatha	Malice	1991	1990	Screaming Bones	Burden, Pat
First Novel	Nominee	Agatha	Malice	1991	1990	Catering to Nobody	Davidson, Diane Mott
First Novel	Winner	Agatha	Malice	1991	1990	The Body in the Belfry	Page, Katherine Hall
First Novel	Nominee	Agatha	Malice	1991	1990	Sea of Troubles	Smith, Janet L.
First Novel	Winner	Macavity	MRI	1991	1990	Postmortem	Cornwell, Patricia
First Novel	Nominee	Macavity	MRI	1991	1990	Catering to Nobody	Davidson, Diane Mott
First Novel	Nominee	Macavity	MRI	1991	1990	Kindred Crimes	Dawson, Janet
First Novel	Winner	Edgar	MWA	1991	1990	Postmortem	Cornwell, Patricia
First Novel	Nominee	Shamus	PWA	1991	1990	Kindred Crimes	Dawson, Janet
First Novel	Winner	SMP/MD	SMP/MD	1991	1992	Winter Widow	Weir, Charlene
First Novel	Nominee	Anthony	B'con	1990	1989	Grime and Punishment	Churchill, Jill
First Novel	Nominee	Anthony	B'con	1990	1989	The Mother Shadow	Howe, Melodie Johnson
First Novel	Winner	Anthony	B'con	1990	1989	Katwalk	Kijewski, Karen
First Novel	Nominee	Anthony	B'con	1990	1989	The Mark Twain Murders	Skom, Edith
First Novel	Winner	Creasey	CWA	1990	1990	Postmortem	Cornwell, Patricia
First Novel	Nominee	Agatha	Malice	1990	1989	Working Murder	Boylan, Eleanor

Awards List 2 – Winners and Nominees by Award Category

Includes awards through 1998 for series novels only

Category	Status	Name	Conf'd by	Award	Pub	BOOK TITLE	Last, First
First Novel	Winner	Agatha	Malice	1990	1989	Grime and Punishment	Churchill, Jill
First Novel	Nominee	Agatha	Malice	1990	1989	A Question of Guilt [U.S. edition]	Fyfield, Frances
First Novel	Nominee	Agatha	Malice	1990	1989	The Mother Shadow	Howe, Melodie Johnson
First Novel	Nominee	Agatha	Malice	1990	1989	The Mark Twain Murders	Skom, Edith
First Novel	Winner	Macavity	MRI	1990	1989	Grime and Punishment	Churchill, Jill
First Novel	Nominee	Macavity	MRI	1990	1989	The Mark Twain Murders	Skom, Edith
First Novel	Nominee	Edgar	MWA	1990	1989	The Mother Shadow	Howe, Melodie Johnson
First Novel	Winner	Shamus	PWA	1990	1989	Katwalk	Kijewski, Karen
First Novel	Winner	Anthony	B'con	1989	1988	A Great Deliverance	George, Elizabeth
First Novel	Nominee	Anthony	B'con	1989	1988	The Killings at Badger's Drift	Graham, Caroline
First Novel	Nominee	Anthony	B'con	1989	1988	Random Access Murder	Grant, Linda
First Novel	Winner	Creasey	CWA	1989	1989	A Real Shot in the Arm	Roome, Annette
First Novel	Winner	Agatha	Malice	1989	1988	A Great Deliverance	George, Elizabeth
First Novel	Nominee	Agatha	Malice	1989	1988	The Killings at Badger's Drift	Graham, Caroline
First Novel	Nominee	Agatha	Malice	1989	1988	The J. Alfred Prufrock Murders	Sawyer, Corinne Holt
First Novel	Nominee	Agatha	Malice	1989	1988	Goodbye Nanny Gray	Stacey, Susannah
First Novel	Nominee	Agatha	Malice	1989	1988	Dead Men Don't Give Seminars	Sucher, Dorothy
First Novel	Nominee	Macavity	MRI	1989	1988	A Great Deliverance	George, Elizabeth
First Novel	Winner	Macavity	MRI	1989	1988	The Killings at Badger's Drift	Graham, Caroline
First Novel	Nominee	Edgar	MWA	1989	1988	A Great Deliverance	George, Elizabeth
First Novel	Nominee	Anthony	B'con	1988	1987	Murder at the War	Pulver, Mary Monica
First Novel	Winner	Anthony	B'con	1988	1987	Caught Dead in Philadelphia	Roberts, Gillian
First Novel	Winner	Creasey	CWA	1988	1988	Death's Bright Angel	Neel, Janet
First Novel	Winner	Macavity	MRI	1987	1986	A Ritual Bath	Kellerman, Faye
First Novel	Nominee	Macavity	MRI	1987	1986	Unquiet Grave	LaPierre, Janet
First Novel	Winner	Macavity	MRI	1987	1986	A Case of Loyalties	Wallace, Marilyn
First Novel	Winner	Ellis	CWC	1986	1985	Murder on the Run	Sale, Medora
First Novel	Nominee	Edgar	MWA	1986	1985	The Glory Hole Murders	Fennelly, Tony
First Novel	Nominee	Anthony	B'con	1985	1984	The Gemini Man	Kelly, Susan
First Novel	Nominee	Edgar	MWA	1985	1984	Sweet, Savage Death	Papazoglou, Orania
First Novel	Nominee	Edgar	MWA	1985	1984	Someone Else's Grave	Smith, Alison
First Novel	Nominee	Edgar	MWA	1984	1983	Dead Man's Thoughts	Wheat, Carolyn
First Novel	Nominee	Creasey	CWA	1981	1981	Corridors of Death	Edwards, Ruth Dudley
First Novel	Winner	Creasey	CWA	1980	1980	Dupe	Cody, Liza
First Novel	Nominee	Edgar	MWA	1977	1976	The Big Pay-Off	Law, Janice
First Novel	Winner [tie]	Edgar	MWA	1969	1968	The Bait	Uhnak, Dorothy
First Novel	Nominee	Edgar	MWA	1965	1964	In the Last Analysis	Cross, Amanda
First Novel	Winner	Edgar	MWA	1962	1961	The Green Stone	Blanc, Suzanne
First P.I. Novel	Winner	SMP/PWA	SMP/PWA	1991	1993	A Sudden Death at the Norfolk Cafè	Sullivan, Winona
First P.I. Novel	Winner	SMP/PWA	SMP/PWA	1989	1990	Kindred Crimes	Dawson, Janet
First P.I. Novel	Winner	SMP/PWA	SMP/PWA	1988	1989	Katwalk	Kijewski, Karen
Lesbian Mystery	Winner	Lambda	LBR	1998	1997	Father Forgive Me	Lordon, Randye
Lesbian Mystery	Winner	Lambda	LBR	1997	1996	Robber's Wine	Hart, Ellen
Lesbian Mystery	Winner	Lambda	LBR	1996	1995	The Intersection of Law and Desire	Redmann, J.M.
Lesbian Mystery	Winner	Lambda	LBR	1994	1993	A Small Sacrifice	Hart, Ellen
Lesbian Mystery	Winner [tie]	Lambda	LBR	1993	1992	Crazy for Loving	Maiman, Jaye
Lesbian Mystery	Winner [tie]	Lambda	LBR	1993	1992	The Two-Bit Tango	Pincus, Elizabeth
Lesbian Mystery	Winner	Lambda	LBR	1992	1991	Murder by Tradition	Forrest, Katherine V.
Lesbian Mystery	Winner	Lambda	LBR	1991	1990	Gaudi Afternoon	Wilson, Barbara
Lesbian Mystery	Winner [tie]	Lambda	LBR	1990	1989	Ninth Life	Douglas, Lauren Wright
Lesbian Mystery	Winner	Lambda	LBR	1990	1989	The Beverly Malibu	Forrest, Katherine V.
Lifetime	Winner	Grand Master	MWA	1998	1998	Lifetime Achievement	Peters, Elizabeth
Lifetime	Winner	Lifetime	Malice	1997	1997	Lifetime Achievement	Lathen, Emma
Lifetime	Winner	Grand Master	MWA	1997	1997	Lifetime Achievement	Rendell, Ruth
Lifetime	Winner	The Eye	PWA	1993	1993	Lifetime Achievement	Muller, Marcia
Lifetime	Winner	Diamond Dagger	CWA	1991	1991	Lifetime Achievement	Rendell, Ruth
Lifetime	Winner	Diamond Dagger	CWA	1987	1987	Lifetime Achievement	James, P.D.

Awards List 2 – Winners and Nominees by Award Category
Includes awards through 1998 for series novels only

AWARD				YEAR		BOOK TITLE	AUTHOR NAME
Category	Status	Name	Conf'd by	Award	Pub		Last, First
Lifetime	Winner	Grand Master	B'con	1986	1986	Lifetime Achievement	Peters, Elizabeth
Lifetime	Winner	Grand Master	MWA	1985	1985	Lifetime Achievement	Davis, Dorothy Salisbury
Novel	Nominee	Ellis	CWC	1999	1998	Next Week Will Be Better	Ruryk, Jean
Novel	Winner	Anthony	B'con	1998	1997	No Colder Place	Rozan, S.J.
Novel	Nominee	Agatha	Malice	1998	1997	Hocus	Burke, Jan
Novel	Nominee	Agatha	Malice	1998	1997	Dreaming of the Bones	Crombie, Deborah
Novel	Nominee	Agatha	Malice	1998	1997	Goose in the Pond	Fowler, Earlene
Novel	Nominee	Agatha	Malice	1998	1997	Seeing a Large Cat	Peters, Elizabeth
Novel	Winner	Agatha	Malice	1998	1997	The Devil in Music	Ross, Kate
Novel	Nominee	Macavity	MRI	1998	1997	Hocus	Burke, Jan
Novel	Winner	Macavity	MRI	1998	1997	Dreaming of the Bones	Crombie, Deborah
Novel	Nominee	Edgar	MWA	1998	1997	Dreaming of the Bones	Crombie, Deborah
Novel	Nominee	Shamus	PWA	1998	1997	Down For the Count	O'Callaghan, Maxine
Novel	Nominee	Shamus	PWA	1998	1997	No Colder Place	Rozan, S.J.
Novel	Nominee	Anthony	B'con	1997	1996	Lethal Genes	Grant, Linda
Novel	Nominee	Anthony	B'con	1997	1996	Hearts and Bones	Lawrence, Margaret
Novel	Winner	Silver Dagger	CWA	1997	1997	Three To Get Deadly	Evanovich, Janet
Novel	Nominee	Ellis	CWC	1997	1996	Nice Girls Finish Last	Hayter, Sparkle
Novel	Nominee	Agatha	Malice	1997	1996	Kansas Troubles	Fowler, Earlene
Novel	Nominee	Agatha	Malice	1997	1996	The Grass Widow	Holbrook, Teri
Novel	Nominee	Agatha	Malice	1997	1996	Hearts and Bones	Lawrence, Margaret
Novel	Winner	Agatha	Malice	1997	1996	Up Jumps the Devil	Maron, Margaret
Novel	Nominee	Agatha	Malice	1997	1996	Strong as Death	Newman, Sharan
Novel	Nominee	Macavity	MRI	1997	1996	The Grass Widow	Holbrook, Teri
Novel	Nominee	Macavity	MRI	1997	1996	Hearts and Bones	Lawrence, Margaret
Novel	Nominee	Edgar	MWA	1997	1996	With Child	King, Laurie R.
Novel	Nominee	Edgar	MWA	1997	1996	Hearts and Bones	Lawrence, Margaret
Novel	Nominee	Edgar	MWA	1997	1996	Pentecost Alley	Perry, Anne
Novel	Nominee	Edgar	MWA	1997	1996	Mean Streak	Wheat, Carolyn
Novel	Nominee	Anthony	B'con	1996	1995	Hard Christmas	D'Amato, Barbara
Novel	Winner	Anthony	B'con	1996	1995	Under the Beetle's Cellar	Walker, Mary Willis
Novel	Winner	Ellis	CWC	1996	1995	Mother Love	Wright, L.R.
Novel	Winner	Hammett	IACW	1996	1995	Under the Beetle's Cellar	Walker, Mary Willis
Novel	Nominee	Agatha	Malice	1996	1995	Miracles in Maggody	Hess, Joan
Novel	Winner	Agatha	Malice	1996	1995	If I'd Killed Him When I Met Him	McCrumb, Sharyn
Novel	Nominee	Agatha	Malice	1996	1995	The Wandering Arm	Newman, Sharan
Novel	Nominee	Agatha	Malice	1996	1995	Twilight	Pickard, Nancy
Novel	Nominee	Macavity	MRI	1996	1995	Hard Christmas	D'Amato, Barbara
Novel	Nominee	Macavity	MRI	1996	1995	A Wild and Lonely Place	Muller, Marcia
Novel	Winner	Macavity	MRI	1996	1995	Under the Beetle's Cellar	Walker, Mary Willis
Novel	Winner	Shamus	PWA	1996	1995	Concourse	Rozan, S.J.
Novel	Winner	Nero Wolfe	Wolfe Pack	1996	1995	A Monstrous Regiment of Women	King, Laurie R.
Novel	Nominee	Anthony	B'con	1995	1994	"K" is for Killer	Grafton, Sue
Novel	Winner	Anthony	B'con	1995	1994	She Walks These Hills	McCrumb, Sharyn
Novel	Nominee	Anthony	B'con	1995	1994	Crack Down	McDermid, Val
Novel	Winner	Gold Dagger	CWA	1995	1995	The Mermaids Singing	McDermid, Val
Novel	Nominee	Gold Dagger	CWA	1995	1995	A Piece of Justice	Paton Walsh, Jill
Novel	Winner	Ellis	CWC	1995	1994	A Colder Kind Of Death	Bowen, Gail
Novel	Nominee	Hammett	IACW	1995	1994	Shinju	Rowland, Laura Joh
Novel	Nominee	Agatha	Malice	1995	1994	Scandal in Fair Haven	Hart, Carolyn G.
Novel	Nominee	Agatha	Malice	1995	1994	The Beekeeper's Apprentice	King, Laurie R.
Novel	Nominee	Agatha	Malice	1995	1994	Angel of Death	Krich, Rochelle Majer
Novel	Winner	Agatha	Malice	1995	1994	She Walks These Hills	McCrumb, Sharyn
Novel	Nominee	Agatha	Malice	1995	1994	Night Train to Memphis	Peters, Elizabeth
Novel	Winner	Macavity	MRI	1995	1994	She Walks These Hills	McCrumb, Sharyn
Novel	Nominee	Macavity	MRI	1995	1994	The Red Scream	Walker, Mary Willis
Novel	Nominee	Edgar	MWA	1995	1994	Miami, It's Murder	Buchanan, Edna
Novel	Winner	Edgar	MWA	1995	1994	The Red Scream	Walker, Mary Willis
Novel	Winner	Shamus	PWA	1995	1994	"K" is for Killer	Grafton, Sue
Novel	Nominee	Shamus	PWA	1995	1994	The Killing of Monday Brown	Prowell, Sandra West
Novel	Winner	Nero Wolfe	Wolfe Pack	1995	1994	She Walks These Hills	McCrumb, Sharyn
Novel	Nominee	Anthony	B'con	1994	1993	Murder on a Kibbutz	Gur, Batya
Novel	Nominee	Anthony	B'con	1994	1993	O Little Town of Maggody	Hess, Joan
Novel	Nominee	Anthony	B'con	1994	1993	Old Enemies	LaPierre, Janet
Novel	Nominee	Anthony	B'con	1994	1993	Southern Discomfort	Maron, Margaret

Awards List 2 – Winners and Nominees by Award Category

Includes awards through 1998 for series novels only

Category	Status	Name	Conf'd by	Award	Pub	BOOK TITLE	Last, First
Novel	Winner	Anthony	B'con	1994	1993	Wolf in the Shadows	Muller, Marcia
Novel	Nominee	Anthony	B'con	1994	1993	To Live and Die in Dixie	Trocheck, Kathy Hogan
Novel	Nominee	Anthony	B'con	1994	1993	Consider the Crows	Weir, Charlene
Novel	Nominee	Gold Dagger	CWA	1994	1994	"K" is for Killer	Grafton, Sue
Novel	Nominee	Gold Dagger	CWA	1994	1994	Crack Down	McDermid, Val
Novel	Nominee	Gold Dagger	CWA	1994	1994	Tunnel Vision	Paretsky, Sara
Novel	Nominee	Ellis	CWC	1994	1993	A Touch of Panic	Wright, L.R.
Novel	Winner	Agatha	Malice	1994	1993	Dead Man's Island	Hart, Carolyn G.
Novel	Nominee	Agatha	Malice	1994	1993	O Little Town of Maggody	Hess, Joan
Novel	Nominee	Agatha	Malice	1994	1993	Fair Game	Krich, Rochelle Majer
Novel	Nominee	Agatha	Malice	1994	1993	Southern Discomfort	Maron, Margaret
Novel	Nominee	Agatha	Malice	1994	1993	To Live and Die in Dixie	Trocheck, Kathy Hogan
Novel	Nominee	Macavity	MRI	1994	1993	To Live and Die in Dixie	Trocheck, Kathy Hogan
Novel	Nominee	Edgar	MWA	1994	1993	Wolf in the Shadows	Muller, Marcia
Novel	Nominee	Shamus	PWA	1994	1993	Wolf in the Shadows	Muller, Marcia
Novel	Nominee	Shamus	PWA	1994	1993	The Lies That Bind	Van Gieson, Judith
Novel	Nominee	Nero Wolfe	Wolfe Pack	1994	1993	Hard Women	D'Amato, Barbara
Novel	Nominee	Anthony	B'con	1993	1992	Southern Ghost	Hart, Carolyn G.
Novel	Winner	Anthony	B'con	1993	1992	Bootlegger's Daughter	Maron, Margaret
Novel	Nominee	Anthony	B'con	1993	1992	The Hangman's Beautiful Daughter	McCrumb, Sharyn
Novel	Winner	Gold Dagger	CWA	1993	1993	Cruel and Unusual	Cornwell, Patricia
Novel	Winner	Silver Dagger	CWA	1993	1993	Fat Lands	Dunant, Sarah
Novel	Nominee	Gold Dagger	CWA	1993	1993	Death Among the Dons	Neel, Janet
Novel	Nominee	Hammett	IACW	1993	1992	By Evil Means	Prowell, Sandra West
Novel	Nominee	Agatha	Malice	1993	1992	The Alpine Advocate	Daheim, Mary
Novel	Nominee	Agatha	Malice	1993	1992	Southern Ghost	Hart, Carolyn G.
Novel	Winner	Agatha	Malice	1993	1992	Bootlegger's Daughter	Maron, Margaret
Novel	Nominee	Agatha	Malice	1993	1992	The Hangman's Beautiful Daughter	McCrumb, Sharyn
Novel	Nominee	Agatha	Malice	1993	1992	Defend and Betray	Perry, Anne
Novel	Nominee	Agatha	Malice	1993	1992	The Snake, the Crocodile and the Dog	Peters, Elizabeth
Novel	Winner	Macavity	MRI	1993	1992	Bootlegger's Daughter	Maron, Margaret
Novel	Nominee	Edgar	MWA	1993	1992	Backhand	Cody, Liza
Novel	Winner	Edgar	MWA	1993	1992	Bootlegger's Daughter	Maron, Margaret
Novel	Nominee	Anthony	B'con	1992	1991	Rogue Wave	Dunlap, Susan
Novel	Nominee	Anthony	B'con	1992	1991	Love Nor Money	Grant, Linda
Novel	Nominee	Anthony	B'con	1992	1991	The Christie Caper	Hart, Carolyn G.
Novel	Nominee	Anthony	B'con	1992	1991	I.O.U.	Pickard, Nancy
Novel	Nominee	Anthony	B'con	1992	1991	A Single Stone	Wallace, Marilyn
Novel	Winner	Silver Dagger	CWA	1992	1992	Bucket Nut	Cody, Liza
Novel	Nominee	Agatha	Malice	1992	1991	The Christie Caper	Hart, Carolyn G.
Novel	Nominee	Agatha	Malice	1992	1991	An Owl Too Many	MacLeod, Charlotte
Novel	Nominee	Agatha	Malice	1992	1991	The Last Camel Died at Noon	Peters, Elizabeth
Novel	Winner	Agatha	Malice	1992	1991	I.O.U.	Pickard, Nancy
Novel	Nominee	Macavity	MRI	1992	1991	The Christie Caper	Hart, Carolyn G.
Novel	Winner	Macavity	MRI	1992	1991	I.O.U.	Pickard, Nancy
Novel	Nominee	Edgar	MWA	1992	1991	Prior Convictions	Matera, Lia
Novel	Nominee	Edgar	MWA	1992	1991	I.O.U.	Pickard, Nancy
Novel	Nominee	Shamus	PWA	1992	1991	Where Echoes Live	Muller, Marcia
Novel	Winner	Anthony	B'con	1991	1990	"G" is for Gumshoe	Grafton, Sue
Novel	Nominee	Anthony	B'con	1991	1990	The Good Fight	Matera, Lia
Novel	Nominee	Anthony	B'con	1991	1990	If Ever I Return Pretty Peggy-O	McCrumb, Sharyn
Novel	Nominee	Anthony	B'con	1991	1990	New Orleans Mourning	Smith, Julie
Novel	Winner	Silver Dagger	CWA	1991	1991	Deep Sleep	Fyfield, Frances
Novel	Nominee	Agatha	Malice	1991	1990	Real Murders	Harris, Charlaine
Novel	Nominee	Agatha	Malice	1991	1990	Deadly Valentine	Hart, Carolyn G.
Novel	Nominee	Agatha	Malice	1991	1990	The Face of a Stranger	Perry, Anne
Novel	Winner	Agatha	Malice	1991	1990	Bum Steer	Pickard, Nancy
Novel	Nominee	Macavity	MRI	1991	1990	Deadly Valentine	Hart, Carolyn G.
Novel	Winner	Macavity	MRI	1991	1990	If Ever I Return Pretty Peggy-O	McCrumb, Sharyn
Novel	Nominee	Macavity	MRI	1991	1990	The Good Fight	Matera, Lia
Novel	Winner	Edgar	MWA	1991	1990	New Orleans Mourning	Smith, Julie
Novel	Winner	Shamus	PWA	1991	1990	"G" is for Gumshoe	Grafton, Sue
Novel	Winner	Anthony	B'con	1990	1989	The Sirens Sang of Murder	Caudwell, Sarah
Novel	Nominee	Anthony	B'con	1990	1989	Pious Deception	Dunlap, Susan
Novel	Nominee	Anthony	B'con	1990	1989	A Question of Guilt [U.S. edition]	Fyfield, Frances
Novel	Nominee	Anthony	B'con	1990	1989	A Little Class on Murder	Hart, Carolyn G.
Novel	Nominee	Anthony	B'con	1990	1989	Corpus Christmas	Maron, Margaret

Awards List 2 – Winners and Nominees by Award Category

Includes awards through 1998 for series novels only

	A W A R D			Y E A R			AUTHOR NAME
Category	Status	Name	Conf'd by	Award	Pub	B O O K T I T L E	Last, First
Novel	Winner	Ellis	CWC	1990	1989	A Chill Rain in January	Wright, L.R.
Novel	Nominee	Agatha	Malice	1990	1989	The Sirens Sang of Murder	Caudwell, Sarah
Novel	Nominee	Agatha	Malice	1990	1989	A Little Class on Murder	Hart, Carolyn G.
Novel	Nominee	Agatha	Malice	1990	1989	Corpus Christmas	Maron, Margaret
Novel	Winner	Agatha	Malice	1990	1989	Naked Once More	Peters, Elizabeth
Novel	Nominee	Agatha	Malice	1990	1989	Philly Stakes	Roberts, Gillian
Novel	Winner	Macavity	MRI	1990	1989	A Little Class on Murder	Hart, Carolyn G.
Novel	Nominee	Edgar	MWA	1990	1989	A Question of Guilt [U.S. edition]	Fyfield, Frances
Novel	Nominee	Shamus	PWA	1990	1989	The Shape of Dread	Muller, Marcia
Novel	Nominee	Anthony	B'con	1989	1988	The Widow's Club	Cannell, Dorothy
Novel	Nominee	Anthony	B'con	1989	1988	"E" is for Evidence	Grafton, Sue
Novel	Nominee	Anthony	B'con	1989	1988	Mischief in Maggody	Hess, Joan
Novel	Nominee	Anthony	B'con	1989	1988	Blood Shot	Paretsky, Sara
Novel	Nominee	Anthony	B'con	1989	1988	Dead Crazy	Pickard, Nancy
Novel	Nominee	Agatha	Malice	1989	1988	The Widow's Club	Cannell, Dorothy
Novel	Winner	Agatha	Malice	1989	1988	Something Wicked	Hart, Carolyn G.
Novel	Winner	Agatha	Malice	1989	1988	Mischief in Maggody	Hess, Joan
Novel	Nominee	Agatha	Malice	1989	1988	Paying the Piper	McCrumb, Sharyn
Novel	Nominee	Agatha	Malice	1989	1988	Dead Crazy	Pickard, Nancy
Novel	Nominee	Macavity	MRI	1989	1988	Murder Unrenovated	Carlson, P.M.
Novel	Nominee	Shamus	PWA	1989	1988	Blood Shot	Paretsky, Sara
Novel	Nominee	Anthony	B'con	1988	1987	A Trouble of Fools	Barnes, Linda
Novel	Nominee	Anthony	B'con	1988	1987	Trojan Gold	Peters, Elizabeth
Novel	Nominee	Anthony	B'con	1988	1987	Marriage is Murder	Pickard, Nancy
Novel	Winner	Silver Dagger	CWA	1988	1988	Toxic Shock [U.S.-Blood Shot]	Paretsky, Sara
Novel	Nominee	Macavity	MRI	1988	1987	Death on Demand	Hart, Carolyn G.
Novel	Winner	Macavity	MRI	1988	1987	Marriage is Murder	Pickard, Nancy
Novel	Nominee	Edgar	MWA	1988	1987	A Trouble of Fools	Barnes, Linda
Novel	Nominee	Shamus	PWA	1988	1987	A Trouble of Fools	Barnes, Linda
Novel	Winner	Anthony	B'con	1987	1986	"C" is for Corpse	Grafton, Sue
Novel	Winner	Macavity	MRI	1987	1986	A Taste for Death	James, P.D.
Novel	Nominee	Edgar	MWA	1987	1986	The Corpse in Oozak's Pond	MacLeod, Charlotte
Novel	Nominee	Shamus	PWA	1987	1986	"C" is for Corpse	Grafton, Sue
Novel	Winner	Nero Wolfe	Wolfe Pack	1987	1986	The Corpse in Oozak's Pond	MacLeod, Charlotte
Novel	Winner	Anthony	B'con	1986	1985	"B" is for Burglar	Grafton, Sue
Novel	Nominee	Anthony	B'con	1986	1985	Strangled Prose	Hess, Joan
Novel	Nominee	Anthony	B'con	1986	1985	No Body	Pickard, Nancy
Novel	Nominee	Gold Dagger	CWA	1986	1986	Under Contract	Cody, Liza
Novel	Winner	Silver Dagger	CWA	1986	1986	A Taste for Death	James, P.D.
Novel	Nominee	Edgar	MWA	1986	1985	An Unkindness of Ravens	Rendell, Ruth
Novel	Winner	Edgar	MWA	1986	1985	The Suspect	Wright, L.R.
Novel	Winner	Shamus	PWA	1986	1985	"B" is for Burglar	Grafton, Sue
Novel	Winner	Gold Dagger	CWA	1985	1985	Monkey Puzzle	Gosling, Paula
Novel	Winner	Silver Dagger	CWA	1985	1985	Last Seen Alive	Simpson, Dorothy
Novel	Nominee	Edgar	MWA	1985	1984	Emily Dickinson Is Dead	Langton, Jane
Novel	Winner	Nero Wolfe	Wolfe Pack	1984	1984	Emily Dickinson Is Dead	Langton, Jane
Novel	Winner	Anthony	B'con	1983	1982	"A" is for Alibi	Grafton, Sue
Novel	Nominee	Shamus	PWA	1983	1982	"A" is for Alibi	Grafton, Sue
Novel	Winner	Nero Wolfe	Wolfe Pack	1983	1983	The Anondyne Necklace	Grimes, Martha
Novel	Winner	Silver Dagger	CWA	1982	1982	Ritual Murder	Haymon, S.T.
Novel	Nominee	Edgar	MWA	1982	1981	Dupe	Cody, Liza
Novel	Nominee	Gold Dagger	CWA	1981	1981	Murder Has a Pretty Face	Melville, Jennie
Novel	Winner	Nero Wolfe	Wolfe Pack	1981	1981	Death in a Tenured Position	Cross, Amanda
Novel	Nominee	Edgar	MWA	1979	1978	A Sleeping Life	Rendell, Ruth
Novel	Winner	Silver Dagger	CWA	1975	1975	The Black Tower	James, P.D.
Novel	Nominee	Edgar	MWA	1974	1973	An Unsuitable Job for a Woman	James, P.D.
Novel	Nominee	Edgar	MWA	1974	1973	Dear Laura	Stubbs, Jean
Novel	Nominee	Edgar	MWA	1972	1971	Shroud for a Nightingale	James, P.D.
Novel	Winner	Silver Dagger	CWA	1971	1971	Shroud for a Nightingale	James, P.D.
Novel	Nominee	Edgar	MWA	1971	1970	Many Deadly Returns [Brit.-Who Saw Her Die]	Moyes, Patricia
Novel	Winner	Edgar	MWA	1971	1970	The Laughing Policeman	Sjöwall, Maj & Per Wahlöö
Novel	Nominee	Edgar	MWA	1970	1969	When in Greece	Lathen, Emma

Awards List 2 – Winners and Nominees by Award Category

Includes awards through 1998 for series novels only

Category	Status	Name	Conf'd by	Award	Pub	BOOK TITLE	Last, First
Novel	Nominee	Edgar	MWA	1969	1968	Picture Miss Seeton	Crane, Hamilton
Novel	Winner	Gold Dagger	CWA	1967	1967	Murder Against the Grain	Lathen, Emma
Novel	Winner	Silver Dagger	CWA	1965	1965	Accounting For Murder	Lathen, Emma
Novel	Winner	Gold Dagger	CWA	1961	1961	The Spoilt Kill	Kelly, Mary
Novel-Europe	Winner	CWA '92	CWA	1991	1991	Gaudi Afternoon [U.K. ed.]	Wilson, Barbara
Novel-Funniest	Winner	Last Laugh	CWA	1996	1996	Two for the Dough	Evanovich, Janet
Novel-Funniest	Nominee	Last Laugh	CWA	1995	1995	Ten Lords A-Leaping	Edwards, Ruth Dudley
Novel-Funniest	Nominee	Last Laugh	CWA	1995	1995	One For The Money	Evanovich, Janet
Novel-Funniest	Nominee	Last Laugh	CWA	1994	1994	Written in Blood	Graham, Caroline
Novel-Funniest	Nominee	Last Laugh	CWA	1993	1993	Poseidon's Gold	Davis, Lindsey
Novel-Funniest	Nominee	Last Laugh	CWA	1992	1992	Clubbed to Death	Edwards, Ruth Dudley
Novel-Historical	Winner	Gargoyle	Historicon	1994	1993	A Broken Vessel	Ross, Kate
Novel-Romantic	Winner	Kiss of Death	RWA	1998	1997	Hidden Agenda	Alexander, Skye
PB Original	Nominee	Anthony	B'con	1998	1997	Charm City	Lippman, Laura
PB Original	Nominee	Edgar	MWA	1998	1997	Home Again, Home Again	Cooper, Susan Rogers
PB Original	Nominee	Edgar	MWA	1998	1997	The Prioress' Tale	Frazer, Margaret
PB Original	Winner	Edgar	MWA	1998	1997	Charm City	Lippman, Laura
PB Original	Nominee	Edgar	MWA	1998	1997	Sunset and Santiago	White, Gloria
PB Original	Winner	Shamus	PWA	1998	1997	Charm City	Lippman, Laura
PB Original	Nominee	Shamus	PWA	1998	1997	Father Forgive Me	Lordon, Randye
PB Original	Nominee	Shamus	PWA	1998	1997	Sunset and Santiago	White, Gloria
PB Original	Winner	Anthony	B'con	1997	1996	Somebody Else's Child	Grimes, Terris McMahan
PB Original	Nominee	Anthony	B'con	1997	1996	The Grass Widow	Holbrook, Teri
PB Original	Nominee	Edgar	MWA	1997	1996	Silent Words	Drury, Joan M.
PB Original	Nominee	Edgar	MWA	1997	1996	The Grass Widow	Holbrook, Teri
PB Original	Nominee	Shamus	PWA	1997	1996	Natural Death	Furie, Ruthe
PB Original	Nominee	Anthony	B'con	1996	1995	Bad Medicine	Dreyer, Eileen
PB Original	Nominee	Anthony	B'con	1996	1995	A Far and Deadly Cry	Holbrook, Teri
PB Original	Nominee	Anthony	B'con	1996	1995	Charged With Guilt	White, Gloria
PB Original	Nominee	Edgar	MWA	1996	1995	Charged With Guilt	White, Gloria
PB Original	Nominee	Shamus	PWA	1996	1995	Interview With Mattie	Singer, Shelley
PB Original	Nominee	Shamus	PWA	1996	1995	Charged With Guilt	White, Gloria
PB Original	Winner	Edgar	MWA	1995	1994	Final Appeal	Scottoline, Lisa
PB Original	Nominee	Shamus	PWA	1995	1994	Lament for a Dead Cowboy	Dain, Catherine
PB Original	Nominee	Shamus	PWA	1995	1994	Dead Ahead	McKenna, Bridget
PB Original	Nominee	Shamus	PWA	1995	1994	Deadly Devotion	Wallace, Patricia
PB Original	Nominee	Edgar	MWA	1994	1993	The Servant's Tale	Frazer, Margaret
PB Original	Nominee	Edgar	MWA	1994	1993	Everywhere That Mary Went	Scottoline, Lisa
PB Original	Nominee	Edgar	MWA	1993	1992	The Good Friday Murder	Harris, Lee
PB Original	Nominee	Edgar	MWA	1993	1992	Principal Defense	Hartzmark, Gini
PB Original	Winner	Edgar	MWA	1993	1992	A Cold Day for Murder	Stabenow, Dana
PB Original	Nominee	Shamus	PWA	1993	1992	Lay it on the Line	Dain, Catherine
PB Original	Winner	Shamus	PWA	1993	1992	The Last Tango of Delores Delgado	Day, Marele
PB Original	Nominee	Edgar	MWA	1992	1991	Murder in the Dog Days	Carlson, P.M.
PB Original	Nominee	Edgar	MWA	1992	1991	Fine Distinctions	Valentine, Deborah
PB Original	Nominee	Shamus	PWA	1992	1991	House of Cards	Hooper, Kay
PB Original	Nominee	Anthony	B'con	1991	1990	Not a Creature Was Stirring	Haddam, Jane
PB Original	Nominee	Anthony	B'con	1991	1990	Dead in the Scrub	Oliphant, B.J.
PB Original	Nominee	Edgar	MWA	1991	1990	Not a Creature Was Stirring	Haddam, Jane
PB Original	Nominee	Edgar	MWA	1991	1990	Dead in the Scrub	Oliphant, B.J.
PB Original	Winner	Anthony	B'con	1990	1989	Honeymoon with Murder	Hart, Carolyn G.
PB Original	Nominee	Anthony	B'con	1990	1989	Murder by Deception	Meredith, D.R.
PB Original	Nominee	Anthony	B'con	1990	1989	A Collector of Photographs	Valentine, Deborah
PB Original	Nominee	Edgar	MWA	1990	1989	A Collector of Photographs	Valentine, Deborah
PB Original	Nominee	Shamus	PWA	1990	1989	A Collector of Photographs	Valentine, Deborah
PB Original	Nominee	Anthony	B'con	1989	1988	Murder Unrenovated	Carlson, P.M.
PB Original	Winner	Anthony	B'con	1989	1988	Something Wicked	Hart, Carolyn G.
PB Original	Nominee	Anthony	B'con	1989	1988	A Radical Departure	Matera, Lia
PB Original	Nominee	Anthony	B'con	1989	1988	Paying the Piper	McCrumb, Sharyn
PB Original	Nominee	Anthony	B'con	1989	1988	Murder by Impulse	Meredith, D.R.

Awards List 2 – Winners and Nominees by Award Category
Includes awards through 1998 for series novels only

| AWARD | | | | YEAR | | BOOK TITLE | AUTHOR NAME |
Category	Status	Name	Conf'd by	Award	Pub		Last, First
NPB Original	Nominee	Anthony	B'con	1989	1988	Primary Target	Wallace, Marilyn
PB Original	Nominee	Edgar	MWA	1989	1988	A Radical Departure	Matera, Lia
PB Original	Nominee	Anthony	B'con	1988	1987	The Cat Who Played Brahms	Braun, Lilian Jackson
PB Original	Nominee	Anthony	B'con	1988	1987	Death on Demand	Hart, Carolyn G.
PB Original	Nominee	Anthony	B'con	1988	1987	Where Lawyers Fear to Tread	Matera, Lia
PB Original	Nominee	Anthony	B'con	1988	1987	Bimbos of the Death Sun	McCrumb, Sharyn
PB Original	Nominee	Macavity	MRI	1988	1987	Where Lawyers Fear to Tread	Matera, Lia
PB Original	Nominee	Edgar	MWA	1988	1987	Bullshot	Kraft, Gabrielle
PB Original	Winner	Edgar	MWA	1988	1987	Bimbos of the Death Sun	McCrumb, Sharyn
PB Original	Nominee	Edgar	MWA	1987	1986	The Cat Who Saw Red	Braun, Lilian Jackson
PB Original	Nominee	Edgar	MWA	1987	1986	Shattered Moon	Green, Kate
PB Original	Nominee	Shamus	PWA	1987	1986	Dark Fields	MacGregor, T.J.
PB Original	Nominee	Anthony	B'con	1986	1985	Murder Is Academic	Carlson, P.M
PB Original	Winner	Anthony	B'con	1986	1985	Say No To Murder	Pickard, Nancy
Police Novel	Winner	Grand Prix	Acad Fran	1971	1970	The Ledger	Uhnak, Dorothy

Awards List 3 – Winners and Nominees by Author's Last Name
Includes awards through 1998 for series novels only

| AUTHOR NAME | | YEAR | | AWARD | | | |
Last, First	BOOK TITLE	Pub	Award	Conf'd by	Name	Status	Category
Adams, Deborah	All the Great Pretenders	1992	1993	Malice	Agatha	Nominee	First Novel
Adams, Jane	The Greenway	1995	1995	CWA	Creasey	Nominee	First Novel
Albert, Susan Wittig	Thyme of Death	1992	1993	B'con	Anthony	Nominee	First Novel
Albert, Susan Wittig	Thyme of Death	1992	1993	Malice	Agatha	Nominee	First Novel
Alexander, Skye	Hidden Agenda	1997	1998	RWA	Kiss of Death	Winner	Novel-Romantic
Andreae, Christine	Trail of Murder	1992	1993	MWA	Edgar	Nominee	First Novel
Barnes, Linda	A Trouble of Fools	1987	1988	B'con	Anthony	Nominee	Novel
Barnes, Linda	A Trouble of Fools	1987	1988	MWA	Edgar	Nominee	Novel
Barnes, Linda	A Trouble of Fools	1987	1988	PWA	Shamus	Nominee	Novel
Barr, Nevada	Track of the Cat	1993	1994	B'con	Anthony	Winner	First Novel
Barr, Nevada	Track of the Cat	1993	1994	Malice	Agatha	Winner	First Novel
Bell, Nancy	Biggie and the Poisoned Politician	1996	1997	Malice	Agatha	Nominee	First Novel
Benjamin, Carol Lea	This Dog for Hire	1996	1997	PWA	Shamus	Winner	First Novel
Blanc, Suzanne	The Green Stone	1961	1962	MWA	Edgar	Winner	First Novel
Bowen, Gail	A Colder Kind Of Death	1994	1995	CWC	Ellis	Winner	Novel
Boylan, Eleanor	Working Murder	1989	1990	Malice	Agatha	Nominee	First Novel
Braun, Lilian Jackson	The Cat Who Played Brahms	1987	1988	B'con	Anthony	Nominee	PB Original
Braun, Lilian Jackson	The Cat Who Saw Red	1986	1987	MWA	Edgar	Nominee	PB Original
Buchanan, Edna	Miami, It's Murder	1994	1995	MWA	Edgar	Nominee	Novel
Burden, Pat	Screaming Bones	1990	1991	Malice	Agatha	Nominee	First Novel
Burke, Jan	Hocus	1997	1998	Malice	Agatha	Nominee	Novel
Burke, Jan	Hocus	1997	1998	MRI	Macavity	Nominee	Novel
Burke, Jan	Goodnight, Irene	1993	1994	B'con	Anthony	Nominee	First Novel
Burke, Jan	Goodnight, Irene	1993	1994	Malice	Agatha	Nominee	First Novel
Cannell, Dorothy	The Widow's Club	1988	1989	B'con	Anthony	Nominee	Novel
Cannell, Dorothy	The Widow's Club	1988	1989	Malice	Agatha	Nominee	Novel
Carlson, P.M.	Murder in the Dog Days	1991	1992	MWA	Edgar	Nominee	PB Original
Carlson, P.M.	Murder Unrenovated	1988	1989	B'con	Anthony	Nominee	PB Original
Carlson, P.M.	Murder Unrenovated	1988	1989	MRI	Macavity	Nominee	Novel
Carlson, P.M.	Murder Is Academic	1985	1986	B'con	Anthony	Nominee	PB Original
Caudwell, Sarah	The Sirens Sang of Murder	1989	1990	B'con	Anthony	Winner	Novel
Caudwell, Sarah	The Sirens Sang of Murder	1989	1990	Malice	Agatha	Nominee	Novel
Churchill, Jill	Grime and Punishment	1989	1990	B'con	Anthony	Nominee	First Novel
Churchill, Jill	Grime and Punishment	1989	1990	Malice	Agatha	Winner	First Novel
Churchill, Jill	Grime and Punishment	1989	1990	MRI	Macavity	Winner	First Novel

Awards List 3 – Winners and Nominees by Author's Last Name

Includes awards through 1998 for series novels only

Last, First	BOOK TITLE	Pub	Award	Conf'd by	Name	Status	Category
Clark, Carol Higgins	Decked	1992	1993	B'con	Anthony	Nominee	First Novel
Clark, Carol Higgins	Decked	1992	1993	Malice	Agatha	Nominee	First Novel
Cody, Liza	Backhand	1992	1993	MWA	Edgar	Nominee	Novel
Cody, Liza	Bucket Nut	1992	1992	CWA	Silver Dagger	Winner	Novel
Cody, Liza	Under Contract	1986	1986	CWA	Gold Dagger	Nominee	Novel
Cody, Liza	Dupe	1981	1982	MWA	Edgar	Nominee	Novel
Cody, Liza	Dupe	1980	1980	CWA	Creasey	Winner	First Novel
Cooper, Susan Rogers	Home Again, Home Again	1997	1998	MWA	Edgar	Nominee	PB Original
Cornwell, Patricia	Cruel and Unusual	1993	1993	CWA	Gold Dagger	Winner	Novel
Cornwell, Patricia	Postmortem	1990	1991	B'con	Anthony	Winner	First Novel
Cornwell, Patricia	Postmortem	1990	1991	MRI	Macavity	Winner	First Novel
Cornwell, Patricia	Postmortem	1990	1991	MWA	Edgar	Winner	First Novel
Cornwell, Patricia	Postmortem	1990	1990	CWA	Creasey	Winner	First Novel
Crane, Hamilton	Picture Miss Seeton	1968	1969	MWA	Edgar	Nominee	Novel
Crombie, Deborah	Dreaming of the Bones	1997	1998	Malice	Agatha	Nominee	Novel
Crombie, Deborah	Dreaming of the Bones	1997	1998	MRI	Macavity	Winner	Novel
Crombie, Deborah	Dreaming of the Bones	1997	1998	MWA	Edgar	Nominee	Novel
Crombie, Deborah	A Share in Death	1993	1994	Malice	Agatha	Nominee	First Novel
Crombie, Deborah	A Share in Death	1993	1994	MRI	Macavity	Nominee	First Novel
Cross, Amanda	Death in a Tenured Position	1981	1981	Wolfe Pack	Nero Wolfe	Winner	Novel
Cross, Amanda	In the Last Analysis	1964	1965	MWA	Edgar	Nominee	First Novel
Daheim, Mary	The Alpine Advocate	1992	1993	Malice	Agatha	Nominee	Novel
Daheim, Mary	Just Desserts	1991	1992	Malice	Agatha	Nominee	First Novel
Dain, Catherine	Lament for a Dead Cowboy	1994	1995	PWA	Shamus	Nominee	PB Original
Dain, Catherine	Lay it on the Line	1992	1993	PWA	Shamus	Nominee	PB Original
D'Amato, Barbara	Hard Christmas	1995	1996	B'con	Anthony	Nominee	Novel
D'Amato, Barbara	Hard Christmas	1995	1996	MRI	Macavity	Nominee	Novel
D'Amato, Barbara	Hard Women	1993	1994	Wolfe Pack	Nero Wolfe	Nominee	Novel
Dams, Jeanne M.	The Body in the Transept	1995	1996	Malice	Agatha	Winner	First Novel
Dams, Jeanne M.	The Body in the Transept	1995	1996	MRI	Macavity	Nominee	First Novel
Davidson, Diane Mott	Catering to Nobody	1990	1991	B'con	Anthony	Nominee	First Novel
Davidson, Diane Mott	Catering to Nobody	1990	1991	Malice	Agatha	Nominee	First Novel
Davidson, Diane Mott	Catering to Nobody	1990	1991	MRI	Macavity	Nominee	First Novel
Davis, Dorothy Salisbury	Lifetime Achievement	1985	1985	MWA	Grand Master	Winner	Lifetime
Davis, Lindsey	Poseidon's Gold	1993	1993	CWA	Last Laugh	Nominee	Novel-Funniest
Dawson, Janet	Kindred Crimes	1990	1991	B'con	Anthony	Nominee	First Novel
Dawson, Janet	Kindred Crimes	1990	1991	MRI	Macavity	Nominee	First Novel
Dawson, Janet	Kindred Crimes	1990	1991	PWA	Shamus	Nominee	First Novel
Dawson, Janet	Kindred Crimes	1990	1989	SMP/PWA	SMP/PWA	Winner	First P.I. Novel
Day, Dianne	The Strange Files of Fremont Jones	1995	1996	MRI	Macavity	Winner	First Novel
Day, Marele	The Last Tango of Delores Delgado	1992	1993	PWA	Shamus	Winner	PB Original
Dobson, Joanne	Quieter Than Sleep	1997	1998	Malice	Agatha	Nominee	First Novel
Douglas, Lauren Wright	Ninth Life	1989	1990	LBR	Lambda	Winner [tie]	Lesbian Mystery
Dreyer, Eileen	Bad Medicine	1995	1996	B'con	Anthony	Nominee	PB Original
Drury, Joan M.	Silent Words	1996	1997	MWA	Edgar	Nominee	PB Original
Dunant, Sarah	Fat Lands	1993	1993	CWA	Silver Dagger	Winner	Novel
Dunlap, Susan	Rogue Wave	1991	1992	B'con	Anthony	Nominee	Novel
Dunlap, Susan	Pious Deception	1989	1990	B'con	Anthony	Nominee	Novel
Dymmoch, Michael Allen	The Man Who Understood Cats	1993	1992	SMP/MD	SMP/MD	Winner	First Novel
Edwards, Grace F.	If I Should Die	1997	1998	B'con	Anthony	Nominee	First Novel
Edwards, Ruth Dudley	Ten Lords A-Leaping	1995	1995	CWA	Last Laugh	Nominee	Novel-Funniest
Edwards, Ruth Dudley	Clubbed to Death	1992	1992	CWA	Last Laugh	Nominee	Novel-Funniest
Edwards, Ruth Dudley	Corridors of Death	1981	1981	CWA	Creasey	Nominee	First Novel
Evanovich, Janet	Three To Get Deadly	1997	1997	CWA	Silver Dagger	Winner	Novel
Evanovich, Janet	Two for the Dough	1996	1996	CWA	Last Laugh	Winner	Novel-Funniest
Evanovich, Janet	One For The Money	1995	1995	CWA	Creasey	Winner	First Novel
Evanovich, Janet	One For The Money	1995	1995	CWA	Last Laugh	Nominee	Novel-Funniest
Evanovich, Janet	One For The Money	1994	1995	Malice	Agatha	Nominee	First Novel

Awards List 3 – Winners and Nominees by Author's Last Name

Includes awards through 1998 for series novels only

AUTHOR NAME		YEAR		AWARD			
Last, First	BOOK TITLE	Pub	Award	Conf'd by	Name	Status	Category
Evanovich, Janet	One For The Money	1994	1995	MWA	Edgar	Nominee	First Novel
Evanovich, Janet	One For The Money	1994	1995	PWA	Shamus	Nominee	First Novel
Fairstein, Linda	Final Jeopardy	1996	1997	MRI	Macavity	Nominee	First Novel
Fennelly, Tony	The Glory Hole Murders	1985	1986	MWA	Edgar	Nominee	First Novel
Forrest, Katherine V.	Murder by Tradition	1991	1992	LBR	Lambda	Winner	Lesbian Mystery
Forrest, Katherine V.	The Beverly Malibu	1989	1990	LBR	Lambda	Winner	Lesbian Mystery
Fowler, Earlene	Goose in the Pond	1997	1998	Malice	Agatha	Nominee	Novel
Fowler, Earlene	Kansas Troubles	1996	1997	Malice	Agatha	Nominee	Novel
Fowler, Earlene	Fool's Puzzle	1994	1995	Malice	Agatha	Nominee	First Novel
Frazer, Margaret	The Prioress' Tale	1997	1998	MWA	Edgar	Nominee	PB Original
Frazer, Margaret	The Servant's Tale	1993	1994	MWA	Edgar	Nominee	PB Original
Furie, Ruthe	If Looks Could Kill	1995	1996	PWA	Shamus	Nominee	First Novel
Furie, Ruthe	Natural Death	1996	1997	PWA	Shamus	Nominee	PB Original
Fyfield, Frances	Deep Sleep	1991	1991	CWA	Silver Dagger	Winner	Novel
Fyfield, Frances	A Question of Guilt [U.S. edition]	1989	1990	B'con	Anthony	Nominee	Novel
Fyfield, Frances	A Question of Guilt [U.S. edition]	1989	1990	Malice	Agatha	Nominee	First Novel
Fyfield, Frances	A Question of Guilt [U.S. edition]	1989	1990	MWA	Edgar	Nominee	Novel
George, Anne	Murder on a Girl's Night Out	1996	1997	Malice	Agatha	Winner	First Novel
George, Elizabeth	A Great Deliverance	1988	1989	B'con	Anthony	Winner	First Novel
George, Elizabeth	A Great Deliverance	1988	1989	Malice	Agatha	Winner	First Novel
George, Elizabeth	A Great Deliverance	1988	1989	MRI	Macavity	Nominee	First Novel
George, Elizabeth	A Great Deliverance	1988	1989	MWA	Edgar	Nominee	First Novel
Gosling, Paula	Monkey Puzzle	1985	1985	CWA	Gold Dagger	Winner	Novel
Grafton, Sue	"K" is for Killer	1994	1995	B'con	Anthony	Nominee	Novel
Grafton, Sue	"K" is for Killer	1994	1994	CWA	Gold Dagger	Nominee	Novel
Grafton, Sue	"K" is for Killer	1994	1995	PWA	Shamus	Winner	Novel
Grafton, Sue	"G" is for Gumshoe	1990	1991	B'con	Anthony	Winner	Novel
Grafton, Sue	"G" is for Gumshoe	1990	1991	PWA	Shamus	Winner	Novel
Grafton, Sue	"E" is for Evidence	1988	1989	B'con	Anthony	Nominee	Novel
Grafton, Sue	"C" is for Corpse	1986	1987	B'con	Anthony	Winner	Novel
Grafton, Sue	"C" is for Corpse	1986	1987	PWA	Shamus	Nominee	Novel
Grafton, Sue	"B" is for Burglar	1985	1986	B'con	Anthony	Winner	Novel
Grafton, Sue	"B" is for Burglar	1985	1986	PWA	Shamus	Winner	Novel
Grafton, Sue	"A" is for Alibi	1982	1983	B'con	Anthony	Winner	Novel
Grafton, Sue	"A" is for Alibi	1982	1983	PWA	Shamus	Nominee	Novel
Graham, Caroline	Written in Blood	1994	1994	CWA	Last Laugh	Nominee	Novel-Funniest
Graham, Caroline	The Killings at Badger's Drift	1988	1989	B'con	Anthony	Nominee	First Novel
Graham, Caroline	The Killings at Badger's Drift	1988	1989	Malice	Agatha	Nominee	First Novel
Graham, Caroline	The Killings at Badger's Drift	1988	1989	MRI	Macavity	Winner	First Novel
Grant, Linda	Lethal Genes	1996	1997	B'con	Anthony	Nominee	Novel
Grant, Linda	Love Nor Money	1991	1992	B'con	Anthony	Nominee	Novel
Grant, Linda	Random Access Murder	1988	1989	B'con	Anthony	Nominee	First Novel
Green, Christine	Deadly Errand	1991	1991	CWA	Creasey	Nominee	First Novel
Green, Kate	Shattered Moon	1986	1987	MWA	Edgar	Nominee	PB Original
Grimes, Martha	The Anodyne Necklace	1983	1983	Wolfe Pack	Nero Wolfe	Winner	Novel
Grimes, Terris McMahan	Somebody Else's Child	1996	1997	B'con	Anthony	Winner (tie)	First Novel
Grimes, Terris McMahan	Somebody Else's Child	1996	1997	B'con	Anthony	Winner	PB Original
Grimes, Terris McMahan	Somebody Else's Child	1996	1997	Malice	Agatha	Nominee	First Novel
Gur, Batya	Murder on a Kibbutz	1993	1994	B'con	Anthony	Nominee	Novel
Haddam, Jane	Not a Creature Was Stirring	1990	1991	B'con	Anthony	Nominee	PB Original
Haddam, Jane	Not a Creature Was Stirring	1990	1991	MWA	Edgar	Nominee	PB Original
Hamilton, Lyn	The Xibalba Murders	1997	1998	CWC	Ellis	Nominee	First Novel
Harris, Charlaine	Real Murders	1990	1991	Malice	Agatha	Nominee	Novel
Harris, Lee	The Good Friday Murder	1992	1993	MWA	Edgar	Nominee	PB Original
Hart, Carolyn G.	Scandal in Fair Haven	1994	1995	Malice	Agatha	Nominee	Novel
Hart, Carolyn G.	Dead Man's Island	1993	1994	Malice	Agatha	Winner	Novel
Hart, Carolyn G.	Southern Ghost	1992	1993	B'con	Anthony	Nominee	Novel
Hart, Carolyn G.	Southern Ghost	1992	1993	Malice	Agatha	Nominee	Novel
Hart, Carolyn G.	The Christie Caper	1991	1992	B'con	Anthony	Nominee	Novel

Awards List 3 – Winners and Nominees by Author's Last Name

Includes awards through 1998 for series novels only

Last, First	BOOK TITLE	Pub	Award	Conf'd by	Name	Status	Category
Hart, Carolyn G.	The Christie Caper	1991	1992	Malice	Agatha	Nominee	Novel
Hart, Carolyn G.	The Christie Caper	1991	1992	MRI	Macavity	Nominee	Novel
Hart, Carolyn G.	Deadly Valentine	1990	1991	Malice	Agatha	Nominee	Novel
Hart, Carolyn G.	Deadly Valentine	1990	1991	MRI	Macavity	Nominee	Novel
Hart, Carolyn G.	Honeymoon with Murder	1989	1990	B'con	Anthony	Winner	PB Original
Hart, Carolyn G.	A Little Class on Murder	1989	1990	B'con	Anthony	Nominee	Novel
Hart, Carolyn G.	A Little Class on Murder	1989	1990	Malice	Agatha	Nominee	Novel
Hart, Carolyn G.	A Little Class on Murder	1989	1990	MRI	Macavity	Winner	Novel
Hart, Carolyn G.	Something Wicked	1988	1989	B'con	Anthony	Winner	PB Original
Hart, Carolyn G.	Something Wicked	1988	1989	Malice	Agatha	Winner	Novel
Hart, Carolyn G.	Death on Demand	1987	1988	B'con	Anthony	Nominee	PB Original
Hart, Carolyn G.	Death on Demand	1987	1988	MRI	Macavity	Nominee	Novel
Hart, Ellen	Robber's Wine	1996	1997	LBR	Lambda	Winner	Lesbian Mystery
Hart, Ellen	A Small Sacrifice	1993	1994	LBR	Lambda	Winner	Lesbian Mystery
Hartzmark, Gini	Principal Defense	1992	1993	MWA	Edgar	Nominee	PB Original
Hathaway, Robin	The Doctor Digs a Grave	1998	1997	SMP/MD	SMP/MD	Winner	First Novel
Haymon, S.T.	Ritual Murder	1982	1982	CWA	Silver Dagger	Winner	Novel
Hayter, Sparkle	Nice Girls Finish Last	1996	1997	CWC	Ellis	Nominee	Novel
Hayter, Sparkle	What's A Girl Gotta Do?	1994	1995	CWC	Ellis	Winner	First Novel
Henry, Sue	Murder on the Iditarod Trail	1991	1992	B'con	Anthony	Winner	First Novel
Henry, Sue	Murder on the Iditarod Trail	1991	1992	MRI	Macavity	Winner	First Novel
Hess, Joan	Miracles in Maggody	1995	1996	Malice	Agatha	Nominee	Novel
Hess, Joan	O Little Town of Maggody	1993	1994	B'con	Anthony	Nominee	Novel
Hess, Joan	O Little Town of Maggody	1993	1994	Malice	Agatha	Nominee	Novel
Hess, Joan	Mischief in Maggody	1988	1989	B'con	Anthony	Nominee	Novel
Hess, Joan	Mischief in Maggody	1988	1989	Malice	Agatha	Nominee	Novel
Hess, Joan	Strangled Prose	1985	1986	B'con	Anthony	Nominee	Novel
Hightower, Lynn S.	Satan's Lambs	1993	1994	PWA	Shamus	Winner	First Novel
Holbrook, Teri	The Grass Widow	1996	1997	B'con	Anthony	Nominee	PB Original
Holbrook, Teri	The Grass Widow	1996	1997	Malice	Agatha	Nominee	Novel
Holbrook, Teri	The Grass Widow	1996	1997	MRI	Macavity	Nominee	Novel
Holbrook, Teri	The Grass Widow	1996	1997	MWA	Edgar	Nominee	PB Original
Holbrook, Teri	A Far and Deadly Cry	1995	1996	B'con	Anthony	Nominee	PB Original
Holbrook, Teri	A Far and Deadly Cry	1995	1996	Malice	Agatha	Nominee	First Novel
Holbrook, Teri	A Far and Deadly Cry	1995	1996	MRI	Macavity	Nominee	First Novel
Holtzer, Susan	Something To Kill For	1994	1993	SMP/MD	SMP/MD	Winner	First Novel
Hooper, Kay	House of Cards	1991	1992	PWA	Shamus	Nominee	PB Original
Howe, Melodie Johnson	The Mother Shadow	1989	1990	B'con	Anthony	Nominee	First Novel
Howe, Melodie Johnson	The Mother Shadow	1989	1990	Malice	Agatha, Nominee		First Novel
Howe, Melodie Johnson	The Mother Shadow	1989	1990	MWA	Edgar	Nominee	First Novel
Jaffe, Jody	Horse of a Different Killer	1995	1996	Malice	Agatha	Nominee	First Novel
Jaffe, Jody	Horse of a Different Killer	1995	1996	MRI	Macavity	Nominee	First Novel
James, P.D.	Lifetime Achievement	1987	1987	CWA	Diamond Dagger	Winner	Lifetime
James, P.D.	A Taste for Death	1986	1987	MRI	Macavity	Winner	Novel
James, P.D.	A Taste for Death	1986	1986	CWA	Silver Dagger	Winner	Novel
James, P.D.	The Black Tower	1975	1975	CWA	Silver Dagger	Winner	Novel
James, P.D.	An Unsuitable Job for a Woman	1973	1974	MWA	Edgar	Nominee	Novel
James, P.D.	Shroud for a Nightingale	1971	1972	MWA	Edgar	Nominee	Novel
James, P.D.	Shroud for a Nightingale	1971	1971	CWA	Silver Dagger	Winner	Novel
Jennings, Maureen	Except the Dying	1997	1998	B'con	Anthony	Nominee	First Novel
Jennings, Maureen	Except the Dying	1997	1998	CWC	Ellis	Nominee	First Novel
Kellerman, Faye	A Ritual Bath	1986	1987	MRI	Macavity	Winner	First Novel
Kelly, Mary	The Spoilt Kill	1961	1961	CWA	Gold Dagger	Winner	Novel
Kelly, Susan	The Gemini Man	1984	1985	B'con	Anthony	Nominee	First Novel
Kijewski, Karen	Katwalk	1989	1990	B'con	Anthony	Winner	First Novel
Kijewski, Karen	Katwalk	1989	1990	PWA	Shamus	Winner	First Novel
Kijewski, Karen	Katwalk	1989	1988	SMP/PWA	SMP/PWA	Winner	First P.I. Novel
King, Laurie R.	With Child	1996	1997	MWA	Edgar	Nominee	Novel
King, Laurie R.	A Monstrous Regiment of Women	1995	1996	Wolfe Pack	Nero Wolfe	Winner	Novel
King, Laurie R.	The Beekeeper's Apprentice	1994	1995	Malice	Agatha	Nominee	Novel

Awards List 3 – Winners and Nominees by Author's Last Name

Includes awards through 1998 for series novels only

Last, First	BOOK TITLE	Pub	Award	Conf'd by	Name	Status	Category
King, Laurie R.	A Grave Talent	1993	1994	B'con	Anthony	Nominee	First Novel
King, Laurie R.	A Grave Talent	1995	1995	CWA	Creasey	Nominee	First Novel
King, Laurie R.	A Grave Talent	1993	1994	MWA	Edgar	Winner	First Novel
Knight, Phyllis	Switching the Odds	1992	1993	PWA	Shamus	Nominee	First Novel
Kraft, Gabrielle	Bullshot	1987	1988	MWA	Edgar	Nominee	PB Original
Krich, Rochelle Majer	Angel of Death	1994	1995	Malice	Agatha	Nominee	Novel
Krich, Rochelle Majer	Fair Game	1993	1994	Malice	Agatha	Nominee	Novel
Langton, Jane	Emily Dickinson Is Dead	1984	1985	MWA	Edgar	Nominee	Novel
Langton, Jane	Emily Dickinson Is Dead	1984	1984	Wolfe Pack	Nero Wolfe	Winner	Novel
Lanier, Virginia	Death in Bloodhound Red	1995	1996	B'con	Anthony	Winner	First Novel
Lanier, Virginia	Death in Bloodhound Red	1995	1996	Malice	Agatha	Nominee	First Novel
Lanier, Virginia	Death in Bloodhound Red	1995	1996	MRI	Macavity	Nominee	First Novel
LaPierre, Janet	Old Enemies	1993	1994	B'con	Anthony	Nominee	Novel
LaPierre, Janet	Unquiet Grave	1986	1987	MRI	Macavity	Nominee	First Novel
Lathen, Emma	Lifetime Achievement	1997	1997	Malice	Lifetime	Winner	Lifetime
Lathen, Emma	When in Greece	1969	1970	MWA	Edgar	Nominee	Novel
Lathen, Emma	Murder Against the Grain	1967	1967	CWA	Gold Dagger	Winner	Novel
Lathen, Emma	Accounting For Murder	1965	1965	CWA	Silver Dagger	Winner	Novel
Law, Janice	The Big Pay-Off	1976	1977	MWA	Edgar	Nominee	First Novel
Lawrence, Margaret	Hearts and Bones	1996	1997	B'con	Anthony	Nominee	Novel
Lawrence, Margaret	Hearts and Bones	1996	1997	Malice	Agatha	Nominee	Novel
Lawrence, Margaret	Hearts and Bones	1996	1997	MRI	Macavity	Nominee	Novel
Lawrence, Margaret	Hearts and Bones	1996	1997	MWA	Edgar	Nominee	Novel
Lawrence, Martha	Murder in Scorpio	1995	1996	B'con	Anthony	Nominee	First Novel
Lawrence, Martha	Murder in Scorpio	1995	1996	Malice	Agatha	Nominee	First Novel
Lawrence, Martha	Murder in Scorpio	1995	1996	MWA	Edgar	Nominee	First Novel
Lee, Barbara	Death in Still Waters	1995	1994	SMP/MD	SMP/MD	Winner	First Novel
Lippman, Laura	Baltimore Blues	1997	1998	PWA	Shamus	Nominee	First Novel
Lippman, Laura	Charm City	1997	1998	MWA	Edgar	Winner	PB Original
Lippman, Laura	Charm City	1997	1998	PWA	Shamus	Winner	PB Original
Lippman, Laura	Charm City	1997	1998	B'con	Anthony	Nominee	PB Original
Lordon, Randye	Father Forgive Me	1997	1998	LBR	Lambda	Winner	Lesbian Mystery
Lordon, Randye	Father Forgive Me	1997	1998	PWA	Shamus	Nominee	PB Original
Lordon, Randye	Brotherly Love	1993	1994	PWA	Shamus	Nominee	First Novel
MacGregor, T.J.	Dark Fields	1986	1987	PWA	Shamus	Nominee	PB Original
MacLeod, Charlotte	An Owl Too Many	1991	1992	Malice	Agatha	Nominee	Novel
MacLeod, Charlotte	The Corpse in Oozak's Pond	1986	1987	MWA	Edgar	Nominee	Novel
MacLeod, Charlotte	The Corpse in Oozak's Pond	1986	1987	Wolfe Pack	Nero Wolfe	Winner	Novel
Maiman, Jaye	Crazy for Loving	1992	1993	LBR	Lambda	Winner [tie]	Lesbian Mystery
Maron, Margaret	Up Jumps the Devil	1996	1997	Malice	Agatha	Winner	Novel
Maron, Margaret	Southern Discomfort	1993	1994	B'con	Anthony	Nominee	Novel
Maron, Margaret	Southern Discomfort	1993	1994	Malice	Agatha	Nominee	Novel
Maron, Margaret	Bootlegger's Daughter	1992	1993	B'con	Anthony	Winner	Novel
Maron, Margaret	Bootlegger's Daughter	1992	1993	Malice	Agatha	Winner	Novel
Maron, Margaret	Bootlegger's Daughter	1992	1993	MRI	Macavity	Winner	Novel
Maron, Margaret	Bootlegger's Daughter	1992	1993	MWA	Edgar	Winner	Novel
Maron, Margaret	Corpus Christmas	1989	1990	B'con	Anthony	Nominee	Novel
Maron, Margaret	Corpus Christmas	1989	1990	Malice	Agatha	Nominee	Novel
Massey, Sujata	The Salaryman's Wife	1997	1998	B'con	Anthony	Nominee	First Novel
Massey, Sujata	The Salaryman's Wife	1997	1998	Malice	Agatha	Winner	First Novel
Massey, Sujata	The Salaryman's Wife	1997	1998	MRI	Macavity	Nominee	First Novel
Matera, Lia	Prior Convictions	1991	1992	MWA	Edgar	Nominee	Novel
Matera, Lia	The Good Fight	1990	1991	B'con	Anthony	Nominee	Novel
Matera, Lia	The Good Fight	1990	1991	MRI	Macavity	Nominee	Novel
Matera, Lia	A Radical Departure	1988	1989	B'con	Anthony	Nominee	PB Original
Matera, Lia	A Radical Departure	1988	1989	MWA	Edgar	Nominee	PB Original
Matera, Lia	Where Lawyers Fear to Tread	1987	1988	B'con	Anthony	Nominee	PB Original
Matera, Lia	Where Lawyers Fear to Tread	1987	1988	MRI	Macavity	Nominee	PB Original
McCrumb, Sharyn	If I'd Killed Him When I Met Him	1995	1996	Malice	Agatha	Winner	Novel
McCrumb, Sharyn	She Walks These Hills	1994	1995	B'con	Anthony	Winner	Novel

Awards List 3 – Winners and Nominees by Author's Last Name

Includes awards through 1998 for series novels only

AUTHOR NAME		YEAR		AWARD			
Last, First	BOOK TITLE	Pub	Award	Conf'd by	Name	Status	Category
McCrumb, Sharyn	She Walks These Hills	1994	1995	Malice	Agatha	Winner	Novel
McCrumb, Sharyn	She Walks These Hills	1994	1995	MRI	Macavity	Winner	Novel
McCrumb, Sharyn	She Walks These Hills	1994	1995	Wolfe Pack	Nero Wolfe	Winner	Novel
McCrumb, Sharyn	The Hangman's Beautiful Daughter	1992	1993	B'con	Anthony	Nominee	Novel
McCrumb, Sharyn	The Hangman's Beautiful Daughter	1992	1993	Malice	Agatha	Nominee	Novel
McCrumb, Sharyn	If Ever I Return Pretty Peggy-O	1990	1991	B'con	Anthony	Nominee	Novel
McCrumb, Sharyn	If Ever I Return Pretty Peggy-O	1990	1991	MRI	Macavity	Winner	Novel
McCrumb, Sharyn	Paying the Piper	1988	1989	B'con	Anthony	Nominee	PB Original
McCrumb, Sharyn	Paying the Piper	1988	1989	Malice	Agatha	Nominee	Novel
McCrumb, Sharyn	Bimbos of the Death Sun	1987	1988	B'con	Anthony	Nominee	PB Original
McCrumb, Sharyn	Bimbos of the Death Sun	1987	1988	MWA	Edgar	Winner	PB Original
McDermid, Val	The Mermaids Singing	1995	1995	CWA	Gold Dagger	Winner	Novel
McDermid, Val	Crack Down	1994	1995	B'con	Anthony	Nominee	Novel
McDermid, Val	Crack Down	1994	1994	CWA	Gold Dagger	Nominee	Novel
McKenna, Bridget	Dead Ahead	1994	1995	PWA	Shamus	Nominee	PB Original
Melville, Jennie	Murder Has a Pretty Face	1981	1981	CWA	Gold Dagger	Nominee	Novel
Meredith, D.R.	Murder by Deception	1989	1990	B'con	Anthony	Nominee	PB Original
Meredith, D.R.	Murder by Impulse	1988	1989	B'con	Anthony	Nominee	PB Original
Monfredo, Miriam Grace	Seneca Falls Inheritance	1992	1993	Malice	Agatha	Nominee	First Novel
Monfredo, Miriam Grace	Seneca Falls Inheritance	1992	1993	MRI	Macavity	Nominee	First Novel
Moyes, Patricia	Many Deadly Returns [Brit.-Who Saw Her Die]	1970	1971	MWA	Edgar	Nominee	Novel
Muller, Marcia	A Wild and Lonely Place	1995	1996	MRI	Macavity	Nominee	Novel
Muller, Marcia	Wolf in the Shadows	1993	1994	B'con	Anthony	Winner	Novel
Muller, Marcia	Wolf in the Shadows	1993	1994	MWA	Edgar	Nominee	Novel
Muller, Marcia	Wolf in the Shadows	1993	1994	PWA	Shamus	Nominee	Novel
Muller, Marcia	Lifetime Achievement	1993	1993	PWA	The Eye	Winner	Lifetime
Muller, Marcia	Where Echoes Live	1991	1992	PWA	Shamus	Nominee	Novel
Muller, Marcia	The Shape of Dread	1989	1990	PWA	Shamus	Nominee	Novel
Munger, Katy	Legwork	1997	1998	PWA	Shamus	Nominee	First Novel
Neel, Janet	Death Among the Dons	1993	1993	CWA	Gold Dagger	Nominee	Novel
Neel, Janet	Death's Bright Angel	1988	1988	CWA	Creasey	Winner	First Novel
Neely, Barbara	Blanche on the Lam	1992	1993	B'con	Anthony	Winner	First Novel
Neely, Barbara	Blanche on the Lam	1992	1993	Malice	Agatha	Winner	First Novel
Neely, Barbara	Blanche on the Lam	1992	1993	MRI	Macavity	Winner	First Novel
Newman, Sharan	Strong as Death	1996	1997	Malice	Agatha	Nominee	Novel
Newman, Sharan	The Wandering Arm	1995	1996	Malice	Agatha	Nominee	Novel
Newman, Sharan	Death Comes as Epiphany	1993	1994	B'con	Anthony	Nominee	First Novel
Newman, Sharan	Death Comes as Epiphany	1993	1994	Malice	Agatha	Nominee	First Novel
Newman, Sharan	Death Comes as Epiphany	1993	1994	MRI	Macavity	Winner	First Novel
North, Suzanne	Healthy, Wealthy & Dead	1993	1994	CWC	Ellis	Nominee	First Novel
O'Callaghan, Maxine	Down For the Count	1997	1998	PWA	Shamus	Nominee	Novel
O'Connell, Carol	Mallory's Oracle	1994	1995	B'con	Anthony	Nominee	First Novel
O'Connell, Carol	Mallory's Oracle	1994	1995	MWA	Edgar	Nominee	First Novel
Oliphant, B.J.	Dead in the Scrub	1990	1991	B'con	Anthony	Nominee	PB Original
Oliphant, B.J.	Dead in the Scrub	1990	1991	MWA	Edgar	Nominee	PB Original
Padgett, Abigail	Child of Silence	1993	1994	B'con	Anthony	Nominee	First Novel
Padgett, Abigail	Child of Silence	1993	1994	Malice	Agatha	Nominee	First Novel
Padgett, Abigail	Child of Silence	1993	1994	MRI	Macavity	Nominee	First Novel
Page, Katherine Hall	The Body in the Belfry	1990	1991	Malice	Agatha	Winner	First Novel
Papazoglou, Orania	Sweet, Savage Death	1984	1985	MWA	Edgar	Nominee	First Novel
Paretsky, Sara	Tunnel Vision	1994	1994	CWA	Gold Dagger	Nominee	Novel
Paretsky, Sara	Blood Shot	1988	1989	B'con	Anthony	Nominee	Novel
Paretsky, Sara	Blood Shot	1988	1989	PWA	Shamus	Nominee	Novel
Paretsky, Sara	Toxic Shock [U.S.-Blood Shot]	1988	1988	CWA	Silver Dagger	Winner	Novel
Parker, Barbara	Suspicion of Innocence	1994	1995	MWA	Edgar	Nominee	First Novel
Paton Walsh, Jill	A Piece of Justice	1995	1995	CWA	Gold Dagger	Nominee	Novel
Penman, Sharon Kay	The Queen's Man	1996	1997	MWA	Edgar	Nominee	First Novel
Perry, Anne	Pentecost Alley	1996	1997	MWA	Edgar	Nominee	Novel

Awards List 3 – Winners and Nominees by Author's Last Name

Includes awards through 1998 for series novels only

AUTHOR NAME		YEAR		AWARD			
Last, First	**B O O K T I T L E**	**Pub**	**Award**	**Conf'd by**	**Name**	**Status**	**Category**
Perry, Anne	Defend and Betray	1992	1993	Malice	Agatha	Nominee	Novel
Perry, Anne	The Face of a Stranger	1990	1991	Malice	Agatha	Nominee	Novel
Peters, Elizabeth	Seeing a Large Cat	1997	1998	Malice	Agatha	Nominee	Novel
Peters, Elizabeth	Lifetime Achievement	1998	1998	MWA	Grand Master	Winner	Lifetime
Peters, Elizabeth	Night Train to Memphis	1994	1995	Malice	Agatha	Nominee	Novel
Peters, Elizabeth	The Snake, the Crocodile and the Dog	1992	1993	Malice	Agatha	Nominee	Novel
Peters, Elizabeth	The Last Camel Died at Noon	1991	1992	Malice	Agatha	Nominee	Novel
Peters, Elizabeth	Naked Once More	1989	1990	Malice	Agatha	Winner	Novel
Peters, Elizabeth	Trojan Gold	1987	1988	B'con	Anthony	Nominee	Novel
Peters, Elizabeth	Lifetime Achievement	1986	1986	B'con	Grand Master	Winner	Lifetime
Pickard, Nancy	Twilight	1995	1996	Malice	Agatha	Nominee	Novel
Pickard, Nancy	I.O.U.	1991	1992	B'con	Anthony	Nominee	Novel
Pickard, Nancy	I.O.U.	1991	1992	Malice	Agatha	Winner	Novel
Pickard, Nancy	I.O.U.	1991	1992	MRI	Macavity	Winner	Novel
Pickard, Nancy	I.O.U.	1991	1992	MWA	Edgar	Nominee	Novel
Pickard, Nancy	Bum Steer	1990	1991	Malice	Agatha	Winner	Novel
Pickard, Nancy	Dead Crazy	1988	1989	B'con	Anthony	Nominee	Novel
Pickard, Nancy	Dead Crazy	1988	1989	Malice	Agatha	Nominee	Novel
Pickard, Nancy	Marriage is Murder	1987	1988	B'con	Anthony	Nominee	Novel
Pickard, Nancy	Marriage is Murder	1987	1988	MRI	Macavity	Winner	Novel
Pickard, Nancy	No Body	1985	1986	B'con	Anthony	Nominee	Novel
Pickard, Nancy	Say No To Murder	1985	1986	B'con	Anthony	Winner	PB Original
Pincus, Elizabeth	The Two-Bit Tango	1992	1993	LBR	Lambda	Winner [tie]	Lesbian Mystery
Prowell, Sandra West	The Killing of Monday Brown	1994	1995	PWA	Shamus	Nominee	Novel
Prowell, Sandra West	By Evil Means	1993	1994	PWA	Shamus	Nominee	First Novel
Prowell, Sandra West	By Evil Means	1992	1993	IACW	Hammett	Nominee	Novel
Pulver, Mary Monica	Murder at the War	1987	1988	B'con	Anthony	Nominee	First Novel
Redmann, J.M.	The Intersection of Law and Desire	1995	1996	LBR	Lambda	Winner	Lesbian Mystery
Reichs, Kathy	Déjà Dead	1997	1998	CWC	Ellis	Winner	First Novel
Rendell, Ruth	Lifetime Achievement	1997	1997	MWA	Grand Master	Winner	Lifetime
Rendell, Ruth	Lifetime Achievement	1991	1991	CWA	Diamond Dagger	Winner	Lifetime
Rendell, Ruth	An Unkindness of Ravens	1985	1986	MWA	Edgar	Nominee	Novel
Rendell, Ruth	A Sleeping Life	1978	1979	MWA	Edgar	Nominee	Novel
Richman, Phyllis	The Butter Did It	1997	1998	Malice	Agatha	Nominee	First Novel
Roberts, Gillian	Philly Stakes	1989	1990	Malice	Agatha	Nominee	Novel
Roberts, Gillian	Caught Dead in Philadelphia	1987	1988	B'con	Anthony	Winner	First Novel
Roberts, Lillian M.	Riding for a Fall	1996	1997	Malice	Agatha	Nominee	First Novel
Roome, Annette	A Real Shot in the Arm	1989	1989	CWA	Creasey	Winner	First Novel
Ross, Kate	The Devil in Music	1997	1998	Malice	Agatha	Winner	Novel
Ross, Kate	A Broken Vessel	1993	1994	Historicon	Gargoyle	Winner	Novel-Historical
Rothenberg, Rebecca	The Bulrush Murders	1991	1992	B'con	Anthony	Nominee	First Novel
Rothenberg, Rebecca	The Bulrush Murders	1991	1992	Malice	Agatha	Nominee	First Novel
Rowland, Laura Joh	Shinju	1994	1995	IACW	Hammett	Nominee	Novel
Rozan, S.J.	No Colder Place	1997	1998	B'con	Anthony	Winner	Novel
Rozan, S.J.	No Colder Place	1997	1998	PWA	Shamus	Nominee	Novel
Rozan, S.J.	Concourse	1995	1996	PWA	Shamus	Winner	Novel
Ruryk, Jean	Next Week Will Be Better	1998	1999	CWC	Ellis	Nominee	Novel
Sale, Medora	Murder on the Run	1985	1986	CWC	Ellis	Winner	First Novel
Sawyer, Corinne Holt	The J. Alfred Prufrock Murders	1988	1989	Malice	Agatha	Nominee	First Novel
Scottoline, Lisa	Final Appeal	1994	1995	MWA	Edgar	Winner	PB Original
Scottoline, Lisa	Everywhere That Mary Went	1993	1994	MWA	Edgar	Nominee	PB Original
Shaber, Sarah R.	Simon Said	1997	1996	SMP/MD	SMP/MD	Winner	First Novel
Simpson, Dorothy	Last Seen Alive	1985	1985	CWA	Silver Dagger	Winner	Novel
Singer, Shelley	Interview With Mattie	1995	1996	PWA	Shamus	Nominee	PB Original
Sjöwall, Maj & Per Wahlöö	The Laughing Policeman	1970	1971	MWA	Edgar	Winner	Novel
Skom, Edith	The Mark Twain Murders	1989	1990	B'con	Anthony	Nominee	First Novel
Skom, Edith	The Mark Twain Murders	1989	1990	Malice	Agatha	Nominee	First Novel
Skom, Edith	The Mark Twain Murders	1989	1990	MRI	Macavity	Nominee	First Novel

Awards List 3 – Winners and Nominees by Author's Last Name
Includes awards through 1998 for series novels only

AUTHOR NAME Last, First	BOOK TITLE	Pub	Award	Conf'd by	Name	Status	Category
Smith, Alison	Someone Else's Grave	1984	1985	MWA	Edgar	Nominee	First Novel
Smith, Barbara Burnett	Writers of the Purple Sage	1994	1995	Malice	Agatha	Nominee	First Novel
Smith, Janet L.	Sea of Troubles	1990	1991	Malice	Agatha	Nominee	First Novel
Smith, Julie	New Orleans Mourning	1990	1991	B'con	Anthony	Nominee	Novel
Smith, Julie	New Orleans Mourning	1990	1991	MWA	Edgar	Winner	Novel
Spring, Michelle	Every Breath You Take	1993	1994	CWC	Ellis	Nominee	First Novel
Stabenow, Dana	A Cold Day for Murder	1992	1993	MWA	Edgar	Winner	PB Original
Stacey, Susannah	Goodbye Nanny Gray	1988	1989	Malice	Agatha	Nominee	First Novel
Staincliffe, Cath	Looking for Trouble	1994	1994	CWA	Creasey	Nominee	First Novel
Stubbs, Jean	Dear Laura	1973	1974	MWA	Edgar	Nominee	Novel
Sucher, Dorothy	Dead Men Don't Give Seminars	1988	1989	Malice	Agatha	Nominee	First Novel
Sullivan, Winona	A Sudden Death at the Norfolk Café	1993	1991	SMP/PWA	SMP/PWA	Winner	First P.I. Novel
Trocheck, Kathy Hogan	To Live and Die in Dixie	1993	1994	B'con	Anthony	Nominee	Novel
Trocheck, Kathy Hogan	To Live and Die in Dixie	1993	1994	Malice	Agatha	Nominee	Novel
Trocheck, Kathy Hogan	To Live and Die in Dixie	1993	1994	MRI	Macavity	Nominee	Novel
Trocheck, Kathy Hogan	Every Crooked Nanny	1992	1993	B'con	Anthony	Nominee	First Novel
Trocheck, Kathy Hogan	Every Crooked Nanny	1992	1993	MRI	Macavity	Nominee	First Novel
Uhnak, Dorothy	The Ledger	1970	1971	Acad Fran	Grand Prix	Winner	Police Novel
Uhnak, Dorothy	The Bait	1968	1969	MWA	Edgar	Winner [tie]	First Novel
Valentine, Deborah	Fine Distinctions	1991	1992	MWA	Edgar	Nominee	PB Original
Valentine, Deborah	A Collector of Photographs	1989	1990	B'con	Anthony	Nominee	PB Original
Valentine, Deborah	A Collector of Photographs	1989	1990	MWA	Edgar	Nominee	PB Original
Valentine, Deborah	A Collector of Photographs	1989	1990	PWA	Shamus	Nominee	PB Original
Van Gieson, Judith	The Lies That Bind	1993	1994	PWA	Shamus	Nominee	Novel
Walker, Mary Willis	Under the Beetle's Cellar	1995	1996	B'con	Anthony	Winner	Novel
Walker, Mary Willis	Under the Beetle's Cellar	1995	1996	IACW	Hammett	Winner	Novel
Walker, Mary Willis	Under the Beetle's Cellar	1995	1996	MRI	Macavity	Winner	Novel
Walker, Mary Willis	The Red Scream	1994	1995	MRI	Macavity	Nominee	Novel
Walker, Mary Willis	The Red Scream	1994	1995	MWA	Edgar	Winner	Novel
Wallace, Marilyn	A Single Stone	1991	1992	B'con	Anthony	Nominee	Novel
Wallace, Marilyn	Primary Target	1988	1989	B'con	Anthony	Nominee	PB Original
Wallace, Marilyn	A Case of Loyalties	1986	1987	MRI	Macavity	Winner	First Novel
Wallace, Patricia	Deadly Devotion	1994	1995	PWA	Shamus	Nominee	PB Original
Warner, Penny	Dead Body Language	1997	1998	Malice	Agatha	Nominee	First Novel
Warner, Penny	Dead Body Language	1997	1998	MRI	Macavity	Winner	First Novel
Weir, Charlene	Consider the Crows	1993	1994	B'con	Anthony	Nominee	Novel
Weir, Charlene	Winter Widow	1992	1993	B'con	Anthony	Nominee	First Novel
Weir, Charlene	Winter Widow	1992	1993	Malice	Agatha	Winner	First Novel
Weir, Charlene	Winter Widow	1992	1991	SMP/MD	SMP/MD	Winner	First Novel
Wesley, Valerie Wilson	When Death Comes Stealing	1994	1995	PWA	Shamus	Nominee	First Novel
Wheat, Carolyn	Mean Streak	1996	1997	MWA	Edgar	Nominee	Novel
Wheat, Carolyn	Dead Man's Thoughts	1983	1984	MWA	Edgar	Nominee	First Novel
White, Gloria	Sunset and Santiago	1997	1998	MWA	Edgar	Nominee	PB Original
White, Gloria	Sunset and Santiago	1997	1998	PWA	Shamus	Nominee	PB Original
White, Gloria	Charged With Guilt	1995	1996	B'con	Anthony	Nominee	PB Original
White, Gloria	Charged With Guilt	1995	1996	MWA	Edgar	Nominee	PB Original
White, Gloria	Charged With Guilt	1995	1996	PWA	Shamus	Nominee	PB Original
White, Gloria	Murder on the Run	1991	1992	B'con	Anthony	Nominee	First Novel
Whitney, Polly	Until Death	1994	1995	Malice	Agatha	Nominee	First Novel
Wilson, Barbara	Gaudi Afternoon [U.K. ed.]	1991	1991	CWA	CWA '92	Winner	Novel-Europe
Wilson, Barbara	Gaudi Afternoon	1990	1991	LBR	Lambda	Winner	Lesbian Mystery
Wilson, Barbara Jaye	Death Brims Over	1997	1998	Malice	Agatha	Nominee	First Novel
Wright, L.R.	Mother Love	1995	1996	CWC	Ellis	Winner	Novel
Wright, L.R.	A Touch of Panic	1993	1994	CWC	Ellis	Nominee	Novel
Wright, L.R.	A Chill Rain in January	1989	1990	CWC	Ellis	Winner	Novel
Wright, L.R.	The Suspect	1985	1986	MWA	Edgar	Winner	Novel

Mystery Book Awards Glossary

The **Agatha Awards**, in honor of Dame Agatha Christie, are conferred at Malice Domestic, the annual author and fan convention held annually since 1989, in late April or early May in the Washington, D.C. area. Registered attendees are sent nominating ballots in February, for consideration of books published the prior year. Voting takes place at the convention. Dedicated to cozy and traditional mysteries, the award is in the form of a teapot. St. Martin's Press and Malice Domestic also sponsor a Best First Novel contest for unpublished cozy mysteries. The prize includes publication by St. Martin's Press the following year and a $10,000 advance.

Anthony Awards, voted by the membership of the World Mystery Convention, are presented annually at Bouchercon for work published during the prior year. Named in honor of Anthony Boucher (William Anthony Parker White), the prize categories change from year to year at the discretion of the convention organizing committee, along with the actual shape of the award, and location of the convention itself. Typical award categories include Best Novel, Best First Novel, Best Paperback Original, Best Short Story, Best Critical/ Biographical and Best Fanzine.

Given by the Crime Writers of Canada since 1984, the **Arthur Ellis Awards** are named after the nom de travail of Canada's official hangman. Categories include Best Novel, Best First Novel, Best Short Story, Best True Crime, Best Juvenile and Best Play published by a Canadian author. The award statuette is a wooden gallows with its own rope and hanging puppet.

The British Crime Writers' Association (CWA), formed in 1953, was patterned after its U.S. counterpart, the Mystery Writers of America. In 1955 CWA began awarding special honors to the best crime novel of the year. Originally named the Crossed Red Herrings Award, the prize later became known as the **Gold Dagger**. A **Silver Dagger** has been awarded to the runner-up since 1969. As of 1973, the association began conferring the **John Creasey Memorial Award** for best first novel, in honor of the famous British mystery writer (1908-1973) who produced almost 600 titles of mystery, crime, romance, western and suspense under 28 pseudonyms. Sponsored by Cartier since 1986 is the **Diamond Dagger Award** for lifetime achievement. Since 1989 the **Last Laugh** award has gone to the funniest crime novel of the year. Hazel Wyn Jones created the **CWA '92** award (1990-1992) for best crime novel set partly or wholly in Europe. From 1985 to 1987, *The Police Review* sponsored an award for the crime novel that best portrayed police procedure. CWA awards, typically announced in December for books of the current year, are awarded in person several months later at a ceremony usually held at the House of Lords.

Each year since 1945, Mystery Writers of America (MWA) has conferred the **Edgar Awards** (named for Edgar Allen Poe) in a variety of categories, including Best Novel, Best First Novel, Best Short Story, Best Paperback Original, Best Juvenile, Best Television Episode, Best Fact Crime, Best Television Feature, Best Critical/ Biographical Work, Best Motion Picture, Best Young Adult and Best Children's. An overall awards chair selects individual committee chairs for each category. The committee chairs, in turn, select the members of their committees, who vote on the top five works in each category. At the time nominations are announced in early February, the identity of the award winner in each category is known only to the committee chair and select MWA board members.

Beginning with its selection of Agatha Christie in 1955, MWA began naming **Grand Masters** which now include 43 best-of-the-best:

1999	**P.D. James**
1998	**Barbara Mertz (Elizabeth Peters)**
1997	**Ruth Rendell**
1996	Dick Francis
1995	Mickey Spillane
1994	Lawrence Block
1993	Donald Westlake
1992	Elmore Leonard
1991	Tony Hillerman
1990	**Helen McCloy**
1989	Hillary Waugh
1988	**Phyllis A. Whitney**
1987	Michael Gilbert
1986	Ed McBain
1985	**Dorothy Salisbury Davis**
1984	John le Carré
1983	**Margaret Millar**
1982	Julian Symons
1981	Stanley Ellin
1980	W.R. Burnett
1979	Aaron Marc Stein
1978	**Daphne du Maurier**
	Dorothy B. Hughes
	Ngaio Marsh
1977	*no award given*
1976	Graham Greene
1975	Eric Ambler
1974	Ross Macdonald
1973	Judson Phillips and Alfred Hitchcock
1972	John D. MacDonald
1971	**Mignon G. Eberhart**
1970	James M. Cain
1969	John Creasey
1968	*no award given*
1967	Baynard Kendrick
1966	Georges Simenon

1965	*no award given*
1964	George Harmon Coxe
1963	John Dickson Carr
1962	Erle Stanley Gardner
1961	Ellery Queen (Frederic Dannay and Manfred B. Lee)
1960	*no award given*
1959	Rex Stout
1958	Vincent Starrett
1957	*no award given*
1956	*no award given*
1955	**Agatha Christie**

The Academie Francaise awards **Le Grand Prix de Littérature Policière** for the Best Police Novel published in France the prior year. The first American woman to win this award was Dorothy Uhnak in 1971 for *The Ledger*. The award has also been won by Patricia Cornwell and Elizabeth George.

The International Association of Crime Writers (North American Branch), established in 1987, has presented the North American **Hammett Prize** annually since 1992 for the best work (fiction or nonfiction) of literary excellence in crime-writing by a U.S. or Canadian author. The trophy is a bronze sculpture of a falcon-headed thin-man symbolizing the literary spirit of Dashiell Hammett.

The Kiss of Death award, created in 1998, is given by the Romance Writers of America (RWA) for the best romantic suspense novel published the prior year. RWA bestows its lifetime achievement honors with induction into the Romance Writers of America Hall of Fame. Two RWA Hall of Fame honorees–Nora Roberts and Eileen Dreyer–also write mysteries.

The Lambda Literary Awards, sponsored by the *Lambda Book Report* since 1989, are given annually to recognize excellence in gay and lesbian writing and publishing in the United States during the previous year. Including Best Lesbian Mystery and Best Gay Men's Mystery, Lambda awards are given in a total of 20 categories. The annual awards dinner is usually held at Book Expo (former the American Booksellers Association national convention) in May or June.

Mystery Readers International (MRI) has presented the **Macavity Awards** annually since 1987. Named for T.S. Eliot's mystery cat in *Old Possum's Book of Practical Cats*, these awards are voted by MRI membership in four categories—Best Novel, Best First Novel, Best Non-Fiction and Best Short Story. Awards are usually presented at Bouchercon.

In 1996 Crime Writers' Association of Australia conferred its first **Ned Kelly Awards** named for the notorious 19th century Australian outlaw. Best Australian Crime Novel was shared by Barry Maitland (*The Malcontenta*) and Paul Thomas (*Inside Dope*), while John Dale (*Dark Angel*) won for Best First Australian Novel. Jon Cleary was the first recipient of the Lifetime Contribution Award.

Since 1979 the **Nero Wolfe Award** has been given to the novel that best captures the spirit and fair play of the work of Rex Stout, creator of Nero Wolfe, America's foremost armchair detective. This award is conferred by a group of Rex Stout aficionados known as the Wolfe Pack at their Black Orchid Dinner in New York each December.

The Private Eye Writers of America (PWA), founded by Robert J. Randisi in 1981, gave its first **Shamus Awards** (for works published in 1981) at Bouchercon XIII in San Francisco. Shamus award categories include Best Private Eye Novel, Best Private Eye Paperback Original, Best Private Eye Short Story (beginning in 1983), Best First Private Eye Novel (beginning in 1984) and The Eye Life Achievement Award. In recent years the private eye category has been expanded to include investigators who are paid for services rendered as part of their investigative work, such as news reporters and attorneys who do their own investigating. In 1986 **St. Martin's Press and PWA (SMP/PWA)** launched a contest for Best First Private Eye Novel which has become an annual event. The award-winning P.I. novel is published simultaneously in the U.S. by St. Martin's Press and in England by Macmillan.

Appendices

Appendix A – Dead Authors Dropped from Detecting Women 2

Author	Born	Died	Series Character	#1	Titles
Allingham, Margery	1904	1966	Albert Campion	1929	22
Armstrong, Charlotte	1905	1969	MacDougal Duff	1942	3
Barber, Willetta Ann	1911	1993	Christopher "Kit" Storm	1940	7
Bell, Josephine	1897	1987	Amy Tupper	1979	2
Bell, Josephine	1897	1987	Claude Warrington-Reeve	1959	3
Bell, Josephine	1897	1987	Dr. David Wintringham	1937	14
Bell, Josephine	1897	1987	Dr. Henry Frost	1964	2
Bell, Josephine	1897	1987	Steven Mitchell	1938	1
Brand, Christianna	1907	1985	Inspector Cockrill	1941	6
Bridge, Ann	1889	1974	Julia Probyn Jamieson	1956	7
Burton, Anne	1922	1985	Richard Trenton	1980	3
Challis, Mary	1922	1985	Jeremy Locke	1980	4
Christie, Agatha	1890	1976	Hercule Poirot	1920	35
Christie, Agatha	1890	1976	Miss Jane Marple	1930	12
Christie, Agatha	1890	1976	Tommy & Tuppence Beresford	1922	4
Crane, Frances	1896	1981	Pat & Jean Abbot	1941	26
Daly, Elizabeth	1878	1967	Henry Gamadge	1940	16
DeLaTorre, Lillian	1902	1993	Dr. Sam Johnson & James Boswell	1946	4
Disney, Doris Miles	1907	1976	Jeff DiMarco	1946	8
Disney, Doris Miles	1907	1976	Jim O'Neill	1943	5
Dolson, Hildegarde	1908	1981	Lucy Ramsdale & James McDougal	1971	4
Eberhart, Mignon G.	1899	1996	Sarah Keate & Lance O'Leary	1929	7
Egan, Lesley	1921	1988	Jesse Falkenstein	1961	13
Egan, Lesley	1921	1988	Vic Varallo	1962	13
Erskine, Margaret	na	1984	Septimus Finch	1938	21
Fenisong, Ruth	1904	1978	Gridley Nelson	1942	13
Ferrars, E.X.	1907	1995	Andrew Basnett	1983	8
Ferrars, E.X.	1907	1995	Supt. Ditteridge	1971	2
Ferrars, E.X.	1907	1995	Toby Dyke	1940	5
Ferrars, E.X.	1907	1995	Virginia & Felix Freer	1978	9
Foley, Rae	1900	1978	Hiram Potter	1955	11
Ford, Leslie	1898	1983	Col. Primrose & Grace Latham	1934	16
Frome, David	1898	1983	Evan Pinkerton	1930	11
Gardiner, Dorothy	1894	1979	Moss Magill	1956	3
Gardiner, Dorothy	1894	1979	Mr. Watson	1933	2

Appendix A – Dead Authors Dropped from Detecting Women 2

Author	Born	Died	Series Character	#1	Titles
Gilbert, Anthony	1899	1973	Arthur G. Crook	1936	50
Gilbert, Anthony	1899	1973	Scott Egerton	1927	9
Green, Anna Katharine	1846	1935	Caleb Sweetwater	1899	3
Green, Anna Katharine	1846	1935	Ebenezer Gryce	1878	12
Hall, Mary Bowen	1932	1994	Emma Chizzit	1989	4
Hart, Jeanne	1919	1990	Carl & Freda Pedersen	1987	3
Heberden, M.V.	1906	1965	Desmond Shannon	1939	17
Heberden, M.V.	1906	1965	Rich Vanner	1946	3
Heyer, Georgette	1902	1974	Supt. Hannasyde	1935	4
Heyer, Georgette	1902	1974	Insp. Hemingway	1939	4
Highsmith, Patricia	1921	1995	Torn Ripley	1955	5
Hitchens, Dolores	1907	1973	Jim Sader	1957	2
Huxley, Elspeth	1907	1997	Supt. Vachell	1937	3
Johns, Veronica Parker	1907	1988	Agatha Welch	1940	2
Johns, Veronica Parker	1907	1988	Webster Flagg	1953	2
Knight, Kathleen Moore	1890	1984	Elisha Macomber	1935	16
Knight, Kathleen Moore	1890	1984	Margot Blair	1940	4
Komo, Dolores	c.1940	c.1992	Clio Browne	1988	1
Leek, Margaret	1922	1985	Stephen Marryat	1980	3
Leonard, Charles L.	1906	1965	Paul Kilgerrin	1942	11
Linington, Elizabeth	1921	1988	Sgt. Ivor Maddox	1964	13
Livingston, Nancy	1935	1995	G.D.H. Pringle	1985	8
Lockridge, Frances	1896	1963	Insp. Merton Heimrich	1947	24
Lockridge, Richard	1898	1982	Pam & Jerry North	1940	26
Marsh, Ngaio	1895	1982	Roderick Alleyn	1934	32
McCloy, Helen	1904	1993	Dr. Basil Willing	1938	13
McGerr, Patricia	1917	1985	Selena Mead	1964	2
Millar, Margaret	1915	1994	Inspector Sands	1943	2
Millar, Margaret	1915	1994	Dr. Paul Prye	1941	3
Millar, Margaret	1915	1994	Tom Aragon	1976	3
Mitchell, Gladys	1901	1983	Beatrice Lestrange Bradley	1929	66
Morice, Anne	1918	1989	Tessa Crichton	1970	23
Offord, Lenore Glen	1905	1991	Bill & Coco Hastings	1938	2
Offord, Lenore Glen	1905	1991	Todd McKinnon & Georgine Wyeth	1943	4
Olsen, D.B.	1907	1973	Professor A. Pennyfather	1945	6
Olsen, D.B.	1907	1973	Rachel & Jennifer Murdock	1939	13
Olsen, D.B.	1907	1973	Lt. Stephen Mayhew	1940	2
Peters, Ellis	1913	1995	Brother Cadfael	1977	20
Peters, Ellis	1913	1995	The Felse Family	1951	13
Popkin, Zelda	1898	1983	Mary Carner	1938	5
Porter, Joyce	1924	1990	Eddie Brown	1966	4
Porter, Joyce	1924	1990	Hon. Constance Burke	1970	5
Porter, Joyce	1924	1990	Wilfred Dover	1964	21
Reilly , Helen	1891	1962	Christopher McKee	1930	31
Rice, Craig	1908	1957	Bingo Riggs & Handsome Kusak	1942	3
Rice, Craig	1908	1957	John J. Malone	1939	14
Rich, Virginia	1914	1985	Eugenia Potter	1982	4
Rinehart, Mary Roberts	1876	1958	Miss Pinkerton	1932	3
Sayers, Dorothy L.	1893	1957	Lord Peter Wimsey	1923	14
Scherf, Margaret	1908	1979	Emily & Henry Bryce	1949	4
Scherf, Margaret	1908	1979	Dr. Grace Severance	1968	4
Scherf, Margaret	1908	1979	Lt. Ryan	1945	2
Scherf, Margaret	1908	1979	Rev. Martin Buell	1948	6
Shannon, Dell	1921	1988	Luis Mendoza	1960	38
Taylor, Phoebe Atwood	1909	1976	Asey Mayo	1931	24
Tey, Josephine	1896	1952	Inspector Alan Grant	1929	6
Tilton, Alice	1909	1976	Leonidas Witherall	1937	8
Torrie, Malcolm	1901	1983	Timothy Herring	1966	6

Appendix A – Dead Authors Dropped from Detecting Women 2

Author	Born	Died	Series Character	#1	Titles
Venning, Michael	1908	1957	Melville Fairr	1942	3
Wells, Carolyn	1869	1942	Fleming Stone	1909	61
Wells, Carolyn	1869	1942	Kenneth Carlisle	1929	3
Wells, Carolyn	1869	1942	Pennington Wise	1918	8
Wells, Tobias	1923	1985	Knute Severson	1966	16
Wentworth, Patricia	1878	1961	Insp. Ernest Lamb	1939	2
Wentworth, Patricia	1878	1961	Maud Silver	1928	32
Woods, Sara	1922	1985	Anthony Maitland	1962	48
Wynn Jones, Hazel	1941	1990	Emma Shaw	1988	2
Yates, Margaret Tayler	1887	1952	Annie Davenport McLean	1937	4

Total Dropped Titles   **1136**

Appendix B – Other Authors and/or Titles Dropped from Detecting Women 2

Author	Main Character	37 Dropped Titles...Reason Dropped
Allingham, Margery	Albert Campion	No Love Lost...not part of this series
Ayres, Noreen	Samatha 'Smokey' Brandon	The Long Slow Whistle of the Moon...not published
Ballard, Mignon	Eliza Figg	Minerva Cries Murder...a non-series mystery
Berenson, Laurien	Gwen Harding	Deep Cover...a non-series mystery
Blackmur, L.L.	Galen Shaw & Julian Baugh	Loves Lies Slain...a non-series mystery
Blackmur, L.L.	Galen Shaw & Julian Baugh	Loves Lies Bleeding...not published
Bradley, Lynn	Cole January	Stand-in for Murder...a non-series mystery
Clark, Carolyn Chambers	Megan Baldwin	Deadlier Than Death...a non-series mystery
Clark, Carolyn Chambers	Theresa Franco	Dangerous Alibis...a non-series mystery
Collins, Anna Ashwood	Abigail Doyle	Deadly Resolutions...standalone in the U.S.
Collins, Anna Ashwood	Abigail Doyle	Red Roses for a Dead Trucker...published only in Japanese
Dunant, Sarah	Marla Materson	Snowstorms in a Hot Climate...a non-series mystery
Florian, S.L.	Delia Ross-Merlani	Born to the Purple...a non-series mystery
Froetschel, Susan	Jane McBride	Alaska Gray...a non-series mystery
Grant-Adamson, Lesley	Laura Flynn	Too Many Questions...a non-series mystery
Grant-Adamson, Lesley	not Laura Flynn	The Dangerous Edge...a non-series mystery
Hollingsworth, Gerelyn	Frances Finn	Murder at St. Adelaide's...a non-series mystery
Jackson, Muriel Resnick	Merrie Lee Spencer	The Garden Club...a non-series mystery
Karr, Leona	Addie Devore	Murder in Bandora...a non-series mystery
Knight, Phyllis	Lil Ritchie	Lost to Sight...not published
Kreuter, Katherine E.	Paige Taylor	Fool Me Once...a non-series mystery
Kunz, Kathleen	Terry Girard	Murder Once Removed...a non-series mystery
Kunz, Kathleen	Terry Girard	Death in a Private Place...not published
Logue, Mary	Laura Mallloy	Still Explosion...a non-series mystery
McFall, Patricia	Nora James	Night Butterfly...a non-series mystery
Moffat, Gwen	not Melinda Pink	The Buckskin Girl...not a mystery
O'Connell, Catherine	Karen Levinson	Skins...a non-series mystery
Porath, Sharon	Kendra MacFarlane	Dead File...a non-series mystery
Rowlands, Betty	Melissa Craig	Murder in the Cotswolds...not published
Schenkel, S.E.	Ray & Kate Frederick	Death Days...a non-series mystery
Scott, Rosie	Glory Day	Glory Day...a non-series mystery
Sedley, Kate	Roger the Chapman	The Hanged Man...British title of The Weaver's Tale
Smith, Evelyn E.	Susan Melville	Miss Melville Runs for Cover...not published
Thompson, Joyce	Frederika Bascomb	Bones...a non-series mystery
Vlasopolos, Anca	Sharon Dair	Missing Members...a non-series mystery
Wilhelm, Kate	Sarah Dexter	Justice for Some...a non-series mystery
Wolfe, Susan	Sarah Nelson	The Last Billable Hour...a non-series mystery

Appendix C - Pocket Guide Corrections

32 Title Changes

DW3PG Page	Author	Series Character	Series Number & Title in Pocket Guide	Series Number & Title in Full-Text Edition
34	Churchill, Jill	Jane Jeffry	11-The Rite Stuff	11-A Groom With a View
34	Churchill, Jill	The Brewsters	01-Ain't Misbehavin'	01-Anything Goes
53	Dixon, Louisa	Laura Owen	02-What You Don't See	02-Outside Chance
53	Dixon, Louisa	Laura Owen	03-Cold Treatment	03-No Chance
64	Farmer, Jerrilyn	Madeline Bean	02-Murder Hymm	02-Immaculate Reception
70	French, Linda	Teddy Morelli	03-The Pig War	03-Steeped in Murder
82	Greenwood, Kerry	Phryne Fisher	09-Ashes and Almonds	09-Raisins and Almonds
84	Guiver, Patricia	Delilah Doolittle	02-Delilah Doolittle and the Purloined Pooch	02-Delilah Doolittle and the Motley Mutts
88	Hamilton, Lyn	Lara McClintock	04-The Amairgen Puzzle	04-The Celtic Riddle
92	Hathaway, Robin	Andrew Fenimore	02-The Doctor and the Doll House	02-The Doctor Makes a Dollhouse Call
98	Holt, Hazel	Sheila Malory	08-Dead and Buried	08-Mrs. Malory and the Only Good Lawyer
103	Jackson, Hialeah	Annabelle & Dave	02-Farewell, Butterfly Sue	02-Farewell, Conch Republic
110	Kennett, Shirley	P.J. Gray	04-Wild Justice	04-Cut Loose
113	Knight, Kathryn L.	Calista Jacobs	04-Dark Swain	04-Dark Swan
119	Laurence, Janet	Darina Lisle	09-Death at the Table	09-Appetite for Death
122	Lin-Chandler, Irene	Holly-Jean Ho	03-Soul Exile	03-Hour of the Tigress
123	Lippman, Laura	Tess Monaghan	04-Gone to Texas	04-In Big Trouble
126	MacKay, Amanda	Hannah Land	01-Murder is Academic	01-Death is Academic
148	Morrone, Wenda W.	Lorelei Muldoon	02-Millennium Bridges Falling Down	02-The Year 2000 Killers
151	Murray, Donna Huston	Ginger Barnes	05-Illegal Procedure	05-A Score to Settle
151	Murray, Lynne	Josephine Fuller	03-Lucille at Large	03-Murder at Large
153	Nadelson, Reggie	Artie Cohen	03-Bloody Sunday	03-Bloody London
156	O'Callaghan, Maxine	Anne Menlo	02-Ashes to Ashes	02-Only in the Ashes
166	Peters, Elizabeth	Amelia Peabody	11-Serpent on Your Brow	11-The Falcon at the Portal
167	Petit, Diane	Kathryn Bogert	02-Take Two	02-Goodbye, Charli--Take Two
167	Petit, Diane	Kathryn Bogert	03-Third Time's A Charm	03-Goodbye, Charli--Third Time Lucky
169	Powell, Deborah	Hollis Carpenter	01-Bayou City Streets	01-Bayou City Secrets
177	Roe, Caroline	Isaac of Girona	03-Salve for a Sore Conscience	03-Antidote for Avarice
177	Rogow, Roberta	Dodgson & Doyle	02-The Problem of the Spurious Spiritualist	02-The Problem of the Spiteful Spiritualist
186	Sherman, Beth	Anne Hardaway	02-Acting Is Murder	02-Death at High Tide
199	Tesler, Nancy	Carrie Carlin	03-Sticks & Stones and Other Deadly Things	03-Shooting Stars and Other Deadly Things
211	Whitney, Polly	Ike & Abby	04-Until Pigs Fly	04-Until the Twelfth of Never

60 Title Additions (+)

DW3PG Page	Author	Series Character	Series Number & Title in Pocket Guide	Series Number & Title in Full-Text Edition
86	Hadley, Joan	Theo Bloomer		01-Night Blooming Cereus (1986)
86	Hadley, Joan	Theo Bloomer		02-Deadly Ackee (1988)
29	Butler, Gwendoline	John Coffin		26-Coffin's Game (1998)
37	Coburn, Laura	Kate Harrod		04-A Missing Suspect (1998)
47	Dain, Catherine	Freddie O'Neal		07-Dead Man's Hand (1997)
48	Danks, Denise	Georgina Powers		02-Better Off Dead (1991)

Appendix C - Pocket Guide Corrections

60 Title Additions (+)...continued

DW3PG Page	Author	Series Character	Series Number & Title in Pocket Guide	Series Number & Title in Full-Text Edition
53	Dewhurst, Eileen	Tim Le Page		01-Death in Candie Gardens (1992)
53	Dewhurst, Eileen	Tim Le Page		02-Alias the Enemy (1997)
53	Dewhurst, Eileen	Phyllida Moon		03-Roundabout (1998)
57	Duffy, Margaret	MacKenzie & Carrick		04-A Fine Target (1998)
63	Evans, Geraldine	Rafferty & Llewellyn		03-Death Line (1995)
67	Fletcher, Jessica	Jessica Fletcher		01-Gin & Daggers (1989)
67	Fletcher, Jessica	Jessica Fletcher		11-A Little Yuletide Murder (1998)
70	Frazer, Margaret	Dame Frevisse		08-The Maiden's Tale (1998)
77	Gosling, Paula	Blackwater Bay		01-The Body in Blackwater Bay (1992)
79	Granger, Ann	Fran Varady		03-Running Scared (1998)
80	Graves, Sarah	Jacobia Triptree		02-Triple Witch (1999)
84	Gunning, Sally	Peter Bartholomew		07-Deep Water (1996)
86	Haddad, C.A.	Becky Belski		01-Caught in the Shadows (1992)
86	Haddad, C.A.	Becky Belski		02-Root Canal (1994)
86	Haddam, Jane	Gregor Demarkian		14-Add Baptism in Blood (1996)
88	Hamilton, Laurell K.	Anita Blake		08-Blue Moon (1998)
94	Hebden, Juliet	Clovis Pel		20-Pel and the Patriarch (1996)
100	Huff, Tanya	Vicki Nelson		05-Blood Debt (1997)
104	Jakeman, Jane	Ambrose Malfine		03-Fool's Gold (1998)
108	Kaewert, Julie Wallin	Alex Plumtree		03-Unprintable (1998)
111	Kershaw, Valerie	Mitch Mitchell		04-Juicy Lucy (1996)
122	Linscott, Gillian	Birdie Linnet		03-Knightfall (1986)
131	Martin, Lee	Deb Ralston		12-Genealogy of Murder (1996)
133	Mathews, Francine	Meredith Folger		04-Death in a Cold Hard Light (1998)
137	McCrumb, Sharyn	Spencer Arrowood		05-The Ballad of Frankie Silver (1998)
139	McKevett, G.A.	Savannah Reid		04-Cooked Goose (1998)
149	Meek, M.R.D.	Lennox Kemp		02-The Sitting Ducks (1984)
145	Moffat, Gwen	Melinda Pink		12-Raptor Zone (1990)
145	Moffat, Gwen	Melinda Pink		14-The Lost Girls (1998)
145	Monfredo, Miriam Grace	Glynis Tryon		05-The Stalking Horse (1998)
153	Nabb, Magdalen	Salvatore Guarnaccia		11-The Monster of Florence (1996)
156	O'Connell, Carol	Kathleen Mallory		04-Stone Angel (1997)
158	O'Shaughnessy, Perri	Nina Reilly		03-Obstruction of Justice (1997)
158	O'Shaughnessy, Perri	Nina Reilly		04-Breach of Promise (1998)
159	Oliphant, B.J.	Shirley McClintock		07-Here's to the Newly Deads (1997)
165	Penn, John	Richard Tansey		01-Outrageous Exposures (1988)
165	Penn, John	Richard Tansey		06-A Legacy of Death (1992)
165	Penn, John	Richard Tansey		07-A Haven of Danger (1993)
165	Penn, John	Richard Tansey		08-Widow's End (1993)
165	Penn, John	Richard Tansey		09-A Guilty Party (1994)
165	Penn, John	Richard Tansey		11-Bridal Shroud (1996)
165	Penn, John	Richard Tansey		12-Sterner Stuff (1997)
169	Porter, Anna	Judith Hayes		03-The Bookfair Murders (1997)
169	Pugh, Dianne G.	Iris Thorne		04-Foolproof (1998)
172	Rayner, Claire	George Barnabas		05-Fifth Member (1997)
179	Rowe, Jennifer	Tessa Vance		01-Deadline (1997) U.S.-Suspect (1999)
179	Rowe, Jennifer	Tessa Vance		02-Something Wicked (1998)
184	Sedley, Kate	Roger the Chapman		08-The Weaver's Inheritance (1998)
187	Silva, Linda Kay	Delta Stevens		05-Tropical Storm (1997)
190	Smith, Cynthia	Emma Rhodes		05-Royals and Rogues (1998)
194	Stacey, Susannah	Robert Bone		08-Hunter's Quarry (1997)
195	Stallwood, Veronica	Kate Ivory		06-Oxford Blue (1998)
216	Wren, M.K.	Neely Jones		01-Neely Jones: The Medusa Pool (1999)
220	Zaremba, Eve	Helen Keremos		06-White Noise (1997)

Appendix C - Pocket Guide Corrections

28 Title Deletions (-)

DW3PG Page	Author	Series Character	Series Number & Title in Pocket Guide	Series Number & Title in Full-Text Edition
33	Charles, Kate	Lucy & David	Free Among the Dead...not part of this series	
33	Charles, Kate	Lucy & David	Unruly Passions...not part of this series	
52	Dengler, Sandy	Joe Rodriguez	Fatal Fishes...not published	
62	Epstein, Carole	Barbara Simons	Perilous Consequences...not published	
67	Fiedler, Jacqueline	Caroline Canfield	Batscape...not published	
97	Hoff, B.J.	Daniel & Jennifer	Mists of Danger...not part of this series	
106	John, Katherine	Trevor Joseph	By Any Other Name...not part of this series	
106	Johnston, Jane	Louisa Evans	Pray for Ricky Foster...not part of this series	
106	Johnston, Jane	Louisa Evans	Paint Her Face Dead...not part of this series	
123	Logan, Margaret	Olivia Chapman	Deathampton Summer...not part of this series	
124	Lucke, Margaret	Jessica Randolph	A Relative Stranger...non-series mystery	
124	Lucke, Margaret	Jessica Randolph	Bridge to Nowhere...not published	
140	Meier, Leslie	Lucy Stone	Mistletoe Murder...re-release of Mail-Order Murder	
145	Moffat, Gwen	Melinda Pink	The Buckskin Girl...not a mystery	
145	Moffat, Gwen	Melinda Pink	Miss Pink's Mistake...not published	
154	Neely, Barbara	Blanche White	Blanche in the 'Hood...working title for book 3	
155	Nielsen, Helen	Simon Drake	A Killer in the Street...not part of this series	
169	Pugh, Dianne G.	Iris Thorne	Body Blow...British title of Fast Friends	
171	Quinn, Elizabeth	Lauren Maxwell	Dead by a Whisker...not published	
172	Radley, Sheila	Quantrill & Lloyd	New Blood...not part of this series	
185	Shaw, P.B.	Abe Rainfinch	The Seraphim Kill...not a series mystery	
185	Shaw, P.B.	Abe Rainfinch	The Water Cannibals...not published	
199	Tell, Dorothy	Poppy Dillworth	Wilderness Trek...not a mystery	
205	Walker, Mary Willis	Kate Driscoll	Zero at the Bone...not a series mystery	
205	Wallace, Marilyn	Theresa Gallaher	Current Danger...not a series mystery	
208	Weir, Charlene	Susan Wren	Lethal Promise...working title for Murder Takes Two	
214	Wolzien, Valerie	Susan Henshaw	Deck the Halls with Murder...not part of this series	

Bibliography

The Armchair Detective, Vols. 27-30, Kate Stine, Editor-in-Chief. New York: The Armchair Detective, Inc., 1994-1997.

The Armchair Detective Book of Lists, Revised Second Edition. Kate Stine, Editor. New York: Otto Penzler Books, 1995 by The Armchair Detective.

AZ Murder Goes...Classic, Conference Papers. Edited by Barbara Peters and Susan Malling. Scottsdale AZ: The Poisoned Pen Press, 1997.

The Big Book of Noir. Edited by Ed Gorman, Lee Server, and Martin Greenburg. New York: Carroll & Graf, 1998.

Bloody Words Program Book, 1999. The Arts & Letters Club, Toronto ON Canada.

Bouchercon 25-30 Program Books, 1994-1999.

BuffCon '95 Program Book, 1995. Medaille College, Buffalo NY.

By a Woman's Hand, A Guide to Mystery Fiction by Women. Jean Swanson and Dean James. New York: Berkley Books, 1994.

By a Woman's Hand, A Guide to Mystery Fiction by Women, Second Edition. Jean Swanson and Dean James. New York: Berkley Prime Crime, 1996.

CADS, Crime and Detective Stories, Nos. 20-35, 1993-1999. Geoff Bradley, Editor and Publisher. Essex, England.

Canadian Crime Fiction, An Annotated Comprehensive Bibliography of Canadian Crime Fiction from 1817 to 1996. Compiled by L. David St C. Skene-Melvin. Shelburne ON Canada: The Battered Silicon Dispatch Box, 1996.

Cluefest, Dallas Mystery Readers Book Fair Program Books, 1996-1998.

Crime Fiction II, A Comprehensive Bibliography 1749-1990. Vols. 1-2. Allen J. Hubin. New York & London: Garland Publishing, Inc. 1994.

Crime Fiction III, A Comprehensive Bibliography 1749-1995. CD-ROM. Allen J. Hubin Oakland CA: Locus Press. 1999.

Crime In Store, London's Crime and Mystery Store Catalogues Nos. 2-15, 1996-1999.

Crimes of the Scene. A Mystery Novel Guide for the International Traveler. Nina King with Robin Winks and other contributors, New York: St. Martin's Press, 1997.

The Crown Crime Companion, Compiled by Mickey Friedman. New York: Crown Publishers, 1995.

Deadly Pleasures, Nos. 1-24, 1993-1999. George A. Easter, Editor and Publisher. Bountiful UT.

Deadly Serious, References for Writers of Detective, Mystery and Crime Fiction. Sharon Villines, Editor and Publisher. 1995.

Deadly Women, The Women Mystery Reader's Indispensable Companion. Jan Grape, Dean James and Ellen Nehr, Editors. New York: Carroll & Graf, 1998.

Detectionary. A biographical dictionary of leading characters in mystery fiction. Compiled by Otto Penzler, Chris Steinbrunner, Marvin Lachman, Charles Shilbuk, Francis M. Nevins, Jr. Edited by Otto Penzler, Chris Steinbrunner, Marvin Lachman. Woodstock, NY: The Overlook Press, 1971.

Doubleday Crime Club Compendium, 1928-1991. Ellen Nehr, Martinez CA: Offspring Press, 1992.

The Drood Review of Mystery, Nos. 133-160. Jim Huang, Editor and Publisher. Kalamazoo, Michigan: The Drood Review, 1994-1999.

The Drood Review's 1990 Mystery Yearbook. Edited by Jim Huang. Kalamazoo MI: Crum Creek Press, 1990.

The Drood Review's 1991 Mystery Yearbook. Edited by Jim Huang. Kalamazoo MI: Crum Creek Press, 1991.

The Drood Review's 1997 Mystery Yearbook. Edited by Jim Huang. Kalamazoo MI: Crum Creek Press, 1997.

Encyclopedia Mysteriosa, A Comprehensive Guide to the Art of Detection in Print, Film, Radio, and Television. William L. De Andrea, New York: Prentice Hall General Reference, 1994.

EyeCon Program Books, 1995 and 1999. Private Eye Writers of America.

Fine Art of Murder, The Mystery Reader's Indispensable Companion. Ed Gorman, Martin H. Greenburg, Larry Segriff, Editors with Jon L. Breen. New York: Carroll & Graf, 1993.

Genreflecting, A Guide to Reading Interests in Genre Fiction. Edited by Betty Rosenberg and Diana Tixier Herald, Third Edition, 1991. Englewood, Colorado: Libraries Unlimited, Inc.

Gun in Cheek, An Affectionate Guide to the "Worst" in Mystery Fiction. Edited by Bill Pronzini. New York: The Mysterious Press, 1982.

Hawk's Authors' Pseudonyms II. A Comprehensive Reference of Modern Authors' Pseudonyms, Second Edition. Compiled by Pat Hawk. Southlake, TX. 1995.

How To Write Crime. Edited by Marele Day. St Leonards NSW, Australia: Allen & Unwin Pty Ltd., 1996.

The Howdunit Series: Amateur Detectives, A Writer's Guide To How Private Citizens Solve Criminal Cases. Elaine Raco Chase and Anne Wingate, Ph.D. Cincinnati OH: Writers' Digest Books, 1996.

The Howdunit Series: Deadly Doses, A Writer's Guide To Poisons. Serita Deborah Stevens, R.N., B.S.N., with Anne Klarner. Cincinnati OH: Writers' Digest Books, 1990.

The Howdunit Series: Scene of the Crime, A Writer's Guide To Crime Scene Investigations. Anne Wingate, Ph.D. Cincinnati OH: Writers' Digest Books, 1992.

Left Coast Crime Program Books, 1996-1998.

Magna Cum Murder Program Books, 1995-1998. Ball State University, Muncie, Indiana.

Malice Domestic I-XI Program Books, 1989-1999.

Mid Atlantic Mystery Book Fair and Convention Program Books, 1995-1997.

Mostly Murder: Your Guide to Reading Mysteries. Jay W.K. Setliff, Editor and Publisher, 1994-1997. Dallas, Texas: Mostly Book Reviews, Inc.

Murder Ink, The Mystery Reader's Companion. Edited by Dilys Winn. New York: Workman Publishing, 1977.

Murderess Ink, The Better Half of Mystery. Edited by Dilys Winn. New York: Workman Publishing, 1979.

Murderous Intent. A Magazine of Mystery & Suspense, 1995-1997. Edited by Margo Power. Vancouver WA: Madison Publishing Co.

Mysterious Women, A Quarterly Newsletter for Fans of Women Mystery Writers. 1995-1999. Kathleen Swanholt, Editor and Publisher. Walnut CA.

Mystery & Detective Monthly, 1995-1999. Robert S. Napier, Editor and Publisher. Tacoma WA: Snapbrim Press.

Mystery & Suspense Writers, The Literature of Crime, Detection, and Espionage. The Scribner Writers Series. Vols. 1 and 2. Robin W. Winks, Editor in Chief and Maureen Corrigan, Associate Editor. New York: Charles Scribner's Sons, 1998.

Mystery News, 1994-1996. Harriett Stay, Editor, Port Townsend WA.

Mystery News, 1997-1999. Lynn Kaczmarek and Chris Aldrich, Editors and Publishers. Buffalo Grove IL: Black Raven Press.

Mystery Readers Journal, The Journal of Mystery Readers International. Vols. 10 through 15, 1994-1999. Janet A. Rudolph, Editor and Publisher. Berkeley CA.

The Mystery Review, A Quarterly Publication for Mystery Readers. Vols. 2-7, 1994-1999. Edited by Barbara Davey. Colborne, Ontario, Canada.

Mystery Scene Magazine, Nos. 41-62, 1994-1998. Martin H. Greenburg, Publisher. Cedar Rapids IA: Mystery Enterprises.

Mystery Women, An Encyclopedia of Leading Women Characters in Mystery Fiction, Volume 1: 1860-1979. Colleen A. Barnett. South Bend IN: Ravenstone Books, 1998.

Mystery Writers Market Place and Sourcebook. Edited by Donna Collingwood. Cincinnati OH: Writer's Digest Books, 1993.

Novel Verdicts: A Guide to Courtroom Fiction. Edited by Jon L. Breen. Metuchen NJ and London: The Scarecrow Press, Inc., 1984.

OCLC Online Computer Library Center, Inc., WorldCat Database, 1999.

100 Great Detectives. Edited by Maxim Jakubowski. New York: Carroll & Graf Publishers, Inc., 1991.

1001 Midnights, The Aficionado's Guide to Mystery and Detective Fiction. Bill Pronzini and Marcia Muller. New York: Arbor House, 1986.

Private Eyes: One Hundred and One Knights. A Survey of American Detective Fiction 1922-1984. Robert A. Baker and Michael T. Nietzel. Bowling Green OH: Bowling Green State University Popular Press, 1985.

Publishers Weekly, The International News Magazine of Book Publishing and Bookselling. 1995-1999. A Cahners/R.R. Bowker Publication.

The Purloined Letter, A monthly publication of The Rue Morgue Mystery Bookstore. Volumes 17-21, Boulder CO, 1996-1999.

A Reader's Guide to the American Novel of Detection. Marvin Lachman. New York: G. K. Hall & Co., 1993.

A Reader's Guide to the Classic British Mystery. Susan Oleksiw. New York: Mysterious Press, 1989. Originally published by G.K. Hall & Co., Boston, 1988.

A Reader's Guide to the Police Procedural. Edited by Jo Ann Vicarel. New York: G.K. Hall & Co., 1995.

A Reader's Guide to The Private Eye Novel. Gary Warren Neibuhr. New York: G.K. Hall & Co., 1993.

St. James Guide to Crime and Mystery Writers. Fourth Edition. Edited by Jay P. Pederson. Detroit, New York, Toronto and London: St. James Press, An Imprint of Gale, 1996.

St. Martin's Press Catalogues. Fall 1993-Winter 2000.

The Shamus Awards 1982-1996. Compiled by Jan Grape and Dick Higgins. Private Eye Writers of America, 1996.

Silk Stalkings, More Women Write of Murder. Victoria Nichols and Susan Thompson. Lanham MD: Scarecrow Press, Inc., 1998.

Sisters in Crime Books in Print. Compiled by Vicki Cameron. Blacksburg VA: Rowan Mountain Literary Associates, 1998 and 1999.

Sisters in Crime Membership Directory. Blacksburg VA: Rowan Mountain Literary Associates, 1999.

Sisters in Crime Newsletter. Edited by Sunnye Tiedemann. Lawrence KS: Sisters in Crime, 1995-1999.

Speaking of Murder, Interviews with Masters of Mystery and Suspense. Edited by Ed Gorman and Martin H. Greenburg. New York: Berkley Prime Crime, 1998.

Speaking of Murder, Interviews with Masters of Mystery and Suspense, Volume II. Edited by Ed Gorman and Martin H. Greenburg. New York: Berkley Prime Crime, 1999.

The Subject is Murder. A Selective Subject Guide to Mystery Fiction. Edited by Albert J. Menendez. New York and London: Garland Publishing, Inc., 1986.

Twentieth-Century Crime and Mystery Writers. Second Edition. Edited by John M. Reilly. Chicago and London: St. James Press, 1985.

Twentieth-Century Crime and Mystery Writers. Third Edition. Edited by Leslie Henderson. London and Chicago: St. James Press, 1991.

The Ultimate Movie Thesaurus. A Henry Holt Reference Book. Christopher Case. New York: Henry Holt and Company, 1996.

www.Amazon.com, On-line catalogue and author interviews.

What About Murder? A Guide to Books About Mystery and Detective Fiction. Edited by Jon L. Breen. Metuchen NJ and London: The Scarecrow Press, Inc., 1981.

What About Murder? (1981-1991) A Guide to Books About Mystery and Detective Fiction. Edited by Jon L. Breen. Metuchen NJ and London: The Scarecrow Press, Inc., 1993.

What Do I Read Next? A Reader's Guide to Current Genre Fiction, 1990-1994. Detroit and London: Gale Research Inc.

Who Done It? A Guide to Detective Mystery and Suspense Fiction. Ordean A. Hagen, New York and London: R.R. Bowker Co., 1969.

Writing Mysteries. A Handbook By The Mystery Writers of America. Edited by Sue Grafton. Cincinnati OH: Writer's Digest Books, 1992.

Index

C

D

PURPLE
MOON
PRESS

About the Author

Willetta L. Heising is the author and publisher of the Macavity Award-winning *Detecting Women, A Reader's Guide and Checklist for Mystery Series Written by Women* (1995) and its popular successor, *Detecting Women 2* (1996), the 1997 Agatha, Anthony and Macavity Award winner for nonfiction, as well as an Edgar nominee. She is also the author and publisher of *Detecting Men, A Reader's Guide and Checklist for Mystery Series Written by Men* (1998). Purple Moon Press is the sponsor of Mystery Series Week, created in 1997, and held during the first week of October (since 1998) to celebrate continuing characters in detective fiction.

Before establishing Purple Moon Press in 1994, Willetta spent twenty years in the business world, chiefly at Michigan's largest bank where she held positions in facilities planning, market research, product management and private banking. A former Certified Financial Planner and one-time instructor in economic geography at Wayne State University, Willetta earned a B.A. degree in geography and sociology from Valparaiso University. She also worked briefly as a Detroit city planner and site location analyst for a Michigan supermarket chain.

A popular speaker, workshop leader and panel moderator, she is a member of Publishers Marketing Association (PMA), Sisters in Crime (SinC), Small Press Association of North America (SPAN), and the Women's National Book Association (WMBA), Detroit Chapter. She is also a Life member of the St. Louis Genealogical Society. Born in Coronado, California and growing up in a large Navy family, she attended schools in six states, Norway and France, before moving to Michigan where she has lived since graduate school days.

You can reach her at:

Purple Moon Press
3319 Greenfield Road, Suite 317
Dearborn MI 48120-1212

phone 313-593-1033 or fax 313-593-4087
e-mail purplemoon@prodigy.net or willetta@purplemoonpress.com

Visit Purple Moon Press and Mystery Series Week at www.purplemoonpress.com
and www.mysteryseriesweek.com